A RABBINIC ANTHOLOGY

Selected and Arranged with Comments and Introductions by

C. G. MONTEFIORE

and

H. LOEWE

With a Prolegomenon by

RAPHAEL LOEWE

SCHOCKEN BOOKS • NEW YORK

First SCHOCKEN edition 1974

Reprinted by arrangement with Raphael Loewe.

Library of Congress Catalog Card No. 73-91340

Manufactured in the United States of America

Second Printing, 1977

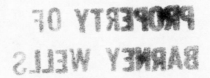

CONTENTS

PROLEGOMENON

by Raphael Loewe

It seems right that the reissue of *A Rabbinic Anthology* some forty years after its compilation should be prefaced with a few remarks suggesting how the passage of time and the advance of scholarship make it appropriate to read the book somewhat otherwise than the two editors could reasonably have expected their original public to have approached it. It is possibly the case that I myself am not the right person to offer a new set of guidelines, for in my boyhood I witnessed much of the editorial work, and by listening to the discussion of texts and topics that took place between my father ז"ל and his colleagues in Cambridge I was able to learn something of a modern, positive approach to rabbinic literature that avoided hero worship and could look below the surface of folk tale and phantasia. My own professional life having been devoted to work within the same general area, I hope that after a generation's lapse I may essay an assessment of the work in which the inevitable element of *pietas* shall not frustrate critical appraisal. The sustained demand for the book is testimony to its continuing value, but the purpose of the two scholars who planned it would be ill-served were its readers not to have their attention drawn to new perspectives within which it ought now be reviewed.

Its impact in the late 1930s, and more particularly in the years of scholarly recovery from World War II, was considerable, and it would, I think, have surprised both editors had they lived to witness it–Montefiore, who died in 1938, lived just long enough to handle an advance copy, and Loewe died in 1940. I suspect that the book also deserves a notable share of the credit for having introduced to rabbinic literature a number of then young theologians and New Testament scholars, as well as many amateur and professional students of Judaism, who have since become leading exponents of their several academic fields and have evinced in their writings a competent use of rabbinic evidence and insight into rabbinic attitudes. There is also the factor of world history since 1938, of which somewhat more must be said below; and the circumstance that the early postwar years, when the *Anthology* was being carefully studied by those able to learn from it, witnessed the discovery of the Dead

Sea Scrolls. Although the contents of these might make essential no more than slight revision of the editorial treatment of the texts here selected, the emergence of an unsuspected body of Jewish writing from an archaeological source has imposed on the student of Judaism the necessity of rethinking his appraisal of the position occupied by rabbinism within Jewry in late antiquity, even though his assessment of the values of rabbinism may emerge intact. Moreover, since 1972 the modern reader has had available an easily accessible work of reference in the new (English) *Encyclopaedia Judaica;* this constitutes a landmark, embodying as it does (besides much else) a magnificently indexed statement of the findings of Jewish scholarship in the two generations since the *Jewish Encyclopaedia* of 1901–6. Clearly, we have an obligation to take a new look at the *Anthology* in the light of all this: and while we gratefully don the spectacles of the original editors, superimposing on them corrective lenses as far as is appropriate, we should also endeavor to see the editors themselves within their own historical context. Indeed, it will be best to deal with the latter item at the outset, and thereafter in the light of it to consider the two elements in the book—the body of the work and the explication of the extracts, and the outlook revealed in the editorial treatment and in the two introductions.

Claude Montefiore (1858–1938), articles on whom will be found in the *Dictionary of National Biography* and in the *Encyclopaedia Judaica*, was deeply influenced while at Balliol College, Oxford, by its Master, Benjamin Jowett; and it may be noted that among the Fellows during Montefiore's years of residence was H. H. Asquith. Montefiore had owed his early education in Hebrew and Jewish matters to his mother, and after Oxford he proceeded to Berlin to study Judaism at the *Hochschule*. It was in Berlin that he came into contact with Solomon Schechter, whom he brought with him to England and who put Montefiore's Jewish scholarship on a sound basis; after Schechter's departure for America at the beginning of the present century he entered into collaborative association with Israel Abrahams, Schechter's successor as Reader in Rabbinics at Cambridge, and after Abrahams' death in 1925 with Herbert Loewe. The three main, interpenetrating factors in Montefiore's life and work may be identified as English 19th-century liberalism, Hegelian Germany, and Jewish spirituality as communicated through rabbinic (or rather midrashic) literature. If his scholarly work reflects all these, they also underlay (with varying emphases) both his substantial and sometimes secret philanthropic activity within the Jewish community generally, and the creation of the Liberal Jewish Synagogue in England, in which Montefiore's was probably the major share. His great capacity for sympathy led him always to seek out what was best in the subject of his attention or enquiry and, when he had identified it, to cultivate greater insight into it. Thus his work on the New Testament in the light of rabbinic Judaism contrasts markedly with the much more heavily documented study by Strack and Billerbeck, the bias in which was exposed by him in his *Rabbinic Literature and Gospel Teachings* (p. 198) and by Loewe in his *Appendix II* to the same work (pp. 380ff.). Although Montefiore could never have compromised over his own Jewish conception of monotheism, his understanding of the teaching of Jesus and of emergent Christianity was sufficiently sympathetic for him to be able to feel that their teaching had something to contribute to the fashioning of the progressive Judaism that he himself propounded—an attitude to Christianity which elicited from the Hebrew philosophical essayist Asher Ginsberg ("Ahad Ha'am") a repudiation, as allegedly being incompatible with a genuine comprehension of Judaism and Jewishness. Personal discussion with Herzl left him unpersuaded that Zionist aspirations had any proper place in Judaism, and he remained convinced that nationalism was a wrong turning for it to take. While it was thus consistent on his part positively to regret, and to endeavor to oppose the British Government's issue of the Balfour Declaration, it would be a misconception to ascribe his position (as has been done) to "assimilationism," or to any supposed concern regarding the specter of divided Jewish loyalties. His attitude was coherent with his own version of Victorian liberalism, born of an age in which it was easy, and perhaps forgivable in an English Jew, to look to a paternally minded *pax Britannica* as the long-term solution of the major political problems of the world, any loose ends being a relatively minor matter for philanthropic endeavor and enlightened administration. Within such a scheme the "political" function of Judaism ought, he reckoned, not be the imitative duplication of the functions of other groups, but rather their complement. And he would make the point succinctly in a quotation from *Isaiah* (xix, 24–5) which, as my father recorded (*The Listener*, 2nd February, 1939) he would frequently cite and liked to use as a motto for his own life's work: "*In that day shall Israel be the third with Egypt and with Assyria, even a bless-*

ing in the midst of the land: whom the Lord of hosts shall bless, saying, Blessed be Egypt my people, and Assyria the work of my hands, and Israel mine inheritance."

Herbert Loewe (1882–1940), regarding whose biography reference may likewise be made to the *Encyclopaedia Judaica*, was born in London and educated at St. Paul's School (towards which he always retained a lively sense of gratitude), and at Queens' College, Cambridge, where he studied Oriental Languages and Theology (being the first, and presumably the only professing Jew so far to sit for the Theological Tripos). Shortly after my father's arrival in Cambridge Schechter left for New York, and although my father was briefly his pupil, he told me that he found himself little attracted by Schechter or influenced by his teaching. Israel Abrahams, on the other hand, who succeeded Schechter, was not only a great teacher, but his nobility of character and spiritual sensitivity exercised a marked influence on Cambridge Jewish undergraduates; and Loewe's own relationship with Abrahams remained particularly close until Abrahams' death. Like Montefiore, Loewe was a child of Gladstonian liberalism, but the atmosphere of liberalism and tolerance in Cambridge has always seemed to me to be of a more welcoming kind than its Oxford counterpart; and the pre-1914 Cambridge as typified by Abrahams and his immediate or wider colleagues—R. H. Kennett, F. C. Burkitt, A. A. Bevan, and others—remained a constant inspiration to him through the years. His educational and cultural background were thus not dissimilar from those of Montefiore, but there was a difference in their respective Jewish backgrounds and the way in which each fashioned his own interpretation of Judaism against them.

Montefiore had been nurtured in the Reform Synagogue by a mother staunch in her Jewish observance, and was led by his own religious development to formulate a progressive Judaism that dealt far more radically with Jewish institutions than had the relatively traditional English variant of the Reform Judaism that began in Germany. Loewe, reared in a full-blooded Jewish orthodoxy, had emerged from a brief period of religious doubt while an undergraduate, having thought his way through the challenge of his faith posed by biblical criticism, to reject fundamentalism as offering an unreliable support for a Judaism that includes in its daily prayers a thanksgiving to God for the gift of knowledge, discrimination, and understanding. His love for institutional Judaism and his utterly unaffected loyalty to its disciplinary demands remained unimpaired: not, indeed, out of any shallow sentimentalism, but because of his conviction that within the biblical texts, be they pentateuchal or prophetic, there can so often be descried the germ of those ethical values or theological notions that later institutional Judaism is concerned to enunciate. Later in life he formulated this thesis as the idea not of progressive revelation so much as intrinsic revelation. He was, I think, able to reach this position (which it would be wrong to regard as a synthesis) because of his capacity for spiritual response to his own sense of historicism—an aptitude that distinguished him most markedly from Montefiore, who (I suppose) realized that this particular reading of Judaism and implementation of its ethical and institutional values could significantly complement his own, largely "de-historicized" approach. There was a close personal rapport between them, as I remember well from the letters (one lies before me as I write) in Montefiore's hand, written obliquely over the notepaper, which would arrive often several times a day, and sometimes be read out over breakfast to the delight of the family. Loewe shared all of Montefiore's great-hearted empathy and generosity of spirit, but he had in addition, I fancy, greater powers of imagination. These are reflected in the frequent situational parallels he drew (occasionally, perhaps, too facilely) in his annotations, not a few of them evoked by a stark awareness of the deteriorating situation of German Jewry under Hitler, the plight of whose refugee victims he was at the time attempting to relieve regardless of the tax on his precarious health, and the presumed similarity of the Jewish situation in times of persecution in antiquity. In this respect we may consider that each of the editors was *felix opportunitate mortis*. It is difficult to imagine how either of them, with their great capacity for compassion, their liberalism, and their 19th-century assumptions as to the general validity of the notion of progress, could have faced the task which history has imposed upon ourselves of trying to make theological sense of the deliberate destruction of European Jewish life and six million dead.

The *Anthology* which Montefiore and Loewe produced is thus already to some extent (despite its continuing usefulness) a period piece—not least in the discursive "chattiness" of its style which, though well suited to the endeavor of reflecting two different approaches, each of them basically positive, to the material, must even at the time of publication have seemed a little unusual. It is also a document of social history in its own right, in that it is the fruit of a type of literary collaboration which, though uncommon, probably attested a wider congruence of attitudes among the Jewish public that welcomed the book than we would be likely to find if a cross section of the corresponding intellectual levels of the Anglo-Jewish and American-Jewish communities were to be canvassed for their views today. The main difference between 1938 and 1973 would, I suspect, be in the numbers of Jewish intellectuals who felt that the book had something of relevance to say for the contemporary Jewish situation. Ours is an age in which, even in theology, de-mythologization is the order of the day: and if rabbinic ideas are to make any impression of relevance, it is no longer enough to demonstrate their consistency with religious values generally acknowledged as noble. If they are to be recognizable to the average educated person as being of potential stimulus to ethical living and spiritual awareness, it is probably necessary to argue that they are capable of surviving a kind of caesarian operation that takes them out of religious categories altogether, while still being other than travesties of themselves. Such a proposition seems to me dubious, to say the least.

We may now return to the book itself, of which there are two aspects to be considered; the body of the work, i.e. the extracts with the explanatory comments that accompany them, and the wider editorial approach as revealed in the two introductions. With regard to the former, there is not a lot that needs to be said. As Montefiore generously volunteered at the end of his preface (p. ix), it remains true despite Loewe's vigorous disclaimer (pp. civff.) that the technical scholarship in the book stemmed essentially from his colleague. Loewe was an accurate and painstaking scholar, with a gift for lucid exposition equally where obscurities were involved and where the general reader or incipient student needed guidance regarding the conventional terms and categories of rabbinic thinking—matters that a specialist, taking them in his stride, might easily have forgotten needed explaining to laymen. The testimony of others, well qualified to judge, consequently relieves his son of the necessity of asserting on his own authority that his father's work may be relied upon as a sound guide. Naturally, scholarship has not stood still since he wrote, and some things in the book would now need qualification. For example, what is said about the angelic name Metatron (pp. 68ff.) needs revision in the light of what Gershom Scholem has written on the subject in *Major Trends in Jewish Mysticism* (pp. 69ff.), and in the English *Encyclopaedia Judaica* (xi, 1445ff.): and the statement that among Jews niece-marriage is rare (p. 508) ought to be elaborated in view of the negative position adopted regarding it in Karaism and also by the Qumran community (see N. Wieder, *The Judean Scrolls and Karaism*, pp. 77, 131). As an introduction to rabbinic thought approached through aggadic rather than halakic categories, the contents of this *Anthology* have stood the test of time thanks to its arrangement, its accompanying comments, and not least its excellent index.

On the other hand, some of the presuppositions of the two introductions certainly call for scrutiny today, and they might possibly not command the assent of persons qualified to make an informed judgment. Foremost, perhaps, as regards Montefiore, is the question of *halakah*, i.e. institutional Judaism, within which is subsumed the whole complex of what western thought categorizes as ethics. It is obvious that the decision having been taken to present rabbinic thinking through the medium of an anthology, the subject matter had to be culled from the aggadic source material that finds its articulation not in law, but in exegesis and lore. Insofar as *halakah* figures in the book it is by way of supplementary comment (e.g. on *havdalah*, pp. lix, 552ff.) introduced by Loewe. Conceivably it ought to have been allowed wider scope and should have been used "contrapuntally." Montefiore's distinction between *halakah* and *haggadah*, even though he recognised the possibility of their interpenetration (p. xvi), was too firm. I imagine, however, that he would have found himself in agreement with my own formulation, *viz*, that whereas the function of *halakah* is to elicit and encourage God-awareness in all practical activities and decision making, including decisions of self-denying discipline and ethical nonparticipation, the function of *haggadah* is to elicit and encourage God-awareness in mental attitudes; and although the latter category is not patient of regulation by codification or enforcement, the former to some extent is. If, therefore, *halakah* is to succeed in protecting group identity and promoting social cohesiveness within it, it must be so regulated, provided always that a sense of proportion is retained. Only so can halakic living proclaim its moral message to the world at large, by laying down guidelines as to how to face issues of God and Mammon, or idolatry disguised as public welfare, and how to prevent fulfillment of religious symbolism degenerating into mere behavior patterns. In such a discipline, the role of example or precedent drawn from the legendary embellishment of the biblical narrative, or from postbiblical anecdotage—i.e. the specific contribution of the *haggadah*—is secondary. Montefiore was fully aware (p. xvi) that for the rabbis of the period with which this book deals—as also for their successors—*halakah* constituted the breath of life, and he certainly understood that *halakah* is a dynamic entity. But—unless I do him an injustice—he seems to have felt that rabbinic reaction to the idea of *miẓwah*, commandment, and the halakic elaboration of the details of its fulfillment, were coextensive with a response (albeit a loving response) to a decree divinely imposed, the validity of which inhered entirely in the divine will, however seemingly arbitrary. That is, of course, true—it corresponds, in fact, to the rabbis' own idea of what is meant by *ḥoḳ, ḥuḳḳah*, i.e. "*statute*," as Montefiore himself explained (p. 148)—but it is hardly the whole truth. It is odd that one who appreciated the fallacy of Paul's negative notion of the yoke of the law (p. 124), apparently himself failed to appreciate that *halakah*, besides being a response expressed in loving obedience that transcends behaviorism, is also an idiom of creative religious expression in its own right. In utilizing symbolic action allied to an explicitly articulated dedication (i.e. *berakah* and *kawwanah*, see index, p. 813), *halakah* is capable of canalizing aesthetic impulses in a manner that can put it, as a category of religious creativity, alongside the soaring spires and stained glass of medieval Christendom. I suppose that Montefiore did, in other contexts, e.g. English academic, parliamentary, royal, and probably also ecclesiastical institutions, appreciate that symbolism is a value in its own right. In view of his early Jewish education it seems strange that he undervalued this dimension in Judaism. It is perhaps significant that the footnote on p. 118 explaining the aesthetic notions implied by the formula *hiddur miẓwah* was interjected over the initials H. L. One must surmise that his shortsightedness here was due to an inadequate feeling for history—a feature which seems to have been not uncommon among the "Greats" of 19th-century Oxford. It is a lacuna that had likewise proved one of the limitations of English puritanism. The parallel is relevant, inasmuch as the Liberal Judaism which Montefiore himself effectively created in England came in due course (especially after the establishment of the State of Israel, and the Six-Day War) to realize its need to express a greater sense of conscious identification with the Jewish past, and it has therefore set itself to redress the effects of its earlier radicalism in regard to the Hebrew language and synagogal institutions.

The foregoing concerns Montefiore alone; but there is another factor, affecting both himself and his colleague, of which account must also be taken. It is scarcely surprising, in view of the background of enlightened tolerance and 19th-century liberalism amid which each of them was reared, that they both spoke in accents of sweet reasonableness. That they were conscious that all religious impulse must have its emotional aspect does not need emphasizing; and Loewe certainly, and Montefiore presumably, was sensitive to poetry and understood its power as a vehicle of spiritual values. But their education had taught them that wherever the human mind sallies forth, reason ought always to hold the reins; and that once the initial *actus fidei* has taken place by which the individual accepts or endorses the religious axioms upon which his own particular religious heritage has been constructed, that heritage must (in the case of a believer who is also an intellectual) be so restated as to inhibit minimally his own rationalist bent of mind, and so allow him to preserve his integrity. Both editors, I surmise, will have felt that Judaism, with its long tradition of encouraging learning, has pre-eminently adapted itself to reducing insofar as is possible the tension between faith and reason, in the resolving of which the intellectual who believes will necessarily encounter problems, and indeed anguish: and from such a proposition I should not myself be deemed to dissent. Neither of them was much attracted towards examining the spiritual potentialities of Jewish mysticism, although Loewe was not unfamiliar with the *Zohar* and the categories with which the *ḳabbalah* operates. Nor was the temperament of either of them such as to react positively to religious revivalism and enthusiasm; and Loewe could write (p. 683) "the commonsense of the Rabbis . . . has saved Judaism from the dangers of uncontrolled ecstasy . . . where such tendencies have occurred, e.g. among the *Ḥasidim*, they have been allied to antinomianism." The last assertion, true enough of the aftermath of Sabbatianism, cannot be maintained in regard to hasidism unless the term "antinomianism" is understood in a sense so attenuated as to make its appositeness dubious; and the whole statement implies a reserve regarding hasidism that those more sympathetic toward it might rather diagnose as prejudice. It is, of course, during the last generation only that the mystical elements in Judaism have been the subject of serious academic study on a large scale, leading to their revised evaluation in the light of other comparable religious phenomena, thanks largely to the work of the school created by Scholem. In the 1930s Scholem's was a lone academic voice, Martin Buber's approach to hasidism being of a different order. Montefiore and Loewe are in no sense exposed to a charge of spiritual obtuseness for having ignored Jewish mysticism, and conceivably they were right in their tacit assumption that kabbalism and hasidism, once they emancipate themselves as substantive movements in their own right, become excrescences that divert energies from the tidily espaliered stock and branches of "Judaism." But they did, I think, misconstrue matters by presupposing that "Jewishness" is equally tidy, and that the reasonableness of Judaism is equally characteristic of the Jewish mind, at the spiritual and speculative levels that transcend the workaday plane on which Jews are on the whole remarkable for their degree of common-sensical steadiness.

The point that I am here making is thrown into sharp relief by the climate of the 1970s. The present age is one, as those who were of an age to fight in World War II and have since come to maturity must be painfully aware, in which a flight from reason characterizes much in economic life, in popular moral attitudes, and to a surprising extent also in speculative endeavor and spiritual search. This is not the occasion to offer any diagnosis—partial explanations, each of them perhaps plausible enough in itself, spring easily to mind. Nor should the foregoing sketch of current trends be considered a mere caricature when it is borne in mind that in the very year in which it is penned university students in England have on several occasions shouted their professors down, and on one occasion have assaulted with physical violence an academic scholar to whom they falsely imputed views with which they themselves were in disagreement. All that concerns us here is that within the context of Jewry and of such popular interest in Judaism as Jews evince, the *Zeitgeist* is no less vigorously operative than it is elsewhere. Just as in periods of the past in which apocalyptic writing flourished, what is now at a premium consists of those elements in the Jewish heritage which allow greatest play to enthusiasm and the cult of the esoteric—almost one might say the occult; and the intellectual self-discipline needed for the perceptive acquisition of the grammar of ascent is nowadays below par. Much enthusiasm and serious lay interest which, in the past, might have been devoted to the classical postbiblical Jewish texts has now been attracted, for reasons that are obvious enough and are not in any sense unworthy, by the archaeology of biblical Israel. If such a subject makes substantial demands on the enthusiast's self-training in the elementary groundwork, the effort is willingly accorded. But where the traditional branches of Jewish learning are concerned, what is wanted at the popular level (I do not, of course, here refer to professional students of Judaism) are quick results, almost the "cheap thrills." At the extreme, we have the paradox of the Jewish hippie type, often quite unfamiliar with Hebrew and the basic institutions of Judaism and Jewish living, and not in the least concerned to study these, or to identify himself with the Jewish people through cultivating a personal response to them, who turns to the English translation of the *Zohar*. If I emphasize this change of atmosphere between the 1930s and the 1970s, it is not for the sake of finding occasion for a tirade against contemporary manners, but precisely because I believe that this irrational element, now so patently potent, was also present—albeit expressed in other forms and being much more subdued—at the time when this *Anthology* was being put together. It is enough to recall that the edtiorial work was substantially lengthened because of the involvement of both Montefiore and Loewe in relief work, made necessary by the release in Germany of irrational forces which stimulated some to make into a routine the perpetration of acts of demoniac savagery against their fellow men, and which dulled the conscience of the majority into the condoning of those acts. Montefiore and Loewe were little interested in, or impressed by Freud, and insofar as they were aware of the potency of the irrational to affect the workings of civilized society, they discounted it as something that must fast atrophy and disappear. They seem, moreover, to have assumed that Jewish life and thinking were either naturally immune to such factors, or else had been inoculated against them by such excesses in Jewish history as the Sabbatian movement. It was, perhaps, a natural error to make at a moment in history when the Jewish people were the avowed target of the forces of unreason; and those who lived through those years, and who must inevitably carry the impact of them throughout their lives, must now experience some emotional anguish in recognizing that it was in fact a fallacy of equivocation on the editors' part. The lore and institutions of Judaism, as they set them forth, are embued with reasonableness and a sense of proportion, and Montefiore and Loewe tacitly assumed that (with negligible exceptions) the same qualities characterize the frame of mind in which Jews in the flesh translate those same institutions and lore into the attitudes and enthusiasms of their day-to-day communal activity and aspiration.

Finally, we must look at the essential arguments in Loewe's own contribution to the work as spelled out in his introduction. His own Judaism being thoroughly impregnated with historical consciousness, he himself found little difficulty in so reinterpreting traditional Jewish material and thought patterns that their ethical and spiritual significance remained uncompromised, although he conceded (pp. lxivff.) that some limits are imposed on this approach by intellectual integrity. Within such an attitude the problems of biblical revelation could be seen in perspective, and we have already glanced at his own concept of what he came to call "intrinsic inspiration" (see also p. lxv). Recognizing as he did that the classical sources of traditional Judaism make no secret of the fact that some change has taken place in Jewish institutional life down the centuries, and that it has been acknowledged, validated, and even initiated jurisprudentially, he concluded that what differentiated the modernist, self-styled "progressive" Judaism of Montefiore and the Liberal Synagogue from so-called "orthodox" Judaism was essentially a matter not of principle, but of degree (pp. lxxvff., especially p. lxxx). I would myself regard that judgment as being fundamentally sound, even though it is liable to be attacked as an oversimplification. It postulates, of course, that an individual Jew's opinion regarding the propriety within Judaism of pentateuchal criticism is not a criterion of his genuineness as a Jew that can be used otherwise than as a mere shibboleth; and Loewe presupposed that not merely all likely readers, but that the intelligentsia within English-speaking Jewry generally, were above slogan bandying.

In this latter estimate he failed, I fancy, to distinguish private opinion from collective reaction, and the individual's behavior where group loyalty is represented (even if incorrectly) as being at issue. He could write (p. lvi) "the combination of Orthodoxy with intellectualism is growing . . . in books of which the authors are unimpeachably orthodox." Even at the time, that was probably an overestimate of a few straws in the wind. It scarcely took account of the extent to which, should a rallying cry go forth from orthodox Jewish ecclesiastical leadership, the open-minded within the orthodox fold were liable to take refuge in abstention or even to compromise with their intellectual conscience, for the sake of what they conceived to be the well-being and inner solidarity of that section of the Jewish community which chooses to give its support to a synagogue whose reputation for orthodoxy is impregnable—even though that same orthodoxy might, if subjected to rigorous intellectual analysis, not bear examination or justify its name. Loewe made no secret of the fact that he was neither a fundamentalist nor a political Zionist (p. lxxv), and even the then Chief Rabbi, J. H. Hertz, who was both, and who himself viewed with misgivings Loewe's influence within university circles, never felt able to challenge his title to orthodoxy (within the contextual meaning of the word), because of Loewe's own staunchly observant Jewish *regimen* combined with his transparent spiritual sincerity. And yet, we must conclude that Loewe underestimated the potentiality of this particular shibboleth to lend itself to an exploitation that flouts logic. He did not, I think, fully realize the extent to which the esteem in which he personally was held throughout the Jewish community in England, and the prestige he enjoyed in that community in virtue of his holding the readership in rabbinics at Cambridge University, afforded his views an indulgence that they would not have elicited from most of the Anglo-Jewish orthodox community had he occupied not a university readership, but a pulpit. Suffice it to say that when, in the early 1960s, an Anglo-Jewish rabbi of equal personal loyalty to institutional Judaism revealed in his publications and his sermons an outlook substantially similar to that of Loewe in regard to biblical inspiration, he was extruded from the ministry of the United Synagogue by a wave of popular orthodox agitation which Hertz's successor felt bound to endorse.

Loewe's own, too reasonable estimate of the case may have been influenced by his experience as a university teacher in Oxford and Cambridge, and his opportunity to observe how some (though by no means all) Jewish students—coming to the university from backgrounds where the issues of orthodoxy *v.* a liberalism assumed to be synonymous with schism seemed simple enough—would mature during their university years and sometimes discover for themselves that the problem has to be addressed in a somewhat less unsophisticated way. He alludes (p. lviii) to his own sense of pastoral responsibility for helping the student confronted with difficulties of this nature. His own work, except as a voluntary prison visitor, and in his last years in connection with Jewish relief work, hardly brought him into contact with the nonintellectual masses of the Anglo-Jewish community, his working life having been spent in Oxford and Cambridge for whose few permanent Jewish residents (themselves mainly academics) he afforded an unofficial religious leadership.

In another, contiguous respect conditions have so changed that the claim to be considered orthodox which was conceded to Loewe by virtually all quarters in the 1930s would probably not go uncontested today. As his remarks on pp. lxxvff. indicate, staunchness in Jewish observance–popularly considered to be at least the hallmark of orthodoxy–is, even by his own rigorous standards, a relative term. This might appear self-evident in the context of American Jewish life of the 1970s, with several varieties of Jewish synagogal life not only independently organized and self-sufficient, but also all enjoying more or less equivalent acceptance in the public view as part of the Jewish establishment. In the case of Anglo-Jewry, the pre-eminent position (and constitutional safeguards) of the orthodox Ashkenazi synagogue with the Chief Rabbi at its head makes a cardinal difference; especially if the climate of Anglo-Jewry today is compared with that of the 1930s, when the degree of Jewish meticulousness that was generally recognised as "[strictly] orthodox" was rather less regimented than is now the case. In the 1930s Jewish groups well to the right of the main body of Anglo-Jewish orthodoxy were of course to be found, as Loewe was perfectly well aware, but they were then more or less social curiosities, and the hasidic movement exercized relatively little influence. The postholocaust psychological trauma of Jewry has, however, had the effect of drawing lines more rigidly than before, with the result that issues tend to be polarized–in defiance of a true sense of realism–into terms of communal solidarity, and of risks to the survival potential of the Jewish people. The consequential *clichés* that gain easy currency are thus liable to delude those who accept them at their face value into treating as *ipso facto* "heterodox" anyone who, recognising them for what they are, does not.

The foregoing assessment should be regarded as sober rather than lugubrious, for in a study of Jewish values as expressed in haggadic sources there should be no place for pessimism. Nothing that has been said here affects the great value of *A Rabbinic Anthology* for the reader, be he professional student or interested layman, who is prepared to take Judaism seriously and is willing to attune his ear to its own natural categories of thought and expression, rather than to assume that the ones which he himself takes for granted are invariably appropriate and useful. Of the factors that we have been considering, which may make the whole approach of this book seem dated, some are due to external circumstances that may be expected ultimately to eliminate themselves. Others will not, for they reflect the inevitable tensions between old and new. Loewe was aware of their inevitability, and was fond of quoting in connection with it the last two verses of *Malachi* (p. lxxi)—it is not until Elijah ushers in the messianic era that father and son will each appreciate completely what the other is trying to do. He was likewise fond of recalling that after the shattering Roman defeat at Cannae the surviving consul C. Terentius Varro received public thanks "because he had not despaired of the state" (Livy, end of Book xxii). Unless one can share that serene optimism there is little point in reissuing this *Anthology*, regarding which, and its editors, it is apposite to conclude with the dictum of Rabbi Simeon b. Yoḥai (T. B. *Yebamoth* 97a), that whenever a scholar is posthumously cited as the source of a rabbinic tradition, his lips so to speak mutter in the grave. For those who essay the task of passing on to their successors the spiritual heritage which they have received, interpreted, and perhaps in so doing enriched, there can be no nobler tribute.

PREFACE

The nature and purpose of this book are sufficiently explained in the first Introduction. For various reasons its production has been somewhat delayed, and this delay may account for a certain unevenness in its composition, for which the indulgence of the reader, or perhaps I should say, the user, is requested. The first sod, so to speak, was turned in March 1932, and this preface is dated 6 June 1938.

It may be desirable to indicate the book's genesis. I had derived much pleasure and profit from the co-operation and assistance of Mr H. Loewe in my book called *Rabbinic Literature and Gospel Teachings*, and after its conclusion and publication I wondered whether there was still one more possible volume, within my capacity, in which that pleasant co-operation, if Mr Loewe's time and duties permitted, could be continued. On reflection I thought that there was. There did not exist in French, German or English any Rabbinic anthology, which, to my mind, was adequate or satisfactory. So Mr Loewe agreed to help me in producing one which should answer better to what I wanted. Perhaps if Dr Cohen's *Everyman's Talmud* had existed at that time, I might have desisted from the attempt. But it appeared considerably after our Anthology had been begun, and after all, his book is conceived on a different plan. It is *not* primarily an anthology, and the Rabbinic quotations, while including some from subjects which are outside the scope of the present volume, are very much less numerous than ours. Our scope is exclusively religious and ethical. Folklore, jurisprudence, legal technicalities and discussions, are excluded.

Every quotation in the present book has been translated from the original. But whatever I have translated has been revised by Mr Loewe, and whatever he has translated has been—not revised!—but considered by me. The whole has been again revised, and many extracts omitted (to make the book less unwieldy), by the two of us together.

All the comments and remarks in the course of the book are by me, except those notes to which Mr Loewe's initials are appended. The thread upon which the extracts are hung is also of my choosing. There are two introductions, one by me and one by him. The reason for this is that, while we agree in many things, we do not agree in all, and, in particular, we do not look upon the religion of the Rabbis in quite identical ways. I believe that it will be greatly to the profit of the reader that in Mr Loewe's notes and in his Introduction he will have another estimate of Rabbinical teaching, and other suggestions as to particular points in that teaching, put before him. The responsibility, however, for what is included in, and for what has been omitted from, the book is entirely mine. Mr Loewe was good enough to leave the choice of the extracts wholly to me. We have not attempted to go through the whole vast compass of the Rabbinic literature or every printed Midrashic writing. That would have taken too long. We have limited our extracts to the books mentioned at the end, where the editions we have used and the method of quotation are given. These in themselves are large enough in all conscience, and a conspectus, by extracts, of Rabbinic views upon religion and morality must surely be based upon them and hardly needs any wider extension.

The book may be much criticised for one particular reason (as well as, doubtless, for many others). It makes no attempt at any chronological arrangement[1] of the extracts upon any particular subject. A quotation from a Rabbi of the second century may be preceded by one of the fourth, and followed by one of the first or third. But, on the other hand, I have indicated where some extract or extracts seem to me to be the general and prevailing Rabbinic view, and where, while striking or beautiful, they seem to me to be more or less exceptional or unusual. It is in accordance with this canon of mine that I have also given a large number of extracts (some readers will, doubtless, think too many) about subjects, such, for instance, as Repentance or Peace or the Evil Inclination, which seem to me prominent or characteristic elements in the general body of Rabbinic teaching taken as a whole.

In the very large majority of quotations the English given is a literal translation from the Hebrew or Aramaic original. I have sought to avoid, and I have urged Mr Loewe to avoid, all modernisations. It is permissible, when using Rabbinic passages for homiletic purposes, to read into them whatever you please: it is not permissible to

[1] For the convenience of the reader a chronological list of Rabbis will be found at the end of the book, and, in addition, a table giving the approximate date of each paragraph where possible. This date may be inferred from that of the Rabbi or Rabbis to which the paragraph refers or from other evidence. Anonymous paragraphs are usually very difficult to date. For these questions the reader is referred to Excursus III, which deals with the groups of Rabbis, their countries and their 'generations', and Excursus IV, which discusses the question of dating.

do so when presenting them in an Anthology, which is intended to tell the English reader what the old Rabbis actually said and thought. One result, however, of this rule is that the extracts are often very bald. They are by no means 'elegant'. The Rabbis, or the men who compiled the Rabbinic literature, were lacking in artistry. Their style is very poor. They use the same sorts of reasoning over and over again till these become a weariness of the flesh. And they have only one or two sorts. 'Is not this an argument from the less to the greater?' 'If, then, so and so is true about *A*, how much more must it be true about *B*.' These two formulae are repeated *ad nauseam*! Nevertheless, it is, in my opinion, not permissible to tinker or to polish. Wherever it is possible, the exact words of the original must be reproduced in the English version. In only a few cases—and then almost always for the sake of compression—has recourse been had to paraphrase.

I must add here that I thought that it would be of great interest if an essay could be written comparing the religious and ethical views of the Rabbis with those of such Church Fathers as were their contemporaries. On the basis of my extracts, this essay has been most kindly written for me by Mr R. H. Snape, to whom I owe my warmest thanks.

For unwearying and generous help in typing and retyping the book from manuscript, as well as for the compilation of the various indexes, I am deeply indebted to six friends. I do not know what I should have done without them. It would, I suppose, have been flippant to have called the book the Octagonal Anthology, but that is what in fact it is.

In conclusion I would like to say that the scholarship of the book is H. L.'s, the arrangement is C. G. M.'s. In other words, H. L., if he had chosen, could have compiled the book without C. G. M., but C. G. M. could not have compiled it without H. L.

C. G. M.

6 *June* 1938.

Mr Loewe's prefatory remarks will be found at the end of his Introduction (pp. civ–cvi).

INTRODUCTION

by C. G. Montefiore

It would be impertinent, and of no interest to anybody, to explain how it has come about, and why, that I, no Rabbinic scholar and very imperfectly acquainted with Aramaic, have yet given much time to, and written many pages about, Rabbinic religious and ethical teaching. I was started on the road by that remarkable Rabbinic scholar, Solomon Schechter. After him, I had the good fortune to be guided and helped by my dear friend, Israel Abrahams. And, lastly, I have been lucky enough to obtain the assistance and supervision of a third scholar of great distinction, Mr Herbert Loewe, in collaboration with whom the present work has been prepared. Thus aided and supported, I have, I hope, made comparatively few blunders, though I have ventured to go my own way in selection, interpretation and comment. In this book, as in a former one (*Rabbinic Literature and Gospel Teaching*, 1930), but this time more fully, Mr Loewe will put forward his own views, and indicate where they differ from mine.

The present volume will be the last of my attempts to put the main facts about the religious conceptions of the old Rabbis, in as simple a form as possible, before the public. The idea struck me, and took my fancy, that there was room, and even need, for one more Anthology from Rabbinic literature. The existing anthologies, so far as I knew them, in French, German and English, were to my mind unsatisfactory and inadequate. Some of them consisted for the most part of brief sayings, adages and reflections, excellent and blameless in themselves, but somehow insufficiently revealing the true nature of Rabbinic teaching and religion. Even when these anthologies contain stories and legends, they too often omit those that are really characteristic. I do not mean by this stricture that what is given in these anthologies is only what is good, and that the bad and the crude are left out, for every anthology is to be a collection of flowers and not of weeds, and my own will be no exception to that universal rule. But the crude and the bad, though absent from the selected quotations, must not be entirely ignored. Where the good is considerably above the average, where it is exceptional, or again where it is habitual and predominant, this must be indicated. And the good need not always be the very respectable. One does not want merely tit-bits and elegant extracts. Ancient and modern tastes differ, and some things which the ancients could easily say and write, we cannot. Nevertheless, we do not (to my mind) want only stories which are very refined and pretty, and in strict accordance with Victorian ideas of propriety or with modern ethical and religious conceptions. An anthology is to be a collection of the best: and yet, though necessarily a brief selection (and, in this case, a selection from an immense mass), it must be a selection which is revealing; it must be characteristic; it must, far so as possible, give no false, no exaggerated, no unfair impression of that whole of which it is a tiny and extracted part. So I thought I would try my hand.

But I must say at once that if I had not begun to collect material for the work a considerable time before Dr Cohen's book, *Everyman's Talmud*, appeared, I should never have begun at all. For *Everyman's Talmud* covers, in a much more systematic and complete form than my own book, much of the same ground. At the same time, though Dr Cohen has many quotations which I have too (I have even added a few of his quotations which I had myself either not noticed or rejected), I have chosen a large number of passages which did not fit in with his plan, or would have made his book too bulky. On the other hand, Dr Cohen has put into his book much which I have not put into mine; moreover, certain subjects (Folklore, Jurisprudence, the Physical Life, pp. 253–366) I have neglected altogether. In fact, Dr Cohen's book is a much more all-round and systematic affair than mine, and much less subjective and impressionist. If people would buy his book (it costs only 4*s.* 6*d.*) as well as mine, I venture to think that they would learn quite a decent amount about the ethical and religious teaching of the ancient Rabbis.

Dr Inge has said: 'Christianity can only be understood from inside' (*The Gate of Life*, p. 52). I can well believe that this is true. But if it be true, a similar saying must be true of other religions as well. It must, for example, be at least as true of Judaism as of Christianity. It may even be true of the various sections of Christianity and of Judaism. It may, for example, be true that Roman Catholicism or Evangelical Protestantism can be understood only from inside. But how ready people sometimes are to accept the saying as regards their own religion, but to deny it about religions which are not their own! Too many Christians imagine that while, shall we say, a Jew cannot understand Christianity, *they* can well understand and evaluate Judaism. Yet the sauce must be the same for both. If the one is incapable, the other is no less incapable. It is no good to say: 'Oh yes; I, as a

Christian, am in much better case. For Christianity is partly based upon Judaism. It is the perfect flower. And whereas imperfection cannot judge perfection, perfection can judge imperfection.' For one thing Judaism was growing when Christianity was born, and it continued to grow after Christianity had diverged from it. And, for another thing, the two religions are distinct, and Christianity did not just quietly and regularly develop out of Judaism. This would be agreed to by passionate advocates of either religion, the New and the Fresh meaning to the one a great difference for the better, and to the other a great difference for the worse. Dr Inge says that a certain remark of Renan 'proves the fundamental frivolity of his outlook upon life'—the remark, namely, that 'in order to understand a religion one ought to have believed [it], and then to have ceased to believe in it'. I think that Dr Inge is right in denying the accuracy of Renan's remark. But still less does the convert from one religion to another understand fully the religion he has left, even as, in spite of all his great genius and originality, no one misunderstood Judaism more profoundly than Paul. There are, nevertheless, exceptions to every rule. For example, no Jew, in my opinion, has written a fairer exposition of Rabbinic Judaism than the non-Jew, G. F. Moore. Yet, perhaps, the rule that to understand a religion one must be inside it, that is, believe in it, is least true as regards religions which have had least to do with, or are farthest off from, one another. If there have been conflicts, if passions come in, if there is room for prejudice and prepossession, understanding becomes more and more difficult. A Christian or Jewish scholar may be able to 'understand' Buddhism better than he can understand the religion which is more akin to his own. So of two different phases of the same religion. Hostile cousins are not good judges of each other's characters. That is why some Liberal Jews may not understand Orthodox Judaism properly, and why some Orthodox Jews may not properly understand Liberal Judaism. In the present undertaking, the co-operation of an Orthodox Jew with a Liberal Jew may help to prevent an inadequate understanding on the one hand, and an uncritical appraisement upon the other. Moreover, there is this advantage in an anthology that, even though it may be accompanied by editorial remarks, yet, if the translation be accurate and honest, the original writers are allowed to speak for themselves.

A great part of the quotations made in this book is assigned to particular Rabbis whose names are given. Scholars hold that, upon the whole, the tradition, which places particular sayings in the mouths of particular Rabbis, is to be trusted. On the other hand, a considerable portion of the quotations is anonymous. The dates of many Rabbis whose names are given can roughly be ascertained. The earliest of them belong to the first century, the latest to the fifth century A.D.[1] The anonymous passages may be spread over an equal, or even a longer, range of time. Thus we get a period of at least some four or five centuries for this anthology. It may be asked whether, in view of this long space of years, one has any right to speak generically of 'the Rabbis', or of 'the Rabbinic religion'. How absurd it would be if, in compiling a religious anthology from English literature between the years 1500 and 1900, one spoke generically of the religion of 'English theologians' or 'English clergymen', as if during these 400 years they had a common religion or the same religious ideas. But, in point of fact, there was far less change and variety as regards the Rabbis between (say) A.D. 100 and 500 than in England between A.D. 1500 and 1900. There was doubtless *some* development, there were doubtless varieties of view between this Rabbi and that; the Rabbis of 500, taken roughly as a group, did, perhaps, in some things, hold religious views which differed from the views of the Rabbis of 100. Historic circumstances, local events, special persecutions, influences of environment, caused particular Rabbis to express particular views. Thus, to take a couple of examples: the circumstances of his age and environment might make one Rabbi express opinions favourable to proselytes, and another Rabbi views unfavourable or hostile. Or they might make one Rabbi more bitter against 'the nations', and another less so. Nevertheless, in spite of such and other differences, due to these and other causes, or due to the fact that one Rabbi might by nature be more 'liberal' or 'progressive', or possessed of a greater mind, than another, in quite a large number of fundamental ideas there was a marked agreement, extending over all these centuries. It is possible that historians might tell us that there was, roughly speaking, a similar agreement among Christian priests and theologians of the years A.D. 600–1000 or 500–900 or 700–1100 in Western or in Eastern Europe. However this may be, I think I am justified in speaking of 'the Rabbinic religion' or of 'Rabbinic religious ideas',

[1] [Some of the Rabbis cited lived B.C. Occasionally a few pre-Christian citations will occur. In any case, many sayings are not the original utterances of the Rabbis who relate them: they are traditional and much older than the date of the authority who records them. For these questions see Excursus III and Excursus IV. (H. L.)]

or justified even in speaking of 'the ancient Rabbis', as if there were a large common measure of agreement between them all.

A Rabbinic anthology must be something more than a Golden Treasury. It must include all that would be naturally included in a Golden Treasury, but it must contain yet more. The subjectivity of the anthologist must come in, not so much by the inclusion of what he thinks the finest and noblest things in the Rabbinic literature (or, perhaps, let me more modestly say, in the main and leading examples or books of that literature), as by the inclusion of what he regards as the most *characteristic* things. He must also say frankly: 'This quotation is fine or interesting, but hardly characteristic. This next quotation is both fine *and* characteristic.' If a Jew of the year, say, A.D. 1000 had made a collection of what *he* regarded as the finest and noblest things in Rabbinic literature, it would have been a very different collection from that which I should make if I were rigidly to include only those things which *I* thought finest and noblest. My contention is that my anthology, strictly so limited, would present a distorted view of the old Rabbis and of their religious opinions. For my own religious ideas and ideals, my own religious beliefs and aspirations, differ widely from theirs. On the other hand, the qualities and limitations of an anthology need not be abandoned. It is not necessary, and there is no intention, to present a *complete* description of Rabbinic religion illustrated by a series of extracts. That would be too long and too difficult. One need not carefully illustrate the weak points of Rabbinic religion, culling 'weeds' as well as 'flowers'. One need not be systematic or complete. One may justly omit a good deal which happens to be uninteresting to oneself. But I am, I think, bound at least to indicate the difference between the religious teaching of the Rabbis and that of modern, and especially of Liberal, Judaism. To be fair to the old Rabbis, I must, I think, indicate the doctrines or the practices which *they* held most dear, about which *they* felt most deeply, which *they* loved most intensely, for which they were ready to die, or about which they would make no compromises or concessions. For if there *are* doctrines and practices central to *their* religion which have disappeared from *my* religion, these, even in an anthology, must, here and there, be alluded to. I must occasionally reveal their dislikes, and what I choose to consider their limitations and their narrownesses. For these may sometimes give an added lustre to the flowers, making them, when they transcend the narrownesses and the intolerances, the more beautiful and fragrant. The shadows show off the light.

The extracts given will sometimes be quite short. But sometimes they must be fairly long: settings as well as jewels, for the settings may be very characteristic. And, for the same reason, I shall include some extracts which are quaint or odd, rather than beautiful or profound. For in these, to us, quaint and odd sayings and stories, much which is of the true Rabbinic spirit may be revealed. Noble ethics may sometimes take queer forms, or be oddly expressed. In all these ways, and not least by indicating what is frequent and what is exceptional, I must try to give a collection of flowers, and yet to suggest a true, and not a false, picture of the Rabbinic religion as a whole.

One, and, to the Rabbis, the most important, aspect of their religion, their most earnest occupation, and I should fancy their chiefest delight, has to be omitted entirely from this anthology. Halakah and Haggadah, we are told, together constitute Rabbinic religion and literature. The interpretations of the Pentateuchal law, the enormous elaborations of it, the immense additions to it, the interminable discussions, arguments, disputations and counter-arguments, all this is Halakah. Upon Halakah all the regulated and orderly intelligence of the Rabbis was spent, all their logic and training. Haggadah was their relaxation and amusement; in Haggadah their fancy and imagination found its occupation. Then, too, their sermons to the congregation, their moral and religious teachings in our modern sense: the reports and records of all these are Haggadah. So, too, their prayers, though not their elaborate rules about prayer. All their vagrant and unsystematic thought and fancy about God and the relations between God and Israel, all that we read of their homiletic, imaginative, uncircumscribed and unregulated interpretation of Scripture on its non-legal side is Haggadah. We find it in a turgid and turbid mass, for the most part a regular, or rather an irregular, jumble and jungle, without artistry or plan. Halakah and Haggadah are sometimes mixed together, so that the latter interpenetrates the former; yet in this book Halakah (with the endless rules and discussions about civil and criminal law, about 'clean and unclean', about sexual life and women's impurities, about Sabbaths and festivals) must be entirely omitted. What I draw upon is almost exclusively Haggadah, with all its freedom and its exaggerations, its variety, its limitations and its disorder, with all its nobilities and absurdities, its excellences and its defects (cp. (16), p. civ).

This total omission of Halakah from my book, though unavoidable, must, I fear, tend to give a false, because one-sided, impression of the

Rabbinic religion, and more certainly, of Rabbinic life. For all these legal discussions, all this 'study of the Law', all these elaborations and minutiae, were to the Rabbis the breath of their nostrils, their greatest joy and the finest portion of their lives. And yet to most of us, it has almost all become distant and obsolete: to most of us the larger part of it seems a waste of mental energy and of time. If a very big percentage of the Halakic portion of the Rabbinic literature were destroyed, archaeology, comparative jurisprudence, and so on, would be the poorer, but our modern religious life would hardly be affected. A gulf separates us from the Rabbis, and this gulf has to be recognised. Their most absorbing interests were not ours. We have also to confess that religion meant, and was, more to them than to us. God was nearer to them in more senses than one, and heaven and hell were more definite and influencing realities. Here too the Rabbis may be compared with the men of the medieval world.[1]

How is the Haggadic portion of the huge Rabbinic literature to be described and judged? It is certainly not first-class literature, though it contains many fine and notable things. It is without form or artistry. The greater part of it is the literature, not of a caste, but of a small set of professional people, of Rabbis and their disciples and of students. It is true that the Rabbis were also preachers. Yet it seems to me that a large part of what has been preserved and written down of Haggadic literature must have been necessarily intended, not for the populace, but for the inner and smaller circles of students and disciples and for the delectation of the Rabbis themselves. Yet they did not by any means lose touch with the community. They were recruited from the people and from all classes. Rich and poor were among them; craftsmen, traders, landowners. After the destruction of the Temple, and after the Hadrianic revolt, all the Jews drew together, learned and unlearned alike. All were Israelites; all felt themselves God's chosen people and children; all seemed nearer and dearer to Him than any other folk on earth; all were partners in a common misfortune; all were heirs to a common glory. The Rabbis cared for the poor, and managed the affairs of the community. Yet they were inclined to look on everything which took them away from the House of Study as a duty

[1] Cp. D. Ogg in Taylor's *Great Events in History*, 1934, p. 335, 'In the past, religion was an overwhelming element in human existence...To-day, when international and economic problems engross the attention of mankind, there is a toleration of creeds, coupled with considerable indifference...Gentlemen now keep their religious views to themselves, and celestial probabilities have been displaced by earthly realities.'

rather than a joy. They did not indulge in games and sports; they took strolls apparently, but no hard 'exercise'. They had no female companionship or friends; they were fond of, and even obedient to, their wives, but these wives did not share with them their studies or interests. Their world was small; they did not look much beyond the Synagogue and the House of Study. They wanted only to be let alone; to study the Law in peace and quiet. The world around was, for the most part, an alien world, an adverse world, which despised them and which they despised.

Modern Jews have used the Rabbinic literature as an unfailing source from which to make elegant extracts for apologetic purposes. But the literature itself is not apologetic. It is entirely honest. It was not written for purposes of propaganda. There is no eyewash about it. One has no need to ask: Is this for outside use? It is wholly sincere. The good and fine and wise things are just as much the expression of the minds of the Rabbis as the things which we regard as crude or cheap or intolerant or silly. Nothing is artificial. As I have said elsewhere, the Rabbis are always in undress.

What I have said about women needs some enlargement. The Rabbinic literature is written by men and for men. The difference in the relations of men and women to each other makes a constant difference between the Rabbis and ourselves. It is always cropping up. Modern apologists tend to ignore or evade it. They quote a few sentences such as 'Who is rich? He who has a good wife'; or they tell of a few exceptional women such as Beruria. It is quite true that wife and mother played a very important part in Rabbinic life; it is true the Rabbis were almost always monogamists; it is true that they honoured their mothers profoundly, and usually honoured and cared for their wives. But that is only one side of the story. 'Women, children and slaves': that familiar and frequent collocation means and reveals a great deal. Women were, on the whole, regarded as inferior to men in mind, in function and in status. Very few women were students of the Law: it was not intended that they should be. Yet the highest and most adorable thing in the world was to study the Law. The greatest and purest joy in the world was to fulfil *all* the commandments and ordinances of the Pentateuch and Rabbinic codes. But women need not, and could not, observe them all. It was not for nothing that the daily blessing was said (the blessing which the modern orthodox Jews have not had the courage and good sense to remove from their prayer books): 'Blessed art thou, O Lord our God, who hast not made me a woman.' This blessing was as sincerely said as the two previous ones: 'Blessed art thou, O Lord our God, who hast not made me a gentile or a slave.' Social intercourse with women was usually taboo. They were the source of moral danger. They were the incitements to depravity and lust. The evil impulse—the *Yetzer ha-Ra*—is especially and mainly the impulse which leads to sexual impurity. The result was not entirely healthy. The Rabbis were prevailingly chaste; there was probably *much* less adultery and fornication among the Rabbis than among us. But this chastity was obtained at a certain cost. The lack of healthy, simple companionship and friendship caused a constant dwelling upon sexual relations and details. In the Rabbinic literature sexual allusions are very frequent. Immense are the Halachic discussions about the details of sex life, and sexual phenomena. 'Repel nature, and it recurs.' Repress it, and it grows up again, and not always in a healthy form. Where we should not dream of thinking that any sexual desire could be evoked, the Rabbis were always on the watch for it, dwelling on it, suggesting it. Though they were almost invariably married men, they yet seem to have often been oddly tormented by sexual desires; perhaps, too, the very absence of natural and healthy social intercourse between men and women drove them to dwell theoretically with double frequency upon every sort of sexual details and minutiae.[1]

Another point to remember in regard to Rabbinic literature is that it comes from men whose outlook was extraordinarily limited. They had no interests outside Religion and the Law. They had lost all historic sense.[2] They had no interest in art, in drama, in *belles lettres*, in poetry, or in science (except, perhaps, in medicine). They had no training in philosophy. How enormously they might have benefited if, under competent teachers, they had been put through a course of Greek philosophy and literature. They had no training in rhetoric or the art of composition. That is one reason why the written precipitate of their teachings and discussions is so formless and shapeless. The Old Testament was practically the only book they possessed, but of an appreciation of the Hebrew Bible as literature we notice little. For them the Bible is a collection of texts and isolated utterances, of injunctions, proofs and teachings. Yet this Bible, with all that it

1 [This tendency was characteristic of the age. Patristic literature is similarly marked. On the other hand, the Rabbinic writings do not eulogise virginity and monasticism. (H. L.)]

2 Cp. Coulton in Taylor's *Great Events in History*, 1934, p. 212 *fin.*, on the Middle Ages, 'The scarcity of books even at the best of times, and the comparatively limited migration of such books as existed, were responsible for a painful rarity of historical sense and method.'

implied, is their world, their one overmastering interest. They picked up, it is true, many current ideas, opinions, superstitions, in a fluid, unsystematic form. But all *that* was by the way and incidental. The total result is very strange. The literature from which my anthology has to be drawn is, I should fancy, unlike any other. It contains a religion—so far as one may speak of a single Rabbinic religion—which, while based upon, and derived from, the Hebrew Bible, is yet, in many ways, higher than the *average* religion of that Bible—higher, purer, and more developed. On the other hand, in some respects, it falls below the finest and noblest portions of the Hebrew Bible, and it has a few infiltrations of superstitions alien to the Old Testament at its best.

It may be asked, what is our present, modern interest in the religious teachings of the Rabbis? There is, obviously, a special Jewish interest, but there is also, I think, a general interest. The Rabbinic literature is required to illustrate the New Testament. This specific New Testament interest I have myself done something to satisfy, so far as the Synoptic Gospels are concerned, in a former volume. But I trust that the Rabbinic religion has a yet wider appeal. Genealogically one may say that from the Judaism of A.D. 20 there sprang all Christianity and all later Judaism. Now the Judaism of A.D. 20 was the offspring of the Hebrew Bible, which is still a living book, and is a portion of the sacred Scripture of Christianity. It is then surely of interest to know something of the direct heir of the Hebrew Bible, for that is what Rabbinic Judaism is. Again, if we examine the Christianity of A.D. 500, we might say it has two main strands: (1) A Jewish strand—the teaching of Jesus and (partly) of Paul, (2) a Greek strand, which, visible already in the Fourth Gospel, became much stronger and more definite later on. But Rabbinic Judaism is purely Jewish. It has no Greek strand. Whether the absence of the second strand was an advantage is disputable. I think it was in many respects a disadvantage, but whether advantage or disadvantage, this purely native development from the Old Testament is certainly interesting.

The Old Testament or Hebrew Bible may be regarded as the parent both of Christianity and of Rabbinic Judaism. The debt of the former to the Old Testament is much less than that of the latter. For there are no such religious geniuses and innovators as Jesus, Paul and the author of the Fourth Gospel among the Rabbis. Moreover, for good and for evil, Christianity owes much to Hellenic and Hellenistic thought and influences, whereas Rabbinic Judaism is almost purely a native growth, and depends upon the Old Testament alone. In its own opinion, it is merely the drawing out and the filling out of the Old Testament, which to it is the undiluted and unchangeable word of God. Nevertheless, Rabbinic Judaism is a development; the child, often for good, sometimes for evil, is different from the parent. And to those who stand a little apart both from Rabbinic Judaism and from Christianity, and contemplate them with a certain amount of impartiality and detachment, it can be of real interest to note, not merely their obvious differences, but their likenesses, and, yet more, the way in which the one is often (in a good sense) the complement or supplement of the other. For, even in their developments beyond the Old Testament, there are likenesses, but more often (I believe) the good development, in ethical and religious (not in dogmatic religious) teaching, of the one is not the same as the good development of the other. Of two brothers one has remained more at home; the other has gone out into the world. Yet even the stay-at-home, though to a less degree, is by no means the copy of his parent. The character of each is a fresh creation, and the excellences of each, though kindred, are yet distinct. As society is the richer for both brothers, so is it, I think, with the teachings both of Rabbinic Judaism and of Christianity. I hope that this anthology may show that we moderns of today are the richer for possessing both. From both we may learn; from both we may go forward, applying, modifying and expanding.

Adapted to modern ideas, or phrased along modern lines, there is possibly some value in the teaching of Maimonides that Christianity and Islam were divinely appointed, though by no means wholly true, religions, intended by God to bring the world by stages to the purest knowledge and worship of Himself.[1] The teaching has many implica-

[1] [In this connection the following lines of Solomon ibn Gabirol are of interest:

Thou art the God of Gods, and the Lord of Lords,
Ruler of beings celestial and terrestrial,
For all creatures are Thy witnesses
And by the glory of this Thy name, every creature is bound to Thy service.
Thou art God, and all things formed are Thy servants and worshippers.
Yet is not Thy glory diminished by reason of those that worship aught beside Thee,
For the yearning of them all is to draw nigh Thee.

The passage cited is from his *Royal Crown* (ed. I. Zangwill and I. Davidson, Philadelphia (1923), VIII, 86, ll. 70–6), a poem which is read after service on the eve of the Day of Atonement. The sentiments recall Wordsworth's *Ode to Duty*:

Glad hearts! without reproach or blot,
Who do thy work, and know it not.

Solomon ibn Gabirol was born in 1021/2. His *Fons Vitae* was a famous text-book of the medieval philosophers and its author was known to them as Avicebron.

'And so, for centuries, Gabirol marched through the philosophic schools of

tions, and can be pushed rather far. It can be expanded so as to include the view that in any one religion there may be development—a shedding of error and an increase of truth, or even an increase and acceptance of error for the sake of the ultimate emergence of a fuller truth. We might conceive of three great Theistic religions all making their long concurrent contributions to the finer and fuller Monotheism of the future. And another familiar thought suggests itself here. It may well be that one religion, and even a particular phase or form of one religion, may be more suited to a given age, a given nation, a given individual, than another. Could any kind of Christianity have been so suited to certain peoples or races in the world as Islam has been or even still is? Could any sort of Judaism have won such conquests as Christianity has won and is still winning? Within Christianity, again, Catholicism may suit some peoples, and Protestantism may suit others. Within the limits of England have we not seen remarkable religious results produced by the Salvation Army? Would or could any other kind of Christianity have produced them? Would any kind of Judaism have produced them? And yet they were partly produced by a combination of doctrines, some of which, at any rate, many Christians today, as well as all Jews, would consider erroneous. So whether we think of the Rabbis, and of any other body of religious teachers, we must be gentle and tender towards doctrines which, however inadequate, or even false, we may ourselves consider them to be, have yet contributed to the religious and moral improvement, refreshment and fortifying of hundreds of our fellow-men whether in the present or in the past.

I have to allow that certain special interests have also prompted me to the attempt of this anthology. I am a Liberal Jew, differing even far more widely than a modern orthodox Jew from the religion of the Rabbis; yet my Judaism comes to me through *them*, and is a development of theirs. Secondly, much of their religious teaching seems to me fine and noteworthy. It contains many 'flowers'; an anthology *is* possible. Some of it, even though *we* can no longer accept it, is yet striking and beautiful. Some of it is capable of adaptation, enlargement and purification. Some of it is pathetic, showing the conflict between higher and lower impulses, or revealing a struggle of ad-

Mediaeval Europe, some taking him for a Christian and some for a Mohammedan, none suspecting that he was a Jew. It was on 12 November, 1846, that the learned world was startled by the announcement of Solomon Munk, in the *Literaturblatt des Orients*, that the well-known scholastic Avicebron was identical with the still better known Solomon ibn Gabirol.' (*Ib.* XXXII.) (H. L.)]

vancing thought against the bonds of a cruel dogma (namely the perfection and inspired character of every Old Testament utterance), which made progress in certain directions difficult or impossible. Thirdly, there is still some prejudice against the Rabbis. Pharisaic, Rabbinic, Jewish, are adjectives still not infrequently used as synonymous, not only for narrow, intolerant, and obsolete, but also for everything and anything in New Testament or early Christian literature which the particular writer happens to dislike. All that is noble and good is original and Christian and new; all that is crude or disagreeable is Jewish and Rabbinic and old. I venture to trust that I have myself been instrumental in removing and lessening some of this prejudice, and I hope that this book may remove and lessen yet more of it. Having given up a considerable portion of my leisure in past years to this effort, I thought I might just as well finish up in the same pathway.

It may be suggested that I should more definitely, if very briefly, deal with the question: How far have the Rabbis advanced beyond the Old Testament? Such a question, so reasonable to us, would to them have seemed blasphemy. As to them, roughly speaking, everything in the Sacred Scriptures was on one level of supreme excellence, so all their religion was for them contained in those Scriptures, and they never expressed any view, or enunciated any doctrine, which they did not seek to justify or substantiate by some biblical passage or utterance. They merely drew out what was already there. To us it would be very doleful to think that there was no religious progress in Judaism for, say, 500 years, and, as a matter of fact, there was a good deal. Not only were several quite new conceptions put forward—an advance direct and clear-cut—but some implicit things in the Scriptures were made explicit, some occasional teachings of value became more frequent, and some indefinite or casually advanced ideas, became definite and dogmatic.

I have already indicated that the drawing out of every biblical idea ran a danger of cutting both ways. For one can obviously draw out the 'low' as well as the 'high', the bad as well as the good. The Rabbis did not entirely escape this danger. Some, at any rate, of the imperfections and crudities in the Hebrew Scriptures were elaborated and hardened by the Rabbis, as for example, the divine partiality for Israel, and the doctrine of tit for tat. This is unfortunate. For when the Old Testament is what we now call 'particularist', it is so usually in a simple, primitive, unreflecting, and 'natural' way, and this is less upsetting to us than when the Rabbis utter *their* particularism with reflection, when they make a theory of it or for it, justifying the, to us, unjustifiable. Again, though for them all the Old Testament is the word of God, and all is Torah, yet the Pentateuch is pre-eminently the word of God and pre-eminently Torah. The legalism and ceremonialism of the Rabbis are in some respects far better than the legalism and ceremonialism of the Pentateuch; they are less priestly, less primitive, freer from superstitions; but they are also more pronounced, theoretic, elaborate and pervasive. Things are said, for example, about circumcision which are positively painful to the modern mind, so that we feel inclined to say: Better than *this* 'advance' is the primitiveness of the Pentateuch. Reflective or justified imperfections are worse than naïve and spontaneous ones. What is said about hell in the Gospels is bad enough; what is said about hell by St Augustine is much worse. The anthropomorphisms of the Hebrew Bible are often crude and glaring; but they are usually naïve, and sometimes grand. Some of the anthropomorphisms of the Rabbis jar upon us more. The things which God is made to say and do and think and feel are sometimes so completely on human level that we are repelled and troubled. Sometimes, too, in doctrine we prefer the primitive spontaneity of the Hebrew Bible. Thus we prefer the simple unreflective tit for tat teachings of the Old Testament to the elaborations of the Rabbis, to the silly idea of such and such divine punishments for such and such sins, of which a shocking and odious instance has found its way from the Mishnah into the orthodox Prayer Book, from which no orthodox authorities have had the manliness or the decency to remove it (*P.B.* p. 121).

In some ways, therefore, the Hebrew Bible is nearer to us than are the Rabbis. It is also nearer because it is more familiar. Moreover, it contains writers and passages much greater than any writers or passages in Rabbinical literature. There is nothing from the Rabbis to compare with the Prophets or with Job or with the nobler Psalms. What is splendidly original and full of genius appeals to us more closely. Because the Old Testament is more creative and original than the Rabbis, we are more drawn to it.

Yet in some respects we are nearer to the Rabbis than to the writers of the Bible. And so far as advance and retrogression are concerned, when all is said, the good outweighs the evil. The advance is more conspicuous than the retrogression: the elaboration, the development, the refinement, of the good are larger than those of the 'evil'.

Moreover—and this is very pleasing—there are not many instances to be found of the elaboration of the 'evil', where we do not also find some flashes of a vivid sense of the inadequacy or questionableness of the 'evil', and some suddenly interjected sayings in the direction of the good. A 'low' doctrine is flatly contradicted by a 'high' utterance, even though the 'low' teaching is not formally renounced or rejected by the man from whom the 'high' utterance proceeds. Such a formal rejection would be impossible for those who, like the Rabbis, fervently believed in the perfection and inerrancy of the Sacred Scriptures. It is only the modernist who is free. We cannot expect the Rabbis to be modernists. The Rabbinic advance will be made manifest and illustrated by the anthology itself. Indeed if there had not been this advance, there would have been no desire to make, and no purpose in making, an anthology. It would never have been begun.

As regards almost all the main teachings of the Pentateuch, and as regards many of the teachings elsewhere in the Sacred Scriptures, we could note some advance. This is so in regard to the doctrine of God, His nearness, His Fatherhood, His immanence, while as regards the Law, though we hear much about 'reward', we hear also much that is new about discipline, purification and joy. 'For its own sake', for 'love's sake', are new teachings. So, virtually, is the sanctification of the Name. The Law says: 'Thou shalt love thy neighbour as thyself'; it is a Rabbi who says that the order is not merely the greatest commandment of the Law, but also its greatest principle. The theory of the Two Inclinations is practically a new theory. A new conception is that of *Kawwanah*. Repentance assumes an importance, and receives a development, which put it upon a fresh plane of significance. The ethics of the Rabbis are based upon the ethics of the Pentateuch, but the advance in refinement and delicacy is very marked. Proselytism forms a new chapter in Judaism, little known in the biblical era, but prominent in the era of the Rabbis, and the same thing is true of the resurrection and the conception of a happy life beyond the grave. The anthology will illustrate these advances and developments. The last 'advance' mentioned, namely the doctrine of the resurrection and of the life beyond death, had naturally an immense influence. It may be said to colour everything else, and tends to make it assume a different complexion. This does not necessarily mean that the doctrine in its Rabbinic form is acceptable to ourselves. Yet it does make the Rabbinic outlook on life not infrequently more like our own than the outlook of the Hebrew Bible. We may add that if the continuous reflections of the Rabbis upon the words of Scripture do sometimes, when those words are crude or poor, repel us, their reflections in *other* instances attract us. By *them* the Rabbis are brought near. They frequently perceive that the Bible speaks with two voices, and in their forced reconciliation of these inconsistencies, which for them are not inconsistencies at all, they often make a religious or ethical advance. Sometimes they realise more fully than the biblical writers the problems and questions which are prominent and pressing to ourselves. It might even be said with some correctness that there are not many fine utterances in the Hebrew Bible which are not developed and enlarged in Rabbinic literature, if sometimes only by a single isolated saying, but sometimes with frequency.

In reading the Rabbinic literature, or even in reading an anthology from it, we have to bear in mind certain grave differences between the Rabbinic view, whether of the world or of the Hebrew Bible, and our own. When I say 'our own', I refer to Jews of modern or liberal opinions in matters of religion. Nevertheless, the most fundamental of these differences would affect all Jews of today, whether modernist or orthodox. Theists we are all, but our God is, in some respects, necessarily other than the Rabbinic God. The Copernican universe is so much vaster and grander than the universe of the Rabbis. God has not necessarily become more remote, but we cannot conceive of Him in the manner of the Rabbis. The interests of the Rabbinic God were concentrated upon earth, and, above all, upon Israel. God was the perfect Rabbi: He too loved and studied the Law. It is not merely on ethical grounds that this special and peculiar love of God for Israel has become unreal, but on metaphysical and theological, I had almost said, on astronomical, grounds as well. Copernicus gave the deathblow to such a conception.

The lack of philosophic training among the Rabbis causes another difference. Only a few of us are philosophers, but yet philosophy has percolated down into our minds without our being aware of it. Let us compare the God of the Rabbis with the God of such a man as St Augustine. He too lived in a pre-Copernican world, and was bound by its limitations. His world was a petty world like the world of the Rabbis: angels, devils and man, and only the last of any interest to God, for the angels were too good and the devils too bad. The Christian doctrine that 'God so loved the world' meant that He so loved *man*; it was only for man that He sent His Son, and the whole Christian doctrine or mythology, whichever word you choose to use, could have arisen only in the tiny pre-Copernican world. Yet, within the limits of such a world, Augustine, I think, conceived of God in *some* respects (I emphasise the word 'some') more philosophically, less anthropomorphically, or anthropopathically, or shall I say, less childishly, than his contemporary Rabbis of the fourth and fifth centuries A.D. In some deeply important respects the Rabbinic conception of God was kept purer and cleaner by the noble and truly beneficent command to represent God under no image or likeness; that, and the rigidity of the doctrine of the divine Unity, and the lack of any incarnational theories, prevented any substantial degradation. But, otherwise, as the Rabbis often took all that is said about God in the Hebrew Bible very literally, and as they were so sadly fettered by the burden of regarding every biblical utterance as good and true and inspired, they seem often to talk about God like so many big children. I do not think it is possible to regard all that they say as conscious 'accommodations'. These childishnesses are too constant and simple for that, and in spite of the famous saying that 'the Torah speaks in the language of men', the Rabbis seldom seem to hint that God cannot *really* be supposed to think and speak and act as they represent Him as thinking, speaking and acting. Even if we suppose that much that the Rabbis say about God is metaphor or pictorial accommodation, you cannot go on speaking about God, and making God speak, as if He were on a par with you or on the same plane—loving the things and people whom *you* love, and disliking the things and people whom *you* dislike, without its affecting, to some extent, your whole conception of God. It may, indeed, be—I think it is—that to most of us God is less vividly realised, less a constant certainty, than He was to the Rabbis, but He is also, if less human, more divine. Our reserve in speaking of Him is good and healthy. A certain austerity and restraint in regard to our conception of, and attitude towards, Him make for increased reverence and awe. Is there a touch of over-familiarity in the Rabbinic attitude towards Him? (Cp. (12), p. ciii.)

Yet other and opposite phenomena in Rabbinic religion deserve notice. We ourselves cling to two doctrines both found in the Hebrew Bible: God, we say, is 'everywhere', and God is 'near'. The Rabbis maintained and deepened both doctrines. With emphasis and power they accentuated the second, and by their important creation of the doctrine of the Shechinah they greatly developed the first. For though the Shechinah is too often used in a particularist fashion, which is alien to us and unsatisfactory, it is, nevertheless, a genuine attempt to teach the divine immanence, to realise God as 'here' as well as 'there', to make the supreme mystery of the divine ubiquity intelligible without interfering with, or trespassing upon, the divine transcendence and 'personality'.

There is, therefore, some vacillation and inconsistency. It was good that the second commandment of the great Ten must have prevented many generations of Jews from habitually forming any definite picture of the Divine Being in a human shape, but probably they, as well as the Rabbis, did, for the most part, believe that God usually resided in a particular portion of space. The Rabbinic images of His throne, of His heavenly court, of the angels and the Torah appearing before Him were, I think, something more than mere images. It may, indeed, be said, that none of all this really matters, any more than it matters for an uneducated lover of God today. It is God's *character* that matters. You may have a God who is regarded as spirit and omnipresent, and yet has a poor or an imperfect character, and you may have a God who lives in 'heaven', and sits on a material throne, who has a fine and noble character. Considering the unfortunate fetters in which the Rabbis were bound—that *all* that is said of, and by, God in the Old Testament is perfect and inspired—they came out of this terrible dilemma very well. We have frankly, though sadly, to admit that the higher, more loving, aspects of God are mainly for the Jews, the fiercer and lower aspects are mainly for the Gentiles. So with contemporary Christians. The higher, more loving, aspects of God are for believers; the condemnatory, punishing and sending-to-hell aspects are for the heretics, the unbelievers, or even for the heathen generally. Both religions, I imagine, attempt to combine and harmonise these differences by saying that the 'fiercer' aspects of God represent His justice, and that justice is not a lower aspect of God, but is merely another side of His love. The modern man is not taken in or satisfied by these attempts to show that a God who annihilates, or sends to eternal hell, a single soul which He has made, is, nevertheless, a God of love. The Rabbis were convinced that all men were God's creatures. 'The Lord is good to all', says the Psalmist, and the Rabbis would heartily subscribe to the doctrine, and even include the animals; yet just as they could honestly think that God liked, or at least ordered, Israelites to worship Him by holocausts of bleeding animals, so they could honestly think that He liked to, or, at least, would, send Gentiles *en masse* to hell, or, at any rate, deprive them of the glorious world to come. We cling with pain and difficulty to the doctrines of 'God in history' and of His impartial love for all men, even though so many of His dealings with men (as, for example, with the aborigines of Tasmania) are utterly mysterious to us; to the Rabbis the particularist and passionate love of God for Israel was adorable indeed, but a *certain fact*, and in no way mysterious.

We may compare the views of the Rabbis about the 'wicked' and their destiny with those of Jesus as regards the men whom *he* thought most especially wicked and detestable. In both cases the most wicked people are usually antagonists; in the one case, they are the oppressors of Israel, in the other the Pharisees, who opposed and mistrusted the new and formidable Prophet. It is not easy to exceed the vituperative language put into the mouth of Jesus in the twenty-third chapter of Matthew. Yet it is likely enough that much of it may be genuine. Both political and religious leaders have had the prevailing habit of speaking ill of those who differed from, and opposed, them. There is no reason to suppose that, as regards such vituperation and condemnation, there was much to choose between Jesus and the Rabbis. Is there much to choose now between the imputations which strong Tories make against the Labour party, and which strong Labour leaders make against the Tories? But this is not to say that because the abuse of the enemy is the same, therefore there is nothing to choose between the *doctrines* of the two contending parties. There may be very much more truth and excellence in the aims and ideals of the Labour party than in those of the Tories. Or vice versa. So too as regards Jesus and the Rabbis. The general teaching of the former may be far greater, more permanent and more inspiring than the teaching of the latter. Or vice versa. The equal condemnation of their opponents does not affect the value and truth of all the other aspects of their teaching, or settle the question of the religious superiority of the one or the other. But this is a digression.

I have already alluded several times to the attitude of the Rabbis towards the Hebrew Scriptures. What was the effect of this 'fundamentalism'? The acuteness of the Rabbis made them perceive many of the contradictions and inconsistencies within the Scriptures. On the whole, their reconcilements of these inconsistencies are in the right direction. They very rarely, I think, explain the pure by the crude, but they do often explain the crude by the pure. Sometimes they even explain away biblical anthropomorphisms. It is mainly in two directions that the burden of the perfect Bible becomes extremely heavy.

First, as regards God's relations with the unrepentant wicked, and' secondly, as regards His relations with Israel and the gentile world. But these two directions merge into one. For to the Rabbis the wicked are predominantly the Gentiles, who are Israel's enemies and oppressors. Within Israel there were doubtless a few heretics, informers, apostates, and high-handed sinners, but to the Rabbis, the percentage of Jews who would go to hell was probably much smaller a percentage than, to the Christian writers of the Middle Ages, the percentage of Christians who would pass on to that undesirable locality. We must remember that the Rabbis knew the Hebrew Bible by heart. Every bit of it was, as it were, constantly before their minds: the good and the bad, the high and the low, the ore and the dross. And all was supposed to be perfect. No wonder, then, when any lower statement suited a human passion, that it was taken at its face value and accepted without demur. Thus the human passion was increased. But when human passions did not come in, the Rabbis tended finely to stress the high, and explain away the low. As the Pentateuch is for them the greatest and divinest portion of the Bible, they are unable to appreciate and understand the Prophetic teaching in its fullness; yet they do absorb and reproduce a great deal of it. Justice and lovingkindness are for them, too, the essential service of God. They *can* reduce the 613 enactments of the Law to two or three ethical precepts, and even to one. Yet the burden is heavy. Sacrifices *were* pleasing to God, in spite of the Psalmist, and they will be pleasing again; to study the ordinances about them is a substitute for offering them; unfortunate children were made to begin their reading of the Bible with Leviticus. The pure children read of the pure sacrifices. So too about circumcision: God delights in it. It is as important as *any* commandment in the whole law, and the moral commandments are *not* excepted. Yet, on the other hand, the Rabbis often rise above the level of the Priestly Law. For its enactments are often regarded as a discipline and a purification, or, again, they are ukases, ordered by God for reasons we know not of, but ordered because He is supremely good and wise. They can say that it can make no difference to *God* whether an animal is killed in one way or in another; they can urge that there is no *magical* efficacy in ordinances such as the Red Cow or the Water of Purification; so far as results follow from them, these results are the direct action of God; God so ordered and arranged; His decrees must not be questioned or criticised. If a modernist Jew could possibly believe that God ordered the Jews never to eat hares and lobsters, and never to wear clothes of mixed linen and woollen, he would be constrained to obey. The Rabbis believed that God had ordered these ordinances just as much, and just as literally and absolutely, as He had ordered the Jews not to commit adultery, or as He had ordered them to love their neighbours and the resident aliens as themselves. Hence they were entirely justified in their observance of these ordinances. Nevertheless, the doubt remains whether to believe that God did fully and directly order these enactments does not in some degree lessen His greatness. I am sure that I love God less deeply than the Rabbis; yet I have a feeling as if my God were somehow a greater, purer God than their God. I can hardly imagine the God of the Copernican age ordering people not to eat lobsters, or bidding them kill an animal for their food in one way rather than in another (cp. p. ciii).

It may be that we moderns, while delighting still to speak of the love and righteousness of God, ignore too much the probability that if there *be* a righteous God, righteousness does not exclude judgment and punishment. Yet the Rabbis, adopting the language and ideas of the Hebrew Bible, talk too much for our taste about God's wrath and His punishments. He appears to show His wrath, and to inflict these punishments, (1) upon all who worship idols (i.e. upon very many non-Jews), (2) upon all enemies of Israel, (3) upon all heretics and sceptics and deniers of the Perfection, Immutability, and Divineness of the Law, (4) upon the high-handed and unrepentant wicked even among the Jews. It would be difficult to say precisely what the Rabbis thought of Christians. Did they fall under class (1) or (2) or (3)? I do not know.

Today the modern religious Jew may, and usually does, believe that the Jews were 'chosen' by God to fulfil a certain task in the religious history of the world. 'Ye are my witnesses.' Not merely, 'Ye *were* my witnesses' till A.D. 29, but 'Ye are still, and will continue to be, my witnesses.' The modern Jew may, and often still does, believe that the Jew's services for Theism are not concluded. But that is all. Any idea that God *loves* the Jews more than He loves Christians is remote. (The bitter joke is, indeed, sometimes made: as, 'whom God loves He chastens', so, by the appalling and continuous measure of Jewish suffering, He must truly love the Jews very deeply!) There is something more. In the personal, individual religious life of the modern Jew, the fact that he *is* a Jew may determine conduct. *Noblesse oblige*; the sanctification of the Name; these may become motives for resisting temptation and for a better life. But in his prayer to God the modern Jew probably thinks of himself more as a human being than as an Israelite. He probably thinks of himself less as a Jew than the modern Christian thinks of himself as a Christian. I do not know the exact meaning of 'through' in the formula 'through Jesus Christ our Lord'; it may mean different things to different people, but I imagine that it includes some such ideas as these: 'As a member of the Christian body or Church, as a believer in Christ, as redeemed and sanctified by him, and through his merits and mediation, may God answer my prayer.' So far as I have noticed, the Rabbis do not say, 'To me, as a member of the house of Israel, may God hearken, and may He answer my prayer,' or 'because of thy love for Israel, do thou help me, an Israelite'. But I think they *feel* like that. God's love is primarily for Israel as a whole. The sense of being an Israelite was more constantly before the mind of an ancient Rabbi in his religious life than it is to a modern Jew of today.

The passionate love of God for Israel, the counterpart and source of Israel's passionate love of God, is found, here and there, in the Hebrew Bible: notably in Deutero-Isaiah (XL–LV). But it is more pervasive and constant and developed among the Rabbis, and it is the more marked and extraordinary because of the completeness of their monotheism. God is the creator of all men, the Lord of the spirits of all flesh, and yet He loves Israel with a peculiar and passionate love, while, as for all the other nations of the world, He is inclined to regard them as of small account, and even, so far as they oppress Israel, actively to *dislike* them. Israel's joy is His joy: Israel's sorrow is His sorrow: 'in all their affliction He is afflicted.' The incongruity of the One God feeling this adoration for one people at the expense of all the other peoples rarely strikes the Rabbinic mind. In fact it would appear that seven-eighths of God's time is taken up by Israel, looking after them, correcting them, grieving for them, listening to their prayers, meditating on the hour and the possibility of their redemption, and so on. The religious life of the Rabbis was greatly affected by these beliefs. The world was created for Israel's sake, and of the overwhelming love of God for Israel every Israelite may claim his share.

One might have thought that these conceptions—so strange and remote to us—would have degraded the entire conception of God. Yet they seldom did so. He is always the God of the universe, small comparatively as that universe is. We find no such idea as: 'I can sin with impunity; I am a Jew; therefore God will pardon my sin.'

In fact we may be sure that such an idea, if the Rabbis had heard of it, would have been strongly reproved by them and repudiated.

The relation of the Law, or I had better say, of the Torah, to God (for the Torah is not limited to the Pentateuch) is very curious. To some extent it purifies the relation of Israel to God. For the love of God for Israel is not merely the chance relation of one particular nation to the One God. God loves Israel, because Israel possesses and accepted the Torah. This idea is often repeated. God loves the Law even more than He loves Israel. Israel was offered the Law and accepted it, and God is grateful. It is not entirely clear why God created the Law. It was regarded, I suppose, as the necessary link between heaven and earth and between man and God. Man required it for his moral and religious well-being. Nevertheless, it seems to have some sort of independent and cosmic existence, even as its creation took place long before the creation of man. Whether this Torah, pre-existent ages before Moses, is to be regarded as the Pentateuch, or as the whole Hebrew Bible, or as something which is not quite one or the other, is not made clear. It is most odd how a book so full of events in time could be regarded as existing before the history of man began. But the sense of history was completely absent, just as there seems to the Rabbis no incongruity in making one biblical hero quote the words of another who lived long after him. But the fact remains that the relation of God to Israel was, on the whole, kept clean and sweet because of the Torah. Israel is loved by God in a way different from that in which Moab was loved by Chemosh. Israel is loved as the possessor and the champion of this inexpressible good: the divine Torah. On the foregoing see [428].

Ideas such as these have become distant to us; yet we can appropriate in some measure another Rabbinic idea which yet is closely allied to Rabbinic particularism. The Rabbis have greatly developed and refined the biblical conceptions of God's sanctification through Israel. In Ezekiel we are mainly repelled by the view that what greatly concerns God is His reputation, His honour, His glory. But the Rabbis, while not entirely free from this lower view, have very considerably improved upon it. The conception of the *Ḳiddush ha-Shem* (the hallowing) with its opposite, the *Ḥillul ha-Shem* (the profanation of the divine Name), had a profound effect upon Jewish morality, which has lasted to the present day. When a Jew in medieval days had the opportunity to cheat a Christian, his oppressor and persecutor, as the Christian usually was, he might, so far as his regard for the Christian was concerned, have been ready, and even tempted, to do so, but the noble doctrine of the sanctification of the Name kept him back. For precisely in the Jew's relation with the non-Jew could God's holy name be either most sanctified or most profaned. That was also why martyrdom (and no religious community can show a higher percentage of martyrs) was the supreme sanctification. The Rabbis make God say, 'When you do my will, my divinity is increased; when you violate it, it is lessened.' God laments over Israel's sins: they grieve Him. His renown is lessened by Israel's shortcomings; it is increased by Israel's good deeds. Here, again, we partly share, and partly have moved away from, Rabbinic ideas. *Judaism* is exalted by Jewish virtue; it is degraded by Jewish sin. That is how *we* put the older conception. The Rabbis felt that way too. In some passages, the notion that human sin, or even Israel's sin, can effect any change in the inner nature or essence of the eternally immutable God is expressly denied. Yet, in other passages, the idea seems to be that, for the fullness of His glory and for His own supremest happiness, God needs the co-operation of His world and especially of Israel. If, through their sin, His chosen witnesses do not witness, if, by their wickedness and frailty, His children deny His Fatherhood, His divinity, on its expansive and forthgoing side, is depressed. We too say, 'God needs us all.' But what *precisely* do we mean by the words?

There are several other points in which Rabbinic religion goes beyond the Old Testament, sometimes for good and occasionally for harm. But when I say for good or harm, these words, I must confess, mainly mean that the development is for good where the modernist or Liberal Jew would agree with it, and for harm where he would not.

(1) There are indications that the Rabbis had given some thought to the question: how far does God help man to be good? On the whole, man's free will is emphasised; yet while man is free both to do well or ill, for sin the door is just left open, for righteousness there is *aid*. Any deeper theological discussion of the difficult questions involved seems to be lacking.

(2) The conception of Repentance is greatly developed, but is still fluid. Sometimes the view is expressed that 'it is never too late to mend'. The power to repent is never lacking to man. Sometimes, though more rarely, the view is taken that if you sin too often, the capacity to repent will be lost. There is the same variety of view about goodness. If you can resist a temptation many times successfully, you may be regarded as immune for ever: or, on the other hand, you are

never safe from the snares of (specially sexual) temptation. 'Alter schützt vor Torheit nicht.'

(3) There is no rigid or worked-out doctrine about Works and Faith. On the whole, the theory of justification by works is strongly pressed. There is a somewhat inadequate appreciation of character. The individual's personality is not well conceived. He is regarded too much as a bundle of deeds. If he has done 720 good deeds and 719 bad ones, he is more righteous than wicked (with due consequences as regards divine punishment and reward); if he has done 720 bad deeds and 719 good ones, he is more wicked than righteous. An unsatisfactory way of looking at human character.[1]

(4) Reward and punishment. Here, while the doctrine of life after death, whether immediately in heaven or in hell, or after the resurrection, greatly relieved biblical difficulties, there was, on the whole, a persistency of biblical conceptions, and in many ways a hardening and systematisation. Here we have, surely for good, moved away from the Rabbis. They seem to be constantly thinking about rewards and punishments, whether in this life or in another. And they do not hesitate to develop the ugly doctrine that such and such punishments are directly sent by God as the punishments of such and such sins.[2] One shocking example, as I have already said, of this doctrine is still allowed to deface the Orthodox Jewish Prayer Book. The Rabbis do not hesitate to say that Tit-for-Tat or Measure for Measure is the greatest of the principles which underlie or govern the divine rule; it is a principle which will never pass away. There are many other illustrations which could be given of the extraordinary emphasis laid by the Rabbis upon punishment and reward, as for example, the constantly repeated remark (in which they seem as far from us moderns as it is possible for men of the same religion to be) that the righteous are punished on earth for the few and trivial sins which they may commit here, in order that they may be the more fully and uninterruptedly rewarded beyond the grave, while the wicked are rewarded here for their few righteous deeds in order that they may be more uninterruptedly and thoroughly

[1] George Eliot could teach the Rabbis here. 'God sees us as we are altogether, not in separate feelings or actions, as our fellow-men see us.' (*Scenes of Clerical Life: Mr Gilfil's Love-Story*, Chapter XIX.)

[2] It is almost inconceivable that any learned men should have spoken and taught such absurdities as are, for example, found in *Aboth* v, 11 (*P.B.* p. 200) or in *Sab.* 32*a*, *b* and 33*a*, *b*. One wonders: how far can all this nonsense have been seriously meant? (Cp. (14), p. ciii.)

punished after their death. Yet it is pleasant to notice that, with hardly a perception of the inconsistency, contrary teachings are also often found. God rewards gratis. He forgives, *not* according to our works. Man has no claim upon God. We must love God purely. Above all, the Law must be fulfilled for its own sake and for the love of God, and *not* for reward. Such sayings are as frequent as the others. So, if the Rabbis go beyond the Hebrew Bible in the *one* direction for evil, they also go far beyond it in the *other* direction for good.

(5) The Rabbis worked out a very strange doctrine concerning Merit (*Zekut*). It is too remote from us to be considered here, and will be little, if at all, illustrated in my anthology. God seems to be always acting, or having to act, upon somebody's, or on something's, merit—the merit of the Patriarchs, of the Messiah, of the Law and so on. This odd conception seems to have wholly passed away from modern Judaism, whether orthodox or liberal.

(6) There was considerable advance (as well as some legalistic retrogression) as regards Prayer. In spite of dull discussions and distinctions as to when you have fulfilled, or not fulfilled, your legal obligations concerning Prayer (both public and private), as to the amount of attention you need legally give to this prayer or to that, and so on, many noble reflections about prayer can be found, and much definite development recorded. Examples of these reflections and of this development will be given (cp. p. 273).

(7) Atonement and forgiveness. Here the advance beyond the Pentateuch, at any rate, is considerable. Doubtless the institution of the Day of Atonement (so enormously altered in Rabbinic times from the purely priestly ceremonial described in Lev. XVI, and yet its lineal descendant) generated a certain amount of evil superstition; yet the Rabbis fought hard against this, and considering the very uncomfortably wide words of Scripture (e.g. Lev. XVI, 30) which yet are perfect and uncriticisable, with very marked success. It was splendid that they could teach: 'For him who thinks he can sin with impunity because the Day of Atonement will bring forgiveness, there will be no forgiveness.' On the other hand, deeper conceptions of forgiveness and atonement are somewhat wanting. To the Rabbis the words mean prevailingly being let off punishment, and no more. But many are the causes which bring atonement, and some are nobler than others. Repentance atones; the Day of Atonement atones, sufferings atone, death atones. Moreover, there is much vicarious atonement. The death of the righteous atones for the sins of the frail. It is

a curious jumble: old and new ideas jostle each other. The anthology will give some examples, but mainly, as an anthology should, of the higher thoughts and conceptions.

(8) In a deeply interesting and admirably clear article in the *Hibbert Journal* (April 1935) Sir Richard Livingstone pointed out that Christianity, on the basis, and as the result, of the teaching of Jesus and of Paul, brought 'a new humanism, a new conception of the supreme human ἀρετή' (excellence) into the world. This new humanism was itself based upon Jewish teaching, upon the highest teaching of the Old Testament. The supreme human excellence or ἀρετή is not reason, as to Aristotle and the Greeks, but love. And this love—this supreme excellence—is 'within the reach of every human being. The philosopher and the artist may achieve it. But so may the illiterate and the unintelligent'.

It is interesting to compare the ideals of Rabbinic Judaism with those of Hellenism, on the one hand, and of Christianity, on the other. Rabbinic Judaism seems to occupy a sort of mid-way position between the two. The contrasts which Sir Richard Livingstone makes between Judaism and Hellenism clearly hold good for Rabbinic Judaism also. The 'Hebraic conception of God as a person', the 'unquestionable imperative of a direct Divine Command', the idea of sin, the conviction that the will of this personal God was 'declared and certain', the 'passion for moral reform' and for righteousness *as* the will of God—all these characteristics of 'Hebraism' are unquestionably characteristics of Rabbinic Judaism too. Yet, as we shall see, the study of the Law is man's highest excellence or glory, and though this study of the Law is, in principle, incumbent upon all, yet, practically, it cannot be realized in its fullness except by a minority. The Rabbis do not deliberately say that the reason or mind is man's highest excellence; they have no word for reason or mind; to them the heart is the seat both of intelligence and of goodness. Yet they can fully accept the saying: 'If you have knowledge, what do you lack? If you lack knowledge, what have you got?', though knowledge, while not *excluding* knowledge in an ordinary sense, means for them something very different from what it meant to Aristotle and the Greeks. The highest happiness to Aristotle lies in the activity of the reason or of the mind. The highest happiness to the Rabbis lies in the study of the Law, which is essentially an activity, not of the will, but of the mind. Nevertheless, it would be hardly true to say that, as with Greek conceptions, so with Rabbinic conceptions, 'there are large classes of men who are born incapable' of the highest happiness. For even the humblest ordinary worker in Rabbinic communities understood *something* about the Law: he loved it, even if he had no leisure to know it thoroughly. He practised it to the best of his ability. He enjoyed the practice of it. Sir Richard Livingstone says: 'What meaning can Hellenism have for the ordinary worker in factory or farm? How many inhabitants of our big cities could understand its ideals, or, if they understood, could achieve them?' Therefore on the basis of Greek conceptions, happiness can only be 'the privilege of a small élite, a tiny fraction of mankind'. On Rabbinic lines this reservation would be only partially true. The gulf between the scholar and the ignorant is not so great as with the Greeks. The ignorant is not, or need not be, *quite* ignorant. There are many links which unite him with the scholar, and which unite the scholar with him. The Rabbinic community may be compared with the Athenian democracy at its best, according to the, perhaps, idealised picture of it in Pericles' great funeral speech in Thucydides. Yet there is a measure of exclusiveness in the Rabbinic ideal, which may also be compared with the exclusiveness of the ideal of Greek philosophers.

The quotations which precede and which follow from Sir R. Livingstone's article in the *Hibbert Journal* can now be more conveniently studied in an enlarged form in his remarkable and delightful book, *Greek Ideals and Modern Life* (Oxford, 1935).[1] To those who have been brought up foolishly and ignorantly to think that Greece gave to the world some fine statues and poems, but nothing else, the book should be a revelation. *How* to think, the free play of the intelligence and the reason, the fearless quest for knowledge in every department of life, the very passion to know and understand—all these things we owe to Greece. 'Modern Europe', says Sir R. Livingstone, 'is mainly the creation of Greece. Open the Bible on any page. In how different a world from our own do we find ourselves.'...For 'though in the Bible we find much that is applicable to our own day, we do not find there people with the same mental outlook as our own. In Greece we find people who think as we do...Socrates, Euripides, Plato, Aristotle would have been perfectly at home in a university common-room or at a meeting of the British Association. The outward forms of our civilization would have been strange to them; its atmosphere, its outlook, its spirit would have been largely their own. But to Amos, even to Isaiah or Jeremiah, even to Paul or John, both outward form

[1] Cp. **Note 9a.**

and inward spirit would have been equally unfamiliar. This is not to say that Socrates or Aristotle are greater than Isaiah, or that we have more to learn from them. I am only pointing out that modern civilization is in a line of direct descent from the former and not from the latter, and that the modern world, though something very like it might have existed apart from the influence of Palestine, is unthinkable without Greece.' But this, again, is not all. We can also learn much from Greek ethical teaching, and something too from Greek religious teaching. The moral idealism of Plato, for example, his reasoned justification of goodness for its own sake, and not for its rewards, his doctrine of the superiority of suffering injustice over the infliction of it, of the imitation of God in the pursuit of justice, wisdom and holiness, can take their place with anything in the Hebrew Bible for noble sublimity and truth. They may even be said to fit in with, and supplement, Rabbinic teaching at its highest and best.

In comparing the Greeks with the Rabbis we may note a certain convergence. The world of the Rabbis was in some ways nearer to the Greeks than was the world of Amos or Isaiah. The Rabbis were hindered in their mental, and to some extent in their moral, advance by the burden of the infallibility of Scripture, and by the narrow environment and the limited intellectual fare upon which their brains were nourished. In some ways the Bible kept them back, and made their thought, too often, rather childish and feeble. They were like squirrels in a cage: they had nothing but one book upon which to exercise their wits. Yet not for nothing, but to some effectiveness, were they the heirs of the Sages as well as of the Prophets, the Psalmists and the Law. They had it in them to become quickly the disciples of reason. One feels that, given a little training, they might soon have become 'at home in a university common-room'. And though in those Hellenic moral and religious supplements to the Hebrew Bible, to which I have alluded, the priority in time belongs to the Greeks, yet it is interesting to find that a good deal of the Rabbis' higher teaching (in its own form and fashion) is congruent with the teaching of the Greeks. Moreover, though they did not realise the implications of the quest for knowledge, they had a reverence, and a sort of unfulfilled yearning, for it. Even though to them knowledge meant little more than Torah, yet the reverence and the yearning were real.

(9) 'In making love the supreme ἀρετή (excellence) of man', says Sir Richard Livingstone, 'Christianity substitutes a democratic spiritual ideal' for one which is aristocratic. 'Thereby it both en-

riched the many whom Hellenism had left in the cold, and enriched and completed the life which Hellenism had given to the few.' For 'while' (like the Rabbis) 'indifferent to the aristocracy of birth, Plato and Aristotle accept the aristocracy of natural endowment, and hold that men rank according to their capacity to lead the life of the reason'. The Rabbis would hold that, speaking generally, men rank according to their capacity to understand, and fruitfully to study and teach, the Divine Law.

There is something to be said for the Rabbis, just as Christianity is incomplete without an Aquinas, on the one hand, and a St Francis, on the other. We want both wisdom *and* righteousness, both reason *and* love. It is this intellectual element in Judaism which enabled the Jews to go through unheard-of degradations and persecutions, and yet never to succumb, never to fall to the level of the gipsy, never to suffer degradation in the soul. And though the Rabbis asserted so loudly that the study of the Law outweighed in merit and value all the other commandments, they were constantly denying the truth of their assertion. The humblest martyr in the cause of the Divine Unity would occupy a higher 'compartment' in the economy of the Blest in heaven than the greatest of the Scholars. R. Akiba declared (and he is quoted repeatedly) that 'Thou shalt love thy neighbour as thyself' was the greatest principle of the Torah, and his view was contested by one Rabbi only, who gave a yet higher place to the simple words, 'These are the generations of Adam,' because they implied or taught the unity of the human race. The indication of a dream sufficed for the belief that an ignorant ass driver who had performed one special deed of love was more fitted to pray for rain in a time of drought than all the Rabbis of the land. Thus, in the last resort, we may say that while the study of the Law was to the Rabbis both the highest human excellence and the highest human happiness, and that, therefore, this excellence and this happiness were within the compass only of a few, yet the range of the 'few' was elastic, and the ideal of Moses, 'would to God that all the Lord's people were prophets', was the ideal of the Rabbis also. And we may also say that goodness, the doing of loving deeds, was not only the duty of all, learned and unlearned alike, but that in the eyes of God (so the Rabbis held) this doing of loving deeds was the highest fulfilment of the Law and scarcely less precious than its study.

Sir Richard Livingstone points out another difference between, not all the Greek teachers but, at any rate, between Aristotle and the

Christian ideal. Aristotle held that the fullest and best life needed a certain duration, and also a certain amount of what he called 'external goods' as well. There are 'some things', he says, in his rather popular vein, 'such as good birth, good looks, and good children, the lack of which takes the lustre from happiness'. Again, some noble deeds can only be done 'through the instrumentality of friends or wealth or potential power'. Thus, as Sir Richard remarks, few persons, according to this view, can be 'fully happy'. 'Ill health, early death, childlessness, unsatisfactory children, low birth, poverty, or any one of them, debar men, not only from being happy in our sense of the word, but from achieving that good which is the aim of life. The earthly paradise is reserved for the fortunate and the well to do.' The Rabbis stand mid-way between the Stoics, who conceived that human good, and, therefore, human happiness, are independent of the external, and the teaching of Aristotle. And they also stand mid-way between those who, by placing all true happiness beyond the grave, deny the value, or even the existence, of any earthly joys. To the Rabbis all the external goods of Aristotle and all his external ills are very real. The one are, indeed, good and delectable: their opposites are, indeed, bad and painful. And yet the truest joys of all, and for many the only joys, are the joys of the world to come. Even from the point of view of sheer happiness, it may be incomparably better to accept every earthly ill than to receive every earthly external good at the risk of being deprived of the eternal felicities beyond the grave (cp. [1511]).

Sir Richard Livingstone points out that Christianity taught 'a new view of the problem of suffering'. For it maintained that 'the highest life ever lived on earth was one of which suffering was an outstanding mark'. Sir Richard thinks that this 'new view' was largely due 'to its conception of a suffering God'. Christianity has 'utilised and transformed suffering and pain'; 'it has made suffering appear as part of the texture of life, and not merely as a destructive and purposeless rent in its fabric.' I think this is true. Rabbinic Judaism (as all subsequent Judaism) denied, in its fullness, the doctrine of 'a suffering God'. Perhaps this denial may be the reason why Rabbinic Judaism has little to say upon the subject of suffering which supplements, or enlarges, or goes beyond, the best teaching of the Old Testament. The Rabbis went willingly to martyrdom, and they extolled it. But the perception of a certain splendour in suffering, or in the endurance of suffering, which most of us now would acknowledge, is wanting in them. Not the glorification of suffering, which is a false emphasis, but a certain glory belonging to it: we may, I think, fitly believe in this, and it may be truthfully ascribed to the teaching and influence of Christianity. The Rabbis have much to their credit. We need not want to ascribe to them more than truth allows. In religions, as in human characters, the words hold: *suum cuique*, to each its own; its own excellences and qualities. The Rabbis were still far too prone to suppose that every suffering (and bodily suffering not least) betokened some previous sin. The purifying and testing property of suffering is constantly referred to. God tries the righteous very specially, for they can endure it. But for anything like the manful protests of the genuine Job, or for any approval of them, we may look in vain. The attitude of the Rabbis seems often to be more in harmony with the attitude of the friends than with that of Job.

There is some truth in a remark made by a writer in the *Guardian* (11 January 1935) in a review of *In Spirit and in Truth: Aspects of Judaism and Christianity*. He says: 'For Christianity the problems of evil, of sin, of atonement, are not only moral, but also metaphysical, problems. They are metaphysical because they imply an apparent conflict in the ultimate constitution of things in which man is involved, and yet to the solution of which he is unequal. The mind of the individual Jew is aware of the metaphysical character of these problems, but for his faith, they are not problems at all. They are simply facts to which God is always equal, to which man is also equal in virtue of his simple unquestioning trust in God.'

I suppose that the contrast is due to this: Christianity came in contact with Greek philosophy, and so acquired this acute perception of the metaphysical nature of the problems. For its greatest teachers, the religion became fused with philosophy at an early stage. The Rabbis, for good or for evil, knew no philosophy. Whether the religion of the historic Jesus was not, however, in this respect, more akin to Judaism than to Christianity could, perhaps, be argued.

(10) There may be said to be a fusion in the Rabbis—not perhaps wholly harmonious—of what might be roughly called the religious points of view of the Pentateuchal Codes, of the Prophets, of the Psalms, and of the Proverbs. As to the first, it is obvious enough. The religion of the Rabbis is emphatically a 'legal' religion. The Law comes first. But the Prophets did not form part of their Bible for nothing. To them too, as to the Prophets, Justice and Compassion and Lovingkindness are the three great moral virtues, and in all the relations of man with his fellow-man these take the front place. Nor

did the ideals of the Prophets concerning the Golden Age, or the ideals of Deutero-Isaiah concerning the 'Mission of Israel', have no part in the make-up of the Rabbinic religion. The universalism of the Great Unknown is often ignored, but it is never entirely forgotten. He had not spoken wholly in vain. Right through the Rabbinic period, and beyond it to our own day, there are echoes of his teaching. Then, thirdly, the Psalms. The individualistic piety of the Psalmists, their passion for God, their yearning to get, and to be brought, near to Him, can all be found again, set, as it were, to a different tune, or expressed in different words, among the Rabbis. Lastly, the Proverbs. The practical, homely wisdom of the Sages, their sometimes utilitarian counsels, their (as we now say) rather bourgeois morality, have also their counterparts among the Rabbis (cp. p. 683). The total result of all these influences strikes us sometimes as strange. Here were men who had undoubtedly a tremendous love for God and for His Law: a complete readiness to sacrifice for God and His Law, if need be, their very lives. Yet, withal, these men were by no means anxious for martyrdom. On the contrary. They wished to avoid it wherever or whenever they legitimately could. They desired, if at all possible, to live their lives in peace and quiet, studying the Law, practising, as judges, the most scrupulous justice, and showing in the intervals of study, and as leaders of the Jewish Communities in Babylonia or Palestine, charity, kindness, and consideration to those around them. Their ethical teaching has very rarely a tone of paradox or excitement. It can infrequently be called heroic. It does not often glow. But it is penetrating; it is delicate; it is very practical; it is detailed; it seeks to cover the ordinary conditions of life, and to make these conditions decent, just, kindly, honourable; it exalts pity, and urges charity and almsgiving, but its ideal, above all, is justice—a life, or a condition of life, in which, because of justice and fair dealing, there should be as much decent comfort and quiet independence and honest industry and study of the Law as possible. Yes, there would be an incredibly happier and lovelier life in the world to come or in the day of the Resurrection of the Dead, but, meanwhile, there was the life on earth, and *this* life, too, had its value and its happiness, its justified blessings and enjoyments, which could be hallowed and sanctified by religion. If the ethics of the Rabbis strike us, now and again, as a little sober and mundane and unexciting, it is partly due to this very feature that their teaching was so thorough, that it sought so earnestly to cover with a network of morality all the circumstances and details of life, and that it was, on the whole, so very fairly successful in covering them. I seem always to come back to an old thesis of mine: namely, that we are richer for possessing both the ethical teaching of the Rabbis and the lofty enthusiasm and paradoxes of the Sermon on the Mount.

(11) As the Rabbis, for reasons already given, fell below the *highest* prophetic teaching about sacrifices and outward ceremonials, so they fell below Deutero-Isaiah's *highest* teaching about the Mission of Israel. They could not, to any large extent, develop the noble conception of the suffering Servant, or the conception that the reason of Israel's election was the conversion of the heathen world to the worship and the knowledge of the true God. On the whole, they did not belong to that section of the Jews who sought actively to disseminate Judaism among the nations. Nevertheless (true to the saying that you can find all possible teachings in the vast Rabbinic literature, even if of some teachings it be but a single example), there are some reachings out towards the larger view that Israel was chosen for service and not for privilege. 'The whole purpose of Israel's dispersion', it is suddenly said, 'was the making of proselytes.' We have to remember that most of the extant Rabbinic literature, huge as it is, comes from periods when to engage in active proselytisation and propaganda was difficult and even dangerous. Yet there are some beautiful and pathetic things said about proselytes, even as (as the result probably of harsh experience) there are also some disagreeable things. And the first category is larger than the second. It is not the case that the Rabbis took the common modern view about proselytes and propaganda. The modern Jew, in a superior sort of way (historically, easily understood), declares that Judaism, unlike Christianity, need not seek to convert non-Jews to Judaism, because Judaism teaches justification by works, and not by belief. Whatever your religious belief, live a good life, and live up to the dictates of your conscience, and you will have every bit as good a time after death as the most orthodox Jew. That was hardly the Rabbinic attitude, for they *did* regard idolatry as sin, and as most Gentiles were idolaters, they would, as I have said, for the most part, according to Rabbinic belief, either be annihilated (at death or at the Resurrection), or would be sent to hell, from which they would either never emerge, or emerge only for final destruction. It is true, and it deserves emphasis, that one distinguished Rabbi called Joshua, in opposition to another distinguished Rabbi called Eliëzer, maintained that the righteous of all nations

would have a share in the blessed world to come. A noble teaching and of the utmost importance, for this teaching of a single Rabbi became in time the accepted doctrine of orthodox Judaism, and has remained so to the present day. But, so far as R. Joshua is concerned, the unfortunate thing is that we have no explanation as to what he meant by 'righteous'. Did he mean a man who, while honest, sober, chaste, charitable and just, was yet a thoroughgoing idolater, or did he mean by righteous a man, who, in addition to his *moral* virtues, was also a monotheist, and *not* a worshipper of idols? I am inclined to believe that he meant the second and not the first. In that case, the number of those who would be admitted to the felicities of the world to come would clearly be much smaller than if R. Joshua had meant that righteous *idolaters* would also enjoy them. Just as to the orthodox Christian the collocation 'righteous unbeliever', 'righteous heretic', 'righteous Jew', was hard to credit, so to the Rabbi the collocation of righteousness with idolatry. But it is the glory of orthodox Judaism to have advanced to the larger hope and the larger doctrine at a comparatively early date, and certainly well before orthodox Christianity attained to them. For I think I am correct in stating that the famous saying: 'The righteous of all nations shall have a share in the world to come' was even by medieval Judaism interpreted to mean and to include the doctrine that the righteous of all *religions* shall have a share in the world to come.

(12) One real trouble in talking about the Rabbis and their religion will always be to gauge correctly the measure of their seriousness in each particular case. One reads a book such as Dietrich's *Die Umkehr*, and one is impressed by its truly German thoroughness. (One is also impressed by its fairness, very seldom impaired. Considering its date, this fairness is both striking and pleasant.) But one wonders: how far are all these divisions and subdivisions of the subject, these distinctions and elaborations, really justified by the sources themselves? How often are poor butterflies broken upon wheels? If only one could—how interesting it would be—like another Witch of Endor, call up a couple of these old gentlemen and cross-examine them. 'Listen, Rabbi Ḥanina or Rabbi Johanan: You said, So and so.' 'Oh, did I? If you say so, doubtless I did.' 'Well then, may I infer that this was your fixed and settled opinion, and that you would certainly not have agreed with R. Pineḥas and R. Ḥama who said something different?' Poor Rabbi Ḥanina and Rabbi Johanan! Would they not reply, 'I see nothing very much wrong with what those other

Rabbis said.' 'But, my dear Sir, don't you see that your opinion is really inconsistent with theirs? And do you not remember that you actually argued *against* Rabbi *X* when he said something very like what R. Pineḥas and R. Ḥama said?' 'Oh, did I? I had forgotten. It was so long ago. And, as you know, we Rabbis in those days loved to argue with one another. We liked to use the words of Holy Scripture to prove our various assertions, as they chanced to crop up in our minds. If one of us said *A*, the other loved to say *B*. It was such *fun*. We had not so many outlets for fun in those days. But you must not take our different and differing sayings so seriously. We never thought of them like that. They were just the outcome of the moment, and we did so enjoy the arguing.' 'I am glad to learn that you had enjoyment and fun. Do you continue this fun in the heavenly places? A poet, long after your time, spoke of mirth in heaven.' 'Our heavenly fun you could not understand while you are on earth, but pray do not pin us too sharply down to the sayings of the moment—in Haggadah—you know. Halachah is a different matter.' So we may imagine the old Rabbis telling us. On the other hand, they *had* beliefs which were deep and rigid. They *had* convictions for which they were ready to die. It needs tact and insight, and perhaps also a certain sense of humour, to know when we must take their sayings very literally, and when we must take them with a grain of salt; when we must regard them as only half-serious exaggerations, not meant to be looked upon as permanent expressions of faith. Sometimes these sayings are the obvious exaggerations of a preacher who wants to stress one particular side or aspect of a complex truth. Sometimes they are just intended to keep the ball of debate rolling between Rabbi and Rabbi. They are never without *some* intention; they are never *wholly* disbelieved at the moment of their utterance, but they are not deliberate convictions from which grave consequences may be legitimately deduced, or which, in the minds of the speakers, excluded other opinions and other consequences which may *seem* to be, and which logically really *are*, at variance with them. I trust that this anthology may perhaps enable the reader to distinguish between the fundamental convictions of the Rabbis and those more lightly held and casually expressed opinions and exaggerations.

(13) The most obvious difference between the religion of the Rabbis and the religion, or rather the religions, of the Hebrew Bible, consists in the doctrine of the world to come. For what is alluded to in a single passage in Daniel, and in a single passage in Isaiah, had now become

an accepted dogma, a doctrine of every day. There would be a resurrection and a judgment. Bliss everlasting for some, and punishment or annihilation for others. There would also be a purgatory, that is to say, some would have to endure Gehenna for a season, and would then be purified and admitted to bliss. Again, what is conceivably alluded to in two or three Psalms is also a commonplace, even though it largely contradicts the other doctrine about the Resurrection. According to this teaching, when men die they go straightway to Bliss or to Pain, to Paradise or to Gehenna (whether Purgatory or Hell). The effect of these doctrines, which were regarded by the Rabbis as unquestioned and unquestionable, was naturally gigantic. The strange thing is that if these beliefs separate the Rabbis from the Hebrew Scriptures, they also separate them, though to a less extent, from ourselves. We may profitably compare what Dr Coulton says about the difference between modern Christian views on these subjects and those of the medieval Church. The difference between us and the Rabbis is not by any means so great, but it is yet on the same lines and very considerable. He says: 'We may safely affirm that the standard medieval ideas of heaven and hell differed more from those of even the most medievally-minded modern theologians, than present-day ideas on that subject differ between any two modern Churches, however far apart they may stand. The present Pope and the Moderator of the Scottish Church—I say this with all personal respect to both—probably differ far less from each other on this point, than both differ from St Gregory the Great or any of the most saintly medieval Popes. This fact seldom receives its full emphasis, and the reminder is especially necessary here. It was a commonplace of medieval theology, and indeed of almost all theology until comparatively recent times, that the last moment of a man's life decided for him between an eternity of unimaginable bliss (with or without preliminary purgatorial suffering) and an eternity of unspeakable horror and torment. This was accepted as an axiom so indisputable that St Gregory the Great, and, after him, almost all the schoolmen, do not attempt to re-consider it even when it is found to lead them by inexorable logic to the conclusion that the Blessed in heaven will find their bliss heightened by the contemplation of the sufferings of the Damned in hell; only indirectly, of course; only as a proof of God's justice and as a reminder of His mercy to themselves—but still, the fatal nexus is there; the full horrors of hell down below will be visible to the Blessed above, and will, for them, sensibly increase the bliss of heaven. Calvin has been mistakenly saddled with beliefs some of which he never held at all, while others are common to him and his medieval predecessors. Concerning this particular medieval tenet there can be no doubt; therefore nobody can realize those times without bearing it constantly in mind. Not only was it held that these unutterably solemn issues depended upon a man's last breath upon earth, but also that the main deciding factor was theological. Nothing, at that supreme moment, would contribute so directly to the upward or the downward turn of the balance as a man's dying faith and his fortification by the rites of the Church. It was a natural complement to this, that even the most moderate and cautious of medieval theologians—even St Thomas Aquinas, for instance—took it for granted that many more men would be damned than saved.' (*Scottish Abbeys and Social Life*, p. 5, cp. the whole passage up to p. 10.) And again he says (and as always he has much chapter and verse to justify his statements): 'It was a commonplace that the majority of the human race went to hell. This is accepted even by St Thomas Aquinas, who among all medieval philosophers is specially remarkable for his balance of judgment; other writers often reckon the saved as only one in a thousand, or in ten thousand, or in more. Unbaptized children, and pagans, however virtuous, must go to hell; Dante's two exceptions prove the rule; as for the rest (although he forsakes Augustine and follows Aquinas in rejecting the idea of bodily torture) the air is thick with their sighs and groans. All orthodox medieval thought rested upon the assumption that the last moment of life marked the man for an eternity of unspeakable bliss or of torment beyond all conception. And, as this was decided by the dying man's state at that last moment, so the decisive factor in this state was his theological belief.' (In Hammerton's *Universal History of the World*, vol. v, Chapter 117, p. 3014.) (Cp. [583] and **Note 15**.)

It would be unfair to the Rabbis to equate exactly *their* beliefs with these miserable beliefs of the medieval Church. So far as Israel was concerned, they were far happier. The main dogma was that *all* Israelites, except grave heretics, apostates, informers, or high-handed and unrepentant sinners, would have a share in the world to come. In spite of one often-quoted story, it is doubtful whether the vast majority of the Rabbis, or of the Jews whom they taught, had any great fear about what would happen to them after death. They rested with confidence upon the goodness, the lovingkindness, and the compassion of God. The effect of the perfervid belief in the life after death was felt in other directions. It fortified in days of trial. It stiffened endurance of persecution. It enabled hundreds to undergo martyrdom. It constituted a powerful motive for the avoidance of sin. It explained away all difficulties in the otherwise unequal distribution of prosperity and adversity. It prevented scepticism. And it stimulated, while it purified, the hope of reward, and while fear of the hereafter was far less usual among the Rabbis than among the men of medieval Christianity, yet God *was* just as well as merciful; a *judge*, as well as a dispenser of forgiveness. We, too, believe in a life to come. But it is, to most of us, a wistful hope, the needful corollary to our belief in God. We are not greatly moved by any conceptions or anticipations of reward or of punishment. They have become unreal to us. The ideas of a final judgment or of a resurrection have passed away. So, too, with the conception of a great catastrophe, a divine intervention, of a Messiah, and of a prolonged Messianic age upon earth, when the people of Israel would be triumphant and the position of Top Dog and Under Dog (in relation to themselves and the nations) would be reversed. Perhaps we have dropped the conception of punishment too much, but, by way of compensation, we think far less of reward, and that is surely to the good. With the Rabbis reward is always cropping up, and seems to be constantly before their minds. God Himself is anxious that His beloved Israelite children should enjoy the everlasting felicities of the life to come. The reward, as I have said, is not conceived as in strict accordance with desert. It will be out of proportion to human excellence. But be it retributional or of grace, it is equally longed for. Yet with equal emphasis it is urged that in order to obtain this reward, it should not be the *motive* of human endeavour. To love the Law and to fulfil it for its own sake, to love God because He is truly lovable—this will bring reward far more surely than to try to be good for the sake of getting a reward. What are the rewards of the righteous? I do not think that the large majority of the Rabbis had any clear idea as to the exact nature of these rewards. 'Eye has not seen and ear has not heard,' as they like to say. But they would be exceedingly great, and would make those who received them exceedingly blissful. And the Rabbis liked and wished to be blissful and happy. It is strange that the particular and special feature of the hope for the life to come which is so prominent with all ordinary people today, namely reunion, in some inconceivable way, with those they most loved upon earth, and who have passed on before them, is, so far as I know, never mentioned by the Rabbis. Is the same difference between us and them characteristic of Christian writers between A.D. 30 and A.D. 600?

It is very striking that so few touches of doubt as to the goodness of God are found in the Rabbinic literature. We hear of one or two great heretics; but of any poignant or agonising doubts passing through the minds of the men who compiled, or whose sayings are recorded in, this literature, we hear hardly anything at all. And yet these men were familiar with suffering: they passed through persecutions; they knew about martyrs and martyrdom. It is true that many of the sore problems which weigh upon us were unknown to them. Questions of hereditary tendencies to sin; puzzles about idiots and mental deficients; sore afflictions caused by the wickedness of others; these, and many other troubles, had hardly risen upon their horizon. They were still influenced and helped by the old views of national solidarity. Whatever befell them, or whatever pain or suffering they underwent themselves, or witnessed in others, two explanations sufficed to maintain their faith. Their own sins, or the sins of their forefathers, merited all which had come, or came, upon them. That, on the one hand, and, on the other, the absolute conviction of the felicities of the future, the world beyond the grave, which would compensate, or more than compensate, for any pains or sufferings in this world, which would even be all the greater and more glorious because of, or in proportion to, these sufferings and these pains, enabled them to withstand unflinchingly any amount of tribulation, and prevented the smallest suggestions or whisperings of doubt. The Rabbis would entirely have agreed with Paul when he wrote: 'I reckon that the sufferings of this present time are not worthy to be compared with the glory which shall be revealed to us.'

It is noteworthy that the Rabbis held the balance curiously between this life and the next. It is true that contrasts are sometimes made between the two, as that one is all darkness, and the other all light. Sometimes, too, there is a note of weary sadness. This life is full of persecution and trouble; the next life will be one of felicity and joy. Yet, in the main, we may say that they, as it were, *added* the life to come on to the Old Testament view of *this* world, without rejecting that view as obsolete and superseded. They still thought that long life on earth was an undoubted blessing, and death, though the prelude to that other life of bliss, was still, somehow, an evil. They did not abandon this world or cheapen it. Even in *this* world the Law could be studied and fulfilled, and such study and practice gave pleasure indescribable and peculiar. But, in addition, the Rabbis were not impervious to other clean and healthy, if mundane, pleasures which God has allowed His creatures to enjoy. They could thank Him for the beauties of nature: they could enjoy a good dinner. They definitely taught that the pleasures of this world must not and should not be despised: so long as they are enjoyed in moderation, sanctified by religion, by gratitude to God, and, above all, not allowed to interfere with the study and fulfilment of the Law, it is wrong to pass them by. It might be *necessary* to practise some asceticism for the sake of *study*. Then one should do so; but if one can combine the lower with the higher joy without detriment to the full obtainment of the higher, *that* is the best manner of life which is possible for man. The Rabbis were resilient optimists: persecution and trouble never daunted their spirits for long. Doubtless this optimism sprang from some causes which we reject. If all calamity, whether public or private, betokens some sin, whether of the individual or of the community, or if the troubles of the righteous are sent to them in order that they may more fully enjoy unclouded felicity and triumph in the life beyond the grave, the perplexities which harassed Job, and which still harass ourselves, are greatly diminished. The problem of evil is practically solved. The Rabbis were unwavering in their faith and in their conviction of God's justice, God's mercy and God's love.

For the commandment of the *Shema* was attained. These Rabbis *did* intensely love God. And they reverenced Him. Did they also fear Him? Perhaps they did; for could He not send you, if you rebelled against His revealed will, to hell? (cp. Matt. x, 28). But their love was far greater than their fear. There was some danger, as they themselves felt and said, lest the conviction of God's immense affection for Israel, of His mercy, His forgiveness, and His tenderness, should lead to some loosening of the moral fibre, lest that fear of God, which is the beginning and foundation of religion, should be obliterated by an over-mastering reliance upon His pity and His love. Of these thoughts, too, the anthology may have something to tell us.

(14) In taking leave of the Rabbis I feel how difficult it is to know precisely, or even to feel precisely, how they really thought, and what they really believed, about many religious fundamentals. Fifteen hundred years and more separate us from them. With sympathy, impartiality, detachment, we may achieve something, but the gap may be too great for any bridge to be thrown across between us. After all,

how hard it is to be *sure* that one appreciates or understands properly the religion of any other person than one's own. And even one's own! How many of us could give a clear account of what we mean by God, or what we take to be the nature of the Divine Being? Again, how far was the religion of the fully trained Rabbi different from the religion of the ordinary Jewish labourer, shopkeeper or artisan? Yet it is one, I think, of the distinctive excellences of the Jewish religion that in it the difference between the religion of the believing philosopher and the religion of the ordinary or uneducated man is almost bound to be less than the difference between two such persons in Christianity. This excellence does not by any means prove that Judaism is truer than Christianity. On the contrary, the reverse may be the fact. For the full truth may be more complicated and difficult than the half truth. The Christian doctrine of the Divine Unity which is also a Trinity all would allow to be a more complicated and difficult theory than the Jewish theory of the Unity which is just a Unity. But its complication or difficulty is no valid argument against its truth. Nevertheless, the excellence of which I have spoken remains. Some modern Christian writers do not hesitate to say that the religion of a vast number of uneducated Christians in all ages, including our own, has been little better or other than Tritheism. I fancy that the simpler Jewish doctrine of the Divine Unity was the means, not only of lessening the difference between trained Rabbi and uneducated labourer as regards the conception of God, but also, in some degree, of binding all the generations of Jews more closely to each other. Because of it we, today, just as we are all nearer to one another, may be also nearer to our forefathers than at first thought one might suppose to be the case. The truly magnificent command to make no outward material representation of God may have helped to this end. When the uneducated man in the Rabbinic period heard about God's arm or eyes or throne, these terms were, doubtless, less of a metaphor, or of an accommodation, or of a survival, to him than to the trained Rabbi, but they were *not wholly* real. For he heard also that God was 'everywhere', that He was spirit and not flesh, and that (in spite of the 'arm' and the 'eyes' and the 'throne') he must not think of or figure God to himself in the likeness of man or beast or of anything material. However confused and vague his conceptions of God may have been, he was, nevertheless, ready to die for the doctrine of that Divine Unity which included His immateriality. To-day it is the same. The ordinary uneducated Jew could not tell what he means by the divine omnipresence; he, too, uses the old metaphors, but he, too, believes in the Unity and the immateriality. The trained Rabbi of the fourth century A.D. and the trained Rabbi of to-day may, perhaps, have been, and may perhaps be, able to tell us a *little*—to give us a slightly more rational *account*—of what they mean by omnipresence and Unity and immateriality, but, perhaps, for them, too, as for their uneducated brothers and sisters, these terms express rather the negation of their opposites than positive and clear-cut conceptions, well expressible in words, which all who read can understand. If this be so, the Jews of old, and the Jews of today, both educated and uneducated, are, perhaps, more truly linked together by a common bond of belief than may possibly be the case in any other historic religion. At least as regards the Divine Unity and the conception of God, educated and uneducated can feel in prayer very close to each other, and, to some extent, the walls of separation between the ages may melt away.

I have a hope that my Anthology, in addition to providing some interesting and curious reading for students and others, may also help a little towards the dispelling of certain old prejudices and prepossessions in Christian minds which still linger here and there, even in England. The Rabbis are an inconvenient lot of people, because their views and beliefs are such an odd mixture. Their religion is inconvenient, because (if you care to examine it at first-hand) it will not readily fit into a nice system: you cannot classify it comfortably; the results which ought to follow from your label are, as a matter of fact, seldom to be found. It is all uncomfortably different. I hope that the Anthology may show something of this inconvenience. For the old comfortable classifications are still occasionally met with today. We are still, sometimes, presented with the contrasted labels of religions of Law and religions of Redemption. And if you happen to belong to a religion of redemption, you can easily show how very superior it is to a religion of law. A favourite logical and necessary result of a religion of law is that God becomes 'far' from those, or to those, who are the adherents of such a religion. So the God of legal Judaism must logically have ever been far from every Rabbi, or, indeed, from every Jew. But, alas, for the facts. 'God is near with every kind of nearness', said the ancient Rabbi, and he probably knew more about the character of his own religion than divines of another faith, writing some sixteen hundred years after his death. In the religion of Law, God obviously has to reward or punish according as man fulfils or violates the Commands of an external

Code. A promised heaven of happiness, a threatened hell of torment are what prompts to obedience, or what keeps back from transgression. The religions of redemption, on the other hand, give inward peace and inward joy. Man is 'redeemed from himself'. But is it not a *little* odd that throughout the nineteen centuries of the life of the greatest of the religions of redemption, hell has been much more a reality and a terror to *its* adherents than to those of the religion of Law? A deep craving for God is not the prerogative of any one type of religion. God and His Torah were a very present help in time of trouble to Jewish Rabbis as well as to Christian Church Fathers. The Rabbis 'found' God no less often or less vividly than the Fathers. Amid persecution and sorrow their religion was to them a source of power and of gladness. Logically, perhaps, it ought not to have been so. Logically, as a religion of law, it ought not to have produced consequences strictly reserved for a religion of redemption. But life is inconveniently inconsequent, and recks little of our categories, or classifications or prejudices. As that truly gracious and open-minded Christian scholar, Crawford Toy in his *Judaism and Christianity*, p. 186, said as long ago as 1890, 'in point of fact the result was different'. The intensely legal religion of the Rabbis produced results which ought to be peculiar to the religions of redemption. It poached on the preserves of others. Such are the vagaries of the religions. Such is actual life as distinct from theory.

There is much more that one might be tempted to say in an introduction. But it is, perhaps, better to make an end, and not to linger overlong 'around the memory of a world which has passed away'.[1]

[1] The *Dialogues* of Plato: translated into English with analyses and introduction by B. Jowett, 3rd ed., 1893, vol. V, p. CCXXXVIII.

INTRODUCTION

by H. Loewe

Two introductions to one book may seem odd and needless. But my colleague has indicated the reasons for this course. Our Anthology is not a mere collection of extracts, without criticisms and comments. Mr Montefiore's criticisms and comments are written from a Liberal Jewish point of view. Now it so happens that we two, who have worked for nearly six years very happily together in the compilation of this Anthology, belong to different schools of Jewish thought. This being so, Mr Montefiore has thought that it might be interesting to the reader (more especially to the Christian reader) if I, from a somewhat different angle, were to add my own comments and criticisms to his. It would also, perhaps—so he says, though of this I am by no means certain—be fairer to the Rabbis, the men who spoke and wrote the passages of which our book is composed. Mr Montefiore is a Liberal Jew. I am an Orthodox Jew, but I am not a fundamentalist.

It might seem strange for a Roman Catholic to join forces with a Plymouth Brother in order to compile a critical anthology of Christian doctrine and thought. Their task would be deemed impossible: shall two walk together save they be agreed? Would not the book be composed either of platitudes or of conflicts? Could a unity emerge? Such fears are, I fancy, superficial. The collaborators would undoubtedly differ about certain obvious and important subjects, but upon many more, no less obvious and no less important, they would agree, and it is mainly upon their points of agreement that their book would be based. The one might hold and the other reject Papal Infallibility: to both, the resurrection of Jesus would be a vital and basic fact. And an anthology of Christian thought would be more concerned with primitive fundamentals than with modern practice or ecclesiastical pronouncements.

That this proposition is true I am in a position to prove by quoting a quite recent experiment. Great as may be the gulf between Roman Catholic and Plymouth Brother, it is surely narrower than that which separates the Jew from the Christian. Two volumes of essays on Judaism and Christianity have just been published by the Sheldon

Press,[1] written by a body of writers drawn from the two faiths. It is a noteworthy fact that, with one exception, the reviewers of these essays have drawn attention to two characteristics. On the one hand they agree that each book breaks new ground, that it deals with vital questions and does not merely confine itself to the obvious: the outstanding points of difference are frankly recognised and no attempt is made to underestimate them or to represent them as trivial. Secondly, the reviewers of each book draw attention to the unity of spirit that underlies it, to the fidelity of the various authors to their respective faiths and to their appreciation of the faith to which they do not belong. Only one critic, writing with sympathy and with insight, has declared that the writers failed because their task was impossible; in other words, that it is impossible to deal with origins unless developments are also considered, or, to put it bluntly, only an insider can be objective. In this view, so far at least, the reviewer stands alone. If, now, we may argue as the Rabbis did, *a fortiori* (*Ḳal wa-Ḥomer*), may we not say that if Jews and Christians can combine to produce a book on the common elements in their respective religions, how much more possible is it for a Liberal Jew and an Orthodox Jew to write about the Rabbinic religion which is, in varying degree, the basis of their spiritual lives? It will not be a case of sinking individualities or of permanent discord. There will be occasional reservations by one or the other. But the bulk of the material will be common property.

That there is homogeneity in this book will be obvious to the reader. If I draw attention to this circumstance and to the fact that each contributor has preserved an independent outlook, it is for a particular reason, and for a reason which concerns me rather than Mr Montefiore. For his independence is unchallenged: mine may be challenged. If my views were merely personal to me, this would matter little. But a bigger issue is concerned. I have already stated that I am not a fundamentalist. Now in England, as contrasted with Germany and America, many Orthodox Jews are either completely unfamiliar with modern biblical exegesis or partially familiar and actively opposed to it. But the combination of Orthodoxy with intellectualism is growing. One now reads of 'Maccabaean Psalms' in books of which the authors are unimpeachably orthodox. More

[1] *Judaism and Christianity*: vol. I, *The Age of Transition*, ed. by W. O. E. Oesterley; vol. II, *The Contact of Pharisaism with other Cultures*, ed. by H. Loewe, London, 1937.

and more Jews are finding that their religious beliefs and orthodox practices are strengthened by the new learning. No longer can it be said that intellectualism is the monopoly of the Liberals. The water-tight era is passing. I am by no means a voice crying in the wilderness. Moreover, I cannot—nor do I desire to—take refuge in privacy or in anonymity. As the holder of an academic position, my words possess a certain authority that they would not otherwise deserve. Now my Readership is free from all dogmatic tests. It might be held by anybody. But in all University posts there must be congruence between the official and the personal views of the teacher in regard to the subject which he teaches. Thus, while there is no reason why the Professor of Botany should not be a Buddhist, the Professor of Physics could hardly become an ardent member of the 'Flat Earth' Society and yet, in his University lectures, teach that the earth is round. Now Rabbinics can be taught as objectively as can botany or physics, and I trust that I am just as true to my charge and just as free from partisan bias as a Christian holder of the Readership would be. Rabbinics, like Hellenism or Islam, can be expounded and understood without being followed in practice. The teacher is not in the position of a pleader: it is his business to state facts only. If he chooses to mould his life on the lives and principles of those about whom he lectures, he is certainly free to do so. But he is not bound to do so. His private life is his own and he is not forced to make any choice at all, he can do as he likes. There are, however, very definitely two things which he must not do, at any cost, if he has chosen to follow in his private life the principles which he describes in the lecture-room. First, he must see to it that his private life does not intrude: his lectures must remain objective: he must not become an advocate: he must not over-emphasise the views which he holds or omit those which he dislikes. Secondly, he must be consistent; he must be bound to the choice that he has once made.

If he says that he is a Liberal in private life, he cannot very well decry Liberalism in his lectures. Such inconsistency would be as gross a breach of trust as though he were to wrest evidence to support Liberal Judaism in his lectures. Since, therefore, I profess, in my private life, to be an Orthodox Jew, it would be unseemly if I wrote and taught things incompatible with Orthodoxy in public. This would offend all students. Above all it might injure my Jewish students. Christian students of theology can turn to their spiritual advisers. I have always endeavoured to be of help to Jewish undergraduates who may find a divergence between their Orthodox faith, in which they have been reared, and the new learning which the University offers them. I have endeavoured to show them that this apparent divergence can be eliminated by further study and by sincerity of thought. The famous words of Erasmus, that he who declares knowledge to be heresy, makes orthodoxy synonymous with ignorance, represent the primitive Jewish view: the Rabbis, much earlier, declared that the combination of Torah with *Derek Ereẓ* was a 'fine thing' and destructive of sin. And so I hope that what I have to say will be a help to the undergraduate who may feel that his beliefs have been shaken by the criticism of his supervisors. He comes up in the October term in time for the first Sabbath of the Jewish year, when the lesson is read from the beginning of Genesis. And on the following Monday he enters his laboratory or lecture room and is taught evolution, geology, and a heliocentric explanation of the universe. He finds in philosophy, anthropology, comparative religion or in biblical studies, views which may, at first, seem to him antithetical to those which he has heard in Synagogue. But when he is brought to realise that all truth is from God and that its parts must be congruent, the knowledge will help him in his efforts to reconcile apparent contradictions. Hence I feel it necessary to reiterate my unswerving loyalty to traditional Jewish life and practice, and to the teachings of Judaism as they have developed and as they are developing. So I feel it incumbent on me to write this Introduction and to attempt to show how Orthodox and Liberal may co-operate, without one of them absorbing the other. Having done so, by sketching the ground which they have in common, it will be necessary to deal in greater detail with those points on which the two attitudes differ. Mr Montefiore, when he suggested this Introduction, said, 'I may often have misconceived the religion of the Rabbis and have given expression to opinions from which you dissent and which you think unfair, erroneous and misleading.' These words are exaggerated. Mr Montefiore has never misconceived the religion of the Rabbis and he has never been unfair. That there may be two views on certain topics is quite a different thing. But judgment is surely subjective. It will be necessary for me to record certain differences, but the extent and significance of these differences must not be overrated. And a positive exposition—which I shall endeavour to give—will, I believe, be more useful to everybody than an enumeration of points of variance, though these will not be neglected: they will follow the positive exposition and be subordinated to it.

To my mind, a not inconsiderable part of the problem is the product of mistaken terminology. Labels are a great convenience: they prevent luggage from going astray. But labels and luggage are not synonymous: if the luggage gets lost and the labels, *sans* luggage, are delivered, the passenger is not unreasonably discontented. Labels, therefore, are admittedly of the highest importance, but the sphere of their importance is strictly circumscribed. The point that I wish to make is that 'labels' are not religion and must not be mistaken for religion. The Hebrew equivalent for 'labels' is *Havdalah*,[1] discrimination, distinction. For the grace of this critical faculty we pray, during the week, three times daily; the very first petition in the *Amidah* is for discrimination. We ask for this gift before we ask pardon for our sins. The order of the paragraphs (cp. *P.B.* p. 46) is deliberate and logical. Without the possession of discrimination between good and evil, between right thinking and wrong thinking, we cannot tell whether we have erred or how we have erred. Hence our need for 'labels' is imperative. But it is interesting to note that this need makes itself felt only on weekdays (cp. [502] and [1547]). On Sabbaths and Festivals, when the religious aspects of life are more obvious, the petition is omitted. Instead, a special *Havdalah* prayer (cp. *P.B.* p. 216 and p. CLXXXII), accompanied by striking ceremonial, such as the kindling of light, is introduced at the termination of Sabbath, to mark its passing and to usher in the working days. Then we thank God for creating the warmth and light of fire: then, when we are about to be engrossed in our worldly occupations, we need illumination and discrimination, for we have to distinguish between light and darkness, between Judaism and assimilation. And this distinction is specifically correlated in the *Havdalah* formula, to the distinction between Sabbath and weekdays. For on Sabbaths and Festivals our days are wholly surrounded by a religious environment, our lives are totally devoted to worship and study: then we are not called upon to exercise discrimination, for during that time we are particularly at one with God, in Whose light we see light. And when we are so united, then the prayers of individuals, which differ enormously in their formulation, become merged in those of the environment and form a congregational whole, just as the

[1] The term literally means 'making a distinction', and is based on Gen. I, 4, 'God divided the light from the darkness' and 7, 'God divided the waters'. According to *Ber.* V, 2, *Havdalah* is to be said in the blessing 'Thou favourest man with knowledge' (*P.B.* p. 46). In this petition we pray for 'knowledge, understanding and discernment' as an act of grace from God. It is only thereby that we can acquire the critical faculty.

light of the sun embraces all the lesser rays which it draws towards itself.

The moral of this is plain. Labels, dogmas, practices and the like are of fundamental importance for safeguarding and delimiting the religious life, but with that life they are not coterminous. A Jew is first of all a Jew, *sans phrase*. If, further, he styles himself 'Orthodox' or 'Liberal', he should regard the adjective as referring to that aspect of Judaism which he and his friends desire to emphasise, not as separating him and his friends from other Jews. The adjective is domestic: its purpose is to keep his special duty before his eyes, not to endow him with a mark of superiority. Too often we find some Jews using the terms 'Orthodox' and 'religious' as synonyms, other Jews regarding 'Liberal' and 'sincere', or 'Liberal' and 'intellectual', as interchangeable. Such a practice is analogous to the introduction of the King's name into politics or the abuse of the Union Jack on election posters. The 'label', which should be an incitement to higher ends, thus tends to debase those ends. The 'Brotherhood of Israel' (*Ḥaverim Kol Yisrael* or *Kelal Yisrael*) is degraded to serve party needs: the ideal is shattered by the very instrument that was intended to enhance it. The skeleton is an essential without which the body cannot stand erect, but the life of the body is not in its bones: the bones need the force of the spirit to clothe them with sinews and vivify them. Yet this obvious truism is often neglected and much harm arises from such misuse. Taunts and exaggerations are mutually exchanged: misconceptions spread rapidly: the essentials are frequently veiled and obscured, because of coverings which are sometimes quite false and, more often than not, quite irrelevant. To understand the essentials, the accretions must be removed and disregarded. When we examine these essentials themselves, we shall understand the Orthodox and Liberal attitudes in their proper perspectives, appreciate their differences, which are considerable, and their likenesses, which are also considerable. We shall judge which preponderate and which have permanent validity. I think that then we shall be able to see how it is possible for advocates of each view to co-operate and to produce a book of this nature. So long as we are content with parrot cries, such as that the Orthodox are fundamentalists and obscurantists, or that the Liberals jettison the Torah and reject Divine Revelation, so long will the composition of this book remain incomprehensible.

All exponents of Judaism would agree that it rests upon the belief in the existence of one God, His Fatherhood and His Sovereignty. Without an acceptance of a unique, yet personal deity, accessible to man yet dominating the universe, there can be no Judaism. But this definition, the *sine qua non*, is not the whole. Without the necessary corollary which it implies, Judaism—though its monotheistic conception is unique—would not necessarily be distinct from Christianity. And if it be interjected that trinitarian Christianity is tritheism and not monotheism at all—an assertion which is certainly unjust to true Christianity—there would still remain Unitarian Christianity and Islam, which are based, as no one can deny, upon a pure combination of the divine immanence and transcendence, just as Judaism is, but which are not Judaism. The corollary to this belief is obedience to that Being, manifesting itself in a life lived in accordance with His Will. Here, again, amplification is needed, for would not Christianity and Islam likewise accept the corollary? It is, indeed, natural that they should do so, in view of their Jewish origins or connections. The definition, then, must take account of the divergences, if it is to be a real definition. We return to the corollary. How is the Will of God to be known? How is it to be obeyed? It is to be known, as all three religions agree, by Revelation. It is over the interpretation of Revelation and the form of obedience that the three differ. It is over the same point that Orthodox Judaism differs from Liberal.

All exponents of Judaism would agree that God has manifested His Will to us. In what manner He has done so, is, philosophically speaking, incomprehensible. Contact between the Infinite and the finite seems inexplicable. In the Bible itself we find two distinct styles of narrative in the accounts. In Exodus, the theophany on Sinai is depicted with considerable anthropomorphism. In Deuteronomy, at the giving of the Decalogue, the warning is emphasised that no form was visible. And in Rabbinic literature the same variety of description can be traced.[1] On the one hand, 'God inclined the heavens like a vault or tub' (cp. *Ab.Zar.* 2*b*): on the other, 'God did not descend: Moses did not ascend' (cp. [56]). Maimonides, who finally decides in favour of an audible voice on Sinai, mentions that others held that Revelation was subjective. But though the method of Revelation be hidden from us, and we cannot think of it save in metaphor, each according to his own ways of thought, of the central, unalterable fact of Revelation, none has any doubt. This is what we term *Torah min ha-Shamayim*. We are not concerned so much with

[1] E.g. cf. *Pes.K.* f. 156*a*.

the channel as with the product. 'The Law which Moses commanded is an inheritance, O Congregation of Jacob.' *In some sense* we all accept a Mosaic Law: 'Blessed be He Who, in His Holiness, gave the Torah to His people Israel' will be found both in the Liberal Prayer-Book (p. 335) and in Singer (p. 143): on this cardinal point there is no ambiguity: in both rites the wording of the declaration is the same.

Yes, *in some sense.* Here, differences of interpretation and belief make themselves manifest: these are, generally speaking, concerned with three issues, for the adequate consideration of which space is here lacking: a bare outline alone can here be given. These issues are:

(1) The relation of the Pentateuch, in its *textus receptus*, to the Sinaitic Revelation.

(2) The scope of Revelation and its content.

(3) The immutability of Revelation.

The first point is, briefly stated, the question of biblical criticism. If we still retain the outlook and phraseology of the Colenso era, then no progress is possible. But we surely are not content to repeat these parrot cries automatically and without examining their validity. For these slogans are almost a century old; slogans are productive of controversy alone, and are destructive alike of faith and of scholarship. The Liberals of old would maintain that the Orthodox were tied to literal inspiration: the Orthodox of old would accuse the Liberals of repudiating Moses' Law *in toto.* Both charges are unreal: both may be neglected. If one opens at random a page of Kennicott's Hebrew Bible, any verse which may be examined will be found to contain variants. The Hebrew Bibles do not agree: no two examples necessarily tally, word for word. It is true that the overwhelming majority of these variants can be regarded as of minor critical importance: but a principle is at stake. The doctrine of literal inspiration is mechanical: it stands or falls by an absolutely uniform text. If the manuscripts of the *textus receptus* differ in one single iota, the doctrine is irreparably shattered. Which, in that case, was the reading revealed to Moses and recorded by him? In the fifteenth century, Elias Levita demonstrated that the vowel-points were a post-Talmudic invention: in the Talmud they are neither mentioned nor implied. On the contrary, their non-existence is evident. Our earliest dated Hebrew Bible goes back to the year 916 C.E. Kennicott's collected variants, therefore, are based on relatively late codices. Even after the discovery of printing, errors crept into the text and were perpetuated (I Sam. XVII, 34). The work of the Massorites, the differences between Ben Asher and

Ben Naphtali, can be regarded as carrying the testimony to textual variation into earlier centuries. It is obvious that we cannot talk of literal inspiration, that is to say, we are not in a position to guarantee that the vowels and consonants in every case mechanically represent the Law as revealed to Moses.

Moreover, when we bear in mind that the stichometry of the Talmudic times does not tally with that to be found in our text,[1] that the numbers of words and the divisions of verses do not always—if at all—correspond with our present numbers and divisions, that the *Ḳere*, or 'read' text, is often the only possible one, we cannot fall back even upon verbal inspiration. We notice that the place of certain verses (Josh. XXI, 35) is uncertain, as the Massoretic note testifies, and that the Massoretic accents imply that others are incomplete (Num. XXV, 19; Gen. XXXV, 22). We have, moreover, Talmudic evidence of textual variants, afforded by the *puncta extraordinaria* (e.g. in Gen. XXXIII, 4 and elsewhere, where the dots denote the conflation of two readings) and by the tradition that the manuscripts in the Temple contained variants (e.g. *Ma'on*, in Deut. XXXIII, 27; cp. [39] note). Biblical citations in the Talmud and Midrash—and also in medieval commentators and writers—differ from our texts. Variety of reading in the versions is a well-known fact: not all the Septuagint variants are errors: not all the Samaritan variants are deliberate changes.

If, then, we may no longer speak either of literal or of verbal inspiration, may we conscientiously accept the eighth article of the Maimonidean creed, which declares that 'the whole of the Torah which is in our possession is that which was given to Moses'? I think we can justifiably do so. Maimonides was not interested in textual problems, but with spiritual values. What he wished to stress was the equal importance of all parts of the Pentateuch. 'There is no difference between verses like "and the sons of Ham were Cush and

[1] Thus, in *Ḳid.* 30*a* an anonymous *Baraita* states: 'The Pentateuch has 8888 verses; the Psalter 8 more; Chronicles, 8 less.' (Some texts read 5888, 5896, 5880.) All these figures differ from the Massoretic totals. L. Goldschmidt points out that the suggestion that Pentateuch, Psalter and Chronicles have substantially the same number of verses is quite unintelligible on the basis of our figures, for our Psalter has about half and Chronicles about a quarter of the number of verses in the Pentateuch. In discussing the *Baraita*, the statement is made that exact knowledge of the numbers of verses no longer existed. It is clear that various systems prevailed, each with different divisions and combinations and, no doubt, additions and omissions. See L. Blau, 'Massoretic Studies', *J.Q.R.* (Old Series), vol. IX, 1897, pp. 122–44 and 471–90; see also his earlier articles.

Mizrayim" (Gen. x, 6) and the Decalogue or the *Shema*.' Each has a lesson to teach, it may be one of historical incident or it may be one of spiritual injunctions. We can learn from both, not least from the frank description of the frailties of heroes and the sins of the wicked, for our conscience tells us which are recorded for our imitation and which for our avoidance. 'They are all equally of divine origin and all belong to the Torah.' How Maimonides would have dealt with critical questions does not concern us: we cannot speculate how Newton would have dealt with the 'quantum theory'. We can be certain that neither the one nor the other would have shirked investigation. Maimonides was fearless. His principles, if not his results, abide, but we must carry them further. It seems to me irrelevant here to discuss how much or how little of the Pentateuch is Mosaic, how much Mosaic material was transmitted orally, how much is editorial. I shall say a brief word about this later. I am here concerned with the so-called creed and its declaration of belief in a revelation to Moses, a declaration which, as has been seen, is to be found also in the Liberal prayer-book. And if the wording of the creed is too dogmatic for our liking, we must remember that it does not emanate from Maimonides himself, it is based on his commentary on the Mishnah: it has become popular as a convenient formula, but the so-called creed has never been adopted, practically, by any Jewish authority as a test of faith (cp. Abrahams, p. CIV foot). We can be fairly safe in asserting that had the question of biblical criticism presented itself to Maimonides, he would have treated it as rationally and as sympathetically as he treated the question of the eternity of matter.

But if we still feel unhappy about Maimonides, we can turn to his predecessor, Abraham ibn Ezra, who, as so unimpeachably orthodox a scholar as Bacher states, held that the origin of the Pentateuch was Mosaic, though it received minor additions in later times. He also regarded Isa. XL–LXVI as not being Isaiah's work.

Reinterpretation is justifiable with ancient formulas that possess a value that is both intrinsic and historic and of which certain parts seem obsolete. The parts must not outweigh the whole. Thus Christians do not scruple to repeat the Apostles' Creed, containing the words 'I believe in the resurrection of the body'. Reinterpretation is the price we pay for a historic religion: it is the safeguard against spiritual and intellectual stagnation, for it implies constant watchfulness in teaching and alertness in thought. But it must not be overdone. We cannot say 'white' with our lips and mean 'black' in our hearts. Reinterpretation has its limits.

If we are prepared to accept the term 'Intrinsic Inspiration' in place of literal or verbal inspiration, we shall find no antagonism between Reason and Revelation. The oft-cited saying 'What is true history is true religion' holds good.[1] We begin with a Torah revealed to Moses and, as the *Perek* continues, 'handed down through Joshua to the Elders and Prophets'. The transmission was in human hands, for the revealed 'Torah belongs to us and our children' (Deut. XXIX, 29): it was not given into the hands of angels, but to flesh and blood. Flesh and blood is fallible, and it is this fallibility that produced varied forms of tradition. During the troublous periods of the Conquest and the Monarchy, tradition faltered, sometimes texts were lost. There can be no holier tradition in Israel than that of the Passover, yet it was forgotten from the days of the Judges until it was reinstituted by Josiah. The Book of the Law itself—however we interpret the phrase—was lost, until it was recovered by Hilkiah. Small wonder then, that when Ezra and his followers 'restored the Crown to its pristine glory' (cp. *Judaism and Christianity*, vol. II, p. 9; vol. I, p. 111), they were faced with divergences. Such is the tale which the Scriptures themselves have to tell: is it so widely different from the verdict of scholars to-day?

Moreover, questions of date call for very serious consideration and theories will need readjustment. On the one hand, the evidence of archaeology must not be abused for party purposes. We have seen what false conclusions, in favour of fundamentalism, have been drawn from the wonderful discovery of the Lachish letters. These have been proclaimed as 'confirming the Bible and confuting the critics'. That they do, in certain respects, conform to—rather than confirm—the Bible narrative is true: that they 'confute the critics' is false. Similar newspaper slogans accompanied the finding of the Moabite Stone and the Siloam inscription. On the other hand, we have travelled a long distance from the Graf-Wellhausen era which relegated so much to a late epoch. Two examples will make this clear. Among the Elephantine papyri there is a rescript of Darius II which permits his Jewish soldiers to keep the Passover and seal up their leaven: yet this custom has usually been regarded as Rabbinic. Again, many

[1] This wise remark of Prof. S. A. Cook is attributed by him to Dean Stanley and by him said to be adapted from Scotus Erigena. See Prof. Cook's inaugural lecture, *The Place of the O.T. in Modern Research*, Camb. 1932, p. 4.

of the Ras Shamra terms relating to sacrifice and ritual occur in the part of the Hebrew Bible assigned to the P Code on the surest grounds. Facts of this nature will have to be reckoned with. The documentary hypothesis may be modified, as Volz and Reider are attempting to do. That it will be swept away, as Jacob or Marston suggest, is unlikely in the extreme.

It is scarcely needful to issue a caveat against giving a blank cheque to all that goes by the name of modern scholarship. 'Not everyone who uses the name is entitled to do so.' Schechter once spoke of certain aspects of biblical criticism as 'the Higher Anti-Semitism'. The remark is sometimes justified, for certain well-known tendencies are both destructive of the idea of Revelation in general and, in particular, are also intended to demonstrate that no ethical good can come out of Israel. We sometimes hear too much of the terms 'Monolatry', 'Henotheism'. We sometimes read commentaries and text-books which seek to show that almost all religious thought before the time of Jesus was narrow and tribal. But with aberrations we are not concerned. Moreover, current biblical scholarship has seceded from the ultra-radicalism of the eighties. The pendulum has swung towards the centre, not to the extreme opposite. Central facts remain but with important modifications. There are few today who would deny that Moses existed and that he was a recipient of Revelation in some form. The case which we would set out is simply that our attitude towards Holy Scripture must be based on the acceptance of Revelation and be guided by the teachings of history and archaeology. For these, too, have been vouchsafed to us by Revelation. Treatment of this kind will be found in Mr Montefiore's recent *Introduction to the Hebrew Bible*, a book which is of great value to every Jew, irrespective of the party to which he belongs. It is as well, in this connection, to recall his *Hibbert Lectures* on much the same topic, with the bulk of which Schechter would have found himself in agreement.

The foregoing arguments may therefore thus be summarised. On the basic fact—though not on the extent—of Revelation, there is no difference between Liberal and Orthodox Jews. Both accept a Mosaic Torah. Both admit that in the course of human transmission, variants have entered the text; where there is divergence, is in the scope of the documentary hypothesis, in the priority of certain prophetical teaching over Mosaic, in the role conceded to variation and in the extent of editorial influence. This divergence is not absolute, it is personal and subjective. It may be enormous, it may be slight. But, in any case, it is a divergence of degree and not of principle. Therefore, though it may sunder individuals, it is not necessarily a line of demarcation between the two parties which automatically renders any intercourse impossible.

Secondly, there is the scope of Revelation and its content. Here, again, we find no clear boundary between Liberal and Orthodox bodies: between individuals, such a dividing line may often be found. Throughout Jewish history the emphasis laid on the greatness of the Torah is unquestionable. But the attitude towards the rest of the Bible was not always uniform. On the one hand, there were periods when it was regarded as heretical to base authority for religious practice on the prophetical books and the Hagiographa (cp. p. civ); on the other hand, at times, those who maintained that Prophets and Hagiographa were not Torah were called 'sinners of Israel' (*Tanḥ.*, Re'eh, § 1, f. 318*a*), for 'whoever busies himself in Torah and fulfils it, is accounted as though he had received it on Sinai' (*ib.*). Now for the stress laid on the 'Speaking' Prophets (e.g. Elijah), see the order of service laid down in *Ta'an.* II, 4. For the stress on the 'Written' Prophets and their association with Torah, see the benedictions to the *Hafṭarah* (cp. *P.B.* pp. 148–51), which may go back to Temple days, if they are the blessings used by the High Priest, and to the contemporary Synagogue, as is possibly suggested by *Yoma* 70*a*. It is clear that since Judaism contains certain post-Mosaic tenets which were derived from the Prophets, the absolute and permanent supremacy of the Law of Moses, over the rest of the Bible, needs some qualification. Thus, even *Meg.* 14*a*, which declares categorically that the Prophets added nothing to the Law of Moses, makes an exception with regard to the Megillah (cp. Abrahams, p. ccv). As will be seen, Judaism regards the Torah as capable of expansion. Hence the Pentateuch possesses what may be termed a potential supremacy, since it is the source of later development (cp. [432–3]). Some Liberals may prefer to stress the development rather than the source. This, again, is a matter rather of subjective decision than of principle. As is somewhat naïvely stated in *Ned.* 22*b*, the prophetical books and Hagiographa would not have been needed had Israel not sinned, the Hexateuch would have sufficed. Here, already, we see the germ of this idea of potential supremacy: even the Pentateuch itself needs the book of Joshua, to be complete.

The terms 'development' and 'source', that have just been used, need explanation. In one sense, Amos, Hosea and Isaiah precede the Law; in another sense, the Law precedes them. If we are concerned with the date of redaction, no doubt priority belongs to these prophets. But if we mean certain oral and, possibly, written traditions which underlie the codified law, then it is at least arguable that these have precedence. And it is these that we mean when we speak of a Mosaic revelation. The interrelation of the two traditions, Law and Prophets, is extremely significant. The connection between Deuteronomy and Jeremiah is a problem in point. Both source and development are indispensable: as we have just said, the Hexateuch rounds off the Pentateuch: Joshua and Moses are linked.

This idea has two implications. It binds the new to the old, investing the new with the authority of the old; but it also prevents the old from remaining static and checking development. It proclaims a line of continuity. The path of progress is straight: the tree of tradition is neither barren nor productive of strange fruit. Thus, on the one hand, we read, 'All that the prophets are destined to prophesy, they received at Sinai, for it says that the divine covenant was made both with "Him who is here, standing with us this day" (Deut. XXIX, 14; A.V. 15) and, as the verse continues, also with "Him that is not here with us this day", that is to say, with those already in existence and with those destined to be created, the souls that were to be born in the future' (*Tanḥ.*, Yitro, §11, f. 124*a*). The passage continues to demonstrate this in detail, by taking Isaiah and Malachi as examples. In a sense Isaiah precedes the Torah, for Isaiah said, 'At the hour when the Torah was given, I received this prophecy;...till this moment, I did not receive the command to utter it.' And this applies 'not alone to the prophets but also to all the sages who will arise in the future, for immediately after the Decalogue, we read (Deut. V, 22), "these words did God speak to *all* your Congregation"'.

And, on the other hand, we read, also in the *Tanḥuma* (wa-yelek, §1, f. 338*b*), that this tradition will take diverse forms, since the minds of men, and consequently their ideas of God, are diverse. But so long as their minds are directed honestly to God, His inspiration will mould their several ideas. All will be produced by the outpouring of His Spirit: there will be no heresy or schism, no heterodoxy, no orthodoxy, 'The words of the wise are like nails, firmly implanted, all given by one shepherd' (Eccles. XII, 11). This means that 'though some Rabbis declare unclean and some clean, though some forbid and some permit, all draw their authority from Moses who derived it from the Almighty' (cp. [436]).

This second issue, however, cannot be separated from the third, mentioned above (p. lxii), i.e. the immutability of the Torah. On p. 406 of the Liberal Prayer-Book the editors deemed it necessary to add a footnote to the ninth verse of *Yigdal*. The verse reads: 'God will never alter nor change His Law, to everlasting, for any other.' The note states: '"His Law" is here taken in a larger sense than it has in the original.' It may be questioned whether the footnote was needed. It may be that the original was intended to repudiate the specifically Christian contention that the old dispensation was to be replaced by the new one. If so, that repudiation would be endorsed by Liberal no less than by Orthodox Jews, by medieval no less than by modern. In that case no note is needed. That 'His Law' meant that the Torah was static for ever and incapable of development is impossible. That 'His Law' may mean the universal Law of God, natural as well as ethical, is, I believe, possible, if not, indeed, probable. For the nineteenth Psalm, which proclaims the unity of the law of nature and the Torah, is significantly selected in the Sefardic rite to be the first daily psalm (the Ashkenazim reserve it, in the same place in the liturgy, p. 20, for Sabbaths and festivals). Both rites introduce the *Shema* by passages of poetic imagery (cp. pp. 37–9, 128–9, XLII–XLVIII, CXXIII, CXLIII foot, CXLV), in which the luminaries are represented as joining man in a combined praise of God. The universal law of nature and the Torah are each equally God's (cp. [563]). This extended meaning of the phrase 'God's Law' may well have been the thought underlying the verse in *Yigdal*. But whether this be so or not, we, Orthodox and Liberals alike, do so interpret it. In my opinion, the dogmatic 'has' of the note should be mitigated by a qualification, such as 'may have had'. Then the note may usefully serve as a source of devotion.

Judaism, whether Orthodox or Liberal, old or modern, teaches that God's Law is universal as well as immutable. What is true in nature is true in religion: what is false in science cannot be true in religion. Truth is one and indivisible. God is bound by His own laws (cp. [454–5]). It is indeed ironical to note that the unity of the XIXth Psalm has been impugned by some people for the very reason that it asserts, first, God's supremacy alike in the natural and in the religious spheres and, secondly, the congruence of those spheres. The sun, in going forth on its daily round, is fulfilling Torah as much as is a human being who worships God, as much as is a Jew when he performs the commandments, which are 'pure and enlightening to the eyes' (Ps. XIX, 8). This, the central element in the Angelology of the Blessing before the *Shema* (cp. *P.B.* p. 38), occurs again in Nehemiah's prayer and is likewise introduced into the morning service on every day in the year (*ib.* p. 34).

And yet there is in Judaism a basic principle of the most potent mutability, the doctrine of progress. God's Torah is immutable, be it manifested in the movements of the heavens or in the ethics given to men. The standards of love, justice and truth are permanent and unchangeable. It is in the operation of the qualities among human beings and by human beings that development is possible, that progress becomes one of God's most cherished promises to man. God gave man reasoning powers capable of expansion, as well as Torah. Without reason, man cannot appreciate Torah (cp. [268]); without Torah, man cannot use his reason rightly (cp. *Aboth* III, 21; *P.B.* p. 194). The two ideas are mutually complementary and inseparable. As reason grows, the appreciation of Torah grows: the Torah constantly reveals itself anew. 'Fresh with the mornings, great is Thy Truth.' God's word is not an antiquated διάταγμα, but one which is ever new, which men run to read (cp. *Sifre Deut.*, Wa'ethanan, § 33, f. 74*a*). In other words, the doctrine of the Messiah, or the belief in the ultimate improvement of the human race, is a correlative to the doctrine of an immutable Torah. The Torah is 'your life' and, like life, it grows. If there are no standards, or if the standards shift, no progress is possible. How can mankind improve if, five thousand years hence, good and evil will have interchanged their meanings? What, on the other hand, is the value of a remote, abstract idea of goodness, preserved in heaven and unattainable by man, unless man reaches out to attain it and unless man knows that he can, in the end, attain it and that every effort he makes brings him nearer to it? What, finally, can a static idea of goodness achieve that is anchored to one generation? It is because the Torah contains the germs of expansion (cp. [426–9]) that it can be termed both immutable and progressive: it is self-sufficing. Eve was the mother of all living: her womb contained the seed of all future humanity. Similarly the Torah possesses 'autarky', for it is ever-developing. 'So Leibnitz presents an infinite system of perfectly distinct though parallel developments, which, on their mental side, assume the aspect of a scale, not through any mutual action but solely through the determination of the Deity' (*Encyc. Brit.* 11th ed. vol. x, p. 27). The Torah extends its influence as needs arise; to correspond with human development, wants and comprehension, it develops new phases immanent in its essence. So God fulfils Himself in many ways, πολυμερῶς καὶ πολυτρόπως.

Throughout Jewish history these two elements have been visible, in harmonious equipoise. On the one hand, Moses appealed to his brethren in the name of the God of their fathers, just as Jacob, at a moment of particular solemnity, testified by Him whom his father Isaac revered. So, too, Elijah, at the supreme crisis, invokes the ancestral God. But when the crisis was past and the victory won, the second element makes its appearance. 'Now, O Lord, take away my life, for I am no better than my fathers.' Life without progress is worthless. Unless we are better than our fathers, why should we struggle, what have we achieved? Elijah's great utterance has had incalculable effect. He becomes the harbinger of the Messiah (cp. [664]), the type of progress, the same Elijah who overthrew Baal worship and brought his people back to the God of their fathers. Malachi ends his prophecy with a climax of hope, God's assurance that He would send Elijah the prophet to turn the hearts of children to fathers and the hearts of fathers to children. In other words, until the Messiah come, the two forces of youth and age, tradition and progress, experience and venture, Orthodoxy and Liberalism, will continue in equipoise—nay, in apparent conflict. He will reconcile them, for it is only in the end that the truth will become manifest: it needs infinity for parallel lines to converge. Every conflict that is in the name of heaven is destined to endure, for God's world would be the poorer, would be incomplete, if one of the two forces were spent. And so, on Sabbath night, when we usher in the working days, we repeat Malachi's promise (cp. Gaster, vol. I, p. 139), and we pray for the gift of discrimination, so that we can learn to judge between the false and the true, whether it be in the traditions of the past or in the innovations which progress would essay.

Revelation, as it seems to the present writer, is something infinitely more magnificent and mysterious than the mechanical system which the doctrine of literal inspiration would make of it. A free Torah connotes free will. 'See I have set before you this day life and death, good and evil, and thou shalt choose life.' There is a tremendous significance in the wording of benedictions spoken when commandments ordained by Rabbinic authority are fulfilled: just as in the case of scriptural commandments, we thank God 'Who hast sanctified us by Thy Commandments and commanded us to...' (cp. Abrahams, p. ccv). The Rabbinic ordinances, framed according to the needs of the day, are as incumbent as the ordinances of the Torah, for 'according to their words shall ye do'. Discussions and differences of opinion among the Rabbis, the dialectics of Raba and Abbaye, like the controversies of the Hillelites and the Shammaites, are, 'these and those alike, the words of the living God' (cp. [436]). No miracles are required: neither falling walls nor moving carob tree (cp. [890]): Birnam Wood need not come to Dunsinane. The Torah is with us, we decide the Law.

But though we have free will, there is yet a providence that shapes our ends and guides our choice. We decide the Law not by caprice. In this fact, it seems to me, lies the wonder of Revelation and the secret of free will. If we review the course of history, from the Pekin man onward, we note how the human race has climbed upward, slowly, painfully, yet progressively. Certain things have dropped off, even as, millenniums before the Pekin man, our tails, it is said, atrophied into appendixes, to be a worry to the patient and a source of income to the surgeon. Mankind has improved. No moral shudder seems to have passed over decent society in Rome when Crassus crucified six thousand slaves along the Appian Way: Europe was not horrified at the enormity of Jenghiz Khan's massacres, it merely dreaded his advent westwards. Yet today, Mussolini's cruelties in Abyssinia do harrow the consciences of men and women, even though these consciences seem somewhat sluggish, if we may contrast the more vigorous days when Gladstone roused England against Turkish atrocities.

Now it might so easily have been different. Things might just as well have gone the other way. If we look at Israel alone, the change is amazing. Already in the dim past, the high places, the human sacrifices, the sacred prostitutions disappeared: they might have endured. The horrors of early days, when each man did as was right in his own eyes, ceased. Gradually, polygamy passed away. Gradually, certain commands, such as the extermination of witches and sorcerers, became obsolete. The crudities of ancient warfare became mitigated and war itself restricted. The private vendetta, which was the only method of upholding justice in lawless days, was circumscribed: the *Lex Talionis* was a step forward in civilisation: the unbounded power of the avenger was curbed and the innocent homicide given a chance of escape. When settled and central justice was established, the vendetta itself was abolished: the *Lex Talionis* gave place to compensation. The change of the name of *Azaz-el* to *Aza-zel* marks the suppression of demon worship and the substitution of a symbolic act of public atonement. And so on.

Why did all this happen? Why did human society choose these lines? Why did not the evil that men do live after them? Was it sheer accident? Man has had the choice, why has he chosen life? For slow though his upward progress may have been, the stages through which he has passed, the shreds which he has discarded, are plainly visible. That he has chosen life we cannot deny. The unavoidable answer seems to be Revelation. Revelation is the silent, imperceptible manifestation of God in history. It is the still, small voice: it is the inevitableness, the regularity of nature. Not the whirlwind or earthquake, but the orderly movements of the heavens, the successions of harvests. God reveals Himself by the fact that while man has freedom to choose evil, yet he has, in fact, chosen good, though he knew not that his choice was guided. Revelation, then, is the denial of chance. Almighty God, through His Shechinah, influences man, who may even be unconscious of the Spirit that is moving him. The Elders of Israel saw God, as they ate and drank, seemingly unmindful of His Presence. He made His Will known to Moses and the Prophets, He caused men to abandon this and to lay hold of that. The Nature festivals gained historical *motifs* and spiritual associations. In primitive times, lads and girls danced in the vineyards on the tenth of Tishri (cp. [1132]): in historical times, the day became the holiest in the year, when a united people sought national and personal atonement from God. The credal paragraphs which, morning and evening, follow the *Shema*, enunciate this doctrine. The power of God is manifested by His works in the past, by His guidance exercised, *'al ha-Rishonim we-'al ha-aḥaronim*, over the men who have been and over the men who are; in other words, God in history is the definition of Revelation.

Without discussing fundamental issues, these few, terse sentences can do no more than sketch the outlines of principles that need to be developed at great length. But this faint adumbration may be enough to show that, broadly speaking, on the question of Revelation and its corollary, there is not an inherent incompatibility between Orthodox and Liberals, that is to say, between those adherents of these two aspects of Judaism who are prepared, *sine ira et studio*, to examine and to discuss the principles which they hold. Between fanatical extremists there can be no approximation. Heresy-hunters are, unfortunately, to be found in both camps. To such, this book will be an irritation and a gnashing of teeth.

This plea for an undenominational, comprehensive Judaism, which shall concentrate on realities and disregard labels, is nothing new. Maimonides did not call himself a Liberal, Judah hal-Levi a Zionist, or Joseph Caro an upholder of Orthodoxy: each was content to be called Jew and 'entitled himself by the name of Israel'. The same name, unadorned and unqualified, should suffice for us.

It is when we pass from the theory of Revelation to its implications that divergences naturally arise. Since men are not vegetables, different conceptions of duty are inevitable. Mass-produced or enforced religion means unreal religion. In the heart of the Maranno, Judaism lived: Torquemada and compulsory baptism could not kill it. Under the stress of a great emergency, the issues may be plain: on Carmel, the alternative, God or Baal, could unite the populace in one cry, 'The Lord, He is God.' But such emergencies are rare. Man does not live all his life at fever heat: issues are not always plain. Life is made up of details and contradictions. Individuality must make itself felt. *Plurimi pertransibunt et multiplex erit sapientia.* The discipline of life takes many forms. The changes of time create ever-increasing demands. *Der Mensch wächst mit seinen höheren Zwecken.* So it is that different conceptions of the best means of obeying the Divine Will, i.e. of interpreting the message of Revelation, are multiplied. Here the conflict between the old and the new is joined. When we contrast the practice of Judaism in Orthodox and in Liberal Congregations, we come to grips with the problem. But we must be extremely careful to avoid generalisation. When we come to examine these two groups even superficially, the inadequacy of the suggested division becomes patent, for within each group wide diversity exists: there is no absolute uniformity, though in each there is an underlying unity, in the broadest sense. Heterogeneity is a symptom of vigorous vitality, of the prevalence of sincerity and independence in thought. These conditions can be observed among Liberal and Orthodox equally. They are natural, since the Jewish unit is the Congregation. History shows this. There have been temporary combinations, sometimes enduring for considerable periods, such as the 'Council of Four Lands' (*Wa'ad Arba' 'Arazot*), which existed in Poland from the sixteenth to the eighteenth century, for certain specific purposes.

But general centralisation has been alien to the Jewish spirit, for in it there lies a danger to local autonomy. Congregationalism has been a source both of weakness and of strength, because feebleness here was counterbalanced by strength there. But that the unit has been always the Congregation is clear from history. (See **Note 73**.)

Now it simply will not do to say that the difference between the Orthodox and the Liberals is that the former do, and the latter do not, obey the rulings of the *Shulḥan 'Aruk*. This is commonly said, but it is inexact. What we mean is that the Liberals keep less of that code than do the Orthodox. I have yet to find a Jew who observes every detail of the *Shulḥan 'Aruk*: I think that there is one in my Congregation; he is a man of great wealth and is able to live his own life, practically in isolation from the outer world. How many Rabbis of so-called Orthodox Congregations refuse to wear garments made of linsey-woolsey? And *Sha'atnez* is a biblical and not even a Rabbinic prohibition! Here, again, as in the case of biblical criticism, a principle is at stake. The test of the *Shulḥan 'Aruk* must be applied with accuracy and thoroughness. Once we consider ourselves at liberty to pick and choose, our definition fails; our actions are dictated not by principle but by subjective choice. Instead of differences of principle or of kind, we are confronted by differences of degree.

That the question of degree is of very considerable—nay, of immense—importance I do not for a moment contest. But the change of definition makes this significant difference. We are now forced to the conclusion that our verdict must be subjective. Logic is gone. We cannot say, definitely and authoritatively, that Judaism is Judaism only when it conforms exactly to the *Shulḥan 'Aruk*. What we, of the Orthodox party, are entitled to say is that, on the whole, the closer Jews adhere to the *Shulḥan 'Aruk*, the better will their Judaism be. But even we feel obliged to have recourse to a qualifying clause, 'on the whole'. And, in the same way, Liberals may deem themselves content with a less degree of conformity. This degree may seem quite inadequate to us, but seeing that we each 'make our own *Shulḥan 'Aruk*', as the saying goes, I fail to see how we can deny the right to others, unless we are disposed to impugn the freedom and mutual toleration that have been the pride of Judaism in the past. This by no means spells indifference. Somehow or other, we have succeeded in combining this toleration with fidelity to tradition: we have enjoyed liberty without suffering disintegration. But advance there has been, and by such advance, Orthodox Judaism has thrived. If Judaism had always remained static and incapable of so moulding new conditions to old institutions as to maintain stability and renew vitality, how poor should we have been![1] Would the Synagogue have survived the fall of the Temple? Would prayers have replaced sacrifices? Were the Pharisees wrong in their fight to impose the belief in the future life, nay, what is more important still, in their contention that this doctrine was immanent in the Torah? Was such an innovation as the *Ketubbah* (see p. c below) a bad thing? And when consecrated wedlock (*Ḥuppah we-Ḳiddushin*) superseded legalised cohabitation (*Bi'ah*) was not the advance a moral one? Was Hillel at fault when he saved Jewish economic society by his introduction of the *Prosbul*, even though, by this legal fiction, he really ran counter to a Deuteronomic injunction? It is an adage in Judaism that potent though the *Din* (Law) may be, though it 'cleave the mountain', yet custom (*Minhag*) prevails over *Din*, for it is in the guidance of the people that Revelation operates: *vox populi* emphatically is *vox Dei*. Is there not a tremendous significance in this? Do we not here see the divine Revelation manifested in the evolution of history? How is it that, if we take long views, we notice that the good *Minhag* has prevailed, the bad *Minhag* has disappeared? *Vox populi* might so easily be *vox diaboli*.

It is true that, as Schechter pointed out, the '613 Commandments' are, for all practical purposes, now reduced to about a hundred (*Studies*, vol. I, p. 302: cp. [525], [538]), if we exclude those unnoticed prohibitions which we 'take in our stride'—murder, adultery, etc.—and those commands which are specifically connected with Palestine. Yet we cannot fail to observe—and, as Orthodox Jews, to deplore—how much of value has been dropped by our Liberal brothers—or rather, one should say, by some of them. The use of Hebrew in the liturgy has been reduced, often to a minimum. What has happened to Sabbath observance and the dietary laws? Does daily prayer, does thanksgiving for food and for countless divine benefits remain? But if we look within the Orthodox fold are not similar symptoms visible? True, these are the shortcomings of individuals, whose adherence to Orthodoxy is but technical. The regulations and conduct

[1] One is reminded of the use made of Ps. CXIX, 126, 'It is time, for thee, Lord, to work: for they have made void thy law', in *Ber.* 63*a*. This was used to prove that in order to revive the religious spirit, the divine name should be mentioned in salutations although its pronunciation was prohibited. Here, to save the Law, the Law is abrogated. (Cp. (12), p. ciii.)

of Orthodox Congregations remain Orthodox. But corporately, Orthodoxy has its faults too. It tends to be content, not infrequently, with superficial conformity; it too often tolerates prayers in an unknown tongue, ceremonies that are unexplained and, because unexplained, devoid of reality. It is slack in some cases, in bringing devotion into the Synagogue, in making worshippers familiar with the Hebrew language, in making the reason for time-honoured rites understood by those who carry them out. But the faults of Liberalism are in the opposite direction. It drops valuable elements unnecessarily: it transfers to the Synagogue official acts which should belong to the home; the father's *Ḳiddush* and *Havdalah*, the mother's Sabbath lights, the family's daily prayers and grace at meals: the palm branch of the individual, the tabernacle of each household, the family *Seder* at Passover. All these beautiful rites are carried out by the Congregational leader alone. What should be a real act by the individual becomes a vicarious symbol. Instead of lighting his lights on the Maccabaean Feast of Dedication in his own home, amid his kinsfolk, the householder watches this historic ceremony in the Synagogue. The worshipper becomes passive: his personal function is gone. He listens, while prayers are read. He comes to service to attend, not to take part, nor to contribute. But he does come!

Now all these Liberal tendencies can be regarded in either of two ways. The old metaphor of the label can usefully be resumed. Let us take an example. Orthodox Jews observe the first and second days of Tishri as the New Year: they blow the *Shofar* (ram's horn) on both the days, unless one of them falls on the Sabbath. That is universal Orthodox custom. Individuals there are who keep only one day—or none at all: this is a private affair with which we are not concerned: there is quite a number, unfortunately, of such individuals, who are nominally associated with Orthodox Synagogues, as we must regretfully admit, in spite of the numerous overflow services arranged for this festival. Now certain Liberal Congregations observe New Year on much the same lines as do the Orthodox. Others make great changes. The name New Year is eschewed, in favour of Day of Memorial: one day alone is observed: the *Shofar* is sounded, even if the day falls on Sabbath. With regard to such procedure, we can make one of two observations. We can say that, in our opinion, it is positively disastrous. The Day of Memorial is a biblical title: New Year is Talmudic: it is the name of a treatise in the Mishnah. It goes back nearly two millenniums, it is time-honoured; there can be no ethical or aesthetic objection to it, such as might be raised against *Ḥaliẓah* (cp. p. 149). Why, then, make this gratuitous breach with tradition? Again, the second days of Festivals were an institution of the Diaspora, but New Year was always excepted since the days of Johanan b. Zakkai.[1] Why drop the second day? Finally, the omission of the *Shofar* on Sabbath practically marked the difference between Temple and Synagogue.[2] To override that distinction means a reversal of progress, a return to the sacrificial era. It is needed only because the Second Day has been dropped. In short, all these changes seem to us Liberal innovations that are perilous in the extreme.

This verdict belongs to the 'label' category, if we use it to belittle Liberals rather than to strengthen ourselves. Another verdict would be based on the circumstance that the Liberal services have made very many Jews acquainted with the Day of Memorial—a title to which no Jew can take exception, since it is Mosaic—with the Liturgy, including the *Abinu Malkenu* (cp. *P.B.* p. 55) and the *Musaf* (*ib.* pp. 245 ff.), and with the *Shofar* itself. But for the Liberal Services, to all these 'absentee' Jews these things would have remained unknown. And since Johanan b. Zakkai ordained that the *Shofar* should be sounded on Sabbath (*Rosh ha-Shanah* 29*b*) as a public sign that the Synagogue replaced the Temple, the Liberal practice has orthodox precedent. Orthodoxy has remained uncompromising. It has lifted no finger to help the drifters. And if it be urged that what Liberalism has given them is but trivial—and this is but an *ipse dixit*—surely even a trivial gift is better than none at all. It is better to say the *Abinu Malkenu* in English than to omit it altogether. One day is better than none.

Here, then, we can appraise the purpose of labels. Labels are for our own convenience. They tell us where to go. Our Orthodox label tells us how *we* should keep New Year; the Liberal label indicates how they should keep the Day of Memorial. If we maintain a strict watch over the functions of labels, their utility will be incalculable. They make for precision and check sloppiness. We need them. But we do not confuse them with the luggage. Luggage that has gone astray can, after all, be traced, even without a label. By itself, the label is a piece of pasteboard.

[1] By the time of the Gemara it was accepted, see *Meg.* 31*a* and Buber's note 1 in his ed. of *Pes.K.* f. 149*b*.

[2] For other reasons, see *Rosh ha-Shanah* IV, §§ 1, 2; Maimon., *Yad.*, *Hilk. Shofar* II, § 6.

Yes, *by itself* a mere piece of pasteboard, but it does not stand *by itself*. To us Orthodox Jews it is much more, it represents divine guidance in a tangible form. Whether we are fundamentalists and believe in mechanical revelation or whether we belong to the school of historic tradition and believe in what I have termed intrinsic revelation, the word revelation remains, therefore the method by which we observe Tishri 1 *be-kol perateha ubekol dikdukeha*, is indeed of paramount importance and is not to be brushed aside lightly. True. But do not our Liberal brothers make precisely the same claim? No doubt, it may be said in reply; but their claim is subjective, whereas ours is not. That is the stock fundamentalist argument, and no more need be said about it. If, however, we take a line more in accordance with genuine Jewish tradition, we shall allow to both sides the right to invest the label with something higher than a mere convenience value. We shall speak of the differences in terms of strictness of observance. Here we are on familiar ground. Here we have a case of Halakic interpretation, and here we can fall back on safe and unambiguous examples, ready to hand, for us to follow. The rule is clear. Rabbi Me'ir used to say, 'If I have ruled for others leniently, for myself I decide with stringency' [1330]. And, conversely, in branding excess, Rabbi Huna describes the Pharisee who belongs to the class of 'Crafty Scoundrels' as the man who, lenient to himself, teaches others to obey the hardest rules [1385]. There are things done and said in the Liberal rite which irritate us: there are omissions which horrify us. But is not the converse true? If we are shocked that in certain Liberal Synagogues men—and also women—go up bareheaded to the open Torah, are we entitled to deny to Liberals a certain feeling of repugnance at *Ḥaliẓah* or weariness of the second days of Festivals, neither of which institutions, by the way, I am prepared to abandon?

We must be fair in our judgment about differences of outlook and labels. A thing is not good or bad merely because it is Orthodox or Liberal, according to our viewpoint. It is good for us or bad for us, as the case may be, and according to the case, so must we act. We must follow the directions on our own label implicitly, without imposing it on the luggage of others.

These distinctions, then, are internal. Their use is limited. Their function is to tell us what we ought to do, not to deprecate the work of others, whose views differ from ours in degree but not in principle. Because, Orthodox and Liberal alike, we are all *Kelal Yisrael*,

Catholic Israel, Jews can discuss the most sacred and the most tremendous issues, sometimes in agreement, sometimes in disagreement, but always conscious of the principle of Catholic Judaism. Each speaks of the other as *Aḥenu Bet Yisrael*, our brothers of the house of Israel. It is upon such a basis that this Anthology was possible.

One of my friends, to whose criticism I attach particular significance, says: 'I cannot help feeling that there is more than a difference of degree between Progressive-Orthodox and Liberal Judaism. Surely one represents a normal development, the other a definite break-away and restatement?' To this I would reply that in some cases it is true, but that extremes are not typical; it is principles that matter, and the fact that in some cases principles have been pushed to too great lengths is not a relevant argument. Between normal orthodoxy and normal liberalism I see but a difference of degree, for they have a common foundation, a common past, and a common future. On the other hand, between any sort of Judaïsm and Nationalism I see an immense difference, a cleavage which can never be repaired. I am not speaking now of the question of Palestine but of the so-called 'National Idea' which maintains that a Jew is a Jew by blood, whether he believes in God or not, whether he has adopted the Christian faith or not: that it is impossible for a Gentile to become a proselyte, since he cannot change his blood, and that a belief in God—though no doubt harmless, nay, even desirable, for those who care to hold it—is not an essential in the definition of Judaism. Again, we must beware of labels; many Jews call themselves Zionists merely because they wish to further Palestinian development or because, being lax in their religious observances, they desire some other link to bind them to their fellow-Jews. Here, in each case, we have confused issues: (1) the question of Palestine has nothing to do with Nationalism; (2) the amount of conformity is a question which every individual must settle with his conscience. Neither of these views represents Nationalism. Nationalism is the declaration that racial descent is equal to belief in God as a test of Judaism. But Judaism teaches 'Thou shalt have no other gods'.

Here, then, we have a gulf which is not to be bridged. Here there is no question of keeping or ignoring the second days of Festivals and the like, here is a vital issue. Is the Jew to be separated from his God or not? On this point there can be no compromise; for this, Jews have died, and for this, Jews must live. But the declaration that blood prevails over ideals is the very antithesis of Judaism. It is the motto of the swastika.

After this preliminary sketch, a few points may now be considered in detail. It is not my present purpose to deal with technical matters. Liturgical, textual, archaeological and historical questions are outside the scope of this Introduction, since they are outside the scope of the book itself. When such information is necessary, e.g. to render the meaning of an extract clear to the general reader, it has already been given, either in conjunction with the extract (e.g. [1], the number of passages which constituted the *Shema* originally (cp. *P.B.* p. 8) and subsequently (*ib.* pp. 40–2)), or in the form of a longer note at the end, when further discussion is needed (e.g. [1] and my **Note 1** on p. 641). Here I am concerned with cases where I consider qualifying clauses necessary, where I feel that perhaps a softer adjective would be more appropriate than Mr Montefiore's, or where a somewhat different verdict may be conjoined to his. I do not pretend to have been systematic. There are not many cases of real divergence. A continuous *Box and Cox* treatment would be wearisome, intolerable. And one cannot expect that readers will agree about the places where comment is added. Some may deem every one of the following remarks irrelevant, intrusive and purposeless: some may call them special pleading. Others will hold that they are meagre and insufficient. Here and there, I may have missed a point. Here and there, a subject comes up twice, and when I have interpolated a caveat once, I may not have repeated it elsewhere. I would stress the importance of the general principles which I have already outlined. In their light should the whole be judged.

The details may now be considered *seriatim*.

(1) *Progress*. As has already been mentioned, the idea of progress is fundamental in Judaism. The conception of a Messiah would be impossible without it. It follows that there are occasions when we must agree with Elijah that we are better than our fathers. There is a notable ambiguity in Ps. XLV, 17, according to our way of rendering the Hebrew preposition *taḥat*. We can follow the A.V., which has 'instead of thy fathers shall be thy children'. Or, with equal justification, we can say, 'Below thy fathers shall thy children be.' The continuation, that we are to regard them as exemplars (lit. princes) in the land, will refer either to the men of old or to the men of today, in accordance with the version which we adopt. And sometimes we must adopt the one, sometimes the other. But unless we

deny progress, we must be prepared to pay the price of it, that is, to jettison some of our inheritance: only, the degree to which we allow this operation needs careful supervision. It is so easy to cast cargo overboard: it is so hard to bring it back. We are not bound by the utterance of every single Rabbi who is mentioned in the Talmud. The Christian theologian feels a moral obligation to justify every saying and action of Jesus because, in some sense at all events, he regards Jesus as divine and the divine cannot be fallible. Hence the frequent attempts to separate the humanity of Jesus from his divinity. But since even Moses had his shortcomings, which Scripture does not conceal, we may readily admit the possibility that a Rabbi has erred. There is a great difference between the authority which Christians ascribe to the Gospels and that which Jews assign to Rabbinic literature. Naḥmanides, in 1263, did not hesitate to proclaim that a Jew was at liberty to reject haggadic interpretations, though, naturally, he allowed to Haggadah great ethical value. But this means that no individual Rabbi possesses Papal infallibility: no Rabbi has claimed to possess it. Therefore, we need not shrink from calling a weed a weed. But we can say that the general tendency is noble: the higher views about God and His nature did, as Mr Montefiore says, generally predominate (cp. pp. xxiii–xxv and [8]). Ups and downs are inevitable in every religion, but these changes must not be given undue importance.

What is important is, which element had the greater influence? This question must be associated with another. Mr Montefiore frequently calls attention to the difference in Old Testament levels. The question therefore is, how far are these levels different and what use of the differences did the Rabbis make?

I do not think that between 'us' and the 'Rabbis' there is as great a difference as Mr Montefiore sometimes suggests (cp. [148], [1500] and [1532]). 'We' too often make the mistake of regarding the Bible as solely a repository of ethics. But the Rabbis realised that it was, in addition, a history book, recording many other things. The Scriptures recall the faults of Israel's heroes, and the Rabbis would not palliate their faults. But they did strain every nerve to reduce the number of faults to the inevitable minimum. If they could clear a hero, so much the better, even if the case for acquittal seems to us rather thin. The part of the Devil's advocate they reversed. They did not recognise, as we do, that scribes who recorded history sometimes ascribed their own sentiments to the Deity. But they were anxious to represent actions which are abhorrent, as facts that happened but which are not to be imitated. They did endeavour to mitigate the stories of Phineas (cp. [608–9]), the slaughter of the Amalekites, etc. They did not always succeed. But, and this is the important thing, they never—or hardly ever—made of these stories morals for conduct in the present, certainly never for the future. Eschatology may demand the elimination of wickedness before the establishment of the Kingdom of God. But the defeat of Gog is left to the divine power.

I am not, therefore, much worried by expressions of opinion on the part of individual Rabbis or by occasional instances of what Mr Montefiore rightly called 'lower' views of God, e.g. [608–9], [9], [73] and [141–4]; pp. xxiiiff. As he says, the higher views prevail (e.g. [9] and [754–6]).

(2) *Particularism* (pp. xxix and xxxii; [95], [128], [142–4], [259–60], [304] and [1034]). I agree that not infrequently there was no clear thinking in regard to the problem presented by [95]. We may cut the Gordian knot. The problem was not often squarely faced, because it was not often realised. Sometimes attention was aroused by the dilemma and various solutions were propounded, as Mr Montefiore says (cp. [144]). It was held to be best not to call the divine justice into question. But that, in this way, divine justice might be injustice, was not remarked. Yet we must not over-estimate this particularist element: one must also take the other view (cp. [143]) into account.

Further, as Mr Montefiore justly remarks, a preacher very often is lost in his audience: he forgets the outside world unless he is, at the moment, concerned with it. And this is right. *Qui trop embrasse, mal étreint*. A sermon dealing with the special needs of a given congregation should not wander over the face of the globe in search for material. Mrs Jellyby is no model for imitation. Naturally sermons which always concentrate on domestic issues tend to become parochial, narrow and particularist. But there is something in the argument I have adduced and I venture to cite a few words that I have written elsewhere on this subject:

Very often 'all good Israelites' is tantamount to 'all good men'; it merely happened that the speaker was thinking in terms of his environment. Recently (22 March 1936) there were three expositions of Christianity on the wireless: Father D'Arcy, S.J., Canon H. C. Robins, of Portsea, and the Rev. W. Taylor Bowie, of the Acton Baptist Church. Each of these emphatically proclaimed the Christian morality to be the only one, generally proving his case by quotations from the Old Testament. As I listened to these eloquent and devout preachers, I did not feel estranged by their narrowness, for that was but seeming and superficial. I pictured them in their pulpits, addressing packed congregations of their own co-religionists, oblivious of any stray Moslems or Jews whom their voices might reach. And I both understood and admired them. I ask for similar consideration for similar Pharisaic utterances.[1]

Again, in the Liturgy, practical steps were taken to prevent portions of Scripture which might give rise to particularist interpretation from being so interpreted (cp. [142]).

As regards [259], I need not add to the note which I have written to [260].

We must not take [304] by itself: the parallels, in [214–15] and [906], must be considered with it, since they complete the picture. In [215] we see that at least one motive is to impress upon Israel the duty of walking in God's statutes, for then God will give rain to Israel and, in consequence, the Gentiles will also benefit. We can see from the conclusion of [215] that the Gentiles, here referred to, are both sinful and persecutors. Hence, if it were not for Israel, who do God's will, they would have no rain. With the eudaemonism of the argument we are not here dealing: the point is that the rain passage in [304] is not necessarily particularistic, especially if we take the pro-Gentile sentiments of [214] into account. And in all three extracts Joshua b. Levi is concerned.

Nor must we take [304] literally. It is hyperbole (see below, p. ci), and Rabbinic hyperbole corresponds to paradox in the Gospel. Neither is meant to be pressed. Did Jesus mean that His disciples alone were, in all circumstances, the salt of the earth? And Jesus' qualifying clause, though absent in [304], is so frequently emphasised in Rabbinic speech that it may here tacitly be taken for granted: the Rabbis, as the Prophets, were outspoken about Israel's shortcomings. They so often state that the choice of Israel is conditional upon Israel's conduct, that the idea can be regarded as implicit even when it is not actually expressed. Here, in [304], we cannot do otherwise. If ever there was a universalist, it was Joshua b. Levi: he would not have uttered a particularist saying. We have had some examples. In [228] he speaks of the divine image in man: in [76] that God hears the prayers of all, face to face: in [1342] that a man with a humble mind is as though he had offered all the sacrifices in the Law: in all

[1] *Judaism and Christianity*, vol. I, p. 157.

these instances Joshua is referring to men in general, not merely to Jews. And in [1582] he takes Judah's view that a proselyte can say 'God of our Fathers' because he is a full Jew (cp. also [116]). Joshua's love of peace was well known: so were his intercourse with Gentiles and his behaviour towards Jewish Christians, who very often harassed him. He refused, under severe provocation, to curse them (cp. [1314]), and so great was his leniency that when a schismatic deliberately omitted one of the test benedictions (*J. Ber.* v, §4, f. 9*c*, lines 39 ff.), he refused to debar him from leading in prayers. Joshua's final remark (in [304]), was clearly meant to apply to the ideal Israel of the future, just as, in [1034], an obedient Israel, hallowing the divine Name by righteous behaviour, is contemplated.

And finally, as Mr Montefiore also remarks, we must take conditions into account and we must judge by date. A naïve *obiter dictum* of the third century is bad enough. Deliberate particularism, uttered by a victim of persecution, is bad enough, though it can be understood. But a cold-blooded treatise,[1] written on behalf of the persecutor, in arm-chair security, and consciously formulated so as to promote hatred and strengthen the case for tyranny, is inexcusable. This remark is prompted by what Mr Montefiore says (p. xxxi) about the bitter jest, 'Whom God loveth He chasteneth.' Mr Montefiore rightly calls this 'a bitter jest'. Is it conceivable that in the year 1934 a German theologian, a Rabbinic scholar of great distinction, should have taken this in earnest! Professor Kittel's thesis is, roughly, that as the Jew claims to be the Suffering Servant, it is the Christian's duty to make him suffer and fulfil his function.[2] No one for a moment takes such extravagances seriously: no Jew would attribute them to responsible Christian thought. But there are not a few cases in current theological literature which seem to us ungenerous and particularist. Most of us feel impelled 'to judge them on the scale of merit', to take the writer's nobler and more usual attitude as characteristic of him. It is sometimes right to have a blind eye and a deaf ear. Jews are said to be hypersensitive: they have reason to be. But, *per contra*, we have a right to ask for some indulgence in return. Not every remark that is to be regretted should be treated

[1] For example, the Homilies of Aphraates, which rejoice in the misfortunes of the Jews and which are inspired by bitter hatred. The same applies to a great part of the material collected by Dr Lukyn Williams in his Corpus *Adversus Judaeos*.

[2] So unbelievable will this be to future generations, that the late Professor Burkitt caused two copies of Kittel's book to be placed in the University Library, as an awful warning of the lengths to which Kittel's hypothesis could go.

as a slogan. For example, in [1524] there is an unpleasant piece of particularism, in the remark said to be made by God to Job, 'Art thou greater than Isaac, whose eyes I dimmed because he loved Esau?' This is not in our taste; it is childish, it is ineffective, and it is casual. But what Ḥanina b. Papa meant was no more than this: Isaac was punished because he made friends with criminals of the deepest dye. To us, Isaac's affection for his elder son seems far from blameworthy. We are, however, not concerned with the real Esau of Genesis but with the 'ideal' Esau, who, already in Malachi (I, 3) had become the type of consummate sinner. Ḥanina conceived of Isaac as weak, indulgent and deficient in moral scruples by accepting gifts from the wicked. Whether his estimate of the Patriarch was correct or not does not matter. What does matter is that his remark, in such circumstances, was not particularistic. For Ḥanina identified Esau with Rome, and we know, from *Ab.Zar. 2a*, what Rome meant to Ḥanina. He there says that Rome has 'constructed many roads, built many baths, amassed silver and gold...'. But Rome has done all this for self-interest; 'the roads are for harlots to ply in, the baths are for luxury, the silver and gold is robbed from God.' Ḥanina knew what martyrdom Roman persecution could involve [677], but none the less he could stress the important function exercised by Gentile proselytes [1605]. (See **Note 78**.)

We must be careful, then, of seeing particularism where it is not really to be found. But that does not mean that Ḥanina's remark is to be an exemplar for us, who view the circumstances in a different light.

(3) *Sacrifices* (pp. xxviii and xxx; [55–7], [111], [311–13], [1145] and **Notes 3 and 4**). Although a few observations on sacrifices have already been made in **Notes 3 and 4** and in the remarks appended to certain extracts on which Mr Montefiore has commented, yet something remains to be said, in view of a sentence in Mr Montefiore's Introduction. Since his Introduction was—like the present one—written after the body of the book was in page-proof, the sentence to which I refer—and which I have only just seen—could not have been treated in my previous remarks. The sentence (p. xxviii) runs thus:

'"The Lord is good to all", says the Psalmist, and the Rabbis would heartily subscribe to the doctrine, and even include the animals; yet just as they could honestly think that God liked, or at least ordered, Israelites to worship Him by holocausts of bleeding animals, so they could honestly think that He liked to, or, at least, would, send

Gentiles *en masse* to hell, or, at any rate, deprive them of the glorious world to come.'

Here, it seems to me, are two incongruities which require separate consideration: (1) the concurrent love of animals and holocausts; (2) the belief that God loves all men and yet acquiesces in—or delights in—the sending to hell of Gentiles *en masse*.

As regards the love of animals existing side by side with their sacrifice, it must be admitted at once, that there was this paradox. That God loved animals, on the one hand, was undeniable. So great is the stress laid on God's all-embracing love, that Ps. CXLV, which contains this doctrine, is regarded as of paramount importance. And yet this very Psalm contains also the paradox. Verse 9 says that God is good to all and His love extends over all that He has made—including the animal kingdom—and verses 15, 16 declare that God opens His hand and satisfies every living thing by providing its food at the due time. Verse 16 is called the *'iḳḳar* or *mafteaḥ shel parnasah*, the 'root' or 'key of sustenance': it is quoted in the Grace before meals by Christians and in the Grace after meals by Jews, for it refers to food, God's gift, and food implies animal food. Thus, in a way, the verses contradict each other. God loves all His works yet He gives some of them to be eaten by others. And sacrifices are but another form of food, for, as I have already written, the institution of the abattoir has had enormous influence on our conception of what is and what is not suitable to be an offering to God.

So profound is the teaching of the Psalm, that it became a model of the *imitatio dei*: it was held that he who recited it devoutly thrice daily would be assured of the world to come (see *Ber.* 4*b* and Abrahams, p. XXXVI) because of these verses; the Psalm would so mould a man's character that he would become a saint. And in fact the Psalm comes three times in the Daily Liturgy (*P.B.* 29, 71, 94): on no day of the year, be it fast or feast, is it omitted. So, likewise, are passages reminiscent of the sacrifices, included in the Orthodox Liturgy. As I have already said, there are three different attitudes to the sacrificial passages. The Liberals have dropped them. At the other extreme, there are those in the Orthodox camp who recite the passages because of their belief in, and prayers for, their literal and physical restoration. But to many Orthodox Jews—probably to the majority of those who reflect on the passages—their value lies in their historical teaching and in their symbolism of a golden age to come. They help us to maintain touch with the past, without injuring our most spiritual hopes for the coming of the Kingdom. They serve to bridge the gulf of time and to mark the path of progress. To those who formulated these prayers, the restoration of the altar symbolised the coming of God's kingdom: it is in that symbolic sense that we repeat their words (see below).

As to the origin of sacrifices I have already written two lengthy notes (3 and 4), and I feel it necessary to apologise for adding to them. But it is, I fancy, inevitable.

To primitive man in almost every place animal blood appeared to be something specially precious and therefore apt for presentation to the deity. Is this because man was carnivorous and felt that the best of food, the life-stream itself, should be offered as a gift? On the other hand, is horror at the sight of blood instinctive, or is it the result of education and aesthetic development? We notice how, in some places, the blood-theme fades away, it yet tends to become refined: it grows into a metaphor. The Hebrew dictionary illustrates this. *Dam*, actual blood, passes, in the plural, through several stages, since it is one of those words which signify both cause and effect. It comes to mean bloodshed in the abstract, blood-guilt, fine for homicide, fine in general, price, value. In Hindustani, *dam* has no other meanings than the last few; no association with blood remains. It even becomes the name of a small copper coin and enables us to say, without the slightest impropriety of speech, 'I don't care a *dam*', which is parallel to 'not worth a Kerse', i.e. cress, in Chaucer and *Piers Plowman* (see H. Yule and A. C. Burnell, *Hobson-Jobson*, 2nd ed., London, 1903, pp. 293–4), so far has the word travelled from its original source.[1]

In Judaism the very idea of blood excited the profoundest horror. 'To eat with the blood' was heinous: sevenfold was the prohibition against it. Sacrifices gave place to prayer and henceforward blood defiled, instead of purifying. And yet Streicher accuses Jews of using blood, human blood, and not merely animal blood, in worship! It is ironical to note how inconsistent the Nazis are. On the one hand, human sacrifice is attributed to Jews and, therefore, bad; on the other, jumping through the fire and other pagan or Moloch rites, reminiscent of living human victims, are Scandinavian or Aryan, and, therefore, good: hence they are revived and fostered. Again, Streicher imagines that to Jews blood is the holiest of holies, hence it must be bad:

[1] It is possible that the Indian coin gets its name from some non-Semitic source. But that *Dam* = value is Semitic, there can be little doubt.

Hitler, however, places blood above ideals and declares it to be the only force that has reality, therefore, good.

While the fall of the Temple and the rise of the Synagogue eliminated the sacrificial idea from Judaism, in Christianity the idea was radically changed to that of the self-surrender of Jesus on behalf of humanity. Hence the blood-theme tended to be symbolised as 'a vivid expression of the ultimate truth of a consecration of life to God, even at the cost of death' (Canon Knox). This idea of consecration by martyrdom is called in Judaism *Ḳiddush ha-Shem*, 'Sanctification of the Name' (see p. 261).

Owing to the fact that Jewish sentiment bans pictorial representations in worship, while Christian sentiment regards them as devotional aids, it has come about that the Christian worshipper, by means of pictures and reliefs, is made familiar with the suffering, death and blood of the crucifixion story in forms that are sometimes exceedingly realistic. There is absolutely nothing to correspond to this on the Jewish side, and the connection of blood with worship is utterly inconceivable to a Jew.

True, on Passover night we repeat the words of Akiba the Martyr, who, praying for the Messianic advent, besought God that our eyes might behold the blood of animals dripping at the rebuilt altar. The prayer is too old, too deeply fraught with meaning, to be dropped as the Liberals do. But we say it in a different sense, giving the words the main, the wider meaning which their author intended. In this there is no intellectual dishonesty. Just in the same way do Christians, repeating the Creed, assert their belief in the resurrection of the body when they actually mean the survival of the soul.

Or again, one thinks of the phrase in the Litany, 'By thy bloody sweat...deliver us'; it is not here a question whether a Jew can ever comprehend the Christian idea of God suffering physically: it is rather a question of the emphasised use of the metaphor of blood. Here, as in the Communion wine, one has known types of exegesis and worship that seem to concentrate on the physical. There is Cowper's hymn of the fountain of blood drawn from Emmanuel's veins. And on the High Church side there are parallels. As an example the rock tomb at Walsingham may be cited. At that shrine, there is a garden and a chapel of which the aesthetic beauty and spiritual purpose are unspeakably wonderful. Every scene in the life of Jesus is most feelingly, most devoutly represented. And then, the climax, is a rock tomb, containing a life-size recumbent model of the bleeding body of Jesus that concentrates on the horror of mangled flesh and gore. It is true that many a French Calvary or an Italian Primitive represents blood vividly. My point is that it is the degree of realism which counts. This, no doubt, is a purely personal opinion. But the fact remains that here at Walsingham a body of men of the highest piety have carried the blood-theme to the furthest lengths imaginable. That is what matters. I feel that there is now—and there always has been, and possibly always will be—even in the best of us, a concentration on blood which I, for my part, call unhealthy. But in view of the saintly character of those who think otherwise, I am prepared to admit that my attitude is subjective; that it is wrong, does not necessarily follow.

We must remember that when we are considering martyrdom, be it Jewish or Christian, the blood-theme may 'be used as a vivid expression of the ultimate truth of a consecration of a life to God even at the cost of death'. These words, cited already previously, are those of Canon Knox, who has kindly discussed this point with me. He goes on to say, 'In Christian devotion it would be easy to find expressions in art or language which might suggest a morbid concentration on the horror of blood. Actually, these are no more than conventional expressions.' This view of Canon Knox seems, if one may say so, eminently sound. It is akin, on the Jewish side, to what some may hold today, who take Akiba's words in the Passover Service in their literal sense. But it is not the only view. Several of my Christian friends feel that such representations as that in Walsingham do imply an undue emphasis on blood. It is noteworthy that Jewish art—which is, in the main, verbal—eschews blood. The poetical dirges recounting the deaths of martyrs narrate them without elaboration. The iron combs that tore Akiba's flesh from him are mentioned in the *'Eleh 'Ezkerah* but details are left to the imagination. Pictures or reliefs of them would be unthinkable. Even when the sentence on criminals—such as Haman's ten sons are assumed to be—is carried out, so far from there being any gloating, the reader has to rush the sentence through in one breath. Such a phrase as 'the blood is the life' is not the motif of hymns. Here and there, in a stray *Seliḥah* on the Day of Atonement, one may come upon such a thought as 'May my flesh and fat, diminished by fasting, be accounted as a burnt offering'. But such ideas are few and far between. They belong to the hymnal and have no authority: they are due to the taste prevailing in the Middle Ages, when they were written, and they may be—and often are—dropped today.

But the circumstance that we find these two views about blood strong and vigorous today, helps us to understand the question with which we started and solves Mr Montefiore's first paradox. So we can realise that there could be men, great and good men, who found no difficulty in believing that God liked blood. To them, the spectacle of blood streaming from the altar was as natural a theme of worship and devotion as is the Walsingham tomb today to the great and good men who created it. Every human institution can be judged in two ways: its essential soul may be obvious to some, whom it raises to God, but incomprehensible to others, to whom it is empty and meaningless. Some see only its faults—if faults there be—others, its values. Judgment is subjective and even biased. So is it with Walsingham: so is it with Jewish institutions. To some, circumcision suggests totemism, initiation rites, mutilation, a relic from the stone age. To others, it is a sacred covenant, sealed in the flesh, typifying the subjugation of passion, and the consecration of the body. To institutions sacred to ourselves we must apply the same moral standards as we use in considering those sacred to others: and we must view their institutions with that sympathy which we extend to our own.

So, too, is it the case with sacrifices. These often stand, as we have seen, for a symbol. We must remember all that the sacrificial system implied to those who lived while it prevailed. It will not do to isolate one feature that is so prominent to us. It must also be borne in mind that, as Mr Montefiore says [111], the Rabbis who took the system for granted also knew by heart the prophetical passages that were opposed to sacrifices and used them, liturgically, as a counterweight. The end of *Menaḥot* is a useful illustration of this tendency (but see also my remarks on the choice of the *Hafṭarah* to *Ẓaw* in **Note 74**). The stress laid on Hos. XIV, 2, 'We will render the service of our life for calves,' which occurs so frequently in the penitential services [897, 909, 904, 902, 951], is very heavy.

Again, the sacrificial theme was often utilised as a homiletic vehicle for teaching ethical conduct [1145] and inculcating charity: he who gives to the poor, gives to God (*ib.*).

But did not the sacrificial system tend to make man callous to suffering and, in consequence, cruel to animals?[1] If we say that it is cruel to kill animals for food, then the answer must be 'yes'. But no one who eats meat is entitled to ask the question for, in that sense, he

[1] Canon Knox is kind enough to remind me that Theophrastus stood alone in his attitude to animals in the ancient world and that we must not look for modern ideas in early times.

is as cruel as the man who offered a paschal lamb. If, however, we exclude the slaughter of animals for food, regarding it as a thing apart, and take the phrase 'cruelty' to mean the infliction of wanton suffering, then the answer is 'no'. It is noteworthy that the utmost care was taken to prevent animals from being ill-treated. *Ẓa'ar ba'al ḥayyim* (cruelty to anything possessed of life) was a crime [123–4]. The slaughter of beasts for food was hedged by the most elaborate precautions to minimise, if not to suppress, pain completely. To eat a 'limb of the living animal' was regarded as a mark of barbarism: today eels are still skinned alive, cod is crimped and lobsters are boiled unpithed. It is remarkable that Jews did not kill animals for sport. Fish had to be netted. Mr William Radcliffe, in his great book *Fishing from the Earliest Times* (London, 1921), blames Jews for lacking the sporting spirit. They caught fish by the net, they did not play them with the rod. This is perfectly true. The word 'hook' occurs in the Bible only as a metaphor of cruelty, or as an instrument used by foreigners. In Rabbinic times, the hook, which entered the mouth of the fish, typified cruelty and with it was compared the terrible disease of croup which similarly attacks and chokes infants: this was the 'evil net' of Eccles. IX, 12 (see *Eccles.R. in loc.*). It can safely be said that the system of sacrifices did not promote cruelty to animals, a fault from which Jews have been remarkably free. Nevertheless this last statement, which is commonly repeated, must not be exaggerated. It is somewhat of an overstatement on the part of Dr Cecil Roth to say that the R.S.P.C.A. 'owes its very existence as well as its inspiration to a professing Jew', just as it is equally unfair of the Society today to decry—if not to deny altogether—Gompertz's share in its original creation, and the present Society acts very unworthily in repudiating its just debt. The truth lies midway. The services of Gompertz were very great; he was a pioneer and indefatigable but he was not the only one to whom the Society owed its existence. Again, Dr Roth further says (p. 299 of *The Jewish Contribution to Civilisation*, London, 1938) that in regard to care for animals 'the Old Testament is in advance of the New': his proof is the contrast between Deut. XXV, 4 ('Thou shalt not muzzle the ox when he treadeth out the corn') and I Cor. IX, 9 ('Doth God care for oxen?'). It is true that the contrast is not his but Paul's (*ib.*). Yet such contrasts of specially selected verses lead nowhere. One thinks instinctively of others, e.g. of Matt. X, 29 ('Not one sparrow shall fall to the ground without your Father'). That love for animals has always been strong among Jews is undeniable and needs no demonstration. Still less does it need advocacy on a partisan basis: such advocacy is often the outcome of an inferiority complex.

We now come to the second paradox to which Mr Montefiore has drawn attention, that God, Who loves all mankind, can consign Gentiles *en masse* to hell. Here Mr Montefiore has really raised two unreal alternatives. First it must be said that consigning Gentiles to hell is not consigning them to eternal punishment, since the *locus classicus*, *R.H.* 17*a* (also *'Eduyot* II, 10, etc.) says that the punishment of the wicked—whoever they be—in hell is limited to twelve months. And when R. Jose, in the second century, interpreted the last verse of Isaiah to mean that hell existed for ever (*Tos.Ber.* VI, § 7 (Z. p. 14, line 7)), this may just as well imply that, so long as the world endures, hell will be needed for successive generations of sinners, as that the individual sinner's punishment was to be eternal. In any case, whatever view be adopted, it can first be said that certain Rabbis did not believe that all Gentiles would be sent to hell for ever but that sinners would be sent there for twelve months, and secondly, that Israelite sinners would also suffer.

Naturally, at different times and in different places, different views prevailed, according to the environment. A Rabbi who lived in completely vicious surroundings, among Gentiles addicted to murder and bestiality and devoid of finer feelings, might well be tempted to draw categorical conclusions as to the utter baseness of the Gentile nature. But I have yet to meet a statement which declares, *sans phrase*, that all Gentiles go, automatically, to hell. The fact that unkind suggestions are occasionally found, does not justify so strong an indictment as that with which we started. (See **Note 75**.)

(4) *Halakah*. On p. xvi Mr Montefiore correctly points out the immense range and influence of Halakah. He remarks that it lacks arrangement and that it is jumbled. This is partly true. The lack of arrangement strikes us immediately and forcibly: yet to the specialist of the past—and even to the specialist today—the path through the jungle is quite clear. The reason is that Halakah was for long periods preserved orally. To write down even the formula for benedictions was tantamount to 'burning the Torah' (*Sab.* 115*b*): the same is said of *Halakot* (*Tem.* 14*b*). For reduction to writing tends to deaden. The letter killeth. Is this why the early Gospel stories circulated by word of mouth and why Q or Ur-Marcus seem to have so many forms? The same may be said of the *Logia*, for 'the

writers of Haggadah have no share in the world to come': neither the preacher who reads Haggadah from a book, nor the hearer, derives profit (*J.Sab.* XVI, § 5, f. 15*c*, line 38). Hence the stress on daily repetition; 'thou shalt teach incisively' (*ve-shin-nantam*), in the *Shema*, was taken as though the root were *Shanah* and not *Shanan*, and rendered 'thou shalt repeat them' daily. Hence, to assist memory, numerous mnemonics were introduced. It is the principle of association by catchwords or outstanding features that rendered oral preservation possible: it is this very device that makes Halakah look 'jumbled'. If one groups together all things that go in tens (e.g. *Ethics*, ch. V; *P.B.* p. 199), they will be easy to recall to mind, but they will present a strange appearance on the printed page. In the same way we might speak of the 'four Georges'. Four farthings make a penny; four parts of the British Isles; the four seasons; the 'Big Four' railways; the four quarter days, etc. This method would now be as absurd as it was useful formerly, because we have invented the index. What should we do without an index to a book? Nevertheless, though we may possess orderly arrangements, we prefer short-cuts. Bradshaw is a model of orderly arrangement, yet when we are in a hurry, we turn to the ABC.

Halakah could be more lively and more capable of development so long as it was oral: the written code is orderly but it is rigid. We have a striking example in the latest code of all, the *Shulḥan 'Aruk*. As Abrahams used to point out, this was the first code produced after the invention of printing: it has been the last. Its sway is unchallenged. The great good it has achieved, in establishing uniformity, is counterbalanced by its bar to progress. No such danger existed in Talmudic times, when Halakah was fluid. The price we pay for such fluidity is the 'jumble'.

On p. xvii Mr Montefiore says that if the whole mass of Halakah disappeared, archaeology, etc., would be the poorer but religious life would hardly have suffered a loss. This statement, it seems to me, tends to make Halakah purely legal and divest it of its ethical elements. It is difficult to make an accurate division and say that such a concept falls on one side of the line rather than on the other. But if we take such a subject as *'Ona'ah*, of which numerous examples are given (cp. pp. 403 ff.), can we divorce this either from Halakah, since it is argued with much casuistry, or from Haggadah, since it is so vitally ethical? When do the *minutiae* of Sabbath observance cease to be Halakic and become Haggadic? When their effect is unmistakably ethical and not legal? But unmistakable to whom? The decision is subjective. To some extent Mr Montefiore is right, but I plead for a qualifying clause. (See p. c footnote.)

Halakah is a necessary discipline for life. In his new Commentary to Ezekiel, Professor Cooke says (p. vi), 'the discipline of ordered rite and obligation is needed to train the spiritual outlook and to save Prophecy from self-will and the empty fate of dreams'. Law needs accurate terminology, definite provisions. In the propounding of abstract principles, precision is uncalled for: in fixing rules of conduct there is no room for vagueness. The late Sir George Lewis used to remark that if a marriage settlement were drawn up on the assumption that all the parties concerned were decent people, the seeds of trouble in the future were planted. If the assumption were that all the parties were rogues, no trouble ever could occur that could not be settled, promptly and amicably. In Europe today, Gentlemen's Agreements are not particularly successful: there is something to be said for the thoroughgoing precision of the Victorian Foreign Office. Bye-laws are not a burden: they are essential. Yet dull they certainly are. No one would take as his light reading a Memorandum on Public Health, or a report on the administration of Local Option. One cannot make an entertaining anthology out of Blue Books or Local Government By-Laws. In his choice of material, Mr Montefiore was clearly right. Yet, in the past, history shows no such clash. Legislation and mysticism could go hand in hand: Safed could produce both poetry and law books, Cabbala and Codes, as Schechter, in his famous essay, has demonstrated. It is scarcely necessary to remind the reader that the author of the *Shulḥan 'Aruk*, Joseph Caro, himself was a profound mystic, for the fact is commonplace, and Caro was far from being exceptional in this respect.

The dialectics which Halakah involved made up, to no small extent, for the lack of philosophy. The Rabbis were no philosophers (cp. [8] and [737]) and, as Mr Montefiore says, their outlook was limited (cp. pp. xix and xlii). They had but a casual acquaintance with Greek thought (*Judaism and Christianity*, vol. I, pp. 121 ff.). This profound system of logical discussion was a substitute. Till the present day it has served to sharpen the wits of the youths taught in the *Ḥeder*, where the curriculum was limited almost exclusively to Rabbinic subjects. But it is true that Haggadah has always been more popular than Halakah (see *ibid.* vol. I, p. 140).

For Mr Montefiore's remarks on legalism (p. xxxvi) see p. 273.

What is said on p. xxvii about 'Conscious accommodation' is very largely true, in my opinion. We must remember that many Rabbis, in spite of their learning, were simple folk; it was with simple folk that they had to deal. Anthropomorphisms were unavoidable. But they were often mitigated by such caveats as *Kebayakol* ('If it be proper to say so' (cp. p. 587)). To generalise is difficult. There were many differences of type, individuality and circumstance.

I would say that the combination of ceremonial and moral which is the aim of Halakah, tends to raise the former, not to cheapen the latter (cp. [273] and [322–3]). This theme is too detailed and too controversial to be discussed at length. It is the ceremonial element that is protective: it prevents the disappearance of Judaism in its environment (cp. [307–8]). When David Rahabi came to India and found some people whom he rightly thought to be Jews, though they were scarcely distinguishable from their Indian environment, it was not the *Shema* which proved that they belonged to the house of Israel, but the fact that they eschewed fish lacking scales and fins. For the discipline of the Torah (cp. p. xxxi) is so powerful a shield that it could be laid aside only at grave risk. It may not matter to God whether we eat or avoid pig: to us it does matter, just as it matters to us whether we clean our teeth or not. The old gibe at the Breslau school, 'Think what you like but carry out the Commands', has always seemed to me most unjust. It really means a combination of progress and tradition. It allows intellectual development and freedom of thought, while it safeguards the Jewish life and strengthens the brotherhood of Israel.

In any disciplined life there are regulations which seem to outsiders to be superfluous and ludicrous. Foreigners make fun of Oxford and Cambridge for granting degrees by pernoctation: we make fun of American universities for granting degrees by credits, a test which we choose to consider mechanical. Both systems work. In neither case is the facile gibe justified: in each case it may easily be justified. As has been said before, institutions can be regarded from two aspects, there is always scope for criticism, genuine or specious, just as there is always an element of value. For the question of ridicule of the Commandments by Gentiles, cp. [400] and [407]. As Mr Montefiore says, the view that the *Miẓwot* are God's arbitrary decrees tended to destroy superstition (cp. [410] and [527]).

That there was a possibility of danger from a mechanical legalism is not to be denied (cp. [553]), but I do not think that it was very real:

a system of discipline makes the danger inevitable. When operative among simple folks, there is also the danger of a wrongful use of *zekut* and of 'Tit-for-tat' (cp. [583 ff.], [601] and [632]): I have said a word on this matter already (cp. [1641]). And, finally, with regard to Mr Montefiore's *bête noire* of 'Tit-for-Tat' (p. xxxv) which 'defaces' the Orthodox Liturgy (*Sab.* II, § 6; *P.B.* p. 121), I find that since I wrote my note about women, my remarks receive support from Pool's new Prayer-Book which, on p. 134, renders the passage thus: '(It was held that) women may die in childbirth for the following three transgressions.' This seems to me perfectly adequate. Nobody has ever been known to take the remark literally: as an old superstition, in a piece of historical reading, it is not uninteresting. And it does not really belong to the service at all, though it is included in the *P.B.* But so are many other passages, such as the Ethics of the Fathers, the Royal Crown, Ps. CXIX and many other Psalms, *Pereḳ Shirah* (Songs of Nature praising God), the *Ma'amadot*, etc., all of which will be found in different prayer-books, according to the editor's choice. These are meant for private study or devotion. In the same way many liturgies have extracts of Halakah, for reading before or after service. The *bête noire*, however, appears to have invaded the service proper. Really, according to the Sephardic rite, it intervened between Afternoon and Evening Service and was intended for private study. At this period the reference to the Sabbath lamp was peculiarly appropriate. According to the Ashkenazic rite, it intervened between Evening Service and *Ḳiddush*, and was also intended for the individual, if he desired to read it. But the Evening Service has overflowed its limits in both directions and has caught up the offending chapter, much as London has absorbed the outlying suburbs, and so the passage is now actually read in many Orthodox Synagogues. It is, however, omitted in many. But the most orthodox of all rites, that of Isaac Lurya the Cabbalist (*Nusaḥ 'Ari*), lacks the passage in Synagogue and in liturgy altogether.[1] The Yemenites, I believe, also lack the passage, since it is usual among them not to read a set piece but to have a text read through, chapter by chapter. So Mr Montefiore must join the Lurya group, since there is not, to my knowledge, a Yemenite Synagogue in London!

But there is one important factor which I have reserved to the end. Superstitions are often employed as means of inculcating morals. Not to spill the salt teaches economy and so on. People are, un-

[1] See, for example, *Siddur 'or 'olam*, Wilna, 1909 (*in loc.*).

fortunately, more prone to fear a supposed bad luck than a real blemish. This particular superstition was intended as an old wives' adage, preaching chastity and self-control. It was appropriate to Friday night, which was regarded as the proper time for husband and wife to meet in love. I cannot feel as indignant as Mr Montefiore is about this point.

(5) *Women.* To what Mr Montefiore says on p. xviii, I have, to some extent at least, replied on pp. 656ff. I revert to the question because Mr Morris, in his book *The Jewish School*, to which I have referred in **Note 4**, discusses it (Woman and her education, pp. 24ff.). Mr Morris takes rather a gloomy view, in my opinion. His array of facts is accurate and well chosen, but I cannot help feeling that some of his conclusions are over-statements. I doubt whether the position of women was generally so unenviable as he would suggest. For example, too much stress must not be laid on phraseology and collocation. Thus, the collocation of women and fields does not prove that in practice women were always regarded as chattels. An obvious parallel suggests itself. The Church of England Marriage Service applies to the wife the *habendum* clause customary at the taking possession of property ('to have and to hold'). Our *Ketubbah* contains analogous legal terms. But neither in Church nor in Synagogue is woman regarded as a chattel today. Mr Morris ends his suggestive chapter with the following sound conclusion: 'In the writings of the rabbis we find something of both these moods [i.e. of appreciation and depreciation], but a characteristic sense of reality helped them to escape from either extreme.'

(6) *The Spatial Conception of God's Dwelling* (p. xxvi; [48], [158] and [25]). What Mr Montefiore says is, it seems to me, very fair. But I do not think that the Rabbis troubled about metaphysical questions. God was the Great Unknown, the Unknowable save by metaphor. I very much doubt whether they pursued the subject far enough to inquire into the literal applicability of the metaphors. The Pharisees objected strongly to the localising of the Divine Presence. Hence they prohibited the Sadducean procedure of kindling the incense *outside* the Veil, an act which was based on the theory that God was, in some special sense, more present within the Veil than without (see *Judaism and Christianity*, vol. I, p. 135). Again, the *Targumim* are permeated by a strong antipathy to anthropomorphism, which is but another aspect of a spatial Deity.

(7) *Works and Faith* (p. xxxv). The Rabbinic antithesis is not

between faith and works but between learning and works. The Apostles were missionaries, who had to bring the Gentiles to faith. Of the Rabbinic missionary epistles or arguments, we have little, if any, knowledge, though we know of their missionary activity. It is an accident that nothing Rabbinic, outside Palestine, has survived, for in this sense Philo is hardly representative of Rabbinic thought. Now the Rabbis in Palestine worked among people who already had faith but who lacked learning. Hence the difference in the two sets of alternatives.

(8) 'There are no such religious geniuses and innovators as Jesus, Paul and the author of the Fourth Gospel among the Rabbis' (p. xx). I wonder. If we count heads, then these three persons undoubtedly influenced more people than did the Rabbis. I should be inclined to say that, in this manner of reckoning, Socrates had a still greater influence than these three, since they influenced Christians, whereas the influence of Socrates was and is acknowledged not only by Christians but also by many more people. But if we take the religious genius to refer to his own faith, to his own place and to the extent and abiding value of his work, then surely we may cite Rabbis like Johanan b. Zakkai or Judah the Prince.

There is, however, another consideration to be borne in mind. Burkitt used to say, 'Judaism is a religion of ideals; Christianity, of an ideal person.' I have drawn attention to the significance elsewhere, but it cannot be emphasised too often. Judaism stresses the message but neglects the messenger. Hence we have so few biographies of great men: how many do we know? Glückel von Hameln, Sabbathai Zebi, Ber of Bolechow, Hayyim David Azulai, etc., a rather meagre lot in truth. There is no article 'Biography' or 'Autobiography' in the *Jewish Encyclopaedia*. It is against the Jewish genius. That is why there is no 'Gospel according to John Zacchaeus, alias Johanan b. Zakkai'. I have always said that his disciples could have written one, had they wished to do so; I have often said that it could be done today, in view of the material available. And now such a work has been undertaken. Dr Finkelstein's *Akiba* is a splendid example for others to follow. After reading it one can hardly deny to Akiba the title of a religious genius or innovator.

This may be conceded, but still the extent of the influence may be denied. This denial is, I believe, due to a misconception of the far-reaching influence of the work of Rabbis as religious innovators. Jews and Christians alike take it for granted, because it was effective before Judaism and Christianity parted. Two examples will make this clear, they may be taken from the social rather than from the purely ethical sphere. Think how Hillel's *Prosbul* has affected Christian and Jewish society! But for this, Jesus could not have uttered the parable of the talents. Neither Christians nor Jews could engage in commerce, and the Ecclesiastical Commissioners could not hold a single share that paid a dividend. Was not the *Prosbul* a religious innovation as far-reaching as the abolition of the dietary laws?

Again, take the case of Simeon b. Sheṭaḥ. He made the *Ketubbah* a safeguard of the rights of married women and a check to hasty divorce. Does not the introduction of this covenant mark an important stage in the progress of female emancipation?[1]

These instances are selected at haphazard. Very few Jews and still less Christians realise what a debt society owes to these 'religious innovators'.

(9) *Zekut* (p. xxxvi). No doubt this idea arose from the ancient conception of corporate solidarity. The individual was merged in his unit, for better or for worse. Then the doctrine of personal responsibility grew up and saved the innocent individual from being involved in the punishment of his guilty kinsman. Fathers were not to be put to death for children: 'The sons of Korah died not.' For an example of the development of this idea, cp. [1093]. It may well be that the doctrine of 'Tit-for-tat', which Mr Montefiore dislikes so greatly, was the first mitigation of the older belief that a man and his household were one and indivisible. Personal responsibility disposed of the belief that sin was a force that could spread far and wide and entrap helpless man, as Orestes was entrapped. That is possibly one explanation of the mysterious proverb in Deut. XXIX, 19, which may be translated 'lest the wet sweep away the dry', i.e. that rain be not a boon to the parched ground but a destruction.

So much for the side of evil. On the other, it was sometimes held that good was indestructible. Probably before the idea of immortality grew up, this heritage of good applied to this life, 'that your days and those of your children be long in the land'. Hence arose, later, the idea of a storehouse of grace. The widow of a V.C. may wear his

[1] Dr Rabinowitz rightly draws attention to the importance of Simon's action. This importance is not generally recognised. People think of Simon in connection with his sentencing women to death at Ascalon but they overlook this great innovation of which the credit is his. Here again we see that the Halakah proves a valuable source for estimating advance in social ethics.

medal. So, the merit of an ancestor avails his descendants. To some extent this may be explained as training and heredity. A careful upbringing may transmit paternal virtues: whether acquired characteristics are transmissible is a theme of controversy to biologists.

The idea of *Zekut* received support from the doctrine of the Suffering Servant. When that doctrine was given a Christological interpretation in the Church, the reaction in the Synagogue was strange. It made the doctrine of *Zekut* far stronger than before, but it transferred it to the Patriarchs and heroes. A good example is furnished by the theme of the '*Akedah* (binding of Isaac). The original lesson which the story of Gen. XXII conveyed was that human sacrifices were detested by God. When the era of human sacrifices had long passed, the story lost much of its topical interest: it became a piece of antiquarianism. The stress laid in the Church on the *Agnus Dei motif*, however, made Jews look for a parallel. Under the influence of the adage *Maḥshabah ke-Ma'aseh* (the will for the deed), Abraham's obedience and Isaac's submission became cardinal points. It was as though the sacrifice had actually been consummated. Therefore, the readiness of Abraham and Isaac to follow the divine command at all costs was elevated to a liturgical theme—as it still remains. The poems in the Liturgy on the '*Akedah* and the appeals to the merit of the Patriarchs are, in fact, regarded as prayers to God to make us worthy of our ancestors and capable of following their example. This conception would, I fancy, not be absent from the Liberal Liturgy, and so I would like to qualify Mr Montefiore's remark that it 'seems to have wholly passed away from modern Judaism, whether Orthodox or Liberal'. I fancy it would be more accurate to say that it has survived in a much modified form. As regards Isa. LIII, see [1529]. For the idea of *Zekut* in Christianity, see p. xxxii.

(10) *Hyperbole* ([1093]; p. lxxxiv), as Mr Montefiore says, must not be taken literally: we may compare the use of paradox in the Gospels. A Rabbi would exaggerate one aspect of a case, in order to drive home his moral, quite oblivious of the fact that on the previous day he had stressed the other side. He might, on Monday, be teaching the lesson of God's omnipotent mercy and say that it could prevail over all. On Tuesday, when emphasising the evils of perjury, he might declare that it was the unforgivable sin. As we have so often said, the Rabbis were not philosophers. See what Mr Montefiore writes on p. xlv.

(11) *The name of God* ([9], [17], [158], etc.). I venture to differ from Mr Montefiore in regard to the use of the divine name in

English. I reject, naturally, the erroneous form, wrongly said to be the invention of Petrus Galatinus (1518) (but occurring in MSS. of the fourteenth century), and I prefer to follow the American-Jewish Version in Exod. XVII, 15, which has Adonai-Nissi. The incorrect form of the E.V. is used in [158].

But I object also to the use of the conventional modern form, as given in [9], for three reasons:

(*a*) I agree with Canon Lukyn Williams that the form is more probably Yaho. Therefore I do not, as a student, wish to use a wrong form. See (1) *Journal of Theol. Stud.* XXVIII, April 1927, pp. 276–83; (2) Burkitt's note, *ib.*, July 1927, pp. 407–9; (3) 'The Tetragrammaton, Name or Surrogate', *Zeitschrift f. d. A. T. Wiss.*, 1936, pp. 262–9; (4) 'The Lord of Hosts', *Journal of Theol. Stud.* XXXVIII, January 1937, pp. 50–6.

(*b*) But if (*a*) is correct, then, as a human being, I must avoid it. If I were to address an earthly monarch—even one whose moral character commanded no respect—I should be obliged to employ a periphrasis, an abstract noun, out of common decency. In the case of the Deity, then, *a fortiori*, or, as the Rabbis would say, *'al aḥat kammah ve-kammah*.

(*c*) Finally, as a Jew, I take exception to the form, since it is very often used to depreciate the Jewish conception of God and to create an artificial and unreal antithesis, between a so-called Christian conception of God, Maker of heaven and earth (alleged to be unknown to Israel although it is to be found in Gen. XIV, 19, a chapter considered to be adapted from a cuneiform source, from some annalist's account), and a so-called Jewish tribal, particularist god (with a small *g*) devoid of ethical attributes. There is no denying the fact that this sentiment is to be found in many a text-book of Old Testament History. I have heard it expounded in lecture-rooms and I have raged and rebelled against its inherent falseness.

But the converse tendency is equally to be shunned. The progress of revelation is an established fact. We would not go back to the miraculous conception of the birth of Juno, fully armed. The middle course is the best. I think it safer to adopt a non-committal policy and retain the old-fashioned equivalents of the divine name.

With regard to the name of God I take this very strong line which I have outlined. On other points I consider that concessions to convenience and conventional usage are justifiable; for example, I always avoid the terms 'Old Testament' and 'Anno Domini' when speaking to a purely Jewish audience or when writing for Jews only. In such cases the terms would be unreal and unsuitable. But when I am writing for general readers I have no objection to referring to the Old Testament or giving the date as A.D. One can carry scrupulousness to undue extremes.

(12) On p. xxvii Mr Montefiore speaks of 'our reserve in speaking of God', and he wonders whether the Rabbinic attitude is overfamiliar. I would refer to my previous remarks on p. cii (*b*), also to p. lxxvi footnote and [350]. Here we have an interesting example of the conflict between 'reserve' and 'familiarity'. The holiness of the Divine Name demands reserve, but reserve may make for remoteness from God. To reinforce the religious spirit it was proposed to introduce the pronunciation of the Name. But this led to familiarity and the proposal was soon abortive.

(13) (p. xxxi). What Mr Montefiore says about abstaining from lobsters and the method of killing animals is capable of being put in another way. I have defined Revelation as that factor which causes certain customs to survive for a moral purpose which may or may not be clear to any particular generation at a given stage in time (pp. lxxii ff.). The survival of the dietary laws seems, to me at least, to indicate that they have a purpose. It is no less intellectual to obey them than it is to remain attached to other ancient symbols, e.g. of royalty or law (see my remarks on p. 356). Why should a Jew be silly if he eschews pork when it is not considered silly, in fact it is laudable, for a Scot to eat haggis? And during the time of Antiochus IV—or again under the Inquisition—many a Jew went to his death rather than eat pork and pass as a renegade. The enormous momentum which the dietary laws have thus gathered cannot be overlooked. They have become an epitome of fidelity to Judaism. That is why they survived. The Rabbis knew, quite as well as any scientist or philosopher, that it does not matter to God what we eat and what we avoid (cp. [403–4]); but it will matter to us. Are Christians any better than we are because they eat pork? Are we any better than they because we do not? I am no advocate of what is called 'Pot-and-Pan theism', but I see that these laws have survived for good reason, and because they have survived, they are divinely approved for Jews.

And as to slaughter of animals, so long as the horrors I have mentioned on p. xcii continue, the Jewish method of humane slaughter needs no defence.

(14) (p. xxxv, footnote 2). Mr Montefiore thinks it inconceivable

that learned men should utter absurdities. Absurdities is a relative term. He expects too much. Some of the extracts which Mr Snape cites seem equally absurd, if we judge by modern standards. Yet the Church Fathers were learned men and had an advantage, in this respect, over the Rabbis, in that they—or some of them—had contact with Greek philosophy. The point that matters, it seems to me, is that these absurdities left no mark in either case. Sometimes they had their use, e.g. the use of numerical arrangement for convenience and for mnemonics (p. xciv).

(15) (p. lxvii). With regard to the Halakic authority of Prophets and Hagiographa, called *Ḳabbalah*, see [428]. On the one hand, *R.H.* 7*a* maintains that Zechariah and Esther have Pentateuchal authority. On the other, *Ḥag.* 10*b* will not permit the Pentateuch to be interpreted by Amos; *Gen.R.* VII, § 2 (Th. pp. 51–2), similarly rejects Nehemiah; *T.J. Ḥal.* I, § 1, f. 57*b*, line 16 refuses to allow Halakah to be deduced from Isa. XXVIII, 25. Isa. is called *Ḳabbalah* in *Sifre Num.*, Shelaḥ, § 112, f. 33*a* (H. p. 120).

(16) (p. xvi). The 'turgid and turbid mass' offers a striking contrast to the orderliness of the N.T. documents. Rabbinic literature was not 'edited', and in contrast to Patristics no book was the planned creation of one author. The stylistic inelegance is therefore an argument for trustworthiness.

There are just a few things that I would like to add to Mr Montefiore's Preface, before I lay down the pen finally and bid the Printers release the Press, which has been waiting so patiently to be quit of the authors. These things are not intended to complete deficiencies in my Introduction, conscious as I fully am of its many shortcomings and of its unfitness to follow that of my Colleague. For that the time is gone by: *Quod scripsi scripsi*.

But the moment of bidding farewell to this book is indeed a solemn one. It marks the conclusion of a delightful quest, of many hours spent in intimate contact with the Rabbis of old, of numerous attempts to understand them, to unravel their obscurities and to estimate their worth, and, above all, of daily letters from and frequent visits to one whom I am proud and grateful to call, in David's words, 'My master, my guide and my intimate friend.' If I have in any small degree contributed something to these pages, it is insignificant, as a 'drop from a bucket', compared with what he has given. The last sentence of *his* Preface is therefore just fantastic—no other term will do. Over this, he and I differ far more than over any Rabbinic controversy, including even his *bête noire* which, with my attempts at whitewashing, the reader has discovered by now. And it is not simply to Mr Montefiore's critical insight and sense of values that the book owes—and I, too, owe—so much. His admirable grasp of Rabbinic thought, his facility in handling texts, his familiarity with Rabbinic idiom and language, have taught me more than I can put into words.

Before, I spoke of deficiencies in my Introduction. Alas, there are loose ends, not a few, there and elsewhere. Mr Montefiore has been very seriously ill and I have been incapacitated less seriously, but none the less my movements have been gravely hampered, precisely at the time when he and I would normally have been putting the finishing touches to our work, eliminating unintentional doublets, filling gaps and checking references for the last time. As I write these lines the hour of danger is past, and the joy that the thought of Mr Montefiore's recovery brings makes the fear of blemishes less awesome than perhaps it should be.

I must mention, too, our deep sense of gratitude to three friends who have stepped into the breach so nobly and given us such precious help; I name these in alphabetical sequence for we would not differentiate the various forms of aid so generously offered us: the Rev. H. St John Hart, Chaplain and Fellow of Queens' College; Mr W. C. Piggott of the University Press; and Dr L. Rabinowitz, Rabbi of the Cricklewood Synagogue. To these three friends our sense of obligation is very real. The Cambridge University Press, too, deserves our warmest thanks for constant help. This book has presented problems of its own, but no trouble has been too great for the printers. Mr Lewis has been amazingly patient. In difficulties, which have been frequent, he has never failed to find a way out. Our wishes—often unreasonable, I fear—have had his sympathetic consideration, and his staff have given us of their best. The Hebrew term by which printing was originally known is 'The Holy Work', a phrase applied in Exodus to the construction of the sacred Tabernacle. To diffuse knowledge is to build a sanctuary. Till quite recent times, the compositors and correctors of a Hebrew book printed their names, towns and dates, at the end, as a colophon. We fain would follow this excellent tradition, and so we thank our unknown friends and fellow-workers, whose anonymity the etiquette of modern typography imposes.

This night is doubly appropriate for the conclusion of this book.

It is a book about the Torah, and today has been the anniversary of the Giving of the Torah. Pentecost is just over. As I write, the date is still 6 June, according to the prevailing Gregorian Calendar: by Hebrew reckoning, it is already 8 Siwwan. But 6 June is Mr Montefiore's birthday.

And now, as I lay down the pen, I am conscious of the time-honoured custom that when the Pentateuchal cycle is ended, it begins instantly anew. No sooner has Deut. XXXIV been read than a new Scroll is opened at Gen. I. 'If a man begins a good work, They say to him "Carry on".' As we say good-bye to this Anthology, I would reveal a secret. Two years ago Mr Montefiore gave me a copy of Mrs M. W. Tileston's *Great Souls at Prayer*, and lamented that there was no Jewish parallel. I told him then—and I have remembered this daily—that he could provide one. Since this Preface is dated on his eightieth birthday, and since 'Eighty years are for strength' is the Rabbinic version of Ps. XC, 10, may we express the hope that renewed health and strength will bring yet another addition to the B.M. Catalogue, s.v. 'C. G. M.'?

HERBERT LOEWE

The night of $\frac{6\ \textit{June}\ 1938}{8\ \textit{Siwwan}\ 5698}$

SYSTEMS OF TRANSCRIPTION, ABBREVIATIONS, ETC.

(1) Biblical references are nearly always to the Authorised Version: the Hebrew text is generally indicated, when necessary, by (M.T.).

(2) In the indexes it is convenient to refer sometimes to the numbers of the extracts in square brackets ([ ], 'square' numbers) and sometimes to the pages; a line at the head of each page of the index indicates which method has been used in that particular index.

(3) Transcription:

(i) All biblical proper names and all Hebrew words occurring in the English Bible follow the spelling of the A.V.

(ii) In other cases the system of the *Jewish Encyclopaedia* has generally been adopted:

א = ' (smooth breathing): usually omitted when initial

ע = ' (rough breathing)

ח = Ḥ	ט = Ṭ	ס = S	צ = Ẓ
ק = Ḳ	שׂ = S	שׁ = Sh	

(iii) Absence of weak *dagesh* is not indicated by *h*, thus וּבְכָל = *u-be-kol*, not *u-bhe-khol*. Nor is *sheva*, whether simple or compound, written over the line (*asher*, not *'^{a}sher*). *Dagesh forte*, after the article, is omitted (*ha-din*, not *had-Din*). פ is sometimes *F* and sometimes *Ph*: ב is sometimes *B* and sometimes *V*.

(iv) Certain common conventional spellings have been retained, e.g. Aboth (not *'Abot*); Akiba (not *'Aḳiba*); *Yetzer ha-ra* (not *Yeẓer ha-ra'*); *Am ha-Aretz* (not *'Am ha-'Areẓ*), *Derek eretz*, etc. The same applies to abbreviations, e.g. *Ab.Zar.* for *'Ab.Zar.*

(v) Certain inevitable inconsistencies will be observed, thus: we write Phinehas (Aaron's grandson), because the name occurs in the A.V. But the lesson from the Pentateuch is *Pineḥas*. We have thought that occasional divergencies, in the interest of simplification, are preferable to a rigid scheme of transcription.

(4) A glossary has been compiled of Hebrew words of which the sense is not explained in the text; in the index an asterisk is prefixed to such words.

(5) Some of the doublets, mentioned on p. cv, are intentional. Certain passages seemed applicable in more than one section, and it was thought preferable to repeat them, for the reader's convenience. In many cases, cross-references have sufficed.

(6) Abbreviations: (i) Names of tractates of the Mishnah, Tosefta, Jerusalem Talmud or Babylonian Talmud:

Ab.R.N.	= *Aboth de Rabbi Nathan*	*Mak.*	= *Makkot*
Ab.Zar	= *'Abodah Zarah*	*Meg.*	= *Megillah*
'Arak.	= *'Arakin*	*Men.*	= *Menaḥot*
Bab.B.	= *Baba Batra*	*M.Ḳ.*	= *Mo'ed Ḳaṭon*
Bab.Ḳ.	= *Baba Ḳamma*	*Ned.*	= *Nedarim*
Bab.M.	= *Baba Meẓia'*	*Nid.*	= *Niddah*
Ber.	= *Berakot*	*Pes.*	= *Pesaḥim*
Beẓ.	= *Beẓah*	*R.H.*	= *Rosh ha-Shanah*
Bik.	= *Bikkurim*	*Sab.*	= *Sabbath, Shabbath*
Dem.	= *Dema'i*	*San.*	= *Sanhedrin*
Der.Er.Z.	= *Derek 'ereẓ Zuṭṭa*	*Sheḳ.*	= *Sheḳalim*
'Erub.	= *'Erubin*	*Soṭ.*	= *Soṭah*
Giṭ.	= *Giṭṭin*	*Suk.*	= *Sukkah*
Ḥag.	= *Ḥagigah*	*Ta'an.*	= *Ta'anit*
Ḥal.	= *Ḥallah*	*Tam.*	= *Tamid*
Hor.	= *Horayot*	*Tem.*	= *Temurah*
Ḥul.	= *Ḥullin*	*Ter.*	= *Terummot*
Ker.	= *Keritot*	*Yeb.*	= *Yebamot, Yabmut*
Ket.	= *Ketubbot*	*Zeb.*	= *Zebaḥim*
Ḳid.	= *Ḳiddushin*		

The reader who is not a Hebraist but who wishes to refer to translations of passages cited will note:

(*a*) References to the Mishnah are by chapter and section, thus, *Ber.* IV, I. These may be found in Danby.

(*b*) References to the Tosefta are prefixed by *T.*, thus, *T.Ber.* IV, I (Z. page and line). As there is no translation to the Tosefta, these references cannot be verified by him.

(*c*) References to the Babylonian Talmud are to folio and side, thus, *Ber.* 59*a*: these may be found in Goldschmidt.

(*d*) References to the Jerusalem Talmud are prefixed by *T.J.* and are to chapter, section, folio, column and line, thus, *T.J.Ber.* I, § 4, f. 27*d*, line 6. These may be found in Schwab.

(ii) Other abbreviations:

Mek.	= *Mekilta*	*Pes.R.*	= *Pesiḳta Rabbati*
P.B.	= Prayer Book. Unless an editor's name follows (e.g. *P.B.* Gaster), the reference is to Singer	*R.*	= *Rabbah*, e.g. *Gen.R.* = *Genesis Rabbah*
		Tanḥ.	= *Tanḥuma*
		Tanḥ.B.	= *Tanḥuma*, ed. S. Buber
Pes.K.	= *Pesiḳta Kahana*		

(7) For list of editions cited, see p. 745.

Chapter I

THE NATURE AND CHARACTER OF GOD AND HIS RELATIONS WITH MAN

The guiding principle of selection for this Rabbinic anthology has been to choose passages which (1) go beyond or lie outside O.T. teaching, or (2) which illustrate and develop that teaching at its best. The religious and ethical teachings of the O.T. are at various levels of excellence. Here it is proposed to illustrate only the higher or highest levels. Therefore, as is but right in an anthology, my purpose is to present flowers, not weeds.[1] For just as the O.T. contains weeds, so too does the Rabbinic literature. These I neglect. Yet it will be necessary to mention some weeds here and there, if only to set off the flowers more sharply. And besides the actual 'weeds', I shall have also occasionally to quote, or allude to, passages which cannot properly be called weeds, and which are certainly not flowers, but which are needed for the better *understanding* of the flowers, and in order not to give a false picture of the Rabbinic religion as a whole. For though the main object of this book is to collect flowers, yet, in presenting such a collection to the reader, care should be taken not to exaggerate, or to give a false impression. The total literature of *any* religion, more especially when that literature is of enormous size, is far from being nothing more than an assemblage of gems. Again, in a Rabbinic anthology the reader must be prepared for oddities, quaintnesses, queer stories, differences of taste between the Rabbis and ourselves, and yet these oddities may justly find a place in an anthology, so far as they are truly characteristic of Rabbinic religion, or illustrate some fine and peculiar Rabbinic teaching. They may, indeed, often illustrate that teaching far better than a brief copy-book utterance. Hence the limits of the anthology have to be drawn fairly wide.

We have also always to bear in mind that to the Rabbis the O.T. was inspired and excellent from end to end: more especially was the Pentateuch regarded as the word of God in the very fullest degree. Thus the lower levels of the O.T. were in their eyes no less divine than the higher levels, and no inconsistencies could ultimately be admitted or allowed. How did the Rabbis get over this basic trouble and dilemma? Did they explain the higher in the light of the lower, or the lower in the light of the higher? Did they drag down the

1 'Amidst the weeds of Pharisaism are flowers, amidst the Evangelic flowers are weeds. I cannot overcome my preference for the flowers. I am no gatherer of weeds' (I. Abrahams, *Studies in Pharisaism and the Gospels*, Second Series, p. vii).

second, or elevate the first? Or did they simply, without realising the inconsistencies of the O.T. or their own, adopt and expand both high and low? Did they make the high yet higher, and the low yet lower? The answer, I think, is that *all* these methods of treatment, *all* these varieties of teaching, can be discovered. Illustrations can be found of them all, and it is probable that, even in this anthology, indications of all of them will be included before the end.

Like Dr Cohen, in his admirable book, *Everyman's Talmud*, I too will begin my anthology with passages about the nature of God and His relation to the world, to man and to Israel. It is hardly necessary to let any Rabbinic quotations emphasise the O.T. doctrine that there is only one God. But the following passage is noteworthy:

[1] When God gave the Law, no bird sang or flew, no ox bellowed, the angels did not fly, the Seraphim ceased from saying, 'Holy, holy', the sea was calm, no creature spoke; the world was silent and still, and the divine voice said: 'I am the Lord thy God....' If you wonder at this, think of Elijah: when he came to Mount Carmel, and summoned all the priests of Baal, and said to them, 'Cry aloud, for he is a god,' God caused all the world to be still, and those above and those below were silent, and the world was, as it were, empty and void, as if no creature existed, as it says, 'There was no voice nor any answer' (I Kings XVIII, 27, 29). For if anyone had spoken, the priests would have said: 'Baal has answered us.' So, at Sinai, God made the whole world silent, so that all the creatures should know that there is no god beside Him, and so He spoke: 'I am the Lord, thy God,' and so too, in the days to come, He will say, 'I, and I alone, am He that comforts you' (Isa. LI, 12). (*Exod.R.*, Yitro, XXIX, 9.)

We need hardly go beyond—we *can* hardly go beyond—the emphatic utterances of Deutero-Isaiah, or the Deuteronomic assertion (IV, 39): 'Know therefore this day, and lay it to thine heart, that the Lord He is God in heaven above and upon the earth beneath: there is none else.' One God only: monotheism; but how about the divine unity? The actual verse of the *Shema*, which is not particularly stressed in the book of Deuteronomy, had, by the time of the Rabbis, become the watchword of Judaism.[1] The growth of the importance of the *Shema* as a creed cannot be accurately traced. Its position by, say, A.D. 30, is assured by the stories in the Gospels. It had become a confession of faith, and as such had to be recited by every Jew twice a day. To the Rabbis the *Shema* in its fuller meaning included not only Deut. VI,

[1] *P.B.* p. 40. The word *Shema* means 'Hear', and is the first word of the passages there quoted and here alluded to.

4–9, but also the two passages Deut. XI, 13–21 and Num. XV, 37–47, which are always grouped with it in orthodox prayer-books (**Note 77**). The full repetition of the *Shema* meant the repetition of all three passages. The reciting of the first section, and thus to acknowledge the One God, was called: 'to take upon oneself the yoke of the Kingdom of Heaven' (cp. [693]). Therefore it says in the Mishnah:

[2] R. Joshua b. Ḳarḥa said: Why does the section, 'Hear, O Israel' (Deut. VI, 4–9), precede 'And it shall come to pass, if ye shall hearken' (Deut. XI, 13–21)? So that a man shall first receive upon himself the yoke of the Kingdom of Heaven, and afterwards receive upon himself the yoke of the commandments.[1]

(*Ber.* II, 2.)

[3] R. Judah said in the name of Rab: He who has to say the *Shema* while he is out walking must stand still, and receive the Kingdom of Heaven. And what is the Kingdom of Heaven? The Lord our God, the Lord is One.

(*Deut.R.*, Wa'etḥanan, II, 31.)

[4] The Rabbis say that when Moses went up to God, he heard the angels of the service say to God, 'Blessed be the name of the glory of His Kingdom for ever,' and he brought this utterance down to the Israelites.[2] Why do the Israelites not say it out loud? R. Assi said: The matter is like as if a man stole a jewel from the King's palace, and gave it to his wife, and said to her, 'Do not deck yourself with it publicly, but only within the house.' But on the Day of Atonement, when the Israelites are as guiltless as the angels of the service, they say out loud, 'Blessed be the name of the glory of His Kingdom for evermore.' (**Note 11 *a*.**)

(*Deut.R.*, Wa'etḥanan, II, 36.)

[It is still the custom in orthodox synagogues to say the words 'Blessed, etc.' more or less quietly after the recitation of the opening verse of the *Shema*. But on the Day of Atonement, in the morning and evening services, it is said aloud by the congregation. The above passage refers to this custom (cp. [290]).

This doxology is the response to the first verse of the *Shema* (*P.B.* p. 40) and was uttered in the Temple on the Day of Atonement when the High Priest pronounced the Ineffable Name. V. Aptowitzer, in an interesting article in the *Monatsschrift f. Gesch. u. Wiss. d. Jud.* vol. LXXIII, Heft 3/4, for March/April 1929, pp. 93 ff.,

[1] See also **Notes 1 and 2.**

[2] See the line in small type on *P.B.* p. 40.

explains this formula as arising from various scriptural doxologies (e.g. Ps. LXXII, 18, 19; Neh. IX, 5; Ps. CXLVII, 20), and as having been introduced in public worship as a protest against the Hasmonean assumption of kingship and the Sadducean denial of the future life. This introduction he places in the reign of Alexander Jannaeus. The article deserves careful study; it deals also with the *Shema* (cp. [693]). (H. L.)]

[5] Jacob on his death-bed wanted to reveal to his sons the End of the Days [i.e. when the Messiah would come]. Then the Shechinah departed from him. Then he said: 'Perhaps there is a blemish in my household, as Ishmael was to Abraham and as Esau was to Isaac.' Then his sons said to him, 'Hear, O Israel, the Lord, our God, the Lord is One. Even as in *your* heart there is only One, so in *our* heart there is only One.' Then Jacob said: 'Blessed be the name of the glory of His Kingdom for ever and ever.' (**Note 78.**) (*Pes.* 56*a.*)

[6] Since when have the Israelites had the privilege to recite the *Shema*? From the day when Jacob was on his death-bed: he summoned the tribes, and said to them, 'When I am removed from the world, perhaps you will worship another god.' So it is written: 'And Jacob called his sons and said, Gather yourselves together, and hear, O sons of Jacob, and hearken unto Israel, your father' (Gen. XLIX, 1, 2). For Jacob said to them, 'Is Israel your father?' They said: 'Hear, O Israel, the Lord our God, the Lord is One.' Then he said softly, 'Blessed be the name of the glory of His Kingdom for ever and ever.' R. Levi said: What do the Israelites say *now*? 'Hear, Israel, our father, The word which thou didst command us is still abidingly with us: The Lord our God, the Lord is One.'

(*Deut.R.*, Wa'ethạnan, II, 35 (cp. [22]).)

What the exact meaning of the *Shema* may have been to the original writer is, like its right translation, extremely doubtful.[1] What did it mean to the Rabbis? Did it mean more than that there was only one God? The 'unity' doctrine is sometimes used in a way which to us may seem hardly appropriate:

[7] 'But He is in One, and who can turn Him? And what His soul desires even that He does' (Job XXIII, 13).[2] R. Pappos expounded

[1] See Abrahams, *Companion*, p. LI and R.V. The translation in A.V. and R.V. (Text), 'Hear, Israel, Yahweh, our God, is one Yahweh,' is probably the more correct rendering. [2] This is the literal translation, but cf. [8].

this verse thus: Seeing that He is unique in the universe and none can restrain Him, therefore, whatsoever He seeks, that He does. Akiba said to him: 'Enough, Pappos; not thus is the true exposition. But all that He does, is done by justice. The procedure in the heavenly court is governed by law as in an earthly court: mercy and justice are equated on either side. What then is the meaning of, "Since He is One"? It is that because God is unique in the universe, He knows the character of every single creature and their minds.' (*Tanḥ.B.*, Wayera, 49*a*.)

There is a second version of the same story, which runs thus:

[8] 'But He is in one mind, and who can turn Him, and what His soul desires, even that He does' (Job XXIII, 13). R. Pappos thus expounded the verse: Since He is alone in the world, and none can withstand Him, therefore whatsoever He seeks to do, that He does. Akiba said to him: 'It is enough, Pappos: not so do we expound the verse. There is judgment above just as there is below (Dan. IV, 17): there too they plead with arguments of law, and all is done in justice (*ib.* X, 21). God Himself deals justice. He says, "How fares the suit of such a one?" And they answer, "So it fell out," and God agrees with their verdict. This you learn from Micaiah, who said: "I saw the Lord seated on His throne, and all the host of heaven on His right and left" (I Kings XXII, 19). Is there a physical right and left in heaven? "Right" therefore means "inclining to right or acquitting", and "left" must mean "inclining to the left or condemnation": all, then, is done in justice. But what does Job mean? It means that since God is alone in the world, He knows the minds of His creatures.' (**Note 12.**) (*Tanḥ.B.*, Shemot, 4*b* (cp. [139] and [368]).)

Did God's unity also mean to the Rabbis that this only God was also in His nature, in His essence, one? I think it did, yet it can hardly be said that the Rabbis touch upon the more metaphysical aspects of the divine unity. The Rabbis were no theologians.[1] They had no training in philosophy. What they are really concerned to emphasise is that God's nature is ever the same: His deeds may vary, but *He* does not change. It is the whole God, and the same God, who expresses Himself in different ways according to different requirements and occasions; or again, it is *we* who perceive different aspects, or, as we say, different attributes, of God, but it is the same God, and the whole

[1] Cp. [100], [692], and [1641].

God, and the one God, who acts in many diverse ways, yet ever remains changeless and constant and the same:

[9] R. Abba b. Memel said: God said to Moses, 'Thou desirest to know my name. I am called according to my deeds. When I judge my creatures, I am called Elohim; when I wage war against the wicked, I am called Sabaoth; when I suspend judgment for a man's sins, I am called El Shaddai (God Almighty); but when I have compassion upon my world, I am called Yahweh, for Yahweh means the attribute of mercy, as it is said, "Yahweh, Yahweh (the Lord, the Lord), merciful and gracious" (Exod. xxxiv, 6). [It is interesting that the Rabbis, unlike Philo, regard what was to them the highest, most sacred, and, in some strange sense, most intimate, name of God as specially identified with the attribute of mercy or compassion. It is pleasant that though, to our minds, the Rabbis, in their human frailty, dwelt too much upon divine vengeance against Israel's enemies, and, perhaps, also too much upon the divine punishment of unrepentant sinners, yet, nevertheless, the essence, the inmost core, so to speak, of the divine nature was not for them vengeance or punishment, but mercy and compassion.] This is the meaning of the words, "I am that I am," namely, I am called according to my deeds.'

(*Exod.R.*, Shemot, III, 6 (cp. [19]).)

The Rabbis try to indicate that, in spite of the varieties of metaphor with which God is spoken of in Scripture, He is always the same God. There is no breach in the unity. If God is represented as a man of war, or as a teacher giving instruction, or as an ancient of days (Daniel), He is, nevertheless, ever the same:

[10] God said to Israel, 'Because ye have seen me in many likenesses, there are not therefore many gods. But it is ever the same God: I am the Lord thy God.' R. Levi said: 'God appeared to them like a mirror, in which many faces can be reflected: a thousand people look at it; it looks at all of them. So when God spoke to the Israelites, each one thought that God spoke individually to him. So it says, "I am the Lord *thy* God"; not collectively, "I am the Lord *your* God."' 'The word of God', said R. Jose b. Ḥanina, 'spoke with each man according to his power. Nor need you marvel at this. For the manna tasted differently to each: to the children, to the young and to the old, according to their power. [Proof passages follow.]

If the manna tasted differently according to men's power, how much more the word. David said, "The voice of the Lord with power" (Ps. XXIX, 4). It does not say "with His (God's) power", but "with power", that is, according to the power of each. And God says, "Not because you hear many voices are there many gods, but it is always I; I am the Lord thy God."'

(*Pes.K.* 109*b*–110*a*; *Tanḥ.B.*, Yitro, 40*a fin.*–40*b* (cp. [689]).)

[11] 'And the Lord spake unto Moses, saying: Speak unto the children of Israel, and say unto them, I am the Lord your God' (Lev. XVIII, 2), that is, 'I am the Lord who spake, and the world was; I am the Judge; I am full of compassion. I am the Judge who punishes; I am faithful to give a full reward.' (*Sifra* 85*c*.)

Without in any way perceiving any weakening thereby of the doctrine of the Unity, the Rabbis are able, if they please, every now and then, to make a distinction, even as the Hebrew Bible occasionally does, between God and the Holy Spirit (**Note 50**). Thus in one passage Jacob is said not to have been able at first to bless Ephraim and Manasseh:

[12] Then he rejoiced over them, for he said, 'Perhaps in my joy the Holy Spirit will rest upon me, and I shall be able to bless them.' [For the Holy Spirit rests only upon the joyful.] But the Holy Spirit did not return to Jacob. Then God said to the Holy Spirit, 'How long shall Jacob be distressed? Reveal thyself quickly, and enter into Jacob, that he may bless Joseph's sons.' (*Pes.R.* 12*a*.)

It would, however, be quite inaccurate and illegitimate to use a clearly rhetorical passage like the above as an argument for the separate existence of the Holy Spirit.

I have not come across any passage which seriously tackles the Christian conception of the Trinity, or which attempts to show that a Unity, which is a simple and pure Unity, is a higher or truer conception of the divine nature than a Unity of a Trinity or than a Trinity in a Unity. Where the Rabbis reply to the *minim* (heretics, sectaries, and sometimes Christians), they always represent these *minim* as believing in many gods. In other words, the doctrine of the Trinity (if that is referred to) is construed to mean Tritheism, which indeed was, and perhaps still is, its vulgar corruption. Hence the 'replies' are to-day of no particular interest, being somewhat obvious and commonplace. As against the arrogance of man, and the deification of the emperors, there are many stories, but they are rather crude and heavy:

[13] When Hadrian conquered the world and returned to Rome, he said to his courtiers, 'As I have conquered the world, I desire you to treat me as God.' They answered, 'But you have not yet prevailed against His city and temple.' So he went and succeeded in destroying the temple and driving Israel out. He then returned and announced his success and repeated his request. Now he had three philosophers. The first said to him, 'No man who is inside the palace can rebel: go outside the palace, and then you will be God: He made heaven and earth, you must first get beyond these, His palace.' The second said, 'It cannot be done, for He has said, "The gods that have not made the heavens and the earth shall perish under the heavens"' (Jer. x, 11). The third said, 'Be pleased to stand by me in this hour of need!' Hadrian said, 'How?' He replied, 'I have a ship three miles out at sea, and it contains all my fortune.' Hadrian said, 'I will send my legions and ships there to rescue it.' The philosopher said, 'Why trouble your legions and your ships, send a puff of wind.' Hadrian said, 'Whence can I get wind to send?' The philosopher retorted, 'How then can you be God who created the wind?' Hadrian went home displeased.

(*Tanḥ.*, Bereshit, §7, f. 10*b*–11*a*.)

[14] Moses and Aaron arrived on their mission to Pharaoh on the day when he was receiving ambassadors. Kings were coming and crowning him, for he was the supreme ruler. Pharaoh's servants said to him, 'Two old men are standing at the door.' He said, 'Have they brought crowns?' They said, 'No.' 'Then', said Pharaoh, 'let them come in last of all.' When all the kings had crowned Pharaoh, Moses and Aaron entered. He asked them what they wanted. They replied, 'The God of the Hebrews has sent us to you saying, Let my people go.' He said, 'Who is the Lord that I should hearken? He did not even know that He ought to send me a crown, for with mere *words* do you come. I know not the Lord.' Then he produced the parchment list of the gods, and began to read, 'God of Edom, god of Moab, god of Sidon,' etc., to the end of the list. He said, 'I have read through my list, and the name of your god is not in it.' Moses and Aaron said, 'Those gods of thine are dead, but our God is true, our God is

eternal, our God is living.' Pharaoh replied, 'Is He young? Is He old? How old? How many cities has He taken? How many provinces has He subdued? How many years have passed since He ascended the throne?' They replied, 'As for our God, "His power and His might fill the universe".[1] He was before the universe came into being, and at the end of all things He will still be there. He formed you, and gave you the breath of life.' Pharaoh said, 'What are His works?' They said, 'He stretched out the heavens and the earth. His voice cleaves the torches of fire, splits the mountains, shatters the rocks; His bow is fire, and His shafts are flashes; His javelin is the brand, and His shield the clouds. His sword is the lightning. He formed the mountains and the hills: He covers the heavens with clouds, brings down the rain and the dew, makes the grass to spring up, ripens the fruits. He causes kings to pass away, and He establishes others.' Pharaoh said, 'Ye speak falsely, for it is I that am lord of the world. "I created myself[2] and the Nile"' (Ezek. XXIX, 3). Then he gathered all the sages of Egypt and asked them, 'Have ye ever heard the report of this god?' They said, 'We have heard that He is the son of wise men, the son of ancient kings.' God said, 'Yourselves ye call wise men, but me only a son of the wise! As ye live, I will destroy your wisdom, as it says, "Surely the wisdom of Pharaoh's counsellors is brutish, how say ye unto Pharaoh that I am but the son of the wise!" (Isa. XIX, 11). Therefore "the princes of Egypt are become fools"' (*ib.* 13). (*Tanḥ.*, Wa'era, § 5, f. 95*a.*)

There are some curious allusions to people who hold that there are two powers in heaven. These people may be Jewish heretics, or also, sometimes, Christians, at a stage when the divinity of Jesus was a well-known doctrine of the Church, but when the doctrine of the Trinity had not yet become familiar to Jews as an essential feature of Christianity:

[15] 'I, even I, am He, and there is no God beside [or with] me; it is I that kill, and it is I that make alive; I wound and I heal' (Deut. XXXII, 39). This verse is an answer to those who say, 'There is no Power in heaven,' or to those who say, 'There are two Powers in heaven,' or to those who say, 'There is no Power who can make alive or kill, do evil or do good.'

(*Sifre Deut.*, Ha'azinu, § 329, f. 139*b* (cp. [69]).)

[1] See **Note 61.**

[2] This is the literal translation. See R.V.

One can imagine that this verse might be used against those who say that there are two powers, because such persons might also acknowledge the divine authority of Scripture. But it is exceedingly curious that the Rabbis, who are not wanting in great acuteness when it comes to making legal distinctions, or indeed to anything juristic, should not have seen that for those who deny that there is any God at all or any God of omnipotence, the verse is valueless, as such people would obviously deny any authority to the book from which the verse comes. Its value would be limited to Jews who were in danger of succumbing to pagan arguments. (Cp. Moore, I, 364–7; III, 116.)

Apparently some childish, or possibly magical, use was made by the *minim* of the various names of God in the O.T., and especially of El, of Elohim, and of Yahweh. Hence R. Simlai's statement to his disciples:

[16] The three words are just mere different names for one and the same God, even as you may call one and the same monarch, Basileus, Caesar, or Augustus.

(*Gen.R.*, Bereshit, VIII, 9 (Th. p. 63 n.); *E.T.* p. 6.)

Analogous to this passage is the following:

[17] [The 50th Psalm begins in Hebrew thus: 'El, Elohim, Yahweh has spoken.' Now El means God, and so does Elohim: thus we have three words for God, one after the other.] The heretics [very possibly Jewish Christians] asked R. Simlai, 'Why does it say, "El, Elohim, Yahweh has spoken"?' He replied, 'It does not say, "They spoke, and they called," but in the singular, "He spoke, and He called."' Then his disciples said to him, 'These men you have driven away with a broken reed.[1] But how would you answer *us*?' He said, 'All three appellations are only one name, even as one man can be called workman, builder, architect.' 'But why does the Psalmist mention the name of God three times?' 'To teach you that God created the world with three names, corresponding with the three good attributes by which the world was created, namely, wisdom, understanding and knowledge, even as it says, "The Lord by wisdom has founded the earth, by understanding has He established the heavens, by His knowledge the depths were broken up"' (Prov. III, 19, 20).

(*Midr.Ps.* on L, 1 (139*b*, § 1).)

The Hebrew word for God, Elohim, has a plural form, and sometimes the adjective which qualifies it is also in the plural. So in Deut.

[1] For the meaning of this phrase see [18].

IV, 7: 'For what nation is there so great that has God so nigh unto them as the Lord our God is in all things that we call upon Him for?'—the adjective 'nigh', or 'near', is in the plural. [This may be because it should be translated, not 'God', but 'a god', or even 'gods'. The Rabbis, however, suppose, like the A.V., that it means God, i.e. the one true God, the God of Israel.] Heretics, or unbelievers, or perhaps Christians, seem often to have worried the Rabbis about these plural forms, as if they proved that the Scriptures taught that there was more than one God, or that God was not one. So here:

[18] Heretics [*minim*, cp. [269]] asked R. Isaac, 'Why is the adjective "near" in the plural?' He replied, 'It is not written, "In all things that we call upon *them* for," but, "In all things that we call upon *Him* for."' [Therefore the One God, who is One, is meant, in spite of the plural of 'near'.] His disciples said, 'Master, you have dismissed these heretics with a reed [i.e. you have given them an inadequate reply (cp. [17])], what reply do you give to us?' He said to them, 'The plural means that God is near with every kind of nearness.'[1]

(*T.J.Ber.* IX, §1, f. 13*a*, line 13.)

We may note also this:

[19] Moses said to God, 'When I come to the children of Israel and they ask me who sent me, what shall I say?' For Moses wished to ask God to reveal His great name to him. God replied, 'Moses, is it my name that thou seekest to know? According to my acts am I called. When I judge my creatures, I am called Elohim or Judge (Exod. XXII, 27); when I punish my enemies, Lord of Hosts; when I suspend judgement over man's sin, El Shaddai (Almighty God); when I sit with the attribute of mercy, I am called the Compassionate One. According as my acts are, so is my name.' (*Tanḥ.*, Shemot, §20, f. 88*b* (cp. [9]).)

[20] An earthly king is wont to have dukes and viceroys, who share with him in the burden of rule, and also have a share in the honour with which he is honoured, but God is not so: He has no duke or governor and no lieutenant. No other with Him does His work, but He does it alone. No other bears the burden with Him, but He bears it alone. Therefore He alone is to be praised.

(*Midr.Ps.* on CXLIX, 1 (270*a*, §1).)

[1] It is the plural of intensification. See Gesenius, *Hebr. Gr.* ed. Oxford, 1910, § 124.

The type of anti-Christian polemic, which the next quotation illustrates, occurs, in one form or another, pretty frequently:

[21] R. Abbahu said: An earthly king has a father, a brother or a son; with God it is not so. For God says, 'I am the first, for I have no father; I am the last, for I have no brother; and there is no god beside me, for I have no son' (Isa. XLIV, 6).

(*Exod.R.*, Yitro, XXIX, 5; *E.T.* p. 6.)

There must be some allusion to polemics in the following. The *Shema* is getting a more distinctive meaning:

[22] 'Hearken unto (*el*) Israel your father' (Gen. XLIX, 2) [*el*, unto, means also *El*, God; so the Midrash says] R. Elazar b. Aḥwai said: From this verse the Israelites received the privilege of reading the *Shema*. When Jacob, our father, was about to die, he called his twelve sons and said to them, 'Hearken unto the God of Israel, your heavenly Father; perhaps there may be in your hearts a controversy about God.' Then they said, 'Even as your heart is whole and undivided towards God, so too is our heart: the Lord our God, the Lord is One.' Then Jacob too pronounced the divine name with his lips, and said, 'Blessed be the name of the glory of His Kingdom for ever and ever.' R. Berechiah and R. Ḥelbo in the name of R. Samuel said: Since, then, the Israelites are wont morning and evening, every day, to say: 'Hear, O Israel, the word which Abraham, our father, from the cave of Machpelah, ordered us to say *then*, we say regularly *still*: the Lord our God, the Lord is One.'

(*Gen.R.*, Wayeḥi, XCVIII, 3 (Th. p. 1252).)

In this extract, the *Shema* is traced back to Abraham (contrast [5] and [6]).

It is, I suppose, hardly possible to enunciate the doctrine of the divine ubiquity or omnipresence more beautifully or adequately than in the 139th Psalm, or in such O.T. verses as I Kings VIII, 27 or Jer. XXIII, 24. Nevertheless, some quaint or fine things which the Rabbis say about this doctrine are worth quoting:

[23] A gentile lady said to R. Jose: 'My god is greater than your god, for when your god appeared to Moses in the thorn bush, Moses hid his face, but when he saw my god, the snake, he fled before it' (Exod. IV, 3). R. Jose said: 'When our God appeared to Moses in the thorn bush, there was no place to which Moses could have fled. Whither could he have fled? To the heaven?

To the sea? To the land? For our God says, "Do I not fill heaven and earth?" (Jer. XXIII, 24). But from your god, the snake, a man has to run only a few steps to save himself.'

(*Exod.R.*, Shemot, III, 12.)

[24] A heathen asked R. Joshua b. Ḳarḥa: 'Why did God speak to Moses from the thorn bush?' R. Joshua replied: 'If He had spoken from a carob tree or from a sycamore, you would have asked me the same question. But so as not to dismiss you without an answer, God spoke from the thorn bush to teach you that there is no place where the Shechinah is not, not even a thorn bush.' (*Exod.R.*, Shemot, II, 5.)

During the joyous ceremony of the water libation, at the close of the first festival day of Tabernacles, Hillel was wont to say as follows:

[25] 'If I am there, all are there, and if I am not there, who is there?' Hillel used also to say: 'To the place where I wish to be, there do my feet bring me. If thou comest to my house, I will come to thy house; if thou dost not come to my house, I will not come to thy house, as it says, "In all places where I cause my Name to be mentioned, I will come unto thee and bless thee"' (Exod. XX, 24). (*Suk.* 53*a* (cp. *Lev.R.*, Beḥuḳḳotai, XXXV, § 1).)

[Hillel's saying seems, on the face of it, bizarre and egotistical. It is, however, esoteric, and when Hillel said 'I' (*Ani*) he meant 'God' (*Adonai*). Some commentators hold that 'I' here refers to Israel, but this is not likely. '*Ani*' is used for *Adonai* (cp. [38] *fin.*) one example will be found in *Aboth* I, 14. Another occurs in this same tractate (*Suk. M.* IV, 5, *T.B.* 45*a*), in connection with the rite of the willow-branch during Tabernacles, where we read that the procession round the altar cried out 'Save, prithee, O Lord' (Ps. CXVIII, 25). R. Judah, however, relates that the cry was not 'Save, prithee, O Lord', but 'Save, prithee, I and He' (*Ani wa-hu* for *Anna Adonai*). This may well be for *Adonai Yhwh*, to avoid pronouncing the Tetragrammaton. Or else, it may be explained as a Kabbalistic substitute for one of the seventy-two divine names: indeed, in *Ber.* 104*a* it is stated that '*He-Waw* (i.e. *Hu*) is the name of God'. It is to be noted that the numerical equivalents (see [716]) of *Anna YHWH* and *Ani wa-Hu* are identical. In the same way Hillel's cryptic remark gains all the more force from the fact, pointed out by Goldschmidt, that his name is numerically equivalent to *Adonai*. He therefore means 'If God is not here, no one is here.' The crowds thronging the Temple were bent on pleasure: Rabbis performed tricks to show their joy and amuse the people. Thus Simeon b. Gamaliel used to conjure with eight torches, throwing them up and catching them in succession without one of them touching another (*Suk.* 53*a*, where similar feats are described). All the more was Hillel drawn to warn the people that unless a religious spirit prevailed, the great ceremonial was valueless. Just because of the general merry-making, he would be likely to avoid pronouncing the Tetragrammaton. But apart from this, esoteric teaching was a known device (cf. Matt. XIII, 3), and it was natural for a teacher to make use of it. (H.L.)]

[In this connection, the following passage may be noted:

[26] Raba, son of bar Ḥanah reported, from R. Johanan: Once in seven years—or, according to others, twice—the Sages entrusted to their disciples the secret pronunciation of the Tetragrammaton... for 'this is My Name for concealing' [Exod. III, 15; *le 'Olam*, 'for ever', taken as *le 'Allem*].... The Rabbis taught: Originally, the twelve-lettered Name was entrusted to everyone. But when the indiscreet [*periẓim*; Rashi, those who abused it for thaumaturgical purposes] multiplied, the Sages entrusted it only to pious [*ẓenu'im*, chaste, discreet] priests, who, when giving the benediction, would gulp the name in the singing. R. Ṭarfon said: Once I followed my mother's brother to the platform, whence the benediction was given, and I bent my ear so as to listen to the High Priest. I heard him gulp the pronunciation amid the singing of his brethren. R. Judah reported in the name of Rab: The forty-two lettered Name is entrusted only to him who is chaste, humble, middle-aged; who is neither prone to anger nor a drunkard; who does not insist upon his due [i.e. only to a responsible man, who is not likely to divulge the secret in anger, drink, etc.]. He who knows the secret, who is careful of it, who preserves it, in purity, is beloved by God and esteemed among men. Respect for him rests on his fellow-creatures, and he inherits both worlds, this and the next. (*Ḳid.* 71*a*.)

The description of the priest who knows the secret is like that of a Freemason, for the mysteries of the Craft are entrusted only to men of probity, and membership of the Craft is an accepted testimonial to character.

To this day, in giving the Priestly Benediction in the Synagogue (*P.B.* p. 238*a*), the *Kohanim* keep up a chant reminiscent of the singing of the Temple priests.

The twelve-lettered Name is not easily to be identified, for there is no evidence to suppose that it is, necessarily, the twelve-lettered Name used by the later Kabbalists, who claim to have it by tradition. It would seem to have been a combination of letters or names (so

Maimonides), like the forty-two and forty-five lettered names. For an explanation of these, and of the seventy-two lettered name, in Kabbalistic usage, see *J.E.* IX, 164. (H. L.)]

The Rabbis, who believed every story about God in the Hebrew Bible, but whose deepest convictions about God were often in conflict with, and far superior to, those stories, were hard put to it to reconcile the omnipresence of God with the stories of His manifestation within a limited space. For the trouble of the O.T. is that there are so many passages and stories which appear to, and some of which indubitably do, teach a very different conception of God from that of Ps. CXXXIX. The Rabbis were in the painful position of having to accept both sets of passages as equally true. So they tried, more or less successfully, to invent some theory which would *partially*, at any rate, relieve the inconsistency, and make of the discordant a harmony. They conceived the idea of a God who, as it were, is able, at will, to expand and to contract, to concentrate Himself into a small space, or to fill all space *and more*, and who (this, I think, must be added) remains always, in His final and ultimate essence, eternally one and the same. They were helped in the development of this idea (as we shall see) by their creation of the doctrine of the Shechinah, or the Indwelling of God. Most useful were these doctrines of contraction and expansion, and of the Shechinah, in relation to the Temple. For the Rabbis grieved over the fallen Sanctuary. Some of them had seen it still uninjured; they had witnessed the sacrifices and, inexplicable as it is to us, had felt no disgust, but only joy, in all the blood and the killings of goat and sheep and bull.[1] They took all that is said of the Temple in the O.T. at its face value; God *did* 'dwell' in the Temple. It *was* His earthly 'house'. In some true, if mysterious, sense, He actually *was* within the Holy of Holies. For all this conception, the doctrine of the Shechinah was of great assistance. A very famous passage runs thus:

[27] It is written, 'And Moses was not able to enter into the tent of meeting, because the glory of the Lord filled the sanctuary' (Exod. XL, 35). R. Joshua of Sikhnin said in the name of R. Levi: The matter is like a cave which lies by the sea shore: the tide rises, and the cave becomes full of water, but the sea is no whit less full. So the sanctuary and the tent of meeting were filled with the radiance of the Shechinah, but the world was no less filled with God's glory. (*Num.R.*, Naso, XII, 4.)

[28] R. Phinehas said: If an earthly king is in his bedchamber, he is not in his dining-room, and *vice versa*, but God fills the upper and the lower regions at one and the same time, as it is said,

[1] But see **Notes 3 and 4**, and Introduction, pp. lxxxvi ff.

'His glory is over the earth and the heaven' (Ps. CXLVIII, 13) and, 'Do I not fill heaven and earth?' (Jer. XXIII, 24).

(*Midr.Ps.* on XXIV, 1 (103*a*, § 5).)

[29] R. Annaniel said: God says, 'If I choose, my glory fills the whole world, as it is said, "Do I not fill heaven and earth?" (Jer. XXIII, 24). And if I choose, I speak with Job out of the whirlwind (Job XXXVIII, 1) or with Moses from the thorn bush.'

(*Exod.R.*, Shemot, III, 6.)

Yet the Shechinah was also supposed not to 'rest' 'upon' or 'within' the second Temple as it had 'rested' 'within' or 'upon' the first. Thus we find the saying:

[30] When the Temple was rebuilt, the Shechinah did not rest upon it. For God had said, 'If *all* the Israelites return [from Babylonia], the Shechinah shall rest upon it, but if not, they shall be served only by the Heavenly Voice [*Bat Ḳol*].' (*Pes.R.* 160*a*.)

[This interesting passage implies (1) that there can be no full revelation when Israel is divided, and (2) that the post-Exilic revelation was non-prophetical and of a lower level. (H. L.)]

Striking is the following:

[31] When God said, 'Make me a dwelling place,' Moses wondered, and said, 'The glory of God fills the upper and the lower worlds, and yet He says to me, Make me a dwelling place....' God said, 'Not as thou deemest so do I deem, but twenty boards to the north, and twenty to the south, and eight to the west (are enough for me) (Exod. XXVI, 18, 20, 25). And not only that, but I will come down and confine my Shechinah within a square yard.... Ye are the children of the Lord your God, and I am your Father (Deut. XIV, 1; Jer. XXXI, 9). It is an honour to children to be near their father, and an honour to a father to be near his children; therefore, make a house for the Father that He may dwell near His children.' (*Exod.R.*, Terumah, XXXIV, 1, 3 (cp. [216]).)

At the beginning of Leviticus it says that God spoke to Moses from the Tent of Meeting, i.e. from between the two cherubim:

[32] Simeon b. Azzai said: It is said of God, 'The heavens and the earth do I fill' (Jer. XXIII, 24). See how potent was the love of God for Israel in that this divine glory was constrained, so as to appear speaking from upon the Mercy Seat between the two cherubim. **(Note 19.)** (*Sifra* 4*a*.)

These passages, too, are suggestive:

[33] When God said to Moses, 'Let them make me a sanctuary that I may dwell among them' (Exod. xxv, 8), Moses said, 'Who can do so? Is it not written, "Do I not fill heaven and earth?" (Jer. xxiii, 24) and, "The heaven is my throne, and the earth is my footstool"' (Isa. lxvi, 1). Then God said, 'I do not ask according to *my* capacity, but according to *their* capacity, for if I were to ask for all the world, it could not contain my glory, or one of the suns[1] which are mine.' (*Num.R.*, Naso, xii, 3.)

[34] A Samaritan asked R. Me'ir: 'How is it possible that He of whom it is said, "Do I not fill heaven and earth" (Jer. xxiii, 24) should have spoken to Moses between the two staves of the ark?' (Exod. xxv, 13). R. Me'ir said: 'Bring me a large [or, magnifying] mirror.' And he said to the man, 'Look at yourself in it.' He did so, and saw his face magnified. Then R. Me'ir said: 'Bring me a small [or, diminishing] mirror.' And he said, 'Look at yourself in it.' He did so, and saw his face made small. Then R. Me'ir said: 'If you, a mortal man of flesh and blood, can change your appearance at will [without altering your substance], how much more can God!'

(*Gen.R.*, Bereshit, iv, 4 (Th. p. 27).)

Again, if God be 'everywhere', how could Jonah possibly even *think* of fleeing from His presence? The puzzle is solved in one passage by the theory that though God is everywhere, yet He, or the Shechinah, does not reveal Himself except in Palestine:

[35] How could Jonah 'flee from the presence of the Lord'? Does it not say, 'Whither shall I flee from thy presence, etc.' (Ps. cxxxix). But Jonah said, 'I will go beyond Palestine to a land where the Shechinah does not reveal itself, for the nations are near to repentance, and I would not make Israel guilty.' (*Mek.*[2], *Pisḥa*, Bo, §1, p. 3; *Mek.*[1] 1*b* (cp. [1562]).)

Cp. Lauterbach's note (vol. i, p. 7): 'For since the Gentiles are more inclined to repent, I might be causing Israel to be condemned, so, by contrast with the Ninevites, who would readily listen to the prophet and repent, Israel would stand condemned for not so readily listening to the prophets.'

[1] [So, according to Ze'eb Einhorn (comm. *in loc.*) and, possibly, also according to David Lurya (*in loc.*). Cp. *Ḥullin* 60*a*, top. But it would be better to read *Shammash* for *Shemesh*, and to render 'one of my ministers'. (H. L.)]

[This passage must not be over-estimated or taken too literally, for it is a paradox. The speaker is, at the moment, thinking only of finding a way out of the difficulty presented by Jonah's action; that the suggested solution limits God's omnipresence does not matter to him, for if he were dealing with that subject, he would be equally emphatic and equally regardless of consequences. There are passages which are in direct opposition to this, e.g. that God revealed Himself at Sinai just because it was in the desert, in no-man's land, and outside Palestine (see [442–6]). The words 'I would not make', or, 'so as not to make, Israel guilty', mean that, by contrast with the repentant Gentiles, Israel would show up badly, and would incur punishment. 'To make guilty' is equivalent to 'make them appear guilty', a declarative use of the Piel conjugation. If, therefore, Jonah 'flees', and does not deliver his message, Israel would not be liable to punishment. (H. L.)]

The presence of God was not *limited* to the Temple. Even as He was in the Temple, so is He in the synagogues when Israelites pray therein:

[36] God says, 'Who has ever come into a synagogue, and has not found my glory there?' 'And not only that', said R. Aibu, 'but if you [individually] are in a synagogue, God stands by you' (Ps. LXXXII). (*Deut.R.*, Ki Tabo, VII, 2.)

[37] 'My love is like a gazelle' (Cant. II, 9). As the gazelle leaps from place to place, and from fence to fence, and from tree to tree, so God jumps and leaps from synagogue to synagogue to bless the children of Israel. (*Num.R.*, Naso, XI, 2.)

God followed Israel into exile; the conception is illustrated by the following story:

[38] R. Aḥa said: Nebuchadnezzar gave three commands to Nebuzar-adan concerning Jeremiah, 'Take him and look well to him' (Jer. XXXIX, 12), that is, him, but not his people. 'Do him no harm'; *him*, but as for his *nation*, do unto them evil, as it may please thee. 'As he shall say unto you, that do'; that is as *he* shall say, but not as his *people* shall say. When Jeremiah saw a band of young men with iron collars round their necks, he put his neck within their fetters, but Nebuzar-adan removed him from them. And so when he saw a band of old men chained with chains, he put his neck into their chains, but Nebuzar-adan removed him from them. And he said to Jeremiah, 'One of

three things: You are a false prophet, or you despise sufferings, or you are a shedder of blood. A false prophet, for all these years you prophesied against this city that it would be laid waste, and now that it has happened, you are very displeased. Or you despise sufferings, for I desire to do you no evil, and you desire to bring evil upon yourself, as if to say to me that sufferings from my hand would be accounted by you as nothing. Or you are a shedder of blood, for the king has given me strict charge about you that no evil should befall you, and you seek to do evil to yourself, so that the king, if he hears of it, may kill me.' At the last he said to him, 'If it be good in your eyes, I will show you special favour.' But Jeremiah would not accept the offer until God had spoken to him, as it says, 'The word that came to Jeremiah after Nebuzar-adan had let him go from Ramah' (Jer. XL, 1). What was that word? God said to him, 'If *you* remain here, I will go with *them*, and if *you* go with *them*, I will stay here.' Then Jeremiah said, 'If I go with them, what can I benefit them? Let their King and Creator go with them, for He alone can benefit them greatly.' Hence it says, 'After Nebuzar-adan had let him go from Ramah, and when he was bound in chains' (the Midrash makes the 'he' refer to God). R. Aḥa said: God was then, as it were, also bound in chains, in accordance with what is said in Ezek. I, 1, 'I was among the captives.' (*Lam.R.*, Introduction, 34.)

Yet the Rabbis go beyond the author of Ps. CXXXIX in their not infrequent assertion that God is, as it were, beyond, or above, and more than, His universe; He is 'transcendent' as well as 'immanent', as we should say. Their thought struggles with its expression. So we get:

[39] 'O Lord thou hast been a dwelling-place to us in all generations' (Ps. XC, 1), and in Deut. XXXIII, 27 it says, 'The God of old is a dwelling-place.' R. Isaac said: We should not know whether God were the dwelling-place of the world, or whether the world were His dwelling-place, had not Moses come [the author of Ps. XC] and said, 'The Lord is for us a dwelling-place.' R. Jose b. Ḥalafta said: We should not know if God were an appendage to the world, or if the world were His appendage, had not He Himself said, 'Behold, there is a place by me' (Exod. XXXIII, 21). He is the place of the world [i.e. He includes the world]; the

world is not His place. So the world is an appendage to Him; He is not an appendage to the world (cp. *R.T.* p. 267).

(*Midr.Ps.* on XC, 1 (195*b*, § 10).)

[The discussion on this page is seen in clearer light, and found to be of greater importance, when we recall that different forms of the word translated 'dwelling-place' are used in the Psalm, which has *ma'on*, and in Deuteronomy, which has the feminine, *me'onah*. The form used in Deuteronomy was the subject of ancient controversy. Resh Laḳish (see *Soferim* VI, 4; *T.J.Ta'an.* IV, 2, f. 68*a*, line 46; etc.) said: 'There were three pentateuchal scrolls (containing variants) found in the Temple Court. One was the scroll which had *ma'on* in Deuteronomy. But the other two had *me'onah*, which was therefore adopted.' Now *me'onah* may well have been a mistake. The true reading was possibly *ma'on*+*he*, the abbreviation of the Tetragrammaton. Similar cases can be seen in Ps. CXVIII, 5 and Cant. VIII, 6. The distinction is evident to the English reader by comparing the English versions:

Ps. CXVIII, 5.

A.V. and R.V.: The Lord answered me and set me in a large place.

American-Jewish version: He answered me with great enlargement.

Here, A.V. and R.V. take *merḥav Yah* as two words, the latter being the divine name. The American-Jewish version takes the two words as one, as an intensitive, feminine form of *merḥav*, enlargement.

Again, in Cant. VIII, 6:

A.V. and R.V margin.: a most vehement flame (*shalhevethyah*).

R.V. text and American-Jewish version: a very flame of the Lord (*shalheveth Yah*).

It may be that the true reading in Deuteronomy contained the divine name, and that this was the reason for the choice of the verse as a proof text in *Midrash Psalms*, i.e. 'Abode of God', God is the abode. (H. L.)]

God is sometimes called *Maḳom*, i.e. place, in Rabbinical literature. How is this?

[40] R. Ammi said[1]: Why is God given the appellation of 'place'? Because He is the place of the world, and the world is not His place [i.e. He fills the world, but the world does not contain Him]. R. Abba b. Yudan said: The matter is like a warrior who rides upon a horse, and his weapons hang down on each side; the

[1] Cited by Huna.

horse is an adjunct and secondary to the rider, but the rider is not an adjunct and secondary to the horse.

(*Gen.R.*, Wayeẓe, LXVIII, 9 (Th. p. 777).)

God is in heaven, yet still more truly can it be said that none knows His place:

[41] As no man knows the place of the soul, so no man knows the place of God. So let the soul, of which no man knows the place, praise God who is exalted above His world, and whose 'place' no man knows. (*Midr.Ps.* on CIII, 1 (217*a*, § 5).)

God in His full nature and glory cannot be understood by man:

[42] 'Riding upon the Heavens' (Deut. XXXIII, 26). The Israelites came to Moses, and asked him to tell them the nature (*middah*) of the upper, that is, of the divine glory. He said, 'You belong to the lower realms and cannot know it. It is like a man who wished to see the King's face. They said to him, "Enter the city and thou wilt see him." He came to the city, and beheld a veil spread over the gate, and precious stones and pearls were affixed to it. At the sight, he fell to earth. They said to him, "Before you could feast your eyes, you fell to earth. If you had entered the city itself and seen the face of the King, how much less could you have endured the sight."'

(*Sifre Deut.*, Berakah, § 355, 148*a fin.*)

The comparison of the relation of God to the world with the relation of the soul to the body is frequent. For example:

[43] It is written, 'Praise the Lord, O my soul' (Ps. CIII, 1). Why did David think of praising God with his soul? He said, 'The soul fills the body and God fills the world (Jer. XXIII, 24), so let the soul which fills the body praise God who fills the world. The soul carries the body, and God carries the world (Isa. XLVI, 4), so let the soul which carries the body praise God who carries the world. The soul outlives the body, and God outlives the world (Ps. CII, 27); so let the soul which outlives the body praise God who outlives the world. The soul is one and alone in the body, and God is one and alone in the world (Deut. VI, 4); so let the soul which is one and alone in the body praise God who is one and alone in the world. The soul does not eat in the body, and there is no eating with God (Ps. L, 13), so let the soul which eats

not in the body praise God with whom is no eating. The soul sees, and is not seen; God sees, and is not seen (Zech. IV, 10); so let the soul which sees, and is not seen, praise God who sees, and is not seen. The soul is pure in the body, and God is pure in the world (Hab. I, 13); so let the soul which is pure in the body praise God who is pure in the world. The soul sleeps not in the body, and with God there is no sleep (Ps. CXXI, 4); so let the soul which sleeps not in the body praise God with whom is no sleep. (*Lev.R.*, Wayiḳra, IV, 8; cp. *Deut.R.*, Wa'etḥanan, II, 37 and *Midr.Ps.* on CIII, 1 (217*a*, § 4).)

[44] As God fills the whole world, so also the soul fills the whole body. As God sees, but cannot be seen, so also the soul sees, but cannot be seen. As God nourishes the whole world, so also the soul nourishes the whole body. As God is pure, so also the soul is pure. As God dwells in the inmost part of the Universe, so also the soul dwells in the inmost part of the body. (*Ber.* 10*a*.)

God is 'immanent' in the world, but He is 'nearest' to man. Thus we find this somewhat mysterious utterance:

[45] 'Behold I will stand before thee there upon the rock in Horeb' (Exod. XVII, 6). God said to Moses, 'In every place where you find a trace of the feet of man, there am I before you.' (**Note 79.**) (*Mek.*², *Wayassa'*, Beshallaḥ, § 6, p. 175; *Mek.*³, § 7, vol. II, p. 133.)

God is near to all who call upon Him.

[46] The idol is near, and is yet far. God is far [for is He not in the heaven of heavens?], and yet He is near.... For a man enters a synagogue, and stands behind a pillar, and prays in a whisper, and God hears his prayer, and so it is with all His creatures. Can there be a nearer God than this? He is as near to His creatures as the ear to the mouth. (*T.J.Ber.* IX, § 1, f. 13*a*, line 17.)

[47] A man has a protector [*patronus*]. If he worries him too much, the protector says, 'I will forget him, he worries me.' But God is not so; however much you worry Him, He receives you. (*T.J.Ber.* IX, § 1, f. 13*b*, line 10.)

No need to invoke the mediation of angels: let man go direct to God.

[48] If a man is in distress, let him not call on Michael or Gabriel, but let him call direct on me, and I will hearken to him straightway. (*T.J.Ber.* IX, § 1, f. 13*a*, line 69.)

It may be noted here that angels, however abundant, have small religious importance. 'They were not objects of veneration, much less of adoration; in orthodox Judaism they were not intermediaries between man and God' (Moore, I, 410, 411, 438; III, 134).

It is obvious that the familiar phrase, 'Our Father who art in heaven', would never have been coined had not there been a rather general belief that God *did* dwell (with His angelic court) in heaven. The phrase is not a *mere* metaphor: I do not suppose it is a mere metaphor to millions of simple believers even at the present day; the Rabbis were, for the most part, 'simple believers', and their universe, we have always to remember, was the tiny universe of pre-Copernican days. But God, if in heaven, is also 'near' to man:

[49] R. Judah b. Simon said: 'An idol is near and far; God is far and near.' 'How?' 'An idolater makes an idol, and sets it up in his house. So the idol is near. But one may cry unto the idol, and it will not answer, therefore the idol is far. But God is far and near.' 'How?' R. Judah b. Simon said: 'From here to heaven is a journey of five hundred years: therefore God is far; but He is also near, for if a man prays and meditates in his heart, God is near to answer his prayer.' (*Deut.R.*, Wa'etḥanan, II, 10.)

When the Israelites study the Law, God or His Shechinah is among them:

[50] R. Ḥanina b. Teradion said: If two sit together, and words of Torah are between them, the Shechinah rests between them, and if even *one* sits and occupies himself with the Torah, God fixes for him a reward. (*Aboth* III, 3; cp. III, 7.)

So, too, when men are busied with that which, to the Rabbis, was, perhaps, the holiest of human actions—the administration of justice—God is among them:

[51] When three sit and judge, the Shechinah is in their midst. (*Ber.* 6*a*.)

[52] When Abraham was recovering from the circumcision, God visited him in his sickness (Gen. XVIII, 1). As the Almighty revealed Himself, Abraham was seated (*ib.*), but attempted to

stand. God said to him, 'Trouble not thyself, remain seated,' as it says, 'The Lord said to my lord, Sit at my right hand' (Ps. CX, 1). Abraham replied: 'But is it respectful for me to sit whilst Thou standest?' God said again 'Trouble not thyself, thou art an old man, a hundred years old. As thou livest, because thou, in thy old age, sittest while I stand, thy descendants, when they are little children, three years old, four years old, shall sit in synagogues and schools, and I will stand among them, for "God stands in a godly congregation"' (Ps. LXXXII, 1).

(*Tanḥ.B.*, Wayera, 43*b* (cp. [721]).)

The Rabbis were not averse to using the most daring, and to our taste, the most unsuitable, anthropomorphisms about God, more particularly in dealing with the relations of God to Israel or to the Law or to Moses. I will give here one example out of very many. Others may have to be quoted in other connections later on (cf. Cohen, *E.T.* p. 8):

[53] R. Joshua b. Levi said: When Moses went up to God, he found God weaving crowns for the letters of the Law. God said to him, 'Moses, do men give no greeting in your city?' Moses said, 'Does a slave greet his Master?' God replied, 'You ought to have wished me success.' Then Moses said, 'May the power of my Lord be great, according as *thou* hast spoken' (Num. XIV, 17).

(*Sab.* 89*a*.)

The point of the last sentence is that Moses feels himself unworthy to wish God success, and therefore quotes what are here, for the purpose of the argument, taken to be God's own words. At bottom, the Rabbi means that no human praise of God is adequate.

If in one Rabbinic passage it is said that God is spoken of as having a voice like the rushing of many waters, or as roaring like a lion (Ezek. XLIII, 2; Amos III, 8, where the Midrash regards the lion as a metaphor for God), the reason is:

[54] We compare Him (to one or other of His creatures) in order that men may understand better.

(*Mek.*[2], *Baḥodesh*, Yitro, § 4, p. 215; *Mek.*[3], vol. II, p. 221.)

Cf. Cohen, *E.T.* p. 6 *fin.* who renders: 'We borrow terms from His creatures to apply to Him in order to assist the understanding.'

But there are many warnings against drawing false inferences. God, who is no creature, or king, of 'flesh and blood', is *not* like man. For example:

[55] It says: 'Command the children of Israel that they bring unto *thee* pure olive oil for the light' (Lev. XXIV, 2). God says: 'For thee, Moses, not for me, God. I need no light.' The table was at the north side [of the Sanctuary]; the light on the south side (Exod. XXVI, 35). God says: 'I need no eating, I need no light.' [In a man's house the table and the lamp are close to each other.] (*Men.* 86*b*.)

Here is a curious attempt to explain away the 'coming down' of God upon Mount Sinai:

[56] 'And the Lord came down upon mount Sinai.' You might suppose that the divine glory came down in its reality, and was spread over mount Sinai. Therefore it says: 'It was from *heaven* that I spoke to you.' This teaches you that God bent the lower and the upper heavens upon the top of the mount, and the glory descended, and was spread over mount Sinai, as a man lays the bolster on the head of the bed....Moses and Elijah did not go up, and the glory did not come down, but you are to understand that God said to Moses: 'Behold I call to thee from the top of the mount, and thou shalt come up.'
(*Mek.*[2], *Baḥodesh*, Yitro, § 4, p. 216 *fin.*; *Mek.*[3], vol. II, p. 224 (cp. *Suk.* 5*a*).)

The burden of the O.T. is apparent whenever the sacrifices and offerings are mentioned. With their views about the Temple as the dwelling-place of God and as the most visible sign of His grace, the Rabbis could not but believe that the sacrifices were enormously important. As, after the destruction of the Temple, they could not be rendered, the next best thing was to study them. So the Rabbis make God say:

[57] If you study the laws about sacrifice, that is to me as if you had offered them. (*Pes.K.* 60*b*.)

The unfortunate children had to begin their Pentateuchal lessons with Leviticus![1]

[58] For God said, As the sacrifices are pure, so are the children pure. (*Pes.K.* 60*b fin.*–61*a init.*)

On the other hand, any coarse archaism as to God actually eating the offerings was as far from the Rabbis as from the author of Ps. L,

[1] [Leviticus was used as an elementary reading-book, but the *Shema* and its moral lessons were emphasised from the earliest possible moment in the child's life. See also **Note 4.** (H. L.)]

whose words they quote in close conjunction with quotations about the sacrifices, and without the smallest sense of any incongruity between them. (See **Notes 3, 4 and 20*e*.**)

It was impossible for the Rabbis to adopt the Prophetic depreciation of sacrifices. For they are commanded in the perfect Pentateuch, and so we get a mixture of high appreciation and devotion together with ethical and religious warnings or lessons. The following are samples:

[59] Abraham said to God, 'If the Israelites sin before thee, thou mightest do unto them as with the generations of the flood and of the Tower of Babel.' God replied, 'No.' Abraham said, 'How can I know this?' Then God said, 'Take a heifer of three years old', etc. (Gen. xv, 9) [i.e. sacrifices will appease me]. Abraham said, 'That is all very well for the time when the Temple exists, but when it does not, what will become of them then?' God said, 'I have appointed for them the chapters about the sacrifices: whenever they read them, I will reckon it to them as if they had brought the offerings before me, and I will forgive them their sins.' (*Meg.* 31*b*.)

Mention in Lev. I, 10 is made of sheep and goats only, so that a man may not say to himself:

[60] I will do what is ugly and unseemly, and *then* I will bring an ox on which there is much flesh, and I will offer it upon the altar, and God will have compassion on me, and accept me in penitence. (*Lev.R.*, Wayiḳra, II, 12.)

[61] It is written in Lamentations (II, 7): 'God has cast off His altar.' R. Haggai said in the name of R. Isaac: It is like the inhabitants of a province who prepared banquets for a king; they angered him, but for a time he bore with them. But at last he said: 'You think you may continue to anger me because of the banquets you have prepared for me. Behold, I hurl down your banquets before your eyes.' So God said to Israel, 'You think you may provoke me because of the sacrifices which you offer to me. Behold, I hurl them down before your face.' (*Lam.R.* II, 11 on II, 7.)

[62] A Rabbi said: In all other places it is said, 'Ye shall *offer* a burnt offering,' but in Num. XXIX, 2 [on the New Year offerings] it is said, 'Ye shall *make* an offering.' Why? God says, 'Since

ye have come before me this day for judgment, and have gone forth in peace, I regard you as if you were created as new creatures before me.' Another Rabbi said: In all other places about burnt offerings the word sin is mentioned, but in the regulations about the burnt offerings for Pentecost the word sin is not mentioned (Num. XXVIII, 27). God says: 'Since you have assumed the yoke of the Law, I regard you as if you had never sinned.' **(Note 81.)** (*T.J.R.H.* IV, § 8, f. 59*c*, line 60.)

[63] It is written, 'My offerings and my bread for my sacrifice.' It is not that *I* need offerings, for all the world is mine, and the animals which you offer I created, as it is said, 'If I were hungry, I would not tell thee, for the world is mine and the fullness thereof' (Ps. L, 12): with me there is no eating and drinking. R. Simeon said: Thirteen modes of compassion are ascribed to God, as it is said, 'The Lord, the Lord, merciful and gracious', etc. (Exod. XXXIV, 6). Would a compassionate being assign the feeding of himself to one who is cruel? [The quaint meaning is that if God, the merciful One, needed food, He would not hand over the supplying Him with food to man, who, as compared with Him, is cruel.] R. Ḥiyya b. Abba said: God says, 'My creatures do not need my creatures. Have you ever heard men say, "Give this vine wine to drink that it may give much wine; drench this olive tree with oil, that it may give much oil? My creatures do not need my creatures; should *I* need my creatures?"'

(*Num.R.*, Pineḥas, XXI, 16, 17 (cp. *Pes.R.* 80*a*; [1145]).)

[It must not be forgotten that the Rabbis, as did the Prophets and Psalmists, regarded sacrifices as subordinate to prayer. The following passage is in no way exceptional:

'God said to Israel: "Be steadfast (*zehirin*) in prayer, for no quality (*middah*) is fairer than prayer, it is greater than all the sacrifices" (Isa. I, 11–15: yet this passage ends, "Yea, though ye multiply prayers, I will not hearken, for your hands are full of blood"): hence prayer, which comes last in the list, is superior to sacrifice. And even if a man be unworthy that his prayer should be answered, and that lovingkindness be wrought for him, yet, if he pray and supplicate much, I will, nevertheless, grant him lovingkindness, as it says, "All the ways of the Lord are lovingkindness and truth" (Ps. XXV, 10). I have put lovingkindness before truth and righteousness before justice, for "righteousness and justice are the foundation of His throne"' (Ps. LXXXIX, 14) (*Tanḥ.*, Wayera, § 1, f. 31*b*). (H. L.)]

God is the creator and sustainer:

[64] Abraham said to the men of the generation of the Tower of Babel: What do you seek from God? Has He said to you, 'Come and provide for me?' He created and He provides; He made and He sustains. (*Tanḥ.B.*, Wayera, 50*a*.)

An ancient blessing in the Prayer Book runs thus:

[65] Blessed art thou, O Lord our God, King of the Universe, who formest light and createst darkness, who makest peace and createst all things, who in mercy givest light to the earth and to them that dwell thereon, and in thy goodness renewest the work of creation every day continually.
(*P.B.* p. 37; Moore, I, 384; III, 120.)

Man cannot fully understand God, not even His attributes (*middot*):

[66] Moses said to God, 'Show me now thy ways' (Exod. XXXIII, 13). And He showed them to him, as it is said, 'He made known His ways unto Moses' (Ps. CIII, 7). Then Moses said, 'Show me now thy glory' (Exod. XXXIII, 18), that is, 'the attributes wherewith thou governest the world'. Then God said, 'Thou canst not comprehend my attributes.' (*Midr.Ps.* on XXV, 4 (106*a*, § 6).)

The Rabbis are, indeed, often at pains, by all kinds of contrasts and comparisons, to indicate the unlikeness of God to man, and I suppose they were all the more anxious to do this because the O.T. constantly talks of God, and makes God act, as if He were just a powerful man with man's passions and man's changes of mood. Perhaps, too, they were anxious to point out God's unlikeness to man (though I am by no means sure that they thought of this), because they knew that they themselves were often guilty of the same sort of anthropomorphisms, and indeed sometimes made God talk more humanly, and even more colloquially and familiarly, than anything that is to be found in the Hebrew Bible.

Thus we get passages like the following:

[67] There may be a mighty man in a country who, when passion and prowess overcome him, will smite his father and mother and his nearest relatives, but God is not like him. The Lord is a man of war when He fought against the Egyptians; but the Lord is His name; that is, He has compassion upon His creatures, as it is said, 'The Lord, the Lord, gracious and merciful.' A mighty man, when he shoots forth his arrow cannot get it

back again, but with God it is not so. When the Israelites do not perform His will, then the decree of doom goes, as it were, forth from Him, as it is said, 'If I whet the lightning of my sword' (Deut. XXXII, 41), but if they repent, He at once takes it back, as it is said, 'My hand holds back the judgment' [Midrashic rendering of Deut. XXXII, 41]. [And then the nationalistic, particularistic emotions of the Rabbis, and their longing for the fall of their oppressors, make themselves felt again, and in odd unconsciousness of any inconsistency with the previous saying that the Lord is merciful to His creatures, they continue thus:] But does the hand return empty? No, for it says, 'I will render vengeance to mine enemies, and I will recompense them that hate me' (*ib.*). And who are these? The nations of the world. A human king goes forth to war, and the provinces by which he passes draw near to him, and tell him their needs, but they are told, 'He is excited, he is going forth to war; when he returns victorious, come *then*, and ask of him your needs.' But God is not like that. The Lord is a man of war, He fights against the Egyptians; but the Lord is His name; He hearkens to the cry of all the inhabitants of the world, as it is said, 'To thee who hearest prayer, all flesh comes' (Ps. LXV, 2). A human king, when he goes forth to war, is unable to feed and to supply provisions for all his troops, but God is not like that. The Lord is a man of war; He fights against the Egyptians, as it is said, 'To Him who divided the Red Sea in sunder' (Ps. CXXXVI, 13); but the Lord is His name; He feeds and provisions all the inhabitants of the world, as it is said, 'He gives food to all flesh, for His mercy endures for ever' (Ps. CXXXVI, 25). (*Mek.*², *Shirata*, Beshallaḥ, § 4, pp. 130–1 (see **Note 5**); *Mek.*³, vol. II, pp. 32–4.)

The phrase 'The Lord is a man of war' strikes the Rabbis as strange, not because of the words 'of war', but because of the words 'a man'; yet contrast the following:

[68] 'The Lord is a *man* of war' (Exod. XV, 3 in the Song of Moses). Is it possible to say this, when it is said, 'Do I not fill heaven and earth, says the Lord?' (Jer. XXIII, 24). And is it not said, 'One cried unto the other, and said, "Holy, holy, holy, is the Lord of Hosts: the whole earth is full of His glory."' What, then, mean the words, 'The Lord is a *man* of war'? Because of your love and your holiness I sanctify my name through you, as it is said,

'I am God, and not man, the Holy One of Israel in the midst of thee' (Hos. XI, 9). [When God fights for, or delivers, Israel, He is sanctified through Israel in the eyes of the nations (cp. Ezek. XX, 41).]

(*Mek.*², *Shirata*, Beshallaḥ, § 4, p. 131; *Mek.*³, vol. II, p. 34.)

[69] God revealed Himself at the Red Sea as a hero waging war, and at Sinai (Exod. XXIV, 10), as an old man full of compassion, even as it speaks in Daniel (VII, 9) of the Ancient of Days; but to the words, 'The Lord is a man of war', the Scripture adds, 'The Lord is his *name*' [i.e. His true essence]: it is the same God in Egypt, the same God at the Red Sea, the same God in the past, the same God in the future, the same God in this world, the same God in the world to come, as it says, 'See now that I, even I, am He' [i.e. ever the same] (Deut. XXXII, 39), and 'I, the Lord, the first, and with the last I am the same' (Isa. XLI, 4).

(*Mek.*², *Shirata*, Beshallaḥ, § 4, p. 130; *Mek.*³, vol. II, p. 31 (cp. [15]).)

If man should be humble, there is a sense in which God is strangely humble too:

[70] If a pupil is ill, and the teacher goes to visit him, the other pupils go before to announce the coming of the teacher. But when God went to visit Abraham in his illness, He went first, before the angels (Gen. XVIII, 1, 2). Is there anyone more humble than He?

(*Tanḥ.*, Wayera, § 2, f. 31 *b*.)

So too:

[71] R. Johanan said: Wherever in the Scripture you find the power of God mentioned, there too you find mention of His humility.

(*Meg.* 31 *a*; see in full in *P.B.* pp. 214 *fin.*–215.)

His humility, to the Rabbis, is manifested because He has regard to the humble:

[72] R. Elazar b. Pedat has said: You can find seven passages wherein God Almighty equated Himself with those of humble heart. First, in Deut. X, 17, we read of Him as 'the God of gods and the Lord of lords'; see, what power! what praise! But what follows: 'He does justice for the fatherless and the widow.' Again, 'the Lord is on high,' but 'He regards the humble' (Ps. CXXXVIII, 6). So Isa. LVII, 15, 'Thus says the high and lofty

One, that inhabits eternity: I dwell with him that is of a humble and contrite spirit.' Again (*ib.* LXVI, 1, 2), 'Thus says the Lord, The heaven is my throne; the earth is my footstool: but I look to him that is humble and of a contrite spirit.' Once more, 'The Lord is King for ever and ever' (Ps. X, 16). 'He judges the fatherless and oppressed' (*ib.* 18); 'He who rides upon the heavens' (*ib.* LXVIII, 4) is 'the Father of the fatherless and the champion of widows' (*ib.* 5). Finally, 'He made heaven and earth' (*ib.* CXLVI, 6), and 'He executes judgment for the oppressed' (*ib.* 7). (*Tanḥ.B.*, Wayera, 42*b*.)

The trouble is that where the 'low' conceptions[1] of God in the O.T. appeal to the human passions of the Rabbis, they are too ready to adopt them. Moreover, to have been compelled to regard as perfect what is so often and obviously imperfect must have had an unfortunate effect upon the *totality* of the Rabbinic religion. It produced some weeds. Nevertheless, the weeds are, in the circumstances, fewer than one would expect. It is mainly the limitations of man, in contrast to the unlimited power and capacity of God, on which the Rabbis delight (sometimes rather quaintly) to dwell. For example:

[73] 'God spake all these things, saying' (Exod. XX, 1). God can do everything simultaneously. He kills and makes alive at one and the same moment; He strikes and heals; the prayer of the woman in travail, of them who are upon the sea, or in the desert, or who are bound in the prison, He hears them all at once; whether men are in the east or west, north or south, He hearkens to all at once. (*Exod.R.*, Yitro, XXVIII, 4.)

[Mr Montefiore's 'too ready' seems to me somewhat over-emphatic, though the balance is, in a certain degree, restored by his subsequent words 'the weeds are fewer than one would expect'. Still, I cannot help feeling that the reader might justifiably gain the impression from 'too ready' that the 'weeds' tend to overgrow the flowers. With this subject I have dealt in my Introduction. Not for a moment would I deny the existence of weeds or condone their sentiment, but my impression—it is purely subjective, and I state it for what it is worth, since I have not made a botanical census—is that the weeds are not so frequent after all. Their influence certainly was not great, and they were regarded as personal expressions of opinion rather than as *ex cathedra* pronouncements, to be accepted *de fide*. And I agree with Mr Montefiore [95] that such faults are inherent in human nature, common to theistic religions, and also [127] that they are paralleled

[1] **Note 19.**

in Patristic literature. But practically there are certain important differences to be observed between Rabbinic and Patristic weeds. First, some, at least of the Rabbinic, were wild and impassioned *obiter dicta*; they were outbursts against persecution: they were not coldly deliberate arguments, penned in scholarly treatises by ecclesiastics who had nothing to fear from those against whom they wrote. If a Judah ben Baba, who, with his disciples, lived in hourly danger merely on account of his religion, and who, to ensure the escape of his disciples, actually perished, was occasionally guilty of a harsh generalisation about the wickedness of Gentiles, we may well deplore it; if we cannot excuse it, we can at least understand it. But can we, in the same way, palliate in an Ambrose, powerful enough to defy the Roman Emperor, a calculated incitement to persecution, not a mere heated and purposeless generalisation? Incidentally, it is well worth noting, and noting in humility and gratitude, that when it comes to the supreme moment, martyrs, Christian and Jewish alike, seem to forget their persecutors: they utter no words of bitterness, their last thoughts are of God. Secondly, we must bear the following phenomenon in mind. Patristic weeds are 'spurlos versenkt', certainly as far as Jews are concerned. Most Jews are ignorant of the Patristic literature altogether: they certainly have not had their attention drawn to handfuls of weeds specially collected to illustrate the superiority of Judaism over Christianity. Unfortunately, in spite of noble correctives, the converse is still not true. What then, is to be the Jewish attitude to Jewish 'weeds'? We must, I think, steer a plain middle course. We must not, as is sometimes done—possibly I myself have to plead guilty occasionally—seek to justify where absolute condemnation is called for without equivocation. But we must not, on the other hand, lose our sense of proportion and we certainly must not condemn everything which others condemn. Mr Montefiore—εἴ τις καὶ ἄλλος—avoids his Scylla and Charybdis, and if, instead of 'too ready', he had said 'somewhat ready' or 'sometimes ready', this note would not have been written. (H. L.)][1]

[74] 'And God spake *all* these words'—all at one and the same moment. At one and the same moment He slays and brings to life, smites and heals, answers the woman in travail, those in peril on the sea, those who wander in the desert, those imprisoned in dungeons, one in the east, one in the west, one in the north, one in the south. He 'forms the light, creates darkness, makes peace and creates evil',[2] all these at one and the same instant; dust is turned into man, and man into dust. He turns the shadow of death into the morning (Amos v, 8), water to blood and blood to

[1] I am so glad I wrote 'too ready', for therefore has the reader secured this excellent note.

[2] Isa. XLV, 7.

water, living flesh to carrion, which again He revives; the staff was transformed to a serpent and the serpent to a staff, the sea to dry land, and the dry land to sea—this is the meaning of 'and God spake *all* these words'. (*Tanḥ.*, Yitro, § 12, f. 125*a*.)

[75] Not as man's capacity is God's capacity. A man cannot say two words at one and the same moment, but God said all the Ten Commandments at one and the same moment. Man cannot hearken to two people who cry before him together, but God can hearken to all the inhabitants of the world if they cry before Him simultaneously, as it is said, 'O thou that hearest prayer, unto thee does all flesh come' (Ps. LXV, 2).
(*Mek.*[2], *Shirata*, Beshallaḥ, § 8, p. 143; *Mek.*[3], vol. II, pp. 62–3 (cp. [901]).)

[76] 'The Lord talked with you face to face in the mount' (Deut. V, 4). Rabbi Johanan said: A thousand people look at a statue, and each one says, 'It is at me that the statue is looking.' So God looks at every single Israelite, and says, 'I am the Lord *thy* God.' R. Levi said: You can learn the same lesson from everyday life. One voice can enter ten ears, but ten voices cannot enter one ear. Yet God hears the prayers of all His creatures as if they were one prayer, as it says, 'O thou that hearest prayer, unto thee does all flesh come' (Ps. LXV, 2). It does not say 'prayers', but 'prayer'. R. Jose b. Abin said in the name of Joshua b. Levi: Face to face, like a hero who whirls his sword and shows its blade in every direction. (*Pes.R.* 100*b*.)

[77] The ways of God are not as the ways of man. A human king does not both wage war and teach children, but God is not so; one day He wages war, as it is said, 'The Lord is a man of war' (Exod. XV, 3), and the next day, at the giving of the Law, He comes down to teach the Law to His children.
(*Exod.R.*, Yitro, XXVIII, 5.)

But while God's power is unlimited, and while in His inmost nature there is never change, yet in the close relation of God to man, and far more in the far closer relation of God to Israel, the actions of man affect the power, even as they affect the happiness, of God. They affect His power, that is, so far as it is manifested in the world.

A fine general passage is the following:

[78] 'Not for victory [R.V. 'for ever'] will he contend' (Ps. CIII, 9).

Did I not contend with the generations of the flood and the dispersion and the men of Sodom, and because I was victorious, did I not suffer loss? But when Moses won the victory over me [i.e. when God pardoned Israel's sin of the Golden Calf], did I not gain profit in my world? That is why it says, 'Not for victory will He contend, and for the sake of the world He will bear no grudge' (cp. *R.T.* p. 107; cp. also [103] and [627]).
(*Midr.Ps.* on CIII, 9 (218*b*, § 12).)

More frequent are passages like these:

[79] R. Azariah in the name of R. Judah b. Simon said: When the Israelites do God's will, they add to the power of God on high. When the Israelites do not do God's will, they, as it were, weaken the great power of God on high. [The Biblical proofs are too forced to quote.] (*Lam.R.* I, 33 on I, 6.)

[80] 'Ye are my witnesses, saith the Lord, and I am God' (Isa. XLIII, 12). That is, when ye are my witnesses, I am God, and when ye are not my witnesses, I am, as it were, not God.
(*Midr.Ps.* on CXXIII, 1 (255*a*, § 2); cp. *Pes.K.* 102*b*. For the converse see [83–5].)

[81] When the Israelites do God's will, they make His left hand as His right hand; but when they do not do His will, they make, if one may say so, His right hand as His left. If they do God's will, He sleeps not, but if they do not do His will, then, if one may say so, He sleeps. If they do His will, wrath is not by Him, but if they do not do His will, wrath is by Him. If they do His will, He fights for them; if they do not do His will, He fights against them, and even, if one may say so, they make the Merciful One cruel. [I omit the proof texts. The passage is one of many of the same kind. It begins better than it ends. It begins on the frequent note that, in a certain sense, man can make greater or weaker the power, or, rather, the results of the power, of God. It ends in a piece of particularism which I omit.]
(*Mek.*^{2}, *Shirata*, Beshallaḥ, § 5, p. 134; *Mek.*^{3}, vol. II, p. 41.)

Israel's frequent lack of faith or idolatry weakens God's power.

[82] 'Thou didst forget God that formed thee' (Deut. XXXII, 18). Each time that I sought to do you good, you weakened the Power on high. You stood by the Red Sea and said, 'This is my God,

and I will praise him' (Exod. XV, 2), and then you returned and said, 'Let us make a captain, and let us go back to Egypt' (Num. XIV, 4). You stood at Mount Sinai and said, 'All that the Lord has spoken to us we will do,' and I sought to do you good, but you returned and said to the calf, 'This is thy God, O Israel.' Lo, whenever I seek to do you good, you weaken the Power which is on high. (*Sifre Deut.*, Ha'azinu, § 319, f. 136*b fin.*–137*a init.* (Moore, I, 472; *R.T.* p. 339).)

[83] 'Unto thee do I lift up my eyes, O thou that sittest in the heavens' (Ps. CXXIII, 1). This implies that when I do *not* lift up my eyes, thou wouldst not be sitting in the heavens (cp. [80]). (*Midr.Ps.* on CXXIII, 1 (255*a*, § 2) (Moore, II, 104; III, 181).)

The idea is softened down in passages like the following:

[84] R. Simeon b. Yoḥai said: Like as when a man who brings together two ships, and binds them together with ropes and cords, and builds a palace upon them; while the ships are lashed together, the palace stands; when they drift apart, it cannot stand. So only when Israel does God's will is His heavenly palace secure. And it also says, 'Unto thee, O Lord, do I lift up my eyes, O thou that sittest in the heavens.' Nevertheless, R. Simeon b. Yoḥai also quoted Exod. XV, 2 ('This is my God and I will make Him lovely'), and he said: When I praise Him, He is lovely, and when I do not praise Him, He is, so to speak, lovely in Himself. (**Note 64.**)
(*Sifre Deut.*, Berakah, § 346, f. 144*a*.)

[85] R. Simeon b. Elazar said: When the Israelites do God's will, His name is exalted in the world; when they do not do His will, His name is, as it were, profaned in the world, even as it says, 'And they profaned my holy name' (Ezek. XXXVI, 20) (cp. [80]). (*Mek.*[2], *Shirata*, Beshallaḥ, § 3, p. 128; *Mek.*[3], vol. II, p. 28.)

And yet, in a deeper sense, God's holiness (His holiness as He is in Himself) is unaffected by Israel's sin:

[86] 'And the Lord spake unto Moses saying, Speak unto all the congregation of Israel, and say unto them, Holy shall ye be, for I, the Lord your God, am holy.' Why was this section of the Law to be said before all the congregation? Because the majority of the most important commandments of the Law are contained

in it. 'Be ye holy, for I am holy'; that is, if you sanctify yourselves, I reckon it as if you sanctified me, and if you do not sanctify yourselves, I regard it as if you did not sanctify me. It does not mean to say, 'If you sanctify me, I am sanctified, and if you do not do so, I am not sanctified,' for it says, 'I am holy.' I abide in my holiness, whether you sanctify me or not (cp. *R.T.* p. 36). (*Sifra* 86*c*.)

The paradox is found that there is a sense in which man can even prevail over God.

[87] The words in II Sam. XXIII, 3 ('He that rules over men must be just,' A.V.) are quoted. What do they mean? R. Abbahu said: They mean, 'I, God, rule over man; who rules over me? The just; for I ordain a decree [of punishment], and he annuls it [by his just life or by his intercessory prayers].' (*M.K.* 16*b*.)

The great supplicators for Israel, Moses more especially, often cause God to 'forgive', or to cancel a decree of doom, where otherwise He would not have done so. In all such cases, the Rabbis, like most teachers of religion, ascribe human methods of action to the Deity, but, concurrently with such ascription, they always maintain God's unlikeness to man—His omniscience, for example, and His foreknowledge. Thus a sentence like the following is a commonplace:

[88] Before a thought is framed in a man's heart, it is known already to God. Even before a man is fully formed, his thought is made manifest to God. (*Gen.R.*, Bereshit, IX, 3 (Th. p. 69).)

After all, this sort of saying hardly goes beyond Ps. CXXXIX, 4, which is quoted in this very connection. That man's free will—so important a doctrine to the Rabbis—seems to conflict with God's foreknowledge did not escape their observation. They could only assert both sides of the puzzle, and leave it at that. Hence R. Akiba's famous saying:

[89] Everything is foreseen, yet freedom of choice is given; and the world is judged by grace, yet all is according to the amount of the work. (**Note 11 *b*.**) (*Aboth* III, 19 (*P.B.* p. 194).)

God created the world and created man. For what purpose? To what end? In the last resort, the Rabbinic answer would, I suppose, be: 'He created the world for His own glory.'

[90] All that God created in His world He created only for His glory, as it is said, 'All that is called by my name, for my glory I created and fashioned and made it' (Isa. XLIII, 7). (*Aboth* VI, 11.)

Again, God created the world for His own pleasure, even as a king might build a palace for his own happiness. He 'saw all that he had created, and it was very good' (Gen. I, 31). For God had once 'created worlds and destroyed them' (*Gen.R.* III, 7 (Th. p. 23); cp. **Note 6**). So:

[91] God said to His world, 'My world, my world, would that thou wouldst ever find favour before me, as thou findest favour before me now' [i.e. at the time of creation].

(*Gen.R.*, Bereshit, IX, 4 (Th. p. 69).)

[92] God said, 'All creatures have been created to praise me,' as it is said, 'All the work of God is for His own sake' (Prov. XVI, 4) (literally, 'God has made everything for its own end' (cp. [992])).

(*Tanḥ.B.*, Wayiḳra, 5*b* (cp. *Ab.R.N.* (vers. I), XLI *fin.*, f. 67*b*).)

God would have wished that all men should have been and remained righteous. Indeed, He *hoped* they would be righteous: to be righteous was the 'end' of man and the reason of their creation.

[93] 'A God of faithfulness and without perversity' (Deut. XXXII, 4). 'Faithful', because He had faith in the world, and created it: 'without perversity', for men were not brought into the world to be wicked, but to be righteous. 'God made man upright, but *they* sought out many (sinful) devices' (Eccles. VII, 29 (cp. [401])).

(*Sifre Deut.*, Ha'azinu, § 307, f. 132*b fin.*)

But, more narrowly, God might, I suppose, be said to have created the world for man's sake, or again, that there might be a field for the exhibition of His own greatest qualities or attributes—justice, beneficence, compassion, lovingkindness. For man is the noblest being:

[94] 'I will sing unto the Lord for He has glorified himself gloriously' (Exod. XV, 1). R. Abin ha-Levi said: There are four glorious creatures in the world; among wild beasts the most glorious is the lion; among cattle, the bull; among birds, the eagle; but man exceeds them all. So God, who is glorious over the glorious, took them all, and fixed them on His throne (Ezek. I, 10 and 26).

(*Tanḥ.B.*, Beshallaḥ, 31*a*.)

And more narrowly still, but, I think, we must admit, most truly of all, God created the world for the sake of the Torah or for the sake of Israel, the people of His choice, the people of His special and overwhelming love. In a way this last reason for the world's creation coalesces with the reason that He created it for His glory, seeing that Israel's function is to display His glory.

The great attributes of God are, to the Rabbis, what I have mentioned: in other words, they are the great attributes of the highest teachings of the O.T. But the particularism of the Rabbis usually prevented them (even as it prevented the writers of the O.T.) from realising that when God, for example, delivers the Israelites by the ruin and slaughter of their foes, there is any difficulty in regarding such a deliverance as anything more than a signal example of God's goodness, mercy or compassion. (Similar instances of the weakness of human nature could, I fancy, be cited from the records of all theistic peoples down to the present day.) Thus, after a passage dealing with the deliverance in the days of Esther and the slaughter of the Persians, we get a perfectly sincere utterance such as this:

[95] You will find that the 'good' attributes of God are mentioned in the Bible repeatedly and in abundance. This is so as regards beneficence, lovingkindness, mercy, righteousness, faithfulness, redemption, blessing, peace. [Then follow a number of scriptural verses, ending up with the familiar, 'The Lord will give strength unto His people, the Lord will bless His people with peace' (Ps. XXIX, 11).] (*Esther R.* X, 15 on VIII, 15.)

[96] R. Yudan said: The world was created for the sake [lit. because of the merit] of the Torah. R. Joshua b. Nehemiah said: For the sake of the tribes of Israel.

(*Gen.R.*, Bereshit, XII, 2 (Th. p. 70).)

[97] R. Joshua b. Ḳarḥa and R. Azariah said: The world was created for the sake of Abraham. As to this great mass [i.e. the earth], for what end is it here? For the sake of Abraham, as it is said, 'Thou hast made the heaven and the earth, and thou didst choose Abraham' (Neh. IX, 6, 7).[1]

(*Gen.R.*, Bereshit, XII, 9 (Th. p. 107).)

[98] God created man for the sake of Abraham.

(*Gen.R.*, Bereshit, XV, 4 (Th. p. 137).)

It is sometimes said that God created man in order that there might be creatures who could fulfil His pre-existing Law; but we also find the view expressed that the Law was created for the sake of Israel:

[99] When God wanted to create man, the angels of the service said,

[1] [This citation from Nehemiah is considered of great importance, and it is included in the daily passages of Praise (*P.B.* p. 34). Abraham is almost a cosmic type because of his linking 'earth' up to 'heaven' through the making of proselytes. Hence Melchizedek commended Abraham to God, the 'Maker of heaven and earth' (Gen. XIV, 19). (H. L.)]

'What is man that thou art mindful of him? What dost thou seek to get from him?' God said, 'He will fulfil my Law and my Commandments.' They said, '*We* will fulfil it.' He said, 'You cannot.' They said, 'Why?' He said, 'It is written, "When a man dies", etc. You do not die. "When a woman bears a child." You do not bear children. It is written, "This shall ye eat." You do not eat.' (*Tanḥ.B.*, Beḥuḳḳotai, 56*b*.)

[100] Was Israel created for the sake of the Law, or the Law for the sake of Israel? Surely the Law for the sake of Israel. Now if the Law which was created for the sake of Israel will endure for ever, how much more Israel which was created by the merit of the Law. (*Eccles.R.* I, § 4, I, f. 2*b*.)

'It cannot be said too often that such variations are not differences of opinion, still less conflicting teachings, but casual exegetical or homiletical conceits' (Moore, I, 451, n. 1). If Moore be right, it makes any attempt to ascertain the real opinions and beliefs of the Rabbis very baffling and difficult.

[101] [If the whole world was created for the sake of Israel, some passages also occur in which it is said that it is only through, or because of, Israel that the Gentiles exist. Israel is compared to the sand on the seashore and the Gentiles to lime (I Kings IV, 20 and Isa. XXXIII, 12).] If sand is not put into the lime, the lime will not last. Thus, if it were not for Israel, the Gentiles could not last. But for Joseph, the Egyptians would have died of hunger: but for Daniel, the wise men of Babylon would have perished.... Again, Israel is compared to the dust of the earth, without which the world could not abide. Without dust there would be no trees and no produce from the earth; so if it were not for Israel, the Gentiles would not exist, for 'in thy seed shall all the Gentiles be blest' (Gen. XXII, 18). (*Pes.R.* 45*b*.)

It is not needful to quote more than a few passages about God's goodness and loving care for man. When the Rabbis in quiet mood are not thinking about Israel and Israel's enemies, they often speak of God's goodness to all mankind—even to the wicked sometimes!—and also to the animals.

[102] 'Thy righteousness is like the mountains of God: thy judgments are a great deep' (Ps. XXXVI, 6). R. Josiah the Great interpreted the verse by transposition: Thy righteousness is above thy

judgments, as the mountains of God are above the great deep. As the mountains press upon the deep, so that it cannot rise up and overflow the world, so do the good deeds of the righteous press down the iniquities of the wicked, so that they may not cause the inhabitants of the world to perish on the day of judgment, as Micah says, 'He will turn again, and have compassion upon us; he will press down our iniquities.'

(*Midr.Ps.* on XXXVI, 6 (125*b*, § 5) (cp. *Lev.R.*, Emor, XXVII, 1).)

A similar thought is expressed by R. Jonathan in [605].

[103] 'Not for ever will I strive and not for eternity will I be wroth' (Isa. LVII, 16). [The word *neẓaḥ*, eternity, can also mean victory, as in 'He will destroy death for ever,' or 'He will swallow up death in victory.'] Read then thus: To be conquered I strive. God said, 'When I conquer, I lose: When I am conquered, I gain. I conquered the generation of the flood. But did I not lose, for I destroyed my world? So, too, with the generation of Babel. So, too, with the Sodomites. But at the sin of the golden calf I was conquered; Moses prevailed over me, and I gained, in that I did not destroy Israel.' Therefore the Psalm-title *Lamnaẓeaḥ* [To the chief musician] should be rendered, 'To him who seeks to be conquered.' (*Pes.R.* 32*b fin.*–33*a init.* (cp. also [78]).)

[104] If a man, when he examines his bonds, finds that others owe him debts, he produces his bonds and exacts the debt; but if he finds that *he* owes a debt, he keeps back the bond, and does not produce it. But God is not so: if we owe Him, He suppresses the bond, as it is said, 'He will suppress our iniquities' (Micah VII, 19); but if He finds any merit in us, He produces it, as it is said, 'The Lord has brought forth our righteous acts' (Jer. LI, 10). [Many other quaint differences are given between God's ways and man's ways, and finally these.] With men, the slave washes his master, dresses him, helps him on with his shoes, but with God it is the reverse, as it is said, 'I washed thee with water, I shod thee' (Ezek. XVI, 9, 10). With men, when the master sleeps, the slave stands by his side, but of God it is said, 'The guardian of Israel neither slumbers nor sleeps' (Ps. CXXI, 4).

(*Exod.R.*, Beshallaḥ, XXV, 6 (cp. [1652]).)

[105] 'For his mercy endures for ever' (Ps. CXVIII, 1). This is like a man who lent money to all the inhabitants of his city, and

they said, 'We are grateful to him, for he supplies us with our needs in the rainy season, and takes from us only three *denarii* as interest in the hot weather.' Then came another man and said, 'I will give you the same for one *sela'*'; so they left the first man, and thanked the second. Then came a third man, who said, 'I will give you the same for nothing.' Was it not fitting to thank *him* most who gave it for nothing? So God sustains all His creatures for nothing. Is it not fitting to praise and give thanks to Him? (*Midr.Ps.* on CXVIII, 1 (240*a fin.*, § 5).)

[106] R. Judah said in the name of Rab: The day has twelve hours. In the first three God sits and busies Himself with the Torah; in the next three He sits and judges the whole world, and whenever He sees that the whole world is guilty [i.e. deserves to be condemned], He arises from the throne of justice, and sits on the throne of mercy; in the next three He sits and feeds the whole world from the horned buffalo to the eggs of the louse; in the last three He sits and sports with the leviathan, as it says, 'The leviathan whom thou hast made to sport with' (Ps. CIV, 26). (*Ab.Zar.* 3*b* (cp. *Sab.* 107*b*; *R.T.* p. 229).)

[107] R. Ḥama said, 'Long-suffering' (Exod. XXXIV, 6). The Hebrew uses idiomatically a dual form which Ḥama interpreted to mean, 'Long-suffering both to the righteous and the wicked.' (*Bab.Ḳ.* 50*b* (cp. *R.T.* p. 109; [849] and [1652]).)

[108] Moses called God, 'The great, mighty and awful God.' Jeremiah said, 'The heathen ramp in His temple, where is His awfulness?' So Jeremiah in his prayer omitted 'awful' (Jer. XXXII, 16–18). Daniel said, 'His children are enslaved. Where is His might?' So he omitted 'mighty' in his prayer (Dan. IX, 4). Then came the men of the Great Synagogue, and said: On the contrary: that is the culmination of His power that He represses His passion, and is long-suffering toward the wicked. And if He were not awful, how could this one nation endure among all the nations of the world? (*Yoma* 69*b*.)

When Moses summoned all Israel before God, he said, 'Your captains, your judges, your elders' (Deut. XXIX, 10). But God made him add the words: 'All the people of Israel':

[109] Now a man is more merciful to men than to women, but God's mercies are over all His creatures (Ps. CXLV, 9), so Moses added

the words, 'all the people of Israel', and continued, 'Your little ones, your wives, and the stranger that is in thy camp,' since God's mercies are on male and female alike, on the wicked equally with the righteous, as it says 'From the hewer of thy wood to the drawer of thy water.' All are equal before God; hence it says, 'All the people of Israel.'

(*Tanḥ.B.*, Niẓẓabim, v, 25*a* (cp. [1439]).)

[110] If men make a sea voyage, and take cattle with them, should a storm arise, they jettison the animals to save mankind, because people do not love animals as much as they love human beings. Not so is God's love. Just as He is merciful to man, so is He merciful to beast. You can see this from the story of the Flood. When man sinned, and God determined to destroy the world, He treated man and beast alike. 'I will destroy man and beast' (Gen. VI, 7). But when He was reconciled, He was reconciled to both, and He pitied both, man and beast alike, as we read in the narrative, 'God remembered Noah and the animals that were with him in the ark' (Gen. VIII, 1). (*Tanḥ.B.*, Noaḥ, 17*a*.)

[The story of the Ark was often used as the medium for inculcating kindness to animals (cp. [124], [150] and [1172]):

[111] Abba bar Kahana said: Noah took with him a supply of vine-tendrils for the elephants; *cistus* (or ivy) for the gazelles, and glass for the ostriches. (*Gen.R.*, Noaḥ, XXXI, 14 (Th. p. 287).)

It may be thought strange that with this divine pity for the animals, the commands about the sacrifices of animals and about God's *pleasure* in those sacrifices, should never have seemed inconsistent to the Rabbis.

It may seem all the more strange when we recall that the Rabbis equally believed and taught the pronouncements of Psalmists and Prophets that God has *no* pleasure in animal sacrifices (cp. pp. 25–6). We must, however, remember that, originally, no animal could be killed for food unless it was sacrificed, and, subsequently, Deuteronomy limited sacrifices to Jerusalem, permitting animals to be killed for food elsewhere. Unless we take the vegetarian point of view, and regard all eating of animal food as unethical, we are scarcely entitled to see any inconsistency. (H. L.)]

[112] 'The Lord supports those that have fallen and raises those that are bowed' (Ps. CXLV, 14). It does not say, 'those who stand erect' but 'those who are bowed', even the wicked He raises. R. Ḥiyya said: God's attributes are not those of man. For a man

who has a wealthy friend cleaves to him and pines for him, but mocks at him as soon as the friend's power declines.[1] God is far different. When He sees a man who has fallen into misfortune, He stretches His hand out and raises him, for it says, 'all those who have fallen', not 'all those who stand'.

(*Tanh.B.*, Wayeze, 76*a*, 76*b*.)

[113] R. Joshua b. Nehemiah said: Have you ever seen it happen that the rain fell on the field of *A* who was righteous, and not on the field of *B* who was wicked? Or that the sun arose and shone upon Israel who was righteous, and not upon the wicked [the nations]? God causes the sun to shine both upon Israel and upon the nations, for the Lord is good to all. [The passage goes on to say that man is often kind to his slaves and cruel to his animals, and *vice versa*, but that God is merciful both to man and beast.] (*Pes.R.* 195*a fin.*–195*b*.)

Cp. 'Who in mercy givest light to the earth and to them that dwell thereon' (*P.B.* p. 37 *fin.*), 'blessed art thou, O Lord, who givest light to the whole world in thy glory' (*ib.* p. 293). These are respectively the first words of the Congregational portion of the Daily Morning Prayer, and the benediction on retiring to rest.

Famous is the enumeration of the thirteen norms, or divisions, or kinds, of God's attribute of Mercy which were found in the great passage of Exod. XXXIV, 6, 7. These were obtained by omitting two words at the end of the half-verse; for of *nakkeh lo ye-nakkeh*, the last two words are omitted. The three words mean: 'He will surely not acquit' (i.e. the guilty); the Rabbis use only the first of the three words, which they take to mean acquitting, or purifying, thus turning the words from their original meaning into their opposite! Thus we get: '(1) The Lord, (2) The Lord (for Yahweh is God as the Merciful One), (3) God (usually God [Elohim] is the judge, God in his attribute of just severity, but here that usual interpretation of Elohim is ignored), (4) merciful, and (5) gracious, (6) longsuffering, and abundant in (7) lovingkindness and (8) fidelity, (9) keeping mercy to a thousand generations, forgiving (10) iniquity, (11) transgression and (12) sin, and (13) acquitting':

[114] R. Johanan said: Thirteen kinds of mercy are written in the Scripture about God. (*Pes.K.* 57*a*.)

[1] In order to heighten the contrast between man and God, the Rabbis frequently take this cynical view of human nature. It is probable that these cynical utterances must not be pressed too hard, as if they were the regular and permanent Rabbinic view.

[There are several lines of exegesis in the interpretation of this difficult list of the 'Thirteen Attributes'. One of these is 'according to the literal sense', i.e. to make the words a saving clause, lest the complementary quality of divine justice be neglected—although this attribute follows immediately on the words under consideration. Thus the Septuagint has 'and he will not clear the guilty' (*καὶ οὐ καθαριεῖ τὸν ἔνοχον*), and this interpretation persisted for several centuries: it is to be found even in the late and paraphrastic 'fragmentary' (so-called Jerusalem) Targum, which has, 'Assuredly he will not acquit the guilty on the Great Day of Judgment.' It will be noted that this latter rendering takes account of the emphasised double verb in the original, which the Greek appears to overlook. But the other two *Targumim* take the double verb differently. Onḳelos renders, 'He forgives those that return to His Torah, but those who do not return He does not acquit' (מזכי). As this is a literal Targum, the interpretation can be regarded as representing, not Midrash, but the actual sense as it seemed to the Meturgeman. The more paraphrastic Pseudo-Jonathan follows Onḳelos, adding at the end 'on the great day of Judgment' or, 'in the day of great judgment'. Nathan Adler, in his commentary (*Netinah la-Ger*) on the Targum, *in loc.*, says: 'The Targum Onḳelos separates the first Hebrew verb (*we-naḳḳeh*, the emphasising infinitive) from the finite verb *lo yenaḳḳeh*, i.e. "...acquitting. He will not acquit (*sc.* sinners)...." Onḳelos thus considers that only *we-naḳḳeh* (and not *lo yenaḳḳeh*) belongs to the Thirteen Attributes. *Lo yenaḳḳeh* must, Onḳelos thinks, go with the following "visiting the iniquity". According to this method, the initial three words "Lord, Lord, God" would be two attributes, as the exegetes have regarded them.' Rashi says: 'Taken literally, the words mean that God is not indulgent to sin entirely (or, all at once), but He exacts retribution for it little by little: the Midrash follows the lines of the Targum.' Ibn Ezra discusses both ways, i.e. taking the infinitive as the end of the Attributes and taking it in its literal sense. Sforno adds a new thought: 'He will not pardon those who repent merely to avoid punishment'; but this is hardly an early concept. (For Meturgeman cp. [434] and [1215].)

Lo yenaḳḳeh could be expounded as a rhetorical question, but since *naḳḳeh* is not a finite verb, this cannot have been the original meaning. The same objection can be urged against the Targum as well. Even if a participle or a finite verb be read for the infinitive, it is not possible to get the Targumic interpretation out of the Hebrew. But in any case the Hebrew is unusual, since *naḳḳeh lo yenaḳḳeh* has no object. Hence the liturgy ends the Thirteen Attributes at *naḳḳeh* and renders 'Forgiving sin...and acquitting' (Gaster, de Sola, Davis and Adler: see also Heidenheim's note and citation from Naḥmanides in his Atonement, vol. *in loc.*). For the double verb cp. [659]. (H. L.)]

In Ps. CXXXVI God is praised and thanked for His wonders which He has wrought for Israel and especially for the cleaving of the Red Sea. But the same refrain, 'for His lovingkindness is for ever', is applied also to the words 'who gives bread to all flesh' (*ib.* 25):

[115] So Hillel said that this juxtaposition showed that the two deeds of God were equal in greatness, and that the giving to man of his daily bread was as wonderful a marvel as the cleaving of the Red Sea. And, very ingeniously, it is said that the same equivalence is shown by Isa. LI, 14, 15, where after the words 'his bread fails not', come the words, 'I am the Lord who divided [A.V. lit. 'stirs up'] the Red Sea.' (*Pes.R.* 152*a*.)

[116] My Father who art in heaven, may Thy great Name be blessed from all eternity, and may Israel Thy servants give Thee pleasure. Thou art He who redeems and rescues all the inhabitants of the world and all the work of Thy hands. (*Tan.d.b.El.* p. 53.)

I may quote here some stories about animals:

[117] While Moses was feeding the sheep of his father-in-law in the wilderness, a young kid ran away. Moses followed it until it reached a ravine, where it found a well to drink from. When Moses reached it, he said, 'I did not know that you ran away because you were thirsty. Now you must be weary.' He carried the kid back. Then God said, 'Because thou hast shown pity in leading back one of a flock belonging to a man, thou shalt lead *my* flock, Israel.' (*Exod.R.*, Shemot, II, 2.)

[The rendering 'ravine' is uncertain. The word in the ordinary text is obscure and may be corrupt. (H. L.)]

[118] Once R. Judah the Prince sat and taught the Law before an assembly of Babylonian Jews in Sepphoris, and a calf passed before him. It came and sought to conceal itself, and began to moo, as if to say, 'Save me.' Then he said, 'What can I do for you? For this lot [i.e. to be slaughtered] you were created.' Hence R. Judah suffered toothache for thirteen years....After that a reptile [perhaps a weasel] ran past his daughter, and she wanted to kill it. He said to her, 'Let it be, for it is written, "His mercies are over all His works".' So it was said in heaven, 'Because he had pity, pity shall be shown to him.' And his toothache ceased.

(*Gen.R.*, Noaḥ, XXXIII, 3 (Th. p. 305); *Bab.M.* 85*a*.)

As regards Exod. XII, 29, 'And all the firstborn of cattle', it is said:

[119] If the human beings sinned, what was the sin of the cattle? But the Egyptians worshipped certain animals, and so that they should not say, '*our* god brought this punishment upon us; [or] how strong is our god, for he stood up for himself, so that the plague should not have power over him', therefore the cattle were included. (Cp. [144].) (*Pes.K.* 65*b*.)

[120] R. Phinehas b. Jair went to a place where they said, 'The mice eat our grain.' He conjured the mice, and they gathered together and squeaked. He said to the men, 'Do you know what they say?' They replied, 'No.' He said to them, 'They say it has not been properly tithed.' They said to him, 'Pledge thyself to us (that the mice will not eat our grain if we tithe it properly),' and he did pledge himself to them, and they suffered no longer.

(*T.J.Dem.* I, § 3, f. 22*a*, line 7.)

Phinehas b. Jair was noted for stories of this type (cp. [889], [1066] and [1359]).

[121] Some robbers stole the ass of R. Phinehas b. Jair, and kept it hidden for three days, during which time it ate nothing. After that time they decided to restore it to its master. 'It is better', they said, 'to send it back than that it should die here and make our cave smell.' So they let it go, and it went to the gate of its master and began to bray. 'Open the gate', he said, 'to this poor animal which has eaten nothing for three days.' They put barley before it, but it would not eat. They said to R. Phinehas, 'It refuses to eat.' He said, 'Have you properly sifted the barley?' They said, 'Yes.' He said, 'Have you tithed that part of the barley which possibly was not tithed?' They said, 'No, for you have taught us that he who buys cereals for sowing, or to give to animals, or rough flour for tanning skins, or oil for lamps or for cleansing vessels, is free from the obligation of tithing the doubtfully-untithed.' He said, 'Yes, but this poor animal imposes upon itself a very strict rule.' So they took away the doubtful tithe, and it ate.

(*T.J.Dem.* I, § 3, f. 21*d*, line 69 to 22*a* *init.* (cf. [120]).)

[122] Once upon a time an Israelite, who owned a ploughing-heifer, became poor and sold her to a pagan. He took her and ploughed with her during the weekdays. On the Sabbath, he brought her

out, as before, to plough, but she lay down under the yoke. Though he beat the heifer, she would not budge. Seeing this, he went to the Israelite who had sold the heifer, and said, 'Come and take your heifer, perhaps she is grieving for her former owner, for though I beat her, she will not move.' The Israelite understood that the reason why the heifer would not plough was because it was the Sabbath day, on which she was accustomed to rest, so he said to the pagan, 'I will come and raise her.' When he came, he whispered into her ear, 'Heifer, heifer, you know well that when you were mine, you ploughed all the week and you rested on the Sabbath, but now, through my sins, you have passed to a pagan master. I beseech you, rise and plough.' The heifer did so at once. The pagan then said to him, 'I beg you take your cow away, because I cannot always come to fetch you to raise her. But now I will not leave you until you tell me what you did to her in her ear. I wearied myself with her and beat her, but she would not get up.' The Israelite then began to appease him and said, 'It was neither witchcraft nor magic that I did, but thus and thus did I whisper in her ear, so that she rose and ploughed.' At once the pagan was struck by fear, and said, 'If a heifer, which has no speech and no sense, could recognise her Maker, shall not I, whom my Creator formed in His own image and to whom He gave understanding, acknowledge Him?' Straightway he went and became a proselyte. He studied and acquired the merit of Torah, and they used to call him, 'John, son of the heifer,' and to this day our Rabbis pronounce rulings which he gave. Now if you are astonished that a heifer should bring a man under the wings of the Shechinah, reflect that it is through a heifer that Israel can be purified (Num. XIX, 1–10).

(*Pes.R.* 56*b fin.*–57*a.*)

[123] R. Judah said in the name of Rab: A man is forbidden to eat anything until he has fed his beast. (*Giṭ.* 62*a fin.*)

[Cruelty to animals was given a special term by the Rabbis, *ẓa'ar ba'al ḥayyim*, which literally means: 'Afflicting anything possessed of life.' (H. L.)]

[124] R. Tanḥuma b. Abba cited Proverbs (XI, 30), 'He that is wise, wins souls.' The Rabbis said: This refers to Noah, for in the Ark he fed and sustained the animals with much care. He gave to each animal its special food, and fed each at its proper period, some

in the daytime and some at night. Thus he gave chopped straw to the camel, barley to the ass, vine tendrils to the elephant, and glass to the ostrich. So for twelve months he did not sleep by night or day, because all the time he was busy feeding the animals.

(*Tanḥ.B.*, Noaḥ, 15*a* (cp. [111], [150] and [1172]).)

[125] In every hour the Shechinah provides sustenance for all the inhabitants of the world according to their need, and satisfies every living thing, and not only the pious and the righteous, but also the wicked and the idolaters.

(*Mek.*², *Amalek*, Yitro, § 1, p. 195; *Mek.*³, § 3, vol. II, p. 178.)

[126] R. Elazar said: Sustenance is put side by side with redemption, and redemption with sustenance, as it is said, 'He has redeemed us from our enemies,' and immediately afterwards, 'He gives food to all flesh' (Ps. CXXXVI, 24, 25). As redemption is marvellous, so sustenance is marvellous; as sustenance is day by day, so redemption is day by day. R. Samuel b. Naḥmani said: Sustenance is even greater than redemption, for the latter can be effected through an angel, as it is said, 'The angel which redeemed me from all evil' (Gen. XLVIII, 16), but sustenance comes only through God, 'Thou openest thy hand, and in thy favour satisfiest every living thing' (Ps. CXLV, 16).

(*Gen.R.*, Bereshit, XX, 9 (Th. p. 192).)

Naturally the details of God's goodness are often pictured in terms of the Law, even when the Israelites as such are not specifically mentioned.

[127] A difficult verse in Job XLI, 11, is quoted: 'Who has anticipated me that I should pay him?' That is, who purposed in his heart to do a command, and I did not previously requite him? Who circumcised, and I had not given him a son? Who made fringes, and I had not before given him a mantle? Who made a railing to his roof, and I had not previously given him a house? Who purposed in his heart to do a command, and was prevented from doing it, and I did not reckon it to him as if he had done it?

(*Midr.Ps.* on XXX, heading (117*a*, § 2).)

The Rabbis usually, it is true, speak as members of the people of Israel. They usually have Israel consciously before their minds, and, prevailingly too, the opposition between Israel and the nations of the world, who are Israel's enemies, and as idolators are also God's enemies. That is the Rabbinic particularism to which the particularism of the Church Fathers is a close parallel. But God is also the Creator and Lord of the whole world. And so the Rabbis, forgetting or ignoring for the time being the opposition between Israel and the nations, frequently speak about human beings generally and of God's relation to them. On such occasions they often employ the word 'biryah', creature, as in the following:

[128] R. Phinehas b. Ḥama ha-Kohen, quoted the words of Isa. XLVI, 10, 'All my pleasure I will do.' What do these words mean? They mean that God's pleasure is to justify His creatures [or, to lead His creatures to righteousness], as it says, 'The Lord was pleased for His righteousness' sake to magnify the Law and make it honourable' (Isa. XLII, 21). And He has no pleasure in condemning a creature, as it says, 'I have no pleasure in the death of the wicked, but that the wicked turn from his way and live' (Ezek. XXXIII, 11). (*Exod.R.*, Wa'era, IX, 1.)

[The word *biryah* is strikingly used in *Aboth* VI, 2 (*P.B.* p. 205). Here the 'woe' to mankind (*Biryoth*) for the contempt of the Torah, and the rest of the two sections, would imply that all mankind can learn from Torah, and derive perfection therefrom, not merely Israel alone. (H.L.)]

[129] God is on the watch for the nations of the world to repent, so that He may bring them under His wings. (*Num.R.*, Naso, X, 1.)

This phrase, which means 'to become a proselyte' (*ger*), is derived from Ruth II, 12 (cp. [1574]).

[130] It is written: 'His mouth is most sweet' (Cant. V, 16). See what it says: 'Seek ye me and live' (Amos V, 4). Can there be a sweeter mouth than this? And it says: 'I have no pleasure in the death of the wicked' (Ezek. XXXIII, 11). Can there be a sweeter mouth than this? 'Yea, let the wicked turn from his way and live' (*ib.*). Can there be a sweeter mouth than this? (*Num.R.*, Naso, X, 1.)

In a well-known and remarkable passage from the Mishnah, it is Israelite criminals who, no doubt, may be referred to, but it is, perhaps, not unfair to give to the words a wider reference:

[131] R. Me'ir said: When man is sore troubled, the Shechinah says, 'How heavy is my head, how heavy is my arm.' If God suffers so much for the blood of the wicked, how much more for the blood of the righteous. (*San.* VI, 5; Danby, p. 390 *fin.*)

If the world were ruled by God according to the strictest dictates of justice, man could not endure:

[132] 'Shall not the judge of all the earth do right?' (Gen. XVIII, 25). R. Levi said: Abraham said to God, 'If thou desirest to maintain the world, strict justice is impossible; and if thou desirest strict justice, then the world cannot be maintained. Thou canst not hold the cord at both ends at once. Thou desirest the world, and thou desirest justice. Take one or the other. Unless thou art a little indulgent, the world cannot endure.'

(*Gen.R.*, Lek leka, XXXIX, 6 (Th. p. 368; cp. [198]).)

[133] 'Shall not the judge of all the earth do right?' (Gen. XVIII, 25). R. Judah b. Simeon said: Abraham pleaded thus, 'Among mortal men an appeal lies from the *dux* to the *eparch*, and from the *eparch* to the commander-in-chief; but as no appeal lies from thee, shall not the judge of all the world do right? When thou didst desire to judge thy world, thou didst deliver it into the hands of two, Remus and Romulus, so that if one sought to do anything [wrong], the other could restrain him; but seeing that none can restrain thee, shall not the judge of all the world do right?' (*Gen.R.*, Wayera, XLIX, 9 (Th. p. 510).)

The reference seems to be to the power of one consul to veto the decisions of his colleague.

[134] R. Yudan in the name of R. Azariah said: When Abraham prayed to God to show compassion upon the men of Sodom, he said, 'Thou hast sworn never to bring again a flood of water upon the earth. Dost thou now propose to bring a flood of fire, and so cleverly to evade the oath? Thou canst not get out of the oath, as it is said, "Far be it from thee to do after this manner." Shall not the judge of all the earth do justice? Yet if thou wantest justice, then the world cannot stand, but if thou wantest the world [to endure], then justice cannot stand [i.e. then thou canst not have perfect justice]. Thou seekest to grasp the cord by both ends at once: thou desirest [to maintain] the world, and thou desirest truthful judgment; if thou dost not yield a little, thy world cannot endure.' Then God said to Abraham: 'Thou lovest justice and hatest evil' (Ps. XLV, 7); thou lovest to justify my creatures, and thou hatest to declare them guilty, 'therefore hast God anointed thee with the oil of gladness above thy fellows' (Ps. XLV, 7). (**Note 21.**) (*Lev.R.*, Ẓaw, X, 1.)

On the other hand, the Rabbis, just because they so constantly emphasise the mercy of God—how His 'compassion' exceeds His 'justice'—and just because they speak so often, as we shall hear, of His exceeding love for Israel, are very anxious to point out that we must not presume upon this compassion and love; God's goodness is something very different from mere lax good nature. Such remarks as the following are not infrequent:

[135] R. Ḥanina said: He who says, God is indulgent, his life shall be outlawed. (*Bab.Ḳ.* 50*a fin.*)

[136] R. Ḥanina said: He who says that God is lax, his bowels shall be relaxed; God is long-suffering, but He exacts His due. He is particular to a hair's breadth. His strictness is greater for the near than for the far [i.e. for the righteous than for the sinful]. (*T.J.Sheḳ.* v, § 2, f. 48*d*, line 35.)

God is not only the merciful Father, but He is the just judge. The saying of Akiba is famous. He used to say:

[137] Everything is given on pledge, and a net is spread for all the living; the shop is open; and the dealer gives credit; and the ledger lies open; and the hand writes; and whosoever wishes to borrow may come and borrow; but the collectors regularly make their daily round, and exact payment from man whether he be content or not; and they have that whereon they can rely in their demand; and the judgment is a judgment of truth; and everything is prepared for the feast. (*Aboth* III, 20; *P.B.* p. 194.)

For an explanation of the various metaphors in this passage, see Charles Taylor's note in his 2nd ed. of *Aboth*. (**Note 11*c*.**)

Famous, too, and solemn is the following:

[138] R. Elazar ha-Ḳappar said: They that are born are destined to die; and the dead to be brought to life again; and the living to be judged, to know, to make known, and to be made conscious that He is God, He the Maker, He the Creator, He the Discerner, He the Judge, He the Witness, He the Complainant; He it is that will, in future, judge, blessed be He. (*Aboth* IV, 29; *P.B.* p. 198.)

God's ways and methods are often incomprehensible, but in the last resort they are absolutely just (**Note 11*d***):

[139] R. Akiba used to argue with a man called Pappos (or Papias). Pappos quoting Job XXIII, 13, 'Who can turn [or reply] to Him,

and what He wishes, that He does,' said, 'Being one, He judges all the inhabitants of the world, and there is none who can reply to Him.' Akiba said, 'Enough, Pappos. It is true that none can reply to Him who spake and the world was, but He judges all in truth and in justice.' (*Mek.*[1], Beshallaḥ, § 6, f. 40*a*; *Mek.*[2], p. 112; *Mek.*[3], § 7, vol. I, p. 248; *Mek.*[4], f. 33*a* (cp. [7, 8]).)

[140] God says, 'All I do, I do in justice. If I sought to pass beyond justice but once, the world could not endure.' Then, quoting the obscure verse Isa. XXVII, 4: 'If I were to overstep justice by a single step, I should set all on fire, and the world would be burnt up.' (*Tanḥ.B.*, Mishpaṭim, 41 *b fin.*)

God may be more indulgent towards a sin against Himself than to a sin of a man against his neighbour.

[141] (It is written: 'The Lord lift up His countenance upon thee' (Num. VI, 26). And also 'The Lord regards not persons' (Deut. X, 17). Now the Hebrew idiomatic wording for 'he regards not persons' is 'he does not lift up (his) countenance'.) R. Jose b. Dosetai asked: How are these two statements to be reconciled? He lifts up His countenance [i.e. is lenient] in a matter between you and Him: He does *not* lift up His countenance [He is unbending] in a matter between you and your neighbour. (*Num.R.*, Naso, XI, 7.)

But in how many O.T. passages are we told of God's anger, of His jealousy, of His fierce punishments! And the Rabbis had to regard all such passages as also divine and accurate. The Bible even seems to imply that God rejoices at the destruction or death of the wicked. The 'natural man' of the Rabbis tended to acquiesce. But attempts were made to rise above this conception. The first part of the following passage is quoted in every anthology. It must be confessed that it is isolated, but its influence was great:

[142] (R. Johanan expressed the view that God does not rejoice in the downfall of the wicked.) The ministering angels wanted to sing a hymn at the destruction of the Egyptians, but God said: 'My children lie drowned in the sea, and you would sing?' R. Elazar said: He does not rejoice, but He causes others to rejoice (cf. *R.T.* pp. 106, 214, 262). (*Meg.* 10*b* (cp. [1313]).)

[This passage has influenced the liturgy. To this day the Hallel is abbreviated on Passover (see rubric on pp. 220 and 221 of *P.B.*)

in accordance with Prov. XXIV, 17 (other reasons, mentioned in *'Arak.* 10*a*, are discussed by Rabbi Gaguine on p. 504 of his *Keter Shemṭob*). *Midrash Proverbs* (on XXV, 21: 'if thine enemy be hungry, feed him') has 'even if he be coming to slay thee...then God will reconcile him to thee' (f. 25*b* in ed. Stettin, 1861). Similarly, in reading the book of Esther on Purim, the execution of the ten sons of Haman is rushed through in one breath: the reason given in *Meg.* 16*b* is inadequate, no doubt the object was to hurry over an unpleasant bit of history. For, in the same way, only the initials of the Ten Plagues and not the whole words were inscribed on the Rod of Moses (*Exod.R.*, Shemot, v, 6; VIII, 3), and only the initials are recited in the domestic service of the Passover (for the usual explanations of this, see Abudarham, *in loc.*). With one exception the 'imprecatory Psalms' are absent from the synagogue liturgy, and even that exception does not apply to the Ashkenazi rite: the psalm in question, 'By the waters of Babylon', is read silently in the Sephardic rite, before evening service opens on the Ninth of Ab, an occasion when the Psalm is so appropriate that it can hardly be ignored. But many omit the last verses (cp. [260]). (H. L.)]

The Rabbis, with their vivid and abiding recollection of the words of the Bible, noticed that in one place where the phrase, 'Give thanks unto the Lord, for His mercy endures for ever' occurs, the usual words 'for He is good' are wanting. This omission is in II Chron. XX, 21, in connection with a great destruction of Israel's enemies, who, from the Rabbis' point of view, are identified with the wicked. Why are the words here omitted?

[143] There is, if one may say so, no rejoicing before God at the destruction of the wicked. But if there is no rejoicing before Him at the death of the wicked, how much less at the death of the righteous, of whom even one is worth the whole world.

(*Mek.*², *Shirata*, Beshallaḥ, § 1, p. 118; *Mek.*³, vol. II, p. 5 (cp. [267]).)

The burden of the 'ugly' Biblical passages is reflected in remarks which I summarise thus:

[144] 'Be not righteous overmuch.' The Rabbis use this verse to mean, 'Try not to be more righteous than God.' They had to meet criticism of the cruelties ordered by God, e.g. in I Sam. XV, 3. The Bible itself attempts in Samuel's words some sort of excuse in I Sam. XV, 22, and the Rabbis could only follow suit. Yet they saw the horror pretty clearly, for they make Samuel say: 'If the men have sinned, how have the women, the children

and the animals sinned?' All they can do is to repeat, 'Seek not to be more righteous than your Maker,' and, again, 'He who is merciful when he should be cruel, will be cruel when he should be merciful,' which sounds well, but is really foolish, even in spite of the example of Saul's cruelty to Nob, the city of the priests (I Sam. XXII, 19). The criticism which Saul is supposed to have made against the law of Deut. XXI, 4: 'If the man has sinned, what has been the sin of the animal?', is rebuked along the same lines. But the very mention of the criticism is itself a moral and religious advance. It paved the way for the time when men could realise that deeds of senseless cruelty could not have been ordered by the good God. (Cp. [119].)
(*Eccles.R.* VII, § 16, 1, f. 20*b*; see **Note 8.**)

It is, indeed, not wonderful that the Rabbis generally sought to concentrate all the cruel aspects of God's character in the Bible upon Israel's enemies. Nevertheless, attempts are made to teach that God—in this, too, unlike man—never loses control over His jealousy and anger.

[145] 'I am a jealous God [so in the second Commandment]. I rule over jealousy, but jealousy does not rule over me. I rule over slumber, but slumber does not rule over me. With jealousy, or with passion, I punish the idolaters for their idolatry, but in other matters I am merciful.'

A philosopher said to R. Gamaliel, 'It is written in your Law, "I am a jealous God." But what is there in an idol to be jealous about? A strong man, a wise man, a rich man, may be jealous in respect of another strong, wise or rich man. But what is there in an idol to be jealous about?' R. Gamaliel said: 'If a man calls his dog by his father's name, and if he makes a vow, saying, "By the life of this dog", will the father be angry with the dog, or with the son?' [God is angry with the idolaters, not with the idols.] (*Mek.*[2], *Baḥodesh*, Yitro, § 6, p. 226; *Mek.*[3], vol. II, p. 244, on Exod. XX, 5.)

[146] Man's anger controls him, but God controls His anger—He is master of His wrath; man's jealousy controls him, but God controls His jealousy. (*Midr.Ps.* on XCIV, 1 (209*a*, § 1) (cp. *R.T.* p. 106).)

[147] Gen. XVIII, 24: 'Wilt thou also destroy the righteous with the

wicked? [A.V. 'also', in Hebrew '*af*'. The same word means anger, wrath: so the Midrash, punning on the word, says:] R. Huna in the name of R. Aḥa said: Thou controllest anger, but anger does not control Thee. R. Judah said: A mortal man is conquered by his anger, but God conquers anger, as it says, 'The Lord is a master of wrath' (Nahum I, 2) [lit. the Hebrew merely means, The Lord is wrathful. See A.V. and R.V.].

(*Gen.R.*, Wayera, XLIX, 8 (Th. pp. 507–8; cp. [201], [248]).)

The burden of such metaphors and conceptions as those of Deut. XXXII, 41, 42, lay heavy upon the Rabbis. *We* can pass them by, for our conception of God is other than theirs. To the Rabbis, being part of the Pentateuch, they were as perfect and divine as any other verses in the Bible, yet sometimes by a little touch they do what they can:

[148] The words in Deut. XXXII, 41 read, 'If I whet my glittering sword, *and* mine hand take hold on judgment' [i.e. retribution]. But a Rabbi said: Punishments go forth from God swift as lightning, *but* His hand has hold of justice [i.e. He is never carried away by punishment: He remains cool; He is always just].

(*Sifre Deut.*, Ha'azinu, § 331, f. 140*a init.*)

We may note also passages like the following:

[149] 'The righteous knows the soul of his beast' (Prov. XII, 10). God, the righteous One of the World, knows even the soul of His beasts, nay, even when He is angered. For His attributes are not those of man. A king sends his legions against a rebellious province and devastates it, slaying good and bad alike. There is none to say: 'So and so was loyal, spare him!' He slays them all. But not so God. Should an entire generation rebel and rouse His wrath, if there be but one righteous man there, He saves him, as it says: 'The righteous knows the soul of his beast,' or, again, 'Good is the Lord as a refuge in the day of distress, He knows those that trust in Him' (Nahum I, 7).

(*Tanḥ.B.*, Noaḥ, 18*a*.)

[150] God does not withhold the due reward of any of His creatures, even of the mouse which preserved its family and mated with its kind, not like the men of the generation of the flood who were promiscuous. (*Tanḥ.B.*, Noaḥ, 18*b* (cp. [111], [124]).)

[151] When God sent Moses on his mission to deliver Israel, He said 'I have seen,' twice in one verse (Exod. III, 7: lit. 'Seeing I have seen,' i.e. 'I have indeed seen'). 'Two things', said God, 'have I seen: I have seen Israel's sufferings, and I redeem them now. And, furthermore, I have also seen this people to be stiff-necked. They are destined to provoke me by making the golden calf (yet I redeem them none the less).'

(*Tanḥ.*, Shemot, § 20, f. 88*b*.)

[152] 'God is not a man that He should lie, or a mortal that He should repent' (Num. XXIII, 19). Samuel son of Naḥmani said: When God promises good, He does not change His promise, come what may, unlike a mortal king who may withhold a promised gift to his son, if the son provokes him. God keeps His promise in spite of man's sin. In Ps. CV, 44 it says: 'He gave them lands of nations that they might keep His statutes.' They did not keep His statutes, but He gave them the land. After the Golden Calf, God said to Moses, 'I am not a man to make a promise and retract.' But when God swore in His wrath, He did retract, for He swore to punish. For God said: 'I am not a mortal man to swear to punish and to exult in doing so.'

(*Tanḥ.*, Wayera, § 13, f. 36*a fin.*–36*b init.*)

[153] Because Ham's eyes gazed at his father's nakedness, Ham's eyes were reddened. Because his mouth told of it, his lips were made curved. Because he turned his face [to gaze again], his hair and beard became singed. Because he did not cover his father's nakedness, he went naked and shamed, for God's principle is measure for measure. But since God's 'mercies are over all His works' (Ps. CXLV, 9) God went back [on Ham's punishment], and said, 'Since he has delivered himself over to slavery, let him go free in return for the eye which saw and the mouth that spake, for a slave is released if his master injures his eye or his tooth' (Exod. XXI, 26).

(*Tanḥ.*, Noaḥ, § 13, f. 21*b*.)

[154] 'Is there ever anger before the Holy One, blessed be He?' 'Yes; for there is a teaching: "A God that has indignation every day"' (Ps. VII, 12). 'But how long does His anger last?' 'A moment' (*ib.* XXX, 6). 'And how long is a moment?' 'The minutest fraction of time [lit. of an hour].' (*Ber.* 7*a*.)

[155] When Balaam went with the princes of Moab against God's will, God was angry, 'and the angel of the Lord stood in his path as an adversary against him' (Num. XXII, 22). Thus the angel of mercy turned into an adversary. So God says to the sinner: 'Thou hast caused me to take up a trade that is not mine.'

(*Tanḥ.B.*, Balaḳ, 69*a fin.*)

[156] Before He brought on the flood, God Himself kept seven days of mourning, for He was grieved at heart (Gen. VI, 6).

(*Tanḥ.B.*, Shemini, 11*a.*)

Whatever befalls themselves or Israel or the world, the Rabbis are convinced believers in the unfailing justice and lovingkindness of God:

[157] R. Berechiah said in the name of R. Levi: It is written, 'Thou, O Lord, art ever on high' (Ps. XCII, 8), that is, Thou art always right (lit. 'For ever is Thy hand raised'). If a king among men sits in judgment, when he acquits, all the people praise him; when he condemns to death, none praises him, for they know he has given sentence in passion or blindness, but with God it is not so; whether He remits or punishes, He is always just and right. R. Huna, in the name of R. Aḥa, quoted Ps. CI, 1: 'I will sing of mercy and judgment, unto thee, O Lord, will I sing.' David said: Be it one way or the other [i.e. whether God acquits or condemns me] to thee, O Lord, will I sing. So the Rabbis, quoting Ps. CXVI, 3, 4, 13, say: Be it this way or that, I will call on the name of the Lord. R. Judah b. Ilai quoted Job I, 21: The Lord gave, the Lord took; may the name of the Lord be blessed. If He gave, He gave in mercy; if He took, He took in mercy. (*Lev.R.*, Ḳedoshim, XXIV, 2.)

Chapter II

GOD'S LOVE FOR ISRAEL

In all honesty and sincerity the Rabbis believed that God and Israel were united together by a passionate love on both sides. Though Yahweh had become the One God of the whole world, yet throughout the O.T. He remained in a peculiar sense the God of Israel. Deutero-Isaiah is the prophet of Monotheism, and he may be justly called universalist in his tendencies: yet no O.T. writer emphasises more than he the peculiar love which God feels for Israel. 'Can a woman forget her sucking child, that she should not have compassion on the son of her womb? Yea, she may forget, yet will not I forget thee. Behold, I have graven thee upon the palms of my hands: thy walls are continually before me. For thy Maker is thine husband...the God of the whole earth.' Such passages, hard for us to fit in with the God of the Copernican universe, or with our ideas of the supreme impartiality of God, were adopted and fully accepted by the Rabbis. They even improved upon them, and enlarged them, and one must admit that many of their enlargements have a tender beauty of their own. Moreover, the love of God for Israel produced, or corresponds with, a most intense love of the Rabbis for God. Let me now quote some of the passages dealing with God's exceeding love for Israel:

[158] It is written in Exod. XVII, 15, 'And Moses built an altar and called the name of it Jehovah-nissi' (cp. p. ci). [Nissi means 'my banner', but it could also mean 'my miracle'.] There was a king whose wife provoked him to anger, so he went to the market, entered a goldsmith's shop, and bought her an ornament. Now if, when she provoked him, he bought her an ornament, what would he not have done for her, had she obeyed his will! So was it with Israel. When they provoked God and said, 'Is the Lord indeed in our midst or not?' (Exod. XVII, 7), He wrought miracles for them; had they but done His will, how much more would He have done for them! (*Pes.R.* 50*b*.)

[159] 'Many waters cannot quench love' (Cant. VIII, 7). If the idolatrous nations of the world were to unite to destroy the love between God and Israel, they would be unable to do so.
(*Exod.R.*, Wayaḳhel, XLIX, 1.)

[160] 'The crown wherewith his [Solomon's] mother crowned him' (Cant. III, 11). R. Simeon b. Yoḥai asked R. Elazar b. R.

Jose: 'Did you hear from your father what crown this was?' R. Elazar said: 'Yes.' R. Simeon said: 'How is it?' He replied: 'It is like a king who had an only daughter whom he loved exceedingly, and he called her, "my daughter", and his love for her did not cease growing till he called her "my sister", and it did not cease growing till he called her "my mother". So God loves the Israelites exceedingly, and He calls them "My daughter ', as it says: "Hearken, O daughter" (Ps. XLV, 10), and His love for them did not cease growing till He called them "My sister", as it says: "Open to me, my sister, my love" (Cant. V, 2), and His love grew till He called them "My mother", as it says: "Give ear unto me, O my mother"' (Isa. LI, 4. For *ammi*, my people, the Midrash reads punningly, *immi*, my mother). Then R. Simeon arose, and kissed R. Elazar upon his head, and said to him: 'If I had come to hear only this one interpretation from you, it would have sufficed me.'

(*Cant.R.* III, § 11, 2, on III, 11; f. 22*b*.)

[161] 'And the angel of God removed and went behind them' (Exod. XIV, 19). It is like a man who on his journey let his son walk in front of him. Robbers came in front to take the son captive. Then he set the son behind him. A wolf came behind; he put the son in front; when robbers came in front and wolves behind, he took the son up in his arms. When the son was distressed because of the sun, he spread his cloak over him; when he was hungry, he gave him to eat; when he was thirsty, he gave him to drink. [Then follow ingenious proof texts to show that God did all these things for Israel.]

(*Mek.*[2], Beshallaḥ, § 4, p. 101; *Mek.*[3], § 5, vol. I, p. 224.)

[162] When Israel came out of Egypt and approached Sinai, God, before proclaiming the Decalogue, said, 'I bare you upon the wings of eagles and brought you unto me' (Exod. XIX, 4). The *Mekilta* asks: 'Why eagle's wings? How does the eagle differ from all other birds?' The answer is that all other birds carry their young in their claws, because they fear to be swooped upon from above [in which case the young can escape, while the dam is caught]. But the eagle [which flies higher than any bird] fears man alone, lest he shoot an arrow at her. The mother eagle says 'Better that the shaft pierce me than that it pierce my child.'

[So the dam carries the young bird on its wings. Such is God's love for Israel.]

(*Mek.*[2], *Baḥodesh*, Yitro, § 2, p. 207 *fin.*; *Mek.*[3], vol. II, p. 202.)

[163] 'His mouth is most sweet' (Cant. v, 16). R. Aḥa said in the name of R. Johanan: When the Israelites at Sinai heard the word 'I am' [the first word of the Ten Commandments], their soul fled from them, as it says, 'My soul failed when he spake' (Cant. v, 6). Then the word returned to God, and said, 'Lord of the world, thou livest for ever, and thy Law lives for ever, but thou hast sent me to the dead.' Then God made the word sweet to them.... It is like a king, who spoke to his son, and he was afraid, and his soul fainted within him. Then the king embraced and kissed him, and coaxed him, and said to him, 'What is the matter with you? Are you not my only one? Am I not your father?' So when God said 'I am', the soul of the Israelites fled from them. Then the angels began to embrace them and kiss them, and said to them, 'What ails you? Fear not; are you not sons of the Lord your God?' And the Lord made the word sweet in their mouths, and He said to them, 'Are you not my sons? Am I not the Lord your God? Beloved are you to me.' And so He coaxed them, till their souls returned to them, and they began to pray before Him, as it says, 'His mouth is most sweet.' Or, again, the Law besought God's mercy upon Israel, and said, 'Did ever a king give his daughter in marriage and kill his son-in-law? All the world rejoices because of me, and are thy children dead?' At once their soul returned to them, as it says, 'The law of the Lord restores the soul' (Ps. XIX, 8).

(*Cant.R.* VI, § 16, 3, on v, 16; f. 32*b*.)

The Rabbis noticed that in Num. VIII, 19 the words 'the children of Israel' occur five times. So they say:

[164] See how God loves the Israelites: in one single verse He names them five times! R. Simeon b. Yoḥai said: Like a king who entrusted his son to a tutor, and kept asking him, 'Does my son eat, does he drink, has he gone to school, has he come back from school?' So God yearns to make mention of the Israelites at every hour. (*Pes.K.* 17*a* (cp. [218]).)

The Rabbis seek to represent in every conceivable way the intimacy of the relation between God and Israel, and the fervour of the passion with which Israel loves God, and with which God loves Israel. The final redemption will be brought about, not through Israel's merit or virtues or 'works', but because God, who shares Israel's distresses, and even Israel's captivity or banishment, has, as it were, to deliver Himself:

[165] 'My salvation is near to come' (Isa. LVI, 1). '*My* salvation', not '*your* salvation': if the word had not been written, it would have been impossible to say it. But God says to Israel, 'If you have no merit, I do it for my own sake', as if He said, 'All the days that you are in distress, I am with you' [i.e. I too am in distress], even as it is said, 'I am with him in distress' (Ps. XCI, 15), and as it is said, 'Behold, thy king comes to thee; he is righteous and "saved"' (Zech. IX, 9), for the word is not 'saving', but 'saved'. Even if there are no works in your hands, God does it for His own sake. [The word *nosha*', which does literally mean 'saved', has actually in Zech. IX, 9 the signification of 'victorious'.] (*Exod.R.*, Mishpaṭim, XXX, 24.)

The Rabbis, who knew their Bible by heart, and had every sentence they required on the tip of the tongue, were quick to see how constantly Israel is attacked by the prophets, and how constantly it is blessed and praised. It is true that the attacks are of the present, the praises mainly of the future, but owing to the nature of Hebrew tenses, this is less marked in the Hebrew than it is in the English translation. In the following passage this dual aspect of the references to Israel is prettily emphasised:

[166] The way [or the method, or the character] of God is unlike the way of men. In a suit before a king, one man is prosecutor, and one man is counsel for the defence: the prosecutor cannot be the counsel for the defence, or the counsel for the defence the prosecutor. But with God it is otherwise. He can be both prosecutor and counsel for the defence. The same mouth which said, 'Woe to the sinful nation', said also, 'Open the gates that the righteous nation may enter in' (Isa. I, 4; XXVI, 2). The same mouth which said, 'A people laden with iniquity', said also, 'My people shall be all righteous' (Isa. I, 4; LX, 21). The mouth which said, 'Yea, though ye make many prayers, I will not hear,' said also, 'Before they call, I will answer' (Isa. I, 15; LXV, 24). The same mouth which said, 'Your new moons my soul hates,' said also, 'From one new moon to another shall all flesh come to worship before me' (Isa. I, 14; LXVI, 23). (*Exod.R.*, Bo, XV, 29.)

[167] 'My dove, my undefiled' (Cant. V, 2). [The Midrash puns on the word for undefiled, which in Hebrew is *Tammati*.] R. Yannai said: Read *Teummati*, my twin, as if God said, 'I am not greater than she, and she is not greater than I.' R. Joshua of Sikhnin said in the name of R. Levi: As with twins, if one has a headache, the other feels it too, so God says of Israel, I am with him in his distress (Ps. XCI, 15).

(*Cant.R.* V, § 2, 2, on V, 2; f. 30*a*.)

[168] 'The Lord is my helper' (Ps. CXVIII, 7). The matter is like two men who come to the judgment seat, and they are afraid of the judge. It is said to them, 'Fear not, let your hearts take courage.' So Israel will stand at the judgment before God, and will be afraid because of the Judge. Then the angels of the service will say to them, 'Fear not; do you not recognise Him? He is your fellow-citizen, as it is said, "It is He who will build my city"' (Isa. XLV, 13); and then they will say, 'Fear not the Judge; do you not recognise Him? He is your kinsman, as it says, "The children of Israel, the people related to Him"' (Ps. CXLVIII, 14). Then they will say, 'Do you not recognise Him? He is your brother, as it says, "For my brethren and friends' sake" (Ps. CXXII, 8). And even more, He is your Father, as it is said, "Is not He thy father?"' (Deut. XXXII, 6).

(*Midr.Ps.* on CXVIII, 7 (242*b*, § 10).)

[169] God said to Moses: Am I not He whose sons ye are, and whose Father I am? Ye are my brethren, and I am your brother: ye are my companions, and I am your companion: ye are my beloved, and I am yours. Have I caused you loss in any wise? I seek nothing from you save that just as I have examined myself and found eleven qualities [in myself], so I seek from you but eleven qualities, viz. walking in perfection, acting righteously, etc. (Ps. XV). And God said: Is there any respect of persons with me? The reward for fulfilling each command is beside it, whether the doer be Gentile or Israelite, man or woman, bondman or bondwoman. Hence they say that if a man enhances the glory of heaven, his own glory is enhanced with that of heaven. But whoso diminishes the glory of heaven while enhancing his own, will find his own diminished, while the glory of heaven remains in its place. (*Tan.d.b.El.* p. 65 (cp. [182]).)

[170] The Lord appeared of old unto me, saying, 'I have loved thee with an everlasting love' (Jer. XXXI, 3). It does not say, 'with abounding love', but 'with everlasting love'. For you might think the love with which God loves Israel was for three years or two years or a hundred years. But it was a love for everlasting and to all eternity. (*Tan.d.b.El.* p. 31.)

[This would appear to be an allusion to the wording of the old prayer which immediately precedes the *Shema*. According to the German and Polish liturgy, this prayer has, in the morning, the words 'with abounding love' (*P.B.* p. 39), but in the evening the words are 'with everlasting love' (*ib.* p. 96). In the Spanish and Portuguese liturgy the wording in each case is 'with everlasting love', as in Jeremiah (cp. [973–4]). (H. L.)]

[171] Galbanum was to be mixed with the incense (Exod. XXX, 34), although it stank, because God's mercies are always manifold over Israel—over those that are wicked among them and over those that are upright. (*Tan.d.b.El.* p. 62.)

[172] Hadrian said to R. Joshua: 'Great indeed must be the lamb, Israel, that can exist among seventy wolves.' He replied: 'Great is the Shepherd who rescues and protects her.'

(*Tanḥ.*, Toledot, § 8, 45 *a fin.*–46 *b init.*)

[173] 'And let those that hate thee flee before thee' (Num. X, 35). Are there, then, any who hate Him who spake and the world was? But it means that he who hates Israel is as if he hated God.... And he who helps Israel is as if he helped God. Whenever Israel is enslaved, the Shechinah is enslaved with them, as it says, 'In all their afflictions He was afflicted' (Isa. LXIII, 9).[1] And if you say this verse shows only that God is afflicted when the *community* of Israel is afflicted, how do we know that He is afflicted when an *individual* Israelite is afflicted? Because it says, 'I will be with *him* (the singular) in distress' (Ps. XCI, 15). R. Akiba [homiletically interpreting an obscure and corrupt verse, II Sam. VII, 23] said: If it were not written in Scripture, it would be impossible to say it: Israel says to God, 'Thou hast redeemed thyself.' [The Hebrew has the words, alluding to Israel, 'Thou hast redeemed for thyself.' The Midrash ignores the 'for', and renders, 'Thou hast redeemed thyself'.] And it says: 'Thus says

[1] Following the *Ḳere*, as opposed to the written Hebrew text (cp. [255]).

the Lord of Hosts: He that touches you touches the apple of His eye' (Zech. II, 8). R. Judah said: It does not say 'the apple of the eye', but 'the apple of *His* eye', that is, of God's eye, for, if one may say so, the Scripture refers to Him who is above, only that it paraphrases [to avoid too great an anthropomorphism]. Whithersoever Israel was exiled, the Shechinah went with them: and when they return, the Shechinah will return with them. (*Sifre Num.*, Beha'aloteka, § 84, f. 22*b* (the order has been slightly changed) (H. p. 81; *Mek.*[2], pp. 51 *fin.*–52 *init.*).)

[There is little doubt that the original reading in Zechariah was either 'apple of my eye' or, possibly, 'apple of the eye', referring to God in either case. The alteration is one of the deliberate changes introduced by the Scribes to avoid too bold anthropomorphisms (*Tiḳḳune Soferim*), see *Ab.R.N.* (vers. II), f. 62*a* and Schechter's note *in loc.* (See **Note 69.**) For a scholarly treatment of this and similar passages, as well as of the *puncta extraordinaria*, see L. Blau, *Masoretische Untersuchungen*, Strassburg, 1891. For the Zechariah passage, see *ib.* p. 51. (H. L.)] (**Note 11*e*.**)

[174] God says: I testify by heaven and earth that I sit and hope for Israel more than a father for his son or than a mother for her daughter, if only they would repent, so that my words could be fulfilled. (*Tan.d.b.El.* p. 163.)

[175] 'Beloved are the Israelites to God, for even when they are unclean, the Shechinah dwells among them' (Num. v, 2, 3). [Lev. XVI, 16 is interpreted to mean, 'Who [God] dwells among them in the midst of their uncleanness.'] (*Sifre Num.*, Naso, § 1, 1*b* (H. p. 4; cp. [271]).)

[176] A heretic said to R. Ḥanina: 'Now that the Temple is destroyed, and you cannot cleanse yourselves from your uncleanness, you are defiled, and God no longer dwells among you.' He replied: 'It is written, "He dwells among them in the midst of their uncleanness"' (cp. Levertoff, *Sifre Num.* p. 1, n. 3). (*Yoma* 56*b fin.*)

[177] God says: Why do the nations of the world say that I will not return to the Israelites because they worshipped idols, as it is said, 'Thy people have corrupted themselves; they have quickly become rebellious'? (Deut. IX, 12). Even if they have become rebellious, I do not abandon them; but with them I dwell, as it

is said, 'Yea, for the rebellious also, that the Lord God might dwell among them' (Ps. LXVIII, 18, A.V., a very corrupt verse). (*Exod.R.*, Terumah, XXXIII, 2.)

(For the reading 'nations of the world' cp. Marmorstein's 'Judaism and Christianity in the middle of the third century', in *Hebrew Union College Annual*, vol. x, p. 239, n. 87, 1935.)

[178] God said to Israel, 'You have made me the only object of *your* love in the world, so I shall make you the only object of *my* love in the world.' (*Ber.* 6*a fin.*)

[179] On the seven days of the feast of Tabernacles, the Israelites offered seventy bullocks for the seventy nations of the world. God said: 'Therefore on the eighth day there shall be an assembly for yourselves' (Num. XXIX, 35). It is like a king who made a feast for seven days, and invited all the citizens. When the feast was over, he said to his friend: 'Now that we have both done our duty towards the citizens, let us revel in a feast for ourselves.' (*Tanḥ.B.*, Pineḥas, 78*b*.)

[180] My Father who art in heaven, be thy great Name blessed for all eternity. Mayest thou have pleasure from Israel, thy servants, wherever they dwell. For in spite of all the hateful and improper things which Israel have done, thou hast towards them neither passion nor vengeance: thou hast not acted proudly towards them. The words of the Torah hast thou not withheld from them, but only the good, and not the evil, done by them hast thou remembered, as thine own lips have said, 'Let not the former things be recalled or come to mind' (Isa. LXV, 17). (*Tan.d.b.El.* p. 83.)

[181] David said: My Father, who art in heaven, be thy great Name blessed for all eternity, and mayest thou find pleasure from Israel, thy servants, wheresoever they dwell! For thou didst rear us up and make us great, thou didst sanctify us and grant us praise, thou didst bind [on us] the crown of Torah, of which the words spread from end to end of the world! If I have fulfilled aught of Torah, then it is only through thee that I have fulfilled it. Any charity I have given, from that which is thine have I given it. And in return for the little Torah which I have done, thou hast granted me to possess this world, the days of the Messiah, and the world to come. (*Tan.d.b.El.* p. 89.)

The reciprocity of the love of Israel for God to the love of God for Israel is prettily indicated in the following:

[182] 'My beloved is mine and I am his' (Cant. II, 16). Israel says: He is my God, and I am His people; He is my Father, and I am His son; He is my Shepherd, and I am His flock; He is my Guardian, and I am His vineyard. R. Judah b. Ilai said: He sings of me, and I sing of Him; He praises me, and I praise Him; He calls me 'My sister, my friend, my dove, my perfect one,' and I say to Him, 'He is my beloved, my friend'; He says to me, 'Thou art fair, my friend,' and I say to Him, 'Thou art fair, my beloved, and pleasant.' He says to me, 'Happy art thou, Israel, who is like unto thee?' And I say to Him, 'Who is like unto thee, O Lord, among the gods?' He says to me, 'Who is like unto Israel, a unique people on the earth,' and I confess the Unity of His name twice every day. [I omit, as too long, the scriptural proof passages.]

(*Cant.R.* II, § 16, 1, on II, 16; f. 18*b*.)

[Cp. [169]. This theme is the subject of a famous Atonement hymn in the Ashkenazi rite: text and translation will be found at foot of p. 45 in Davis and Adler's P.B., *Atonement* Volume, Part I. See also Davidson, *Thes. of Med. Heb. Poetry*, II, p. 470, No. 186†. (H. L.)]

[183] 'Thou art our father' (Isa. LXIII, 16; LXIV, 8). God says, 'You have abandoned your fathers, Abraham, Isaac and Jacob, and call me Father.' The Israelites say, 'Yea, thee we recognise as Father. Like an orphan girl, who was brought up by a good and faithful guardian, who looked after her well. He sought to give her in marriage, and the scribe came to write the marriage contract. He said to her, "What is your name?" She told him. "What is your father's name?" She was silent. "Why are you silent?" said her guardian. She said, "Because I know none other than you as my father, for he who brings up is father, not he who begets."' Such orphans are the Israelites, as it is said, 'We are orphans (Lam. V, 3); our good and faithful guardian is God.' So they call God father, and say to Him, 'He who brings up is father, not he who begets, as it is said, "Thou art our Father, Abraham knows us not."' (*Exod.R.*, Ki Tissa, XLVI, 5.)

Even though Israel's troubles and misfortunes may have been due to Israel's sins, and the punishment which God, as the God of justice, had to inflict upon Israel, yet God grieves in respect of these troubles none the less. The following is characteristic of the Rabbinic view (cp. [648]); note that God and the Shechinah are distinct (**Note 50**):

[184] In the hour when God determined to destroy the Temple, He said, 'So long as I was in its midst, the nations could not touch it; now I will hide my eyes from it, and I will swear that I will not connect myself with it until the end; then the enemy can come and destroy it.' At once God swore with[1] His right hand, and drew it back, as it is said, 'He drew back his right hand on account of the enemy' (Lam. II, 3). Then the enemy entered the Temple and burnt it. When it was burnt, God said, 'Now I have no dwelling-place in the land; I will withdraw my Shechinah from it, and ascend to my former place, as it is said, "I will go and return to my place till they acknowledge their sins"' (cp. [225]) (Hos. V, 15). Then the Lord wept, and said, 'Woe is me, what have I done? I caused my Shechinah to descend because of Israel, and now that they have sinned, I have returned to my former place. Far be it from me that I should be a laughing stock to the nations and a scorn to men.' Then Metatron came, and fell on his face, and said, 'I will work, but thou must not weep.' Then God said, 'If thou sufferest me not to weep, I will go to a place where thou hast no power to enter, and I will weep there, as it is said, "My soul shall weep in secret places"' (Jer. XIII, 17). Then God said to the angels of the service, 'Come, we will go, you and I, and we will see what the enemy has done to my house.' So God and the angels of the service set forth, and Jeremiah went in front of them. When God saw the Temple, He said, 'Assuredly, that is my house, and that is my place of rest, into which the enemy has come and worked his will.' Then God wept and said, 'Woe is me for my house. Where are you, my sons? Where are you, my priests? Where are you, my friends? What can I do to you? I warned you, but you did not repent.' Then God said to Jeremiah, 'I am to-day like a man who had an only son, and he set up for him the marriage canopy, and he died under it. Do you not grieve for me and my sons? Go, call Abraham, Isaac and Jacob and Moses from their graves, for they know how to weep.' Then Jeremiah said, 'I do not know where Moses is buried.' God said, 'Go to the border of the Jordan, and lift up your voice and cry: "Son of Amram, stand

[1] Or, by: see commentary *Yefeh 'Anaf in loc.* See also note to [637].

up, and see how the enemy has devoured your flock."' So Jeremiah went to the cave of Macpelah, and he said to the Patriarchs, 'Arise, for the time has come when you are summoned before God.' They said, 'Why?' He replied 'I know not,' because he was afraid lest they should say, 'So it is in *your* days that this evil has befallen our sons.' Then Jeremiah went, and stood by the border of Jordan, and cried, 'Son of Amram, arise, the time has come that you are summoned before God.' He said, 'Why is it to-day more than on other days that I am summoned before God?' Jeremiah replied, 'I do not know.' Then Moses left Jeremiah, and went to the angels of the service, for he knew them ever since the giving of the Law. He said to them, 'You ministers of God on high, do you know at all why I am summoned before God?' They said, 'Do you not know that the Temple is laid waste, and Israel driven into exile?' Then Moses cried and wept till he came to the Patriarchs. Then they, too, rent their clothes, and they laid their hands on their heads, and they wept and cried till they came to the gates of the Temple. When God saw them, He 'called to weeping and to mourning and to baldness and to girding with sackcloth' (Isa. XXII, 12). If this verse were not written, one could not dare to say it (**Note 69**). Then they all went weeping from one gate of the Temple to another, as a man whose dead lies before him. And God mourned and said, 'Woe to the King who prospers in His youth, and not in His old age.'

(*Lam.R.*, Introduction, 24, f. 6 *b* (foot of outer column) (cp. [649]).)

[Metatron was a Talmudic archangel in the 'wisdom' hierarchy, being superior to Yofiel, Uriel and Yefehfiyyah. The name is best to be derived from *Metator*, 'He who delimits', rather than from μετὰ θρόνον, 'after the throne'; μεταθρονίος, 'one who shares the throne'; μετὰ τύραννον, vice-gerent; *metatrion* or *metatrium* (palace, hence connected with *maḳom*); or from Mithras. It is sometimes held that the function of Metatron was to be a substitute for the Alexandrine Logos, which had tended to become too materialised in the opinion of Palestinian Rabbis. Metatron was, therefore, definitely subordinated, and, like Michael and Gabriel, denied any share in the work of the Creation (cp. *Gen.R.* I, 3 (Th. p. 5), and V, 4 (Th. p. 34 and Theodor's note *in loc.*): the former passage cited supports the derivation from *metator*, which, in classical Latin, means a military marker, cp. *castrorum antea metator, nunc urbis* (Cicero, *Philippics*, XI, 5, 12). The latter passage almost equates the function of Metatron with that of the Logos. In several instances Metatron is an intermediary designed to prevent too intimate a contact between God and the material world and his activity manifests itself in intellectual operations, e.g. he shows Palestine to Moses (*Sifre Deut.*, Ha'azinu, f. 141 *a*, § 338): he follows God in teaching Torah to children (*Ab.Zar.* 3 *b*), and he is described as the 'Great scribe' (Targ. Pseudo-Jonathan to Gen. v, 24) identified with Enoch. It has been noted as significant, by Grünwald (cited in *J.E.*), that the numerical equivalents of Metatron and Shaddai are equal (= 314). This equation precludes the alternative, if rarer, spelling *Mītatron*, with *yod*. In the later Kabbalistic literature, Metatron developed other functions. (**Note 22.**) (H. L.)]

Not less expressive of Rabbinic feeling is this:

[185] By an exegetical device, Isaiah XL, 1 is read thus: 'Comfort, comfort [me], O my people.' For the matter is like as if a king had a palace or a vineyard, which enemies had destroyed. The king needs comfort, not the palace or the vineyard. But the Temple is God's palace, and it lies waste, and Israel is His vineyard [which went into exile]. Therefore, comfort me, comfort me, O my people. (*Pes.K.* XVI, 128 *a fin.*)

But what of Israel's sins? The Rabbis were very conscious of these, and they did not forget the numerous passages in the O.T. in which God expresses His wrath and indignation at Israel's iniquities, or the passages in which punishment is threatened, or the facts that such punishments have taken place. Sometimes they speak as if God could regard Israel as His people only when they do His will; more often they hold that Israel is still His people even if, and when, they sin, and that they will never be wholly cut off; most often of all they, like the prophets, speak of repentance as the means by which, at any time, Israel can 'return', and find forgiveness and favour from their heavenly Father. Such passages, for example, are the following:

[186] It is said in Deut. XXXII, 6, 'Is He not thy father and thy owner?' If thy father, why thy owner? If thy owner, why thy father? When the Israelites do God's will, He has pity upon them, as a father has pity on his children. When they do not do His will, He rules over them, as an owner rules over his slaves. As the slave, whether voluntarily or involuntarily, has to serve his master, and even against his will, so you shall accomplish God's will, whether voluntarily or involuntarily, and even against your will. (*Exod.R.*, Beshallaḥ, XXIV, 1 (cp. [195]).)

[187] The prophets prayed to God when Israel was in distress that

He should have compassion upon them. God said, 'For whom do you pray?' They replied, 'For thy children.' God said, 'Only when they do my will are they my children; when they do not do my will, they are not my children.' The prophets said, 'Even by their faces they are recognised as thy children, as it is said, "All that see them recognise that they are a seed blessed by the Lord" (Isa. LXV, 23). As it is the manner of a father to have pity upon his children, even if they have corrupted themselves, so must thou have pity upon them.'

(*Exod.R.*, Ki Tissa, XLVI, 4.)

[188] R. Levi said: God said to Jeremiah, 'Go, bid the Israelites repent.' He did so, and they said to him, 'How can we repent? With what countenance can we come before God? Have we not provoked Him? Have we not angered Him? Those hills and mountains upon which we practised idolatry, do they not still stand?' As it is said, 'They sacrifice upon the tops of the mountains, and burn incense upon the hills' (Hos. IV, 13); so, 'Let us lie down in our shame and let confusion cover us' (Jer. III, 25). Jeremiah reported what they said to God, who replied, 'Say to them, Did I not write in my Law, I will set my face against that man, and I will cut him off from among his people. Have I done so? No, I have not caused mine anger to fall upon you, for I am merciful, and I do not keep anger for ever' (Jer. III, 12). R. Isaac said: God replied, 'If you come back to me, is it not to your Father in heaven that you come back?' As it is said, 'For I am a father to Israel' (Jer. XXXI, 8). (*Pes.K.* 165*a*.)

[189] R. Joshua b. Levi said: A king left his wife before her child was born, and went away over seas, and remained there many years. The queen bore a son, and he grew up. Then the king returned, and she brought her son into the presence of the king, his father. The son gazed at a duke, and then at a provincial governor, and kept on saying, 'This is he; this is he.' The king reflected, and said, 'Why do you gaze at these? From them you have no profit. You are my son, and I am your father.' So when God descended on Mount Sinai, there came down with him Michael and his band and Gabriel and his band. The Israelites gazed at each of them in turn, and said, 'This is he, this is he.' God said to Israel, 'My children, why do you look at these, from them you have no profit, but you are my children, as it says,

"Children are ye to the Lord your God" (Deut. XIV, 1), and I am your father, as it says, "And I will be a father to Israel" (Jer. XXXI, 8), You are my people, and I am your God.' (*Pes.R.* 104*b*.)

[190] It is said in Isa. LXIV, 8, 'But now, O Lord, thou art our father.' God says to Israel, '*Now* I am your father; when you are in trouble, *then* you call me your father.' Like the son of a chief physician, who met a quack, and he greeted him, and called him, 'My master, my father.' His father heard of this and was angry, and said that his son should not see his father's face, because he had called the quack his father. After a time the son became ill, and asked that his father should be called to come and see him. When they told his father, his compassion was stirred, and he went to him, and the son said, 'I pray of you, my father, look upon me.' Then the father said, '*Now* I am your father, but erstwhile you called the quack your father. Now that you are in trouble, you call *me* your father.' So God says to Israel, 'Now you call me father, but erstwhile you worshipped idols, and called them father, as it is said, "Saying to a stock, Thou art my father," but in your trouble you say to God, "Arise and save us"' (Jer. II, 27). (*Exod.R.*, Ki Tissa, XLVI, 4.)

[191] 'Be thou like a gazelle' (Cant. VIII, 14). As the gazelle, when it sleeps, has one eye open and one eye shut, so when Israel does the will of the Holy One, He looks upon them with two eyes, but when they do not do His will, He looks upon them only with one eye. [The proof passages from Ps. XXXIV, 15 [eyes of the Lord] and Ps. XXXIII, 18 [eye of the Lord] are, I suppose, meant to indicate that even when the Israelites do not do His will, they are still His children, and still beloved.]

(*Cant.R.* VIII, § 12, 1, on VIII, 14; f. 41*b*.)

[192] Even if a sharp sword be laid upon a man's neck, let him not despair of [the divine] mercy. (*Ber.* 10*a fin.*)

So even the individual Israelite need not despair. God is good and merciful. He is to be 'accepted' and relied on always, whether He 'judges' or 'forgives'. Even in His judgments mercy is close behind.

[193] David said: If you judge me with the attribute of Judgment, I accept thee; and if you judge me with the attribute of Mercy, I accept thee. (*Midr.Ps.* on LVI, 10 (148*a*, § 3).)

[194] R. Simeon b. Laḳish said: Happy are the men to whom God imputes not guilt. Who are these? They are those whose transgressions God forgives. They are the Israelites who are made pure [meritorious] on the Day of Atonement, who specify all their sins, and God forgives them. 'On this day He will make an atonement for you to clean you, from all your sins shall He clean you.' Dost thou say, 'So, too, he cleans another nation?' No: he does thus to Israel only. He forgives Israel only.... On the Day of Atonement Satan comes to accuse Israel, and he enumerates their sins. He says, 'Lord of the World, there are adulterers among the nations, and also in Israel; there are thieves among the nations, and also in Israel.' God enumerates the merits [good deeds] of Israel. He takes the handle of the scales, and weighs the merits against the sins, and the two are equal in weight, and the scales hang down equally. Then Satan goes to find [some more] iniquities, so as to put them in the pan of guilt in order to make it go down. What does God do? Before Satan returns, God takes the iniquities from the pan and hides them under His purple. Satan returns, and finds no iniquities there, as it is said, 'The iniquity of Israel shall be sought for, and there is none' (Jer. L, 20). Then Satan says, 'Lord of the World, thou hast taken away the sin of thy people: wonderful!'

(*Pes.R.* 185*b*–186*a* (the order is slightly changed).)

[195] Hearken to thy Father who is in heaven. He deals with thee as with an only son [if thou obeyest Him], but, if not, He deals with thee as a slave. When thou doest His will, He is thy Father, and thou art His son, but if not, against thy will, and opposed to thy consent, He is thine owner, and thou art His slave.

(*Pes.R.* 132*b* (cp. [186]).)

God is a Father to Israel and to every Israelite. The term 'Father in heaven', found so frequently in Matthew, is also very common among the Rabbis. Moore says: 'The words "who is in heaven" have in them no suggestion of the remoteness of God, exalted above the world in His celestial habitation: they remove the ambiguity of the bare word "father" by thus distinguishing between God and an earthly father' (vol. II, p. 215).

[196] 'If ye shall diligently keep all this commandment, etc.' (Deut. XI, 22). Perhaps you might say, I will learn a difficult section, and neglect an easy one; therefore it says: 'it is not an empty

thing for you' (Deut. XXXII, 47); a matter which you might think to be empty is not 'empty'; it is your life (*ib.*), and the light of your days. So, too, you might, perhaps, say, I have learnt Halakah; this is enough; therefore it says: '*all* this commandment'; so you must learn Bible, Halakah and Agada. So it says: 'Not by bread alone does man live'; that is Bible [exegesis], but 'from everything which issues from the mouth of the Lord does man live', that is Halakah and Agada (Deut. VIII, 3). So it says: 'My son, be wise, and make my heart glad, that I may answer him who reproaches me' (Prov. XXVII, 11). And it says: 'My son, if thine heart be wise, my heart shall rejoice, even mine' (Prov. XXIII, 15). R. Simeon b. Yoḥai says: It is clear about his father on earth; how do I know that he will also make glad his Father in heaven? Because it says: 'even mine'; to include his Father in heaven.

(*Sifre Deut.*, 'Eḳeb, § 48, 84*b* (cp. 140*b fin.*; Hd. p. 113).)

Halakah means Canon Law; Haggadah or Agada, homily and parable (cp. [350]). **(Note 94.)**

Even to the wicked God is long-suffering:

[197] 'And Moses bowed down and worshipped' (Exod. XXXIV, 8). What did Moses see? R. Ḥanina said: He saw [the attribute of] Long-suffering; the Rabbis say, He saw Truth. In accordance with the former view, it is taught that when Moses went up the Mount, he found God sitting and writing 'Long-suffering'. Moses said to him, 'Long-suffering to the righteous.' God replied, 'Also to the wicked.' Moses said, 'May the wicked perish.' God said, 'You shall see what you have asked.' When the Israelites sinned, God said, 'Did you not say to me, Long-suffering to the righteous?' Moses replied, 'But did you not reply to me, Long-suffering also to the wicked?'

(*San.* 111*a fin.*)

[198] The matter is like a king who had some empty goblets. The king said, 'If I put hot water in them, they will burst; if I put cold water, they will crack.' So the king mixed cold and hot water together, and poured it in, and the goblets were uninjured. Even so, God said, if I create the world with the attribute of mercy, sin will multiply; if I create it with the attribute of

justice, how can it endure? So I will create it with both, so that it may endure.

(*Gen.R.*, Bereshit, XII, 15 (Th. p. 112; cp. [132]).)

[199] It is said, 'I will stand upon my watch' (Hab. II, 1). Habakkuk drew a circle and stood in the middle of it, and said to God, 'I will not come out till thou tellest me for how long thou art long-suffering to the wicked in this world.' God said, 'You have cried unto me, and you have not criticised me. So I will answer and tell you. I am long-suffering to them in this world so that they may return and repent, and so that their deliberate sins may become as involuntary offences.'

(*Midr.Ps.* on LXXVII, 1 (171 *b fin.*, § 1).)

[For this practice of circle-drawing, as an impetuous means of securing consent, cp. the story of Onias the 'circle-drawer' in *Ta'an.* 23 *a*, Malter, p. 167, cited in [984] and [987], or the action of Gaius Popilius against Antiochus in Egypt in 168 B.C. (cp. note to [984]). (H. L.)]

[200] 'Blow the Shofar on the New Moon' (Ps. LXXXI, 3). 'On the New Moon' (*Ḥodesh*), that is, make new (*ḥaddeshu*) your deeds. God says, 'If you cleanse your deeds before me, then I will arise from the throne of Judgment, and sit upon the throne of Mercy, and have mercy upon you, and the attribute of Judgment shall be changed for you into the attribute of Mercy.'

(*Pes.K.* 154 *a*.)

A somewhat similar pun on the same subject can be seen in [632].

[201] 'God is long-suffering.' [In the Hebrew the second of the two words (*af*), which we translate by 'long-suffering', has a dual affix.] R. Jonathan said: That is because God is long-suffering, both to the righteous and to the wicked. Rabbi Johanan said: The dual means that God is slow to begin to punish, and when He does begin to punish, He is slow in the doing of it. (**Note 53**.)

(*T.J.Ta'an.* II, 1, 65 *b*, line 45 (cp. [147], [248]).)

[202] R. Samuel b. Naḥmani said: Woe to the wicked, who turn the attribute of pity into the attribute of judgment. Wherever the word Yahweh is used of the divine Being, the attribute of pity is meant; and wherever the word Elohim is used, the attribute of judgment is meant. Happy are the righteous who turn the

attribute of judgment into the attribute of pity. [The chief proof passage about the meaning of Yahweh is the familiar 'Yahweh, Yahweh, merciful and gracious God', etc. in Exod. XXXIV, 6. The proof passage about the meaning of Elohim depends upon the view that Elohim sometimes means 'judges,' e.g. Exod. XXI, 6.] (*Gen.R.*, Wayeẓe, LXXIII, 3 (Th. p. 847).)

[203] It is the custom among men when they appear before a court of justice to put on black clothes, and to let the beard grow long because of the uncertainty of the issue. Israelites do not act so. On the day when the judgment opens (the New Year), they are clad in white and shave their beards; they eat and drink and rejoice in the conviction that God will do wonders for them. (*T.J.R.H.* I, § 3, f. 57*b*, line 6.)

Very often it is Moses, or the Patriarchs, who are represented, either in their earthly lives, or after their deaths, as pleading for Israel's forgiveness and effecting it. They become intercessors for Israel before God.

[204] It is written, 'How long shall I bear this evil congregation?' (Num. XIV, 27), and 'My name is great among the nations, says the Lord' (Mal. I, 12). God said: The nations honour me, and you, for whom I have wrought many miracles, provoke me. I carry you; how long shall I bear you? God said, It is, as it were, as if a man brought a slave so that the slave should carry the lantern before him and make the way light, but I, though you are my slaves, as it is said, 'For unto me the children of Israel are slaves' (Lev. XXV, 55), have taken the lantern and given you light. Usually when a man buys a slave, and he goes a journey, the slave precedes him, and provides for him a well-provisioned resting place, but I did not act thus, for though you are my slaves, I provided for you a well-provisioned resting place, as it is said, 'The ark of the covenant of the Lord went before them to search out a resting place for them' (Num. X, 33). Usually a man buys a slave so that he may bake bread for him, but though ye are my slaves, I baked for you bread from heaven, as it is said, 'Man did eat angels' food' (Ps. LXXVIII, 25). So God said to Moses, 'I will destroy them from before me.' Moses replied: 'Thou art long-suffering; if a slave acts well and listens to his master, and his master looks upon him with a friendly and favourable counte-

nance, no credit is gained by the master. When does he get credit? When the slave acts badly, and *yet* his master looks upon him with a friendly and favourable countenance. So do thou not look upon their stiff-neckedness, as it is said, "Look not unto the stubbornness of this people"' (Deut. IX, 27). Then God said, 'For thy sake I will pardon them, as it is said, "I have pardoned according to *thy* word"' (Num. XIV, 20).

(*Num.R.*, Shelaḥ leka, XVI, 27.)

[205] [The Midrash says, 'There were three occasions when Moses spoke to God, and God said, You have taught me.' Two of these are here given.] Moses said: 'How should the Israelites know that they did wrong in the matter of the Golden Calf? Were they not brought up in Egypt, and are not all the Egyptians idolaters? And then, when thou gavest the Law, thou didst not give it to *them*, and they were not really present at Sinai, for it says, "And the people stood afar off" (Exod. XX, 21). So thou gavest the Law not to them, but to *me*, as it says, "And the Lord said unto Moses, Come up unto the Lord" (Exod. XXIV, 1). And when thou gavest the Ten Words, thou didst not give them to the Israelites, for thou didst not say, I am the Lord *your* God, but I am the Lord *thy* God; thou didst speak to *me*; perhaps *I* have sinned.' Then God said: 'You have spoken well; you have taught me; henceforth I will say, I am the Lord *your* God.' Then, again, when God said, 'He visits the iniquity of the fathers upon the children,' Moses said: 'Lord of the world, many wicked fathers beget righteous sons. Should these bear the iniquities of their fathers? Terah was an idolater, Abraham was righteous; Ahaz was a sinner, Hezekiah was righteous; Amon was a sinner, Josiah was righteous. Is it fitting that the righteous should be punished for the sins of their fathers?' Then God said: 'You have taught me; I abrogate my word, and confirm your word, as it is said, "The fathers shall not be put to death for the children, nor the children for the fathers" (Deut. XXIV, 16). And I will ascribe it to your name, as it is said, "But the children of the murderers he slew not, according to that which is written in the book of the law of Moses, The fathers shall not be put to death for the children, nor the children be put to death for the fathers"' (II Kings XIV, 6). (*Num.R.*, Ḥuḳḳat, XIX, 33.)

[206] It is written in Exod. XXXII, 11, 'Moses said, Lord, why does

thy wrath wax hot against thy people? Why art thou angry with them? Is it that they have made an idol? But thou hast not commanded them not to do so.' God said to Moses, 'Have I not said in the Second Word, Thou shalt not make unto thee a graven image?' Moses replied, 'Thou didst not command *them*, thou didst command *me*. [The commandments are given in the singular, 'thou'; hence Moses ingeniously argues that they referred only to him.] If *I* have made an idol, blot *me* out of thy book.' When God saw that he gave his life for them, He said, 'For thy sake I will give them the Law, as it is said, "Write thou these words"' (Exod. XXXIV, 27).

(*Exod.R.*, Ki Tissa, XLVII, 9.)

[207] Moses saw that there was no continuance for Israel, so he united his life with their life, and he broke the Tables, and he said to God, 'They have sinned, and I have sinned. If thou wilt pardon them, pardon me too; but if thou wilt not pardon them, then pardon not me; blot me out of thy book' (Exod. XXXII, 32).

(*Exod.R.*, Ki Tissa, XLVI, 1.)

[208] When Moses asked God that he might enter the Promised Land, God said that He had cancelled His decree to destroy Israel after the sin of the Golden Calf, at Moses's request; He could not grant *two* requests. Let Moses choose; let the old request be cancelled, then the new request could be granted, or let the old request stand, and then the new request must be refused. When Moses heard this, he said, 'Lord of the world, let Moses and a hundred such as he die rather than a nail of one of the Israelites be harmed.' (*Deut.R.*, Ki Tabo, VII, 10.)

There is a certain feeling of discomfort every now and then as to God's amazing love and partiality for Israel. What caused it? A theory is invented that the Law was refused by other nations and accepted by Israel. Here are three examples of this theory:

[209] R. Berechiah said: It is like a judge who had a cloak, and bade his servant shake it and fold it, and give much heed to it, and the servant said, 'My lord judge, of all the cloaks that you possess you enjoin me only about this one.' The judge replied, 'That is because this was the cloak which I wore when I was first appointed a judge.' So Moses said to God, 'Of all the seventy great nations thou has created in the world thou givest

me commands only about Israel.' God replied, 'That is because they took upon themselves the yoke of my Kingdom at Sinai, for they said, "All that the Lord has said we will do, and we will be obedient"' (Exod. XXIV, 7).

(*Pes.K.* II, 17*a* (cp. [210] and [320].)

[210] The nations of the world were asked to receive the Law, in order not to give them an excuse for saying, 'Had we been asked, we might have accepted it.' They were asked, but they did not accept it, as it is said, 'The Lord came from Sinai and rose up from Seir unto them' (Deut. XXXIII, 2), that is, He revealed Himself to the children of Esau, the wicked, and said to them, 'Will you receive the Law?' They said, 'What is written therein?' He said, 'Thou shalt do no murder.' They said, 'That is the inheritance which our father left to us, as it is said, "By thy sword shalt thou live"' (Gen. XXVII, 40). Then He revealed Himself to the children of Ammon and of Moab, and said to them, 'Will you receive the Law?' They said, 'What is written in it?' He said, 'Thou shalt not commit adultery.' They said, 'We all spring from one adulterer, as it is said, "And the daughters of Lot became with child by their father" (Gen. XIX, 36); how can we receive the Law?' Then He revealed Himself to the children of Ishmael, and said, 'Will you receive the Law?' They said 'What is written in it?' He said, 'Thou shalt not steal.' They said, 'Our father was given this blessing, "He will be a wild ass among men, his hand will be against every man" (Gen. XVI, 12); how can we receive the Law?' But when He came to Israel, they all said with one accord, 'All that the Lord has said, we will do, and we will be obedient' (Exod. XXIV, 7). Again, if the children of Noah could not abide [i.e. observe] the seven commandments which were enjoined upon them, how much less could they have accepted and fulfilled all the commandments of the Law.

(*Mek.*[2], *Baḥodesh*, Yitro, § 5, pp. 221, 222; *Mek.*[3], vol. II, p. 234.)

[211] 'The Lord came from Sinai' (Deut. XXXIII, 2). When God revealed Himself to give the Torah, He did so in four tongues. 'He came from Sinai,' that is Hebrew. 'He rose up from Seir,' that is Latin (Seir = Edom = Rome). 'He shone forth from Mount Paran,' that is Arabic (Paran is said to be in Arabia). 'He came from Kadesh,' that is Aramaic (the word *atha*, 'he came,' is

Aramaic). For God offered the Law to all the nations in turn (cp. *R.T.* p. 77). It is like a man who sent his ass and his dog into his barn. He loaded the ass with a *lethek* (5 seahs weight) and the dog with three seahs. The ass went on with its burden, but the dog panted. So he took off from the dog first one, then a second and finally a third seah, and put them on the ass. So Israel received the whole Law, with all its details and developments, including the seven commands which the Noachides took upon themselves, but could not bear.

(*Sifre Deut.*, Berakah, § 343, 142*b*.)

[212] 'The Lord came from Sinai' (Deut. XXXIII, 2). Hence we learn that God went about from nation to nation to see whether they would receive the Law, and they would not receive it; as it says, 'All the Kings praise thee, O Lord, for they have *heard* the words of thy mouth' (Ps. CXXXVIII, 4). One might think, that since they heard, therefore they were *also* willing to *receive* the Law. But Micah came and explained, saying, 'I execute vengeance in anger upon the nations which have not hearkened' (V, 15). Hence we may learn that they *did* hear, but would not receive the Law. David came and gave thanks, as it is said, 'Thou art the God that doest wonders, in that thou hast shown thy might among the peoples' (Ps. LXXVII, 14). For David said: 'Thou hast done wonderful things in thy world, in that thou hast made known thy Law to all the peoples of the world. For by the word "might" is meant the Law, as it is said, "The Lord gives might to His people"' (Ps. XXIX, 11). R. Abbahu said: 'As it was known and revealed unto God that the nations would not accept the Law, why did He seek to be justified in regard to them? Because such is God's character. He never punishes till He is justified in regard to His creatures. Only then does He drive them from the world, for God does not act as a tyrant towards His creatures.' [Thus, in this particular case, God gave the nations the choice and possibility of accepting the Law. Only when they refused to do so, did He punish them.]

(*Pes.K.* 199*b fin.*–200*a* (see **Note 7**).)

[213] God gave the Torah in the third month (Exod. XIX, 1). Why in this month? Because it is in the Zodiacal division of the Twins, so that the Gentiles should not have an excuse for saying, 'If He had offered us the Torah, we would have fulfilled it.'

So God said, 'See, I have given the Torah in the Twins, so that Esau, Jacob's twin, may come and learn Torah and become a proselyte.' (*Tanḥ.B.*, Yitro, 38*b*.)

[214] If only the nations knew what a benefit the Tabernacle was to them, they would surround it with tents and forts to protect it. Why? Before the Tabernacle was set up, the divine speech was wont to enter the tents of the nations, and they would be terrified, for 'who of all flesh has heard the voice of the ever-living God, as thou didst hear it, and live?' (Deut. v, 26). *Thou* couldst hear it and live, but not *they*. [But from the Tabernacle God's voice was heard gently.] Still better for the nations than the Tabernacle was the sanctuary, as Solomon said in his prayer with reference to the foreigner (I Kings VIII, 41): 'Also the prayer of the foreigner, who is not of thy people Israel, mayest thou hear from heaven.' Of an Israelite who comes to pray, Solomon says: 'Mayest thou give each man according to his ways' (*ib.* 43), 'for thou knowest his heart' (*ib.* 39). But with regard to foreigners, he says simply: 'Grant them according to their desire, so that all the earth may know that thou art God.'

(*Tanḥ.B.*, Terumah, 47*a* (cp. [304] and [906]).)

[215] It says, 'If ye walk in my statutes, I will give you rain in its due season (Lev. XXVI, 3), but if not, I will make the heavens as iron' (*ib.* 4, 14, 19). So the prophet says, 'It is on your account that the heavens are restrained from dew' (Hag. I, 10). Thus it is on your account that the Gentiles suffer. Joshua b. Levi said: If the Gentiles only knew that they would suffer through Israel's sin, they would establish two armies so as to guard every Israelite from wrong-doing. Yet it is not enough that the Gentiles do not guard Israel, but they even induce them to abandon the commandments. But if Israel sin not, the whole world is blessed (Gen. XXVI, 4).

(*Tanḥ.B.*, Beḥuḳḳotai, 55*a*.)

[216] A man said to me, 'My Master, why do the Gentiles enjoy this world?' I replied, 'My son, this is their reward because God separated Israel from among them. It is like a king who found that one man, out of a large family, did his will. The king sent gifts to all the members of the family for the sake of that single man who did the king's will. So is it with the Gentiles. They

enjoy this world as a reward that God separated Israel from among them.' (*Tan.d.b.El.* p. 174.)

Such theories or stories seemed partially to explain and justify the peculiar relation and 'nearness' of God to Israel and of Israel to God. This nearness of God is half physical, half spiritual. The conception of the Shechinah was of great value to the Rabbis in their emphasis on the belief that wherever Israel is, there too is God. For, in one sense, if God is everywhere, He is no 'nearer' to one bit of space than to another. But yet He dwelt (as we have seen) in the sanctuary, and He is ever close to Israel, accompanying them in their pilgrimages and exiles from land to land. For the Shechinah, as God's more concentrated presence, can both contract and expand (cp. [12], [31]). A striking saying of R. Akiba's has been already quoted in a somewhat similar connection (cp. [173]).

The thought of the last passage is frequent. Again, the idea occurs that it was not till, and only through, the deliverance from Egypt that Israel really became God's people. So one gets a passage like this:

[217] Zabdai ben Levi, using Ps. LXVIII, 6, 'God sets the solitary in their houses,' said: You will find that till the Israelites were redeemed from Egypt, they dwelt by themselves, and the Shechinah dwelt by itself, and when the Israelites went into captivity, then again the Shechinah dwelt by itself, and the Israelites dwelt by themselves, as it is written, 'The rebellious dwell in a dry land: how does she sit solitary?' (Ps. LXVIII, 6; Lam. I, 1). (*Lam.R.*, Introduction, 29.)

Or, again, it was only when Israel had accepted the Law that it became God's people:

[218] 'Why is Israel called God's people?' 'Because of the Torah.' R. Jose b. Simon says: Ere you stood at Sinai and accepted my Torah, you were called 'Israel', just as other nations, e.g. Sabtekhah and Raamah, are called by simple names, without addition. But after you accepted the Torah at Sinai, you were called 'My People', as it says, 'Hearken, O my people, and I will speak' (Ps. L, 7). (*Tanḥ.B.*, Wa'era, 9*a*.)

[The remark that Israel became God's people only by the acceptance of the Torah is exemplified by the following allegory on Exod. XIII, 17, 18: 'When Pharaoh let the people go, God did not lead them by way of the Philistines...the children of Israel went up harnessed,' R.V. 'armed'. The word translated 'harnessed' (A.V. 'in battle array') (*ḥamushim*) is unusual: the Targum renders it by *zerizin* (zealous in service; cp. [359]) and it is connected with *ḥummesh*, lit. a fifth, i.e. the Pentateuch. So, says the allegory, six times in succession do the Scriptures either style them '*am* or use a pronoun. It is only after they become *ḥummashim*, possessed of the Torah, that they are termed Bene Yisrael. The higher title was given them only because of their acceptance of God's Law. I regret that the source of the allegory is no longer known to me and I shall be glad if a reader can enlighten me as to its origin (cp. [164]). (H. L.)]

[219] First acknowledge (or accept) God's Kingship [over you], and then only seek for His compassion.

(*Sifre Num.*, Beha'aloteka, § 77, 19*b fin.* (H. p. 71 *fin.*).)

It is also said that God did not 'dwell below' till the Sanctuary was built:

[220] From the first day on which the world was created God yearned to dwell with His creatures below, but He did not do so till the Sanctuary was erected, and then God caused His Shechinah to rest upon it, and when the princes came to make their offering, God said, 'Let it be written that on this day the world was created, as it is said, On the first day' (Num. VII, 12).

(*Num.R.*, Naso, XIII, 6.)

[Into the ancient controversy, whether the year began in the spring (i.e. in Nissan) or in the autumn (i.e. in Tishri), we need not now enter. The beginning of *T.B. Rosh ha-Shanah* speaks of four different 'New Years', just as we have different dates for reckoning financial, judicial, academic and civil years. It is interesting that the recent Ras Shamra evidence is held to point to the spring beginning. This is the view of *Numbers R.* and is illustrated by this passage. In the ancient chronicle *Seder 'Olam* (Ch. VII, ed. Neubauer, p. 37, in vol. II of *Mediaeval Jewish Chronicles*) we read that on 23 Adar Moses began to set up the Tabernacle and perform the ceremony of consecration: this was completed on 1st Nissan. 'That day was the first of creation, of the consecration of the Twelve Princes of the Tribes, of the order of the months, of the dwelling of the Shechinah in Israel, of the prohibition to sacrifice on high places, of the Priesthood, of the blessing, of the temple-service etc.... and to that day applies Cant. IV, 16, "Arise, North Wind (i.e. the holocaust, slaughtered in the North) and come, South Wind (i.e. the peace-offerings, slaughtered in the South), and let my Beloved (i.e. the Shechinah) come to His Garden."' In consequence of this interpretation, the passages in Num. VII relating to the consecration of the Twelve Princes are read, day by day, after morning service, from

Nissan 1 to 12. But another tradition puts the beginning of the world on 1st Tishri: see the hymn on p. 157 of the New Year Service in Davis and Adler's edition (for sources, see Heidenheim's note *in loc.*). (H. L.)]

The immense importance of the Sanctuary to the Rabbis is illustrated by the following:

[221] What was the world like up to the building of the Sanctuary? It was like a chair with two legs, which cannot stand firmly, but shakes: when a third leg is made for it, it stands firmly. So when the Sanctuary was made, the world became secure, for at the beginning, the world stood on two legs only, namely, on lovingkindness and the Torah, and it shook, but when the third leg was made for it, namely, the Sanctuary, it stood firm.... At the time when God bade the Israelites build the Sanctuary, He indicated to the angels of the service that they too should make a Sanctuary; so when the Sanctuary below was set up, the upper Sanctuary was set up also, and it is the Sanctuary [dwelling] of the youth whose name is Metatron (cf. [184]), and in it he offers up the souls of the righteous to atone for the Israelites in the days of their exile. (*Num.R.*, Naso, XII, 12.)

In making the altar, iron might not be used.

[222] 'For if thou lift thy tool over it, thou dost pollute it' (Exod. XX, 25). For the altar was made to add to the length of human life, but the iron blade shortens human life. It is not right, then, to wield the shortener over the lengthener.

(*Tanḥ.*, Yitro, § 17, 126*b fin.* (cp. [1508]).)

[223] God said to Israel, 'Make me a dwelling (Exod. XXV, 8; XXVI, 1), for I desire to dwell amid my sons.' When the ministering angels heard this, they said to God, 'Why wilt thou abandon the creatures above, and descend to those below? It is thy glory that thou shouldst be in heaven, "O Lord our God, who hast set thy majesty in the heavens"' (Ps. VIII, 2). But God said, 'See how greatly I love the creatures below that I shall descend and dwell beneath the goats' hair.' Hence it says: 'Make curtains of goats' hair for the Tabernacle' (Exod. XXVI, 7).

(*Tanḥ.B.*, Terumah, 47*b*.)

[224] 'I have loved you, saith the Lord, and ye say, Wherewith hast thou loved us?' (Mal. I, 2). See with what love God loves you!

From earth to heaven is five hundred years' distance, from the first heaven to the second there is yet more, and so between each of the seven heavens. And we need not reckon beyond the footsteps of the angels. Above them all is the divine throne. 'See, then, how I have loved you in that I have left all this sublime glory and said to you, "Make me goatskin curtains (Exod. XXVI, 7), and I will abide among you."'
(*Tanḥ.B.*, Terumah, 47*a init.* (cp. *Yalkuṭ*, Terumah, §369 (? 370), f. 109*b* on Exod. XXVI, 1).)

Another view is that the Shechinah came to earth at the Creation, but through human sin removed itself farther and farther from earth. Then Abraham and successive righteous Israelites gradually brought it down again, till Moses finally brought it back again to earth:

[225] R. Aibu said that when Adam sinned, the Shechinah withdrew to the first (and lowest) heaven, when Cain sinned to the second, in the generations of Enoch to the third, in the generations of the flood to the fourth, in the generation of the Dispersion of Tongues to the fifth, through the sin of the men of Sodom to the sixth, and through the sin of the Egyptians to the seventh [and highest] heaven. Then six righteous men arose, and they brought the Shechinah back to the earth. For Abraham brought it back to the sixth heaven, Isaac to the fifth, Jacob to the fourth, Levi to the third, Kehat to the second, and Amram to the first. Moses finally brought it back from the upper world to the lower world [i.e. to earth]. For indeed the wicked cause the Shechinah to ascend from the earth, while the righteous cause it to dwell on the earth. When exactly did the Shechinah come down upon the earth? On the day when the Sanctuary was set up, as it is said, 'Then the cloud covered the tent of meeting, and the glory of the Lord filled the Sanctuary' (Exod. XL, 34).
(*Num.R.*, Naso, XIII, 2 (cp. [184]).)

[This theme is the subject of a beautiful poem, of which the authorship is uncertain. The poem is included in the series of dirges recited on the Ninth of Ab, in the Sephardic rite, and it will be found, with an English translation, on p. 114 of *The Order...of Prayers for the Fast Days....* David Levi, London, A.M. 5570 (i.e. A.D. 1810). For details as to authorship, etc., see I. Davidson, *Thes. of Med. Heb. Poetry*, New York, 1930, vol. III, p. 461, No. 1167. (H. L.)]

The mixture of God's spiritual presence with His semi-material presence in the final quotation is quite characteristic.

Sometimes the Rabbis are also ready to generalise, and to say quite simply that the Shechinah ever accompanies the righteous. Doubtless *they* thought of *their* 'righteous' almost wholly as Israelites, just as the Church Fathers thought of *their* righteous as almost wholly composed of orthodox Christians:

[226] R. Simeon b. Yoḥai said: Whithersoever the righteous go, the Shechinah goes with them.

(*Gen.R.*, Wayesheb, LXXXVI, 6 (Th. p. 1058).)

Chapter III

MAN'S NATURE AND GOD'S GRACE

Let me now quote a few passages in which the Rabbis speak more generally about the nature of man:

[227] R. Tafdai[1] in the name of R. Aḥa said: The upper beings [the angels] are created in the image and likeness of God, but they do not increase and multiply [there is no begetting and giving birth among them]. The lower beings [the animals] increase and multiply, but they are not created in the image and likeness of God. So God said, 'I will create man in the image and likeness of the angels, but he shall increase and multiply like the animals.' And God said, 'If I were to create him entirely according to the nature of the angels, he would live for ever, and never die; if I were to create him entirely according to the nature of the animals, he would die, and not live again; so behold I will create him with something of the natures of both; if he sins, he shall die, if he does not sin, he shall live.'

(*Gen.R.*, Bereshit, VIII, 11 (Th. p. 65).)

[228] R. Joshua b. Levi said: When a man goes on his road, a troop of angels proceed in front of him and proclaim: 'Make way for the image of the Holy One, blessed be He.' (*Deut.R.*, Re'eh, IV, 4.)

I have taken this quotation from an interesting essay by Rabbi Max Katten of Bamberg in the *Monatsschrift für Geschichte und Wissenschaft des Judentums*, May–June, p. 221, 1935 (cp. [940]).

A righteous man ranks almost above the angels:

[229] If man does worthily, they[2] say to him, 'Thou wast created before the angels of the service'; if he does not, they say to him, 'The fly, the gnat, the worm were created before thee.'

(*Gen.R.*, Bereshit, VIII, 1 (Th. p. 56).)

[The saying is missing in Theodor's text. For sources see his notes. (H. L.).]

[230] It is the righteous, for whose sake blessing comes to the world. It is a Sanctification of the Name that when the righteous are

[1] The name is uncertain.

[2] Cp. p. 179 footnote.

in the world, blessing comes to the world; when [or, if] the righteous are removed from the world, blessing leaves the world. The house of Obed-Edom was blessed because of the Ark (II Sam. VI, 10). If because of the Ark, which could receive neither reward nor punishment, blessing came to a household, how much more does blessing come because of the righteous for whose sake the world was created.

(*Sifre Deut.*, 'Eḳeb, § 38, 77*b* (H. p. 76).)

Extraordinary praises are given to the 'righteous':

[231] 'They that turn many to righteousness are like the stars for ever' (Dan. XII, 3). As among the stars there is no enmity, jealousy and contention, so too with the righteous. They who love God are as the sun when he goes forth in his might (Judges V, 31). Who are greater, they who love, or they who cause [others] to love Him? Surely the latter. If those who love God are as the sun, how much more those who cause others to love Him. 'As the stars.' As their light is seen from one end of the world to the other, so is the light of the righteous seen from one end of the world to the other. And as the number of the stars is uncountable, so is the number of the righteous uncountable. [This seems rather strong; contrast Matt. VII, 14. But perhaps one must not press the statement too far, because the passage continues:] Is this so, whether they do the will of God, or do not do it? [The righteous are becoming synonymous with Israel, and there is a blurring of definite outline, so characteristic of the Rabbis.] So it says: 'Thy seed shall be as the dust of the earth' (Gen. XXVIII, 14). When Israel does the will of God, they are as stars, but if they do not do it, they are as dust. 'As the days of the heavens above the earth' (Deut. XI, 21 and cp. Isa. LXVI, 22). If the heavens and the earth, which were created only for the glory of Israel, are to continue for ever, how much more the righteous for whose sake the world was created.

(*Sifre Deut.*, 'Eḳeb, § 47, 83*a* (H. pp. 105, 106).)

But it is realised that the deliberate creation by God of a creature who could (and would) sin—in this strange and mournful quality unlike either angel or animal—presented its difficulty:

[232] R. Berechiah said: In the hour when God was about to create the first man, He saw that both righteous and wicked men would

issue from him. He thought: 'If I create him, wicked beings will issue from him: if I do not create him, how can the righteous issue from him?' What did God do? He removed the way of the wicked out of His sight, and united Himself with the attribute of mercy, and He created man, as it is said, 'The Lord knows the way of the righteous, but the way of the wicked He destroys' [A.V. 'shall perish'] (Ps. I, 6). R. Ḥanina said: No, it was thus: When God was about to create the first man, He consulted the angels of the service, and He said to them, 'We will make a man in our image and likeness.' They said to Him, 'What is to be the nature of this man?' He said to them, 'Righteous beings shall issue from him,' as it says, 'The Lord knows the way of the righteous,' for He made known the way of the righteous to the angels of the service, but He suppressed from them the way of the wicked. He revealed to them that righteous beings should issue from Adam; but that wicked persons should also issue from him He did not reveal to them. For if He had revealed this to them, the attribute of judgment would not have permitted Adam to be created.

R. Simeon said: In the hour when God was about to create Adam, the angels of the service were divided into different groups. Some said, 'Let him not be created', others, 'Let him be created,' for 'Love and Truth met together; Righteousness and Peace kissed each other' (Ps. LXXXV, 10). For Love said, 'Let him be created, he will do loving deeds'; but Truth said, 'Let him not be created, for he will be all falsity'; Righteousness said, 'Let him be created, for he will do righteous deeds'; Peace said, 'Let him not be created, for he will be all quarrelsomeness and discord.' What did God do? He seized hold of Truth, and cast her on to the earth, as it is said, 'Thou didst cast down Truth to the ground' (Dan. VIII, 12). Then the angels of the service said to God, 'Lord of the world, how dost thou despise thine angel of truth; let truth arise out of the earth,' as it is said, 'Truth springs out of the earth.'

(*Gen.R.*, Bereshit, VIII, 4, 5 (Th. p. 59).)

One might almost say that man was created in order to give opportunity for God to display His forgiveness, His lovingkindness, His mercy, His grace—the last three words translating indifferently the one Hebrew word *ḥesed*. God expects a man to be and do good, and He ascribes merit to, and rewards, the man, and more especially the

Israelite, who does good and fulfills the Commandments, but beyond all human merit and deed are His compassion and His grace. And God is especially ready to receive the smallest indication of genuine repentance, and is never weary of listening to the cry of His human creatures in their various distresses:

[233] 'Cast thy burden upon the Lord, and he will sustain thee' (Ps. LV, 22). A man has a protector (*patronus*). He applies to him once or twice, and is received. The third time the protector will not see him, the fourth time he turns from him altogether. But God is not thus; whenever you worry Him, He receives you.

(*Midr.Ps.* on LV, 22 (147*a*, § 6).)

[234] 'Have mercy upon me, O Lord, according to thy loving-kindness' (Ps. LI, 1). With whom may we compare David? With one who had a wound in his hand. He went to the doctor, who said, 'I cannot heal you; your wound is too big, and the fee that you offer is too small.' The man replied, 'I pray you take all I have, and the rest supply from what you possess; act charitably with me, and have compassion upon me.' So David said, 'Have mercy upon me according to thy lovingkindness; thou art compassionate, and according to thy compassion, blot out my sins. From thee comes healing; as the wound is large, give me a large plaster' (cf. *R.L.* p. 362).

(*Midr.Ps.* on LI, 1 (140*b fin.*, § 2).)

[235] 'Thou didst lead them in thy mercy' (*ḥesed*) (Exod. XV, 13). Thou hast wrought grace (*ḥesed*) for us, for we had no works, as it is said, 'I will mention the lovingkindnesses of the Lord' (Isa. LXIII, 7), and again, 'I will sing of the mercies of the Lord for ever' (Ps. LXXXIX, 1). [In both these texts the Hebrew is *ḥesed*, but in the plural.] And, from the beginning, the world was built only upon grace (*ḥesed*), as it is said, 'I declare the world is built upon grace' (Ps. LXXXIX, 2. A.V. 'I have said, "Mercy (*ḥesed*) shall be built up for ever"').

(*Mek.*[2], *Shirata*, Beshallaḥ, § 9, p. 145; *Mek.*[3], vol. II, p. 69.)

[236] 'I said, the world is built upon *ḥesed*' (Ps. LXXXIX, 2). And not only the world, but also the throne of God, as it is said, 'The throne is founded on *ḥesed*' (Isa. XVI, 5). To what is the matter like? To a chair which had four feet, and one shook because it was too short. Then they took a pebble [as a wedge] and sup-

ported it. So the throne above, as one might say, shook, but God supported it. And with what did He support it? With *ḥesed*. And the heavens stand upon *ḥesed*, as it says, 'To Him that by wisdom made the heavens, for His *ḥesed* endures for ever' (Ps. CXXXVI, 5). (*Midr.Ps.* on LXXXIX, 2 (191 *a*, § 2).)

[237] R. Haggai said in the name of R. Isaac: All need grace, for even Abraham, for whose sake grace came plenteously into the world, himself needed grace. (*Gen.R.*, Ḥayye Sarah, LX, 2 (Th. p. 641).)

[238] It says, 'Say ye of the righteous that he is good, for they shall eat the fruit of their doings' (Isa. III, 10). R. Judah the Levite (see Buber's note) son of R. Shallum said: Who is it who is called righteous? It is God, as it is said, 'For the Lord is righteous and loves righteousness' (Ps. XI, 7). If we have merit, and if we possess good deeds, He gives us of what is ours; if not, then He acts charitably and lovingly towards us from what is His. Can there be any one more righteous than this?

(*Midr.Ps.* on LXXII, 1 (162 *a fin.*, § 1).)

The unintentional man-slayer, who took even one step outside the city of refuge in which he was interned, before the death of the High Priest, was liable to be put to death by the Avenger of Blood (Num. XXXV, 26). On this fact the following saying is based:

[239] R. Elazar b. Azariah said: The range of punishment is restricted; yet he who takes one step within its limit endangers his soul, how much more then (must a man benefit his soul by taking one step) within the sphere of good, which is vast?

(*Sifre Num.*, Masse'e, § 160, 62 *a* (H. p. 220).)

[God is unwilling to punish but eager to reward, (e.g. 'visiting the iniquities...to the third and fourth generation but showing mercy unto thousands'). Man has assistance from God to do good and it should therefore be easier for him to gain reward than to incur punishment. This is characteristically Rabbinic and not Pauline. (H.L.)]

[240] 'Through thy righteousness deliver me' (Ps. LXXI, 2). Israel says to God, 'If thou save us, save us not through our righteousness or good deeds, but, be it to-day or be it to-morrow, deliver us through thy righteousness.'

(*Midr.Ps.* on LXXI, 2 (161 *b fin.*, § 2).)

The Biblical word for 'righteousness' in Rabbinic Hebrew often means 'charity' or 'almsgiving'. Here it is applied to God's charity, His 'almsgiving', His grace.

[241] 'Deal with thy servant according to thy *ḥesed* (grace)' (Ps. CXIX, 124). Perhaps thou hast pleasure in our good works? Merit and good works we have not: act towards us in *ḥesed*. The men of old whom thou didst redeem, thou didst not redeem through their works: but thou didst act towards them in *ḥesed*, and didst redeem them. So do thou with us (cf. *R.T.* p. 362) (cp. [752] end). (*Midr.Ps.* on CXIX, 123 (250*b*, §55).)

[242] R. Berechiah said: God said to the Israelites, 'My children, if you see the merit of your fathers failing, or the merit of your mothers tottering, come and cling to my love' [i.e. God's *ḥesed* or *grace*]. (*T.J.San.* X, § 1, f. 27*d*, line 60.)

For the meaning of the phrase 'the merit of the fathers' and for further references see below, p. 219.

[243] R. Elazar quoted Ps. LXII, 13: Thine, O Lord, is lovingkindness (*ḥesed*), for it is Thou who requitest each man according to his work. But if the man has no *ḥesed* (lovingkindness), thou givest of *thy ḥesed* (grace). (*T.J.Pe'ah*, I, § 1, f. 16*b*, line 46.)

[Play on the word *ḥesed*, which can mean both the human virtue of lovingkindness and God's mercy or grace. (H.L.)]

[244] There are ten words for Prayer. One of them is appeal for grace. Of all the ten, Moses used only this one, as it is said, 'And I appealed for grace [A.V. besought] with the Lord at that time' (Deut. III, 23). R. Johanan said: Hence you may learn that man has no claim upon God; for Moses, the greatest of the prophets, came before God only with an appeal for grace. R. Levi said: Why did Moses do so? The proverb says, 'Be careful lest you be caught by your words.' God said to Moses, 'I will be gracious to whom I will be gracious. To him who has anything to his account with me, I show mercy, that is, I deal with him through the attribute of mercy; but to him who has nothing I am gracious, that is, I deal with him by gift and gratis.' (*Deut.R.*, Wa'etḥanan, II, 1.)

Here the Hebrew word for 'grace' is *ḥen*, from which is derived the adverb *ḥinnam*, gratis or for nothing. Thus even 'mercy' (Hebrew *raḥamim*) is here subordinated to *ḥen*, grace.

In the case of Israel, this divine 'grace' may sometimes be given, not entirely for Israel's sake, but for God's sake and for His glory. The one reason merges into the other.

[245] It was not for their works that the Israelites were delivered from Egypt, or for their fathers' works, and not by their works that the Red Sea was cloven in sunder, but to make God a name, as it says, 'Dividing the water before them to make Himself an everlasting name' (Isa. LXIII, 12). So Moses told the Israelites, 'Not through your works were you redeemed, but so that you might praise God, and declare His renown among the nations.' 'Arise for our help; redeem us for thy mercy's sake' (Ps. XLIV, 26). If we have works, do thou arise for our help; and if not, do so for thy name's sake. (*Midr.Ps.* on XLIV, 1 (134*b*, § 1).)

Chapter IV

ISRAEL'S LOVE FOR GOD

In this chapter I return again to God's love for Israel, and deal also with Israel's love for God. Pathetic are the passages which speak of Israel's clinging to God, and of its devotion to Him, in spite of suffering and persecution.

[246] R. Joshua b. Levi said: Not even an iron wall can separate Israel from their Father in Heaven. (*Sot.* 38*b fin.*)

[247] 'I am sick of love' (Cant. II, 5). The congregation of Israel says to God, 'Lord of the world, all the sicknesses which thou bringest upon me are only for the purpose of making me love thee....All the sicknesses, which the nations bring upon me are only because I love thee.'

(*Cant.R.* II, § 5, 1, on II, 5; f. 15*a.*)

[248] 'Thou art fair, my beloved, yea pleasant' (Cant. I, 16). ['Yea', in Hebrew *af*, can also mean 'wrath', as in [147], [201].] So Israel says to God, 'Lord of the World, even thy wrath which thou bringest upon me, is pleasant, because thus thou causest me to return, and bringest me back to virtue.'

(*Cant.R.* I, § 16, 1, on I, 16; f. 13*a.*)

[249] It is written, 'As the lily among thorns' (Cant. II, 2). R. Ḥanina b. R. Abba interpreted the thorns to be the nations of the world. As the north wind blows and bends the lily southwards, and the thorns prick it, and then the south wind blows and bends the lily northwards, and the thorns prick it, and yet, for all that, the centre of it tends upward, so Israelites, though they are harried by levies and forced supplies [*aggereia* and *annonae*], yet direct their heart to their Father in heaven.

(*Lev.R.*, Aḥare Mot, XXIII, 5.)

[250] 'We will be glad and rejoice in thee[1]' (Cant. I, 4). It is like a queen, whose husband, the king, had gone with her sons and her sons-in-law upon a journey. When they returned, it was said

[1] The word 'thee' is emphasised, and made to mean 'in thee alone'.

to her, 'Your sons have come back.' She said, 'What is that to me? Let my daughters-in-law rejoice.' They said, 'Your sons-in-law have returned.' She said, 'What is that to me? Let my daughters rejoice.' They said, 'Your lord, the king, has returned.' She said, 'Now there is a complete rejoicing, joy upon joy.' So, in the time to come, prophets will say to Jerusalem, 'Thy sons come from far,' and Jerusalem shall say, 'What is that to me?' And they will say, 'Thy daughters are at thy side' (Isa. LX, 4). She will answer, 'What is that to me?' But when they say, 'Behold, thy King comes to thee,' then she will say, 'Now there is a complete rejoicing,' as it says, 'Rejoice greatly, O daughter of Jerusalem' (Zech. IX, 9), and she says, 'I will greatly rejoice in the Lord' (Isa. LXI, 10). (*Cant.R.* I, § I, 2, on I, 4; f. 8*a*.)

We think involuntarily of Heine's wonderful poem, as we read the following:

[251] It is written, 'The righteous shall flourish like the palm tree' (Ps. XCII, 12). As the palm tree directs its heart upward, so the Israelites direct their heart to their Father in heaven. As the palm tree has its yearning, so the righteous among them have their yearning. Towards what is this yearning? Towards God, the Holy One. R. Tanḥuma said: There was a palm tree which stood in Ḥamethan, and it bore no fruit, and they fertilised it, but it bore no fruit.[1] Then a palm-planter said to them: 'It sees a palm tree of Jericho, and it yearns after it in its heart.' So they brought some of the palm tree from Jericho, and they fertilised the first palm tree, and it bore fruit at once. So all the yearning and the hope of the righteous are turned towards God. (*Num.R.*, Bemidbar, III, I (cp. [803]).)

Jericho was famous for its palms (Deut. XXXIV, 3 and II Chron. XXVIII, 15).

There is a frequent contrast, or rather a sort of see-saw, between the ideal Israel—Israel as it should be, and, as represented by its martyrs and righteous men, it even is—and the Israel of fact, too often sinful and negligent of its supreme duty. The suffering and poverty, which press so hard upon Israel, have yet their uses in causing the Israelites to repent of their sins:

[252] R. Joshua b. Levi said: The Israelites are compared to an olive tree, because as the olive never sheds its leaves whether in

[1] According to Neubauer (*Géographie du Talmud*, 1868, p. 115), Ḥamethan is Emmaus.

winter or in summer, so will the Israelites never cease to be, whether in this world or in the world to come. R. Johanan said: The Israelites are compared to an olive tree, because as the olive yields its oil only by hard pressure, so the Israelites do not return to righteousness except through suffering.

(*Men.* 53*b.*)

[253] R. Aḥa said: When the Jew has to eat the fruit of the carob tree, then he repents. Poverty suits the Jew as a red bridle on a white horse. (*Lev.R.*, Shemini, XIII, 4.)

The simile will be found again in the section dealing with Riches and Poverty. The carob bean was the food of the poor and hungry (cp. Mark I, 6; Luke XV, 16) (cp. [363]).

Meanwhile, in spite of all Israel's earlier shortcomings of which we hear in the O.T.—shortcomings from the grosser sort of which it had emerged—God is united to Israel by an indissoluble bond.

Whether the bond was in all circumstances indissoluble was a matter of some discussion. Thus, in Deut. XIV, 1, the former half of the verse ('Ye are the children of the Lord your God') seems incongruous with the latter ('ye shall not cut yourselves etc.'). What, then, is the connection between the two parts? The following views are taken:

[254] 'If you behave as children [i.e. by abstaining from cutting yourselves like the heathen], then you are called "children": if you do not so behave, you are not called His "children".' This was the opinion of R. Judah b. Ilai [who held that the verse was a conditional sentence, the former clause being the protasis]. 'But', said R. Me'ir [who, more accurately than the A.V., took account of the emphasis in the Hebrew which the A.V. neglects, since 'children' stands at the head of the sentence], 'the meaning is that "children", and nothing but "children", are you called. In any case, this name is applied to you, even though you are "foolish" (Jer. IV, 22), "untrustworthy" (Deut. XXXII, 20), or "corrupt" (Isa. I, 4). In each instance the word "children" is employed. And even after you have been repudiated, you are yet again called "children" (Hos. I, 10).' (*Ḳid.* 36*a.*)

Somewhat similar to the metaphor of the twins in [167] is the following:

[255] 'In all their afflictions he was afflicted' (Isa. LXIII, 9). [No verse from the Prophets is more frequently quoted by the Rabbis and more frequently made use of. It is strange to think

that it is probably not the original reading, but a corruption of the text; cp. [173].] So God said to Moses, 'Dost thou not notice that I dwell in distress when the Israelites dwell in distress? Know from the place whence I speak with thee, from the midst of thorns, it is as if I stand in their distresses.'

(*Exod.R.*, Shemot, II, 5.)

[256] God weeps for Israel in exile. It is like a king whose wife and son became corrupt, and he drove them forth from his house. But year by year he would go to the place whence he had expelled them, and prostrate himself lengthwise on the ground. If this were not written, we might not say it (**Note 69**). Like a father who says, 'My sons, my sons,' or like a hen who cries for her brood, so God declares, 'Look away from me, I will weep bitterly' (Isa. XXII, 4). (*Tan.d.b.El.* pp. 154, 155 top.)

[257] 'The covenant and the love' (Deut. VII, 12). R. Simeon b. Ḥalafta said: The matter is like a king who married a lady who brought to him two precious ornaments, and the king also added two precious ornaments to match them. But when his wife abandoned her two ornaments, the king took away his. After a time she arose and purified herself, and brought back her two ornaments, and then the king brought back his two. And the king said, 'The four together shall be made into a crown, and shall be put upon the queen's head.' So you may find that Abraham gave his descendants two precious ornaments, as it is said, 'For I know him that he will command his children after him, that they keep the way of the Lord to do righteousness and justice' (Gen. XVIII, 19). Then God set up two ornaments to match those other two, namely love and pity (Deut. VII, 12; XIII, 17). When the Israelites abandoned their two, as it is said, 'Ye turned justice into gall and righteousness into hemlock' (Amos VI, 12), God also took away His two, as it is said, 'I have taken away my peace from this people, even love and pity' (Jer. XVI, 5). Then Israel arose and purified itself, and brought its two back, and God restored His two likewise (Isa. I, 27; LIV, 10). For when Israel brings its two, God gives His two, and God says, 'The four together shall be made into a crown, and shall be placed upon Israel's head,' as it is said, 'I will betroth thee unto me in justice and in righteousness and in love and in pity' (Hos. II, 19). (*Deut.R.*, 'Eḳeb, III, 7.)

[258] R. Ḥalafta, the son of Dosa, of the village of Ḥananya, said: When ten people sit together and occupy themselves with the Torah, the Shechinah abides among them, as it is said, 'God stands in the congregation[1] of the godly' (Ps. LXXXII, 1). And whence can it be shown that the same applies to five? Because it is said, 'He has founded his band[2] upon the earth' (Amos IX, 6). And whence can it be shown that the same applies to three? Because it is said, 'He judges among the judges'[3] (Ps. LXXXII, 1). And whence can it be shown that the same applies to two? Because it is said, 'Then they that feared the Lord spake one with the other; and the Lord hearkened, and heard' (Mal. III, 16). And whence can it be shown that the same applies even to one? Because it is said, 'In every place where I cause my name to be remembered, I will come unto thee and I will bless thee' (Exod. XX, 24).

(*Aboth* III, 7, in Singer's translation, *P.B.* p. 191 foot.)

The following passage indicates that in relation to God the very angels are subordinate to Israel:

[259] The ministering angels do not [dare to] mention the name of Him who is on high, until Israel, who are below, mention it, for it says, 'Hear, O Israel, the Lord is our God, the Lord is One' (Deut. VI, 4), and it says also, 'When all the morning stars sang together' (Job XXXVIII, 7). Only then, as the verse continues, did 'all the sons of God shout for joy' (*ib.*). The 'morning stars' are Israel, who are compared with the stars in Gen. XXII, 17, and the 'sons of God' are the 'ministering angels' mentioned in Job I, 6. (*Sifre Deut.*, Ha'azinu, § 306, 132 *b.*)

The legends with which *Esther R.* enlarges and fills out the biblical text are not entirely pleasant reading. However much the circumstances of the time in which they were written may explain them, there is too much unqualified delight in the downfall and punishment of Haman, and also in the awful revenge of the Jews upon their enemies (Esther IX, 5–16). No nation is near to God except Israel. All other peoples but Israel are foreigners unto God. Only the Israelites are his children. The particularism is only slightly modified by the reappearance of the familiar conception that the world cannot

1 Ten are the minimum to form a 'congregation' (*'edah*) (cp. [280] and [1214]).
2 Five, the minimum to constitute a 'band' (*aguddah*).
3 The smallest judicial tribunal was composed of three judges.

exist without Israel, and that the worth of Israel lies in its acceptance of the Law, because, somehow or other, the continuance of the world is dependent upon the divine Law being in operation among, at least, one small portion of humanity. These bizarre theories were doubtless themselves invented partly by national pride and national exclusiveness; yet they were also partly due, I fancy, to an uneasy sense that the particularism needed some religious veneer and justification, and partly to the higher, if inarticulate, feeling that the world exists for the sake of religion and the glory of God, and that religious truth is of ultimate and inexplicable value. Some of the legends, in spite of their particularism, have a certain pathos and beauty, as, for example, the legend of the days and the months pleading before God for the preservation of Israel, the legend how Haman sought to compass the destruction of Israel by tempting them to sin, the legend of the wood of the gallows upon which Haman was to hang, and of God's consultation with the trees as to which of them should supply the wood, and the legends of the children coming from school and of the children in the house of study. Part of the second of these legends runs as follows:

[260] R. Isaac, the smith, said: Haman the wicked came with great craft against Israel. For when it says (Esther I, 5) that the king made a feast unto all the people, Israel is meant. For Haman said to Ahasuerus the king, 'The God of this people hates libidinousness. Arrange for them harlots, and make for them a banquet, and bid them to come to eat and drink, and do as they please.' When Mordecai heard of this, he bade them not to go to the banquet, 'to which,' he said, 'the king has invited you only in order to destroy you, and to find an opening with the Attribute of Justice to accuse you before God.' Nevertheless, they would not listen to Mordecai, and they all went to the banquet, to the number (according to R. Ishmael) of 18,500 persons, and they ate and drank, and became intoxicated, and acted unchastely. Then Satan arose and denounced them before God, and he said, 'How long wilt thou cleave to this people, who are separating their heart and their faith from thee? If it be thy will, destroy them from the world, for they do not come in repentance before thee.' God said, 'What is to become of the Law?' Satan replied, 'Let the heavenly beings suffice thee.' And God acquiesced to destroy Israel. Then God said, 'What is this people any more to me for whose sake I have multiplied my signs and my wonders upon all who rose up against them? I will make the memory of them to cease from among men' (Deut. XXXII, 26). Then God said

to Satan, 'Bring me a scroll, and I will write the destruction of Israel upon it.' And Satan did so, and God wrote upon the scroll. Then the Law came in widow's weeds, and lifted up her voice before God in weeping, and the angels of the service also cried and wept. They said, 'If Israel is destroyed, of what use are we in the world,' as it is said, 'Behold the valiant ones cry without; the ambassadors of peace weep bitterly' (Isa. XXXIII, 7). When the sun and moon heard the weeping, they withheld their light, as it is said, 'I clothe the heavens with blackness' (Isa. L, 3). Then Elijah went in haste to the Patriarchs and to Moses, and said to them, 'How long will you be sunk in sleep, and pay no heed to the trouble which has befallen your children. The angels of the service, and sun and moon and stars and planets, and earth and heaven, and all the host on high are weeping bitterly, and you remain afar and pay no heed?' They said, 'For what are they weeping?' Then Elijah replied, 'Because the Israelites took their enjoyment at the banquet of Ahasuerus, and therefore the decree is passed to destroy them from the world and to blot out their remembrance.' Then Abraham, Isaac and Jacob said, 'If they have transgressed against the law of God and the decree is sealed, what can we do?' Then Elijah turned to Moses, and said, 'You, faithful shepherd, how many times did you stand in the breach for Israel, and caused the decrees to be annulled so that Israel was not destroyed (Ps. CVI, 23). What say you in this present trouble?' Moses said, 'Is there no upright man in this generation?' Elijah said, 'Yes, there is, and his name is Mordecai.' Then Moses said, 'Go and tell him, Let him stand in prayer *there*, and I will stand *here*, and we will beseech God for mercy upon them.' Elijah said, 'Faithful shepherd, the decree of destruction is already written.' Moses said, 'If it is sealed with clay, our prayer will be heard; if it is sealed with blood, it will stand.' (*Esther R.* VII, 13 on III, 9.)

For a corrective and criticism of what I have said about Haman cp. Mr Loewe's note on [142] and the following ingenious plea.

[As mentioned before [142], the 'cruelty' *was* felt, and the account of the execution of Haman's sons read over hurriedly in one breath. But there were other reasons for reading the book. It is Esther's self-sacrifice, and the miracle of the divine preservation, which are the *raisons d'être*. It is usually pointed out that Esther stands in a different category from the other books. Twice it is called an *Iggeret* (IX, 26, 29), i.e. an 'Epistle', and, hence, as a letter, it lacks the name of God. To make this character clear, the scroll is unwound before it is read, and folded into strips, like a letter. It is not turned, column by column, like the Pentateuch. And when the Reader comes to the word 'epistle', he raises the scroll and shakes it slightly to show that it is a letter that he is reading and not a book. But lest this treatment should appear to reflect on a book which, after all, was canonical, we find other views as to its sanctity as well, because the memory of God's miraculous intervention must never be forgotten. Nevertheless, the discussions in *Meg.* 7*a* point to objections to the book's canonicity which would seem to demand answer. It is also well to remember that what Esther asked from the king was the right of self-defence, not of attack, and the fact that IX, 13 asks for the execution of Haman's sons, which has already been recorded in verse 6, points to IX, 13 being a doublet, and this verse is the gravamen of the charge of cruelty brought against Esther. All this is not special pleading *ad hoc*; it is what Jewish children are taught with regard to the scroll of Esther and the feast of Purim. I have no doubt that in older generations the young were similarly taught. In the main, it is always the two ideas of self-sacrifice and divine intervention which recur to the child's mind even though Haman was often burnt in effigy, exactly like Guy Fawkes. Yet 5 November is not usually regarded (now, at all events) as a celebration of particularism. (H. L.)]

The end of the previous legend, which is not given in its place, is implied in the second story about the children, part of which runs much as follows:

[261] After Haman made the gallows, he went to Mordecai, and he found him sitting in the house of study, and the children sat before him with sackcloth on their loins and busy with the Law, and they cried and wept. He counted the children, and he found twelve thousand, and he cast upon them chains of iron, and set watchers over them, and he said, 'To-morrow I will kill these children first, and after that I will hang Mordecai.' Then their mothers brought them bread and water, and said to them, 'Children, eat and drink before you die to-morrow; do not die hungry.' Then the children laid their hands upon their books, and swore, 'By the life of Mordecai, our teacher, we will neither eat nor drink, but we will die fasting.' They wept and wept, till their weeping arose on high, and God heard their weeping in the second hour of the night. Then the compassion of God was moved, and God arose from the throne of judgment, and sat upon the throne of compassion, and He said, 'What is

this great cry that I hear as of kids and lambs?' Then Moses came and stood before God, and he said, 'The cry is not from kids and lambs, but it comes from the little ones of thy people who have fasted three days and three nights, and to-morrow the enemy intends to slaughter them, as if indeed they were kids and lambs.' Then God took the decree which He had sealed with clay, and He tore it up. (*Esther R.* IX, 4 on V, 12.)

[262] 'The Lord is my strength and my song' (Exod. XV, 2). God is a helper and support to all inhabitants of the world, but yet more to me [i.e. to Israel]. All the nations of the world tell the praise of God, but my praise is more pleasant and more beautiful in His eyes than theirs. The Israelites say, 'Hear O Israel, the Lord thy God, the Lord is One' (*eḥad*). And the Holy Spirit calls from heaven and says, 'Who is like unto thee, O Israel, a people unique (*eḥad*) upon the earth?' (I Chron. XVII, 21). The Israelites say, 'Who is like unto thee, O Lord, among the gods?' (Exod. XV, 11). And the Holy Spirit calls from heaven and says, 'Happy art thou, O Israel, who is like thee?' (Deut. XXXIII, 29). The Israelites say, 'Who is like the Lord, who answers us whenever we call upon Him?' (Deut. IV, 7), and the Holy Spirit cries out and says, 'What nation has God near it like Israel?' (*ib.*). The Israelites say, 'Thou art the glory of their strength' (Ps. LXXXIX, 17), and the Holy Spirit cries out and says, 'Israel, in thee I will be glorified' (Isa. XLIX, 3). [The parity is complete.]
(*Mek.*[2], *Shirata*, Beshallaḥ, § 3, p. 126; *Mek.*[3], vol. II, p. 23
(cp. *Sifre Deut.*, Berakah, § 355, f. 148*a*, 148*b*).)

[263] R. Akiba said: I will speak of the beauty and praise of God before all the nations. They ask Israel and say, 'What is your beloved more than another beloved that "thou dost so charge us" (Cant. V, 9), that you die for Him, and that you are slain for Him,' as it says, 'Therefore till death do they love Thee' [a pun on Cant. I, 3], and, 'For thy sake are we slain all the day' (Ps. XLIV, 22). 'Behold,' they say, 'You are beautiful, you are mighty, come and mingle with us.' But the Israelites reply, 'Do you know Him? We will tell you a portion of His renown; my beloved is white and ruddy; the chiefest among ten thousand' (Cant. V, 10). When they hear Israel praise Him thus, they say to the Israelites, 'We will go with you,' as it is said, 'Whither has your beloved turned him that we may seek him with you?'

(Cant. VI, 1). But the Israelites say, 'You have no part or lot in Him,' as it is said, 'My beloved is mine, and I am His' (Cant. II, 16). (**Note 11 *f*.**)

(*Mek.*[2], *Shirata*, Beshallaḥ, § 3, p. 127; *Mek.*[3], vol. II, p. 23.)

[264] 'Is He not thy Father, who has bought thee?' (Deut. XXXII, 6). God says to Israel, 'Beloved are you unto me; you were bought by me, and not inherited.' Like a man who inherited ten fields or ten country seats from his father, and then bought one. This one he loved more than all the ten which his father had bequeathed to him. (*Sifre Deut.*, Ha'azinu, § 309, 133 *b fin.*)

There seems to have been an occasional feeling as if God's unity should, perhaps, have prevented Israelites from saying 'our God'. For the words 'our God' would seem to imply that Israel's God was not the God of other nations and the God of all the world, and as if, therefore, there must be more than one God:

[265] Why is it said [in the *Shema* (Deut. VI, 4)] 'the Lord our God' as well as 'the Lord is One'? 'The Lord our God' means that His name has been made to rest on Israel especially....'The Lord is One' implies that He is the God of all the inhabitants of the world. (*Sifre Deut.*, Wa'ethḥanan, § 31, 73 *a init.* (Hd. p. 54).)

The following is a curious passage in which the Angel Princes and Protectors of the Nations are represented as addressing God at the time of the last Judgment, and claiming that if 'the nations' have to be despatched to hell because of their idolatry, their immorality and their murders, the Israelites should also go to hell, because they have been guilty of the same offences; Michael, the Angel Protector of the Israelites, is silent:

[266] God says to Michael, 'Thou art silent, and makest no defence for my sons. Then I will tell of a deed of charity (lit. "I that speak in righteousness, mighty to save" (Isa. LXIII, 1)) which they have done, and I will save my sons.' R. Elazar said: The deed of charity—so God will say—was that which you wrought to my world in that you received my Torah, for if you had not received my Torah, I should have caused the world to become again without form and void. (*Ruth R.*, Introduction, 1, on I, 1, f. 1 *a*.)

Yet man as such is beloved of God. But how much more Israel!

[267] Before God one righteous man is equal to the whole world, for

it says, 'The righteous man is the foundation of the world' (Prov. x, 25). (*Tanḥ.*, Beshallaḥ, § 10, f. 113*a* (cp. [143]).)

[268] R. Akiba used to say: Beloved is man, for he was created in the image of God; but it was by a special love that it was made known to him that he was created in the image of God, as it is said, 'For in the image of God made He man' (Gen. IX, 6). Beloved are Israel, for they were called children of the All-present; but it was by a special love that it was made known to them that they were called children of the All-present, as it is said, 'Ye are children unto the Lord your God' (Deut. XIV, 1). Beloved are Israel, for unto them was given the desirable instrument; but it was by a special love that it was made known to them that that desirable instrument was theirs, through which the world was created, for 'I give you good doctrine; forsake ye not my law' (Prov. IV, 2). (**Note 11 *g*.**) (*Aboth* III, 18; *P.B.* pp. 193–4.)

[269] Only one single man was created in the world, to teach that, if any man has caused a single soul to perish, Scripture imputes it to him as though he had caused a whole world to perish, and if any man saves alive a single soul, Scripture imputes it to him as though he had saved a whole world. Again, but a single man was created for the sake of peace among mankind, that none should say to his fellow, 'My father was greater than your father'; also that the heretics (*minim*) should not say, 'There are many ruling powers in heaven.' Again, but a single man was created to proclaim the greatness of God, for man stamps many coins with one die, and they are all like to one another; but God has stamped every man with the die of the first man, yet not one of them is like his fellow. Therefore every one must say, 'For my sake was the world created.' (**Note 82.**)
(*San.* IV, 5 (Danby's translation). (For *minim*, cp. [18]).)

[270] R. Me'ir said: Even though the Israelites are full of blemishes, they are still called 'His sons' (Deut. XXXII, 5). Isaiah calls them 'sons who act corruptly' (Isa. I, 4). If they are called 'sons' when corrupt, how much more would they be His sons did they not act corruptly! Jeremiah calls them 'sons, wise to do evil' (Jer. IV, 22). If they did good, how much more would they be his sons! Beloved are Israel, for whether they do God's will or no, they are called His sons. (*Sifre Deut.*, Ha'azinu, § 308, f. 133*a fin.*–133*b init.* (cp. *R.T.* p. 114 and [823]).)

[271] 'Defile not the land which ye shall inhabit, wherein I dwell, for I dwell among the children of Israel' (Num. XXXV, 34). Beloved are Israel, for, even when they are defiled, the Shechinah is among them, as it says, 'wherein I dwell'. Whithersoever they go into exile, the Shechinah accompanies them. It is like a king who said to his servant, 'Whenever you seek me, I shall be with my sons,' and so it says of the Shechinah, 'It dwells among them in the midst of their uncleanness' (Lev. XVI, 16). [It really says this of the Tent of Meeting.] (Levertoff, p. 150.)

(*Sifre Num.*, Masse'e, § 161, f. 62*b*–63*a* (H. pp. 222–3; cp. [175–6]).)

[272] When the Israelites went into exile, the angels of the service said to God, 'When Israel were in their land, they were addicted to idolatry. Now that thou hast exiled them among the Gentiles, surely they will serve idols all the more.' God answered the angels, 'I trust my sons that they will not abandon me and cleave to idols. They will give their lives for my sake every hour. And it is not enough that they will become martyrs, but they will bring others under my wings. Come and consider the case of Egypt. Ten plagues alone I brought upon Egypt, and they were not able to stand, they are extinct and quenched as tow (Isa. XLIII, 17). But a few troubles did I bring on Babylon, yet they could not stand them, and disappeared (Isa. XXIII, 13). But though I bring all the troubles and sufferings in the world upon Israel, they will not be driven away from me, but they will abide for ever. See...(Prov. XXXI, 12)...the righteousness of my sons; how many troubles and sufferings I bring upon them in every generation, and they do not kick at them, but they call themselves wicked and me righteous, saying, "Verily it is we that have sinned, and done perversely; it is we who have transgressed, committed iniquity and rebelled and departed from thy commandments, for thou art righteous in all that has come upon us, for thou hast done faithfully, but we have done evil."'

(*Pes.R.* 160*a*.)

The metaphor of kicking is derived from Deut. XXXII, 15 (cp. [1003]).

Israel is a holy nation, severed from others to be holy and pure and separate, even as God is holy and pure and separate (*Parush* (cp. [719]): the same root as in Pharisees). Stress is laid upon passages such as Lev. XX, 22–6, and the holiness and separateness of Israel are to be shown both by outward and ceremonial laws as well as by inward and moral laws. They are often all jumbled together in the Rabbis' minds, even as in Lev. XIX they are all jumbled together in the Code:

[273] And ye shall be holy unto me, for I, the Lord, am holy. Even as I am holy, so be you holy. As I am separate, so be you separate. And I have severed you from the other peoples that you should be mine. If you sever yourselves from the other peoples, then you belong to me; but if not, then you belong to Nebuchadnezzar and his fellows. R. Eliezer said: How can we know that a man must not say, 'I have no desire to eat pig, I have no desire to have intercourse with a woman whom I may not marry': but he must say, 'Yes, I would like to do these acts, but what can I do? My Father who is in heaven has forbidden them.' Because it says, 'I have severed you from among the nations to be mine.' He who is separated from iniquity receives to himself the Kingdom of heaven. (*Sifra* 93*d* (cp. [584]).)

The words of R. Eliezer must obviously not be taken at the foot of the letter. They are intended by a deliberate exaggeration to show and bring out his point that the highest virtue is to obey the Law even if, or just because, it may involve some struggle. Kant would, I suppose, agree with him, though Aristotle would not. Cp. my remarks in *R.T.* pp. 127 and 193.

[274] 'Ye shall be holy unto me, for I the Lord am holy, and I have severed you from other peoples that ye should be mine' (Lev. XX, 26). R. Yudan in the name of R. Ḥama b. Ḥanina and R. Berechiah in the name of R. Abbahu said: If God had separated the other nations from you, there would have been no hope of survival[1] for these nations, but he separated you from the nations. If a man picks out the fair from the foul, he comes and picks again, but if he picks the foul from the fair, he does not come to pick again. (*Pes.R.* 69*b* (cp. [299]).)

[This passage, which occurs in various parallels, e.g. [299], contains several difficulties, see Friedmann's notes. One suggestion is that 'these nations' is a euphemism for Israel, like 'the enemies of Israel' (cp. [464]), for 'Israel', in such a sentence as *Suk.* 29*a*, 'An eclipse of the moon is a bad sign for the enemies of Israel, for Israel reckons by the moon.' This suggestion is unlikely for two reasons. First, the use of such an unusual euphemism as *ummot ha'olam* for Israel; secondly, in some of the parallels, e.g. [299], God awaits the conversion

[1] *Teḳumah*, cp. [464].

of the nations. The real difficulty is to understand the metaphor; this Dr Hyamson explains as follows:

If a man picks out the fair, when he has enough for his purpose, the residue remains for another occasion; he does not throw the residue away, since it contains fair as well as foul. Therefore the foul remain where they are, preserved by the presence of the fair. But if he reverses the process, the foul are thrown away as each one is picked out and found wanting, so that, in the end, only the fair remain. Hence by the selection of Israel—we must assume that the 'Remnant' of Israel is meant—the residue of bad Jews and Gentiles gains a respite, and so God can 'wait for the conversion of the Gentiles'. Or if, not the Remnant, but all Israel is meant, the conclusion still remains. (H. L.)]

[275] R. Simeon b. Yoḥai said: As the Israelites accepted God's sovereignty in Egypt, so God says, 'Let them accept my decrees. As you accepted my sovereignty at Sinai, so receive my decrees.' (*Sifra* 85*d*.)

[Cf. *P.B.* p. 99: 'When His children beheld His power at the Red Sea, they willingly accepted His sovereignty.']

The value of even one Israelite to God is sometimes spoken of with oriental exaggeration. (**Note 82.**)

[276] Citing Exod. XIX, 21, it is said: If only one of them should fall, it would be to God as though all of them fell. Everyone of them that might be taken away is to God as valuable as the whole work of creation, even as it says, 'The Lord has an eye upon all men, and upon all the tribes of Israel' (Zech. IX, 1 (R.V.M.)). (*Mek.*[2], *Baḥodesh*, Yitro, § 4, p. 217; *Mek.*[3], vol. II, p. 225.)

[Lauterbach's note runs thus: 'To God one Israelite is as valuable as all the tribes of Israel. The work of creation was for the sake of Israel. One Israelite, being equal to all the tribes of Israel, is, therefore, also as valuable as the whole work of creation.']

[277] 'Israel is a scattered sheep' (Jer. L, 17, A.V.). Why are the Israelites compared to a sheep? Just as if you strike a sheep on its head, or on one of its limbs, all its limbs feel it, so, if one Israelite sins, all Israelites feel it. R. Simeon b. Yoḥai said: It is like as if there are men in a boat, and one man takes an auger, and begins to bore a hole beneath him. His companions say, 'What are you doing?' He replies, 'What business is it of yours? Am I not boring under myself?' They answer, 'It *is* our business, because the water will come in, and swamp the boat with us in it.' (*Lev.R.*, Wayiḳra, IV, 6 (Moore, I, 471).)

[278] 'And they shall stumble, one man by his brother' (Lev. XXVI, 37). This means that one man will stumble because of the sin of his brother. Hence learn that every Israelite is surety for every other. (*Sifra* 112*b* (cp. [1550] and [1554]).)

[279] A Rabbi said that as fire does not burn when isolated, so will the words of the Torah not be preserved when studied by oneself alone. Another said that the learned who are occupied in the study of the Law, each one by himself, deserve punishment, and they shall become fools. (*Ta'an.* 7*a* (cp. [494]).)

[280] 'Now the brothers of Joseph, being ten, went down to Egypt' (Gen. XLII, 3). [Note how the emphasis in the Hebrew is neglected both in A.V. and R.V.; it is precisely the emphasis which was noted in the *Tanḥuma* and which is the basis of the homily.] Why 'Being ten in number'? Because they had the power to cancel the sentence ['thy seed shall be a sojourner and they will afflict them'] and annul the decree. Similarly, you will observe that, in regard to Sodom, Abraham reduced his pleading from 'for the sake of fifty' to 'for the sake of ten'. When ten righteous men could not be found, Abraham was silent. Because the generation of the Flood could not muster ten righteous souls, they were not saved, for there were among them only Noah and his sons and their wives, eight altogether.

(*Tanḥ.B.*, Miḳḳeẓ, 98*a*.)

Ten is the fixed congregational quorum (see [258] and [1214]). Hence the power of not less than ten to act as representing all Israel and of cancelling the sentence.

As the years grew on during the Rabbinic period, there was, I suppose, much more unity among the entire body of Israelites than in the days, shall we say, of R. Akiba. The antagonism between the Learned and the Ignorant, between those who meticulously observed the laws of Tithing and external Purity and those who did not, between *Ḥaber* and *Am ha-Aretz*, gradually ceased. Israel grew one, and its solidarity was emphasised (cp. [945]).

[The second chapter of Demai, both in the Mishnah and in the Tosefta, is interesting as throwing light on the *Am ha-Aretz* and their relation to the *Ḥaberim* (members of a *Ḥaburah*, or brotherhood). The chapter gives the conditions required for becoming a *Ḥaber* and these conditions are concerned with tithing. It is probable that it was mainly in connection with this question that the brotherhoods grew up, though there were other causes. Finkelstein (*Journal of Bib. Lit.*

XLIX, Part I, 1930, pp. 32 ff.) shows how, in the third pre-Christian century, the 'second tithe' (Deut. XIV, 22) had become burdensome. The author of Jubilees would have abolished it: John Hyrcanus modified it by introducing the system of 'Demai', which placed on the claimant, and not on the purchaser of grain, the burden of proof that tithe was liable. Now this compromise had to be observed loyally and to create a sense of honour was the object of the brotherhoods. *T. Dem.* II (Z. p. 48), gives the conditions under which a man could join a brotherhood. We note that so far from being exclusive, the *Ḥaberim* were eager to enlist adherents from the *Am ha-Aretz* class.

Ordinary citizens, neither *Am ha-Aretz* nor *Ḥaberim*, would be called *Ba'ale Battim*, 'householders' (cp. [296]); these might or might not be further qualified by the adjective *Ne'eman* (reliable, faithful).

The relation between *Am ha-Aretz* and *Ḥaberim* might be close. Sentences like 'A *Ḥaber's* son who is being educated by an *Am ha-Aretz*' (II, §18 (Z. p. 48, line 20)) or vice versa (*ib.*): 'A *Ḥaber's* son who marries the daughter of an *Am ha-Aretz*' (*ib.* 15, line 13) are significant. Moreover, even a scholar (*Talmid Ḥakam*) was received in a brotherhood only if he undertook to observe the conditions, though a teacher with a 'chair in a seminary' was exempt (*ib.* 13, line 10). (H. L.)]

[281] Israel's reconciliation with God can be achieved only when they are all one brotherhood. (*Men.* 27*a.*)

To the Rabbis Israel forms one whole throughout all its generations. Thus we find passages such as the following:

[282] When Moses summoned the people before God, he said: 'Not with you alone do I make this covenant' (Deut. XXIX, 14). All souls were present then, although their bodies were not yet created. (*Tanḥ.B.*, Niẓẓabim, VIII, 25*b.*)

There are laws in the Mishnah about violence against the person (beating, pulling out the hair, spitting upon a man, loosening a woman's hair in the street), and about the penalties to be inflicted, which are in accordance with a person's position and rank. Yet:

[283] R. Akiba said: Even the poorest in Israel are looked upon as freemen who have lost their possessions, for they are the sons of Abraham, Isaac and Jacob. It once happened that a man unloosed a woman's hair in the street, and she came before R. Akiba, and he condemned him to pay her 400 *zuz*. He replied, 'Rabbi, give me time.' And he gave him time. The man perceived her standing at the entry of her courtyard, and he broke before her a cruse that held an *issar's* worth of oil She unloosed

her hair [a sign of lack of good breeding, if not of low conduct] and scooped up the oil in her hand, and laid her hand on her head. He had set witnesses in readiness against her, and he came before R. Akiba and said to him, 'Rabbi, should I give such a one as this 400 *zuz*?' He answered, 'Thou hast said naught at all, since he that wounds *himself*, even though he has not the right to do so, is not culpable; but if others have wounded him, they are culpable. If a man cut down his own plants, even though he has not the right, he is not culpable; but if others cut them down, they are culpable.'[1] [The 'plant' sentence refers to the law of Deut. xx, 19 which was generalised.] (*Bab.Ḳ.* VIII, 6.)

There were indeed certain virtues which came to be regarded as the characteristics of all Israelites. Such passages as the following are frequent:

[284] David said: God gave three good gifts to the Israelites: to be pitiful, bashful, and charitable. Pitiful, for it says, 'And God will show thee pity' [the Talmud translates, 'Make thee pitiful'] (Deut. XIII, 17). Bashful, for it says, 'That His fear may be before you, that you do not sin' (Exod. xx, 20). Those words are an indication that the bashful man is free from sin, and of him who is not bashful, it may be affirmed that his ancestors were not at Sinai. Charitable, for it says, 'The Lord will keep to you the covenant and the charity (*ḥesed*), etc.' (Deut. VII, 12).
(*T.J.Kid.* IV, 1, f. 65*c*, line 25 (cp. *Num.R.*, Naso, VIII, 4).)

Sometimes, too, we hear of Israel's humility towards God.

[285] God said to Israel, 'I love you, because even when I shower greatness upon you, you make yourselves small before me. I gave greatness to Abraham, and he said, "I am dust and ashes" (Gen. XVIII, 27); I gave greatness to Moses and Aaron, and they said, "What are we?" (Exod. XVI, 8). I gave greatness to David, and he said, "I am a worm and no man"' (Ps. XXII, 6).
(*Ḥul.* 89*a*.)

A curious passage, unusual as regards what it says about the Gentiles, is the following:

[286] God said to Israel, 'I love you, but it is not because you are more than the Gentiles, and not because you do more commandments [*miẓwot*, cp. [753]] than they, for they magnify my name more than you do (Mal. I, 11), and you are the smallest of all nations

[1] Cp. the Latin maxim, *volenti non fit injuria* (**Notes 11 *h* and 14**).

(Deut. VII, 7). But because you make yourselves small before me, therefore I love you.' (*Tanḥ.B.*, 'Eḳeb, 9*a fin.*)

Though they are humble, Israelites have no terror before God. It is only when they sin, that they are fearful:

[287] 'Before Israel sinned, the appearance of the glory of the Lord was a burning fire at the head of the mountain in the sight of all Israel' (Exod. XXIV, 17). R. Abba b. Kahana said: Seven divisions of fire could not terrify Israel, but after they had sinned, they could not look even on the face of the intermediary; they feared to approach him, as it says, 'They were afraid to come nigh to Moses for his face shone' (Exod. XXXIV, 30).... Before David sinned, he wrote 'The Lord is my light and my salvation: whom shall I fear?' (Ps. XXVII, 1), but after he had sinned, it says, 'I will come upon him while he is weary, and will make him afraid' (II Sam. XVII, 2). Before Solomon sinned he ruled over the demons [by a pun on Eccles. II, 8]. After he sinned, he brought sixty warriors to protect his couch from the terror by night, as it says, 'Behold, Solomon's bed; sixty mighty men are about it of the mighty men of Israel' (Cant. III, 7). (*Pes.R.* 69*a*.)

Yet there is a sense in which obstinacy may be a virtue:

[288] It is said in Exod. XXXII, 9, 'I have seen this people, and, behold it is a stiffnecked people.' R. Johanan said: There are three impudent creatures: among beasts, it is the dog; in birds, it is the cock; among people, it is Israel. But R. Ammi said: Do not suppose that this is said in blame; it is said in praise, for to be a Jew means a readiness to suffer crucifixion. (*Exod.R.*, Ki Tissa, XLII, 9.)

We are often told of the Prophets' readiness to accept suffering:

[289] Isaiah answered (VI, 8), 'Here am I; send me.' R. Phinehas said: God said, 'My children are wearisome and rebellious. If you will take it upon yourself to be despised and beaten by them, then go forth on my mission, but if not, accept it not.' And Isaiah said, 'Upon this condition I go forth, namely, my back I give to the smiters, my cheeks to them that pluck off the hair (Isa. L, 6), and even so, I am not worthy to go forth on thy mission to thy children.' (*Lev.R.*, Ẓaw, X, 2.)

In comparing Israel with other peoples the Rabbis accept the Biblical saying, 'Who is like unto thee, O Israel,' and they improved upon it! Yet the praise of Israel is usually made in relation to the observance of the Law, as in the following striking passage:

[290] 'It is a people which rises up as a lion' (Num. XXIII, 24). There is no people which resembles them. In sleep they are unconscious of the Torah and the Commandments, but they rise up from sleep like lions, and hurry to the reading of the *Shema*, and proclaim the sovereignty of God, and, strengthened by their prayers like lions, they separate each to his occupations and business; and if one among them stumbles [sins], or if temptation [lit. evil spirits] assail one of them, he proclaims the sovereignty of God; he does not 'lie down till he eats of the prey' (*ib.*); for when he says, 'The Lord is One,' the temptations [i.e. the evil spirits] are overpowered before him, and they whisper[1] after him, 'Blessed be the name of the glory of His kingdom for ever and ever,' and they take flight, and he relies upon the reading of the *Shema* from the time of the morning watchman till the time of the night watchman. And when he comes to sleep, he commends his spirit to God, as it is said, 'Into thy hands I commend my spirit' (Ps. XXXI, 5), and when he wakes up, he proclaims the sovereignty of God, and the angel watchers of the night deliver him over to the angel watchers of the day, as it is said, 'My soul waits for the Lord from the time of the watchers of the morning' (Ps. CXXX, 6). (*Num.R.*, Balaḳ, XX, 20.)

Through the Law the true Israelites will love God:

[291] It is noticed as two of the marks of the Israelite that he should 'penetrate to the very essence of the Law and love God with a perfect love, whether good befall him or evil.'

(*Lev.R.*, Wayiḳra, III, 7.)

The very purpose of Israel's life is to do honour to God by the observance of His Law.

[292] R. Levi said: As the bee gathers everything which it gathers for its owner, so whatever the Israelites gather of commandments and good works, they gather for their Father in heaven.

(*Deut.R.* I, 6.)

[1] The idea is that the evil spirits are overcome and respond unconsciously. For 'whispering' in this connection see note to [4].

[293] R. Judah b. Shallum said: God said to the Israelites, 'When are you called my sons? When you accept my words.' It is like as if the son of a king said to his father, 'Distinguish me in the land to make me as your son.' The king said, 'If you wish all to know that you are my son, put on my robe of purple, and place my crown upon your head, and then all will know that you are my son.' So God said to the Israelites, 'If you wish to be marked out as my sons, busy yourselves with the Torah and the Commandments, and then all will see that you are my sons.' (*Deut.R.*, Berakah, XII, 9.)

[294] God said to the Israelites, 'If the words of the Law are near to you, then I call you [my] "near ones",' as it says, 'The children of Israel, the people near to Him' (Ps. CXLVIII, 14). (*Deut.R.*, Niẓẓabim, VIII, 7.)

In such an Israel God delights.

[295] 'In the multitude of people is the King's glory' (Prov. XIV, 28). R. Ḥama b. Ḥanina said: Though God has before Him thousands and tens of thousands of angels of the service, who serve Him and praise Him, He delights not in their praise, but only in the praises of Israel, as it is said, 'For the multitude of the people is the King's glory.'...The people is Israel, and God is the King....R. Simeon said: When is God exalted in His world? When the Israelites are gathered together in their synagogues and houses of study, and they offer praise and laud to their Creator. R. Ishmael said: When the Israelites are gathered together in their houses of study, and hear *Agada* from a wise man, and they answer 'Amen, may His name be blessed,'[1] in that hour God rejoices and is exalted in His world, and He says to the angels of the service, 'Come and see how this people whom I have formed in my world praise me.' So in that hour they clothe Him with honour and glory. (*Midr.Prov.* XIV, 28, 38*a*.)

If the Israelites sometimes enjoy prosperity in this world, this is a just reward for the sufferings they more often undergo: but the full reward for their fidelity and love of God is reserved for them in the world to come.

[1] This is the response in the Rabbis' *Ḳaddish* which is recited after study; see *P.B.* p. 86 and Abrahams' note in *Companion*, p. C. (H. L.)

[296] It is written in Deut. VII, 12, 'The Lord will store up unto thee [A.V. keep] the covenant and the love.' R. Ḥelbo said: It is like an orphan who was brought up by a householder,[1] and ate and drank of, and was clad with, what belonged to him, and was taught a craft. The orphan thought: 'My food and drink and my clothing are my wages,' but the householder said, 'Your food and clothing you receive in virtue of the pitcher of water you fill for me and the wood which you cleave; your *wages* are stored and remain for you.' Even so all that the Israelites enjoy in this world they receive in virtue of the sufferings which befall them, but their *reward* is stored up and preserved for them in the world to come. (*Deut.R.*, 'Eḳeb, III, 4.)

Like the nations among whom they dwelt, the Jews and the Rabbis believed in astrology, and in the influence of the planets. But it is rather fine to notice that their very particularism enabled them, as regards Israel, to rise to some extent above this current superstition:

[297] R. Ḥanina said: Upon the planets depend wisdom and wealth, and there is a planet for Israel. But R. Johanan said: Israel is not subject to the planets [or signs of the Zodiac], for it is said, 'Learn not the ways of the nations, and tremble not at the signs of the heavens: let the nations tremble at them' (Jer. X, 2). Let the nations tremble; let Israel tremble not. And Rab agreed with R. Johanan, for R. Judah said in Rab's name: Whence do we learn that the Israelites are not subject to the planets? Because it says, 'And God brought Abraham forth into the open and said, Look now towards heaven, and tell the stars, if thou be able to number them: and He said unto him, So shall thy seed be' (Gen. XV, 5). Abraham said, 'I have seen in astrological books that I am not fit to beget a son'; God replied, 'Come forth out of your astrology; the Israelites are not subject to the planets; you think that, because Jupiter is in the west, I will turn him round, and make him stand in the east, even as it is written, "Who has raised up Jupiter from the east?"' (Isa. XLI, 2). [The word 'righteousness', *ẓedeḳ*, means also Jupiter.] (**Note 83.**) (*Sab.* 156*a fin.*)

[298] So long as Israel busy themselves with Torah, they need not be troubled as regards eclipses and the like, as it says: 'Thus says the Lord, Learn not the way of the nations, and be not dismayed

[1] Cp. p. 108.

at the signs of heavens; for the nations are dismayed at them' (Jer. x, 2). (*T.Suk.* II, 6 (Z. p. 194, line 10 (cp. *Suk.* 29*a*)).)

The Rabbis were not impervious to the higher thought of the 'Second Isaiah'. Thus we get a few passages like the following:

[299] It is written, 'I separated you from the nations' (Lev. xx, 24). Had it said, 'I separated the nations from you,' there would have been no hope for the nations. But it says, 'I separated you from the nations, to be for me and for my name for ever.' R. Aḥa said: Hence we learn that God bade the nations repent, that He might bring them under His wings.

(*Cant.R.* VI, § 16, 5, on V, 16; f. 32*b* (cp. [274]).)

[300] 'Thou hast dove's eyes' (Cant. I, 15). As the dove is chaste, so the Israelites are chaste. As the dove stretches out her neck to the slaughterer, so do the Israelites, for it is said, 'For thy sake are we killed all the day long' (Ps. XLIV, 22). As the dove atones for sins, so the Israelites atone for the nations, for the seventy oxen which they offer on the festivals represent the seventy peoples, so that the world may not be depopulated of them; as it says, 'In return for my love they are become my adversaries, but I pray' (Ps. CIX, 4). As the dove, from the hour when she recognises her mate, does not change him, so the Israelites, from the time when they recognised the Holy One, have not changed Him. (*Cant.R.* I, § 15, 2, on I, 15; f. 13*a*.)

[301] R. Elazar said: God scattered Israel among the nations for the sole end that proselytes should wax numerous among them. R. Hoshaiah said: God did Israel a benefit when He scattered them among the nations. (*Pes.* 87*b*.)

The use of the term *ger* or proselyte is explained in [1574].

It may perhaps be said that to-day the *gerim* comprise more classes than one. For not only is he a *ger*, who formally joins the religious brotherhood of the house of Israel, but he too is a *ger* who believes in the One God, Father and King—the God to whom men pray. Or shall we call him the *ger* in incompleteness, the *ger* who is on the road? For all who can say Father and King in sincerity are allies and akin to one another.

[302] It is written, 'If he do not utter it, then he shall bear his iniquity' (Lev. V, 1). If you do not proclaim my Godhead to the nations, I will punish you. (*Lev.R.*, Wayiḳra, VI, 5.)

As we shall hear, Abraham was a great maker of proselytes, and this was reckoned unto him as a great merit:

[303] R. Isaac said: Abraham received the passers-by, as they came and went: after they had eaten and drunk, he would say to them, 'Say the blessing.' Then they would say to him, 'What shall we say,' and he would say to them, 'Say, Blessed be the Lord of the world, of whose gifts we have eaten.'[1] So God said to Abraham, 'My name was not known to my creatures: as you made me known to my creatures, so I regard it as if you had been in partnership with me in the creation of the world.'

(*Gen.R.*, Lek leka, XLIII, 7 (Th. p. 421).)

In the next quotation the pride of race and the particularism of the Rabbis are strangely combined with a certain curious universalism. It is for us hardly possible to conceive a state of mind which could honestly produce a statement such as that about the sun and the rain in this passage, and yet there is a religious touch about it which redeems it, and gives to it a certain distinction of its own:

[304] R. Joshua b. Levi said: If the nations had known how valuable the Temple was for them, they would have surrounded it with forts in order to protect it. It was even more valuable to them than to the Israelites, for Solomon in his prayer of dedication said, 'And concerning the foreigner...do according to all that the foreigner calls to thee to do' (I Kings VIII, 41–3), but when he touches on the Israelites, he says, 'Render unto everyone according to his ways,' that is, give to him what he asks if it is fitting for him, and if it is not fitting, give it him not. And indeed one could go further and say, 'If it were not for Israel, no rain would fall, and the sun would not shine, for it is through Israel's merit that God gives assuagement to His world, and in time to come, i.e. in the Messianic age, the nations will see how God dealt with Israel, and they will come to join themselves unto them,' as it is said, 'In those days it shall come to pass that ten men shall take hold, out of all the tongues of the nations, of the skirt of him that is a Jew, saying, "We will go with you, for we have heard that God is with you"' (Zech. VIII, 23).

(*Num.R.*, Bemidbar, I, 3.)

Most of this passage is given in [214] and [906].

[1] This is still the introduction to the grace after meals, *P.B.* p. 279 (cp. [725]).

Chapter V

THE LAW

There is yet more to quote about Israel—of its earlier sins and of its later martyrdoms—but I now turn to the Law—a long section!—and to Israel's relation to that Law. For the real value of Israel in the eyes of God, as also in its own, is that it is the people who accepted, and lovingly fulfil, God's Law. Israel, in other words, is a religious people, a religious community: apart from its religion it is nothing, and has no value whatever. A secular, non-religious Israel is a monstrosity. The following brief passage is fundamental:

[305] If it were not for my Law which you accepted, I should not recognise you, and I should not regard you more than any of the idolatrous nations of the world. (*Exod.R.*, Ki Tissa, XLVII, 3.)

[306] 'Yet for all that, in spite of their sins, when they have been in the lands of their enemies, I have not rejected them utterly' (Lev. XXVI, 44). All the goodly gifts that were given them were taken from them. And if it had not been for the Book of the Law which was left to them, they would not have differed at all from the nations of the world. (*Sifra* 112*c*.)

The purpose of Israel's election by God is that it shall sanctify God's name, and be a holy people dedicated to God's service:

[307] It is written, 'Keep my statutes: through them shall a man live' (Lev. XVIII, 5). R. Ishmael said: How can one know that if [in a time of persecution] they say to an Israelite in private, 'Serve the idol, and you shall not be killed,' he should serve the idol, and not be killed? Because it says, 'A man shall *live* through them,' and it does not say, 'A man shall *die* through them.' But if he is told in public, is he to obey? No, for it says, 'Ye shall not profane my holy name, but I will be hallowed among the children of Israel' (Lev. XXII, 32). If you sanctify my name, I will sanctify my name through you, even as Mishael, Hananiah, and Azariah did, for when all the nations of the world bowed down to the idol, they stood erect as palm trees. Of them it says in the Kabbalah [i.e. the holy Writings], 'This, thy standing upright, is like unto a palm tree' (Cant. VII, 8). To-day

I am exalted [=sanctified] through them in the eyes of the nations who deny the Torah, this day will I punish their enemies, this day I will quicken the dead; I am the Lord; I punish, and I am faithful to reward. (**Note 11 *i*.**) (*Sifra* 86*b*.)

[308] It says in Lev. XI, 45, 'For I am the Lord your God who brought you up out of the land of Egypt to be your God: ye shall, therefore, be holy, for I am holy.' That means, I brought you out of Egypt on the condition that you should receive the yoke of the commandments: he who acknowledges the yoke of the commandments acknowledges that I have brought Israel out of Egypt, and he who denies [or rejects the obligation of] the yoke of the commandments, denies that I brought Israel out of Egypt. When it says, 'to be your God', it means even against your will. 'Ye shall be holy': even as I am holy, so be you holy: as I am separate, so be you separate [*perushim*] (cp. [719]). 'On a condition I brought you out of Egypt: namely, on the condition that you should surrender yourselves to the Sanctification of my Name' (Lev. XXII, 33). (*Sifra* 57*b*, 99*d* (cp. [688]).)

[309] 'A holy people art thou unto the Lord thy God' (Deut. XIV, 2). The holiness which is upon you compels you [i.e. it should drive or urge you to be holy]. Do not compel another people to be holy [i.e. do not compel God to choose another people in your stead]. (*Sifre Deut.*, Re'eh, § 97, f. 94*a* (H. p. 158).)

[310] Why is the Exodus from Egypt mentioned in connection with every single commandment? The matter can be compared to a king, the son of whose friend was taken prisoner. The king ransomed him, not as son, but as slave, so that, if he should at any time disobey the king, the latter could say, 'You are my slave.' So, when he came back, the king said, 'Put on my sandals for me, take my clothes to the bath house.' Then the man protested. The king took out the bill of sale, and said, 'You are my slave.' So when God redeemed the children of Abraham His friend, He redeemed them, not as children, but as slaves, so that if He imposed upon them decrees, and they obeyed not, He could say, 'Ye are my slaves.' When they went into the desert, He began to order them some light and some heavy commands, e.g. Sabbath and incest commands, and fringes and phylacteries. They began to protest. Then God said, 'You are

my slaves. On this condition I redeemed you, that I should decree, and you should fulfil.' [Nevertheless, God's slaves are unlike man's slaves.] God's ways are not like those of 'flesh and blood'. For a man acquires slaves that these may look after and sustain *him*, but God acquires slaves that He may look after and sustain *them*.

(*Sifre Num.*, Shelaḥ, § 115, f. 35*a*; *Sifre Deut.*, 'Eḳeb, § 38, f. 77*a* (H. p. 127; H. p. 74).)

The Law is Israel's beauty, its strength, its comfort, and its adornment:

[311] 'Thou art beautiful, my love' (Cant. I, 15). [The following passage is vividly illustrative of the attitude of the Rabbis to the Law. Whether the commands concerned morality or ritual, whether they seem *to us* moderns petty or important, ugly or beautiful, to the Rabbis all were fair, all a glory, all a privilege.] 'Thou art beautiful' through the commandments, both positive and negative, beautiful through loving deeds, beautiful in thy house with the heave-offerings and the tithes, beautiful in the field by the commands about gleaning, the Forgotten Sheaf and the Second Tithe; beautiful in the law about mixed seeds and about fringes, and about first fruits, and the fourth year planting; beautiful in the law of circumcision, beautiful in prayer, in the reading of the *Shema*, in the law of the door-posts and the phylacteries, in the law of the *Lulab* and the Citron; beautiful, too, in repentance and in good works; beautiful in this world and beautiful in the world to come.[1]

(*Cant.R.* I, § 15, 1, on I, 15; f. 12*b*.)

[312] As the lily dies only with its scent, so Israel will not die so long as it executes the commands, and does good deeds. (**Note 37**.)

(*Cant.R.* II, § 2, 6, on II, 2; f. 14*a*.)

The Law acts as a surrogate for the Temple. Where sacrifices would have atoned for certain classes of sins, now that the Temple has gone, the Law, if Israelites occupy themselves with its study, serves as an equivalent (**Note 51**).

[1] [But, conversely, Israel 'beautifies' God by performing the commandments in the most 'beautiful' manner, e.g., by buying the choicest *Lulab* obtainable, see *Mek.* ed. Weiss, 44*a*, on Exod. xv, 2. This is called *Hiddur Mizwah* (*Bab.K.* 9*b*, top). That the conception was common may be inferred from the fact that three words for 'beauty' are used, *yafeh* (in Cant.), *na'eh* in Exodus and *Hiddur* in *Bab.K.* (cp. [714]) (H. L.)]

[313] God foresaw that the Temple would be destroyed, and He said, 'While the Temple exists, and you bring sacrifices, the Temple atones for you; when the Temple is not there, what shall atone for you? Busy yourselves with the words of the Law, for they are equivalent to sacrifices, and they will atone for you.'

(*Tanḥ.B.*, Aḥare Mot, 35*a* (Moore, III, 155).)

The Israelites are fair and acceptable to God, only when they fulfil the commandments of the Law:

[314] It is like a king who said to his wife, 'Deck yourself with all your ornaments that you may be acceptable to me.' So God says to Israel, 'Be distinguished by the commandments so that you may be acceptable to me.' As it says, 'Fair art thou, my beloved, when thou art acceptable to me' [a playful mistranslation of Cant. VI, 4].

(*Sifre Deut.*, Wa'ethḥanan, § 36*fin.*, f. 75*b* (Hd. p. 68).)

[315] 'I, even I, am He that comforts you' (Isa. LI, 12). R. Abba b. Kahana in the name of R. Johanan said: The matter is like a king who betrothed himself to a lady, and wrote for her a large marriage covenant. 'Thus and thus I give to thee; so much jewellery I give thee, so many treasures I give thee.' Then he left her, and went to a far country by the sea, and stayed there many years; her companions taunted her, and said to her, 'How long will you sit here? Take to you a husband while you are yet young and are strong.' But she returned to her house, and took the covenant and read it, and was comforted. After a long time the king came back, and said to her, 'My daughter, I wonder that you waited for me after all these years.' She said, 'My Lord, if it had not been for the large marriage covenant you wrote for me, my companions would long ago have made me give you up.' So in this world the nations taunt the Israelites and say to them, 'How long will you die for your God, and give your lives for Him, and be slaughtered for Him? How much pain does He not bring upon you, how much contempt and suffering? Come with us, and we will make you generals and prefects and governors.' Then the Israelites go into their synagogues and houses of study, and they take up the book of the Law, and they read in it, 'And I will turn unto you, and make you fruitful and multiply you, and will establish my covenant

with you' (Lev. XXVI, 9), and they are comforted. When the end shall have come, God will say to the Israelites, 'My sons, I marvel that you have waited for me all these years,' and Israel will say, 'Lord, if it had not been for the book of the Law which thou didst write for us, the nations would long ago have caused us to abandon thee.' So it is said, 'Unless the Law had been my delight, I should have perished in my affliction' (Ps. CXIX, 92), and 'This [i.e. the Law] I recall to my mind, therefore have I hope' (Lam. III, 21). (*Pes.K.* XIX, 139*b*.)

Elsewhere, following the quotation from Ps. CXIX, 92, we read that the Israelites say:

[316] Therefore we hope in Him, we wait for Him, and we confess the Unity of His Name twice a day, as we repeat the words, 'Hear, O Israel, the Lord our God, the Lord is One' (Deut. VI, 4). (*Lam.R.* III, 7, end, on III, 19.)

[317] If affliction overtakes a man who has words of Torah, he is resigned: if he has no words of Torah, he is embittered. What does the former do? He acknowledges that God's decree is righteous. If he hungers, he says, 'Such and such a thing is said about hunger in the Torah' [so, too, about thirst and nakedness and poverty, Deut. XXVIII, 48–51]. So with David: Had not words of Torah consoled him when affliction befell him, he would have uprooted himself from the world, as it says, 'Unless thy Law had been my delight, I should have perished in my affliction' (Ps. CXIX, 92). (*Tan.d.b.El.* p. 137.)

[318] Beloved is the Torah, for when David, the King of Israel, asked God [to give him something], it was the Torah that he desired, as it is said, 'Thou art good and doest good, therefore teach me thy statutes' (Ps. CXIX, 68) [which, being interpreted, means:] 'Thy goodness is exceeding great towards me, and towards all those who come into the world. May thy goodness be ample towards me, in that thou wilt teach me thy statutes.'
(*Sifre Num.*, Ḳoraḥ, § 119, f. 39*b* (H. p. 143).)

The Israelites accepted the Law voluntarily. Therefore they doubtless receive special rewards for its fulfilment, but also special punishments for its violation. The magnificent utterance of Amos (III, 2)—his terrible 'therefore'—was not forgotten.

[319] God said to the Israelites, 'I am the Lord thy God; thou shalt have no other gods besides me,' that is, I am He whose sovereignty you accepted in Egypt. They said, 'Yes'; then God said, 'As you then accepted my sovereignty, so now accept my decrees.'

(*Mek.*[2], *Baḥodesh*, Yitro, § 6, p. 222; *Mek.*[3], vol. II, p. 238 (cp. [305]).)

The Midrash explains the declaratory statement of the First Commandment (Exod. XX, 2) by regarding it as Israel's acceptance of God's rule and sovereignty:

[320] When God determined to give the Law, none of the nations except Israel would receive it. [This is a favourite theory of the Rabbis and serves many purposes, of some of which we may well approve, of others less.] A king had a field, and he wanted to give it to tenants to till. He called the first and said, 'Will you take over this field?' The man replied, 'No, the labour is too hard for me.' Similarly did he ask the second, third and fourth man, and they refused. He called the fifth man, and said, 'Will you take over the field?' He replied, 'Yes.' 'Upon the condition of tilling it?' He said, 'Yes.' But when he received the field, he left it untilled. With whom will the king be angry? With them who said, 'We cannot take it over,' or with him who accepted it, but then left it fallow? Surely with him who accepted it. So when God revealed Himself upon Mount Sinai, there was not a nation at whose doors He did not knock, but they would not accept the Law and keep it. But when He came to Israel, they said, 'All that the Lord has spoken we will do, and we will hearken' (Exod. XXIV, 7). Therefore He is justified if, should you hearken not, He punish you. (**Note 35**.)

(*Exod.R.*, Yitro, XXVII, 9 (cp. [209–10]).)

Israel sometimes confesses a strange alternation as regards the Law:

[321] 'I sleep, but my heart wakes.' The congregation of Israel speaks unto God, 'Lord of the world, I am asleep [negligent] as regards the commandments, but my heart wakes [yearns] to do deeds of lovingkindness; I am asleep [careless] about righteous deeds, but my heart is awake [i.e. stirs me up] to do them. I sleep as regards the sacrifices, but my heart is awake for the *Shema* and the Prayer; I sleep as regards the Temple, but my heart is awake for the synagogue and the houses of study; I sleep as regards the End, but my heart is awake for the redemption; my heart sleeps

about the redemption, but the heart of the Holy One is awake to redeem me.' (*Cant.R.* v, § 2, 1, on v, 2; f. 30*a*.)

To the Rabbis morality and religion form a single whole. They cannot separate the one from the other. He who is 'good' must believe in God. He who is bad must deny or ignore Him. Goodness implies faith in God. Faith in God implies, at the least, the obligation to be 'good', for God has commanded the Israelite to be 'good', that is, to fulfil the ordinances of the Law. Wickedness produces the denial or forgetfulness of God; and we may also say that, to the Rabbis, the denial or forgetfulness of God is the cause of wickedness:

[322] 'If a man sin, and lie unto his neighbour about a deposit' (Lev. vi, 2). R. Hananiah b. [Ḥa]kinai said: No man lies to his neighbour until he has denied the Root [i.e. disbelieves in God]. It happened once that R. Reuben was in Tiberias on the Sabbath, and a philosopher asked him: 'Who is the most hateful man in the world?' He replied, 'The man who denies his Creator.' 'How so?' said the philosopher. R. Reuben answered: 'Honour thy father and thy mother, thou shalt do no murder, thou shalt not commit adultery, thou shalt not steal, thou shalt not bear false witness against thy neighbour, thou shalt not covet.' No man denies the derivative [i.e. the separate commandments] until he has previously denied the Root [i.e. God], and no man sins unless he has denied Him who commanded him not to commit that sin. (*T.Shebu'ot* iii, 6 (Z. pp. 449 *fin.*, 450 *init.*); cp. Moore, i, 467; iii, 144.)

So the Law is the Israelites' life: the cause of their continuance in this world; their *true* life in this world, and the cause of their eternal life in the world to come:

[323] It is written 'That ye seek not after your own eyes and after your own heart' (Num. xv, 39). The heart and the eyes are the panders for the body, for they lead the body to be unchaste. 'That ye may remember and do all my commandments' (Num. xv, 40). Like a man thrown into the water: the steersman threw him a rope, and said to him, 'Grasp the rope with your hand, and do not let it go, for if you do, you will lose your life.' So God says to the Israelites, 'So long as you cleave to the commandments, you are alive, every one of you, this day' (Deut. iv, 4), even as it says, 'Take fast hold of instruction, let it not go; it is thy life' (Prov. iv, 13), and 'Be holy unto your God' (Num.

xv, 40). As long as you execute the commandments, you are sanctified, but if you separate yourselves from the commandments, you are profaned. And God says, In this world the evil inclination separates you from the commandments, but in the world to come I will root it out from you, as it is said, 'I will put my spirit within you, and I will take away the stony heart out of your flesh, and I will give you a heart of flesh, and I will put my spirit within you, and cause you to walk in my statutes and do them' (Ezek. xxxvi, 26, 27).

(*Num.R.*, Shelaḥ, xvii, 6 (cp. *Tanḥ.B.*, Shelaḥ, § 31, 37*b*).)

[324] With regard to the commandment of the fringes (Num. xv, 39) it says, 'Ye shall see it' ['it' and 'him' are the same in Hebrew]. So when the Israelites glance at the fringes, it should seem to them as though the Divine Presence were resting upon them.

(*Tanḥ.B.*, Shelaḥ, § 31, 37*b*.)

The Israelites have been chosen by God to be His sons and His servants. There is no escape. God will use them for His purpose whether they will or no:

[325] 'I am the Lord your God' (Num. xv, 41, twice in the one verse). Why twice? So that the Israelite shall not say: 'Did not God give us commandments that we should receive reward? Well, then; we will not do them, and we will receive no reward.' So they said to Ezekiel: 'When a master has sold his slave, has the slave not passed out of his master's power?' He said, 'Yes.' Then they said to him, 'Because God has sold us to the nations, we have passed out of His power.' He said to them, 'Has a slave whom his master has sold with the intention of reacquiring him [lit. that the slave should return to him either by repurchase or at the seventh year], passed out of the master's power?' Even as it says: 'That which has come into your minds shall not be at all, when ye say, we will be as the nations, as the families of the lands, to serve wood and stone. As I live, says the Lord, surely with a mighty hand, and with a stretched out arm, and with fury poured out, will I rule over you' (Ezek. xx, 32, 33). The mighty hand, that is the sword; and the stretched out arm, that is, famine. 'After I have brought these three punishments upon you, one after the other, the sword, famine, exile, then I will reign over you even against your will.'

(*Sifre Num.*, Shelaḥ, § 115, f. 35*a fin.*–35*b init.* (H. p. 128).)

[The argument in the *Sifre* looks as though it were directed against Jews who, after the destruction of the Temple or, perhaps, the Bar Kochba catastrophe, imagined that all was lost and that assimilation with pagans was the only course available. (H. L.)]

Yet the Law (contrast the theory of Paul!) helps the Israelite to conquer the evil impulse and temptation:

[326] All the time that the words of the Law find free entrance into the chambers of the heart, the words of the Law can rest there, and the evil inclination cannot rule over them, and no man can expel them. As if a king went into the steppe, and found dining halls and large chambers, and went and dwelt in them. So with the evil inclination; if it does not find the words of the Law ruling (in the heart), you cannot expel it from the heart.

(*Midr.Prov.* XXIV, 31, f. 48*b*.)

[327] R. Alexander proclaimed, 'Who wants life, who wants life?' Then all the world came gathering around him, and said, 'Give us life.' He quoted Ps. XXXIV, 12, 13, 'Who is the man that desires life, etc.' 'Perhaps some may say, I have kept my tongue from evil, and my lips from speaking guile. So now I will indulge in sleep. Therefore it says: [not only] "Depart from evil," [but also] "Do good," and by good is meant Torah.'

(*Ab.Zar.* 19*b* (cp. [705]).)

The Rabbis were well aware that both goodness and sin need not necessarily consist of actual deeds. To help others to virtue is even better than to do virtuous deeds oneself. To cause others to sin is worse than to sin oneself (cp. p. 289):

[328] R. Aḥa said: He who has learnt Torah, taught it, kept it and done it, but who, having the opportunity to encourage and abet others, did not do so, is accursed. R. Jeremiah said: He who has neither learnt nor taught, neither kept nor done, Torah, but who, having the opportunity to encourage and abet others, availed himself of it, is blessed.

(*T.J.Soṭ.* VII, § 4, f. 21*d*, line 9.)

[329] 'I am the Lord who heals thee' (Exod. XV, 26). God said to Moses, 'Say to the children of Israel, The words of the Law which I have given you are a source of healing for you and of life,' as it is said, 'They are life to those who find them, and healing to all their flesh' (Prov. IV, 22), and it says, 'It [i.e. the Law] will be healing to thy flesh and refreshment to thy bones'

(Prov. III, 8). R. Isaac said: If they have no sicknesses [for it says, 'I will put none of these diseases upon thee' (Exod. XV, 26)], why do they need healing? But the words mean: 'I will put no disease upon thee in this world, and I will heal thee in the world to come.'

(*Mek.*[2], *Wayašša'*, Beshallaḥ, § 1, p. 158; *Mek.*[3], vol. II, p. 96.)

[330] The evil *yetzer* has no power over against the Law, and he who has the Law in his heart, over him the *yetzer* has no power (cf. *R.T.* p. 182). (*Midr.Ps.* on CXIX, 10 (246*b*, § 7).)

[331] R. Levi b. Ḥama said in the name of R. Simeon b. Laḳish: A man should always oppose the good impulse to the evil impulse, as it is said, 'Stir up (A.V. Stand in awe) and sin not' (Ps. IV, 4). If he conquer it, well and good; but if not, let him occupy himself with Torah, as it goes on to say, 'Commune with your heart.' Should this gain him the victory, well and good; but if not, let him read the *Shema*; as it continues, 'Upon your bed' (for the *Shema* is to be said when you 'lie down'). If he conquer it, well and good; but if not, let him reflect upon the day of death, even as the verse ends, 'And be still.'

(*Ber.* 5*a*.)

[332] The words of the Law are likened to a medicine of life. Like a king, who inflicted a big wound upon his son, and he put a plaster upon his wound. He said, 'My son, so long as this plaster is on your wound, eat and drink what you like, and wash in cold or warm water, and you will suffer no harm. But if you remove it, you will get a bad boil.' So God says to the Israelites, 'I created within you the evil *yetzer*, but I created the Law as a medicine. As long as you occupy yourselves with the Law, the *yetzer* will not rule over you. But if you do not occupy yourselves with the Torah, then you will be delivered into the power of the *yetzer*, and all its activity will be against you.'[1]

(*Sifre Deut.*, 'Eḳeb, § 45, f. 82*b* (*R.T.* p. 182; Hd. p. 103).)

[The point of the parable is derived from the *Shema*, where, in Deut. XI, 18, it says, 'And ye shall set (*we-sam-tem*) these my words upon your heart.' By a change of one vowel, the verse means 'And a perfect drug (*we-sam tam*) shall these my words be upon your heart.'

[1] [It is interesting to note that evil is ascribed directly to God: contrast *P.B.* p. 37, where 'createst all things' is a moderating substitute for 'creating evil' in Isa. XLV, 7 which is quoted. 'All things' includes evil. See Abrahams' note, p. XLIII. (H. L.)]

The word *sam*, like the Greek *pharmakon*, means either a poison or a drug, and the double meaning is the basis of the parable. It is possibly directed at the Pauline argument that through the Torah came death: according to the *Sifre*, it brings life (cp. [399], [441] note, [705], [760] and [762]). (**Note 41.**) (H. L.).]

But the Law should be loved and studied for its own sake, and not for its rewards. No worldly use must be made of it:

[333] R. Abba bar Kahana said: Thou shalt not sit and weigh the commands of the Law. Thou art not to say, 'Because there is a greater reward for this command, I will do it, and because there is only a small reward for that command, I will not do it.' What has God done? He has not revealed to the creatures [i.e. to men] the particular reward for each particular command, in order that they might do all the commands in integrity. The matter is like a king who hired labourers, and brought them into his garden; he hid, and did not reveal, what was the reward of [working in] the garden, so that they might not neglect that part of the work for which the reward was small, and go and do that part for which the reward was great. In the evening he summoned them all, and said, 'Under which tree did you work?' The first answered, 'Under this one.' The king said, 'That is a pepper tree; its reward is one gold piece.' He said to the next, 'Under which tree did you work?' He said, 'Under that one.' The king said, 'It is a white flower tree; its reward is half a gold piece.' He asked a third, 'Under which tree did you work?' He said, 'Under this one.' The king replied, 'That is an olive tree; its reward is 200 *zuzim*.' The labourers said to him, 'Ought you not to have told us the tree under which the reward was the greatest?' The king replied, 'If I had done that, how could all of my garden have been tilled?' Even so, God has not revealed the reward of the commandments, except of two—one, the heaviest of the heavy, the other, the lightest of the light, viz. Exod. XX, 12, 'Honour thy father and thy mother,' and Deut. XXII, 7, 'Thou shalt let the mother bird go.' For both the reward is the same, namely, long life.

(*Deut.R.*, Ki Teẓe, VI, 2.)

[With Abba's remark, compare the famous saying of R. Judah the Prince in *Aboth* II, 1 (*P.B.* p. 187, top): 'Be as heedful of a light precept as of a grave one, for thou knowest not the reward for each.'

It is noteworthy that the word 'creatures' (*biryot* or *beriyyot*) is here used and this is usually of general application. The present passage might possibly be of universal import, since kindness to animals and honouring of parents are incumbent on all mankind: Abba has not chosen commands like the Sabbath or dietary laws, which would necessarily limit the parable to Jews. (H. L.)]

[334] It says in Ps. CXII, 1, 'Happy is the man that fears the Lord and delights greatly in his commandments.' Happy is the *man*; but is not the *woman* who fears the Lord happy too? [That is obvious. What, then, does 'man' mean?] R. Amram in the name of Rab said: It means, Happy is he who repents while he is yet a man. R. Joshua b. Levi said: Happy is he who masters his inclination like a man. (*Ab.Zar.* 19*a*.)

[335] Antigonos of Soko, a disciple of Simeon the Just, used to say, 'Be not like servants who minister to their master upon the condition of receiving a reward; but be like servants who minister to their master without the condition of receiving a reward; and let the fear of Heaven be upon you.'
(*Aboth* I, 3; *P.B.* p. 184.)

Other passages about reward will be quoted, later on, in another connection.

[336] R. Johanan b. Zakkai said: If thou hast learned much Torah, take not credit to thyself, for thereunto wast thou created. R. Jose said: Let all thy deeds be done for the sake of Heaven [i.e. for God's sake].
(*Aboth* II, 9, 17 (Herford's ed. of *Pirke Aboth*, 2nd ed., 1930, pp. 49, 58 *fin.*).)

Mr Herford is not unfair when he says, 'The principle here implied lies at the heart of Pharisaism, viz. that any given act only has worth, moral or religious, when it is done with the purpose of serving God thereby. Merely to do it as an *opus operatum* is nothing; and the only ground on which such action is to be excused or even recommended is that it may lead to action from the higher motive, even as it says, "Ever let a man be occupied with Torah and precepts, even though it be not for its own sake; for while he is doing it not for its own sake, he comes to do it for its own sake"' (*Pes.* 50*b*).

[337] Hillel used to say: Whoso makes great his name loses his name, and whoso adds not, makes to cease, and he who does not learn deserves killing, and one who serves himself with the Crown, passes away. So R. Zadok said: Make not of the Torah a crown where-

with to aggrandise thyself, or a spade wherewith to dig.... Whoever derives a profit for himself from the words of the Torah is helping on his own destruction.

(*Aboth* I, 13; IV, 7 (cp. [710]).)

The first sentence is given in Mr Herford's translation.

[338] Teach the Law gratis, and take no fee for it: for the words of the Law no fee must be taken, seeing that God gave the Law gratis. He who takes a fee for the Law destroys the world.

(*Der.Er.Z.* IV, 2.)

[339] Raba said: As for him who does not fulfil the Torah for its own sake, it were better had he never been created. (*Ber.* 17*a*.)

[340] Do the words of the Law for the doing's sake; speak of them for their own sake. Perhaps you might say, 'I will learn Torah so that I may be called wise, or sit in the College, or gain long days in the world to come'; therefore it says, 'Thou shalt love the Lord thy God' [i.e. the learning must be only done from love].

(*Sifre Deut.*, 'Eḳeb, §48, f. 84*b* (*R.T.* p. 324; H. p. 113) (cp. [374]).)

[341] Learn Torah: the honour will come at the end of itself. R. Eliezer b. Zadok said: Do the words of the Law for the doing's sake; speak of them for their own sake. If Belshazar, because he made use of the vessels of the Temple, was deprived of this world and the world to come, how much more will this be the case with him who makes use of [i.e. uses as a means to another end] that for which both this world and the world to come were created.[1]

(*Sifre Deut.*, 'Eḳeb, § 48, f. 84*b*; *Ned.* 62*a* (H. p. 114; cp. [709]).)

Yet great are the benefits of the Law and its rewards. It makes a man truly free:

[342] When Law came into the world, freedom came into the world.

(*Gen.R.*, Wayera, LIII, 7 (Th. p. 562).)

[343] It says, 'And the tables were the work of God, and the writing was the writing of God, graven upon the tables' (Exod. XXXII, 16). Read not *ḥarut* (graven), but *ḥerut* (freedom), for no man is free but he who labours in the Torah. (See **Note 66.**)

(*Aboth* VI, 2; *P.B.* p. 205.)

[1] Even the use of the secular vessels of the Temple apparently deserved this appalling punishment (*Bekorot* 50*a* foot, based on Ezek. VII, 22 (**Note 84**)).

[344] R. Jeremiah said to R. Ze'era: It says in Job of Sheol (III, 19), 'Small and great are there, and the slave is free of his master.' Is it not obvious that small and great are there? It means, 'He who, for the sake of the words of the Torah, makes himself small in this world, will be great in the world to come, and he who, for the sake of the words of the Torah, makes himself as a slave in this world, will be a free man in the world to come.'

(*Bab.M.* 85*b*.)

[A similar moral is deduced from Eber's younger son in Gen. x, 25, where it says that Eber had two sons, the elder being called Peleg, which means division, because it was in his days that the earth was divided into small and great, 'and the name of his brother was Joktan' (he belittles himself). No explanation of the name is given in Genesis, and it is a Rabbinic axiom that when a name is unexplained, but, none the less, distinctively mentioned in a clause of its own, and not merely enumerated in a catalogue, there is a reason for the choice of name which must be looked for and interpreted homiletically:

[345] Therefore, asks the Midrash, why was he called Joktan [he belittles]? Because he belittled himself and his affairs [i.e. he was humble in demeanour and modest in his enterprises, never exalting himself]. What was his reward? To raise twelve families of descendants. Now if this is the reward of a small man who makes himself small, what will be the reward of a great man who does so? A similar story is learnt from the fact that Jacob stretched out his hand on to the head of Ephraim, though 'he was the younger' [lit. the insignificant one] (Gen. XLVIII, 14). But why the last clause? Do we not know this from the pedigree? The answer is that he made his needs insignificant, and so his reward was the right of primogeniture. If a younger son thus abases himself, and is then rewarded, what will be the reward of an elder son who does likewise? (See **Note 67**.)

(*Gen.R.*, Noaḥ, XXXVII, 7 (Th. p. 349).) (H. L.)]

The Law is for all Israelites: each of them may apprehend it, or partake of it, according to his capacity (cp. [10] and [689]):

[346] There are three crowns, the crown of the Torah, the crown of the Priesthood and the crown of the Kingdom. Aaron was worthy of the crown of the Priesthood and obtained it, David was worthy of the crown of the Kingdom and obtained it. The crown of the Torah remains over, so that no man shall have the pretext

to say: 'If the crown of the Priesthood and the crown of the Kingdom were yet available, I would have proved myself worthy of them and have obtained them.' For the crown of the Torah is available for all. For God says: 'Of him who proves himself worthy of *that* crown, I reckon it to him as if all the three were yet available, and he had proved himself worthy of them all. And of every one who does not prove himself worthy of the crown of the Law, I reckon it unto him as if all three crowns were yet available, and he had proved himself worthy of none of them.'

Which is the greatest [do you ask] of the three crowns? R. Simeon b. Elazar said: Who is greater; he who makes a king or the king? Surely he who makes a king. Who is greater, he who appoints rulers or the rulers? Surely he who appoints them. But the other two crowns come to be only in virtue of the Torah. Even as it says: 'By me kings reign, by me princes rule' (Prov. VIII, 15, 16).

(*Sifre Num.*, Ḳoraḥ, § 119, f. 40*a* (H. p. 144; cp. [1386]).)

There is, perhaps, an occasional perception that revelation is progressive:

[347] When God revealed His presence to the Israelites, He did not show forth all His goodness at once, because they could not have borne so much good; for had He revealed His goodness to them at one time they would have died. Thus, when Joseph made himself know to his brethren, they were unable to answer him, because they were astounded by him (Gen. XLV, 3). If *God* were to reveal Himself all at once, how much more powerful would be the effect. So He shows Himself little by little.

(*Tanḥ.B.*, Debarim, 1*a*.)

A prophet may even order the violation of a Law, if the exigencies of the moment demand it:

[348] 'A prophet...shall the Lord raise up...to him shall ye hearken' (Deut. XVIII, 15). Even though he bid thee transgress one of the commands ordained in the Torah, as did Elijah on Mount Carmel, yet according to the need of the hour listen to him. (*Sifre Deut.*, Shofeṭim, § 175, f. 107*b*; *Yeb.* 90*b*.)

[349] Resh Laḳish said: There are times when the suppression [or cancellation] of the Torah [perhaps, rather, 'of a command-

ment in the Torah'] may be the [firmer] foundation of the Torah. (*Men.* 99*b*.)[1]

[350] [There seems once to have been a Rabbinical ruling that ordinances [*halakot*] of the Oral Law must not be written down.] R. Johanan said: The writing down of halakot is equal [in wrongdoing] to the burning of the Torah. Yet R. Johanan and Resh Laḳish used on Sabbaths to read Agadic books. They taught, 'At a time of working for the Lord, they broke thy Law' [a playful mistranslation of Ps. CXIX, 126]. For they said, 'It is better that the Law should be broken than forgotten.' (Cp. (12), p. ciii.) (*Temurah* 14*b*.)

For the term Halakot cp. [196].

[While collections of Haggadah seem to have been current at an early period, the writing down of Halakah was deprecated. So also was the writing down of Blessings, the same phrase being used in *Sab.* 115*b* top, with regard to Blessings. The objection was based on the fear that a stereotyped blessing or Law would lack spontaneity and the 'writing down' would check development. The leader in prayer had certain subjects assigned to him, to be alluded to in a certain order. The phrasing was, within certain limits, left to him (see *Ber.* 48*b* and 49*a*). Similarly, the codification of law was held to imperil the continuance of living and expanding law: Maimonides was careful to state that his code was but a convenience, not a substitute for original authorities or a seal on future activity.

The Haggadah was highly esteemed by reason of its ethical value: it did not, however, possess the binding authority of the Halakah. But the Rabbis saw that through Haggadah the hearts of the people could be reached, and so they realised that the Haggadist was fulfilling a valuable function. A good example of the relation of Haggadah and Halakah is furnished by *Sot.* 40*a*: R. Abbahu and R. Ḥiyya bar Abba once chanced to come to a certain place where the former gave Haggadic and the latter Halakic addresses. Everyone left Ḥiyya, and flocked to listen to Abbahu, so that Ḥiyya felt discouraged. Abbahu said to him: 'I will tell you a parable: we are like two traders, one a jeweller and one a haberdasher: which of the two will attract the greater number of customers? Surely he who sells cheap articles.' Now day by day Ḥiyya was in the habit of accompanying Abbahu up to his inn, as a sign of respect, because of the esteem in which the Government regarded him. (Abbahu was

[1] [Thus the verse cited in [350] was used at the end of *Berakot* as a justification for re-introducing the prohibited pronunciation of the divine name in greetings ('The Lord be with you,' 'May the Lord bless you') in order to revive religion. (H. L.)]

very wealthy, and had great influence with the Government, with whom he would intercede for his co-religionists in cases of need: see *Ḥag.* 14*a*; *San.* 14*a*; *Ket.* 17*a*.) But on this day it was Abbahu who accompanied Ḥiyya to his inn, and yet even this did not restore Ḥiyya's composure. (H. L.)] Cp. [435].

The Law gives life, above all, life in the world to come:

[351] R. Samuel b. Naḥmani said: The words of the Law are compared to wine. For as wine strengthens, so the Law strengthens those that toil in it with all their will, as it is said, 'The praises of God in their mouths, and a two-edged sword in their hands' (Ps. CXLIX, 6). R. Judah said: A two-edged sword means the written and the oral Law. R. Nehemiah said: It is a sword which cuts on both sides, that is, a Law which gives life in this world and life in the world to come. (*Pes.K.* 102*a fin.*–102*b init.*)

[352] Resh Laḳish said: Over him who occupies himself with the Torah in this world, which is like night, God extends the cord of His grace in the world to come, which is like day, as it is said, 'The Lord will command His lovingkindness in the day time, while in the night His song shall be with me' (Ps. XLII, 9). (*Ab.Zar.* 3*b*.)

[353] Even though Israel be in exile among the nations, if they occupy themselves with Torah, it is as though they were not in exile. (*Tan.d.b.El.* p. 148.)

[354] 'Ye shall keep my ordinances to walk therein' (Lev. XVIII, 4), that is, you are to make them the main purpose of your life, and not a subsidiary thing; all thy business is with them alone, and other matters must not be mixed up with them. Do not say, 'Now that I have learnt the wisdom of Israel, I will go and learn the wisdom of the nations of the world,' for the Torah says, 'To walk in them.' You are not permitted to separate from them, as it says, 'Let them be thine only ones, and let no strange things be with thee' (Prov. V, 17) (A.V. 'Let them be only thine own, and not strangers' with thee'). (*Sifra* 86*a fin.*–86*b init.*)

[355] It is written, 'If thou seekest her as silver, and searchest for her as for hid treasures' (Prov. II, 4). R. Phinehas said: If you seek after the words of the Law as for hid treasures, God will not withhold from you your reward. If a man loses some money or

even a small coin in his house, how many lamps and wicks does he not kindle till he finds it! If for that which gives the life of an hour in this world, a man kindles all these lamps and wicks, how much more should you search, as for hidden treasure, after the words of the Law which gives life in this world and life in the world to come. (*Cant.R.* I, § 1, 9 on I, 1; f. 2*b*.)

[356] 'Happy is he who makes himself as an ox to the yoke, as an ass to the burden, as the cow to the plough in the hollow. Happy are ye who sow beside all waters' (Is. XXXII, 20) [for 'the waters' mean Torah; cp. *Sifre* 84 *a*, ed. Fr. and [437]]. How is this? He who reads the Torah, then the Prophets, then the Writings, then the *halakot* [i.e. the Mishnah], then the Midrash, who attends the Seminary, and does little business—to such a man, God says, 'My son, this world and the next world are mine and thine: the Sanctuary is mine and thine: the days of the Messiah are mine and thine.' (**Note 94**.) (*Tan.d.b.El.* p. 198.)

[357] Artaban sent to Rabbenu[1] a priceless pearl, and said to him, 'Send me a precious object of equal value.' R. Judah sent him a *mezuzah*. He said to him, 'I sent you a priceless gift, and you send me something worth a penny.' R. Judah replied, 'Our respective gifts cannot be compared. Moreover, you sent me something which I must guard, but I sent you something which, when you sleep, will guard you, as it is said, "When thou walkest, it will lead thee, when thou liest down, it will watch over thee, and when thou awakest, it will talk with thee" (Prov. VI, 22); it will lead thee in this world, it will watch over thee in the hour of death; it will talk with thee in the world to come.' (**Note 23**.) (*Gen.R.*, Noaḥ, XXXV, 3 *ad fin.* (Th. p. 333, notes; *Aboth* VI, § 9, *P.B.* p. 208).)

To fulfil each precept at its hour and as soon as possible is the delight of the pious:

[358] R. Judah and R. Elazar [b. Shammua'] said: Precious [or lovely] is a command fulfilled at its proper time. (*Sifra* 25 *a*.)

[1] [The reading 'Rabbenu', i.e. R. Judah the Prince, is usually held to be incorrect. It should be Rab, i.e. Abba Arika; Artaban V was the last of the Parthian Kings, who died A.D. 227: he favoured his Jewish subjects. In the parallel *T.J.Pe'ah* I, § 1, f. 15 *d*, line 54 the reading is also wrong, viz. *Rabbenu ha-Ḳadosh*, but it is marginally corrected to Rab (cf. [419]). (H. L.)]

[359] The zealous hasten to fulfil the commandments, as it is said, 'And Abraham rose up early in the morning' [to fulfil God's command] (Gen. XXII, 3). (*Sifra* 58*c* (cp. *Pes.* 4*a*).)

[The Hebrew for 'zealous', *zariz*, is a very strong word, and is even stronger than the English 'zealous' (cp. [218]). This phrase has had much influence in later Judaism. (H. L.)]

[360] R. Josiah said: Just as you must not allow the *mazzah* [unleavened bread] to get sour [i.e. as you must be quick to make the *mazzah* lest it leaven], so you must not let the commandment get sour [by delay]. If a command comes your way, do it at once. (*Mek.*[2], *Pisha*, Bo, § 9, p. 33; *Mek.*[3], vol. I, p. 74.)[1]

It is worth while to accept poverty, and to study and love the Law. One must be ready even for death sooner than abandon the Law:

[361] R. Johanan was going for a walk from Tiberias towards Sepphoris, and R. Ḥiyya b. Abba supported him. They came to a field, and R. Johanan said, 'This field was mine, and I sold it to entitle [enable] me to acquire the Law.' They came to a vineyard and to an olive garden, and R. Johanan said the same. R. Ḥiyya began to weep. 'Why do you weep?' said R. Johanan. R. Ḥiyya said, 'Because you have left nothing for your old age.' Then R. Johanan said, 'Is it a light thing in your eyes what I have done? I have sold what was created in six days, and acquired what was given in forty days, as it is said, "Moses was there with the Lord forty days and forty nights." (Exod. XXXIV, 28).' (*Lev.R.*, Emor, XXX, 1.)

[362] R. Me'ir said: Let a man always have his son taught a decent [respectable] and easy handicraft [or occupation], and pray to Him to whom riches and property belong, for there is no occupation from which poverty or riches may not come; for neither wealth nor poverty comes from the occupation, but all is according to desert. R. Simeon b. Elazar said: Have you ever seen an animal or a bird which has an occupation [craft]? Yet they are nourished without worry; and they have been created only to serve me; how much more should I, who have been created to serve my Maker, be nourished without worry. But I have corrupted my deeds, and I have impaired [injured] my sustenance.

[1] [The saying is based on the fact that *mazzot*, unleavened bread, and *mizwot*, commandments (cp. [753]), have the same consonants. (H. L.)]

R. Nehorai said: I have put aside every occupation in the world, and teach my son nothing but the Law. For the reward [interest] of it a man enjoys in this world, and the capital remains for him in the world to come. It is not so with all other occupations. If a man is sick and old or suffering, he cannot practise his occupation, and he dies of hunger. But the Law keeps a man from all evil in his youth, and gives him hope and an assured outlook in his old age. [This is all from the Mishnah. In the Gemara the words are as follows.] R. Simeon b. Elazar said: In my life I never saw a stag as a dryer of figs, or a lion as a porter, or a fox as a merchant, yet are they all nourished without worry. If they who are created only to serve me are nourished without worry, how much more ought I, who am created to serve my Master, to be nourished without worry, but I have corrupted my ways, and so I have impaired my sustenance.

(*Ḳid.* IV, 14; *Ḳid.* 82*b* (cp. [1223]).)

[363] Ben Azzai said: If any man humiliates himself for the Law, eats dry dates and wears dirty clothes, and sits and keeps guard at the doors of the wise, every passer-by thinks him a fool, but at the end you will find that all the Law is within him.

(*Ab.R.N.* (vers. I), XI, 23*b*.)

[The reading is probably wrong. Dates, even when dried, are far from being a poor man's food. The collocation is unusual, and the word (*ḥarubin*) rendered 'dried' is probably the carob, which was a symbol of poverty, e.g. in *Lev.R.* XXXV, 6, where there is a play on the words *ḥarob*, carob, and *ḥereb*, sword, as in Isa. I, 20, 'Ye shall be made to eat the sword', where probably for 'sword' we should read 'carob' (cp. [253]). (H. L.)]

[364] Moses said to Israel: Know you not with what travail I gained the Torah! What toil, what labour, I endured for its sake. Forty days and forty nights I was with God. I entered among the angels, the Living Creatures, the Seraphim, of whom any one could blast the whole universe in flame. My soul, my blood, I gave for the Torah. As I learnt it in travail, so do you learn it in travail, and as you learn it in travail, so do you teach it in travail. (*Sifre Deut.*, Ha'azinu, § 306, f. 131*b*.)

[365] 'Bless ye the Lord, all ye His angels, mighty in strength, that do His commandments' (Ps. CIII, 20). R. Isaac Nappaḥa said: This refers to those who keep the seventh year. Why is such

a man called 'mighty in strength'? If a man is content without complaint to see his carefully tended field made free to all and sundry, and his trees the property of all who pass by, and his fence broken down and his fruit consumed, and in spite of all this he suppresses his feelings, and does not say a word, because it is the seventh year of release, such a man is angelic in temper and strong, for it is said (*Aboth* IV, 1), 'Who is mighty? He who subdues his evil inclination.' (*Tanḥ.B.*, Wayiḳra, 1*b init.*)

[366] The words of the Torah endure only with him who would suffer death on their behalf. (*Ber.* 63*b.*)

[367] God gives Torah only to him who puts himself in pain for it. (*Tan.d.b.El.* p. 156.)

[368] Our Rabbis have taught: Once the wicked government decreed that Israel should no longer occupy themselves with Torah. Then came Pappos b. Judah (cp. [139]) and found R. Akiba holding great assemblies and studying Torah. He said to him, 'Akiba, are you not afraid of the wicked government?' He replied, 'I will tell you a parable. To what is the matter like? To a fox who was walking along the bank of the stream, and saw some fishes gathering together to move from one place to another. He said to them, "From what are you fleeing?" They answered, "From nets which men are bringing against us." He said to them, "Let it be your pleasure to come up on the dry land, and let us, me and you, dwell together, even as my fathers dwelt with your fathers." They replied, "Are you he of whom they tell that you are the shrewdest of animals? You are not clever, but a fool! For if we are afraid in the place which is our life-element, how much more so in a place which is our death-element!" So also is it with us: If now, while we sit and study Torah, in which it is written, "For that is thy life, and the length of thy days" (Deut. XXX, 20), we are in such a plight, how much more so, if we neglect it.' (**Note 24**.) (*Ber.* 61*b.*)

Let the Law always be fresh, 'like a new enactment which *all* run to read' (*Pes.K.* 102*a*):

[369] 'On this day Israel came to Mount Sinai' (Exod. XIX, 1). Why on *this* day? Because, when thou learnest Torah, let not its commands seem old to thee, but regard them as though the

Torah were given *this* day. Hence it says, 'On *this* day', and not, 'On that day'. (*Tanḥ.B.*, Yitro, 38*b*
(cp. *Sifre Deut.*, Wa'ethanan, § 33, f. 74*a* (H. p. 59).)

The Law's enactments must be, in one sense, *not* an obligation; in another sense, they must be performed, just *because* they are ordered, and *because* you are bidden to fulfil them:

[370] R. Jonathan said that the famous words in Joshua I, 8, 'Thou shalt meditate therein [the Law] day and night,' were not command or obligation, but blessing. They meant that because Joshua loved the words of the Law so much, therefore they should never depart out of his mouth. In the school of R. Ishmael it was taught that 'the words of the Law are not to be unto you an obligation, but, on the other hand, you are not free to dispense yourself from them' (cp. Ṭarfon's saying in *Aboth* II, 21, *P.B.* p. 190, quoted elsewhere [579]). (*Men.* 99*b*.)

[371] R. Ḥanina said: It is finer to do what is commanded than to do the same thing when it is not commanded. (*Ḳid.* 31*a*.)

There may be a sense in which we may honour the divine Lawgiver more by admitting that His injunctions are hard to fulfil, demanding—'costing' as Baron von Hügel would say—our fullest resolution, than by a too ready acceptance, as if we were capable of doing very much more than is asked of us, and as if what was asked of us were so much child's play. Some such idea as this is contained in the following parable.

[372] A king had two servants. He ordered them not to drink wine for thirty days. The one said, 'Why only thirty days? I am ready not to drink it for a year or even for two years.' But in saying this he weakened the words of his master. The other said, 'Can I possibly do without wine even for a single hour?' By saying this he honoured his master.
(*Sifre Deut.*, Wa'ethanan, § 28, f. 71*b* (H. p. 44).)

Help others also to perform the commandments.

[373] R. Elisha b. Abuyah (cp. [469]) said: If a man causes another to do a commandment the Scripture regards him as if he had done it himself. (*Ab.R.N.* (vers. I), XXIV, 39*b*.)

The Law is to be studied and fulfilled for its own sake, but also even not for its own sake!

[374] Who are the true guardians of the city? Not the senators and the chief of the city guard, but the teachers of the Law and the teachers of the Mishnah... God is more lenient towards idolatry, unchastity and murder than towards contempt of the Law. It says in Jer. XVI, 11, 'They have deserted me, and have not kept my Law'; God says, 'Would that they had deserted me, and kept my Law, for if they had occupied themselves with the Law, the leaven [other reading, 'light'] which is in it would have brought them back to me.' That is why R. Huna said: Study the Law even not for its own sake, for through being occupied with the Law, even not for its own sake, you will come to fulfil it for its own sake.

(*Pes.K.* XV, 120*b fin.*–121*a init.* (cp. [340] and [1460]).)

[This passage is a good example of Rabbinic ways of thought, rather than of hyperbole. In Rabbinic homiletics, the preacher is always ready to emphasise the topic with which he is at the moment dealing, even, as it seems to us, to the extent of going beyond his brief. Neither Samuel b. Isaac, nor Huna, and R. Jeremiah who quoted him, would have denied that the three sins mentioned here were cardinal, and if these sins had chanced to be their *theme*, their denunciation would have stigmatised them as the worst man could commit (**Note 84**). But here they happen to be speaking of the Torah, and so neglect of the Torah is put in the limelight. Such rapid changes of thought can be paralleled in biblical style. What we call a 'mixed metaphor' is good Hebrew writing. The Israelites can declare to Moses 'You have caused us to stink in the eyes of Pharaoh.' The late Professor Kennett used to say that the vivid brain of the Hebrew caused him to utilise a metaphor instantaneously, and then drop it: to utilise it twice would have seemed tedious to him. This, I think, explains such a passage as this. One could, of course, point out that, according to the parable, the civic guardians' function is negative, i.e. to suppress breaches of the civil law, while that of the teacher is positive, i.e. to inculcate an active moral attitude, which would so influence public and private life that the need of the guardians would disappear. This almost Pauline sentiment is not excluded here. For 'leaven' see **Note 85**. (H. L.)]

The knowledge or study of the Law, or rather of Torah, divine Revelation, is the true purpose or end of the Israelites' life. But not only must it be *combined* with practice. It needs moral goodness even for its acquisition, and it *promotes* moral goodness. Righteousness and knowledge, in pursuit and in product, are strangely combined and intertwined with one another. Thus we read:

[375] The Torah is greater than the priesthood and than royalty,

seeing that royalty demands thirty qualifications [see *Sanhedrin*, ch. ii], the priesthood twenty-four [see *Baba Ḳamma*, 110*b*, and *Mid. Tanḥuma*, section *Bemidbar*], while the Torah is acquired by forty-eight. And these are they: By audible study; by distinct pronunciation; by understanding and discernment of the heart; by awe, reverence, meekness, cheerfulness; by ministering to the sages, by attaching oneself to colleagues, by discussion with disciples; by sedateness; by knowledge of the Scripture and of the Mishnah; by moderation in business, in intercourse with the world, in pleasure, in sleep, in conversation, in laughter; by long-suffering; by a good heart; by faith in the wise; by resignation under chastisement; by recognising one's place, rejoicing in one's portion, putting a fence to one's words, claiming no merit for oneself; by being beloved, loving the All-present, loving mankind, loving just courses, rectitude and reproof; by keeping oneself far from honour, not boasting of one's learning, or delighting in giving decisions; by bearing the yoke with one's fellow, judging him favourably, and leading him to truth and peace; by being composed in one's study; by asking and answering, hearing and adding thereto [by one's own reflection]; by learning with the object of teaching, and by learning with the object of practising; by making one's master wiser, fixing attention upon his discourse, and reporting a thing in the name of him who said it. (*Aboth* VI, 6; *P.B.* pp. 206–7.)

[376] R. Ḥanina b. Dosa said: He in whom the fear of sin comes before wisdom, his wisdom will endure; but he in whom wisdom comes before the fear of sin, his wisdom will not endure.

(*Aboth* III, 11 (cp. [466]).)

[377] It is as though a man went into a shop, and asked for a pint of wine. The shopkeeper says to him, 'Give me your vessel.' But the man opens his bag. Then he says to the shopkeeper, 'Give me some oil.' When the shopkeeper asks for the vessel, he offers the corner of his garment. The shopkeeper says to him: 'You have not got a vessel, and yet you want to buy wine and oil.' So God says to the wicked: 'You are destitute of good deeds, yet you want to learn Torah. My statutes you keep not; how then would you talk of them?' (Ps. L, 16).

(*Ab.R.N.* (vers. II), XXXII, 35*a*.)

[378] R. Me'ir said: Whosoever labours in the Torah for its own sake merits many things; and not only so, but the whole world is indebted to him: he is called friend, beloved, a lover of the All-present, a lover of mankind; it clothes him in meekness and reverence: it fits him to become just, pious, upright and faithful; it keeps him far from sin, and brings him near to virtue. R. Joshua b. Levi said: No man is free, but he who labours in the Torah. (*Aboth* VI, 1, 2; *P.B.* p. 204.)

[379] This is the way that is becoming for the study of the Torah: a morsel of bread with salt thou must eat, and water by measure thou must drink, thou must sleep upon the ground, and live a life of trouble, the while thou toilest in the Torah. If thou doest thus, 'Happy shalt thou be and it shall be well with thee' (Ps. CXXVIII, 2); happy shalt thou be in this world, and it shall be well with thee in the world to come. Seek not greatness for thyself, and crave not honour more than is due to thy learning; and desire not the table of kings, for thy table is greater than theirs, and thy crown greater than theirs; and faithful is He, the master of thy work, to pay thee the reward of thy labour.
(*Aboth* VI, 4, 5; *P.B.* pp. 205–6 (cp. ed. Herford, p. 155; cp. [1380]).)

[380] 'Wisdom cannot be found in the land of the living' (Job XXVIII, 13). This cannot be taken literally, for is Torah to be found in the land of the dead? Therefore 'living' must mean 'good living', 'luxury'. The Torah is not to be found with him who seeks the lusts of the world, pleasure, glory, greatness in this world, only with him who kills himself, so far as living in this world is concerned, as it says, 'This is the Law, if a man dies' (Num. XIX, 14). (*Tanḥ.*, Noaḥ, § 3, f. 15*b*.)

[381] The right character for a scholar is to be modest and humble, eager and bright, submissive, beloved by all, gentle to the members of his household, sin-fearing, judging everyone according to his deeds. He should say: 'I have no pleasure in the things of this world, for it does not concern me.' Let him sit at the feet of the wise, and let no one perceive in him an evil quality. Let him ask aptly and answer properly. (*Der.Er.Z.* I, I.)

Choose Torah rather than riches.

[382] R. Jose b. Ḳisma said: I was once walking by the way, when

a man met me and saluted me, and I returned the salutation. He said to me, 'Rabbi, from what place art thou?' I said to him, 'I come from a great city of sages and scribes.' He said to me, 'If thou art willing to dwell with us in our place, I will give thee a thousand thousand golden dinars and precious stones and pearls.' I said to him, 'Wert thou to give me all the silver and gold and precious stones and pearls in the world, I would not dwell anywhere but in a home of the Torah'; and thus it is written in the book of Psalms by the hands of David, King of Israel, 'The law of thy mouth is better unto me than thousands of gold and silver' (Ps. CXIX, 72); and not only so, but in the hour of man's departure neither silver nor gold, nor precious stones nor pearls accompany him, but only Torah and good works, as it is said, 'When thou walkest, it shall lead thee; when thou liest down, it shall watch over thee; and when thou awakest, it shall talk with thee' (Prov. VI, 22); when thou walkest, it shall lead thee—in this world; when thou liest down, it shall watch over thee—in the grave; and when thou awakest, it shall talk with thee—in the world to come. (*Aboth* VI, 9; *P.B.* p. 208.)

[383] Words of Torah are like golden vessels, the more you scour them and rub them, the more they glisten and reflect the face of him who looks at them. So with the words of Torah, whenever you repeat them, they glisten and lighten the face, as it says, 'The Commandment of the Lord is pure, enlightening the eyes.' But if you neglect them, they become like vessels of glass which are easily broken, as it says, 'Gold and glass cannot be put side by side' (Job XXVIII, 17) [A.V. 'The gold and the crystal cannot equal it,' i.e. equal wisdom]. (*Ab.R.N.* (vers. II), XXXI, 34*b*.)

[384] Words of Torah are compared with garments of delicate wool, which are not quickly acquired, but are speedily torn. So, words of Torah are hard to acquire, but easy to lose. Words of foolishness, on the other hand, are like sackcloth, easy to buy, but not easy to tear. So words of folly are easy to acquire and hard to lose. (*Ab.R.N.* (vers. II), XXXI, 34*b*.)

It is no easy thing to acquire, or to keep one's hold on, Torah.

[385] As a man has to take heed of his money that it should not be lost, so must he take heed of what he has learnt so that it should not be lost. As silver is hard to acquire, so are the words of the

Torah hard to acquire. Moreover, if they are hard to acquire like silver and gold, it is also easy to lose them, as it is easy to lose vessels of glass. (Cp. Bacher, *Agada der Tannaiten*, II, 21 and I, 298, ed. 2.)

(*Sifre Deut.*, 'Eḳeb, § 48, f. 83*b* (Hd. p. 108).)

Torah is all sufficient for man:

[386] Ben Bag Bag said: Turn it [the Torah], and turn it over again, for everything is in it, and contemplate it, and wax grey and old over it, and stir not from it, for thou canst have no better rule than this. Ben He He said: According to the labour is the reward.

(*Aboth* V, 25, 26; *P.B.* p. 204.)

The Rabbinic idea of a friend is a companion who studies the Law with you:

[387] A companion can be gained only with the greatest difficulty. Hence they say, 'Let a man gain a companion for himself, one who will read with him, learn with him, eat and drink with him, and share his secrets, for two are better than one' (Eccles. IV, 9).

(*Sifre Deut.*, Niẓẓabim, § 305, f. 129*b*.)

To study Torah is good; to teach it is a grade yet higher. Even so, to fulfil a command is good; to cause another to fulfil it is a grade yet higher:

[388] 'He has despised the word of the Lord' (Num. XV, 31). R. Me'ir said: This is the man who studies [the Torah], but does not teach it to others. R. Nathan said: This is he who could study the Law, but does not.

(*Sifre Num.*, Shelaḥ, § 112, f. 33*a* (H. p. 121).)

[389] If a man teaches the son of his fellow-student the Torah, the Scripture accounts it to him as if he had created him. R. Elazar says: As if he had created the Law itself. For if a man induces his fellow to fulfil a *miẓwah* (cp. [753]), it is reckoned to him as if he had done it himself.... He who endures hunger for the Law in this world shall be satisfied in the world to come. (**Note 25**.)

(*San.* 99*b*, 100*a*.)

[390] R. Johanan said: He who learns the Torah, and does not teach it, is like a myrtle in the desert. But some say, He who learns

the Torah, and teaches it in a place where there is no learned man, is like a myrtle in the wilderness, for it is beloved there.

(*R.H.* 23*a*.)

[391] 'I hate them that are of a double mind' (Ps. CXIX, 113). These are they who ponder over the fear of God because of their sufferings, but not from love. David said, 'I am not like them; not from compulsion, or from fear, but from love, do I fulfil thy commands,' as it says, 'Thy law do I love. I hate what thou hatest; I love what thou lovest. An earthly ruler publishes his decrees, and all obey them, but though they obey them, they do so out of fear only; but I am not so: from love of the Law I fulfil the Law.' (*Midr.Ps.* on CXIX, 113 (250*a*, §46).)

We might feel that if David had said that, he would have been very self-righteous. But we must remember that it is not David who is really speaking; it is the Rabbis who use him for the purpose of putting forth their ideals of morality and religion (cp. Abraham's remark in [613]).

[392] David said, 'O how I love thy Law' (Ps. CXIX, 97). It is always with me. I have not neglected it at all. And because I have not neglected it, it has been to me not a burden, but a song (cp. Ps. CXIX, 54; *R.T.* p. 240). 'Thy commandments are ever mine' (Ps. CXIX, 98), because I have not busied myself with other books, but only with thy Law. The Law may be compared with a jar full of honey; if you pour water into it, the honey trickles out. So, if you let other things enter your heart, the words of the Law go out. (*Midr.Ps.* on CXIX, 97 (249*b*, §41).)

[393] Rab quoted the verse, 'Make known to me mine end and the measure of my days, and what time I have here' (Ps. XXXIX, 4). David said to God, 'Tell me my end' [i.e. when I shall die]. God replied, 'It is my decree not to make known to man his end.' David said, 'Tell me the number of my days.' God said, 'It is my decree that the number should not be made known to man.' Then David said, 'Tell me on what day I shall die.' God said, 'Thou shalt die on a Sabbath.' David said, 'Let me die the day after a Sabbath.' God said, 'The kingdom of Solomon, thy son, has drawn nigh, and one kingdom cannot delay another kingdom even by a hair.' David said, 'Then may I die on the eve of Sabbath?' God said, 'A day in thy courts is better than a thousand elsewhere. A single day which thou spendest in the study of

the Torah is better to me than all the burnt offerings which Solomon will offer upon the altar.' So David sat every Sabbath, and studied the Torah all the day. On the day when his soul was to go to its rest, the angel of death came, but could do nothing with him because his mouth never ceased from studying. Then the angel of death said, 'What am I to do?' There was a garden behind David's house, so the angel went and shook the trees. David got up to look, and ascended the stairs, which broke under him, and he became silent, and his soul passed to its rest.

(*Sab.* 30*a fin.*–30*b init.*)

None can be excused from the study of the Law on the score of poverty or wealth. David again can be an example:

[394] The dawn did not find David sleeping, as it says, 'Awake my honour [A.V. glory: the word is often used in the Psalms to mean 'soul', e.g. XXX, 12], awake psaltery and harp; I myself will awake early' (Ps. LVII, 8); that is, 'Awake, my honour, before the honour of my Creator; my honour is nothing before His honour; therefore I awake the morning, and the morning does not awake me.' R. Phinehas said in the name of R. Elazar b. Menahem: There was a harp under David's head, and he arose and played upon it in the nights. R. Levi said that the harp hung over his bed, and when midnight came, and the north wind blew on it, the harp played by itself, and when David heard it, he arose and occupied himself with [i.e. studied] the Law, and when the Israelites heard the voice of David busying himself with the Law, they said, 'If King David busies himself with the Law, how much more must we.' And they did so.

(*Lam.R.* II, 22, on II, 19.)

The Rabbis did not encourage their disciples to study anything beside the beloved Torah. [But see H. L.'s note on p. 145.]

[395] 'And thou shalt speak of them when thou liest down, etc.' (Deut. VI, 7). That is, make them the principal thing, and not a bywork [a *parergon*] so that all your business may be with them, and that you do not mix up other things with them, or say, 'I have learnt the wisdom of Israel; now I will go and learn the wisdom of the nations of the world.'

(*Sifre Deut.*, Wa'etḥanan, § 34, f. 74*a fin.* (Hd. p. 61 *fin.*; cp. [1232]).)

[The end of [394] needs qualification. It is hardly accurate to say that study other than Torah was *quod nunquam, quod nusquam, quod a nullis*. Greek learning, for example, was sometimes deprecated, sometimes encouraged. It is not to be expected that when Antiochus Epiphanes was using every effort to destroy Judaism, Greek learning would be favoured, since at that time circumstances made the two antithetical and even mutually incompatible; when the High Priest himself changed his Hebrew name for a Greek one and, in addition, sent a deputation to sacrifice to Herakles, it was obvious that to a loyal Jew, anything Greek was, *eo ipso*, anti-Jewish. Hellenisation stood for apostasy. Thus, the 'thick darkness' which fell on Abraham (Gen. XV, 12) was interpreted to mean Greece, 'which darkened the eyes of Israel with her decrees, saying to Israel "write ye on the bull's horn (said to be a Seleucid emblem) that ye have no part in Israel's God"' (*Gen.R.*, Bereshit, II, 4 (Th. p. 16): also XLIV, 17 (Th. p. 440 n.) etc.). At other times, Greek learning might be considered less deadly, merely useless. Thus, when R. Joshua was asked whether it was desirable for a man to teach his son Greek, he replied 'in the time when it is neither day nor night, for "thou shalt meditate in it [the Torah] day and night" (Josh. I, 8)' (*T.J.Soṭ.* IX, § 16, f. 24*c*, line 8). He does not say that to study Greek was treachery, he implies that it was a waste of time. Yet the Gemara will not have this: it continues 'you might say the same of any occupation'. A grudging tolerance for Greek is noticeable in connection with the Septuagint (or other Bible translations), though there were those who deemed that its appearance would be prejudicial to Hebrew. *Meg.* 8*b*, 9*a*, also *Mishnah* I, 8, would imply that even in Palestine non-Hebrew-speaking Jewish communities read the Scriptures in Greek, no other language but Greek being a permissible substitute for Hebrew (see Rabbinowitz, ed. of *Mishnah Meg.* p. 63). Gradually Greek came into its own. Greek was an 'adornment' in a girl's education (*T.J.Sab.* VI, § 3, 7*d*, line 58). But it is doubtful whether 'Books of Homer' is correct in *Yadayim* IV, 6 (**Note 20*j***). Finally, Judah the Prince, who was a good Greek scholar, went so far as to say that there was no room for Aramaic or Syriac in Palestine, either Hebrew or Greek should be spoken (*Bab.Ḳ.* 83*a*, top) (see **Note 63**). Other evidence could be cited, but enough has been given for the present. For an objection to Greek, on the ground that the Gentiles—i.e. Christians—translated the Scriptures into Greek and thereby claimed to be the true Israel, see *Pes.R.* 14*b* and *Tanḥ.*, Wayera, § 5, 33*a*.

In early Christianity, as in Judaism, philosophy was sometimes deprecated and regarded as superfluous or even as directly antithetical to religion; here, also, it had to fight for recognition. For this parallel, I am indebted to the Rev. W. L. Knox. He says: 'Clement of Alexandria, *Stromata*, Book I, is mainly a defence of philosophy and a plea for the study of Greek letters—especially ch. 2. For the opposite view, see Tertullian, *De Praescriptione Hereticorum*, 6–9. See for the whole subject, Harnack, *Mission und Ausbreitung des Christentums*, ed. 1902, f. 161 ff. Clement is interesting, since he differentiates literature from pure philosophy. For the view of the ordinary Christian, Origen, *c. Celsum* (cited in Harnack), is important.' (H. L.)]

[396] Let not a man withdraw himself from the house of study and from the words of the Law, even up to and at the hour of his death.... The words of the Law abide only with him who gives his life for them. (*Sab.* 83*b fin.* (cp. [332]).)

[397] The poor who study the Law are richly rewarded after death by God. Why are they poor in this world? So that they may not occupy themselves with vain things and forget the Torah, for one must neglect one's business and occupy oneself in the Torah, for the Torah goes before everything (*Midr.Ps.* on v, 1 (26*a*, §3)). So it is said that the poor, the rich and the wicked [here equivalent to the rake] come to the judgment. They ask the poor man why he has not occupied himself with the Law. If he says, 'I was poor, and I was busy in getting my livelihood,' they say, 'Were you poorer than Hillel?' (For they tell of Hillel that he used to gain by work a *stater* a day, and half of it he gave to the porter at the house of study, and half he used for his own maintenance and that of his family. One day he had earned nothing, and the porter would not let him in. So he climbed up, and sat by the edge of the window on the roof, so that he might hear the words of the living God from the mouth of Shemaiah and Abtalion. And it happened that it was a Friday in winter, and the snow from the sky fell upon him. At the break of dawn, Shemaiah said to Abtalion, 'My brother, usually it is light; to-day it is dark; perhaps the day is cloudy.' They looked up, and saw the shape of a man against the window, and they found three cubits of snow upon him. They took off the snow, and washed him, and anointed him, and put him by the fire, for they said, 'He is worthy that the Sabbath be profaned for his sake.') They ask the rich man, 'Why did you not occupy yourself with the Law?' If he says, 'I was rich, and I was busy with my possessions,' they say, 'Were you richer than R. Elazar?' (For they say of R. Elazar b. Ḥarsom that his father left him a thousand cities on the land and a thousand ships on the sea. Every day he took a sack of meal upon his shoulder, and went from city to city to

study the Law. Once his own slaves found him, and made him do forced service. Then he said to them, 'I beseech you set me free that I may go and study the Law.' They said, 'By the life of R. Elazar b. Ḥarsom we will not let you go.' For he never saw them in his life, but was always day and night studying the Torah.) They ask the rake, 'Why did you not occupy yourself with the Torah?' If he answers, 'I was beautiful, and I was pressed by my *yetzer*,' they say, 'Were you more beautiful than Joseph?' (For the wife of Potiphar sought daily to persuade him with words; she put on fresh garments by day and by night; she said to him, 'Yield to me.' He refused. She said, 'I will put you in prison.' He said, 'The Lord sets free the prisoners.' She said, 'I will crush you.' He said, 'The Lord lifts up the bowed.' She said, 'I will blind you.' He said, 'The Lord opens the eyes of the blind.' Then she offered him a thousand talents of silver that he might yield to her, 'to lie by her and to be with her' (Gen. XXXIX, 10), but he would not yield. He would not be with her in this world, so as not to have to be with her in the world to come.) Thus Hillel accuses the poor, R. Elazar the rich, and Joseph the rakes. (*Yoma* 35*b*.)

[398] R. Judah b. R. Ilai said: Come and see that the later generations are not like the former generations. The former generations made their Torah their principal concern and their work only occasional, and both flourished in their hand; whereas the later generations made their work their principal concern and their Torah only occasional, and neither flourished in their hand. (*Ber.* 35*b*.)

Yet it is said that a certain caution is required. The Law, falsely studied, may lead to heresy and death:

[399] Raba said: For those who make a right use of the Law, it is a drug for life; for those who make a wrong use, it is a drug for death. (*Sab.* 88*b* (cp. [332]).)

[400] A disciple of the wise [i.e. a man of learning], whose inside is not as his outside, is no disciple of the wise: he is an abomination. Woe to the disciples of the wise who occupy themselves with the Torah, but have no fear of God. Woe to him who has no house, but makes a door for it. R. Joshua b. Levi said: Is his intent pure [be he worthy], the Law is made for him a medicine of life: if it is not, it is made for him a medicine of death. Resh

Laḳish said, in reference to Ps. XIX, 9: 'The word of the Lord is pure': if his intent is pure, the Law purifies him to life; if his intent is not pure, it purifies him to death. (*Yoma* 72*b*.)

The Rabbis knew well enough that many of the enactments of the Law were the subject of Gentile ridicule. The law of circumcision, for example, which to them was so precious and divine (they knew nothing of its true origin, or of its wide diffusion among many savage races, and they believed implicitly in the account of its origin as given in Genesis), was laughed at by the cultivated Hellenists and Romans. The same was the case with many other enactments, some of which, even to the Rabbis themselves, may have seemed (like the law of the Red Cow) to bear a resemblance to the customs of the heathen. They, therefore, invented the theory that certain ceremonial enactments of the Law were just arbitrary rules of God, which the Israelites must obey without criticism. The general purpose of these enactments *was* indeed to induce unquestioning obedience: secondly, they tended to discipline and self-control and purification: any criticism of them, any questioning, destroyed their effect and was rebellion against God. For such an enactment the technical term was *ḥuḳḳah* or *ḥoḳ*, rendered by 'statute' in A.V. and R.V. See *Num.R.* XIX, 5, 'I have ordained a statute,'...'There are four things to which *ḥuḳḳah*, rule without a reason, is applied' (cp. [405] ff.):

[401] 'The Rock, his work is perfect; all his ways are just; a God of faithfulness' (Deut. XXXII, 4). His work is perfect in regard to all who come into the world; and one must not at all criticise His ways, and a man must not ponder, and say, 'If I had three eyes or three hands or three feet, if I could walk on my head, if I had eyes at my back, how nice it would be.' He is a God of justice: He judges each one justly and gives him his due: a God of faithfulness; He had faith in the world and so He created it; for He did not create men that they should be wicked, but that they should be righteous, as it is said, 'God made man upright, but they sought out many inventions' (Eccles. VII, 29 (cp. [93])). (*Sifre Deut.*, Ha'azinu, § 307, f. 132*b*.)

[402] It often says in the Law, 'Take,' 'And ye shall take,' as, for example, 'And they shall take a red heifer' (Num. XIX, 2). Do you think it is for my sake? No, it is for your sakes, to purify you....And it says, 'And thou shalt take thee pure olive oil beaten for the light, to cause the lamp to burn always' (Exod. XXVII, 20). Do I need your light? Does it not say, 'Light dwells with Him' (Dan. II, 22)? But it is to purify you, and to atone for your

souls, which are compared to a light, as it is said, 'A light of the Lord is the soul of man' (Prov. xx, 27).

(*Lev.R.*, Emor, xxx, 13 (cp. [1050]).)

[403] What does God care whether a man kills an animal in the proper way and eats it, or whether he strangles the animal and eats it? Will the one benefit Him, or the other injure Him? Or what does God care whether a man eats unclean animals or clean animals? 'If thou art wise, for thyself art thou wise, but if thou scornest, thou alone shalt bear it' (Prov. ix, 12). So thou learnest that the Commandments were given only to purify God's creatures, as it says, 'God's word is purified, it is a protection to those who trust in Him' (II Sam. xxii, 31). (*Tanḥ.B.*, Shemini, 15*b*.)

[404] Rab said: The commandments were given to Israel only in order that men should be purified through them. For what can it matter to God whether a beast is slain at the throat or at the neck? (**Note 56**.) (*Gen.R.*, Lek leka, xliv, 1 and *Lev.R.*, Shemini, xiii, 3 (Th. pp. 424, 425).)

[405] In one passage it is said that there are four enactments concerning which the Evil Inclination (*Yetzer ha-Ra'*) makes objections, namely, *yibbum* [levirate marriage], linen and woollen (Deut. xxii, 11), the scapegoat and the red heifer. Yet each of them is called a statute (cp. [401]). Then the passage adds: God said to Moses, The reasons for my Law I will reveal to *you*, but to others it is a statute [i.e. it must be obeyed without criticism]. But the things which are hidden from you in this world will be revealed to you in the world to come.

(*Pes.R.* 64*a* (cp. *Pes.K.* 38*b fin.*–39*a* and Moore, iii, 85).)

[406] It says in Lev. xviii, 4, 'Ye shall observe my judgments and execute my statutes.' The Rabbis teach: 'My judgments'; these are the things which, if they had not been written, would have had to be written, such as idolatry, unchastity, bloodshed, robbery, blasphemy. 'My statutes'; these are the things to which Satan and the Gentiles raise objections, such as not eating pig, not wearing linen and woollen together, the law of *ḥaliẓah* (Deut. xxv, 5–10), the scapegoat. Should you say, 'These are empty things,' the Scripture adds, 'I am the Lord, I have made decrees; you are not at liberty to criticise them.'

(*Yoma* 67*b* (cp. *Sifra* 86*a*).)

In the *Sifra* parallel the Evil Inclination is put instead of Satan.

The reply of R. Johanan b. Zakkai to the argument of the heathen critic became famous.

[407] A heathen said to R. Johanan b. Zakkai, 'What you do [in the matter of the Red Cow] looks like sorcery. You take a red cow and kill it, and burn the corpse, and crush its ashes, and take (care of) them, and if one of you becomes unclean by touching a dead body, you sprinkle upon the man two or three drops of the water into which the ashes have been cast, and you say to him, "You are clean."' R. Johanan said to him, 'Has the demon of madness ever entered into you?' He said, 'No.' 'Have you ever seen a man into whom that demon had entered?' He said, 'Yes.' 'What do they do to him?' He replied, 'They take roots, and make a smoke underneath the man, and sprinkle water on him, and the demon flies away from him.' R. Johanan said, 'Let your ears hear what your mouth has said [i.e. you are condemned out of your own mouth]. This spirit was a spirit of uncleanness, as it is said, "I will cause the unclean spirit to pass out of the land" (Zech. XIII, 2). They sprinkle upon him the "waters of separation" (Num. XIX, 21), and the unclean spirit flies away.' When the heathen had gone, his disciples said to R. Johanan, 'You drove off this man with a reed [i.e. you gave him an inadequate answer], what do you say to us?' He said, 'The dead body does not really defile; the water does not really purify; but God has said, I have ordained an ordinance, I have decreed a decree; it is not permitted to you to transgress it.'

(*Num.R.*, Ḥuḳḳat, XIX, 8.)

Thus superstition is avoided and magic too. These laws are just simply the inscrutable and mysterious will of the perfect God.

[408] It is written, 'This is an ordinance of the Law' (Num. XIX, 2). Who has made it? Who has ordered it? Who has decreed it? Is it not the Unique Only One of the world? And He has said, 'I have enjoined an ordinance; I have decreed a decree; it is not permitted to you to transgress my decree.'

(*Num.R.*, Ḥuḳḳat, XIX, 1.)

Playing upon Eccles. II, 12, the Rabbis say that Solomon, in his old age, exclaimed, 'When I argued subtly about the words of the Law, and sought to prove to myself that I knew the reasons of the Law, my knowledge and understanding became "madness and folly", for who is he who is permitted to criticise the ways of God?... Because I criticised His ways, I stumbled and fell.' In the same way, the Rabbis remarked about Exod. v, 23, where Moses complains to God that since he (Moses) had begun to announce God's words to Pharaoh, the servitude of the Israelites had become worse, and no deliverance had come.

[409] Moses began to argue about God's decisions, and to contend with God, and to criticise His ways....Therefore the Attribute of Justice sought to punish Moses, but when God reflected that it was because of Israel's distress that Moses spoke thus, God dealt with him according to His Attribute of Mercy. The Rabbis also point out that Abraham, Isaac and Jacob, in spite of many trials, did not 'criticise God's ways'; they did not do so, even though God did not reveal Himself to them by His true name of Yahweh, the Merciful One, as He revealed Himself to Moses. They did not even ask God what His name was, as Moses had asked Him (Exod. III, 13). And, later, when God said that He had hearkened to the groaning of the children of Israel, this was because they had not criticised Him.

(*Exod.R.*, Wa'era, VI, 1–4.)

[410] R. Simeon b. Azzai said: Notice that in all the ordinances in the Law about sacrifices, the terms 'God', or 'thy God', or 'Almighty' or 'Sabaoth' are not employed, but only 'Yahweh' [the Lord], so as not to give an opening to the heretics to mock. And notice that the words 'sweet savour unto the Lord' are used equally in the case of an ox or a sheep or a bird, to show you that the big and the little sacrifice are equal before God, for before Him is no eating or drinking, but He has ordained, and we must execute His will.

(*Sifre Num.*, Pineḥas, § 143, f. 54*a* (H. p. 191).)

The view that the Commandments are God's arbitrary ukases tended to destroy superstition, cp. [404]. It was not the ceremonies which produced certain results; it was *God* who produced them.

The Day of Atonement is a divine ordinance. But behind it is God. In the last resort, it is not the *Day* (cp. [837]) which purifies Israel, and so causes the divine forgiveness, but *God* Himself who purifies and forgives. Thus the tractate of the Mishnah on the Day of Atonement ends fitly with the words:

[411] R. Akiba said: Blessed are ye, O Israel. Before whom are ye made clean, and who makes you clean? Your Father in heaven;

as it is written, 'And I will sprinkle clean water upon you and ye shall be clean' (Ezek. XXXVI, 25). And again it says, 'O Lord the hope [*miḳweh*] of Israel' (Jer. XVII, 13)—as the *miḳweh* cleanses the unclean, so does the Holy One, blessed be He, cleanse Israel. [A play upon words. *Miḳweh* means also the 'Immersion-pool' prescribed for the cleansing of those who contract [ceremonial] uncleanness.]

(*Yoma* VIII, 9 (Professor Danby's translation, p. 172).)

I would like to quote here some excellent passages from Moore which bear upon the Rabbinic view of the 'ceremonial' portion of the Law.

'The Jewish teachers recognised the distinction between acts which the common conscience of mankind condemns as morally wrong and such as are wrong only because they are made so by statute; but the former are not the more properly sin because of their moral quality nor the latter less so because in themselves they are morally indifferent. The sin is in either case the same, violation of the revealed will of God' (vol. I, p. 462), cp. [401].

'In the logic of a revealed religion—Judaism is not peculiar in this respect—the ground of obligation is the will of God as known through revelation; moral precepts have not an independent ground of obligation in what we call ethical principles. The religious man believes that in giving those particular statutes for which he discerns no rational or moral reason God was actuated by a wisdom and goodness that pass our understanding; he does not exempt himself from them because of the limitations of his own understanding' (vol. III, p. 142).

'The Scripture gives no warrant whatever for dividing the law into ceremonial and moral, and attributing to the latter perpetuity and superior obligation, while regarding the former as of less moment in the eyes of God, and negligence in the observance of it as a venial offence on the part of men. Jewish teachers were quite aware of the intrinsic difference between laws which the common intelligence and conscience of mankind recognise apart from revelation, things which "if they were not written in the law would on grounds of reason have to be written"—idolatry, incest, homicide, robbery, blasphemy—and such laws as the prohibition of eating pork, or wearing garments of linsey-woolsey (Deut. XXII, 11; Lev. XIX, 19), loosing the shoe in the refusal of levirate marriage (Deut. XXV, 7–10), the ritual of purification of the leper (Lev. XIV) and the scapegoat (Lev. XVI), which men might be tempted to call futile performances.... That is the logical attitude of a revealed religion. Its observances—the ceremonial law in the widest extension of the term—are statutory. It is not for man to cavil about its prescriptions or interdictions, or to exempt himself from any of them because he can discover no rational or moral ground for them. It should be observed also that what we call the moral law is delivered in statutory form, and that its obligation in such a religion rests, not on the consensus of men, however unanimous, that certain acts are intrinsically right and others wrong, but on the fact that they are commanded or forbidden by divine law. Obedience to God's law in its entirety is the supreme *moral* obligation of man, irrespective of the subject matter of the particular article. The modern distinction of duties to God as *religious* obligations, and those to our fellow men or in our personal conduct as *moral* obligations, is, from the point of view of revealed religion, a false division of an indivisible unity. Even ignorant or inadvertent deviations from the law are offences which demand expiation, while knowingly and purposely to violate it is to "throw off the yoke" of the sovereign whose will it is —to rebel against God' (vol. II, pp. 6–8).

'In a revealed religion which includes both kinds of duties or prohibitions the ground of obligation is the same for both, namely that thus and so is the revealed will of God. The gravity of the offence in case of neglect or transgression is dependent not on our natural notions, but upon revelation, which affixes the doom of extirpation not solely to vile crimes such as incest, but to eating flesh with a remainder of blood in it or the suet of certain animal kinds. It belonged to the Jewish faith in God's wisdom and goodness to believe that in prohibiting the flesh of a "hare" and in similar cases for which there was no reason apparent to men, God had reasons which were beyond human understanding, but that all such things were ordered for the good of his people' (vol. III, p. 167).

It is very satisfactory to note that the Rabbis had freed themselves from all sacerdotalism. The rules about priests had to be maintained, because they were in the Law, but it was God who blessed Israel: there was no mediation through priests.

[412] When God ordered Aaron and his sons, 'Thus shall *ye* bless the children of Israel' (Num. VI, 23), the Israelites said, 'Lord of the world, thou biddest the priests to bless us; we need *thy* blessing only, and to be blessed from *thy* mouth.' God said, 'Even though I have told the priests to bless you, I stand by you, and bless you with them.' Therefore the priests spread out their hands to indicate that God stands behind them. (*Num.R.*, Naso, XI, 2.)

[413] It says at the end of the priestly benediction, 'And it is I that will bless them' (Num. VI, 27). One might think that if the priests choose to bless the Israelites, then they are blessed, and if they do not choose, they are not blessed. Therefore it says, 'And it is *I* that will bless them. *I* will bless my people.'[1]

(*Num.R.*, Naso, XI, 8.)

[1] In the Hebrew, the 'I' is a special pronoun and emphatic. To the Rabbis, this added pronoun was of great significance, ethically as well as grammatically.

Similarly:

[414] 'And *I* will bless them' (Num. VI, 27). These words are added so that the Israelites should not think that their blessings [i.e. the divine benedictions] depend on their priests, and so that the priests should not say, 'It is we who bless Israel.'

(*Sifre Num.*, Naso, § 43, f. 13*b* (H. p. 49).)

A bad priest has no value or power.

[415] When Torah issues from the priests' mouth, then God speaks of them as if they were angels of the service (Mal. II, 7), but when Torah does not issue from their mouths, then they are as wild animals, and as beasts which do not know their owner.

(*Sifre Num.*, Koraḥ, § 119, f. 39*b* (H. p. 143).)

In fact, the foregoing refers to Israel who, just before the passage cited, are likened to priests on the basis of Isa. LXI, 6 (**Note 42**).

[416] 'My beloved gazes through the windows; he peeps through the lattices' (Cant. II, 9). That is God, who gazes through the shoulders, and between the fingers, of the priests. 'My beloved speaks unto me': God says, 'The Lord bless thee and keep thee.'

(*Pes.R.* 72*a fin.*)

[The number and position of the extended fingers was of very considerable importance. According to Jewish custom, the five fingers of both hands were raised, the two hands being placed side by side and the ten fingers paired, so as to form five groups. In Sabazios worship, two fingers of one hand were raised. Gressmann and Oesterley hold that some Jews succumbed to this cult. In Christianity, the *Benedictio Latina* was a symbol of the Trinity: in it, the thumb and first two fingers of the right hand were raised. In the *Benedictio Graeca*, the third finger was turned down, with the thumb crossed over it, the other three fingers being held up. Some excellent pictures of the Sabazios hand are given by Oesterley (pp. 139 ff. of *The Labyrinth*, S. H. Hooke, London, 1935). The attention of scholars may well be directed to this controversial and interesting subject. For the extension of the fingers of the priests—through which the Shechinah 'peeps'—see *Sot.* 39*b* and *Pes.K.* 49*a*. For the use of the right hand in the paternal blessing, see *Midr. Sekel Ṭob*, p. 308, on Gen. XLVIII, 14. For the custom—said to be a mark of the unintelligent—of using one hand only, see the remarks in the *Derek ha-Ḥayyim* P.B. (the pagination differs in the various editions: the passage will be found after the Friday evening service, before the formula of blessing) and, above all, Rabbi Gaguine's excellent essay on the whole question, in his *Keter Shem Ṭob*, p. 212 (London, 1934). (H. L.)]

[417] God says, 'In this world, in the chapter of the red heifer, you are made clean and are purified by the mouth of the priest' (Num. XIX, 7–9). But in the world to come it shall not be so. Then God Himself will purify you from all your sins and impurities, as it says, 'And I will sprinkle over you clean water, and cleanse you from all your sins and impurities, and from all your defilement will I purify you' (Ezek. XXXVI, 25). (*Pes.R.* 66*a*.)

All are equal before the Law:

[418] 'Ye shall diligently keep all these commandments' (Deut. XI, 22). All are equal before the Law. The duty of observance is for all. For the Law is 'the inheritance of the congregation of Jacob' (Deut. XXXIII, 4). It does not say 'priests' or 'Levites' or 'Israelites', but 'the congregation of Jacob'.

(*Sifre Deut.*, 'Eḳeb, § 48, f. 84*b* (cp. [1570]; Hd. p. 112).)

[419] 'Let my doctrine drop as rain' (Deut. XXXII, 2). R. Judah used to say: Ever let a man gather words of Torah in mass, but give them out in details, like dew-drops, which are smaller than raindrops (Deut. XXXII, 2), like showers upon the grass (*ib.*) which come down and permeate the grass, so as to prevent it from rotting. So you permeate yourself with words of Torah, lest you forget them. So used R. Jacob b. Ḥanina to say to Rabbi: Come, let us permeate ourselves with *Halakot*, lest they get rusty, and just as showers permeate the grass and enrich it, so let us stuff ourselves with words of Torah, and rehearse them thrice and four times (cp. [498]).

(*Sifre Deut.*, Ha'azinu, § 306, f. 131*b*.)

['Rabbi', used alone in this way, is the 'short' for Rabbi Judah I ha-Nasi (the Prince), born A.D. 135 (when Akiba died), died 219. He was the final redactor of the Mishnah, completing the work begun by Akiba and continued by Me'ir. Judah was the sixth direct descendant of Hillel, his father being Simeon II b. Gamaliel II. Hillel's grandson, Gamaliel I, who is mentioned in Acts V, 34, was thus Judah's great-great-grandfather. The title *Nasi*, or prince, was originally given to the chief of the Great Sanhedrin in Jerusalem and of its successors in other parts of Palestine (*T.B.R.H.* 31*a*, foot), the second being the *Ab Bet Din*. From *Nasi* was derived *Nesiah*, which was used practically as a family name of Hillel's

Palestinian successors, thus Judah *Nesiah* was the cognomen of Judah II, the grandson of Judah I ha-Nasi, and of Judah III, the grandson of Judah II *Nesiah* (end of the third century). The sources do not distinguish clearly between Judah II and III (both *Nesiah*).

Sometimes, e.g. *Ḥul.* 124*a*, Nesiah is used also of the Exilarch in Babylon, the more usual designation of whom was *Rosh Golah* or *Resh Geluta*. He was the head of the Babylonian Jews and enjoyed great authority. The Exilarch was a hereditary office in a family which claimed Davidic descent. The first historical evidence about the Exilarchate dates from Parthian times: the office continued under the Arabs, but the title persisted even after the cessation of the office. An interesting impression of the Exilarch and his court, by a traveller, may be read in Benjamin of Tudela's itinerary. Benjamin travelled between 1165 and 1167. In M. N. Adler's edition (London, 1907, pp. 39 ff., republished from the *Jewish Quart. Rev.*, XVI, 453 ff., the text and translation can be conveniently studied. For a full account, see the *Jewish Encyclopaedia*, s.v., and Jacob Mann's *Texts and Studies* (Cincinnati, 1931). (H. L.)]

All the words of the Law are sweet and delightful:

[420] Why does it say, 'A heap of wheat set about [fenced] with lilies' (Cant. VII, 2)? This refers to Torah. Have you ever heard of a man who made a fence of lilies? People hedge their fields and vineyards with thorns or brambles. But the words of Torah are soft and gentle. (*Pes.R.* 35*b init.*)

[Cp. [503], [508]. The use of the 'fence' metaphor in Rabbinics is interesting. Both the biblical *gader* and the rarer (biblical) *seyag* (Cant. VII, 3; Isa. XVII, 11) are used; a 'fence' has two functions; (*a*) to keep a bad object in check, cf. the 'fence of chastity' (*Lev.R.* XXIV, 6). It can be said that God 'fences' wrath, but wrath does not 'fence' Him (*Gen.R.* XLIX, 8 (Th. p. 507)). (*b*) The 'fence' preserves a good object, as here. One can speak even of a 'fence within a fence' (*T.J.San.* II, § 4, f. 20*b*, line 52). For the protective 'fence of the Wise' round the commandments, see *T.J.Ab.Zar.* II, § 2, f. 41*a*, line 1. The 'fence of the world', which the serpent broke through (*Lev.R.* XXVI, 2; Eccles. X, 8), is fundamental decency (cp. [1510]). (H. L.)]

Only very occasionally do we hear a warning against making the fence (i.e. the Rabbinic enactments) to the Pentateuchal Law too high:

[421] 'And make a fence for Torah' (*Aboth* I, 1). A vineyard with a fence is better than one without it. But a man should not make a fence higher than the object which it is to guard, lest the fence fall and crush the plants. This is what Adam did [really

Eve], who added the prohibition against touching the tree (Gen. III, 3); he made a fence higher than the object, and the fence fell and crushed the plants [i.e. he broke the command; he began by touching the tree, then he ate and fell].

(*Ab.R.N.* (vers. II), I, 2*a*.)

[422] Basing his words upon the severe verse, Num. XV, 31, R. Elazar of Modi'im[1] said: If a man says, 'I accept all the Torah with one exception,' or if he says, 'All the Torah was spoken by God, with the exception of one passage which was spoken by Moses,' he has despised the word of the Lord, and is worthy to be thrust out of the world [i.e. of the world to come]. (Cp. [1585–6], but contrast [1610].) (*Sifre Num.*, Shelaḥ, § 112, f. 33*a* (H. p. 121).)

[This was, possibly, directed against an arrogant sectarian (see the context in [423]) or against a proselyte who wished to dictate his terms of admission, for proselytes were initiated into the commandments gradually. In the same way, however tolerantly a Bishop might treat his clergy, he would, we may presume, be compelled to refuse Ordination to a candidate who expressly excepted one of the XXXIX Articles from his Declaration. (H. L.)]

[423] R. Elazar of Modi'im said: He who profanes the holy things [i.e. the Sanctuary], and despises the festivals, and breaks the covenant of Abraham our father, even if he has in his hand many commandments ['good deeds'] is worthy to be thrust out of the world [i.e. the world to come] (cp. [536] and [857]). (*Sifre Num.*, Shelaḥ, § 112, f. 33*a* (H. p. 121; cp. *Aboth* III, 15).)

[424] Let the light command be as beloved to thee as the weighty one.

(*Sifre Deut.*, Re'eh, § 79, f. 91*a* (H. p. 145).)

[425] If you become slack about one commandment, you will end by becoming slack about another; if you despise one, you will end by despising another. (*Der.Er.Z.* III, 5.)

Contact with Christians, and the arguments of those who accepted the teaching of Paul, made the Rabbis cling the more devotedly to the Law. It was immutable: it was given as a whole: no new Law or new Covenant was to follow it:

[426] It is written, 'For this commandment is not in heaven' (Deut. XXX, 11, 12). Moses said to the Israelites, 'Lest you should say,

[1] [Or, Modin, the home of the Maccabees: said to have been 15 miles from Jerusalem. According to Neubauer, *op. cit.* p. 99, it is el-Mediyeh, by Lydda. (H. L.)]

Another Moses is to arise, and to bring us another Law from heaven, therefore I make it known to you now that it is not in heaven: nothing is left of it in heaven.' R. Ḥanina said: The Law and all the implements by which it is carried out have been given, namely, modesty, beneficence, uprightness and reward. (*Deut.R.*, Niẓẓabim, VIII, 6.)

The polemical intention is obvious and interesting. The Prophets and the Sages only draw out the implications of the Law (i.e. the Pentateuchal Code):

[427] R. Isaac said: The Prophets drew from Sinai the inspiration of all their future utterances, for God spoke 'with him that stands here with us this day' (Deut. XXIX, 15), that is, with those who were already created, 'and also with him that is not here with us this day'; these are the souls which are destined to be created. So, too, it does not say, 'the burden of the Lord *to* Malachi' (Mal. I, 1), but 'by the hand of Malachi', to show that the prophecy was already in his hand at Mount Sinai. So, too, in Isa. XLVIII, 16, it says: 'From the time that it was, there am I'; that is, 'From the hour when Torah was given, I received this prophecy.' Not only to the Prophets alone does this apply, but to all the sages that are destined to arise in after days, for the Decalogue is described in Deut. V, 22 as 'One great voice', and this was divided into seven, and then into seventy, tongues for all mankind. (*Tanḥ.*, Yitro, § 11, f. 124*a fin.*–124*b*.)

[428] Asaph said: 'Give ear, O my people, to my Law' (Ps. LXXVIII, 1), and Solomon said, 'Forsake ye not my Law' (Prov. IV, 2). Israel said to Asaph, 'Is there then another law, that thou speakest of *my* Law? We have already received the Law at Sinai.' He said to them: 'There are sinners in Israel who say that the Prophets and the Holy Writings are not Torah, and we will not obey them'[1] (Dan. IX, 10). But the Prophets and the Holy Writings are Torah. Hence it says, 'Give ear, O my people, to my Law.' (*Tanḥ.B.*, Re'eh, 10*a*.)

Torah, indeed, is often very inadequately translated by 'Law'. The word does often mean the Pentateuch or its codes; it means, too, the Rabbinic or 'Oral' Law; it means, as in the last passage, all Scripture, and it must also 'be taken to include the whole of revelation—all that God has made known of His nature, character and purpose, and of

[1] This illustrates the growth of the Canon; cp. [1060].

what He would have man be and do. To the unwritten Law the religious and moral teachings of the Haggadah belong no less than the juristically formulated rules of the Halakah. In a word, Torah in one aspect is the vehicle, in another and deeper view, it is the whole content of revelation' (Moore, vol. I, p. 263). See also p. 7 of R. Travers Herford's *Talm. and Apoc.* London, 1933. (Cp. (15), p. civ and **Note 70.**)

[429] Let not a man say, the Psalms are not Torah; they are Torah, and the Prophets too are Torah, and the riddles and the parables are also Torah. (*Midr.Ps.* on LXXVIII, 1 (172*b*, § 1).)

The Oral Law was, in one sense, even more precious than the written Law, for it was Israel's unique possession. The Pentateuch formed part of the Christian Bible: but the Oral Law was the exclusive privilege of Israel:

[430] God gave the Israelites the two Laws, the Written Law and the Oral Law. He gave them the Written Law with its 613 ordinances, to fill them with commandments, and to cause them to become virtuous, as it is said, 'The Lord was pleased for His righteousness' sake to increase the Law and make it glorious.' And He gave them the Oral Law to make them distinguished from the other nations. It was not given in writing so that the nations should not falsify it, as they have done with the Written Law, and say that they are the true Israel. Therefore it says, 'If I were to write for him the many things of my Law, they would be counted as strange' (Hos. VIII, 12). The many things are the Mishnah, which is larger than the Law, and God says, If I were to write for Israel the 'many things', they would be accounted as strange (by the Gentiles). (*Num.R.*, Naso, XIV, 10.)

[This passage and [431] and [434] are clearly Jewish replies to the Christian claim to be the true Israel, on the basis of the possession of the Scriptures. Dr Parkes (*Conflict of Church and Synagogue*, London, 1934, pp. 97, etc.) has much to say about this controversy. Particularly significant is p. 105. (H. L.)]

[431] God said to Moses: 'Write thee these things, for it is by means of these things that I have made a covenant with Israel' (Exod. XXXIV, 27). When God was about to give the Torah, He recited it to Moses in due order, Scriptures, Mishnah, Agada, and Talmud, for God spake *all* these words (XX, 1), even the answers to questions which distinguished scholars in the future are destined to ask their teachers did God reveal to Moses, for He

spake *all* these things. Then, when God had ended, He said to Moses 'Go and teach it to my sons'....Moses said, 'Lord, do thou write it for them.' God said, 'I did indeed desire to give it all to them in writing, but it was revealed that the Gentiles in the future will have dominion over them, and will claim the Torah as theirs; then would my children be like the Gentiles. Therefore give them the Scriptures in writing, and Mishnah, Agada and Talmud orally, for it is they which separate Israel and the Gentiles.' (**Notes 26 and 94**.)

(*Tanḥ.B.*, Ki Tissa, 58*b* (cp. *Tanḥ.*, Wayera, § 5, f. 33*a*).)

[432] No man should say, 'I will not observe the precepts of the elders' [i.e. the Oral Law], since they are not of Mosaic authority [lit. contained in the Torah]. For God has said, 'Nay, my son, but whatsoever they decree for thee, do thou perform,' as it says, 'According to the Torah which they [i.e. the elders in days to come] *shall* teach thee, shalt thou do' (Deut. XVII, 11): for even for me do they make decrees, as it says, 'when thou [i.e. the elders] dost decree a command, it shall be fulfilled for thee, i.e. by me, God' [a playful interpretation of Job XXII, 28].

(*Pes.R.* 7*b*.)

Sometimes development or plasticity seems to be recognised as possible as regards new rulings in the Oral Law. (**Note 27**.)

[433] R. Joshua b. Ziruz, the son of the father-in-law of R. Me'ir, testified before R. Judah the Patriarch that R. Me'ir had eaten a leaf of a herb at Beth Shean[1] [without having tithed it], wherefore R. Judah declared all Beth Shean's produce as permitted [i.e. the produce of Beth Shean was to be regarded as having been tithed already]. Then his brothers and his father's house protested against him, and said, 'A place which your father and your fathers' fathers regarded as forbidden, would you treat as permitted?' Then he taught them how Hezekiah broke the 'brazen serpent which Moses had made, for unto those days the Israelites had burnt incense to it' (II Kings XVIII, 4), and he said, 'How could Asa and Jehoshaphat not have removed it, seeing that they removed all the idols from the land? (I Kings XV, 12).

[1] [In the Decapolis, by Mt Gilboa and Jezreel: Jos. XVII, 11 and I Sam. XXXI, 10 (Beth Shan); later called Scythopolis. According to Josephus (*Vita* 6) it was inhabited by pagans, but the Jewish citizens were strict in their observances (*Pes.* 50*b*), as this passage indicates. Neubauer, *op. cit.* p. 174. (H. L.)]

But as *his* fathers left room for Hezekiah to distinguish himself, so too, *my* predecessors left me room to distinguish myself.' Hence we may learn that if a scholar pronounces a new rule [*Halakah*], they do not make him give up his opinion [or, as some read, 'They do not reject him,' or, as some read, 'They do not reproach him as being haughty']. (*Ḥul.* 6*b fin.*–7*a.*)

[434] When the Scriptures were read in Synagogue a translator stood beside the reader, and rendered the Hebrew into the vernacular. The reader was forbidden to take his eyes off the scroll—i.e. to improvise or trust to memory, or use a written version; for only the Torah was given in writing, as it says, 'I will write upon the tables' (Exod. XXXIV, 1). Judah b. Pazzi said: 'Write thee these words' (*ib.* 27) is a pregnant verse: the Scriptures were given in writing. But the translator was forbidden to look into the scroll, since the Targum [translation] was oral, for it goes on to say 'According to [lit. by the mouth of] these words.' R. Judah, the son of R. Shalom, remarked: Moses desired that the Oral Law [lit. Mishnah] should be written also. But God foresaw that the Gentiles would one day translate the Torah and read it in Greek, and say, 'They [the Jews] are not [the true] Israel.' God said to Moses, 'The nations will say, We are [the true] Israel, we are the sons of God, and Israel will say, We are the sons of God. And now the scales are evenly balanced.' So God said to the Gentiles, 'Why do you claim to be my sons? I know only him who has my mystery in his possession; he is my son.' Then the Gentiles ask, 'What is thy mystery?' God replied, 'It is the Mishnah' [i.e. the Oral Law]. (*Pes.R.* 14*b.*)

[The translation[1] of the lectionary was a very important element in public worship. Since a literal rendering would sometimes be unintelligible and sometimes misleading, the introduction of a certain amount of exegesis was inevitable.[2] This amount was considerably less in the Pentateuch than in the Prophets. In the latter, far more freedom and expansion were permitted. But this opportunity for exegesis naturally became the medium for the affirmation of doctrine and the repudiation of heresy. Hence the Scripture translations became centres of controversy. We read of marginal glosses, which probably indicated christological proof-texts and contained arguments for opinions deemed heretical. When Christianity had definitely parted from Judaism, the provision of a canon became imperative.

[1] Cp. pp. 44 and 437. [2] E.g. in Lev. XXIII, 15.

But once it was settled which books were included and which were to be excluded, Jews and Christians found themselves in common possession of a written Bible, that is to say of the Old Testament: therefore neither could claim to be the 'Chosen People' on the basis of the ownership of the sacred writings alone. It was the exegesis in each case that was regarded as the special distinction and the title to true belief. So, among the Jews, the Oral Law was the sign that Israel was God's people: it was the 'mystery' to which this passage refers. It is sometimes a secret password or a king's private sign. It must not be published. Thus, the angels of the Presence were expelled for revealing the mystery, i.e. God's purpose (*Gen.R.*, Wayera, L, 9 (Th. p. 524)). The dying Jacob, like a 'king's friend on his death bed who wishes to reveal the king's mystery to his friends' sees the Shechinah; i.e. the redemption of Korah through Hannah's prayer (*ib.* XCVIII, 2 (Th. p. 1251)). The mystery is esoteric, thus 'mystery' messages are written in a solution of gall-nuts (*T.J.Sab.* XII, § 4, 13*d*). But sometimes the 'mystery' is a token, as in this passage of the *Pesiḳta Rabbati*. Conversely, among Christians, this gave rise to the idea of a pre-incarnation Church, claiming all the Old Testament heroes as Christian Saints and leaving to Judaism only the Sinners, Israelites and Gentiles irrespectively. Thus David and Samuel were Christian; Amalek and Korah were Jews. This mode of interpretation gave rise, according to Parkes, to Anti-Semitism. See his essay in *Judaism and Christianity*, vol. II, ed. H. Loewe, 1937, pp. 127 ff.

There is an excellent note on Scriptural translation and translators in Rabbinowitz's ed. of *Mishnah Megillah*, pp. 121–3. For the pre-incarnation Church and Anti-Semitism, see Parkes, pp. 105–6 and cp. [430]. (H. L.)]

The Rabbis, however, valued the Haggadah—the non-legal portions of the Oral Torah—only a little less than the strictly legal portions (cp. H. L. in [350]):

[435] 'They who searched out the implications'[1] of the Scripture said, 'If you wish to know the Creator of the World, learn Haggadah: for from it you will learn to know God and to cleave to His ways.' (*Sifre Deut.*, 'Eḳeb, § 49, f. 85*a* (H. p. 115).)

The Rabbis realised that the chief men among them had not always agreed among themselves. Nevertheless, the spirit of God was with them all. For example, the school of Shammai and the school of

[1] [The people alluded to here (*Doreshe Reshumot*) were a particular group of preachers, of whom little is known, though they are mentioned several times. See Cohen, *Ber.* p. 158 and note, and *Judaism and Christianity*, vol. II, ed. H. Loewe, p. 7 and footnote. (H. L.)]

Hillel differed on many rulings. But both were the words of the living God (see p. 656):

[436] 'The words of the wise are as goads [*Kedorbonot*]...which are given from one shepherd' (Eccles. XII, 11). R. Berechiah said: What is the meaning of 'like goads' [*Kedorbonot*]? It means *Kaddur Banot*, a girl's ball, which maidens toss in sport from one to another, one hither, one thither. So it is when the sages enter the house of study, and are occupied with the Law. One says its meaning is this, and another says its meaning is that. One gives such an opinion, his fellow a different one. But they all were 'given from one shepherd' (*ib.*)—that is from Moses, who received the teaching from Him who is One and unique in the world. (See **Note 71**.) (*Pes.R.* 8*a* and cp. 8*b*.)

For the reading 'toss', see Bacher's note on the passage, on p. 66 in *Studies in...honor of K. Kohler*, Berlin, 1913.

Many are the things to which, for homiletic purposes, the Law is compared: oil, wine, honey are among the most frequent:

[437] The words of the Law are compared with water, wine, oil, honey and milk (cp. [356]). With water, as it says, 'Ho, everyone that thirsts, come ye to the waters' (Isa. LV, 1); as the waters extend from one end of the earth to the other, for it says, 'To him that stretched out the earth above the waters' (Ps. CXXXVI, 6), so the Law is to extend from one end of the world to another, as it is said, 'The measure thereof is longer than the earth and broader than the sea' (Job XI, 9). As water gives life to the world, so the Law gives life to the world, as it says, 'It is life to those who find it' (Prov. IV, 22). As the water covers the nakedness of the sea, so the Law covers the nakedness of Israel, as it says, 'Love covers all sins' (Prov. X, 12). As the water comes down in drops and becomes streams, so a man learns two Halakahs a day until he becomes a bubbling spring. As water is pleasant only to the thirsty, so the Law is pleasant only to the man who toils in its study. As water leaves the high places and rests in the lowlands, so the Law leaves him whose disposition is haughty, and cleaves to him whose disposition is lowly. As water is not kept fresh in vessels of silver and gold, but in vessels of earthenware, so the Law is not maintained firmly except in him who makes himself as a vessel of earthenware; as a great man is not ashamed to ask a small man, 'Give me water to drink,' so the great man

must not be ashamed to say to the small man, 'Teach me a chapter, a verse, a saying, or even a letter.' As water, if a man knows not how to swim, swallows him up, so the words of the Law, if a man knows not how to swim in them and to teach them, end by swallowing him up. But lest one should suppose that as water, if it is kept for long in a jar, becomes foul and sour, so it is with the words of the Law, therefore the Law is also compared with wine. For wine, which grows old in a bottle, becomes more valuable, so the words of the Law, as a man grows older, become more precious to him. Or, because water does not make the heart rejoice, therefore the Law is also compared to wine, which makes the heart rejoice, for the Law rejoices the heart (Ps. XIX, 8). But because wine is sometimes bad for head and body, therefore the words of the Law are also compared to oil, for, like oil, they refresh and brighten the head and the body. But because oil is half bitter and half sweet, therefore the Law is also compared with honey; as honey is sweet, so are the words of the Law (Ps. XIX, 10). But as in honey there is wax, lest one should suppose that it is so with the Law, it is also compared with milk; as milk is pure, so is the Law, but as milk is tasteless, therefore the Law is compared to milk and honey combined, for as these two combined are good for the body, so with the Law, as it says, 'It shall be health to thy body, and healing to thy flesh' (Prov. III, 8; IV, 22).

(*Cant.R.* I, § 2, 3, on I, 2; f. 6*a* (cp. [506]).)

[438] As water is gratis for all, so is the Torah gratis for all. As water is priceless, so is the Torah priceless. As water brings life to the world, so the Torah brings life to the world. As water brings a man out of his uncleanness, so Torah brings a man from the evil way into the good way. As wine cannot keep good in vessels of gold and silver, but only in cheap earthenware vessels, so the words of the Torah keep good only with him who makes himself lowly. Like wine, words of the Torah rejoice the heart; as wine grows better by keeping, so the words of the Law become better as a man grows older.

(*Sifre Deut.*, 'Eḳeb, § 48, f. 84*a* (H. pp. 110, 111; cp. *R.T.* p. 37).)

[439] Just as water forms a purifying bath, so do words of Torah purify all. Torah purifies the sinners in Israel, when they repent, even if they have served idols, as it says, 'I will sprinkle clean

water upon you, and you shall be clean,' and by water is meant words of Torah. (*Tan.d.b.El.* p. 105.)

[440] As oil is made good only by heating, so only through sufferings does Israel repent. As oil on the top of another liquid, when the cup is full, does not flow over with the other liquids, so the words of the Law do not flow over the lips in connection with words of frivolity. As oil in a full cup drives out a drop of water which has fallen into the cup, so the words of the Law drive out frivolous words from your heart; and so, too, frivolous words drive out words of the Law; as the oil brings light to the world, so Israel gives light to the world, as it says, 'The nations shall come to thy light' (Isa. LX, 3).

(*Cant.R.* I, § 3, 2, on I, 3; f. 6*b*.)

[441] 'From His right hand went a fiery law for them' (Deut. XXXIII, 2). The words of the Torah are compared to fire, for both were given from heaven, both are eternal. If a man draws near the fire, he is burned;[1] if he keeps afar, he is frozen, so with the words of the Torah, if a man toils in them, they are life to him, if he separates from them, they kill him; fire is made use of both in this world and the next, and so too with the Torah. Fire leaves its mark on him who makes use of it, so does the Torah. As those who work with fire are recognised,[2] so are they who toil in the Torah. For students of the Law are recognised in the street by their walk, their speech, and their dress.

(*Sifre Deut.*, Berakah, § 343, f. 143*a fin.*–143*b init.*)

The idea that 'fire' is made use of in the world to come is very strange. It might, on the one hand, indicate a belief in a very material heaven. Or, possibly, the world of the resurrection may still be conceived of as earth, but a finer earth than now. Or, fire may be regarded as a metaphor of God, 'the consuming fire', or a reminiscence of the fire at the lawgiving on Sinai.

About the giving of the Law there are endless stories and reflections. Why, for instance, it is often asked, was the Law given in the wilder-

[1] [This is in Friedmann's text but it gives a poor sense. It would be an unusual remark. In his note, Friedmann suggests that for *nikweh* (he is burned) we should read *neheneh* (he derives benefit), and this gives a better sense. The reading 'burnt' would mean 'Be careful, beware! If you are incautious in your treatment of the Torah, it may burn you up.' In this case, 'close' would be 'too near'. The misuse or neglect of Torah is compared with a poison (*sam*), in [332]. (H. L.)]

[2] This would seem to suggest humility, since artisans who work with fire and coals would presumably be soiled in person and raiment.

ness? One answer is to the effect that the Law is, in one sense, for all (proselytes may accept its yoke). Or, again, the scene being laid in the wilderness shows that the Law was in the first instance offered to all:

[442] The wise have taught that the Law was given in three things, in fire, in water and in the desert. In fire, as it is said, 'And Mt Sinai was altogether on a smoke' (Exod. XIX, 18); in water, as it is said, 'The clouds dropped water' (Judges V, 4); and in the desert, as it is said, 'And the Lord spake unto Moses in the wilderness of Sinai' (Num. I, 1). And why was it given thus? To show that as these three things are given gratis to all the inhabitants of the world, so the words of the Law were given gratis, as it is said, 'Ho, all that thirst, come to the waters' (Isa. LV, 1). 'In the wilderness of Sinai.' He who does not make himself free as the wilderness [i.e. humble to learn from all and ready to teach all] cannot acquire wisdom and the Torah. (*Num.R.*, Bemidbar, I, 7.)

[443] The Law was given in the wilderness and in fire and in water. As these three are free to all the inhabitants of the world, so are the words of the Law free to all the inhabitants of the world. (*Mek.*[2], *Baḥodesh*, Yitro, § 5, p. 222; *Mek.*[3], vol. II, p. 237.)

[444] The Law was given publicly and openly, in a place to which no one had any claim. For if it had been given in the land of Israel, the nations of the world could have said, 'We have no portion in it.' Therefore it was given in the wilderness, publicly and openly, and in a place to which no one had any claim. Everyone who desires to accept it, let him come and accept it (cf. *R.T.* pp. 76, 77). (*Mek.*[2], *Baḥodesh*, Yitro, § 1, p. 205, § 5, p. 222; *Mek.*[3], § 5, vol. II, p. 236.)

Other explanations are such as these:

[445] Why was the Law given in the wilderness? Because if it had been given in the Promised Land, the tribe on whose territory it had been given might have said of the other tribes, 'I am better than you.' It was given in the wilderness because there all were equal. Or, again, as in the wilderness there is no sowing or tilling, so from him who receives the yoke of the Law they remove the yoke of worldly occupations....Or, again, he who fulfils the Law makes himself like unto an empty wilderness, and disregards all other influences. (*Num.R.*, Ḥuḳḳat, XIX, 26.)

[446] Why was the Law given in the desert? To teach you that if a man does not make himself free to all as the desert, he is not worthy to receive the Law....And as the wilderness has no limit, so the words of the Law have no limit, as it is said, 'The measure thereof is larger than the earth and broader than the sea' (Job XI, 9). And as the words of the Law have no limit, so has their reward no limit, as it says, 'How great is thy goodness which thou hast laid up for them that fear thee' (Ps. XXXI, 19). (See **Note 44** and p. 18.)

(*Pes.K.* 107*a* (cp. '*Erub.* 54*a*; cp. [1341]).)

The word for 'free to all' is not without some difficulty. Mr Loewe says it may mean 'makes himself free from prepossessions', 'empties himself of prejudices', i.e. receives the Law in simple and open faith.

To the Rabbis the Law was a sort of binding link between man and God. Moreover, it existed in heaven ages before it was given to man. It was one of the earliest of God's creations. It was adored by the angels and by God Himself:

[447] When God created the world, He decreed that 'the heavens are the heavens of the Lord and the earth is for men' (Ps. CXV, 16), but when He intended to give the Law, He repealed the former decree, and He said, 'The Lower shall ascend to the Upper, and the Upper shall descend to the Lower, and I will make a beginning,' as it is said, 'And the Lord came down upon Mount Sinai, and he said unto Moses, Come up unto the Lord' (Exod. XIX, 20). (*Exod.R.*, Wa'era, XII, 3.)

There are strange passages in the Rabbinic literature which speak of God Himself as a student and teacher of the Law. But if we remember that, to the Rabbis, Torah meant and included all wisdom, the strangeness is lessened. Perfect wisdom must, as it were, think wisdom, even as to Aristotle, God, the thinker, thinks thought. Besides being a student, God is also a teacher, of the Law:

[448] God said to Israel, 'On this day I have given you the Law, and individuals toil at it, but in the world to come I will teach it to *all* Israel, and they will not forget it.' (**Note 28**.)

(*Tanḥ.B.*, Yitro, 38*b*.)

Moore quotes *T.J.Sab.* 8*d*, line 27, where God teaches the souls of the righteous in heaven. 'The picture of God teaching the Law, like the head of a Rabbinical academy (*Bab.M.* 85*b*, 86*a*) has been the occasion of some rather witless pleasantries. But instruction in religion is not the most unbecoming occupation that can be imagined

for God in heaven or in the World to Come' (vol. III, p. 85). Again, 'In the hour when Moses went up to heaven he found God sitting and weaving crowns for the letters' (*Men.* 29*b*). (The crowns are the little flourishes with which some letters of the alphabet are ornamented in the Scrolls of the Law.) 'To many,' says Moore, with his genial sarcasm, 'in whose imagination of God portentous dignity is a dominant attribute, such occupations seem unbecoming, and, for want of a sense of humour, they have set them down to the "rabbinical idea of God", all the more absurd in association with the "transcendence" which the rabbis were supposed to ascribe to Him' (vol. III, p. 135).

[449] God said, 'If you read the Law, you do a kindness,[1] for you help to preserve my world, since if it were not for the Law, the world would again become "without form and void"' (as before creation, Gen. I, 2).... The matter is like a king who had a precious stone, and he entrusted it to his friend, and said to him, 'I pray you, pay attention to it and guard it, as is fitting, for if you lose it, you cannot pay me its worth, and I have no other jewel like it, and so you would sin against yourself and against me; therefore, do thy duty by both of us, and guard the jewel as is fitting.' So Moses said to the Israelites, 'If you keep the Law, not only upon yourselves do you confer a benefit, but also upon God,' as it is said, 'And it shall be a benefit for us' (Deut. VI, 25). [The Midrash takes 'us' to mean God and Israel, and the word *ẓedaḳah*—A.V. righteousness—it takes to mean benefit, which led to its later signification of 'alms'.]

(*Deut.R.*, Niẓẓabim, VIII, 5.)

[450] When Moses came down from God, Satan came before God and said, 'Where is the Torah?' God said, 'I have given it to the earth.' Satan went to the earth and said, 'Where is the Torah?' The earth replied, 'God [alone] knows the way thereof' (Job XXVIII, 23). Then he went to the sea and to the deep, and they said, 'It is not with us' (Job XXVIII, 14). Then he returned and said to God, 'I have enquired all over the earth, and have not found it.' God said, 'Go to the son of Amram.' So he went to Moses, and said to him, 'Where is the Law which God gave to you?' Moses said, 'What am I that God should have given the Torah to me?' Then God said, 'Moses, are you a liar?' Then

[1] [*Miẓwah* is here used in an unusual sense (i.e. as '*kindness*'): see the commentaries: *Mattenot K.* and note of Einhorn. The passage is hardly capable of Wuensche's rendering: see Fürst's note in Wuensche, p. 130 (cp. [753]). (H. L.)]

Moses said, 'This lovely and hidden thing in which day by day thou tookest thy pleasure, should *I* take the credit of it?'... Then God said, 'Because you have made yourself small, therefore it shall be called by thy name,' as it says, 'Remember the Law of Moses, my servant' (Mal. III, 2). (*Sab.* 89*a.*)

[451] When the Law was about to be given to the Israelites, a loud noise went forth from one end of the earth to the other; terror seized the peoples in their palaces, and they sang, as it is said, 'In their palaces [A.V. his palace] all say Glory' (Ps. XXIX, 9). They gathered together to Balaam and said, 'What is this tremendous noise which we have heard? Is a new flood coming upon the earth?' He replied, 'God has sworn that He will never bring another flood.' Then they said, 'But, perhaps He is going to bring a flood, not of water, but of fire?' He replied, 'He has sworn that He will never again destroy all flesh.' Then they said, 'What then was the noise?' He replied, 'God has a precious treasure in His storehouse which has been stored up there for 974 generations before the creation of the world, and now He proposes to give it to His children.'...Then they said, 'May God bless His people with peace' (Ps. XXIX, 11). (*Zeb.* 116*a.*)

[The Torah was in existence a thousand generations before the Creation (Ps. CV, 8) and there were 26 generations from Adam to Moses: 1000 – 26 = 974. Further, the creation of man was postponed for 1000 years—both man and Torah having been contemplated 1000 years before the Creation. Several explanations, too long to be cited here, endeavour to show why 974 is right and 1026 would be wrong: but none seems clear or satisfactory. See, for example, Rashi on the two *T.B.* passages [451–2]; *Gen.R.* I, 10 (Th. I, 11, p. 10), XXVIII, 4 (Th. p. 262), where see the commentaries *Mattenot K.*, Pseudo-Rashi, *Yefeh To'ar*, Wolf Einhorn, etc. (H. L.)]

[452] R. Joshua b. Levi said: When Moses went up to God, the angels said, 'What has a son of woman to do among us?' God said, 'He has come to receive the Law.' Then they said, 'The beautiful Torah, which thou hast hidden away since creation and for 974 generations before creation, dost thou purpose to give it to one of flesh and blood?' Then God said, 'Moses, answer them!' Moses replied, 'I fear they may burn me with the breath of their mouths.' God said, 'Hold fast to my throne of glory, and answer them....' Then Moses said, 'What is written in the Law which thou gavest me, "I am the Lord your God who brought

you forth from Egypt," Did you'—he said to the angels—'go down to Egypt? Were you enslaved by Pharaoh? What need have you of the Law? It is written, "Ye shall have no other gods." Do you dwell among the uncircumcised who practise idolatry? It says, "Remember the Sabbath day." Do you do any work, so that you need a day of rest?...It says, "Honour thy father and mother." Have you any fathers and mothers? It says, "Do no murder, do not steal or commit adultery"; is there any envy, is there any Evil Inclination among you?' Then they praised God, and became the friends of Moses. (*Sab.* 88*b*–89*a*.)

[453] When God gave the Torah to Israel, the earth rejoiced and the heavens wept. Why was this? It is like a king who celebrated the marriage of his daughter. The men of the cities did not attend the feast or give praise, but the villagers came singing praises and songs with many musical instruments. The king's herald came forth and spoke, 'It is customary for the men of the cities to know how to honour the king; would it not have been right for them to praise the king's daughter?' So it was when God gave the Torah to Israel, earth gave praise, but the heavens were silent. God said to the heavens, 'You, whose place is above, should have given praise to my glory and to my daughter, even more than the earth has done.' They said, 'Sovereign of the Universe, the earth may well give praise since it is to her that the Torah has been given; but we, from whom the Torah goes forth, how can we give praise and not be grieved?' **(Note 51.)** (*Pes.R.* 95*a*.)

[454] God created the world by the Torah: the Torah was His handmaid and His tool by the aid of which He set bounds to the deep, assigned their functions to sun and moon, and formed all nature. Without the Torah the world falls. So sang the sons of Korah, 'The earth and all the inhabitants thereof would be dissolved, did I not bear up the pillars' (Ps. LXXV, 3). The Torah is God's handmaid, whom Moses was saintly enough to receive. For as for the Torah, humility is her imprint and Godfearingness is her crown, as it says, 'The end of humility is the fear of the Lord' (Prov. XXII, 4) and 'The beginning of wisdom is the fear of the Lord' (Ps. CXI, 10). These two gifts were combined in Moses, who was 'exceedingly humble' (Num. XII, 3), and who 'feared to behold God' (Exod. III, 6). Hence for three acts of

humility, he was accorded three marks of distinction. Because 'he hid his face' (*ib.*), his face shone (Exod. XXXIV, 29): because he feared to approach God, the people feared to approach him (*ib.* 30): because he refrained from gazing at God (*ib.* III, 6), he was granted a vision of the divine similitude (Num. XII, 8).[1] So, because Moses was humble, he was worthy to receive the Torah (cp. [1015], [1357] and [1377]). (*Tanh.*, Bereshit, § 1, f. 6*b*.)

[The pre-existence of the Torah is very often merely tantamount to an expression that God Himself is bound by His own Laws. The world was made 'by law', not arbitrarily. Even miracles are within the Law and not without. Thus, the cleaving of the Red Sea was foreordained when the sea was created. 'God made conditions with the sea, that it should split before Moses, and with the sun that it should pause at Joshua's bidding' (*Gen.R.*, Bereshit, V, 5 (Th. p. 35)). (H. L.)]

God, Israel and the Law form a sort of triad, linked together by the closest ties of affection. This idea is often to the fore. While the particularism may jar upon us, the tenderness and intimacy of the conception cannot be gainsaid, or the fact that it kept the Rabbinic religion living and warm. The conception may be illustrated by the following:

[455] Can there be a sale in which the seller sells himself along with the object he sells? God says, 'I sold you my Torah, and with it I, as it were, sold myself.' The matter is like a king who had an only daughter, and another king sought her and got her in marriage. The father said, 'My daughter is an only child; I cannot be parted from her, and yet to say to you, Do not take her away, is also not possible, for she is your wife. Do me, therefore, this kindness; whithersoever you go, prepare for me a chamber, that I may dwell with you, for I cannot forsake my daughter.' So God says to Israel, 'I have given you my Torah; I cannot be separated from her; yet I cannot say to you, Do not take her; therefore in every place whither you go, make me a house, wherein I may dwell.'...When a man buys a desirable object in the market, does he usually buy also its owner? But God, when He gave the Law to Israel, said, 'With the Torah you, as it were, take also me.' [The Midrash plays on Exod. XXV, 2, 'Bring for me an offering,' i.e. take me in exchange for your offering.] (*Exod.R.*, Terumah, XXXIII, 1, 6.)

[1] The same Hebrew verb for 'behold' is used here as in Exod. III, 6.

Though, from one point of view, the Rabbis specially adored all the ceremonial enactments of the Law because they were so exclusively intended for Israel, yet, as we may also see later on, they realised well enough that, from another point of view, the moral took precedence over the ceremonial. They spoke of heaviest commands and lightest commands, and distinguished between them. Here I may quote the famous and familiar passage in which the unity of the human race—the brotherhood of man—and the love of neighbour are called the greatest and most inclusive principles of the Law:

[456] Ben Azzai quoted the verse, 'This is the book of the generations of Adam' (Gen. V, 1), and said: This is the greatest principle in the Law. R. Akiba said: 'Thou shalt love thy neighbour as thyself' (Lev. XIX, 18) is the greatest principle in the Law. Do not say, 'Because I am despised, so may my neighbour be cursed with me.' If you act thus, said R. Tanḥuma, know whom you despise, namely, a being made in the image of God. [The word for neighbour in R. Akiba's comment is not the same as the word (*rea'*, cp. [1068]) in the quotation from Lev. XIX, 18. It is *ḥaber*. Cf. *R.T.* pp. 71 f. See also Travers Herford, *Talmud and Apocrypha*, pp. 145–149.

(*Gen.R.*, Bereshit, XXIV, 7 (Th. pp. 236, 237).)

[457] 'Thou shalt love thy neighbour as thyself' (Lev. XIX, 18). R. Akiba said: That is the greatest principle in the Law. Ben Azzai said: The sentence, 'This is the book of the generations of man' (Gen. V, 1), is even greater than the other. (*Sifra* 89*b*.)

[458] It is related that an ass-driver came to R. Akiba and said to him, 'Rabbi, teach me the whole Torah all at once.' He replied, 'My son, Moses our teacher stayed on the Mount forty days and forty nights before he learned it, and you want me to teach you the whole of it at once! Still, my son, this is the basic principle of the Torah: What is hateful to yourself, do not to your fellow-man. If you wish that nobody should harm you in connection with what belongs to you, you must not harm him in that way; if you wish that nobody should take away from you what is yours, do not take away from another what is his.' The man rejoined his companions, and they journeyed until they came to a field full of seed-pods. His companions each took two, but he took none. They continued their journey, and came to a field full of cabbages. They each took two, but he took none. They asked him why he had not taken any, and he replied,

'Thus did R. Akiba teach me: What is hateful to yourself, do not to your fellow-man. If you wish that nobody should take from you what is yours, do not take from another what is his.'

(*Ab.R.N.* (vers. II), XXVI, f. 27*a* (*E.T.* p. 228) (cp. [539]).)

[Akiba's teaching was not new. Hillel had already taught, 'What is hateful to you, do not to your fellow-creature' (*Sab.* 31 *a*, following the stories of Hillel's patience). Hillel, again, re-echoes Tobit IV, 15 (see the variants in the critical notes in Charles' *Apocrypha and Pseud.*). There is an excellent article by G. Brockwell King, *The 'Negative' Golden Rule*, on pp. 268 ff. of *The Journal of Religion*, VIII, No. 2, April 1928. (H. L.)]

Chapter VI

STUDY, PRACTICE AND GOODNESS

Keen as were the Rabbis on the study of the Law, they realised and taught that study without practice, and especially without moral practice, was absurd. A sinful learned man was an abomination. And a mere *abstention* from sin was not enough. The learned man must also be the good man. He must accomplish deeds of charity and love:

[459] 'Ye shall diligently guard these commandments to *do* them' (Deut. VI, 17; XI, 22). Lest a man might suppose, if he guard the words of the Law, he can sit quiet and need not *do* them, it says: 'To *do* them.' If a man learns the words of the Torah, he has fulfilled one command, if he learns and guards them, he has fulfilled two; if he learns and guards and does them, there is no one greater than he.

(*Sifre Deut.*, 'Eḳeb, § 48, f. 84*b* (H. p. 113; *R.T.* p. 159.)

[460] When Rabbi Elazar b. Peraṭa I and R. Ḥanina[1] b. Teradion were arrested, Elazar said to Ḥanina, 'Happy are you that you have been arrested on one count, whereas I have been arrested on five.' Ḥanina answered, 'Happy are you, who will be set free; woe is me, who will not be delivered. You occupied yourself with the study of the Law, and with deeds of charity, whereas I occupied myself with the study of the Law only.' Ḥanina said this according to the teaching of R. Huna, who declared, 'He who occupies himself with the study of the Law only, is as if he had no God'[2] (*R.T.* p. 373). But had he really not occupied himself

[1] So in the ordinary texts: Hananiah is more probable. See [683] and *J.E.*, v, 103.

[2] [It is interesting to note that in Judaism the antithesis is generally not 'Faith or Works', i.e., 'Believing or Doing', but 'Learning or Doing'. The Christian antithesis was due to the fact that the missionaries were concerned, mainly, with Gentiles who had as yet no faith, and who had to be won to faith, though they might be decent and kindly, even though pagans, none the less. We have not much evidence of what the Rabbis said to such Gentiles. What there is, e.g., 'Any man who repudiates idolatry is called a Jew,' seems to be on similar lines. But what we do know of the Rabbis is their method of dealing with those who already had faith, but who were ignorant of the Bible and religion. For such people, learning was often the essential need, for 'learning leads to doing', as we have seen. (Cp. end of *Pe'ah* I, I, *P.B.* p. 5, cited from *T.J.Pe'ah* in [739].) Barren learning was regarded as useless, as the present passage indicates. (H. L.)]

with deeds of love? Is it not taught that R. Eliezer b. Jacob said, 'Let no man put his money in the almsbox unless a scholar like R. Ḥanina is its superintendent'? They trusted in him, for he was trustworthy, but he did not *practise* charity himself. But is it not taught that he said, 'Special Purim money for the poor has got mixed up with the ordinary alms money? I gave both to the poor, and I put back the Purim money from my own money.' He *did* practise charity, but not as much as he ought. (*Ab.Zar.* 17*b*.)

This precision is illustrated by the following:

[461] R. Huna had four hundred casks of wine that went sour. R. Judah, the brother of R. Sala the saint, and certain other Rabbis, came to see him. They said to him: 'Sir, examine your actions [and confess the sin to which this is to be attributed].' He replied, 'Am I then suspected by you of sin?' They answered, 'Is then the Holy One, blessed be He, to be suspected of punishing without just cause?' Huna said, 'Let anyone who has heard anything against me speak out.' They remarked, 'Well, it has been said that you do not give your tenant-gardener [his due share of] vine-tendrils.' Huna retorted, 'But he has left me none! He steals them all!' They answered, 'The proverb runs 'Steal from a thief, and you will get a taste of the theft.' Huna said, 'I undertake to give him the vine-tendrils.' Some say that the vinegar became wine again; others, that vinegar appreciated to the cost of wine. (*Ber.* 5*b*.)

[A tenant-gardener or farmer (*Aris*) was a man who tilled the ground in return for a share in the produce: he did not pay rent. (H. L.)]

Reverting to the question of worldly occupations:

[462] Rabban Gamaliel, the son of Rabbi Judah the Prince, said: An excellent thing is the study of the Torah combined with some worldly occupation [*Derek ereẓ*; cp. p. 176 note], for the labour demanded by them both makes sin to be forgotten. All study of the Torah without work must in the end be futile, and become the cause of sin. (*Aboth* II, 2; *P.B.* p. 187.)

[463] It is written, 'Mingled with oil' (Num. VII, 19). This is the Law, which must be mingled with good works, as it is taught, 'Beautiful is the study of the Law, combined with good manners.' Man gives pleasure to his Maker when he busies himself

with the study of the Law, does good deeds, and refrains from sin.[1] (*Num.R.*, Naso, XIII, 16.)

[464] It is written, 'Wisdom [to the Rabbis, wisdom is the Law] is a tree of life to those who lay hold upon her' [that is, who fulfil her, who do the commands contained in the Law] (Prov. III, 18). If it said, 'The Law is a tree of life for those who *labour* in it,' there would be no safety for Israel,[2] but it says, 'Those who lay hold upon it.' If it said, 'For those who *learn* it,' there would be no safety for Israel, but it says, 'All the words of this Law to *do* them' (Deut. XXVII, 26). (*Lev.R.*, Ḳedoshim, XXV, 1.)

[For this difficult passage, see *Comm. in loc.* 'Labour' has two interpretations: (*a*) those who study without fulfilling; (*b*) those who study without supporting themselves by manual or other labour. 'Lay hold of' implies, as in Prov. III, 18, that both alternatives should be grasped equally. For 'safety' (*teḳumah*), cp. p. 105 footnote. (H. L.)]

[465] R. Johanan b. Zakkai said: The wise man who is a sin-fearer is like a craftsman who has the tools of his craft ready in his hand. The wise man who is not sin-fearing is like a craftsman who has no tools. And, finally, the sin-fearer who has no wisdom is like a man who has the tools, but is no craftsman. [He has the will, but does not know what he ought to do.] (*Ab.R.N.* (vers. I), XXII, 37*b fin.*–38*a init.*)

[466] R. Ḥanina b. Dosa said: He in whom the fear of sin comes before wisdom, his wisdom will endure; but he in whom wisdom comes before the fear of sin, his wisdom will not endure. He used to say, 'If a man's works exceed his wisdom, his wisdom shall endure; but if his wisdom exceeds his works, his wisdom will not endure.' [What is fear of sin? Mr Travers Herford says: 'Fear of sin is the attitude of the sensitive conscience towards God; sin is feared, not because of any penalty attaching to it but from pure love to God' (Herford, *Aboth*, 2nd ed. 1920, p. 76). Fear of sin is the negative form of the virtue of which good deeds is the positive form. I doubt whether the Rabbis conceived the idea of a man constantly afraid of committing a sin, but never actually doing any good deed. That sort of anxious scrupulosity constitutes a character the like of which they had not met many in real life.] So too, R. Elazar b.

[1] ['Good manners', as in the well-known phrase 'Manners maketh Man', implies more than polite deportment. *Derek ereẓ* can imply decency, sexual restraint, a worthy secular occupation, and so on. Cp. [462]. (H. L.)]

[2] Cp. [274] and [606].

Azaryah used to say: He whose wisdom exceeds his works, to what is he like? To a tree whose branches are many, but whose roots are few; and the wind comes and plucks it up and overturns it upon its face....But he whose works exceed his wisdom, to what is he like? To a tree whose branches are few, but whose roots are many, so that even if all the winds in the world come and blow upon it, it cannot be stirred from its place.

(*Aboth* III, 11, 12, and 22; *P.B.* pp. 192–3, 194 (cp. [376]).)

[467] Rabbah b. Rab Huna said: He who has knowledge of the Law, but no fear of God, is like a keeper of a treasury, who has the inner keys, but not the outer keys. He cannot enter.

(*Sab.* 31*b init.* (cp. [465], [473]).)

[468] A man may learn *Halakot*, *Midrashim*, *Haggadot*, but if he has no fear of sin, he has nothing. It is like a man who says to his neighbour, 'I have a thousand measures of corn, wine and oil.' His neighbour says to him, 'Have you storehouses in which to put them? If yes, you have all, if no, you have nothing.' So with the man who has learnt everything; only if he has the fear of sin is it all his. (**Note 94**.) (*Exod.R.*, Mishpaṭim, xxx, 14.)

[469] R. Elisha b. Abuyah said that a man who has learnt much Torah and has good deeds is like a horse which has reins. The man who has the first, but not the second, is like a horse without reins:[1] it soon throws the rider over its head.

(*Ab.R.N.* (vers. I), xxiv, 39*a*.)

[470] Let a man first do good deeds, and then ask God for [knowledge of] Torah: let a man first act as righteous and upright men act, and then let him ask God for wisdom: let a man first grasp the way of humility, and then ask God for understanding.

(*Tan.d.b.El.* p. 31.)

[471] R. Ḥiyya said: If a man learns the Law without the intention of fulfilling that Law, it were better for him had he never been born. And R. Johanan said: If a man learns the Law without the intention of fulfilling the Law, it were better for him had he never seen the light. R. Aḥa said: He who learns in order to do is worthy to receive the Holy Spirit.

(*Lev.R.*, Beḥuḳḳotai, xxxv, 7; cp. *R.T.* p. 118 (cp. [475]).)

[1] On Elisha b. Abuyah see T. Herford's note in his second ed. of *Aboth* IV, 25, p. 120.

[472] R. Elisha b. Abuyah said: He who studies the words of the Law and does them, his face shines like gold, but he who studies them, and does them not, his face is dark like crystal (cf. Job XXVIII, 17). (*Ab.R.N.* (vers. I), XXIV, 39*b*.)

[473] R. Hoshaiah said: He who possesses knowledge, but has not the fear of sin, possesses nothing. Every craftsman who has no tools is no craftsman. The key which unlocks the Law is the fear of sin. (*Exod.R.*, Ki Tissa, XL, 1.)

[474] Study is not the principal thing, but doing, for we have been taught that deeds make atonement for a man, and that repentance and good deeds are a shield against punishment.
(*Num.R.*, Naso, XIV, 10 (cp. *Aboth* IV, 13; *P.B.* p. 197).)

[475] One learns to do; one does not learn not to do: he who does not learn to do, it were better for him that he had not been born.
(*Sifra* 110*c* (cp. [471]).)

Sometimes even, though perhaps not very frequently, the Rabbis are willing to allow, not only that one can be good with little or no study, but that simple goodness may be regarded by God as of great value:

[476] It was a favourite saying of the Rabbis of Jabneh: I am a creature [of God] and my neighbour is also His creature; my work is in the city and his in the field; I rise early to my work, and he rises early to his. As he cannot excel in my work, so I cannot excel in his work. But perhaps you say, I do great things, and he does small things. We have learnt that [it matters not whether] a man does much or little, if only he direct his heart to heaven. (*Ber.* 17*a*.)

[477] '...If thou doest what is right in God's sight' (Exod. XV, 26). That is, what is right in business, or in buying and selling. And hence you may learn that he who conducts business, and buys and sells, in truth and fidelity, and in whom the mind of man finds pleasure, is regarded as if he had fulfilled the whole Law.
(*Mek.*[2], *Wayassa'*, Beshallaḥ, § 1, p. 158 *init.*; *Mek.*[3], vol. II, p. 96.)

[478] R. Joshua said: If a man learns two ordinances (*Halakot*) in the

morning and two in the evening, and is busy at his work all the day, 'they'[1] reckon it to him as if he had fulfilled the whole Law. (*Mek.*[2], *Wayašša'*, Beshallaḥ, § 2, p. 161; *Mek.*[3], § 3, vol. II, p. 103.)

[479] R. Elazar said: What was the blessing which Moses said over the Law when he received it? Blessed art thou, O Lord, King of the Universe, who hast chosen the Law, and hast sanctified it, and hast pleasure in those who fulfil it. He did not say, In those who labour to study it, or in those who meditate on it, but in those who fulfil it. A man may say, I have not learnt wisdom, I have not studied the Law, what am I to do? God said to the Israelites, All wisdom and all the Law is a single easy thing: he who fears me, and *fulfils* the words of the Law, he has all wisdom and all the Law in his heart. (*Deut.R.*, Berakah, XI, 6.)

[480] Two Rabbis sat together: a third passed by. One said to the other, 'Let us rise, for he is a sin-fearer.' The other said, 'Let us rise, for he is a learned man in the Law.' Then the first said to the second, 'I tell you that he is a sin-fearer, and you tell me that he is learned.' God receives to Himself nothing else in His world except only the fear of Him. (*Sab.* 31*b*.)

I am very fond of the following stories:

[481] [In a time of drought] it was revealed to the Rabbis in a dream that a certain man in a certain village should pray that rain might come. So they sent and fetched him. They asked him what his trade was, and he replied that he was an ass-driver. Then they said, 'Have you ever done any good deed in your life?' [Ass-drivers were not much esteemed.] He answered, 'Once I hired an ass to a woman who began to weep on the road. I asked her why she wept, and she told me that her husband was in prison, and that she was going to the city to sell her chastity to obtain his ransom. When we came to the city, I sold my ass, and gave her the money I received, and I said to her, "Take this, free your husband, and do not sin."' The Rabbis said to him, 'Worthy indeed art thou to pray for us and be answered.' And the man prayed, and the rain fell. (**Note 86.**) (*T.J.Ta'an.* I, 4, 64*b*, line 48.)

[1] The impersonal plural 'they' is often used for the Deity to avoid needless use of the words 'God' or 'the Holy One', etc. The reader will at once be reminded of Dolly Winthrop in *Silas Marner* (cp. [580], [754–6] and note following [756]).

[482] [In a time of drought] it was revealed to Abbahu in a dream that Pentekaka [i.e. the man of five sins] should pray for rain. Abbahu sent and fetched him. He asked him what his trade was. Pentekaka replied, 'Five sins does this man[1] do daily; I hire out[2] harlots; I deck the theatres; I take the harlots' garments to the baths; I clap and dance before them; and I beat the tympanum for their orgies.' Abbahu said to him, 'Have you ever done one good deed?' He said, 'Once I was decking out the theatre when a woman came and wept behind one of the pillars. When I asked her why she was weeping, she told me that her husband was in prison, and that she was going to sell her honour to obtain his ransom. So I sold my bed and coverlet, and gave her the price, and said, "Go, redeem thy husband, and sin not."' Abbahu said to him, 'Worthy art thou to pray and to be answered.'

(*T.J.Ta'an.* I, 4, 64*b*, line 54.)

[483] Abba[3] the Bleeder received every day a greeting from the heavenly academy, while Abbaye received one every Friday, and Raba every year on the eve of the Day of Atonement. Abbaye felt discouraged on account of the greater distinction of Abba the Bleeder. Abbaye was therefore told, 'Thou canst not perform deeds like those of Abba the Bleeder!' What were the deeds of Abba the Bleeder? When he performed the operation [of bleeding], he had a separate place for men and another for women. He had a garment ready in which there were numerous slits, and when a woman came, he made her put it on, so that he should not have to look upon her bare body. Outside of his office he had a place [box] where his fees were to be deposited. Whoever had money could put it in, but those who had none could come in

1 ['This man', i.e. 'I'. A frequent idiom. The reading of the text in part is not clear, and it is rendered according to the marginal gloss. (H. L.)]

2 [Although most commentators so explain this rather difficult phrase, the rendering does not make good sense: (*a*) it makes Pentekaka a principal, whereas in the other sins he is but an agent; (*b*) even if the story is meant to show that one single good deed can atone for a life of crime, yet this particular good deed is merely a momentary abstention from sin committed habitually and, presumably, subsequently. Why should this one woman be excepted? Merely because she wept? The text, at this point, is not clear. I should prefer to read the *ethpa'al* form of the verb and, with an added preposition, translate 'I work as a labourer for the harlots,' i.e. 'I hire myself out to them,' i.e. to do their odd jobs for them. (H. L.)]

3 [The point of the story is that Abba was an ordinary artisan: Abbaye was head of the school at Pumbeditha: while Raba, head of the school at Maḥoza, was, in a way, greater than Abbaye, since, except in six instances, the Halakah decided in his favour against Abbaye. (H. L.)]

without feeling embarrassed. When he saw a person who was in no position to pay, he would offer him some money, saying to him, 'Go, strengthen thyself.' One day Abbaye sent a pair of scholars to him to find out the truth about him. When they came to his house, he gave them to eat and drink, and laid cushions before them to sleep on. The next morning the scholars took the cushions with them, and brought them to the market place. Abbaye then sent for Abba, and the scholars requested him to appraise the value of the cushions. Abba said, 'They are worth so and so much.' 'But, perhaps, they are worth more?' the scholars inquired. 'This is what I paid for them,' he replied. 'Of what did you suspect us?' the scholars asked. 'I thought', he said, 'the gentlemen happened to be in need of money for some charitable purpose, and were ashamed to tell me.' 'Take them back now,' they said. 'No,' he replied, 'from that moment I diverted my mind [from them], considering them consecrated to charity.' (*Ta'an.* 21*b*, 22*a* (Malter, pp. 157–8).)

The heavenly academy or tribunal [*yeshibah*] corresponds to the earthly tribunal, and consists of God and His angels. A greeting from this heavenly tribunal may be taken to mean a vision:

[484] R. Baruka of Ḥuza frequented the market of Lapet. One day Elijah appeared to him there, and R. Baruka asked him: 'Is there among the people of this market any one that is destined to share in the world to come?' Elijah replied, 'There is none.' In the meantime there came a man who wore black shoes, and had no fringes on his garment. 'This man', Elijah remarked, 'is one who will share in the world to come.' R. Baruka thereupon called to the man, and asked him what his occupation was. 'I am a jailer,' the man declared, 'and I keep men and women separate. At night I place my bed between the men and women, so that no wrong be committed.' R. Baruka then asked him, 'Why do you wear black shoes?' 'Because I mourn for Jerusalem.' 'And why did you not put fringes on your garment?' 'In order that the people should not recognise me as a Jew, so that when they have some secret plot against us, and are about to issue hard decrees, they may reveal it to me, and I could advise the Rabbis thereof, in order that they may pray to God, and avert the menace.' Then two other men appeared on the scene, and Elijah said to R. Baruka, 'These two will also share

in the world to come.' R. Baruka then asked them, 'What is your occupation?' They said, 'We are merry-makers; when we see a man who is downcast, we cheer him up; also when we see two people quarrelling with one another, we endeavour to make peace between them.' (*Ta'an.* 22*a* (Malter, pp. 158, 159, 160).)

[The black shoes are explained in the Gemara as a sign of mourning, but Rashi, *in loc.*, says that it was not a Jewish custom to wear black shoes. This, and the omission of the fringes, would suffice to make the man pass for a Gentile. (H. L.)]

The quaintness of Rabbinic thought is shown by the following:

[485] An epidemic once broke out in Sura, but in the neighbourhood of Rab's residence the epidemic did not appear. The people thought that this was due to Rab's merits, but in a dream they were told that the miracle was too slight to be attributed to Rab's great merit, and that it happened because of the merits of a man who willingly lent hoe and shovel to a cemetery [for the digging of graves]. A fire once broke out in Drokeret, but the neighbourhood of R. Huna was spared. The people thought that it was due to the merit of R. Huna, but they were told in a dream that R. Huna's merits were too great, and the sparing of his neighbourhood from fire too small a matter to attribute the marvel to him, and that it was due to the merits of a certain woman who used to heat her oven, and place it at the disposal of her neighbours. (*Ta'an.* 21*b* (Malter, p. 155).)[1]

Any good deed is of value. Any sin is a loss.

[486] 'By ten sayings the world was created.' To teach you that him who fulfils one command, or keeps one sabbath, or preserves one human life, the Scripture regards as if he had preserved the whole world. And him who commits one sin, desecrates one sabbath, and destroys one human life, the Scripture regards as if he had destroyed the whole world....

(*Ab.R.N.* (vers. I), XXXI, 45*b*, 46*a*.)

By an ingenious interpretation of Gen. IV, 10, the inference is made that 'One human life is as important as the whole creation.' The text, as most commonly cited, is 'any Israelite soul'. But the word 'Israelite' is bracketed by Schechter: it did not form part of the

[1] Sura was an important town on the Euphrates, the seat of a Rabbinic academy established by Rab. Cp. Neubauer, *op. cit.* p. 343 and for Drokeret (or Tekrit) p. 390.

original saying. The example from Cain shows this clearly, for 'Israelite' would make no sense at that biblical period. (**Note 82.**)

For deed done man is more responsible than for teaching given:

[487] 'But the man who acts in presumption...shall die' (Deut. XVII, 12). For an act, but not for [false] teaching or for a [false] judicial decision, is a man guilty [i.e. to be condemned to death]. (*Sifre Deut.*, Shofeṭim, § 155, f. 105*a* (cp. *Hor.* 2*a*).)

Famous and familiar is the following, which attempts to solve the problem as to the relative merits of study and practice:

[488] Once R. Ṭarfon and the elders sat in the upper chamber of the house of Nitzah in Lydda, and the question was raised, 'Is study greater, or doing?' R. Ṭarfon said, 'Doing was greater.' Akiba said, 'Study was greater.' Then they all said that study was greater, for it led to doing (cf. *R.T.* pp. 158–9). (**Note 11*j*.**) (*Ḳid.* 40*b*.)

So far as happiness is concerned, any occupation may ensure it:

[489] God makes every occupation pleasant to those who follow it. (*Ber.* 43*b*.)

I will not allude here to the difficult question of the *Am ha-Aretz*, or to the Rabbis' view of the ignorant man, or of those who were careless in the observance of the Law. Dr Abrahams' essay in my *Synoptic Gospels*, 2nd ed. vol. II, pp. 647–69, should be read by the curious. It repays study. Two kindly sayings about the *Am ha-Aretz* may, however, be quoted:

[490] Resh Laḳish compared Israel to a vine; the stems are the householders, the clusters are the 'disciples of the wise' the leaves are the *Amme ha-Aretz*, the dry suckers are the empty ones [apparently those who have neither learning nor morals]. The Palestine saying was, 'Let the grapes pray for the leaves, for without leaves there would be no grapes.' (**Note 91.**) (*Ḥul.* 92*a*.)

[491] R. Aḥa said of an ignoramus [*Am ha-Aretz*] who mixes up Love [*Ahabah*] with Hate [*Aybah*], and says, 'Thou shalt hate' [*ayabta*] instead of, 'Thou shalt love' [*ahabta*], God says, 'Even his jumping [his confusion of letters] is dear to me.' (*Cant.R.* II, § 4, 1, on II, 4; f. 15*a*.)

This is a pun upon Cant. II, 4, 'His banner (*diglo*) over me is love.' The Midrash reads '*dillugo*', his skipping, his jumping (cp. [1470]).

Perhaps, however, I may in justice, before passing from this vexed, difficult and painful subject of the *Am ha-Aretz*, quote a passage from Moore, which, because of the impartiality and objectivity of this author, and his great desire to give to the Rabbis *all* the due that is rightly theirs, is all the more significant. 'The educated (i.e. the Rabbis and their disciples) had the common pride of learning in double measure because it was religious learning. It was impossible to obey the divine laws without knowledge of the Law, written and traditional. Hillel had put it in a word, "No ignorant man (*Am ha-Aretz*) is religious." They were no less proud of the pains they took to keep the laws in all their refinements, and particularly, as we have seen above, those about which common men were most careless. They were led in this way to lay especial stress on articles in the laws which from our point of view seem of the smallest religious significance—the taxation of agricultural produce for the support of a hereditary clergy who after the destruction of the temple no longer had any sacerdotal functions, and the various kinds of uncleanness which, detached from their relation to participation in the cultus, were extended to social intercourse.

'The large development of these sides of the Law long antedates the Christian era, and pre-occupation with such things is the only notion many have of Pharisaism. So far as that is concerned, the Pharisee or the Schoolman would have replied: God gave these laws for reasons sufficient to Himself; it is not for men to set them aside as antiquated or unimportant. In the application of them many cases arise which require a definite ruling and a practice in conformity to it. You may think them small commandments by the side of those whose obligation the reason and conscience of all men recognise; but fidelity to the revealed will of God is not a small matter, and the crucial test of it is precisely solicitude about keeping the commandments whose obligation is solely positive—God has commanded thus and so. It is, as has been repeatedly remarked, the unimpeachable logic of revealed religion.

'The effect of such a situation as we have been considering goes farther than this putting of all obligations in principle on the same plane. In all sects, and in every *ecclesiola in ecclesia*, it is the peculiarities in doctrine, observance, or piety, that are uppermost in the minds of the members; what they have in common with the great body is no doubt taken for granted, but, so to speak, lies in the sectarian subconsciousness.

'Worse than this displacement of values by emphasis on the differential peculiarities is the self-complacency of the members of such a party or association, and the self-righteousness that comes of believing that their peculiarities of doctrine or practice make them singularly well-pleasing to God. With this goes censoriousness towards outsiders, which often presumes to voice the disapprobation of God. The Pharisees and the Associates, who seem to have numbered among them in the second century most of the learned and their disciples, conspicuously illustrate these faults. It is not without detriment to himself that a man cherishes the consciousness of being superior to his fellows, and the injury to his character is not least when he has the best reason for his opinion.' (Vol. II, pp. 160, 161.)

To go back to study and the Law, we may notice that one must sometimes not turn aside from study to do even the most primary good deeds. Thus R. Abbahu sent his son to Tiberias to study; the son, it was reported, occupied his time in 'good works' (burying the dead, visiting the sick, etc.). R. Abbahu sent to him to say, 'Are there no graves in Caesarea that I sent you to Tiberias?' But R. Abbahu's colleagues said, that if there were no one else to do the 'deeds of love', then the son was justified in neglecting his study.[1] So we hear that three young Rabbis were late one day in coming to the lecture room of their master.

[492] R. Elazar said, 'Where were you?' They said, 'We were occupied in performing a pious deed.' He said, 'Were there no others to do it?' They said, 'No, for the man was a stranger.'

(*T.J.Pes.* III, § 7, f. 30*b*, line 58.)

The pious deed must have been a burial.

Here is a legend of R. Akiba's devotion to the study of the Law and of his wife's unselfishness:

[493] R. Akiba was the shepherd of Ben Kalba Sabua'. When his daughter saw how pious and capable Akiba was, she said to him, 'If I became betrothed to you, would you go to the house of study?' He said, 'Yes.' So she became secretly betrothed to him, and sent him off. When her father heard of it, he expelled her from his house, and vowed that she should inherit none of his property. Akiba went and stayed twelve years in the house of study, and when he returned, he brought twelve thousand disciples with him. He heard an old man say to his [Akiba's] wife, 'How long yet will you live a life of living widowhood?' She replied, 'If he listened to me, he would stay away another twelve years.' Then he thought, 'It would happen with

[1] [It has been suggested that the (original?) Aramaic of Matt. VIII, 22 was 'Let the Sexton (*Ḳabora*) bury the dead', so that the intention of Jesus would be that of Abbahu. On the one hand, to bury the dead was 'true lovingkindness' (see Gen. XLVII, 29: this is the usual Midrashic interpretation); on the other, a *met miẓwah*, i.e., a corpse, of which the duty of burial devolved on the first person who found it, was an unattended corpse. Burial might thus raise a conflict of duties or interruption of prayer: such contingencies are discussed in *Ber.* III, 1–2 and *Ber.* 14*b*. For the various meanings of *miẓwah* see [753]. (H. L.)]

her permission.' So he returned and stayed in the house of study another twelve years, and when he came back he brought twenty-four thousand disciples with him. When his wife heard of his coming, she went out to meet him. Her neighbours said to her, 'Borrow some clothes and dress up in them.' She said, 'The righteous man knows the soul of his beast' (Prov. XII, 10). When she came to him, she fell down and kissed his feet. His disciples began to push her away; but he said, 'Let her be, what is mine and what is yours is hers.' When her father heard that a learned man had come to the city, he said, 'I will go to him; perhaps he will annul my vow.' He came to Akiba, and Akiba said to him, 'If you had known that he was a learned man, would you have made the vow?' He said, 'If he had known only one section or one *halakah*, I should not have made the vow.' Then Akiba told him who he was. Then he fell down and kissed Akiba's feet, and gave him half his possessions. (*Ket.* 62*b*, 63*a*.)

The next saying of R. Judah is very familiar:

[494] As a little wood can set light to a great tree, so young pupils sharpen the wits of great scholars. Hence said Rabbi Ḥanina: Much Torah have I learnt from my teachers, more from my colleagues, but from my students most of all.

(*Ta'an.* 7*a* (cp. *Mak.* 10*a*; cp. [279]).)

The latter saying is ascribed in *Ta'anit* to Ḥanina and in *Makkot* to 'Rabbi' (cp. [419]).

Sometimes, indeed, study is definitely put above 'doing':

[495] It is written 'That ye may learn them and observe to do them' (Deut. V, 1). The Scripture shows here that doing depends upon learning, and not *vice versa*; and we find that the punishment for not learning is heavier than that for not doing. And even as the punishment for not studying is greater than that for not doing, so too is the reward for study greater than the reward for doing. R. Jose of Galilee said: Study is greater than doing.

(*Sifre Deut.*, 'Eḳeb, § 41, f. 79*a*–79*b* (*R.T.* pp. 158, 159; H. p. 85).)

Study may take precedence even of prayer:

[496] Raba noticed that R. Hamnuna prolonged his prayer. He said: Such men neglect the eternal life, and busy themselves with the

life of the hour: for he thought, 'There is a set time for prayer, and a set time for study of the Law.' R. Jeremiah sat before R. Ze'era, and they were busy in the study of a legal question; the time for saying the evening prayer passed; R. Jeremiah hastened to say it. R. Ze'era quoted concerning him, 'He who turns his ear from hearing the Torah, his very prayer is an abomination.' (*Sab.* 10*a.*)

But one must not keep one's study to oneself. One must also teach.

On the strength of Lev. XXVI, 14, 15 a sort of chain is set up, and it is argued:

[497] One who refuses to learn will not fulfil [the commandments]. He who neither learns nor fulfils will despise others [who do fulfil]: such a one will hate the wise; such a one will seek to prevent others from fulfilling; such a one will end by denying [the obligation of fulfilling] the commandments; and lastly, such a one will end by denying the Root [i.e. God]. (*Sifra* 111*b fin.*–111*c init.*)

[498] 'Observe and learn [lit. hear] all these things which I command thee, that it may go well with thee, and with thy children after thee for ever, when thou doest that which is good and right in the sight of the Lord thy God' (Deut. XII, 28). ['To hear' often means 'to learn' or 'to understand'.] If thou hast learnt [lit. heard] a little, in the end thou wilt learn much: if thou hast kept a little, thou wilt end by keeping much. If thou keepest what thou hast learnt, thou wilt end by keeping what thou hast not learnt. If thou keepest that which is in thy power to keep, thou wilt end by keeping this in the life to come...for what is not learnt, will not be performed. (*Sifre Deut.*, Re'eh, §79, f. 91*a* (H. p. 145).)

The reference to the life to come is based upon the biblical words 'for ever', though the idea of doing the commandments in the world to come is unusual.

[499] 'How goodly are thy tents, O Jacob,...like watercourses [A.V. valleys] are they spread forth, like gardens by the river's side' (Num. XXIV, 5, 6). [Tents are interpreted to mean houses of study or synagogues.] What have watercourses to do with houses of study and synagogues? Just as those that are defiled go down to the watercourses, bathe therein and come up clean, so is it with the houses of study and with the synagogues:

men enter them full of sin, and come out from them clean and full of commandments. (*Tan.d.b.El.* p. 116 (cp. [1469]).)

[500] R. Ḥama b. Ḥanina said: Why are there found associated 'tents' and 'streams'—for it is written, 'As streams stretched out, as gardens by the river's side, as tents planted by the Lord, as cedars by the waters' (Num. XXIV, 6)? Its intention is to tell you that as streams bring a man up from impurity to purity, so do tents bring a man up from the scale of guilt to the scale of merit. (*Ber.* 16*a init.* (Cohen's trans. p. 102).)

Here too 'tents' are taken to mean 'houses of study'.

Sometimes, in place of 'study of the Law', we get a praise of knowledge, as for example:

[501] Abbaye said: We have received the teaching that 'poor' is he who is poor in knowledge. In the west they say, 'He who has knowledge has all; who has no knowledge, what has he? He who has got knowledge, what does he lack? Who has no knowledge, what has he?' (cp. *R.T.* p. 6). (*Ned.* 41*a.*)

'West', in the *Babylonian Talmud*, refers to Palestine, as opposed to Mesopotamia (cp. [1432]).

Knowledge is simply a wider term than study of the Law, and includes it. The main part, and the greatest part, of knowledge is always the study of the Law:

[502] Rabbi said: I am astonished that the prayer for knowledge (*P.B.* p. 46) is omitted on Sabbaths, for without knowledge how can one pray? R. Isaac said: Great is knowledge, for it is placed between the divine names, as it is said, 'For Yahweh is of knowledge the God' (I Sam. II, 3).

(*T.J.Ber.* IV, 3, f. 8*b*, line 10.)[1]

The Rabbis believed in a connection between wisdom and goodness. There was a certain intellectual element in their conception of righteousness. A pious fool, or even a virtuous fool, was not a combination to which they could have been sympathetic.

[503] 'And God gave Solomon wisdom and understanding, exceeding much, even as the sand which is on the sea shore' (I Kings IV, 29). R. Levi said: The sand surrounds the sea, and makes a fence, and is as a rampart and wall, and prevents the sea from coming

[1] A special prayer for knowledge has been inserted at the conclusion of Sabbaths. *P.B.* p. 94*d*. See too *Ber.* 33*a*. For 'Rabbi' cp. [419].

up over the land. So Solomon's wisdom surrounded him as a rampart and wall. How is this? When a man wishes to do something unseemly, if his wisdom does not surround his evil inclination, and stand before him as a wall, every evil will be found within him. For, as Solomon says, 'A man who has no rule over his spirit is like a broken down city without walls' (Prov. xxv, 28). Into such a city every evil thing can enter, robbers and wild beasts. So a man whose wisdom does not surround his *yetzer*, how many unseemly things does he not do.

(*Pes.R.* 59*a fin.*–59*b init.*)

Sometimes wisdom is given a very practical turn!

[504] It is written, 'They that are wise shall shine as the brightness of the firmament' (Dan. XII, 3). These are the judges who give a just and truthful judgment. 'And they that turn many to righteousness [i.e. to almsgiving] are as the stars for ever,' or again they are the teachers of little children. [Here righteousness is taken in its literal sense.] (*Bab.B.* 8*b.*)

The highest and best thing is the *combination* of doing and study. The following passage is very famous:

[505] 'And thou shalt make known to them the way wherein they must walk, and the work that they must do' (Exod. XVIII, 20). 'The way', that is, the study of the Law, and 'the work', that is, good deeds. So said R. Joshua. R. Elazar of Modi'im said, 'make known to them', that is, the house of study; 'the way', that is, visiting the sick; 'they should walk', that is, the burial of the dead; 'therein', that is, deeds of lovingkindness; 'and the work', that is, the letter of the Law (*shurat ha-Din*); 'and the work which they are to *do*', that is, *beyond* the letter of the Law [or, as we might say, equity] (*lifnim mish-shurat ha-Din*). [The interesting conceptions of *shurat ha-Din* and *lifnim mish-shurat ha-Din* are spoken of in *R.T.* pp. 191, 282 (cp. [1063]).]

(*Mek.*[2], *Amalek*, Yitro, § 2, p. 198; *Mek.*[3], § 4, vol. II, p. 182.)

There seems to have been a high ideal as regards preaching:

[506] 'Thy lips, O my bride, drop as the honey from the comb; honey and milk are under thy tongue' (Cant. IV, 11). R. Jose b. Ḥanina said: He who speaks words of Torah in public, if his words are not as pleasant to his hearers as honey from the comb,

had better not speak at all. The Rabbis say: He who speaks words of Torah in public, if his words are not as pleasant to his hearers as honey and milk mixed together, had better not speak at all. R. Johanan said: He who speaks words of Torah in public, if his words are not as pleasant to his hearers as a bride under the canopy is pleasant to the sons of men, had better not speak at all. Resh Lakish said: He who speaks words of Torah, if his words are not as pleasant to his hearers as a bride in the bridal chamber is pleasant to her husband, had better not speak at all.

(*Cant.R.* IV, § 11, 1, on IV, 11; f. 28*a* (cp. [437]).)

Chapter VII

THE COMMANDMENTS, THE SABBATH, AND THE LAW

The study and the practice of the commandments of the Law form the glory, the distinction, the beauty and the happiness of the life of the Israelites.

So, the more commandments, the more the Israelite's life can be sanctified and beautified:

[507] Beloved are the Israelites, for God has encompassed them with commandments: *tephillin* on head and arm, fringes on their garments, *mezuzot* on their doors. (*Men.* 43*b*.)

[508] R. Phinehas said: Whatsoever you do, the commandments accompany you. If you build a house, there is Deut. XXII, 8 (battlements); if you make a door, there is Deut. VI, 9 (text on door); if you buy new clothes, there is Deut. XXII, 11 (linsey-woolsey); if you have your hair cut, there is Lev. XIX, 27 (corners of beard); if you plough your field, there is Deut. XXII, 10 (ox and ass together); if you sow it, there is Deut. XXII, 9 (mixed crop); if you gather the harvest, there is Deut. XXIV, 19 (forgotten sheaf). God said, 'Even when you are not occupied with anything, but are just taking a walk, the commands accompany you,' for there is Deut. XXII, 6 (bird's nest). (*Deut.R.*, Shofeṭim, V, 3.)

The Rabbis regard this ubiquity of the commandments, not as a burden and a nuisance, but as a wonderful privilege and glory, perhaps also, too, a little as a safeguard, to remind a man everywhere of duty and of God.

[This passage is based on Prov. I, 9, 'For they (*sc.* instruction and law) shall be an ornament of grace unto thy head.' This is, as Mr Montefiore points out, the sense in which the commandments were regarded. But R. Phinehas' saying was founded on the other meaning of the word rendered 'ornament', i.e. 'accompaniment'. From different roots with the same radicals (*lavah*) come 'Levi', 'Leviathan', 'to accompany', 'to borrow or to lend', 'chaplet', 'ornament'.

There are many passages of similar import. *Pes.R.* 14*b* has already been cited [434], where the Oral Law, i.e. the Rabbinic system of jurisprudence, is regarded as God's mystery which differentiates Israel from the Gentiles, i.e. the Christians. Another well-known example is [585].

See also note in Abrahams, p. CLXXVIII. (H. L.)]

So far as any of the commandments are, as it were, gifts rendered to God, they are far smaller than God's gifts to man:

[509] God said to Israel, My children, when I gave you the omer of manna, I gave one omer for each single member of your households (Exod. XVI, 16), but when I ask you for an omer, I ask only for a single omer from you all (Lev. XXIII, 10). (*Pes.R.* 91*b*.)

The more commandments the more joy:

[510] He who loves the commandments is never satiated [or satisfied] with them. [He always longs for more and more, as the fulfilment of each is a joy to him.]

(*Deut.R.*, Wa'ethanan, II, 27 (in some edd. II, 18).)

[511] Once a certain pious man forgot a sheaf in the midst of his field. He said to his son: 'Go, offer a bullock as a burnt offering for me, and also a bullock for a peace offering.' The son said: 'My father, why do you rejoice in the fulfilment of this command especially, more than over all the other commands in the Torah?' He replied: 'All the commands in the Torah were given us by God to be observed knowingly, but this one we can observe only unknowingly. For if we seek to keep it deliberately, it cannot be kept, since it is ordained only for forgetfulness' (Deut. XXIV, 19). (*T.Pe'ah* III, 8 (Z. p. 22, line 1; cp. [556]).)

The story has been told in verse in the *Jewish Year* by my sister, Mrs Henry Lucas, 2nd ed. p. 166.

Perhaps the most delightful and joy-giving of all the commandments of the Law is the observance of the Sabbath:

[512] The Emperor asked R. Joshua b. Hananiah, 'What gives your Sabbath-meat such an aroma?' He replied, 'We have a spice called Sabbath, which is put in the cooking of the meat, and this gives it its aroma.' The Emperor said, 'Give me some of this spice.' He replied, 'For him who keeps the Sabbath the spice works, for him who does not keep it, it does not work.'

(*Sab.* 119*a*.)

[513] It is written, 'If thou turn away thy foot from doing thy business on my holy day' (Isa. LVIII, 13). Hence, a man is forbidden to

walk out to his field upon the Sabbath in order to see what it may need. It happened that a certain pious man walked out to his vineyard upon the Sabbath to see what it needed, and he found a break in its fence, and he thought about repairing it, and it was the Sabbath. Then he said, 'Now I will not do it at all, because I thought about it on the Sabbath day.' What did God do? God prepared a caper bush, and it made a fence for his vineyard, and the man sustained himself from it all the days of his life. (*Lev.R.*, Behar, XXXIV, 16.)

[514] R. Jose b. Judah said: The angels of the service accompany a man on Friday evening from the Synagogue to his house, one good and one bad angel; and if, when he comes to his house, the lamp is lit, and the table spread, and the couch arranged, the good angel says, 'May it be God's will that the next Sabbath may be as this one,' to which the bad angel, even against his will, says, 'Amen.' But if it is not so, then the bad angel says, 'May it be God's will that thus it may be on the next Sabbath also,' and the good angel, against his will, says, 'Amen.'[1] (*Sab.* 119*b*.)

[515] R. Ḥanina said: A man should always have two suits of clothes, one for workdays, and one for the Sabbath. R. Simlai taught publicly the same. The disciples wept and said, 'As our clothes are on weekdays, so are they on Sabbaths' [i.e. we have each only one suit]. He replied, 'Then make, at least, some little change upon the Sabbath.' (*Ruth R.* v, 12 on III, 3, f. 10*a*.)

[516] R. Ḥisda and R. Hamnuna said that it is permissible to make plans for good deeds on the Sabbath; and R. Elazar said that one may arrange about alms to the poor on Sabbath. R. Johanan said: One may transact business which has to do with the saving of life or with public health on Sabbath, and one may go to synagogue to discuss public affairs on Sabbath. R. Jonathan said: One may even go to theatres and circuses on Sabbath for such a purpose. And in the school of Manasseh it was said that one may talk about the future marriage of one's children on Sabbath, or about the children's education, or about teaching them a handicraft, for the Scripture forbids '*thy* business', but *God's* business is permitted (cp. *R.T.* p. 327).

(*Sab.* 150*a fin.* (cp. *Tanḥ.*, Bereshit, § 2, f. 8*a*).)

[1] [On this passage see my *Mediaeval Hebrew Minstrelsy*, pp. 25f. The subject is treated more fully in the forthcoming ed. (H. L.)]

[517] He who makes the Sabbath a delight shall have the wishes of his heart fulfilled. [The delight is here explained to mean special food.] Even a little is regarded as 'Sabbath delight', if it is prepared to honour the Sabbath. (*Sab.* 118*b*.)

[518] On Sabbath a man should always walk with an easy and leisurely gait, but to do a good act, interposed R. Joshua b. Levi, a man should always run, even on Sabbath. (*Tanḥ.*, Bereshit, § 2, f. 8*a init.*)

[The word *gas* ('run with a *hasty* step') is used also of a *proud* spirit, of a *large* domestic animal (e.g. a cow as opposed to a goat) or a *full* meal. With regard to 'steps', it implies the large, hasty step of the soldier or civilian pursuing his daily avocations, hence it was a characteristic of the working day. One sometimes sees those who are called to the Reading of the Law come up to the lectern with a short symbolical run, but leave the lectern with leisurely deliberation, in contrast. (H. L.)]

[519] R. Ḥanina used, on the eve of the Sabbath, to put on his best clothes, and to say, 'Come, let us go and meet the Queen Sabbath.' R. Yannai used on Friday evening to put on his best clothes, and to say, 'Come, O bride; come, O bride.'[1]
Rabba b. R. Huna once happened to visit Rabba b. R. Naḥman on the eve of the Sabbath, and they offered him three special cakes. He said, 'Did you know I was coming?' They said to him, 'Are you more distinguished than she?' ['She' meant the Sabbath.]...Him who lends to the Sabbath, the Sabbath will repay. (*Sab.* 119*a*.)

Frivolous talk on the Sabbath was discountenanced, but, on the other hand, any action which, in itself not unpraiseworthy, might cause a passing sadness, was also not looked on with favour:

[520] R. Ḥiyya b. Abba said: When the mother of Simeon b. Yoḥai talked too much on the Sabbath, he would say to her, 'Mother, it is Sabbath'; and she would stop. (*Pes.R.* 116*b*.)

[521] R. Ḥanina said: Only with reluctance did they [the Rabbis] allow mourners to be comforted, or the sick to be visited, on Sabbaths. (*Sab.* 12*b* (cp. Moore, II, 37, 39).)[2]

[1] See *P.B.* p. 111 and Abrahams' note p. CXXIV. For English verse renderings see Alice Lucas, *Jewish Year*, 2nd ed. p. 19 and David de Sola Pool, *Book of Prayer*, New York, 1936, p. 134.

[2] [The fixed saying is: 'On Sabbath we do not sorrow; help is nigh.' For the greeting to mourners on their entry into the Synagogue, see *P.B.* p. 112, in the new edd. (Cp. [1537].) (H. L.)]

[522] R. Ḥiyya b. Abba said: The Sabbath was given for enjoyment. R. Samuel b. Naḥmani said: The Sabbath was given for studying the Torah. The one saying does not contradict the other. R. Ḥiyya referred to scholars who spend the week studying the Torah; when the Sabbath comes, they enjoy themselves, whereas R. Samuel was thinking of labourers, who are busy with their work all the week, and on the Sabbath they come and study the Torah. (*Pes.R.* 121*a*.)

[523] 'Therefore the Lord blessed the Sabbath day and sanctified it.' [The literal meaning of 'sanctify' is 'to separate'. So God separated the Sabbath.] It has no partner. All the other days of the week go in pairs, but the seventh day has no partner. The Sabbath said to God, 'The other days have partners; I have no partner.' God said, 'Israel shall be thy partner.' (*Pes.R.* 117*b*.)

The Day of Atonement was naturally regarded as an extraordinary Sabbath of Rest (Lev. XXIII, 32), and it was honoured by a special meal before its opening. The following story illustrates the custom, and illustrates also the dangers which, in spite of the warnings of the Rabbis, the Day was bound to bring with it to the minds of simple and even pious folk, like the tailor, who naïvely says, 'Of all sins which we commit in the year this day absolves us' (cp. [837]):

[524] R. Phinehas said: It happened that a pious man in Rome was wont to honour the Sabbath and the Festivals. On the afternoon before the Day of Atonement he went into the market to make his purchases, and he found only one fish for sale. Now the Governor's servant was standing there, and they bid against each other for the fish. In the end the Jew bought it at a denarius per pound. At dinner time the Governor said to his servant, 'There is no fish here.' He answered, 'To-day only one fish came to market, and a Jew bought it at a denarius the pound.' He said, 'Would you recognise him?' He said, 'Yes.' The Governor replied, 'Go and accuse him of having in his house a hidden treasure belonging to the king.' He did so. The Jew said, 'I am a tailor.' The servant replied, 'And do you, a tailor, eat fish at a denarius a pound?' So he brought him before the Governor. The Jew said, 'Will my Lord give me permission to say something?' The Governor said, 'Speak.' The Jew said to him, 'We have one day in the year which is dearer to us than

all the rest; of all sins which we commit in the year this day frees us and absolves us. Therefore we honour that day more than all the rest of the year.' The Governor said, 'Since you have brought a proof for your words, you are acquitted.' How did God reward the tailor? God prepared for him a pearl of great price in the fish, and on the proceeds of the pearl he lived ever afterwards.

(*Pes.R.* 119*a*.)

All the commandments should be fulfilled in joy. The next quotation is curious:

[525] On the prohibition against eating meat containing blood, Rabbi (cp. [419]) observes: Every single command which Israel accepted at Sinai in joy, they observe in joy to this day. Those which they then accepted without joy they do not now observe with joy. R. Simeon b. Gamaliel says: Every command for which the Israelites gave their lives in the times of the persecution, they now carry out openly: the others have grown effete [lit. weak] among them. ['The persecution' usually refers to the great persecution under Hadrian.] (*Sifre Deut.*, Re'eh, §76, f. 90*b* (H. p. 141).)

[526] Ever let a man fulfil the commands [or, possibly, 'study'] of the Torah in joy, and it will be accounted unto him for righteousness. Let him separate his leave-offerings and give his tithes in joy, and it will be accounted unto him for righteousness.

(*Tan.d.b.El.* p. 144.)

It is to the Israelites' praise and honour that they received the Law in simplicity, and asked neither about the reason of the commands nor about their reward:

[527] God said, 'I gave them positive commands, and they accepted them; I gave them negative commands, and they accepted them and I did not specify their reward, and they said nothing, and how many commands there were!' Israel received the Law in perfect sincerity. God said to them, 'Thou shalt not seethe the kid in its mother's milk,' and they did not say, 'Why?', but received it. And He said to them, 'Ye shall eat no manner of fat,' and they did not say, 'Why?', but received it. Though they received and accepted the commands, they did not say, 'What is their reward? *then* only we will do them.'

(*Midr.Ps.* on CXIX, 1 (244*b*–245*b*, §§1–6).)

So all commandments should be fulfilled, whether heavy or light, whatever may, or may not, be their reward:

[528] The wise say, 'Keep you far from a light sin, for perhaps a light sin may bring you to a heavy sin. Run to fulfil a light commandment, for it will bring you to fulfil a heavy one....' When the Israelites fulfil the light commandments, these bring them to the life of the world to come.
(*Ab.R.N.* (vers. I), II, 5*a* (cp. [532]).)

[529] Whoever begins a commandment, but does not finish it, forfeits his life. (*Tan.d.b.El.* p. 188.)

For the last three words we may compare R. Jacob's saying in *Aboth*. Mr Singer's rendering of them is followed.

[530] R. Jacob said: He who is walking by the way and studying, and breaks off his study and says, 'How fine is that tree, how fine is that fallow,' him the Scripture regards as if he had forfeited his life. (*Aboth* III, 9.)

The meaning is, I suppose—to be taken *cum grano salis*, as Oriental exaggeration—he has lost his chance of a place in the world to come.

Man's responsibility for his actions is strongly maintained:

[531] It is written, 'See, I set before you this day a blessing and a curse' (Deut. XI, 26), and 'From the mouth of the Most High proceeds there not evil and good?' (Lam. III, 38). R. Elazar said: When God proclaimed the former words [i.e. Deut. XI, 26] on Sinai, in that instant 'from the mouth of the Most High good and evil did *not* go forth' (Lam. III, 38), but they came forth from themselves: evil came upon the doer of evil, and good upon the doer of good. R. Haggai said: Not merely did I set before you two ways [i.e. evil and good], but I have gone beyond the line of strict justice in that I have said to you, 'Do thou choose life' (Deut. XXX, 19). [For the 'way' cp. [505].] (*Deut.R.*, Re'eh, IV, 3.)

Very famous is the following saying, that one good deed, or fulfilled command, will induce, or help, a man to do another; that one sin will make another sin more likely and easy:

[532] Ben Azzai said: Run to do even a slight precept, and flee from transgression; for precept draws precept in its train, and transgression, transgression; for the recompense of a precept is

a precept, and the recompense of a transgression is a transgression. (*Aboth* IV, 2 (cp. [528]).)

[533] Rabbi Me'ir said: If you neglect the Torah, many causes for neglecting it will present themselves to you. (*Aboth* IV, 12.)

God helps a man to keep in the good path; but He allows a man to sin, and it may even be said that He is the author of the rule that one lapse hastens another lapse:

[534] 'And it shall come to pass that if thou hearkenest hearkening [i.e. diligently] to the voice of the Lord thy God, and do what is upright in his eyes' (Exod. XV, 26). Why does it say, 'thou hearkenest hearkening'? It means that if *thou* hearkenest, there will be a hearkening for thee. If a man wishes to hearken to God's voice at the time when he hears it, God will cause him to hearken ever afterwards. If a man wishes to forget, God similarly aids him, for it also says, 'And it shall be if thou forgetting forget' (Deut. VIII, 19). Thus it comes that if a man is ready and willing to hearken, God causes him to hearken even when he is unready or even unwilling. For in man's own hand is free will [i.e. to make the first choice, but then], 'Surely the scorners does He scorn, but to the lowly He gives grace' (Prov. III, 34). So, if a man hearkens to one command, God gives him the power to hearken to many; and so also is the case with forgetfulness, as it says, 'if thou forgetting forget' [i.e. utterly]; if thou forgettest once, there will come more forgetting.

(*Tanḥ.*, Beshallaḥ, § 19, f. 117*a* (cp. [752]).)

[535] All who [of their own accord] draw near to God, God draws near to Him [i.e. He helps man to draw near to Him, when man seeks to draw near].

(*Sifre Num.*, Beha'aloteka, § 78, f. 20*b fin.* (H. p. 75).)

Goodness draws goodness in its train, just as sin incites to sin:

[536] Isaiah said: 'Woe to those that draw iniquity with cords of falsehood, and sin as it were with a cart rope' (V, 18). That is, the beginning of sin is like a thread of a spider's web; its end is like a cart rope. Rabbi said: He who fulfils one command for its own sake should not rejoice because of that one [fulfilled] commandment, but because in the end this one [fulfilled] commandment will draw after it the fulfilment of many command-

ments; so he who commits one sin should not grieve over that one sin, but rather grieve that in the end the commission of one sin may mean the commission of many sins, for commandment incites to commandment and sin incites to sin. [For 'Rabbi' cp. [419].] (*Sifre Num.*, Shelaḥ, § 112, f. 33*a* (H. p. 120).)

[537] He who violates a light command will ultimately violate a heavy one; he who violates, 'Love thy neighbour as thyself,' will ultimately violate, 'Thou shalt not hate thy brother in thy heart, and thou shalt not take vengeance nor bear any grudge'; and even 'He shall live with thee' (Lev. xxv, 35), till at the end he will come to shedding blood.

(*Sifre Deut.*, Shofeṭim, § 187, f. 108*b* (cp. [1068]).)

To regard the command to 'love thy neighbour as thyself' as in any sense a 'light' command, seems passing strange. It would seem (so Mr Loewe thinks) that it is considered light in the sense of being comparatively easy to fulfil, because it is natural to man to love. The absence of love leads to hate, and so finally to murder.

Once again let me remind the reader of the pleasant fact that the Rabbis usually kept their heads as to primaries and secondaries. The following passage is quoted in every anthology, but it must not, on that account, be left out in mine:

[538] R. Simlai said: Six hundred and thirteen commandments were given to Moses, 365 negative commandments, answering to the number of the days of the year, and 248 positive commandments, answering to the number of a man's members. Then David came and reduced them to eleven [eleven commands are found in Psalm xv]. Then came Isaiah, and reduced them to six [as one may count in Isa. xxxiii, 15]. Then came Micah, and reduced them to three [as is seen in the great saying of Micah vi, 8]. Then Isaiah came again, and reduced them to two, as it is said, 'Keep ye judgment and do righteousness.' Then came Amos, and reduced them to one, as it is said, 'Seek ye me and live.' Or one may say, then came Habakkuk (ii, 4), and reduced them to one, as it is said, 'The righteous shall live by his faith.'

(*Mak.* 23*b*–24*a* (cp. [667]).)[1]

[1] [See Schechter's essay on 'The Law and recent criticism' in his *Studies in Judaism*, 1896, pp. 283 f., 301 and 302. Also Montefiore, *Origin and Development of the Religion of the Ancient Hebrews*, Hibbert Lectures, 1892 (a book which is as valuable now as in 1892), in Chapters vii–ix, especially pp. 503 f. (H. L.)]

[539] A heathen came to Shammai, and said to him, 'Accept me as a proselyte on the condition that you teach me the whole Law while I stand on one foot.' Then Shammai drove him away with the measuring rod which he held in his hand. Then he went to Hillel, who received him as a proselyte and said to him, 'What is hateful to you do not to your fellow: that is the whole Law; all the rest is its explanation; go and learn.'

(*Sab.* 31*a* (cp. [458]).)

[540] 'If they had been wise, they would have understood this' (Deut. XXXII, 29). If the Israelites had understood the words of the Torah which was given to them, no people or kingdom would have ruled over them. And what did the Torah say to them? 'Take upon you the yoke of the Kingdom of Heaven, and excel one another in the fear of God, and do deeds of loving-kindness one towards the other.'

(*Sifre Deut.*, Ha'azinu, § 323, f. 138*b init.*)

[541] Let all your doings be done for the sake of God. Fear God and love Him. Feel reverence and joy towards all the commandments. (*Der.Er.Z.* II, 1.)

[542] Learn to receive the words of the Law in trouble; and seek not [recompenses for] the insult you receive. For there is an exact reckoning of reward and punishment. Love the Torah and honour it; love your fellow-men and honour them; love the righteous and the upright and reproof. (*Der.Er.Z.* II, 2.)

[543] Bar Ḳappara taught: Which is the shortest passage in Scripture upon which all the essentials of the Law (*gufe Torah*) depend? [Dr Cohen renders, 'All the principles of the Torah.'] It is: 'In all thy ways acknowledge God, and He will direct thy paths' (Prov. III, 6). (*Ber.* 63*a*.)

A curious passage is the following:

[544] R. Judah said: Let a man always acquire his knowledge of Torah in the form of general principles, for, if he acquires it in the form of many details, they will weary him, and he will not know what to do [with them]. It is like a man going to Caesarea and needing a hundred or a couple of hundred *zuzim* [shillings] for expenses. If he takes them as separate coins, they will weary

him, and he will not know what to do, but if he changes them for pieces of higher denominations, i.e. *sela'im* (crown pieces), he can take them about from place to place at will.

(*Sifre Deut.*, Ha'azinu, § 306, f. 132*a*.)

[545] Let not a man say, 'I will follow hateful ways, and do things which are unseemly, and then will I bring a meat offering mingled with oil to show the love which I have for God.' God says to him, 'My son, wherefore hast thou not mingled thy actions with words of Torah, for there is no better oil than Torah and good deeds.' (*Tan.d.b.El.* p. 37.)

Chapter VIII

REWARD, MERIT AND ATONEMENT

It is often alleged against the Rabbis that they attached an undue importance to reward. It is said that the motive for right-doing and for fulfilling the commandments of the Law was the hope of reward, whether on earth, or in the life to come at the resurrection, or in heaven. There is, undoubtedly, a measure of validity in this criticism. One of God's primary duties, so to speak, as regards Israel was to punish and to reward, to reward even far more than to punish. When the Law was violated, the Israelites had to be punished; when it was observed, it was God's delight to reward them. Indeed it may be said that one purpose of the giving of the Law was to enable God to reward Israel for its acceptance and fulfilment of the Law. There is an extremely significant, just because it is an entirely casual, remark, in *Pes.R.* 107*a*. Israel is there made to say, 'If I had not accepted the Law, I should have been just as one of the nations, for whom there is neither reward nor punishment.' This casual utterance shows the important place assigned to punishment and reward. Yet the view mentioned above is *not* entirely just to the Rabbis. They *did* believe in 'reward'; they *did* expect that the righteous would be 'rewarded', more particularly after death. For the constant troubles and persecutions under which the Jews suffered made them convinced that the reward of the righteous must be after death, if at all! Yet the fulfilment of the Law on earth was, in one sense, its own reward. The 'joy of the commandment' is an idea which constantly recurs. The Rabbis were keen about joy. Religion must create joy; the fulfilment of the Law was pure joy. God's inspiration, His very presence, rests only upon the joyful.

[546] Our Rabbis have taught: One must not stand up to say the [statutory] prayer from the midst of sorrow, idleness, jocularity, frivolous conversation, levity or idle chatter, but from the midst of the joy of the commandment. (*Ber.* 31*a*.)

[547] 'I said of laughter, It is to be praised' [A.V. 'it is mad'] (Eccles. II, 2). That is, the joy of the commandment. (*Sab.* 30*b*.)

[548] The Holy Spirit does not rest where there is idleness, or sadness, or ribaldry, or frivolity, or empty speech, but only where there is joy. (*Midr.Ps.* on XXIV, 3 (102*b*, § 3) (cp. *Sab.* 30*b*).)

[549] It is written that Moses said, 'I have done according to all

that thou hast commanded me' (Deut. XXVI, 14). That means, I have rejoiced, and caused others to rejoice.

(*Sifre Deut.*, Ki Tabo, § 303, f. 129*a*.)

[550] It says, 'Serve the Lord with gladness' (Ps. C, 2), and it says, 'Serve the Lord with fear' (Ps. II, 11). If with gladness, how with fear? If with fear, how with gladness? R. Aibu said: All your life you should rejoice in your prayer, and yet have fear before the Lord. (*Midr.Ps.* on C, 2 (213*a*, § 3).)

[551] The Holy Spirit rests on him only who has a joyous heart.

(*T.J.Suk.* V, § 1, f. 55*a*, line 68.)

[552] R. Eliezer said: On festivals let a man eat and drink, or sit and study. R. Joshua said: Divide your time; devote half to God, and half to yourselves. [Both views were supported by Pentateuchal verses.] R. Eliezer quoted the verse in Neh. VIII, 10, 'Go your way, eat the fat, and drink the sweet, and send portions unto him for whom nothing is ready; for this day is holy unto our Lord; neither be grieved, for the joy of the Lord is your strength.' What do the last words mean? R. Johanan said: God said to the Israelites, 'My sons, borrow on my account, and sanctify the sanctification of the day, and trust in me; I will repay.' (*Beẓ.* 15*b*.)

[553] Rab said: A man will have to give account in the judgment day of every good thing which he might have enjoyed and did not [lit. which his eyes saw, and he did not eat]. [The saying must have been interpreted quite literally, for the Talmud goes on to say:] R. Elazar gave heed to that teaching, and he used to collect together small coins, and he ate from them [he bought with them] every possible food once in every year.

(*T.J.Ḳid.* IV, § 12, f. 66*d*, line 32.)

[This apparently refers to the custom—still observed—of making a point on the Festivals of eating, and offering guests, a variety of fruits and other dainties, each of which has its special and appropriate form of blessing and thanksgiving. (H. L.)]

Of *external* reward on earth for the fulfilment of the commands there was, too frequently, very little! It was, I think, possible for the Rabbis, as it has been possible for many millions of simple believers in more religions than one, to look forward, with complete confidence and hope and pleasurable anticipation, to heavenly reward, and *yet* to fulfil the commandments purely, for their own sake, and for the love of God. Such a combination is real. It was real in olden times: it is real to-day.

On the other hand, their legalism had a certain mechanical side. To the fulfilment of every command they believed that God allotted reward, just as for the committal of sin (putting repentance and forgiveness and other matters on one side) He inflicted punishment. Hence, nothing is more frequent in the Rabbinical literature than the view that the righteous are punished for their few sins by punishments in *this* world, in order that they may be free from all punishment, and receive nothing but 'reward', in the world to come; whereas the wicked are rewarded for their few virtues in this world, in order that they may be punished the more completely in the world to come. The same doctrine is often found as regards the well-being of the Gentiles and the sufferings of the Israelites. This world's happiness is for the nations; the next world's happiness is for the Israelites. No doubt a few Israelites will have a bad time hereafter, and a few non-Israelites will have a good time, but for the great majority the rule is as I have stated. Here we see manifested the Rabbinic particularism. But of these weeds no examples need be given. The particularism of orthodox Christians in mediaeval times was precisely on all fours. **(Note 87.)**

Of the general doctrine of reward I quote the following as specimens:

[554] Rabbi Judah the Prince (Rabbi, cp. [419]) said: Be heedful of a light precept as of a grave one, for thou knowest not the grant of reward for each precept. Reckon the loss incurred by the fulfilment of a precept against the reward secured by its observance, and the gain gotten by a transgression against the loss it involves. Reflect upon three things, and thou wilt not come within the power of sin: Know what is above thee—a seeing eye, and a hearing ear, and all thy deeds written in a book. (*Aboth* II, 1.)

The 'loss' could refer, for example, to the material or pecuniary loss involved, say, in keeping the Sabbath, and the 'gain' to the profit obtained by its violation. I doubt whether we can accept Mr Travers Herford's view as to the meaning of reward in such passages as the above. 'Reward', he says, 'in connection with conduct means an expression of divine approval, it does not mean a concrete benefit which could be claimed and earned by the fulfilment of a precept.' (His ed. of *Aboth*, p. 40).

[555] R. Aḥa quoted Prov. v, 6, 'Canst thou find the path of life? Thou canst not know it', and said: God has made the reward

of those who fulfil the commands irregular, so that they may do them in sincerity. R. Aḥa said: Take heed of all that is written in the Law, for you do not know from the doing of which commandment life may come to you.

R. Abba b. Kahana said: The Scripture has made the lightest command in the Torah equal to the heaviest command; for the reward of length of days is attached to both of them [to the command about the young birds and the mother in Deut. XXII, 6, 7, and to the command about the honour of parents]. R. Abun said: If in a command, which is, as it were, the payment of a debt, the reward of length of days is appended, how much more should it be appended to commands which involve loss of money or danger of life (cp. p. 215).

(*T.J.Ḳid.* I, § 7, f. 61*b*, line 62; *T.J.Pe'ah* I, § I, f. 15*d*, line 12.)

[556] R. Elazar b. Azariah said: He who, in reaping his field, leaves the forgotten sheaf for the stranger, the fatherless and the widow (Deut. XXIV, 19), is assured of God's blessing. So the Scripture attaches blessing even to one who unwittingly fulfils a commandment. So, if a man drops a coin from his garments, and a poor man finds it and sustains himself with it, the Scripture ordains that the same blessing will rest on him who dropped the coin as on him who forgets his sheaf in his field.

(*Sifra* 27*a* (cp. [511]).)

[557] R. Jose said: If you wish to know of the reward of the righteous in the world to come, consider the case of Adam. One single negative command was given him. This he violated, and see how many deaths have been decreed for him and for all his generations unto the end of time. Now which is greater, the attribute of reward [lit. of goodness] or that of punishment? Surely the attribute of reward. If, then, the attribute of punishment, which is less, caused all those deaths, of him who repents from sin, and fasts on the Day of Atonement, how much more will he bring blessing to himself and to all his generations to the end of time. ['Bring blessing', lit. cause *zekut*.] (*Sifra* 27*a*.)

The character of the teaching of many Rabbis as regards reward and punishment is illustrated by the following passage:

[558] There was a disciple of R. Simeon b. Yoḥai who went abroad, and came back rich. His fellow-disciples saw him, and were

jealous of him, and they too wanted to go abroad. R. Simeon noticed it, and he took them into a valley, and he prayed and said, 'Valley, valley, be filled with golden coins.' And golden coins began to pour in upon them. Then he said to them, 'If you seek gold, here it is, take it; but know that he who takes it, takes his portion of the world to come [i.e. he will receive no reward in the world to come], for the reward of the Torah is only in the world to come.' (**Note 97**.) (*Exod.R.*, Peḳude, LII, 3.)

[559] It is written, 'What profit has a man of all the labour with which he labours under the sun' (Eccles. I, 3). R. Benjamin b. Levi said: They sought to store away the book of Ecclesiastes because they found in it words which tended to heresy. They said, 'Was it fitting for Solomon to say, "Rejoice, O young man, in thy youth, and let thy heart cheer thee in the days of thy youth" (Eccles. XI, 9). Had not Moses said, "Seek not after your own heart and your own eyes" (Num. XV, 39)? But Solomon said, "Walk in the ways of thine heart and in the light of thine eyes." Then is the bridle loosened; there is no judgment and no judge.' But when they read the end of the verse, 'But know that for all these things God will bring thee into judgment,' they said that Solomon spoke well. R. Samuel b. Naḥmani said: They sought to store away the book of Ecclesiastes because they found in it words which tended to heresy. They said, 'Need Solomon have said, "What profit has a man of all his labour?" One might think that he meant, Even for labour in the Law there was no profit to a man.' But they changed their minds and said, 'If Solomon had said, For *all* labour, and had stopped there, one could have thought that he meant even for all labour upon the Law. But Solomon says, For all *his* labour; that is, for all *his* labour there is no profit, but for labour spent on the Law there *is* profit.' R. Yudan said: *Under* the sun there is no profit, but *above* the sun there *is* profit. (*Lev.R.*, Emor, XXVIII, 1 (cp. [1400]).)

[560] R. Simeon b. Ḥalafta on one Sabbath eve had nothing to eat. He went outside the city, and prayed to God, and a precious stone was given him from heaven. He gave it to the money-changer, and he got provisions for the Sabbath. His wife said to him, 'Whence have you obtained these things?' He said, 'God has provided me with them.' She said to him, 'If you

do not tell me whence you got them, I will not taste a thing.' He then told her, 'I prayed to God, and it [the stone] was given me from heaven.' She said, 'I will eat nothing until you promise me to restore the stone when the Sabbath is over.' He said, 'Why?' She said, 'Do you wish that your table should be empty, and the table of your fellows should be full?' Then Rabbi Simeon went and told the whole story to Rabbi (cp. [419]) [i.e. Judah the Prince]. Rabbi said, 'Go and tell your wife that if your table is defective, I will supply the deficiency from mine.' She said, 'Come with me to him who has taught thee Torah.' She said to Rabbi, 'Does one man see his fellow in the world to come? Has not each one his world to himself?' [As a proof she quotes Eccles. XII, 5, 'Man goes to the house of his world' (A.V. 'his long home').] When R. Simeon heard that, he went and gave the stone back, and the Rabbis said: The second miracle was greater than the first. For no sooner had he stretched out his hand to give it back, straightway an angel from heaven came down, and took it from him. And why? Because the reward of the Law is only in the world to come. (**Note 97**.)

(*Exod.R.*, Pekude, LII, 3.)

[561] R. Levi said: What profit have men who lay by good deeds and commandments? 'It is enough', God says, 'that I cause a light to rise upon them.' The Rabbis say, What profit have the righteous that they lay by for themselves commandments and good deeds? 'It is enough', God says, 'that in the world to come I shall renew their countenance like the face of the sun,' as it says, 'They that love him are as the sun when he goes forth in his might' (Judges V, 31). (*Eccles.R.* I, § 3, 1, on I, 3 (2*a*).)

[562] It says in Prov. XI, 21, 'Though hand join in hand, the wicked man shall not go unpunished.' R. Phinehas said: This is said of him who gives alms, and seeks to get an immediate reward. Such a one, said R. Simeon, is like a man who says, 'Here is the sack, here is the weight, here is the measure; mete out.' Behold, if the patriarchs had sought to obtain reward in this world for their good deeds, how could their merit have been stored up for their descendants after them? (*T.J.San.* X, § 1, f. 27*d*, line 40 (for other interpretations of this proof text cp. [586] and [637]).)

[563] 'Give ear, ye heavens' (Deut. XXXII, 1). God said to Moses,

'Say unto Israel; Consider the heavens which I made to serve you, Have they ever failed in their duty?' [lit. changed their nature]. Does not the sun rise in the east and give light to the inhabitants of the earth? It rises and it sets with regularity (Eccles. I, 5), nay, more, it rejoices in doing its Creator's will (Ps. XIX, 5). 'And let the earth hear my mouth's words' (*ib.*). Consider the earth which I created for your service. Has it ever changed its nature? Have you ever sown without its sprouting forth? Have you ever sown wheat, and has it produced barley? Or does the cow not thresh and plough? or the ass not bear his load and walk? Does not the sea observe the limits which I have assigned to it (Jer. V, 22)? If *these* have not changed their nature, these which, unlike you, were created neither for profit nor for loss; if, unlike you, when they do well, they receive no reward, if when they sin, they are not punished: they have no care for their sons and their daughters, yet these have not changed their nature: but you if you do well, you receive reward, if you do evil, you receive punishment, and you have care for your sons and daughters. How much more ought you in no wise to change your characters? [I.e. from good to bad, in view of Deut. XXXII, 5, 'You have corrupted yourselves.'] (**Note 98**.)

(*Sifre Deut.*, Ha'azinu, § 306, f. 131*a*.)

[564] It says in Ps. XXXVII, 'Fret not thyself because of evildoers: trust in the Lord, and do good.' God said to David, 'If you see that I do good to the wicked, let it not seem evil in your heart, but go on doing good. If to the wicked who provoke me and do not profit me, I do good, how much more shall I do good to you who trust in me, and occupy yourself with the Law?' David was like a workman who worked for a king all his life, and had been given no hire; and he was grieved, and said, 'Perhaps I shall never get anything at all.' Then the king hired another workman for one day only, and gave him food and drink and his full wage. Then the first workman thought, 'If this has happened to the man who laboured only one day, how much more will it be so with me, who have laboured for him all my life.' And he began to rejoice. R. Elazar said: From the prosperity of the wicked in *this* world, you can judge the reward of the righteous in the world to come. If the wicked fare thus, how much more the righteous! (*Midr.Ps.* on XXXVII, 3 (127*a*, § 3).)

[565] 'At thy right hand there are pleasures for evermore' (Ps. XVI, 11). David said to God, 'Lord, make known to me which is the class that of all the classes is the most beloved and lovely.' One Rabbi said: It is they who come before God because of their knowledge of the Law, and because of their good deeds. Another Rabbi said: It is the class of those teachers of Scripture and Mishnah who teach the children faithfully, for they will sit at God's right hand. (*Pes.K.* 180*a*.)

[566] R. Aḥa said: God has made uncertain the reward of those who perform the commands of the Law, so that they may do them in fidelity. (*T.J.Pe'ah* I, §1, f. 15*d*, line 13 (see comm. *Pene Mosheh*).)

But the O.T., and the Pentateuch in particular, speak of earthly rewards (e.g. long life) too plainly, too definitely, and too frequently, for the Rabbis to ignore or explain away such passages altogether. They often asserted the doctrine themselves. For example:

[567] R. Ḥiya b. Abba said in the name of Ula: Greater is he who profits from the labour of his hands than he who fears God, for of the latter it says, 'Happy is he who fears the Lord'; but of the former, 'If thou eat the labour of thy hands, happy art thou, and it shall be well with thee; happy in this world, and it shall be well with thee in the world to come.'
(*Midr.Ps.* on CXXVIII, 1 (257*a*, §1).)

[568] When R. Haggai appointed and instituted officers, he was wont to put a roll of the Law in their hands, and say that all rule which is given to men is given from the Torah. While R. Eliezer was a *Parnas* [communal administrator], he one day went to his house, and he said to the members of his household, 'How have you fared?' They replied, 'A band of travellers came here and ate and drank, and prayed for you.' He said, 'Then there will be no good reward' [i.e. because the men thanked me, therefore God will not reward me]. On a similar occasion the reply was, 'Another band of travellers ate and drank, and cursed you.' He said, 'Then the reward will be good.' When it was desired to make R. Akiba a communal officer, he said, 'I will consult my wife.' Those who followed him to his house heard her say, 'Take it on condition that you are cursed and despised' [because you will not be able to satisfy everybody, and then you will gain reward from God]. (*T.J.Pe'ah* VIII, § 7, f. 21*a*, line 29.)

Incidentally it may be noticed that office was regarded as so unpleasant that it was in itself supposed to cause forgiveness of all sins!

[569] When they wanted to appoint R. Ze'era as Nasi (cp. [419]), he did not want to accept the office. When he heard this teaching: 'As regards the scholar, the bridegroom, the Patriarch, the office atones for sin,' he accepted it. How is the teaching proved? As regards the scholar, it says, 'Thou shalt rise up before the hoary head, and honour the face of an old man, and fear thy God: I am the Lord' (Lev. XIX, 32). And immediately after follows the verse, 'If a stranger [proselyte] sojourns in thy land, thou shalt not oppress him' [i.e. reproach him for his former idolatry]; even as the proselyte is forgiven his former sins, so the scholar appointed to an office is forgiven his iniquities. As to the bridegroom, it says: 'Esau took Mahalath (i.e. forgiveness), the daughter of Ishmael, to wife.' But her original name was Bashemath [daughter of shame]; the new name shows that Esau was forgiven all his iniquities. (See Gen. XXVIII, 9 and XXXVI, 3.) As to the Nasi, it says, 'Saul was one year old when he began to reign' [corrupt Hebrew text]. Was he really one year old? No, it means, his sins were forgiven him, and he became as if he were a sinless child of a year old (I Sam. XIII, 1). (**Notes 57 and 78**.) (*T.J.Bik.* III, 3, 65*c fin.*–65*d init.* (cp. [1106]).)

The office bearer was the servant of the community:

[570] He who receives office in order to profit from it is like an adulterer, who gets his pleasure from a woman's body. God says, 'I am called holy, you are called holy; if you have not all the qualities which I have, you should not accept leadership.'

(*Pes.R.* 111*a*.)

[571] R. Gamaliel was told of two Rabbis who were very clever and very poor. He determined to appoint them to a salaried post. He sent for them, but they did not come. He sent again, and they came. He said to them, 'You thought I was going to offer you rule. [And so in humility they wanted to evade the honour.] It is service that I am giving you,' and he quoted I Kings XII, 7, 'If thou wilt be a servant unto this people this day.'

(*Hor.* 10*a fin.*)

The following bizarre story also reflects the Rabbinic point of view. It is interesting because it likewise reveals a certain humility and broad-mindedness on the part of the Rabbi, which, in all the circumstances of the case, is rather surprising:

[572] R. Nathan said: There is no commandment in the Law, however light, for which there is not a reward in this world; the reward in the world to come, I know not. Learn this from the command of the fringes. There was a man who was very careful about the law of the fringes. He heard that there was a courtesan in a city beyond the sea who demanded 400 gold pieces for her hire. So he sent her these, and fixed an appointment with her. When the time came, he went and sat at her door. Her maid said, 'The man who sent you the 400 gold pieces is here.' She said, 'Let him come in.' Now she had prepared seven couches, six of silver and one of gold, and she lay down upon the topmost couch. So the man entered. [He was about to sin with her, when he noticed the fringes on his garment.] Then he sat on the ground, and she did the same. Then she said, 'I swear I will not let you go till you tell me what blemish you have discerned in me.' He said, 'I swear I have never seen a woman as beautiful as you, but God has given us a commandment called fringes, and in the wording of this commandment it is twice said, "I am the Lord your God," that is, "I am He who will surely punish and who will surely reward." And now the four fringes have seemed to me like four witnesses.' Then she said, 'I will not let you go till you tell me your name and that of your city, and of your Teacher, and of your house of study where you learn the Law.' He wrote them down and gave them to her. Then she arose and sold all her possessions. One-third of the proceeds she gave to the government, a third she gave to the poor, and a third she took with her, but she did not sell the couches. Then she came to the house of study of R. Ḥiyya, and said to him, 'Master, make me a proselyte.' He said to her, 'Have you cast your eye upon one of my disciples?' Then she took out the writing of that disciple, and gave it to him. He said to her, 'Go and enjoy your purchase.' And those couches which she had prepared for him in a forbidden manner, she now prepared for him in a permitted manner. Such was the reward of the fringes in this world, but how great the reward in the world to come, I know not.

(*Men.* 44*a*.)

The story of Monobaz and his treasure is very familiar:

[573] Monobaz distributed all his treasures to the poor in the year of trouble [famine]. His brothers sent to him, and said, 'My

fathers gathered treasures, and added to those of *their* fathers, and you have dispersed yours and theirs.' He said to them, 'My fathers gathered treasures for below, I have gathered treasures for above; they stored treasures in a place over which the hand of man can rule, but I have stored treasures in a place over which the hand of man cannot rule; my fathers collected treasures which bear no fruit [interest], I have gathered treasures which do bear fruit; my fathers gathered treasures of money (mammon), I have gathered treasures in souls; my fathers gathered treasures for others, I have gathered treasures for myself; my fathers gathered treasures in this world, I have gathered treasures for the world to come, even as it says, "Righteousness [i.e. charity, *ẓedaḳah*] delivers from death."' Does this mean that a charitable man does not die? No, it means that he does not die a death for the world to come. (*T.J.Pe'ah* I, § I, f. 15*b*, line 63.)

The simple confidence of the Rabbis in the certainty of heavenly reward is well illustrated by the following stories:

[574] Once R. Gamaliel, R. Elazar, R. Joshua and R. Akiba were journeying, and they heard the tumult of the city of Rome from afar, and the first three wept, but Akiba laughed. They said, 'Why do you laugh?' He said, 'Why do your weep?' They said, 'These heathen, who pray and burn incense to idols, dwell in peace and security, whereas in our case the house, which was the footstool of our God's feet, is burnt with fire; how should we not weep?' He replied, 'That is why I laugh: if this is the lot of those who transgress His will, how much more glorious shall be the lot of those who perform His will.'

Again, on another occasion, they were going to Jerusalem, and when they came to Mount Scopus, they rent their clothes. And when they came to the Temple-mount, they saw a fox coming out of the Holy of Holies. Then the first three wept, but Akiba laughed. They said, 'Why do you laugh?' He said, 'Why do you weep?' They said, 'In and out of the place of which it is said, "The foreigner that comes near to it shall be put to death," now foxes run (Lam. v, 18; Num. I, 51). How should we not weep?' He said, 'That is why I laugh, for it says, "I will take unto me faithful witnesses, Uriah the priest, and Zechariah the son of Jeberechiah" (Isa. VIII, 2). How came Uriah and Zechariah together? Uriah lived during the first Temple and

Zechariah during the second. But the Scripture made the prophecy of Zechariah dependent upon the prophecy of Uriah. For Uriah said, "Zion shall be ploughed as a field, and Jerusalem shall become heaps" (Mic. III, 12 and Jer. XXVI, 18–20), and Zechariah said, "Yet again shall the streets of Jerusalem be full of boys and girls playing in its streets" (Zech. VIII, 5). If Uriah's prophecy had not been fulfilled, I might fear that Zechariah's prophecy would not be fulfilled, but now that Uriah's prophecy has been fulfilled, it is certain that Zechariah's prophecy will also be fulfilled.' Then they said to him, 'Verily, Akiba, you have comforted us.'

(*Mak.* 24*b* (cp. *Lam.R.* V, 18).)

Nevertheless, the famous adage in *Aboth* is constantly repeated, as at the end of the next passage:

[575] It says in the Psalms, 'Happy is the man who fears the Lord, and delights greatly in his commandments.' R. Elazar said: In his commandments, but not in the reward of his commandments. As it is taught (*Aboth* I, 3), 'Be not as servants who minister to their master upon the condition of receiving a reward, but be like servants who minister to their master without the condition of receiving a reward.' (**Note 80.**) (*Ab.Zar.* 19*a*.)

The next quotation is also rather significant:

[576] 'Be not like servants that serve the master for the sake of receiving a reward.' It would have been fitting for a part of the reward of the righteous in this world to have been revealed [but for their reward in the next world to have been concealed]. But because of those who were wanting in faith, God was fain to reveal some part of the reward of the righteous in the world to come. (*Ab.R.N.* (vers. II), X, 13*b*.)

The Rabbis tried as much as they could to shift the 'earthly' reward of the Bible on to the world to come:

[577] The reward for obedience to the Law is not in this world, but in the world to come, for it says, 'The commands which I bid you do this day' (Deut. VII, 11). 'To do' this day, but not 'to receive their reward' this day. So says David, 'How great is the reward which thou hast stored away for them that fear thee' (Ps. XXXI, 19). (*Tanḥ.*, Bereshit, § 1, f. 7*a* (cp. [1555]).)

[578] You find that, in the hour of death, God shows to those who study the Law the reward they will receive. It happened that when R. Abbahu was passing out of this world, God showed him thirteen rivers of balm, and as his death approached, he began to say to his disciples, 'Happy are you, who busy yourselves with the Law!' They said, 'Our Master, what dost thou see [that thou sayest this]?' He told them of the rivers of balm; 'These has God given me, and I had thought, "I had laboured in vain, for nothing and vanity had I wasted my strength, but truly my judgment is with the Lord, and my reward with my God"' (Isa. XLIX, 4). (*Tanḥ.*, Bereshit, § 1, f. 7*a*.)

So were prevented doubts. For as nobody can say what happens to a man after death, faith in future reward need not be shaken by the *facts* and happenings of earth. Thus:

[579] R. Ṭarfon said: The day is short, and the work is great, and the labourers are sluggish, and the reward is much, and the Master of the house is urgent. He used also to say: It is not thy duty to complete the work, but neither art thou free to desist from it; if thou hast studied much Torah, much reward will be given thee; and faithful is thy Employer to pay thee the reward of thy labour; but know that the grant of reward to the righteous will be in the time to come. (*Aboth* II, 20, 21 (**Note 88**.))

The following long passage is famous. It also illustrates the 'mechanical' view of goodness and reward to which I have already alluded, and the ingenuity and joy of the Rabbis in raising objections and in finding answers to them:

[580] 'He who fulfils a command, they (cp. [478]) do good to him, they prolong his days, they cause him to inherit the land [i.e. the world to come]. He who does not fulfil a command, they do not do good to him, they do not prolong his days, he does not inherit the land.' The Gemara points out that this Mishnah appears to be in contradiction with the teaching: 'Of the following things a man enjoys the fruit and interest in this world, while the stock remains for him in the world to come, namely, the honour of father and mother; the doing of loving deeds; hospitality; making peace between man and his fellow; but the study of the Law weighs as much as all of them together.' R. Judah said: The meaning of the Mishnah is that if a man's sins and good deeds balance one another, then if he does one good deed more,

to him 'they' do good, as if he had fulfilled the whole Law. But, then, are we to understand that, of the commandments mentioned above, if a man does only one of them and is otherwise sinful, to him they do good? R. Shemaiah said: No, it means that when sins and good deeds are equal, one of the good deeds mentioned turns the scale. Another apparent contradiction [to the teaching that to him who does one extra good deed they do good, etc.] seems to be given in the *Baraita*, that to him whose good deeds are [just] greater than his sins, they 'do evil', as if he had burnt the whole Law, and left not a letter behind; whereas to him whose sins are [just] greater than his good deeds, they 'do good', as if he had kept the whole Law and every letter of it [i.e. the sins of the one are punished in this world, so that he may inherit the world to come; the good deeds of the other are rewarded in this world, so that he may be excluded from the world to come]. Abbaye said: The Mishnah means that both his good deeds are rewarded, and his bad deeds punished, in *this* world. Raba said: The *Baraita* quoted above is in accordance with the view of R. Jacob, who said that there is no reward in this world for the fulfilment of the commandments. For R. Jacob said: There is no command of the Law to which a reward is attached with which the resurrection of the dead is not connected [i.e. the reward is in the world to come]. In the command to honour father and mother it is said, 'That you may live long, and that it may be well with you,' and in the command about the bird and its young it is said, 'That it may be well with you, and that you may live long' (Deut. XXII, 7). Now if a father say to his son, 'Ascend to the top of yonder castle, and bring me down some young pigeons,' and he goes up, and lets the mother bird escape, and takes the young birds, and on coming down he falls and dies, how is it well with him, and where is his long life? But the meaning is that it may be well with you in the world which is all good, and that you may live long in the world which is everlasting. But perhaps such a case never happened? R. Jacob saw it happen. But perhaps the man had sinful intentions? God does not count the evil intentions if there be no evil deed. But perhaps he had idolatrous intentions? For it is said, 'That I may take the house of Israel in their own heart, because they are all estranged from me through their idols.' [This verse from Ezek. XIV, 5 seems to indicate that even the idolatrous *intention* is punishable by God.]

But if the reward of the commandments is in this world, then surely they should have protected him that he did not have sinful thoughts? But R. Elazar said: They who carry out a command are not injured in their going forth to do it. But it was different here, for the death occurred upon the *return*. But R. Elazar really said that they who carry out a command are not injured upon their return as well as on their going forth. It was perhaps a broken ladder, and where there is an injury to be expected, one must not rely on a miracle. (*Ḳid.* 39*b*; *Ḳid.* I, 10 (cp. [555]).)

['Our Rabbis have taught' (*teno Rabbanan*) is one of the phrases which indicates a citation from a *Baraita* (cp. [830]); others are *tene*, *tanya*, 'it has *been taught*, there is a teaching'. In contradistinction, the phrases *tenan*, *teneyna*, 'we have learnt', denote citations from the Mishnah. *Baraita*, lit. external matter, is haggadic or halachic material taught in 'external' or private schools, as opposed to the academies. The title *Tanna Bara*, 'Teacher of the External School', was applied to the Rabbi cited as responsible for the *Baraita*. These external teachings, some of which go back to the time of Shammai, were not included by Judah ha-Nasi in his Mishnah: not all, however, are pre-Mishnaic. But very frequently the *Baraita* preserves the old Halakah, while the Mishnah gives the later development. The post-Mishnaic *Baraita* usually elucidates the *halakah* of the Mishnah. Readers of this book can generally regard the passages cited as *Baraita* as old; hence the need for this elucidation. *Baraitot* are preserved in the Gemara: they are introduced by special formulas, e.g. 'There is a teaching' or 'Our Rabbis have taught', cp. Gaster's *P.B.* p. 9. (H. L.)]

Illustrative is also this story:

[581] Two pious men [or, in the variant, two disciples of the wise, or two Rabbis] lived in Ashkelon. They ate and drank together, and occupied themselves with the Torah. One died, and no one accompanied his body to the grave. The tax collector Mayan [or his son] died, and the whole town followed his body. The surviving pious man said, 'Woe, nothing evil happens to the wicked.' He saw a vision in a dream. A voice said, 'Despise not the sons of your Lord'; the one had committed one sin [and so by his unaccompanied burial his iniquity is atoned for, or he has received his punishment]; the other had performed one good deed [and so by his grand funeral he has received his reward]. What sin had the one committed? Far be it that he had ever committed a [serious] sin. But once he put on the *Tefillin*

for the head before the *Tefillin* for the hand. And what good deed had the other performed? Far be it that he had ever done a [really fine] deed. But once he had arranged a meal for the *Bouleutai* [the municipal councillors] of the city, and they did not come. And he said, 'Let the poor eat it, that it be not wasted.' Others say, 'He once went through the market place, and he dropped a loaf, and a poor man picked it up, and he said nothing, so as not to make him blush for shame.' After some days the pious man saw in a dream his companion walking in the garden [Paradise] under trees and by wells of water; and he saw the tax collector, and his tongue sought to drink at the brink of a river; he tried to reach the water, but he could not.

(*T.J.San.* VI, § 9, f. 23*c*, line 31; *T.J.Ḥag.* II, § 2, f. 77*d*, line 43.)

The reward of learning and love of God on *earth* may be martyrdom. The following strange story is justly famous:

[582] R. Judah said in the name of Rab: When Moses went up to God, he found God sitting and putting little crowns on the top of the letters of the Law. He said to God, 'Who is it that forces thee to put crowns to the letters of the Law' [which thou hast already written]? He replied, 'A man is to appear on earth after many generations, Akiba b. Joseph by name, who will expound for each tip of every letter of the Law heaps and heaps of rulings' [*Halakot*]. Then Moses said, 'Show him to me.' God replied, 'Turn round.' So he did, and he went and sat at the end of the eighth row [of the students listening to R. Akiba], and he did not understand anything of what was being said, and his strength abated. When Akiba came to a certain matter [which needed proof], and his disciples asked him how he knew this, Akiba replied, 'This is a teaching which was delivered to Moses on Sinai.' Then the mind of Moses was quieted. Then he went back to God, and said, 'Thou hast a man like this, and thou givest the Torah through *me*?' Then God said, 'Be silent; thus it has seemed good to me.' Then Moses said, 'Thou hast shown me his knowledge of the Torah; show me now his reward.' Then God said, 'Turn round.' He did so, and he saw the flesh of Akiba being weighed in the meat market. Then he said, 'Such is his knowledge of the Law, and such is his reward?' Then God said, 'Silence, so it has seemed good to me.'

(*Men.* 29*b*.)

The doctrine of Merit (*zekut*), for which the Rabbis are much attacked, especially by Lutheran theologians, is important, but complicated. It is not of great interest for the general reader. I give, therefore, only a few characteristic quotations out of a possible multitude:

[583] The Rabbis say: Let a man ever regard himself as if he were half-guilty and half-deserving; then, if he fulfils one command, happy is he, for he has inclined the scale towards merit [*zekut*]; if he commits one sin, woe to him, for he has inclined the scale to guilt; as it is said, 'One sin [really 'sinner'] destroys much good' (Eccles. IX, 18). By the one sin which he has committed he has caused himself to lose much good. R. Elazar b. Simeon said: The world is judged by the majority, and the individual is judged by the majority. If a man fulfils one command, happy is he, for he has caused the scale for himself and for the whole world to incline towards the pan of merit [*zekut*]; if he has committed one sin, woe to him, for both for himself and for the whole world he makes the pan of guilt the heavier. By his one sin he has made himself and the world lose much good. R. Simeon b. Yoḥai said: Nevertheless, if he has been perfectly righteous all his life, and at the last rebels, he destroys [the effect of] all his former good deeds; and if he has been a complete sinner all his life, and repents at the last, his evil deeds are not remembered against him. (*Ḳid.* 40*b* (cp. [617]).)

The subject of *zekut* has been exhaustively treated by Dr A. Marmorstein, *The Doctrine of Merits in old Rabbinical Literature*, Jews' College Publications, No. 7, London, 1920. For the question of vicarious merit, see note to [617]. (**Note 15**.)

[584] R. Ḥanina b. Gamaliel said: If he who has committed one sin thereby forfeits his life, how much more shall he who fulfils one command be given life! R. Simeon [through an ingenious collocation and interpretation of Lev. XVIII, 29 and XVIII, 5) said: Hence it is proved that God rewards a man who sits passively, and does no sin, as much as him who actively fulfils a commandment. R. Simeon b. Rabbi, quoting the command not to eat blood, said: If a man who refrains from eating blood, against which a man revolts, is rewarded, how much more shall he who refrains from robbery and unchastity, which a man may desire to do, be rewarded and earn merit for himself and all his descendants. (*Mak.* III, 15 (cp. [273]).)

From one point of view the whole purpose of the Law with its large number of enactments was to enable the Israelites to acquire 'merit', and through 'merit', reward:

[585] R. Hananiah b. 'Akashya said: It pleased God to make Israel able to acquire merit. Therefore He multiplied to them Torah and commandments, as it is said, 'It pleased the Lord for his righteousness' sake to make the Law large' (Isa. XLII, 21).

(*Mak.* III, 16 (cp. [508]).)

This passage is added in the Prayer Book to be recited in the synagogue after the reading of each chapter of *Aboth* (*P.B.* p. 186). Professor Danby translates the opening words, 'God was minded to give merit to Israel.'

'Merit' can be stored up. The 'merits' of the Patriarchs helped their descendants. They form a sort of treasury upon which Israel can claim to draw. Even the 'merit' of an ordinary good man can help his children or the world at large (cp. [611]).[1]

[586] R. Phinehas the Priest said in reference to Prov. XI, 21: If you have fulfilled a command, do not seek its reward from God straightway, lest you be not acquitted of sin, but be regarded as wicked, because you have not sought to cause your children to inherit anything. For if Abraham, Isaac and Jacob had sought the reward of the good deeds which they performed, how could the seed of these righteous men have been delivered, and how could Moses have said, 'Remember Abraham, Isaac and Jacob, so that God repented of the evil which he thought to do unto his people' (Exod. XXXII, 13, 14)?...Why did Moses mention the Patriarchs? R. Levi said: Moses said, 'Lord of the world, will the dead live?' God replied, 'Moses, are you a heretic?' Moses said, 'If the dead are not to live in the world to come, then it is fair that thou shouldst deal with thy people as thou mayest wish; but if the dead live, what wilt thou say to the Patriarchs in the world to come, when they arise and seek from thee the fulfilment of the assurance in which thou didst cause them to trust; how wilt thou answer them? Didst thou not assure them

[1] [Sometimes *zekut Aboth* (the merits of the Patriarchs) seems to mean no more than the effect of training and heredity, expressed in simple terms which the multitude could comprehend, for the Rabbis, like Jesus, lacked a scientific terminology and the philosophic outlook which Greek gave to Paul. Good discipline and example may bear fruit and thus the 'merit' of ancestors or parents may be said to avail their descendants. As S. Levy says (*Original Virtue and other Short Studies*) (cp. [242] and [643]), *zekut Aboth* is the Jewish antithesis to original sin But it was sometimes materialised. (**Notes 46, 95 and 96.**) (H. L.)]

that their seed should be as the stars in heaven for multitude, and now thou seekest to destroy them!' And Moses said also to God, 'Were the Patriarchs wicked or righteous? Make a distinction. If they were wicked, then it is fair that thou shouldst destroy their descendants, for then their ancestors have no works of merit [*zekut*] with thee; but if they were righteous, then give their descendants the benefit of their works.' (**Note 47**.)

(*Exod.R.*, Ki Tissa, XLIV, 3, 6, 9 (for another interpretation of this proof text cp. [562]).)

[587] 'A bundle of myrrh (*kofer*) is my well-beloved' (Cant. I, 14). This refers to Isaac, who was tied up like a bundle upon the altar. *Kofer*, because he atones for the sins of Israel.

(*Cant.R.* I, § 14, I, on I, 14; f. 12*b* (cp. [612]).)

['*Kofer* or Camphor', Hebrew *Kofer*, and 'atonement', 'ransom', also *Kofer*, are from different roots which are outwardly similar. Our 'Camphor' is, in fact, identical with the Hebrew, via the Arabic *Kafúr*, Spanish *Canfora*, French *Camphre* (cf. Italian *Cafura* and Middle High German *gaffer*). The word 'tie' is used of twisting the four feet of a sacrifice, of tying the red heifer to a post, and of various forms of physical and moral restraint. It is several times used of Isaac in this connection. Thus, according to one reading, 'As much as Abraham bound his son in this world, so did God restrain the genii of the Gentiles in the world above' (*Gen.R.*, Wayera, LVI, 5 (Th. p. 600)). Isaac said 'tie me firmly' (*ib.* 8 (Th. p. 603 n.)). The Gentiles are 'tied', i.e. restrained from sin, by the seven Noachide laws. The same root is used of tying bundles and posies. It is therefore very appropriate here. The Commentary *Yefeh Ḳol* remarks that the reference to Isaac's atonement must be supplemented by a citation from Abraham's prayer, when he bound Isaac, 'May it be thy will that when Isaac's sons fall into sin and commit evil deeds, this... binding may be remembered by thee and thou mayest be filled with mercy towards them' (*ib.* 10 (Th. p. 607)). (H. L.)]

[588] 'Thou shalt not take the mother bird with the young. Thou shalt surely let the mother bird go free, and take the young to thee' (Deut. XXII, 7). R. Elazar said: It was not necessary to add the words, 'Thou shalt surely let the mother bird go free,' but because she was busy with beautifying the world and with its maintenance, it is right that she should be preserved. R. Hiyya said: If in the case of a bird, where there is no question of merit [*zekut*], or of ancestors or of covenants or of oaths, her young

atone for her, how much more in the case of the descendants of Abraham, Isaac and Jacob, if one of them sins, will the merits of these patriarchs atone for him.[1] (*Deut.R.*, Ki Teẓe, VI, 5.)

The first part of the above passage does not strictly belong here, but is worth citation, and is therefore given.

[589] 'Ye stand this day, all of you, before the Lord, all the men of Israel' (Deut. XXIX, 10). All of you are pledges one for the other: if there be but one righteous man among you, you exist all of you through his merit, and not you alone, but the whole world, as it says, 'And the righteous is the foundation of the world' (A.V. 'an everlasting foundation') (Prov. X, 25). If one man sins, the whole generation suffers, as was the case with Achan (Josh. XXII, 20). How much more will the good done by an individual benefit his environment!

(*Tanḥ.B.*, Niẓẓabim, 25*a*.)

Yet one must not rely upon *zekut* too much (cp. [597]):

[590] A man must not trust in the work of his ancestors. If a man does not do good in this world, he cannot put his trust in the work of his fathers. No man will eat in the time to come of his father's works, but only of his own. (*Midr.Ps.* on CXLVI, 3 (267*b*, §2).)

I would like to state here that the great scholar, Moore, holds that *zekut* 'is often used in a prepositional way, without thinking of the desert, or merit, of the object, as we use "by virtue of" without any thought of the usual meaning of the noun'. He contends that when we read, for example, that 'the world was created by the merit (*zekut*) of the Torah' or by the merit (*zekut*) of Israel, the natural rendering is 'for the sake of the Torah, or for the sake of Israel'. So, too, the *zekut* of the Fathers is frequently best translated in the same way: for the sake of the Patriarchs God did this or that (vol. III, p. 164) (cp. p. xxxii).

[1] [I do not think that this, the conventional rendering of R. Elazar's remark, is correct; *nit'assek*, rendered 'she was busy', is masculine, while *tinnaẓel*, 'she should be preserved', is feminine. Fürst, in his comments on Wünsche (p. 129), would alter the former verb to the feminine. In all deference I would suggest that *nit'asseḳ* can stand, but that it be taken as the first plu. *hithpa'el* imperfect, not as a *nithpa'el* perfect. I should render thus:

'God said: "seeing that we [i.e. God and the man who finds the nest] are busying ourselves with the maintenance of the world, do thou indeed let her go."' The argument is derived from the double verb, 'releasing shalt thou release'. One of the verbs is taken to refer to God and the other to man, thus suggesting a partnership. Examples of deductions from double verbs have been given before, e.g. [534]. (H. L.)]

[591] Rabbi Gamaliel, the son of R. Judah the Prince, said: Let all who are employed with the congregation act with them for heaven's sake, for then the merit [*zekut*] of their fathers sustains them, and their [i.e. the Patriarchs'] righteousness endures for ever. 'And as for you,' God says, 'I account you worthy of great reward as if you had wrought it all yourselves.'

(*Aboth* II, 2.)

This is Mr Singer's translation. Moore renders: 'All who exert themselves in the interest of the community should do so with a religious motive, for the virtue (*zekut*) of their fathers helps them, and their (i.e. the Patriarchs') righteousness abides for ever. And as for you, I, God, will reckon to you a reward as though you (alone) did the work.' (**Note 48**.)

Occasionally the Rabbis realise that the doctrine of merit will not account for the hard facts of life. One Rabbi fell back upon luck. You cannot account for the divergences of human lot:

[592] Raba said: Life, sons and wealth do not depend upon merit, but upon luck. Rabbah and R. Ḥisda were both righteous Rabbis: when either prayed for rain, it came. Yet R. Ḥisda lived for 92 years, and Rabba only for 40; in the house of R. Ḥisda there were 60 weddings, in the house of Rabba 60 deaths; in the house of R. Ḥisda the very dogs were given bread of finest flour, and had no lack of it; in the house of Rabba there was only barley bread for men, and even this was wanting.

(*M.K.* 28*a* (cp. [1511]).)

The Rabbis believed intensely in the doctrine of measure for measure as the method of divine action.[1] Endless passages occur on the same lines as the following:

[593] When Joseph's brethren were arrested and accused of stealing his cup, 'they rent their garments' (Gen. XLIV, 13). God said to them, 'Because you caused your father to rend his garments for a lie, so do you now rend your own garments for a lie.'

(*Tanḥ.B.*, Miḳḳeẓ, 99*b*.)

They go so far as to say that this rule of God's working will never be abolished. Their insistence upon measure for measure is one of their weaknesses. But it is pleasant to note that the doctrine is crossed by several other considerations. It is a modification of tit for tat (**Note 68**) that 'to him who has shall be given'.

[1] [So a section of the *Wisdom of Solomon* (XI, 2ff.) is devoted to the *lex talionis* in the Egyptian plagues. 'By what things a man sins, by these is he punished' (XI, 16) and 'By what things their foes were punished, by these they in their need were benefited' (XI, 5). For this idea, see *Sot.* 11*a*. (H. L.)]

[594] Not as with man is the method of God. With men a full vessel receives no more; an empty vessel gets filled. With God, the full is filled, the empty is not filled. If you have heard, you will continue to hear; if you have not heard, you will not hear [subsequently]. If you have heard the old, you will also hear the new; if you have turned your heart away, you will hear no more (cp. *R.T.* p. 252). (*Ber.* 40*a.*)

[595] R. Johanan said: The Holy One, blessed be He, gives wisdom only to him who has wisdom. (*Ber.* 55*a.*)

[596] Once a Roman lady put this question to R. Jose b. Ḥalafta: Is it a fact that all God's praise consists in his 'giving wisdom to the wise'? (Dan. II, 21). It should rather be by giving wisdom to fools! Jose said to her, 'Have you any jewels?' 'Certainly.' 'If someone comes and wishes to borrow them, will you lend them to him?' 'Yes, I will, if he is a man of responsibility.' 'Then', said Jose, 'you will not lend your jewels save to a worthy borrower, and shall God give his wisdom to fools?' For Elihu meant, 'Not to all who seek does God give [wisdom], but only to those in whom there is spiritual aptitude' (A.V. 'But there is a Spirit in man, and the inspiration of the Almighty gives them understanding') (Job XXXII, 8).
(*Tanḥ.B.*, Miḳḳeẓ, 97*a fin.*–97*b.*)

Again, God forgives, God gives freely, 'gratis', as the Rabbis say: He supplies, by His own grace, what is wanting to man's merits. Again, man repents, and all is changed. Or, again, man dies, and his death has not only atoning power for himself, but also, if he be righteous, for others.

[597] 'Lord, I cry unto thee; make haste unto me' (Ps. CXLI, 1). David said, 'As I hasten to do thy word, so hasten thou to me.' To what is the matter like? To a man who has a suit before a lord. He sees that all the others have advocates to plead for them. He called to the lord and said, 'All have their advocates; I have none. There is no one to plead for me. Be thou my advocate and my judge.' So David said, 'Some trust in their fair and upright deeds, and some in the works of their fathers, but I trust in thee. Although I have no good works, yet because I call upon thee, do thou answer me.' (*Midr.Ps.* on CXLI, 1 (265*b*, §1) (cp. [590]).)

[598] 'I will be gracious to whom I will be gracious' (Exod. XXXIII, 19). In that hour God showed Moses all the treasuries of the rewards which are prepared for the righteous. Moses said, 'For whom

is *this* treasury?' And God said, 'For him who fulfils the commandments.' 'And for whom is *that* treasury?' 'For him who brings up orphans.' And so God told him about each treasury. Finally, Moses spied a big treasury and said, 'For whom is that?' And God said, 'To him who has nothing I give from *this* treasury'; as it is said, 'I will be gracious to whom I will be gracious and I will show mercy on whom I will show mercy' (*ib.*). (*Exod.R.*, Ki Tissa, XLV, 6.)

[599] It is written in Daniel (IX, 7), 'To us belongs shame of face: to God belongs righteousness [*ẓedaḳah*].' R. Yudan said: It is written, 'The house of Joseph went up to Bethel, and the Lord was with them' (Judges I, 22). They went to serve idols, and God was with them! Can there be a charity [grace, generosity] greater than this? (*Pes.K.* 99*a*.)

[600] It is written in Can icles: 'The voice of my beloved! Behold, he comes.' R. Judah said: That is Moses, when he said to the children of Israel, 'In this month you shall be redeemed.' They said, 'How can we be redeemed? Did not God say to Abraham, You shall serve them, and they shall afflict you four hundred years, and now only two hundred years have passed?' Moses replied, 'Because God desires to redeem you, He pays no heed to your reckonings.' Again they said, 'How can we be redeemed? Egypt is full of our idols.' Moses replied, 'Because God desires your redemption, he pays no heed to your idolatry.' They said, 'How can we be redeemed? We have no good deeds.' He replied, 'Because God desires your redemption, He looks not upon your evil deeds, but only on the deeds of the righteous, as for example, on Amram and his court of justice.' (*Pes.K.* 47*a*, *b*.)

[601] R. Jose said: God said, 'I spake not unto the seed of Israel: Seek me in a waste place' (Isa. XLV, 19): I did not give the Law to them on a commercial basis (lit. 'as a pledge', [of which you cannot have the usufruct[1]]), for I, the Lord, speak righteousness; while I had not yet given the Law, I accorded to them its rewards. [The proof is the manna.]

(*Mek.*[2], *Baḥodesh*, Yitro, § 1, p. 206; *Mek.*[3], vol. II, p. 199.)

[1] The words 'as a pledg etc., are omitted by Lauterbach in his translation, but see his Hebrew note on p. 199 of vol. II. They occur in the *Mekilta* of R. Simeon b. Yoḥai: see Jastrow, *s.v. Pignus*, p. 1186, also note in Horovitz, p. 206, where ὑποθήκη occurs for *pignus*.

The next, and very important doctrine which crosses and upsets the teaching of tit for tat in its crudest and sharpest form—i.e. that the exact measure of Jones's iniquity falls upon Jones and only upon Jones, that the measure of your divine punishment is in precise proportion to your sin—is the doctrine of atonement, and more especially of vicarious atonement. We know how according to the Pentateuch certain sins—mainly unintentional and involuntary and 'ceremonial' sins—can be wiped out and their effects cancelled by sacrifices. Far more powerful and wide-reaching as an agency for the cancellation of sin is repentance, with which we shall deal later on. Yet even repentance has to do only with the individual's own case. But, according to the Rabbis, the individual, or, more specifically, the individual Israelite, is a portion of the living organism which we know as the community, or the people, of Israel. What the community does, or, as the community as a whole acts, can affect for good or for evil the individuals of whom the community is composed. So, as regards atonement, with which we are now concerned, the sacrifices of the community are, in their degrees, an atonement even for the private sins of the individuals who make up the community (see p. 328). Israel's united devotion to the Law has the atoning power of sacrifices, especially since the cessation of sacrifices through the destruction of the Temple. The Day of Atonement, somewhat mysteriously, has atoning power for the individual and for the community at one and the same time. According to the Rabbis, death, which, in spite of the doctrine (practically unknown to the O.T. writers) of the resurrection and of the blessed life beyond the grave, is still an evil, and therefore a punishment, is also an atonement for the sins of him who dies. But what is much more striking is that the death of the righteous and the innocent is an atonement for the sinners: the good Israelites help the bad Israelites. The unity of the community is a unity which is an advantage to its evil members.

[602] As the Day of Atonement atones, so the death of the righteous atones. (*Lev.R.*, Aḥare Mot, xx, 12.)

[603] The question is asked, 'Why is the death of Miriam mentioned immediately after the passage about the Red Heifer?' The reply is that as the Red Heifer makes atonement, so, too, does the death of the righteous.

(*M.Ḳ.* 28*a* (cp. *T.J.Yoma* I, § 1, f. 38*b*, line 15).)

[604] It is written, 'God has set the one over against the other. God has made the righteous and the wicked' (Eccles. VII, 14). Why? That the one should atone for the other.

(*Pes.K.* XXX, 191*a fin.*)

[605] 'Thy righteousness is like the mountains of God; thy judgments are a great deep' (Ps. XXXVI, 6). R. Jonathan transposed the verse thus: 'Thy righteousness is over thy judgments as the mountains of God are over the great deep.' As these mountains press down the deep, that it should not rise and engulf the world, so the deeds of the righteous force down the punishments that they should not come upon the world. (*Pes.K.* 73*b*.)

The same thought is expressed by R. Josiah in [102], where the same proof text occurs in two parallels.

In the middle of the chapters devoted to the plan of the Tabernacle (*mishkan*, lit. abiding place, hence *shechinah*, presence), the order is given 'And thou shalt make the boards for the Tabernacle' (Exod. XXVI, 15). Nowhere else are the words 'for the Tabernacle' used; minute descriptions have been given of the different parts of the *mishkan* and of its various articles of furniture and ritual. That these were all intended for the Tabernacle and for nothing else is obvious, and the words in question would seem to be redundant. But in the Bible nothing is redundant, therefore the consonants must be read differently, not as *mishkan* but as *mishken* or *mashkon*, i.e. he pledged, or, a pledge. So R. Hoshaiah said:

[606] It was unnecessary to say 'boards for the Tabernacle'; the verse means that the boards [i.e. the Sanctuary] stood up as a pledge. For if Israel ever deserved annihilation, it would be their security with God. Then said Moses to God, 'But will there not come a time when they have neither Tabernacle nor Temple? What then shall be [the pledge] for them?' God replied, 'I will take one righteous man from among them, and hold him as pledge for them, and I will atone for them on account of all their sins.' Hence, 'He slew all that were pleasant to the eye in [return for] the Tabernacle' (Lam. II, 4) (to atone for the rest of Israel). (For 'Israel', cp. [274].) (*Exod.R.*, Terumah, XXXV, 4.)

[607] 'And His land shall atone for its people' (Deut. XXXII, 43: R.V. 'And will make expiation for His land, for His people'). How canst thou know that the martyrdom [lit. slaying] of Israel at the hands of the Gentiles is an atonement in the world to come? Because it says 'O God, the heathen have come into thine inheritance...they have given...the flesh of thy saints to the beasts of the earth' (Ps. LXXIX, 1, 2). (Because they are called 'Saints' ['holy ones'], therefore the *Sifre* assumes that they had

by their death an atoning efficacy for the rest of their brethren in faith.) (*Sifre Deut.*, Ha'azinu, § 333, f. 140*a fin.*)

The saying with regard to Phinehas, 'because he was zealous for his God, and made atonement for the children of Israel' (Num. xxv, 13) is to be compared with 'because he has poured out his soul unto death' (Isa. LIII, 12):

[608] It does not say 'so as to make atonement', but 'and he made atonement'. Even till now, he does not cease, but he stands and makes atonement until the dead revive. (*Sifre Num.*, Pineḥas, § 131, f. 48*b*, Balaḳ (= H., § 131, p. 173) (cp. [1500]).)

[Friedmann, in his note, says that some words are missing, and he thinks that the *Sifre* interpreted the rest of the passage in Isaiah, 'He bare the sins of many and made intercession for transgressors', as referring to Phinehas. The Targum Pseudo-Jonathan, which is always discursive and homiletical, makes Phinehas 'pray with his mouth for the house of Israel,' in addition to slaying Zimri and Kozbi. *Num.R.*, Pineḥas, XXI, 3, applies to Phinehas Mal. II, 5, 'My covenant was with him (cf. Num. xxv, 12), for the fear wherewith he feared me.' An entire chapter in the *Pirke de R. Eliezer* (Chap. XLVII) is devoted to Phinehas: see G. Friedlander's annotated translation (London, 1916, pp. 367–73). (H. L.)]

The cruel and repugnant nature of the passage in Num. xxv, 1–18, is characteristically ignored by the Rabbis, who fasten only upon verse 13 as an illustration of their doctrine of atonement (cp. [1500]):

[609] [Thus the death of the righteous atones. Yet the Rabbis are also willing to accept the doctrine of Ps. XLIX, 7, 8, and they can say:] If men give all the world's wealth, they cannot ransom another's soul: for the soul with which a man sins no indemnity can be paid by another. (*Sifre Deut.*, Ha'azinu, § 329, f. 139*b*.)

The death of innocent, and therefore virtuous, children (as in [639], [1215] and **Note 36**) has also an atoning efficacy:

[610] R. Gorion, or R. Joseph, said: In an age when there are righteous men in a given generation, the righteous are taken for the generation; in a generation where there are no righteous men, school children are taken (cf. *R.T.* p. 301). (*Sab.* 33*b*.)

[611] 'They have no comforter' (Eccles. IV, 1). R. Judah b. Ilai said: These are the children who are removed away because of the iniquities of their fathers in this world. In the world to come they

will stand in the troop of the righteous, and their fathers in the company of the wicked, and they will say to God, 'We died because of our fathers' sins; let now our fathers come to us through our merits.' Then God replies, 'Your fathers sinned after your death; their sins accuse them.' Then Elijah will make defence, and he will tell the children, 'Say to God, Which is the greater? The attribute of goodness or the attribute of punishment?' He will reply, 'The attribute of goodness.' 'Then,' say the children, 'if we died because of the sins of our fathers, even though the attribute of goodness is greater, how much more should they now come over to us?' Then God will reply, 'Your defence is excellent; they *shall* come over to you,' as it says, 'They shall live with their children and return' (Zech. x, 9). (*Eccles.R.* IV, § 1, 1, on IV, 1 (12*b*).)

The Patriarchs' virtues are of great avail for the sins of their descendants (cp. [586–7]); not least the readiness of Abraham to sacrifice his son at the bidding of God, and the readiness of Isaac to suffer death:

[612] Abraham prayed unto God, and said, 'Thou knowest that when thou didst say unto me, "Take now thine only son Isaac and offer him for a burnt offering," it was in my heart to answer, "Yesterday thou didst say to me, 'In Isaac shall thy seed be called', and to-day thou biddest me offer him up as a burnt offering." But though I could have answered thus, I suppressed my inclination, and did not do so, as it is said, "As a dumb man, who opens not his mouth"' (Ps. XXXVIII, 13). If then Isaac's descendants fall into sin and evil deeds, do thou make mention of the binding of Isaac, and get up from the throne of judgment, and sit down upon the throne of compassion, and be filled with pity, and turn the attribute of judgment into the attribute of mercy. (**Note 20 *a*.**) (*Lev.R.*, Emor, XXIX, 9; *Gen.R.*, Wayera, LVI, 10 (Th. p. 607; cp. [587]).)

[613] Abraham had a worrying thought, and he said to God, 'Lord, thou didst make a covenant with Noah that thou wouldst not destroy his children. Then I arose, and I heaped up commandments and good works more than he, so that my covenant expels his covenant.[1] Thou mayest arrange that another shall arise after me who will heap up commandments and good works more than

[1] Cp. the note on David's apparent self-righteousness in [391].

I, and his covenant will expel my covenant.' Then God said, 'From Noah I did not cause to arise righteous protectors, but from thee I will cause to arise righteous protectors, and not only so, but when thy children fall into sin and evil deeds, I will arrange for a righteous man who will cause the balance to sink in their favour, for he will be able to say to the attribute of Justice, "Enough, I will take *him*, and I will make him atone for *them*."'

(*Gen.R.*, Lek leka, XLIV, 5 (Th. pp. 428, 429).)

[614] 'Boughs of goodly trees, branches of palm trees, and the boughs of thick trees and willows of the brook' (Lev. XXIII, 40). 'Boughs of goodly trees': these are the Israelites. As the citron has taste and smell, so among the Israelites some have both Torah and good works. 'Branches of palm trees': these are the Israelites. As the date has taste, but no smell, so are there Israelites who have Torah, but no good works. 'Boughs of thick trees': these are the Israelites. As the myrtle has smell, but no taste, so there are Israelites who have good works, but no Torah. 'Willows of the brook': these are the Israelites. As the willow has neither taste nor smell, so there are Israelites who have neither Torah nor good works. What is God to do with them? It is not possible to destroy them. God says, 'Bind all together into one bundle, and the one will atone for the other.'

(*Lev.R.*, Emor, XXX, 12 (cp. *Pes.K.* 185*a*).)

Thus, in a certain sense, the sinners are needed as well as the righteous:

[615] Rabbi Simeon the Pious said: No fast is a true fast unless some of the sinners in Israel participate therein, for the smell of the frankincense is bad, yet the Scripture enumerates it together with the other spices. Abbaye proved this from Amos IX, 6, 'His band is established upon the earth' [i.e. the earth is established only when all things, good and bad, are united together].

(*Ker.* 6*b*.)

In the Biblical period there often stood between human sin and divine forgiveness certain material media. They worked atonement, and the atonement, one might, I think, say, then automatically brought about forgiveness. But the two ideas of atonement and forgiveness tended to run and merge into one another, and this they continued to do in the Rabbinical period likewise. We may indeed say that all the various and unsystematic Biblical ideas about Atonement continued into the Rabbinical period, but they tended to become purified, and (as many quotations already given show) they tended also to become more 'inward'.

The disappearance of sacrifices, and of the whole Temple ritual, after A.D. 70 helped, doubtless, in the accomplishment of this process. Nevertheless, the words of the Old Testament and, more especially, of the Pentateuch, remained, and to the Rabbis these words were all true and all perfect and all divine. Hence we cannot expect, and we do not find, complete consistency or a completed process of spiritualisation. The external media, though spiritualised, and sometimes almost evaporated, abide. They are of various kinds. We have come across some of them already. The Day of Atonement is, perhaps, the greatest of the media, the *piacula*. But there are several others. For each individual Israelite, bodily sufferings have atoning power. Great poverty is mentioned more rarely. Fasting is also named, but no great or frequent stress is laid on it. Almsgiving, charity (cp. [870]), deeds of love, are powerful *piacula*. Prayer, too, has atoning efficacy, and so has the study of the Law. Death is regarded for the individual as perhaps the strongest *piaculum* of all.

Hence is reached the conception of vicarious atonement. As we have already seen, the death (as well as the sufferings) of the righteous are helpful for those who are less righteous than they. Their deaths have strong atoning power. Israel's sufferings, e.g. its exile from its land, and the persecutions which it undergoes, are also of atoning efficacy to every Israelite. Lastly, God Himself purifies Israel, so that He can pardon Israel. Atonement becomes the destruction of sin and sinfulness, the creation of a new being, a sort of being who is born again, the breaking of the barrier between sinful man and his Maker, so that God can then freely forgive. (**Note 81**.)

I think that the Rabbis may have felt that there was something beyond forgiveness (i.e. the letting off of punishment). They may have felt that Atonement went beyond, and was more than, forgiveness. They speak of turning to God and of God turning to them. They speak of God's 'nearness' and of His 'farness'. He is far from the sinner. Did they mean that the sinner *feels* Him to be far? I hope so. That repentance and amendment of life bring man near again to God they would certainly assert, and perhaps this renewed nearness and sense of nearness is what they mean by atonement.

We may, I think, say that to the author of the 51st Psalm forgiveness, or atonement, involved something much more than the letting off of punishment. The 'joy or gladness' of verse 8, 'the clean heart', the presence of the 'holy spirit' in verses 10 and 11, surely go beyond the mere request that his 'transgressions may be blotted out'. He wants to be pure and clean, and to have the sense of God within him, quite apart from the letting off of punishment. He wants, in other words, atonement, not merely forgiveness. I hope that the Rabbis realised and appreciated the difference, like the author of the Psalm.

It is certain, at any rate, that the Rabbis take Biblical statements such as, 'Precious in the sight of the Lord is the death of the pious', very seriously:

[616] The death of the righteous weighs as heavily as the burning of the Temple. (*R.H.* 18*b*.)

[God is equally unwilling to destroy even the wicked. Thus: '"The angels came to Sodom" (Gen. XIX, 1): what do we read previously, "Abraham drew near and said, Wilt thou destroy" (Gen. XVIII, 23)? R. Phinehas the Priest, son of R. Ḥama, said: God does not desire to condemn a single creature, as it says, "I have no pleasure in the death of him that is guilty of death" (Ezek. XVIII, 32). [Further proofs are found in Ps. V, 5 and Ezek. XXXIII, 11.] In what then does God take pleasure? In justifying His creatures. [The proof is from Isa. XLII, 21.] And a proof of this is to be found in the circumstance that when men sin and provoke God so that He is angry with them, He sends them an Advocate who pleads their merits....' (*Tanḥ.*, Wayera, §8, f. 34 *b*.)

The whole of the section should be noted as well as §10 on f. 35 *b*. (H. L.)]

[617] Even for the sake of *one* righteous man the world would have been created, and for the sake of *one* righteous man it will continue. (**Note 82**.) (*Yoma* 38*b* (cp. [583]).)

[This idea that one individual can, by his merit, sustain the world, is similar to the conception of the 'Thirty-six', i.e. *Lamed-waw* (=36). There is a whole series of legends relating to these thirty-six hidden saints, who exist in every generation, unknown to their contemporaries, to one another, and possibly even to themselves, since, if asked, they would deny that they belong to this band. It is natural that the genuine saint should repudiate such a title. But God never leaves the world without the full complement (cp. [797]): when one dies, *non deficit aureus alter*. Otherwise, the world could not continue. They belong to every rank of society, and are often humble craftsmen, just as, in the cycle of stories relating to prayers for rain, it is often the meanest—and, sometimes, the apparently sinful—whose supplications are accepted by God on behalf of the Community. The stories of the ass driver and the jailer have been given above ([481] and [484]). But in process of time the function of the '*Lamed-vov-nik*' or 'Thirty-sixer' (*-nik* is a Russian adjectival ending) changed. Instead of being merely a passive agent, diffusing virtue which upholds a sinful world, he develops—without losing this function—into a saviour in a crisis, such as are the Heavenly Twins at the battle of Lake Regillus: like the Twins, too, he retires into obscurity when his work is accomplished.

The number 36 is said in the Gemara (*San.* 97*b*; *Suk.* 45*b*) to be derived from the word *Lo* 'to him' (which is spelt *Lamed-waw*), in Isa. XXX, 18: Abbai said, 'The world never has less than six and thirty saints, that daily receive the face of the Shechinah, as it is said "Happy are they that hope on Him"'. (The two letters make up 36 (L=30, V=6).) The passage occurs in a discussion on the number of the saints, who 'hope on' God. Now it is clear that the counting of the letters did not give rise to the belief: on the contrary, it was found to be a convenient proof for a belief that already existed. Father Wilfred Knox points out that the number 36 is significant as being the square of 6, the symbol of the created, finite and imperfect world, in Alexandrian Jewish philosophy, contrasted with 7, which, since it includes the Sabbath, represents the complete and eternal *cosmos*. The square of six therefore represents the consummation of imperfection, which needs a special make-weight of virtue, if it is to exist. Such an idea may well have been the source of the legend, but since the conception of an evil world was not favoured by the Rabbis, the underlying motive would easily disappear.

It is noteworthy that in later times the number was doubled, there being an additional thirty-six secret saints in Palestine. Here, the 'evil world' *motif* has vanished, since Palestine would be considered *per se* holy enough not merely to survive, but to help the rest of the world to survive. For the tradition, and for the sources, of thirty saints in Palestine see *Ba'al ha-Ṭurim* on Deut. XXVI, 1. See also M. Buber, *Die Chassidischen Bücher*, Berlin, 1928, pp. 413 and 687.

A similar tradition is found in connection with the number thirty. Thus: 'R. Tanḥum in the name of R. Aḥa said: "The world can never lack thirty righteous, for God promised Abraham, 'Thus shall be thy seed' and thirty is the numerical equivalent of *shall be*"' (*Tanḥ.*, Wayera, §13 end, f. 36*b*). (H. L.)]

[618] The whole world was created only for the sake of the righteous man. He weighs as much as the whole world. The whole world was created only to be united to him. (**Note 82.**) (*Sab.* 30*b*.)

[In the passage cited, the 'righteous man' is not expressly specified; the word *zeh* (this) is used, in connection with Eccles. XII, 13. But the context may imply that the righteous man is referred to, though perhaps the passage gains in point if it is interpreted generally. (H. L.)]

[619] It is not necessary to erect monuments for the righteous: their teachings are their memorial. (*T.J.Sheḳ.* II, 7, f. 47*a*, line 11.)

[The saying, as usually cited, is 'their deeds are their memorial'. But the reading, both here and in *Gen.R.* LXXXII, §10 (Th. p. 988 n.), is as above. The commentator in the Krot. ed. of the *T.J.* regards 'deeds' and 'words' as synonymous. (H. L.)]

Chapter IX

DIVINE MERCY AND DIVINE JUDGMENT, IDOLATRY, MARTYRDOM

It would not be easy to construct a consistent statement of God's principles of judgment, or of His principles of reward, punishment and forgiveness, according to the Rabbis. In any case, no such exhaustive and consistent account can be attempted here. So far as the Israelites or Jews are concerned, it would seem that there was a sort of twofold judgment passed upon them. The idea was fashioned that on each New Year there was a yearly judgment which ended upon the Day of Atonement. Apparently this judgment affected only those who died between the Day of Atonement and the next New Year, for, on that next New Year, the whole affair, with the opening of the heavenly books and the examination of each man's 'account', began all over again.

The vivid conception, however, of God's mercy constantly breaks through these and other statutory imaginings.

[As Mr Montefiore points out, there is a double strain of opinion with regard to the occasion for repentance. This is natural and inevitable. On the one hand, we have such well-known sayings as 'repent one day before your death, i.e. at once and always' (cited below [839]). On the other, what can and should be done at any moment is liable to be put off till the Greek Kalends. Hence the need for stated times when the atmosphere of the Synagogue and home is full of penitential associations. Such a need was met by the New Year and Day of Atonement festivals, and if their primitive origins were different from their characteristics in the Mishnaic period, the change is significant. It supplied what was required. But the Rabbis were on their guard lest the Day of Atonement should become a formal apotropaic institution, or even lest the idea of an annual judgment should become materialised. A good example is furnished in the Ashkenazic prayer book for the Day of Atonement (Davis and Adler, p. 149), where, as an introduction to the *Ḳedushah* (*Trisagion*), the famous prayer of Meshullam b. Kalonymos (*u-netanneh tokef*) is introduced. Now this beautiful prayer, all the more solemn because of its tragic memories (see *J.E.* s.v.) tends at the end to become somewhat deterministic, in that it stresses the idea that on this day each man's destiny is sealed. This idea (cf. *Rosh ha-Shanah* I, 2, 16*b*) is developed at some length. But the counterbalance follows immediately, in the form of a citation (*T.J.Ta'an.* II, § 1, 65*b*, l. 3): 'But Penitence, Prayer and Charity avert the evil decree.' These words are printed prominently, so as to stand out by themselves, and usually in large type. They form, in some congregations, the congregational response to Kalonymos' prayer which is chanted by the Reader. And then come the verses which proclaim that God is slow to anger and does not desire the death of the sinner (cp. [868]). (H. L.)]

[620] Israel had two good leaders, Moses and David: they could have had their own sins cancelled through their good deeds, but they asked God that He should give them [forgiveness] only by grace, gratuitously; how much more should he, who is not even one of their least disciples, ask that God should forgive him by grace, gratuitously.

(*Sifre Deut.*, Wa'ethanan, § 26, f. 70*b* (H. p. 38; cp. *R.T.* p. 363, where the translation is inaccurate, and p. 364).)

[621] It is written, 'In the seventh month, in the first day of the month, shall ye have a solemn rest, a memorial of blowing of trumpets' (Lev. XXIII, 24). And it is said, 'God has gone up with a blowing of trumpets, the Lord with the sound of the Shofar' (Ps. XLVII, 5). In the hour when the Israelites take up their *shofarot*, and blow them before God, He gets up from the throne of judgment and sits down upon the throne of mercy, and He is filled with compassion for them, and He turns the attribute of Judgment into the attribute of Mercy. (*Lev.R.*, Emor, XXIX, 3.)

[622] Which attribute [*middah*] is greater: the attribute of goodness or the attribute of punishment? The attribute of goodness.

(*Sifre Num.*, Naso, § 8, f. 4*b* (H. p. 15).)

The attribute of 'goodness' is equivalent to the attribute of mercy. God's goodness is His compassion.

[623] If God [in the instance given] is thus pitiful towards those who transgress His will, how much more pitiful is He towards those who do His will. (*Sifre Num.*, Naso, § 11, f. 5*a* (H. p. 17).)

[624] R. Simeon said: What skilled craftsmen are the Israelites. They know how to appease and win the favour of the Creator. R. Yudan said: Like those gipsies [Cuthaeans] who are clever at begging. One of them came to a woman and said to her, 'Have you an onion? Give it to me.' When she gave it to him, he said, 'Can one eat an onion without bread?' When she gave it to him, he said, 'Can one eat without drinking?' So he got food and

drink. R. Aḥa said: Some women are clever at asking; some are not. A woman who is clever at asking comes to her neighbour; the door is open, but she knocks and says, 'Peace be with you, neighbour; how fare you? How fares your husband? How are your children? May I come in?' The other answers, 'Come in. What do you want?' She rejoins, 'Have you such and such an article? Will you give it to me?' She replies, 'Yes.' The woman who is not clever at asking comes to her neighbour; the door is shut, she opens it, and says, 'Have you such and such an article?' The reply is, 'No!' R. Ḥanina said: Some tenant-farmers are clever at asking, some are not. The clever one observes that he is going downhill in his farm, he plucks up heart of grace, he combs his hair, he whitens his clothes, and with a bright countenance, and with stick in hand and rings on his fingers, he goes to his landlord, who says, 'How is the land, will you be able with joy to eat of its fruits? How are the oxen? Will you be able to enjoy their fat? How are the goats? Will you sate yourself with the kids? What do you want?' The farmer says, 'Have you ten denarii? Will you give them to me?' He replies, 'If you want twenty, take them.' He who does not know how to ask, goes with unkempt hair, dirty clothes, and miserable face to his landlord, who says to him, 'How is the land?' He replies, 'O that it produced what we have put into it.' 'How are the oxen?' 'They are weak.' 'What do you want?' 'Can you give me two denarii?' He replies, 'Bring me first what you owe me.' R. Onias said: David was one of the clever farmers. He first sang God's praises, and said, 'The heavens declare the glory of God' (Ps. XIX, 1). God said, 'Perhaps you want something?' He said, 'And the firmament shows his handiwork.' God said, 'Perhaps you want something?' He said, 'Day upon day utters speech.' Then God said, 'What do you require?' Then David replied, 'Who can understand his errors? The errors which I have done before thee, pardon.' God said, 'They are dismissed and forgiven.' Then David said, 'Cleanse thou me from secret faults, from the hidden sins which I have committed before thee.' God replied, 'These, too, are dismissed and forgiven.' Then he said, 'From the presumptuous sins keep back thy servant—the premeditated sins. Let them not have dominion over me; then shall I be innocent—these are the big iniquities—and pure of great transgression.' For David said to God, 'Thou art a great God, and my trespasses are great'; it befits the great God to pardon the great trespasses, as it is written, 'For the sake of thy name [which is great], pardon my iniquity, for it is great' (Ps. XXV, 11). (*Lev.R.*, Wayiḳra, v, 8.)

Constant use is made of the verses in Job (XXXIII, 23–5), 'If there be for him an interpreter', etc. So it is said:

[625] 'Even though there be nine hundred and ninety-nine accusers against a man, and only one who ascribes to him merit, God, as it were, inclines [the scale] to merit....' The angel [A.V. messenger], who informs God of the man's merit, says to God, 'Punish him with sufferings, and so do thou bring him to repentance.' (*Pes.R.* 38*b*.)

The righteous and the wise are an atonement for their generation.

[626] The scholars in each generation bear in secret the sins of that generation, yet not a soul notices that they do so. (*Tan.d.b.El.* p. 136.)

[627] R. Abba b. Kahana said: On New Year God judges His creatures, and finds merit in them, for He desires to acquit, and not to condemn them, as it says, 'As I live I desire not the death of the wicked' (Ezek. XXXIII, 11). God desires to justify His creatures, as it says, 'It pleased the Lord to justify him' (Isa. XLII, 21, a playful mistranslation). Resh Laḳish said: God says, 'In the hour when I conquer, I suffer loss, but in the hour when I am conquered, I gain. I conquered at the generation of the flood, but I lost, for I destroyed all those masses. So it was with the generation of the Tower of Babel, and with the men of Sodom. But when the Golden Calf was made, Moses conquered me, and I gained all those masses. So I acquit all my creatures, so that I may not suffer loss.' (*Pes.R.* 166*b* (cp. [103]).)

Innumerable must be the number of times in which the Ezekiel verses are quoted, 'I have no pleasure in the death of him that dies,' and 'I have no pleasure in the death of the wicked; therefore repent' (XVIII, 32; XXXIII, 11). Frequently, too, is quoted Ps. V, 4, 'Thou art not a God that has pleasure in wickedness.' This Psalm teaches us that God has no pleasure in condemning a creature. On the contrary, He has pleasure in pronouncing His creatures righteous (or 'in justifying, or in acquitting, His creatures'). So with Adam. When he sinned, God pronounced sentence upon him, but when the Sabbath came, He set him free. He began to talk to him, hoping he would repent, as it says, 'And the Lord God called to Adam.' For the Lord (Yahweh) is the attribute of mercy. So God made the attribute of mercy take precedence over the attribute of judgment. (Partly from *Yalkuṭ* on Pss. v and xcii.)

[628] R. Johanan said: It is only the angels of peace and of mercy who stand before God; the angels of wrath stand far off. (The proof is Isa. xiii, 5, 'The weapons of His wrath come from the end of heaven.') And he said: God is not dragged behind [attracted by] evil; evil does not drag [have power over] Him, as it is said, 'Evil does not dwell with thee' (Ps. v, 4). [The result is obtained by a play upon words.]

(*Tanḥ.B.*, Tazria', 20*a fin.* (cf. Moore, I, 392).)

[629] Moses said to God, 'Show me the attribute wherewith thou governest thy world.' God said, 'I will do so.' And He said, 'I will cause all my goodness to pass before thee.' And He said, 'I owe no creature anything, but I give to them gratuitously,' as it is written, 'I will be gracious to whom I will be gracious.'

(*Tanḥ.B.*, Wa'ethạnan, 5*a*.)

Moses prayed, 'O Lord God, thou hast begun to show thy servant thy greatness and thy strong hand' (Deut. iii, 24).

[630] 'Thy strong hand.' For thou subduest with thy compassion the attribute of justice, as it is said, 'Who is a God like thee that pardons iniquity? He will subdue our iniquities' (Mic. vii, 18, 19). (*Sifre Num.*, Pineḥas, § 134, f. 50*b* (H. p. 180).)

The compassion of God, as it were, fights with His justice and subdues it, and in the success of this contest is shown God's strength.

[631] Esau wept. R. Elazar declared: God said, 'Behold this sinner weeps to me for his very life, I cannot turn him away in vain,' and at once He bade Isaac bless him.

(*Tanḥ.B.*, Toledot, 72*b init.*)

Esau, however unjustly, is always regarded as the prototype and representative of the wicked. (**Note 78.**)

There was also a frequent attempt to weaken superstition. The Rabbis, in spite of the burden of their Biblical fundamentalism, yet tried to make the statements of the Pentateuch more ethical. So in the following passage, by means of two clever puns. *Ḥodesh* means month, but the verb *ḥadash* (*ḥiddesh*) can mean 'renew'. *Shofar* is the Trumpet or Ram's Horn, but the verb *shafar* can mean 'cleanse'.

[632] In this month you shall renew your deeds [i.e. you must seek to amend them]. On this month blow the *shofar*, that is, cleanse your deeds. God says, 'If you cleanse your deeds, then will I be to you like the *shofar*. As the *shofar* draws in the air from the narrow end, and emits it from the wide end, so I will get up from the throne of judgment, and sit down upon the throne of mercy, and turn for you the attribute of judgment into the attribute of mercy. (*Lev.R.*, Emor, XXIX, 6 (cp. [200]).)

Here the purely mechanical or magical effect of the *shofar* as stated in the previous passage is given an ethical condition or basis.

[633] 'Regard not them that have familiar spirits, neither seek after wizards, to be defiled by them: I am the Lord your God' (Lev. XIX, 31). Seek not: these things do not come upon a man unless he has turned his mind towards them, and has become defiled by them. So if you defile yourself with these things, know what you are changing for what [i.e. wizards and familiar spirits for God]. (*Sifra* 91 *a*.)

[634] You might think that the Day of Atonement does not atone without the sacrifices and the goat: it does, because it says, 'It is the Day of Atonement, to make an atonement for you' (Lev. XXIII, 28); or you might think that the Day of Atonement atones for the penitent and impenitent alike, since both sacrifices and the Day of Atonement are efficacious in obtaining atonement. But just as sin offerings and trespass offerings atone only for those who repent, so, too, the Day of Atonement atones only for those who repent. (*Sifra* 102 *a*.)

As to what happened after a man's death there seems to have been a good deal of confusion. I conclude that the general view gradually came to be that the Judgment passed upon the man at the last New Year took immediate effect after death. And yet that could not be so entirely. For a man might genuinely repent at or before the Day of Atonement, and then he might be forgiven. Or his very death might secure his forgiveness. It depended upon the nature of his sin. But crossing this idea of an immediate punishment or reward, there was the doctrine of the resurrection. That doctrine was that, at some point in the future, all the dead would 'rise' (from their graves, mostly, I suppose), and then be finally judged. It is clear that these two conceptions are really opposed to each other: they have probably different origins, and cannot, except somewhat arbitrarily or artificially, be reconciled and harmonised. What is important to notice is that the

Day of Atonement tended to lose its magical or mechanical power. It was only a sort of vehicle for the divine forgiveness, a sort of yearly impetus for human repentance. The official doctrine was:

[635] To a man who says, 'I will sin and repent, the Day of Atonement brings no forgiveness. For sins against God the Day of Atonement brings forgiveness; for sins against a man's neighbour, the Day of Atonement brings no forgiveness till a man has become reconciled with his neighbour.

(*Yoma* VIII, 9.)

Without repentance there is no atonement for committed sin.

[636] Abbaye said: He who dies in his wickedness has no atonement. Raba said: He who dies in his wickedness in an ordinary way has no atonement, but he who is executed, and dies in his wickedness, does have atonement. Abbaye denied this: Those who are executed justly by a Jewish tribunal have no atonement [i.e. if unrepentant]; those executed by the Government [i.e. martyrs] have atonement. (*San.* 47*a fin.*)

Nor can man hope to cheat God. The following passage is significant.

[637] 'From hand to hand the wicked shall not be unpunished' (Prov. XI, 21). Man has two hands. If he steal with one hand, and give charity with the other, he shall not remain unpunished. In the time to come, God will say to the wicked, 'I created two worlds, one for men to do good works therein, and one to receive the reward of them.' As you have done no good works in this world, do you seek reward in the other? If a man sins with one hand, and gives alms with the other, he shall not be unpunished....R. Johanan said: Like to a man who went to a harlot and sinned with her, and gave her her hire, and as soon as he left her house, he met a poor man who asked for alms, and he gave the poor man alms, and he said to himself, 'If it had not been God's will to offer me atonement for my sins, He would not have sent this poor man for me to give him alms, so that He should cause atonement for me in respect of what I have done.' God says to him, 'Learn from the Proverbs: "From hand to hand the wicked shall not be unpunished"' (cp. [562] and [586]).

If a man, in respect to something between him and his neighbours, swears with his mouth, but annuls it in his heart, shall he be unpunished? No: hand to hand, he shall not remain unpunished.[1] (*Midr.Prov.* XI, 21, f. 34*b fin.*–35*a*.)

For some sins there is no forgiveness, though whether this signifies that the Rabbi who enunciated the statement meant that such sinners would be annihilated or punished everlastingly is uncertain.

[638] Five classes of men will not be forgiven: he who repents repeatedly; he who sins repeatedly; he who sins in a righteous generation; and he who sins with the intention of repenting; and he who profanes the Name (cf. *R.T.* p. 245).
(*Ab.R.N.* (vers. I), XXXIX, 58*b* (cp. Moore, III, 155).)

[It is interesting to note how, in the famous tenth chapter of *Sanhedrin* which deals with the world to come ('All Israel have a share in the world to come except...') efforts are made to rehabilitate the excluded, one by one. Extenuating circumstances are looked for. Sometimes God's mercy, or the intercession of a saint secures pardon; thus Korah was 'brought up' by Hannah's prayer, 'It is the Lord who leads down to Sheol, but who also brings up' (I Sam. II, 6). Here, too, the redeeming factor is God's mercy, for the order of the Hebrew, as translated above, places emphasis on the subject (see *Gen.R.*, Wayeḥi, XCVIII, 2 end). Thus the effort was made to retain two irreconcilable concepts: the unforgivable sin, and the omnipotence of mercy and penitence over any possible sin. (H. L.)]

Strange ideas occur about God's forgiveness and about vicarious punishment.

[639] A Rabbi taught in the presence of R. Johanan: Whoever occupies himself with Torah and benevolent acts, or who buries his children, all his sins are forgiven him. (*Ber.* 5*a fin.*)

The death of the children is due to the sins of the parents, and the suffering incurred by their loss causes forgiveness, i.e. no further punishment. Forgiveness plainly meant here remission of punishment (see Cohen, *Ber.* p. 23, n. 3). A man's death (for death was still regarded as a punishment) can atone for his sins, and is often spoken of as doing so.

[To some extent these attempts to explain suffering may be *ex post facto*. They do not look like a theory formulated by itself. To a man who has lost children such a thing may have been said by way of consolation, curious though it seems to us. The crudity is slightly mitigated if we take this view (cp. [610]). (H. L.)]

[1] For the connection between 'hand' and 'oath' cp. Exod. XVII, 16, A.V., 'The Lord has sworn', but the Hebrew is: 'Yea, the hand on [*or* towards] the throne (?) of Jah' (cp. Gen. XXIV, 2, 3 and [184]).

Even for a criminal, if he confesses his sin before his execution, confession and death together secure him a place in the future world. So we find in the Mishnah:

[640] When he is ten cubits from the stoning-place they say to him, 'Confess'; for it is the custom of all about to be put to death to make confession;. and every one who confesses has a share in the world to come; for Joshua induced Achan to confess, and his confession expiated his crime, as it is said, 'And Joshua said, Why hast thou troubled us? The Lord shall trouble thee this day;—this day thou art to be troubled, but in the time to come thou art not to be troubled' (Josh. VII, 25). (*San.* VI, 2.)

Hence a frequent death-bed prayer is: 'May my death be an atonement for all my transgressions,' e.g. *Ber.* 60*a* (cp. *P.B.* p. 317).

The Tosefta says the same as the Mishnah, and then tells a story:

[641] Those who are put to death by the court have a share in the world to come, because they confess all their sins. Ten cubits from the stoning-place they say to the condemned man, 'Confess!' It happened to one who went out to be stoned, that when they told him to confess, he said, 'May my death be an expiation of all my [other] sins; but if I have done *this* sin [for which I am to be executed], let it *not* be forgiven me; yet let the court of Israel be innocent.' When this was reported to the judges, their eyes trickled with tears, but they said, 'It is not possible to reprieve him, for then there would be no end to the matter; but his blood is hung on the neck of the witnesses against him.'[1]

(*T.San.* IX, 5 (Z. p. 429, line 9).)

The worst sins, as the highest virtues, are moral sins and moral virtues. There is, indeed, a third class of sins, as there is a third class of virtues, namely sins and virtues which have to do with man's direct relation to God. In Israel's past, the flagrant sin was idolatry:

[642] R. Elazar b. Azariah said: Idolatry is like a man saying to his neighbour, 'Thou hast scooped out the dish, and left too little in it.' R. Issi b. 'Aḳabya said: It is like a man who has scooped out the whole dish, and left nothing in it.

(*Sifre Num.*, Shelaḥ, § 112, f. 33*a* (H. p. 120).)

The readings in this passage are difficult and various. The passage

[1] The meaning is that, if he were let off, every one sentenced to death would attempt this means of exculpation, but if he be really innocent, then may the false witnesses be punished in the world to come.

has been explained in three ways: (1) a Jew who commits idolatry can do no good deed; (2) he impairs, so to speak, the divine nature itself, or, (3) though he has thus sinned, he has *not* impaired the divine nature itself.

The worst, or most typical, instance of Israelite idolatry was the making of the Golden Calf (Exod. XXXII, 4):

[643] R. Isaac said: There is no calamity which has ever since happened [to Israel] which does not contain one twenty-fourth part of a *litra* as an adjunct for the sin of the Golden Calf [i.e. as Mr Levy renders the words, 'which does not contain a small ingredient of retribution for the sin of the Golden Calf'. (*Original Virtue and other Short Studies*, by the Rev. S. Levy, 1907, p. 47) (cp. [585] and **Note 96**)]. (*San.* 102*a*.)

Very numerous are the Rabbinical stories about the Calf, and very curious are some of the arguments put into the mouth of Moses to induce God to forgive the Israelites:

[644] It is said in Exod. XXXII, 11, 'Moses said, Lord, why does thy wrath wax hot against thy people whom thou hast brought out of the land of Egypt?' Moses said to God, 'Is it not from Egypt that thou hast brought them out? In Egypt they all worship lambs.' R. Huna said: It is like a sage, who opened a shop of perfumes for his son in the street of the harlots. The locality did its part, the trade did its part, and the youth of the young man did its part, and so he corrupted his way. His father came and caught him with a harlot, and cried out, 'I shall kill you.' But a friend of the sage was there, and said to him, 'It is you who have ruined the young man, and now you cry out against him. You have neglected all other trades and handicrafts, and you taught him only about perfumes; you avoided all other localities, and opened for him a shop only in the street of the harlots.' So Moses said, 'Lord of the world, thou didst avoid all other places, but didst cause thy people to be enslaved in Egypt, where all the inhabitants worship lambs. Thy children learnt this worship from the Egyptians, and therefore it is that they made this calf.' (*Exod.R.*, Ki Tissa, XLIII, 7.)

[645] R. Nehemiah said: When the Israelites did that wicked deed, Moses sought to appease God, and he said, 'Lord of the world, they have only made for thee an assistant: why shouldst thou be angry with them? This calf which they have made will

assist thee; thou wilt cause the sun to shine, and the calf will cause the moon; thou wilt look after the stars, the calf after the zodiac; thou wilt cause the dew to fall, the calf will make the winds to blow; thou wilt bring down the rain, and the calf will cause the herbs to sprout.' God said, 'Moses, Do you err like them? In this calf is there any reality?' Then Moses replied, 'If not, why shouldst thou be angry with thy children?' (*Exod.R.*, Ki Tissa, XLIII, 6.)

The Rabbis are ready to let Moses, as it were, catch God out! If the calf is a mere mass of matter, why make such a fuss about it? But we also get passages like the following:

[646] R. Berechiah, in the name of R. Levi, said: A king had a vineyard which he entrusted to a tenant. When the wine was good, he said, 'How good is the wine of my vineyard'; when it was bad, he said, 'How bad is the tenant's wine.' The tenant said, 'Be the wine bad or good, it is yours.' So, at first, God said to Moses, 'I will send you to Pharaoh that he may let *my* people go.' But after the making of the calf, God said, 'Go, get thee down, for *thy* people have corrupted themselves.' Moses said, 'So then, when they sin, they are mine; when they are virtuous, they are thine. Nay, be they sinful or virtuous, they are thine.' (*Pes.K.* 128*b*.)

[647] God said to Hosea, 'Your children have sinned.' He should have replied, 'They are thy children, the children of Abraham, Isaac and Jacob: roll thy mercy upon them.' But not only did he not say this, but he said, 'The whole world is thine; change them for another people.' God said, 'What shall I do with this old man? I will tell him to take a harlot unto himself in marriage, and let her bear unto him children of harlotry, and then I will tell him to send her away; if he brings it over himself to send her away, then I will send Israel away.'...So after she bore unto him two sons and a daughter, God said to him, 'You should learn from Moses thy Master, for when I began to speak to him, he separated himself from his wife (Exod. XVIII, 2); so do you separate yourself from your wife.' Then Hosea said, 'I have children from her, and I cannot bring it over myself to send her away or to divorce her.' Then God said, 'If that is so with you, whose wife is a harlot, and whose children are of harlotry, so that you know not if they are from you or from others, how can I send away

Israel, who are the children of my tried ones, the children of Abraham, Isaac and Jacob, and who are one of the three acquisitions which I have acquired for myself in the world? The Torah is one, heaven with earth is another, and Israel is the third. And do you say, Exchange them for another nation?' Then Hosea saw that he had sinned, and he prayed God for compassion. God replied, 'Sooner than ask for mercy for yourself, ask for mercy for Israel, seeing that because of you I have decreed three decrees against them.'[1] Then he prayed unto God for compassion, and God annulled the decrees. (*Pes.* 87*a–b*.)

Sometimes Israel makes its own excuse, and pleads its own cause:

[648] 'We are the clay, and thou art our Father' (Isa. LXIV, 8). Israel says, 'Therefore even though we sin, and thou art angry, thou shouldst not desert us. For see, the potter, if he makes a jug and leaves a pebble in it, then, when the jug comes out of the oven, if liquid is poured into it, it drips where the pebble is, till all the liquor is lost. What is the cause that the jug drips and loses the liquor? The potter who left the pebble in it.' So the Israelites say to God, 'Thou didst create in us from our childhood the evil inclination, as it is said, "The inclination of man's heart is evil from his childhood" (Gen. VIII, 21). It is the evil inclination which causes us to sin, and thou dost not remove the sin from us, wherefore we beseech thee, cause it to pass away from us that we may do thy will.' And God replies, 'I will do so in the time to come' [the biblical proof is an untranslatable play upon words in Mic. IV, 6, where 'I will gather her that I have afflicted' is interpreted to refer to the removal of the evil inclination. Also, the evil inclination is in Hebrew *yetzer*, and the potter is *Yotzer*].

(*Exod.R.*, Ki Tissa, XLVI, 4.)

The destruction of the Temple, the expulsion of the Israelites from their country, and their exile, whether to Babylon or through the Roman Empire, exercised the minds of the Rabbis very sorely. The

[1] [According to Rashi, God's three promises in Hos. II cancel the three punishments of Hos. I, which are connected with the names of Hosea's three children, thus:

II, 2 'I will gather' annuls I, 4, Jezreel (God scatters); Hosea's first son.

II, 20 'I will compassionate' annuls I, 6, Lo-Ruchamah (not compassionated); Hosea's daughter.

II, 20 'My people art thou' annuls I, 9, Lo-Ammi (not my people); Hosea's second son. (H. L.)]

Patriarchs are made to plead Israel's cause. The following extract is long, but curious and interesting (cp. [184] (**Note 52**)):

[649] R. Samuel b. Naḥmani said that when the Temple was destroyed, Abraham came before God, weeping, plucking out his beard, tearing out the hair of his head, striking his face, rending his garments, and with ashes on his head; then he went to the Temple, and mourned and cried. He said to God, 'Wherein am I different from any other people and tongue, that I have come to this reproach and shame?' When the angels saw him, they arranged a mourning in serried ranks, and they said, 'The highways are waste, the wayfaring man ceases; He has broken the covenant; He has despised the cities; He regards no man' [Man, in Hebrew, *Enosh*] (Isa. XXXIII, 8). For they said, 'The highways to Jerusalem, which were prepared so that the pilgrims might not be stopped on the way, have become waste. The paths on which the Israelites passed to and fro on the festivals—they are desolate. Broken is the covenant which thou didst make with Abraham their father, through which the order of the world was established, and through whom men recognised thee as the most high God, creator of heaven and earth. Thou hast despised Jerusalem and Zion, which aforetime thou chosest. Thou hast not regarded Israel, even as much as thou didst regard the generation of Enos who first began the worship of idols' (Gen. IV, 26, according to a Midrashic interpretation). Then God gave heed to the angels, and said to them, 'Why do you hold a mourning in your serried ranks concerning this matter?' They said, 'Because of Abraham, thy friend, who has come to thy house weeping and mourning, and thou payest no attention to him.' God replied, 'Since my friend has been parted from me and gone to his eternal home, he has not come to my house, and now what has my beloved to do in my house?' (Jer. XI, 15). Then Abraham said, 'Why hast thou sent my sons into exile, and delivered them into the hands of the nations, who have killed them with unnatural deaths, and why hast thou laid waste the Temple, the place where I offered up my son Isaac as an offering before thee?' God said, 'Thy sons sinned, and transgressed the whole Law—all the twenty-two letters that are in it.' Then Abraham said, 'Who testifies against them that they have transgressed thy Law?' God said, 'Let the Law come and testify against Israel.' Then the Law came to testify

against them. Then Abraham said, 'My daughter, you come to testify against Israel that they have violated your commandments. Are you not ashamed before me? Remember the day when God made you pass before every nation and tongue, and they were unwilling to receive you, until my sons came to Mount Sinai, and they received you and honoured you. And now you come to testify against them in the day of their distress!' When the Law heard this, the Law stood on one side, and did not testify against them. Then God said, 'Let the twenty-two letters come and testify against them.' So they all appeared, and the first letter came to testify against Israel that they had broken the Law. Then Abraham said, 'You, Aleph, the first letter of the alphabet, do you come to testify against Israel in the day of their distress? Remember the day when God revealed Himself upon Mount Sinai, and He began with you, "I am the Lord thy God." [The Hebrew word *Anokhi*, I, begins with an Aleph.] No nation and tongue received you except my sons, and now you come to testify against them.' Then Aleph stood aside, and did not testify against them. Then arose the second letter, Beth, to testify against them; and Abraham said, 'You come to testify against my sons who were zealous in [the study of] the five books of the Law, which begin with you.' [The Hebrew for 'In the beginning', the first word of Genesis, begins with Beth.] Then the second letter stood aside, and did not testify against them. Then came the third letter (*g*) to testify against them. But Abraham said, 'You, Gimel, come to testify against my sons that they have transgressed the Law. Is there any nation save my sons which observe that command of the fringes with which you begin?' [Deut. XXII, 12 opens with the word *Gedilim*, of which Gimel, *g*, is the first letter.] Then Gimel too stood aside, and did not testify against them. When all the other letters saw how Abraham had silenced the first three, they were ashamed, and they refrained, and they did not testify against Israel. Then Abraham said to God, 'Thou gavest me a son when I was a hundred years old, and when he had acquired intelligence, and was thirty-seven years old, thou badest me offer him up for a burnt offering before thee. Then I made myself cruel, and had no pity upon him, but I myself bound him; wilt thou not remember this, and have pity upon my sons?' Then Isaac began and said, 'When my father said to me, "God will provide the lamb for the burnt offering, my son,'' I did not cavil at his words, but I let myself willingly be bound upon the altar, and I stretched out my neck under the knife. Wilt thou not remember this for me, and have pity on my sons?' Then Jacob began and said, 'Did I not remain twenty years with Laban, and when I left him, the wicked Esau met me, and sought to kill my sons, and I delivered myself to die in their stead; and now they are delivered into the hands of the enemy as sheep for the slaughter, after I had brought them up as the chickens of a hen, and I bore for them the troublous responsibility of bringing up children, for through most of my days I was in great trouble for their sakes. Now wilt thou not remember this for me, and have compassion on my sons?' Then Moses began and said, 'Was I not a faithful shepherd for Israel during forty years? Like a horse I ran before them in the wilderness. And when the time came that they should enter the land, thou didst decree that my bones should be consumed in the wilderness, and now that the Israelites have been carried into captivity, thou hast sent for me to mourn and to weep over them. Like the proverb which men use, ''Of my Lord's good, I do not partake; of his evil, I do.''' Then Moses said to Jeremiah, 'Go before me, for I will go and see who lays his hands upon them.' Jeremiah said, 'I cannot pass upon the way because of the slain.' Moses said, 'Nevertheless, proceed.' So they went on till they reached the rivers of Babylon. When the Israelites saw Moses, they said, 'The son of Amram has risen from his grave to deliver us from our enemies.' Then a heavenly voice went forth and said, 'It is a decree of God.' Then Moses said, 'My sons, I cannot bring you back, for the decree has been announced, but God will soon restore you.' Then he left them. Then they lifted up their voices in weeping till their cry came up to God, as it is said, 'By the waters of Babylon we wept' (Ps. CXXXVII, 1). Then Moses came to the Patriarchs, and they said to him, 'What have the enemies done to our sons?' He said, 'Some they have killed, the hands of some they have tied behind their backs, some they have bound with fetters of iron, some they have stripped naked, some have died on the way, and their corpses have been left to the birds of the air and to the beasts of the earth, and some, hungry and thirsty, have been exposed to the heat of the sun.' Then they all began to weep and lament: 'Woe for that which has befallen our sons. How have you become as orphans without a father. How had you to sleep in the sun and in the heat, without covering or raiment. How had you to walk over rocks and gravel without shoes or sandals. How were you laden with heavy burdens of sand. How were your hands tied behind your backs. How have you not been suffered to swallow the spittle in your mouths.' Then Moses said, 'Cursed be you, O sun, that you did not become dark in the hour when the enemy entered the Temple.' Then the sun answered and said, 'Moses, faithful shepherd, when I would have become dark, they did not allow me to do so, and they ceased not to strike me with sixty scourges of flame, and they said to me, Go forth, and shine with thy light.' Then Moses said, 'Woe, how is your radiance, O sanctuary, become dark; woe, that the time has come for the Temple to be laid waste and the Sanctuary destroyed, and that the school children are killed, and that their parents are driven into exile and captivity and desolation. I adjure you, O captors, do not commit merciless slaughter, do not make a complete destruction; do not kill the son in the presence of the father, and the daughter in the presence of the mother, for a time will come when the Lord of heaven will call you to account.' But the wicked Chaldeans did not act thus, but they put the son by the side of his mother, and said to his father, 'Arise and kill him.' The mother wept, and let tears fall upon him, and the father slew him. Then Moses said to God, 'In thy Law it is written of ewe or cow, "Ye shall not kill it and its young both in one day" (Lev. XXII, 28), and now they have slaughtered ever so many sons and their mothers together, and thou art silent.' Then Rachel, our mother, leapt up before God, and said, 'It is known to thee that Jacob, thy servant, loved me with a special love, and that he served my father because of me seven years, and when the seven years were over, and the time of my nuptials was at hand, my father determined to give my sister to my husband instead of me, and the thing was so dreadful to me when I got to know of his plan that I revealed it to my husband, and I gave him a sign that he should distinguish between me and my sister, so that my father should not be able to substitute her for me. But afterwards I repented, and I overcame my desire, and I had pity on my sister that she should not come to shame. And in the evening, when they substituted my sister for me, then I entrusted to my sister all the signs which I had given to my husband, so that he might think that it was I. And not only that, but I crept under the bed in which he lay with my sister, and when he spoke to her, she was silent, and I answered him throughout, so that he might not recognise my sister by her voice, and I acted lovingly towards her, and I was not jealous, and did not expose her to shame. And if I, who am flesh and blood and ashes, was not jealous of my rival, and did not expose her to shame and reproach, why shouldst thou, eternal King, the loving and merciful One, be jealous of idols who have no reality in them, so that thou hast sent my children into exile, and let them be slain by the sword, and suffered their enemies to do unto them according to their pleasure?' Then the compassion of God was stirred, and He said, 'For thy sake, Rachel, I will restore Israel to their land,' as it is said, 'Thus says the Lord, A voice is heard in Ramah, lamentation and bitter weeping; Rachel weeping for her children refuses to be comforted, because they are not. Thus says the Lord, Refrain thy voice from weeping, and thine eyes from tears, for thy work shall be rewarded, and they shall come again from the land of the enemy' (Jer. XXXI, 15, 16).

(*Lam.R.*, Introduction, 24, f. 6*b*, inner col. foot.)

Israel's ultimate redemption can be attributed to many causes. Curious is the idea that the pre-ordained End of itself, as it were, helps to bring about Israel's salvation:

[650] R. Elazar said: Israel will be redeemed through by five things only, through distress, through prayer, through the merits of the fathers, through repentance, and through the End.

(*Midr.Ps.* on CVI, 44 (229*a*, § 9.)

Sometimes God is made to *wish* that there should be a petition put up before Him for Israel's forgiveness:

[651] R. Samuel b. Naḥmani quoted the verse, 'Doubtless thou art our Father, for Abraham is ignorant of us, and Israel does not acknowledge us' (Isa. LXIII, 16). In the days to come God will say to Abraham, 'My children have sinned against me'; Abraham will reply, 'Let them, then, for the sanctification of thy Name, be blotted out.' Then He will say, 'I will say it to Jacob, for he has felt the pain of bringing up children; perhaps he will supplicate me for compassion upon them.' But Jacob answered like Abraham. Then God will say, 'With the old one

there is no sense, and with the young one no counsel.' Then He will say to Isaac, 'Thy children have sinned against me.' Isaac will say, 'My children! Are they not also thy children? When they said, "We will do", even before, "We will hearken" (Exod. XXIV, 7), didst thou not call them "Thy first-born son" (*ib.* IV, 22), but now thou speakest of my children and not of thy children, and, after all, how much have they sinned against thee? Man's life has seventy years. Remove twenty, for the which thou dost not punish, there remain fifty.[1] Remove half for the nights, and there remain twenty-five. Take away twelve and a half for praying and for eating and other bodily needs, and there remain twelve and a half. If thou wilt take the whole [of the sin which remains], it is well; but if not, let us each take half; but if thou goest further, and sayest that I must take the whole—did I not offer myself before thee?' Then they will all exclaim, 'Thou art our Father,' and Isaac will say to them, 'Instead of praising me, praise God,' and he will cause them to see God with their own eyes, and they will raise their eyes to the heavens, and say, 'For thou, O Lord, art our Father, our Redeemer from of old.' (*Sab.* 89*b*.)

The only respect in which idolatry was still, in their actual life, important to the Rabbis was in relation to the world around them. Sometimes we hear of arguments between Rabbis and gentile philosophers. One sometimes reads to-day how in a fire, or in an earthquake, a church is singularly preserved. The same thing must have happened in antiquity with heathen temples. A 'philosopher' is made to argue with R. Gamaliel on this point. If, after a fire, the temple is preserved, does it not show that the idol is, at any rate, not a *pure* nonentity? The reply apparently is that God does not bother about the idols, but only about the idolaters. Again, if the idols are so objectionable, why does God not destroy them? The reply is that the idols are too various.

[652] Ye worship sun and moon and stars and plants and hills and valleys and springs, and even *men*. Is God to destroy His world because of the fools?

(*Mek.*[2], *Baḥodesh*, Yitro, § 6, p. 226; *Mek.*[3], vol. II, p. 245.)

The same argument is used from a different point of view in the following:

[653] The elders in Rome were asked, 'If your God has no pleasure

[1] [Of the generation in the wilderness, God punished only those over twenty years old (Num. XIV, 29): this is taken to denote God's usual practice. (H. L.)]

in the worship of idols, why does He not destroy them?' They replied, 'If men had worshipped the things which the world does not need, He would have destroyed them. But they worship sun, moon, stars and planets; is He to destroy His world because of the fools?' [Quoting this, the Gemara adds, 'The world maintains its course, but the fools who have corrupted their ways, will be judged hereafter.'] The questioners replied, 'Then He ought at least to destroy the things which the world does not need, and leave the others.' The elders said, 'Then the worshippers of the stars, sun and moon would be strengthened in their idolatry, for they would say, "Behold, these verily are true gods, for they have not been destroyed."'

(*Ab.Zar.* IV, 7; *Ab.Zar.* 54*b*.)

The Gemara adds this example: 'If a man steals some wheat and plants it in his field, you might argue that it ought not to grow up; the world pursues its course, but the fools will be judged hereafter.' A sort of hardness is here apparent; no trace of any yearning desire to convert the fools to the true worship of the true God.

The following passage may perhaps be interjected here:

[654] R. Naḥman said in the name of Rabbah b. Abuha: There are no heretics among the nations. 'But we see that there *are* heretics among them.' 'Say rather that the majority of the nations is not composed of heretics.' R. Naḥman was of the opinion of R. Ḥiyya b. Abba, who said in the name of R. Johanan: The peoples who live outside Palestine are not idolaters, but they follow the customs of their fathers. (*Ḥul.* 13*b init.*)

[The environment of this passage is somewhat similar to that of Acts XV, 20, 29 and XXI, 25 (see p. 141 of Foakes-Jackson's *Acts* in the Moffatt Series, London, 1931). Animals slaughtered by Gentiles could not be eaten by Jews, but 'advantage' could be derived from commerce in them. Thus, a Jewish tanner might buy and sell their skins. If, however, the animals had not merely been slaughtered, but also sacrificed, then no 'advantage' might be derived from them. Such animals are called 'strangled' in Acts. Thus, a Jew may not buy leather of animals when the skin shows an incision at the heart (*Ab.Zar.* II, 3, with Elmslie's note, and V, 9), since these must have come from a Mithraeum or other temple. A 'heretic among the Gentiles' may, therefore, be assumed to have killed his animal for commercial, and not for religious, reasons, since, *ex hypothesi*, he rejects the idols. R. Eliezer, just before our passage opens, had declared that a pagan, when slaughtering a beast, always had idolatry in mind. Who could these heretics be? Clearly not Judaeo-Christians.

Of the authorities cited in this extract, Naḥman and Rabbah b. Abuha were Babylonians. Rabbah, an Amora of the Second Generation, was Naḥman's father-in-law and teacher. They lived at Nehardea on the Euphrates till it was destroyed in 259, when they moved to Maḥoza, on the Tigris. They lived all their lives in Mesopotamia, where the Jews enjoyed a kind of autonomy under the Parthians, until, in 226, the Sassanians rose to power, and these, being fanatical Zoroastrians, caused the greatest apprehension to the Jews. The Magi attempted to prohibit Jews from killing animals for food. But in spite of temporary anxieties, and though they suffered during the Roman Wars, the lot of the Jews was a happy one. No doubt the contrast between the Zoroastrian worship and that of the ordinary pagan altar, prompted the remark of Rabbah. It is very doubtful whether the Rabbis understood the theology of their neighbours: to them a heathen who repudiated images might seem a heretic *qua* pagan—even though elsewhere he is said to be equivalent to a Jew, and even to fulfil the Torah. Therefore a Zoroastrian, *vis à vis* a worshipper of Diana or Isis, may have been to them but heretic 'writ large'. Ḥiyya b. Abba was a Palestinian Amora, at the end of the third century. He was a disciple of Johanan. Here we have the Palestinian outlook. Gentiles, remote from Palestine, have not come in contact with Judaism. They serve idols as their fathers did. And a few lines lower down, the Gemara concludes from Lev. XXII, 18, that vows from Gentiles are as acceptable as from Israelites. (H. L.)]

Sometimes the Rabbis conceive that just because there is nothing real in an idol, therefore idolatry is a less serious offence than (say) sexual licence or some other grave moral sin:

[655] When the Israelites sinned against the second commandment, they were forgiven [as in the crucial case of the Golden Calf], for there is nothing substantial and real in idols; idolatry only provokes God's jealousy. But when the Israelites sinned at Shittim in unchastity, there fell of them twenty-four thousand men; for in unchastity there *is* something substantial and real; therefore they were punished, but for their idolatry they were forgiven. (*Exod.R.*, Mishpaṭim, XXX, 21.)

This passage represents one mood of the Rabbis, while in another passage idolatry might be represented as worse than unchastity. As we might say, no sin is worse than idolatry, and at another moment, no sin is worse than unchastity. And against Num. XXV, 1 (Shittim) we may set Exod. XXXII, 28, where three thousand men *were* slain because of the Golden Calf! (**Note 84.**)

Sometimes, indeed, the mere rejection of idolatry would seem enough to justify a man being called a Jew.

[656] He who renounces idol worship may be called a Jew.

(*Meg.* 13*a*.)

[657] Whoever acknowledges idols, repudiates the whole Torah, but whoever repudiates idolatry is as though he accepted the whole Torah.

(*Sifre Deut.*, Re'eh, § 54, f. 86*b* (H. p. 122; cp. *Ned.* 25*a*).)

[658] 'Thou shalt have no other gods besides me' (Exod. xx, 3). The Rabbis said: If there is nothing real in the idols, why are they called gods? R. Phinehas b. Ḥama said: In order to reward all who separate themselves from them. For God said, 'Though there is nothing real in the idols, yet directly a man separates himself from them, I account it to him as if he served Him in whom *is* reality, and as if he had drawn near to me.'

(*Deut.R.*, Wa'ethanan, II, 18.)

[659] He who commits idolatry denies the Ten Commandments, and all that was commanded to Moses, to the Prophets and to the Patriarchs.... He who renounces idolatry is as if he professed the whole Law.... But R. Ishmael said that the words 'his sin shall be upon him' (Num. xv, 31) show that the sin of idolatry [when an Israelite commits it] is not visited upon the third and fourth generation.... Moreover, R. Ishmael, as against R. Akiba, said that the words, 'his soul shall be *utterly* cut off' (*ib.*) [i.e. the twofold use of the verb (cp. [1316] and p. 44)] do not refer to a cutting-off in the world to come as well as to a cutting-off in this world. In this verse the Law speaks in the tongue of men [i.e. it is a mere idiom]. (*Sifre Num.*, Shelaḥ, § 111, f. 31*b fin.*–32*a*, 33*a fin.*–33*b init.* (H. pp. 116, 121; cp. [857]).)

There is yet hope for an Israelite, if he commits the sin of idolatry and repents, grave as the sin of idolatry is.

It is clear that, at a time of persecution, any smallest concession to idolatry might be regarded as apostasy. The Rabbis were men who valued life: they did not seek, or bid others seek, martyrdom. On the contrary: they ruled that, in order to save his life, a Jew might violate any commandment in the Law, except the three great prohibitions: murder, unchastity, idolatry (**Note 11 *k***). Moreover, they bade the Israelites, so far as possible, to obey the decrees of the government.

[In connection with R. Ishmael's first remark, Num. xv, 31, cited above, must be considered. As just quoted (from the A.V.), the verse does not accurately represent the Hebrew original, which not only lacks 'his' (really, 'her', since 'soul' is feminine), but is at pains to show that 'his' must not be inserted. Nevertheless, the A.V., R.V., American-Jewish version, Septuagint and Targum Onḳelos all have the pronoun, and this would be the obvious translation of anyone confronted with an unpointed Hebrew Bible.

Yet the Massoretic text goes out of its way to avoid the pronoun at all possible costs. It invents a word for 'sin' which occurs nowhere else (a feminine form of the usual '*awon*) and it puts a special mark over the final consonant to indicate that it is not the pronoun 'her' but the feminine nominal ending. So astonishing is this form, that some grammarians prefer to treat it as an abnormal pronoun rather than as an unusual noun.

What is at the bottom of this extraordinary insistence of the Massorah that the words must, whatever happens, mean 'sin is in her' and not 'her sin is in her'? Quite possibly we have here a relic of an ancient controversy about inherited sin. Does the Massorah wish to differentiate between sin in general, sinfulness that is always prevalent and to which anyone can fall prone, and 'her' sin, i.e. 'her sin which has come down to her', 'which is hereditary'? This is what the context would suggest, but the actual words imply the contrary. One would expect 'her' sin to be personal, and 'sin', without a pronoun, to be ancestral. Or the controversy may have been whether or no the evil that men do is buried with their bones. That some such difference of opinion existed is clear when we turn to the paraphrastic Targum (Pseudo-Jonathan), which has:

'For the first word that God commanded at Sinai has he despised and the command of the circumcision has he annulled. With destruction in this world shall that man be destroyed [and he shall likewise be destroyed] in the world to come, [in] which he is destined to give an account of his guilt on the great Day of Judgment.' (The bracketed words have to be supplied: the sense is not altogether certain.)

This interpretation of the Targum is thus opposed to that of Ishmael. (H. L.)]

[660] 'Keep the king's command' (Eccles. VIII, 2). The Holy Spirit says, 'I adjure you that if the earthly kingdom decree persecutions, you shall not rebel in all that it decrees against you, but you shall keep the king's command. But if it decree that you should annul the Torah, the Commandments and the Sabbath, then hearken not to the king's command. Thus did Hananiah, Mishael and Azariah. But when deliverance came, they would not come forth till the king bade them' (from the furnace).[1]

(*Tanh.B.*, Noaḥ, 19*b*–20*a*.)

[1] I.e. they showed respect to the king *qua* king, idolater though he was. Mr Loewe thinks that the reference to the Sabbath tends to suggest that the passage is old (cp. I Macc. II, 41).

But if a Jew is ordered to violate even the smallest command as a mark of apostasy, then he must sooner die. Thus we read:

[661] One may violate all laws in order to save life except idolatry, unchastity, murder. But this rule holds only if one is alone, or if less than ten men are present. Otherwise in public one must die rather than violate the lightest law, as the brothers Lulianos and Pappus did, who, being commanded to drink water in a coloured glass, refused and were killed. In the case of the Rabbis who baked bread on the Sabbath for a Roman governor, he did not command them to do this because he wanted them to become apostates, but because he wanted new bread. R. Abba b. Zemina stitched some clothes for a heathen in Rome. The heathen offered him '*ṭerephah*' [forbidden] food, and said, 'Eat.' He refused. The heathen said, 'Eat, or I will kill you.' He replied, 'If you wish to kill me, kill, but I will not eat *ṭerephah* food.' The man said, 'Henceforward, know that if you had eaten, I would have killed you; for one must be either completely Jew or completely heathen.' (*T.J.Shebi'ith* IV, § 2, f. 35*a*, line 49.)

[Lulianus, Lilianus, etc. are variants of the name Julian: they occur chiefly in Syriac and in the Jerusalem Talmud. For the different accounts of the brothers Pappus and Julian, see *J.E.* s.v. Pappus. The Roman governor mentioned in [661] was Arsicinius (or Ursicinus). See Hamburger's *Real-Encyclopädie*, p. 73 and also the lexicons of Levy and Jastrow, s.v., where the difficult passage about the bread is explained. (H. L.)] (**Note 16**.)

[662] It happened once that four hundred youths and maidens were taken captive, and were to be employed in a life of shame. When they realised for what purpose they were wanted, they said, 'If we throw ourselves into the sea, shall we enter into the life of the world to come?' Then the eldest among them quoted the verse, 'I will bring them again from the depths of the sea' (Ps. LXVIII, 22). 'These are they', he said, 'who are drowned in the sea.' When the maidens heard this, they leapt up and jumped into the sea. Then the youths said, 'If *they* act thus, how much more should *we*?' So they too jumped into the sea, and to such as them the verse refers, 'For thy sake are we killed all the day long '(*ib*. XLIV, 22). (*Giṭ*. 57*b* (cp. [678]).)

[663] 'Rest in the Lord and wait patiently for Him' (Ps. XXXVII, 7). By a pun this is said to mean: 'Accept God's decree, even if,

for His name's sake, thou art made a corpse.' As Job said, 'Though He slay me, I will hope in Him' (Job XIII, 15).

(*Tanh.B.*, Debarim, 3*a*.)

The following reflects actual life and its complicated problems:

[664] The Mishnah (VIII, 12) says, 'If women are told by some Gentiles, "Surrender one of you to us, and we will dishonour her; if not, we will dishonour you all," then let no single Israelite woman[1] be surrendered.' This is not to be the rule if she had already been dishonoured. And it is not to be the rule if the woman is a slave. If a company of Israelites on a journey meet a band of heathen who say, 'Deliver us up one of your number, and we will kill him; if not, we will kill you all.' Then they must all be killed, for no Israelite must be delivered up to the heathen. But if they say, 'Deliver us up such a one, mentioning him by name, then they may deliver him up.' One Rabbi said: Yes, but only if he has committed an act for which he is liable to be put to death. R. Johanan said: Even without this restriction. Ulla b. Kosheb was sought for by the government. He fled, and took refuge at Lud with R. Joshua b. Levi. They came and told the inhabitants that the place would be laid waste unless he were given up. R. Joshua went and persuaded Ulla that he should let himself be delivered up. Now Elijah was in the habit of appearing to R. Joshua, and he came no more. Then R. Joshua fasted many days, and at last Elijah appeared. He said to R. Joshua, 'Should I reveal myself to informers?' 'I did but act according to a teaching,' said the Rabbi. 'Is that a teaching for the pious?' said Elijah. (*T.J.Ter.* VIII, § 10, f. 46*b*, line 45 (cp. the variant in *Gen.R.* XCIV, 9 (Th. p. 1184)).)

[The role played by Elijah in Jewish legend is of extreme importance. From the last two verses of Malachi he takes his place as the harbinger of the Messiah, and he is constantly depicted as a messenger of hope and as a deliverer. Because of his zeal for God's 'covenant' in the days of Ahab (I Kings XIX, 10), he is symbolically present at every

[1] [Although the exceptive word 'Israelite' might here seem terribly particularistic, it must be remembered that the antithesis was 'pagan', not 'Christian'. Mainly owing to the groves at Daphne, by Antioch, Jews were presented with the fouler aspects of Gentile life, without the corrective which contact with true Greek culture would have supplied. References to Gentile promiscuity are frequent and we cannot wonder that Rabbis inferred that, to a Gentile woman, rape did not hold out the same horror as to a Jewess. Hence the use of 'Israelite' here. It is to be noted that a raped, i.e. unchaste, 'Israelite', was to be surrendered. (H. L.)]

initiation of a boy into the 'covenant of Abraham' (i.e. at the boy's circumcision), for every boy is a potential Messiah. Elijah is supposed to be seated at the right of the *Sandeḳ* (godfather) and the words 'this is Elijah's chair' are proclaimed (see *P.B.* p. 304). At the conclusion of Sabbath, his name appears frequently in the hymns, for with the return of the working week, with its cares and, sometimes, with its perils, the thought of Elijah is appropriate. (E.g. Gaster, *P.B.* I, 138, 139.) Gradually he becomes a synonym of progress: he is Phinehas, i.e. the phoenix, the Arabic al-Hidr, ever-verdant, for he stands for confidence in the future, the Jewish equivalent to 'a good time coming'. The stories told about his appearances on earth are exceedingly numerous: not a few are cited in these pages. He will solve all doubts, for he is the 'prophet who will arise with Urim and Tummim'. When, in the Gemara, a difficulty is reached that defies elucidation, it is left pending: the technical term is '*teḳu(m)*', i.e. 'it stands'. But the letters are taken to form the sentence, 'The Tishbite will solve all doubts and perplexities.' Elijah is always wandering on earth, and his journeys bear a marked resemblance, in some ways, to those associated with the 'Wandering Jew'. He appears both to Tannaim and to Amoraim. Even as late as the fourteenth century, persons claimed to have had interviews with him (see *J.E.* s.v.). (H. L.)]

One may kill *A* who is attempting to murder *B*. One may kill a man who is attempting to violate a betrothed woman. But if ordered to commit a murder, or threatened with the loss of life, one must lose one's life.[1] If a woman, when betrothed, is ordered to submit to violation, or threatened with death, then she must lose her life:

[665] A man came to Raba and said, 'The prefect of my town has ordered me to kill so and so, or he will kill me.' Raba replied, 'Let him kill you; do you commit no murder. Why should you think that your blood is redder than his? Perhaps his is redder than yours.' (*Pes.* 25*b*.)

[This, and the next two passages, may be regarded as fairly indicative of the Rabbinic attitude towards what is to-day called 'Pacifism'. The love of the Rabbis for peace, and the tremendous emphasis which they attached to it, can be seen from Chapter XXVI and from the prominence assigned to peace in so many portions of the liturgy. This is natural, for who has ever suffered more than the Jews have done from the brutalities of war. But between love of peace and non-resistance there is a great difference. The Rabbis taught that one must hate no man (see [1328]) but this did not mean that one must look on apathetically at the slaughter of the innocent and helpless. The Jews are probably the only people who have given this

[1] For no man can say that his own life is more valuable than his neighbour's (cp. [665]).

extreme pacifism a trial (I Macc. II, 34 f.). The Saints (*Ḥasidim*), who decided that a man must defend himself and succour the weak (*ib.* 39 f.), had as strong a sense of duty and as active a conscience as have the pacifists of to-day. 'A man must do God's commands, and live thereby, and not die' [1401] was a general principle. (H.L.)] **(Note 58.)**

[666] Two disciples[1] changed their garments in the time of the Great Persecution (i.e. they dressed as Gentiles). A Roman soldier, himself an apostate Jew, met them and said, 'If you are children of the Torah, give your lives for it. If you are not, why should you be killed because of it?' They replied, 'We are its children, and we are ready to be slain for its sake; but it is unnatural for men to destroy themselves deliberately.'

(*Gen.R.*, Wayishlaḥ, LXXXII, 8 (Th. pp. 984, 985).)

[667] One who is attacked by robbers may break the Sabbath in order to save his life. Once it happened that letters from the Roman Government, containing evil tidings for the Jews, reached the elders of Sepphoris. They came and asked R. Elazar b. Peraṭa what to do. It was on the Sabbath, and they said, 'Shall we flee?' He was frightened to tell them directly to flee on the Sabbath, so he said, 'Do you ask me? Ask Jacob (Hos. XII, 12) or Moses (Exod. II, 15) or David' (I Sam. XIX, 18). Danger to life annuls the Sabbath, for man is to live by doing God's commandments, and not to die by them. The law of circumcision annuls the Sabbath. Now if something affecting a single one of man's members annuls the Sabbath, how much more must the Sabbath be annulled when his life, which concerns all his 248 members, is affected. **(Note 20 *i*.)** (*Tanḥ.B.*, Masse'e, 81*a* (cp. [538]).)

[668] 'Ye shall make you no idols: my Sabbaths shall ye keep, and my Sanctuary shall ye revere' (Lev. XXVI, 2). So if a Jew is sold [as a slave] to an idolater, he must not say: 'As my master is an idolater, I will worship idols. As my master is unchaste, I will be unchaste; as my master profanes the Sabbaths, I will profane the Sabbaths.' For Scripture warns him about all the commandments, and it says, 'I am the Lord; I am faithful to pay a full reward.' (*Sifra* 110*c init.*)

The following legend is also a reflection of life. Whatever befall, God's name must not be profaned:

[1] Of R. Joshua (b. Hananiah ?).

[669] Nebuchadnezzar set up an image, and he chose three men from every people to worship it. The three men from Israel were Hananiah, Mishael and Azariah. They protested that they would not worship the idol. They asked Daniel whether they should bow down to it or not. He referred them to Ezekiel, the prophet. Ezekiel quoted to them the verse of Isaiah, his master, 'Hide thyself a little moment till the wrath shall be overpast' (Isa. XXVI, 20). They said to him, 'What do you wish? That they should say that *all* nations have worshipped that image?' He replied, 'What do *you* wish?' They said, '*We* desire to discredit the idol by not bowing down to it, so that men may say that all nations bowed down to that idol, except Israel.' He said, 'If *that* is your mind, wait while I enquire of God.' So he said to God, 'These three men wish to give their lives for the sanctification of thy Name. Wilt thou stand by them or not?' He replied, 'I will not, as it says, "Do ye come to enquire of me? I will not be enquired of by you" (Ezek. XX, 3). You caused me to burn my temple and to exile my sons among the nations, and after that, do you come to enquire of me? I will not be enquired of by you.' Then Ezekiel lamented, and said, 'Woe to Israel, the remnant of Judah is lost.' And he wept. When he came back to them, they said, 'What did God say to you?' He replied, 'He will not stand by you.' They said, 'Whether he deliver us or no, we will not worship the idol' (Dan. III, 17, 18). And this reply they made to Nebuchadnezzar. When they left Ezekiel, God revealed himself to Ezekiel and said, 'Do you suppose that I shall not stand by them? Verily, I shall stand by them, even as it says, "I will yet be enquired of by the house of Israel to do it for them" (Ezek. XXXVI, 37). Nevertheless, leave them alone; tell them nothing from me. I will let them alone to go forward in their purity, as it says, "He that walks purely walks securely."' What did they do? They scattered themselves among the crowd, and repeated their defiance to Nebuchadnezzar.

(*Cant.R.* VII, § 8, 1, on VII, 8; f. 37*b*.)

The story of the mother and her seven sons (II Macc. VII) is told also in the Talmud, though somewhat differently:

[670] R. Judah told the story of the woman and her seven sons. They brought the eldest before the Emperor; he said to him, 'Worship the idol.' He replied, 'It is written, "I am the Lord thy God."'

Then they took him away and killed him. They did the same to the second, and he said, 'It is written, "Thou shalt have no other god besides me."' They took him away and killed him. The third said, 'He that sacrifices unto any god save unto the Lord only, shall be destroyed.' He, too, was killed. Then they brought the fourth before the Emperor, and the Emperor said, 'Worship the idol'; he replied: 'Thou shalt bow down to no other god than the Lord.' He, too, was killed. Then they brought forth the fifth, and he replied, 'Hear O Israel, the Lord thy God, the Lord is One.' He, too, was killed. The sixth said, 'Know this day, and lay it to thine heart, that the Lord He is God in heaven above and on the earth beneath: there is none else.' He, too, was killed. Then they brought out the seventh son, and said to him, 'Worship the idol.' He replied, 'Thou hast avouched the Lord this day to be thy God, and the Lord has avouched thee this day to be a peculiar people unto Himself. We have sworn to God that we will not exchange Him for any other god, and He has sworn to us that He will not exchange us for any other people.' Then the Emperor said, 'I will throw down my signet ring. Bend down, and pick it up, that they may say you have accepted the authority of the King.' He replied, 'Woe to you, O Emperor; if you are so solicitous about your honour, how much more must I be solicitous about the honour of God.' When they took him away to kill him, his mother said, 'Give him to me that I may kiss him a little.' Then she said, 'My son, go and say to Abraham your father, "You erected one altar, I have erected seven altars."' Then she went upon the roof, and threw herself down and died. And a heavenly voice said, 'Joyful mother of sons' (Ps. CXIII, 9).

(*Giṭ.* 57*b*.)

The allusions to martyrdom, and especially to the martyrs of the Hadrianic persecution, are very numerous. For example:

[671] '*Thy* dead shall live: with *my* dead body shall they arise' (Isa. XXVI, 19). Isaiah cried out to God, 'Let *thy* dead live. Who are *thy* dead? Those who let themselves be made corpses for the sake of God. Such a one was crucified. Why? For circumcising his son. Another was burnt for keeping the Sabbath, a third was slain for reading the Bible. These are *thy* dead.'

(*Tanḥ.B.*, Toledot, 69*b*.)

[672] 'All thy saints are in thy hand' (Deut. XXXIII, 3). These are Israel's leaders who stand up for Israel, and give their lives for Israel. (*Sifre Deut.*, Berakah, § 344, f. 143*b*.)

[673] 'As the wings of a dove covered with silver' (Ps. LXVIII, 13). Why is Israel compared to a dove? As the dove, when it is slaughtered, does not struggle, so the Israelites do not struggle when they are slaughtered for the sanctification of the Name, and as the dove saves herself only by her wings, so the Israelites are saved only by the merit of the Torah, which is compared to silver, as it says, 'The words of the Lord are pure words, like silver purified seven times' (Ps. XII, 6).

(*Midr.Ps.* on LXVIII, 13 (159*a*, § 8).)

[674] It is written in Exod. XX, 6, 'They who love me and keep my commandments.' R. Nathan said: These are the Israelites who gave their lives for the commandments. 'Why were you brought out to be killed?' 'Because I circumcised some Israelites.' 'And why were you brought forth to be burnt?' 'Because I read the Law.' 'And why were you brought out to be crucified?' 'Because I ate unleavened bread.' 'And why were you scourged?' 'Because I carried the *lulab* on Tabernacles. These wounds have caused me to be loved by my Father who is in heaven.'

(*Mek.*[2], *Baḥodesh*, Yitro, § 6, p. 227; *Mek.*[3], vol. II, p. 247.)

There is considerable interest in the account of the fall of Bethar, the last stronghold to hold out against Rome:

[675] Rabbi could preach four and twenty sermons on 'The Lord has swallowed up and not pitied' (Lam. II, 2), but R. Johanan (b. Nappaha) could preach sixty on the same verse. What! R. Johanan could preach more than R. Judah (cp. [419])! Yes, but R. Judah (A.D. 135–220) lived nearer the time of the Destruction than R. Johanan (died 279), and when R. Judah used to preach, there were present old men who remembered the Destruction, and when he preached about it [and mentioned things that happened], they would weep, and were so afflicted that they would depart: therefore R. Judah shortened his addresses [and did not say all that he might, so as not to trouble them]. [See parallel in *Lam.R.* II *in loc.* ed. Buber, 50*b*, with slight variants, some of which have been adopted in the following.] R. Judah [b. Ilai] said that R. Judah the Prince used to expound 'The voice is the

voice of Jacob, but the hands are the hands of Esau' (Gen. XXVII, 22) thus: Hark! the voice of Jacob, crying out for what Esau's hands have wrought in Bethar. R. Simeon b. Yoḥai said, 'My teacher Akiba used to expound Num. XXIV, 17 ("A star has gone forth from Jacob") as "A liar has gone forth from Jacob."' [The verse was taken as a Messianic prophecy and 'star' = *kokab*, was applied by Bar Kokba to himself. Akiba must have said this after his disillusionment by Bar Kokba.] Nevertheless, when R. Akiba [first] saw Bar Koziba [=liar, i.e. Bar Kokba], he said, 'This is King Messiah.' Johanan b. Torta said to him, 'Akiba, grass will sprout through your cheeks [i.e. you will be dead] ere the son of David comes.' R. Johanan said: Hark! the voice of Hadrian Caesar slaying eighty thousand myriads in Bethar! R. Johanan said: Eighty thousand pairs of trumpeters surrounded Bethar, each one of whom was set over countless hosts. And there was Bar Koziba, with two hundred thousand men who had cut off their fingers [i.e. who were exceptionally bold: Bar Kokba tested his warriors by bidding them cut off their fingers, and he accepted only those who obeyed without demur]. The Sages sent word to him: 'How long wilt thou continue to turn all Israel into maimed men!' He replied, 'How, then, can I test them?' They answered, 'Let no man be enrolled in thine army who is unable to uproot a cedar of Lebanon as he rides on his horse.' So Bar Kokba had two hundred thousand of each kind. When Bar Kokba set out to fight he said: 'Sovereign of the Universe! Neither aid us nor destroy us' [but leave things to take their natural course]. 'Who will lead me into Edom? Wilt not thou, O God, who hadst cast us off, and thou, O God, who didst not go out with our armies?' (Ps. LX, 9, 10).

[The translation of the last five lines is based on the commentary in the ed. Krotoschin and David Fränkel's *Ḳorban ha-'Edah*: it contains two difficulties.

(1) There is no proof that *tiksof*, rendered 'destroy', can bear this meaning. The root means 'to be pale as silver', and it usually means 'to grow pale with eagerness', 'to desire anxiously' (Gen. XXXI, 30), and, in Rabbinic Hebrew, 'to grow pale with shame'. Possibly it has this last meaning in Zeph. II, 1. Since both the Krot. and Petrikov editions spell the word with *waw*, it can be inferred that they intended the *ḳal* to be read, and not the *hif'il*, which, in Rabbinic Hebrew, can mean 'to frighten' or 'to cause to deteriorate'. Moses

Margalith, in his commentary *Pene Mosheh*, has 'Do not desire anxiously to help us, for thou wilt not go out....'

(2) The application of Ps. LX, 9, 10 is incongruent with 'destroy', for although verse 11 says 'God has cast us off', there is no hint of His neutrality: on the contrary, His help is implored in verse 13. And if, according to Margalith, the remark of Bar Kokba is defiant, he would hardly have cited verse 14. It is probable that the text is corrupt: several corrections suggest themselves. (H. L.)]

The extract continues:

> For three years and a half did Hadrian surround Bethar. R. Elazar of Modi'im sat in sackcloth and ashes, and prayed daily: 'Sovereign of the Universe! Take not this day thy judgment seat.' Hadrian desired to abandon the siege, but a Samaritan said to him, 'Do not depart. For as long as the hen [i.e. R. Elazar] sits on her brood in sackcloth and ashes, you will not be able to take the city. But I see what needs to be done, and I will deliver the city to you.' So he entered the city by means of a drain, and found R. Elazar standing in prayer. The Samaritan made as though he were whispering in Elazar's ear [but Elazar did not notice him]. The citizens saw the Samaritan, and brought him to Bar Koziba, and said to him, 'Your uncle wishes to betray the city; we have seen this old man conversing with your uncle.' Bar Koziba said to the Samaritan, 'What did you say to him, and what did he say to you?' The Samaritan replied, 'If I tell you, Hadrian will kill me: if I do not tell you, you will kill me. Better that Hadrian kill me than that you should.' So he said, 'Elazar told me that he wished to deliver the city to Hadrian.' Then Bar Koziba went to Elazar, and asked what the Samaritan had said to him. He answered 'Nothing.' 'What did you say to him?' 'Nothing': so Bar Koziba trampled him to death. Instantly a heavenly voice went forth, saying, 'Woe to the worthless shepherd that leaves the flock; the sword shall be upon his arm, and upon his right eye: his arm shall be clean dried up, and his right eye shall be utterly darkened (Zech. XI, 17). Thou hast slain R. Elazar, the arm of all Israel and their right eye, therefore shall thine arm be clean dried up, and thy right eye utterly darkened.' At once Bethar was captured and Bar Koziba slain. They brought his head to Hadrian who asked, 'Who slew this man?' A Samaritan said, 'It was I.' Hadrian said, 'Show me his body.' He showed it him, and there was a snake entwined round it. Hadrian said, 'Had God not slain him, no man could have done

so.' And he applied the verse of Deut. XXXII, 30, 'Except their Rock had sold them.'

The Romans continued the slaughter till horses were plunged in blood to their nostrils, and the blood-stream whirled weights of forty seahs, till it reached the sea, forty miles distant. They say that on one stone they found the brains of three hundred infants. They found also three piles of capsules of phylacteries, each pile weighing nine seahs....

Simeon b. Gamaliel said: 'There were in Bethar five hundred schools, the smallest of which had not less than five hundred infants, who said, "If the foe come, with these styluses[1] will we march against them and blind them." But sin brought it to pass that the Romans wrapped each child in its scroll, and burnt it, and of all the children, I alone survive,' and he applied to himself Lam. III, 51 [i.e. 'alone, out of all the daughters of the city']. (*T.J.Ta'an.* IV, § 8, f. 68*d*, line 43.)

[The style and contents of this passage suggest that it was not written down until some time after the fall of Bethar, so that it was possible for legends to grow up around the historical facts. (H. L.)]

[676] R. Ḥiyya b. Abba said: If a man said to me, 'Give your life for the sanctification of God's Name,' I would give it, but only on the condition that I should be killed at once. But the tortures of the "Time of the Persecution" I could not endure. What was then done? They brought iron balls and made them white hot upon the fire, and put them under the armpits, and so they took their lives, or they drove pieces of reed under their nails, and so they took their lives; as David said, 'To thee, O Lord, I lift up my soul' (Ps. XXV, 1). [For *Essa*, I lift up, the Midrash reads, *Assi*, I cause to take, I take away.] They let their souls [lives] be taken away for the sanctification of the Name of God.

(*Cant.R.* II, § 7, 1, on II, 7; f. 16*a*.)

[677] R. Ḥanina b. Papa, commenting on Ps. XVII, 14, 'From men which are thy hand' (A.V.), said: This must be translated differently, not 'from men', but [by a pun] 'from those who allow themselves to be slain' for the Torah. Because the Israelites surrender their lives for the Torah and the sanctification of the Name, God makes them a blessing in the world.

(*Tanḥ.B.*, Ki Tabo, 24*a*.)

[1] See **Note 62**.

There are also many stories connected with the capture of Jerusalem in A.D. 70 and with the horrors which followed it:

[678] Vespasian filled three ships with the great ones of Jerusalem to place them in a Roman house of prostitution. They said, 'Was it not enough that we provoked God in God's sanctuary; should we also do so outside Palestine?' They said to their wives, 'Would *you* consent to this?' They replied, 'No.' The men said, 'If our wives refuse, how much more should we. Do you think that if we throw ourselves into the sea, we shall come to the life of the world to come?' Then God enlightened straightway their eyes by the verse, 'I will bring them again from the depths of the sea' (Ps. LXVIII, 22). So, then, the first band arose, and said, 'Shall we forget the name of our God, and stretch out our hands to a strange god?' (Ps. XLIV, 20). And they hurled themselves into the sea. Then the second band arose, and said, 'Yea, for thy sake we are killed all the day long' (*ib.* 22). And they hurled themselves into the sea. Then the third band arose, and said, 'Will not God search this out? for He knows the secrets of the heart' (Ps. XLIV, 21). And they hurled themselves into the sea. And the Holy Spirit cried and said, 'For these things I weep' (Lam. I, 16). (*Lam.R.* I, 45 on I, 16 (cp. [662]).)

[679] It happened that two children of Zadok the priest, one a youth, and one a girl, came into the hands of two officers. The one officer went to a harlot and gave the youth to her. The other went to a shopkeeper and exchanged the girl for wine. So were the words of Joel fulfilled, 'They have given a boy for a harlot, and sold a girl for wine' (III, 3). After a time that harlot who had the youth went to the shopkeeper, and said to him, 'Since my youth is like your girl, I would desire that we unite them together, and what comes from them we will have between us.' He said, 'Yes.' So they were fetched and taken together into a house. Then the girl began to weep. The youth said to her, 'Why do you weep?' She replied, 'How should I not weep that I, the daughter of the High Priest, am to be united to a slave?' He said, 'Whose daughter are you?' She said, 'Of Zadok, the priest.' He said, 'And where, if so, did you live?' She said, 'In the upper market place.' He said, 'And what was the sign of your courtyard?' She told it to him. He said, 'Had you a brother or a sister?' She said, 'I had one brother, who had a mole on his

shoulder, and whenever he came back from school, I used to uncover it and kiss it.' He said, 'If you saw it, would you recognise it?' She said, 'Yes.' He uncovered himself, and they recognised one another, and they embraced and kissed each other till their souls departed from them. And the Holy Spirit cried and said, 'For these things I weep' (Lam. I, 16).

(*Lam.R.* I, 46 on I, 16.)

Perhaps the story about R. Johanan b. Zakkai is almost *too* familiar to be omitted here, even though it has no special religious or ethical content:

[680] When Vespasian came to destroy Jerusalem, he said to them, 'Fools, why do you seek to destroy this city, and to burn the Temple? All I want is that you deliver up to me one single bow and arrow, and then I will raise the siege.' They said, 'As we repelled the first and second attacks, and slew your men, so we will repel the next attack, and slay them.' When R. Johanan heard this, he sent for the men of Jerusalem and said to them, 'Why would you lay waste this city and burn the Temple? All he seeks from you is one bow and arrow, and then he will retire.' They replied, 'As we repelled the first two attacks and killed his soldiers, so we will now go out against him and kill him.' Vespasian had men who watched beside the walls, and whatever they heard, they wrote upon arrows and threw them over the wall. So they told Vespasian that R. Johanan was a friend of the Emperor. When R. Johanan urged them for three days, and they refused, he called his disciples, R. Eliezer and R. Joshua, and said, 'Up and carry me out of the city. Make a coffin and I will sleep in it.' They did so, and R. Eliezer took up one side and R. Joshua the other, and at the setting of the sun they brought it to the gates of Jerusalem. The gate-keeper said, 'What is this?' They said, 'A corpse is in it, and, as you know, a corpse must not be left in the city overnight,' so they said, 'If it be a corpse, carry it forth.' So they carried him forth, and brought him to Vespasian. Then they opened the coffin, and he stood before Vespasian. He said, 'Are you R. Johanan b. Zakkai? What shall I give you?' He replied, 'All I ask of you is that I may go to Jabneh, and teach my disciples there, and fix a place of prayer there, and carry out all the commandments.' He answered, 'Go, and all that it pleases you to do there, do.' (*Ab.R.N.* (vers. I), IV, 11*b*–12*a*.)

There are many stories about individual martyrs.

[681] In the hour when the enemy had captured Jerusalem, and sought to enter the Temple, they said, 'Let an Israelite enter first.' So they said to R. Jose, 'Go in, and what you bring out shall be yours.' He went in, and brought out the golden candlestick. They said to him, 'This is no object which a private person can use; go in a second time, and what you bring out shall be yours.' But this second time he refused to go in. R. Phinehas said that they offered him [a remission of] tax for three years, but he still refused. He said, 'Is it not enough that I have provoked my God once that I should provoke Him a second time?' What did they do? They put him on a carpenter's sawing jack, and sawed his body. He kept crying out, 'Woe, woe, that I have provoked my Maker.' And Jakim of Ẓerorot, who was the nephew of R. Jose b. Joezer, rode on a horse, and came past the beam on which R. Jose was to be hung. And it was the Sabbath Day. Then Jakim said to Jose, 'Behold the horse on which my master lets me ride, and behold the horse on which your Master makes you ride.' Jose said, 'If such things happen to those who provoke Him, how much better things shall happen to those who do His will?' Then Jakim said, 'Did any man ever do His will more than you?' Then Jose said, 'If such things [as what is happening to me] happen to those who do His will, how much worse things will happen to those who provoke Him.' The word entered into Jakim's soul like the poison of a snake. He went and executed upon himself all the four kinds of death which the court can inflict, stoning, burning, decapitation and strangling. For he brought a beam, and fastened it in the ground, and tied a cord to it, and placed wood on the ground, and made a fence of stones around the wood, put brushwood under the stones, and stuck a sword in the middle of the circle, and kindled a fire under the wood which was under the stones, and hanged himself on the beam, and strangled himself. The fire broke the beam, he fell into the fire, and then upon the sword, and the wall collapsed, and he was burnt. Then, as he died, R. Jose b. Joezer saw the bed of Jakim flying aloft into the air and he said, 'By a little space of time Jakim has entered even before me into Paradise.'

(*Gen.R.* LXV, 22 (Th. pp. 741–4).)

[This passage must refer to Maccabean times, for Jose b. Joezer of Ẓeredah, Jakim's uncle, lived *circa* 200–162 B.C. See *Aboth* I, 4.

Jakim is said to have been Alcimus, the Hellenizer (I Macc. VII, 6 f.), whom Josephus (*Ant.* XII, ch. IX, § 7 (385)) calls Iakeimos (for Eliakim, II Kings XVIII, 18; equivalent to Jehoiakim). Travers Herford (comm. on *Aboth*, *in loc.*) raises the question whether Jose perished in 162 B.C. in the massacre perpetrated by Alcimus (I Macc. VII, 16). (H.L.)]

[682] When they seized R. Simeon b. Gamaliel and R. Ishmael and took them to be executed, Simeon was dazed, and said to Ishmael, 'Woe to us, we are to be killed like profaners of the Sabbath, or idolaters, or incestuous persons, or murderers.' Then Ishmael said, 'May I say something?' He said, 'Speak.' Ishmael said, 'Perhaps when you sat in your house, poor people came, and they stood outside, and you did not let them in, and give them food.' Then Simeon said, 'I swear to heaven, I never did so. For I kept watchers before my house that they should at once bring in any poor who came to my door, and the poor ate and drank and blessed the name of God.' Then Ishmael said, 'Perhaps, when you sat upon the Temple Hill, and taught, and all the bands of the Israelites were before you, your mind was puffed up.' Then Simeon said, 'My brother, a man must be prepared to receive his fate.' Each besought the executioner to let him die first. One said, 'I am a priest, son of a high priest; let me die first, that I shall not see the death of my friend.' The other said, 'I am a prince, the son of a prince, let me die first.' The executioner said, 'Draw lots.' The lot fell on Simeon, and the executioner cut off his head. Ishmael took it up, put it on his bosom, and wept and cried, 'Holy mouth, faithful mouth, mouth that brought forth precious stones, who has rolled you in the dust, and filled your tongue with ashes? For you was it said, "Awake, O sword, against my friend"' (Zech. XIII, 7). He had not finished the words when his head fell. (*Ab.R.N.* (vers. I), XXXVIII, 57*b*.)

[683] When R. Ḥanina[1] b. Teradion was arrested, they asked him, 'Why did you occupy yourself with the study of the Law?' He answered, 'Because God commanded me to do so.' Then they sentenced him to be burnt alive. He carried a scroll of the Law in his bosom. Then they took him, and wrapped the scroll round him, heaped bundles of willow wood about him, and set fire to them. Then they took tufts of wool, soaked them in water, and laid them on his heart that he might not die quickly. Then

[1] Usually called Hananiah. See note to [460].

his daughter said, 'Father, that I should have to see you thus!' He replied, 'If I were to be burnt alone, it would have been hard for me, but now that the scroll of the Law is being burnt with me, He who will avenge His own humiliation in the burning of the scroll, will also avenge my humiliation.' His disciples said to him, 'What do you see?' He replied, 'The sheets of the scroll are being burnt, and the letters are flying' [up to heaven. The idea is that the divine word has an indestructible existence of its own, independent of the material to which it is temporarily attached]. Then they said to him, 'Open your mouth that the fire may enter into it.' [The object was that his tortures should be shortened.] He replied, 'It is better that He who gave me my soul should take it rather than that [I should break the rule] "Let no man do himself an injury [or let no man do violence to himself]."' Then the executioner said to him, 'Master, if I increase the flame, and remove the tufts of wool from your heart, will you bring me into the life of the world to come?' Ḥanina replied, 'Yes, I will.' He said, 'Swear it to me.' Then Ḥanina swore it. At once the executioner increased the flame, and removed the tufts of wool from his heart, and his soul departed quickly. Then the executioner himself leaped into the fire. Then a heavenly voice was heard to say, 'R. Ḥanina b. Teradion and the executioner are appointed for the life of the world to come.' And Rabbi wept and said, 'Some attain their world [to come] in an hour, and some win it [only] after many years.'

(*Ab.Zar.* 17*b*–18*a* (cp. *R.T.* pp. 374–5).)

The shortest, and perhaps oldest, version of R. Akiba's martyrdom runs thus:

[684] When Akiba was being tortured, the hour for saying the *Shema* arrived. He said it and smiled. The Roman officer called out, 'Old man, art thou a sorcerer, or dost thou mock at thy sufferings, that thou smilest in the midst of thy pains?' 'Neither,' replied Akiba, 'but all my life, when I said the words, "Thou shalt love the Lord thy God with all thy heart and soul and might," I was saddened, for I thought, when shall I be able to fulfil the command? I have loved God with all my heart and with all my possessions [might], but how to love Him with all my soul [i.e. life] was not assured to me. Now that I am giving my life, and that the hour for saying the *Shema* has come, and my resolution

remains firm, should I not laugh?' And as he spoke, his soul departed.

(*T.J.Ber.* IX, § 7, f. 14*b*, line 59 (cp. *T.J.Soṭ.* V, § 7, f. 20*c*, line 53).)

It must not, however, be supposed that the Rabbis sought to make ordinary life too hard, or that they taught that, in order to obtain entrance into the life to come, God demanded more of man than the ordinary man could render. God gives in no proportion to what He demands. The last of the next three passages is often repeated.

[685] When God gives, He gives according to *His* power; when He demands, He demands according to *our* power.

(*Num.R.*, Pineḥas, XXI, 22 (cp. [10] and [689]).)

[686] God says to Israel, 'For all the wonders and mighty deeds which I have wrought for you, the only reward I ask is that you should honour me as my children, and call me your Father.'

(*Exod.R.*, Mishpaṭim, XXXII, 5.)

[687] When R. Gamaliel read the verse in Ezek. XVIII, 19 ('When the son has done that which is lawful and right, and has kept all my statutes, and has done them, he shall surely live'), he was wont to weep, for he said, 'Shall only he who ḥas kept *all* God's statutes live, not he who does any one of them?' But Akiba said to him, 'It says, "Defile not yourselves in all these things" (Lev. XVIII, 24); here "all" means "in any one of these things", and so in Ezekiel.' (*San.* 81*a*.)

Interesting are the following:

[688] After the Temple was destroyed, the Separated Ones [*Perushim*] increased in Israel; they ate no meat, and drank no wine.[1] Then R. Joshua went to them and said, 'Why do you eat no meat and drink no wine?' They said, 'How can we eat meat, when it was offered daily on the altar, or drink wine which was poured out on it? And now all this has ceased.' He said to them, 'In that case we ought to eat no figs and grapes, for they were offered as firstlings, and we ought to eat no bread, because they used to bring two loaves on Pentecost, and the shewbread on every Sabbath, and we ought to drink no water, for there was a libation of water at the feast of Tabernacles.' They were silent. He said,

[1] *Perushim* would not necessarily mean *Pharisees* (cp. [719]). One authority renders, 'they who practised self-restraint'; another, 'the abstemious'; or one might say, 'the ascetics' (cp. [1359]).

'Not to mourn at all is impossible; to mourn more than is adequate is also not possible.' For R. Joshua had said before, 'Only such decrees must be issued which the majority of the community can endure.' (**Note 20 *b*.**)

(*Midr.Ps.* on CXXXVII, 5 (262*b fin.*, § 6) (cp. [1477]).)

[689] God's voice went forth to each one in Israel according to his powers of obedience. The elders heard the voice according to their capacity, the adolescents, the youths, the boys, the sucklings, each according to his capacity, the women, too, according to their capacity, and also Moses according to his capacity, for it says, 'Moses kept speaking, and God would answer him with *the* voice' (Exod. XIX, 19), i.e. with that voice which Moses was able to hear.

(*Tanḥ.*, Shemot, § 25, f. 90*b* (cp. [10] and [685]).)

Chapter X

THE IMPORTANCE OF MOTIVE OR INTENTION. *KAWWANAH*, AND *LISHMAH*. THE LOVE, THE FEAR, AND THE PRAISE OF GOD

Rabbinic Judaism is a 'legal' religion, but though the Rabbis laid enormous stress upon the fulfilment of the commandments, whether of the Written or of the Oral Law, yet they realised that the motive was often more important than the deed—even though the doing of a commandment as a mere duty might lead to its fulfilment in joy and in love. God looks to the intention and the purity of the deed rather than to its amount: to quality rather than to quantity.

The following brief sentence occurs again and again:

[690] It matters not whether you do much or little, so long as your heart is directed to heaven. (*Ber.* 17*a et saepe.*)

Famous is the following story:

[691] A woman once brought a handful of meal as an offering. The priest despised it. He said, 'What sort of offering is that? What is there in it for eating or for a sacrifice?' But in a dream it was said to the priest, 'Despise her not; but reckon it as if she had offered *herself* as a sacrifice.' [Playing upon the verbal fact that in Lev. II, 1, the Hebrew word for 'anyone' is *nefesh* (lit. 'soul', 'life', 'person'), the Midrash goes on to say], If in regard to anyone who does *not* sacrifice himself, the word *nefesh* is used, how much more fitly of one who does!

(*Lev.R.*, Wayiḳra, III, 5.)

The word 'directed' is of much importance. The verb suggested a noun, *kawwanah*, which is one of the fine religious creations of the Rabbis. It depends upon Biblical verses such as I Chron. XXIX, 18, but is a new conception all the same. *Kawwanah* (intention, concentration, collectedness) is especially required in prayer, though the legalism of the Rabbis could not prevent them from delightedly discussing when it was necessary, and when it was not necessary, in the recitation of the statutory daily prayers, whether in the synagogue, or at home, or elsewhere:

[692] R. Me'ir said: All depends upon the *kawwanah* of the heart (cf. *R.T.* p. 187). (*Meg.* 20*a.*)

['Delightedly discussing' needs some qualification. The predominant view of the Rabbis, as opposed to Raba's remark in [697] (see also *Ber.* 13*a*; *Meg.* 20*a*, etc.) is that intention is certainly necessary. The question is not altogether like that of *ex opere operato* or *operantis*. For example, in the case of the *Shema*, the existence of devotion on the part of the individual is not challenged; it is assumed. The man under consideration chances to be studying the Bible, and happens actually to be at Deut. IV, when the time for the *Shema* has arrived. He reads the passage with devotion, but the problem arises: has he read the passage for edification, as a pious act, or has he thereby fulfilled his legal obligation to recite the *Shema*? Is his devotion tantamount to intention? Or is the technical difference between intention and edification negligible? A somewhat similar instance, in connection with the blowing of the *Shofar*, is discussed in *R.H.* 28*b* (cp. [694]). But so far as attuning the mind is concerned, the Rabbis were emphatic in regarding this as essential. Hence the institution of *kawwanot*, or meditations introduced before the performance of a sacred duty or the recitation of a prayer, so as to attune the mind of the agent or worshipper. These *kawwanot* sometimes precede the prayer or act, and begin, 'Behold, I am intent on...' (see *P.B.* pp. 14, 15, 218), and sometimes are interwoven in the body of the prayers or in the margins, in small type. Most are late in origin (Abrahams, p. LXXXIV), but for an earlier statement on *kawwanah* see Maimonides, *Yad*, *Hilk. Tefil.* X, 1; IV, 15 ff.: 'No prayer without *kawwanah* is a prayer...if a man's mind is disturbed he should first compose himself, and then pray: one who is back from a journey and tired should not pray....' Finally it should be remarked that some seemingly irrelevant and interminable discussions were nothing but exercises in dialectic. Without these, the lack of Greek philosophical training would have left Rabbinic thought jejune. These arguments were often divorced from reality. Nevertheless, like Euclid, they sharpened the wits, and inculcated logic almost as well as an Attic rhetorician could have done. Yet logic is only the preliminary instrument of higher philosophical thought, the absence of which is so marked, e.g. [737], and this absence is reflected by the limitations of Rabbinic terminology. (H. L.)]

[693] How is a wayfarer to pray? He must not take the Kingdom of heaven upon himself while he is walking, but he must pause, direct his heart to God with awe and fear, trembling and quaking, at the proclamation of the divine Unity, as he utters the *Shema*, every single word with heartfelt sincerity (*kawwanah*), and then he should recite the doxology [i.e. 'Blessed be the name of His glorious kingdom for ever and ever']. But when he begins the following paragraph, he may, if he so desire, resume his journey

and pray as he walks (for it says, 'when thou walkest by the way', Deut. VI, 7). (*Tanḥ.*, Lek leka, § 1, f. 24*a*.)

[To take upon oneself the Kingdom of heaven means here, as frequently (see [1–4]), to recite the first sentence of the *Shema*, i.e. Deut. VI, 4. (H. L.)]

[The date of this passage is doubtful, since it is somewhat strange for R. Huna to cite the *Tanna* R. Judah b. Ilai. Further, R. Samuel is either the Palestinian *Amora* Samuel b. Nahmani or else the Babylonian *Amora* Samuel b. Abba, in which case the designation is incorrect. Some texts have *Rav* not *Rabbi* Judah. (H. L.)]

[694] If a shepherd pastures his flock behind a synagogue, and hears the *Shofar* [on New Year], then, if he has directed his heart, he has fulfilled his religious duty, but if he has not directed his heart, then he has not fulfilled his duty. The same applies to a sick man whose bed is placed behind the synagogue, or again to one who hears the *Megillah* [Book of Esther] [on the feast of Purim]. All depends upon whether the man has directed his heart or not. (*T.R.H.* III, 6 (Z. p. 212, line 1).)

[695] 'And it came to pass when Moses held up his hand that Israel prevailed, and when he let down his hand, Amalek prevailed' (Exod. XVII, 11). But could the hands of Moses promote the battle or hinder the battle?—it is, rather, to teach you that such time as the Israelites directed their thoughts on high, and kept their hearts in subjection to their Father in heaven, they prevailed; otherwise they suffered defeat. After the like manner it says, 'Make thee a fiery serpent, and set it upon a standard, and it shall come to pass that if a man is bitten, when he sees it, he shall live' (Num. XXI, 8). But could the serpent slay, or the serpent keep alive?—it is, rather, to teach you that such time as the Israelites directed their thoughts on high, and kept their hearts in subjection to their Father in heaven, they were healed; otherwise they pined away. (*R.H.* III, 8.)

[696] He who prays must direct his heart.

(*T.Ber.* III, 6 (Z. p. 6 (**Note 65**), line 11).)

The best thing is to fulfil a command with joy and love, with full intention, and with heart directed to God; yet better than total omission or violation is its fulfilment without these. On the other hand, a sinful deed is regarded as no sin, if it be done accidentally. Thus:

[697] Raba said: For *doing* a commandment, *kawwanah* is *not* required; for committing a sin, *kawwanah is* required (cf. *R.T.* p. 184). (*R.H.* 28*b fin.*)

So, once again, the intention is all important.

[698] R. Johanan quoted Hos. XIV, 10, 'The ways of the Lord are right, and the righteous shall walk in them, but transgressors shall fall therein,' and he said: So of two people who cook their paschal lamb, one eats it to fulfil the commandment, and one eats it out of gluttony. (*Hor.* 10*b.*)

The next quotation is characteristically Rabbinic:

[699] 'For the sake of this word [A.V. 'thing'] the Lord thy God shall bless thee' (Deut. XV, 10). If a man decides to give [alms] and gives them, God gives him the reward for deciding and for doing: if a man decides to give, and then finds he has not the means, God gives him such a reward for deciding as is equivalent to the reward of doing. If he has decided not to give, but has asked others to give, or if he has neither given nor asked others to give, but has been kindly to the poor man in words, God still gives him a reward, for it says, 'For the sake of this *word* God will bless thee.' (*Sifre Deut.*, Re'eh, § 117, f. 98*b* (H. p. 176).)

The Rabbis could see that a man who, as it were, fulfilled the commandments in sin, was doubly reprehensible. A difficult half-verse in the Psalms says (probably), 'The covetous renounces, yea, despises the Lord' (R.V.). But it can also playfully be rendered, 'The robber, in blessing, blasphemes the Lord' (Ps. X, 3). So we find:

[700] They told a parable: To what can this be compared? It is like to a man who had stolen a *se'ah* of wheat; he ground it, and baked it, and set apart the *ḥallah*, and fed his children. When such a one recites the blessing, he does not bless, but he blasphemes. (*T.San.* I, 2 (Professor Danby's trans. p. 27; Z. p. 415, line 11).)

[*Se'ah* is a measure; about one and a half pecks. For the *ḥallah*, see the law in Num. XV, 20, 21 and Gaster's *P.B.* p. 79. (H. L.)]

[701] R. Nehemiah said: If a man purpose to commit a sin, God does not reckon it to him till he has done it, but if he purpose to fulfil a command, then, although he has had no opportunity to do it, God writes it down to him at once as if he had done it. (*Midr.Ps.* on XXX, heading (118*a*, § 4).)

To the Rabbis, the love of God is both the supreme command of the Torah and the supreme motive:

[702] 'And thou shalt love the Lord thy God' (Deut. VI, 5). Act from love. The verse makes a distinction between him who acts from love and him who acts from fear. If a man fears his fellow, then, if that other troubles [*v.l.* acts subtly towards] him, he leaves him and goes his way. But do you act from love, for there is no love where there is fear, or fear where there is love, except in relation to God. 'Love the Lord thy God': that is make Him beloved among all creatures as did Abraham [i.e. seek to gain proselytes]. 'With all thy heart': that is with both the good and the evil inclination. 'With all thy heart': let not your heart be divided—i.e. not wholly one—as regards your love for God. 'And with all thy soul': even if He takes your soul [i.e. your life]. So it says, 'For thy sake we are slain every day' (Ps. XLIV, 22). R. Simeon b. Menasya said: Can a man be killed every day? But God accounts it to the righteous as if they were killed every day. R. Simeon b. Azzai said: 'With all thy soul': that is, love Him to the pressing out of the last drop of your life. 'With all thy might.' [The Midrash takes this to mean with all thy substance.] If with all thy substance, why with all thy life, and if with all thy life, why with all thy substance? To some men their bodies [life] are more precious than their money: to some, their money is more precious than their life (cp. [1246]). So it says, 'With all thy life and with all thy substance.' R. Jacob—by similarity of sound of *me'ōd* and *middah*—said: 'With all thy might' means: with whatever measure God metes out to you, be it the measure of good or of chastisement, love Him. Love Him with all your heart, like Isaac, who himself bound himself upon the altar (cp. *R.T.* pp. 190, 191, 228, 31). 'To love the Lord thy God' (Deut. XI, 13). So that you shall not say [i.e. think to yourself], "I will learn Torah to become rich, or to be called Rabbi, or to receive reward." No. All that you do, do only from love. 'With all thy heart and with all thy soul.' The words occur twice (Deut. VI, 5 and XI, 13). Why? The first passage has reference to the congregation; the second to the individual; the first to study, the second to doing.

(*Sifre Deut.*, Wa'ethạnan, § 32, f. 73*a–b*, 79*b fin.*–80*a*
(H. pp. 54, 55, 58, 87, 88; cp. [1000]).)

[703] Of them who are oppressed and do not oppress, who are reviled and do not [in reply] revile, who act only from love [to God], and rejoice in their sufferings, the Scripture says: 'They who love him are like the sun when it rises in its might.' R. Joshua b. Levi said: What means the verse, 'My beloved is unto me as a bundle of myrrh that lies between my breasts.' The congregation of Israel speaks before God and says, 'Lord of the world, though my Beloved oppresses me, and makes my life bitter, yet shall He dwell between my breasts' (cp. *R.T.* p. 32). (*Sab.* 88*b*.)

Another great Rabbinical conception is that of *lishmah*, 'for its own sake'. The right fulfilment of the Law must be *lishmah*.

[704] The Torah [that is practised and studied] for its own sake is a law of love; the law [that is practised and studied] not for its own sake is a law without love. The Torah which is studied in order to teach, is a law of love; the Torah which is not studied in order to teach, is a law without love. (*Suk.* 49*b fin.*)

[705] R. Banna'ah used to say: If one studies the Torah for its own sake, it becomes to him an elixir of life; but if one studies the Torah not for its own sake, it becomes to him a deadly poison. (*Ta'an.* 7*a* (Malter, p. 40; cp. *Yalkuṭ*, § 934, on Prov. III, 18) (cp. [332]).)

There are two etymologically different Hebrew verbs in the Bible spelt and pronounced in the same way. One means to drop down; the other, to break the neck; so, in their punning way, the Rabbis say:

[706] R. Banna'ah said: The Scripture says, 'Let my doctrine drop down as rain' (Deut. XXXII, 2). If you fulfil the words of the Law for their own sake, they are life for you, as it says, 'They are life unto those that find them' (Prov. IV, 22), but if you fulfil them *not* for their own sake, they are death to you, for it says, 'Let my doctrine *kill* like rain,' for breaking the neck is killing, as it says, 'They shall break the heifer's neck in the valley' (Deut. XXI, 4). (*Sifre Deut.*, Ha'azinu, § 306, f. 131*b fin.*)

[707] He who busies himself with the Law for its own sake causes peace in the upper and the lower family [965]; he is as if he had built the upper and the lower palace; he protects the whole world; he brings near the redemption. (*San.* 99*b*.)

[708] R. Dosetai b. R. Yannai[1] said: Why did God not create warm springs in Jerusalem as He has done in Tiberias? So that one Israelite should not say to another, 'Let us go up to Jerusalem. If we go up just for one warm bath only, it will be enough.' Then there would be a going up[2] which would not be 'for its own sake'.[3] (*Sifre Num.*, Beha'aloteka, § 89, f. 25*a* (H. p. 90).)

[709] One day, at the close of the fig harvest, R. Ṭarfon was walking in a garden, and he ate some figs which had been left behind. The custodians of the garden came up, caught him, and began to beat him unmercifully. Then Ṭarfon called out, and said who he was, whereupon they stopped, and let him go. Yet all his days did he grieve, for he said, 'Woe is me, for I have used the crown of the Law for my own profit.' For the teaching ran: 'A man must not say, I will study, so as to be called a wise man, or Rabbi, or an elder, or to have a seat in the College, but he must study from love; the honour will come of itself.'

(*Ned.* 62*a* (cp. [341]).)

For God's sake, out of love, and *lishmah*, are really all equal to one another.

[710] He who makes use of the crown of the Law is rooted out of the world. Do the words of the Law for the doing's sake, and speak of them for their own sake. Make them not a crown with which to exalt thyself, or a spud with which to weed.

(*Ned.* 62*a* (cp. [337]).)

[711] It is written, 'Ye shall see the difference between him that serves God and him who serves him not' (Mal. III, 18), that is, between him who has faith and him who has not; between him who serves God for God's sake, and him who does not. For a man must not make the words of the Torah an axe to cut with, or a garland to crown himself with them. 'The Lord plentifully requites the proud doer' (Ps. XXXI, 23). These are the students who learn Torah to make a proud boast of their learning in this world, and not for the sake of God; they hope for their reward in this world; but of them who study the Torah and hope for their reward in the world to come, it says, 'Be of good courage, and let your heart gather strength, all ye who hope in the Lord.' For they who hope in the Lord are they who store up their reward for the world to come. (*Midr. Ps.* on XXXI, 23 (120*b*, § 9).)

[1] Or Jose. [2] To Jerusalem for the festivals. [3] **Note 20 *c*.**

[712] Happy is the man whose every action is in the name of Heaven [i.e. pure and selfless]. But the heart of the man alone knows whether his action is straight or crooked. (*Tan.d.b.El.* p. 121 *fin.*)

Curious is the paradox:

[713] R. Naḥman b. Isaac said: Better is a sin which is done *lishmah* than a commandment which is not done *lishmah*. [A sin with a good intent is better than a commandment not done in purity and for its own sake (cf. *Nazir* 23*b* and *R.T.* p. 188). But the criticism is added:] Say that they are equal, but not that the sin is superior. (*Hor.* 10*b*.)

The fulfilment of the Law was to be the Israelite's joy, and this very fulfilment was a joy to God. God studies the Law, and in many ways fulfils it. For *His* beneficence is also the very beneficence which is enjoined in the Law. The loving deeds on which the Rabbis lay most stress—comforting the mourners, visiting the sick, clothing the naked, burying the dead, joining in the rejoicing of the bride and bridegroom—were all said to be deeds which, in the Biblical story, had been done by God Himself. The truest rule or principle for human goodness was the Imitation of God.

[714] 'This is my God, and I will praise Him' (Exod. xv, 2) [lit. and I will beautify, or adorn Him, i.e. with praises]. R. Ishmael said: Can a man beautify the Creator? But I will make myself beautiful to Him through the commandments. I will make a beautiful *lulab*, a beautiful *succah*, beautiful fringes, beautiful *tefillin*...or scrolls of the Law, and write the scrolls for His sake with beautiful ink and a beautiful pen by the hand of practised scribes, and wrap them in beautiful silk. (*Mek.*[2], *Shirata*, Beshallaḥ, § 3, p. 127; *Mek.*[3], vol. II, p. 25; *Sab.* 133*b* (cp. [311]).)

[715] 'Ye shall walk after the Lord your God' (Deut. XIII, 4). But how can a man walk after God who is a devouring fire? (Deut. IV, 24). It means, walk after His attributes [*middot*], clothe the naked, visit the sick, comfort the mourner, bury the dead. [Each with its verse-proof to show that God did all these things.] (*Soṭ.* 14*a*.)

By a pun or paronomasia upon the word for 'and I will praise him'—Exod. xv, 2—*Weanwehu*, Abba Saul makes it read *Ani wa-Hu*, 'I and He' (cp. [25]), and these words, again, he interprets as 'I as He'. So:

[716] Abba Saul said: Let us become like Him; as He is merciful and gracious, so be you merciful and gracious. (*Mek.*[2], *Shirata*, Beshallaḥ, § 3, p. 127; *Mek.*[3], vol. II, p. 25.)

[717] R. Simeon b. Yoḥai said: What means the verse, 'I the Lord love justice; I hate robbery with a burnt offering' [really 'robbery with violence', or 'with iniquity'] (Isa. LXI, 8). It is like a king who passed by the toll house, and said to his servants, 'Pay the toll to the toll-keepers.' Then they said to him, 'But all the toll is thine!' He said, 'From me shall wayfarers learn not to evade the toll.' So God says, 'From me let my children learn to keep far from robbery [or, not to have anything to do with what has been stolen].' (*Suk.* 30*a*.)

[718] 'The Lord is good to all, and His mercies are over all His works.' R. Levi said: The Lord is good to all, because all are His works. R. Samuel said: The Lord is good to all, and His mercies are over all His works. His nature is to be merciful. R. Joshua of Sikhnin, in the name of R. Levi, said: The Lord is good to all, and He gives of His mercy to His creatures. R. Tanḥuma and R. Abba b. Abbin said in the name of R. Aḥa: When, in a year of drought, human beings show mercy towards one another, God will be filled with mercy towards them. In the days of R. Tanḥuma, the Israelites wanted to have a fast [for rain]. They came to R. Tanḥuma and said, 'Rabbi, appoint a public fast to-day.' He did so. But after three days no rain fell. He preached to them, and said, 'Do you show abundant mercy to one another, and God will have abundant mercy upon you.' (Ps. CXLV, 9; *Gen.R.*, Noaḥ, XXXIII, 3 (Th. p. 304).)

[719] God said to Moses, 'Go and tell the Israelites, My children, as I am pure, so be you pure; as I am holy, so be you holy, as it is said, "Holy shall ye be, for I, the Lord your God, am Holy"' (Lev. XIX, 2). (*Lev.R.*, Ḳedoshim, XXIV, 4 (cp. [308]).)

The passage is interesting, because the word translated by 'pure' is *parush*, separated, and is the same word as in Pharisee. Clearly the writer regarded *parush* as parallel to, or as a synonym for, holy (cp. [688] and p. 104).

[720] It is written in Exod. XVII, 2 that the people murmured against Moses, and Moses cried unto God, 'They are almost ready to stone me.' Moses said to God, 'Make known to me if they are going to kill me.' God said to him, 'What is that to thee? Pass over [A.V. 'go on'] before the people' (Exod. XVII, 5). R. Me'ir said: These words mean, 'Be like unto me. As I return

good for evil, so do thou return good for evil,' as it is said, 'Who is a God like thee, forgiving sin, and *passing over* transgression' (Mic. VII, 18). (*Exod.R.*, Beshallaḥ, XXVI, 2.)

[721] R. Simlai said: Thou canst learn that the verse, 'All the paths of the Lord are loving-kindness' (Ps. XXV, 10) is indeed true. For, at the very beginning of the Law, we read that He decked the bride. It says (Gen. II, 22; see R.V.M.) that God 'built up' the rib to become Eve, and He brought her to Adam, for in the seaside towns this word 'build up' means 'to braid the hair', and they use the word 'built up' for the bride in her wedding garb. Again, at the very end of the Law, we read that He, God Himself, brought Moses to burial (Deut. XXXIV, 6). And in the middle of the Law, we read how He and His angels visited the sick, when they appeared to Abraham after his circumcision (Gen. XVIII, 1; cp. [52]). (*Tanḥ.*, Wayera, 1, p. 62.)

For the metaphor of 'building up the bride' see [1214].

[722] God decked Eve, and brought her to Adam. How did He bring her? Do you imagine that He brought her under a sprig of olive or a fig leaf? No, thirteen bowers did God construct for Adam and Eve. [The ingenious proof, given in Buber's note, is too difficult to be reproduced here (H. L.).] R. Ḥama b. Ḥanina said: God crowned Eve with four and twenty ornaments, nay more, He took her by the hand, and brought her to Adam (Gen. II, 22). (*Tanḥ.B.*, Ḥay. Sar., f. 58*b*.)

[723] By a change of vowel points the Rabbis take Joel II, 32 (M.T. III, 5) to mean, 'Whoever shall be called by the name of the Lord,' and so they say: How is it possible for a man to be called by the name of God? But the words mean: As God is called merciful and gracious, so do thou be merciful and gracious, offering gifts gratis to all; as the Lord is called righteous and loving, so be thou righteous and loving.

(*Sifre Deut.*, 'Eḳeb, § 49, f. 85*a* (H. p. 114; *R.T.* p. 105).)

Thus all man's good deeds must be done in conscious relation to God, and with the thought and love of Him continually in his mind. To Him alone is the glory, and He must ever be praised.

[724] Abraham caused God's name to be mentioned by all the travellers whom he entertained. For after they had eaten and drunk, and when they arose to bless Abraham, he said to them, 'Is it of mine

that you have eaten? Surely it is of what belongs to God that you have eaten. So praise and bless Him by whose word the world was created.' (*Soṭ.* 10*b*.)

The Hebrew word for 'bless' is almost equivalent to our 'thank'. A somewhat similar example of its use may be seen in *Ber.* 54 *a*. The word rendered 'thank' in A.V. and R.V. (e.g. in Ps. CXVIII, 1) means rather 'to give thanks in worship', 'to confess', than to render gratitude to a human benefactor. In *Ber.* IX, 1–3 Danby has 'bless'.

[725] 'To do justice (=charity) and judgment (=justice)' (Gen. XVIII, 19). R. Azariah said: The first word is charity, the second word is justice. What is meant? Abraham used to entertain the passers-by. When they had eaten and drunk he said to them, 'Speak the blessing.' They said, 'What are we to say?' He replied, 'Say, Blessed be the Lord of the world, of whose gifts we have eaten.' If they did so, he suffered them to go their way. But if any one refused, he would say to him, 'Pay what you owe.' The man would say, 'What do you ask of me?' He replied, 'One quart of wine for ten pennies (*phollarion, follis*), one pound of meat for ten pennies, one loaf of bread for ten pennies. Who gave you wine, meat or bread in the desert?' When the man saw the dilemma in which Abraham had placed him, he said, 'Blessed be the Lord of the world, of whose gifts I have eaten.' (*Gen.R.*, Wayera, XLIX, 4 (Th. pp. 502, 503).)

The dilemma was, 'Pray or Pay': 'Pray' = charity, 'Pay' (*sc.* what you owe) = justice.

The words which Abraham made the passers-by speak are still the basis of the introductory formula of the grace (*P.B.* p. 279, cp. [303]).

There are many interesting passages about the praise of God, some of which may find a place here:

[726] 'To thee, O Lord, will I sing' (Ps. CI, 1). R. Huna in the name of R. Aḥa said: David said to God, 'If thou showest me grace, I will sing to thee; and if thou dealest me out judgment, I will sing to thee; whether this way or that, to thee, O Lord, will I sing.' R. Judah b. Palia said: So too said Job, 'The Lord gave and the Lord took; may the Lord's name be blessed; if He gave, it was He alone; if He took, it was He and His tribunal; blessed be He when He gave, and blessed be He when He took; whether this way or that, the Lord's name be blessed' (cp. [1001]).
(*Midr.Ps.* on CI, 1 (213*b*, § 1) [for the doubtful name Palia, see Buber's note *in loc.* (H. L.)].)

Yet even of praise there may be excess.

[727] R. Abbahu said in the name of R. Johanan: If a man seeks to praise God excessively, he is banished from the world, as it is said, 'Who can utter the mighty acts of the Lord, and show forth all His praise?' (Ps. CVI, 2). R. Ḥanina and R. Jonathan went on business to a city of the south; they went into a Synagogue, and they saw the reader get up and say, 'The great, mighty and awful God, the glorious, the powerful, the majestic.' They bade him be silent, and said to him, 'You must not add to the formula of the blessings which the wise have fixed. For Moses said, "The great, mighty and awful God" (Deut. X, 17). To this was added the formula of Abraham, "God most high, maker of heaven and earth"' (Gen. XIV, 22). R. Abin said: Jacob, a man of the village of Neboria near Tyre, was wont to render the opening words of Ps. LXV thus: 'To thee silence is praise' (see R.V.M.). Silence is a medicine for everything. It is like a jewel of priceless value; however high a price you set upon it, you undervalue it.... The Men of the Great Synagogue restored the old formula, as it is said, 'Now therefore, our God, the great, mighty and awful' (Neh. IX, 32), because He is exalted above all the praise wherewith men can praise Him. R. Jacob said: They knew of their God that He is truth-loving, they did not flatter Him; the praise with which Moses had praised Him was enough for them.

(*Midr.Ps.* on XIX, 1 (82*b*, § 3) (cp. *T.J.Ber.* VII, § 4, f. 11*c* and [729]).)

[728] R. Johanan said: He who recounts the praise of God more than is fitting will be torn away from the world (cf. *R.T.* p. 120).

(*Meg.* 18*a*.)

[729] A certain man went down to the Ark [to act as precentor] in the presence of R. Ḥanina. He said, 'O God, the great, the mighty, the revered, the glorious, the powerful, the feared, the strong, the courageous, the certain, the honoured.' R. Ḥanina waited until he had finished. When he had finished, he said to him, 'Have you exhausted all the praises of your Lord? What is the use of all those adjectives? The three which we do say [great, mighty, and revered], if Moses had not used them in the Torah, and if the men of the Great Synagogue had not come and instituted them in the *Tefillah* [prayer], we should not have been

able to say; and you go on saying all these! A parable: The matter may be likened to a human king, who possessed a million gold *denarii*, and people kept praising him as the possessor of a million *denarii* of silver; is it not an insult to him?'

(*Ber.* 33*b* (Cohen, p. 226; cp. *Meg.* 25*a*).)

It is always God who is the ultimate motive of the pious Israelites' action. The love of Him and also the fear of Him: these are fundamental.

[730] 'Praise Him all ye peoples; laud Him all ye nations.' R. Simeon, the son of R. Judah the Prince, asked his father, 'What is the difference between peoples and nations?' He replied, 'The peoples are they who have enslaved Israel; the nations are they who have not enslaved Israel. The nations say, "If the peoples who have enslaved Israel praise God, how much more should we who have not." And the Israelites say, "And how yet much more should we."' (*Midr.Ps.* on CXVII, 1 (240*a*, § 2).)

[731] 'I will praise Thy name for ever and ever.' Not as now will it be then. *Now*, if God has wrought for them a miracle, they sing a song to Him; if not, they are silent; but in the time to come, they will never cease, but they will keep on saying songs and blessings continually; for they will say, 'We have no other task than to bless thee with ever new blessings.'

(*Midr.Ps.* on CXLV, 1 (267*b init.*, § 1).)

[732] To an earthly king, if a poor man greets him, or one who has a burn on his hand, it is a disgrace, and the king does not reply, but God is not so, everybody is acceptable to Him, and He says, 'Praise me, and it is acceptable to me.'

(*Midr.Ps.* on CXLVII, 1 (269*a*, § 2).)

The sin, trespass, and burnt-offerings were instituted for sins in thought and deed, but the thanksgiving offering was to atone for nothing, but simply to give thanks:

[733] God said, 'This offering is more precious to me than all the rest, as David sang, "He who brings a sacrifice of thanksgiving assuredly honours me" (Ps. L, 23). [In the Hebrew the emphasis is expressed by the so-called energetic mood of the verb 'to honour'.] Such a man honours me twice; in this world, and in the world to come.' (*Tanḥ.B.*, Ẓaw, 9*a*.)

[734] R. Samuel[1] went to Rome when the queen lost her bracelet. He found it. A crier went about the kingdom and said, 'Whoever returns the bracelet within 30 days shall receive such and such a reward, but if it is found upon him after 30 days, his head shall be cut off.' He did not return it within 30 days. After the 30 days he returned it. She said to him, 'Have you not been in the kingdom?' He said, 'Yes.' She said, 'Have you not heard the proclamation?' He said, 'Yes.' She said to him, 'What did the crier say?' He told her. She said, 'And why did you not return it within the 30 days?' He said, 'So that you should not say, I feared *you*, but I returned it because I feared God.' Then she said, 'Blessed be the God of the Jews.'

(*T.J.Bab.M.* II, § 5 (?), f. 8*c*, line 35.)

[735] God said to Moses: 'Do not fear' (Num. XXI, 34), and yet it says in Prov. XXVIII, 14, 'Happy is the man who fears always.' It is a quality of the righteous that although they have received God's assurance, they never cast off the fear of Him.

(*Tanḥ.B.*, Ḥuḳḳat, 65*b*.)

[736] R. Ḥanina said: Everything is in the hand of heaven [i.e. of God] except the fear of heaven, as it is said, 'And now, Israel, what does God require of thee but to fear Him?' (Deut. X, 12). Is then the fear of heaven a small thing? R. Ḥanina said, in the name of R. Simeon b. Yoḥai: God has in His storehouse nothing but the treasure of the fear of heaven, as it is said, 'The fear of the Lord is His treasure' (Isa. XXXIII, 6). (*Ber.* 33*b*.)

Moore, II, 93, adds: 'It is perhaps not pressing the words too hard if we put on them the meaning, What God prizes in men's good works is not the acts themselves but the religious motive from which they spring.'

Yet the right relation to God involves and includes goodness to man. So it is of importance to note that, apart from idolatry, the emphasis is constantly laid upon the commandments which have to do with the duties of man to his fellow. The Rabbis had obviously a difficulty in expressing themselves in these matters. But the following cumbersomely worded passage is significant:

[737] One who is 'good' towards God and 'good' towards men is a good righteous man: and one who is 'good' towards God but 'bad' towards men is a not good righteous man. Similarly: one who is bad towards God and bad towards men is a bad

[1] ? b. Sustra or Susreta.

bad man; one who is bad towards God but not bad towards man is a not bad bad man. (*Ḳid.* 40*a*.)

In these strange words, the Talmud seeks to distinguish between the commands in the Law which are ordered by God, but which do not relate to our fellow-men, and those commands which do relate to our fellow-men. The former set of commands are less weighty than the latter. Thus one might say that, from this point of view, the Jew who violates the Sabbath, does not observe the Day of Atonement, etc., but who honours his parents, and is charitable, just and kind towards his fellows is a 'not bad bad man', whereas he who does just the reverse, is 'a not good righteous man'.

[The difficulty to which Mr Montefiore refers was a very real one. One might say that the cause of it was the absence of abstract terms, a deficiency which is very remarkable in classical and post-classical Hebrew. Syriac is far better equipped in this respect, often by borrowing from Greek. The fact that abstract adjectives in the Bible have to supply many diverse connotations hardly needs mention (p. 659). But this paucity of terms may be regarded, perhaps, as a symptom rather than as a cause, for had the Jews had a bent for philosophy, they could surely have created the requisite vocabulary. They did so in the concrete sphere, to a remarkable degree. The language of the Mishnah contains a large number of scientific terms and of names of objects in the material world: it is in the world of abstract thought that the poverty is obvious. The Rabbis tended to express themselves practically rather than philosophically, because their main interest lay with the practical details of life rather than with speculation (cp. [692] and p. xcv). (H. L.)]

The following legend is also suggestive in showing that for a loving deed a ceremonial law might conceivably be violated:

[738] After R. Akiba had died, they did not permit his body to be buried, but the body was brought back to the prison, and the overseer of the prison was there to watch over it. Then Elijah went and stood at the door of R. Joshua, the groats maker (who had ministered before to R. Akiba in the prison), and R. Joshua said to him, 'Peace be with you, my master.' Elijah replied, 'Peace be with you, my master and teacher.' R. Joshua said, 'Do you need anything?' Elijah said, 'I am a priest, and I come to tell you that R. Akiba lies dead in the prison.' Then they went to the prison, and they found the gate of the prison open, and the governor and all the warders asleep. So they placed R. Akiba upon a bier, and went out. Then Elijah took up the body, and carried it on his back. When R. Joshua saw him doing so, he

said, 'My master, you said you were a priest, and a priest is forbidden to make himself unclean with a dead body.' Then Elijah said, 'Let it suffice you, R. Joshua, my son, surely uncleanness does not apply to the righteous, or to their disciples.' So they carried the body all the night till they came to Antipatris.[1] When they arrived, thrice they ascended and thrice they descended, and a cave lay open before them, and they saw there a chair and a bench and a table and a lamp, and they placed R. Akiba upon the bier and went out. As soon as they had gone out, the cave closed, and the light in the lamp was kindled. Then Elijah, when he saw this, said, 'Happy are you, O you righteous, and happy are you who labour in the Torah, and happy are you who fear God, for a place in Paradise in the time to come is hidden and preserved for you. Happy are you, R. Akiba, that you have found so pleasant a lodging place in the hour of your death.' (*Midr.Prov.* IX, 2, 31 *a fin.*)

Speaking generally, however, it might, perhaps, be rightly said that for the Rabbis goodness and piety were hardly distinguishable. The good man must be also the pious man, and the pious man fulfils the ceremonial, no less than the moral, enactments of the Law. We can gather the Rabbinic point of view from the following passage in the Mishnah:

[739] These are the things which have no exact measure or limit. The 'corners' of the field [i.e. the law in Lev. XIX, 9 and 10, 'And when ye reap the harvest of your land, thou shalt not wholly reap the corners of thy field, neither shalt thou gather the gleanings of thy harvest: and thou shalt not glean thy vineyard, neither shalt thou gather every grape of thy vineyard; thou shalt leave them for the poor and the stranger; I am the Lord your God']; the first fruits; the offerings brought by pilgrims at the three statutory visits to the Temple; the practice of loving-deeds; and the study of the Law. These are the things of which a man eats the fruit in this world, but the capital remains for him in the world to come: the honour of parents; the practice of loving-deeds; making peace between a man and his neighbour; the study of the Law, which is equal to them all (cp. p. 174, note 2).

The Gemara explains:

No limit for loving-deeds. This is said for the body, but for money there *is* a limit. It is reported that this is in accordance

[1] See Buber's note *in loc.*

with what R. Simeon b. Laḳish said in the name of R. Judah b. Ḥanina: It was decided at Usha that a man should give a fifth of his possessions for good works (in charity).... But R. Gamaliel b. Inninia (*sic*) said, in the presence of R. Mana: If this means a fifth of his whole possessions, then in five years he would have nothing left. It was replied, The first year a fifth of the capital, afterwards a fifth of the revenue. [It does not appear that this arrangement was seriously meant or actually carried out. Anyway, it was intended as a maximum levy by oneself upon oneself.] R. Jeshebab, we are told, gave all his possessions to the poor. R. Gamaliel sent to him to say, Do you not know that the Rabbis have ordered that a man should not give more than a fifth?

(*T.J.Pe'ah* I, § I; f. 15*b*, line 22 (cp. *R.T.* pp. 56, 57).)

[740] Merit [*zekut*] [goodness] has a stock [capital], and bears fruit [interest]. Sin has a stock, but bears no fruit [i.e. sin is punished according to its degree and sinfulness, and there is an end of it]. But if so, how is this to be reconciled with the verse, 'They [the wicked] shall eat of the fruit of their own way, and be filled with their own devices' (Prov. I, 31)? There are sins which bear fruit, and there are sins which bear no fruit. [The sin which bears fruit is the sin which spreads over to others beyond the sinner, causing them to sin likewise.]

(*Ḳid.* 40*a*; *T.Pe'ah* I, 1–3 (Z. p. 18, line 1).)

In this passage the fruit and the stock do *not* apparently, as in the Mishnah, refer to this world and the world to come.

[741] The good intention is united by God to the deed [i.e. He rewards a man for both]. R. Assi said: If a man intended to do a good deed and was prevented, the Scripture reckons it to him as if he had done it. The evil intention God does not unite to the deed [i.e. if a bad deed is intended, but not accomplished, God does not punish a man for the unaccomplished intention]. How can this be reconciled with the verse, 'I will bring evil upon this people, even the fruit of their thoughts [intentions]' (Jer. VI, 19)? The intention which issues in a deed, God unites with a deed; the intention which does not issue in a deed, He does not unite with the deed. But R. Assi said: The intention to commit idolatry is reckoned as equivalent to committing it, for idolatry is so grave a sin that he who rejects it is regarded as if he had agreed to the whole Law. (*Ḳid.* 40*a*; *T.Pe'ah* I, 4 (Z. p. 18, line 9).)

[742] R. Huna said: If a man commits a sin repeatedly, it becomes permitted to him. It becomes permitted to him! What an idea! Say rather: it *seems* to him to be permitted. (*Ḳid.* 40*a*.)

There is not infrequently some discussion whether abstention from evil, or the fulfilment of negative commands, is adequate goodness in the eyes of God (cp. [327]).

To corrupt the soul is worse than to kill the body:

[743] R. Simeon said: How can it be shown that to cause another to sin is worse than to murder him? Because if you murder him, you kill him as regards this world, but a portion remains for him in the world to come, but if you cause him to sin, you deprive him both of this world and of the world to come.

(*Num.R.*, Pineḥas, XXI, 4.)

[744] Whosoever causes the multitude to be righteous, through him no sin shall be brought about; but he who causes the multitude to sin shall not have the means to repent [the sins of others being beyond the remedial action of his repentance].

(*Aboth* V, 21; *P.B.* pp. 202–3.)

Sin in thought is as bad as, or worse than, sin in deed:

[745] Evil thoughts [i.e. lustful thoughts] are even worse than lustful deeds. (*Yoma* 29*a init.* (cf. *R.T.* p. 41 *fin.*).)

[746] R. Ammi said: He who gives himself up to sensual thoughts is not allowed to draw near to the Presence [lit. 'they'[1] do not let him enter God's compartment [*meḥiẓah*]]. (*Nid.* 13*b init.* (cp. p. 588).)

[747] From the hour that a man thinks in his heart to commit a sin, he is faithless to God. (*Num.R.*, Naso, VIII, 5.)

[748] There is no greater adultery than when a woman, while her husband has intercourse with her, thinks of another man.

(*Tanḥ.B.*, Naso, §13, f. 16 *a* (cp. [1447] and [1453]).)

[Though not expressly stated, it seems clear from the anecdote (which follows in § 13) that this remark was intended to apply equally to a man who acted in this way towards his wife. (H. L.)]

The Rabbis, as I have suggested, just because there was with them no healthy simple comradeship and intercourse between the two sexes, were often plagued by sensual thoughts and temptations. For an example see [1123]. See also [769 ff.] See also *Ḳid.* 81 *a* (cited below) for comradeship with or without 'chaperonage'.

[1] Cp. p. 179 note.

[Examples (e.g. [770] ff.) show how prone even the greatest were to these thoughts, how they wrestled with them and how they overcame them. The greater the man, the stronger the temptation (cp. [782]). No one is exempt (cp. [1123]). But this recognition of human frailty is not exceptional, nor is it limited to Rabbinic literature or to Rabbis. It will be found just as prominently stressed in Patristic and in other literatures: the story of St Anthony is proverbial. But the Rabbinic and Patristic literatures are noteworthy for their condemnation of sexual laxity, in contrast, say, to Boccaccio or even to Shakespeare, where it is regarded as venial or even as customary. William the Conqueror was known as 'the Bastard', the description being merely the recognition for fact, not an expression of horror. Curiously enough his title, *Manserus*, is the Hebrew *Mamzer* (on this see *Starrs and Charters in the B.M.* II, note 902*b*; for the strange history of this word see the rest of the note).

It is not unnatural that, in our eyes, this detestation of sexual licence should lead to exaggeration. This tendency is natural at most periods and in most circles. The golden mean is indeed hard to preserve. Nevertheless, we do find occasional glimpses of normal friendship between the sexes. As regards married women, we read in *Ḳid.* 81*a* of what we may call the question of 'chaperonage'. A wife can talk to a male friend, that is to say, she can be alone with him in her house, if the door is open, or if her husband is in town. This, as a general rule of conduct, does not strike one as being unreasonable or as a regulation of Mrs Grundy: in fact, it was, till recently, in force at women's colleges, where, however, younger unmarried men and women would be concerned. But the policy of the 'open door' does seem to indicate that married women had men friends. Or again, in *Pes.* 113*a*, R. Joshua b. Levi records three sayings of the 'Men of Jerusalem', which, therefore, may be taken as indicative of public opinion. The third saying is: 'Be careful in regard to your wife's first (or erstwhile) fiancé.' Such a saying was liable to be misunderstood. R. Ḥisda attributed it to a fear of impropriety; R. Kahana, to financial reasons (Rashi, *in loc.*, says: 'She will be prodigal of your money in entertaining him'). The Gemara admits the force of both arguments. But the fact remains that the woman could invite her former fiancé to dinner; otherwise the saying is meaningless. The number of instances of 'Roman matrons'—usually rendered 'Gentile ladies' in this book—who converse with Rabbis is evidence for the existence of friendship between the sexes.

Nor is it altogether correct to say that the rule of conduct or etiquette which says that one should not walk four paces behind a woman is the mark of a nasty mind. One does not follow women to whom one has not been introduced.

As regards the relationship of unmarried people of different sexes, particularly of youths and maidens, there is an interesting remark of

R. Johanan, in *Baba Bathra* 91*b*. This occurs amid a string of reminiscences of the 'good old days', when food was so plentiful that if a crow stole a bit of meat, it left a trail of fat down the wall, or of the 'bad old days', when bread was cheap but men died, because they could not afford to buy it. In such varied circumstances, Johanan recalls that there was a day when youths and maidens of sixteen or seventeen years of age could go out for walks without sinning. Is there not a modern touch about this remark? Certain passages in the birth-control controversy, relating to automatic machines in garages, have a very similar ring. But in each case the conclusion would rather be that there were transient periods of sexual laxity than that boys and girls never went on excursions together. Did they not dance in the woods, once upon a time, on the Day of Atonement and the 15th Ab, and pick their sweethearts! (Cp. [782].)

But all this, true enough as it well may be, is but one side of the picture. The other side could give us examples deprecating intercourse which, to our eyes, is both reasonable and desirable. (H. L.)]

[749] [Nevertheless it is stated that] R. Johanan said: When the majority of a man's years have passed without sin, he will never sin. And it was taught that when the opportunity for sin comes to a man once and twice and is resisted, he will never sin (cf. *R.T.* p. 20). (*Yoma* 38*b*.)

God *permits* a man to sin—such seems to be the prevailing doctrine—for free will is given: but God actively *helps* a man to be good. It is in man's free choice whether he will be good and pious or the reverse. The following sentence has been already quoted on p. 285:

[750] All is in the hand of heaven except the fear of heaven. (*Ber.* 33*b*.)

[751] R. Levi said: There are six things which serve man; three are in his control, and three are not. Eye, nose and ear are not. He must see, smell and hear what he may not want to see, smell and hear. A man may be passing through a street when they are burning incense to an idol, and he has no wish to smell the incense, but his nose forces him to do so. So, too, his eye brings him sinful sights, and his ear blasphemous words, against his will, for they too are not under his control. But mouth, hand and foot are in his power. He need not desire with his mouth to labour in the Law. He need not wish to slander or curse or blaspheme. He need not wish with his hand to fulfil the commandments. He need not wish to steal or murder. With his foot

he can visit the theatres or circuses, or he can go to the synagogues or houses of study.

(*Tanḥ.B.*, Toledot, 70*b* *fin.*–71*a* (cp. *Gen.R.*, Toledot, LXVII, 3 (Th. p. 756) and *Tanḥ.B.*, Miḳḳeẓ, 96*b*).)

It may seem curious that the 'mouth' is the organ which is connected with the study of the Law. With us it would be the eye. But the men of the ancient world held that all true study must be reading out loud. Reading with them was almost always reading out loud.[1]

There is an idiom in biblical Hebrew by which a verb in the infinitive is put for emphasis' sake before the verb in the imperfect or perfect. The A.V. translates this idiom variously, e.g. in Exod. XV, 26, for 'If to hear, you will hear', it has, 'If ye will diligently hearken'. The Rabbis use the idiom for many interpretations (cp. [1316]):

[752] If a man hearkens to [i.e. obeys] one command, they cause him to hearken to many. If a man forgets [i.e. neglects] one commandment, 'they'[2] cause him to forget [i.e. neglect] many. Simeon b. Azzai said: If a man desires to hearken at once, they cause him to hearken even subsequently; if a man desires to forget at once, they cause him to forget even subsequently. If a man desires to hearken freely, they cause him to hearken also even against [i.e. without] his will; if a man desires to forget freely, they cause him to forget even against his will: [initial] free will is given, yet, as it is said, 'He gives to the mockers mockery, and to the humble grace' (Prov. III, 34). (*Mek.*[2], *Wayaṡṡa*', Beshallaḥ, § 1, pp. 157–8; *Mek.*[3], vol. II, p. 97 (cp. [241], [534]).)

(For the text, translation and meaning of the above, cp. Bacher, *Agada der Tannaiten*, vol. I, ed. 2, pp. 412 and 412 n. 4.)

[753] Ben Azzai used to say: Be startled on account of a light sin, so that you may be startled by reason of a heavy sin: execute a commandment as early as possible, lest the punishment [for its neglect] anticipate you: if you sin, grieve not for that sin, but for the sin which may succeed it, and if you execute a commandment, rejoice not over *it*, but over the commandment which may follow it, for commandment leads on to commandment, and sin leads on to sin, for the reward of commandment is commandment, and the reward of sin is sin. (*Ab.R.N.* (vers. II), XXXIII, 36*b*.)

[1] [Thus what we term 'Scripture', they termed 'Reading out loud', 'Lecture', *Miḳra*. (H. L.)]

[2] 'They' is very frequently used to mean God (see p. 179 note).

The word *miẓwah* can be equally well translated commandment or good deed; to the Rabbis the two are identical. Every good deed in our modern sense is also the fulfilment of a commandment, and every fulfilment of a commandment is a good deed.

The more habitual doctrine would appear to be the following:

[754] Resh Laḳish said: Him who would be pure, 'they'[1] help; to him who would pollute himself, the door is open. (*Men.* 29*b*.)

[755] If a man comes to defile himself, 'they'[1] open the door for him, but him who comes to purify himself, they help. In the school of R. Ishmael it was taught: It is as when a man sells naphtha and balm: when a purchaser for naphtha comes, the shopman says, 'Measure it out for yourself'; but if one comes who asks for balm, he says, 'Wait till I help you measure, so that we may each become perfumed.' (*Yoma* 38*b fin.*–39*a init.*)

In this striking and noble passage it is not only said that God helps a man to be good: the mystical idea is brought in that God is made more beautiful or more beatific by man's righteousness.

On the other hand, where we would say, 'If a man takes five steps with sin with some resistance, he will take the next five more quickly' (or the like), the Rabbis are sometimes inclined to bring in God:

[756] Do not defile yourselves lest you become unclean. If a man defiles himself a little, 'they'[1] [= God] defile him much. If a man defiles himself below, they defile him from above; if he defiles himself in this world, they defile him in the world to come. If a man sanctify himself below, they sanctify him above; if he sanctify himself in this world, they sanctify him in the world to come. (*Yoma* 39*a*.)

The meaning of the saying is not by any means wholly clear in all its parts. The first two sentences seem to mean the same thing, namely, that if a man begins to sin, then God *makes* him sin the more. This sounds a terrible doctrine; yet it may mean little more than that sin tends to be progressive and cumulative. The sentence, 'If he defile himself in this world, they defile him in the world to come,' is very hard. Dr Cohen translates 'for the world to come'. The Hebrew can bear either rendering. But what would either rendering *mean*? Does it mean that a man is made to sin in the world to come? Hardly, because in the world to come there is no 'sin': there is only punishment in Gehenna, which cannot be signified by the world to come. Or does it mean that they (i.e. God) make him unfit to attain

[1] See p. 179 note and [746].

to the world to come by causing him to sin yet more? Nor is the 'hallowing' sentence clear. What precisely does hallowing 'for' or 'in' the world to come mean? Does it mean that the man is helped to become more and more righteous, so that he may enter the world to come? These verbal paradoxes tend to become unclear and dubious n meaning. Mr Loewe says that the difficult words might have a declarative sense; that is: If a man defiles himself in this world (and dies unrepentant, *bien entendu*), God, in the world to come, declares him defiled, or God declares him too sinful to enter the world to come. Dr Cohen quotes also the saying in *Sab.* 104*a*: 'If a man would purify himself (i.e. be good), they help him: if a man would defile himself, an opening or a door is there for him.' This would mean that while goodness is helped, sin is only permitted. A saying in *Mak.* 10*b* goes further: 'R. Elazar said: On the way that a man wishes to walk they cause him to walk.'[1] One of the proof passages quoted is Prov. III, 14, 'Surely He scorns the scorners, but He gives grace unto the lowly.' So it seems that both ways are intended in the statement, the way of good and the way of evil. Down either road—whether to righteousness or wickedness—there is a push from God. On the other hand, just before, R. Elazar's saying, Ps. xxv, 8, 'God instructs sinners in the way,' is quoted by R. Ḥama b. Ḥanina, in order to indicate that God helps the sinner to *overcome* his sin, and the Rabbi adds: 'If He teaches the way to sinners, how much more to the righteous.' Here we must leave it: and, perhaps, the Rabbis themselves would have been hard put to it, if we had asked them, 'Do you *really* mean that God *pushes* man sinward?' We must, however, remember that whatever *we* regard, under God, as a natural or psychological tendency, *they* attributed to the direct agency of God. And as sin does lead to sin, they could hardly do otherwise than say that God, as the creator of these tendencies, does induce the early sinner to sin more and more. But they happily did not make much use of the doctrine. And it was crossed and mitigated by the doctrine of repentance.

[1] *Suk.* 53*a*, in name of R. Johanan.

Chapter XI

THE DOCTRINE OF THE EVIL INCLINATION. RIGHTEOUSNESS AND SIN

In this chapter I propose to illustrate, by means of quotations, the Rabbinic doctrine of the good and the evil *yetzer* (*Yetzer ha-Ra*), and more especially of the evil *yetzer*. The word *yetzer*, inclination (lit. form), is biblical, and in addition to its literal meaning is used to signify purpose, device, imagination. The salient passages are I Chron. XXIX, 18, XXVIII, 9, Gen. VI, 5, VIII, 21, Deut. XXXI, 21 and Isa. XXVI, 3. In all these passages except the last the A.V. renders the word by 'imagination', but it may be questioned whether 'inclination' would not convey the meaning more accurately. It would be impossible by means of mere quotations to give a full account of the very elaborate theory of the Rabbis about the two *yetzers*. I can present only a few passages showing the Rabbis' views about the evil *yetzer* and its power, and of the best means with which to combat and overcome its solicitations.

[757] This is the device of the evil *yetzer*: To-day it says, 'Do this'; to-morrow 'Do that,' till at last it says, 'Worship an idol,' and the man goes and does it. (*Sab.* 105*b*.)

[758] R. Simeon b. Levi said: The evil *yetzer* of a man waxes strong against him day by day, and seeks to kill him, and if God did not help him, man could not prevail against it.

(*Ḳid.* 30*b* (cp. *Suk.* 52*b*).)

The proof of both these statements is found in Ps. XXXVII, 32, 33, where 'the wicked' is taken to mean the evil *yetzer*.

[759] 'Thou deliverest the poor from him that is too strong for him, and the needy from him that spoils him' (Ps. XXXV, 10). The poor is Israel: the spoiler is the Evil Inclination. How does the Good Inclination strive [to do right], and then the Evil Inclination comes and causes loss! There is no brigand stronger than the Evil Inclination. But God delivers Israel from the Evil Inclination. (*Pes.R.* f. 32*b*.)

[760] Raba said: Though God created the *Yetzer ha-Ra*, He created the Law, as an antidote [lit. spice] against it.

(*Bab.B.* 16*a* (cp. [332]).)

[761] R. Yannai said: He who hearkens to his evil *yetzer* is as if he practised idolatry; for it is said, 'There shall be no strange God within thee: thou shalt not worship any foreign God' (Ps. LXXXI, 9). (*T.J.Ned.* IX, § 1, f. 41*b*, line 48.)

[762] The words of the Law are likened to a medicine of life. Like a king who inflicted a big wound upon his son, and he put a plaster upon his wound. He said, 'My son, so long as this plaster is on your wound, eat and drink what you like, and wash in cold or warm water, and you will suffer no harm. But if you remove it, you will get a bad boil.' So God says to the Israelites, 'I created within you the evil *yetzer*, but I created the Law as a drug. As long as you occupy yourselves with the Law, the *yetzer* will not rule over you. But if you do not occupy yourselves with the Torah, then you will be delivered into the power of the *yetzer*, and all its activity will be against you.'

(*Ḳid.* 30*b* (cp. [332]).)

[763] If the Evil Inclination says to you, 'Sin, and God will forgive you,' believe it not. (*Ḥag.* 16*a*.)

[764] The Rabbis taught: We should not put opportunity to sin even before an honest man, much less before a thief, for the sages say this is like putting fire next to tow.

(*Tanḥ.B.*, Meẓora', 26*b init.* (cp. *ib.*, Wayishlaḥ, 85*b*, § 12).)

[765] The Israelites say to God, 'Lord of the world, thou knowest how hard is the strength of the Evil Inclination.' God says, 'Remove it a little in this world, and I will rid you of it altogether in the world to come.' (*Num.R.*, Beha'aloteka, XV, 16.)

[766] R. Simai said: The evil *yetzer* is like a big rock, which stands at the cross-roads, and people stumble against it. The king said, 'Crush it little by little, till I come and remove it altogether'; so God says, 'The Evil Inclination is a great stumbling block; crush it little by little, till at the last I remove it from the world.'

(*Pes.K.* 165*a*.)

[767] In the school of R. Ishmael it was taught: If this abomination meet you, drag it to the House of Study; if it is hard as stone, it will be crushed; if it is hard as iron, it will be broken in pieces.

(*Ḳid.* 30*b*.)

[768] Simeon the Just said: I have only once in my life eaten the guilt offering of a Nazarite.[1] Once a man from the south came to me, and I looked at him; he was ruddy in countenance and with beautiful eyes, and goodly to see, and his hair hung from his head in curly locks. I said to him, 'Wherefore do you propose to cut off this lovely hair?' He said to me, 'I was a shepherd in my city, and I went to fill the trough from the well, and I saw my image in the water. Then my evil inclination seized me, and sought to destroy me out of the world. Then I said, Thou wicked one, why dost thou boast thyself of that which is not thine, which belongs to the dust, to the worm: I will consecrate thee to heaven, and I will cut thee off for heaven's sake.' Then I bowed my head and kissed him, and I said, 'Like you, who do the will of God, may there be many in Israel.'

R. Muna said: Why did Simeon the Just not eat the offering of the Nazarite? Was it because the Nazarite committed a sin in that he refrained from drinking wine?...No, it was because he thought that men often took the Nazarite vow in haste, and therefore ended by repenting it. But this young man took the vow with calmness and on full reflection: mouth and mind were at one. (*Num.R.*, Naso, x, 7.)

[769] R. Ḥiyya b. Ashi, when he fell on his face in prayer, was wont to say: May God deliver me from the evil inclination. When one day his wife heard him, she thought, 'It is now many years that we have lived apart: why does he say this?' One day he was studying in his garden; his wife decked herself out, and passed up and down before him twice. He said to her, 'Who are you?' She said, 'I am Ḥirta [a famous courtesan], and have returned to-day.' He solicited her, and she yielded to him. Then she said, 'Fetch me the pomegranate on the top of the palm tree'; he hastened, and went, and brought it to her. When he went home, his wife was heating the oven; he went and sat in it. She said to him, 'What means this?' He said to her, 'Thus and thus have I done.' She said to him, 'It was I.' He did not believe her till she gave him the token. Then he said to her, 'Nevertheless I intended what is forbidden.' All his days did that religious man thereafter fast, till he died therefrom. (*Ḳid.* 81 *b.*)

[1] Simeon, being a priest, had a right to sacrificial portions: he was, in fact, High Priest.

['Fasting' in this case does not mean total abstinence from food but abstention during the daytime. Other instances of such prolonged fastings occur, e.g. R. Zadok fasted for forty years in an endeavour to prevent the destruction of the Temple which he foresaw (*Giṭ.* 56 *a*; *Lam.R.* I, § 31, on I, 5); cf. also Elazar of Modi'im in *Lam.R.* II, § 4, where presumably fasting is implied (cp. p. 263).

'Sitting in the oven' was not usually a means of suicide, but a self-inflicted punishment (cp. [785], [1130] and [1161]). (H. L.)]

[770] Some[1] women redeemed from captivity were brought to Nehardea, and they took them to the house of R. Amram the pious, and they took away the ladder from the room in which they were put. While one of them was walking up and down in the room, a ray of light fell from the skylight on to the ground, and revealed her. R. Amram took the ladder which ten men could not lift up, and he lifted it by himself. When he had got half-way up the ladder, he forced himself to stop, and called out with a loud voice, 'Amram's house is on fire.' Then the Rabbis came and said, 'You frightened us by a false alarm.' He said, 'It is better that you should be falsely alarmed about the house of Amram in this world than that you should be ashamed of Amram in the world to come.' Then he conjured it [i.e. the evil inclination] to go forth from him. Then it went out of him in the guise of a pillar of fire. Then he said, 'I perceive that thou art fire, and I am flesh, but I am stronger than thou.' (*Ḳid.* 81 *a.*)

Here the Evil Inclination is half-personified as an evil spirit or demon, separate from the man, of which he is possessed, but of which he can, by conjuration or effort, be rid.

[771] R. Me'ir[1] used to mock at sinners. One day Satan appeared in the likeness of a woman on the other side of the river. As there was no ferry boat, he seized the rope bridge, and went across. When he was half-way, Satan vanished saying, 'If they had not called out from heaven, "Beware of R. Me'ir and his Torah," I would not have assessed your blood at two farthings.' (*Ḳid.* 81 *a.*)

A similar story is told of R. Akiba. Satan appears in the form of a woman on the top of a palm tree. Akiba climbs up, and when he is half-way, Satan vanishes, making the same remark as to Me'ir.

[772] Mattithiah b. Ḥeresh[1] was a wealthy man and God-fearing. He possessed excellent qualities, and was devoted to all kinds of good

[1] See pp. 289 foot to 291.

deeds. He supported many scholars from his property, and widows and orphans were always sustained at his table. In all his ways he was perfect, and his whole time was devoted to study like his teacher R. Me'ir. His face shone like the sun. They say about him that all his days he had never cast a glance at another man's wife, or indeed at any woman at all. Once when he was sitting and studying, Satan passed by, and was jealous at the sight of him. He said, 'Is it possible that there can be a righteous man without sin in the world?' At once he went up to heaven and, standing before God, said, 'Sovereign of the Universe, what is Mattithiah b. Ḥeresh before thee?' God said, 'He is a perfectly righteous man.' Satan said, 'Then give me permission to test him.' God gave him permission, and at once he went to Mattithiah whom he found studying as usual. He appeared to him in the form of a woman more beautiful than any since the days of Naamah, Tubal Cain's sister, for whom even the ministering angels went astray. When Mattithiah saw her, he turned his face backwards, so Satan came to him from behind. Wherever he turned, Satan was facing him. Then he said to himself, 'I fear lest the evil inclination may prevail against me.' What did that righteous man then do? He called his disciple, who was his attendant, and told him to bring him some nails and a brazier. Mattithiah then heated the nails in the brazier and blinded himself with them. When Satan saw this, he hastily departed in fear, and came to God, and told Him what had happened. At once God called Raphael, the angel of healing, and bade him go and heal Mattithiah's eyes. So Raphael went and stood before Mattithiah, who said to him, 'Who art thou?' He replied, 'I am Raphael the angel, God's messenger, sent to heal thine eyes.' Mattithiah answered, 'I do not desire it; what has been, has been.' Raphael returned to God, and told him what Mattithiah had said. God said, 'Go and say to him: Henceforward fear no more: I am thy pledge that temptation will never prevail against thee all thy life long.' When Mattithiah heard this from the angel, he accepted the healing, and was healed. Hence, say the sages, 'Whoever has never glanced at a woman is safe from the evil inclination; in the world to come God will remove it altogether, and replace it by his Holy Spirit' (Ezek. XXXVI, 26). (*Tanḥ.B.*, Ḥuḳḳat, 66*a*.)

[773] The *yetzer* at first is weak as a woman, afterwards it becomes

strong as a man. R. Akiba said: At first it is like a spider's thread and at last it is like a rope of a ship. R. Isaac said: At first it is a wayfarer and lodger, at last it becomes the master of the house.... R. Ammi said: The evil *yetzer* does not walk at the side, but in the middle of the street, and when it sees a man who winks with his eyes, and dresses his hair elegantly, and lifts up his heels, it says, 'This man is mine.' R. Abin said: If a man indulges his *yetzer* in his youth, it will be his ruler in his old age. R. Ḥanina b. Papa said: If the *yetzer* comes and would jest with you, drive it away with words of Torah; and if you would say, 'It is not in my power to do so,' then the Scripture says, 'In yourself should be your trust' (Isa. XXVI, 3), and remember that God wrote for you the words of the Law, 'The desire of the evil *yetzer* is to rule over you, but you are to rule over it' (Gen. IV, 7).

(*Gen.R.*, Bereshit, XXII, 6 (Th. pp. 210–12); *Suk.* 52*a*.)[1]

Sometimes the Rabbis venture to complain that God Himself has acknowledged that the evil *yetzer* is a sore calamity. Why then was it created?

[774] The Rabbis say: So hard is the evil *yetzer* that even its Creator (*Yotzer*) calls it evil, as it is said, 'For the *yetzer* of man's heart is evil from his youth' (Gen. VIII, 21). (*Ḳid.* 30*b*.)

[775] 'It repented the Lord that He had made man on the earth and it grieved Him at His heart' (Gen. VI, 6). R. Abbahu said: God mourned only over the heart of man, as one does who has made something bad, and knows that he has not made a good thing, and says, 'What have I made?' So God said: 'It was I who put the bad leaven in the dough, for the *yetzer* of the heart of man is evil from his youth.' So the words in Gen. VI, 6 mean 'man's heart', not 'God's'. God grieved over man's heart.

(*Tanḥ.B.*, Noaḥ, 15*b*.)

The verse in Genesis means God's heart, as the Rabbi knew well enough. It is for homiletic, and one might even say for theological, purposes that he suggests this other interpretation.

[1] The last three Hebrew words in Isaiah XXVI, 3 (A.V. 'Because he trusts in thee') are playfully rendered by the Midrash as above. It will be noticed that in this passage man's Free Will and his (unaided) power to conquer temptation are strongly emphasised. Nevertheless, this may be regarded as only one aspect of the complete Rabbinic doctrine. Man is not wholly unaided: the Torah and God help him in his fight for righteousness.

[776] R. Ḥana b. Aḥa said: In the school of Rab it was said, 'There are four things which God regretted to have made, The Exile, the Chaldeans, the Ishmaelites and the Evil Inclination.'

(*Suk.* 52*b* (Moore, I, 480, 481).)

[777] God said, 'The *yetzer* of man's heart is evil from his youth' (Gen. VIII, 21). R. Ḥiyya said: Poor must be the dough, which the Baker himself calls evil. R. Abba Jose, the potter, said: Poor is the leaven of which its Owner testifies that it is bad, as it is said, 'For He knows our *yetzer*; He remembers that we are dust' (Ps. CIII, 14). The Rabbis say: Poor must be the plant which the Gardener himself testifies to be bad, as it is said, 'The Lord who has planted thee has spoken of thee as bad' (A.V. 'has pronounced evil against thee') (Jer. XI, 17).

(*Gen.R.*, Noaḥ, XXXIV, 10 (Th. p. 320).)

[778] R. Aibu said: God said, 'I made a mistake that I created the evil *yetzer* in man, for had I not done so, he would not have rebelled against me.' This is said in relation to Gen. VI, 6, 'It repented the Lord that He had made man on the earth.'

(*Gen.R.*, Bereshit, XXVII, 4 (Th. p. 258).)

[779] God regretted the evil inclination, and He said, 'What damage have I wrought! I regret that I have created it in my world.' In that hour the gate of mercy was opened for the sinners in Israel, so as to receive them in repentance. They say, 'It is revealed and known unto thee that it was the evil inclination which incited us; in thy great mercy receive us in perfect repentance before thee.' (*Tan.d.b.El.* p. 62.)

The difficulty sometimes, somewhat unsatisfactorily, is sought to be got over like this:

[780] It is written, 'God made man upright' (Eccles. VII, 29), and also Gen. III, 22, 'Man is become like one of us.' God, who is righteous and upright, created man in order that he should be upright and righteous like Himself. But if you say, 'Why did God create the *yetzer*?' or, 'No man can keep himself (from the power of the *yetzer*),' the reply is: 'Why does a child of five, six, seven, eight or nine years not sin, but only at ten years and upwards? He himself makes his *yetzer* big. *You* make your *yetzer* bad. Why did you, when you were a child, not sin? But when you grew up, you sinned. There are many things in the world harder

and bitterer than the *yetzer*, such as lupin, mustard and capers, but by soaking them in water, etc., you know how to make them soft and sweet. If the bitter things, which I have created, you can make sweet, to meet your own needs, how much more the *yetzer*, which has been delivered into your hand.'

(*Tanḥ*., Bereshit, § 7, f. 10*a* (*R.T.* p. 180 *fin*.).)

The Rabbis insist that the only effective remedy for the Evil Inclination is the study or the fulfilment of the Law. Yet they sometimes seem to realise (in this, at least like Paul!) that the *yetzer* is stirred up by the prohibitions of the Law. Such, perhaps, would seem to be the suggestion of the following story:

[781] The evil inclination desires only that which is forbidden. R. Mena [on the Day of Atonement] went to visit R. Haggai who was ill. R. Haggai said, 'I am thirsty.' R. Mena said, 'Drink.' Then he left him. After an hour he came again, and said, 'How about your thirst?' He said, 'No sooner had you permitted me to drink than the desire left me.'

(*T.J. Yoma* VI, § 4, 43*d*, line 21.)

Though the study of the Law is the sovereign remedy against the evil *yetzer*, yet the learned in the Law are specially subject to its attack. This is an illustration of the rule that the bigger a man's whole nature, the more powerful too is the *yetzer* within him:

[782] The evil *yetzer* attacks the scholars most of all. Abbaye once heard a man say to a woman, 'We will go away together,' as their road was the same. He thought, 'I will go and keep them back from sin.' He went after them for three parasangs along a meadow. When they separated from one another, they said, 'The way has been long, our companionship has been sweet.' [They had walked together in innocence.] Then Abbaye said, 'If he who hates me [the *yetzer*] had thus encountered *me*, I could not have withstood him.' Then he went and leant against the bar of the door of his house, and was grieved. Then an old man came and said, 'He who is greater than his neighbour, his *yetzer* is also greater.' (*Suk*. 52*a* (cp. p. 290, [748] and [801]).)

[783] Once R. Ḥanina and R. Jonathan were walking along a road when they came to a fork. One path led to the door of an idolatrous temple and one to the door of a brothel. One said to the other, 'Let us pass the door of the temple, for its *yetzer* is slain' [i.e. its effectiveness is non-existent, since idols have no

reality; or, it has no lure to us. But see Rashi]. The other replied, 'No, let us pass the brothel and subdue our own *yetzer* [temptations], and gain the reward.' But when the Rabbis passed, the women retired into their rooms. The former Rabbi then asked his colleague, 'How did you know this [i.e. that you may come into proximity with sin]?' He replied, 'Prudence will guard thee, intelligence will protect thee' (Prov. II, 11)....Prudence, i.e. Torah. (*Ab.Zar.* 17*a* foot.)

Even the righteous are never completely secure from the solicitations of the *yetzer*:

[784] God never unites His name with the righteous during their lifetime, only after their death, as it says, 'To the holy that are [buried] in the earth' (Ps. XVI, 3). When are they 'holy'? When they are in the earth. While they are alive, the evil inclination may prevail over them. But when they are dead, God unites His name with them. Yet He did so to Isaac during his lifetime, for He said to Jacob, 'I am the God of thy father Isaac' (Gen. XXVIII, 13). Why was this? The Rabbis held that God counted Isaac's willingness to die on the altar as though he had already died for God's sake. R. Berechiah said: Isaac was blind, (Gen. XXVII, 1), and one who is blind is as though he were dead, for he is hidden in the house, and cannot see the temptations that are without. (*Tanḥ.*, Toledot, § 7, f. 46*a* (cp. [1337]).)

The following two stories are told to illustrate 'excelling in strength to do His Commandments' (Ps. CIII, 20):

[785] So was R. Zadok and so were his companions. A certain Roman *matrona* pressed R. Zadok to sin with her. He said, 'My heart is weak, and I cannot: is there anything to eat here?' [i.e. he did not 'excel in strength' physically]. She said, 'Yes, there is something unclean here.' He replied, 'What matters it! He who does this, may eat that.' [Rashi observes that the *matrona* was a member of the nobility, from whose power Zadok could not escape, and who could have him put to death.] She had the oven heated and put the dish on it. Zadok went and sat in the oven (cp. [769]). She said to him, 'What means this?' He answered, 'He who does this falls into that [i.e. Hell].' She said, 'Had I known it [that this meant so much to you; Rashi], I would not have persecuted you so much'; [so, 'in doing God's Commandments', Zadok 'excelled in strength'].

R. Kahana peddled osier baskets. A certain Roman *matrona* importuned him to sin with her. He said, 'Let me go and deck myself.' He went up to the roof, and threw himself down. Elijah came and caught him, saying, 'You have put me to the trouble of coming four hundred parasangs.' Kahana said, 'What save my poverty was the cause, [which made me take up a trade so risky]?' So Elijah gave him a potful of *denarii*.

(*Ḳid.* 40 *a.*)

[786] R. Johanan said: There are three whose virtue the Holy One, Blessed be He, Himself proclaims daily. These are, the bachelor who lives sinless in a city, the poor man who restores lost property to the owner, the rich man who pays tithes secretly. Now R. Safra was a bachelor who lived in a city, and it happened that a Tanna once taught this very passage in his presence and in that of Raba. R. Safra's face shone [this may have been with delight or embarrassment]. Raba said to him: 'The saying does not apply to bachelors like you, but to bachelors like R. Ḥanina and R. Osha'ya, who were shoemakers, in Palestine, and who dwelt in the harlots' street, making shoes for them and carrying them to their houses. And while the women inspected the shoes, they did not raise their eyes to glance at the women. So people would swear 'by the lives of the holy Rabbis of Palestine'. (Cp. [1231].) (*Pes.* 113 *b.*)

[787] 'When a man's ways please the Lord, He makes even his enemies to be at peace with him' (Prov. XVII, 7). R. Joshua b. Levi said: This refers to the evil inclination, than which man has no greater enemy. Now if a man live in close intimacy with his fellow for one year, even if, at the outset, he is his enemy, at the end he becomes his friend. But the evil inclination grows up with man from youth to old age: day by day it seeks to overthrow him. If it cannot overthrow him within ten years, it seeks to overthrow him within twenty years. If it can find an opportunity within eighty years, it will seize it. Thus, they relate that John [Hyrcanus], the High Priest, ministered for eighty years in the sacred office, yet at the end he became a Sadducee.

(*Tanḥ.B.*, Beshallaḥ, 28 *a* (with adaptations from *Exod.R.*).)

The above is an instance in which the evil inclination has nothing to do with sexual desire.

Yet there is also a sense in which the evil *yetzer* can be regarded as good. Since it is largely identified with sexual passion, and since without sexual passion the race of man could not continue, and since even sanctified marriage is dependent upon it, the evil *yetzer* is also good. Again, since business and trade depend (as the Rabbis conceived) upon competition and rivalry, which, in their turn, depend upon the instigations of the *yetzer*, it may be said that the evil *yetzer* is good:

[788] 'It was very good' (Gen. I, 31). R. Naḥman b. Samuel said: That is the evil inclination. But is the evil inclination very good? Yes, for if it were not for the evil inclination, man would not build a house, or take a wife, or beget a child, or engage in business, as it says, 'All labour and skilful work comes of a man's rivalry with his neighbour.' (*Gen.R.*, Bereshit, IX, 7 (Th. p. 72).)

The weakness of human nature is recognised by the Rabbis, and some allowance is made for it. As the Jew is, as one might say, the earthly keeper of God's honour, the sanctifier of His Name, the enormously important thing is that Jews should not sin publicly. For instance, unchastity is a sin, whether known or unknown. Suppose, let us say, a Jew commits an unchaste act with a Jewess, and nobody knows about it but themselves, it is a sin, and remains a sin: but if all the world knows about it, then God's name is profaned, and the sin is very greatly accentuated. That is the meaning of the following well-known and much-discussed passage:

[789] R. Ilai said: If a man finds that his evil inclination overmasters him, let him go to a place where nobody knows him, dress and cover himself in black, and act as his passion desires, but let him not profane the Name of God in public. Is this a contradiction to the teaching that he who does not spare the honour of his Creator had better never have been born, a teaching which R. Joseph interpreted to refer to the man who sins in secret? The solution of the contradiction is to be found in the fact that the second teaching must be regarded as referring to the man who *could* control his inclination, and the first to the man who cannot possibly do so. (*Ḳid.* 40*a*.)

For as the sanctification of the Name is the supreme virtue or duty, so the profanation of the Name is the supreme sin.

[790] R. Ḥanina said: Better that a man should commit a sin in secret than that he should profane the Name in public. (*Ḳid.* 40*a*.)

[791] No *loan* on time is granted [i.e. no chance for repentance is allowed] when the Name of God is profaned. [Or, perhaps:] No

comparing [balancing of good deeds against sins] is granted when the Name of God is profaned. (*Kid.* 40*a fin.*)

[792] It says in Num. XX, 12, 'Because he believed not in me', after the striking of the rock. Hence Moses was not allowed to enter the land. But did Moses never show a greater lack of faith? Did he not say, 'If flocks and herds were slaughtered for them, it would not suffice?' (*ib.* XI, 22). Why did not God pass sentence on him *then*? It is like a king who had a friend who behaved overbearingly to him in private, but the king paid no attention to him. Some days afterwards, he acted similarly to him in the presence of the legions. Then the king sentenced him to death. So God said to Moses, 'I took no account of thy first action because it was in private; but now I cannot overlook it, because this sin was before the multitude,' as it says, 'In that ye did not sanctify me in the sight of the children of Israel' (Num. XX, 12). (*Tanḥ.B.*, Ḥuḳḳat, 61*a.*)

Yet the Name of God *can* be profaned in secret as well as in public!

[793] R. Johanan, the son of Baroḳa, said: Whosoever profanes the Name of Heaven in secret will suffer the penalty for it in public; and this, whether the Heavenly Name be profaned in ignorance or wilfulness. (*Aboth* IV, 5 (cp. *P.B.* pp. 195–6).)

[794] Wherever the profanation of the Name might be involved, no respect must be paid even to a Teacher. (*Ber.* 19*b.*)

The Rabbis did not propound any theory as to the corruption of man's heart or the incapacity of man to do and be good without a preliminary regeneration. They did, indeed, speak of a poison or dirt which the serpent injected into Eve, and which continued among her descendants (*Yeb.* 103 *b*). But this 'dirt' was removed from the Israelites by the acceptance of the Law. It is to be regarded as a peculiar propensity to sexual, or even to unnatural, lust (cp. *R.T.* p. 164). We also find the statement that there is no generation to which at least one ounce of the sin of the Golden Calf does not inhere (*T.J.Ta'an.* IV, § 8, f. 68 *c*, line 5; **Note 96**). Yet neither theory is often alluded to. Even a heathen, if he chose, could be righteous—and, apparently, this righteousness did not always involve his becoming a proselyte. Righteousness was not exclusively a matter of birth:

[795] 'The Lord loves the righteous' (Ps. CXLVI, 8). If a man wishes to become a priest or a Levite, he cannot, if his father was not

one. But if he wishes, he can become righteous, even if he be a heathen, because the righteous do not depend on ancestry, but of themselves they resolve to be righteous and love God.

(*Midr.Ps.* on CXLVI, 8 (268*b*, § 7).)

Though the Rabbis would have certainly accepted the biblical statement, 'There is no man who does not sin', they often spoke inconsistently of the 'completely righteous', and there are several reported sayings of one particular Rabbi who was particularly convinced of his own righteousness (cp. *R.T.* p. 167, n. 1). Reference is made, for example, to the completely righteous in the following passage:

[796] R. Aḥa b. Ḥanina said: God said to Gabriel (Ezek. IX, 4), 'Go and mark a *Tau* of ink upon the foreheads of the righteous, so that the angel of destruction may have no power over them. But mark a *Tau* of blood upon the forehead of the wicked, so that the angel of destruction may have power over them.' Then the Attribute of Justice said to God, 'How do the former differ from the latter?' God replied, 'The former are completely righteous, the latter are completely wicked.' The Attribute said, 'The former could have rebuked [prevented] the latter, and they did not do so.' God replied, 'I know that they would not have accepted reproof.' The Attribute of Justice said, 'Though *you* may know it, did the righteous know it?' [This means that some responsibility rests upon the righteous for the sins of the wicked.] As it is said, 'The aged, the young, the virgin, infants and women, shall ye slay for the destroyer, but to none shall ye draw nigh that has the mark (*Tau*) upon him, and with my sanctuary shall ye begin' (Ezek. IX, 6). R. Joseph said: Read not 'my sanctuary' [*miḳdashi*] but 'my consecrated ones' [*meḳuddashai*]: these are the men who have fulfilled all the Torah from *Aleph* to *Tau* (beginning to end) (cp. *R.T.* pp. 271, 272, 166, 167).

(*Sab.* 55*a*.)

[The *Tau*, in Ezek. IX, 4, 6, is a mark of exemption from judgment: the word occurs again in Job XXXI, 35, of a written mark in attestation, Petosiris, a slave belonging to Mibtahyah, a Jewess in Elephantine in 411 B.C., had the mark of a *Yod* on his right arm (Cowley, *Aramaic Papyri*, p. 104). The *Tau* is the conclusion of God's seal, which is *emeth*, truth, and which is composed of the first, middle and last letters of the alphabet (*T.J.San.* I, § 1, f. 18*a*, line 64). But the *Tau*, as a sign of acquittal, is meant in *Sab.* 55*a* (cited above) which is based on the Ezekiel passage. Ḳimḥi, commenting on Ezekiel, remarks that, as stated by Rab, *Tau*, in a judicial pronouncement, could stand for *Tiḥyeh*, 'Thou shalt live', or, equally well, for *Tamut*, 'Thou shalt die', since both words have the same initial: hence the difference between the *Tau* of blood (for sinners) and the *Tau* of ink (for saints). This *motif* is used in the Synagogue hymns, the most noted example being Solomon Gabirol's 'Judge of all the earth' (in stanza 3), which occurs in the New Year Liturgy of the Sefardic rite (*Gaster*, p. 75). The Ashkenazic rite has this hymn on *Kippur* and Nina Salaman's verse translation will be found on p. 86 of the Davis-Adler *Atonement* volume. Her rendering of the *Tau* line is 'Inscribe the seal of life, to be upon their brow for ever.' Michael Sachs (*Festgebete*, *Kippur*, Breslau, 1898, p. 193) gives a German verse rendering: 'O präg ihm auf das Lebensmal! Auf seiner Stirne lass es leuchten alle Zeit.' (H. L.)]

In any case, the righteous stand apart as a separate class, just as the wicked stand apart as a separate and distinct class likewise. Just so do we get the two classes in the Psalms. God knows the righteous, and tries them, and uses them, and rewards them.

[797] A righteous man is not removed from the world till another righteous man like him is created. (*Ḳid.* 72*b* (cp. [617]).)

[798] R. Ḥiyya b. Abba and his disciples [or, as some say, R. Akiba or R. Joshua] used to go and teach under a certain fig tree, and every day the owner of the fig tree used to get up very early and gather the figs. Then they said, 'Let us change our place; perhaps he suspects us.' So they went and sat elsewhere. The owner of the fig tree got up early, and did not find them. He went and looked for them till he found them. He said, 'My masters, you conferred upon me just one privilege, and now you withdraw it from me.' They said, 'Far be that from us.' 'Then why,' he replied, 'did you leave your place, and go elsewhere?' They said, 'We thought you might suspect us.' He said, 'Far be it from me; why I get up early and gather the figs is because, when the sun shines upon them, they become wormy.' So they returned to the old place, and one day they found that he had not gathered the figs. Then they took some, and opened them, and found them wormy. Then they said, 'The owner of the fig tree spoke well; if he knows the season of the figs and when to gather them, so God knows the season of the righteous, and when to take them away, and then He takes them.'

R. Samuel b. Naḥman said: It is like a king who had a garden, and he planted in it a row of nut trees, of apple trees and of pomegranates, and he entrusted the garden to his son. When the son did the will of his father, his father would look and find a beautiful plant somewhere, and would pluck it out by its roots, and would bring it and plant it in the garden. But when the son did not do the will of his father, the father would look for a beautiful plant in the garden, and would tear it out. So, when the Israelites do the will of God, He looks for a righteous man among the nations and joins him to Israel, but when they do not do His will, He looks for a righteous man among Israel, and takes him away. (*Cant.R.* VI, § 2, 2, on VI, 2; f. 33*a*.)

[799] 'I said in mine heart, concerning the estate of the sons of men that God might prove them, and that they might see that they themselves are cattle' (Eccles. III, 18). Concerning the lot of the righteous in this world, in privations, fasts and sufferings, why is this? It is that God might manifest their righteousness. 'And that they might see that they themselves are cattle', means that the nations of the world may see how the Israelites not only follow after God like sheep [cattle] after their shepherd, as it says, 'Ye are the flock of my pasture' (Ezek. XXXIV, 31), but even as the sheep stretches out its neck to the slaughter, so do the righteous, as it says, 'For thy sake are we killed all the day' (Ps XLIV, 22). (*Eccles.R.* III, § 18, 1, on III, 18 (12*a*).)

[800] R. Johanan said: He who conducts himself righteously here below, is judged strictly in the heaven above.

(*Ta'an.* 8*a* (Malter, p. 53).)

Malter's note, *in loc.*, is as follows: 'The thought is that the actions of a prominent man are judged more severely than those of the ordinary man.'

The sufferings of the righteous are to purify them, or to enable them the more assuredly to inherit the life of the world to come:

[801] R. Jonathan said: 'The Lord tries the righteous' (Ps. XI, 5). The potter does not test cracked vessels; it is not worth while to tap them even once, because they would break; but he taps the good ones, because, however many times he taps them, they do not break. Even so God tries, not the wicked, but the righteous. R. Jose b. Ḥanina said: The flax dealer who knows that his

flax is good, pounds it, for it becomes more excellent by his pounding; and when he knocks it, it glistens the more. But when he knows that his flax is bad, he does not knock it at all, for it would split. So God tries, not the wicked, but the righteous. R. Elazar said: A man had two cows, one strong and one weak. Upon which will he lay the yoke? Surely upon the strong. So God tests the righteous.

(*Gen.R.* XXXII, 3 (Th. p. 290; cp. *Tanḥ.B.*, Shemot, x, 3*b* and *Tanḥ.* Wayera, § 20, f. 38*a*); [792] and [1542].)

[802] R. Elazar b. Zadok said: With what may the righteous in this world be compared? To a tree whose trunk stands entirely in a pure place, but its branches extend over to an unclean place. If those branches are cut off, then all the tree is in a pure place. So God imposes sufferings on the righteous in this world that they may inherit the world to come. Similarly, the wicked are like a tree standing in an unclean place, some of whose branches spread over to a clean place. If these are cut down, the entire tree stands in an unclean place. So God gives the wicked abundant good in this world, to drive them down into, and cause them to inherit, the lowest depths of hell. (*Ḳid.* 40*b*.)

The life of the righteous is concentrated on God:

[803] 'The righteous shall flourish like the palm tree: he shall grow like the cedar in Lebanon' (Ps. XCII, 12). As the palm and the cedar have neither crookedness nor excrescences, so the righteous have neither crookedness nor excrescences. As the palm and the cedar throw their shade afar, so the reward of the righteous extends far. As the palm and the cedar strain upwards, so the heart of the righteous is directed towards God. As the palm and the cedar have a desire, so the righteous have a desire, and their desire is God.

(*Gen.R.*, Lek leka, XLI, 1 (Th. p. 386; cp. [251]).)

I may here intercalate the following. The Hebrew noun which we translate by 'righteousness' has in Rabbinical Hebrew various shades of meaning. Sometimes it truly means righteousness, sometimes it means justice, sometimes charity, sometimes mere almsgiving. In the following paean on *Ẓedaḳah* it must have now one meaning and now another, and sometimes it is difficult to say which is the exact meaning intended.

[804] R. Johanan said: Come and see how great is the power of righteousness, for it is placed in the right hand of God, as it is said, 'Thy right hand is full of righteousness' (Ps. XLVIII, 10). Great is righteousness, for God is praised with it in the hour when He brings salvation to Israel, as it is said, 'I that speak with righteousness, mighty to save' (Isa. LXIII, 1). Great is righteousness, for it brings honour and life to those who practise it, as it is said, 'He that follows after righteousness shall find life, righteousness and honour' (Prov. XXI, 21) in the day of judgment. But how does he who follows after righteousness find righteousness? Because God will give him money to do charity with it to men worthy of charity, so that he may receive reward. Great is righteousness, for our father Abraham is praised with righteousness, as it is said, 'And he believed in the Lord, and it was accounted to him as righteousness' (Gen. XV, 6). And it is said, 'For I know him that he may command his children and his household after him, that they may keep the way of the Lord, to do righteousness and justice' (Gen. XVIII, 19). Great is righteousness, for David is praised with righteousness, as it is said, 'And David wrought justice and righteousness to all his people' (II Sam. VIII, 15). Great is righteousness, for with it Solomon is praised, as it is said, 'Because the Lord loved Israel, therefore He made the king to do righteousness and justice' (I Kings X, 9). Great is righteousness, for it reaches to the throne of glory, as it is said, 'Righteousness and justice are the foundations of thy throne' (Ps. LXXXIX, 14). Great is righteousness, for with it Israel is praised, as it is said, 'And it shall be our righteousness, if we observe to do all these commandments' (Deut. VI, 25). Great is righteousness, for with it God will be praised on the day of judgment, as it is said, 'And the holy God shall be sanctified in righteousness, and in justice shall He be exalted' (Isa. V, 16). Great is righteousness, for it accompanies him who practises it in the hour of his departure from the world, as it is said, 'Thy righteousness shall go before thee, and the glory of the Lord shall be thy rereward' (Isa. LVIII, 8).

(*Midr.Prov.* XIV, 34, f. 38*b*.)

The Rabbis do not ascribe the evil inclination specifically to the flesh. We cannot say that they definitely ascribe righteousness to the soul, and sin to the body or to the flesh. On the other hand, the soul is often regarded as in itself pure and sinless. It comes pure from God.

The old Rabbinic prayer, still recited daily, runs thus: 'O my God, the soul which thou gavest me is pure; thou didst create it, thou didst form it, thou didst breathe it into me; thou preservest it within me; and thou wilt take it from me, but wilt restore it unto me hereafter. So long as the soul is within me, I will give thanks unto thee, O Lord my God and God of my fathers, Sovereign of all works, Lord of all souls! Blessed art thou, O Lord, who restorest souls unto dead bodies' (*P.B.* p. 5). We find passages like the following:

[805] R. Phinehas and R. Ḥilkiah in the name of R. Simeon said: When does the spirit return to God who gave it? (Eccles. XII, 7). When the dust returns to the earth as it was, but it is also said, 'The souls of thine enemies He will sling out' (I Sam. XXV, 29). R. Ishmael b. R. Naḥman taught in the name of R. Abdimi of Haifa: It is like a learned and particular priest who gave an ignorant priest a portion of the heave offering, and said, 'I am clean, and my house is clean; if you return it to me in the same condition, all is well; if not, I will throw it down before you.' So God says to man, 'Behold, I am pure, and my dwelling-place is pure, and my ministers are pure, and the soul which I have given you is pure. If you return it to me in the same condition, all is well; but if not, I will tear it in pieces before you.'

(*Lev.R.*, Meẓora', XVIII, 1.)

[806] The Rabbis say: As the spirit was given to thee pure, so return it pure. (*Sab.* 152*b.*)

The relation of soul and body is discussed in a well-known argument:

[807] R. Ishmael said that the matter resembled a king who had a garden with fine early figs. He put two keepers in it, one was blind, and one was lame, and he bade them to look well after the figs. After a time the lame man said to the blind man, I see some fine figs in the garden. The blind man said, 'Bring me to them, and we will eat.' The lame man said, 'I cannot walk.' The blind man said, 'I cannot see.' Then the lame man got on the shoulders of the blind man, and they went and ate the figs. After a time the king came to the garden, and he asked, 'Where are the figs?' The blind man said, 'Can I see?' The lame man said, 'Can I walk?' But the king was clever; he set the lame man on the shoulders of the blind man, and made them walk a little, and he said, 'Even so have you managed, and you have eaten the

figs.' So, in the world to come, God says to the soul, 'Wherefore have you sinned before me?' The soul replies, 'I have not sinned; the body has sinned; since I have come out of the body, I have flown about like an innocent bird in the air; what is my sin?' Then God says to the body, 'Why have you sinned before me?' The body replies, 'I have not sinned; it is the soul which has sinned; from the hour that the soul went out of me, I lie prone like a stone cast upon the ground. How can I have sinned against thee?' What does God do? He brings the soul and casts it into the body, and judges the two together.

R. Ḥiyya said: It is like a priest who had two wives, the one was the daughter of a priest, the other of a layman. He gave them some dough which belonged to the heave offering, and they allowed it to become unclean. He asked, 'Which of you did this?' Each accused the other. Then the priest let the daughter of the layman alone, and began to condemn the daughter of the priest. She said, 'Why do you leave her alone and condemn me? You gave the dough to the two of us together.' He replied, 'She is the daughter of a layman, and was not taught about these things in the house of her father, but you are the daughter of a priest, and were taught in the house of your father. Therefore I leave her alone, and condemn you.' So will it be in the world to come with the body and the soul when they come to judgment. God will let the body alone, and condemn the soul. Then the soul will say, 'We have sinned together, why dost thou leave the body alone, and condemn me?' God answers, 'The body belongs to the lower sphere, to the place where they sin; but you belong to the upper sphere, where they do not sin; therefore I leave the body alone and condemn you.'

(*Lev.R.*, Wayiḳra, IV, 5.)

[This story is one of the comparatively rare indications of the existence of polygamy: it is a story, and not a fact, and it must not be pressed. No Rabbi is known to have had more than one (living) wife, but the legal possibility is discussed at length. For the Rabbinic aversion to the custom, see *J.E.* s.v. 'Polygamy' (cp. [1431)]. (H. L.)]

[808] It says in Lev. IV, 2, 'If a soul sins in ignorance.' But the soul comes from a place where there is no iniquity or sin. So the Scripture marvels that a soul can sin in ignorance. Two men sinned against a king, one a villager, and one a man brought up

in the palace. The king let the villager go, and pronounced sentence on the other. His courtiers said to him, 'Both committed a similar sin; yet you let one go, and sentenced the other.' He replied, 'I let the villager go, because he did not know the laws of the kingdom, but the courtier was continually with me, and knew what the laws of the kingdom are, and what judgment is pronounced against one who offends against me.' So the body is a villager—'God fashioned man from the dust of the ground'—but the soul is a courtier from above—'He breathed into his nostrils a soul of life.' And they both sin; for there is [on earth] no soul without body, and no body without soul. 'The soul that sins, it shall die' (Ezek. XVIII, 20).

(*Tanḥ.B.*, Wayiḳra, 4*a fin.*, 4*b* (Moore, I, 488).)

[809] R. Simai says that in regard to all the creatures who were created from the heavens, their bodies and souls are heavenly, and as to all the creatures that were created from the earth, their bodies and souls are earthly; man is the exception, for his body is earthly, but his soul is heavenly; therefore if man fulfils the Law, and does the will of his Father in heaven, then he is like the creatures above; but if not, then he is like the creatures below. (*Sifre Deut.*, Ha'azinu, § 306, f. 132*a*.)

Interesting too are the following:

[810] 'All the labour of man is for his mouth, yet the soul [A.V. 'appetite'] is not filled' [i.e. satisfied] (Eccles. VI, 7). R. Ḥanina b. Isaac said: 'The soul is not filled,' for the soul knows that all its travail is for itself, therefore it is insatiable for Torah and good works. It is like a villager who married the daughter of a king; whatever he brings her she regards as nothing, for she is a king's daughter. So with the soul; if all the delights of this world are brought to her, they are to her as nothing, for she belongs to the world above.

(*Eccles.R.* VI, § 6 (in some edd. 7), 1, on VI, 7 (17*a*).)

[811] Once when Hillel left his disciples, they said to him, 'Whither are you going?' He replied, 'To do a kindness to a guest in the house.' They said, 'Have you every day a guest?' He said, 'Yes, is not the soul[1] a guest in the body? To-day it is here, to-morrow it is gone.' (*Lev.R.*, Behar, XXXIV, 3 (cp. [1271].)

[1] *Mattenot Kehunnah* says: 'The soul which is oppressed by the conduct of the body.' See Levy's rendering of '*Aluv*.

Chapter XII

MAN'S REPENTANCE AND GOD'S COMPASSION

On the whole, the Rabbis take a wholesome view of life and of man's relation to God and of God's relation to man. So far from the ordinary view being accurate that the Jewish God is a God of stern justice, the very opposite would be nearer the truth. The Rabbinic God is a God of tender compassion. Unrepentant and high-handed must be the sinner whom God finally and irretrievably condemns. There are, indeed, sometimes, notes of stern severity and pitiless hardness in the Rabbinic God's attitude to the wicked, but we have to make diverse qualifications as regards this severity and hardness. They are, I think, found largely in passages where it is sought to make and bring out a sharp contrast between the righteous and the wicked. If the former go to heaven, the latter must go to hell; if the former are rewarded exceedingly, the latter are punished exceedingly, and so on. We have also to admit that for certain definite Israelite sinners, such as apostates, heretics, informers, there was, generally speaking, in the eyes of the Rabbis, no place after death but hell, though even to this rule there are exceptions. The same would be true as regards the oppressors of Israel, the nations who were enemies of Israel and of God. But the Rabbis have far more often Jews in their minds than non-Jews. Their teaching is for Jews, not for Gentiles. As we have already seen, there was a certain fear that the lovingkindness of God might be stressed so greatly that it might be misinterpreted, and even tempt lower natures to wrongdoing. 'God will forgive. It is His *métier*.' Nevertheless, the compassion of God is much more often insisted on than His severity. The attribute of lovingkindness is more powerful than the attribute of justice. The essential tenderness, the desire to bring back, to save, to forgive, of the Rabbinic God are most strikingly shown in the endless passages about repentance. We hear, indeed, a good deal about *repentance* (*teshubah*, lit. return) in the O.T., but the subject is enormously developed and deepened by the Rabbis.

Here are some passages taken largely at random, but all more or less interesting or beautiful. The story about R. Elazar b. Durdaya is one of the finest and most dramatic of all the Rabbinic stories. It is a pity that a few lines in it, owing to a difference between our modern and western ideas of good taste and Rabbinic and oriental ideas, have to be omitted.

[812] Be not like the fools who, when they sin, bring an offering, but do not repent. They know not the difference between good and evil, and yet venture to make an offering to God. (*Ber.* 23*a*.)

[813] As soiled garments can be cleansed, so the Israelites, albeit they sin, can return by repentance unto the Lord.

(*Exod.R.*, Beshallaḥ, XXIII, 10.)

[814] R. Helbo said to R. Samuel b. Naḥmani: 'Since I have heard that you are a good Haggadist, tell me the meaning of Lam. III, 44, "Thou hast covered thyself with a cloud that our prayers should not pass through."' He replied, 'Prayer is likened to a bath, repentance to the sea. As the bath is sometimes open and sometimes shut, so the gates of prayer are sometimes shut and sometimes open, but as the sea is always open, so the gates of repentance are always open. When a man wishes to bathe in the sea, he can bathe in it at any hour he likes. So with repentance, whenever a man wishes to repent, God will receive him.' But R. Anan said: The gates of prayer, too, are never shut.

(*Lam.R.* III, 60, on III, 43 (cp. *Midr.Ps.* on LXV, 5 (157*a*, § 4)) (cp. [1105]).)

[815] These are man's intercessors: repentance and good deeds.

(*Sab.* 32*a*.)

Then, on the basis of Job XXXIII, 23, it is said that if nine hundred and ninety-nine 'messengers' accuse him, and only one tell of his merits, he is saved.

[816] 'And Cain went out' (Gen. IV, 16). On his way Cain met Adam, who said to him, 'What has happened as regards the judgment passed upon you?' Cain replied, 'I repented, and I am pardoned.' When Adam heard that, he smote his face and said, 'Is the power of repentance as great as that? I did not know it was so.' (*Lev.R.*, Ẓaw, X, 5 (cp. [858]).)

[817] In II Chron. XXXIII, 11–13 it is said of Manasseh that the king of Assyria took Manasseh and 'bound him with fetters and carried him to Babylon. And when he was in affliction he besought the Lord his God, and humbled himself greatly before the God of his fathers, and prayed unto Him. And He was intreated of him, and heard his supplication, and brought him again to Jerusalem into his kingdom. Then Manasseh knew that the Lord He was God.' The Midrash develops this legend as follows: They prepared for him a bronze cauldron (lit. mule), and threw him within it, and kindled under it a fire, and he was scorched inside. Then he called upon all the gods of the world to whom he had sacri-

ficed, and they did not answer him. Then in his distress he called on the Lord, and said, 'I have called on all the gods of the world, and I realise that there is no reality in them. Thou art God over all the gods, but if thou answerest me not, I may think that all the gods, including thee, are equal.' God said to him, 'You wicked one; you deserve that I should not answer you, for you have provoked me to anger, but so as not to shut the door upon the repentant, lest they should say, "Manasseh sought to repent, but was not received," therefore I will answer you.' The angels of the service stopped up the windows of the firmament, so that Manasseh's prayer should not ascend to heaven, but God broke through the firmament under the throne of His glory, and received his prayer. [There is an untranslatable pun upon the Hebrew word for 'he was entreated', which in sound closely resembles the word 'he broke through'.] (*Deut.R.*, Wa'etḥanan, II, 20.)

[818] If a man were to come and say that God does not receive the penitent, Manasseh would come and testify against him, for there was never a man more wicked than he, and yet, in the hour of his repentance, God received him, as it is said, 'He prayed unto God, and God was entreated of him' (II Chron. XXXIII, 13). (*Num.R.*, Naso, XIV, I (cp. [1655]).)

[819] R. Jose ben Ṭarṭos said: Whence can it be proved that he who repents is regarded as if he had gone up to Jerusalem, built the Temple and the altar, and offered upon it all the sacrifices mentioned in the Law? From the verse, 'The sacrifices of God are a broken spirit' (Ps. LI, 17). (*Lev.R.*, Ẓaw, VII, 2.)

The practical, and, one might say, the common-sense, side of the Rabbis is shown in R. Judah's definition as to what constitutes full and genuine repentance. 'The proof of the pudding' is to be shown, not in a man's emotions and contritions, but in his refraining from sin when the old opportunity and situation recur:

[820] 'Who is the penitent man?' R. Judah said: The man who, when the same opportunity for sin occurs once or twice, refrains from sinning. He added: The same woman, the same season, the same place. (*Yoma* 86*b*.)

[821] 'Open to me, my sister.' R. Issi said: God says to the Israelites, open to me, my children, the gate of repentance as minutely as the point of a needle, and I will open for you gates wide enough

for carriages and waggons to enter through them. R. Levi said: If the Israelites would but repent for one day, they would be redeemed, and the son of David would come straight away, as it says, 'To-day, if ye would hear his voice' (Ps. XCV, 7). (*Cant.R.* V, § 2, 2, on V, 2; 30*a* (cp. [1617]).)

The law of Deut. XXIV, 1–4 about divorce is quoted. If *A* divorces his wife and she marries *B*, and *B* also divorces her, she may not return to *A* to be his wife anew:

[822] But God is not so. Even though Israel has deserted Him, and served other gods, He says, 'Return unto me, repent, and I will receive you.' So Jeremiah, too, applies the same contrast, and says, 'Though thou hast played the harlot with many lovers, yet return again to me and I will receive you' (Jer. III, 1). (*Pes.R.* 184*a*.)

[823] It says in the [very corrupt] verse (Deut. XXXII, 5), 'They are not His children: it is their blemish': *when* their blemish is in them, they are not His children, but when their blemish is *not* in them, they *are* His children.
(*Sifre Num.*, Shelaḥ, § 112, f. 33*a fin.*–33*b init.* (H. p. 121; cp. [270]).)

The famous sentence from *Yoma* is quoted that the Day of Atonement does not bring forgiveness of sins to any man till he has appeased, and sought pardon from, his neighbour whom he has wronged. But suppose that neighbour refuses to forgive him, what then?

[824] R. Samuel b. Naḥman said: Let him bring ten men, and set them in a row, and say before them, 'There was a quarrel between me and so-and-so, and I sought to be reconciled to him, yet he would not receive me, but abides in his refusal, whereas I have humbled myself before him.' Then God will see that he has humbled himself, and God will forgive him; but so long as a man stays in his stiffness, God does not forgive him. And Job was forgiven by God only when he forgave, and prayed for, his friends. (*Pes.R.* 165*a* (cp. p. 97 and [836]).)

[825] R. Alexander said: If a mortal man uses broken vessels, it is a disgrace, but with God it is otherwise, for all His servants [lit. service] are broken vessels, as it is said, 'The Lord is nigh to the broken-hearted, and the contrite in spirit will He save' (Ps. XXXIV, 18; CXLVII, 3). (*Pes.K.* 158*b*.)

[826] It is written, 'Good and upright is the Lord, therefore He will instruct sinners in the way' (Ps. xxv, 8). They asked Wisdom, 'What shall be the punishment of the sinner?' Wisdom answered, 'Evil pursues sinners' (Prov. xiii, 21). They asked Prophecy. It replied, 'The soul that sins shall die' (Ezek. xviii, 4). They asked the Law. It replied, 'Let him bring a sacrifice' (Lev. i, 4). They asked God, and He replied, 'Let him repent, and obtain his atonement. My children, what do I ask of you? Seek me and live.' (*Pes.K.* xxv, 158*b*.)

It may be worth while to give an instance of the ingenious way in which the Rabbis play with the words of Scripture:

[827] 'The Lord' [Yahweh] is the name of the Deity as the Merciful One: Elohim [God] is the Deity as judge. The consonants of '*od*, 'while' can also be read as '*ad*, 'unto'. Hosea (xiv, 2) says: 'Return *unto* the Lord, thy God.' So, R. Me'ir said: Repent while ['*od*] He is standing upon the attribute of mercy: if not, He will be 'thy God' [i.e. Judge]; repent while the advocate has not yet become the accuser. (*Pes.K.* 164*a* (Moore, i, 387).)

[828] God says to the Israelites, 'Repent before I return to the attribute of judgment, for then I should not know how to act; repent while I stand upon the attribute of mercy, and then I can receive you.' (*Pes.R.* 182*b fin.*)

[829] It is written, 'Commit thyself unto the Lord' (Ps. xxii, 8; the Hebrew word is *gol*). So too it says, 'Commit unto the Lord thy way' (Ps. xxxvii, 5, where the Hebrew word is again *gol*). R. Bebai, in the name of Rab, said: The word *gol* comes either from *galah*, in which case the words mean, reveal, i.e. confess, your sins, as it says, 'Whoso confesses and forsakes his sins shall obtain mercy' (Prov. xxviii, 13), or it comes from *galgel* [it really is the imperative of *galal*, to roll], in which case it means, 'Roll them upon me, and I will carry them,' as it is said, 'Cast thy burden upon the Lord, and He shall sustain thee' (Ps. lv, 22). R. Johanan said: It is like the son of a king, to whom they gave a thick beam to carry. His father saw it and said, 'Lay upon me all that you wish, and I will carry it.' So God says to the Israelites, 'Roll your sins upon me, and I will carry them.' (*Midr.Ps.* on xxii, 8 (96*b*, § 22).)

[830] Our Rabbis have taught: If a man is guilty of a sin and confesses it, but does not change his way, unto what is he like? He is like a man who holds a reptile in his hand, to whom, though he should immerse himself in all the waters of the world, it will avail nothing; but as soon as he throws away the defiling reptile, an immersion in forty *se'ah* of water will be accounted to him as a cleansing bath, as it is said, 'But whoso confesses and forsakes them shall obtain mercy' (Prov. XXVIII, 13), and as it is further said, 'Let us lift up our heart with our hands unto God in the heavens' (Lam. III, 41).

(*Ta'an.* 16*a* (Malter's translation, p. 112).)

For 'Our Rabbis have taught' (*Baraita*) cp. p. 216.

[831] R. Bebai b. Zabdai, R. Tanḥum bar Ḥanilai and R. Josiah went out together on a fast day, and R. Bebai explained the verses, 'Let us search and try our ways, and turn again to the Lord.' 'Let us lift up our heart with our hands unto God in the heavens.' He said: Is it possible for the heart of a man to be taken out of him and put back again? But the verse means: Let us make our hearts like our hands in cleanness, and then let us return to the Lord. If a man holds an unclean thing in his hand, he may dip in all the seas of creation, and he will never become clean. Let him throw away the unclean thing, and a very small amount of water will suffice. Then R. Tanḥum spoke on II Chron. XII, 6, where it is said that the princes of Israel humbled themselves, and God was gracious to them. It is not said that God saw that they fasted, but He saw that they humbled themselves. [The sound of the two verbs is in Hebrew much alike.] Lastly, R. Josiah spoke on Zeph. II, 1, 'Correct yourselves.' First, let us correct *ourselves*; then only let us seek to correct others.

(*Lam.R.* III, 50 on III, 40 (cp. *T.J.Ta'an.* II, § 1, f. 65*a*, line 66).)

[832] R. Judah Nesiah said in the name of R. Judah b. Simeon: If a man shoots an arrow, it may reach one field's length or two, but greater is the power of repentance, for it reaches unto the throne of glory. (*Pes.K.* 163*b*.)

[833] If your sins are as high as heaven, even unto the seventh heaven, and even to the throne of glory, and you repent, I will receive you.

(*Pes.R.* 185*a*.)

[834] To an earthly king, a man goes full, and returns empty; to God, he goes empty, and returns full. (*Pes.R.* 185*a*.)

[835] A king had a son who had gone astray from his father a journey of a hundred days; his friends said to him, 'Return to your father'; he said, 'I cannot.' Then his father sent to say, 'Return as far as *you* can, and *I* will come to you the rest of the way.' So God says, 'Return to me, and I will return to you.'

(*Pes.R.* 184*b fin.*–185*a init.*)

[836] R. Elazar said: If a man treats his fellow with contempt in public, and afterwards seeks to be reconciled with him, the other says, 'You treated me contemptuously in public, and now you want to be reconciled with me between ourselves. Go and bring the men before whom you treated me contemptuously; then I will be reconciled with you.' But God does not act thus. A man stands and reviles and blasphemes Him in the open street, and God says, 'Repent between ourselves, and I will receive you.'

(*Pes.K.* 163*b* (cp. [824]).)

[837] It is written, 'They shall be ashamed who deal treacherously' (Ps. XXV, 3). These are they who fast without repentance.

(*Midr.Ps.* on XXV, 2 *fin.* (106*a*, § 5 *fin.*).)

This saying shows that the Rabbis clearly realised a danger to which the observance of the Day of Atonement was exposed (cp. [524] and [411]).

[838] Let not a man after he has sinned say, 'There is no restoration for me,' but let him trust in the Lord and repent, and God will receive him. Let him not say, 'If I confess, I shall lose my office,' but let him hate office, and humble himself, and return in repentance. (*Midr.Ps.* on XL, 4 (129*a fin.*, § 3).)

[839] 'Teach us to number our days' (Ps. XC, 12). R. Joshua said: If we knew exactly the number of our days, we should repent before we die. R. Eliezer said: Repent one day before you die. His disciples said, 'Who knows when he will die?' 'All the more, then, let him repent to-day, for peradventure he will die to-morrow. The result will be that all his life will be spent in repentance.' (*Midr.Ps.* on XC, 12 (197*a*, § 16) (cp. p. 233).)

[840] 'My heart bubbles up with a good matter' (Ps. XLV, 1). This verse tells you that men can make right confession with their

mouths only when their hearts bubble up with repentance, and then God will receive them. (*Midr.Ps.* on XLV, 1 (135*b*, §4).)

[841] 'He that covers his transgressions shall not prosper, but whoso confesses and forsakes them shall obtain mercy' (Prov. XXVIII, 13). R. Simeon said: If a man confesses his sin to a human tribunal, he is punished; if he does not, he may be acquitted; but God acts otherwise; if a man does not confess, he is punished; if he confesses, he is acquitted. (*Midr.Ps.* on C, 1 (213*a*, §2).)

[842] R. Elazar b. Durdaya was a great sinner, and much addicted to sexual offences. On one occasion he heard of a beautiful courtesan in a distant land who demanded a purse full of *denarii* as her price. So R. Elazar took a purse full of *denarii*, and crossed seven rivers to the place where she lived. [While he was with her, something happened at which, in the story, the courtesan—very incongruously and out of character!—called out that R. Durdaya would never be received in repentance by God.] Then he went away, and sat between two hills, and said, 'Ye hills and mountains, pray for compassion upon me.' But they said, 'Before we seek for compassion for you, we must seek compassion for ourselves,' as it is said, 'For the mountains shall depart and the hills be removed' (Isa. LIV, 10). Then he said, 'Earth and heaven, seek for mercy upon me.' But they said, 'Before we seek mercy for you, we must seek it for ourselves,' as it is said, 'For the heavens shall vanish away like smoke, and the earth wax old like a garment' (Isa. LI, 6). Then he said, 'Sun and moon, seek for mercy upon me.' But they said, 'Before we seek mercy for you, we must seek it for ourselves,' as it is said, 'The moon shall be confounded and the sun ashamed' (Isa. XXIV, 23). Then he said, 'Ye stars and planets, seek for mercy upon me.' But they said, 'Before we seek mercy for you, we must seek it for ourselves,' as it is said, 'All the host of heaven shall be dissolved' (Isa. XXXIV, 4). Then he said, 'The matter depends wholly on me.' And he sank his head between his knees, and he cried out and wept until his soul passed out of his body. Then a heavenly voice was heard to say: 'R. Elazar b. Durdaya is appointed for the life of the world to come.' And Rabbi Judah the Prince wept and said, 'There are those who can but attain the world to come in how many years, and there are those who attain it in an hour!' And he said, 'It is not

enough that the repentant are received into the life to come, but they are even called Rabbis.' (**Note 38**.) (*Ab.Zar.* 17*a*.)

[843] Sin offering and guilt offering and death and the Day of Atonement, all of them together, do not expiate sin without repentance. (*T.Yoma* v, 9 (Z. p. 190, line 22).)

This is the best, and, probably, the most prevailing, Rabbinic view (cp. *R.T.* p. 396, n. 4).

[844] God says, 'My hands are stretched out towards the penitent; I reject no creature who gives me his heart in penitence.' Therefore it says, 'Peace, peace, to the far and to the near. To all who draw near to me I draw near, and I heal them.' (*Midr.Ps.* on CXX, 7 (253*a*, §7).)

[845] It is difficult for repentant tax and custom collectors to make restitution [of fraudulent exactions]. They should recompense those whom they know they have defrauded, and the balance should be devoted to public needs. (*T.Bab.M.* VIII, 26 (Z. p. 390).)

[846] There is nothing greater than repentance. It is written in Deut. XXX, 2, 'If thou return unto the Lord.' R. Me'ir said: To what is the matter like? To a king's son who turned to evil courses. The king sent his tutor to him to say, 'Turn again, my son.' But the son sent to his father to say, 'With what face can I return? I am ashamed before thee.' Then the father sent to him again to say, 'Can a son be ashamed to return to his father?' So God sent Jeremiah to the Israelites in the hour of their sin, and He bade the prophet, 'Tell my children to return' [i.e. to repent] (Jer. III, 12). The Israelites said, 'With what face can we return,' as it is said, 'We lie down in our shame' (Jer. III, 25). Then God replied to them, 'My children, if you return, is it not to your Father that you return?' As it is said, 'I am a Father to Israel' (Jer. XXXI, 9). (*Deut.R.*, Wa'ethanan, II, 24.)

[847] There is no man who is not in debt to [i.e. guilty before] God, but He is gracious and compassionate, and forgives our former sins, as it is said, 'Thou rememberest not against us former iniquities' (Ps. LXXIX, 8). Like a man who borrowed from a moneylender, and forgot. After a time he came again, and said to him, 'I know I am in debt to you,' and the moneylender

replied, 'Why do you remind me of this former debt? It had passed from my mind.' So when men sin before God, and He notices that they repent not, He allows the former sins to slide, for when they *do* at last repent and come before Him, and recall their former sins, He says, 'Do not remember former things.' Whence can it be shown that if a man returns and repents, even if he has committed many iniquities, they are regarded as merits? Because (Ezek. XXXIII, 19) 'If the wicked turn from his wickedness and do justly and righteously, *by them* he shall live.' [The Midrash playfully takes 'them' to refer to the 'sins'; if he 'lives' by them, that means that they are regarded as virtues.]

(*Exod.R.*, Mishpaṭim, XXXI, 1 (cp. *Pes.R.* 184*a*).)

[848] 'Against thee only have I sinned, that thou mightest be justified' (Ps. LI, 4). With whom may we compare David? With a man who has sustained an injury, and gone to the doctor. The doctor marvels, and says to him, 'How great is your wound; I am distressed about you.' The man replies, 'You are distressed about me? Is it not for your advantage that I have been wounded, for the fee is yours?' So David said to God, 'For thee, thee only, have I sinned, so that thou mayest say to transgressors, Why do you not repent? If thou receivest *me*, then all transgressors will surrender to thee, and all will look at me, and I shall be a witness that thou receivest the penitent.'

(*Midr.Ps.* on LI, 4 (141*a*, §3).)

This passage depends upon the Hebrew preposition meaning both 'against' and 'for', 'to thy advantage'.

[849] R. Hezekiah b. Ḥiyya said: When Moses fell before the Lord, and sought pardon for Israel on account of the calf, God listened to his plea, because he invoked the merits of the patriarchs, who, like Abraham, interceded for the guilty. What[1] did God do? He wrapped Himself in his *ṭallit* [mantle used during prayers], like a precentor who 'passes before' the Ark to read the *Amidah*, and He said to Moses, 'Thus shalt thou pray, saying, "The Lord, merciful and gracious", etc.' (Exod. XXXIV, 6). For it says there, 'The Lord passed before.' See, therefore, how the righteous entreat grace for the whole world and plead for Israel, and not

[1] The following is related by R. Phinehas b. Ḥama in the name of R. Simeon and by R. Abin in the name of R. Aḥa.

for Israel alone, but even for the wicked, as it says, 'As I live, I desire not the death of any sinner' (Ezek. XXXIII, 11). Why? Peradventure he may repent. This we see from the story of Sodom, when God took counsel with Abraham, who pleaded for the men of Sodom because they might repent.[1]

(*Tanḥ.B.*, Wayera, 46*a* (cp. [104] and [1652].)

[850] See how wonderful a thing is repentance! God says, 'If ye return unto me, I will return unto you' (Mal. III, 7). For however many sins a man may have committed, if he return to God all are forgiven; He accounts it to him as though he had not sinned (Ezek. XVIII, 22). But if he does not return, God warns him once, twice, thrice. *Then*, if the man return not, God exacts punishment. (*Tanḥ.B.*, Wayera, 47*b*.)

[851] Isaiah said, 'Peace, peace, to him that is far and to him that is near, says the Lord, and I will heal him' (Isa. LVII, 19). Who is he that is far? He that has made himself far from God. But what healing does the man need who is near to God? The words refer to the wicked man who *was* far from God, but who repented, and so brought himself near. (*Pes.R.* 184*b*.)

[852] A king's son was sick, and the doctor said that if he would eat a certain thing, he would be healed. But the son was frightened to eat it. His father said to him, 'So that you may know that it will not harm you, I will eat of it.' Thus God said to Israel, 'You are ashamed to repent; behold, I will be the first to repent,' as it says, 'Behold I repent' [a playful mistranslation of Jer. XXX, 18]. Now if one in whom there is neither sin nor corruption says, 'Behold I repent,' how much more must the sons of men repent. (*Pes.R.* 184*a*.)

[853] One of the disciples of Rabbi Akiba, who sat at the head of Akiba's four and twenty [thousand] pupils, was once passing through the street of the harlots, and he saw a woman there and loved her. He sent a go-between to her, and made an appointment for that evening. Towards evening the woman went on to the roof of her house, whence she beheld this disciple sitting at the head of the rest as a prince over a host, and Gabriel was at his right hand. She said to herself, 'Woe to me that all the

[1] To pass before the Ark is a technical term for reading, not *any* part of the Service, but only the *Amidah* (*P.B.* p. 44).

punishments of hell are waiting for me. Such a great man, like unto a king! And shall I bring him to ruin, so that when I die, and leave this world, I inherit hell? But he will listen to me, I will rescue both him and me from hell.' When he came to her, she said to him, 'My son, why wouldst thou lose the life of the world to come for one hour of this world?' But his passion was not diminished until she said to him, 'My son, what thou desirest is the foulest of all things.' At last he listened to her persuasion, and was chaste from that moment, and a heavenly voice went forth saying, 'That man and that woman are appointed for the life to come.'

(*Tan.d.b.El.* (Pseudo-Seder Eliahu Zuṭa, p. 39).)

[854] R. Eliezer said: God sits upon His glorious throne with His hands outstretched beneath the wings of the living creatures (Ezek. I, 8) towards the penitent, and He says, 'O, when will Israel repent perfectly before me?' But day by day the Attribute of Justice stands in his might before God Almighty, and says, 'Sovereign of the Universe, it is written in the Torah, "Ye shall not swear by my name falsely" (Lev. XIX, 12), yet Israel rise early and go into the streets and swear falsely: they covet their neighbours' wives: they slander their fellows: dost thou respect persons[1] [that thou dost not punish them?' But God replies, 'Yes], but Israel rise from their beds, and sanctify My name twice each day: scholars go early to the Synagogue and the houses of study: the common folk go to the Synagogue, and the children to school: they circumcise their flesh, and they are full of commandments. And, moreover, I have created for them repentance which is equal to the Torah, and yet you say that I respect persons.'

(*Tan.d.b.El.* (Pseudo-Seder Eliahu Zuṭa, p. 37).)

[855] Repentance is greater than prayer, for Moses' prayer to enter the land was not received, but the repentance of Rahab the harlot was received.... Repentance is greater than almsgiving, for in almsgiving there is loss, but in repentance there is no loss, and God seeks from Israel only repentance and words, as it says, 'Take words, and repent unto the Lord' (Hos. XIV, 2).

(*Tan.d.b.El.* (Pseudo-Seder Eliahu Zuṭa, p. 37).)

[1] There is a gap in the text, but the portion in square brackets may be inferred.

[856] Balaam said to the angel: 'I have sinned' (Num. XXII, 34), for he knew that nothing can stand between a man and punishment save repentance. For the angel has no power to touch any sinner who says, 'I repent.' (*Tanḥ.B.*, Balaḳ, 70*a*.)

[857] A marked tendency of the Rabbis is to limit, in every possible way, the number of those Israelites who will have no share in the world to come. For those who repent no sin is a bar to the everlasting felicities. Thus it says in Num. XV, 30, 31, that the man who 'does anything presumptuously, who, despising the word of the Lord, breaks the Lord's commandments', *he* shall be utterly cut off: his iniquity shall be upon him. On these verses the *Sifre* observes: Even if he has repented? No, it means: His iniquity is upon him so long as he has *not* repented, but not when he *has* repented.

(*Sifre Num.*, Shelaḥ, § 112, f. 33*a* (H. p. 121; cp. [659]).)

[858] Cain at first attempted to exculpate himself. Among other pleas he said, 'Lord of the universe! All my days I have never known or seen one slain. Could I have known that if I smote him with a stone [from the ground] he would die?' God at once answered him, 'Then cursed art thou from the ground.' Cain said again, 'Then hast thou informers who slander man to thee? My own father and mother, who are on earth, know not that I slew him, and thou, who art in heaven, whence knowest thou?' God said to him, 'Fool, the entire world do I bear' (Isa. XLVI, 4). 'Then if thou canst bear the whole world, canst thou not bear my sin? Truly, too great is my sin to be borne!' Then said God, 'Since thou repentest, go forth into exile.' When Cain went forth, the earth shook beneath him, the beasts rose up to devour him, saying, 'This is Cain who slew Abel; against him God has decreed exile, let us destroy him.' At that hour tears welled forth from Cain's eyes, and he cried out, 'Whither shall I go from thy spirit...even in the uttermost parts of the sea may thy hand uphold me' (Ps. CXXXIX, 7).

(*Tanḥ.*, Bereshit, § 9, f. 12*b* (cp. [816]).)

The Hebrew for 'informers' is the Latin *delatores*, as frequently. The evil done by these imperial informers was as great in the provinces as in Rome, and the choice of this Latin word indicates their activity against Jews also.

[859] R. Joshua b. Levi said: The Israelites made the Golden Calf only to give an opening [defence] to the repentant. R. Simeon b. Yoḥai said: David was not suited for his sin, and the Israelites were not suited for their sin. Why did they commit them? In order that if an individual sin, he may say, 'Look at that individual' [i.e. at David], and if the community sin, they may say, 'Look at that community' [i.e. my repentance may be accepted by God who accepted David's and the Israelites']. Both were needed, for if we knew only of the forgiveness of the individual [David], we might say, 'His sin was not in public, but the sin of the community is open and public': and if we knew only of the forgiveness of the community, we might say, 'This does not hold for the individual, for the good deeds of the community are many, but the merit of the individual is small.' (*Ab.Zar.* 4*b fin.*–5*a init.* (cp. pp. 225, 351).)

Let me here quote the following illuminating passages from Moore: 'The Law stands first among the seven things which were created before the creation of the world, and repentance is next to it. This collocation is not accidental. That God did not make the Law, with all its commandments and prohibitions and its severe penalties, without knowing that no man could keep it, nor without creating a way by which his fault might be condoned, is as firm a conviction as there is in all the Jewish thought of God. Repentance must therefore be coeval with Law.' (Vol. I, p. 266.)

'The reflection which thus gives repentance a premundane existence in the plan of God is obvious from the other members of the group—the Law, paradise, hell. God knew that the man He purposed to create, with his freedom and his native evil impulse, would sin against the revealed will of God in His law and incur not only its temporal penalties in this life, but the pains of hell. He must therefore have provided beforehand the remedy for sin, repentance.' (Vol. I, pp. 526, 527.)

'Shame' is a sort of equivalent or synonym for repentance:

[860] Rab said: Whoever commits a transgression, and is filled with shame thereby, all his sins are forgiven him. (*Ber.* 12*b*.)

So, too, to confess your sins is looked upon as repentance, and was supposed to bring forgiveness.

The more prevailing and usual doctrine seems to be that 'it is never too late to mend', and so, 'it is never too late to repent', but sometimes the view is taken that there comes a point when, by habitual lapses or uninterrupted sin, a man cannot repent. The power of repentance is taken from him. The biblical story of the hardening of Pharaoh's heart is explained in that way. It is also said that God gave extension of time or delay to the generation of the Flood, to the builders of the tower of Babel, and to the inhabitants of Sodom, in order that they might repent, but they did not do so, and God did not finally decide on their destruction till they had made their wickedness full and complete before Him (*Mek.*[2] p. 133; cp. the biblical phrase in Gen. xv, 16):

[861] God strengthens the power of the righteous to do His will. 'Who is a teacher like unto Him' (Job xxxvi, 22), in that He teaches the way to repentance? So did God teach the wicked Pharaoh to repent, in that He was pleased to send no plague until He had warned Pharaoh to repent.

(*Exod.R.*, Wa'era, xii, 1 (cp. *Exod.R.*, Wa'era, ix, 9).)

[862] 'God hardened the heart of Pharaoh.' R. Johanan said this verse gives an opening to heretics to say, 'It was not in his power to repent.' But R. Simeon b. Laḳish quoted Prov. iii, 34, 'Surely He scorns the scorners,' and said: God warns men once, twice and thrice, and if then they do not repent, He shuts their heart, so that they cannot repent, and so that He may punish them for their sin. So after God had sent five times to Pharaoh, and Pharaoh had paid no heed to God's words, God said, 'Thou hast stiffened thy neck, and hardened thy heart; behold, now I add uncleanness to thy uncleanness.'

(*Exod.R.*, Bo, xiii, 3 (cp. ix, 9).)

[863] R. Phinehas b. Ḥama ha-Kohen said: After God has waited for the wicked to repent, and they do not, then, if at the last they desire to repent, He removes from them the power. Even if they wish to return to the Lord, and seek to pray, they are unable to repent, for He shuts the door upon them.

(*Exod.R.*, Wa'era, xi, 1.)

After death the usual doctrine is that there can be no repentance. Then it is, indeed, too late.

[864] It is said, 'The crooked cannot be made straight, and the wanting cannot be supplied' (Eccles. i, 15). In this world he who is crooked can become straight, but not in the world to come. There may be two sinners in partnership in the world; one repents before his death, and one does not. One is with the company of the righteous, and the other with the company of the

wicked. The second sees the first, and says, 'Woe is me. Is there partiality here? We both stole; we both murdered; yet he is with the righteous, and I am with the wicked.' They reply, 'You fool! You were corrupt, and you were cast out after your death for three days, and dragged with cords to your grave. Worms are spread under you, and maggots cover you (Isa. XIV, 19, 11). When your partner noted this, he turned from his evil way; but you had opportunity to repent, yet you did not.' He said to them, 'Suffer me to go and repent.' They answered, 'Fool, do you not know that this world is like the Sabbath, and the world from which you came is like the Sabbath eve? If a man does not prepare on the sixth day, what shall he eat on the seventh? Or this world is like the sea, and the world from which you came is like the dry land. If a man does not provide on the dry land, what shall he eat on the sea? Or this world is like the desert, and the world from which you came is like the inhabited land. If a man does not provide his victuals when he is in the cultivated land, what shall he eat in the desert? What then does he do? He wrings his hands and eats his own flesh' (Eccles. IV, 5). Then the sinner said, 'Let me at least see my partner in his glory.' They reply, 'Fool, we are commanded by God that in this world the wicked should not stand near the righteous, nor the righteous with the wicked. The pure must not stand near the polluted, nor the polluted with the pure, and we are appointed over this gate,' as it is said, 'This is the gate of the Lord, the righteous [alone (the Hebrew is emphatic)] shall enter therein' (Ps. CXVIII, 20).

(*Ruth R.* III, 3 on I, 17, f. 6*a*.)

This is a cheerless and heartless doctrine, exactly parallel to that of Luke XVI, 19–31. Cp. my remarks and those of Mr Loewe in *R.T.* pp. 357–60.

Does God help man to repent? Sometimes it looks as if all was left to man and his free will:

[865] God said, 'All depends on you. As the lily blooms and looks upward, so when you repent before me, let your heart be directed upward, and then I will bring the Redeemer,' as it says, 'I will be as the dew unto Israel; he shall blossom as the lily; that is, *when* he blossoms like the lily' (Hos. XIV, 5).

(*Midr.Ps.* on XLV, 1 (135*b init.*, § 3).)

But the general idea is that if man, by an effort of will, move a little forward on the right road, God will aid him, and come, as it were, to meet him. This view we have already met. Or again, God's grace and man's will can act simultaneously.

[866] The Israelites say, 'Turn thou first,' as it says, 'Return, O Lord, how long yet?' (Ps. XC, 13), and God says, 'No, but do thou, Israel, turn first.' So, do thou not return first, and let us not return first, but let us return together simultaneously.

(*Midr.Ps.* on LXXXV, 3, (186*b*, §3).)

Who is the more beloved of God? The repentant sinner, or the righteous who had no need to repent? There is more than one opinion:

[867] R. Ḥiyya b. Abba said in the name of R. Johanan: All the prophets have prophesied only about [the rewards of] the repentant, but concerning the perfectly righteous, eye has not seen [the reward laid up for them. God only knows it]. There he is at variance with R. Abbahu, who said in the name of Rab: In the place where the repentant stand, the righteous stand not, for it says, 'Peace, peace, to the far and the near.' First the far, next the near. The far is he who was originally far; the near is he who was ever near. R. Johanan said: The far is he who is far from sin; the near is he who was near sin, and made himself far from it. (*San.* 99*a* (cp. *R.T.* p. 260; cp. *Ber.* 34*b*).)

Sometimes the efficacy of repentance for the obtaining of forgiveness is combined with other means:

[868] R. Yudan said in the name of R. Elazar: Three things[1] annul the evil decree: prayer, repentance and almsgiving, and all are contained in this one verse: 'If my people shall humble themselves, and pray and seek my face, and turn from their evil ways, then will I forgive their sins' (II Chron. VII, 14), for to seek my face is almsgiving, as it says, 'Through almsgiving [A.V. 'righteousness'] shall I behold thy face' (Ps. XVII, 15).

(*Pes.K.* 191*a*.)

[869] Which is more powerful, prayer or repentance? R. Judah b. Ḥiyya said: Repentance annuls half the decree of punishment, whereas prayer annuls the whole. But R. Joshua b. Levi said: Prayer annuls half, repentance annuls the whole. [There follow biblical proofs and instances for either view.] (*Pes.R.* 188*b*.)

[1] For the 'three things' see p. 233.

Charity is supposed to be a means of atonement:

[870] R. Johanan said: So long as the Temple was in existence, the altar used to atone for Israel, but now a man's table atones for him. [The poor may be fed from his table, or he may have them as guests.] (*Ber.* 55*a*.)

Sometimes, too, the power of repentance is combined with the power of the Day of Atonement:

[871] When the Israelites are immersed in iniquities because of the evil inclination within them, if they return in repentance, God forgives them their iniquities year by year, and gives them a new heart to fear Him, as it is said, 'A new heart will I give you' (Ezek. XXXVI, 26). (**Note 99**.) (*Exod.R.*, Bo, XV, 6.)

[872] 'The people which shall be created shall praise the Lord' (Ps. CII, 18). Is there another people to be created in the future? The Rabbis say that 'people' means 'the generations which have made themselves guilty by their evil deeds, and they come and repent, and pray before God on New Year and the Day of Atonement, and if they make their deeds new, then God creates them, as it were, into new creatures.' (*Midr.Ps.* on CII, 18 (216*a*, §3).)

One must never despise the penitent:

[873] If a wicked man abandons his wickedness and repents, do not despise him. (*Midr.Prov.* VI, 30, f. 29*a*.)

It is right to help the sinner to repent:

[874] In the neighbourhood of R. Ze'era there lived some coarse [or bad] men, but he drew near them [had some intercourse with them], so that they might repent. His colleagues the Rabbis were angry with him. When R. Ze'era died, the men said, 'Till now we had R. Ze'era who besought compassion for us; who will do so now?' They pondered upon this in their hearts [or they took this to heart], and repented. (*San.* 37*a*.)

[875] The Rabbis say: Always drive away with the left hand, but bring near with the right. Do not act like Elisha, who drove away Gehazi with both hands. Elisha had three illnesses, one because he incited the bears on the children, one because he drove away Gehazi with both hands, and the one of which he died. (*San.* 107*b* (cp. [1578] and [1609]).)

[On this passage, the sequel of which was sometimes held to refer to Jesus, see p. 50 of Travers Herford's *Christianity in Talmud and Midrash*, London, 1903, and Bacher's remarks in his criticism of Herford, on p. 180 of the *Jewish Quarterly Review* (Old Series), XVII, 1905. (H. L.)]

The reader is recommended to study further passages (here omitted for the sake of brevity) cited in Strack-Billerbeck, vol. I, pp. 162–72; vol. II, pp. 215, 249 top and 250; vol. IV, pp. 474 and 1069. Also *Mekilta*, Baḥodesh, § 1, ed. Lauterbach, vol. II, p. 196.

Chapter XIII

HOPE AND FAITH; MIRACLES

The Rabbinic conception of God as the author of life and death, as the omnipotent King, and as the supremely wise and supremely righteous Father, who loves His human children, or, at any rate, His Israelite children, and wishes them to 'live' (both in this world and the next) is fundamentally simple and childlike. Man should have implicit trust in God: he should pray to Him, he should reverence and love Him. For all that he enjoys, and even for all that befalls him, he should thank God. As an Israelite, his duty is so to order his life that it should tend to the sanctification, and never to the profanation, of God's holy Name. It was an extremely simple faith, and the doctrine of the world to come prevented any amount of trouble and calamity from clouding or weakening this faith. For trouble and calamity were always explicable as a test and purification, or as a temporary punishment; all the greater would be the joys and raptures of the world to come. Fulfil the commandments: then God will help you.

[876] 'And the blood shall be for a token' etc. (Exod. XII, 13). What benefit could the blood be to the angel or to Israel? But because the Israelites fulfilled the command, God had pity upon them.
(*Mek.*², *Amalek*, Beshallaḥ, § 1, p. 180; *Mek.*³, vol. II, p. 144 (cp. *R.H.* III, 8).)

Never lose hope and faith in God's redemption:

[877] It says, 'I hoped for the Lord, and He heard my cry' (Ps. XL, 1). There is nothing left for Israel but to hope that God may deliver them. So it says, 'Hope in the Lord, yea, hope in the Lord' (Ps. XXVII, 14); one hope after the other. 'Be of good courage and let your heart be strong' (*ib.*): if you have hoped, and have not been saved, hope and hope again....And it says: 'He set my feet upon a rock' (Ps. XL, 2). Why did He do so? Because of the hope which I [David] hoped. For God has pleasure not in burnt offerings or in peace offerings or in sacrifices, but in hope.
(*Midr.Ps.* on XL, 1 (129*a*, § 1).)

[878] 'O love the Lord all his saints' (Ps. XXXI, 23). These are the righteous in Israel; 'The Lord preserves the faithful': these are

the proselytes. Or, the words may also be rendered, 'The Lord keeps faith': this refers to the transgressors in Israel, for they answer 'Amen', against their will, in faithfulness, and say, 'Blessed is He who quickens the dead.' Or, 'The Lord preserves the faithful': these are the Israelites who say, 'Blessed is He who quickens the dead,' and in faith they answer 'Amen', for with all their strength they have faith in God that He will quicken the dead, even though the resurrection of the dead has not yet come, and they say, 'Blessed is He who redeems Israel,' though they are not yet redeemed, and they say, 'Blessed is He who rebuilds Jerusalem,' though it is not yet rebuilt.

(*Midr.Ps.* on XXXI, 23 (120*b*, §8).)

[The three blessings mentioned above occur in the *Amidah*, see *P.B.* pp. 45, 47, 49 and Abrahams' note on p. LXIV. The blessings on pp. 45 and 49 were 'test benedictions'. The synagogue being free, and it being open to anyone to lead in prayer, there was a danger that heretical prayers might be recited by a reader who held heretical views. His reluctance to recite one of the 'tests' preserved the orthodoxy of the pulpit. A Sadducee would be deterred by having to proclaim that 'God quickens the dead' and a Samaritan would hesitate to pray for Jerusalem. But in this passage there is no mention of the paragraph repudiating Jewish-Christian belief (*P.B.* p. 48, paragraph 3). This was introduced about A.D. 100.[1] This passage may, therefore, be of earlier date. The prayer for the rebuilding of Jerusalem is not according to the pre-70 form, but it may have been so originally in the passage, and then changed after the year 70. Or this passage may belong to the period A.D. 70–90.

For 'test benedictions' see also [979]. (H. L.)]

[879] 'And they believed in the Lord and in His servant Moses' (Exod. XIV, 31). If they believed in Moses, how much more in God! But the words are to teach you that anyone who believes in the faithful shepherd is as if he believed in God. And so, contrariwise, where it is said, 'And the people spake against God, and against Moses' (Num. XXI, 5) and you might argue that, if they spoke against God, obviously they would have spoken against Moses, the words are to teach you that he who speaks against the faithful shepherd is as if he spoke against God. 'And they had faith in the Lord. Great is faith, for as a reward that the Israelites had faith in God, the Holy Spirit rested upon

[1] On this see S. Krauss, in *J.Q.R.* (O.S.), vol. IX, April 1897, pp. 515–17.

them and they sang the Song (Exod. xv). And Abraham inherited both this world and the world to come only through the merit of faith, as it is said, 'And he believed in the Lord and He counted it to him for righteousness' (Gen. xv, 6). R. Nehemiah said: Everyone who executes a single command in faith deserves that the Holy Spirit should rest upon him. [There is a play upon the words *shirah* (song) and *sharetah* (rests).] And the Israelites were delivered from Egypt only as a reward of faith, as it is said, 'And the people believed' (Exod. IV, 31). And it says, 'The Lord preserves the faithful' [the word can also be rendered 'Them that have faith'] (Ps. XXXI, 23). And it says, 'Open ye the gates that a righteous nation which keeps faith [i.e. has the virtue of faith] [A.V. and R.V. 'truth'] may enter therein' (Isa. XXVI, 2). [Thus righteousness is equated with faith.] Through this gate all the men of faith do enter. And it says, 'It is a good thing to give thanks unto the Lord, and to sing praises unto thy name, O Most High, to show forth thy lovingkindness in the morning, and thy faithfulness in the night.... For thou, O Lord, hast made me glad through thy work; I will rejoice in the works of thy hands' (Ps. XCII, 1–4). And what caused us to have this joy? The reward of the faith which our fathers had in God in this world, which is all night, is that we are counted worthy for the world to come, which is all morning. [As the Israelites in the night showed forth God's faithfulness, i.e. manifested their faith by showing forth God's faithfulness, so shall they show forth, and rejoice in, God's love in the morning, that is, in the world to come.] And so Jehoshaphat said, 'Have faith in the Lord, and ye shall be established; have faith in his prophets, and ye shall prosper' (II Chron. XX, 20). And so the exiles of Israel will be gathered back only as a reward of faith, as it says, 'I will betroth thee unto me, through thy faith' [A.V. and R.V., 'in faithfulness'] (Hos. II, 20).

(*Mek.*[2], Beshallaḥ, § 6, pp. 114–15; *Mek.*[3], § 7, vol. I, p. 252.)

[880] In Rabbinic quotations, the word *emunah* [faith] may often be more fitly translated, trust [in God]. The verse 'And the people trusted in [A.V. 'believed in'] the Lord and in his servant Moses' (Exod. XIV, 31) was constantly upon the Rabbis' lips: the verses Gen. XV, 6, 'And Abraham trusted in [A.V. 'believed in'] the Lord, and the Lord counted it to him for righteousness' and

Hab. II, 4, 'The righteous shall live through his trust' [A.V. 'faith'], are also frequently quoted.

Rabbi (cp. [419]) said: God said, 'The trust which Israel put in me was worthy that I should cleave the Red Sea for them, in that they did not say to Moses, "How can we go backward [for 'the land entangles us and the wilderness will shut us in', Exod. XIV, 1–3], and break the heart of our children and our wives?" but they trusted in me, and went after Moses.'

(*Exod.R.*, Beshallaḥ, XXI, 8.)

[881] R. Nehemiah said: The Israelites were privileged [*zaku*] to sing the Song of the Red Sea only by the merit [*zekut*] of trust, as it is said, 'They trusted in the Lord,' and it is said, 'And the people trusted' (Exod. IV, 31). But R. Isaac said: They saw all the wonders which were wrought for them: how should they not have trusted? R. Simeon b. Abba said: Yet it was by the merit [*zekut*] of Abraham's trust that they were privileged [*zaku*] to sing the Song of the Sea.

(*Exod.R.*, Beshallaḥ, XXIII, 5.)

[882] In the time to come the Israelites will sing a fresh song, as it is said, 'Sing unto the Lord a new song' (Ps. XCVIII, 1). By whose merit [*zekut*] will they do so? By the merit of Abraham, because he trusted in God, as it is said, 'And Abraham trusted in God' (Gen. XV, 6). (*Exod.R.*, Beshallaḥ, XXIII, 5.)

Trust in God implies resignation and acceptance of God's will.

[883] When Aaron heard of the death of his two sons, he 'held his peace' (Lev. X, 3); he acknowledged the justice of the divine decree. With the righteous it is habitual to act thus. So did Abraham, when he said, 'I am but dust and ashes' (Gen. XVIII, 27); so did Jacob and David. (*Sifra* 45*a*.)

So the mourner at a funeral justifies the (divine) judgment (*ẓidduḳ ha-Din*: he acknowledges the judgment as righteous) by saying:

[884] Lord of the Universe, I have often sinned before thee, and thou hast not exacted punishment from me for one in a thousand. May it be thy will, O Lord our God, to repair our breaches and the breaches of all thy people, the house of Israel, in mercy.

And so, in the Prayer Book, a particular portion of the Burial Service is called *ẓidduḳ ha-Din*—the justification, or the acknowledgment of the righteousness of the judgment, and God is invoked in it as 'the faithful Judge' (*P.B.* pp. 318, 319; see also 'The Mourner's Grace', p. 283).

The Rabbis, in spite of their faith in a future life, still strangely clung to the old idea that death was an evil, and, in some sort of sense, a punishment or a doom. So, too, 'on hearing evil tidings' the appropriate and right blessing to say is: 'Blessed art thou, O Lord our God, King of the universe, the true Judge' (*P.B.* p. 292).

[885] It is written, 'Fear not, my servant Jacob' (Jer. XXX, 10), and 'Jacob dreamed, and behold a ladder set up on the earth, and the top of it reached to heaven' (Gen. XXVIII, 12). R. Samuel b. Naḥman said: The ladder stands for the Princes of the peoples of the world, for God showed to our father Jacob the Prince of Babylon rising seventy rungs, the Prince of Media fifty-two, the Prince of Greece one hundred and eighty, and the Prince of Edom rising, but how many rungs was not known. In that hour Jacob feared, and he thought, 'Perhaps for Edom it will be all rising and not falling.' Then God said, 'Fear not, Jacob; even if he rises, and sits near me, from there I will cast him down,' as it is said, 'Though thou exalt thyself as the eagle, and though thou set thy nest among the stars, thence will I bring thee down, says the Lord' (Obad. 4). R. Berachyah said: Hence one may learn that God showed to Jacob the Princes of Babylon, Media, Greece and Edom rising and falling. And God said to Jacob, 'Thou too wilt rise.' And Jacob was afraid, for he thought, 'Perhaps I too shall fall.' God said, 'Fear not, Jacob, for though thou risest, thou shalt never fall.' But he believed [or trusted] God not; therefore he did not rise. And God said, 'If you had believed, and had risen, you would never have fallen; but now as you did not believe and did not rise, your descendants will be enslaved by four kingdoms of the world with taxes and forced supplies and fines and poll taxes.'

(*Lev.R.*, Emor, XXIX, 2.)

[886] He who created the day, created the sustenance thereof. R. Elazar of Modi'im said: If a man has food for the day, but says, 'What shall I eat to-morrow?' such a one is deficient in faith. R. Eliezer the Great said: He who has yet bread in his basket, and says, 'What shall I eat to-morrow?' belongs to those who are small in faith.

(*Tanḥ.*, Beshallaḥ, § 20, f. 117*b init.*; *Soṭ.* 48*b fin.*)

[887] R. Huna related this tale: A proselyte who was an astrologer once wished to go on a journey. 'But,' he said, 'how can I go forth now [for he saw that the hour was unpropitious]?' Then he said, 'Since I have joined this holy nation, should I not abandon these practices of mine? Let me then sally forth in God's name.' He drew near to a part where there were wild beasts, so he gave them his ass, and they ate it. [So he escaped.] What was the reason of his falling into danger? [His astrological belief in this very danger.] What caused him to be saved? His reliance on his Creator. And so Levi said: All those who predict their end by divination reach that end.

(*T.J.Sab.* VI, § 8, f. 8*d*, line 15.)

[888] R. Abun said: We have heard that the earth has wings, as it is said, 'From the wings [A.V. 'uttermost parts'] of the earth have we listened to songs' (Isa. XXIV, 16). The sun has wings, as it is said, 'The sun of righteousness shall arise with healing in his wings' (Mal. IV, 2). The 'creatures' have wings, as it is said, 'I heard the noise of the wings of the living creatures' (Ezek. III, 13). The Cherubim have wings, as it is said, 'The Cherubim spread forth their two wings' (I Kings VIII, 7). The Seraphim have wings, as it is said, 'Above it stood the Seraphim, each one had six wings' (Isa. VI, 2). Come and see how great is the power of the righteous, how great the power of those who do charity, how great the power of those who do loving deeds; they do not put their trust in the shade of the morning, or in the shade of the wings of the earth or of the sun, or in the shade of the wings of the 'creatures', or in the shade of the Cherubim or of the Seraphim, but in the shade of Him who spoke, and the world was, as it is said, 'The children of men put their trust under the shade of *thy* wings' (Ps. XXXVI, 7).

(*Ruth R.* V, 4 on II, 12, f. 9*a*.)

The Rabbis lived at a time when there were no troubles about miracles. God manipulated nature as He chose. Many Rabbis worked miracles. I give just one example:

[889] R. Phinehas b. Jair went to a place, and they said, 'Our fountain no longer yields us water.' He said, 'Perhaps you are not particular [about your tithes].' They said, 'Pledge yourself to us' [that if we do so, all will be well], and he pledged himself to them, and the fountain yielded its water (cp. note to [120]).

Once R. Phinehas was going to the House of Study, and the river Ginai which he had to pass was so swollen that he could not cross it. He said, 'O river, why do you prevent me from getting to the House of Study?' Then it divided its waters, and he passed over. And his disciples said, 'Can we too pass over?' He said, 'He who knows that he has never insulted an Israelite can pass over unharmed.'

R. Haggai in the name of R. Naḥman told this tale. There was a pious man who was wont to dig wells and cisterns for passers-by and travellers. One day his daughter, who was about to be married, was drowned in a river. Everybody went to console him, but he would not receive their consolations. Then R. Phinehas went to console him, and he too was not received. He said, 'Is that your man of piety?' They said, 'These are his deeds, and this is what befell him.' Then R. Phinehas said, 'Is it possible that he who has honoured his Maker through water should be overwhelmed in affliction through water?' Then the rumour ran through the city that the daughter had returned. Some said, 'She was saved by a projecting peg'; others said, that an angel came down in the likeness of R. Phinehas and delivered her. (*T.J.Dem.* 1, § 3, f. 22*a*, line 14.)

But because miracles were so common, the Rabbis were not particularly impressed by them:

[890] On a certain occasion R. Eliezer used all possible arguments to substantiate his opinion, but the Rabbis did not accept it. He said, 'If I am right, may this carob tree move a hundred yards from its place.' It did so.... They said, 'From a tree no proof can be brought.' Then he said, 'May the canal prove it.' The water of the canal flowed backwards. They said, 'Water cannot prove anything.' Then he said, 'May the walls of this House of Study prove it.' Then the walls of the house bent inwards, as if they were about to fall. R. Joshua rebuked the walls, and said to them, 'If the learned dispute about the Halakah [the rule, the Law], what has that to do with you?' So, to honour R. Joshua, the walls did not fall down, but to honour R. Eliezer, they did not become quite straight again. Then R. Eliezer said, 'If I am right, let the heavens prove it.' Then a heavenly voice said, 'What have you against R. Eliezer? The Halakah is always with him [his view is always right].' Then

R. Joshua got up and said, 'It is not in heaven' (Deut. xxx, 12). What did he mean by this? R. Jeremiah said, 'The Law was given us from Sinai. We pay no attention to a heavenly voice. For already from Sinai the Law said, "By a majority you are to decide"' (Exod. xxiii, 2 as homiletically interpreted). R. Nathan met Elijah and asked him what God did in that hour. Elijah replied, 'He laughed and said, "My children have conquered me."' (*Bab.M.* 59*b*.)

The naïve, but daring, anthropomorphism at the end of this last extract may seem almost flippant to modern readers. The apparent flippancy is not due to any Rabbinic lack of deep reverence for God or of fervent love; it may rather be said that this very reverence and love produced a certain intimate familiarity, which may be compared to the familiarity of a loving son who is on very intimate terms with his father, and can even make jokes about him to his face.

[On R. Joshua's refusal to accept the miracle of the carob tree Abrahams says: 'Liberals have no interest in R. Joshua's point of law, but his assertion of the rights of private judgment interests Liberals very much' (*Permanent Values*, p. 84 (Oxford, 1924)). (H. L.)]

Another view of miracles and of man's account or merit-book with God is reflected in the following:

[891] R. Yannai said: One should never stay in a place of danger, and say, 'I shall be saved by a miracle,' for perhaps no miracle will be wrought, and even if one *is* wrought, it will be deducted from his merits. R. Ḥanan as proof of this quoted Gen. xxxii, 11, 'I am not worthy of [lit. I have become smaller, i.e. poorer in merits, on account of] all the mercies [i.e. the miracles] which thou hast done for me.'

(*Ta'an.* 20*b* (Malter, p. 47; cp. *Sab.* 32*a*; Moore, iii, 119).)

The general attitude of the Rabbis towards the miraculous and the position of miracles in Rabbinic theology are briefly discussed in **Note 97**.

Chapter XIV

ON PRAYER

I now proceed to give some quotations about Prayer. For prayer became all important when the Temple was destroyed, and all sacrifices ceased. Sincere prayer brought forgiveness for sin.

[892] 'Thou art not a God who has pleasure in wickedness' (Ps. v, 4). Thou hast no pleasure in the guilt of the world, as it is said, 'God has no pleasure in the death of the wicked, but that he should turn from his way and live.' Yea, God seeks that the creatures should pray before Him, and He will accept them. R. Isaac said: We have now no prophet or priest or sacrifices or Temple, or altar which can make atonement for us: from the day whereon the Temple was laid waste, nought was left to us but prayer. Therefore, O God, hearken and forgive.

(*Midr.Ps.* on v, 4 (27 *a*, §7).)

Prayer is always acceptable to God, but it should come from the heart.

[893] 'And the children of Israel feared and cried unto the Lord' (Exod. xiv, 10) when they saw Pharaoh approach. They betook themselves to their ancestors' weapons. When Abraham was in need, he 'cried upon the name of the Lord' (Gen. xiii, 4). So, too, Isaac prayed in the field (Gen. xxiv, 63), and Jacob prayed at night (Gen. xxviii, 11). For prayer, the weapon of the mouth, is mighty. Why is Israel called 'thou worm, Jacob' (Isa. xli, 14)? The worm's only weapon is her mouth, but with it she fells mighty cedars. (*Tanḥ.*, Beshallah, §9, f. 111*a* (cp. [948]).)

[894] 'To serve the Lord your God with all your heart' (Deut. xi, 13). What is a service with the heart? It is prayer.

(*Sifre Deut.*, 'Eḳeb, §41, f. 80*a* (H. p. 88; cp. [903]).)

'To serve' is also study. As the tending of the altar is called service, so both study and prayer are 'service'.

[895] Why is the prayer of the righteous like a rake? As the rake turns the grain from place to place, so the prayer of the righteous

turns the attributes of God from the attribute of wrath to the attribute of mercy. (*Yeb.* 64*a*.)

The power of prayer is boundless.

[896] If, so might one say, a man were to ask for the whole world in one hour, it would be granted him, as it says, 'Ask of me; I will give thee the uttermost parts of the earth' (Ps. II, 7, 8). (*Tan.d.b.El.* p. 107.)

[897] The congregation of Israel says, 'We are poor; we have no sacrifices to bring as a sin offering.' God replies, 'I need only words,' as it says, 'Take with you words' (Hos. XIV, 2). 'Words' mean 'words of the Law'. The congregation says, 'We do not know anything [we are not learned].' God replies, 'Weep and pray, and I will receive you.' (*Exod.R.*, Teẓawweh, XXXVIII, 4.)

[898] God says to Israel, 'I bade you pray in the synagogue in your city, but if you cannot pray there, pray in your field, and if you cannot pray there, pray on your bed, and if you cannot pray there, then meditate in your heart and be still.' (**Notes 20 *d* and 43**.) (*Pes.K.* 158*a*.)

[899] How long must a man persist in prayer? R. Judah said: Till his heart faints, as it says, 'A prayer of an afflicted one when he faints' (Ps. CII, 1). (*Midr.Ps.* on LXI, 2 (153*b*, §2).)

[900] R. Johanan said: Would that man could pray all day, for a prayer never loses its value (cf. *R.T.* p. 368). (*T.J.Ber.* I, § I, f. 2*b*, line I.)

[901] 'O thou that hearest prayer, unto thee shall all flesh come' (Ps. LXV, 2). Why does it say, 'all flesh', and not all men? The wise have used this verse to teach that man's prayer is heard only if he make his heart soft as flesh. A human king can hearken to two or three people at once, but he cannot hearken to more; God is not so, for all men may pray to Him, and He hearkens to them all simultaneously. Man's ears become satiated with hearing; but God's ears are never satiated with hearing. [He is never wearied by men's prayers.] (*Midr.Ps.* on LXV, 2 (156*b*, §2) (cp. *Exod.R.*, Beshallaḥ, XXI, 4; cp. [75–6]).)

[902] 'In the morning my prayer comes before thee' (Ps. LXXXVIII, 13). R. Phinehas said: The angel who is appointed to prayer [i.e. a sort of heavenly secretary of state for the department of prayer]

waits till the Israelites in the last Synagogue have finished their prayers, and then he takes all the prayers, and makes them into a chaplet, and places them upon God's head, as it says, 'Blessings are upon the head of the just, that is, upon Him who is the life of the worlds, who lives for ever' (Prov. x, 6).

(*Midr.Ps.* on LXXXVIII, 4 (190*b*, § 2).)

[903] R. Johanan said: What is the service of God? Prayer.

(*Midr.Ps.* on LXVI, 1 (157*b*, § 1) (cp. [894]).)

[904] It says, 'To love the Lord your God, and to serve him with all your heart and with all your soul' (Deut. XI, 13). ['Service' is prayer. You say it is prayer; may it not be [sacrificial] service? No, Scripture says, 'with all your *heart*'; what service is that of the heart?] You must say that it is prayer.

(*Ta'an.* 2*a fin.* (Malter, p. 6).)

[The words in brackets do not occur in the Talmudic passage cited, although Malter includes them: they are to be found in the parallel in *Sifre Deut.*, 'Eḳeb, §41, f. 80 *a* (H. p. 88). (H. L.)]

[905] R. Ḥiyya of Palestine entered the Synagogue to pray. R. Kahana [from Babylon] entered after him, and stood behind him to pray also. When R. Ḥiyya had finished his prayer, he sat down to wait till R. Kahana had finished, so as not to pass R. Kahana while he was praying. He prolonged his prayer, and when at last he finished, R. Ḥiyya said to him, 'Is it the custom with you thus to trouble your Rabbis?' R. Ḥiyya said, 'I am of the house of Eli, and it is written about the house of Eli, "The iniquity of the house of Eli shall not be expiated either with sacrifice or with offerings for ever" (I Sam. III, 14). It shall not be expiated by sacrifices or offerings, but it *shall* be expiated by prayer.' Then R. Ḥiyya prayed for him, and to R. Kahana was given the privilege of becoming so old that his nails became as red as those of a young child (cf. *R.T.* p. 122).

(*T.J.R.H.* II, § 6, f. 58*b*, line 10.)

The pious Rabbis, in full sincerity of heart, believed that if God did not 'answer' a prayer, it was because the request, if granted, would not have been for the asker's good. Indeed, it is the mark of the true Israelite not to murmur if the request be denied:

[906] When Isaac blessed Jacob, he said, 'May God [Elohim] give thee of the fatness of the earth' (Gen. XXVII, 28). 'May God

[Elohim] give thee' means: May He give thee according to the attribute of justice. If it is fitting for thee, He will give it thee. If it is not fitting for thee, He will not give it thee. But to Esau He said, 'Thy dwelling shall be the fatness of the earth' (Gen. XXVII, 39). Whether he were righteous or wicked, God would give him that. For Isaac thought: 'Esau is wicked; but as for the righteous Jacob, if he fulfils the commandments, and yet is chastened, he will not accuse the attribute of justice'; but as for the wicked, if he executes a single commandment, or prayer, and is not answered, he says at once: 'Even as I prayed before an idol, and found no response, so I have prayed before God, and found no response.'

So Solomon prayed, 'If an Israelite comes to the Temple and prays, give him what he asks, if it is fitting for him, and if it is not fitting, do not grant it,' and he also said: 'Give to every man [i.e. every Israelite] according to his ways' (I Kings VIII, 39). But if a foreigner comes and prays, give to him whatever he asks, even as it says, 'Do according to all that the foreigner calls to thee for' (I Kings VIII, 43). For if not, he will say, 'This is Solomon's Temple, and I have come from one end of the earth to the other, and I have grown weary in my journeyings, and I have come and prayed in this Temple, and I have found no response, even as I found no response before any idol.' That is why Isaac made a difference between what he said to Esau and to Jacob, for Esau was wanting in faith, while Jacob was a past master of faith and righteous. (**Note 78**.)

(*Tanḥ.B.*, Toledot, 67*b* (cp. [214] and [304]).)

This is a very curious instance of Rabbinic indifference to what is the actual sense of the biblical narrative. For when Isaac said, 'May God give thee of the fatness of the earth', he thought he was blessing, not the wicked deceiver Jacob, but Esau! Yet to the Rabbis, Jacob is righteous Israel, while Esau represents wicked Rome, the wicked nations. So the cruel deception of Jacob is entirely ignored.

[907] Simon the Pious said: In his prayer a man should think that the Shechinah is before him. (*San.* 22*a*.)

[908] When Moses prayed to God that he might enter the promised land, God said, 'Let it suffice thee; speak no more unto me of this matter.' Yet did Moses not cease to seek compassion from God. How much less should the rest of mankind cease to keep

on praying....One hour in prayer is better than good works; not because of his good works was it said to Moses, 'Go up and view the land,' but because of his supplication.

(*Sifre Deut.*, Wa'ethạnan, § 29, f. 71*b* (*R.T.* p. 148 *fin.*; H. pp. 46, 47).)

[909] In the law of the sacrifices it says, 'If a man has a bullock, let him offer a bullock; if not, let him give a ram, or a lamb, or a pigeon; and, if he cannot afford even a pigeon, let him bring a handful of flour. And if he has not even any flour, let him bring nothing at all, but come with words of prayer' (Hos. XIV, 2).

(*Tanḥ.B.*, Ẓaw, VIII, 9*a*.)

[910] R. Judah b. Shalom said: If a poor man comes, and pleads before another, that other does not listen to him; if a rich man comes, he listens to, and receives, him at once: God does not act thus: all are equal before Him, women, slaves, rich and poor.

(*Exod.R.*, Beshallaḥ, XXI, 4.)

As we have already heard, prayer needs *kawwanah*, concentration of mind, direction towards God, collectedness, calm.

[911] Rab said: He whose mind is not quieted should not pray. R. Ḥanina was wont not to pray when he was irritated.

(*'Erub.* 65*a*.)

[912] R. Samuel b. Naḥmani said: If you have directed your heart in prayer, be assured that your prayer will be heard by God.

(*Midr.Ps.* on CVIII, 1 (232*a*, § 1).)

[913] It is written in Cant. VIII, 13, 'O thou that dwellest in the gardens, thy companions hearken to thy voice; cause me to hear it.' [The Midrash takes the dweller in the gardens to be Israel.] When the Israelites are gathered together in their synagogues, and read the *Shema* with reverent intention and in unison, and with one mind and one intention, then God says, 'Thou that dwellest in the gardens, when thou readest thus, as one band, then I and my retinue (*familia*)[1] hearken to thy voice'; but when the Israelites read the *Shema* with distracted minds, not in unison, some before the others and some after, and with no reverent intention, then the Holy Spirit cries out, 'Flee away, my Beloved.'

(*Cant.R.* VIII, § 11, 2, on VIII, 13; f. 41*b* (cp. [965]).)

God's *familia* are the angels. The 'Beloved' is God. Here again the Holy Spirit and God are artlessly distinguished (see **Note 50**).

[1] [The form *famalia*, from *famulus*, is also used in Hebrew (cp. [965]). (H. L.)]

[914] One must not stand up to say the *Tefillah* except in a serious frame of mind. The pious men of old used to wait an hour, and then say the *Tefillah*, in order to direct their hearts to their Father in Heaven.

(*Ber.* v, 1 (cp. p. 349; *T.J.Ber.* v, § 1, f. 8*d*, line 22).)

The *Tefillah* is the statutory daily prayer of the eighteen benedictions (cp. *P.B.* p. 44).

[915] R. Ammi said: Man's prayer is not accepted unless he puts his heart in his hands. (*Ta'an.* 8*a* (Malter, p. 52).)

[916] Prayer needs *kawwanah* (cp. *R.T.* p. 186).

(*T.J.Ber.* iv, § 1, f. 7*a*, line 50.)

[917] A man must purify his heart before he prays.

(*Exod.R.*, Beshallaḥ, xxii, 3.)

[918] Let him who prays cast his eyes downwards, but turn his heart upwards. (*Yeb.* 105*b*.)

[919] R. Elazar said: Always let a man test himself: if he can direct his heart, let him pray; if he cannot, let him not pray.

(*Ber.* 30*b*.)

[920] If a man is riding on an ass [and the time for prayer comes], if there is anyone who can hold his ass, let him get off and pray; but if not, let him remain on the ass and pray. Rabbi (cp. [419]) said: In either case let him remain on the ass and pray; the only important thing is that his heart should be directed.

(*T.Ber.* iii, 18 (Z. p. 8 (**Note 65**), line 11); *R.T.* p. 186.)

[921] A load carrier, even when the burden is on his shoulders, may recite the *Shema*. But while he is either putting on or taking off the load, he may not recite it, because he cannot direct his heart [i.e. properly fix his attention upon the prayer]. The *Amidah* he may not say [lit. he may not pray] until he has taken off his load.

(*T.Ber.* ii, 7 (Z. p. 4 (**Note 65**), line 6); cp. *R.T.* pp. 117, 118.)

The words 'because he cannot direct his heart' show that the fundamental condition of prayer was never forgotten. There are various technical reasons for the distinction made between the *Shema* and the *Amidah*. Moore gives an excellent account of Rabbinic views about Prayer, ii, pp. 212–25.[1]

[1] [The *Shema* may be repeated while 'walking by the way' or 'lying down'; the *Amidah* must be recited erect and 'standing to attention'. (H. L.)]

Prayer can be long or short; its length is no guarantee of its excellence:

[922] R. Me'ir said: A man's words should always be few towards God (Eccles. v, 2). (*Ber.* 61 *a.*)

[923] 'And he cried unto the Lord, and the Lord showed him a tree, etc.' (Exod. xv, 25). Hence you can learn that the righteous have no difficulty [in getting their prayers answered], and incidentally you may learn also that the prayers of the righteous are short.[1] It happened once that a disciple was reading the *Amidah* in the presence of R. Eliezer, and curtailed his benedictions. The other disciples said, 'Master, do you see how he has shortened the benedictions?' And they mocked him and said, 'Here is a disciple of the wise, who is a shortener.' But Rabbi Eliezer said, 'He has not been shorter than Moses, who said, "Heal her, O Lord, I pray"' (Num. XII, 13). And another one, on another similar occasion, prolonged the benedictions, and the disciples said, 'Master, did you notice him, how he prolonged his benedictions?' And they called him the prolonger. But R. Eliezer said, 'He did not prolong more than Moses, who said, "I fell down in prayer before the Lord for forty days and forty nights" (Deut. IX, 18), for Moses said to himself, "There is a time to shorten and a time to prolong."'
(*Mek.*[2], *Wayassa'*, Beshallaḥ, § 1, p. 155; *Mek.*[3], vol. II, p. 91; *Sifre Num.*, Beha'aloteka, § 105, f. 28 *b* (H. p. 104).)

[924] And the Lord said unto Moses, 'Wherefore criest thou unto me?' (Exod. XIV, 15). R. Eliezer said: God said to Moses, 'My children are in trouble; the sea shuts them off on one side, the enemy pursues them on the other, and you stand and make long prayers.' And God said, 'There is a time to lengthen prayer, and a time to shorten it.' (*Mek.*[2], Beshallaḥ, § 3, p. 97; *Mek.*[3], vol. I, p. 216.)

[925] R. Ḥiyya b. Abba said in the name of R. Johanan: Whoever prolongs his prayer, and calculates on it, [i.e. anticipates its fulfilment as a reward for its length], will eventually come to pain of heart. (*Ber.* 32 *b* (Cohen, p. 215).)

[926] R. Akiba when he prayed with the congregation, was short; when he prayed by himself, you could leave him on one side of

[1] Lauterbach in his edition and translation of the *Mekilta* has a different explanation of the first part of this sentence.

the room, and find him on the other, because of his genuflexions and prostrations. (*T.Ber.* III, 7 (Z. p. 6 (**Note 65**), line 13).)

Prayers should be spontaneous.

[927] Prayer should not be recited as if a man were reading a document. R. Aḥa said: A new prayer should be said every day.

(*T.J.Ber.* IV, § 3, f. 38*a*, line 64.)[1]

[928] R. Eliezer said: If a man makes his prayer a fixed task [*ḳeba*ʿ], his prayer is no supplication. So the Mishnah. The Gemara asks: What means *ḳeba*ʿ? R. Jacob b. Idi said in the name of R. Oshaya: Anyone whose prayer seems to him a burden. The Rabbis say: Anyone who does not recite it in the language of supplication. Rabbah and Rab Joseph both said: Anyone who is not able to add something new thereto.

(*Ber.* IV, 4; *Ber.* 29*b* (cp. *T.J.Ber.* IV, § 4, f. 7*a*, line 23; *Aboth* II, 18; *P.B.* p. 190; also [948–9], [952 ff.], [1112]).)

['Fixed Task' (*ḳeba*ʿ) is here used in a bad sense because mechanical prayers, uttered by rote, are valueless. But the word can be used in a good sense also. *Aboth* II, 18, which declares that prayers must *not* be *ḳeba*ʿ, complements I, 15, which declares that study *should* be *ḳeba*ʿ; regularity in study is essential. For prayer, one should have a fixed or *regular* place (*Ber.* 7*b*). The root is used also in connection with *regular* sleep, a *regular* meal, or a *regular* place of burial. Prayer, too, was to be regular, in the sense that it was not to be casual: there was a communal obligation devolving on the individual Israelite to recite daily, to the glory of God, *the* 'prayer', i.e. the *Tefillah* [914], also called *Amidah*, or 'standing' [921]. But it must be 'fresh' [927], and it should contain 'supplications', i.e. private petitions or meditations, called *taḥanunim* etc., and repeated in silence. An example will be found at the end of the *Amidah* (*P.B.* p. 54, the paragraph beginning 'O my God...') which is never said aloud. The term *taḥanunim* (*taḥanun*, *teḥinnot*, etc.) does not happen to be used in Singer on p. 57: it will be found in the corresponding part of the service in Pool's *P.B.* (p. 61).

The leader in prayer had to mention certain subjects in a certain order, but the formulation was left to him. Some phrases were regarded as essential, thus 'the great, the mighty and the awful God', for which there was Mosaic authority (see p. 357). Exaggerated adjectives were deprecated (see [727–9]). In this way, the services tended to acquire stability without the sacrifice of spontaneity. The writing down of blessings was also deprecated, it was tantamount to

[1] See Luncz' text, f. 45 *b* for different reading.

'burning the Torah' (see above, [350]). But in course of time this step was inevitable. According to *Tanh.*, Shemot, 2, 81*b*, the Men of the Great Synagogue expanded existing benedictions, and the context, especially their association with the passage cited from Nehemiah, suggests that the Men of the Great Synagogue and the prototypes of the benedictions were of early date. The writing down of the Mishnah involved the writing down of the Blessings, and to a large extent stabilised the liturgy. But the final stage—initial, when viewed from another standpoint—belongs to the Geonic Age, with the prayer books of Amram and others. (H. L.)]

Quaint is this:

[929] He who makes his voice heard during prayer is of the small of faith. Rab Huna said: This teaching applies only to one who is able to direct his heart when whispering [the words of prayer]; but if he is unable to do so, he is permitted [to pray aloud]. This holds good only of one praying alone, but with a congregation it would cause disturbance to others. (*Ber.* 24*b*.)

[Moderation is to be observed. Absolute silence may lead to the slurring over of prayers or to inattention. Hence 'the ears must hear what the lips utter' (*Ber.* 13*a*), i.e. the words must be spoken distinctly—though not loudly, so as to disturb others—and a pause must be made when one word begins with the same consonant as that with which the previous one ended: they must not be run together (*ib.* 15*b*; see also 15*a*). But *kawwanah* is essential (*ib.* 16*a*).

It is interesting to observe that the Hebrew word 'to read' (*kara*) also—and no doubt originally—meant 'to call out', thus pointing to audible reading as being general. Of Augustine it is told that, quite by accident, he discovered the art of reading inaudibly, to the amazement of his pupils, who noticed that his lips moved not, and no sound issued from them. Whether this story has any foundation, I am unable to say. Sometimes silent prayer can be misunderstood. Hannah was accused of drunkenness. Yet 'the highest service is the service of the heart' [894], for 'to Thee silence is praise' (Ps. LXV, 2). (H. L.)]

To thank God is prayer:

[930] R. Phinehas, R. Levi, and R. Johanan, in the name of R. Menaḥem of Galilee, said: In the time to come all other sacrifices will cease, but the sacrifice of thanksgiving will not cease. All other prayers will cease, but thanksgiving will not cease. (*Lev.R.*, Ẓaw, IX, 7 (cp. *Midr.Ps.* on LVI, 12 (148*a*, §4)).)

One must pray for others as well as for oneself, and one must pray with Israel in the Synagogue.

[931] Rab said: Whoever has it in his power to pray on behalf of his neighbour, and fails to do so, is called a sinner. (*Ber.* 12*b*.)

[932] God says, 'If a man occupies himself with Torah, practises benevolent acts, and prays with the congregation, I will ascribe it to him as though he had redeemed me and my son [Israel] from [exile] among the peoples of the world.' (*Ber.* 8*a*.)

It must be remembered that the community of Israel, and even each local congregation, were more important to the Rabbis, and, as they believed, more important even to God, than any individual Israelite. The Rabbis never abandoned the 'collective' point of view of the O.T., even though they had also adopted and intensified the later individualism. The community of Israel (*kelal Yisrael*) forms a sort of real, if mystical, personality. It is because the community is known to, and beloved by, God that God knows and loves each individual who composes it:

[933] R. Judah said: I once walked behind R. Akiba and R. Elazar b. Azariah, and the time came for saying the *Shema*, and it seemed to me that they forbore to say it because they were engaged on affairs of the community.
(*T.Ber.* I, 4 (Z. p. 1, line 11).)

The last quotation induces me to add some extracts about the community and its service (cp. [859]).

[934] Moses said to God, 'I am one, and Israel is six hundred thousand. Often have they sinned, and I have prayed for them, and thou hast forgiven them: thou hast had regard for the six hundred thousand, wilt thou not have regard to me?' God replied, 'The doom of a community cannot be compared with the doom of an individual.' (*Tanḥ.*, Wa'etḥanan, § 36, f. 313*a*.)

[935] The sacrifices of the community are acceptable to God, and make atonement between Israel and its Father in heaven.
(*T.Sheḳ.* I, 6 (Z. p. 174, line 5).)

[936] God does not reject the prayer of the multitude.
(*Sifre Num.*, Pineḥas, § 135, f. 51*a* (H. p. 181).)

[937] 'In an acceptable time' (Ps. LXIX, 13). When is that? When the community prays. (*Ber.* 8*a init.* (cp. [949]).)

[938] 'Get thee down' (Exod. XXXII, 7). What does this mean? R. Elazar said: God spake to Moses, 'Get you down from your

greatness: I gave you greatness only because of Israel; now that Israel has sinned, what art thou to me?' (*Ber.* 32*a*.)

[939] Israel will be redeemed only when it forms one single band: when all are united, they will receive the presence of the Shechinah. Therefore Hillel said (*Aboth* II, 5), 'Separate not thyself from the community.'

(*Tanḥ.B.*, Nizzabim, 25*a* (cp. *Ber.* 49*b*).)

[940] The Rabbis teach: When Israel is in trouble, and one among them separates himself, the two angels of the Service who accompany a man lay their hands on his head, and say, 'This man, who has separated himself from the community, shall not see its consolation.' And it is taught: If the community is in trouble, a man must not say, 'I will go to my house, and eat and drink, and peace shall be with thee, O my soul.' But a man must share in the trouble of the community, even as Moses did. He who shares in its troubles is worthy to see its consolation.

(*Ta'an.* 11*a* (Malter, p. 74; cp. *Tan.d.b.El.* p. 112) (cp. [228]).)

[941] When R. Assi was dying, his nephew saw him weeping. He said, 'Why do you weep? Is there any part of the Law which you have not learnt? Your disciples sit before you. Is there any deed of lovingkindness which you have not done? And over and above all these qualities, you have kept yourself far from the judge's office, and you have not brought it over yourself to be appointed as an official for the needs of the community.' He replied, 'That is why I weep. Perhaps I shall have to give an account [i.e. be condemned], because I was able to be a judge, and did not judge.' A man who retires to his house, and says, 'What have I to do with the burden of the community, or with their suits, why should I listen to their voice? Peace to thee, O my soul'—such a one destroys the world. (*Tanḥ.*, Mishpaṭim, § 2, f. 127*a fin.*)

[942] It is to the praise of the righteous that, even when they are on the point of death, they do not think of their own affairs, but concern themselves with the needs of the community. So when God told Moses that he must die (Num. XXVII, 12–14), Moses' immediate concern was that God should appoint a leader in his place (*ib.* 16). (*Sifre Num.*, Pineḥas, § 138, f. 52*a* (H. p. 184).)

[943] He who sacrifices himself for Israel is worthy of greatness and the Holy Spirit. (*Num.R.*, Beha'aloteka, XV, 20.)

[944] R. Jeremiah said: He who occupies himself with the affairs of the community is as one who studies the Law.

(*T.J.Ber.* v, § 1, f. 8*d*, line 43.)

[Office was regarded, variously, as an honour desired by all; as a burden or temptation, to be shunned by the prudent (cp. [1059]); as a responsibility, not to be evaded by those endowed with a sense of duty. Such differences of outlook are natural at all times and depend on circumstances and temperaments. One of the Hebrew terms for 'office' is *Rabbanut*. This sometimes means 'government', in general. Its etymology naturally suggests the connection with the office of Rabbi. Shemaya, in the time of Herod, taught his disciples to love work and hate office (*Aboth* I, 10: see Travers Herford, *in loc.*). R. Johanan, in the third century, reiterated the sentiment, in the warning that 'office buries its holder' (*Pes.* 87 *b*), since 'every prophet survived four kings' (*ib.*). R. Nehemiah pointed out the responsibilities of office; the office holder becomes the 'surety' for his fellow (Prov. VI, 1). Before appointment, a scholar (*Ḥaber*) is care-free: when invested with the robe (*Ṭallit*) of office, 'all the burden of the community is upon him. Should he see a man constraining his neighbour or committing a sin, and check him not, he, the official, is punished on his account, for the Holy Spirit proclaims "My son, if thou be surety for thy friend, thou hast then struck thy hand for a stranger" (Prov. VI, 1)' (*Exod.R.* XXVII, 9). Akabya b. Mahalalel was one of the earliest Tannaim (for his date, see Travers Herford's note to *Aboth* III, 1). He 'testified to four opinions', i.e. he took an adverse view from his colleagues on four points, two of which were matters of medical hygiene. His colleagues said, 'Retract these four decisions, and we will make thee *Ab Bet Din*' (Vice-President of the Rabbinical Court). He replied, 'Better is it for me to be called a fool all my life long, than to be made a godless man before God even for a single hour, so that people shall not say of me "For the sake of office, he went back on his word"' ('*Eduyot* v, 6). He was excommunicated, possibly in consequence of his firmness, and he died under the ban. But the circumstances are not quite clear (see Travers Herford's note, cited above). On his death-bed he said to his son, 'Retract those four opinions of mine.' His son replied, 'But why did you yourself not retract' (*sc.* and be released from the ban)? Akabya answered, 'I heard those teachings from a majority of authorities, and therefore I am bound to them; my opponents heard their views from a majority of their teachers, and they, likewise, are bound. But you, my son, have heard these views from me, an individual, and the contrary opinions, from a majority, my opponents, as well. It is better to abandon the opinion of an individual in favour of the opinion held by the majority.' His son said: 'Father, commend me to your colleagues.' Akabya replied: 'Nay, I will not do so.' 'Have you any cause for complaint against me?' 'None,' said Akabya, 'but it is your own deeds that will prove your commendation or your rejection' (*'Eduyot* v, 7). (H. L.)]

[945] So long as a man is only a simple *Ḥaber*, he is not bound to the community [he need not concern himself with its affairs], and he is not punished for its sins, but when he is appointed to a post, and receives the *ṭallit* of investiture, then he must not say, 'I am concerned only with my own good, I am not bound to the community.' On the contrary. All the burden of the community is upon him. If he sees a man doing wrong to his neighbour, or committing a sin, and he does not stop him, he will be punished for his neglect; the Holy Spirit says to him, 'You are responsible for your neighbour'; God says to him, 'You have entered the arena, and he who enters the arena must either be conquered or conquer.' God says to him, 'You and I stand in the arena; either you conquer, or I conquer you.'

(*Exod.R.*, Yitro, XXVII, 9 on XVIII, 1.)

[The general reader may perhaps need some explanation of the word *Ḥaber*, cited above. For his purposes, the excellent article in Levy, from which the following references have been extracted, will suffice:

The word is derived from a root meaning 'to bind'. Its primary meaning is 'companion', thus *Aboth* II, 5, 'judge not thy associate till thou be come unto his place': *ib.* 13, 'a good companion'. In *Sab.* 63*a* top, it is used of a wife and in *T.J.Sheḳ.* III, § 1, f. 47*b*, line 30, in an academic sense: 'Ben Azzai was the colleague and disciple of Akiba.' Hence comes the special use of the word, in contradistinction to *Am ha-Aretz*, a member of a brotherhood, scrupulous in tithing and other religious observances. Sometimes the *Ḥaber* was not a learned man, e.g. 'Ye are sages, I am but a *Ḥaber*' (*Ḳid.* 33*b*). The four conditions necessary for acceptance as a *Ḥaber* are specified in *T.Dem.* II. (Cp. p. 107.) (H. L.)]

[946] When the small obey the great, but the great do not carry the burden of the small, God will come to judgment.

(*Ruth.R.*, Introduction, 6 on I, 2, f. 2*a*.)

[947] About the choosing of the seventy elders (Num. XI, 16) it is said: God said to Moses: 'First speak to them words of praise: Happy are you that you have been chosen; then say unto them harsh words: Know that the Israelites are troublesome and disobedient; on *this* condition you have been chosen, namely,

that you suffer them to curse and stone you; the condition I made with *thee*, I make with *them*.'...For God had previously, 'in sending Moses and Aaron to the Israelites' (Exod. VI, 13), said to them, 'Know that the Israelites are stubborn and rebellious, and I give you a charge to them only on the condition that you receive it knowing that they will curse you and stone you.'

(*Sifre Num.*, Beha'aloteka, § 92, f. 25*b*, 25*a* (H. pp. 93, 91).)

Returning to prayer, there are many rules about it, partly because the Rabbis, unfortunately, could not help making rules and fine distinctions about everything, partly because by prayer they often mean statutory prayer—the fixed prayers which a pious Jew is bound, or ordered, or expected, to repeat two or three times a day (cp. [928]). Thus we get:

[948] How many times daily ought a man to pray? So taught our teachers: One should not pray more than thrice daily, for the three patriarchs instituted the three statutory prayers: Abraham, the morning service (Gen. XIX, 27), Isaac, the afternoon service (*ib.* XXIV, 63), and Jacob, the evening service (*ib.* XXVIII, 11). Daniel, too, prayed thrice daily on his knees (Dan. VI, 10). But Daniel did not specify the hours. David, however, did so, when he said, 'evening, morning and noonday' (Ps. LV, 17). Therefore, man should not pray more often than thrice daily. R. Johanan said: Would that man were capable of praying continuously all day long! Antoninus asked R. Judah the saint, 'What about praying at every hour?' Judah said, 'It is forbidden.' He said, 'Why should it be forbidden?' Judah replied, 'So as not to treat the Almighty with frivolity.' Antoninus was dissatisfied. What did Judah do? Early next morning he went to Antoninus and said to him, 'Hail, O Lord.' After an hour he went in again, and hailed Antoninus as Imperator. After a third hour he said, 'Peace, O King!' Antoninus said, 'Why do you mock at Majesty?' Judah replied, 'Let your ears hear what your mouth uttered. If you, a king of flesh and blood, say this when greeted hourly, what shall be said of one who mocks the supreme King of kings, the Holy One, blessed be He? Should one importune Him at every hour?'

(*Tanh.B.*, Mikkez, 98*a fin.*–98*b* (cp. [893]).)

[949] R. Jose b. Ḥalafta taught: There are proper times for prayer, as it says, 'As for me, let my prayer come before thee at an

acceptable time' (Ps. LXIX, 13). What is an 'acceptable time'? When the community is at prayer. Therefore a man should rise early to pray, for nothing is greater than the power of prayer.
(*Tanḥ.B.*, Miḳḳeẓ, 98*b fin.* (cp. [937]).)

Public morning prayer was always held at a very early hour.

An interesting way in which, among the Rabbis, the inward and outward are blended together is shown by the following:

Rules are laid down about the place towards which a man must turn in prayer (i.e. towards Palestine, Jerusalem, the Temple, etc.). To us moderns all this seems very needless, as if it mattered a pin whether our bodies face one way or the other. And yet these rules are prefaced thus:

[950] A blind man, or one who is unable to locate the directions, should direct his heart to his Father in heaven. (*Ber.* 30*a.*)

[Mr Montefiore's pin' sticks in my gizzard! In one sense, it certainly does not matter which way we face, when we pray, so long as our hearts, as the Rabbis said, are set towards our Father in Heaven. Still worse, if such a detail as direction is given undue importance! And yet the Christian has his 'Eastward Position' and the Muslim his *Ḳiblah*. Turning to a given place is an old and natural idea. Solomon, when he dedicated the Temple, said, 'Hearken to the supplication...of thy people Israel when they shall pray toward this place' (I Kings VIII, 30), and the previous verse gives the reason, 'that thine eyes may be open toward this house night and day, even toward the place of which thou hast said, My Name shall be there: that thou mayest hearken unto the prayer which thy servant shall make toward this place.' We see, then, a mystic symbolism in this action of turning: it was a gesture of aligning oneself with God, a kind of *imitatio dei*, since God, too, was anthropomorphically supposed to be looking to the place. Gestures and symbols may be exaggerated sometimes, but such misuse does not condemn their essential worth, when properly employed. If we abandon all such symbols in our different spheres of activity, military, juristic, academic and civic, in the Church and in the palace, then we can certainly be very modern, but our life will be the poorer; it will become very drab and commonplace. And in our process of elimination where shall we stop? To many people, unfortunately, the sanctity of an oath would be diminished if the time-honoured ceremonial were no longer associated with it: the sense of duty towards the state is linked very largely to the monarchical idea, and so on. Assuming that symbols are not misapplied, and assuming also that they are picturesque and instructive, then surely any one is, in principle, as valuable or as valueless as any other, and it is nothing but subjective reasoning to say 'this must stay' and 'this must go'. And I am sure that Mr Montefiore does not want them all to go! (Cp. (13), p. ciii.) (H. L.)]

Prayer is better than sacrifice:

[951] God said to Israel, 'Be assiduous in regard to devotion, for there is no finer quality than prayer. Prayer is greater than all the sacrifices (Isa. I, 11, 13). Even if a man is unworthy that his prayer be answered, and mercy shown him, none the less, if he pray much, and supplicate for grace, I grant him mercy, as it says, "All the paths of the Lord are lovingkindness and truth" (Ps. XXV, 10). I put lovingkindness before truth [strictness], and righteousness [i.e. mildness] before justice' (*ib.* LXXXIX, 15). (**Note 20*e*.**) (*Tanḥ.*, Wayera, § 1, f. 31*b*.)

[952] 'And this is the blessing which Moses...' (Deut. XXXIII, 1). Moses did not begin with Israel's needs, until he had opened with God's praise. He was like an orator, standing by the judge's seat, who was hired by a client to plead for him. But before speaking of the client's needs, the orator opened with the praises of the king, saying, 'Happy is the world by reason of his rule, by reason of his justice': all the people joined in the praise. Then he opened his client's case; he ended, too, with praise of the king. So did Moses. So, too, did David and Solomon. So, too, did the Elders who composed the Eighteen Benedictions for Israel to use in prayer. They did not open with Israel's needs, but with, 'The great, mighty, and awful God,' 'Holy art thou and awful is thy name.' Only then came, 'Thou loosest the bound and healest the sick.' Finally they ended with, 'We give thee thanks.' (**Note 20*f*.**) (*Sifre Deut.*, Berakah, § 343, f. 142*a*, *b*.)

This early reference to the Eighteen Benedictions is interesting. For the prayers concerned, see, e.g. *P.B.* pp. 44, 45, 51 (cp. [928]).

It would fill too much room to quote many of the old Rabbinic prayers, which can easily be found in *P.B.*, published by Eyre and Spottiswoode at 2*s*. 6*d*. Yet for those who do not possess that book, I will quote some of the prayers here.

Here is part of the abstract of the Eighteen Benedictions—the *Tefillah*, i.e. prayer, *par excellence*:[1]

[953] Give us understanding, O Lord our God, to know thy ways; circumcise our hearts to fear thee, and forgive us so that we

[1] In the Bible the word *tefillah* really meant prayer in general, e.g. Isa. I, 15.

may be redeemed. Keep us far from sorrow. Satiate us on the pastures of thy land, and gather our scattered ones from the four corners of the earth. Let the righteous rejoice in the rebuilding of thy city and in the establishment of thy Temple, and in the flourishing of the horn of David thy servant, and in the clear-shining light of the son of Jesse, thine anointed. Even before we call, do thou answer. Blessed art thou, O Lord, who hearkenest unto prayer. [The date of this prayer is probably pre-Christian; for a chronological analysis of the Eighteen Benedictions, see L. Finkelstein, in *J.Q.R.* (N.S.), vol. XVI, Nos. 1 and 2.] (*Ber.* 29*a* (*P.B.* p. 55).)

Here is a night prayer:

[954] Blessed art thou, O Lord our God, King of the universe, who makest the bands of sleep to fall upon mine eyes, and slumber upon mine eyelids. May it be thy will, O Lord my God and God of my fathers, to suffer me to lie down in peace and to let me rise up again in peace. Let not my thoughts trouble me, nor evil dreams, nor evil fancies, but let my rest be perfect before thee. O lighten mine eyes lest I sleep the sleep of death, for it is thou who givest light to the apple of the eye. Blessed art thou, O Lord, who givest light to the whole world in thy glory. (*Ber.* 60*b* (*P.B.* p. 293).)

A prayer for the morning:

[955] O my God, the soul which thou gavest me is pure; thou didst create it, thou didst form it, thou didst breathe it into me; thou preservest it within me; and thou wilt take it from me, but wilt restore it unto me hereafter. So long as the soul is within me, I will give thanks unto thee, O Lord my God and God of my fathers, Sovereign of all worlds, Lord of all souls! Blessed art thou, O Lord, who restorest souls unto the dead. (*Ber.* 60*b* (*P.B.* p. 5).)

Prayer of R. Yannai's disciples on awakening:

[956] Blessed art thou, O Lord, who quickenest the dead. May it be thy will, O Lord my God, to give me a good heart, a good *yetzer*, a good hope, a good name, a good eye, a good soul, a lowly soul, and a humble spirit; may thy name not be profaned among [or through] us, and make us not a mockery in the mouth

of men; may our end not be cut off, nor our hope be a vexation, and may we not need the gifts of flesh and blood, and put not our sustenance into their hands, for their gifts are small, and the shame [which they inflict] is great; and place our portion in thy Law, with those who do thy will; build up thy house, thy sanctuary, thy city, thy temple, speedily in our days.

(*T.J.Ber.* IV, § 2, f. 7*d*, line 49.)

A very ancient morning prayer:

[957] May it be thy will, O Lord our God and God of our fathers, to make us familiar with thy Law, and to make us cleave to thy commandments. O lead us not into sin, or transgression, iniquity, temptation or shame. Let not the evil inclination have sway over us: keep us far from a bad man and a bad companion. Make us cleave to the good inclination and to good works; subdue out [evil] inclination so that it may submit itself unto thee, and let us obtain this day, and every day, grace, favour and mercy in thine eyes, and in the eyes of all who behold us; and bestow lovingkindnesses upon us. Blessed art thou, O Lord, who bestowest lovingkindnesses upon thy people Israel.

(*Ber.* 60*b* (*P.B.* p. 7).)

Another very ancient morning prayer which goes back to Talmudic times is the following:

[958] Sovereign of all worlds! Not because of our righteous acts do we lay our supplications before thee, but because of thine abundant mercies. What are we? What is our life? What is our piety? What our righteousness? What our helpfulness? What our strength? What our might? What shall we say before thee, O Lord our God and God of our fathers? Are not all the mighty men as nought before thee, the men of renown as though they had not been, the wise as if without knowledge, and the men of understanding as if without discernment? For most of their works are void, and the days of their lives are vanity before thee, and the pre-eminence of man over the beast is nought, for all is vanity, save only the pure soul which will hereafter render its judgment and account before the throne of thy glory.

(*P.B.* p. 7, and Abrahams' *Companion*, p. XXI.)

The words from 'save' to 'glory' occur only in the rite of the Spanish and Portuguese Jews—the *Sephardim*. 'Because of' might better be rendered: 'relying on.' Dr Abrahams says that: 'In this passage we have the true Rabbinic spirit on the subject of "grace" and "works". The Rabbis held that reward and punishment were meted out in some sort of accordance with a man's righteousness and sin. But nothing that man, with his small powers and finite opportunities, can do constitutes a *claim* on the favour of the Almighty and the Infinite. In the final resort all that man receives from the divine hand is an act of grace.'

God rewards obedience; this, as Moore says, is the constant teaching of the Hebrew Bible, and it is also the constant teaching of the Rabbis. Yet, as Moore also says, 'man's good deeds do not of themselves lay God under an obligation; God does not *owe* him a recompense for doing his duty. But God has put Himself under obligation by this promise of reward; and in this sense man, in doing what God requires of him, deserves the recompense' (vol. II, p. 90). There is, in my opinion, little *fundamental* difference between the doctrine of reward as held by the Rabbis and as stated by Jesus in the Synoptic Gospels. Act in a given way, 'and thou shalt have treasure in heaven' (Mark X, 21). Act in a given way, and so 'lay up treasures for yourselves in heaven' (Matt. VI, 20). Endure persecution, 'for great will be your reward in heaven' (Matt. V, 12). Do not act in a particular manner, or 'else ye shall have no reward with your Father in heaven' (Matt. VI, 1). He who does a certain good deed 'shall in no wise lose his reward' (Mark IX, 41). 'Love your enemies...and your reward shall be great' (Luke VI, 35). 'Well done, good and faithful slave. Enter thou into the joy of thy Lord' (Matt. XXV, 21). It is true that the Rabbis made larger use of the doctrine of reward, and pressed and emphasised it more eagerly and frequently than Jesus. On the other hand, the Rabbis, as we have seen, and as the prayer shows, were fully alive to the higher motives for right action. We have heard their insistence upon *lishmah*, upon 'love', upon 'doing the commands for their own sake', and so on. And we have heard, too, how they taught that man has no true *claim* upon God, and that though man may expect recompense, he must not send up his good deeds as a sort of cheque which God is bound to honour in the guise of reward.

Another summary of the Eighteen Benedictions:

[959] The needs of thy people Israel are many, but their knowledge is small. May it be thy will, O Lord our God and the God of our fathers, to give to every creature his need, and to every human frame what may be lacking to it. Blessed be thou, O Lord, who hast heard the voice of my supplications. Blessed art thou, O Lord, who hearkenest to prayer.

(*T.J.Ber.* IV, § 4, f. 8*b*, line 25.)

A prayer before going on a journey:

[960] May it be thy will, O Lord my God, to conduct me in peace, to direct my steps in peace, to uphold me in peace, and to deliver me from every enemy and ambush by the way. Send a blessing upon the work of my hands, and let me obtain grace, lovingkindness and mercy in thine eyes, and in the eyes of all who behold me. Blessed art thou, O Lord, who hearkenest unto prayer. (*Ber.* 29*b* (*P.B.* p. 310).)

A brief prayer in a moment, or place, of danger:

[961] R. Elazar said: Do thy will in heaven above; grant tranquillity of spirit to those who fear thee below, and do that which is good in thy sight. Blessed art thou, O Lord, who hearkenest unto prayer. (*Ber.* 29*b*.)

Various prayers which were often on the lips of individuals are preserved in the Talmuds. Some of these (e.g. [970]) became incorporated into the daily prayer-book:

[962] R. Elazar, on concluding his prayers, used to say: May it be thy will, O Lord our God, to cause love and brotherhood, peace and comradeship to abide in our lot, to enlarge our border with disciples, to prosper our goal with a [happy] end and with hope, to set our portion in the Garden of Eden, and fortify us in thy world with good companionship and with the good impulse, so that we may rise [day by day: Rashi] and feel [lit. find] the longing of our heart to fear thy name; and may the satisfaction of our souls come before thee for good.
(*Ber.* 16*b* (cp. *T.J.Ber.* IV, § 2, f. 7*d*, line 42).)

[963] R. Elazar b. Zadok said: My father used to pray a short prayer on the evening of Sabbaths, 'Of thy love, O Lord our God, with which thou hast loved Israel thy people, and of thy compassion, O our King, with which thou hast had compassion on the sons of thy covenant, thou hast given to us, O Lord our God, this great and holy seventh day in love.' (*T.Ber.* III, 7 (Z. p. 6, line 22; Davis and Adler's *Atonement* volume, p. 238).)

[964] R. Johanan was wont to say: May it be thy will, O Lord our God, to glance at our shame and look upon our evil plight; and do thou clothe thyself in thy mercy, cover thyself with thy might, enfold thyself with thy piety, and gird thyself with

thy grace, and may thy attribute of goodness and gentleness come before thee. (*Ber.* 16*b*.)

[965] R. Safra used to pray: May it be thy will, O Lord our God, to grant peace in the household above and the household below, and among the students who occupy themselves with thy Torah, whether they devote themselves thereto for its own sake, or not for its own sake; and as for them that devote themselves thereto not for its own sake, may it be thy will that they shall [at last] devote themselves thereto for its own sake. (*Ber.* 16*b fin.*–17*a*.)

['Household above': this is Dr Cohen's rendering. I prefer 'retinue', as in [913], above, for the Hebrew *famalya* or *familya* is not 'family', in the modern English sense, but it retains the idea of *famulus*. I observe that Goldschmidt has 'in der oberen und in der unteren Familie' and so does Pinner, who adds a note that the reference is to the angelic hosts (cp. [707] and [1643]). (H. L.)]

The 'household below' are the sages.

[966] Rab was wont to say: May it be thy will, O Lord our God, to grant us long life, a life of peace, a life of good, a life of blessing, a life of sustenance, a life of bodily vigour, a life marked by the fear of sin, a life free from shame and reproach, a life of prosperity and honour, a life in which the love of Torah and the fear of heaven shall cling to us, a life wherein thou fulfillest the desires of the heart for good. (*Ber.* 16*b* (cp. *P.B.* p. 154).)

The prayer of R. Tanḥum b. Eskolastiḳai:

[967] May it be thy will, O Lord our God and God of our fathers, that thou break, and cause to cease, the yoke of the evil *yetzer* in our hearts, for thou hast created us to do thy will, and we are bound to do thy will: thou desirest it, and we are desirous, and what prevents? The dough in the leaven [i.e. the evil *yetzer*]. It is revealed and known before thee that we have not within us the strength to resist it: therefore may it be thy will to cause it to cease from us, and to crush it; and then we will do thy will with a perfect heart. (*T.J.Ber.* IV, § 2, f. 7*d*, line 61.)

Two prayers of R. Ḥiyya b. Abba:

[968] Let our hearts be united in the fear of thy name; bring us near to what thou lovest; keep us far from what thou hatest.

May it be thy will, O Lord our God and the God of our

fathers, that thou put it into our hearts to perform a perfect repentance before thee, so that we be not ashamed before our fathers in the world to come. (*T.J.Ber.* IV, § 2, f. 7*d*, line 46.)

R. Pedat's prayer:

[969] May it be thy will, O Lord my God and God of my fathers, that no hatred against any man come into our hearts, and no hatred against us come into the hearts of any man, and may none be jealous of us, and may we not be jealous of any; and may thy Law be our labour all the days of our lives, and may our words be as supplications before thee.

(*T.J.Ber.* IV, § 2, f. 7*d*, line 57 (cp. Gaster, *P.B.* p. 140).)

Mar bar Rabina's prayer:

[970] O my God! Guard my tongue from evil and my lips from speaking guile, and to such as curse me let my soul be dumb, yea, let my soul be unto all as the dust. Open my heart to the Torah, and let my soul pursue thy commandments. If any design evil against me, speedily make their counsel of none effect, and frustrate their designs. Let the words of my mouth and the meditation of my heart be acceptable before thee, O Lord my Rock and Redeemer. (*Ber.* 17*a* (*P.B.* p. 54).)

Mar Zuṭra used this prayer in a house of mourning, at the grace after meals:

[971] Blessed art thou, O Lord our God, King of the universe, O God, our Father, our King, our Creator, our Redeemer, our Holy One, the Holy One of Jacob, the Living King, who art kind and dealest kindly, true God and Judge, who judgest with righteousness, and in judgment takest the souls [of men unto thyself], who rulest in the world, doing therein according to thy will, for all thy ways are judgment and all is thine. We are thy people and thy servants, and in all circumstances it is our duty to give thanks unto thee and to bless thee. O thou who repairest the breaches in Israel, mayest thou also repair this breach in Israel, granting us life. (*Ber.* 46*b*.)

This prayer is still used. See *P.B.* p. 283.

R. Hamnuna's prayer on the Day of Atonement was incorporated in the Prayer Book (*P.B.* p. 263):

[972] O my God, before I was formed I was nothing worth, and now that I have been formed, I am but as though I had not been

formed. Dust am I in my life: how much more so in my death. Behold I am before thee like a vessel filled with shame and confusion. O may it be thy will, O Lord my God and God of my fathers, that I may sin no more, and as to the sins I have committed, purge them away in thine abounding compassion, though not by means of affliction and sore diseases.

(*Yoma* 87*b*.)

A very ancient prayer, alluded to in the Talmud (*Ber.* 11*b*), is said immediately before the *Shema* at the evening service:

[973] With everlasting love[1] thou hast loved the house of Israel, thy people; a Law and commandments, statutes and judgments hast thou taught us. Therefore, O Lord our God, when we lie down, and when we rise up, we will meditate on thy statutes: yea, we will rejoice in the words of thy Law and in thy commandments for ever; for they are our life and the length of our days, and we will meditate on them day and night. And mayest thou never take away thy love from us. Blessed art thou, O Lord, who lovest thy people Israel. (*P.B.* p. 96.)

Another and longer form of the same prayer is recited in the morning service:

[974] With abounding love[1] hast thou loved us, O Lord our God, with great and exceeding pity hast thou pitied us. O our Father, our King, for our fathers' sake, who trusted in thee, and whom thou didst teach the statutes of life, be also gracious unto us and teach us. O our Father, merciful Father, ever compassionate, have mercy upon us; O put it into our hearts to understand and to discern, to mark, learn and teach, to heed, to do and to fulfil in love all the words of instruction in thy Law. Enlighten our eyes in thy Law, and let our hearts cleave to thy commandments, and unite our hearts to love and fear thy name, so that we be never put to shame. Because we have trusted in thy holy, great and revered name, we shall rejoice and be glad in thy salvation. O bring us in peace from the four corners of the earth, and make us go upright to our land; for thou art a God who workest salvation. Thou hast chosen us from all peoples and tongues, and hast brought us near unto thy great name for ever in faithfulness, that we might in love

[1] For an interesting reference to this prayer, see above [170].

give thanks unto thee and proclaim thy unity. Blessed art thou, O Lord, who hast chosen thy people Israel in love.

(*P.B.* pp. 39, 40.)

An ancient and famous prayer, at least as old as the Talmud, is known by its opening Hebrew word as the '*Alenu* prayer. A good deal of information about it will be found in Abrahams' *Companion*, pp. LXXXVI–LXXXVIII, and in Moore, I, 434, and II, 373. The undisguised pride in the supposed privileged and peculiar position of Israel in the eyes of God, and the no less undisguised disdain of the heathen in the opening lines of the prayer, are unpleasant to us moderns, but the universalistic hope in the latter part of the prayer is no less characteristically Rabbinic:

[975] It is our duty to praise the Lord of all things, to ascribe greatness to Him who formed the world in the beginning, since He has not made us like the nations of other lands, and has not placed us like other families of the earth, since He has not assigned unto us a portion as unto them, nor a lot as unto all their multitude. For we bend the knee and offer worship and thanks before the supreme King of kings, the Holy One, blessed be He, who stretched forth the heavens and laid the foundations of the earth, the seat of whose glory is in the heavens above, and the abode of whose might is in the loftiest heights. He is our God; there is none else: in truth He is our King; there is none besides Him; as it is written in His Law, 'And thou shalt know this day, and lay it to thine heart, that the Lord He is God in heaven above and upon the earth beneath: there is none else.'

We therefore hope in thee, O Lord our God, that we may speedily behold the glory of thy might, when thou wilt remove the abominations from the earth, and the idols will be utterly cut off, when the world will be perfected under the kingdom of the Almighty, and all the children of flesh will call upon thy name, when thou wilt turn unto thyself all the wicked of the earth. Let all the inhabitants of the world perceive and know that unto thee every knee must bow, every tongue must swear. Before thee, O Lord our God, let them bow and fall; and unto thy glorious name let them give honour; let them all accept the yoke of thy kingdom, and do thou reign over them speedily, and for ever and ever. For the kingdom is thine, and to all eternity thou wilt reign in glory; as it is written in thy Law, 'The Lord shall reign for ever and ever.' And it is said, 'And the Lord shall be king over all the earth: in that day shall the Lord be One, and His name One.' (*P.B.* pp. 76, 77.)

[In regard to the translation of '*Alenu*, I venture, in all humility, to differ from the late Mr Singer who has here given a literal translation which obscures the real meaning of the prayer. Let me cite from other Prayer Books. The Sephardic rite has, 'Since He has not made us like *some* nations of *other* countries, nor established us like *other* families of the earth.' This is from de Sola, second ed., 1852, vol. I, p. 51. It is substantially the same in A. Haliva's Prayer Book (London, 1852), and partially the same in Gaster. It is so rendered in A. P. Mendes' Ashkenazic liturgy (London, 1864). A. ben B. Créhange and E. A. Astruc, in the French Prayer Book (Paris, 1864), have 'Il ne nous a pas traité comme les peuples de certaines contrées: il ne nous a pas confondus avec toutes les tribus de la terre.' Finally let me cite what I consider the best and most accurate rendering, that in Pool's *P.B.* p. 90:

It is for us to praise the universal Lord,
To acclaim the greatness of the God of creation,
For He has not made us heathens,
Nor allowed us to be a pagan people,
Nor given us their inheritance,
And the destiny of their masses,
That bow down to vanity and hollowness,
'And pray to a god that saves not'.

The object of these qualifying clauses is to make the original meaning clear, namely, that it is a thanksgiving to God for having been favoured with a knowledge of Him instead of having grown up amid idolatrous surroundings. True, the idolater who finds God is more praiseworthy than the Jew who worships Him because his father and mother have taught him to do so. The esteem in which proselytes are held is shown by passages in Chapter xxx. This prayer, however, is concerned, not with proselytes, but with Israel. It is a joyful recognition of privilege and a humble declaration of duty. In this there is nothing particularist or offensive.

It *would* be offensive if the prayer, as its literal interpretation might be misconstrued to imply, were an arrogant assertion of superiority over contemporaries, in this case, monotheists and our spiritual equals. But the prayer, by reason of age and environment, did not refer to Christians (for details, see Abrahams' note: art. in *J.E.*, s.v.: and Elbogen, *Der Jüd. Gottesdienst*, refs. in index). As usual, it was a convert to Christianity who was responsible for this fable, and who discovered that the numerical value of 'and nothingness' could amount to that of 'Jesus', just as another hit upon the fact that the initials of '*Akum* (worshippers of stars and the zodiac, '*ovede kokabim umazza-*

lot) could represent '*ovede Cristus u-Maria*, 'worshippers of Christ and Mary'. The words in question ('and nothingness') do not occur in the version given by Mr Montefiore. For after 'their multitude' and before 'For we bend the knee', a verse is omitted in the Ashkenazic rite. It runs thus: 'For they bow down to vanity and nothingness and worship a god that cannot save,' from Isa. XXX, 7 and XLV, 20. It will be found in other rites. In Moslem lands, where there was no Inquisition, the misrepresentations of converts would have been ineffectual, and the verse, therefore, has survived. On this, and on the libels of converts, see William Popper's *Censorship of Hebrew Books*, New York, 1899 (refs. in index) and illustrations in *J.E.* s.v. 'Censorship'.

The history of this prayer and its association with martyrs deserve study (see *J.E.* and Abrahams). This association, and the fact that it comes originally from the liturgy of New Year (*P.B.* p. 247), invests it with special solemnity. No Jew who recites it ever thinks of it in relation to Christians: the chief thought in his mind is the noble conclusion. It is, in fact, a universalist pronouncement of the Messianic hope, and with this idea every Service concludes. (H. L.)]

A fine ancient prayer is that found in the liturgy for the New Year (cf. Abrahams' *Companion*, p. CXCVII, and Moore, II, 64, 210):

[976] Our God and God of our fathers, reign thou in thy glory over the whole universe, and be exalted above all the earth in thine honour, and shine forth in the splendour and excellence of thy might upon all the inhabitants of thy world, that whatsoever has been made may know that thou hast made it, and whatsoever has been created may understand that thou hast created it, and whatsoever has breath in its nostrils may say, the Lord God of Israel is King, and His dominion rules over all. Sanctify us by thy commandments, and grant our portion in thy Law; satisfy us with thy goodness, and gladden us with thy salvation: O purify our hearts to serve thee in truth, for thou art God in truth, and thy word is truth, and endures for ever. Blessed art thou, O Lord, King over all the earth, who sanctifiest Israel and the Day of Memorial. (*P.B.* p. 249.)

Highly curious in its realism is a recorded prayer of the High Priest on the Day of Atonement. The last words mean: The travellers (or, more probably, the pilgrims returning from Jerusalem) may pray for fine weather, but rain is a greater general need:

[977] How ran the prayer of the High Priest on the Day of Atonement? When he left the Holy of Holies, he said, 'May it be thy will

that this year be a year of rain and warmth and dew, a year of grace and blessing, a year of cheapness and of plenty, a year of good trade, and may thy people not need the help of one another [i.e. may all be independent], and let them not assume lordly power one over the other, and do thou pay no heed to the prayers of travellers [i.e. the returning pilgrims from Jerusalem].' (*Lev.R.*, Aḥare Mot, xx, 4 (cp. *Yoma* 53*b*; Gaster, *Atonement* volume, p. 175).)

[The High Priest was in a position of some difficulty, and we can well understand that he uttered a 'short' prayer. For he was a Sadducee, and the Sanhedrin was predominantly Pharisee. The latter, urban inhabitants in Jerusalem, needed rain badly and immediately, for at the end of summer, when the Day of Atonement was celebrated, their cisterns were empty. The Sadducean farmers, however, had their wells and springs, and were not in such a hurry. And the pilgrims wanted to reach home in safety. The first rainfall made the roads impassable. One must not pray for something which one does not desire whole-heartedly. Hence arose the compromise, which has lasted till this day. Very soon after the Day of Atonement, that is, at the conclusion of Tabernacles, 12 days later, the orthodox Jews 'mention' the rain (see *P.B.* p. 44 foot and rubric). From 4 December, that is, 60 days after the autumnal equinox, they 'pray' for rain (*P.B.* p. 47; see the variant in Gaster, p. 32 and see Abrahams' notes in each case; see also the beginning of *Ta'an.* and *Ber.* v, 2. On the whole question, see L. Finkelstein, in *Harvard Theol. Rev.* XXII, No. 3, July 1929, p. 194). (H. L.)]

By a fanciful interpretation of Isa. LVI, 7 it was argued that God Himself prays! What is His prayer? Rab said it ran thus:

[978] May it be my will that my compassion may overcome mine anger, and that it may prevail over my attributes [of justice and judgment], and that I may deal with my children according to the attribute of compassion, and that I may not act towards them according to the strict line of justice. (*Ber.* 7*a*.)

In Palestine or Babylonia rain was of enormous importance. We can gather that from the praise of rain of which I may quote a few samples:

[979] R. Abbahu said: The day of rain is more important than the day of resurrection, for the day of resurrection is for the righteous only and not for the wicked, while the day of rain is for the righteous and for the wicked. (*Ta'an.* 7*a* (Malter, p. 39).)

[The connection between the rain and the resurrection goes back to the *Amidah*, or even earlier, since the *Amidah* gives expression to an idea which is much older than itself. The first blessing of the *Amidah* (*P.B.* p. 44), is called *Aboth* or patriarchs, since it invokes the 'God of Abraham, God of Isaac, God of Jacob'. The second, which begins 'Thou, O Lord, art mighty', is called 'Mights', or 'Powers', and deals with two manifestations of God's *might*, the rain and the resurrection. The blessing was the first of the three 'tests'. The Synagogue being free to all, it might well happen that the leader of prayers held heretical views, and so, if the *Amidah* was being recited by a Sadducee, he would be forced to avow his belief in the resurrection. The reference to rain would also be in the nature of a test to him (see note to [878] above). But already in Isa. XXVI, 19, dew and resurrection are combined. It was a natural union, for as soon as the first rainfall comes, after summer, the parched land of Palestine revives with such amazing rapidity that the most casual observer cannot fail to be struck by the connection. Now the 'God of Abraham' phrase comes from Moses at the Burning Bush (Exod. III, 6), and was a Midrashic proof of the resurrection, 'God of the living, not of the dead.' It is so used also by Jesus (Mark XII, 27). And when he says 'Ye err, that ye know not the Scriptures nor the power of God' (*ib.* 24), he means that the resurrection is taught in the Scriptures (i.e. Moses at the bush) and in the *Amidah*, for 'power of God' is, in my opinion, a reference to the second blessing, called 'Powers, Mights' (*Geburot*). The Hebrew root from which *Geburot* is derived is often rendered in the Septuagint by the Greek root which is used in the Gospels for 'power'. (H. L.)]

[980] For four sins rain is held back, (1) idolatry, (2) unchastity, (3) bloodshed, (4) because of those who promise publicly to give charity, and do not give it. For the merit of three things rain comes down: for the merit of the earth, for the merit of lovingkindness, for the merit of sufferings, and all three are indicated in the one verse of Job XXXVII, 13: 'He causes it to come whether for correction, or for His land, or for mercy.'

(*T.J.Ta'an.* III, § 3, f. 66*c*, line 28.)

[981] A philosopher asked R. Joshua b. Hananiah, 'At what time are all men equal, and when do the nations worship God?' He replied, 'On the day when all rejoice.' 'When is that?' said the other. 'When the heavens have been shut up, and all are in distress, and the rain comes down, and all rejoice and praise God.' R. Tanḥum b. Ḥiyya said: The falling of the rain is greater than the giving of the Law, for the giving of the Law was

a joy only to Israel, while the falling of the rain is a rejoicing for all the world, including the cattle and the wild beasts and the birds. (*Midr.Ps.* on CXVII, 1 (240*a*, §1).)

[982] R. Hoshaiah said: Great indeed is the force of rain, for it is equal to the whole creation....R. Isaac said: Rain wins God's favour like the sacrifices. R. Tanḥum b. Ḥanilai said: Rain atones for sins: R. Ḥiyya bar Abba said: Rain is as important as the resurrection of the dead...nay, it is even greater than the resurrection of the dead. For the resurrection applies only to man, rain to both man and beast; the resurrection only to Israel, rain both to Israel and the heathen. A heathen once asked R. Joshua b. Ḳarḥa, 'You have festivals and we have festivals, but when you rejoice, we do not; when we rejoice, you do not. When do we *all* rejoice?' He replied, 'When it rains,' as it is said, 'The meadows are clothed with flocks; the valleys are covered with corn; they shout for joy, yea, they sing' (Ps. LXV, 13). And immediately after it says, 'Shout with joy before God, all the earth' (Ps. LXVI, 1). It does not say, 'Priests, Levites and Israelites', but 'shout for joy, all the earth'.

(*Gen.R.*, Bereshit, XIII, 4–6 (Th. pp. 115–17).)

For the question whether the resurrection was limited to Israel or whether it applied also to Gentiles see [1563–4].

The sayings of R. Isaac and R. Tanḥum are apparently an abbreviated form for: 'Rain is a sign that God's favour has been won; it is a sign that Israel's atonement has been accepted.'

'Aforetime, in Jerusalem, when public fasts were proclaimed under stress of scarcity [i.e. supplications for rain], no man was allowed to lead in prayer unless he, too, had an empty larder at home' (Abrahams, *Studies in Pharisaism*, II, 110).

[983] They stood up in prayer, and sent down before the Ark an old man, well versed [in prayer], one that had children, and whose house was empty [of sustenance], so that he might be whole-hearted in prayer.

(*Ta'an.* II, 2 (Professor Danby's translation).)

In the daily *Amidah* for half the year, in the prayer about the resurrection ('Thou, O Lord, art mighty for ever, thou quickenest the dead, thou art mighty to save'), after the words 'Thou art mighty to save' are inserted the words: 'Thou causest the wind to blow and the rain to fall.' Many are the stories about the men who prayed successfully for rain.

[984] Our Rabbis have taught: It happened once that the greater part of the month of Adar had passed, and no rain had yet fallen. Honi the Circle-drawer was, therefore, asked to pray that rain should fall. He did so, but rain did not fall. He then drew a circle, and placed himself in its centre, as did the prophet Habakkuk, who said (Hab. II, 1): 'I will stand upon my watch,' and said before God: 'Master of the world! Thy children have set their face upon me, because I am, as it were, thy intimate.[1] I swear by thy great name that I will not move from here until thou showest mercy to thy children.' Rain began to trickle. The people therefore said to him: 'Master, we see thee, and this is a warranty to us that we shall not die, but it seems to us that this rain comes only in order to free thee from thy oath.' 'Ye have seen me, and ye shall not die,' Honi replied, and continuing his prayer, he said, 'Not for such rain did I pray, but for rain sufficient to fill the cisterns, ditches and caves.' The rain then came down with vehemence, each drop as big as the opening of a barrel, and the Rabbis estimated that none of them contained less than a *log*. The people again said to him: 'Master, we see thee, and this is a warranty that we shall not die, but it seems to us that this rain comes only to destroy the world.' 'Ye have seen me, and ye shall not die,' he replied, and then continued: 'Not for such rain did I pray, but for a rain of benevolence, blessing and graciousness!' The rain then continued coming in proper measure so that the Israelites had to go up from the streets of Jerusalem to the Temple Mount on account of the rain. They then said to him: 'Just as thou hast prayed for the rain to come, so pray now that it should stop.' He, however, replied, 'I have a tradition that it is not proper to pray for the cessation of too much good; however, bring to me a bullock for the confession of my sins!' They brought him a bullock, upon which Honi laid both his hands, and said: 'Master of the world! Thy people Israel, whom thou hast brought out of Egypt, can stand neither too much good, nor too much punishment; when thou becamest wroth [withholding rain], they could not stand it; let it be thy will that there be ease in the world.' Immediately the wind blew, the clouds dispersed, and the sun began to shine, and the people

[1] Lit. a son of the house.

went out into the fields and brought home morils and truffles. Thereupon Simeon b. Sheṭaḥ sent word to Honi, saying: 'Wert thou not Honi, I would order thy excommunication; if these years were like those of Elijah, would not the name of God be profaned through thee? However, what can I do since thou behavest petulantly before God as a son behaves before his father, who then grants the son's desire, so that if the son says to him, Bathe me in warm water, the father bathes him in warm water; if the son says, Wash me with cold water, he washes him in cold water; if he says, Give me nuts, peaches, almonds and pomegranates, he gives him nuts, peaches, almonds and pomegranates.' (*Ta'an.* 23*a* (Malter, p. 167).)

For circle drawing cp. [199].

[For Honi (Onias) and his 'miracle', see Gaster, *Atonement* volume, p. 12: 'circle-drawer' is sometimes interpreted as 'wheel-wright' or 'geometer'. Onias was the hero of a fable of the 'seven sleepers' type: for this see *Ta'an.* 23*a* and Malter's note on p. 171 of his ed. Onias died as a martyr. During the civil war between Hyrcanus and Aristobulus, after the death of Queen Salome, Onias refused to pray for the victory of either side, for 'these and those are thy people'. He was stoned to death. The story has been suppressed in Rabbinic sources, but is narrated by Josephus (*Ant.* XIV, 2, § 1, 22–4), who states that each side was eager for the prayer of Onias because his prayers for rain were so successful (cp. note to [199]). (H. L.)]

[985] It happened that R. Eliezer went before the ark, and said the twenty-four benedictions, but his prayer was not answered. R. Akiba then succeeded him before the Ark and said: 'Our Father, our King, we have sinned before thee. Our Father, our King, we have no king beside thee. Our Father, our King, have compassion upon us!' His prayer was answered, and the Rabbis therefore began to utter suspicion against R. Eliezer. However, a heavenly voice came forth and proclaimed: 'R. Akiba is not greater than R. Eliezer, but the one is of a forbearing disposition, while the other is not.' [The words for 'forbearing disposition' one might also render 'more yielding', 'more conciliatory', 'less insistent upon his rights, or claims'.] (*Ta'an.* 25*b* (Malter's translation, p. 193).)

[986] Our Rabbis have taught: It once happened that the Israelites went up to Jerusalem for the festival, and there was not enough water in the city for drinking. Naḳdimon [Nicodemus, cp. [1168]]

b. Gorion therefore betook himself to a general who possessed water, and said to him: 'Lend me twelve wells of water, and I will return to you twelve wells of water, or, in case I cannot do so, I will give you twelve talents of silver.' He stipulated the sum of money, and fixed the day for payment. When the time arrived, the general sent word to Naḳdimon that he should deliver either the water or the money. The latter replied, 'The day is not yet over.' At noon he sent to him again, saying, 'Deliver the water or the money.' Naḳdimon again replied, 'I have still time.' In the afternoon the general sent again the demand that either the water or the money be delivered, and Naḳdimon again replied, 'The day is not yet over.' The general said: 'There has been no rain for a whole year, and you expect it to come now?' He then went in good spirits to the bathhouse. But while the general was on his way to the bathhouse, Naḳdimon went to the Temple, wrapped himself in his cloak, and prayed: 'Master of the world! It is well known before thee that I did not do it for my own glory or for that of my father's house, but for thy glory, that the pilgrims should have water.' Immediately the skies became clouded, and rain began to fall, so that all wells overflowed with water. While the general was coming from the bathhouse, Naḳdimon came from the Temple, and when they met, the former said to the latter: 'I know that it is for you alone that your God disturbed His world. However, I can still maintain my claim against you, so as to get my money from you, for the sun has set, and the rain came during the time that belonged to me.' Naḳdimon returned to the Temple, wrapped himself, and again stood in prayer, saying: 'Master of the world! As thou hast performed a miracle for me before, do it also now!' Immediately the wind blew, the clouds were dispersed and the sun shone. The general then said: 'Were it not that the sun shone, I would have had a claim against you, to collect my money from you.' (**Note 90**.) (*Ta'an.* 19*b*–20*a* (Malter, p. 141).)

[987] Ḥanin ha-Neḥba was the son of the daughter of Honi the Circle-drawer. When the world needed rain, the Rabbis would send schoolchildren to him, who would pull him by the corners of his garments, and say to him: 'Father, father! Give us rain!' Said Ḥanin: 'Master of the world! Do it for the sake of these, who do not distinguish between the Father who

gives rain and a father who does not give rain.' And the rain came. (*Ta'an.* 23*b* (Malter, p. 175).)

For Honi or Onias the Circle-drawer see [984].

[988] Rab happened to come to a certain place, where he ordered a fast. The reader of the congregation then went down to the praying desk and recited, 'He causes the wind to blow,' and immediately a wind blew, and when he recited, 'He causes the rain to fall,' rain fell. Rab therefore asked him: 'What is your occupation?' 'I am a teacher of young children,' he replied, 'and I teach the children of the poor as well as those of the rich, and if anyone is so poor that he is unable to pay, I take no fee from him. I possess a fish-pond, and if a child is careless in his studies, I bribe him by giving him some of the fish, and thus win him over to study.' (*Ta'an.* 24*a* (Malter, p. 181).)

[989] Abba Hilkiah was the grandson of Honi the Circle-drawer. Once the Rabbis sent to him a pair of scholars to ask him to pray for rain. When they came to his house, they did not find him at home. They went to see him in the field, and found him ploughing the ground. They greeted him, but he did not heed them. He was picking up chips of wood and, towards evening, on his way home, he carried the chips on one shoulder and his cloak on the other. The whole way along he did not put on his shoes, but when he had to cross the water, he put them on. When he came across thorns and shrubs, he lifted up his garments, and when he reached the city, his wife came to meet him bedecked with her finery. When he arrived at the door of his house, he let her enter first, then he followed. He sat down to eat, but did not invite the scholars to join him. Distributing cakes to the children, he gave to the older child one, and to the younger two. Turning to his wife, he said: 'I know that these scholars came to see me on account of rain; let us go up to the roof and pray; the Holy One, blessed be He, will, perhaps, accept our prayer, and there will be rain.' When on the roof, he stood praying in one corner, and she in another. The clouds appeared first over the corner where his wife stood. He came down and asked the scholars: 'Why did the Rabbis come?' 'The Rabbis sent us to the Master, that you might pray for rain,' they replied. Said he: 'Blessed be the Lord who put you beyond the need of Abba Hilkiah's prayer!' They, however, replied:

'We know well that this rain is come through you, but be that as it may, we should like you to explain to us those actions of yours that greatly surprised us. Why, when we greeted you, did you not heed us?' 'I had hired myself out for the day, so I thought I had no right to interrupt my work.' 'Why did you carry the chips of wood on one shoulder and your cloak on the other?' 'It is a borrowed garment,' he said, 'and it was loaned to me for the purpose of wearing, but not for the purpose of placing wood on it.' 'Why did you not put on your shoes the entire way,' the scholars continued, 'but when you had to cross the water you put them on?' 'Because the entire way,' he replied, 'I could see [what I was stepping on]. In the water I could not see.' 'Why did you lift up your garments when you came upon thorns and shrubs?' 'Because a scratch on the body heals up, a rent in the garment does not heal up.' 'Why did your wife come to meet you so well dressed?' 'In order that I should not cast my eye upon another woman.' 'Why did your wife enter the house first and you after her?' 'Because you are not known to me.' 'Why did you not invite us to eat with you?' 'Because there was not enough food, and I did not want to get your thanks for nothing.' 'Why did you give one cake to the older child and two to the younger?' 'The older one stays at home, while the younger goes to school.' 'Why did the clouds appear first over the corner where your wife was standing?' 'Because the woman is usually in the house, and the good she does is direct.'[1] [Or it may be: 'Because there were some highwaymen living in my neighbourhood; I prayed that they should die, while she prayed that they should improve their ways.' Cp. Beruriah's exegesis in **Note 40**.] (*Ta'an.* 23 *a*, *b* (Malter, p. 172).)

[990] Levi b. Sisi fasted and prayed for rain in vain. Said he: 'Master of the world! Thou hast gone up, and taken thy seat in heaven, and showest no consideration for [the suffering of] thy children.' Rain fell, but Levi became lame. R. Elazar said: One must never reproach God. (*Ta'an.* 25 *a* (Malter, p. 190).)

In *P.B.* pp. 287–92 will be found a number of 'blessings on various occasions'. Most of them go back to ancient times. There are blessings for partaking of different kinds of food, for the teaching ran:

[991] Our Rabbis have taught: A man is forbidden to enjoy anything

[1] The hungry find immediate relief by her supply of food.

of this world without a benediction, and whoever does so commits sacrilege. (*Ber.* 35*a*.)

Similarly in the *Tosefta* we find:

[992] Let not a man taste anything until he pronounces a benediction, for it is said: 'The earth is the Lord's, and the fulness thereof; the world and they that dwell in it' (Ps. XXIV, 1). He that gets enjoyment out of this world without a benediction, behold, he has defrauded [the Lord] to such a degree that at last all the commands are loosed for him. [This means that they are considered of no account.] Let not a man make use of his face, his hands, and his feet, save for the honour of his Owner, for it is said: 'The Lord has made everything for His own purpose' (Prov. XVI, 4) (the literal meaning is: 'for *its* own purpose').

(*T.Ber.* IV, 1 (Z. p. 8, line 20; cp. [92]).)

[This rendering is the traditional one: it is followed by Lukyn Williams (p. 45 of his *Tractate Berakhoth, Mishna and Tosefta*, S.P.C.K. 1921). It is, however, possible to suggest an alternative, on the basis of *Sab.* 50*b*, which cites the verse of Proverbs, used here, as its authority. The passage is a *Baraita* and runs thus: 'A man should daily wash his face, hands and feet in honour of [lit. for the sake of] his Maker,' as it says in Proverbs XVI, 4. (H. L.)]

It is characteristic of the Rabbinic joy in life and in God's gifts that a blessing is to be said 'on seeing trees blossoming the first time in the year':

[993] Rab Judah said: He who goes out during the days of Nissan and sees the trees budding, should say, 'Blessed be He who has caused nothing to be lacking in His universe, and created therein beautiful creations and beautiful trees, wherefrom men may derive pleasure.' (*Ber.* 43*b*.)

This, and most of the following blessings, may be found in *P.B.* p. 292.

[994] If a man sees beautiful persons and beautiful trees, he should say: 'Blessed be He who created beautiful creatures in His world.'

(*T.Ber.* VII, 7 (Z. p. 16 (**Note 65**), line 21).)

It is pleasant that the Rabbis were broad-minded enough to utter a blessing on the knowledge and wisdom of Gentiles:

[995] Blessed art thou, O Lord our God, King of the universe, who hast given of thy wisdom to flesh and blood.

(*Ber.* 58*a*; *P.B.* p. 291.)

A blessing in constant use on festivals and all joyful occasions is this:

[996] Blessed art thou, O Lord our God, King of the universe, who hast kept us in life, and hast preserved us, and hast enabled us to reach this season.

On hearing good tidings one must say:

[997] Blessed art thou, O Lord our God, King of the universe, who art good and dispensest good.

On hearing evil tidings the following:

[998] Blessed art thou, O Lord our God, King of the universe, the true judge.

[999] R. Me'ir said: Whence do we learn that as you should say a blessing over the good, so you should say a blessing over the evil? Because it says, 'Which the Lord thy God [*Eloheka*] gives thee' (Deut. VIII, 10; XXVI, 11; XXVIII, 53). And 'thy God' means 'thy judge'; in every judgment with which He judges you, whether with the attribute [or measure] of good or with the attribute of punishment, bless God.

(*T.Ber.* VII, 3 (Z. p. 16 (**Note 65**), line 3); *Ber.* 48*b*.)

The teaching of the Rabbis was that one must bless God for sorrow as well as for joy:

[1000] A man is in duty bound to utter a benediction for the bad even as he utters one for the good; as it is said, 'And thou shalt love the Lord thy God with all thy heart, and with all thy soul, and with all thy might' (Deut. VI, 5)—'with all thy heart', i.e. with thy two impulses, with the good and with the evil impulse; 'with all thy soul', even if He take thy soul; 'with all thy might', i.e. with all thy wealth. Another explanation of 'with all thy might' [*me'odeka*]—with whatever measure [*middah*] He metes out to thee, do thou return Him thanks [*modeh*].

(*Ber.* IX, 5 (cp. [702]).)

[1001] David said: 'If thou actest in mercy towards me, I will sing to thee, and if thou actest in judgment towards me, I will sing to thee. Whether so or so, I will sing to thee' (Ps. CI, 1). So Ps. CXVI, 3, 4, 13: 'I will call upon God in sorrow as in deliverance.' Job said: 'The Lord gave, the Lord has taken away,

blessed be the name of the Lord' (I, 21). When He gave, it was in compassion; when He took, it was in compassion.
(*T.J.Ber.* IX, § 7, f. 14*b*, line 34 (cp. [726]).)

There is a blessing to be said on entering a cemetery:

[1002] R. Johanan used the formula: He who knows your number, He will awaken you, and will remove the dust from your eyes.[1] Blessed art thou, O Lord, who quickenest the dead. R. Ḥana said: He who formed you in justice, sustained you in justice, and took you away in justice, will thereafter quicken you in justice. He who knows your number will remove the dust from your eyes. Blessed art thou, O Lord, who quickenest the dead. (*T.J.Ber.* IX, § 3, 13*d*, line 53 (cp. *P.B.* p. 320).)

In fine, God must be ever reverenced and loved.

[1003] Fear God and love God; the Law says both; act both from love and fear; from love, for, if you would hate, no lover hates, and from fear, for, if you would kick, no fearer kicks.
(*T.J.Ber.* IX, § 7, f. 14*b*, line 45 (cp. [272]).)

[1004] One verse says: 'Thou shalt love the Lord thy God,' and one verse says: 'Thou shalt fear the Lord thy God.' So act both from love and from fear. Act from love; then, if thou wouldst hate, know that thou lovest, and no lover hates; act from fear; for, if thou wouldst rebel, no fearer rebels (cp. *R.T.* p. 228).
(*T.J.Soṭ.* V, § 7, f. 20*c*, line 38.)

[1005] R. Eliezer says: If it is stated 'with all thy soul', why is it stated 'with all thy might'? And if it is stated 'with all thy might', why is it stated 'with all thy soul'? But should there be a man whose body is dearer to him than his money, therefore it is stated 'with all thy soul', and should there be a man whose money is dearer to him than his body, therefore it is stated 'with all thy might'. R. Akiba says: 'With all thy soul' [means] even if He take thy soul. (*Ber.* 61*b* (cp. [1000]).)

[1006] Judah, the son of Tema, said: Be strong as a leopard, light as an eagle, fleet as a hart, and strong as a lion, to do the will of thy Father who is in heaven. (*Aboth* V, 23 (*P.B.* p. 203).)

[1] 'Who knows your number' means: who knows the total number of the dead, none being lost (cp. Isa. XL, 26).

[1007] Raba said: When men are brought to the Judgment, they will be asked, 'Have you been honest in your business? Have you set aside fixed times for the study of the Law? Have you fulfilled the duty of procreation? Have you hoped for the salvation of Israel [i.e. did you believe in the coming of the Messiah]? Have you searched after wisdom? Have you deduced one thing from another [in study]? And yet, if the fear of God is your treasure, all is well, and if not, it is not well' (Isa. XXXIII, 6). [The fear of God is the preponderant test in the Judgment.] (*Sab.* 31*a fin.*)

[1008] As to the God-fearing man, the whole world was created for his sake. He is equal in worth to the whole world. (*Ber.* 6*b fin.*)

[1009] R. Judah b. Tema was wont to say: Love and fear God; tremble and rejoice when you perform the commandments; if you have done a little wrong to your neighbour, let it seem to you large; if you have done him a big kindness, let it seem to you small; if he has done to you a big evil, let it seem to you small; if he has done to you a small kindness, let it seem to you large. (*Ab.R.N.* (vers. I), XLI, 67*a*.)

[1010] Let a man love God with a perfect love, whether it go well with him or ill. (*Tan.d.b.El.* p. 63.)

[1011] The reward of the lover is two portions: that of the fearer is one. Hence the Gentiles [who fear God without loving Him] enjoy only this world, while Israel, who both loves and fears God, enjoys this world and the next. (*Tan.d.b.El.* p. 141.)

[1012] How can a man acquire his Father in Heaven? He may acquire Him by his good deeds and by the study of the Torah. God will cause him to acquire this world and the world to come and the days of the Messiah. God acquires man through [man's] love, brotherliness, through reverence, through amity, truth, peace, lowliness and humility, through study, through little worldly business, through attendance on scholars, and discussions with pupils, through gladness of heart, seemly behaviour and by man's nay being nay and his yea being yea. (*Tan.d.b.El.* p. 128.)

The antithesis—verbal rather than real—of God acquiring man may be taken to mean that through the virtues mentioned God obtains the service of man.

[1013] 'Therefore the Gentiles [lit. the virgins] love thee' (Cant. I, 3). Even the Gentiles recognise the wisdom, understanding and discernment [which God's words impart], and they attain to the root principles of the Law: they love God with a perfect love, whether He do good to them or evil. (*Tan.d.b.El.* p. 37.)

[With this passage we may compare *Yalkuṭ*, Lek leka, §76: God said to Moses: 'Is there respect of persons with me? Whether it be Israelite or Gentile, man or woman, slave or handmaid, whoever does a good deed (*miẓwah*), shall find the reward at its side, as it says, "Thy righteousness is like the everlasting hills: man and beast alike thou savest, O Lord" (Ps. XXXVI, 6).' (H. L.)]

Some of these passages are given in H. L.'s essays in the two volumes of *Judaism and Christianity*, ed. by W. O. E. Oesterley and H. Loewe (S.P.C.K. 1937).

It is noteworthy that in the *Tanna*, passages of a markedly universalistic character alternate with others of an entirely contrary tendency (cp. [1561]).

[1014] Rabban Gamaliel[1] said: Do His will as if it were thy will, that He may do thy will as if it were His will. Nullify thy will before His will, that He may nullify the will of others before thy will. (*Aboth* II, 4.)

[1015] That fear of the Lord, which wisdom makes the crown of her head, humility makes the imprint of her shoe.[2]

(*T.J.Sab.* I, § 5, f. 3*c*, line 17.)

[1016] One must not behave with levity in a Synagogue, nor enter the building merely to escape heat or cold or rain. One must not eat or drink in a Synagogue, or go to sleep in it, or walk about in it. But the building may be used for learning Torah or Mishnah, for lectures and for public funeral orations.

(*T.Meg.* III, 7 (Z. p. 224, line 7).)

[The Synagogue was much more than a place for divine service. It was a centre for study and charity and social work. Strangers were fed there, hence *Ḳiddush* was recited on Friday and Festival evenings during the service (cf. *P.B.* p. 122), save on the first two nights of Passover, when strangers would be given hospitality not in the Synagogue but in private homes because of the domestic paschal ritual. Sometimes the social side was unduly stressed, and irreverence crept into the service, which might follow immediately on a joyous meal or

[1] Son of R. Judah the Prince.

[2] Cp. [454] and [1377]. Cp. also *Judaism and Christianity*, vol. II, pp. 227–9.

a contentious business meeting. The same problem exists to-day for social workers, who are divided between the advantages of maintaining a special room for conducting divine worship and of concluding an evening's activities with prayer in the place where these activities have been carried on. R. Ishmael b. Elazar (in *Sab.* 32*a*) refers to irreverence on the part of women and of the *Am ha-Aretz*, who call the Holy Ark a cupboard and the Synagogue 'People's House' (*Bet 'Am*). And this is also said to have been one of the reasons which led to the destruction of Jerusalem. (H. L.)]

Chapter XV

JUSTICE, HONESTY, TRUTH IN OATHS

Some of the last excerpts lead on naturally to a series of quotations dealing with the favourite Rabbinic virtues—to those, I mean, upon which they would seem to lay most stress and to dwell upon with greatest fervour. And, perhaps, the virtue which one can most fitly begin with is justice, though, frequently, justice is not a completely adequate translation. What one wants, but has not got in English, is an equivalent for the German *das Recht*.

[1017] One of the three recommendations of the Men of the Great Synagogue, the supposed successors of the prophets, was, 'Be deliberate in judging.' (*Aboth* I, 1.)

[1018] R. Simeon b. Gamaliel said: Do not sneer at justice, for it is one of the three feet of the world, for the sages taught that the world stands on three things: justice, truth and peace. Therefore reflect that if you pervert justice, you shake the world, because justice is one of its three feet.... It is written, 'To do justice and righteousness is better than sacrifice' (Prov. XXI, 3). For sacrifices could be brought only when the Temple existed, but justice and righteousness can be applied both then and after. Sacrifices atone only for involuntary sins, but justice and righteousness atone both for voluntary and involuntary sins; sacrifices are brought only by men, but justice and righteousness are used also by the world above [i.e. in heaven, among the angels]. Sacrifices can occur only in this world, but righteousness and justice are for this world and for the world to come. (*Deut.R.*, Shofeṭim, V, 1 and 3.)

[1019] R. Simeon b. Gamaliel used to say: On three things the world rests, on justice, truth and peace. And all three are contained in Zech. VIII, 16: 'These are the things ye shall do: speak ye every man the truth with his neighbour; with truth, with peace, and with justice, judge in your gates.' And the three are one. If truth is wrought, peace is wrought; where justice is wrought, peace and truth are wrought also. (*Pes.K.* 140*b*.)

[1020] As God is urgent concerning the Ten Commandments, so is He urgent about justice, for on justice the world depends.
(*Exod.R.*, Mishpaṭim, xxx, 15.)

[1021] To every judge who judges truly, even for an hour, the Scripture reckons it as if he had been a partner with God in the work of creation. (*Sab.* 10*a* (cp. *Mek.*², *Amalek*, Yitro, § 2, p. 196; *Mek.*³, § 4, vol. II, p. 179).)

[1022] R. Elazar said: The whole Torah depends upon justice. Therefore God gave enactments about justice (Exod. XXI, 1) immediately after the Ten Commandments, because men transgress justice, and God punishes them, and He teaches the inhabitants of the world. Sodom was not overthrown till the men of Sodom neglected justice, and the men of Jerusalem were not banished till they disregarded justice (Ezek. XVI, 49; Isa. I, 23).
(*Exod.R.*, Mishpaṭim, xxx, 19.)

[1023] 'According to the sentence...of the judges shalt thou act, thou shalt not decline...to the right or to the left' (Deut. XVII, 11). Even if they demonstrate that that which seems to you right is left, and that that which seems to you left is right, hearken to them. (*Sifre Deut.*, Shofeṭim, § 154, f. 105*a*.)

[1024] When the judge judges truthfully, God, as it were, leaves the heaven of heavens, and lets His Shechinah rest by the judge's side, but when He sees that the judge has 'respect of persons', then He, as it were, removes His Shechinah, and rises up into heaven, and the angels say to Him, 'Lord of the world, how is it with thee?' And God replies, 'I saw a judge who had respect of persons, and I removed myself from him,' as it is said, 'Because of the oppression of the poor and the sighing of the needy, now do I rise up, says the Lord' (Ps. XII, 5). And God draws His sword against that judge to make known that there is a judge on high. (*Exod.R.*, Mishpaṭim, xxx, 24.)

[1025] 'Thou shalt not take a bribe, for a bribe blinds the eyes of the wise' (Deut. XVI, 19). R. Ḥama b. Osha'ya says: If a man suffers from his eyes, he pays much money to a doctor, but it is doubtful whether he will be healed or not. But he who takes a bribe, overturns justice, blinds his eyes, brings Israel into exile, and hunger into the world.
(*Tanḥ.B.*, Shofeṭim, 15*b fin.*)

[1026] 'Thou shalt not take a bribe' (Deut. XVI, 19). Obviously not to acquit the guilty or condemn the innocent, but not even to acquit the innocent or condemn the guilty.

(*Sifre Deut.*, Shofeṭim, § 144, f. 103*a*.)

[1027] Let a case about a small matter be as important to you as a case about a big matter. A case in which a penny is involved is as important a case as one in which £100 is involved.

(*Ab.R.N.* (vers. I), X, 22*a* (cp. *T.B.San* 8*a*).)

For the judge's duty to keep his colleagues' opinions secret see [1038].

[1028] 'In righteousness shalt thou judge thy neighbour' (Lev. XIX, 15). You must not let one litigant speak as much as he wants, and then say to the other, 'Shorten thy speech.' You must not let one stand and the other sit. (*Sifra* 89*a*.)

[1029] You must not say [when you are acting as judge], 'This defendant is rich or of noble birth, I will not put him to shame, or look on with indifference at his disgrace, much less will I, personally, be the cause of his dishonour.' For it says, 'Thou shalt not honour the mighty' (Lev. XIX, 15). (*Sifra* 89*a*.)

[1030] 'Thou shalt not respect the person of the poor' (Lev. XIX, 15). When a poor man is one of the parties, you must not say, if you are a judge, 'This is a poor man, and I and the rich man [the other in the suit] are bound to support him; so I will acquit him, in order that he may be supported as an innocent man.' For it says, 'Thou shalt not favour the poor.'

(*Sifra* 89*a*.)

[1031] 'Ye shall do no unrighteousness in judgment' (Lev. XIX, 15). A judge who perverts justice is called unrighteous, hateful, abominable, a cursed thing and abhorred. [These terms, as well as the consequences which follow, are all derived from biblical quotations.] Moreover, he is the cause of five misfortunes; he defiles the land, profanes the Name of God, causes the Shechinah to depart, Israel to fall by the sword, and to be exiled from their land. (*Sifra* 88*d fin.*)

[1032] R. Akiba said that a court which has pronounced a sentence of death, should taste nothing all that day, for it says: 'Ye shall not eat anything with the blood' (Lev. XIX, 26). (*Sifra* 90*b*.)

[1033] 'Then both the men shall stand before the Lord' (Deut. XIX, 17). They may think that it is before flesh and blood that they are standing, but it is before God.

(*Sifre Deut.*, Shofeṭim, § 190, f. 109*b*.)

The naïve, frank particularism of the Rabbis is presented here in a pleasant combination:

[1034] It is written, 'Judges shalt thou make thee in all thy gates' (Deut. XVI, 18). R. Levi said: The matter is like a king who had many sons, and he loved the youngest more than all the others. And he had a garden which he loved more than all his other possessions. So he said, 'I will give the garden, which I love more than all the rest of what I have, to the son whom I love more than all my other sons.' So God says, 'Of all the peoples I have created I love only Israel,' as it is said, 'Because [A.V. 'when'] Israel was young, I loved him' (Hos. XI, 1), 'and of all things that I have created, I love only justice,' as it is said, 'I, the Lord, love justice' (Isa. LXI, 8), 'so I will give the thing which I love to the people whom I love.'...God says to the Israelites, 'By the merit [which you win] in maintaining justice, I am exalted,' as it is said, 'I, the Lord, am exalted by justice' (Isa. V, 16), 'and if you exalt me by justice, then I execute righteousness, and let my holiness dwell among you,' as it is said, 'The Holy God is sanctified by righteousness' (Isa. V, 16), 'and if you keep both righteousness and justice, I will redeem you with a perfect redemption,' as it is said, 'Keep justice and do righteousness, for then will my salvation be near to come' (Isa. LVI, 1). (*Deut.R.*, Shofeṭim, V, 7.)

[1035] [The Midrash quotes the fine words in Deut. I, 17, 'For the judgment is God's,' and the fine words in II Chron. XIX, 6, 'For ye judge not for man, but for the Lord; and He it is who is with you in the judgment,' and continues,] Let not the judges say, 'We sit by ourselves in court,' for God says to them, 'Know that I sit with you, and if you pervert justice, you pervert me.' (*Midr.Ps* on LXXXII, 1 (184*b*, § 1).)

[1036] 'Defend the poor and fatherless, do justice to the afflicted and needy' (Ps. LXXXII, 3). It does not say 'Have pity on', but 'Do justice to'. Give a righteous judgment; not *because* he is an orphan or poor shall you say, 'We will give him what belongs to the rich,' for 'the earth is the Lord's and the fulness thereof,' 'and if you take [unjustly] from the rich in judgment, and give it to the poor, you rob me,' says God, 'for you give him what is mine, for all the earth is mine, and I have appointed him to be rich, and you take what is his.'

(*Midr.Ps.* on LXXXII, 2 (185*a init.*, § 2).)

[1037] Simeon b. Sheṭaḥ said: When you are judging, and there come before you two men, of whom one is rich and the other poor, do not say, 'The poor man's words are to be believed, but not the rich man's.' But just as you listen to the words of the poor man, so listen to the words of the rich man, for it is said, 'Ye shall not respect persons in judgment' (Deut. I, 17).

(*Ab.R.N.* (vers. II), XX, 22*a* (cp. [1044]).)

[1038] After a trial has been concluded, one of the judges, on leaving the court, must not say: 'I acquitted him; my colleagues convicted him. But what can I do? They outvoted me.' Of such a one it is written, 'Thou shalt not go about as a talebearer among thy people,' and 'He that goes about as a talebearer reveals secrets' (Lev. XIX, 16; Prov. XI, 13).

(*San.* 31*a* (cp. [1027]).)

A similar argument is used by R. Nehemiah in *Sifra* 89 *a*.

[1039] 'The wages of a hireling shall not abide with thee till the morning' (Lev. XIX, 13). So, too, in regard to the hire of animals, or of utensils, or of fields. So, too, a man breaks the law [if he withholds the hire], even if the hireling has not come to him to ask for his wages, for it says, 'with thee'. A wage-earner engaged for the day must be given pay for the following night; one engaged for the night, for the following day.

(*Sifra* 88*d* (cp. [1143]).)

[1040] In a lawsuit you stand before God. R. Akiba, when men came with a case before him, said, 'Know before whom you stand; not before me, Akiba, but before the Creator of the world.'

(*T.J.San.* I, § 1, f. 18*a*, line 40.)

Justice is of God. Let both judges and witnesses realise this.

[1041] The judges should know whom they are judging, and before whom they are judging, and who He is who is judging with them. And the witnesses should know against whom they are testifying, and with whom they are testifying, and who He is who bears testimony with them, as it is written: 'Then both the men between whom the controversy is, shall stand before the Lord.' And also it is written: 'God stands in the congregation of God, and in the midst of judges He judges.' So again it is said concerning Jehoshaphat: 'Consider what ye do, for ye judge not for man, but for God' (II Chron. XIX, 6). And lest a judge should say, 'Why do I take this trouble?'—has it not been said, 'He is with you in the matter of judgment? Thy concern is only with what thine eyes see.'

(*T.San.* I, 9 (Z. p. 416 *init.*) (Prof. Danby's translation, p. 30).)

[1042] A judge who gives a true verdict causes the Shechinah to dwell in Israel....A judge must regard himself as if a sword lay between his thighs, and as if hell were open beneath him.

(*San.* 7*a fin.*)

[1043] God does not punish the unjust judge by a money penalty. God exacts his life. A human judge may make an unjust judgment about a little money, but God demands his life, even as it is said, 'Oppress not the needy in the gate, for the Lord will plead their cause, and will despoil of life those that despoil them' (Prov. XXII, 22, 23).

(*Sifre Deut.*, Debarim, § 9, f. 67*a* (H. p. 17).)

[1044] 'Ye shall not respect persons in judgment' (Deut. I, 17). This refers to the man who has to appoint judges. Such a one must not say, 'This man is beautiful, or strong, or my relation, or has once lent me money, or knows many languages, I will appoint him as judge.' Then may he acquit the guilty and condemn the innocent, not because the man is innocent or guilty, but because he [the judge] is ignorant. Yet God will account it to him as if he had 'respected persons' in his judgments.

You shall hear the small as well as the great. You must not say, 'Because this man is poor and that man is rich, and because the rich man is commanded to sustain the poor, therefor I will acquit the poor man,' with the result that he will be helped as if he were innocent. Again, you must not say, 'Why should I injure the honour of this man for the sake of a small sum of money: I will acquit him, and afterwards, out of court, I will say to him, "Give it to the poor man, for you owe it to him."' (*Sifre Deut.*, Debarim, § 17, f. 68*b fin.*–69*a* (H. pp. 27 *fin.*, 28; cp. [1037]).)

[1045] When judgment has been given in a case, justifying him who was in the right, and condemning him who was in the wrong, if it be a poor man who has been condemned, the judge may, afterwards, give him support out of his own pocket. He is thus found acting with charity to the one, and with justice to the other.

(*T.San.* I, 4 (Z. p. 415, line 19) (Prof. Danby's translation, p. 28).)

[1046] God said to David, 'When thy days are fulfilled' (II Sam. VII, 12), that is, Thy days shall not be wanting. It is Solomon, indeed, who shall build the Temple in which sacrifices shall be offered, but I prefer justice and righteousness, which you practise, to sacrifices, even as it says, 'To do justice and judgment is more acceptable to God than sacrifices' (Prov. XXI, 3).

(*T.J.Ber.* I, § 1, f. 4*b*, line 52.)

[1047] The Rabbis noticed that the word *Yahweh* [the Lord] occurs eighteen times in Ps. XXIX, and so they make each occasion correspond with one of the eighteen Benedictions. 'The Lord breaks the cedars' (verse 5) corresponds with 'the blessing of the years', for 'God breaks those who raise prices' (speculating on a coming scarcity) and 'make the weights small', and the rich who are at ease ('the idle rich!'), who are like cedars, and He blesses His world, and brings cheapness to the world, and breaks the staff of iniquity. (*Midr.Ps.* on XXIX, 2 (116*b*, § 2).)

[1048] It is written, 'Thou shalt not respect persons' (Deut. XVI, 19). R. Judah b. Ilai said: I have heard that if a judge desires that the parties to a suit should be seated, he may allow them to be so, but one of two parties to a suit must not sit and the other stand.... R. Elazar said: If you realise at once that one man is in the right, do not show him a favourable countenance, lest he should say, 'He intended from the first to give the verdict in my favour.' R. Samuel said: If you realise at once that one of them is in the wrong, show him a favourable countenance, lest he say, 'He intended from the first to condemn me.'

(*Deut.R.*, Shofeṭim, V, 6 (cp. [1037]).)

[1049] R. Jose b. Elisha said: If there is a generation upon whom many calamities fall, go and investigate the judges in Israel, for all the punishments which befall the world are due only to Israel's evil judges. God will not let His Shechinah rest upon Israel till the wicked judges and rulers are removed from Israel.
(*Sab.* 139*a init.*)

[1050] 'God came down to see [the town of Babel]' (Gen. XI, 5). But did He need to come down? Is not all patent and revealed to Him who knows what is in the darkness and with whom light dwells (Dan. II, 22)? The answer is that God did this as a lesson to mankind, not to pass sentence, yea, even not to utter a word, on hearsay, but to look with their own eyes.
(*Tanḥ.*, Noaḥ, § 18, f. 23*b fin.* (cp. [402]).)

[1051] Whence is it that we may not give exact weight in a place where the practice is to give overweight and vice versa? The text declares, 'A perfect weight.' And whence is it that in a place where the practice is to give overweight, if the seller says, 'I will give exact weight, but I will reduce the price,' or in a place where the practice is to give exact weight, if the seller says, 'I will give overweight, but I will increase the price,' he is not allowed to do so? The text declares, 'A perfect and just weight' (Deut. XXV, 15). (*Bab.B.* 89*a* (Cohen, *E.T.* pp. 241–2).)

Local custom must be observed.

One has to remember that the Rabbis were, by their very professions and office, judges—judges rather than clergymen—and therefore it is not surprising that there are many stories about their work as judges, and about their solicitude for impartiality and fairness.

[1052] The Rabbis say: Thou shalt not take a bribe: this need not be bribery in money: bribery in deed is also forbidden. Thus R. Samuel was getting on to a ferry: a man came, and gave him a hand. When R. Samuel asked him what he was there for, he replied, 'I have a lawsuit.' Then Samuel said, 'I am forbidden to be your judge.' (*Keth.* 105*b.*)

[1053] R. Papa said: A man will not give just judgments to those whom he hates, or to those whom he loves: he does not see the wrongdoing of those he loves, or the just case of those whom he hates.[1] (*Keth.* 105*b.*)

[1] We need not take the word 'hate' too literally. For love put 'like' and for hate 'dislike', and the rendering would be more accurate.

[1054] A man rented the garden of R. Ishmael. This man used to bring him every Friday a basket of fruit. On one occasion he brought it on Thursday, and when the Rabbi asked him why, he replied, 'I have a lawsuit, and I thought that while I was on my way here, I would bring the fruit to you.' The Rabbi would not accept them, and said to him, 'I am disqualified from being your judge.' He appointed two other Rabbis to judge the case; he walked up and down while the case was on, and thought, 'If the man wished, he could bring forward such and such arguments.' And he said, 'May those who take bribes perish! If I, who did not take a bribe, have had these thoughts, how much worse would have been the thoughts of those who had taken a bribe.' (*Keth.* 105*b*.)

[1055] R. Jonathan was a righteous judge. There was a Roman whose house and land adjoined that of R. Jonathan. A tree belonging to R. Jonathan hung over the land of the Roman. One day there came before him a case of this kind. He said, 'Come back to-morrow morning.' The Roman said, 'Because of me he did not pronounce his verdict; to-morrow I will neglect my own affairs, and I will see what sentence he pronounces. If he judges others and not himself, he is no true judge.' At nightfall R. Jonathan sent for his carpenter, and said to him, 'Go, cut down that part of my tree which overhangs the land of the Roman.' The next day the suitor came early to R. Jonathan, and the Rabbi said to him, 'Go and cut down that part of your tree which overhangs the other man's land.' The Roman said, 'But how about your tree?' He replied, 'Go and look at my tree in its relation to your land.' He went and saw, and he said, 'Blessed be the God of the Jews.'

One day a female litigant brought with her some figs as a gift of honour to R. Jonathan. He said to her, 'I request that if you brought these figs uncovered, you take them away uncovered, and if you brought them covered up, you take them away covered up, so that none may say that it was money which she gave to him, but it was figs which he gave to her.'

(*T.J.Bab.B.* II, § 13, f. 13*c*, line 37.)

[1056] R. Yannai had a tree, branches of which leant over the public way, and another man had a similar tree. Then the people came to the other man, and told him to remove it. He came to

R. Yannai, who said to him, 'Go away now, but come again to-morrow.' During the night the Rabbi had his own tree cut down. When the man came again, R. Yannai said, 'Cut down your tree.' Then the man said, 'You have a similar tree.' Then R. Yannai said, 'Go and look. If my tree is not cut down, do not cut yours down.' Why did R. Yannai change his mind? Before, he thought that the people liked the tree, because they could sit in its shade, but when he found that they disliked the tree, he cut his tree down. Why did he not say to the man, 'You cut yours down, and then I will cut mine down?' Because of a teaching of Resh Laḳish who said, 'First clean yourself, and then clean others.' [As it is also said, 'Remove the burrs from yourself before you remove them from others' (*T.J.Ta'an.* II, § 1, f. 65*a*, line 75; cf. *R.T.* p. 146).]

(*Bab.B.* 60*a fin.*–60*b*.)

[1057] A potter delivered some pots to a carrier who broke them. He took away his cloak. He went to R. Jose who said, 'Walk in the way of the good' (Prov. II, 20). So the potter went and returned the cloak to the man. Then R. Jose said to the potter, 'Did you pay the man his hire?' He said, 'No.' Then, said the Rabbi, 'Keep the paths of the righteous' (*ibid.*). So the potter went and gave the man his hire. (*T.J.Bab.M.* VI, § 8, f. 11*a*, line 51.)

[1058] Jethro told Moses to appoint 'Men of truth, hating covetousness' (Exod. XVIII, 21). What does this mean? Men who insisted upon true justice, and who hated even their own wealth: how much more the wealth of others. Such a one would say, 'Even though you burn my standing crops, even though you cut down my vineyard, none the less will I judge you truly.'

(*Tanḥ.*, Yitro, § 2, f. 121*a*.)

Judges, like all other officers and rulers, must regard themselves as the servants of the community:

[1059] When R. Gamaliel II appointed R. Johanan b. Nuri and R. Elazar (or Eliezer) (b.) Ḥisma to be judges, and the disciples did not pay them due regard, they, in dudgeon, sat down among the disciples [instead of in the seats appointed for officers]. When R. Gamaliel entered the college and saw them, he said, 'You have let the community know that you seek to exercise rule over the community. Before [your appointment], you were independent, but from henceforward you are servants of, and subjected to, the community.' (*Sifre Deut.*, Debarim, § 16, f. 68*b* (*R.T.* p. 300; H. p. 26; cp. [944]).)

One Rabbi may rebuke another:

[1060] Some wine carriers for Rabbah b. Bar Ḥana (who was a vintner) broke a cask of his wine. He took away their cloaks. They came and told this to Rab, who said to Rabbah, 'Give them back their cloaks.' He said, 'Is this the Law?' He replied, 'Yes, for it says, "That thou mayest walk in the way of good men."' Then he gave them back their cloaks. Then they said to Rab, 'We are poor, and have toiled all day, and we are hungry, and have nothing.' Then Rab said to Rabbah, 'Give them their hire.' He said, 'Is this the Law?'[1] He replied, 'Yes, for it says, "Keep the paths of the righteous"' (Prov. II, 20[1]). (*Bab.M.* 83*a*.)

It may be a good thing to settle a case out of court:

[1061] R. Joshua b. Ḳarḥa said that it may be positively right to arrange an equitable settlement between two parties, as it is said, 'Judge truth, and the judgment of peace' (Zech. VIII, 16 R.V.M.); the meaning is, 'Wherever there is strict truth, there cannot be peaceful judgment; wherever there is peaceful judgment, there cannot be strict truth. How can one combine both? Only by an equitable settlement, satisfying both parties.' (*T.J.San.* I, § 1, f. 18*b*, line 19.)

The *Tosefta* gives the last passage as well, and it adds:

[1062] It is written of David: 'And David acted with judgment and charity to all his people' (II Sam. VIII, 15: 'charity', lit. 'righteousness', *ẓedaḳah*, but here used in its later Rabbinic sense of almsgiving or charity). And is it not the case that wherever there is judgment, there is not charity? And where there is charity, there is no judgment? Then what is the judgment wherein is charity? This can only be arbitration. (*T.San.* I, 3 (Z. p. 415, line 17) (Prof. Danby's translation, p. 28).)

There is thus sometimes a justice which is higher than the letter of the Law. The Rabbis reached the conception of equity, though

[1] The quotation is valuable as showing how any part of Scripture was regarded as Torah (cp. [428]).

they had no one single word for it. Neither *mesharim* nor *pesharah* is the exact equivalent of 'equity'.

[1063] R. Johanan said: Jerusalem was destroyed only because they judged in it by the letter of the Torah. What! should they have judged by an arbitrary law? Say, rather, they stuck to the strict *letter* of the Torah, and did not advance to equity.... Why were the shops of Beth Hino [Bethany; cp. Neubauer, *Géogr.* p. 150] destroyed three years before Jerusalem was destroyed? Because the shopkeepers stuck to the mere letter of the Law. (For *Shurat ha-Din*, see [505].) (*Bab.M.* 30*b*, 88*a fin.*)

[1064] If a man knows evidence favourable to his fellow, but withholds it, he is not legally liable to compensate his fellow, but Heaven will not pardon him until he does so.
(*T.Sheb.* III, 2 (Z. p. 449, line 7).)

From justice to honesty. The Rabbinical writings have several stock stories, often repeated, about the honesty of certain Rabbis. They are especially fond of stories of honesty shown to Gentiles, bringing glory to Israel's God:

[1065] Simon b. Sheṭaḥ was occupied with preparing flax. His disciples said to him, 'Rabbi, desist; we will buy you an ass, and you will not have to work so hard.' They went and bought an ass from an Arab, and a pearl was found on it. They came to him and said, 'From now on you need not work any more.' He said, 'Why?' They said, 'We bought you an ass from an Arab, and a pearl was found on it.' He said to them, 'Does its owner know of it?' They said, 'No.' He said to them, 'Go and give it back to him.' They said, 'But did not R. Huna, in the name of Rab, report that, even according to him who said that no profit may be made [by a third party] from that which is *stolen* from a heathen, yet all the world agrees that, if you *find* something which belonged to a heathen, you may keep it?' He said, 'Do you think that Simon b. Sheṭaḥ is a barbarian? No, he would prefer to hear the Arab say, "Blessed be the God of the Jews," than to possess all the riches of the world.'
It is also proved, from the story of R. Ḥanina, that lost property should be restored for the sake of the sanctification of the Name. For once, some aged Rabbis bought a heap of corn from some soldiers, and they found in it a bundle of *denarii*,

and they returned it to the soldiers, who said, 'Blessed be the God of the Jews.'

(*T.J.Bab.M.* II, § 5, 8*c*, line 21 (cp. *Deut.R.*, 'Eḳeb, III, 3).)

[1066] It is written in Deut. VII, 9, 'The faithful God.' The Rabbis say, 'From the faithfulness of flesh and blood you can conceive the faithfulness of God.' R. Phinehas b. Jair dwelt in a city of the south, and some men came thither to earn their living. They had two measures of barley which they deposited with him, but when they left, they forgot them. So R. Phinehas sowed them each year, brought the produce to the threshing floor, and collected it. After seven years the men came again to claim their barley. R. Phinehas recognised them at once, and said, 'Come and take your store.' Thus from the fidelity of man you may conceive the [greater] fidelity of God.

(*Deut.R.*, 'Eḳeb, III, 3 (cp. note to [120]).)

[1067] Abba Osha'ya, a laundryman, found some precious jewels in the linen which a queen had given him to wash. He gave them back to her. She said, 'They are yours, I have many others of more value.' He said, 'Our Law orders us to return what we have found.' She said, 'Blessed be the God of the Jews.'

(*T.J.Bab.M.* II, § 5, f. 8*c*, line 34.)

[The text does not state that he was a laundryman (but see note in ed. Krotoschin); he is called *'ish Turya* or *Traya*, 'a man of Turya'. According to Neubauer (*op. cit.* p. 267), Turya was one of two villages in the neighbourhood of Carmel. (H. L.)]

[1068] A man said to me, 'Rabbi, once I sold some dates to a Gentile, and I measured them out to him falsely in a dark room. He said to me, "You alone, and God who is in heaven, are aware of what you measure me." I gave him three *se'ahs* of dates less than his due. With the price of the dates, I bought a jug of oil which I placed in the spot where I had sold the dates to the Gentile. The jug broke, and the oil was spilt and lost.' I said to him, 'My son, it says, "Thou shalt not oppress thy neighbour." Now thy neighbour is as thy brother, and thy brother is as thy neighbour: hence you learn that to rob a Gentile is robbery' (Lev. XXV, 14, 17). (*Tan.d.b.El.* pp. 74 *fin.*–75 *init.*)

The word for 'neighbour' is *rea'*: it is clearly used here in a general sense, and is not limited to Israelites (cp. [456] and [537]).

[1069] R. Elazar leant on the arm of R. Simon b. Kahana, and said to him as they passed a vineyard, 'Bring me a chip of wood for me to pick my teeth': then he changed his mind, and said, 'Do not bring it me, for if everybody went and took a chip, the man's hedge would be destroyed.' So, too, R. Haggai supported R. Ze'era, and a man passed with a load of faggots: R. Ze'era said, 'Bring me a chip to clean my teeth': then he changed his mind, and said, 'Do not do so, for if everybody took a chip, the man's load would disappear.' R. Ze'era was not really so exceedingly pious [or scrupulous], but he wanted to warn people to observe the commandments of God. [The last six words of the original are very obscure.]

(*T.J.Dem.* III, § 2, f. 23*b*, line 70.)

[1070] R. Joshua b. Hananiah said: I was once walking along, and there was a path crossing a field, and as I was entering it, a little girl called out to me, 'Rabbi, this is a field' [i.e. no right of way]. I said, 'There is a trodden path.' She said, 'It is robbers like you who have made it a path.'

(*'Erub.* 53*b* (Abrahams, *Studies*, II, 112).)

Sincerity, honesty, strict integrity and truthfulness are often praised. Some of the sayings reflect actual life.

[1071] After the laws about just weights and measures, the words come, 'I am the Lord who brought you out of the land of Egypt.' God says, 'I brought you out on condition that you should receive the commandments about just weights and measures. He who accepts them, accepts the Exodus from Egypt. He who denies them, denies the Exodus from Egypt.'

(*Sifra* 91*b* (cp. [1082]).)

'Denies the Exodus' may be taken to mean denies the element of overruling, divine providence in the story of the Exodus.

[1072] There is a teaching, 'A man must not plough with his ox at night, and hire it out by day, nor must he himself work at his own affairs at night, and hire himself out by day. And he must not fast or undergo privations of his own accord, for he diminishes [by his consequent weakness] the amount of his work for his master.' R. Johanan went to a place, and found the school teacher was fatigued. He asked the cause. They said to him, 'Because he fasts.' The Rabbi said to the man, 'You are forbidden to act thus.' If it is forbidden to act thus as regards the work rendered to man, how much more is it forbidden as regards the work rendered to God.

(*T.J.Dem.* VII, § 4, f. 26*b*, line 23 (cp. [1486]).)

No Pentateuchal law was exempt from, or did not provide a subject for, Rabbinic casuistry. But a sense of justice and equity informed the casuistry. Thus as regards the law of Deut. XXIII, 24, 'When thou comest into thy neighbour's vineyard, then thou mayest eat grapes thy fill at thine own pleasure; but thou shalt not put any in thy vessel,' it is said:

[1073] The worker in the vineyard may eat grapes, but not figs. If he is collecting his master's figs, he may eat figs, but not grapes. He may wait till he comes to the best fruit, and then eat. R. Elazar (or Eliezer) (b.) Ḥisma said: He may not eat more than his day's wage, but the Sages say that the words 'at his own pleasure' show that he may. On the other hand, 'in thy vessel' is interpreted strictly, for it is said, 'Even when he is filling his master's vessels.' (*Sifre Deut.*, Ki Teẓe, § 266, f. 121*b fin.*)

The phraseology used in Deut. XXV, 2, 3 is cleverly noted:

[1074] R. Hananiah b. Gamla said: Before his beating the criminal is called 'the wicked man', but after his beating he is called 'thy brother'. (*Sifre Deut.*, Ki Teẓe, § 286, f. 125*a*.)

[1075] A shopkeeper is not permitted to make the liquid bubble in the measure or to bound, nor may he lean the vessel on its side.... A shopkeeper who sells oil must wipe his measures once a week: a wine seller's measures must be cleansed as soon as sediment is formed, which diminishes their capacity, and, for the same reason, he should not clean them with salt.

(*T.Bab.B.* V, 5, 7 (Z. p. 404, line 33).)

[1076] It is forbidden to the house of Israel to rob or to snatch anything from any creature, for in all the punishments in the Law, none is more grievous than that for illegitimate gain. R. Eliezer says: All the sins in the Law did the generation of the Flood commit, but the decree that they should be blotted out was not sealed till they put forth their hands to illegitimate gain, for it first says that the world was corrupt (Gen. VI, 12), but 'the end of all flesh' was decreed only when 'the earth was full of violence' (*ib.* 13)....R. Johanan says: He who robs his fellow even of a farthing is as though he took away his life (Prov. I, 19). (*Tanḥ.*, Noaḥ, § 4, f. 16*b*–17*a*.)

[1077] 'Ye shall not steal, neither deal falsely, neither lie one to another' (Lev. XIX, 11). You must not steal, even if it be done merely to annoy, or even to restore double or fourfold or fivefold; Ben Bag Bag said: You must not steal your own property back from a thief, lest you appear to be stealing. (*Sifra* 88*c*.)

[1078] He who deceives or lies to man is as if he deceives or lies to God. (*Sifre Num.*, Naso, § 2, f. 2*a* (H. p. 5).)

[1079] R. Eliezer b. Jacob said: If a man steals some wheat and makes bread from it, and separates the cake [*ḥallah*] [according to the law of Num. XV, 19–21], and says the blessing over it, such a one does not bless, but blasphemes. [For the law of *ḥallah* and the blessing, see *Sephardic Prayer Book*, ed. Gaster, vol. I, p. 79.] (*Bab.Ḳ.* 94*a*.)

[1080] R. Ze'era said: One must not promise to give something to a child, and not give it to him, because thereby he is taught to lie. (*Suk.* 46*b*.)

[1081] What is profanation of the Name? Rab said: I [a scholar] profane it if I buy meat from the butcher, and do not pay him straightway. (*Yoma* 86*a*.)

[The 'I' is emphatic. In a scholar, the trifling neglect, venial in others, is culpable. (H. L.)]

[1082] 'Just balances, just weights, a just *ephah*, and a just *hin*, shall ye have' (Lev. XIX, 36). Appoint a market inspector for this purpose. They said that the wholesale seller should cleanse his measure once in thirty days: the householder once a year. R. Simeon b. Gamaliel said: The shopkeeper must clean his measures twice a week, and wipe his weights once a week, and cleanse his scales after every weighing. This refers to moist goods, but it is not necessary for dry goods. Further, he must allow the pan of the goods to sink one hand-breadth lower than the pan of the weights. But if he gives exact measure, then he must allow an extra overweight, ten per cent for wet goods, and five per cent for dry goods.

(*Sifra* 91*b* (cf. *Bab.B.* 88*b*, and *ib.* Mishnah V, 11; [1071]).)

[1083] R. Simeon said: Theft from an idolater is no less theft than theft from an Israelite. (*Sifra* 110*b*.)

[1084] He who steals from a non-Jew is bound to make restitution to the non-Jew; it is worse to steal from a non-Jew than to steal from an Israelite because of the profanation of the Name. (*T.Bab.Ḳ.* x, 15 (Z. p. 368, line 1).)

[1085] He who robs the public [the many] must restore to the many. Worse is stealing from the many than stealing from an individual, for he who steals from an individual can appease him, and return the theft; the former cannot. (*T.Bab.Ḳ.* x, 14 (Z. p. 367 *fin.*; *R.T.* p. 371 *init.*).)

[1086] R. Gamaliel II was wont to say: No pupil whose 'within' is not the same as his 'without' may enter the house of study. (*Ber.* 28*a*.)

[1087] R. Huna, in the name of Samuel b. Isaac, said: The yea of the righteous is yea, and their nay is nay. (*Ruth R.* VII, 6 on III, 18, f. 12*a*.)

[1088] He who punished the generations of the Flood and the Tower of Babel will also punish him who does not keep his word. Let your yea and nay be both righteous. Do not speak with your mouth what you do not mean in your heart. (*Bab.M.* IV, 2; *Bab.M.* 49*a*.)

[1089] R. Simeon said: The punishment of the liar is that he is not believed even when he speaks the truth. (*Ab.R.N.* (vers. I), XXX, 45*b*.)

[1090] Raba said: I used once to say that there was no such thing as truth in the world [Rashi: that there was no man who spoke the truth in all circumstances], till I was told the following about one of the disciples, by name R. Ṭabuth or R. Ṭabyomi, who would never break his word, even if one offered him all the fullness of the world. Once he came to a place called Kushta [truth]. The inhabitants of this place never broke their word, and none of them ever died prematurely. The disciple married a wife there, who bore him two sons. Once his wife was sitting combing her hair, when a neighbour came and knocked at the door. The husband thought it unseemly to receive her while his wife was so engaged. So he told her that his wife was not at home. Then his two sons died. Then the townsfolk came to him and asked what this [these premature deaths] implied [i.e. what lie he had told]. He related what had happened, and they said, 'We entreat you to leave our place and not to tempt death to come here.'

(*Sanh.* 97 *a.*)

[1091] R. Levi said: God says, 'If you bear false witness against your neighbour, I regard it as if you had declared that I had not created the world.' (*T.J.Ber.* I, § 8, f. 3*c*, line 24.)

[1092] The Ten Commandments correspond to the ten 'sayings' with which God created the world. So, 'Thou shalt not bear false witness against thy neighbour' corresponds to, 'Let us make man in our image,' for God said, 'Behold I have created thy fellow for thee in my image, so that thou hast become a fellow to me and like unto my image. Therefore, do not bear false witness against thy neighbour.' (*Pes.R.* 108*a*, *b.*)

Few sins are greater than perjury, and even a false oath, which is supposed to be true, may be a danger to him who uses it. Better not to swear at all (cp. [1395]).

[1093] The Rabbis taught that the oath in a court of law can be spoken in any language. They say to the man who is about to take the oath, 'Know that the whole world trembled when God declared, "Thou shalt not take the name of the Lord thy God in vain."' With regard to all the other sins mentioned in the Law, it says, 'God will forgive'; but here it says, 'God will not forgive.' For all the other sins, the sinner alone is punished: for the false oath, both he and his family, for it says, 'Suffer not thy mouth to cause thy flesh to sin' (Eccles. v, 6), and by flesh is meant his relatives, as it says, 'Hide not thyself from thine own flesh' (Isa. LVIII, 7). For all other sins, the sinner only is punished: for the false oath, he and all the world, as it says, 'There is nought but swearing and breaking faith' (Hos. IV, 2).

(*Shebu'ot* 38*b fin.*–39*a* (*T.Sot.* VII, 2 (Z. p. 306, line 12)).)

Again, one must beware of taking these statements (like others which are here omitted) too literally. They are homiletic exaggerations and ingenious misinterpretations of biblical texts, in order to show up and emphasise the terrible nature of the sin of perjury:

[1094] 'Come and see: what the fire does not burn, the false oath destroys' (Zech. v, 4). R. Jonah said: Only the oath which a man knows to be false before he swears. R. Jose said: Even the false oath (which a man swears by error). R. Haggai taught according to R. Jose, and he told the following story: A woman went to her neighbour's house to roll the dough. She had fastened two *denarii* in the seam of her bonnet. They fell down, and were rolled into the dough. When she returned, she looked for the *denarii*, and could not find them. She went back, and said to her neighbour, 'Give me the two *denarii* which fell down in your house.' The neighbour said, 'I know nothing of them; may I bury my son if I know about them.' She buried her son. When they returned from the burial, she heard a voice saying, 'Had she not known about the *denarii*, she would not have buried her son.' She said, 'May I bury my other son if I know about them.' And she buried him. They came to comfort her: at the meal a loaf was cut, and the two *denarii* were found in it. So they say, 'Be you guilty or innocent, do not swear.'

(*T.J.Shebu'ot* VI, § 6, 37*a fin.*, line 69–37*b init.* (cp. *Pes.R.* 114*a*).)

[1095] R. Simeon quoted the two prohibitions against false swearing (Exod. XX, 7 and Lev. XIX, 12). Hence he said that the third commandment referred to an oath which is true, but 'vain'. R. Samuel b. Naḥmani said: Four and twenty cities were destroyed in the south on account of true oaths which were vain [or needless]. Hezekiah said: Even if a man swears [lit. says] about an olive tree that it is an olive, and about a fig tree that it is a fig, this is a vain oath. R. Haggai said: If a man walks in the street, and sees the rain falling, and then says [in the Greek tongue], 'By God, it has rained much' [*Kyrie, polu ebrexen*], this is a vain oath. [Possibly the implication is that vain swearing is not limited to Hebrew.] R. Simeon said: We do not administer an oath to one who runs after it. It once happened that a man entrusted a hundred *denarii* to Bartholomew. When he claimed them, Bartholomew said, 'I have given them back into your hand.' The man said, 'Come, and I will make you swear that you have done so.' Bartholomew took a reed, and hollowed it out. He put the *denarii* inside the reed, and began to lean upon it. When he came into the Synagogue, Bartholomew said to the man, 'Take this stick into your hand while I swear.' Bartholomew then swore, 'By the Lord of this good[ly house], I swear that that which has been entrusted into my hand I have given back into your hand.' The other man, finding the stick rather heavy in his hand, dropped it, and the *denarii* fell out. He began to pick them up. Bartholomew said to the man, 'Pick them up, pick them up, it is your own that you pick up'.

(*Pes.R.* 112*b fin.*–113*a* (cp. *R.T.* pp. 48 ff.).)

[The story of the money in the reed is widely known. For parallels, see Friedmann's note. It has possibly come from farther East, and may belong to some cycle like Ahikar, Barlaam and Josaphat, which, in part, can be traced to Buddhist Jatakas. The name Bartholomew is uncommon: by some it was understood to be that of a demon. But Bar Talmiyon may not be the same as Bar Talmai.

The story spread westwards: it occurs in *Don Quixote*, Part II, ch. XLV, and an editor notes that earlier versions are to be found in the following: *Life of San Nicolas of Bari* in the *Golden Legend*, by J. de Voragine: *El Libro de los exemplos*, by Clemente Sanchez de Vercial, No. CLXV. (H. L.)]

[1096] God said to Israel, 'Be careful what you vow, and do not become addicted to making vows, for whoever is so addicted, will, in the end, sin by breaking his oath, and he who breaks his oath denies me without hope of pardon' (Exod. XX, 7).

(*Tanḥ.B.*, Maṭṭot, 79*a.*)

[1097] It says in Deut. X, 20, 'It is the Lord thy God that thou shalt fear. Him shalt thou serve, and to Him shalt thou cleave.' And then the verse continues, 'And by His Name shalt thou swear.' You may swear only if you are God-fearing, even as Abraham, who was so called in Gen. XXII, 12, or Joseph (Gen. XLII, 18), or Job (Job I, 2).

(*Tanḥ.B.*, Wayiḳra, 5*a fin.*)

[1098] When God created the heavens, He created them only by a word. What caused God to swear [as in Deut. XXXII, 40, 'I lift up my hand to heaven,' i.e. I swear]? They who were lacking in faith caused Him to swear. (*Sifre Deut.*, Ha'azinu, § 330, f. 139*b.*)

There is a certain robbery or deception of the mind, as it is called, which is also strongly condemned:

[1099] There are seven sorts of thieves, and the first of them all is he who steals the mind of [i.e. deceives] his fellow-men. For example, he who urges his neighbour to be his guest, when, in his heart, he does not mean to invite him: he who presses gifts upon his neighbour when he knows that his neighbour will not accept them.

(*T.Bab.Ḳ.* VII, 8 (Z. p. 358, line 19; cp. [1263]).)

[1100] A man must not press his neighbour to eat with him, when he knows that his neighbour will not accept the invitation. A man must not open a cask of wine which has already been sold, in order to give a friend a drink.

(*T.Bab.B.* VI, 14 (Z. p. 406, line 13; cp. [1263]).)

[1101] Samuel said: One must not 'steal the mind' of one's fellow-men, not even of a Gentile. (*Ḥul.* 94*a*.)

[1102] R. Me'ir said: One must not utilise for buying vessels a loan obtained for the purpose of buying fruit, or vice versa, because the borrower thereby 'steals the mind' of the lender.

(*T.Meg.* I, 5 (Z. p. 222, line 4).)

[1103] A man must not send his fellow a cask of wine with oil swimming on the top. Once a man did so, and the receiver invited guests, and when they had come, it was found that the cask contained wine, and the man hanged himself.

(*Ḥul.* 94*a*.)

[Wine was relatively cheap, oil was dear. In this case the sender pretended to have sent his friend a valuable present. The receiver invited his friends to share it but, when the trick was discovered, killed himself out of shame at having to disappoint them. (H. L.)]

[1104] As there is a wronging or overreaching in buying or selling, so there is a wronging in words. One must not ask the price of anything, if one has no intention of buying it. One must not say to a man who has repented [and changed his way of life], 'Remember your former deeds.' If a man is a descendant of proselytes one must not say to him, 'Remember the deeds of your ancestors,' for it says, 'A proselyte you shall not vex or oppress.' So the Mishnah. The Gemara enlarges: If a proselyte wants to study the Law, one must not say, 'What! A mouth which ate forbidden food and creeping abominations wants to learn the Law which was spoken by the mouth of God!' If sufferings and sickness befall anyone, or if his children die, one must not say to him, as Job's friends said to Job, 'Who ever perished being innocent? Is not thy piety thy confidence?' If donkey-drivers seek provender, and you have none, you must not say, 'Go to such a one; he sells provender,' when you know that he never does so. R. Judah says: One must not look at goods when one has no money to buy them with. All such things are matters entrusted to the heart, and of things entrusted to the heart it says, 'You shall fear the Lord your God.' R. Johanan said: The wrong in words is a heavier sin than the wrong in money, for it is only in regard to the wrong in words that it says, 'You shall fear the Lord your God.' R. Elazar said: It is worse, because it relates to the personality, and the other only to a man's money. R. Samuel b. Naḥmani said: It is worse, because the one can be paid back and the other cannot. (**Note 86**.) (*Bab.M.* 58*b*; *ib.* Mishnah IV, 10 (cp. *Sifra* 107*d*).)

[1105] R. Elazar said: Since the day the Temple was destroyed, the gates of prayer have been shut (Lam. III, 8). But the gates of tears are never shut (Ps. XXXIX, 12). R. Ḥisda said: The gate of heaven may be shut to all prayers, but never to the prayer of him who has been wounded by the words of his fellow. R. Elazar said: All sins are punished by an angel, except the sin of wounding. R. Abbahu said: The heavenly curtain is drawn back before three things, wounding, robbery and idolatry. (*Bab.M.* 59*a* (cp. [814]).)

The gate means the heavenly gate. God sees to the punishment of wounding Himself; He regards it as so very serious: the punishment of other sins He delegates to angels.

[1106] What is meant by *ona'ah*? The root of this word is used in Lev. XIX, 33. If a stranger sojourn with you, do not vex him (*lo tonu oto*). What do vexation, annoyance, unkindness comprise? This, taught the Rabbis, is *ona'ah*: if a man ask a tradesman the price of an article when he has no intention of buying it. Or, if a man say to a penitent, 'Think of your past deeds,' or to the son of a proselyte, 'Remember your parents' deeds, the swine's flesh is still between their teeth.' God says, 'It is enough for thee to make thyself, as it were, like to me. For when I created my world, I strove not to hurt a single one of my creatures, and I did not publish to any human being the name of the tree of which Adam ate' [so that even the tree should not be put to shame]. (*Tanḥ.B.*, Wayera, 53*a* (cp. [569], [1177] and [1275]).)

[1107] The law, 'Thou shalt not set a stumbling block before the blind,' is extended to mean, 'You must not hide part of your intention in giving advice to a man.' You must not say, 'Sell your field, and buy a donkey,' when you are really intending to circumvent him, and get his field [i.e. by buying his field from him]. Perhaps you will reply, 'I gave him good advice' [i.e. it was *really* to his interest to sell his field and get the donkey]. [No, even so, you must not act thus.] This is a matter delivered to the heart. (*Sifra* 88*d.*)

There is no actual law against such action, but good feeling and the higher justice declare that it must not be done.

It may, therefore, be readily imagined that hypocrisy is one of the sins most strongly condemned.

[1108] R. Elazar said: A man in whom is hypocrisy brings wrath upon the world, and his prayer is not heard. He also said: Him in whom is hypocrisy the children in their mother's womb curse. He also said: The hypocrites fall into Gehinnom (*R.T.* p. 118). (*Soṭ.* 41*b* (cp. [1385]).)

The Hebrew word *ḥanef* means both a flatterer and a hypocrite.

[1109] R. Ḥiyya taught: Hypocrites may be exposed publicly because of the profanation of the Name [as it says in Prov. XXVI, 26, 'His wickedness shall be exposed before the congregation']. And why does God make known his evil way? In order that if any misfortune befall him because of his iniquities, men should not accuse the justice of God. Therefore God exposes the deeds of him who flatters his neighbour hypocritically. Come and learn from Doeg, who was the President of the Sanhedrin, as it says, 'Doeg, the Edomite, the chief of the herdsmen of Saul' (I Sam. XXI, 7). Because of his slander, even though he was learned in the Law, the Scripture makes it publicly known that he was a slanderer, in order to specify to men his deeds, so that when punishment befell him, they should not accuse the divine justice. (*Midr.Ps.* on LII, heading (142*b*, §3).)

[1110] 'They had no comforter' (Eccles. IV, 1). R. Benjamin interpreted the verse to refer to the hypocrites in regard to the Law. People suppose that they can read the Scriptures and the Mishnah, but they cannot: they wrap their prayer shawls around them; they put their phylacteries on their heads, and they oppress the poor. Of *them* it is written, 'Behold the tears of the oppressed, and they have no comforter; it is mine to punish,' says God, as it is said, 'Cursed be they who do the work of the Lord deceitfully' (Jer. XLVIII, 10).

(*Eccles.R.* IV, § 1, 1, on IV, 1 (12*b*).)

[1111] R. Gamaliel used to say: Act in secret as you act in public.

(*Ab.R.N.* (vers. II), XXXII, 36*a init.*)

[1112] Shammai said: Let thy Torah be something fixed (*Aboth* I, 15). [Mr Singer renders the sentence: 'Fix a period for thy study of the Torah.'] Do not make the Law light for thyself and heavy for others, or light for others, but heavy for thyself, but let the light for thee be light for others, and the heavy for thee be heavy for others. (As to fixed study, cp. [928].)

(*Ab.R.N.* (vers. II), XXIII, 24*a* (cp. [1330]).)

[1113] There are four classes of men who do not see the face of the Shechinah: the mockers, the hypocrites, the slanderers, the liars. (*Midr.Ps.* on CI, 7 (214*b*, § 3).)

A sin about which the Rabbis speak with remarkable iteration is slander, a sin which was, perhaps, rather prevalent in some Jewish communities, and was possibly connected with the wickedness of the Informers (*delatores*).

[1114] The slanderer is as if he denied God. His sin is so great that it extends even unto heaven. God says of the slanderer, 'He and I cannot live together in the world.' How can a man cure himself from being a slanderer? Let a disciple of the wise study the Law; let an *Am ha-Aretz* become humble.

('*Arak.* 15*b*.)

[1115] 'A good-for-nothing and wicked man is he that walks with a crooked mouth' (Prov. VI, 12). This is the slanderer. For God has likened him to an idolater. Slander is as serious as idolatry. R. Joshua says: Slander is as bad as murder. Slander is like unto idolatry and murder and incest.

(*Midr.Prov.* VI, § 12, f. 28*a*.)

[1116] God says, 'In this world, because there were slanderers among you, I have withdrawn my Shechinah from your midst, but in the time to come, when I root out the evil inclination from you, I shall cause my Shechinah to return to you. And because

I shall make my Shechinah to dwell among you, you will be worthy to fulfil the Law, and you will dwell in peace.'
(*Deut.R.*, Ki Teẓe, VI, 14.)

Here there seems to be a sort of double and concurrent action. In the Messianic age, because God by His grace removes the evil *yetzer*, and the Israelites are able to do and to be good, the Shechinah can once more rest and dwell among them: and because the Shechinah once again comes down upon them, therefore they are worthy to be enabled to fulfil the Law.

[1117] Why is the slanderous tongue called *shelishi* [Third]? Because it slays three: him who utters the slander, him who receives it, and him of whom it is uttered. (*Num.R.*, Ḥuḳḳat, XIX, 2.)

Evil speaking is sometimes worse than evil doing.

[1118] It was the sin of slander that sealed the fate of our ancestors in the wilderness (Num. XIV, 37). Joshua ben Levi said: No man reaches the sin of slander till after he has repudiated God, for when it speaks of the deceitful tongue (Ps. XII), it says that the slanderers declare, 'Who is Lord over us?' Hard is slander, for it brought death to Adam. The serpent said to him, 'God knows that if you eat the fruit, you will become like Him, and every craftsman is jealous of his fellow'; Adam listened, and death came as a result of slander. (*Tanḥ.*, Bereshit, § 8, f. 11*b*.)

[1119] R. Jose said in the name of R. Johanan: All other sins which man commits have to do with the earth; but slander relates both to earth and to heaven, as it is said, 'They set their mouth against the heavens, and their tongue walks through the earth' (Ps. LXXIII, 9). (*T.J.Pe'ah* I, § 1, f. 16*a*, line 8.)

[1120] There are four great sins which correspond to four great virtues, in that man is punished for them in this world, and their capital, or stock, remains in the form of punishment dealt out to him in the world to come. These four are idolatry, incest, murder, slander, which last is as bad as all the other three put together.
(*T.J.Pe'ah* I, § 1, f. 15*d*, line 60.)

[1121] In the world to come all sinners will be healed save the serpent, because it uttered slander. Therefore it says, 'Cursed art thou above all creatures' (Gen. III, 14); they will all be healed except the serpent, whose food is dust, both in this world and in the next (Isa. LXV, 25). (*Tanḥ.B.*, Meẓora', 24*a*.)

[1122] It says, 'I will take heed to my ways, that I sin not with my tongue. I will keep my mouth with a muzzle' (Ps. XXXIX, 1). Can there be a muzzle for the mouth? But the meaning is, 'I will keep silence, so that I may not busy myself with empty matters, but only with the words of the Torah.' As it says, 'A tree of life is healing for the tongue' (Prov. XV, 4). The tree is the Torah. Hence you may learn that God gave the Law to the Israelites only that they should not busy themselves with vain things and with slander, as it says, '"Thou shalt talk of them" (Deut. VI, 7), that is, of the Law, and not of vain things or slander.' So David said, 'Who desires to acquire [buy] the life of the world to come?' They said to him, 'Man cannot buy it.' He replied, 'But it is cheap,' for it is written, 'Who is the man that desires life?' (Ps. XXXIV, 12). [It depends upon man's will and not his riches.] They said, 'Who can acquire life?' He replied, 'Keep thy tongue from evil, and evil means slander' (*ib.* 13), as it says, 'Let lying lips be put to silence' (*ib.* XXXI, 18).
(*Midr.Ps.* on XXXIX, 1 (128*b*, §4).)

'There is a less serious form of slander which is called "dust of slander", which we may perhaps call uncharitable comment on our neighbours, a thing that even good men find it very hard to avoid' (Moore, II, 150):

[1123] R. Amram said, in the name of Rab: From three sins a man cannot escape every day: wicked [i.e. lustful] thoughts, calculation on, or inattentiveness during, prayer, and slander. Surely not slander? Well, 'dust' of slander. R. Judah said, in the name of Rab: In most men is a little [tendency to] robbery, in a few men to unchastity, and in all to slander. Surely not to slander? Well, to dust of slander. (*Bab.B.* 164*b fin.*)

[The word *abaḳ*, lit. 'dust', is sometimes used in a transferred sense, meaning *something akin to* or *connected with* or a *shade of something else*, or *tantamount to it*; thus 'dust of slander' = 'gossip'.

'Calculation on, or inattentiveness in, prayer.' These are alternative renderings of one phrase, which, owing to its ambiguity, has attracted the attention of commentators. This phrase is '*iyyun tefillah*. The word '*iyyun* (from the same root as '*ayin*, eye) really suggests *attention to*, rather than *inattention*. The root-meaning, i.e. *to look at*, is essentially neutral in significance, though in the Bible already it acquires special connotations, e.g. I Sam. XVIII, 9 (Saul was *eyeing* David) and synonyms, in the sense of *looking askance at*, occur, e.g. Ps. XCII, 11; CXVIII, 7 and on the Moabite Stone, line 7.

In post-classical Hebrew it means 'to consider'; sometimes, *to regard with close attention.* As a noun, our phrase occurs also in *Ber.* 55*a* top, where Cohen renders it by 'calculating in prayer'. The preceding sentence in *Berakot* is 'whoever prolongs his prayer and calculates on it (*me'ayyen*) will, in the end, come to heart-grief', and this phrase is explained by Rashi as 'whosoever says in his heart (i.e. thinks) that his request will be fulfilled, because he has prayed sincerely'. Rashi goes on to say that 'grief of heart' means that 'his request will not be fulfilled'. In *Baba Bathra* Rashi repeats this explanation, but rather elaborates it, and he prefaces it with the words: 'some commentators think that.'

But the Tosafist in *Baba Bathra*, commenting on Rashi, points out that *'iyyun tefillah* is also used in a good sense, i.e. *devotion in prayer*, e.g. *Sab.* 127*a*. The passage has several parallels, of which the best known is the beginning of *Pe'ah*, cited in *P.B.* p. 5. Here Abrahams has, as usual, an excellent note. This, as well as his article in *J.Q.R.* O.S. XX, 276, should be studied. The Tosafist suggests that a man may be praying while thoughts of sin (*hirhur 'averah*) are in his heart.

It would seem that there is little support for the rendering 'inattention in prayer', given by Levy, s.v. *'iyyun*, save in so far as concentration on a material wish is inattention to the real import of the words uttered in prayer. The rendering 'calculation' is to be preferred. (H. L.)]

[1124] There are four 'dusts'; the dust of usury, the dust of the seventh year [i.e. any agricultural occupation not directly related to those forbidden in the Sabbath year], the dust of idolatry, the dust of slander. A man should not do business with money borrowed from his neighbour, nor with seventh year produce, because of the dust of usury and the dust of the seventh year. Because of the dust of idolatry, he should avoid business with his neighbour on a heathen festival, and because of the dust of slander a man should not gossip about his neighbour, even gossip to his neighbour's credit [or, possibly, with his neighbour's approval]. (*T.Ab.Zar.* I, 10–14 (Z. p. 461, line 11).)

Take care even about over-praising a man, for that may lead others to adverse criticism:

[1125] R. Dimi said: Let not a man dilate in praise of his neighbour, lest from his praise there is a passing to his blame.

(*Bab.B.* 164*b fin.* (Moore, II, 150; Prov. XXVII, 14).)

Allied to slander is scoffing and mockery.

[1126] He who mocks [*sc.* at sacred things, the commandments, etc.] will end in hell. (*Ab.Zar.* 18*b.*)

[1127] Scoffing is serious, for its beginning is sufferings, and its end is destruction. (*T.J.Ber.* II, § 8, f. 5*c*, line 71.)

One must be very careful not to hurt one's neighbour's feelings:

[1128] As the folk say, 'If there is a case of hanging in a family, say not to one of them, "Hang this fish up for me."' (*Bab.M.* 59*b fin.*)

To put your neighbour to shame is a cardinal sin according to Rabbinic ethics:

[1129] Why did they ordain that some prayers should be recited in a low voice? So as not to put a sinner to shame in public. (*Soṭ.* 32*b.*)

For this reason the penultimate sentence of Grace after meals, in *P.B.* p. 285 (Ps. XXXVII, 25), is said silently by the Ashkenazic Jews, so as not to put to shame a poor guest who may perchance be present (but cf. *Lev.R.*, Beḥuḳḳotai, XXXV, §2).

[1130] R. Simeon b. Yoḥai said: It were better for a man to fall into a burning oven than to put his neighbour to shame in public. (The burning oven or fiery furnace metaphor is not infrequent, cp. [769], [1161].) (*Soṭ.* 10*b.*)

[1131] Someone taught before R. Naḥman b. Isaac: If a man puts his neighbour to shame in public, it is as if he shed blood. R. Naḥman said to him: Well have you spoken, for we see how the red disappears, and the pallor comes. (*Bab.M.* 58*b.*)

[1132] R. Simeon b. Gamaliel said: There were no happier days for Israel than the fifteenth of Ab and the Day of Atonement, for on them the sons [some texts have, the daughters] of Jerusalem used to go forth in white garments to dance in the vineyards, and these garments were borrowed, so that none who did not possess them should be put to shame....The daughters of Jerusalem, too, used to go out on these days, and dance in the vineyards, saying, 'Young man, lift up thine eyes, and consider whom thou wilt select for thyself [as a wife]; do not fix thine eyes upon beauty, but consider the family.' And the young man replied (Cant. III, 11): 'Go forth, O ye daughters of Zion, and gaze upon King Solomon, even upon the crown wherewith his mother has crowned him in the day of his espousals, and in the day of the gladness of his heart.' (*Ta'an.* IV, 8 (cp. p. lxxiii).)

The quotation in the present connection should end with the words 'put to shame', but the sentences which follow seem worth inclusion.

[The Commentators on this well-known and interesting passage are concerned mainly with the fifteenth of Ab. Why was it a 'joyous day'? Clearly the origin was forgotten. In the Gemara, great uncertainty prevails, and different reasons are offered. Nearly all these reasons are connected with the abrogation of certain bans, e.g. against the intermarriage of the tribes (Num. XXXVI, 6, 7); against giving wives to the Benjamites (Jud. XXI, 2); against the entry into the promised land, for on this day the last of the generation, doomed to wander, died (Deut. II, 16, 17); against Israelite pilgrimages to Jerusalem (II Kings XVII, 2); against the burial of the Bethar Martyrs in the Bar Kokba war. Or, it was the day on which they ceased cutting wood for the Altar. Now any one of these reasons might suffice: cumulatively, they cancel each other. The last are even inherently impossible. How could *they* be responsible for a holiday in ancient Israel? The suggestion of Bethar comes from R. Matnah, who lived in Babylonia about A.D. 320. Can he really have thought that an event which happened in A.D. 135 would explain a practice of ancient Israel? Again, the saying in the Mishnah is recorded by Simeon b. Gamaliel II, who was a youth in Bethar when the Bar Kokba war broke out, and who escaped from the massacre. Is it likely that he, of all people, would have referred so vaguely to an event which must have had poignant memories for him? Moreover, the phrase he uses ('There used not to be such joyous days in Israel') surely points to a long-distant past! It is clear that we have here traditions of an ancient holiday, no longer observed, and but dimly recorded. Both Simeon and the Amoraim are giving us antiquarian information, not a description of current usage.

Still more is this evident in the case of the Day of Atonement. Can we reconcile the 'bank holiday' with the propitiatory character of the day? When would the people have time to dance in the vineyards? The Mishnah tells us that a worshipper who saw the burnings of the bullock and the he-goat could not see the High Priest read the lesson, because the acts were performed at the same time, and the distance between the places where they were performed was great (*Yoma* VII, 2). Moreover, there was so much to witness in the Temple and in the environs, e.g. the High Priest's procession, the sending away of the scapegoat, that there would be no time for the dancing in the vineyards, even if such a celebration were in keeping with the character of the day. There is no trace of it in the *Yoma* programme of ritual.

One cannot escape the conclusion that we have here a reminiscence of the ancient celebration of the day, as it was kept before the time of Ezekiel. There were elements in it that the Pharisees did not like. The controversy over the kindling of the incense is a striking example of their efforts to spiritualise the atonement rites. Had the day been entirely a post-exilic institution, it is doubtful whether the scapegoat would have been introduced. The ritual of the goat was too ancient to be removed, but the Pharisees did their best to elevate it to a symbol. No doubt the dancing in the vineyards is another relic of a joyous national festival which was celebrated during the monarchy, and which was later transformed to a great day of solemn expiation and national reconciliation with God. (See **Note 60**.) (H. L.)]

We find in Lev. VI, 25 (M.T. VI, 18) the words:

[1133] 'In the place where the burnt offering is killed shall also the sin offering be killed.' R. Levi said in the name of R. Simeon b. Laḳish: This was ordained so as not to expose the sinners [to shame]. (*T.J.Soṭ.* VIII, § 9, f. 23*a*, line 31.)

People might think they were bringing, not a sin offering, but a burnt offering.

Sensitive consideration for the feeling of others is, indeed, very characteristic of the Rabbis:

[1134] R. Eliezer b. Jacob invited a blind man to dinner, and he placed him above himself at the table, so that they said, 'This must be a great man, or R. Eliezer would not have placed him above himself at the table.' They showed him therefore much distinction. 'To what do I owe this?' the blind man asked them. They replied, 'Because R. Eliezer placed you above himself at the table.' Then the blind man prayed for him thus: 'Thou hast shown lovingkindness to him who is seen, but cannot see. May He who sees, but cannot be seen, receive thy graciousness, and show lovingkindness to thee.'

(*T.J.Pe'ah* VIII, § 9, f. 21*b*, line 51.)

[1135] R. Hoshaiah employed a blind man as a teacher for his son, and he used to dine with R. Hoshaiah. One day R. Hoshaiah had guests, and he did not invite the blind man to eat with him. In the evening he went to him and said, 'Let not my master be annoyed with me; I had guests, and I did not want you to be held in low esteem, and not receive due honour: hence it was that I did not have you to eat with me to-day.' The blind man said, 'You have appeased him who is seen and sees not: may He who sees and is unseen receive your appeasement.'

(*T.J.Pe'ah* VIII, § 9, f. 21*b*, line 45.)

Chapter XVI

ON CHARITY

Nothing is more marked in Rabbinic ethics than the stress laid upon charity in every sense of the word—from almsgiving to all sorts of lovingkindness. And in the old Jewish communities we may observe a mixture: there was much free giving of alms to all who asked—even to deceivers!—but there was also much systematic and careful 'relief', which might win the approval of the Charity Organisation Society to-day (**Note 89**). There are, I believe, monographs on Rabbinic and medieval charity. Here (in accordance with the general lines of this work) I give only illustrative extracts in no systematic order.

[1136] It is said, 'If thy brother be waxen poor, and his hand fail with thee, then thou shalt strengthen him; that he may live with thee' (Lev. xxv, 35). If your brother be waxen poor, you shall not suffer him to fall. He is like a load resting on a wall; one man can then hold it, and prevent it from falling, but if it has once fallen to the ground, five men cannot raise it up again. And even if you have strengthened [i.e. helped] him four or five times, you must [if he needs it], strengthen him yet again. Yet, lest you should think that it is your duty to help him, even if you cause him injury, by helping him to live a corrupt life, the Scripture says 'with thee' [i.e. that he may live with you, obeying the commandments]. (*Sifra* 109*b*.)

I much prefer the reading 'wall' to the reading 'donkey'. So, too, Moore, II, 178.

[1137] He who gives alms in secret is greater than Moses (cf. *R.T.* p. 112). (**Note 29**.) (*Bab.B.* 9*b*.)

[1138] Almsgiving weighs as much as all the other commandments. (*Bab.B.* 9*a*.)

[1139] R. Levi says: There are three sorts of nuts—*Perek* or soft-shelled, middling, and stony ones. The first variety can be opened of themselves; the second break if you knock them; the third are very hard to break, and if you beat them on a stone and break them, nevertheless you gain no good. So is it with Israel. There are those among them who give charity of themselves, unasked; these are like the soft-shelled nuts. There are some, again, who, if asked for charity, give it at once; these are like the middling nuts. Finally, there are others, from whom, even if you press them any number of times, you get no good. R. Levi quoted the proverb, 'The door which is not open to charity is open to the doctor' [i.e. those who do not give charity when in health, either will fall ill or promise to give when sick]. **(Note 30.)** (*Pes.R.* 42*b*.)

Perek, the modern Ferka, by Samaria, was noted for the quality of its nuts and for their soft shells. According to '*Orlah* III, 7 Perek nuts were usually sold separately, i.e. not in bulk, because of their excellence.

[1140] R. Ḥiyya said: He who turns his eyes away from almsgiving is as if he worshipped idols. (*Ket.* 68*a*.)

[1141] 'God will bring every work into judgment, with every secret thing, whether it be good or whether it be evil' (Eccles. XII, 14). What is the meaning of, 'Whether it be good or evil?' R. Yannai said, 'It is he who gives money to the poor publicly.' For R. Yannai once saw a man give money to a poor man publicly. He said, 'It had been better that you had given him nothing than that you should have given him and put him to shame.'
(*Eccles.R.* XII, § 14, 1, on XII, 14 (31*b*) (cp. *Ḥag.* 5*a*).)

[1142] All the almsgiving and loving deeds which the Israelites do in this world are great advocates between them and their Father in heaven. Great is almsgiving, for it brings the Redemption nearer. (*Bab.B.* 10*a*.)

To put money in the charity box is a very high form of almsgiving, for neither giver nor recipient know each other.

In relation to the Law about a pledge (Deut. XXIV, 10–13) it is said:

[1143] You must restore to him by day [i.e. early in the morning] the things he uses in the day, and by night [i.e. before nightfall] the things he uses in the night: e.g. a blanket before the night, an axe in the day.
(*Sifre Deut.*, Ki Teẓe, § 279, f. 123*b* (cp. [1039]).)

The law of Deut. XXIV, 14, 15, is compared with that of Lev. XIX, 13. It is inferred that stealing and defrauding is a sin, whether the wronged man is rich or poor, but it is especially a sin towards the poor, for:

[1144] God hastens to punish a sin committed against the poor and the needy more than to punish a sin committed against any man whatever. And of the words in Deut. XXIV, 15, 'he sets his soul [his life] upon it,' it is said: This means that he who withholds from the servant his hire is as if he had taken his life.

(*Sifre Deut.*, Ki Teẓe, § 278, f. 123*b*.)

[1145] A poor man who is journeying from place to place should be given not less than one loaf worth a *pondion* [from wheat costing] one *sela*ʿ for four *se'ahs*. If he spends the night [in such a place], he should be given what is needful for the night. [In *T.Pe'ah* IV, 8 (Z. p. 23, line 17), this is said to be lodging, oil and pulse, and for the Sabbath, in addition to the food for the three meals, he should be given oil, pulse, fish and fresh vegetables. Cf. Moore, II, 176.] If he stays over the Sabbath, he should be given food enough for three meals.

(*Pe'ah* VIII, 7 (Professor Danby's translation).)

[So important was the duty of supporting the poor deemed to be, that the prescriptions of the sacrificial system were homiletically utilised to inculcate it (cp. Phil. IV, 18).

The complete annual cycle of sacrifices is set out in Num. XXVIII, and the system is elaborated with full details: the haggadah is correspondingly rich, and many ethical ideas are extracted. Thus, the section begins: 'Command the children of Israel...*my* bread for *my* sacrifices...shall ye observe to offer unto *me*' (*ib.* 2). Here, the pronoun 'my' is stressed, and among the many lessons drawn from the words, it is taught that God has no need for sacrifices: examples have been cited from *Num.R.*, Pineḥas, XXI, 16 (cp. [63]) or from the parallels in *Pes.K.* f. 57*a*, *Pes.R.* 80*a*, *Tanḥ.*, Pineḥas, § 12, 299*b*, *Sifre Num.*, Pineḥas, § 143 end, f. 54*a* see [63]. These mostly repeat each other; in other places, new ideas may be seen. Thus: God says to Israel, 'My sons, whenever you give sustenance to the poor, I impute it as though you gave sustenance to me, for it says, "My bread".' Does, then, God eat and drink? No, but whenever you give food to the poor, God accounts it to you as if you gave food to Him. This is a slight development of the previous passages: it is cited from *Midrash Tannaim*, p. 83 *fin.* and Moore (II, 169) aptly compares Matt. XXV, 40. Somewhat similar is a comment on Ps. L, 8: 'Not for thy sacrifices do I reprove thee.' R. Naḥman, in the name of R. Berechiah, said: If a man intends (or, is privileged) to give alms, God inscribes it as 'opposite to Him' (i.e. given to Him), for the verse continues 'and thy oblations are opposite to me always' (*Midr.Ps.* on L, 8 (140*a fin.*, § 2).) (H. L.)]

[1146] Let your house be open; let the poor be members of your household. Let a man's house be open to the north and to the south and to the east and to the west, even as Job's house was, for Job made four doors to his house, that the poor might not be troubled to go round the house [to the back door], but that each would find a door facing him as he approached. 'Members of your household': that is, let the poor relate what they have eaten and drunk in your house, as happened with Job. For when two poor men met, one said, 'Whence came you?' And the other said, 'Whither go you?' The answers were, 'From and to the house of Job.' When the great suffering came upon Job, he said, 'Lord of the world, have I not fed the hungry and clothed the naked?' But God said, 'So far, you have not reached to the half of the measure of Abraham, for you sat in your house, and when wayfarers came unto you, you gave wheaten bread to him whose wont it was to eat wheaten bread, and meat to him whose wont it was to eat meat, and wine to him whose wont it was to drink wine. But Abraham did not so; he went out and wandered about, and when he found wayfarers, he brought them to his house, and he gave wheaten bread to him whose wont it was *not* to eat wheaten bread, and so with meat and wine. And not only this, but he built large inns on the roads, and put food and drink within them, and all came and ate and drank and blessed God. Therefore quiet [or, appeasement] of spirit was granted to him, and all that the mouth of man can ask for was found in his house. (*Ab.R.N.* (vers. I), VII, 17*a*, *b*.)

[1147] It happened to a man called Bar Bohin that our Rabbis came to him in connection with a collection of contributions for the maintenance of students, and they heard his son say to him, 'What are we to eat to-day?' He said, 'Endives.' The son said, 'Of those which you get one measureful or two measurefuls for a *mina*?' He replied, 'Of those which you get two for a *mina*, for they are withered and cheap.' The Rabbis said, 'How can we come first to such a one? Let us go on, and do our business in the city, and then return to him.' They did so. After they had done their business in the city, they came to him and said, 'Give us a charitable donation.' He said, 'Go to my wife, and she will give you a measure of *denarii*.' They went to her, and said, 'Your husband bids you give us a measure of *denarii*.' She said to them, 'A heaped measure or an exact one?' They said, 'He did not specify which.' She said, 'I will give you

...d measure, and if my husband says, "Why?" I will say, ...ve it to them from my dowry."' They went to the husband ... said, 'May your Creator supply your needs.' He said to ...m, 'How did she give to you? A heaped measure or an exact one?' They replied, 'We did not specify which measure to her, but she said, "I shall give you a heaped measure, and if my husband asks me why I have given it you, I will say, I will deduct it from my dowry."' He said, 'Just so was it my wish to give you. Why did you not come to me at first?' They said to him, 'We heard your son asking you, "What shall we eat to-day," and you said, "Endives," and he said, "Of those that one gets one measureful for a *mina*, or of those which one gets two?" And you said, "Of those which one gets two, because they are withered and cheap." We thought: "Does a man who has much money eat endives of which one gets two measures for a *mina*?"' He replied, 'In what concerns myself I can do as I like, but in regard to that which is commanded me by my Creator, I have no power or authority.'

(*Esther R.* II, 3, on I, 4.)

[1148] He who sustains God's creatures is as though he had created them. (*Tanḥ.B.*, Noaḥ, 16*a*.)

[1149] He said to me, 'Twice did Israel go into exile: for the first exile, a time for return was given, but for the second, none. Why?' I said, 'Though the men of the first Temple practised idolatry, yet there was proper behaviour [*derek erez̧*] among them.' And what was this *derek erez̧*? Almsgiving and deeds of lovingkindness. (*Tan.d.b.El.* p. 71.)

[1150] There was once a widow who lived near a man who owned land, and her two children went to glean the ears of corn. But the landowner did not allow them to do so. Their mother said, 'When will my children return? Perhaps they will bring something to eat.' And the children said, 'Let us return to our mother; perhaps we shall find with her something to eat.' *She* got nothing from *them*, and *they* found nothing with *her*, and they put their heads between the knees of their mother, and they died all three on one day. And God said, 'You have taken their lives; surely I will exact your lives from you, even as it says, "Rob not the poor, oppress not the afflicted, for the

Lord will despoil of life them that despoil them"' (Prov. XXII, 22). (*Ab.R.N.* (vers. I), XXXVIII, 57*a.*)

[1151] 'If thou lend money to my people' (Exod. XXII, 25). The Israelites say to God: 'Who is thy people?' He replies, 'The poor,' as it is said, 'For the Lord comforts His people, and has mercy upon His poor' (Isa. XLIX, 13). If a rich man has poor relations, he does not acknowledge them, as it is said, 'The brothers of the poor hate them' (Prov. XIX, 7), but God is not so, for He cares only for the poor, as it is said, 'The poor of his people take refuge in Him' (Isa. XIV, 32). David said, 'Lord of the world, make equality in thy world.' God replied, 'If I made all equal, who would practise faithfulness and loving-kindness?' [The last two sentences are based on untranslate-able puns on Ps. LXI, 6, 7.] (*Exod.R.*, Mishpaṭim, XXXI, 5.)

[1152] R. Ishmael said: Every 'if' in the Torah refers to a voluntary act with the exception of three. [Of these three, one is:] 'If thou lend money to any of my people with thee who is poor' (Exod. XXII, 25). The 'if' is obligatory, for it says, 'thou shalt surely lend him' (Deut. XV, 8) (cp. [1184 *fin.*]).
(*Mek.*², *Baḥodesh*, Yitro, § 11, p. 243; *Mek.*³, vol. II, pp. 287–8.)

[1153] God glorifies the offering of the poor. (*Pes.R.* 201*b.*)

[1154] Abba b. Abba gave some money to his son to distribute among the poor. When his son set forth, he found one poor man eating meat and drinking wine. He went back and told his father, who said, 'Give him all the more; his soul is bitter within him.'[1]
(*T.J.Pe'ah* VIII, § 9, f. 21*b*, line 20.)

[1155] How do we know that in uncertainty with regard to gleanings and the forgotten sheaf and the corner of the field, the benefit of the doubt should be given to the poor? Because it says, 'Unto the needy and the sojourner shalt thou abandon them' (Lev. XIX, 10). (*Sifra* 88*c.*)

[1156] He who places a basket under his vine when he is gathering the harvest [in order to catch the fruit that drops] is robbing the poor of their due gleanings. (*Sifra* 88*a.*)

[1] [Abba took the view that the man was mourning because he was drinking wine (Prov. XXXI, 6). (H. L.)]

[1157] One day R. Johanan and R. Simeon b. Laḳish went to bathe in the public baths of Tiberias. They met a poor man who asked for charity. They said, 'When we come back.' When they returned, they found him dead. They said, 'Since we showed him no charity when he was alive, let us attend to him now that he is dead.' When they were laying him out for burial, they found a purse full of silver pieces upon him. Then they remembered what R. Abbahu had said, 'We must show charity even to the deceivers, for if it were not for them a man might be asked for alms by a poor man, and he might refuse and be punished.' (*T.J.Pe'ah* VIII, § 9, f. 21*b*, line 13 (cp. [1160]).)

[1158] Samuel left his father, and halted by some huts of the poor. He heard them say: 'Shall we eat to-day off vessels of gold or of silver?' He went back and told his father, who said, 'It is incumbent on us to show gratitude to the deceivers among the poor.' **(Note 89.)** (*T.J.Pe'ah* VIII, § 9, f. 21*b*, line 10.)

[1159] R. Tanḥum, needing only one pound of meat for himself, was wont to buy two, one for himself and one for the poor; two bundles of vegetables, one for himself and one for the poor. 'God has set the one over against the other' (Eccles. VII, 14), namely the rich and the poor, that each may gain a blessing through the other. **(Note 91.)**
(*Eccles.R.* VII, § 14, 2 on VII, 14 (20*b*) (cp. [1218]).)

[1160] R. Ḥanina was wont to send a poor man four *zuzim* every Friday. Once he sent them by his wife, who reported on her return that the man was not in need. 'What did you see?' said the Rabbi. 'I heard how he was asked, "Would he use the silver outfit for his dinner or the gold outfit."' Then R. Ḥanina said, 'This is what R. Elazar said, "We must be grateful to the deceivers, for were it not for them, we might sin every day."'
(*Ket.* 68*a* (cp. [1157–8]).)

[1161] In the neighbourhood of Mar Ukba was a poor man, for whom he was wont to put every day four *zuzim* under his door. One day the poor man said, 'I will go and see who it is who does this good deed.' That day Mar Ukba had tarried late in the house of study, and his wife accompanied him. When the poor man saw the door move, he went after Mar Ukba, who ran into the oven, of which the fire had been raked out. The foot of Mar

Ukba was burnt. His wife said, 'Let my feet support yours.' He fainted. She said to him, ['Better leave charity to me, for] I stay within the house, and what I give is of immediate utility.' Why did he act thus? He acted according to the saying, 'Better for a man to throw himself into a fiery furnace than to put his neighbour openly to shame.' (*Ket.* 67*b* (cp. [1130]).)

[For 'sitting in the oven', see note to [769].]

[1162] Mar Ukba was wont to send a poor man of his neighbourhood every eve of the Day of Atonement four hundred *zuzim*. Once he sent them by his son, who came back and said that the man was not in need. 'What did you see?' said Mar Ukba. The son replied, 'I saw old wine being poured out for him.' Mar Ukba said, 'So spoilt and indulged is he?' He doubled the amount, and sent it him. When he was dying, he said, 'Bring me my charity list,' and he found written in it seven thousand *dinarim*. He said, 'The provision is scanty; the journey is long.' He, thereupon, bequeathed in charity half his fortune. How could he do this? Did not R. Ilai say that they had ordered in Usha that however generous a man wanted to be, he should not give away more than a fifth of his fortune? This rule applies to a man only in his lifetime; it does not apply to what a man chooses to do as regards his fortune after his death. (*Ket.* 67*b*.)

[1163] Though you may have given already, give yet again even a hundred times, for it says, 'Give, yea, give shalt thou...' (Deut. xv, 10, 11). (*Sifre Deut.*, Re'eh, §116, f. 98 *a fin.* (H. p. 175).)

[1164] 'Thou shalt open thy hand wide unto thy brother' (Deut. xv, 11). To him for whom bread is suitable, give bread; to him who needs dough, give dough; to him for whom money is required, give money; to him for whom it is fitting to put the food in his mouth, put it in. (*Sifre Deut.*, Re'eh, § 118, f. 98*b* (H. p. 176).)

[1165] A poor man came to Raba, and Raba asked him what he usually had for his fare. The man replied, 'Fatted chicken and old wine.' 'But do you not,' said Raba, 'feel worried that you are a burden to the community'? 'Do I eat what is theirs?' said the man. 'I eat what is God's' (Ps. CXLV, 15). While they talked, Raba's sister came to see him, whom he had not seen for thirteen years. She brought him a present of a fatted chicken and some old wine. 'That is a token,' thought Raba. 'I apologise,' said he to the poor man. 'Come and eat.' (*Ket.* 67*b.*)

[1166] There were two vestries in the Temple, one called the Vestry of the Secret Ones, the other, the Vestry of the Utensils. In the former, the sin-fearing men used to put their gifts secretly, and the poor of gentle birth were supported from them secretly. (*Sheḳ.* v, 6.)

[1167] Just as there was a 'vestry of secret givers' in the Temple, so was there one in every city, for the sake of respectable people who had come down in life, so that they might be helped in secret. (*T.Sheḳ.* II, 16 (Z. p. 177, line 10).)

[1168] We read in a *Baraita*: R. Johanan b. Zakkai rode an ass outside Jerusalem, and his disciples walked after him. He saw a woman gathering grains of barley from among the dung of the horses of the Arabians. When she saw him, she covered herself with her hair, and stood before him and said, 'Rabbi, feed me.' He said to her, 'Who are you?' She said, 'I am the daughter of Niḳodemos b. Gorion.' He said to her, 'What has become of your father's money?' She replied, 'Was not this a proverb in Jerusalem, "The preservation of money is losing it in charity?"' He then asked her, 'What has become of your father-in-law's money?' She answered, 'That, too, was lost with the other. Do you remember how you signed my marriage covenant?' He said to his disciples, 'I remember how I signed it, and I read in it of a million gold *denarii* of her father, besides what was given to her by her father-in-law.' And R. Johanan wept and said, 'Blessed are you, O Israel, when you fulfil God's will. No people or tongue rule over you, but when you do not, he delivers you into the hand of a degraded people, and even into the power of their horses.' But did not Niḳodemos practise charity? It is related of him that when he left his house to go to the House of Study, shawls were spread under his feet, and the poor folded them and collected them. Well, perhaps he did all this for his own glory, or perhaps he did not practise as much charity as he should have done. As folk say: 'According to the camel should be the burden.' (**Note 90.**) (*Ket.* 66*b.*)

[1169] Nehemiah of Siḥin met a man in Jerusalem who said to him, 'Give me that chicken you are carrying.' Nehemiah said, 'Here is its value in money.' The man went and bought some meat and ate it and died. Then Nehemiah said, 'Come and bemoan the man whom Nehemiah has killed.'

(*T.J.Pe'ah*, VIII, § 9, 21*b*, line 36.)

[Siḥin was near Sepphoris; for its interesting history, see Neubauer, *op. cit.* p. 202. (H. L.)]

[1170] R. Nathan b. Abba said in the name of Rab: The rich Jews of Babylonia will go to hell. Sabbatai b. Marinos went to Babylon and asked for work. They refused to give it him. He asked for sustenance; they refused to give it him. Then he said: These people must be descended from the mixed multitude who went out of Egypt with the Israelites (Exod. XII, 38), for he who has no pity upon his fellow-creatures is assuredly not of the seed of Abraham our father. (*Beẓ.* 32*b*.)

[1171] Nahum of Gimzo was carrying a gift to the house of his father-in-law, when he met a man covered with boils, who said, 'Give me something of what you have with you.' He said, 'When I come back.' When he came back, the man was dead. He said: 'Those eyes which saw thee when I did not give, may they be blinded; may those hands which did not reach out to give thee, be cut off; may those feet which did not hasten to give thee, be broken'; and it happened to him accordingly. R. Akiba went to see him, and said, 'Woe is me that I see thee thus.' Nahum replied, 'Woe is me that I do *not* see thee thus.' Akiba said, 'What, dost thou curse me?' Nahum said, 'Dost thou kick against sufferings?' (*T.J.Pe'ah* VIII, § 9, f. 21*b*, line 39.)

Nahum must mean that sufferings in *this* world prevent much worse suffering in the future world. In the parallel story in *Ta'an.* 21*a*, Nahum's answer is 'Woe to me if you did *not* see me in this condition.' This is a much more preferable and likely reading.

[1172] It says, 'Let not thy heart envy sinners' (Prov. XXIII, 17). [The Hebrew could also mean 'get excited about', 'be passionate about'.] God says: 'Be passionate for me, for if it were not for passion, the world would not continue.' Man would take to himself no wife, and build no house. If Abraham had not shown passion [zeal, eagerness, enthusiasm, yearning], he would not have acquired heaven and earth. How did he acquire them? He said to Melchizedek, 'How did you come out of the ark?'

Melchizedek answered, 'By the charity which we practised there.' Abraham said, 'How could you practise charity in the ark? Were there any poor there? There was nobody there but Noah and his sons. To whom could you show charity?' He said, 'To the tame and wild beasts and to the birds. We never slept, but we gave food now to this one and now to that one, all through the night.' Then Abraham said, 'Seeing that these men, if they had not shown charity to the beasts and the birds, could not have come out of the ark, how much more must I show charity to the children of men?' So then he planted a tamarisk in Beersheba. [Tamarisk in Hebrew is *Eshel*; now the three letters of which the word *Eshel* is composed are the first three letters of the Hebrew words for food, drink, escort or accompaniment. Abraham gave food and drink to the three angels, and 'accompanied' them on their way (Gen. XVIII, 16). He also gave food and drink to many passers-by, and 'accompanied' them on their way. (H. L.)]

(*Midr.Ps.* on XXXVII, 1 (126*b*, § 1) (cp. [111] and [124]).)

[1173] It is written: 'And they shall build up *from thee* the old waste places' (Isa. LVIII, 12). R. Ṭarfon gave to R. Akiba a large sum of money and said to him, 'Go and buy for us this estate, so that we can be supported thereby while we are studying the Law.' He took the money, and divided it among scribes and scholars and students of the Law. Some days after, R. Ṭarfon said to him, 'Have you bought that estate for us about which I spoke to you?' He said, 'Yes.' R. Ṭarfon replied, 'Can you show it me?' He said, 'Yes.' He took him, and showed him the scribes and scholars and students of the Law. Then R. Ṭarfon said, 'Has there ever been a man who gave away his capital for nothing?' He replied, 'Yes, David, who scattered and gave to the poor, and whose charity abode for ever' (Ps. CXII, 9). (*Lev.R.*, Behar, XXXIV, 16.)

[1174] There are people who cause pain whether they give or no. Be thou not so: harden not thy heart. There are people who give, and then draw back: be thou not so: if thou hast opened thy hand four times, thou must do so a hundred times. 'Thou shalt surely lend him,' etc. (Deut. XV, 8, 9): first they give to him, and afterwards they take a pledge from him: so said R. Judah: but the wise say, 'Tell him to bring a pledge so as *to quiet his mind*.'

'According to his need': you are not commanded to make him rich; 'what he wants': even if it be a horse or a slave, as Hillel once gave a poor man of good family [who had come down in the world] a horse and a slave. And once, in Galilee, they gave a man a *litra* of fowl-flesh a day. 'What he wants': 'he' includes his wife. 'Beware', etc.: be careful that thou withhold not pity, for he who withholds pity from his fellow is likened by Scripture to an idolater, and he casts off from him the yoke of heaven. (*Sifre Deut.*, Re'eh, § 116, f. 98*a fin.*–98*b init.* (H. pp. 175–6).)

[1175] 'Take heed lest there be an evil [*beliya'al*] thought in thy heart, and thou close thy hand from thy poor brother' (Deut. xv, 9). Take care lest thou withhold mercy, for whosoever withholds mercy from his neighbour is as though he commits idolatry and breaks off heaven's yoke, for 'belial' means yokeless, i.e. *beli*, without, *'ol*, yoke. (*Sifre Deut.*, Re'eh, § 117, f. 98*b* (H. p. 176).)

[1176] Rabbis Eliezer, Joshua and Akiba went to the neighbourhood of Antioch to make a collection for needy scholars. One Abba Judah lived there who was very liberal in giving. But he lost all his wealth, and when the Rabbis came, he was ashamed and went home, and his visage was dejected. His wife said to him, 'Why do you look so dejected?' He replied, 'The Rabbis have come here, and I do not know what to do.' His wife was even more pious than he, and she said to him, 'You still own one field; sell half of it, and give them the proceeds.' He did so. The Rabbis prayed for him and said, 'May your needs be supplied.' When they left, he went to plough the half of the field that was still his, and as he did so, his cow stumbled and broke her hoof. He bent down to help her up, and God opened his eyes, and he found a treasure. Then he said, 'Surely for my benefit has my cow broken her hoof.' When the Rabbis came again, they asked how Abba Judah fared. The reply was, 'Who can see Abba Judah? So rich is he in cattle and sheep and camels. He is as wealthy as he was before.' Then Abba Judah came to the Rabbis, and he greeted them, and said, 'Your prayer has produced fruit upon fruit.' Then they said, 'Though on the last occasion others gave more than you, we put your name at the head of our list.' Then they took him with them, and made him sit next to them at their dinner, and they applied to him the verse in Proverbs (XVIII, 16), 'A man's gift makes room for him, and brings him before great men.'

(*T.J.Hor.* III, § 7, f. 48*a*, line 44.)

'We put your name at the head of our list': a charming and characteristic touch. Not much less characteristic, perhaps, is the naïve application of the verse in Proverbs to themselves.

[1177] The Egyptians sinned secretly and God made them known publicly. If, as regards the Attribute of Punishment, which is small, he who acts in secret is made known by God publicly, how much more, in regard to the Attribute of Goodness, which is great, [will God make known deeds of goodness done secretly].

(*Sifre Num.*, Shelaḥ, § 115, f. 35*a* (H. p. 127; cp. converse [1106]).)

[1178] In a city where there are both Jews and Gentiles, the collectors of alms collect both from Jews and from Gentiles; they feed the poor of both, visit the sick of both, bury both, comfort the mourners whether Jews or Gentiles, and they restore the lost goods of both—for the sake of peace. (**Notes 31–2.**)

(*T.J.Dem.* IV, § 6, f. 24*a*, line 67 (cp. *R.T.* p. 92).)

Money had better be used in charity than in grand buildings:

[1179] R. Abun erected two grand gates for the House of Study, and he showed them to R. Mina. The latter Rabbi quoted Hos. VIII, 14, 'Israel builds temples, and forgets his Maker,' and went on to say, 'Had you spent this money more piously, would there not have been many labouring in the Law?'

(*T.J.Shek.* V, § 6, f. 49*b*, line 35.)

[1180] One day R. Ḥama b. Ḥanina and R. Hoshaya went about among the Synagogues at Lyd. R. Ḥama said to R. Hoshaya, 'How much money my ancestors have sunk here!' R. Hoshaya replied, 'How many souls thy ancestors have sunk here. For how many men might, through that money, have been toiling in the Law.'

(*T.J.Pe'ah* VIII, § 9, f. 21*b*, line 57.)

The verse in Proverbs that righteousness (*zedakah*: in Rabbinic Hebrew used for almsgiving or charity) delivers from death was taken very seriously by the Rabbis. The 'death' which *they* thought was meant was hell, or long residence in purgatory, or deprivation of the bliss of the happy hereafter. Passages like the following are frequent:

[1181] If a man sees that his means are straitened, let him give alms, and all the more if his means are large. He who cuts down his property, and gives alms, is preserved from the judgment of hell. It is like two sheep swimming over a stream. The one is shorn, the other not. The shorn sheep crosses in safety, the other is swept away. (*Giṭ.* 7*a fin.*)

[1182] It is taught in the name of R. Joshua: The poor man does more for the rich man than the rich man for the poor man. (**Note 91.**) (*Ruth R.* v, 9 on II, 18, f. 10*a.*)

To lend may be better than to give:

[1183] He who gives alms—a blessing is upon him; he who lends is yet better, and he who gives a poor man money to trade with, and becomes a partner with him at half profits, is better than either. [The translation follows Schechter's note *ad. loc.*] (*Ab.R.N.* (vers. I), XLI, 66*a.*)

[1184] He who lends is greater than he who gives alms; and he who provides capital for a useful enterprise is greatest of all. (*Sab.* 63*a.*)

[In connection with Deut. xv, 7, 'If there be among you a poor man of one of thy brethren within any of thy gates in thy land which the Lord thy God gives thee, thou shalt not harden thy heart, nor shut thine hand from thy poor brother: but thou shalt open thine hand wide unto him, and shalt surely lend him sufficient for his need, in that which he wants,' two principles are frequently stressed. First, the extent of the aid to be given is discussed. 'Sufficient for his need' is capable of two interpretations. On the one hand, it means 'you must help him, but you need not enrich him' (*Ket.* 67*b*). On the other hand, you must consider his social status and, if it demands, give him 'a horse for riding and a slave to run before him' (*ib.*). The technical term for such a poor man is *ben ṭovim*, the son of goodly folk, gentry, born of noble descent: the dictionaries thus render it, but Goldschmidt has *verwöhnt*. It is stated that Hillel, having provided such a man with a horse, was unable to find a slave [1174]. Hillel, therefore, himself 'ran before him for three miles' (*ib.* cf. Matt. v, 41, where the injunction to 'go two miles' is in immediate connection with granting loans to the poor). The curious use of the verb *'anaḳ*, in xv, 14, supports this view. The root means 'necklace' and, by a mixed metaphor which is quite in keeping with vivid Hebrew style, the literal translation is, 'thou shalt make a rich necklace for him of thy flock', A.V. 'furnish him liberally'.

The second principle is the preservation of self-respect. Instances are given in *Ket.* 67*b* to show how this was maintained; R. Abba, for example, 'used to wrap money in a *sudarium*, which he trailed over his shoulder when he went to visit the poor (so that they could help themselves secretly), but he used to peep sideways, on account of the deceivers' (*ib.*). A similar convention—though in the opposite direction—survives in the pouch on the back of a barrister's gown, in which clients were supposed to slip their fees without his cognizance. But the best relief was by loan. It was an old saying, 'If a man has nothing, and is unwilling to be supported (which may mean, either that he is too lazy to work, or too sensitive to accept gifts) he should be given something, as a gift, in the first instance, and then be told that he can repay later' [1187]. Or, if a man be not in such desperate need that instant relief is necessary, the procedure may be reversed. He can be given a loan which can subsequently be treated as a gift. On the words 'open wide' R. Ishmael said: 'If a man of good family come, and is ashamed to ask for alms, "open" to him with words, saying, "My son, perhaps thou needest a loan": hence the saying alms are given as a loan' (*Midr.Tann.*, ed. Hoffmann, p. 82). This principle is illustrated by one of the three 'obligatory ifs' [1152]. It is said that three times in the Pentateuch the word *im*, 'if', is not conditional but obligatory, and should be rendered 'when'. The second of these occurs in Exod. XXII, 25, 'if thou lend money to any of my people': this, R. Ishmael takes as a command (*Mekilta*, Yitro, *Baḥodesh*, end, ed. Weiss, f. 80*b* foot: ed. Lauterbach, II, 287). *Ket.* 67*b*; *Sifre Deut.*, Re'eh, 98*b*, ll. 1–5 (H. p. 175). (H. L.)]

[1185] If an individual assigns funds for the relief of the poor in his town, he must give them to the poor of his own town. But if he has assigned them to the poor of another town, he, the donor, may give the money to the poor of his own town. But administrators of charity are not so entitled to vary their distributions: they must give the funds assigned to the poor of a particular city to that city. A donor, who has promised money to a particular charitable object, may not, before the money has reached the administrators, vary the object save with their approval. (*T.Meg.* II, 4 (Z. p. 224, line 17).)

One must be thoughtful in giving to, and helping, the poor:

[1186] To him who has nothing, and refuses to let himself be maintained, one must lend on pledge, and afterwards one must give it him. And he who has something, but from miserliness will not nourish himself, must be maintained, and after his death one must get it back from his property. So said R. Judah. The wise say: One need not bother oneself about him. He who has nothing, and will not be maintained, let him be offered relief first on loan and then as a gift, and afterwards let them demand it back [i.e. it is explained, after his death]. R. Simeon said: The latter man need not be considered, but as to him who has nothing and refuses to take, let him first be asked to give a pledge, and let him then be asked to take, so that his self-respect may be raised. (*Ket.* 67*b*.)

[1187] R. Jonah said: It is not written, 'Happy is he who gives to the poor,' but 'Happy is he who *considers* the poor' (Ps. XLI, 1): i.e. he who ponders how to fulfil the command to help the poor. How did R. Jonah act? If he met a man of good family, who had become impoverished, he would say, 'I have heard that a legacy has been left to you in such a place; take this money in advance, and pay me back later.' When the man accepted it, he then said to him, 'It is a gift.'
(*T.J.Pe'ah* VIII, §9, f. 21*b*, line 29 (cp. *Midr.Ps.* on XLI, 1 (130*b*, §3).)

[1188] 'Blessed is he who considers the poor' (Ps. XLI, 1). R. Huna said: That is he who visits the sick, for he who visits the sick takes away from him a sixtieth part of his sickness. Then they retorted to R. Huna, 'If that be so, let sixty people visit the sick man, and he could go down with them into the street!' 'Ah, but', said R. Huna, 'they must all love him as their own soul. Yet, in any case, they will relieve him.'
(*Lev.R.*, Behar, XXXIV, 1.)

[1189] Thou shalt not harden thy heart from thy poor brother. If you do not give to him, in the end you will have to take from him.
(*Sifre Deut.*, Re'eh, § 116, f. 98*a fin.* (H. p. 175).)

[1190] It has been taught that if a person has become poor and needs public assistance, if he had before been used to vessels of gold, they give him vessels of silver; if of silver, they give him vessels of copper; if of copper, they give him vessels of glass. R. Mena said: They give him vessels of silver or glass only if he employs them for personal use [and not for adornment]. How about that teaching which said that if a man had been wont to wear clothes of fine wool, then give him clothes of fine wool? Again, these are for his own bodily use. It happened that a man of the Patriarch's family had lost his fortune, and they gave him vessels of earthenware: he ate from them and was sick: they sent a doctor to him who said, 'As the food was cooked in an earthenware vessel, so eat it from an earthenware dish!'

(*T.J.Pe'ah* VIII, § 8, f. 21 *a*, line 58.)

[1191] R. Simeon used to say: For four reasons a man, who leaves the corner of his field for the poor (Lev. XIX, 9), should choose the end of his field. First, so as not to rob the poor. For a man might seize a suitable opportunity, and tell a poor relative to take the produce from the near corner. Secondly, so that the poor may not have to wait all day, but may be able to go and gather elsewhere, and come back to him when the end of his field is being cut. Thirdly, for appearances' sake, so that passers-by should not say: 'See how so-and-so has reaped his field, and has not left a corner for the poor.' And fourthly, because the Law says: 'Thou shalt not reap the *end* corner of thy field' (A.V. 'Thou shalt not wholly reap the corners of thy field').

(*Sifra* 87*c*.)

[1192] The poor-tithe money...must not be used to ransom captives or for marriage-expenses [of indigent brides].

(*T.Pe'ah* IV, 16 (Z. p. 24, line 9).)

Charity accounts must be kept carefully, for funds for different purposes are not interchangeable. As the French would say, there must be no *virement*.

The extreme care taken to avoid suspicion falling upon anybody is illustrated by the following:

[1193] Officials who entered the Temple treasury, in order to remove funds that were needed for the ritual, were searched on entering and on leaving. So long as they were inside, people engaged them in conversation. This was done so that, 'Ye shall be guiltless before the Lord and before Israel' (Num. XXXII, 22.)

(*T.Sheḳ.* II, 1 (Z. p. 175, line 9).)

[In this connection and to illustrate the same verse, it is related also that no woman belonging to the Euthinos family ever went out perfumed. The Euthinos family held the monopoly of manufacturing the incense for the Temple, and when they married a woman from some different place (family?), they made it a condition that she was to refrain from the use of perfume, so that no one could suggest that she appropriated the Temple materials for her own use (*T.Yoma* II, 6 (Z. p. 184, line 20)). (H. L.)]

[1194] If a [poor] man says: 'I ought not to be supported by others,' then one should watch over him, and support him, giving him help as a loan, and then letting him regard the loan as a gift. This was R. Me'ir's opinion. But the sages held that the help should be first given as a gift, and then that he should be told that it could be regarded as a loan. R. Simeon said that he should be asked for a pledge, so as to preserve his self-respect. (*T.Pe'ah* IV, 12 (Z. p. 24, line 1).)

Though the Rabbis, as we have seen, thought that even impostors had their uses, they did not admire them:

[1195] He who needs not, and takes, will not reach old age and die before he will really need help from others. He who is in need, and yet does not take, will not reach old age and die before he will be able to help others. He who is not lame or blind, but pretends to be so, will not reach old age and die before he becomes really blind and lame. (*Pe'ah* VIII, 9.)

[1196] R. Akiba said: He who takes even a penny from charity, when he needs it not, will not die before he requires the help of man. He said: He who binds rags on his eyes or on his loins, and says, 'Give to the blind man,' or 'Give to the man who is smitten with boils,' will end by having good cause to utter this cry. (*Ab.R.N.* (vers. I), III, f. 8*a*.)

Loving deeds (*gemilut ḥasadim*) are greater than mere almsgiving (*ẓedaḳah*):

[1197] R. Elazar said: Almsgiving is greater than all sacrifice, for it says, 'To give alms [lit. to do justice] is more acceptable to God than sacrifices' (Prov. XXI, 3). But loving deeds are greater than almsgiving, as it says, 'Sow in almsgiving [lit. righteousness], reap in love' (Hos. X, 12). Of his sowing, a man may eat or no; of his reaping, he will eat assuredly. And he said: Almsgiving becomes increasingly perfect according to the amount of love that is shown in it. (*Suk.* 49*b*.)

[The metaphor of sowing, and the famous verse of Ps. CXXVI are applied to charity in the following Midrash, the source of which I am unable to trace: 'Those who sow', i.e. those who give alms, are of two kinds. Some give 'in tears', some 'in joy'. Both 'shall reap'. If one gives so as to beshame the recipient and so that 'he goes forth and weeps', still, the giver 'bears the seed'. But if the giver gives alms so that the poor man 'doubtless shall come again with rejoicing', such a giver will get, not seed, but 'sheaves'. (H. L.)]

[1198] Almsgiving and loving deeds weigh as heavily as all the other commandments of the law. But almsgiving is done only to the living: loving deeds affect also the dead; almsgiving is done only to the poor; loving deeds can relate both to poor and rich; almsgiving has to do only with money, loving deeds can be wrought by money or by personal service.

(*T.J.Pe'ah* I, § I, 15*c init.* (cp. *Suk.* 49*b*).)

By a consideration of the wording of Ps. CIII, 17 and of Deut. XI, 21, R. Johanan, in the continuation of the passage just cited from *T.J. Pe'ah*, deduces that loving deeds are more beloved in God's eyes, not only than almsgiving, but even also than the study of the Law.

[1199] The highest form of benevolent action is that undertaken towards the dead, for then there can never be any thought of recompense from the recipient. A poor man may one day be in a position to repay his benefactor, but the dead man cannot repay and, moreover, the dead needs the help of the living. This idea is the subject of the Midrashic comment on the request, made by Jacob, on his deathbed, to Joseph, that he should do unto him 'true kindness'. Is there, then, such a thing as 'false kindness'? Why does Jacob ask for 'true kindness'? Because of the common proverb, 'When thy friend's son dies, carry the bier: when thy friend himself dies, put it down.' Jacob said, 'The kindness you do me after my death, that indeed is true kindness.'

(*Tanḥ.B.*, Wayeḥi, 107*a.*)

It is true kindness, because no reward can be expected. The proverb is cynical: put down the friend's bier, because you can get no reward for carrying it.

[1200] Simeon the Just said: 'Upon three things the world is based: upon the Torah, upon the Temple Service, and upon the doing of loving deeds.' As regards the third, it is said, 'I desire love, and not sacrifice.' The world at the beginning was created only by love, as it is said, 'The world is built by love' (A.V. 'Mercy shall be built up for ever,' Ps. LXXXIX, 2). It happened that R. Johanan b. Zakkai went out from Jerusalem, and R. Joshua followed him, and he saw the burnt ruins of the Temple, and he said, 'Woe is it that the place, where the sins of Israel find atonement, is laid waste.' Then said R. Johanan, 'Grieve not, we have an atonement equal to the Temple, the doing of loving deeds,' as it is said, 'I desire love, and not sacrifice.'

(*Ab.R.N.* (vers. I), IV, 11*a*.)

[1201] R. Judah said: He who denies the [virtue of] doing loving deeds is as if he denied the Root [= God: the very foundation of faith]. (*Eccles.R.* VII, § 1, 4, on VII, 1 (18*a* foot).)

[For an explanation of this passage, see *Mattenot Kehunnah*. (H. L.)]

[1202] R. Johanan said: Happy are you, Israelites, when you occupy yourselves with the Law and with deeds of love: then is your evil inclination given into your control, and you are not given into the control of your evil inclination. (*Ab.Zar.* 5*b*.)

[1203] Abba Taḥnah, the pious, was once returning to his city on the Sabbath eve, towards nightfall, with his bundle upon his arm. He met a man stricken with boils lying at the crossing of the roads. The man said, 'Rabbi, act charitably towards me, and carry me to the city.' Abba Taḥnah thought, 'If I leave my bundle here, how can I nourish myself and my household? But if I leave the man with boils, I incur guilt.' His good inclination conquered his evil inclination, and he carried the man into the city. Then he returned, and fetched his bundle, and entered the city with the setting of the sun. And all marvelled and said, 'Is that Abba Taḥnah, the pious?' And he, too, fidgeted in his heart and thought, 'Perhaps I have profaned the Sabbath?' Then God caused the sun of charity to shine, as it is said, 'Unto you who fear my name shall the sun of charity [*ẓedaḳah*] arise with healing in its wings' (Mal. IV, 2). Then he fidgeted in his heart and thought, 'Perhaps I shall receive no reward?' Then a heavenly voice called out and said, 'Go, eat thy bread with joy, and drink thy wine with a merry heart, for God has accepted thy deeds: thy reward will be allotted to thee.'

(*Eccles.R.* IX, § 7, 1, on IX, 7 (23*b*).)

The above is a very characteristic Rabbinic story. The piety of the Rabbi, displayed both in his humanity and in his strictness about the Sabbath, and then again, the frank desire for reward, which is, nevertheless, *not* the motive for his good deed: all is thoroughly Rabbinic.

[1204] R. Elazar b. Shammua was taking a stroll by the shore of the great sea, when he saw a ship tossed about in the sea. In a moment it sank with all on board. Then he saw a man sitting on a plank of the ship, and he was carried from wave to wave till he got to the land. As he was naked, he hid himself on the shore. It happened to be the season when the Israelites went up for the festival to Jerusalem. He said to them, 'I am of the children of Esau, your brother; give me a small garment, that I may cover myself with it; for the sea has stripped me bare, and nothing has been left me.' They said, 'May all thy people be stripped bare likewise.' He raised his eyes, and saw R. Elazar who was walking among them. He said, 'I see you are an old and honourable man, who has regard to the self-respect of all fellowmen; deal charitably with me; give me a garment, that I may cover myself with it, for the sea has stripped me bare.' R. Elazar had seven garments. He took off one, and gave it to him, and he took him to his house, and gave him food and drink, and two hundred *denarii*, and drove him for fourteen *parasangs*, and showed him much honour till he had reached his home. After a while the wicked Emperor died, and this man was appointed to succeed him [see the story of Bar Ḳappara, [1208]]. He made a decree that all the Jews in that province should be killed, and all the women given away as spoil. They asked R. Elazar to go and make supplication for them. He said, 'You know that the Government does not do anything for nothing.' They said, 'Here are 4000 *denarii*, take them, and go, and supplicate for us.' He took them, and went, and came to the gate of the palace, and he said, 'Go and tell the king that a Jew is at the gate, and desires to greet the king.' The king said, 'Let him enter.' When the king saw him, he rose from his seat, and fell down before him, and said, 'What is my lord's business, and why has he troubled to come here?' He replied, 'That you may have pity upon the Jews of that province, and cancel the decree.' The king said, 'Is there anything false in your Law?' He said, 'No.' The king said, 'Is it not written in your Law, "The Ammonite and the Moabite shall not enter the congregation of the Lord?" Why? Because they did not meet you with bread and water in the way (Deut. XXIII, 4). And does it not say, "Thou shalt not hate an Edomite, because he is thy brother?" And am I not a son of

Esau, your brother, and you showed me no lovingkindness? He who transgresses the Law is guilty of death.' R. Elazar replied, 'Though they are guilty, forgive them, and have pity upon them.' 'Do you know', said the king, 'that the government does not do anything for nothing?' He replied, 'I have with me 4000 *denarii*, take them, and have pity.' The king said, 'Let these 4000 *denarii* be given back to you, in exchange for the two hundred you gave me, and let all the Jews of that province be saved for your sake, and in exchange for the food and drink which you gave me, and go to my treasury, and take seven garments in exchange for the one you gave me, and go back in peace to your people, and let them be forgiven for your sake.' To R. Elazar one may apply the verse, 'Cast thy bread upon the waters' (Eccles. XI, 1). (*Eccles.R.* XI, § 1, 1, on XI, 1 (28*b* top).)

[1205] R. Joshua of Sikhnin [Sogane] in the name of R. Levi said: It says in Isa. LI, 16, 'I have put my words in thy mouth,' that is, the Law, and, 'I have covered thee in the shadow of my hand,' that is, the doing of loving deeds; to teach thee that he who occupies himself with the words of the Law, and with the doing of loving deeds, is worthy to take refuge in the shadow of God, as it is said, 'How precious is thy lovingkindness, O God; the children of men take refuge in the shadow of thy wings' (Ps. XXXVI, 7). (*Pes.K.* 140*b*.)

[1206] In the future world, man will be asked, 'What was your occupation?' If he reply, 'I fed the hungry,' then they reply, 'This is the gate of the Lord; he who feeds the hungry, let him enter' (Ps. CXVIII, 20). So with giving drink to the thirsty, clothing the naked, with those who look after orphans, and with those, generally, who do deeds of lovingkindness. All these are gates of the Lord, and those who do such deeds shall enter within them. (*Midr.Ps.* on CXVIII, 19 (243*b*, § 17).)

[1207] David showed lovingkindness to all. He said, 'Whether a man is a murderer or murdered, persecutor or persecuted, I show him lovingkindness as if he were a righteous man.'
(*Eccles.R.* VII, § 1, 4, on VII, 1 (18*a* foot).)

[1208] Bar Ḳappara walked by the cliff of the sea at Caesarea. He saw a ship sink, and a proconsul came out naked. When he saw him, he went up to him and gave him two *sela'im*. Then he took him to his house, and gave him food and drink and three more *sela'im*, for he said, 'A great man like you must need them.' After many days, some Jews were imprisoned [i.e. on the instigation of some official]. They said, 'Who shall go and plead for us?' One said to the other, 'Bar Ḳappara is much thought of by the Government.' He said to them, 'But do you know that the Government does nothing for nothing?' They said to him, 'Here are 500 *denarii*. Go and appease [the Government] for us.' He took them, and went to the Government. When the proconsul saw him, he got up and greeted him, and said to him, 'Why have you troubled to come hither?' He said, 'To ask you to have pity on those Jews.' He said, 'Do you know that a government does not do anything for nothing?' He said, 'I have 500 *denarii*, take them and be appeased.' He said, 'Let those 500 *denarii* be kept by you in pledge for[1] the five *sela'im*, and let your people be saved because of the food and drink which you gave me, and go home in peace and honour.' To him the saying, 'Cast thy bread upon the waters' (Eccles. XI, 1) may be applied. (*Eccles.R.* XI, § 1, 1, on XI, 1 (28*a*).)

[1209] 'Cast thy bread upon the waters.' R. Bebai said: If you seek to do charitable deeds, do them to those who labour in the Torah, for by the 'waters' of this verse the words of the Law are meant. R. Akiba said: I was on the seashore, and I saw a ship founder in the sea, and I was grieved for a learned man who was on it, and who would be drowned. When I came to Cappadocia, I saw the man engaged in answering questions of learners. I said to him, 'My son, how did you escape from the sea?' He said to me, 'Through thy prayer. One wave carried me to the other, and that one to the next, till they brought me to the shore.' I said to him, 'What good deeds had you to show?' He said, 'As I got on the ship, I met a poor man who said to me, "Do me a kindness." And I gave him a loaf of bread. He said to me, "As you have given me my life by your gift, so may your life be given to you."' Then I applied to him this verse, 'Cast thy bread upon the waters.'

(*Eccles.R.* XI, § 1, 1 *init.*, on XI, 1 (28*a*).)

There are certain special deeds, most of which have been mentioned in one or other of the above passages, which are regarded by the

[1] I.e. in exchange for (cp. [1204]).

Rabbis as peculiarly and characteristically 'loving deeds'. These include visiting the sick, comforting the mourners, and even 'accompanying' the bride, i.e. taking part in the marriage festivities:

[1210] There is no limit as regards the visitation of the sick. What does this mean? R. Joseph argued that it meant that there is no limit to its reward. Abbai said to him, 'Is there a limit to the reward of *any* of the commands? Is it not taught, "Be as zealous about a light as about a heavy command, for you know not the reward of the commands"?' 'No limit means', said Abbai, 'that the great must visit the small.' Raba said, 'Even a hundred times a day.'

R. Akiba said: He who does not visit the sick is as if he shed blood. Rab said that the Shechinah hovers over the bed of the sick. So let not him who visits the sick sit on the bed or on a chair or a bench, but let him wrap his head, and sit upon the ground, because the Shechinah hovers over the bed of the sick, for it says, 'God [and no one else] supports the sick on his bed.'

(*Ned.* 39*b*, 40*a*.)

[1211] It happened that R. Ṭarfon was teaching his disciples, and a bride passed before him; he ordered that she should be brought into his house, and he bade his wife and his mother to bathe her, and anoint her, and adorn her, and dance with her till she went to her husband's house.

(*Ab.R.N.* (vers. I), XLI, 67*a*.)

No doubt the bride in this story was a poor orphan.

[1212] What words must be used when dancing before the bride? The school of Hillel said: 'Say, "O bride, beautiful and gracious".' The school of Shammai said: 'If she is lame or blind, is one to say, "O bride, beautiful and gracious"? Does it not say in the Torah, "Keep thee far from lying"' (Exod. XXIII, 7). The Hillelites said, 'Then, if someone makes a bad purchase in the market, is one to commend it, or to run it down? Surely one should commend it.' Hence the wise say, 'Always make your disposition sympathetic to that of your neighbour.'

(*Ket.* 17*a*.)

[1213] R. Samuel b. Isaac used to dance before the bride with three branches of myrtle. When he was dying, great storms and hurricanes arose, and uprooted all the goodly trees in the land of Israel. Why? Because he had plucked branches from them, when he danced before the bride. The Rabbis said, 'Why did he act thus? Why did he despise the Law?' [i.e. the law against bridal wreaths, after the tragedy of the revolt in the days of Hadrian (see **Note 63**)]. R. Ze'era said, 'Let him be; he knew what he was doing.' When he had died, and they had come to pay him the last loving attention [i.e. to attend his funeral], a tongue of fire came down, and assumed the shape of a myrtle branch, and separated the bier from the people. Then they said, 'Look, for this old man who laboured in the Law, the merit of his twigs stood by him at his funeral.'

(*Gen.R.*, Ḥay. Sar., LIX, 4 (Th. p. 632).)

[1214] When scholars are sitting in study, and a funeral procession passes or a wedding, they shall not interrupt their study if there be enough present with the bier or the bride for the appointed duty. But if there be not enough, then the scholars shall break off. It once happened that a bridal procession passed R. Judah and his disciples. He said, 'Colleagues, arise and occupy yourselves with attendance on the bride, as God did at Adam's wedding when He built the rib,' which means that God decked and adorned Adam's bride when He gave her to him, and there are places where they call the bride 'the built one' (Gen. II, 22) (cp. [721]). There should in either case be ten males present (cp. [258] footnote and [280]). (*Ab.R.N.* (vers. II), VIII, 11*b.*)

In the following story, comforting the mourners is presented in a curious guise, and is mixed up with other matters, but the whole tale is characteristically Rabbinic:

[1215] R. Ḥiyya b. Abba taught the son of Resh Laḳish. A young child of R. Ḥiyya died. On the first day Resh Laḳish did not visit him. On the next day, he took the interpreter [his deputy] with him, and he said to the deputy, 'Say something in regard to the child.' Then he began and said, 'The Lord saw it, and was wrathful, because of the provocation of His sons and daughters. It is a generation in which the fathers make God wrathful; so that He is provoked with their sons and daughters, and they die young.' He came to comfort him, and he hurt him!' What he really meant was, 'Thou art worthy to be taken for this generation.' [It was really the child who was taken. But he was taken, not, in this instance, because of his innocence, but because of the 'worthiness' of the father.] Then Resh Laḳish said to the deputy, 'Say something to the glorification of God.' So he said, 'God is great and mighty in His wondrous deeds: by His word He quickens the dead: His mighty deeds cannot be searched out, His marvels are beyond number: blessed art thou, O Lord, who quickenest the dead.' Then Resh Laḳish said to the deputy, 'Say something about the mourners.' Then he said, 'O brethren, who are weary and crushed by your mourning, apply your hearts to understand this: it continues for ever, it is a path since the creation, many have drunk this cup, and many will drink it. As the drinking of the first, so is the drinking of the last. May the Lord of consolation console you. Blessed is He who consoles the mourners....' Then Resh Laḳish said to the deputy, 'Say something for those who are comforting the mourners.' Then he said, 'O our brothers, doers of loving deeds, and the sons of the doers of loving deeds, and who therefore hold fast to the covenant of Abraham our Father, may the Lord of recompense recompense to you your deeds. Blessed art thou, who recompensest deeds of love.' Then Resh Laḳish said to the deputy, 'Say something about all Israel.' Then he said, 'Lord of the Universe, redeem, deliver, and save thy people Israel from pestilence, the sword, plunder, drought, mildew, and from all punishments which befall the world. Before we call, do thou answer. Blessed art thou, who restrainest the plague' (cp. the burial Ḳaddish, *P.B.* Gaster, I, 202). (*Ket.* 8*b*.)

[The word rendered 'interpreter' is *Meturgeman*, which comes ultimately from the Assyrian, and which should, in reality, be *Targeman*. On the name and function of the Meturgeman, see [114] and [434] and J. Rabbinowitz's note on p. 121 of his ed. of *Megillah*. Originally he was the translator of the lesson of the day. When Hebrew ceased to be well understood of the people, the Meturgeman would render the lessons into Aramaic. In course of time the duty devolved on the communal teacher, and a regular salaried office was established. In Babylon, however, in contradistinction to Palestine, there arose a similar practice with regard to the Mishnah. Here the interpreter was termed the *Amora* or Speaker. He would repeat aloud the lectures given in a lower voice by the head of the Academy. It is noteworthy that in some instances these 'Speakers' were not held in high esteem, due to their failure to repeat the gist of the lectures correctly. Hence Abbahu decreed that no one under the age of fifty should be appointed to the post (*Ḥag.* 14*a*). Yet others were distinguished men, such as R. Ḥuẓpit, the Amora of Rabban Gamaliel II; Abdan, the Amora of R. Judah I, who, though arrogant in his demeanour towards R. Ishmael b. Jose, was yet praised by R. Naḥman b. Isaac. Abba Areka himself (Rab) once acted as Amora. Resh Laḳish's Amora was Judah b. Naḥmani (see p. 13 of Strack's *Introduction*, ed. 1931), and from the passage cited it is clear that he was well qualified to be the vehicle of his master's sentiments.

It seems strange—and almost unfeeling—of Resh Laḳish not to have addressed R. Ḥiyya in person. But the presence of the 'Interpreter' suggests that this was a ceremonial, and not a private, visit of condolence, hence the proper formal procedure.

Nevertheless, the strangeness of the passage is not altogether mitigated by what has been written above. Rabbi L. Rabinowitz suggests the following explanation: 'The words of Judah b. Naḥmani were a formal sermon which was delivered by the *Meturgeman*. Judah b. Naḥmani was a good homilist (cf. *Sanh.* 7 *b*), and it is only because Resh Laḳish asked him to deliver the address that he did so: it does not mean that Resh Laḳish himself refrained from offering his condolences....The whole point of the address lies in the word "generation". Not because of the unworthiness of the father, but because of the unworthiness of the old generation was the child taken. "Children die young because of the wickedness of the older generation." Rif (i.e. J. Pinto), commenting on the '*En Ya'aḳob, in loc.* says that "since they are taken away because of the sin of the generation, it might seem as though God, being angry with the generation, takes the sons of a righteous man to punish the sin of the generation". The implication is that Ḥiyya's son was taken because his father was worthy.' (H. L.)] (**Notes 36 and 87**); see also [610] and [639].)

Another signal deed of love is to help widows and orphans:

[1216] R. Jose said: Why does God love widows and orphans? Because their eyes are turned upon Him, as it is said, 'A father of the fatherless and a judge of the widows' (Ps. LXVIII, 5). Therefore, any one who robs them is as if he robbed God, their Father in heaven. (*Exod.R.*, Mishpaṭim, XXX, 8.)

[1217] The Rabbis say that if a male and female orphan have to be maintained, the female takes precedence, for a man can beg, but a woman cannot. And so as regards marriage, the female should be married first, for the shame of a woman is greater than the shame of a man. (*Ket.* 67 *a fin.*–67 *b init.*)

The Rabbis had very simple ideas why, in human society, there are differences between rich and poor.

[1218] It is written, 'In the days of prosperity be joyful, in the day of adversity, consider' (Eccles. VII, 14). R. Tanḥum b. Ḥiyya said: In the happy days of your neighbour, be with him in his happiness; if an evil day befall your neighbour, consider how you can show him lovingkindness to deliver him from the evil. The mother of R. Tanḥum b. Ḥiyya was wont, when she wanted one pound of meat, to buy two pounds, one for him and one for the poor, because God has set the one against the other. Why indeed has God created both rich and poor? That the one might be sustained by the other. **(Note 91.)**

(*Pes.K.* 191*b* (cp. [1159]).)

Chapter XVII

ON INDUSTRY AND INDEPENDENCE: ON POVERTY AND RICHES

In spite of all their insistence on charity, the Rabbis were intensely keen on independence, on industry, and on the rightness of work.

[1219] Three lives are no lives: he who looks for the table of others, he who is ruled by his wife, he whose body is overcome by sufferings. And some say, He who has only one shirt!

(*Beẓ*. 32*b*.)

[1220] It is written, 'The Lord will bless thee in all the work of thy hands' (Deut. II, 7). R. Jacob said: One might think that He will bless us even if we are idle; therefore it says, 'in all the *work* of thy hands'. If a man works, he is blessed; if not, he is not blessed. (*Midr.Ps.* on XXIII, I (99*b*, §3).)

[1221] R. Judah carried a jug, and R. Simeon a basket, into the House of Study. They said, 'Great is handicraft, for it honours those who do it.' (*Ned.* 49*b* (cp. [1230]).)

[1222] Hire yourself out to a work which is strange to you rather than become dependent on others.

(*T.J.San.* XI, § 7, f. 30*b*, line 68.)

[1223] When a man falls into sickness or old age or troubles, and cannot engage in his work, lo, he dies of hunger. But with the Law it is not so; for it guards him from all evil while he is young, and in old age it grants him a future and a hope. Of his youth, what does it say? 'They that wait upon the Lord shall renew their strength' (Isa. XL, 31). Of his old age what does it say? 'They shall still bring forth fruit in old age' (Ps. XCII, 14).

(*Ḳid.* IV, 14 (Prof. Danby's translation) (cp. [362]).)

[1224] Bar Ḳappara said, 'Let a man always teach his son a clean and easy handicraft. What is such?' R. Judah said, 'Embroidery.' Rabbi said, 'There is no handicraft which can disappear from the world. Happy is he whom his parents see engaged in a respected handicraft; woe to him whom his parents see engaged in an inferior handicraft; the world cannot exist without druggists or tanners; happy is he whose handicraft is that of a druggist, and woe to him whose handicraft is that of a tanner. The world cannot exist without men and women; happy is he whose children are sons; and woe to him whose children are women.' R. Me'ir said, 'Let a man ever teach his son a clean and easy handicraft; and let him pray to God to whom belong riches and possessions. For riches and poverty do not come from handicrafts, but from Him to whom riches belong,' as it is said, 'For mine is the silver and gold, says the Lord of Hosts' (Hag. II, 8). (*Ḳid.* 82*a fin.*–82*b.*)

The two 'woes' must not be taken too literally and strictly. Where we should say 'They are fortunate whose children are boys, or whose sons are druggists rather than tanners,' the Oriental uses terms which seem to us strange and exaggerated. For tanners' and druggists' shops cp. [1368]. For 'Rabbi' cp. [419].

[1225] There was a legend that the young man of Judges XVIII, 3 defended himself for serving as an idolatrous priest by saying, 'There is a tradition in our family, "Rather hire yourself out for idolatry than require the help of others."' He, however, mistook the meaning of the term 'strange service,' in the saying which here is not to be taken in the usual applied sense, to mean idolatry, but literally, for the saying means, 'Rather than require the help of your fellows accept work which is strange to you' [i.e. beneath your dignity]. So Rab said to R. Kahana, 'Skin the corpse of an animal in the public street, and accept a wage for doing so, and do not say, "I am a great man, this work does not befit me."' (*Bab.B.* 110*a.*)

[1226] Akiba said: Rather make your Sabbath a weekday than need the help of your fellow-man. (*Pes.* 112*a.*)

[It is laid down in the Mishnah (*Pes.* X, 1 : see further in the Gemara, *Pes.* 112*a*) that on Passover Eve not even the poorest Israelite should sup without reclining at the *triclinium*. For slaves ate their meals sitting upright, while the *triclinium* was the privilege of the free. On this night, everyone was to be free, and by this symbolic action men would demonstrate their gratitude for the divine redemption. Similarly, however poor be the Israelite, he must drink his four cups of wine on Passover Eve, again as a symbol, even though he be dependent on poor relief given in kind (the *tamḥui* or dish of food).

In the Gemara, the discussion begins with the question, 'Why only on Passover Eve?' After various digressions, Akiba's saying is cited, 'Rather make your Sabbath a weekday than need the help of your fellow-men.' This does not mean, 'Work on Sabbath rather than take charity', but refrain from the usual Sabbath luxuries, rather than beg. The Gemara remarks that the adage in the Mishnah about Passover and the poor man is needed because of Akiba's remark. Yet Akiba agrees that on Passover the poor man should buy or receive from the *tamḥui* four cups, because of 'publishing the miracle', i.e. of showing his appreciation of the divine redemption. Now the Sabbath was also a declaration of this kind, since, in the Deuteronomic Decalogue, the reason for Sabbath observance is the Exodus. Special food on the Sabbath, therefore, *also* 'publishes the miracle', as the Gemara puts it.

The same phrase is used in the codes in connection with the deliverance from Haman (*Meg.* 3*b*), and also with regard to the prominent displaying of the Chanuca light. The inquirer who asks why a Jew is lighting the light, or having extra food, or drinking four cups of wine, will be told the reason, and so the 'miracle' in each case will be 'published'. In the 'College of Elijah' it was taught that although Akiba made this remark about the Sabbath, yet one should provide some trifle to differentiate the Sabbath from the weekday meal (i.e. to publish the miracle). 'What sort of a trifle?' promptly asks the Gemara. 'A pie of fish-hash and flour,' said R. Papa, and immediately there follows, most incongruously, the remark of R. Judah b. Tema, given also in *Aboth* v, 20, 'Be fierce as a leopard, swift as an eagle, light as a roe and strong as a lion, to do the will of thy Father in heaven,' i.e. to spend a little money for your Sabbath dinner. (H. L.)]

[1227] Ulla said: Greater is he who enjoys the fruit of his labour than the fearer of Heaven; with regard to the fearer of Heaven it is written, 'Happy is the man that fears the Lord' (Ps. CXII, 1), but with regard to him who enjoys the fruit of his labour it is written, 'When thou eatest the labour of thy hands, happy shalt thou be, and it shall be well with thee' (Ps. CXXVIII, 2)—happy shalt thou be in this world, and it shall be well with thee in the world to come. It is not written, 'and it shall be well with thee', about the fearer of Heaven. (*Ber.* 8*a*.)

[1228] When Laban was overtaking Jacob, God warned him, saying, 'Take heed that thou speak not to Jacob either good or bad' (Gen. XXXI, 24). From this passage we learn that the merit of labour avails where the merit of ancestry cannot. Jacob said, 'Except the God of my father, the God of Abraham and the fear of Isaac, had been with me, surely thou hadst sent me away empty' (*ib.* 42). Thus the merit of ancestry sufficed only to protect Jacob's *property* [and not his life]. But Jacob then went on to say, 'It was my toil and the labour of my hands that God saw when He rebuked thee yesterday and saved my life,' for it was through the merit of labour that God warned Laban not to harm Jacob. Learn, then, that a man should not say, 'I will eat and drink and enjoy good, and I will not burden myself, for Heaven will look after me.' Therefore it says, 'His handiwork hast thou blessed' (Job I, 10). It is incumbent on a man to toil and work with his two hands, and then God sends His blessing. (*Tanḥ.*, Wayeẓe, § 13, f. 52*b*.)

[1229] R. Dosetai b. Yannai said in the name of R. Me'ir: It says, 'I am with thee [i.e. Isaac], and I will bless thee' (Gen. XXVI, 24). Isaac expounded the saying and said, 'No blessing rests on a man except by the work of his hands.' So he arose and sowed, as it says, 'Then Isaac sowed that land' (Gen. XXVI, 12). (*T.Ber.* VII, 8 (Z. p. 15, line 17).)

[1230] 'For stealing an ox, the thief restores fivefold, but for a lamb, only fourfold' (Exod. XXII, 1). R. Me'ir said: See how beloved is labour to Him who spake and the world existed. Fivefold compensation is exacted for the ox, because the thief interrupted its labour. But since the lamb does not labour, the compensation is but fourfold. R. Johanan b. Zakkai said: See how God cares for human dignity. The ox walks on its own feet, but the lamb is picked up and carried.
(*T.Bab.Ḳ.* VII, 10 (Z. p. 359, line 2) (cp. [1221]).)

[1231] R. Judah the Prince said in the name of the Band of Pious Men: Get you a handicraft as well as the Torah, for this is the meaning of, 'Live joyfully with the wife whom thou lovest.' Why did he call them the band of pious men? Because among them were R. Jose and R. Simeon who divided the time thus: A third for the Torah, a third for prayer, and a third for work. Some say that they laboured in the Torah all the winter and at their work all the summer. (For this 'Band' see *J.E.* s.v. '*Edah Ḳedoshah* (cp. [786]).) (*Eccles.R.* IX, §9 *init.*, on IX, 9 (24*a*).)

The wife must here be understood to mean the Torah.

[1232] R. Joshua was asked, 'May one teach one's son the Greek language?' He replied, 'Teach it him when it is neither day nor night,' for it says, 'Thou shalt meditate therein [i.e. in the Law] day and night' (Josh. I, 8). Then one ought never to teach one's son a handicraft. That is not so, for R. Ishmael said, 'Choose life' (Deut. XXX, 19), and 'life' means a handicraft. It was also said that the prohibition of Greek was on account of the informers [whose familiarity with Greek tempted them to treason, and to deliver their fellow Jews into the hands of the Romans]. R. Abbahu said: One may teach one's daughter Greek, because it is an adornment to her. (**Note 63.**)

(*T.J.Pe'ah* I, § I, f. 15*c*, line 7 (cp. [395]).)

[1233] R. Simeon b. Elazar said: Even Adam did not taste food until he had done work, as it is said, 'The Lord God took the man, and put him into the Garden of Eden to till it and keep it' (Gen. II, 15), after which He said, 'Of every tree of the garden thou mayest eat' (*ib.* 16). R. Ṭarfon said: Even the Holy One, blessed be He, did not cause His Shechinah to alight upon Israel until they had done work; as it is said, 'Let them make for me a sanctuary, and then I will dwell among them' (Exod. XXV, 8). (*Ab.R.N.* (vers. I), XI, 23*a*.)

[1234] A man is obliged to teach his son a trade, and whoever does not teach his son a trade teaches him to become a robber. The person who has a trade in his hand is like a vineyard which is fenced in, so that cattle and beasts cannot get into it or passers-by eat of it or look into it; and whoever has no trade in his hand is like a vineyard with its fence broken down, so that cattle and beasts can enter it, and passers-by can eat of it and look into it.

(*T.Ḳid.* I, 11 (Z. p. 336, line 7).)

Here I have translated the Hebrew word *'umanut* (see **Note 20k**) indifferently by trade or handicraft.

[1235] R. Elazar b. Azariah said: Great is work, for every craftsman walks out with the implements of his calling, and is proud of them. Thus the weaver walks out with a shuttle in his ear. The dyer walks out with wool in his ear. The scribe walks out with his pen behind his ear. All are proud of their craft. God speaks of His work (Gen. II, 2); how much more should man. (*Ab.R.N.* (vers. II), XXI, 23*a*.)

[1236] Shemaiah said: 'Love labour or work' (*Aboth* I, 10). A man must always love work, and busy himself with it. For even of God, to whom belong the world and its fullness, it is written that 'He rested from all His work which He had done' (Gen. II, 2); how much more then must human beings work. R. Eliezer said: Great is work, for even Adam did not taste anything till he had worked, for it is said, 'God put him in the garden to work at, and to keep it' (Gen. II, 15). Great indeed is work, for just as Israel were commanded to keep the Sabbath, so they were commanded to work, as it says, 'Six days shalt thou labour and do all thy work' (Exod. XX, 9). R. Judah said: If a man does no work, people speak about him and say, 'How does so-and-so manage to eat and drink?' It is like a woman who has no husband, but who decks herself and goes into the street, and people speak about her. R. Me'ir said: He who does not work in the week will end by working on the Sabbath. How is this? If a man is idle for two or three days, he will have nothing to eat, and he will steal. They will catch him, hand him over to the Government, and cast him into prison, where he will have to work on the Sabbath. (*Ab.R.N.* (vers. II), XXI, 22*b*.)

[1237] R. Jose said: A private individual must not fast excessively [*saggef*], lest he become a burden on the public, and the public should be forced to support him.

(*T.Ta'an.* II, 12 (Z. p. 218, line 15).)

[1238] A hired labourer must not starve himself or undergo privations, because he diminishes his value as a workman to his employer.

(*T.J.Dem.* VII, § 4, f. 26*b*, line 26 (cp. [1486]).)

The Rabbis had no love of poverty. Indeed they thought that grinding poverty (see **Note 92**) was one of the sorest of human afflictions. They regarded riches as a blessing from God. Yet they remembered the temptations of riches, and gave warnings about riches illegitimately acquired, and they often said that Israel was more faithful to God when poor than when rich:

[1239] Gold and silver take a man out of this world and the world to come, but the Torah brings a man to the life of the world to come. (*Sifre Num.*, Ḳoraḥ, § 119, f. 39*b* (H. p. 144).)

[1240] Elijah said, 'God looked about among all good qualities to give to Israel, and he found nothing better than poverty.' So people say, 'Poverty suits Israel as a red bridle suits a white horse.' (*Ḥag.* 9*b*.)

[1241] God examined all the good qualities in the world, but found no quality so good for Israel as poverty, for through poverty they fear the Lord. For if they have no bread to eat, no raiment to wear, no oil for anointing, then they seek the Lord of mercy, and they find Him. (*Tan.d.b.El.* p. 181.)

[1242] Be heedful of the children of the poor, for from them Torah proceeds (cf. *R.T.* p. 270).[1] (*Ned.* 81*a*.)

[1243] There is nothing harder than poverty. It is hardest of all the afflictions of the world.... Our sages say: 'All other sufferings in one pan, and poverty in the other, and the scales would balance.' There is no lot which is harder than poverty, for he who is crushed by poverty is as if he were crushed by all the afflictions of the world, and as if all the curses enumerated in Deuteronomy had befallen him, and our Sages say, 'All afflictions in one pan, and poverty in the other, and the scale of poverty would fall.' (*Exod.R.*, Mishpaṭim, XXXI, 12, 14.)

[1244] 'The poor and the man of means meet together; the Lord lightens the eyes of both' (Prov. XXIX, 13). The poor is he who is poor in [i.e. ignorant of] Torah, the man of means is he who has learnt a few divisions [of the Mishnah]. The first comes to the second, and says, 'Teach me a chapter.' And he does so. Of him it is said, 'The Lord lightens the eyes of both.' They acquire both this world and the world to come.

'Rich and poor meet together; the Lord is the maker of them all' (Prov. XXII, 2). [Rich and poor are interpreted as before.] The poor man comes to the rich man and says, 'Teach me a chapter,' and he does not teach him, but says to him, 'Why should I want to sit and teach you either the last or the first section of the Mishnah? Read and learn with those like yourself.' But God has made both. He who has made the one wise can also make him stupid, and He who has made the other stupid can also make him wise. Or, the poor is he who is [literally] poor in possessions, and the man of means is he who is in work.

[1] [For 'children of the poor' *Sanh.* 96*a* has 'children of the *Am ha-Aretz*.' This saying is introduced by the words 'They sent from there (Palestine)...' which, according to *Sanh.* 17*b*, denotes a dictum of R. Elazar b. Pedat. (H. L.)]

If the first comes to the second and says, 'Give me alms,' and he gives it him, then of them it is said, 'The Lord lightens both their eyes'; that is, the poor man has won the life of to-day, and the other has won the life of the world to come. Or the poor is he who is poor in goods, and the rich is he who is rich in goods. If the first says to the second, 'Give me alms,' and he refuses, then of them it is said, 'The Lord is the maker of both.' He who has made the one poor can also make him rich, and He who has made the other rich can also make him poor. But if the rich man says to the poor man, 'Why do you not work, and then eat? Look at your legs, look at your thighs, look at your belly,' then God says to the rich man, 'Not enough that you give him nothing, but you grudge him even that which has been given him by me.' (**Note 91.**) (*Lev.R.*, Behar, XXXIV, 4.)

[1245] Three gifts were created in the world. If a man has obtained any one of them, he has acquired the desire of all the world: if he has obtained wisdom, he has obtained everything; if he has obtained strength, he has obtained everything; if he has obtained riches, he has obtained everything. But when? When these things are the gifts of God, and come to him through the power of the Torah, but the strength and the riches of flesh and blood are worth nothing at all, and if they come not from God, they will be taken from him at the end. [Proof texts are Eccles. IX, 11, and Jer. IX, 22, 23.] (Cp. [1511].)

(*Num.R.*, Maṭṭot, XXII, 7 (cp. *Tanḥ.B.*, Maṭṭot, VII, 80 *a fin.*).)

[1246] It is written, 'The wise man's heart is at his right hand, but the fool's heart is at his left' (Eccles. X, 2). The wise are the righteous, who apply their heart to the Law, for the Law is at the right hand, as it is said, 'From His right hand came a fiery Law for them' (Deut. XXXIII, 2): the fools are the wicked who apply their heart to get rich, as it says, 'At the left hand are riches' (Prov. III, 16). Or, the wise man is Moses, while the fools are the children of Reuben and Gad (Num. XXXII, 1–32), who made the chief thing the secondary thing, and the secondary thing the chief thing, for they loved their money more than their souls. For they said to Moses, 'We will build sheep-folds here for our cattle, and cities for our little ones' (Num. XXXII, 16). Moses said to them, 'Not so, but make the main thing the main thing: first build cities for your children, and then sheep-folds for your cattle.' And God said to them, 'You love your cattle more than the souls; therein will be no blessing' (cp. [702]).

(*Num.R.*, Maṭṭot, XXII, 9.)

[1247] Happy the man who is firm in his trial. For there is no man whom God does not try. He tests and tries the rich to see whether his hand will be open to the poor: and He tries the poor to see if he can accept sufferings without murmuring. If the rich abides the test, and is charitable, he enjoys his wealth in this world, and the capital [i.e. the merit] of it remains in the world to come, and God delivers him from the judgment of hell; and if the poor abides his test, and does not kick, he receives double in the world to come (Ps. XLI, 1; XVIII, 27; Job XLII, 10). (*Exod.R.*, Mishpaṭim, XXXI, 3.)

Riches must not be acquired illegitimately. It is interesting to hear the Rabbinic opinion of usury, i.e. interest. It is quite on ancient Greek, and even medieval, lines:

[1248] He who takes usury has no fear of God.... God says, 'He who lives on usury in this world shall not live in the world to come.'

(*Exod.R.*, Mishpaṭim, XXXI, 6.)

[On the taking of interest from non-Jews, see pp. C–CII of my essay 'Usury' in vol. II of my *Starrs and Charters in the British Museum* (cp. also [1254]). (H. L.)]

[1249] 'Every one who takes usury from an Israelite has no fear of God....' The Scripture regards him who takes interest, as if he had committed all the evils and iniquities that are in the world, but he who lends without interest is regarded by God as if he had fulfilled all the commandments.

(*Exod.R.*, Mishpaṭim, XXXI, 13.)

'Usury' has to be taken in its old sense, as equivalent to what we call interest. It does not mean here *excessive* interest, but *any* interest.

By a series of fantastic interpretations of scriptural verses, the Midrash establishes the proposition that the works of God in nature lend to one another without interest: only man takes interest from his neighbour and oppresses him:

[1250] He who takes interest says to God, 'Why dost thou not exact payment from thy world and its creatures? Payment from the earth which thou waterest, from the plants which thou makest sprout, from the stars which thou causest to shine, from the soul which thou hast breathed into the body, from the body which thou guardest?' God replies, 'I lend much, but I take no interest, and the earth lends and takes none; I take back only capital which I have lent, and the earth takes back only its own,' as it is said, 'Then shall the dust return to the earth, and the spirit shall return to God who gave it' (Eccles. XII, 7). (*Exod.R.*, Mishpaṭim, XXXI, 15.)

[1251] Whoever takes upon himself the yoke of usury [i.e. undertakes to observe the prohibition against usury], takes upon himself the yoke of heaven, and whoever breaks off the one yoke, breaks off the other. For the verse prohibiting usury (Lev. XXV, 37) is followed by: 'I am the Lord your God who brought you out of the land of Egypt.' And this means: 'I brought you out of Egypt, on condition that you would accept the prohibition against usury.' He who denies [the obligation of] the command against usury is as if he denied the going out of Egypt.

(*Sifra* 109*c*.)

[1252] Come, see how blind are the usurers! A man may call his neighbour idolatrous, unchaste and a shedder of blood: he may persecute him even so far as to deprive him of his livelihood [i.e. his life in this world]. But that fellow, the usurer, fetches the notary, the pen, the ink, the document and the witnesses and says, 'Come and write down that this man has no more share with Him who forbade usury.' He writes out the deed, and takes it to the Courts, and thus repudiates Him who spake and the world existed. So you see that usurers deny the Root [God]. R. Simeon b. Elazar says: They incur more guilt than they gain profit, for they make out the Torah to be a forgery, and Moses to be a fool, saying, 'Had Moses but known how much we earn, he would not have inscribed the prohibition of interest.' R. Akiba said: A hard thing is usury, for it can turn even a greeting to usury. How? If a man has never greeted another all his life, but now, when the other becomes his creditor, he greets him first, then that greeting is usury. R. Simeon said: Whoever owns money, but refrains from lending at interest, to him applies Ps. XV, while usurers sink deeper and deeper and perish (Prov. XXIV, 11).

(*T.Bab.M.* VI, 7 (Z. p. 385).)

[1253] R. Akiba said: A hard thing is usury, for even a good deed can be usury: thus if a man gives money to another, and bids him buy him vegetables in the street, this is usury. R. Simeon also said: Usury is so wicked that if a man who has borrowed money from another greets him, when he had not been accustomed to greet him before, that is usury.

(*T.J.Bab.M.* v, § 13, f. 10*d*, line 11.)

[1254] When Solomon had built the Temple, he prayed to God and said, 'Lord of the world, if a man pray for riches, and thou knowest that they would be bad for him, give them not to him; but if thou seest a man whom riches would become, then grant them,' as it is said, 'Render unto every man according to his ways, for thou alone knowest the hearts of the children of men' (II Chron. VI, 30). For, in this world, the wicked are rich and are at ease, and the righteous are poor, but in the world to come, when God shall open the treasuries of Paradise to the righteous, the wicked, who have eaten of usury shall bite their flesh with their teeth. (*Exod.R.*, Mishpaṭim, XXXI, 5.)

[Later Jewish law made some distinctions between usury (*neshek*) and interest (*marbit*, *ribbit*). The law in Deut. XXIII, 20, 21, made no such distinctions. It uses only the word *neshek*, which is prohibited between Jew and Jew, but allowed to be used by a Jew to a foreigner. In Lev. XXV, 36, 37, both *neshek*, *tarbit* and *marbit* are forbidden to be used by Jew to Jew. For the whole subject, as for the distinction between Jew and foreigner in Deuteronomy see my essay referred to in [1248]. (H. L.)]

In Ps. XV, 1, the pious man is said not to put out his money to usury (*neshek*), and the Talmud says:

[1255] He [who walks in perfection (referring to Ps. XV, 1–5)] is the man who does not lend on interest [*ribbit*] even to a Gentile.

(*Mak.* 24*a*.)

Chapter XVIII

HOSPITALITY, COURTESY AND GOOD MANNERS

Most oriental people and their teachers lay great stress on hospitality. The Rabbis were no exception.

[1256] Great is hospitality; greater even than early attendance at the House of Study or than the reception of the Shechinah.

(*Sab.* 127*a.*)

[1257] God said to Moses, 'I will send thee to Pharaoh.' Moses answered, 'Lord of the world, I cannot; for Jethro has received me, and opened his house door to me, so that I am as a son with him. If a man opens his house to his fellow, his guest owes his life to him. Jethro has received me, and has honourably entertained me; can I depart without his leave?' Hence it says, 'Moses went and returned to Jethro his father-in-law' (Exod. IV, 18). (*Tanḥ.*, Shemot, § 16, f. 87*a.*)

[1258] 'When a man is gentle, and his family is gentle, if a poor man stands at the door, and says, 'Is your father within?' they reply, 'Yes, enter.' Then, hardly has he entered, before the table is prepared, and he comes in and eats, and blesses God. When they are hot-tempered, they reply, 'No,' and they rebuke him, and drive him away with an outcry.

(*Ab.R.N.* (vers. I), VII, 17*b.*)

[1259] Three things conduce to [lit. restore] tranquillity of mind: music [lit. the voice], fair sights, sweet smells. Three things render a man cheerful [lit. widen his mind]: a fair home, a fair wife, fair chattels. (*Ber.* 57 *b.*)

[1260] Ben Zoma used to say: What does a good guest say? Remember the host for good! How many kinds of wine has he brought before us! How many kinds of portions of meat has he brought before us! How many kinds of fine bread has he brought before us! All that he did, he did only for my sake. But what does an evil guest say? Well, what have I eaten of his? One bit of bread have I eaten of his; one portion of meat have I eaten of his; one cup have I drunk of his; all that he did, he did only for the sake of his wife and his children. And so it says: 'Remember that thou magnify His work, whereof men have sung' (Job XXXVI, 24). ['God is the host, who has provided all.' Dr Lukyn Williams' note.] (*T.Ber.* VII, 2 (Z. p. 14, line 30).)

'All that he did': this means, 'All these fine viands and drinks he provided only for the sake of his wife and his children.'

[1261] Guests should not take from what is set before them and give thereof to the host's son or daughter, without asking his leave first. Once, in a year of drought, it happened that three guests were invited by a man, who had but three eggs to offer them. When the host's son entered, one guest took his portion [presumably of an omelet] and gave it to the child and the other guests did likewise. The host, entering, found his son with one piece in his mouth and two in his hands. He beat the child to the ground, and the child died. When the mother saw this, she threw herself from the roof, and then the father, too, threw himself down. Thus, said R. Eliezer b. Jacob, three perished for this thing. (*Ḥull.* 94 *a.*)

[Cf. the Proverb, 'He who gives food to a small child, must tell its mother' (*Sabb.* 10 *b*). This would seem to be an exception to the adage that if you give your friend a present, you need not, nay, you should not, tell him, for 'Moses knew not that his face shone'. But this is really no exception. The present and its source will, ultimately, become known to the recipient. In the case of a child, the mother, in ignorance of the dainties already eaten by the child, may give it the usual food and upset its digestion. But everyone is pleased at kindness shown to one's children and such gifts 'promote love and brotherhood, if known'—not if the doctor has to be summoned in consequence. See Rashi on *Bezah* 16 *a*, where this saying also occurs. Its author, R. Gamaliel, had a sound knowledge of human nature. (H. L.)]

[1262] Rabban Simeon ben Gamaliel said: This was a custom in Jerusalem; a napkin was spread on the top of the doorway; all the time that the napkin was spread, wayfarers could enter; when the napkin was removed, wayfarers were not allowed to enter. (*T.Ber.* IV, 9 (Z. p. 9, line 15).)

One must be sincere in one's offers of hospitality:

[1263] A man must not press his fellow to be his guest when he knows that his fellow does not wish to accept; he must not multiply offers, when he knows that the man will not accept them. What is meant by multiplying offers? When one knows for certain that the man will not come, and yet keeps on worrying him. (*T.J.Dem.* IV, § 6, f. 24*a*, line 62 (cp. [1099] and [1100]).)

The Rabbis were gentlemen: they liked courtesy and good manners; cleanliness of body as well as purity of soul.

[1264] 'And [his brethren] hated him and would not return his greeting' [lit. could not speak peaceably unto him] (Gen. XXXVII, 4). Joseph used to greet them, but they would not respond. It was always his custom to greet them. There are folk who, before rising to greatness, will always greet other people, but when they attain to greatness, their spirit becomes haughty, and they pay no heed to greet fellow-citizens. Joseph was different. After he had risen, he still greeted others (Gen. XLIII, 27). God said to him, 'Joseph, because thou didst take the initiative in greeting thy brethren in this world, though they hated thee, I will reconcile you in the world to come, and remove hatred from among you, and settle you in amity,' as it is said, 'How good it is when brethren dwell peacefully together' (Ps. CXXXIII, 1). (*Tanḥ.B.*, Wayesheb, f. 90*b*.)

[1265] R. Yannai was taking a walk, and he saw a man very neatly dressed [as a student]. Rabbi Yannai said to him, 'Will the Rabbi be pleased to be our guest?' He said, 'Yes.' So R. Yannai took him to his house. He gave him food and drink; then he tested him in Scripture, but he found nothing, and so in Mishnah, Haggadah and Talmud, and the man knew nothing. Then he said, 'Take [the cup], and say the blessing.' The man said, 'Let Yannai say the blessing in his own house.' R. Yannai said, 'Can you repeat what I say to you?' He said, 'Yes.' 'Then say,' rejoined Yannai, 'a dog has eaten Yannai's bread.' The man jumped up, and seized Yannai, and said, 'Would you withhold from me my inheritance?' Yannai said, 'How is your inheritance with me?' He said, 'Once I passed a school, and I heard the voices of the children say, "The Law which Moses commanded us is the inheritance of the congregation of Jacob": they did not say "congregation of Yannai".' Then R. Yannai said, 'What merit have you [what meritorious deed have you done] that you should eat at my table?' The man said, 'I never heard an unkind word, and returned it to its speaker, and

I never saw two men quarrelling without making peace between them.' Then R. Yannai said, 'You have so much good breeding [*derek ereẓ*] [lit. way of the land, a characteristic and important Rabbinic expression and virtue, equivalent to culture, good manners, decency, good taste, good breeding], and I called you a dog!' And to that man he applied Ps. L, 23, 'To him that orders his way aright, I will show the salvation of God.' [The 'way' is interpreted to mean *derek ereẓ*.] (**Note 94**.)

(*Lev.R.*, Ẓaw, IX, 3.)

[Zunz dates the compilation of Leviticus Rabbah in the seventh century: it is therefore quite possible that 'Talmud' was then inserted by the editor, who made use of much older material. If this Yannai be Yannai the Great, he lived at the end of the second century, *before* the codification of the Talmud. But the word may be used in a general way, in the sense of teaching (for instances, see Levy). Since it is here employed antithetically to Mishnah and Haggadah, it is more probably an editorial addition. (H. L.)]

[1266] He who possesses [is versed in] Scripture, Mishnah and good manners will not speedily sin, as it is said, 'A threefold cord is not quickly broken' (Eccles. IV, 12). He who has none of the three is not a civilised man. (*Ḳid.* I, 10.)

[1267] R. Judah said in the name of Rab: three things shorten a man's days and years: the refusal to read the lesson, when invited to do so; to decline the cup of wine which the leader in post-prandial grace drinks; to give oneself out as a Rabbi [or, to assume airs of superiority].

These are three instances of churlish behaviour. The Torah is 'Life' and he who declines to read the lesson keeps 'Life' from himself and his hearers. The Leader of Grace 'blesses' his host: it is churlish to refuse to do so. God says, 'I will bless those who bless thee' (Gen. XII, 3). Joseph gave himself airs of superiority, and died before his brethren (Exod. I, 6) (cp. *Ber.* 55*a*).

[1268] It happened that Rabbi [R. Judah the Prince] entered his lecture room and smelt garlic: so he said, 'Let him who has eaten garlic leave the room.' Then R. Ḥiyya stood up and went out. Whereupon they all got up and went out. (*San.* 11 *a*.)

[The point of the story is that Ḥiyya was Judah's chief pupil and favourite: he was almost a colleague. This is why Ḥiyya set the example.

Garlic was known as a love-philtre (*Bab.K.* 82*a*; *T.J.Meg.* IV, 1, 75*a*, l. 27) and the phrase 'to eat garlic' was therefore a euphemism for the sexual act. But it is probably not used in this sense here. Judah did not suspect any pupil of incontinence: he was merely annoyed by the smell. There is a further moral to the story: Ḥiyya's example induced the rest of the students, not only to emulate his conduct but also, by their action, to stand by him. A similar, but more serious story, about R. Me'ir, follows in the Gemara. (H. L.)]

[1269] If a man gives to his fellow all the good gifts of the world with a grumpy countenance, the Scripture regards it as if he had given him nothing; but if he receives his fellow cheerfully and kindly, the Scripture regards it as if he had given him all the good gifts in the world. (*Ab.R.N.* (vers. I), XIII, 29*a*.)

[1270] From the visits of the angels to Abraham and to Lot, and from the way they behaved and were treated, the Rabbis deduce various rules of hospitality and conduct. Because Lot had been allied to Abraham, he learnt from him the duty of hospitality. The angels declined Lot's invitation at first, though they accepted Abraham's at once. Hence we may learn that from a small man one should let oneself be importuned to accept an invitation [for he may be poor and may feel it his duty to offer hospitality which he cannot afford], but a great man's invitation may be accepted without demur. Lot baked unleavened bread for the angels. But angels do not eat! Well, they made as though they ate, to teach the lesson of politeness. A man should never change the established custom of the place. You can learn this also from Moses who went to heaven, and neither ate nor drank for forty days. Had there been eating and drinking in heaven, Moses would have eaten and drunk. (**Note 20*g*.**)

(*Tanḥ.*, Wayera, § 11, f. 35*b fin.*–36*a init.*)

Here follow a few extracts on behaviour and decency.

[1271] It is written, 'The pious man does good to his own soul' (Prov. XI, 17). That is Hillel the Elder. For once when he left his disciples, they said to him, 'Whither are you going?' He replied, 'To execute a pious deed.' They said, 'What may that be?' He said, 'To take a bath.' They said, 'Is that a pious deed?' He said, 'Yes, for if the man who is appointed to polish and wash the images of kings which are set up in the theatres and circuses, receives his rations for doing so, and is even raised up to be regarded as among the great ones of the kingdom, how much more is it obligatory on me to polish and wash my body, since I have been created in the divine image and likeness' (Gen. IX, 6). (*Lev.R.*, Behar, XXXIV, 3 (cp. [811]).)

[1272] R. Huna asked his son Rabbah why he did not attend R. Ḥisda, whose teaching was said to be very clever. The son replied, 'When I go to him, he speaks of mundane matters: he tells me about certain natural functions of the digestive organs, and how one should behave in regard to them.' His father replied: 'He occupies himself with the life of God's creatures, and you call that a mundane matter! All the more should you go to him.' (*Sab.* 82*a*.)

Each man has his place and his honour:

[1273] R. Eliezer said: Let the honour of thy neighbour be as dear to thee as thine own. As a man has pleasure in his own honour, so let him have pleasure in the honour of his neighbour. (*Ab.R.N.* (vers. I), XV, 30*a fin.*)

[1274] When R. Eliezer was ill, his disciples went to visit him, and they sat down before him, and said, 'Master, teach us something.' He replied, 'Be careful of the honour of your fellow-man, and when you pray, know before whom you stand. Then will you merit the life of the world to come.' (*Ab.R.N.* (vers. I), XIX, 35*b*.)

God is often said to care for the honour of His creatures.

'Even in the infliction of merited punishment God spares the honour of the transgressor' (Moore, I, 394) (cp. *Sifre Deut.* 110*a*, § 192 and Deut. XX, 3–8).

[1275] Why may not a woman suspected of adultery drink the water from a cup belonging to another woman? So that people may not say, 'In that cup did so and so drink, and she died.' The ox that gored must be killed, that men may not say: 'That is the ox which belonged to so and so, who was put to death because his ox had gored a man.' So too, 'When an ox or sheep is born' (Lev. XXII, 27). Is an ox born? Is it not a *calf* which is born? But because the Israelites made the golden calf, therefore the Scripture says 'ox' and not 'calf'. And God has not revealed, and will not reveal, the name of the tree of which

Adam ate. God said, 'If I am going to spare the honour of his descendants, it is only right that I should spare his honour.'

(*Pes.K.* 75*b*, 142*b* (cp. [1106]).)

[1276] Ben Azzai said: Despise not any man, and carp not at any thing; for there is not a man that has not his hour, and there is not a thing that has not its place.

(*Aboth* IV, 3 (*P.B.* p. 195).)

[1277] If you see a great crowd of human beings, say, 'Blessed art thou, O Lord our God, King of the universe, who knowest the secret minds of men'; as the faces of men are unlike one another, so their dispositions are unlike one another; each one has his own disposition. So when Moses was about to die, he besought God and said, 'Known and revealed to thee is the disposition of all men, and the dispositions of thy children are unlike one another; when I am removed from them, I beseech you to appoint over them a leader who may bear with each one according to his disposition.' (*Num.R.*, Pineḥas, XXI, 2.)

To judge men favourably and to harbour no unjust suspicions are virtues often commended.

[1278] Joshua the son of Peraḥyah said, Judge all men in [or by] the scale of merit. (*Aboth* I, 6.)

[1279] Some Rabbis had to transact business with a [Roman] lady with whom all the great ones of the city used to consort. They said, 'Who shall go?' R. Joshua said, 'I will go.' So he went with some disciples. When they got near her house, he took off his *Tephillin*, and went in and shut the door behind him. When he came out, he bathed, and taught his disciples, and said to them, 'When I took off my *Tephillin*, of what did you suspect me?' 'We thought the master felt that holy objects should not be brought into an unclean place.' 'And when I shut the door?' 'We thought perhaps you had a matter of state business to transact with her.' 'And when I bathed?' 'We thought perhaps the spittle from her mouth might have fallen on your clothes.' He replied, 'Thus it was, and as you judged me favourably, so may God judge you favourably.' (**Note 39**.) (*Sab.* 127*b*.)

[1280] He who judges his neighbour favourably will himself be judged favourably by God. Once a man from Galilee hired himself for three years to a man in the south. On the afternoon before the Day of Atonement he said, 'Give me my hire; I will go and nourish my wife and children.' The man said, 'I have no money.' 'Then give me produce.' 'I have none.' 'Give me land.' 'I have none.' 'Give me cattle.' 'I have none.' 'Give me mattresses and coverlets.' 'I have none.' Then the man put his things on his back, and went to his house in despair. After the fast, his master took the man's wages and three asses laden with food, drink and all sorts of delicacies, and went to the man's house. After they had eaten and drunk, and he had given him his wages, he said to the man, 'When you asked me for your wages, and I said I had no money, in what suspicion did you hold me?' He replied, 'I thought you had bought goods cheaply, and so had used up your money.' 'And about the cattle?' 'I thought: perhaps they were hired out.' 'And the land?' 'I thought: perhaps it was rented out.' 'And the produce?' 'I thought: perhaps it had not been tithed.' 'And the mattresses and coverlets?' 'I thought: perhaps he has consecrated all his property to God.' Then the man said, 'And so it was. I had vowed away all my property, because my son does not occupy himself with the study of the Law. But I went to my colleagues, and they freed me from my vow. As you have judged me favourably, so may God judge you.'

(*Sab.* 127*b*.)

[1281] 'Judge every man in the scale of merit' (*Aboth* I, 6). Once a man sent his son to his neighbour, and said to him, 'Go and say, "My father says, Lend me a measure of wheat."' The son went and found his neighbour measuring wheat. The neighbour said, 'I have not got any wheat.' The son told his father, who said, 'Perhaps that wheat belonged to the second tithe.' Then he said to his son, 'Go and say to him, "My father says, Lend me a pound."' The son went to the neighbour and found him counting out money. The neighbour answered, 'I have not got twopence.' The son returned to his father and said, 'Father, I found him counting out money, but he said, "I have not got twopence."' The father said, 'Perhaps he was counting trust money.' When they went into the street, the two neighbours met. One said to the other, 'When your son came to see me, and found me measuring wheat, and I gave him none, what did you think of me?' The other replied, 'I thought that it was wheat of the second tithe.' 'And about the money?' 'Perhaps it was trust money.' The other replied, 'So, indeed, it was, even as you say. You have not turned aside to the right or to the left, but you judged every man in the scale of merit.' (*Ab.R.N.* (vers. II), XIX, 20*b*.)

Chapter XIX

PITY, FORGIVENESS AND LOVE

Let men be forbearing and pitiful and forgiving towards one another.

[1282] If a man has received an injury, then, even if the wrongdoer has not asked his forgiveness, the receiver of the injury must nevertheless ask [God] to show the wrongdoer compassion, even as Abraham prayed to God for Abimelech (Gen. xx, 17) and Job prayed for his friends. R. Gamaliel said: Let this be a sign to you, that whenever you are compassionate, the Compassionate One will have compassion upon you.

(*T.Bab.Ḳ.* IX, 29, 30 (Z. p. 365, line 31; cp. [1289]).)

[1283] If others speak ill of you, let the worst they say seem to you small; if you speak ill of others, let a small thing seem to you big, till you go to appease the man of whom you have spoken ill.

(*Der.Er.Z.* I, 6.)

[1284] If you have done much good, let it be in your own eyes as little. Do not say: 'I have given from my own,' but rather, 'I have given from what others have given to me,' and for which you owe thanks to God. But let a small benefit from others to you seem in your eyes great.... Let a small wrong which you have done seem great to you, but if much wrong has been done to you, let it seem little to you, and say, 'I have been punished less than I deserved: a bigger punishment would have been fitting.' (*Der.Er.Z.* II, 8.)

[1285] Let a man forgive the disgrace to which he has been subjected: let him seek no honour through the disgrace of his neighbour.

(*Der.Er.Z.* VI, 3 *fin.*)

[1286] R. Abba said in the name of R. Alexandri: He who hears himself cursed, and has the opportunity to stop the man who curses him, and yet keeps silence, makes himself a partner with God, for God hears how the nations blaspheme Him, and He is silent. (*Midr.Ps.* on LXXXVI, 1 (186*b*, §1).)

[1287] If you have something to testify to your neighbour's advantage, [when he is accused], you may not keep it back.

(*Sifra* 89*a*.)

[1288] R. Gamaliel said: So long as you are merciful, God will have mercy upon you, and if *you* are not merciful, He will not be merciful unto you. (*T.J.Bab.Ḳ*. VIII, § 10, line 24, 6*c* (cp. *Sifre Deut*., Re'eh, § 96, f. 93*b fin*. (H. p. 157)).)

[1289] If a man seeks to appease one whom he has grieved, the latter should not repel him. So long as you are merciful to your brother, you will find mercy yourself. But if the aggrieved man repels him, what then? Let him assemble ten persons, and stand them in line, and say to them, 'My brothers, there has been contention between me and this man, and I have tried to appease him, but he will not receive me.' Then God will see that he who did the injury has humbled himself, and He will have compassion on him, as it says, 'He looks upon men, and if any say, I have sinned, God will deliver his soul' (Job XXXIII, 27). (*Tanḥ.B*., Wayera, 52*a fin*.–52*b init*. (cp. [1282]).)

[1290] 'Let the sinners be consumed out of the earth, and let the wicked be no more' (Ps. CIV, 35). R. Judah [by a pun and play upon words untranslatable in English] said: Let the sinners become perfect, and then the wicked will be no more. R. Nehemiah said: May wickednesses be consumed, for then there will not be any wicked. (The pun is not the same as the pun in [1291].) (**Note 40**.) (*Midr.Ps*. on CIV, 35 (224*b*, § 27).)

[1291] There were some lawless men living in the neighbourhood of R. Me'ir, and they used to vex him sorely. Once R. Me'ir prayed that they should die. His wife, Beruria, exclaimed, 'What thinkest thou? Is it because it is written, "Let sinners cease out of the earth"? But has the text *ḥaṭṭa'im*? It is written *ḥaṭa'im*. Glance also at the end of the verse, "And let the wicked be no more," i.e. when sins will cease, then the wicked will be no more. Rather shouldst thou pray that they repent, and be no more wicked.' Then R. Me'ir offered prayer on their behalf, and they repented (cp. *R.T*. p. 263). (The unvocalised consonants could be pronounced in either way.) (**Note 40**.) (*Ber*. 10*a*.)

[1292] Belong ever to the persecuted rather than to the persecutors (cf. *R.T*. p. 96). (*Bab.Ḳ*. 93*a*.)

[1293] God loves the persecuted, and hates the persecutors. (*Pes.R.* 193*b*.)

[1294] Learn to receive suffering, and forgive those who insult you (cf. *R.T.* p. 97). (*Ab.R.N.* (vers. I), XLI, 67*a*.)

[1295] 'Thou hast established equity' (Ps. XCIX, 4). A man goes on his way, and he sees the donkey of his fellow fallen beneath his burden; he gives him his hand, and helps him to unload and reload; then they go to an inn together, and the owner of the donkey says, 'How he loves me, and I thought he hated me!' Then they speak to each other, and become reconciled to one another. What brings it about that they become reconciled and are friends? Because the one obeyed the commandment of the Law, 'If thou see the ass of him that hates thee lying under his burden, thou shalt surely help him' (Exod. XXIII, 5). And so it is written, 'Her [Wisdom's] ways are ways of pleasantness, and all her paths are peace' (Prov. III, 17. Wisdom is taken to mean the Law) (cf. *R.T.* p. 93). (*Midr.Ps.* on XCIX, 4 (212*a*, §3).)

[1296] And the people came to Moses and said, 'We have sinned, for we have spoken against the Lord, and against thee' (Num. XXI, 7). At once Moses prayed for them. This shows you the humility of Moses in that he did not delay to seek mercy for them, and it shows further the power of repentance. As soon as they said, 'We have sinned,' instantly he was reconciled to them. For one who pardons can never become cruel. And how do you know that if a man asks pardon of his neighbour whom he has offended, and that if the neighbour refuses to pardon him, he, the neighbour, and not the offender, is called a sinner? Because Samuel said, 'As for me, far be it from me to sin unto the Lord by refraining to pray for you' (I Sam. XII, 23). When was this? When the people came and said, 'We have sinned.' (*Tanḥ.B.*, Ḥuḳḳat, 63*b*.)

[1297] Even though a man pays another whom he has insulted, he is not forgiven by God, till he seeks forgiveness from the man he has insulted. That man, if he does not forgive the other, is called merciless. (*Bab.Ḳ.* VIII, 7.)

[1298] For the long discussions in the *Talmud* and *Tosefta* and *Sifre* about the law of Exod. XXIII, 4, see *R.T.* p. 93. If there are two concurrent cases of need, (1) to help to *unload* the ass of a friend, (2) to help to *load* the ass of an enemy, the enemy takes precedence. Why? In order to crush the evil *yetzer* [i.e. to crush the evil inclination of the man who would be tempted to leave the enemy, and to turn to help the friend]. In the *Tosefta*, however, the purpose of the rule is said to be 'to crush [i.e. change] the heart of the *enemy*'. [The enemy is said to be an Israelite, but the *Tosefta* adds that 'one must help the ass of a non-Jew no less than the ass of a Jew, unless it is laden with libation-wine,' in which case one may not help it, for that would be aiding and abetting in idolatry, which is a greater sin than cruelty to animals.]

(*Bab.M.* 32*b*; *T.Bab.M.* II, 26 (Z. p. 375, line 13).)

Hatred, revenge, grudging and anger are condemned:

[1299] The first Temple was destroyed because of the sins of idolatry, harlotry, and murder. The second, in spite of Torah studied, commandments and deeds of love executed, during its existence, fell because of groundless hatred, and this teaches us that groundless hatred is a sin that weighs as heavily as idolatry, harlotry and murder (cp. [1396]). (*Yoma* 9*b*.)

[1300] R. Johanan b. Torta said: Why was the first Temple destroyed? Because of idolatry, unchastity and murder. But in the days of the second Temple, they were earnest about the Torah, and careful about tithes. Why then did the destruction come? Because they loved money, and hated one another. So learn that the hate of man for his fellow-man is a sore sin before God, and weighs as heavily as idolatry and unchastity and murder. (*T.Men.* XIII, 22, p. 533 *fin.*–534 *init.* (cp. *T.J.Yoma* I, §1, f. 38*c*, line 57).)

[1301] Yield your will to the will of your friend: but let both his will and yours yield to the will of God. (*Der.Er.Z.* I, 8.)

[1302] The Rabbis have taught: It says, 'Thou shalt not hate thy brother in thy heart.' For a man might think, 'I must not strike him or beat him or curse him' [but I may hate him]. Therefore it says, 'In thy heart.' (*'Arak.* 16*b* (cp. also *Sifra* 89*a*).)

[1303] If *A* asks *B*, 'Lend me your scythe,' and *B* refuses, and next day *B* says to *A*, 'Lend me your spade,' and *A* replies, 'I will not, even as you refused to lend me your scythe,' that is revenge [which the Law forbids]. If *A* says to *B*, 'Lend me your spade,' and *B* refuses, and next day *B* says to *A*, 'Lend me your scythe,' and *A* replies, 'Here it is; I am not like you, who would not lend me your spade,' that is bearing a grudge, which also is forbidden. (*Sifra* 89*b* (cp. *R.T.* p. 89).)

[1304] R. Ḥama b. Ḥanina said: Even though your enemy has risen up early to kill you, and he comes hungry and thirsty to your house, give him food and drink. Read not *yeshallem*, 'God will [reward or] repay,' but *yashlimennu*, 'God will make him at peace with you.' [Cp. *R.T.* p. 94. The extract is based on Prov. XXV, 21, 'If thine enemy be hungry, give him bread to eat, and if he be thirsty, give him water to drink: for thou shalt heap coals of fire upon his head and the Lord shall reward thee.'] (*Midr.Prov.* XXV, 21, f. 49*b*.)

[1305] It says in Proverbs (XVII, 13), 'Who requites evil for good, evil shall not depart from his house.' R. Johanan said: If your neighbour offers you lentils, then do you offer him meat. Why? Because he did good to you first. R. Simeon b. Abba said: The verse means even more: it means that if a man requites evil for evil, evils shall not depart from his house. R. Alexander said: The verse applies also to him who contravenes the law of Exod. XXIII, 5 (to help the enemy in unloading the ass). (*Gen.R.*, Noaḥ, XXXVIII, 3 (Th. pp. 352, 353).)

[1306] R. Akiba said: He who tears his clothes, and breaks his furniture in his passion and wrath, will in the end become an idolater, for such is the craft of the evil inclination: to-day it says, 'Tear your clothes,' and to-morrow it says, 'Worship idols.' (*Ab.R.N.* (vers. I), III, 8*a*.)

[1307] All the divisions of hell rule over the angry man (cf. *R.T.* p. 38 *fin.*). (*Ned.* 22*a*.)

[1308] By the angry man even the Shechinah itself is not esteemed (cf. *R.T.* p. 38 *fin.*). (*Ned.* 22*b*.)

[1309] The angry man forgets what he has learnt, and becomes more and more stupid. (*Ned.* 22*b*.)

[1310] It is certain that the iniquities of the angry man outweigh his merits. (*Ned.* 22*b*.)

[1311] Hillel used to say: A passionate man cannot be a teacher.

(*Aboth* II, 6; *P.B.* p. 187.)

[1312] R. Elazar said: Three times did Moses come into the category of error because he gave way to anger (Lev. x, 16; Num. xx, 10; xxxi, 14). [For a similar remark about Hillel, cp. [1331].]

(*Sifre Num.*, Maṭṭot, § 157, f. 60*a* (H. p. 213; cp. *Ab.R.N.* (vers. I and II), I, 2*a*; *Pes.* 66*a*, *b*).)

[1313] [It is noteworthy how a touch of pity occasionally comes over the Rabbis in regard to the enemies of Israel and their destruction. One may get this touch even after a passage full of human satisfaction in the destruction of Israel's enemies and oppressors in the Messianic age. In relation to the Feast of Tabernacles, rejoicing is mentioned three times, Deut. xvi, 14, 15; Lev. xxiii, 40. But concerning Passover, rejoicing is not mentioned at all. Why? Two explanations are given, of which the first is that at Passover it is not yet known whether the harvest will be good or bad. The second explanation is], Because at Passover the Egyptians died. And so you find that during Tabernacles we read the 'Hallel' psalms all the seven days, but on Passover we read them only on the first day and in the evening, even as Samuel was wont to quote Prov. xxiv, 17, 'When thine enemy falls, do not rejoice.'

(*Pes.K.* 189*a* (cp. [142]).)

The rite here alluded to differs slightly, but not in principle, from the modern rite. See *P.B.* p. 221.

[1314] In the neighbourhood of R. Joshua b. Levi there dwelt a heretic who caused him much vexation [in *Berakot*, 'who plagued him with questions about the interpretations of the Scriptures']. He took a cock, and tied it to the foot of his bed. He thought: 'When the comb of the cock grows white, which is the hour when God is wrathful against the wicked, I will curse the heretic.' But when the hour came, he was asleep. When he woke, he thought, 'One learns from this [that I was asleep] that it is not seemly to do thus [i.e. to curse]' even as it is written, 'To punish is not good for the righteous' [Midrashic translation of Prov. xvii, 26], and it is written, 'His tender mercies are over all His works.' Even a heretic it is not fitting to curse.

(*San.* 105*b* (cp. *Ber.* 7*a*).)

[1315] R. Huna said: Strife is like a channel made by a burst of water: it widens continually. Abbaye the Elder said: Strife is like the plank of a landing bridge, which, once it is put in position, remains. (*San.* 7*a.*)

On the other hand, right reproof is much praised:

[1316] How do we know that he who sees anything that is ugly and shameful in his neighbour is bound to reprove him? Because it says, 'Thou shalt surely reprove him.' And if he does not accept the reproof, how do we know that we must reprove him again? Because it says, 'Thou shalt *surely* reprove him.' But one must not go on reproving him if his countenance is changed [i.e. if he feels ashamed], because it says, 'Thou shalt not raise over him his sin.' [The literal meaning is, 'Thou shalt not bear sin because of him' (Lev. XIX, 17).] (For the use of the double verb, 'reproving reprove', cp. [659] and pp. 44 and 292.) (*'Arak.* 16*b.*)

[1317] Rabbi said: Which is the straight [or right] way which a man should choose? Let him love reproofs, for when there are reproofs in the world, appeasement of spirit and good and blessing come into the world, and evil departs from it; as it is said, 'They that rebuke find favour, and a good blessing falls upon them' (Prov. XXIV, 25). ['Rabbi', *par excellence*, denotes R. Judah the Prince (cp. [419]).]

R. Jonathan said: He who reproves his neighbour with pure intent is worthy of a portion from God, as it is said, 'He who rebukes a man finds favour with me' [A.V. and R.V. 'afterwards'], and not only that, but God draws over him a thread of love. [Jastrow translates: 'strings round him a chord of grace,' i.e. protection.] (Prov. XXVIII, 23.) (Cf. on rebuke, *Sifre* 65*b*; *R.T.* p. 265.) (*Tam.* 28*a.*)

[1318] It is written, 'Reprove a wise man, and he will love thee' (Prov. IX, 8). R. Jose b. Ḥanina said: A love without reproof is no love. Resh Laḳish said: Reproof leads to peace; a peace where there has been no reproof is no peace. (*Gen.R.*, Wayera, LIV, 3 (Th. p. 578).)

[1319] R. Ḥanina said: Jerusalem was destroyed only because none reproved his fellow. R. Ṭarfon, who witnessed the destruction, said: I should be surprised if there is anybody in this generation who knows how to give reproof rightly [i.e. without putting his fellow to shame], or how rightly to receive it. If one says to another, 'Take away the splinter from your eye,' he replies, 'Take away the beam from your own eye' (cp. [1396]). (**Note 11 *l*.**) ('*Arak*. 16*b*; *Sab*. 119*b*.)

In the following extract, some of the ideas previously given are slightly varied:

[1320] 'Thou shalt surely rebuke thy neighbour and not suffer sin upon him' (Lev. XIX, 17). How do we know that if a man has rebuked his neighbour four and five times [without succeeding in turning him from sin], he should continue to reprove him? Because it says: 'Thou shalt surely reprove him.' One might infer that the reproof should be carried so far as to change a man's face with shame. But it says, 'Thou shalt not bring guilt upon him.' R. Ṭarfon said: In this generation there is no one capable of reproving [because he is himself a sinner]. R. Elazar b. Azariah said: In this generation there is no one capable of receiving reproof. R. Akiba said: In this generation there is no one who knows how reproof ought to be worded. R. Johanan b. Nuri said: I call heaven and earth to witness that more than four and five times was R. Akiba whipped through me by the order of R. Gamaliel, to whom I had complained about him, but I know that Akiba loved me the more on that account, so that the word of Scripture was fulfilled, 'Rebuke a wise man and he will love thee' (Prov. IX, 8). (**Note 11 *m*.**) (*Sifra* 89*a fin*.–89*b* (cf. *Sifre Deut*., Debarim, § 1, f. 64*a* (H. p. 3) and *R.T*. p. 265).)

[1321] For four reasons a man should rebuke others only just before he dies; so as not to have to reprove him again and again; so that he should not feel shame in the presence of the reprover, whenever he should happen to see him; so that he should feel nothing in his heart against the reprover; and so that the reprover should part from him in peace, for reproof then brings him unto peace (*R.T*. p. 265).

(*Sifre Deut*., Debarim, § 2, f. 65*b fin*. (H. p. 10).)

Love is commended, but I fear that, as with the teachers of other religious communities, love sometimes has its limits.

[1322] Whenever love depends upon some material cause, with the passing away of that cause, the love, too, passes away; but if it be not dependent upon such a cause, it will not pass away for ever (*P.B.* p. 202). (*Aboth* V, 19.)

[1323] A man once said: When our love was strong, we could sleep on a bed no wider than a sword's edge; now that our love is not strong, a bed of sixty ells is too small for us. [For the metaphor, cp. *Gen.R.*, Wayishlaḥ, LXXV, 4.] (*San.* 7*a*.)

[1324] R. Ḥanina b. Dosa said: He in whom the spirit of his fellow-creatures takes delight, in him the Spirit of the All-present takes delight; and he in whom the spirit of his fellow-creatures takes not delight, in him the Spirit of the All-present takes not delight (*P.B.* p. 193). (*Aboth* III, 13.)

I take this last adage to mean simply that the man who is unbeloved by his fellow-man cannot become beloved of God. Piety without human service will not be acceptable to God. Dr T. Herford has a more elaborate explanation.

[1325] Man must love his fellow-creatures, and not hate them; the men of the generation which was dispersed over the earth (Gen. XI, 1–9) loved one another, and so God did not destroy them, but only scattered them, but the men of Sodom hated one another, and so God destroyed them both from this world and from the world to come.

(*Ab.R.N.* (vers. I), XII, 26*b*.)

[1326] God said to Israel, 'My sons have I made you lack aught? What is it that I seek of you? Only that you love each other, honour each other and respect each other: that there be not found among you either sin or theft or anything ugly: that you never become soiled and base.' For, 'He has told thee, O man, what is good...walk humbly [or secretly] with thy God' (Mic. VI, 8), that is to say, 'Walk in secret with thy God, and God will be with thee.' [There is a play upon the word *ẓanua*', which can mean 'humble', or 'secret', or 'hidden'.] So long as you are with Him in secret, He will be with you in secret also.

(*Tan.d.b.El.* p. 143.)

[1327] 'Thou shalt go in His ways' (Deut. XXVIII, 9). What are His ways? Just as it is God's way to be merciful and forgiving to sinners, and to receive them in their repentance, so do you be merciful one to another. Just as God is gracious, and gives gifts gratis both to those who know Him and to those who know Him not, so do you give gifts [freely] one to another. Just as God is longsuffering to sinners, so be you longsuffering one to another. (*Tan.d.b.El.* p. 135.)

[1328] Let not a man accustom himself to say, 'Love the wise, and hate the disciples, love the disciples, but hate the *Am ha-Aretz*,' but rather, 'Love all, and hate [only] the heretics, the apostates, and the informers,' as David says, 'Do I not hate them that hate thee?' 'Thou shalt love thy neighbour as thyself, I am the Lord' [that is, I have created him]? Yes, if he acts as thy people should act, then thou must love him, but if he does not, then thou must [or needst] not love him. R. Simeon b. Elazar said: With a great oath was this word said, 'Thou shalt love thy neighbour as thyself.' 'I, the Lord, have created him; if thou lovest him, I am trustworthy to give thee good reward: and if not, I am a judge to punish thee.'

(*Ab.R.N.* (vers. I), XVI, 32*b* (cp. [665]).)

The Rabbis remember, and enlarge upon, both the good and the cruel injunctions of the Law. They remember the passage about Amalek (Deut. XXV, 17–19), and Amalek became a type of Israel's foes; they remember, too, the kindly law about the Edomite and the Egyptian:

[1329] 'Thou shalt not abhor an Edomite, for he is thy brother'; good or bad, he is thy brother. 'Thou shalt not abhor an Egyptian, for thou wast a sojourner in his land'; good or bad, among them you lived many years. But as to Amalek, 'Remember what Amalek did to you.' (*Pes.R.* 47*b* (cp. [1404]).)

The Law reinforces the good and the evil instincts of the Israelite as regards the Gentile: but it must be remembered that Amalek is the persecutor, the oppressor, the wielder of the sword and the stake.

Chapter XX

ON HUMILITY AND PRIDE

Even as man must be generous in his estimate of his neighbours, so must he be modest as regards himself. The Rabbis are never weary of attacking pride and of praising humility. It may not be too unkind to suggest that with the enormous importance which they attached to their own class and to learning (that is, learning in Torah), they were conscious of the great need for these warnings both for themselves and their colleagues. They knew where the shoe pinched. (Cp. *Aboth* II, 15; *P.B.* p. 189; *Num.R.* III, 1 *init.*)

[1330] R. Me'ir said: If I have ruled for others in the more easy way [in any particular case], I decide for myself in the harder way (cp. p. lxxix, [1112] and [1385]).

(*T.J.Ber.* I, § 2, f. 3*a*, line 14.)

[1331] R. Judah said in the name of Rab: If any learned man is boastful, his learning is removed from him, and from a boastful prophet his prophecy is removed. And so it was in the case of Hillel: he once rebuked his disciples with boastful words, and then had to say, 'This law I once knew, but I have now forgotten it.' Resh Laḳish said: The same is the case with anger (cp. [1312]). (*Pes.* 66*a*, *b.*)

[1332] R. Simeon b. Yoḥai said: Pride is equivalent to idolatry. R. Johanan said: The proud man is as sinful as if he had denied God. R. Ḥama b. Ḥanina said: His sin is as if he had committed every kind of unchastity. Ulla said: It is as if he erected an altar for idolatry. R. Elazar said: The proud man deserves to be cut down, as one cuts down a symbol of idolatry. He also said: Over the proud man the Shechinah makes lament. R. Ḥisda said: God declares, 'The proud man and I cannot live in the world together.' (*Soṭ.* 4*b*–5*a.*)

With the last remark about the proud man we may compare a *Baraita*, which says: Because of three men the Almighty weeps daily; of these three, the last is the President of a Synagogue who acts haughtily towards his congregation. (*Ḥag.* 5*b.*)

[1333] Why was man created on Friday: So that, if he become overbearing, one can say to him, The gnat was created before you.

(*San.* 38*a.*)

[1334] Some righteous men boast how well they fulfil the commandments; then God weakens their strength. So David said, 'Thy statutes are to me as songs' (Ps. CXIX, 54), as if to say that they were as easy and light to him as songs. So God said, 'One day you will err in a matter which the children know.' So when Uzzah was killed, because he touched the Ark, and David was angry (II Sam. VI, 3–8) God said, 'Did you not say, Thy statutes are to me as songs? Have you not learnt that the Service of the Sanctuary belongs to the sons of Kohath, that they should bear [the ark] upon their shoulders?' (Num. VII, 9). (*Num.R.*, Pineḥas, XXI, 12.)

[1335] Job says, 'All high things He beholds' (XLI, 34). But does not God see low things? 'Verily the eyes of the Lord run hither and thither throughout the world' (Zech. IV, 10). R. Berechiah said: This means that the 'high things' are the proud, those whose spirit is overbearing, who raise themselves and deify themselves. What does God do to them? He displays them to His creatures, and makes them abased in the world, as He did with Nebuchadnezzar and Sennacherib. (*Tanḥ.B.*, Wa'era, 12*b*.)

The following may be harsh, but has its grain of truth:

[1336] One coin in a bottle rattles; a bottle full of coins makes no sound; so the scholar who is the son of a scholar is modest; the scholar who is the son of an *Am ha-Aretz* trumpets his knowledge around. (*Bab.M.* 85*b*.)

Let not a man be over-confident in his virtue or in his ability to resist temptations:

[1337] R. Yudan said: Even for the righteous there can be no self-confidence, so long as he lives on earth. (*Gen.R.*, Wayishlaḥ, LXXVI, 2 (Th. p. 898).)

[There is a popular proverb, cited by the poet Immanuel of Rome (*Maḥb.* IX, p. 72, line 19 in ed. Lemberg, 1870; also *Maḥb.* XXI, beginning, p. 168) to this effect: 'After their death—but not before—declare them saints.' The proverb consists of the titles of three successive weekly lessons from Leviticus. 'After their death' = *Aḥare mot* (XVI, 1); 'Saints' = *Ḳedoshim* (XIX, 2); 'declare' = *'emor* (XXI, 1). (Cp. [784].) (H. L.)]

[1338] We are taught: 'Trust not in thyself till the day of thy death.'[1] A man of great piety was once sitting and studying, and when

[1] Cp. Hillel's saying in *Aboth* II, 5.

he came to this verse, he said, 'This verse does not apply to me.' Then there came a spirit in the form of a woman, and tempted him, and his *yetzer* pressed him to desire her, [but he began to repent], and then the spirit said to him, 'Grieve not, for I am only a spirit; but, henceforward, regard thyself as no better than thy neighbour.' (*T.J.Sab.* I, § 3, f. 3*b*, line 64.)

[1339] Resh Laḳish, or, as some say, R. Joshua b. Levi, desired to see R. Ḥiyya the Great in a dream. They said, 'You are not worthy.' He said, 'Why? Have I not laboured in the Law even as he?' They said, 'You have not taught as much Torah as he, and, in addition, he left his home.' He said to them, 'Did I not leave my home?' They said, 'You left it to learn; he left it to teach.' After three hundred fasts, R. Ḥiyya did appear to him in a dream. He said to him, 'If a person is "somebody", and comports himself as "somebody", it were better for him had he never been born.' (*Eccles.R.* IX, § 10, 1, on IX, 10 (24*a*).)

Humility is, therefore, constantly praised.

[1340] R. Johanan said: The words of the Torah abide only with him who regards himself as nothing. (*Soṭ.* 21*b*.)

[1341] R. Joseph had a disagreement with Raba.[1] On the eve of the Day of Atonement, he said, 'I will go and become reconciled with him.' He went and found Raba's servant in the act of mixing for him a cup of wine. R. Joseph said to the servant, 'Allow me to mix it for him.' [The mixing of wine with water to a nicety was a skilled, but menial, task.] The servant gave R. Joseph the wine, and he mixed it. When Raba tasted it he said, 'This mixing is very much like that of R. Joseph.' The latter said, 'It was I who mixed it.' Raba said to him, 'You shall not sit down before you have explained to me the meaning of this verse—'And from the desert to Mattanah [lit. gift], and from Mattanah to Nahaliel [lit. inheritance of God], and from Nahaliel to Bamoth [lit. heights], and from Bamoth to the valley' (Num. XXI, 19). R. Joseph said to him, 'If a man makes himself [lowly] like the wilderness on which all trample, then is the Torah given to him as a gift: if it is given to him as a gift, God confirms it to him as an inheritance, as it says, "And from the gift to the inheritance of

[1] Raba b. Joseph b. Ḥama.

God." When God has confirmed it to him as an inheritance, he rises to greatness, as it says, "And from the inheritance of God to heights." But if he makes his heart proud, God humbles him, as it says, "And from the heights to the valley": but if he returns, then God raises him, as it says, "Every valley shall be exalted"' (Isa. XL, 4). (*'Erub.* 54*a* (cp. [446]).)

[1342] R. Joshua b. Levi said: He who has a humble mind is regarded as if he had offered all the sacrifices of the Law. (*Soṭ.* 5*b*; *San.* 43*b*.)

[1343] 'And Solomon spoke to [A.V. 'of'] trees, from the cedar to the hyssop' (I Kings IV, 33). Can a man speak to trees? It means: he drew teachings from them. Why is the leper cleansed with the highest of the high and the lowest of the low? [cedar and hyssop, Lev. XIV, 4, 6]. Because when a man is haughty like the cedar, he is smitten with leprosy; when he humbles himself like the hyssop, he is healed. (*Pes.R.* 60*b*.)

[1344] Do not resemble a big door, which lets in the wind; or a small door, which makes the worthy bend down; but resemble the threshold on which all may tread, or a low peg on which all can hang their things. (*Der.Er.Z.* I, 3.)

[1345] Those who are despised in their own esteem, and abased before themselves, who humble their spirit, who subdue their evil inclination, of such it is said, 'Thus says the Lord, Of him who is abased in soul, kings shall see and arise.' [A playful translation and use of Isa. XLIX, 7.] (*Tan.d.b.El.* p. 78.)

[1346] Ever let a man be humble in Torah and good works, humble with his parents, teacher and wife, with his children, with his household, with his kinsfolk near and far, even with the heathen in the street, so that he become beloved on high and desired on earth. (*Tan.d.b.El.* p. 197.)

[1347] R. Isaac said: When R. Gamaliel prepared a banquet for the wise, and they were at table with him, R. Gamaliel stood and served them. They said, 'We are not worthy that he should wait on [or serve] us.' Then R. Joshua said to them, 'Permit him to wait on us, for we find that a greater than R. Gamaliel waited on the creatures [i.e. on men].' They said, 'Who was this?' He said, 'Abraham, our father, the greatest in the world, who waited on the angels, but he *thought* that they were men, Arabians, idolaters. How much more should R. Gamaliel wait on the wise who are studying the Law!' R. Isaac said to them, 'We find that one who is even greater than Abraham and R. Gamaliel waits on the creatures [i.e. on men].' They said, 'Who is this?' He said, 'The Shechinah, for in every hour the Shechinah provides sustenance for all the inhabitants of the world according to their need, and satisfies every living thing, and not only the pious and the righteous, but also the wicked and the idolaters. How much more, then, may R. Gamaliel wait on the wise and the students of the Law.'

(*Mek.*², *Amalek*, Yitro, § 1, p. 195; *Mek.*³, § 3, vol. II, p. 177.)

[1348] R. Ḥanina b. Idi said: Why are the words of the Torah likened unto water, as it is written, 'Ho, every one that thirsts, come ye to the waters' (Isa. LV, 1)? In order to indicate that just as water leaves high places and goes to low places, so the words of the Torah leave him who is haughty, and stay with him who is humble. (*Ta'an.* 7*a* (Malter, p. 41).)

[1349] R. Osha'ya said: Why are the words of the Torah likened unto these three liquids: water, wine and milk?...To indicate to you that just as these three liquids can be preserved only in the cheapest kind of vessels, so will the words of the Torah be preserved only in him whose mind is lowly.

(*Ta'an.* 7*a* (Malter, p. 42).)

[1350] 'Thy humility educates me' [A.V. 'Thy gentleness has made me great'] (Ps. XVIII, 35). Abba bar Aḥa said: Is there anyone more humble than God? The disciple who sits before his master, when he ends his lesson, says, 'Master, how much I have wearied you!' But when Israel had been taught of God, and they were leaving His presence, God said to them, 'How much have I wearied you,' as it is written, 'Too long have I made you sit' [A.V. 'have ye dwelt'] (Deut. I, 6).... R. Simeon b. Ze'era said: If the disciple says, 'Teach me a chapter,' the master says, 'Go, wait for me in such a place.' But when God told Ezekiel to go forth to the valley (Ezek. III, 22), Ezekiel, on his arrival, found God awaiting him (*ib.* 23).

(*Tanḥ.B.*, Bereshit, 2*a*.)

[Compare Judah ha-Levi's lines:

Longing I sought Thy presence;
Lord, with my whole heart did I call and pray,
And going out toward Thee,
I found Thee coming to me on the way.

(Mrs Salaman's translation, p. xxv of her ed.) (H. L.)]

[1351] If a man makes himself great, he is not really great, unless one greater than he has made him great. Moses was great, but it was God who raised him to greatness.
(*Ab.R.N.* (vers. II), I, 1*a init.*)

[1352] R. Levitas, of Jabneh, said: Be exceedingly lowly of spirit since the hope of man is but the worm. (*Aboth* IV, 4.)

[1353] The judge must be wise and humble, and the mind of men must be pleased with him. So he, too, is a child of the world to come who is very humble, constantly studies the Law, and does not claim credit for himself (cf. *R.T.* p. 8). (*San.* 88*b*.)

[1354] Him who humbles himself, God exalts; him who exalts himself, God humbles; from him who searches for greatness, greatness flies; him who flies from greatness, greatness searches out: with him who is importunate with circumstances, circumstance is importunate; by him who gives way to circumstance, circumstance stands. (*'Erub.* 13*b*.)

[1355] If King Uzziah (II Chron. XXVI, 16–21), who did not intend to magnify himself, and did not seek his own honour, but that of his Creator, was yet so heavily punished, how much more heavily will he be punished who intends to magnify himself and seeks his own honour, and not the honour of his Creator!
(*Sifre Num.*, Beha'aloteka, § 99, f. 27*a* (H. p. 98).)

[1356] Shamefacedness leads to sin-fearing. It is a good sign if a man is shamefaced. A man who is shamefaced will not easily sin, and the shameless man's ancestors never stood at Mount Sinai.
(*Ned.* 20*a*.)

[1357] R. Samuel b. Naḥmani says: For seven days did God seek to win over Moses at the burning bush, but each time he fled, deeming himself unworthy. Then Moses hid his face out of reverence for the Presence, for he feared to look towards God

(Exod. III, 6). His reward was that he beheld God's similitude immediately (Num. XII, 8).

(*Tanḥ.*, Ḥay. Sar., § 6, f. 43*a* (cp. [454]).)

[1358] It is written, 'Do not glorify thyself in the presence of kings, and stand not in the place of great men' (Prov. XXV, 6). If a man is to bear himself humbly before a king of flesh and blood, how much more before God. They teach, 'Be strong as a leopard, swift as an eagle, to do the will of thy Father, who is in heaven,' in order to instruct you that there should be no pride before God. Elijah taught, 'If a man exalts the glory of God, and diminishes his own glory, God's glory will be exalted and his own too, but if he diminishes God's glory, and exalts his own, then God's glory remains what it was, but the man's glory is diminished.' (*Num.R.*, Bemidbar, IV, 20 *init.*)

[1359] R. Phinehas b. Jair said: The Torah leads to watchfulness, watchfulness to strictness, strictness to sinlessness, sinlessness to self-control, self-control to purity, purity to piety, piety to humility, humility to sinfearing, sinfearing to holiness, holiness to the Holy Spirit, and this last to the resurrection of the dead. Some say piety, and some say humility, is the greatest virtue of all (cp. [1377], [1390] and note to [120]). (*Ab.Zar.* 20*b*.)

[The translation given above follows the interpretation of Rashi, *in loc.*, but there is an alternative rendering, 'cleanliness leads to separation which leads to levitical purity'. The words are, indeed, capable of such a sense, but that adopted seems the more natural.

For *perishûth*, parting, abstinence, self-control, cp. [688] above. (H. L.)]

[1360] R. Abba ben Yudan said: All that God has declared to be unclean in animals He has pronounced desirable [*kasher*] in men. In animals He has declared 'blind or broken or maimed or having a wen' to be unserviceable (Lev. XXII, 22), but in men He has declared the broken and crushed heart to be desirable. R. Alexandri said: If a private person uses broken vessels, it is a disgrace to him, but God uses broken vessels, as it is said, 'The Lord is nigh to the broken-hearted' (Ps. XXXIV, 18).

(*Lev.R.*, Ẓaw, VII, 2.)

[1361] Do not abandon the belief in retribution. When a man sees that his doings prosper, let him not say, 'Because of my virtue and merit, God has given me food and drink in this world, and the capital is stored up for me in the world to come.' Rather let him say, 'Perhaps only one virtue was found in me, and God has given me prosperity in this world, so that He may cause me to be ruined in the world to come.'

(*Ab.R.N.* (vers. I), IX, 21*b*.)

If it is right to be humble, if it is right to feel that, so far as one's duty to the divine Master is concerned, one has never fully come up to the mark, how far should one be confident and cocksure of one's lot in the world to come? Assume that a man believes with the utmost assurance and simplicity that there are to be 'rewards' and 'punishments' after death, assume further that they who receive 'rewards' are roughly called 'righteous', and that they who receive 'punishments' (whether these 'punishments' are to be short or long) are roughly called 'wicked', should decent, humble people be *sure* that they, after their death, will be in the class of the 'righteous', or may they not legitimately have some apprehension that they will be in the class of the wicked? The following passages show varying Rabbinic attitudes towards this question. The German Lutheran theologians (e.g. Rengstorf in *Theologisches Wörterbuch zum Neuen Testament*, p. 524, 1934) regard the first of the next three stories as a proof and example of the Rabbinic lack of *Heilsgewissheit*, assurance of salvation. Ordinary, unprejudiced people may, perhaps, rather regard it as an example of modesty. Why should a man be so certain as to the nature of his reception before the heavenly Judge? Some may prefer R. Johanan's attitude to that of R. Josiah, who seems rather too sure of his immediate place in Paradise [1363]. I think I remember that, together with R. Simeon b. Yoḥai (cp. *R.T.* pp. 271–4, 167), he has been regarded by the German Lutheran theologians as an outstanding example of Rabbinic self-righteousness. Perhaps the truth may be that the average Rabbi had both fear and confidence as regards what would befall him after death. I may quote here some sentences from Lord Rosebery's delightful essay on Dr Johnson: 'None the less did his extreme conscientiousness inspire him with an abnormal fear of death, much more than men of infinitely less virtue. "Death, my dear, is very dreadful," he wrote to his stepdaughter ten months before the end. But when he thought it was near, he displayed a high composure.... And when the shadow was finally on him, he was able to recognise that what was coming was divine, an angel, though formidable and obscure; and so he passed with serene composure beyond mankind' (*Miscellanies*, by Lord Rosebery, vol. I, p. 57). Moore says: 'There is no indication that pious Jews were afflicted with an inordinate preoccupation about their individual hereafter. The anxiety of a few pre-eminently godly men in the hour of death is recorded because exceptional; it was never cultivated as a mark of superior piety' (vol. II, p. 321).

[1362] When R. Johanan b. Zakkai was ill, his disciples went in to visit him. On beholding them, he began to weep. His disciples said to him, 'O lamp of Israel, right-hand pillar (I Kings VII, 21), mighty hammer, wherefore dost thou weep?' He replied to them, 'If I was being led into the presence of a human king, who to-day is here and to-morrow in the grave, whose anger, if he were wrathful against me, would not be eternal, whose imprisonment, if he imprisoned me, would not be everlasting, whose death sentence, if he condemned me to death, would not be for ever, and whom I could appease with words and bribe with money—even then I would weep; but now, when I am being led into the presence of the King of kings, the Holy One, blessed be He, who lives and endures for all eternity, whose anger, if He be wrathful against me, is eternal, whose imprisonment, if He imprisoned me, would be everlasting, whose sentence, if He condemned me to death, would be for ever, and whom I cannot appease with words or bribe with money—nay, more, when before me lie two ways, one towards the Garden of Eden and the other towards Gehinnom, and I know not towards which I am to be led—shall I not weep?' They said to him 'Our master, bless us!' He said to them, 'May it be His will that the fear of heaven be upon you [as great] as the fear of flesh and blood.' His disciples exclaimed, 'Only as great!' He replied, 'Would that it be [as great]; for know, that when a man intends to commit a transgression, he says, "I hope nobody will see me."' (*Ber.* 28*b*.)

The fears of R. Johanan b. Zakkai would not have seemed strange to any Christian, even the most pious, in the Middle Ages, and right up to the Reformation. Indeed, hell was a much greater dread to the average pious Christian than to the average pious Rabbinic Jew. The following passage is taken from an article by Dr Coulton on 'The Faith of St Thomas More' in the *Quarterly Review* of October 1935, pp. 332, 333:

'Not one man in a hundred—shall we say, not one in a thousand?—can now see heaven and hell as More saw them. St Thomas Aquinas, like almost every other Schoolman who ventured upon that ground, concluded that the happiness of the blessed in heaven would be heightened by the sight of the damned writhing below in everlasting torture (*Sum. Theol.* App. q, p. XCIV). Not, of course, that they rejoice in the torture as such—nobody conceived anything so devilish as that—but because it bears continuous witness to them of God's justice and at the same time of His mercy to them. St Bonaventura is even more severe; and his fellow-Franciscan, St Bernardino of Siena, writes how these "bellowings and cries" from hell "shall sing to Paradise with ineffable sweetness", a greater joy than "all the joys of this world melted into one" (*Quadragesimale*, Serm. XII and XIII). More himself, in his last months, thanks God for His mercy in providing hell (*English Works*, p. 1257). And this, though the Schoolmen describe infernal torments with a pitiless detail far beyond the parallel passage in Calvin's *Institutes*, which is ignorantly mis-described by writers who can never have looked at the actual text.

'It is commonly said that men did not so much believe these things, as believe that they believed them. Yet More himself emphasises the extent to which, in most men's minds, the fear of hell fire outweighed the hopes of celestial bliss (*English Works*, p. 1258). Even more significant are the words of his fellow-martyr Fisher, speaking of Henry VII's death-bed terrors:

"As touching his soul, in what agony suppose ye that he was, not for the dread of death only, but for the dread of the judgment of Almighty God; for albeit he might have great confidence, by the reason of his true conversion unto God, and by the sacraments of Christ's Church which he with full great devotion had received before, yet was not he without a dread. *Nemo novit an sit odio an amore dignus*: 'there is no man, be he never so perfect, unless he have it by revelation, that knoweth certainly whether he be in the state of grace or no'; for of another manner be the judgments of God than of men. And the holy abbot Hely said likewise. 'Three things' (said he) 'there be that I much dread; one is what time my soul shall depart out of my body, another is when I shall be presented before my Judge, the third is what sentence he shall give, whether with me or against me.' If these holy fathers which had forsaken this world, and had lived so virtuously were in this fear, no marvel though this great man which had so much worldly business, and daily occupied in the causes thereof, no marvel though he were in great fear" (Fisher's *English Works* (E.E.T.S. Extra Series, 1876, p. 277). Abbot Elias's words are in "Lives of the Fathers" (Migne, *Pat. Lat.* vol. LXXIII, col. 861).

'More, himself, in his *De Quatuor Novissimis*, reckons that not fourteen men in four thousand think on these things with deep earnest during their lifetime, until at the last "the fear of hell, the dread of the devil, and sorrow at our heart in sight of our sins, shall pass and exceed the deadly pains of our body" (*English Works*, pp. 73, 78).' Perhaps I need not have put in the qualifying words 'up to the Reformation'. I quote again from Dr Coulton: 'It was a commonplace of medieval theology, *and indeed of almost all theology until comparatively recent times*,[1] that the last moment of a man's life decided for him between an eternity of unimaginable bliss (with or without preliminary purgatorial suffering) and an eternity of unspeakable horror and torment. This was accepted as an axiom so indisputable that St Gregory the Great, and, after him, almost all the schoolmen, do not attempt to reconsider it, even when it is found to lead them by inexorable logic to the conclusion that the Blessed in heaven will find their bliss heightened by the contemplation of the sufferings of the Damned in hell; only indirectly, of course; only as a proof of God's justice and as a reminder of His mercy to themselves—but still, the fatal nexus is there; the full horrors of hell down below will be visible to the Blessed above, and will, for them, sensibly increase the bliss of heaven. Calvin has been mistakenly saddled with beliefs some of which he never held at all, while others are common to him and his medieval predecessors. Concerning this particular medieval tenet there can be no doubt; therefore nobody can realise those times without bearing it constantly in mind. Not only was it held that these unutterably solemn issues depended upon a man's last breath upon earth, but also that the main deciding factor was theological. Nothing, at that supreme moment, would contribute so directly to the upward or the downward turn of the balance as a man's dying faith and his fortification by the rites of the Church. It was a natural complement to this, that even the most moderate and cautious of medieval theologians—even St Thomas Aquinas, for instance—took it for granted that many more men would be damned than saved.' (*Scottish Abbeys and Social Life*, 1933, pp. 5, 6.)

Here is a different view:

[1363] When R. Johanan was about to be taken from the world, he said to those who had to attend to him, 'Bury me in grey clothes which are neither black nor white: so that if I arise and stand among the righteous, I shall not be ashamed, and if I stand among the wicked, I shall not be confounded.' When R. Josiah was about to be taken from the world, he said to his attendant, 'Call my disciples.' He said to them, 'Bury me in white garments, for I am not ashamed of my deeds, and I am fit to meet the countenance of my Creator.' (*Gen.R.*, Wayeḥi, XCVI, 5.)

There follows the story of R. Johanan in a different form:

[1364] R. Johanan in his last instructions said, 'Do not clothe me in white garments or in black, but in purple garments: if I am summoned with the righteous, the wicked will not know me; and if I am summoned with the wicked, the righteous will not know

[1] Italics mine.

me.' R. Josiah ordered and said, 'Clothe me in white garments and flowing': they said to him, 'Thy master ordered those, and thou orderest *these*': he said, 'Why should I be ashamed of my deeds?' R. Jeremiah said, 'Clothe me in white, flowing garments, and put on my socks, and lay my staff in my hand, and my sandals on my feet, and so set me on my way, so that when summoned, I may be ready.' (*Gen.R.*, Wayeḥi, C, 2 (Th. p. 1285).)

[The word rendered 'flowing' properly means 'bordered' or 'folded': the commentary *Mattenot Kehunnah* states that such robes were worn by travellers. Josiah therefore meant 'prepare me for a journey'. (H. L.)]

We find stories like the following, illustrative of the Rabbinic conception of 'Goodness'. They are indicative rather of naïve simplicity than of self-conscious conceit:

[1365] When R. Adda bar Aḥwah wished for rain to fall, he would take off one of his boots [as a sign that he was getting ready to go barefoot and fast]; if he took both boots off, a flood came upon the land. Where he lived, there was a house in danger of falling, and he placed one of his disciples near by until the house was clear of goods. When the disciple went away from the house, it collapsed. Some say that it was Adda himself who stood close to the house. The Rabbis sent to ask him: 'What good deeds have you done?' He said, 'No man entered the synagogue before me, and none remained there when I left. I never walked four cubits without thinking about Torah; I never made mention of Torah in an unclean place. I never spread my bed in order to have a fixed sleep. I have never strutted among my fellow-scholars, or given one of them a nickname, or rejoiced when one stumbled. No curse of any one of them ever came upon my bed [i.e. he would before nightfall forgive any one of them who did him a wrong]. I never walked by the side of my debtor [so as not to make him feel uncomfortable]. I never got into a passion in my house, so as to fulfil the words of the Psalmist, "I walk within my house with a perfect heart"' (Ps. CI, 2). (*T.J.Ta'an.* III, § 13, 67*a*, line 48 (cp. [1397]).)

There is a certain pride of class which occasionally breaks through, though sometimes it takes a pleasant form:

[1366] A teacher should hold his pupil as dear as he holds himself. The honour of a fellow-student should be as precious to a man as the honour of his master. And the honour of his master should be as precious to a man as the fear of heaven.

(*Mek.*[2], *Amalek*, Beshallaḥ, § 1, p. 178; *Mek.*[3], vol. II, p. 140.)

[1367] Jose, the son of Joezer, of Ẓeredah said, 'Let thy house be a meeting house for the wise; sit amidst the dust of their feet, and drink their words with thirst' (*Aboth* I, 4), for when sages and their disciples enter a man's house, it is blessed through their merit. So Jacob brought blessing to Laban through his merit, Joseph to Potiphar, and the Ark, through its merit, to the House of Obed-Edom. Now this is a case of *a fortiori*. If the Ark, which contained only the two tables of stone, and no more, could bring blessing into a house, how much more can living sages and their disciples do so through their merit!

(*Ab.R.N.* (vers. II), XI, 14*a*.)

[1368] 'He who associates with the wise becomes wise' (Prov. XIII, 20). It is like a man who goes into a scent shop, even if he does not buy anything, the sweet smell clings to his clothes, and does not depart all day. But 'the companion of fools shall be destroyed' (*ib.*): if a man goes into a tannery, even if he buys nothing, he and his clothes are dirtied, and the bad smell does not leave him all day. [For the metaphors cp. [1224] and p. 484 and 1 Cor. XV, 33, 'evil communications,' etc.]

(*Ab.R.N.* (vers. II), XI, 14*b*.)

[1369] The Rabbis said, 'If you see a scholar who has committed a sin to-day, do not disparage him for it to-morrow, for he may have repented of it in the night,' as it is said, 'Love covers all sins' (Prov. X, 12), and love means Torah...so you see that whoever talks [evil] about the shortcomings of scholars is as though he talked [evil] about the Shechinah.

(*Tan.d.b.El.* p. 16.)

[1370] God said, 'I swear by my holy throne that if even a little child at school busies himself with Torah for my name's sake, his reward is stored up before me, so long as he keeps himself from sin. And if a man have nothing more than decent behaviour [*derek ereẓ*], and the knowledge of Scripture, his reward is present before me, so long as he keeps himself from sin. And even if a man knows no Scripture and no Mishnah, but yet attends early and late at Synagogue and House of Study, reciting the *Shema* and praying the statutory Prayer for the sake of my great name, his reward is present before me, so long as he keeps himself from sin.' (*Tan.d.b.El.* p. 13.)

The Rabbis practised humility towards one another, and they held that it should be shown to all regularly constituted authorities (cp. [1372–3]). The next story is rather touching. The fixing of the New Year and of the Day of Atonement depended on the recorded observations of the new moon. R. Gamaliel accepted the evidence of certain men which R. Joshua did not accept. Hence R. Joshua considered that the Day of Atonement in a certain year fell on a given day, while R. Gamaliel held that it fell rather later. But R. Gamaliel was the president of the supreme Rabbinical Court, and, as such, superior to R. Joshua, so:

[1371] R. Gamaliel sent to R. Joshua, and said, 'I charge thee that thou come to me with thy staff and thy money on the Day of Atonement as it falls according to thy reckoning.' [That he was ordered to come with staff and money was a hard condition, for to carry a 'burden', and money not least, would be a sore sin on the Day of Atonement. R. Joshua consults with R. Akiba and R. Dosa b. Harkinas who counsel submission, so:] R. Joshua took his staff and his money in his hand, and went to Jabneh to R. Gamaliel on the day which fell according to his [R. Joshua's] reckoning on the Day of Atonement. R. Gamaliel stood up and kissed him on the head, and said to him, 'Come in peace, my master and my disciple!—my master in wisdom, and my disciple in that thou hast accepted my words.' (*R.H.* II, 9.)

From a certain Pentateuchal verse which R. Dosa quoted, the Gemara draws this conclusion:

[1372] Even the smallest of the small, if he is once appointed as head of a congregation, is to be regarded as equal to the greatest of the great. (*R.H.* 25*b*.)

And in respect of R. Gamaliel's utterance to R. Joshua, the Gemara says:

[1373] Happy the generation where the great listen to the small, for then it follows obviously that in such a generation the small will listen to the great. (*R.H.* 25*b*.)

[1374] No table from which a scholar is not fed, is blessed. (*Tan.d.b.El.* p. 91.)

The Rabbinic conception of the ideal scholar or Rabbi has many attractive points. Its limitation would seem to be precisely where Jesus broke away from the current ideal: he consorted with 'sinners' and people of questionable characters, whose observance of the ceremonial law was dubious. The Rabbis kept close to the adage that 'evil communications corrupt good manners'.[1] They feared lest, touching pitch, they might be defiled. Again, the ideal which Jesus set before his disciples was clearly to give a great deal of time to *seeking* out erring sheep and attempting to reclaim them: the ideal of the Rabbis was to give the largest possible amount of time to 'study'. The disciple of Jesus was, I should imagine, to study very little, if at all: he would seldom enter the *Beth ha-Midrash*: the disciple of the Rabbis would spend a large part of his days within its walls. He would be charitable, and as we have heard, he would regard it as a regular part of his duty to fill the office of judge. He would also have to take part in various communal affairs, more especially in the administration of the communal charities and of the relief of the poor. He would also have to interrupt his studies to attend funerals and to attend weddings. But his most beloved, most essential, duty would ever be the teaching and the 'study' of the Torah, using the word in its widest sense to include biblical exegesis, legal discussions, haggadic sermons, the written and the oral Law. In his behaviour the ideal scholar must be humble, retiring, and well-mannered. He must be scrupulously polite, ready to receive an abusive word without returning it, very good tempered, but cautious with whom he associates. He must be clean and tidy in his personal dress and habits, not given to much laughter or jesting, simple and peaceful. The little ethical treatise called *Derek Ereẓ Zuṭṭa*, from which I have made several quotations, is mainly a rather late compilation from earlier writings. But it clearly represents a sort of written precipitate of the Rabbinic ideal.

[For what it is worth, my personal opinion is that to contrast the pastoral activities of Jesus with those of the Rabbis, in this way, is hazardous and subjective. I consider that the stories of Jesus's work are touching and exemplary, but I am not conscious of any contrast or 'limitation' in this regard. First, I do not think that the phrase 'observance of the ceremonial law' is altogether accurate. The word 'ceremonial' is tendentious. It implies that Hillel would have shunned a man who had committed some ritual peccadillo, but would have consorted with one guilty of mortal sin, while Jesus would have sought the latter out, endeavoured to reclaim him, but would have overlooked the former. The validity of such a distinction seems to me to be open to doubt.

Secondly, there is a difference between social intercourse and social service. People do not invite notorious evil-livers to their dinner table and introduce them to the family. Queen Victoria was censured for

[1] Cp. [1368].

excluding from Court even the innocent party to divorce. But such rigidity is not necessarily due to narrowness of outlook: it may well be founded upon a sense of decency and an abhorrence of evil. The dining-room is not the proper place for sermons: conversation, not conversion, is appropriate between the soup and the savoury. Conversely, a slum parson would be held reprehensible who neglected his duties and who confined his visits to the 'comfortable' members of his flock. Have we any evidence to justify either generalisation—or impression—that Jesus condoned sin or that the Rabbis abandoned the sinner? Is it not far more reasonable to suppose that each held similar ideals? This does not mean that every Rabbi was always true to these ideals. Nor does it imply approval of every single action of Jesus.

Thirdly, Jesus occupied no official position. He was free to come and go without question, where others might have been called upon for explanation. He had no regular duties, so that he could undertake any task that came to hand, without neglecting another. How many a clergyman to-day is faced with a conflict of duties, when the emergency impinges on the daily task, and when the reclaiming of an individual sinner, a task demanding great patience and time, has to yield to communal claims! Jesus had no responsibility: he was not constructive: he was not concerned with the organisation of society. To enunciate principles is not always easy: to apply them, both ethically and efficiently, is a far harder task. For example, his tenderness to the woman taken in adultery is an outstanding example to humanity. But is a judge who pronounces a divorce on a faithless wife thereby to be condemned? Is the sanctity of the marriage to be disregarded? The duty of the judge is to condemn the guilty: the duty of the prison chaplain is to comfort and reclaim them. *Suum cuique.*

Finally, Jesus was not concerned with scholarship at all. Here again, *suum cuique* applies. The spheres of a lay preacher and of a Regius Professor of Divinity differ widely: each has its legitimate purpose, and though these purposes are not essentially incompatible, it would need an exceptionally gifted man to fulfil both to perfection.

But, as I said, the question is one of impression, not of fact. (H. L.)]

[1375] [A man should be careful near whom he lives, with whom he dines, with whom he talks, with whom he signs contracts. So it is said:] 'A man [i.e. a gentleman] is known in three ways: by his behaviour as regards money, and drink, and by the control of his temper, and, some say, by his jokes.' ('*Erub.* 65*b init.*)

The three signs, given above, are cleverly alliterated, i.e. *be-kiso, be-koso, be-ka'aso*, as though we said 'a gentleman is known by his cups, by his cash, by his curses'.

[1376] A scholar is recognised by his conduct as regards money, and drinking; also by the control of his temper, by his dress, and, some say also, by his speech. Four things are unseemly for a scholar: to walk out at night, to smell of scent in the street, to be among the last to enter the synagogue, to dally much with the *Amme ha-Aretz*. Let the scholar be seemly and quiet in his eating, drinking, bathing, anointing, tying his shoes, his gait, his dress, his voice, and in his charitable deeds.

(*Der.Er.Z.* V, 2, 3; VI, 1; VII, 2.)

And we find:

[1377] The adornment of Torah is wisdom, the adornment of wisdom is humility, the adornment of humility is the fear of God, the adornment of the fear of God is [the execution of] the commandments, the adornment of the commandments is modesty [*ẓeni'ut*] (cp. [454], [1015], [1359] and [1390–1]).

(*Der.Er.Z.* V, 4.)

So too:

[1378] The scholar must be modest [*ẓanua'*] in his deeds, and must be recognised by his seemly ways. (*Der.Er.Z.* VII, 3.)

[1379] If a scholar has no good taste, an animal is better than he.

(*Tan.d.b.El.* p. 33.)

The word *de'ah*, literally knowledge, is used here to mean tact, good manners, good taste.

[1380] I call heaven and earth to witness that every scholar who eats of his own, and who enjoys the fruits of his own labour, and who is not supported by the community, belongs to the class who are called happy, as it says, 'If thou eat the fruit of thy hands, happy art thou' (Ps. CXXVIII, 2).

(*Tan.d.b.El.* p. 91 (cp. [379]).)

One must not act in a jarring or inapposite manner in respect of the company and the situation in which one is:

[1381] There are eight warnings: 'Let not a man be awake among those who sleep, or sleep among those who are awake, or weep among the joyful, or be joyful with those who weep. Let him not sit when others stand, or stand when others sit, or read Scripture when others are reading Mishnah, or Mishnah when others read the Scripture'—in fine, the principle is, 'Let not a man depart from the conduct or usages [*minhag*] of his environment.' (*Der.Er.Z.* V, 5.)

The Rabbis were well aware of false piety and of silly exaggerations:

[1382] R. Joshua said: A man of piety who is a fool, a crafty scoundrel, a woman who hypocritically does works of charity, and 'the wounds of the Pharisees', ruin the world. (*Soṭ.* III, 4.)

Moore translates: 'A fool saint, a subtle knave, a woman Pharisee, and the plagues of Pharisees ruin the world.' 'The Palestinian (or Jerusalem) Talmud finds "the plagues of Pharisees" in scholars (lawyers) who give counsel by which, apparently in strict form of law, the law may be circumvented. Nowhere is there any connivance at the pretences of such sham Pharisees, who brought an historically honourable name into disrepute. Nor were the religious teachers blind to the evils of exaggerated self-esteem, or self-righteousness, to which the most sincere were exposed' (vol. II, p. 194).

[1383] The Pharisee woman is she who sits down and quotes biblical phrases in a lascivious manner.
(*T.J.Soṭ.* III, § 4, f. 19*a*, line 28.)

[1384] Who is a man of piety that is a fool? He, for example, who, if a woman is drowning, says, 'It is unseemly for me to look at her, and therefore I cannot rescue her.' Who is the crafty scoundrel? R. Johanan said: He is the man who explains his case to the judge before his opponent appears. (*Soṭ.* 21*b*.)

[1385] Who is the pious fool? He who sees a child struggling in the water, and says, 'When I have taken off my phylacteries, I will go and save him,' and while he does so, the child breathes his last. Who is the crafty scoundrel? R. Huna says: He is the man who, lenient to himself, teaches others the hardest rules (cp. [1330]). (*T.J.Soṭ.* III, § 4, f. 19*a*, line 13.)

It is perhaps desirable to add here the saying about the seven classes of Pharisees of whom only one—he who acts from love—is the true Pharisee acceptable to God. I will first give Moore's summary: 'The motive of love and the motive of fear exemplified by Abraham and Job belong to the schools; the others show us the Pharisees as the people saw them. There is no malice in these characterisations nor in the enlargements in the Talmud; those who drew them evidently found the subjects ridiculous rather than obnoxious in the vanity of the "good works", done to be seen of men (Matt. XXIII, 5)' (vol. II, p. 194).

'The first four are designated by what were perhaps old nicknames at the enigmatic significance of which those who recorded them in the Talmuds could only guess, and did not guess alike. In the

Palestinian Talmud they are the "shoulder Pharisee", who packs his good works on his shoulder (to be seen of men); the "wait-a-bit" Pharisee, who (when someone has business with him) says, Wait a little; I must do a good work; the "reckoning" Pharisee, who when he commits a fault and does a good work crosses off one with the other; the "economising" Pharisee, who asks, What economy can I practise to spare a little to do a good work? the "show me my fault" Pharisee, who says, show me what sin I have committed, and I will do an equivalent good work (implying that he had no fault); the Pharisee of fear, like Job; the Pharisee of love, like Abraham. The last is the only kind that is dear (to God)' (vol. II, p. 193, from *T.J.Ber.* IX, § 7, f. 14*b*, line 48, *T.J.Soṭ.* V, § 7, f. 20*c*, line 49).

In the Babylonian Talmud the enumerations and explanations are somewhat different. One kind is the Pharisee who is so humble that he keeps shuffling or knocking his feet together and wounding them; another walks with his eyes half shut for fear he should see a woman, and so he strikes his head against a wall and makes it bleed (*Soṭ.* 22*b*).

I now give Mr Loewe's summary:

'There are seven classes of Pharisees: (1) The shoulder Pharisee (who carries his good deeds on his shoulder ostentatiously: or, according to another explanation, tries to rid himself of the commandments). (2) The wait-awhile Pharisee (who says, "Wait till I have done this good deed"). (3) The bruised Pharisee (who breaks his head against the wall to avoid looking at a woman). (4) The pestle Pharisee (whose head is bent in mock humility, like a pestle in a mortar). (5) The book-keeping Pharisee (who calculates virtue against vice; or who sins deliberately, and then attempts to compensate for his sin by some good deed). (6) The God-fearing Pharisee, who is like Job. (7) The God-loving Pharisee, who is like Abraham.

'Just as in the first century B.C. King Alexander Jannaeus warned his wife, not against the true Pharisees, but against the "dyed" Pharisees who were like hyenas or chameleons, doing the deeds of Zimri, but expecting the reward of Phineas, so, at the beginning of the second century A.D., Joshua ben Hananiah describes the eccentric Pharisees as "destroyers of the world" (*Soṭ.* III, 4).' (*Ẓebu'im* means both 'dyed' and 'hyenas'.)

Moore's remarks are very judicious: 'Men who make a show of more piety or virtue than they possess are not peculiar to any creed or age, and the higher the value set on religiousness the more they have flourished. The Pharisees had endeavoured by teaching and example to establish a higher standard of religion in Judaism, and had gained the reputation of being more religious than their Sadducean opponents or the ignorant and negligent mass of the people. That many men cared more for the reputation than for the reality, is only what human nature would lead us to expect; and that many sincere

Pharisees thought better of themselves in comparison with other men than is good for any man to think, and that their superior airs were often very disagreeable, may be taken for granted. But that the Pharisees as a whole were conscious and calculating hypocrites whose ostentatious piety was a cloak for deliberate secret villainy is unimaginable in view of the subsequent history of Judaism.[1] For it was men of the Pharisaean party who tided Judaism over the two great crises of the destruction of Jerusalem and the war under Hadrian, and in the three-quarters of a century following consolidated the labors of their predecessors and added their own to create the type of Judaism which it is the aim of this volume to record and interpret. Judaism is the monument of the Pharisees' (vol. II, pp. 192, 193).

[With regard to the preceding sayings, it will be remarked how true to life some of them are. They are easily intelligible to-day, since they deal with foibles to which human nature is ever prone. Others are difficult to understand because they are ephemeral: they relate to special conditions, and are strange in a new environment, where another social order prevails. (H. L.)]

[1] Hypocrisy cannot be more severely condemned than it was by R. Elazar (*Soṭ.* 41*b*–42*a* (cp. [1108])).

Chapter XXI

VARIOUS ETHICAL CONCEPTIONS

I propose to give here a few more passages, in no particular order, illustrative of the ethical conceptions of the Rabbis.

[1386] R. Elazar said: Let the honour of thy disciple be as dear to thee as thine own, and the honour of thine associate be like the fear of thy master, and the fear of thy master like the fear of Heaven. [And yet in the next saying we hear that the crown of a good name excels even the crown of Torah.] R. Simeon said: There are three crowns: the crown of Torah, the crown of priesthood, and the crown of kingdom; but the crown of a good name excels them all. (*Aboth* IV, 15–17 (cp. [346]).)

[1387] Whosoever has three qualities is of the disciples of Abraham, our father: a good eye, a humble mind, and a lowly spirit. (*Aboth* V, 22.)

[1388] Ben Zoma said: Who is wise? He who learns from all men, as it is said, 'From all my teachers I have gotten understanding' (Ps. CXIX, 99). Who is mighty? He who subdues his passions. Who is rich? He who rejoices in his portion. Who is honoured? He who honours others. (*Aboth* IV, 1.)

[1389] R. Levi said: Eye and heart are the two go-betweens [mediators] of sin. So God says, 'If thou give me thy heart and thine eyes, then I know that thou art mine' (Prov. XXIII, 26). (*T.J.Ber.* I, § 8, f. 3*c*, line 19.)

[1390] In the school of R. Anan, in quoting Cant. VII, 1, 'The roundings of thy thighs,' it was taught, 'Why are the words of the Law compared with the thigh? In order to teach you that as the thigh is hidden, so are the words of the Law hidden.' That is what R. Elazar said, for he quoted Mich. VI, 8, 'He has told thee, O man, etc.,' and he said: To do justly, that is, just judgment; to love mercy, that is, doing loving deeds; to walk humbly before God, that is, following the dead to the cemetery and accompanying the bride to the canopy. There is here an argument from less to greater: for if about things which are wont

to be done openly, the Law says, 'Walk humbly,' about things which are usually done unobtrusively, how very much more!
(*Suk.* 49*b*; *Mak.* 24*a* (cp. [1359] and [1377]).)

The famous verse in Micah (VI, 8) ends 'to walk humbly with thy God.' The Hebrew word is *haẓnea*ʿ, the Hiphil infinitive of the verb *ẓana*ʿ, 'to be humble, lowly'. The verb occurs only this once in the O.T. The adjective *ẓanua*ʿ, humble, lowly, occurs once, in Prov. XI, 2, 'with the lowly is wisdom.' The verb, the adjective and the substantive formed from the verb, occur repeatedly in Rabbinic literature, and acquired various shades of meaning. *Ẓeni*ʿ*ut* means chastity, seemliness, modesty, secretiveness (in a good sense), retiredness. In connection with a purely outward matter of cleanliness and seemliness, the remark is made:

[1391] God loves nothing better than modesty [*ẓeni*ʿ*ut*].
(*Pes.R.* 185*b* (cp. [1377–8]).)

[1392] R. Joshua b. Levi said: A man should never let an unseemly expression fall from his mouth, for Scripture makes a paraphrase of many letters to avoid an unseemly word [i.e. in Gen. VII, 8, where, instead of saying 'of unclean beasts', it says, 'of beasts that are not clean']. (*Pes.* 3*a*.)

[1393] R. Ḥanan b. Raba said: Everyone knows why a bride enters the bridal chamber. But if a man sullies his lips by speaking of it, then, even if seventy years' prosperity have been decreed for him, it is reversed. Rabbah b. Shela said, in the name of R. Ḥisda: If a man sullies his mouth with ribaldry, hell is deepened for him, for 'there is a deep pit *for* the mouth of strange [immoral] words' (Prov. XXII, 14). R. Naḥman b. Isaac added, Even if he hear and keep silence, for the verse continues, 'He that is abhorred of the Lord shall fall therein [for the application, see Rashi]....' Wounds and boils follow lasciviousness...dropsy is its mark. (*Sab.* 33*a* (cp. [1438]).)

[1394] Three God loves: him who does not get angry; him who does not get drunk; him who does not stand upon his rights. Three God hates: him who says one thing with his mouth, and thinks otherwise in his heart; one who could give evidence in another's favour, and does not do so; and one who, being alone, sees a bad deed of his neighbour, and gives unsupported evidence against him. (He should reprove, but not accuse, his neighbour.)
(*Pes.* 113*b*.)

[1395] It is written, 'If a man vow a vow, or swear an oath, unto the Lord' (Num. xxx, 2). God said to the Israelites, 'You must not think that you are permitted to swear by my name even truthfully. You are not permitted to swear by my name unless you have the character of one of those who truly feared God, Abraham, Joseph, and Job.'

(*Num.R.*, Maṭṭot, XXII, 1 (cp. [1092–8]).)

The following reasons are given why Jerusalem was destroyed:

[1396] (1) Because the Sabbath was profaned, (2) because the *Shema* was not said morning and evening, (3) because the children were kept back from school, (4) because there was no right shame, (5) because small and great thought themselves equal, (6) because men did not reprove one another, (7) because the Rabbis were despised, (8) because there were no trustworthy men within it (cp. [1299–1300], [1319], and [1458]).

(*Sab.* 119*b*.)

[The authorities for these statements, as given in the Wilna ed. and also in the Munich MS. cited by Goldschmidt, are, in order, Abbaye, Abbahu, Hamnuna, Ulla, Isaac, Simeon b. Abba in the name of Ḥanina, R. Judah (b. Ilai) and Raba. Rabbi Rabinowitz draws attention to the unlikelihood of Judah b. Ilai, the teacher of Judah the Prince, being cited among *Amoraim*. The Vienna ed. reads Rab Judah, i.e. Judah b. Ezekiel (220–299), which is probably correct. (H. L.)]

[1397] God wants the heart. (*San.* 106*b* (cp. [1365] end).)

[This simple sentence of three words has had great influence and had, already at an early date, passed into a popular proverb. It is derived ultimately from I Sam. XVI, 7. The three words of which it is composed should be noted, in view of a citation, given below, which they are made to cap: they are *Raḥmana libba ba'e*. *Raḥmana* may be rendered 'the All-Merciful': it is a term by which is meant not only God, but sometimes also the Torah, or possibly even the other Scriptures. In some versions, the initial word is, however, not *Raḥmana* but 'The Holy One, blessed be He.'

The quotation from *Sanhedrin* is even more striking when considered in its context, which discusses the worth of intellectual supremacy. Thus, Doeg and Ahitophel were said to have been able to ask four hundred questions relative to a swaying tower (the details need not concern us). Whereupon Raba remarked, 'Is, then, the asking of questions in itself such a great thing?' Note that Raba's pithy sentence consists also of three words: *Rebutha lemib'e ba'e*. The Talmud then proceeds to show how studies have developed and how learning has increased, not in the usual tone of a *laudator temporis acti*. Thus, in the days of R. Judah b. Ezekiel (220–99) studies did not reach beyond the sphere of Torts (*Neziḳin*), 'whereas', says Raba (i.e. Joseph bar Hama, 280–352), 'we have now advanced far beyond that. Yet such a saint was R. Judah that if a fast for rain was ordained, he had but to remove his shoes, and at once rain fell (cp. [1365]). But we pour out our supplications and fast in vain: the reason is that God requires the heart, *Raḥmana libba ba'e*' (i.e. learning alone does not avail). Compare these three words with Raba's previous sentence, to which they are clearly intended to be antithetical. If so, the original reading must have been 'The All-Merciful' (*Raḥmana*), as elsewhere, not 'The Holy One, blessed be He.'

In discussing the proper method of reciting the *Shema*, R. Me'ir held that intention was more important than audibility, although the Scripture uses the verb 'Hear, O Israel' (which word R. Elazar b. Azarya took literally and emphasised), for, said Me'ir, 'it is on the direction of the heart that the words depend' (*Ber.* 15*a*; *Meg.* 20*a*). A somewhat similar adage occurs in *T.R.H.* III, § 6 (Z. p. 212, line 4): 'Everything proceeds solely from the impulse (*kawwanat ha-Leb*) of the heart.' Cp. *Midr.Ps.* on CVIII, 1 (232*a*, § 1) and *Pes.R.* 198*b*: 'God wants, not sacrifices, but the impulse (*kawwanat ha-Leb*) of the heart.'

Our sentence is quoted in the Zohar as a well-known saying. Thus: 'R. Isaac chanced to be with R. Elazar and said to him, "Of a truth, the love a man has for God is aroused by the heart alone, and the All-Merciful desires the heart"...hence the Scripture says, "Thou shalt love the Lord thy God with all thy heart," and then, afterwards, "with all thy soul (i.e. intellect)."' (*Terumah*, on Exod. XXVI, 1, line 5 from foot of f. 162*b* in ed. Amsterdam, 1805.) Again (Ki Teẓe, ed. cit., f. 281*b*, line 2), 'And although we know that all is in His power, yet the All-Merciful desires the heart.' Again (Yitro, f. 93*b*, line 6), 'If a man have the opportunity of doing a good act and he does it, while attuning his heart, then worthy is he. If he do it without attuning his heart, then he is worthy in a less degree...for the Holy One, blessed be He, desires the heart.' (See also *Sefer Ḥasidim* (by Judah b. Samuel) (§ 590 ed. Zitomir, 1885, p. 144), *Cusari*, V, § 26 and Ibn Ezra on Exod. XXXI, 18.)

The influence of this saying may also be estimated by its use in the following extract from *The Duties of the Heart*, an ethical treatise, composed in Arabic by Bahya ben Joseph in 1040 and translated into Hebrew by Judah ibn Tibbon, under the title *Ḥobot ha-Lebabot* in the years 1161–80. It has been frequently rendered into other languages. English readers may refer to Edwin Collins' *Selections* (Wisdom of the East Series, John Murray) and to Dr Hertz's *Bachya, The Jewish Thomas à Kempis*. Bachya, in his preface, writes as follows:

'Since the obligation of the duties of the heart was made clear to me alike from the Torah and from the intellect, I searched the writings of our Rabbis and found that the obligation was developed by them more explicitly than in the Scriptures and by the intellect. Sometimes I found this expressed in general terms, e.g. "The All-Merciful desires the heart" or "The heart and the eyes are the two panders of sin." Or again, in more detail, in *Aboth*...' (Preface, p. 8 (top) in M. C. Stern's ed., Vienna, 1853: f. 5*a* in Amsterdam ed. 1738).

Finally it may be added that even at an early date there is evidence that the phrase was abused. Ibn Ezra, in his commentary on Eccles. v. 1, seizes the occasion to protest against interminable, ungrammatical and insincere liturgical poems (his attack on the *piyyuṭim* was answered by Heidenheim in his New Year and Atonement *P.B.*). It is significant that Ibn Ezra's antagonists are represented as saying: 'A man need not understand the meaning of his prayers, since God wants the heart.' Needless to say Ibn Ezra deals faithfully with this plea. (H. L.)]

[1398] Alexander of Macedon asked the Elders of the South, 'Who is a hero?' They said, 'He who controls his evil passion [*Yetzer ha-Ra*]' (cp. *Aboth* IV, 1; *P.B.* p. 195). He said, 'Who is rich?' They replied, 'He who is joyous in his lot.' He said to them, 'What shall a man do, that he may live?' They said, 'Let him kill his lust.' 'And what', he said, 'shall a man do that he may die?' They said, 'Let him keep his lust alive' [lit. not 'his lust' but 'himself'. The interpretation given in the commentary which replaces Rashi is trite, and Mr Loewe thinks that my paraphrase is correct.] Alexander said, 'What should a man do to be liked by his fellows?' They said, 'Let him hate kingship and rule.' He said, 'My thought is better than your thought. I say, Let him love kingship, and rule, and do good to mankind.' (*Tam.* 32*a* (cp. *J.E.* I, 342).)

[1399] R. Ḥiyya b. Ashi said in the name of Rab: The disciples of the wise have rest neither in this world nor in the world to come; as it is said, 'They go from strength to strength, every one of them appears before God in Zion.' (**Note 93**.) (*Ber.* 64*a*.)

[1400] 'The living know that they will die, but the dead know not anything' (Eccles. IX, 5). On a certain occasion R. Jonathan repeated this verse to R. Ḥiyya. 'My son,' said R. Ḥiyya, 'you know the Scriptures, but not their interpretation. "The living", these are the righteous, for even after their death they are called living; "the dead", these are the wicked, for even in their lifetime, they are called dead.' [Then follow the usual proof texts.] Then said R. Jonathan, 'Blessed be he who has taught me the interpretation,' and he kissed him.

(*Eccles.R.* IX, § 5, 1, on IX, 5 (23*a*).)

[This is an interesting example of the Pharisaic method of dealing with Sadducean doctrine contained in the canonical scripture. Here allegory is employed. Ecclesiastes was a Sadducean book, one of the last to be included in the canon. It owed its inclusion to its ascription to Solomon, to Akiba's advocacy, and to the epilogue which made the whole book orthodox. But the final sentence did not give *carte blanche* to all the contents. Instances where Solomon was blamed for his sentiments are not lacking: some have been quoted (see [559]). Here, however, the plain meaning of the text, which denies the future life, is turned by means of metaphor. It must, however, be stated that Dr Lukyn Williams, in his excellent commentary on Ecclesiastes, in the *Cambridge Bible Series*, dissents from the view that the book was Sadducean. (H. L.)]

[1401] Rabbi used to say: If thou hast done God's will as thy will, thou hast not done His will as His will. If thou hast done His will against thine own will, then only hast thou done His will as His will. Is it thy will that thou shouldst not die? Die [i.e. be ready to die, or die to the lower life], while yet thou diest not. Is it thy will that thou shouldst live? Live not, while yet thou livest. It is better for thee to die the death of this world, even against thy will, than to die the death of the world to come, where, if thou wilt, thou need not ever die. (For 'Rabbi' cp. [419].) (*Ab.R.N.* (vers. II), XXXII, 36*a*.)

['To die' is sometimes used in the metaphorical sense of yielding to one's passions and sometimes in the sense of conquering them. The latter is probably intended here. At other times, however, 'to die' is used literally, especially when the question of martyrdom is being considered. The general principle of the Rabbis was to make martyrdom the very last resort and to offer every possible alternative. For God gave His Laws that 'man should live by doing them' (Lev. XVIII, 5) and not die. At times, e.g. during the persecutions following the Bar Kokba war, it was necessary to check the zeal of those burning to die in testimony of their faith. Therefore the verse in Leviticus was made the authority for limiting martyrdom to the three cardinal sins of murder, idolatry and adultery (*T.B.Yoma* 85*b*; *T.B.San.* 74*a*). The element of publicity (*parrhesia*) was the deciding factor in the case of other acts. Again, to abandon the study of the Torah was sometimes regarded as tantamount to idolatry, and so reckoned as a sin to which martyrdom was to be preferred. But, generally, the efforts of the Rabbis had to be directed to restraining, rather than to encouraging, martyrdom. It is clear, therefore, that certain passages dealing with 'death' would be interpreted differently in different circumstances. For rules connected with martyrdom, cp. [665]. (H. L.)] **(Note 11 *n*.)**

[1402] When the Israelites came to Edom they said to the king, 'Let us go through thy land...we will not drink the waters of a well' (Num. xx, 17—the singular is used). The Torah teaches good manners. If a man travels in a strange country, and has all his provisions with him, he should, nevertheless, not eat and drink what he has brought with him, but he should put it aside, and buy his wants from the shopkeepers, in order to improve trade. And so Moses said to the King of Edom, 'The well is with us [referring to the legendary miraculous well which accompanied the Israelites], but we will not drink its waters; and the manna, which we have, we will not eat. Thou shalt not say that we are nothing but a trouble to thee, for thou wilt do business for thyself.' That is why Moses added, 'Food for money shalt thou sell us' (Deut. II, 28). (*Tanḥ.B.*, Ḥuḳḳat, 61*b*.)

[1403] If a man causes a community to do good, he will himself be saved by God from sin [lit. They do not give him the opportunity or power to sin], lest his disciples inherit the world [to come], while he goes to hell, as it says, 'Thou wilt not leave my soul in hell, neither wilt thou suffer thine holy one to see corruption' (Ps. XVI, 10), but, conversely, whosoever leads the community to sin will not have the opportunity or power to repent, lest his disciples go to hell while he inherits the world to come (Prov. XXVIII, 17).

(*T. Yoma* V, 10 (Z. p. 190 *fin.*).)

[N.B. See Jastrow's renderings of *Mezakkeh* on p. 399 of his dictionary. (H. L.)]

[1404] R. Simeon said: One who causes another to sin is worse than a murderer, for a murdered man can have a share in the world to come, but one made to sin is lost in both worlds. Two nations met Israel with the sword, the Egyptians (Exod. XV, 9) and the Edomites (Num. XX, 18), and two met them with sin, Moab and Ammon. With regard to Israel's open foes, it says, 'Thou shalt not detest an Egyptian or an Edomite' (Deut.

XXIII, 7), but with regard to those who sought to make Israel sin, it is said that they should never enter the congregation of the Lord (*ib.* 3). (*Tanḥ.B.*, Pineḥas, 76*a fin.* (cp. [1329]).)

[1405] Isaiah said, 'Sovereign of the Universe, what must a man do to be saved from the doom of hell?' God said to him, 'Let him give charity, dividing his bread to the poor, and giving his money to scribes and their students; let him not behave haughtily to his fellow-men; let him busy himself in the Torah and in its commandments; let him live in humility and not speak in pride of spirit. If he humbles himself before all creatures, then will I dwell with him, as it says, "I dwell with him that is of a humble spirit" (Isa. LVII, 15). I testify that he who has these qualities will inherit the future life; whoever has Torah, good deeds, humility, and fear of heaven, will be saved from doom.

(*Pes.R.* 198*a.*)

[1406] Moses said to Israel, 'Remove the evil inclination from your heart, and be united in one fear of God and in one counsel to minister before Him; as He is unique in the world, so let your service be unique before Him, as it says: "Circumcise your hearts."' (*Sifra* 43*d.*)

Unique service means wholly pure service.

['And Moses said *this* is the thing which the Lord has commanded that ye should do: and the glory of the Lord shall appear unto you' (Lev. IX, 6): this is the verse on which the passage in the *Sifra* ultimately depends. The emphasis on 'one' and the word 'unique' are not easy to understand. Malbim's commentary has the following remarks: 'The *Sifra* takes the word "this" homiletically. God commands each Israelite to perform the special, unique service of the High Priest. What the High Priest does within the Great Sanctuary, let them do in the Lesser Sanctuary, which is the human heart, the abiding place of the divine glory, for God says, "I will dwell in their midst." So, then, as they offered upon the altar the life and force of the sacrificial victims, so let each man offer the life and force of his lustful soul which prompts him to sin, his evil *Yetzer*, upon the lesser altar, and purge it with the fire of the love of God, and so let him make all his powers, and faculties one and unique in the service of the One and Unique God.' (H. L.)]

[1407] Afflictions are doubled for the man who rebels [kicks] against them. (*Tan.d.b.El.* p. 12.)

[1408] David said, 'My fear comes from my joy, and my joy comes from my fear, but my love rises higher than both.'

(*Tan.d.b.El.* p. 13.)

[1409] 'Sanctify yourselves, and be ye holy, for I am the Lord your God' (Lev. xx, 7). This means not only separation from idolatry, but also, as a consequence of this, the holiness of all the commandments [i.e. the holiness which comes from observing them]. 'I am the Lord your God.' That is: 'I am the Judge who punishes; I am He who is faithful to render a full reward.'

(*Sifra* 91 *d init.*)

[1410] Test your words before you utter them, and make your deeds conform to proper behaviour, and let your footsteps lead towards actions which bring merit. Acknowledge always the justice of God, and refrain from murmuring. (*Der.Er.Z.* III, 1.)

[1411] He who utters a curse is cursed [the curse returns to him].
(*Sifre Deut.*, Ki Teẓe, § 250, f. 120*a* (see Friedmann's note *in loc.*).)

[1412] One should not praise a man to his face. R. Elazar b. Azariah said: One should speak only a part of a man's praise to his face. So we find that God said *to* Noah, 'Thee only have I seen righteous before me in this generation,' but in a man's absence [one may praise him], as it is said: Noah was a righteous man and perfect in his generation. R. Elazar b. R. Jose the Galilean said: Even in speaking to *God* one should mention only a part of His praise, for it says, speak *unto* God that 'awful art thou in thy works', but *of* Him it says, 'Praise the Lord, for He is good, and His lovingkindness endures for ever.' [The proof texts are Gen. VI, 9; VII, 1; Ps. LXVI, 3; CXVIII, 1.]
(*Sifre Num.*, Beha'aloteka, § 102, f. 27*b* (H. pp. 100 *fin.*, 101).)

[1413] R. Johanan b. Zakkai said: On account of three sins the householders [i.e. the well-to-do citizens] were delivered over to the [Roman] Empire: because they practised usury, and exacted payment for bills already paid, and because they promised charity in public, but did not give it, and because they removed burdens [lit. the yoke] from themselves, and laid them, and also the taxes, upon the poor and needy.

(*Ab.R.N.* (vers. II), XXXI, 34*a*.)

[In similar lists four sins are mentioned. In *Suk.* 29*b* the authority is Rab. Cp. *T.Suk.* II, §5 (Z. p. 194, line 7); *Derek Ereẓ*, II. (H. L.)]

[1414] Let not a man say to himself, 'I have learned Torah and Mishnah to-day, to-morrow I need not learn; I have done good deeds to-day, to-morrow I need do none; I have given charity to-day, to-morrow I need not.' Let a man rather reflect and realise that after a while comes death. Let him lift his eyes heavenward, and say, 'Who created all these?' Now heaven and earth, sun and moon, stars and planets, early and late do the will of Him who created them. So, too, do you early and late study words of Torah, and ever do the will of your Creator, as it says, 'Let us continue to know the Lord' (Hos. VI, 3).

(*Tan.d.b.El.* p. 195.)

[1415] R. Isaac said: He who sins in secret is as if he drove away the feet of the Shechinah. (*Ḳid.* 31*a*.)

Chapter XXII

THE FAMILY: (*a*) FATHER AND MOTHER

I pass now to some extracts dealing with the family. And first as regards the honour of parents.

[1416] The Rabbis say: Three combine [in the making of] men: God and father and mother. If men honour their father and mother, God says, 'I reckon it to them as if I dwelt among them, and as if they honoured me.' (*Ḳid.* 30*b fin.*)

[1417] Let not a man say to himself: 'Seeing that my Father in heaven was the first cause of my life, therefore will I go and do the will of my Father in heaven, and leave the will of my father and mother.' Hence, 'Honour thy father and mother' Exod. xx, 12), and also, 'Honour the Lord from thy substance' (Prov. III, 9). And let not a man say, 'Seeing that my father was the primary cause of my life, I will do the will of my father, and neglect the will of my mother,' for it says, 'Ye shall fear your mother and father' (Lev. XIX, 3 (cp. [1418])), and 'Ye shall fear thy God' (Deut. VI, 13). If a man curses his parents or strikes or wounds them, God, if one might so say, folds His feet under the throne of glory, and says, 'I have made my honour equal to theirs [for the same word, honour, is used of all three], for all three of us are equal in respect of honour. Had I been beside that man, so would he have done to me. Rightly, then, have I done that I have not lived in the house of that man.' Whoever seeks many years and days and wealth and possessions and life in this world, and long life in the world to come which has no end, let him do the will of his Father in heaven and of his earthly father and mother. (*Tan.d.b.El.* p. 134.)

[1418] The Rabbis noticed that in Exod. xx, 12 the father is put before the mother; in Lev. XIX, 3 the mother is put before the father. So they say: It is known before God that a son [naturally] honours his mother more than his father, because she pets him; therefore God put the honour of father before that of mother; it is known to God that a son reverences his father more than his mother, because his father teaches him the Law; therefore God put the reverence of mother before that of father. (*Ḳid.* 31 *a*; *Mek.*², *Pisḥa*, Bo, § 1, p. 2; *Mek.*³, vol. 1, p. 3.)

[1419] Whenever R. Ṭarfon's mother wanted to get up on to her bed, he bent down, and she would step upon him. When he came to the House of Study and boasted of it, they said, 'You have not fulfilled half of the commandment to "honour". Has she thrown your purse into the sea before your eyes, and you did not put her to shame?' When R. Joseph heard the footsteps of his mother, he said, 'I rise up before the Shechinah which is approaching.' (*Ḳid.* 31 *b*.)

[1420] In what does reverence for a father consist? In not sitting in his presence, and in not speaking in his presence, and in not contradicting him. Of what does honour for parents consist? In providing for them food and drink, in clothing them, in giving them shoes for their feet, in helping them to enter or leave the house [or, possibly, to spend and to earn]. R. Eliezer said: Even if his father order him to throw a purse of gold into the sea, he should obey him. (*Ḳid.* 31 *b fin.*–32 *a*.)

[1421] R. Elazar b. Mattai said: If my father were to say to me, 'Give me some water to drink,' and I had at that moment a command [of the Law] to fulfil, then I should omit the honour due to a father, and fulfil the command....R. Isi b. Judah said: If the command can be executed by others, let it be done by others, and let the son fulfil the honour due to a father....The Halakah is as R. Isi said....Samuel said to R. Judah (who had corrected his father; the incident had been related just before the saying of R. Elazar): Speak not thus to thy father, for it is said, 'If a father makes a mistake in the words of the Law, let not the son say, "Father, you have made a mistake," but let him say, "Father, in the Law it is written thus."' But [it is replied] would not even such a reply pain the father? Rather let the son say, 'In the Law we find the following verse' (*R.T.* p. 250). (*Ḳid.* 32 *a*.)

[1422] R. Abbahu said, 'My son Abimi fulfilled the command, "Honour thy father and mother."' Abimi had five sons ordained as Rabbis in his father's lifetime, but whenever his father came and called out at his gate, Abimi would run to open the door, and called,

'Yes, yes, I am coming to you.' One day his father asked him for some water. When he brought it, his father had fallen asleep. He bent over him, and stood there till his father woke up. (*Ḳid.* 31 *b.*)

[1423] One day R. Ṭarfon's mother's sandals split and broke, and as she could not mend them, she had to walk across the court-yard barefoot. So R. Ṭarfon kept stretching his hands under her feet, so that she might walk over them all the way. One day he was ill, and the Rabbis came to visit him, and his mother said, 'Pray for my son Ṭarfon, for he honours me more than is my due.' 'What has he done to you?' they said. She told them what had happened. They replied, 'If he had done to you a thousand times more, he would not have done half of the honour enjoined in the Law.'

The mother of R. Ishmael came to complain about her son to the Rabbis, and she said, 'Rebuke my son, Ishmael, for he does not show me honour.' Then the faces of the Rabbis grew pale, and they said, 'Is it possible that R. Ishmael should not show honour to his mother? What has he done to you?' She said, 'When he goes to the House of Study, I want to wash his feet, and to drink the water wherewith I have washed them, and he will not permit it.' They said, 'Since that is her wish, honour her by permitting it.' R. Mena said, 'Well do the millers say, "Every man carries his virtues to his own tub" [i.e. methods of showing reverence vary]. R. Ṭarfon's mother spoke to you thus, and you answered her accordingly: R. Ishmael's mother spoke to us thus, and we answered her accordingly.' R. Ze'era had been grieved, and had said, 'Oh that I had father and mother, so that I could honour them and inherit Paradise.' But when he heard of these two stories he said, 'Blessed be God that I have no father and mother, for I could not have acted like R. Ṭarfon, or made myself do like R. Ishmael.' R. Abun said, 'I have been free of the command of honouring parents.' They said, 'How is that?' He said, 'Before I was born, my father died, and soon after I was born, my mother died.'

A man may feed his father on fattened chickens and inherit hell, and another may put his father to treading the mill, and inherit Paradise. In the first case, a son gave his father fattened chickens to eat, and the father said, 'My son, whence did you get these?' The son said, 'Old man, old man, eat and be silent; so the dogs eat and are silent.' He feeds his father on fatted chickens and inherits hell. The other man grinds in his mill; there comes an ordinance for millers to go and grind for the government. The son says, 'Father, come and grind here instead of me; if any ill-treatment should happen, better that it befall me and not you; if there should be scourgings, better that they come to me, and not to you.' Such a one makes his father grind the mill, and will inherit Paradise.

It is written, 'Ye shall reverence father and mother, Thou shalt reverence the Lord thy God.' Thus the Scripture puts the reverence of parents side by side with the reverence of God. And so it does as regards cursing God and cursing parents (Exod. XXI, 17 and Lev. XXIV, 15). And this is just, because all three are partners in man's creation. R. Simeon b. Yochai said: So great is the honour of father and mother that God has made it more important than His own honour. For it says, 'Honour thy father and mother,'[1] without qualification, but it says, 'Honour God with thy substance';[2] that is, by dedicating to Him gleaning, forgotten sheaves, corners of the field, tithes, dough, by making a booth, and a *lulab*, by *shofar* and phylacteries and fringes, by feeding the poor and giving drink to the thirsty. If you have the wherewithal, you are obliged to do all these things; but if not, then you are not obliged. But as regards the honour of father and mother, you must honour them whether you are rich or poor, even if you have to beg for them at the doors of other men's houses. (*T.J.Ḳid.* I, §7, f. 61*b*, line 18; *T.J.Pe'ah* I, § I, f. 15*c*–15*d*, line 35.)

[The remark of R. Abun and such passages as [1419–20], [1424] might create the impression that the Rabbis attached undue importance to money. But they were realists, and understood the mentality of their flock. To most human beings, money is a potent attraction, and a preacher can utilise this attraction for moral purposes, as R. Abun has done. (H. L.)]

It is noteworthy that the stock example of the highest reverence of parents, is taken not from a Jew, but from a heathen:

[1424] An Israelite who is zealous for the honour of parents—what is his reward? The honour of parents, our Rabbis tell us, is

[1] Exod. XX, 12. [2] Prov. III, 9.

one of those commands for the fulfilment of which a man receives the fruit in this world, while the stock [the capital] is reserved for him in the world to come. R. Abbahu said: His disciples asked R. Eliezer the Great, 'Wherein consists the honour of father and mother?' [i.e. how far does it extend?] He replied, 'Go and see what Dama b. Netina did. His mother was a foolish person, and she slapped him in the presence of his fellows, and all he said was, "Let that suffice thee, my mother."' Our Rabbis say that some of our wise men came to him to buy a precious stone in the place of one which had fallen out, and been lost, from the breastplate of the High Priest. He lived at Askelon, and they agreed with him to give a thousand gold pieces for the stone. He went in, and found his father asleep with his leg stretched out upon the box which contained the jewel: he would not disturb him, and came back without it. When the wise men perceived this, they thought that he wanted more money, and they offered ten thousand gold pieces. When his father woke up, he went in, and brought out the jewel. The wise men offered him the ten thousand pieces, but he replied: 'Far be it from me to make a profit from honouring my father; I will take only the thousand which we had agreed on.' And what reward did God give him? Our Rabbis say that in that very year his cow bore a red calf, which he sold for more than ten thousand gold pieces. [The translation at one place follows the text of the *T.J.Pe'ah* I, § I, f. 15*c*, line 15.]

(*Deut.R.*, Debarim, I, 15.)

[The 'red calf' is the 'Red Heifer', free from blemish, out of the ashes of which the waters of purification were prepared (Num. XIX, 1–22 and XXXI, 21–4). According to R. Me'ir (*Parah* III, 5) seven heifers in all were so prepared, one by Moses, one by Ezra and five by Ezra's successors: according to the rest of the Rabbis, seven were prepared after Ezra. In any case, the rite was very rarely performed. And in view of the difficulty of finding a perfectly red calf—even a wen was enough to disqualify an animal (*ib.* II, 2)—the price of a suitable beast was very high, and the owner could get anything that he asked. It will be noted that Dama ben Netina was a heathen, and the Mishnah (*ib.* II, 1) dissents from R. Eliezer's view that the heifer may not be bought from Gentiles.

Among the Samaritans, the rite of the heifer survived for long. Since it has fallen out of use, they consider themselves to be in a state of perpetual impurity, and they will not, in consequence, write scrolls of the Pentateuch. 'As the ashes of the red heifer were not used after the end of the fifteenth century, no Scroll of the Bible has been written on parchment since that date' (p. 104 of M. Gaster, *The Samaritans*, Schweich Lectures, 1926). Hence the striking rarity of Samaritan scrolls, contrasted with the ubiquity of those written by Jews. (H. L.)]

The Rabbis, I may add, had much reverence for old age, though sometimes age is interpreted to mean knowledge of the Torah:

[1425] He who welcomes an old man is as if he welcomed the Shechinah. (*Gen.R.*, Toledot, LXIII, 6 *fin.* (Th. p. 684).)

[1426] R. Judah said: Be careful [to honour] an old man who has forgotten his learning involuntarily [i.e. from old age], for both the second tables and the fragments [of the first tables] were placed in the Ark. (*Ber.* 8*b*; *Bab.B.* 14*b*.)

[1427] Resh Laḳish said: He who puts an old man to shame must give him [or must pay him] a fine in proportion to the special shame he has inflicted [because he is an old man]. A man once insulted R. Judah b. Ḥanina [who was old]. The fact was reported to Resh Laḳish who fined the man a pound weight of gold. (See **Note 14**.) (*T.J.Bab.Ḳ.* VIII, § 8, f. 6*c*, line 13.)

The Rabbis interpreted the ordinance in Leviticus (XIX, 32), 'Thou shalt rise up before the aged', very strictly, and, in accordance with their manner, they liked to discuss casuistically how often one must rise up if an old man passes and repasses before one; whether and how often one must interrupt one's studies to rise up, and many similar minutiae.

[The discussions of the Rabbis ranged far and wide. This instance is as much an exercise in logic as in manners or ethics; more especially the other examples of when to rise up and not to rise up which have not been quoted are such an exercise. (H. L.)]

[1428] R. Me'ir, when he saw even an old *Am ha-Aretz*, would rise up, for he said: It is not for nothing that he has prolonged his days. [Long life is a divine blessing: therefore the man, however ignorant, must have done some good deeds.] (*T.J.Bik.* III, § 3, f. 65*c*, line 62.)

[1429] It is written, 'Thou shalt rise up before the hoary head, and honour the face of the old man, and fear thy God: I am the Lord' (Lev. XIX, 32). One might think one must honour a *bad* old man. But by 'old man' is meant 'wise man', as it says,

'Gather to me seventy elders' (Num. XI, 16). R. Jose the Galilaean says: By old man is meant a man who has acquired wisdom....What is honouring? It means that one should not sit in the seat of the old man, or speak before he has spoken, or contradict him. 'Thou shalt rise up.' One might think that one might shut one's eyes when he passes, as if one had not seen him; this is a matter which is entrusted to the heart; that is why it says, 'Thou shalt fear thy God.' R. Simeon b. Elazar asked: How do we know that an old man must not make himself a nuisance? [By passing and repassing, so that people have constantly to get up.] Because it says, 'Old man' and 'Thou shalt fear thy God.' [The old man, too, must fear God!] R. Issi b. Judah said: Thou shalt rise up before the hoary head: this means that all old men are included [i.e. whether they are wise or not]. (*Ḳid.* 32*b* (cp. *Sifra* 91*a*).)

Chapter XXIII

THE FAMILY: (*b*) THE WIFE

When we come to the wife and her position, we enter controversial ground. No amount of modern Jewish apologetic, endlessly poured forth, can alter the fact that the Rabbinic attitude towards women was very different from our own. No amount of apologetics can get over the implications of the daily blessing, which orthodox Judaism has still lacked the courage to remove from its official prayer book. 'Blessed art thou, O Lord our God, who hast not made me a woman.' At the same time it must be readily admitted that the Rabbis seem to have loved their wives, that they all, apparently, had only one wife each, and that the position of the wife was one of much influence and importance. Here I cite flowers only; no weeds.

On the above see **Note 9** by H. L. I may say here that my words relate to the past. I say nothing of the present Rabbinic and orthodox-Jewish attitude to women.

[1430] R. Jacob said: He who has no wife lives without good, or help, or joy, or blessing, or atonement. R. Joshua of Sikhnin [Sogane], in the name of R. Levi, added that he is also without life. R. Ḥiyya b. Gammada said that he is not really a complete man, and some say that he diminishes the divine likeness. [The proof passages are quaint, but too long to quote.]

(*Gen.R.*, Bereshit, XVII, 2 (Th. pp. 151–2).)

[1431] Job said, 'I made a covenant with mine eyes that I would not look upon a maid' (XXXI, 1). R. Judah b. Bathyra said: Job was entitled to look upon an unmarried woman, since he could have married her himself, or given her as wife to one of his sons or relations, but he said, 'If it had been fitting for Adam to have been given ten wives, God would have given them to him, yet He gave him but one. So I, too, will be satisfied with one wife and my one portion' (cp. p. 313).

(*Ab.R.N.* (vers. II), II, 5*a*.)

[1432] R. Ḥanilai said: A man who has no wife lives without joy, blessing and good.... In the West they said, 'Without Torah and without [moral] protection': Raba b. Ulla said, 'And without peace.'... The Rabbis say: Of him who loves his wife as himself, and honours her more than himself, and brings up his sons and daughters rightly, and marries them early, the Scripture says, 'Thou knowest that thy tent is in peace' (Job v, 24). Of him who loves his neighbours, looks after his relations, marries the daughter of his sister [i.e. when destitute], and lends money to the poor in their distress, the Scripture says, 'Then shalt thou call, and the Lord will answer thee' (Isa. LVIII, 9). R. Elazar said: A man who has no wife, and owns no land, is no man. (For 'west' cp. [501].) (*Yeb.* 63*a*; *San.* 76*b*.)

[Two different cases are here considered. First is the married man, who 'loves his wife' and 'marries', i.e. gives in marriage, his children in their youth. Secondly, there is the bachelor, who himself 'marries' his niece. In all the actions which are here predicated of him, he is fulfilling Isa. LVIII, 7. By marrying his niece he is *not* 'hiding himself from his own flesh': the context in Isaiah shows that the niece is destitute. Hence his reward, Isa. LVIII, 9.

Rashi remarks, curiously, that the love of a man for his sister is stronger than for his brother, hence he will love his wife, her daughter, all the more. But, according to general Semitic custom, it was the paternal uncle who was the natural protector. In time of stress he stood by the widow. The tractate from which this extract is taken, *Yabmut*, deals with this institution, the Levirate marriage, i.e. the marriage of a childless widow to her husband's brother. This function of the paternal uncle, to be the natural protector, exists also among the Arabs. But we seem here to be concerned with an unmarried girl, not with a widow.

Marriage to a niece is illegal in English law, and is strongly deprecated in Rabbinic law—though it is valid. It is rare among Jews. (H. L.)]

[1433] Rab said: Be careful not to hurt your wife, because woman is prone to tears and sensitive to wrong [Rashi takes this differently]. R. Ḥelbo said: Be careful about the honour of your wife, for blessing enters the house only because of the wife. (*Bab.M.* 59*a*.)

[1434] 'All glorious is the king's daughter within' (Ps. XLV, 13). R. Jose says: When a woman keeps chastely within the house, she is fit to marry a High Priest and rear sons who shall be High Priests [for the word 'within' is emphasised]. On the same verse R. Phinehas bar Ḥama ha-Kohen says: This means, when she keeps chastely within the house. Just as the altar atones for the house, so does she atone for her house, as it says, 'Thy wife shall be like a fruitful vine within the sides of the house' (Ps. CXXVIII, 3). [The same word is used for 'sides' here as in the sacrificial regulations with regard to the altar.] Where shall she be as a fruitful vine? When she is within the sides of thy house. If she act thus, then will thy children be like olives (*ib.*); she will rear sons to be anointed with the olive oil of the High Priesthood. (*Tanḥ.*, Wayishlaḥ, § 36, f. 55*a.*)

[1435] There was once a pious man who was married to a pious woman, and they had no children. They said, 'We are no profit to God.' So they divorced one another. The man went and married a bad woman, and she made him bad; the woman went and married a bad man, and she made him good. So all depends upon the woman. (*Gen.R.*, Bereshit, XVII, 7 (Th. p. 158).)

[1436] R. Elazar said: If a man divorces his first wife, even the very altar sheds tears because of him. (*Giṭ.* 90*b.*)

[This passage at the end of *Giṭṭin* comes again in *San.* 22*a* (see below, [1443]), where other sayings about man and wife, some extremely touching, are to be found. The phrase 'First wife' seems, to some extent, to be due to the dialectic use of 'second' in Mal. II, 13, 'This second thing [A.V. 'This again'] have ye done...covering the altar of the Lord with tears...because the Lord has been witness between thee and the wife of thy youth.' But 'first' really means 'wife of thy youth', a phrase well known in the prophets; it is by no means antithetical to a rival wife or even to a second wife, married after the death of the first. The Commentators take it in this sense, 'i.e. the wife with whom thou hast grown up'. In *Sanhedrin* it also says that when a man's wife dies, the world grows dark for him: it is as though the Temple were destroyed in his days: his steps are shortened: his spine is bent. For all save this is compensation possible. A man dies only to his wife, and a wife only to her husband. More curiously expressed is this: 'The bond between man and wife is as strong as the sundering of the Red Sea.' Marriages were foreordained in heaven, before man and wife were born. In *Sanhedrin* this leads on to the thought that the loss of the first wife, i.e. the wife of one's youth, is specially grievous, as in *Giṭṭin.* (H. L.)]

[1437] If a woman is good, there is no limit to her goodness, if she is bad, there is no limit to her badness. Our Rabbis have said, He who is without a wife dwells without blessing, life, joy, help, good and peace. [The usual proof texts follow.] See how important [lit. heavy] a thing marriage is, for God has united His name with marriage, in the Law, in the Prophets, and in the Holy Writings. [Then follow the proof texts: Gen. XXIV, 50; Judges XIV, 4; Prov. XIX, 14.]

(*Midr.Ps.* on LIX, heading (151 *a*, § 2).)

[1438] 'Let my beloved come into his garden' (Cant. IV, 16). The Torah teaches gentle manners: the bridegroom should not enter the marriage-chamber until the bride gives him leave.

(*Pes.R.* 17 *b* (cp. [1393]).)

[1439] When the daughters of Zelophehad (Num. XXVII, 1–12) heard that the land was being divided among men to the exclusion of women, they assembled together to take counsel. They said: 'The compassion of God is not as the compassion of men. The compassion of men extends to men more than to women, but not thus is the compassion of God; His compassion extends equally to men and women and to all, even as it is said, "The Lord is good to all, and His mercies are over all his works"' (Ps. CXLV, 9).

(*Sifre Num.*, Pinehas, § 133, f. 49 *a* (H. p. 176; cp. [109]).)

[1440] The daughters of Zelophehad said to Moses: 'Give unto us a possession among the brethren of our father' (Num. XXVII, 4). R. Nathan said: The strength [of the faith] of the women was, therefore, finer than that of the men. For the men had said: 'Let us make a captain, and let us return into Egypt' (Num. XIV, 4). (*Sifre Num.*, Pinehas, § 133, f. 49 *b* (H. p. 177).)

The women, therefore, excelled the men in faith and trust in God, and in confidence of reaching and obtaining the land which God had promised unto Israel. Cp. Kuhn, p. 539, n. 46.

The general Rabbinic view about women, half-kindly, half-oriental, is aptly shown in the following. Women may be more assured and confident of salvation than men, but how do they acquire the 'merit' which assures them salvation? By being useful to their husbands and children:

[1441] Our Rabbis have taught: Greater is the assurance [Cohen, unliterally, 'promise'] given by the Holy One, blessed be He, to women than to men; as it is said, 'Rise up, ye women that are at ease, and hear my voice; ye confident daughters, give ear unto my speech' (Isa. XXXII, 9). Rab asked R. Ḥiyya: Wherewith do women acquire merit? By sending their children to learn (Torah) in the Synagogue, and their husbands to study in the schools of the Rabbis, and by waiting for their husbands until they return from the schools of the Rabbis. (*Ber.* 17*a*.)

The verse from Isaiah is here used in a friendly sense, not as in the original.

[1442] R. Aḥa said: If a man marries a godly wife, it is as though he had fulfilled the whole Torah from beginning to end. To him applies, 'Thy wife is like a fruitful vine' (Ps. CXXVIII, 3). Therefore the verses of the chapter of the virtuous wife in Proverbs (XXXI) are arranged in complete alphabetical sequence (and no letter is missing, as in other alphabets in the Bible) from *Alef* to *Tau*. It is solely for the merit of the righteous women in each generation that each generation is redeemed, as it is said, 'He remembers His lovingkindness and faithfulness by reason of [A.V. 'towards'] the house of Israel' (Ps. XCVIII, 3). It does not say 'by reason of the children of Israel', but 'by reason of the *house* of Israel'. ['House' is the regular Rabbinic equivalent of 'wife', not in the sense of domicile, but of home.] (*Ruth Zuṭa*, ed. Buber, IV, 11, p. 24*b*.)

[1443] R. Johanan said: If a man's first wife dies, it is as if the Temple were destroyed in his day. R. Alexandri said: If a man's wife dies, the world becomes dark for him. R. Samuel b. Naḥman said: For everything there is a substitute except for the wife of one's youth. (*San.* 22*a* (cp. [1436]).)

[1444] R. Idi said: There was a woman in Sidon, who lived ten years with her husband, and had borne no child. They went to R. Simeon b. Yoḥai, and asked to be divorced. He said to them, 'As your coming together was with a banquet, so let your separation be with a banquet.' They agreed, and made for themselves a holiday and a banquet, and she made her husband drink more than enough. When his mind returned to him, he said to her, 'My daughter, look out what is most precious to you in my house, and take it, and go to your father's house.' What did she do? When he had gone to sleep, she beckoned to her servants and handmaids, and said to them, 'Carry him on the mattress to my father's house.' In the middle of the night he woke up, and he said to her, 'Whither have I been brought?' She said, 'To the house of my father.' He said to her, 'What have I to do there?' She said, 'Did you not tell me last night to take what was most precious to me from your house, and to go with it to the house of my father? There is nothing in the world more precious to me than you.' They went back to R. Simeon b. Yoḥai, and he prayed for them, and they were given a child. Hence you may learn that as God 'visits' (Gen. XXI, 1) the barren woman, so the righteous 'visit' the barren woman. [The meaning apparently is that the influence of the prayer of the righteous Rabbi procured the child.] And, moreover, if this woman, who said to her husband that nothing was to her more precious than he, was blessed by God with a child, how much more will God bless the Israelites who hope day by day for God's salvation, and who say, 'We have nothing more precious in the world than thee: "We will be glad and rejoice in thee"' (Cant. I, 4). (*Cant.R.* I, § 1, 2, on I, 4; f. 8*a*.)

'Hide not thyself from thine own flesh' (Isa. LVII, 7). To appreciate the two stories which follow, one must understand that if a man divorced his wife, it was regarded as suspicious if he had anything more to do with her. The stories illustrate what I regard as the weak point in Rabbinic ethics, namely, the comparative frequency with which even respectable men divorced their wives, and at the same time they illustrate the tender heart of the Rabbis towards those in suffering or in want:

[1445] R. Jacob in the name of R. Elazar said: 'Thine own flesh' means here, 'thy divorced wife'. R. Jose, the Galilean, had a bad wife who despised him in the presence of his disciples. They said to him, 'Divorce her.' One day R. Jose and R. Elazar b. Azarya were sitting and expounding the Law. When they had finished, the disciples said to R. Jose, 'Let the master pay heed to us, and now we will go to your house.' He said to them, 'Yes.' When they got there, his wife lowered her face [in shame] and went out. He looked into the pot upon the stove, and called to her and said, 'Is there anything in the pot?' She said, 'There are bread crumbs and vegetables in it.' He went and opened the lid, and found in it chickens. So R. Elazar b. Azarya knew that she did not behave well to her husband. When they sat down to eat, R. Jose said to her, 'Did you not say that there were vegetables in the pot, and we have found chickens in it?' She said, 'It is a miracle.' When they had eaten, R. Elazar said, 'Divorce your wife: she does not act to your honour.'

He said, 'Her dowry is too great for me: I cannot divorce her.' They said to him, 'We will provide the dowry, and then do you divorce her.' They did so. They provided the dowry, and he divorced her, and they made him marry another wife, who was better than the former one. For her sins the divorced woman married a senator of the town, whom, after a time, sufferings befell, and he became blind, and his wife led him about in all the town [to beg], and she went into every quarter, but into the quarter of R. Jose she did not go. But her husband knew the town, and said, 'Why do you not bring me into the quarter of R. Jose, for I have heard that he is charitable.' She said, 'I am his divorced wife, and I cannot look upon his face.' After a time they came near the quarter of R. Jose, and her husband began to beat her, and their voices were heard far and wide, so that they made themselves contemptible in the whole town. Then R. Jose noticed it, and he saw that she was brought to shame in the street, and he took them, and gave them dwelling in one of his houses, and he provided for them all the days of their lives. (*Lev.R.*, Behar, XXXIV, 14.)

In *T.J.Keth.* XI, § 3, f. 34*b*, line 61, this story ends thus: 'Nevertheless, sounds were heard in the night, and they heard her say, "The pain I suffered in my body was better than the pain I now suffer within me".'

[1446] In the days of R. Tanḥuma the Israelites needed rain. They came to him, and said, 'Rabbi, decree a fast, that rain may fall.' He decreed a fast, and a second one, but no rain fell. Then at the third fast he preached to them and said, 'Let every one do some special good deed.' Then a man arose, and took all that he had in his house, and went out to distribute it. His divorced wife met him and said to him, 'Be charitable to me, for from the day I left your house I have seen no good.' When he saw her naked and distressed, he was filled with pity for her, and he gave to her, because it says, 'Hide not thyself from thine own flesh.' A man saw him, and went to R. Tanḥuma and said, 'You are here, and a sin is there.' He said, 'What have you seen?' He replied, 'I have seen someone conversing with his divorced wife, and not only that, but he gave her money. If his conduct towards her were not suspicious, he would not have given her money.' Then R. Tanḥuma sent for the man, and caused him to come to him, and he said, 'My son, the world is in distress, and the creatures are in distress, and you went and conversed with your divorced wife, and not only that, but you gave her money; and if your conduct towards her were not suspicious, you would not have given her money.' The man replied, 'Have you not preached, "Hide not thyself from thine own flesh"? And did you not say that we were all to do a special good deed? I went out to do as you bade us, and my divorced wife met me and said, "Be charitable towards me, for from the day I left your house I have seen no good." Then since I saw her naked and in great distress, I was filled with pity for her, and I gave her money by virtue of the command, "Hide not thyself from thine own flesh."' Then R. Tanḥuma raised his face heavenwards and said, 'Lord of the world, if this man who is flesh and blood and hard, and who had no call to support this woman, was yet filled with pity for her, and gave to her, how much more is it fitting that thou shouldst sustain us and have pity upon us, who are the children of thy children, the descendants of Abraham, Isaac and Jacob.' Then the rain fell, and the world was refreshed. (*Lev.R.*, Behar, XXXIV, 14.)

Although divorce was not infrequent, there was a high level of chastity, and lewdness was abhorred:

[1447] It is written, 'The eye of the adulterer' (Job XXIV, 15). Resh Laḳish said: The eye: lest you should think, only he who sins with his body is an adulterer: he who sins with his eye is also an adulterer. (*Lev.R.*, Aḥare Mot, XXIII, 12 (cp. [748] and [1453]).)

The Tenth Commandment is commonly interpreted to mean the coveting, or the lusting over, the wife of the neighbour. The connection in which it occurs (too long to be quoted here) shows that this is the case in the following brief utterance:

[1448] R. Yaḳum said: Whoever transgresses, 'Thou shalt not covet,' is as though he has transgressed all the Ten Words.

(*Pes.R.* 107*a*.)

[1449] We find that to every sin God is long-suffering, except to the sin of unchastity. R. Azariah said: All things can God overlook save lewdness.

(*Lev.R.*, Aḥare Mot, XXIII, 9; *Tanḥ.*, Bereshit, §12, f. 13*a*.)

[1450] R. Me'asha, son of R. Joshua b. Levi, said: He who sees something lascivious, and does not feast his eyes upon it, is worthy to receive the face of the Shechinah, as it says (Isa. XXXIII, 15), 'He shuts his eyes from seeing evil.' (*Pes.R.* 125*a*.)

[1451] If you are handsome, do not go astray after lewdness, but honour your Creator, and fear Him, and praise Him with the beauty which He has given you. (*Pes.R.* 127*a*.)

In the law in Deut. XXIII, 12–14 the words '*ervat dabar* mean 'unclean thing'. The Rabbis, taking 'unclean' to mean definitely 'unchaste', say:

[1452] The verse teaches that any unchastity causes the Shechinah to depart. (*Sifre Deut.*, Ki Teẓe, § 258, f. 121*a init.*)

[1453] When husband and wife meet each other in holiness, God gives them righteous children. [This means that the mentality of the offspring can be affected by that of their parents.] We find that Hannah acted thus, when she said, 'For this child have I prayed, and God granted my prayer' (I Sam. I, 27). Because Samuel was begotten and conceived in holiness, he was as saintly as Moses, for it says, 'Moses and Aaron among His priests, and Samuel among them that call upon His name' (Ps. XCIX, 6). (*Tanḥ.B.*, Naso, f. 16*a*, par. 13 (cp. [748] and [1447]).)

[1454] The Ten Commandments correspond to the ten 'sayings' with which God created the world (*Aboth* V, 1; *P.B.* p. 199).... So 'Thou shalt not covet' corresponds with 'And God said, "It is not good for man to be alone"' (Gen. II, 18). For God said: 'I have created for thee thy partner; let each of you cleave to his partner, and not covet his neighbour's wife.' (*Pes.R.* 108*a*, *b*.)

Chapter XXIV

THE FAMILY: (*c*) CHILDREN

Pleasant and characteristic are many sayings about children. Religious education is praised.

[1455] 'They that are planted in the house of the Lord' (Ps. XCII, 13). R. Ḥanan b. Pazzi said: While they are yet saplings, they are in the house of the Lord; these are the little children who are in school. (*Num.R.*, Bemidbar, III, 1 *ad fin.*)

Exod. XXV, 34 describes the golden candlestick in the Sanctuary. The Midrash gives to each part a homiletic interpretation:

[1456] Its flowers: these are the children who learn in school. (*Pes.R.* 29*b.*)

[1457] R. Judah said in the name of Rab: Verily R. Joshua b. Gamla should be remembered for good, for had it not been for him the Torah would have been forgotten in Israel. For at first, the boy who had a father was taught Torah by him, while the boy who had no father did not learn. Later, they appointed teachers of boys in Jerusalem, and the boys who had fathers were brought by them [to the teachers] and were taught; those who had no fathers were still not brought. So then they ordered that teachers should be appointed in every district, and they brought to them lads of the age of sixteen or seventeen. And when a teacher was cross with any of the lads, the lad would kick at him and run away. So then R. Joshua b. Gamla ordered that teachers should be appointed in every district and in every city and that the boys should be sent to them at the age of six or seven years.... Raba said: The number of boys for one teacher should be twenty-five. If there are fifty boys, they appoint two; if there are forty, they appoint an assistant, who is supported by the funds of the town. Raba said: If, of two teachers, one man teaches better than the other, they do not dismiss the less good one, lest the other become slack. R. Dimi said: No, he would teach all the better, for the rivalry of teachers increases wisdom. Raba said: If, of two teachers, one knows more, but is not exact, and one knows less, but is exact, appoint the one who knows more and is less accurate, for this fault goes of itself. R. Dimi said: Appoint the one who is more accurate, for a fault once entered [into the mind] remains there.[1]

(*Bab.B.* 21*a*.)

One of the many reasons given why Jerusalem was destroyed is:

[1458] R. Hamnuna said: Jerusalem was destroyed only because the children did not attend school, and loitered in the streets.

(*T.B.Sab.* 119*b* (cf. Moore, III, p. 104; cp. [1396]).)

[1459] R. Abba b. Kahana said: No philosophers have arisen among the nations to equal Balaam and Abnimos, the weaver.[2] They said to them, 'Can we attack this people?' They replied, 'Go to their house of assembly. If the children are chirping there with their voices, you will not be able to destroy this people, but, if not, then you will, for their fathers made them rely upon this saying: "The voice is that of Jacob; the hands are those of Esau." When the voice of Jacob is heard in their houses of assembly and of study, then the hands of Esau are powerless; but when no voice chirps there, then the hands of Esau can act' (Gen. XXVII, 22). (*Lam.R.*, Introduction, 2.)

[1460] Yuda[3] Nesiah (cp. [419]) sent R. Ḥiyya, R. Assi and R. Ammi to traverse the cities in the land of Israel in order to appoint Bible and Mishnah teachers. They came to a city, and they found no teacher of Bible or Mishnah. They said, 'Bring to us the guardians of the city.' So they brought to them the senators of the town. They said, 'Are these the guardians of the town? They are the destroyers of the town.' 'Who then', they said, 'are the guardians of the town?' They said, 'The teachers of Bible and Mishnah,' as it is said, 'Unless the Lord guard the city, the watchman wakes but in vain' (Ps. CXXVII, 1).

(*T.J.Ḥag.* I, § 7, f. 76*c*, line 30 (cp. [374]).)

[1461] 'He has set the world in their heart' (Eccles. III, 11). R. Jonathan interpreted the words to refer to the love of children which God has put in men's hearts. Like a king who had two sons; the elder honoured him; the younger was corrupt, and yet he loved the younger more than the elder.

(*Eccles.R.* III, § 11, 3, on III, 11 (10*b* foot).)

[1] See **Note 55**. [2] See **Note 45**. [3] Here, Yuda.

[1462] R. Judah said: See how beloved the little children are before God. When the Sanhedrin went into captivity, the Shechinah went not with them; the watchers of the priests went into captivity; the Shechinah went not with them. But when the little children went into captivity, the Shechinah went with them. For it says in Lamentations, I, 5, 'Her children are gone into captivity,' and immediately after (I, 6), 'From Zion her splendour is departed.' [The 'splendour' is interpreted to be God.]

(*Lam.R.* I, 33, on I, 6.)

[1463] 'Eat thy bread with joy' (Eccles. IX, 7). R. Huna b. Aḥa said: When children leave school, a heavenly voice calls out, 'Eat thy bread with joy'; the breath of your lips is received before me as a sweet savour. And when the Israelites leave their Synagogues and Houses of Study, a heavenly voice declares, 'Eat your bread with joy'; your prayers have been heard before me as a sweet savour. (*Eccles.R.* IX, § 7, I, on IX, 7 (23*b* top).)

[1464] R. Huna said: Because twice daily, once in the morning and once in the evening, the children in the Synagogue say, 'Save us, O Lord our God' (Ps. CVI, 47), therefore God also says twice daily, 'O that the time would approach when I could cause your redemption to draw nigh' (cp. Ps. XIV, 7; LIII, 6).

(*Pes.R.* 174*a*.)

[R. Huna's remark depends on two sets of doublets. The verse said by the children is from Ps. CVI, 47, which is very much like I Chron. XVI, 35: that by God is Ps. XIV, 7, which is almost the same as LIII, 6. Huna's saying is therefore of the 'measure for measure' type.

But the reference to the children must be made clear. The custom mentioned by Huna still survives in the Sephardic rite: it is the first privilege which a child has. From the age of five or even four years, he ascends the reading desk at an early stage of the Morning Service (see Gaster, I, 17) and when the Reader concludes Ps. CIII, the child sings the *ha-Shem Melekh*, i.e. the versicle 'The Lord is King: the Lord has reigned: the Lord will reign for ever more': the congregation responds, and then the procedure is repeated. After this the Reader (not the child as in our passage) continues, 'The Lord shall be King over all the earth, in that day shall the Lord be One and His Name One. Save us, O Lord our God, etc.'

This verse is repeated again, after the daily psalm (Gaster, I, 55). In the Evening Service the verse 'O that the time would approach' (Ps. XIV, 7) comes at the beginning (p. 67) and, sometimes, at the end

(p. 75 foot, in rubric), though now only the first three verses on p. 67 are repeated.

It will be seen that though some details have changed, the rite has survived. It is the first introduction of the child to taking an active part in the Service, and it is greatly appreciated. From this the child advances, at the age of six or seven, to reading the *Hafṭarah* or lesson from the prophets. (H. L.)]

[1465] 'My son, if thou art surety for thy friend, if thou hast stricken thy hand with a stranger' (Prov. VI, 1). When God was about to give the Torah to Israel, He asked them, 'Will you accept my Torah?' and they answered, 'We will.' God said, 'Give me surety that you will fulfil its ordinances.' They said, 'Let Abraham, Isaac and Jacob be our pledges.' God answered, 'But the Patriarchs themselves need sureties. Did not Abraham show lack of faith (Gen. XV, 8; cp. [1524]); Isaac, a love for my foe Esau (Mal. I, 3), Jacob, a want of belief in my protection' (Isa. XL, 27)? [Then Israel said, 'Let the prophets be our sureties.' But 'the prophets have sinned against me' (Jer. II, 8, not cited exactly).] Then Israel said, 'Our children shall be our sureties.' [God said, 'Such pledges will I indeed accept.' Straightway the Israelites brought their wives with their children, even infants at the breast, even babes yet unborn. And God gave power of speech even to those yet in the womb. He said to them, 'I am about to give the Torah to your parents, will you pledge yourselves that they will fulfil it?' They said, 'We pledge ourselves.' Then God rehearsed command after command, and to each in succession the children promised obedience. How do we know that it was on the sucklings and babes yet unborn that the Torah was based?] As it says, 'Out of the mouths of babes and sucklings has strength been based' (Ps. VIII, 2), for the 'strength' which God gives His people is Torah (Ps. XXIX, 1). So it is that when Israel neglects the Torah, God demands the penalty from the sureties, as it is said, 'Thou didst forget the Torah of thy God, I, also I, will forget thy children' (Hos. IV, 7). Why 'also I'? God says, 'Also I am grieved for them, the children [to whom the parents have not taught Torah], who say daily, "Blessed be the Lord, who is to be blessed for evermore."' (**Note 46.**)

(*Tanḥ.*, Wayiggash, § 2, f. 67*b*; additions in square brackets from *Midrash 'Asereth ha-Dibroth*, ed. Warsaw, 1924, pp. 10–19.)

[1466] 'Touch not mine anointed, and do my prophets no harm' (I Chron. XVI, 22). The former are schoolchildren; the latter, Rabbis. The world, said Resh Laḳish in the name of R. Judah Nesiah, stands only upon the breath of the schoolchildren. R. Papa said to Abbai, 'How about your breath and mine?' Abbai replied, 'The breath of them that are sinful cannot be compared with the breath of them that are not sinful.' Resh Laḳish in the name of R. Judah Nesiah said: Let not the children be kept back from school, even to help in building of the Temple. (*Sab.* 119*b*.)

For the title Nesiah see [419].

[1467] As soon as a child is free from his mother's care, he is old enough to be under the obligation of dwelling in the Tabernacle, on the Feast of Tabernacles. If he knows how to wave the palm-branch, he must wave one. If he understands the commandments of fringes and phylacteries and can put them on, it is his father's duty to provide him with them. As soon as he can speak, his father teaches him the *Shema*, Torah and the sacred tongue; otherwise, it were better he had not come into the world. (*T.Ḥag.* I, 2 (Z. p. 232, line 2).)

Similarly, when a little girl becomes adolescent, all the commandments of the Torah are incumbent on her except those which have to be fulfilled at a specified time. See p. 656.

[1468] Children are not obliged to fast on the Day of Atonement, but they should be trained a year or two before they are of age, so that they may become versed in the Commandments. (*Yoma* VIII, 4 (cp. *T.Yoma* IV, 2; Z. p. 189, line 18).) [The difficulty in the Tosefta is explained by Weiss, *Dor.* I, 162: see parallel in *Yoma* 77*b*. (H. L.)]

Boys were 'of age' at thirteen and girls at twelve. Then fasting was compulsory. A year or two before coming of age, the plan was that they should have rather less to eat than usual on the fast day.

[1469] 'Like gardens by the river's side' (Num. XXIV, 6). These are the teachers of little children in Israel, who bring forth from their hearts wisdom, understanding and discernment, and teach them to do the will of their Father who is in heaven. [For a somewhat similar use of this text cp. [499].] (*Tan.d.b.El.* p. 116.)

[1470] R. Issachar said of a child who says Masha for Moses, Ahran for Aaron, and for Ephron, Aphron, that God says, 'Even his stammering I love' [a pun on Cant. II, 4. 'His banner (*diglo*) over me is love'; for *diglo* the Midrash reads *dillugo*; cp. [491]]. R. Hunya said: Formerly, if a man pointed to the statue of the king with his finger, he was punished, but now a man puts his finger over and over again upon the sacred Name, and he is not punished, and even more, for God says, 'His very thumb [*godlo*] I love' [*godlo* for *diglo*, another pun]. The Rabbis say: A child may jump over the holy Name of God again and again, and he is not punished; yea, even more, for God says, 'His very jumping I love' [*dillugo* for *diglo*]. (*Cant.R.* II, § 4, I, on II, 4; f. 15*a*; *Num.R.*, Bemidbar, II, 3.)

[1471] Once R. Ḥiyya b. Abba met R. Joshua b. Levi with a cloth thrown over his head, and taking a boy to school; he said to him, 'What does this mean?' He quoted the verses in Deut. IV, 9, 10, and said, 'It is no small thing that after the words, "Thou shalt teach them to thy sons, and thy sons' sons", follow immediately the words, "The day that thou stoodest before the Lord thy God in Horeb."' Henceforward R. Ḥiyya ate no breakfast till he had taught a boy a piece of scripture, repeating with him what he had learnt the day before, and teaching him a new bit. R. Huna ate no breakfast till he had taken a boy to school. (*Ḳid.* 30*a*.)

[1472] There was once a man who made a will saying that his son should inherit nothing of his till he became a fool. R. Jose b. Judah and Rabbi Judah the Prince went to R. Joshua b. Ḳarḥa to ask about this matter. They saw him outside his house, and noticed that he was crawling on his hands and feet with a reed in his mouth, and following after his son. When they saw him, they hid themselves, and then they went to him, and asked him about the will. He laughed and said, 'The matter about which you ask has happened to me! Hence you see that when a man lives to have children, he acts like a fool.'
(*Midr.Ps.* on XCII, 14 (206*b*, § 13).)

[In conclusion the following passages relating to children may be added. It has already been noted that children's reading lessons began with the book of Leviticus (cp. p. 647 foot). We further note that they had lessons on Friday night. Thus, the Tosefta (*T.Sab.* I, § 12 (Z. p. 110, line 22)) deprecates reading by the light of the Sabbath lamp on Friday night, presumably lest the reader should forget and tend the lamp. Yet the Sabbath Day is specially suitable for study. But the Tosefta cites Simeon ben Gamaliel's authority for children to study their 'portions', i.e. the lectionary of the morrow, on Friday night, by the light of the Sabbath lamp, and arrangements may be made on Sabbath with teachers to teach children: marriage-plans for daughters may be discussed (*Sab.* 150*a*).

On the eve of the Day of Atonement, children leave school early, so as to have a proper meal: Akiba used to suspend his classes for this purpose. Children nearing adolescence begin to fast a little more, year by year. A curious story is related of Shammai the Elder, that he wished to feed his son only with one hand, but they decreed that he must feed him with both (*T.Yom ha-Kip.* V, §2 (Z. p. 189, line 20): a parallel to the Shammai story in *Yoma* 77*b*). Weiss (*Dor.* I, 162) takes the passage to mean that Shammai, until overruled, would not feed his son on the Day of Atonement at all (see Weiss' note, *in loc.*). The Gemara gives a different reason. Children, on Passover Eve, were given nuts and parched corn by Akiba, so that they should keep awake and ask questions (*Pes.* 109*a*) and R. Judah thought that this was better for them than the wine (*ib.*). These same dainties were sometimes given as presents to visiting children, by their hosts (*T.Beẓ.* IV, §10 (Z. p. 208, line 12)). We read there that little boys and little girls were taken on visits of joy or condolence in sorrow, and to dinner parties. But a guest should not give of his portion to his host's children (*ib.*) without asking the host's permission because of a terrible calamity that once ensued after such thoughtlessness: the story is told in *Ḥull.* 94*a* (cp. [1261]).

An interesting description of children's rights and duties to their parents is given in *T.Ḥag.* I, §§2 ff. (Z. p. 232): the special case of girls is considered (*ib.* §3, line 12). See also *T.Ḳid.* I, §10 (Z. p. 336, line 2).

Israel, singing a song of praise to God at the Red Sea, is compared to a school-child (*T.Soṭ.* VI, §2 (Z. p. 303, line 16)).

The games of children are mentioned, thus we read of their playing with tame cattle (*T.Bab.Ḳ.* II, §2 (Z. p. 347, line 30)). (H. L.)]

Chapter XXV

ASCETICISM

No doubt the children grew up under strict guidance. Yet, as we have seen, there must have been much joy in the Rabbinic households. The Rabbis rarely despaired of this life, however intensely they believed in another. Asceticism, except in so far as it was useful for the study of the Law, was not favoured. The following extract represents the Rabbinic point of view. Joy, but disciplined joy, is the ideal. Note, however, the delicate ending of the quotation:

[1473] 'For a holy people art thou' (Deut. XIV, 2). Sanctify thyself even in that which is permitted to thee: things allowed to thee, but forbidden to others, do not regard as permissible in their presence. (*Sifre Deut.*, Re'eh, § 104, f. 95*a* (H. p. 163).)

[The Hebrew term which, probably, comes nearest to 'asceticism' is *siggûf*: we have had the verb previously [1072], where it is stated that a workman, who, by undue asceticism, becomes inefficient, robs his employer. For an interesting example of the term, see *Eccles.R.* on III, 18, f. 12*a*. The biblical verse is very difficult—and probably corrupt—and the meaning of the Midrashic adaptation is also, in parts, difficult and uncertain: the following is a possible rendering:

'I said in my heart concerning the estate of the sons of men' (Eccles. III, 18): this refers to the manner in which the righteous conduct themselves in this world, in asceticism, in afflictions and in sufferings. Why do they act thus? 'That God might manifest to them' (*ib.*) the measure of their righteousness 'and that they might see that they themselves are beasts' (*ib.*), i.e. to see and to show forth to the Gentiles that they follow God as a beast follows the shepherd (Ezek. XXXIV, 31). (H. L.)] (Cp. [1486].)

R. Isaac's like R. Joshua's [1477], advice is interesting:

[1474] R. Isaac said: Are not the things prohibited in the Law enough for you that you want to prohibit yourself other things? A vow of abstinence is like an iron collar, such as is worn by prisoners, about a man's neck: one who imposes on himself such a vow is like a man who meets a detachment of soldiers with such a collar, and puts his own head into it. Or he is like a man who drives a sword into his body.

(*T.J.Ned.* IX, § 1, f. 41*b*, line 62.)

[1475] 'On the Day of Atonement, ye shall afflict your souls' (Lev. XVI, 31). You might think that a man should sit in the sun or in the cold, so as to feel pain. No, for it only says, 'No manner of work shall ye do.'...And it says, 'He afflicted thee with hunger' (Deut. VIII, 3). So the affliction of your souls in Leviticus is only an affliction of hunger. (*Sifra* 82 *d*...83 *a*.)

The meaning is that extra supererogatory asceticisms are not desirable.

R. Elazar Ha-Ḳappar uses the wording of the Law in Num. VI, 11, to say:

[1476] If the Nazarite, because he afflicted himself in abstaining from wine, needed atonement, how much more does he need atonement who gives himself pain by abstaining generally [from pleasant and legitimate enjoyments] (see Kuhn's note, and *S.B.* III, 403; IV, 94).

(*Sifre Num.*, Naso, § 30, f. 10*a* (H. p. 36).)

[1477] When the Temple was destroyed, the number of the abstemious in Israel was increased who would neither eat flesh nor drink wine. R. Joshua went to them and asked them why they did so. They said, 'How can we eat flesh, seeing that flesh was offered upon the altar, and how can we drink wine, seeing that wine was used in libations upon the altar, and all has now ceased?' Then he said, 'In that case we should not eat bread, for the meal offerings have now ceased.' They said, 'Well, perhaps we can live on fruit.' He said, 'Then we should eat no fruit, for the offering of the firstfruits has ceased.' They said, 'Perhaps we can manage on fruits, of which the firstfruits were not offered.' He said, 'Then we should drink no water, for water was used in the libations.' Then they were silent. He said to them, 'Not to mourn at all is impossible for us, seeing that the decree has been decreed; but to mourn overmuch is also not possible for us, for a decree is not imposed upon the community which the majority of the community is unable to endure.' R. Ishmael b. Elisha said the same, and he added: From the time that the Roman Government has power over us, and imposes hard decrees upon us, and seeks to cause the Law and Commandments to cease, and to prevent the circumcision of our sons, we ought, perhaps, to ordain that no one should marry and beget children; but then the descendants of Abraham would come to an end; therefore we must allow Israel to marry, for it is better that the Israelite should sin unwittingly than wittingly. (*Bab.B.* 60*b* (cp. [688]).)

The decree mentioned here is one imposed by the rabbinical court. The phrase is a common one, i.e. that too heavy a burden must not be imposed.

Sometimes a mournful tendency is observed:

[1478] Mar b. Rabina made a marriage-feast for his son when he observed that the Rabbis who were present were very merry. So he seized a *Moḳra'* goblet [Rashi; a goblet of fine crystal: *Tosafot*, 'hence the custom of breaking the glass at weddings'], worth four hundred *zuzim* [approximately, shillings], and broke it in their presence and made them sombre. Rab Ashi acted similarly in like circumstances. At Mar's [own] wedding, the Rabbis asked Hamnuna the Small to sing to them. He replied [presumably in song], 'Woe to us, for we die, woe to us, for we die.' They said, 'How shall we sing [lit. say] in response to thee?' He said to them, 'Where is the Torah and where the *Mitzvah* that shall protect us?' In the name of R. Simeon b. Yoḥai, R. Johanan said: A man should not fill his mouth with laughter in this world because it says, '*Then* shall our mouth be filled with laughter' (Ps. CXXVI, 2). When will this be? When, as the verse continues, 'they say among the nations: great things has the Lord done with these.' They tell of R. Simeon b. Laḳish that after hearing this explanation from his teacher, R. Johanan, he never more filled his mouth with laughter. (*Ber.* 30*b* foot.)

As regards wine, one could make quotations both ways. As one who leans towards teetotalism, I give the following:

[1479] R. Isaac said, quoting Prov. XXIII, 31: Wine makes the faces of the wicked red in this world, but pale in the world to come. R. Me'ir said: The tree of which Adam ate was a vine, for it is wine that brings lamentation to man. (*San.* 70*a*, 70*b*.)

[1480] The wine and sleep of the wicked are a benefit to them and a benefit to the world; but the wine and sleep of the righteous are a misfortune for them and for the world. (*San.* VIII, 5.)

Wine induces sleep:

[1481] He who, in order to guard against sin, abstains from wine, is worthy to receive all the blessings contained in the Priestly Benediction. (*Num.R.*, Naso, XI, 1.)

[The point of this saying is that priests might not drink wine before serving at the altar, as is stated in the next extract. The death of Nadab and Abihu, in the biblical account (Lev. X, 1–7), is not directly connected with any sin committed by them. But as the narrative immediately proceeds to forbid an officiating priest, under pain of death, to drink wine, it is assumed that Aaron's two sons perished for this reason. The chief relic of sacerdotal functions in the Synagogue is the pronouncing of the Priestly Benediction (Singer, p. 238*a*). Among the *Sefardim*, or Jews of the Spanish and Portuguese rite, this Benediction is recited in the Morning Service, before which one should not breakfast. But among Jews who follow the Ashkenazic rite, the recital takes place at the Additional Service, as indicated in Singer's rubric. The Additional Service (*Musaf*) now follows immediately on the Morning Service, though in some Congregations the original interval survives. In that case, people would have breakfasted before the Additional Service, and have recited the *Ḳiddush* over the wine (Singer, p. 174, foot), and have drunk wine at Grace after meals (*ib.* pp. 287–8): this applies also to the priest. Hence he should not stand up to bless the people. Therefore, on the Feast of the Rejoicing of the Law, when it may be assumed that most people will have drunk wine, the Benediction is omitted. Line 1 of Singer's rubric is, therefore, incorrect, but this extra page was inserted in the later editions, published after Mr Singer's death.

In this saying, the meaning is that just as the priest abstains from wine, so is it desirable for the worshipper, the recipient of the Benediction, also to do. (H. L.)]

[1482] Wherever there is wine there is unchastity.... It is written, 'It is not for kings to drink wine, lest they forget the Law, and pervert the judgment of the afflicted' (Prov. XXXI, 4, 5). Drink wine, and you will condemn the innocent and acquit the guilty. Hence, it has been said, 'A judge who has drunk a quart of wine must not sit in judgment, and a wise man who has drunk a quart of wine must not teach. Give strong drink to him that is about to die, and wine to those who are troubled in heart' (Prov. XXXI, 6). R. Ḥanan said: Wine was created in this world only to reward the wicked in this world, for they are lost for the world to come. 'Wine to the troubled.' Hence they have told us that all who were condemned to death by the Court in Jerusalem were given strong wine that their consciousness might become confused, and that the word might be fulfilled, 'Give strong drink to him that is about to die....' [The Midrash then contrasts two verses, in both of which 'strength' occurs: in the former it is associated with Torah; in the latter, with wine. The former is] 'Happy art thou, O land, when thy king is free [A.V. 'son of nobles'], and thy princes eat in due season, for strength, and not for drunkenness' (Eccles. x, 17). [Free, son of freedom, son of nobles, is here connected with Torah, on the basis of *Aboth* vi, 2, *P.B.* p. 205, cited above [378]. The second verse is] 'Woe unto them that are strong to drink wine,' says Isaiah (v, 11). The strength of the Law is 'Happy', the strength of wine is 'Woe'....When wine comes in, knowledge goes out. Where there is wine, there is no knowledge. When wine comes in, a secret goes out....[The point of this remark is that the numerical equivalent of 'wine', *yayin*, is 70; 'secret', *sod*, also amounts to 70. On the use of numerical equivalents, see *Judaism and Christianity*, ii, 12. (H. L.)]

[The Hebrew quart is a small measure, and so the Midrash says:] If a man has drunk one quart of wine, a quarter of his intelligence is gone, has he drunk three, three-quarters of his intelligence are gone, and his mind is confused, and he begins to say unseemly things. If he drinks a fourth quart, all his intelligence goes, his mind is confused, his tongue is broken, he seeks to speak and cannot; his tongue is tied. Therefore they say, 'A priest who has drunk one quart is disqualified for the service of the altar, and an Israelite who has drunk one quart is disqualified from judging,' so as to teach you that nothing good comes from wine. [The Midrash is not always so unfavourable to wine, but it recognises its dangers.]

(*Num.R.*, Naso, x, 4, 8.)

[1483] When Noah was about to plant the vine, Satan came and stood before him and asked what he was planting. Noah said, 'A vineyard.' Satan said, 'What is its nature?' He replied, 'Its fruits are ever sweet, whether moist or dry, and from them one makes wine that "rejoices the heart of mortals"' (Ps. civ, 15). Satan then said, 'Come and let us collaborate, the two of us, in this vineyard.' Noah said to him, 'Very good.' So Satan brought successively a lamb, a lion, a pig and an ape, which he slaughtered, and with their blood he fertilised the vineyard. This is a sign that before a man drinks wine, he is ignorant as a sheep, that has no knowledge at all, or as a ewe, dumb before those that shear her. If a man drinks properly, he becomes strong as a lion, whom nothing in the world can withstand. When he drinks more than is proper, he becomes like a pig that wallows in mire, and when he becomes drunk, he dances like an ape, and utters folly before all, and knows not what he does. If all this happened to Noah, that man whom God singled out for praise as 'righteous in his generation' (Gen. VI, 9), how much more will it happen to ordinary folk [who drink to excess]! (*Tanḥ.*, Noaḥ, § 13, f. 21 *b*.)

[1484] If he who refrains from wine is called a sinner [because the Nazarite brings a sin offering], how much more is he a sinner who painfully refrains from everything. Hence, too, he who habitually fasts is called a sinner. (*Ned.* 10 *a*.)

[1485] Samuel said: He that fasts [for self-affliction] is called a sinner. R. Elazar ha-Ḳappar Berebi[1] said: Why is it said (Num. VI, 11), 'And make atonement for him, for that he sinned?' Against what soul did he sin? It can only mean that he denied himself the enjoyment of wine. Now, if a person who denies himself only the enjoyment of wine is called a sinner, all the more so one who denies himself all the enjoyments of life. Yet R. Elazar said: He that fasts is called holy, for it is said (Num. VI, 5), 'He shall be holy.' Now if this man [the Nazarite], who denied himself only the enjoyment of wine, is called holy, all the more so one who denies himself all the enjoyments of life. But did not R. Elazar also say: A man should always consider himself as if the Holy One were within him, because it is said (Hos. XI, 9), 'The Holy One in the midst of thee'? [The idea here is that on account of the presence of the divine within man, he should not be allowed to afflict himself.] This is no contradiction, for in one instance he has in mind one who can stand privations, in the other one who cannot.

(*Ta'an.* 11 *a fin.*–11 *b* (Malter, p. 77).)

[1486] R. Jose said: An individual is not allowed to afflict himself by fasting, for he might become dependent upon the public [by reason of incapacity for work] and find no mercy on their part. R. Judah said in the name of Rab: What is R. Jose's [scriptural]

[1] For an explanation of the title Berebi, see *J.E.* s.v.

reason? It is written (Gen. II, 7), 'And man became a living soul'; the Torah means to say, 'Keep alive the soul which I gave you.' (*Ta'an.* 22*b* (Malter, p. 164).)

For *siggef* (to afflict oneself) cp. [1072], [1238] and [1473].

[1487] R. Jeremiah b. Abba said in the name of Resh Laḳish: A scholar is not allowed to impose fasts upon himself, because it makes him lessen his heavenly work.

(*Ta'an.* 11*b* (Malter, p. 78).)

The 'heavenly work' is the study of the Law.

Let man then be thankful for what God or his neighbour has given him:

[1488] Ben Zoma said: How hard the first man, Adam, must have laboured before he could eat a bit of bread! He had to plough and sow and weed and hoe and reap and thresh, winnow and sift, grind, sift again, knead, moisten and bake, and only after all this eat his bread; whereas I get up in the morning and find the bread all ready for me. What toil Adam had till he could be clothed with the simplest raiment! He had to shear, bleach, beat the wool, dye it, spin it, weave it, wash it, and sew it together, and only after all this was he clothed; whereas I get up in the morning, and find all my clothes prepared for me. How many workmen get up early, and go late to rest! Whereas I get up in the morning, and find all things I need before me.

(*T.J.Ber.* IX, § 2, f. 13*c*, line 12 (*Ber.* 58*a*).)

Even the most commonplace things have their place in life, and therefore have a claim on man's esteem. He must recognise what he owes them:

[1489] Why were the water and the dust smitten by Aaron, as it is written, 'God said to Aaron, Take thy staff' (Exod. VIII, 5)? Because God said to Moses, 'The water which guarded thee when thou wast cast into the Nile, and the dust which protected thee when thou slewest the Egyptian [and covered his body in the dust]—it is not right that they should be smitten by thy hand, therefore let them be smitten by Aaron.'

(*Tanḥ.*, Wa'era, § 14, f. 99*b*.)

Chapter XXVI

PEACE

It may be imagined that to the Rabbis, who lived together amid danger and wars and persecutions and cruelties, there could be no greater blessing than concord and peace, and few greater virtues than peacefulness. By peace is meant most generally peace between man and man, and especially between Jew and Jew.

[1490] R. Simeon b. Gamaliel said: He who makes peace in his house, the Scripture reckons it as if he made peace for every single Israelite in Israel; he who brings jealousy and strife into his house, as if he brought them among all Israel.

(*Ab.R.N.* (vers. I), XXVIII, 43*a*.)

[1491] It is written, 'Seek peace and pursue it' (Ps. XXXIV, 14). The Law does not order you to run after, or pursue, the commandments, but only to fulfil them, when the appropriate occasion comes, i.e. when *A* happens, then you must do *B*. When the occasions come for the commandments, then you are enjoined to fulfil them. But peace you must seek in your own place, and run after it to another. (*Num.R.*, Ḥuḳḳat, XIX, 27.)

[1492] Every Israelite must seek to promote peace in Israel, even as Aaron sought to promote peace. R. Simeon b. Elazar said: If a man sits in his place, and keeps silent, how can he pursue peace in Israel between man and man? But let him leave his place, and roam about in the world, and pursue peace in Israel. Seek peace in your own dwelling place, and pursue it to another place. (*Ab.R.N.* (vers. I), XII, 26*a*.)

[1493] R. Elazar said: Great is peace, for even if Israel commit idolatry, but nevertheless live in peace and brotherhood, judgment cannot touch them, as it says, 'Ephraim is joined in brotherhood to idols, let him be' [an intentional mistranslation of Hos. IV, 17]. He also said: Great is peace, for it is the seal [end] of the priestly benediction (Num. VI, 26). Come and see how great is the reward of one who brings about peace between man and his fellow. It is said, 'Out of peaceful [lit. perfect] stones shalt thou build the altar of the Lord thy God' (Deut. XXVII, 6). Now these stones hear not and see not; they cannot smell, they cannot speak. But since, through the offerings which come upon them, they spread peace between man and his fellow, they are saved from the sword; for it declares concerning them, 'Thou shalt not lift up any iron tool over them' (*ib.* 5). How much more must this apply to a human being who can hear and see, and who can smell and speak, if he promote peace between man and his neighbour! (*Pes.R.* 199*b* (cp. [1508]).)

See also *Sifra* 92*d*, where there is added to the last words: 'husband and wife, family and family, city and city, nation and nation. Iron was created to shorten human life: an altar was created to lengthen it: it is not meet that the shortener should raise a hand against the lengthener.'

[1494] Referring to Mal. II, 6, 'He turned away many from iniquity,' it is said that if Aaron was on the road, and met a bad man, he greeted him [lit. gave him peace, i.e. said '*Shalom* to you', 'Peace be with you']. The next day, if that man wanted to commit a sin, he said, 'Woe is me, how could I then lift up my eyes, and look at Aaron? I should be ashamed before him, for he gave me the greeting of peace'; and so he refrained from sin. If two men had quarrelled, Aaron went and sat near one and said, 'See what your neighbour says: he is tearing his heart and rending his garments, and saying, "Woe is me, how shall I lift up my eyes, and look on my neighbour: I am ashamed because of him, for I have sinned against him": and he sat with him till he had removed hatred from his heart. Then he went, and did and said the same thing to the other man. So when these two men met, they embraced and kissed each other.'

(*Ab.R.N.* (vers. I), XII, 24*b*–25*a*.)

[1495] R. Ishmael said: Great is peace, for concerning the great Name of God which is written in holiness, God has decreed that it may be blotted out in water to produce peace between man and wife (Num. V, 11–31). R. Me'ir used to give every Friday evening a public sermon or exposition of Scripture in a certain synagogue. A certain woman used to go and hear him. One evening his sermon was very long, and when the woman returned, the lamp had gone out. Her husband asked her where she had been. She told him. He said, 'Never shall you enter this house till you have spat in the eyes of the preacher.' Through the Holy Spirit R. Me'ir saw what had happened, and pretended that he was suffering in his eyes. He announced, 'Any woman who knows how to whisper a spell against pains in the eyes, let her come and whisper it.' The neighbours said to the woman, 'The time has come when you can return to your house. Pretend that you are going to whisper a spell, and then spit in his eyes.' She went to R. Me'ir, who said to her, 'Can you whisper a spell?' From nervousness she said, 'No.' He said, 'Spit seven times into my eyes; that will heal them.' She did so, and he said, 'Go and tell your husband, "You told me to spit once, and I have spat seven times."' Then his disciples said to R. Me'ir, 'Should the Law be thus made contemptible? If you had told us, we would have sent for the man, and lashed him with rods till he had made it up with his wife.' R. Me'ir replied, 'Shall it not be with the honour of R. Me'ir as with the honour of his Maker? If the holy name may be washed away in water, in order to make peace between a man and his wife, how much more is this true of the honour of R. Me'ir!'

(*T.J.Soṭ.* I, § 4, f. 16*d*, line 45 (cp. *Lev.R.*, Ẓaw, X, 9; *Deut.R.*, Shofeṭim, V, 15).)

[1496] 'And it came to pass in the days of Amraphel etc.' (Gen. XIV, 1). These four kings introduced war into the world, for before their day there had been no war [i.e. this is the first war mentioned in the Bible], and it was they who made this innovation. God said, 'O you wicked men! Because you have introduced the sword, let the sword come into your own hearts,' as it says, 'Their sword [i.e. which they made their own, or invented] shall enter their heart' (Ps. XXXVII, 14, 15).

(*Tanḥ.B.*, Lek leka, 32*b*.)

[1497] So great is peace, said R. Simeon b. Laḳish, that Scripture speaks fictitious words in order to make peace between Joseph and his brothers. For it says, 'Thy father commanded before his death, saying, Forgive, I pray thee, the trespass of thy brothers' (Gen. L, 16, 17), and we do not find in the Scripture that Jacob had given any such command, but it used fictitious words for the sake of peace. Great is peace, for God has given it to 'the far and to the near' (Isa. LVII, 19). Great is peace for God has 'put it in heaven' (Job XXV, 2).... When God sought to bless

His people, He found no vessel which would contain all the blessings with which to bless them except peace, as it is said, 'The Lord blesses His people with peace' (Ps. XXIX, 11).

(*Deut.R.*, Shofeṭim, V, 15; *Tanḥ.*, Toledot, § 1, f. 44*a*.)

[1498] R. Simeon b. Yoḥai said: Great is peace, for all blessings are contained in it, as it says, 'The Lord will bless His people with peace' (Ps. XXIX, 11). Bar Ḳappara said: Great is peace, for if the beings above, among whom is no jealousy or hate or contention or wrangling or quarrel or strife or envy, need peace, as it is said, 'He creates peace in his high places' (Job XXV, 2), how much more do the beings below, with whom all these bad qualities are present, need peace.... R. Yudan b. R. Jose said: Great is peace for God's name is peace, as it is said, 'And he called it Jehovah-Shalom' (Judges VI, 24). [The Midrash translates, 'And he called Jehovah Shalom,' i.e. 'And he called the Lord, peace.'] (*Lev.R.*, Ẓaw, IX, 9.)

[1499] 'And give thee peace.' 'Peace in thy coming, and peace in thy going out; peace with all men.' Great is peace, for it is equal to everything, as it is said, 'He makes peace and creates all' (Isa. XLV, 7). Great is peace, for even if the Israelites worship idols, and peace is among them, God, as it were, says, 'Satan cannot touch them,' as it is said, 'Ephraim is joined to idols; let it alone' (Hos. IV, 17). But if there are quarrels [divisions] among them, then it is said, 'Their heart is divided; now they shall fear their guilt' (Hos. X, 2). Great is peace, for even the dead need peace, as it is said, 'Thou shalt go to thy fathers in peace' (Gen. XV, 15). Great is peace, for it is given to the penitent, as it is said, 'Creator of the fruit of the lips, peace, peace, to the far and to the near' (Isa. LVII, 19). R. Me'ir said: Great is peace, for God has given no more beautiful gift to the righteous; for when a righteous man passes from the world, three companies of ministering angels go before him, and the first says, 'He shall enter into peace' (Isa. LVII, 2); the second says, 'He shall rest on his bed' (*ib.*), and the third says, 'He walks uprightly' (*ib.*).... Beloved is peace, for the reward which Abraham received for his pious and meritorious deeds was peace, as it is said, 'And thou shalt go to thy fathers in peace' (Gen. XV, 15). The Law is compared only with peace, as it is said, 'And all its paths are peace' (Prov. III, 17). And God comforts Jerusalem only with peace, as it is said, 'And my people shall dwell in a habitation of peace' (Isa. XXXII, 18).

(*Num.R.*, Naso, XI, 7.)

This passage has been considerably contracted; only the best specimens of the praise of peace are given. (Cp. a somewhat similar passage in *Sifre Num.*, § 42, 12*b*–13*a*.)

[1500] It is written, 'I make with him [Phinehas] my covenant of peace' (Num. XXV, 12). Great is the peace which God gave to Phinehas, for the world is governed only with peace, and all the Law is peace, as it is said, 'All her paths are peace' (Prov. III, 17). And if a man comes back from a journey, they greet him with peace, and they ask for peace morning and evening, and after reading the *Shema*, they end with 'who spreads the tent of His peace on His people' (*P.B.* pp. 53, 94*j*, 114). And the daily prayer ends with peace (*ib.* p. 54), and the priestly benediction likewise. R. Simeon ben Ḥalafta said: There is no way to bless except through peace, as it is said, 'The Lord blesses His people with peace' (Ps. XXIX, 11).

(*Num.R.*, Pineḥas, XXI, 1 (cp. [608]).)

The pathetic fundamentalism of the Rabbis is shown in the environment in which this prayer stands. The horrible story of Phinehas and the Midianite woman and the plague and the slaughter (Num. XXV, 1–18) were to them as fully inspired and as true and as commendable as those passages in the Bible which breathe a very different spirit. They could make no distinctions. Sometimes, even as they deepen, and enlarge upon, the good things of Scripture, so they, in a wrong sense, improve upon the bad things, as when, for example, they say in this very section, 'He who sheds the blood of the wicked is as he who brings a sacrifice.' So, too, when they even condemn David because he showed kindness to Hanun the Ammonite, which they regard as against the spirit of Deut. XXIII, 3–6, and they quote Eccles. VII, 16, 'Be not righteous over much', and say, 'A man should not seek to go beyond, or to be more virtuous than, the Law'; David sought to do a kindness to an Ammonite, whereas God had said, 'Thou shalt not seek their peace and their prosperity for ever.' Such was the burden of fundamentalism, but here I am happily concerned to gather flowers not weeds, and the weeds have only to be just occasionally alluded to, and then ignored and passed by.

[On the question of Fundamentalism and its consequences in Ethics (e.g. what Mr Montefiore says about the Phinehas story), see below p. 650 and **Note 8**. (H. L.)]

[1501] Rabbi (cp. [419]) said: Great is peace, for even if the Israelites worship idols, and there is peace among them, God says, 'I have no power, as it were, over them, seeing that peace is among them.' (*Gen.R.*, Noaḥ, xxxviii, 6 (Th. p. 355).)

[1502] Hillel said: Be of the disciples of Aaron, loving peace and pursuing peace, loving thy fellow-creatures, and drawing them near to the Torah. (*Aboth* I, 12.)

[1503] A man should always be keen-witted in the fear [of God], giving the soft answer that turns away wrath (cf. Prov. xv, 1), increasing peace with his brethren and relatives and with all men, even the heathen in the street, so that he may be beloved above and popular on earth, and acceptable to his fellow-creatures. (*Ber.* 17*a*.)

This was a favourite saying of Abbaye.

[1504] There were two men whom Satan incited against each other. Every Friday evening they wrangled with one another. It happened that Rabbi Me'ir came thither, and he restrained them three Friday evenings running, till he made peace between them. Then he heard Satan cry, 'Woe is me; R. Me'ir has driven me away from my house.' (*Giṭ.* 52*a*.)

[In certain versions, e.g. in the Friday night meditations contained in the *P.B. Derek ha-Ḥayyim* (which contains many ethical extracts to illustrate and amplify the liturgy) the story is told not of 'two men', but of husband and wife (p. 298 of ed. Warsaw, 1874: it will be found in most edd. after the conclusion of the Synagogue Service and before the family benedictions). (H. L.)]

[1505] R. Elazar said in the name of R. Ḥanina: The disciples of the wise increase peace in the world; as it is said, 'And all thy children shall be taught of the Lord; and great shall be the peace of thy children' (Isa. liv, 13). Read not *banayik*, 'thy children', but *bonayik*, 'thy builders'. 'Great peace have they that love Thy law; and there is no stumbling for them' (Ps. cxix, 165). 'Peace be within thy walls and prosperity within thy palaces' (Ps. cxxii, 7). 'For my brethren and companions' sake, I will now say, Peace be within thee' (*ib.* 8). 'For the sake of the house of the Lord our God, I will seek thy good' (*ib.* 9). 'The Lord will give strength unto His people, the Lord will bless His people with peace' (Ps. XXIX, 11). (*Ber.* 64*a* (cp. *P.B.* p. 122).)

[This passage has been generally misunderstood. There is a treatise by Isaac Dob Bamberger, called *Sefer Ḳore Emet*, dealing with all the Talmudic passages involving a 'Read not' (Frankfort-on-the-Main, 1871). Bamberger, too, takes the alternative reading as *Bonayik*, 'builders', and he proceeds to show the relevance of the metaphor of 'building'. But such reasoning is *ex post facto*. *A priori*, one does not associate students with building, though we do use the word 'edification'. The truth, I venture to suggest, is that *Bonayik* is an unusual form—not unparalleled however—for *Banayik*, 'thy students', which is an exact homonym of *Banayik*, 'thy sons'. In order to bring out the contrast, the unusual form was essential, otherwise it would appear as though *X* was being explained by *X*. The translation should then be, 'read not "thy children" but "thy students"'. For further details, see my essay in *Orient and Occident* (the volume of essays presented to Dr Gaster), London, 1937. (H. L.)]

[1506] Of the Torah it says, 'its ways are peaceful ways' (Prov. III, 17). God purposed to give the Torah to Israel immediately when they left Egypt, but they were quarrelsome. Hour after hour one said to the other, 'Let us appoint a chief and return to Egypt' (Num. XIV, 4). It says, '*They* (plural) journeyed from Sukkoth, *they* (plural) encamped in Etham, *they* were journeying in contention (Meribah), *they* were camping in contention.' But when they reached Rephidim, they all became reconciled and united into one single band, for when Israel arrived there, '*he* encamped face to face with Sinai' (Exod. XIX, 2), not 'they' encamped, but 'he'. Then said God, 'The Torah, all of it, is peace: to whom can I give it? To a people that loves peace': henceforward 'all its paths [i.e. Israel's] are peace' (Prov. III, 17, continuation of verse cited above). (*Tanḥ.B.*, Yitro, 37*b*.)

[1507] God told Moses to make war on Sihon (Deut. II, 24), but Israel did not make war: they sent messengers of peace (*ib.* 26). God said, 'I ordered you to make war, but you made overtures for peace.' 'There is no peace, says the Lord, for the wicked' (Isa. XLVIII, 22). How great, then, must be words of peace, if Israel disobeyed God for peace's sake, and yet He was not wrath with them. (*Tanḥ.B.*, Debarim, 3*b*.)

For Moses's efforts for peace and their reward see [1522].

[1508] R. Johanan b. Zakkai said: It says, 'Out of peaceful [A.V. 'perfect'] stones shalt thou build the altar, for the altar makes peace between Israel and their Father who is in heaven.' Here is an inference from minor to major. The altar stones cannot see, hear, or speak. Yet because they bring peace, the Torah ordains that iron shall not be wielded over them (Exod. xx, 25). How much more then must one who promotes peace between a man and his fellow, between husband and wife, have his days prolonged. God said: 'In this world, by reason of sin, life is cut short. But in the world to come God will destroy death for ever and wipe away tears from every face' (Isa. xxv, 8; cp. [1493]).

(*Tanḥ.*, Yitro, § 17, f. 126*b fin.*–127*a init.* (cp. [222]).)

[1509] 'Be of the disciples of Aaron, loving peace' (*Aboth* I, 12). If a man quarrelled with his wife, and the husband turned the wife out of the house, then Aaron would go to the husband and say, 'My son, why did you quarrel with your wife?' The man would say, 'Because she acted shamefully towards me.' Aaron would reply, 'I will be your pledge that she will not do so again.' Then he would go to the wife, and say to her, 'My daughter, why did you quarrel with your husband.' And she would say, 'Because he beat me and cursed me.' Aaron would reply, 'I will be your pledge that he will not beat you or curse you again.' Aaron would do this day after day until the husband took her back. Then in due course the wife would have a child, and she would say, 'It is only through the merit of Aaron that this son has been given to me' [and she would call the boy Aaron]. Some say that there were more than three thousand Israelites called Aaron. And so, when Aaron died, it says that *all* the congregation mourned for him. But when Moses died, it says that those who wept were the children of Israel, not *all* the children of Israel (Num. xx, 29; Deut. xxxiv, 8).

(*Ab.R.N.* (vers. II), xxv, 25*b*.)

Chapter XXVII

THIS LIFE IN COMPARISON WITH THE NEXT LIFE

On the whole, the observance of, and the devotion to, the Law were so real and intense and vivid to the Rabbis that long life as such was still to them a mark of God's favour, even as in the O.T., although the Rabbis believed in a much happier life after death, and the writers of the O.T., with hardly an exception, did not. Thus we get passages like the following:

[1510] His disciples asked R. Neḥunya b. ha-Ḳanah the cause of his long life. He said, 'I have never gained honour by the disgrace of my neighbour, and the curse of my neighbour never came upon my bed, and I was generous with my money.' R. Huna carried a rake on his shoulder, and R. Ḥana came and took it from him. R. Huna said, 'If it is your habit to carry it in your town, carry it; but if not, I do not want to be honoured at the expense of your disgrace.' Mar Zuṭra, when he went to bed, was wont to say, 'Forgiven be everybody who may have done me an injury.' Another Rabbi said: 'I never took presents, I never stood upon my rights, and I was generous with my money.' R. Elazar, when they sent presents to him from the house of the Exilarch, would not accept them. And when he was invited, he did not go. He said: Is it not pleasant to you that I should live? For it is said, 'He that hates gifts shall live' (Prov. XV, 27). Raba said: If a man passes by his rights, his sins shall be passed by. For it says, 'He pardons iniquity and passes by transgression' (Mic. VII, 18). Of whom does He pardon the iniquity? of him who passes by an offence [done to him]. (*Meg.* 28*a.*)

As to the Exilarch, see note on p. 156.

What good things of this world were regarded by the Rabbis as specially precious and desirable are summed up in the following passage (but cp. p. xli, [592], [1245]:

[1511] R. Simeon, the son of Judah, said in the name of R. Simeon: Beauty and power and wisdom and wealth and old age and glory and honour and sons are good for the righteous and good for the whole world. [The proof passages are Prov. XVI, 31; XVII, 6; XX, 29; and Isa. XXIV, 23.]

(*T.San.* XI, 8 (Z. p. 432, line 7; Prof. Danby's translation, p. 111).)

A depreciation of this life in comparison with the next occurs only occasionally:

[1512] The Schools of Hillel and Shammai disputed two and a half years whether it would have been better if man had or had not been created. Finally they agreed that it would have been better had he not been created, but since he had been created, let him investigate his past doings, and let him examine what he is about to do. [The meaning is, 'Let him live a righteous life.']

('*Erub.* 13*b*.)

This passage has been quoted as an example of the fundamental pessimism of Rabbinic attitude towards life. That is absurd. The passage is clearly a record of some famous dialectical discussion, without any true bearing upon the arguers' *real* views about actual life. The Rabbis were prevailingly optimists, and whenever circumstances allowed it, they enjoyed life. Their *manner* of enjoyment may not be ours, but that does not make *their* enjoyment less.

[1513] It is said in Ecclesiastes, 'The day of death is better than the day of birth' (VII, 1). When a man is born, none know what his deeds will be; when he has died, men know them....R. Levi said: It is like two ships which sail upon the ocean. The one leaves the harbour, and the other returns to it. People rejoice over the first, and not over the second. But a clever man said: I take the contrary view. For the one which leaves the harbour we should not rejoice, for none know what seas and winds it will have to encounter; but for the ship which has returned to harbour, all should rejoice that it has come back in peace. So with man. When he is born, they regard him as dead, when he is dead they regard him as living.

(*Exod.R.*, Wayaḳel, XLVIII, 1.)

Here there *is* a real touch of pessimism; but it is extremely unusual. It is more Greek than Hebraic. Cf. Jebb's beautiful essay, 'On the melancholy of the Greeks' in *Some Aspects of the Greek Genius*.

Very unusual too is the tone of the next two passages:

[1514] R. Judah the Prince said: He who accepts the pleasures of this world is deprived of the pleasures of the world to come, and vice versa. (*Ab.R.N.* (vers. I), XXVIII, 43*a*.)

[1515] God says to the wicked, 'The righteous do not rejoice in my world, and do you seek to rejoice in my world? Adam did not rejoice in my world, and do you seek to rejoice in my world? Abraham did not rejoice in my world, and do you seek to rejoice in my world?' If one may say so, God Himself does not rejoice in His world, and would you seek to rejoice in His world? For it does not say, 'The Lord rejoices in His works,' but, 'The Lord will rejoice in his works' (Ps. CIV, 31). That is, 'God will rejoice in the works of the righteous in the world to come. The Israelites have not rejoiced in my world, and do you seek to rejoice in my world?' For it does not say, 'Israel has rejoiced in his Creator,' but it says, 'Israel will rejoice in his Creator' (Ps. CXLIX, 2), that is, 'Israel will rejoice in the works of the Lord in the world to come.' (*Pes.K.* XXVII, 170*a*, 171*a*.)

Chapter XXVIII

ON SUFFERINGS

The Rabbinic attitude towards sufferings is, in the main, one of humble resignation to the will of God. But it is a *very* curious thing that by sufferings and chastisements are most frequently meant *bodily* sufferings. The convinced faith in a future life of blessedness and happiness enabled the Rabbis to face sufferings, not indeed, for the most part, with pleasure, but with fortitude, and even *sometimes* with joy, because they were regarded as sure passports to 'heaven'. The old view, now far off and obsolete, that sufferings mean previous sin, was never entirely got rid of. As, then, you *must* be punished for your sins, how much better to be punished by 'sufferings' on earth and before death, and so to *ensure* immediate and eternal felicity in the world to come. Or, again, if sufferings were not a punishment, then they were a purification. 'Whom God loves He chastens', says the verse in Proverbs, a very constantly repeated adage. Tendencies to sin are prevented from becoming actual by 'sufferings', or they are, as it were, combed out and eradicated by sufferings. Sufferings can ennoble man's nature and bring man nearer to God. Into the deeper problem of evil—whether physical or moral evil—as a whole, there is very little to be found in the Rabbinical literature, and what little there is to be found there is, it must be confessed, somewhat trivial and disappointing. For example:

[1516] R. Samuel b. Naḥmani said in the name of R. Jonathan: A visitation of punishment comes upon the world only when there are [many] wicked in the world, and it begins with [i.e. begins by smiting down] the righteous. When the permission [to destroy] is given to the Destroyer [the angel of destruction], he makes no difference between righteous and wicked, and he even *begins* with the righteous. At this R. Joseph wept and said: 'So they are even regarded as nought.' But Abbaye said to him, 'It is a benefit for them,' as it is said, 'The righteous is taken away from the evil to come' (Isa. LVII, 1). (*Bab.Ḳ.* 60*a.*)

Childlike, very frequently, are the ideas of the Rabbis about good and evil and creation. For example:

[1517] Among all the things which God created in His universe, He created nothing that is useless. He created the snail as a cure for a wound, the fly as a cure for the sting of the wasp, the gnat as a cure for the bite of the serpent, the serpent as a cure for a sore, and the spider as a cure for the sting of a scorpion.

(*Sab.* 77*b*; quoted from Cohen, *E.T.* p. 41.)

[1518] 'And God saw everything which He had made, and behold it was very good' (Gen. I, 31). Why does death befall the righteous and not only the wicked? It had to befall the righteous too, or else the wicked might have said, 'The righteous live because they practise the Law and good works: we will do so too,' and they would have fulfilled the commandments deceitfully, and not for their own sake. Again, death befalls the wicked, because they cause vexation to God. But when they die, they cease to vex Him. Death befalls the righteous, because all their life they have to struggle with their evil inclination; when they die, they are at peace.

(*Gen.R.*, Bereshit, IX, 5–9 (Th. p. 70).)

[1519] Why has God created both wicked and good? So that the one should atone for the other.... In the same way He created poor and rich, that one should be supported by the other. (**Note 91.**)

(*Pes.R.* 201*a init.*)

From the pious resignation of the Rabbis, in the view that God, the perfect in wisdom and goodness, knows best, and that His visitations and dispensations must be accepted without murmuring, there *is* something to be admired even by us to-day.

[1520] God gave Israel three goodly gifts, but each was given through suffering: the Torah, the land of Israel and the world to come. The Torah, as it says, 'Happy is the man whom thou chastenest, O God, and whom thou teachest from thy Torah' (Ps. XCIV, 12): the land of Israel, as it says, 'And thou shalt know in thy heart that as a man chastens his son, so the Lord thy God chastens thee' (Deut. VIII, 5), and it continues, 'for the Lord thy God brings thee to a goodly land' (*ib.* 7): the world to come, as it says, 'For the commandment is a lamp, and the Torah is light, and reproofs of chastening are the ways of life' (Prov. VI, 23).

(*Tanḥ.*, Shemot, § 1, f. 81*a*.)

[1521] R. Joshua b. Levi said: He who accepts gladly the sufferings of this world brings salvation to the world.

(*Ta'an.* 8*a* (Malter, p. 54).)

[1522] To him who gives thanks for his afflictions and rejoices over them, God grants life in this world and, in the world to come, life without end, 'for a lamp are the commandments and the Torah is light' (Prov. VI, 23). Why, then, did Moses merit that his countenance should shine, even in this world, with a light destined for the righteous in the next world? Because...he was ever striving, yearning, watching to establish peace between Israel and their Father in Heaven. (*Tan.d.b.El.* p. 17.)

[1523] 'We thank thee, O God, we thank thee: thy name is near.' That is, 'we thank thee when thou givest us benefits, we thank thee when thou smitest us; in either case we thank thee, and thy name is near in our mouth' (Ps. LXXV, 2).
(*Midr.Ps.* on LXXV, 1 (169*a*, §1).)

[1524] Happy is the man who, when afflicted by sufferings, does not cavil against God's justice. If Job had restrained his wrath when sufferings came upon him, and had not cavilled against God's justice, he would have come to great and praiseworthy qualities. R. Ḥanina b. Papa said: Just as we say,' God of Abraham, God of Israel, God of Jacob,' so, [had he not cavilled], we should have added 'God of Job'....God said to Job, 'Thou cavillest because sufferings have come upon thee; art thou greater than Adam, the creation of my hands? For the sake of the one command which he broke, I decreed death upon him and upon his descendants, but he did not cavil. I tested Abraham with many testings, because he said, "Whereby shall I know?" (Gen. XV, 8; cp. [1465]), and I said to him, "Know of a surety that thy seed shall be strangers in a land that is not theirs" (*ib.* 13); yet he did not cavil. Art thou greater than Isaac, whose eyes I dimmed because he loved Esau (Gen. XXVII, 1), or than Moses, whom I would not let enter the promised land, because he said, "Hear now, ye rebels" (Num. XX, 10)? Yet they did not cavil.' (See **Note 49** and Introd. p. lxxxvi.)
(*Pes.R.* 189*b fin.*–190*a*.)

[1525] Beloved are sufferings, for they appease like offerings; yea, they are more beloved than offerings, for guilt and sin offerings atone only for the particular sin for which they are brought in each case, but sufferings atone for *all* sins, as it says, 'The Lord has chastened me sore, but He has not given me over unto death' (Ps. CXVIII, 18). (*Midr.Ps.* on CXVIII, 18 (243*b*, §16).)

[1526] 'Truly, God is good to Israel, even to the pure in heart.' That is, the sufferings which He has brought upon them are good. For whom are they good? For the pure in heart, to purify the heart of the righteous (Ps. LXXIII, 1).

(*Midr.Ps.* on LXXIII, 1 (167*a*, §1).)

[1527] 'Make known to me the path of life' (Ps. XVI, 11). David said to God, 'Lord, make known to me the gate through which one enters the life of the world to come.' R. Yudan said: God replied, 'If you seek life [i.e. in this world], look to the fear of God,' as it is said, 'The fear of the Lord prolongs days' (Prov. X, 27). R. Azariah said: God replied, 'If you seek life [i.e. in the world to come], look for sufferings,' as it is said, 'Reproofs of instruction are the way of life' (Prov. VI, 23). (*Pes.K.* XXVIII, 179*b*.)

[1528] Only for man's good does suffering come upon him, to rid him of what he has done [wickedly]. So the sages teach (*Aboth* I, 7), 'Be not doubtful of retribution.' (*Tan.d.b.El.* p. 67.)

Here the saying is apparently taken to mean, 'Do not grieve over punishment': it is disciplinary.

[1529] R. Huna, quoting Isa. LIII, 10, said: Everyone in whom God delights, He crushes with sufferings, but he added that the scriptural verse showed that this is true only when a man receives the sufferings 'voluntarily and in love'. (*Ber.* 5*a*.)

Quotations from the famous 53rd chapter of Isaiah are rare in the Rabbinic literature.

[Because of the christological interpretation given to the chapter by Christians, it is omitted from the series of prophetical lessons (*Hafṭarot*) for the Deuteronomy Sabbaths. These seven lessons are called the 'Seven (Chapters) of Comfort', and are taken from the preceding and following parts of the book: the omission is deliberate and striking. (H. L.)]

[1530] Not merely should we be ready to receive the evil as well as the good from God, but a man should rejoice over sufferings more than over good, for if a man is in prosperity all his life, his sins will not be forgiven him. But they *are* forgiven him through sufferings. R. Eliezer b. Jacob quoted the verse, Prov. III, 12, 'Whom God loves He chastens, even as the father chastens the son of whom he is fond.' What causes the son to be loved by his father? Sufferings. R. Me'ir quoted the verse, Deut. VIII, 5, 'As a father chastens his son, so God has chastened thee.' God says, 'Thou, Israel, knowest the deeds which thou hast done, and that the sufferings which I have brought upon thee are not in proportion to thy deeds.' R. Jose b. Judah said: Beloved are sufferings before God, for the glory of God rests upon sufferers.

(*Sifre Deut.*, Wa'ethạnan, § 32, f. 73*b* (H. p. 56).)

[1531] Which is the way which brings a man to the life of the world to come? Sufferings. R. Nehemiah said: Beloved are sufferings, for even as the sacrifices brought acceptance, so sufferings bring acceptance. For as to the sacrifices it says: 'And the burnt offering shall be accepted for him to make atonement for him' (Lev. I, 4). And as to sufferings it says: 'They shall win acceptance as regards their iniquity' (Lev. XXVI, 43). And not only so, but sufferings are more acceptable than sacrifices, because sacrifices affect a man's money, but sufferings affect his body. So when R. Eliezer was ill, four elders went to visit him, namely R. Ṭarfon, R. Joshua, R. Elazar b. Azariah and R. Akiba. R. Ṭarfon said, 'More precious are you to Israel than the orb of the sun, for the sun shines in this world, but you give us light in this world and in the world to come.' R. Joshua said, 'More precious are you to Israel than rain, for the rain gives life in this world, but you give life in this world and in the world to come.' R. Elazar said, 'More precious are you to Israel than father and mother, for they bring a man into this world, but you bring us into the world to come.' But R. Akiba said, 'Beloved are sufferings.' Then R. Eliezer said to his disciples, 'Support me that I may hearken to the words of my disciple Akiba.' Then R. Eliezer asked R. Akiba, 'How do you prove what you have said about sufferings?' Then Akiba quoted the verse: 'Manasseh did what was evil in God's sight' and again the verse 'These are the proverbs of Solomon which the men of Hezekiah copied out' (Prov. XXV, 1). And he added, 'Would Hezekiah have taught Torah to all and sundry, and not to Manasseh his son? Yet all the teaching which his father gave to him, and all the trouble which his father spent upon him, did not influence him for good; only sufferings did so,' as it says, 'Manasseh was bound in chains and carried to Babylon, and when he was in distress, he besought the Lord, and humbled himself greatly before God, and prayed unto God, and God heard his supplication, and brought him into his kingdom' (II Chron. XXXIII, 1, 12, 13). 'Beloved are sufferings.' (*Mek.*[2], *Baḥodesh*, Yitro, § 10, pp. 240–1; *Mek.*[3], vol. II, p. 280 (*Sifre Deut.*, Wa'ethanan, §32, f. 73*b* (H. p. 56)).)

[1532] All the punishments for rebellion which God brought upon the Egyptians had the object of purifying them from evil, as it says, 'Wounds cleanse away evil' (Prov. XX, 30). (*Pes.R.* 196*a* (cp. *Tan.d.b.El.* p. 40).)

To the Rabbis, the 'evil' or sin of the Egyptians was that they, or, rather, that Pharaoh, who represents the Egyptians, would not 'let the Israelites go'. When they let them go, they were purified, though it was, I suppose, in view of subsequent events, a very partial and temporary purification! The moral and religious difficulties of the plagues, and especially of the slaying of the firstborn, were occasionally, and to a certain degree, felt by the Rabbis, though their explanation would hardly satisfy us to-day.

[Each generation will find its own solution of old problems and fresh problems calling for solution. I have already pointed out that the importance of these explanations of religious difficulties is that they are stages in progressive thought. The basic point is that there was a need for them and they served their day. Manasseh ben Israel's *Conciliator* (of difficult texts), written in the seventeenth century, was still useful enough in the nineteenth to warrant translation. Its value has not departed even if, in many respects, its function has been fulfilled. (H. L.)]

[1533] If you receive, God says, the chastisements with joy, you will receive reward; but if not, you will receive punishment (cp. *R.T.* p. 219). (*Mek.*[2], *Baḥodesh*, Yitro, § 2, p. 210; *Mek.*[3], vol. II, p. 209.)

[1534] 'Whoso loves correction loves knowledge' (Prov. XII, 1). Four were beaten. One kicked, one laughed, one besought his friend, and one said, 'Why hangs the strap? Beat me with it.' One kicked; that is Job, as it is said, 'I say unto God, Do not condemn me; make me know wherefore thou contendest with me' (Job X, 2). 'Why am I beaten? What have I done to thee? Wherein have I sinned? Make known to me my transgression' (Job XIII, 23). 'I know that thou hast the power, and that thou canst deal thus with me. O earth, cover not thou my blood' (Job XVI, 18). Thus Job kicked. The second was beaten and laughed. That is Abraham, as it is said, 'And Abraham fell upon his face and laughed' (Gen. XVII, 17). The case of Abraham is like the case of a man who beat his son because he had sworn to beat him, and he said to his son, 'I have sworn to beat you.' The son said, 'The power is yours.' So he beat him, thinking that his son would say, 'Enough' [i.e. stop; but the son kept silence]. When the father had beaten him, he said, 'I have beaten him enough.' So God said to Abraham, 'I am God Almighty; I am He who says to my world, It is enough. I am He who says about thy testing, It is enough.' The third besought his friend. That is Hezekiah, as it says, 'He prayed unto the Lord' (Isa. XXXVIII, 2), turning his face to the wall. The fourth said, 'Why hangs the strap? Beat me with it.' That is David, who said, 'Judge me [i.e. make me suffer] O Lord' (Ps. XXVI, 1). (**Note 17**.) (*Midr.Ps.* on XXVI, 1 (108 *a*, §2) (cp. *R.T.* pp. 363–5).)

['I am God Almighty: I am He who says to the world, it is enough.' This Midrash is based on the explanation of *Shaddai*, Almighty, as *She-Dai* (=who+enough). This was the rendering of Aquila, i.e. Self-sufficing God, ἰσχυρὸς ἱκανός or ἄξιος ἱκανός. The conventional translation 'Almighty' is based on conjecture, since the etymology of the word is very difficult to determine (see Brown-Driver-Briggs, *Hebrew Lexicon*). (H. L.)]

[1535] R. Phinehas said in the name of R. Ḥanin of Sepphoris: It is written, 'Happy is the man whom thou chastenest, O Lord' (Ps. XCIV, 12), but if he lose his temper [because of his sufferings] then 'do thou teach him out of thy law' (*ib.*). For when Abraham, at God's behest, left his birthplace, famine befell him, and yet he did not lose his temper and reproach God. So when sufferings fall upon you, do you not lose your temper, or reproach God. R. Alexander said: There is no man to whom no sufferings come; happy he whose sufferings come upon him from the Torah, as it says, 'Teach me from thy Law.' R. Joshua b. Levi said: All sufferings which come upon a man, and keep him back from studying the Law, are sufferings of reproof; the sufferings which do not so keep him back are sufferings of love. R. Ḥama saw a blind man who was studying the Law. He said to him, 'Peace be with thee, O freedman.' The man replied, 'How have you heard that I am a son of slaves?' He answered, 'I have not heard it; I meant that you are a freedman of the world to come.' R. Yudan said: It is written in the Law that if a man knock out the tooth or eye of a slave, the slave shall go free because of the tooth or the eye; if the Law sets a man free for sufferings relating to one single limb, how much more shall a man be set free to whom sufferings befall over all his body (Exod. XXI, 26–7)?

(*Gen.R.*, Miḳḳez̤, XCII, 1 (Th. p. 1137).)

[1536] David said, 'Thy rod and thy staff they comfort me.' 'Thy staff': that is the Law. 'Thy rod': that is sufferings. 'Thou anointest my head with oil'; 'only goodness and mercy shall follow me all the days of my life' (Ps. XXIII, 4, 6). You might think even 'without sufferings'. Therefore it says 'only' [A.V. 'surely'], i.e. only through sufferings wilt thou anoint my head with oil, or only through sufferings shall goodness and mercy follow me, and so too 'only' means that only in the world to come shall goodness and mercy follow me all the days of my life, for '*all*' the days means the days of the world to come.

(*Cant.R.* II, § 1, 3, on II, 1; f. 14*a*.)

[1537] The Rabbis say: He who visits a sick man on the Sabbath must say, 'It is the Sabbath; one must not complain; recovery is near.' R. Me'ir said: May God have pity upon you. R. Judah said: May God have pity upon you and upon all the sick in Israel. (*Sab.* 12*a fin.* (cp. [521]).)

[The first prayer is still in use, although, curiously, it is included neither by Singer not by Gaster. It will be found on p. 174 of A. P. Mendes, *The Daily Prayers*, London, 1864. Another formula is given on p. 80 of D. de Sola's *The Blessings*, London, 1829. (H. L.)]

For those sufferings, which seemed to the Rabbis to suggest rather the mercy, than the severity, of God, they coined the rather charming title of 'chastisements of love':

[1538] 'Happy is the man whom God chastens, whom thou dost teach thy Law' (Ps. XCIV, 12). How can such a man be happy? R. Joshua said: If when sufferings come upon thee, thou canst still study the Law, then thy chastisement is a chastisement of love; if thou canst not study the Law, it is a chastisement for rebellion, as its says '...whom thou chastisest...and teachest'. There is no man in the world to whom suffering does not come. If his eye or his tooth pain him, he cannot sleep, but he is wakeful all night long, and so he can study the Law; happy is he! (*Tanḥ.B.*, Miḳḳez̤, 101 *a fin.*–101 *b*.)

[1539] Bodily suffering is a suffering of love, if it is not sufficient to make a man neglect Torah and prayer. Such sufferings are sufferings of love, for they purge all the iniquities of man. As the salt cleanses meat, so chastisements purify the sins of man. (*Ber.* 5*a* (*R.T.* p. 35).)

[1540] Raba said: Should a man see sufferings come upon him, let him scrutinise his actions, as it is said, 'Let us search and try our ways, and return unto the Lord' (Lam. III, 40). If he has scrutinised his actions without discovering the cause, let him attribute them to neglect of Torah, as it is said, 'Happy is the man whom thou chastenest, and teachest out of thy Law' (Ps. XCIV, 12). If he attributed them to neglect of Torah without finding any justification, it is certain that his sufferings are chastenings of love, as it is said, 'For, whom the Lord loves He chastens' (Prov. III, 12). (*Ber.* 5*a*.)

Or, again, the old argument is used that the woes of the righteous are brief in comparison with the eternal joys which await them, while the beatitudes of the wicked are brief in comparison with the pains which will ultimately befall them:

[1541] It is like one who sat by a cross-road, and before him were two paths, of which one was smooth to start with, and ended in thorns, and the other was thorny to start with, but became smooth. And he told the passers-by, 'You see this path which, at the outset, is smooth: yet only for a few paces will you walk on the smooth: after that, it is thorny. And as to the path which begins with thorns, it soon becomes smooth.' So Moses said to Israel, 'The wicked whom you see prosperous have prosperity but for a brief space in this world, but their end is to fall. And you see the righteous who suffer torments in this world; it is but for a short time that they suffer, but their end is rejoicing.' (*Sifre Deut.*, Re'eh, § 53, f. 86*a* (H. p. 120).)

Stories are told about Rabbis who suffered pain:

[1542] 'He feeds among the lilies' (Cant. II, 16). R. Johanan suffered for three years and a half with fever. R. Ḥanina went to visit him. He said, 'How fares it with you?' He said, 'It is more than I can bear.' He said, 'Do not speak so; say, rather, God is trustworthy.' When the pain was hard, he said, 'God is trustworthy.' But when the suffering became unbearable, R. Ḥanina went again to visit him, and he spoke a word to him, and he took courage. After some while, R. Ḥanina fell ill, and R. Johanan went to visit him. He said, 'How fares it with you?' He replied, 'How hard are sufferings.' R. Johanan replied, 'How great is their reward.' He replied, 'I desire neither them nor their reward.' R. Johanan replied, 'Why do you not say to yourself the word which you said to me, and I took courage?' He said, 'When I was free of sufferings, I could help others; but now that I am myself a sufferer, I must ask others to help me.' R. Johanan said, 'He feeds among the lilies; God's rod comes only upon those whose heart is soft like the lily.' R. Elazar said: Like a man who had two cows; the one was strong, the other was weak. Upon which does he put a burden? Upon the strong. So God does not try the wicked, for they could not endure it, but He tries the righteous. R. Jose b. R. Ḥanina said: The flax worker does not beat the hard flax much, because it would split; but the good flax, the more he beats it, the better it grows. So God tries the righteous. R. Johanan said: The potter, when he examines his kiln, does not test the cracked vessels, because, if he were to hit them, they would break, but he tests the good vessels, because, however many times he hits them, they do not break; so God tries, not the wicked, but the righteous. (*Cant.R.* II, § 16, 2, on II, 16; f. 19*a* (cp. [801]).)

[1543] R. Elazar was ill, and R. Johanan went in to visit him. He saw that he was lying in a dark room, so R. Johanan bared his own arm, and a brightness was radiated therefrom. He then noticed that Elazar was weeping. He said to him, 'Why weepest thou? Is it because thou hast not applied thyself sufficiently to the teaching of Torah? We have learnt that it matters not whether one does much or little, so long as he directs his heart to heaven. Is it because of [the lack of] food? Not everyone has the merit of two tables! Is it because of childlessness? This is the bone of my tenth son!' R. Elazar assured him, 'I weep because of this beauty which will decay in the earth.' R. Johanan said to him, 'Well dost thou weep on that account'; and they both wept. After a while he said to him, 'Are thy sufferings dear to thee?' He replied, 'Neither they nor the reward they bring.' He said to him, 'Give me thy hand.' He gave him his hand, and R. Johanan raised him. (*Ber.* 5*b*.)

R. Johanan was noted for his great beauty (*Bab.M.* 84*a*). 'Two tables'; i.e. prosperity in this world and felicity in the world to come. R. Johanan had lost ten sons. The bone was probably a tooth.

The following quotation is touching:

[1544] The Rabbis taught: 'Who wrote the scroll of the Fasts?' They said, 'Ḥananiah and his band, because they loved the [memory of the great] distresses.' R. Simeon b. Gamaliel said, 'We too love [the memory of] the distresses, but what can we do? They are so many, that if we attempted to write them down, we should not be able to do so.' (*Sab.* 13*b*.)

[Scroll of Fasts. This is an ancient list of thirty-five days on which it is forbidden to fast or mourn, since the days were anniversaries of joyful events. It is in Aramaic, and is accompanied by a scholium. The text may have been written about the seventh century, and according to one account it was compiled by the pupils of Hillel. There are numerous modern editions and translations (e.g. Neubauer, *Med. Jew. Chron.* II, 3–25, Oxford, 1895; S. Zeitlin, Philadelphia, 1922 and H. Lichtenstein, Cincinnati, 1932). The scroll, i.e. *Megillat Ta'anit*, must not be confused with Mishnah (and Gemara) *Ta'anit*.

Since the scroll deals with joyful days, the meaning of the extract must be that there is yet some sorrow involved, since some joyous anniversaries marked the cessation of persecutions, the memory of which was thus renewed. (H. L.)]

[1545] When Moses came down from Mount Sinai, and saw how corrupt Israel had become, he gazed at the Tablets, and saw that the letters which were on them had flown away from the stone. So he broke the Tablets beneath the mountain. Immediately he became dumb, and was unable to utter a word. At that very time a decree was issued concerning Israel that Israel should learn them [i.e. the commandments] through affliction and enslavement, through exile and banishment, through straits and through famine. And on account of that suffering which they have undergone, God will repay their recompense in the days of the Messiah many times over. (*Tan.d.b.El.* p. 117.)

One must bow the head before the visitations of God:

[1546] R. Abbahu had the misfortune to lose a young son. R. Jonah and R. Jose went to visit him. Because of the awe in which they held him, they said no word of Torah to him. He said to them, 'Would you Rabbis say a word of Torah?' They said, 'May our master do so.' He said to them, 'If for the government in the human world, wherein are lying and falsity and deception and respect of persons and taking of bribes, and where a man is to-day and to-morrow is not, the Law [of the Mishnah] is that the relations of a criminal who has been put to death are to greet the judges and the witnesses, and to say, "We have no grudge against you in our hearts, you have given a righteous judgment," how much more should we accept the verdict of the Attribute of Justice of the government above, where there is no lying or deception, and where the judge is He who lives and endures for ever.' (*T.J.San.* VI, § 12, f. 23*d*, line 71.)

[1547] R. Me'ir sat discoursing on a Sabbath afternoon in the House of Study. While he was there, his two sons died. What did their mother do? She laid them upon the bed, and spread a linen cloth over them. At the outgoing of the Sabbath R. Me'ir came home, and said to her, 'Where are my sons?' She replied, 'They went to the House of Study.' He said, 'I did not see them there.' She gave him the *Havdalah* cup, and he said the blessing for the outgoing of the Sabbath. Then he said again, 'Where are my sons?' She said, 'They went to another place, and now they have returned.' Then she gave him to eat, and he ate and said the blessing. Then she said, 'I have a question to ask you.' He replied, 'Ask it.' She said, 'Early to-day a man came here, and gave me something to keep for him; now he has come back to ask for it again. Shall we return it to him or not?' He replied, 'He who has received something on deposit must surely return it to its owner.' She replied, 'Without your knowledge I would not return it.' Then she took him by the hand, and brought him up to the bed, and took away the cloth, and he saw his sons lying dead upon the bed. Then he began to weep, and said about each, 'O my son, my son; O my Rabbi, my Rabbi! My sons, as all men would say; Rabbi, Rabbi, because they gave light to their father's face through their knowledge of the Law.' Then his wife said to him, 'Did you not say to me that one must return a deposit to its owner? Does it not say, "The Lord gave, the Lord took, blessed be the name of the Lord"?' (Job I, 21). So she comforted him and quieted his mind. (*Midr.Prov.* XXXI, 10, f. 54*b*.)

[For the ceremony of *Havdalah* (lit. making a distinction), which marks the outgoing of Sabbath, and 'distinguishes' it from the incoming working days, see *P.B.* p. 216 and Abrahams' note (*Companion*, p. CLXXXII). At this ceremony, wine, spices and lights are used. Probably, as Abrahams suggests, the association of wine was due to the proximity of the evening meal, which could not be cooked until Sabbath was ended. This suggestion is supported by our story, since Me'ir's wife at once gives him his supper after he has pronounced the blessing over the wine. (H. L.)] (**Note 36.**)

[1548] There was a pious pit-digger called Neḥunya. His daughter fell into a pit, but was rescued. R. Ḥanina b. Dosa foretold her rescue, for he said, 'Would it be possible that a child of this pious man would suffer in respect of the very occupation of her father?' 'Nevertheless,' said R. Abba, 'his [Ḥanina's] son died of thirst,' because...God deals particularly strictly with those near to him. (*Yeb.* 121*b*; *R.T.* p. 349.)

[This is deduced by R. Abba from Ps. L, 3, where he renders by a pun 'it shall be very tempestuous round about Him' (A.V.) as 'those round about Him, God judges with a hair's breadth'. R. Ḥanina, the *Amora* (not Ḥanina b. Dosa) deduces the same idea from Ps. LXXXIX, 7 (Heb. 8), where he takes the A.V. 'in reverence' to mean 'judicially severe': cp. Lev. X, 3 and Rashi, *in loc.* (H. L.)]

Does God really visit the sins of the fathers upon the children? The Rabbis were inclined to deny it, in spite of the 'second commandment':

[1549] Like as if there were four chambers in four stories, one above the other. In the first is wine, in the second oil, in the third honey, and in the fourth water. If a light falls in one of them, one extinguishes the other, but if all were full of oil, all would be burnt. So when one generation continues the ill deeds of the former generation, the second is judged like the first, but if there is skipping, one generation being righteous and the next wicked, then the other law applies, namely, that the sons shall not be put to death for the sins of their fathers (Deut. XXIV, 16). Then Moses rejoiced, for he said, 'In Israel a destroyer is not the son of a destroyer; there is no hereditary wickedness in Israel.' (*Pes.K.* 167*a fin.*–167*b*.)

[1550] It says in Deut. XXIV, 16, 'The children shall not be put to death for the fathers. Every man shall be put to death [only] for his own sin.' But it says in Exod. XX, 5, that 'God visits the sins of the fathers upon the children.' This means that He does so only if they hold fast to the deeds of their fathers. But does it not say: 'And they shall stumble one through the agency of [A.V. 'upon'] the other' (Lev. XXVI, 37)? So are they not all responsible one for the other? Only if one could have prevented the other's misdeeds, and if he did not do so.

(*San.* 27*b* (cp. [278] and [1554]).)

[1551] R. Jose b. Ḥanina said that Moses made four declarations [*gezerot*], and then four prophets came after him and annulled them. Of these four, the fourth was Ezekiel, for whereas Moses said, 'He visits the sins of the fathers upon the children' (Exod. XX, 5), Ezekiel came and annulled the assertion, even as it says, 'The soul that sins, that soul [alone] shall die' (Ezek. XVIII, 20). (*Mak.* 24*a*.)

[1552] 'Visiting the iniquity of the fathers upon the children' (Exod. XX, 5). Where there is no skip, but not when there is a skip. How is this? The wicked son of a wicked father, who in turn also was the son of a wicked father. R. Nathan says: A destroyer the son of a destroyer, who in turn was the son of a destroyer.... One might think that just as the measure of punishment extends over four generations, so also the measure of rewarding the good extends only over four generations. But Scripture says: 'Unto thousands.' But: 'Unto thousands' I might understand to mean the minimum of 'thousands', that is, two thousand, but it also says: 'To a thousand generations' (Deut. VII, 9), that is, generations unsearched and uncounted.

(*Mek.*[2], *Baḥodesh*, Yitro, § 6, p. 226; *Mek.*[3], vol. II, p. 246.)

[1553] R. Ammi said: No death without sin; no suffering without iniquity. [But at the end of the discussion on R. Ammi's statement it was held that, after all], There *is* a death without sin, and there *is* a suffering without iniquity. (*Sab.* 55*a fin.*)

In the 'Sayings of the Fathers' (*Aboth* IV, 19) we find the adage, 'It is not in our power to explain either the prosperity of the wicked or the afflictions of the righteous,' but this translation is by no means certain. The saying may mean something quite different. (See Dr Travers Herford's edition of *Aboth*, 2nd ed., 1930, p. 114.) Finally I may quote the two following passages:

[1554] Moses said before God, 'Lord of the universe, why is there a righteous man enjoying prosperity, and a righteous man afflicted with adversity? Why is there a wicked man enjoying prosperity, and a wicked man afflicted with adversity?' He answered him, 'Moses, the righteous man who enjoys prosperity is the son of a righteous father; the righteous man who is afflicted with adversity is the son of a wicked father. The wicked man who enjoys prosperity is the son of a righteous father; the wicked man who is afflicted with adversity is the son of a wicked father.' The above-mentioned teacher[1] said: 'The righteous man who enjoys prosperity is the son of a righteous father; the righteous man who is afflicted with adversity is the son of a wicked father; but it is not so; for lo, it is written, "Visiting the iniquity of the fathers upon the children" (Exod. xxxiv, 7), and it is also written, "The children shall not be put to death for the fathers"' (Deut. xxiv, 16). We set these verses one against the other and conclude that there is no contradiction, because the former passage refers to those children who continue in their fathers' ways. But [we may suppose that] God answered Moses thus: 'The righteous man who enjoys prosperity is perfectly righteous; the righteous man who is afflicted with adversity is not perfectly righteous; the wicked man who enjoys prosperity is not perfectly wicked; the wicked man who is afflicted with adversity is perfectly wicked.'

(*Ber.* 7*a* (cp. [278] and [1550]).)

[1555] God said to Moses, 'Thou canst not see my face' (Exod. xxxiii, 20). Moses wished to understand the mystery of reward and the prosperity of the wicked. God said to him, 'Thou canst not see my face [i.e. comprehend my justice]. I will remove my hand, and thou shalt see my back.' That means, 'In this world I will show thee the reward of the God-fearing, but in the next world I will show thee the great goodness stored up for those that fear me' (Ps. xxxi, 19). [The passage is difficult: Buber gives variants. Possibly the sense is this: 'In this world I show you the principle of reward: in the next the reward itself, which is incomprehensible in this.' (H. L.)]

(*Tanḥ.B.*, Ki Tissa, 58*b* (cp. [577]).)

[1] [This phrase (*amar mar*) is applied to the author of the Mishnah paragraph, or to the *Baraita*, under discussion. In the present instance, it may refer to R. Me'ir, in whose name a *Baraita* had been recited just before, or to the *Tanna* of the first Mishnah of *Berakot* (cp. [1652]). (H. L.)]

Chapter XXIX

THE GENTILES

In this chapter I shall briefly recur to the Rabbinic attitude towards the outside world, and then, in the following chapter, I shall illustrate their attitude to proselytes.

As I have indicated in my book, *Rabbinic Literature and Gospel Teachings*, idolaters, the wicked, the enemies of Israel, are three terms which to the Rabbis were often synonymous. And there is a fourth term, namely, enemies of God, and this fourth term was too often a synonym of the other three. But, nevertheless, the One God was also the One Creator of all mankind, and the lovingkindness of God extends to all His works. Here is a contradiction which the Rabbis were unable to resolve.

[1556] The sons of Noah were given seven commands: in respect of (1) idolatry, (2) incest (possibly, or more generally, unchastity), (3) shedding of blood, (4) profanation of the Name of God, (5) justice, (6) robbery, (7) cutting off flesh or limb from a living animal. R. Ḥanina said: Also about taking blood from a living animal. R. Elazar said: Also about 'diverse kinds' and 'mixtures' (Lev. XIX, 19). R. Simeon said: Also about witchcraft. R. Johanan b. Baroka said: Also about castration [of animals]. R. Assi said: Everything forbidden in Deut. XVIII, 10, 11 was also forbidden to the sons of Noah, because it says, 'Whoever does these things is an abomination unto the Lord.'

(*Gen.R.*, Noaḥ, XXXIV, 8 (Th. pp. 316, 317).)

The sins enumerated here are regarded as repugnant to fundamental human morality, quite apart from revelation.

[1557] The wise men taught: Six commandments were enjoined upon Adam, justice and the prohibitions of idolatry, profanation of the Name, murder, incest, robbery....For the violation of all of them there is forgiveness, except for murder.

(*Deut.R.*, Wa'ethḥanan, II, 25.)

[1558] It says in Isa. LXVI, 23, 'All flesh shall come to worship before me.' It does not say, 'All Israel shall come,' but 'All flesh shall come.' R. Phinehas said: Everyone who makes his *yetzer* [his evil inclination] as flesh [i.e. weakens it] in this world is worthy to see the face of the Shechinah, even as it says, 'He shuts his eyes from seeing evil,' *his* eyes 'shall see the King in his beauty' (Isa. XXXIII, 15, 17) (cp. *R.T.* p. 26). 'All flesh': even the heathen; yet not all the heathen, but only they who have not enslaved Israel, will be received by the Messiah. (**Note 20 *h*.**) (*Pes.R.* 2*a*.)

[1559] R. Johanan said, quoting Jer. XXX, 6, 'All faces are turned into paleness.'...God says, 'Both these [i.e. the Gentiles] and these [i.e. Israel] are my handiwork; why should I let the former perish because of the latter?' (*San.* 98*b*.)

One of the oddest examples of the mixture of universalism and particularism which I have come across is the following:

[1560] 'A land which the Lord cares for' (Deut. XI, 12). Rabbi said: But does He care only for Palestine? Does He not care for *all* lands? It is as if He cared only for Palestine, but as the reward of His caring for it, He cares with it for all other lands. 'The Guardian of Israel.' But is He the Guardian of Israel only? Does He not guard all? (Job XII, 10). It is, as it were, like this. He guards Israel only, but as the reward of guarding them, He guards all with them. (For 'Rabbi' cp. [419].)
(*Sifre Deut.*, 'Eḳeb, § 40, f. 78*b* (H. p. 80).)

[1561] What was Deborah's character that she should have judged Israel, and prophesied to them at a time when Phinehas son of Elazar was alive? I call heaven and earth to witness that whether it be Gentile or Israelite, man or woman, slave or handmaid, according to the deeds which he does, so will the Holy Spirit rest on him. (*Tan.d.b.El.* p. 48.)

The *Tanna debé Eliyahu* contains several anti-Gentile sayings; yet mixed with them are some of an entirely opposite character (cp. [1013]).

[Among such examples is the saying, 'The righteous among the Gentiles are priests of God.' This occurs in *Tan.d.b.El.Zuta*, ed. Lublin, 1897, at the end of ch. XX. The passage is not in the Venice edition, nor in Friedmann's. The same idea is to be found in a comment on Ps. CXXXII, 16, 'Let thy priests be clothed with righteousness.' This is interpreted 'of righteous Gentiles, such as Antoninus, who are God's priests' (see *Yalḳuṭ* on Isa. XXVI, 2, § 429). Antoninus is to head the righteous proselytes in the world to come (*T.J.Meg.* I, § 13, f. 72*b*, line 61).

I venture to cite the following from p. 116 of my essay in *Judaism and Christianity*, vol. I (ed. W. O. E. Oesterley, S.P.C.K. 1937):

'Commenting on the first verse of the *Shema* (Deut. VI, 5, "Thou shalt love the Lord thy God"), the *Yalkuṭ* (§837) says: "See that thou thyself art beloved by human beings (*beriyyot*), and keep thyself far from sin and theft from Jew, Gentile or any man. He who begins by stealing from a Gentile ends by stealing from a Jew, and the same applies to robbery by violence, perjury, circumvention and murder. Now the Torah was given only to sanctify God's great Name, as it says: 'And I will put a sign on them (Israel)...and they shall declare My glory among the Gentiles' (Isa. LXVI, 19)." Also in *Ḥullin*, f. 94*a*, the circumventing of a pagan is forbidden. On Isa. XXVI, 2 ("Open ye the gates, that the righteous Gentiles who keep truth, may enter") the *Yalkuṭ* (§429) has a striking piece of eschatology, based on a paronomasia ("who keep truth" = "who say Amen", *She'omer 'amenim* for *shomer 'emunim*):

'"For the sake of one single Amen which the wicked respond from Gehinnom, they are rescued therefrom. How so? In time to come, the Holy One, Blessed be He, will take His seat in Eden and expound. All the righteous will sit before Him: all the retinue on high will stand on their feet. The sun and the Zodiac [or, constellations] will be at His right hand and the moon and the stars on His left; God will sit and expound a new Torah which He will, one day, give by the Messiah's hand. When God has finished the recital [Haggadah], Zerubbabel, son of Shealtiel, will rise to his feet and say 'Be His Great Name magnified and sanctified' (i.e. the prayer after study, *P.B.* p. 86). His voice will reach from one end of the universe to the other and all the inhabitants of the universe will respond 'Amen'. Also the sinners of Israel and the righteous of the Gentiles, who have remained in Gehinnom, will respond 'Amen' out of the midst of Gehinnom. Then the universe will quake, till the sound of their cry is heard by God. He will ask 'What is this sound of great rushing (Ezek. III, 12, 13) that I hear?' Then the angels of the service make answer, 'Lord of the Universe, these are the sinners of Israel and the righteous of the Gentiles, who remain in Gehinnom. They answer "Amen", and they declare that Thy judgement of them was just.' Immediately God's mercy will be aroused towards them in exceptional measure (*be-yoter*) and He will say: 'What can I do unto them, over and above this judgement, or, what can I do unto them exceptionally, in view of this judgement? For it was but the evil inclination that brought them to this.' At that moment God will take the keys of Gehinnom in His hand and give them to Michael and to Gabriel, in the presence of all the righteous, and say to them, 'Go ye, open the gates of the Gehinnom and bring them up.' Straightway they go with the keys and open the eight thousand gates of Gehinnom. Each single Gehinnom is 300 [parasangs?] long and 300 wide: its thickness is 1000 parasangs and its height 1000 parasangs, so that no single sinner who has fallen therein, can ever get forth. What do Michael and Gabriel do? Immediately they take each sinner by the hand and bring him up, as a man raises his fellow from a pit and brings him up by a rope, as it says: 'And he raised me from the horrible pit' (Ps. XL, 3; 2 in E.V.). Then the angels stand over them, they wash and anoint them; they heal them from the smitings of Gehinnom, clothe them in fair raiment, and bring them into the presence of the Holy One, Blessed be He, and into the presence of all the righteous, when they, the sinners, have been clad as priests and honoured, as it says: 'Let Thy priests be clothed with righteousness and let Thy saints shout for joy' (Ps. CXXXII, 9). 'Thy priests', these are the righteous of the Gentiles, who are God's priests in this world, such as Antoninus and his associates...."'

The following citation comes from pp. 115–16 of the same volume: 'God said to Moses: "Is there respect of persons with Me? Whether it be Israelite or Gentile, man or woman, slave or handmaid, whoso doeth a good deed (*mizwah*), shall find the reward at its side, as it says, 'Thy righteousness is like the everlasting hills: man and beast alike Thou savest, O Lord'" (Ps. XXXVI, 6), *Yalkut*, *Lek leka*, §76. Commenting on Lev. XVIII, 5: "...my commandments, which, if a *man* do, he shall live by them," R. Me'ir said: Hence we know that a Gentile who occupies himself with Torah [here = lives a godly life; it does not mean that he merely studies the Hebrew Pentateuch] is like a High Priest, for it says "a man", it does not say "a priest" or "a Levite" or "an Israelite", but a "man"' (*T.B. Ab. Zar.* 3*a*, top).

With regard to particularism and the relations between Jews and Gentiles, two points should be noted. First, practice is more significant than theory. A generalising statement, often not meant to be taken literally, is less indicative of actual life than are legal provisions, designed to cover contingencies arising in the intercourse of Jews and Gentiles: some of these will be given. Secondly, one observes differences of attitude in the treatment, by different documents, of the same subject. It will be noted that in the relations of Jews to Gentiles and of Jews to Samaritans, the Tosefta of *Aboda Zarah* shows a more friendly spirit than does the Mishnah (compare *Tos.* III, §14 ff. (Z. p. 464, lines 20–5) with the corresponding paragraph in the Mishnah). Probably Tosefta and Mishnah reflect different circumstances and environments and types of Gentiles, hence the divergence of outlook. To-day, the relations between Jews and Gentiles in England and in Germany differ so vastly, that it would not be easy to find much common ground between the estimates formed by English and German Jews of the desirability of being intimate with their Christian neighbours.

Turning now to practical life, the Mishnah and Tosefta contain prescriptions prohibiting intimacy between Jew and Gentile which may lead to idolatry or to other sin: they contain, moreover, some prescriptions which seem, on the face of them, gratuitously unfriendly. But that is not all. They contain many instances of friendship between the two classes and of their co-operation. The following are picked at haphazard.

We read of the payment of tithe on goods bought from a Gentile (*Dem.* v, §9); of fields leased from Gentiles (*ib.* vi, §1); of proselytes and Gentiles as co-heirs (vi, §10). Newly-ploughed land may be hired in the Sabbatical year from a Gentile but not from an Israelite, and Gentiles—but not Israelites—may be helped in their field-labour in the Sabbatical year: greetings may be offered to Gentiles in the interests of peace (*Shebi'it* iv, §3; *T.Ab.Zar.* i, §3 (Z. p. 460, line 19)). Heave-offerings or tithes or dedications to the Temple from Gentiles are valid (*Ter.* iii, §9). Jewish and Gentile farmers in partnership are mentioned in *T.Pe'ah* ii, §9 (Z. p. 19, line 30).

Reference is made to Gentiles and Jews travelling together on board ship (*T.Pes.* i, §24 (Z. p. 157, line 1)), to Jews borrowing from Gentiles (*ib.* i, §21 (Z. p. 156, line 24)). Poor Gentiles may glean and participate in the 'corner of the field' and the 'forgotten sheaf' charities (*Giṭ.* v, §8). The ordinance, cited above, that Gentiles are to be greeted is extended to their festivals (*T.Ab.Zar.* i, §3 (Z. p. 460, line 18)). One may buy from Gentiles Bibles, phylacteries and *mezuzot*, provided that these are properly written (*ib.* iii, §6 (Z. p. 463, line 30)). A case is recorded of a Gentile writer of scrolls (*ib.* §7, line 31). Gentiles and Jews are mentioned as business-partners (*ib.* iii, §14 (Z. p. 464, line 22)) and cattle may belong to Jewish and Gentile owners jointly (*ib. B.K.* iv, §1 (Z. p. 351, line 20)). It is worse to rob a Gentile than a Jew, because of profaning the Name of Heaven (*ib.* x, §15 (Z. p. 368, line 1)). Jews can be guardians and trustees to or of Gentiles (*T.Bab.Meẓ.* v, §20 (Z. p. 382, line 26)). Gifts are made to Gentiles by Jews who are their 'friends and neighbours' (*T.Ab.Zar.* iii, §14 (Z. p. 464, line 20)).

An excellent anthology of passages, illustrating both friendly and unfriendly attitudes, is given by E. G. Hirsch in *J.E.*, s.v. 'Gentile'. (H. L.)]

[1562] Jonah said, 'I will go beyond Palestine to a land where the Shechinah has not revealed itself, for the nations are near to repentance, and I would not make Israel guilty.' It is like the slave of a priest who ran away from his master. He said, 'I will go to a country where my master cannot follow me.' His master said, 'I have substitutes to fill your place.' So when Jonah said, 'I will go beyond Palestine to a place where the Shechinah does not reveal itself,' God said, 'I have messengers to act in thy place,' as it is said, 'And the Lord sent out a great tempest upon the sea.' [The *Mekilta* goes on to speak of three kinds of

prophets; one is solicitous for the honour, both of the Father and of the son (both of God and of Israel); one for the honour of the Father, and *not* of the son; and one for the honour of the son, but not of the Father. Jonah apparently belonged to the third class.] R. Jonathan said that Jonah had intended to destroy himself [for the sake of Israel], as it says, 'Take me up and cast me forth into the sea.' And so you will find that the patriarchs and the prophets were always ready to give up their lives for Israel; so too were Moses and David (Exod. XXXII, 32; II Sam. XXIV, 7). [For the explanation of this passage cp. *R.T.* p. 78.]
(*Mek.*[2], *Pisha*, Bo, § 1, p. 3; *Mek.*[3], vol. 1, p. 7 (cp. [35]).)

Jonah's attempt to escape from God was 'prompted by a presentiment that the heathen were near repentance', and is apparently regarded as an honouring of the son (Israel), but a dishonouring of the Father (God). The Ninevites' repentance would show up by contrast the unrepentance of Israel, and God would hold the Israelites guilty, and punish them for their sins. Jonah did not want to make Israel guilty. Cp. also *R.T.* p. 302 about the readiness of the patriarchs and the prophets to die for the sake of Israel.

[1563] God destroyed Sodom. But in the world to come, when he heals Israel, he will heal her also, as it says, 'I will give her her vineyards' (Hos. II, 15)—her vineyards are her prophets—'and her troubled valley for a gate of hope,' the valley which I troubled in my wrath shall be their gate of hope. And then will Sodom 'sing there as in the days of her youth' (*ib.*), singing songs of thanksgiving to God. (*Tanh.B.*, Wayera, 50*a*.)

[1564] It has been taught: If a man sees an idol, he should say, 'Blessed is He who is long-suffering to those who transgress His will.' If he comes to a place where idolatry has been rooted out, he should say, 'Blessed is He who has rooted out idolatry from our land.' And so may it please thee, O Lord, to root it out from all places, and to turn the hearts of idolaters to serve Thee with a perfect heart. But if one prays thus, is one not praying for the wicked? But R. Johanan [by a fantastic interpretation of Eccles. IX, 4] said: Even for those who have lifted their hands against the Temple there is hope. Yet for them to live again is impossible, because they have lifted their hands against the Temple; to destroy them is impossible because they repented. Of them it is said, 'They shall sleep an everlasting sleep, and shall not wake' (Jer. LI, 39). And so, too, it is taught that the children of the nations and the armies of Nebuchadnezzar do not live again, and are not judged, but they too sleep an everlasting sleep. (**Note 33.**) (*Ruth R.* III, 2, f. 6*a* (cp. [982]).)

Wicked as the Rabbis considered the Empires and especially the Empire of Rome to be, they were not entirely impervious to their merits, or to the value of governments even of the heathen world. We hear a semi-cynical, semi-pessimistic remark:

[1565] 'Thou makest men as the fishes of the sea' (Hab. I, 14). As it is with the fishes of the sea, the one that is bigger swallows the other up, so with man; were it not for the fear of the government, every one that is greater than his fellow would swallow him up. This is what R. Ḥanina, the prefect of the priesthood, said: Pray for the welfare of the government, for were it not for fear of the government, a man would swallow up his neighbour alive. (*Ab.Zar.* 4*a*.)

[1566] 'And behold it was very good' (Gen. I, 31). Resh Laḳish said: 'Behold it was very good.' This is the rule of God. '*And* behold it was very good.' This is the earthly kingdom. But is the earthly kingdom very good? Strange! Yes, for it exacts justice of mankind. As it is said, 'I made the earth and created man upon it' (Isa. XLV, 12). [Man is Adam: here pronounced Edom: Edom is Rome: the unpointed consonants could be read either way.]

(*Gen.R.*, Bereshit, IX, 13 (Th. p. 73 *fin.*; Moore, II, 115, n. 7).)

[1567] [The Rabbis have, as we know, prevailingly, no gentle feelings towards the 'nations', for the nations are mostly and mainly the enemies of Israel, and therefore the enemies of God. So though they cannot deny that some individuals among the nations do good deeds, they are inclined to agree with St Augustine that the good deeds of the 'nations' (he said the 'unbelievers') are only brilliant vices. In this connection the verse in Prov. XIV, 34 gave them a convenient handle. 'Righteousness (or, as *Ẓedaḳah* often meant to them, 'charity' or 'almsgiving') exalts a people.' The people is Israel. 'But the charity [*ḥesed*] of the nations is sin.' So:] R. Johanan said that the 'nations' *do* practise 'charity', but they do so only to boast themselves therewith, and therefore their charity is but sin. For the boaster falls a prey to

Gehenna. [Yet sometimes the verse in Proverbs is given a kinder interpretation; for 'sin' is taken to mean sin-offering, and so it is said:] 'As the sin-offering brings atonement to Israel, so charity atones for the nations.' (*Midr.Prov.* XIV, 34, f. 38*b*.)

One of the finest and most 'universalist' passages in the Rabbinical literature is the following. It is made up of several older parallel passages, the existence of which increases its significance and import. The eighth verse of Ps. IX runs:

[1568] 'He shall rule the world with righteousness, and judge the peoples with uprightness' (Ps. IX, 8). What then is, With uprightness? R. Alexander says: With the uprightness in them. [This perhaps means either (1) according to the upright persons who have so far appeared among them, i.e. giving them the vicarious benefit of the righteousness of these particular persons, or (2) according to the righteousness which they possess, i.e. if any one of them has any good deed to show, or manifests any desire to repent.] [He judges them] through [the uprightness of] Rahab, Jethro, and Ruth. How? God says to [a man who belongs to] the peoples of the world [i.e. to a heathen]: 'Why did you not draw nigh to me?' He answers, 'Because I was a thorough scoundrel, and I was ashamed.' God replies, 'Were you worse than Rahab, who dwelt in the house upon the town wall, where she received robbers, and practised immorality? And did she not draw near to me, and did I not receive her, and did I not cause to descend from her prophets and righteous men? Or were you worse than Jethro, who was priest to an idol: and when he came nigh to me, did I not receive him, and cause to descend from him prophets and righteous men? And when Ruth the Moabitess came to me, did I not receive her, and cause kings to be descended from her?' Again, R. Levi said: God judges the people with uprightness. He judges them by night, when they sleep [and cease from] their iniquities; for by day they commit unchastity, and they rob and oppress: therefore God judges them by night when they are asleep—for then they cease from their sins—so that there may be for them a rising up in the world [to come] (cp. [1656]). (*Pes.R.* 167*b* (cp. *Midr.Ps.* on IX, 9 (44*a*, §11); *T.J.R.H.* I, §3, f. 57*a*, line 47; *R.T.* pp. 337–8).)

[1569] R. Reuben said: The nations of the world slept, and did not come under the wings of the Shechinah. Who woke them up so that they might come? Abraham, as it is said, 'Who has stirred up one from the east?' (Isa. XLI, 2). And not only so, but Abraham woke up charity which slept. For he opened an inn, and received within it the passers-by, as it is said, 'And charity met him at his feet' (*ib.*). [Abraham is regarded as the great maker of proselytes.] (*Midr.Ps.* on CX, 1 (233*a*, §1).)

[1570] R. Jeremiah said: Whence can you know that a Gentile who practises the Law is equal to the High Priest? Because it says, 'Which if a *man* do, he shall live through them' (Lev. XVIII, 5). And it says, 'This is the Law [Torah] of man' (II Sam. VII, 19). It does not say: 'The Law of Priests, Levites, Israelites,' but, 'This is the Law of man, O Lord God.' And it does not say, 'Open the gates, and let the Priests and Levites and Israel enter,' but it says, 'Open the gates that a righteous Gentile may enter' (Isa. XXVI, 2); and it says, 'This is the gate of the Lord, the righteous shall enter it.' It does not say, 'The Priests and the Levites and Israel shall enter it,' but it says, 'The righteous shall enter it' (Ps. CXVIII, 20). And it does not say, 'Rejoice ye, Priests and Levites and Israelites,' but it says, 'Rejoice ye righteous' (Ps. XXXIII, 1). And it does not say, 'Do good, O Lord, to the Priests and the Levites and the Israelites,' but it says, 'Do good, O Lord, to the good' (Ps. CXXV, 4). So even a Gentile, if he practises the Law, is equal to the High Priest. (*Sifra* 86*b* (cp. *San.* 59*a* (cp. [418]); *Bab.Ḳ.* 38*a*).)

[When we take into consideration that this passage is written in connection with Lev. XVIII and especially XVIII, 5, it would seem as if the Law, which the Gentile who equals the High Priest practises, must be the acknowledgment of one God, and the doing of the moral commandments, especially as the fulfilment of the Sabbath and other ceremonial laws by a Gentile who does *not* become a proselyte is vehemently deprecated in *San.* 58*b*. (**Note 34.**) (H. L.)]

[1571] Four times does it say, 'I adjure you, daughters of Jerusalem' (Cant. II, 7; III, 5; VIII, 4). God calls the Gentiles 'Jerusalem's daughters'. R. Johanan said: In time to come God will make Jerusalem a mother-city for the whole world, as it is said, 'And I will give them to thee as daughters, though they be not of thy covenant' (Ezek. XVI, 61). (*Tanḥ.B.*, Debarim, 2*b fin.*)

[1572] 'They shall call the peoples unto the mountain; there shall they offer righteous sacrifices' (Deut. XXXIII, 19). The peoples

and their kings will come together on business to Palestine, and they will say, 'Since we have troubled ourselves to come hither, let us look at the business of the Jews, and what its nature is,' and so they will go to Jerusalem, and they will observe how Israel worships One God only, and eats one sort of food only, while of the nations, each worships different gods, and the food of one is not the food of the other, and they will say, 'It is well to join this people,' and they will not budge from Jerusalem until they are made proselytes, and they will offer sacrifices and burnt offerings.
(*Sifre Deut.*, Berakah, § 354, f. 147*a* (cp. Moore, I, 336, n. 1).)

[1573] 'Give thanks unto the Lord *all* the earth' (Ps. C, 1). R. Jacob in the name of R. Abbahu in the name of R. Aḥa said: God said, 'Let all the nations give thanks unto me, and I will receive them, as it is said: "By myself I have sworn that unto me every knee shall bow, every tongue shall swear" (Isa. XLV, 23). At the time when every knee shall bow to me, and every tongue swear, then will I receive them.' (*Midr.Ps.* on C, 1 (212*b*, §1).)

Chapter XXX

ON PROSELYTES

The last extract of the previous chapter forms a natural transition to a series of quotations about proselytes. We must remember that in Rabbinic Hebrew the proselyte is called *ger*, whereas in biblical Hebrew the *ger* is the resident alien (A.V., R.V. 'stranger'). So all the laws in the Pentateuch enjoining kindness to the *ger* are by the Rabbis applied to the proselyte.

Extracts dealing with proselytes will be found in [301] ff.

[1574] It is written in Hos. XIV, 7, 'They that dwell under his shadow shall return.' R. Abbahu said: These are the proselytes who come and take refuge under the shadow of the Holy One. 'The Lord recompense thy work, and a full reward be given thee of the Lord God of Israel, under whose wings thou art come to trust' (Ruth II, 12). 'They shall revive as the corn.' They shall become as integral a part of Israel as the inborn. And they shall grow as the vine, as it is said, 'Thou hast brought a vine out of Egypt, thou didst cast out the peoples and didst plant it.' [The Midrash apparently intended to use this verse (Ps. LXXX, 8) as if it meant that God took proselytes from the nations and planted them in Israel.] God says, 'The names of the proselytes are as dear to me as the wine which is poured out upon the altar.' (*Lev.R.*, Wayiḳra, I, 2.)

For the reference to Ruth II, 12 cp. [129].

Dr Marmorstein, in an interesting article entitled 'Judaism and Gentile Christianity in the Third Century A.D.' (*London Quarterly and Holborn Review*, July, 1935, p. 370), considers that the correct reading in this passage should be not *gerim* (proselytes), but *goyim* (nations).

[1575] 'The Lord loves the righteous' (Ps. CXLVI, 8). God says, 'I love them who love me.'... Why does God love the righteous? Because they have no inheritance or family. The Priests and Levites form a household, as it is said, 'O house of Aaron and O house of Levi, praise the Lord' (Ps. CXXXV, 19, 20). If a man desires to become a Priest or Levite, he cannot do so, because his father was not one, but if a man wants to be righteous [i.e. a proselyte], he can do so, even if he be a heathen, even though he has no father's house, as it is said, 'Ye that feaı the Lord, bless the Lord' (*ib.* 20). It does not say, 'O house of them that fear the Lord,' but 'Ye who fear the Lord,' that is, they who have no 'house', but of themselves have vowed themselves unto the Lord and love Him. Therefore God loves them.

The Holy One loves the proselytes exceedingly. To what is the matter like? To a king who had a number of sheep and goats which went forth every morning to the pasture, and returned in the evening to the stable. One day a stag joined the flock and grazed with the sheep, and returned with them. Then the shepherd said to the king, 'There is a stag which goes out with the sheep and grazes with them, and comes home with them.' And the king loved the stag exceedingly. And he commanded the shepherd, saying: 'Give heed unto this stag, that no man beat it'; and when the sheep returned in the evening, he would order that the stag should have food and drink. Then the shepherds said to him, 'My Lord, thou hast many goats and sheep and kids, and thou givest us no directions about these, but about this stag thou givest us orders day by day.' Then the king replied: 'It is the custom of the sheep to graze in the pasture, but the stags dwell in the wilderness, and it is not their custom to come among men in the cultivated land. But to this stag who has come to us and lives with us, should we not be grateful that he has left the great wilderness, where many stags and gazelles feed, and has come to live among us? It behoves us to be grateful.' So too spake the Holy One: 'I owe great thanks to the stranger, in that he has left his family and his father's house. and has come to dwell among us; therefore I order in the Law: "Love ye the stranger."'

'The Lord guards the proselytes' (Ps. CXLVI, 9). They are greatly to be protected, so that they should not return to their original evil ways. Beloved are the proselytes, for everywhere the Scripture places them side by side with the Israelites. [The Midrash then shows that in a number of instances the same words are used of 'strangers' (*gerim* = proselytes) as of Israelites, and so it declares:] 'Hence we learn that the proselytes are as the Israelites,'...'Them that honour me I will honour' (I Sam. II, 30).

These are the proselytes who honour God, in that they leave their evil ways, and come and take refuge under the wings of the Shechinah; therefore God honours them.... Who is a God like Him who loves those who love Him, and draws near to Him the far as well as the near?... Nor must you think that God draws near only the proselytes of 'righteousness', who become proselytes for His Name's sake, but in regard to those who become proselytes not for His Name's sake, we find that God requites the wrongs done to them.... God says, 'If you keep far off them that are far, you will end by making far off them that are near.'... God brings near the far, and supports the far as well as the near. And not only that, but He offers peace to the far even before He offers it to the near, as it is said, 'Peace, peace to the far and to the near' (Isa. LVII, 19).

(*Num.R.*, Naso, VIII, 2–4.)

[1576] God commanded the Israelites to do good to proselytes and to treat them with gentleness.

(*Sifre Num.*, Beha'aloteka, § 78, f. 21 *a* (H. p. 76).)

[1577] Dearer to God is the proselyte who has come of his own accord than all the crowds of Israelites who stood before Mount Sinai. For had the Israelites not witnessed the thunders, lightnings, quaking mountain and sounding trumpets, they would not have accepted the Torah. But the proselyte, who saw not one of these things, came and surrendered himself to the Holy One, blessed be He, and took the yoke of heaven upon himself. Can anyone be dearer to God than this man?

(*Tanḥ.B.*, Lek leka, § 6, f. 32 *a*.)

[1578] R. Eliezer said: To Moses was said 'I'; I am He who spake and the world was; I am He who draws near and does not drive far off, even as it is said, 'Am I not a near God, and not a far-off God?' (Jer. XXIII, 23). [An amusing illustration of the Rabbinic method of using Scripture, for the verse, as both R. Eliezer and his hearers well knew, means just the very opposite, namely, that God knows the far as well as the near.] I am He who brings near, and does not keep a man far off. So when a man comes to you to be made a proselyte, and he comes to you with pure intent, draw him near, and do not keep him at arm's length. And learn that if you repel with your left hand, you must draw near with your right, and not act like Elisha who drove away Gehazi for ever. [The right hand is the stronger hand.] (*Mek.*[3], *Amalek*, Yitro, § 1, vol. II, p. 172; *Mek.*[2], p. 193 (cp. *San.* 107*b*; *Soṭ.* 37*a*; cp. [875]).)

[1579] 'And Moses sent his father-in-law away' (Exod. XVIII, 27). R. Elazar of Modi'im said: That is, he gave him many gifts, as we may learn from what Moses said to him, 'Leave us not, I pray thee' (Num. X, 31). He said to him, 'You gave us good counsel, and God approved of it; do not leave us.' But Moses' father-in-law said to Moses, 'Is the lamp of any value except in a place of darkness? Is the lamp of value between the sun and the moon? You are the sun, and Aaron, your brother, is the moon; what can the lamp do between you two? I will go to mine own land, and I will convert all the children of my country, and I will bring them to the Law, and I will draw them near under the wings of the Shechinah.'
(*Mek.*[2], *Amalek*, Yitro, § 2, p. 199 *fin.*; *Mek.*[3], § 4, vol. II, p. 185.)

[1580] Resh Laḳish said: He who turns aside the right of [i.e. oppresses] the *ger* is as if he turned aside the right of God (Mal. III, 5). (*Ḥag.* 5*a*.)

[1581] Timna was a princess (Gen. XXXVI, 10, 12, 29), for her brother was a prince. She wanted to become a proselyte, and she went to Abraham, Isaac and Jacob, and they would not receive her. So then she became a concubine of Eliphaz, the son of Esau, for she said, 'Better to become a handmaid of this nation than a princess of any other.' Her son was Amalek, who wrought great trouble to Israel. Why? Because they ought not to have repelled her. (*San.* 99*b*.)

It says in the Mishnah of *Bikkurim* that a proselyte cannot use the formula given about the firstfruits (Deut. XXVI, 3), because he cannot speak of 'our fathers':

[1582] R. Judah said that he *can*, as it says of Abraham, 'A father of many nations I have made thee' (Gen. XVII, 5); that is, 'Hitherto thou wast a father only in Aram, but henceforth thou shalt be a father for all the nations.' R. Joshua b. Levi said: The rule is according to R. Judah. A case came before R. Abbahu, and he decided it according to R. Judah.
(*T.J.Bik.* I, § 4, f. 64*a*, line 16.)

[1583] Before a proselyte even of the tenth generation do not despise a heathen. (*San.* 94*a*.)

[1584] 'The souls whom they had made [A.V. 'gotten'] in Haran' (Gen. XII, 5). R. Elazar b. Simeon said: If all the inhabitants of the world came together to create even one single fly, they could not put life into it. How, then, can it say, 'The souls which they had made'? But these souls are the proselytes whom they converted. And why does it use the word 'made'? To teach you that if anyone brings near an idolater and converts him, it is as if he had created him. And why does it say '*They* made'? [in the plural]. R. Huna said: Abraham converted the men, and Sarah converted the women. Abraham received them at his house, and gave them food and drink, and dealt lovingly with them, and brought them under the wings of the Shechinah. This is to teach you that he who brings a man under the wings of the Shechinah is regarded as if he had created him.

(*Gen.R.*, Lek leka, XXXIX, 14 (Th. pp. 378, 379; cp. *Cant.R.* I, § 3, 3, on I, 3, f. 6*b*; cp. Acts VII, 2).)

[1585] R. Jose said: If a man desires to become a proselyte, on condition that he accepts the whole of the Torah except one thing, he may not be received, yea, if he rejects even a single detail, Scriptural or Rabbinic. [Mr Loewe thinks that the context shows that this applies to defiant rejection of cardinal principles, or to some form of heresy, and may be directed against the Jewish Christians.] R. Judah bar Shalom said: You will find that in eight and forty places the Torah is urgent about proselytes, and in the same number of places about idolatry. And God says: 'It is enough that the proselyte has abandoned his idolatry, and come to thee, therefore I urge thee to love him,' as it says, 'He loves the proselyte so as to give him bread and raiment' (Deut. X, 18). (*Tanḥ.B.*, Wayiḳra, 2*a fin.*–2*b init.*)

The proselyte is, however, required and expected to be as strict in observance as the born Jew.

[1586] 'The stranger [i.e. the proselyte] that dwells with you shall be unto you as one born among you [*ezraḥ*] and thou shalt love him as thyself' (Lev. XIX, 34). The proselyte is as the *ezraḥ* (home-born): even as the home-born [i.e. the born Israelite or Jew] accepts [the obligations] of all the words of the

Law, so does the proselyte. So they say: 'A would-be proselyte, who is willing to accept all the words of the Law except one, is not received.' R. Jose b. Judah said: 'Even if it be a small matter of the minutiae of the Scribes.' As the home-born is a son of the covenant, so the proselyte is a son of the covenant (cp. [422] and contrast [1610]). (*Sifra* 91 *a* (cp. 84*d*).)

[1587] As it says in Num. IX, 14, 'Ye shall have one ordinance both for the *ger* [A.V. 'stranger', i.e. resident alien] and for the native,' and as, to the Rabbis, *ger* means proselyte, it is said, 'This verse shows that the Scripture makes the proselyte equal to the native as regards all the commandments of the Law.' (*Sifre Num.*, Beha'aloteka, § 72, f. 18*b* (H. p. 67).)

Isa. LVI, 3–6, the grand passage about foreigners, is quoted, and then the sentence from Job, 'The stranger did not lodge in the street.' The Midrash continues:

[1588] God disqualifies no creature [i.e. no man, nobody], but He receives them all. The gates are always open, and all who wish to enter can enter; therefore it says, 'The proselyte did not lodge in the street.'...R. Berechiah said: The verse, 'the proselyte did not lodge in the street,' refers to proselytes who are to serve as priests in the Temple, as it is said, 'And the proselytes shall be joined with them' (Isa. XIV, 1), for the word 'joined' refers to the priesthood, as it says, 'Join me, I pray thee, to one of the priesthoods' (I Sam. II, 36). (*Exod.R.*, Bo, XIX, 4.)

[The rare word for 'join' occurs only in three other places in the Bible, but a similar root furnishes the noun meaning 'scab', 'eruption', i.e. that which 'clings' to something or which joins it (cp. Lev. XIII, 2).[1] (H. L.)]

[1589] It is written, 'Ye that fear the Lord, praise him.' R. Ishmael b. Naḥman said: These are the righteous proselytes. R. Elazar said: When the righteous proselytes enter the world to come, Antoninus will come at the head of them. (*Lev.R.*, Wayiḳra, III, 2.)

[1590] A pagan lady asked R. Jose, 'Can your God draw near to Him whom He wills?' He brought to her a basket of figs. She chose

[1] Hence R. Ḥelbo, churlishly, said that proselytes (let us hope he meant proselytes from impure motives) were as an 'eruption' or 'scab' to Israel (*Yeb.* 109*b*). Cp. *Ḳid.* 70 *b fin.*, which shows that the saying is but a jocular play on words, not meant to be taken literally.

a good one and ate it. He said to her, 'You know how to choose. Should not God know how to choose? Him whom He sees to be a doer of good deeds He chooses and brings near to Him.'

(*Num.R.*, Bemidbar, III, 2.)

[1591] It is written, 'Happy is everyone that fears the Lord' (Ps. CXII, 1). It does not here say, 'Happy are the Israelites or the Priests or the Levites,' but everyone that fears God. These are the proselytes. 'Happy' is said of them, as it is said of Israel (Deut. XXXIII, 29). And it says, 'Thou shalt eat of the labour of thine hands,' that is, the proselyte, who has not the merit of his fathers to lean on, so that he shall not say: 'Woe is me, I have no merit of my fathers; for all the good works which I do I shall have merit only in this world'; therefore the Scripture declares to the proselyte that, by his own merit, he shall enjoy both this world and the world to come. So it says, 'Thou shalt eat the labour of thine hands. Happy shalt thou be in this world, and it shall be well with thee in the world to come.' (*Num.R.*, Naso, VIII, 9.)

[1592] It is written, 'Happy is the man whom thou choosest and causest to approach unto thee that he may dwell in thy courts' (Ps. LXV, 4). Happy is the man whom God has chosen, even if He has not brought him near, and happy, too, is he whom God has brought near, even though He has not chosen him. Whom has He chosen? Abraham, Jacob and Moses [with respect to all of whom the word 'chosen' is found in diverse passages]. But none of these did God bring near, for they brought themselves near. But Jethro and Rahab [i.e. the typical proselytes] God brought near, though He had not chosen them. Happy are they for this very reason. (*Num.R.*, Bemidbar, III, 2.)

[1593] If a man wishes to become a proselyte, but says, 'I am too old; at this time I cannot become a proselyte,' let him learn from Abraham, who, when he was ninety-nine years old, entered God's covenant. (*Tanḥ.B.*, Lek leka, f. 40*b*.)

[1594] Every Israelite should endeavour actively to bring men under the wings of the Shechinah even as Abraham did.

(*Ab.R.N.* (vers. I), XII, 27*a*.)

[1595] Who is greater, he who loves the king, or he whom the king loves? Say: He whom the king loves, even as it says, 'God loves the *ger*' [i.e. the proselyte] (Deut. x, 18).

(*Mek.*², *Mishpaṭim*, Neziḳin, § 18, p. 311; *Mek.*³, vol. III, p. 138.)

[1596] 'Bread to eat and raiment to put on' (Gen. XXVIII, 20). Aquila, the proselyte, went to R. Eliezer and said to him, 'It says, "God loves the stranger [i.e. the proselyte] in giving him food and raiment" (Deut. x, 18). Is that all the remuneration which God gives to the proselyte?' Then R. Eliezer said, 'Is that so light in thine eyes for which the patriarch Jacob begged in prostration? And now this proselyte comes, and God offers it to him straightway.' Then he went to R. Joshua, who appeased him by telling him that by food was meant the Law, and by raiment the praying-shawl. When a man has proved himself worthy in the Law, then he is held worthy of the shawl, and such proselytes may give their daughters in marriage to priests, and their children may become high priests and offer sacrifices upon the altar. It was said, 'Had it not been for the patience which R. Joshua showed to Aquila, he would have returned to his errors.'

(*Gen.R.*, Wayeẓe, LXX, 5 (Th. pp. 802, 803).)

[1597] All the infants that our mother Sarah suckled became proselytes. God said, 'In this world, through the work of the righteous, individuals have become converted. But in the world to come *I* will draw the righteous near [to me] and I [myself] will bring [the nations] beneath the wings of the Shechinah,' as it says, 'For *then* will I turn to the Gentiles a pure speech that they may all of one accord call on God's name' (Zeph. III, 9).

(*Tanḥ.B.*, Wayera, 54*b*.)

[1598] Why does it say, 'Who would have said unto Abraham that Sarah should have given suck to *children*'? (Gen. XXI, 7). [Isaac was her *only* child.] The Gentiles brought their children to Sarah that she might nurse them. Some brought their children in sincerity; others merely to see whether she was able to nurse them. Neither suffered loss. R. Levi said: Those who came in truth became proselytes, they became children *with* Israel; the others became great people in the world. And all the proselytes, and all those who fear heaven, who have ever been, came from the children whom Sarah nursed. She is the joyful mother of children (Ps. CXIII, 9). (*Pes.R.* 180*a*.)

[1599] 'The father of all proselytes was Abraham.' Therefore when a proselyte is named, he is called N., son of our father Abraham. (*Tanḥ.B.*, Lek leka, 32*a fin.*)

So, when a Hebrew name is given to a proselyte, he is, to this day, called, 'N, son of our father Abraham.' A woman is similarly called, 'N, daughter of our mother, Sarah.'

[1600] 'To him that sows righteousness there shall be a sure reward' (Prov. XI, 18). This refers to Abraham who 'sowed righteousness', for he fed travellers. When they had eaten and drunk, they would bless him, but he would refuse their blessing and say, 'Do you rather bless the Master of the house who gives all creatures to eat and drink, and who puts breath in them.' They would say, 'Where indeed is He?' Abraham would answer, 'He rules heaven and earth, He slays and makes men live again, He wounds and He heals. He forms the embryo in the mother's womb, and brings it forth to the air of the world. He rears plants and trees, He brings down to the pit, and leads up therefrom.' On hearing this, they would ask, 'How can we bless Him? How can we thank Him?' He would answer, 'Say, Bless the Lord who is to be blessed for all eternity. Blessed is He that gives bread and sustenance to all flesh,' and so he taught them prayers and good works...the fear of God and the Torah. God said, 'Thou hast sown righteousness, and made me known in the world, thy reward shall be exceedingly great' (Gen. XV, 1). (*Tanḥ.*, Lek leka, § 12, f. 28*a fin.*)

[1601] [Why did the wise Solomon, who was filled with the holy spirit of wisdom and inspiration, marry so many heathen women? This was a puzzle to the Rabbis, and different explanations are given. One of them is as follows.] R. Jose b. Ḥalafta said: The word 'love' in the passage, 'Solomon clave unto them in love' (I Kings XI, 2), means to make them love God, and to draw them near, and to make them proselytes, and to bring them under the wings of the Shechinah. (*Cant.R.* I, § 1, 10, on I, 1; f. 3*a*.)

[1602] Onḳelos, the son of Kalonimos, became a proselyte. The Emperor sent a troop of Romans after him. He attacked them with scriptural quotations, and they became proselytes. Then he sent a second troop after him, and bade them not to say anything to him at all. When they took him, and went along with him, he said to them, 'I will tell you something; the torch-bearer(?) carries the light in front of the chief officer(?); the chief officer carries the light for the *dux*, the *dux* for the *hegemon*, the *hegemon* for the *comes*. Does the *comes* carry the light before the people that follow the procession?' They said, 'No.' Then he said to them, 'But God carried the fire before the Israelites, as it says, "God went before them by night in a pillar of fire"' (Exod. XIII, 21). Then they became proselytes. Then the Emperor sent a third troop after him, and bade them hold no converse with him at all. When they seized him, and took him along with them, he saw a *mezuzah* and pointed to it, and said to them, 'What is that?' They said, 'Tell *us*.' He said, 'In this world, a king dwells in his palace, and his servants guard him outside; but the servants of God dwell within, and He guards them from without, as it is said, "The Lord shall guard thy going out and thy coming in"' (Ps. CXXI, 8). Then they became proselytes. Then the Emperor sent no further troops after him. (*Ab.Zar.* 11 *a*.)

The ranks of the different Roman officials are discussed by I. Ziegler, on p. 32 of his *Königsgleichnisse des Midrasch*..., Breslau, 1903.

[1603] R. Simeon b. Gamaliel said: I was once on a journey, and a man came up to me with outstretched arm, and he said to me, 'You say that seven prophets have arisen among the nations, and they warned them [but they hearkened not], and they went down into hell.' I said to him, 'My son, so it is.' [He said,] 'From the seven generations and henceforth, the nations can say, "The Law was not given to us, and no prophets warn us; why should we go down into hell?"' I replied to him, 'My son, thus it is: our sages have taught in the Mishnah: "To anyone who desires to become a proselyte they stretch out a hand, in order to bring him under the wings of the Shechinah." So from henceforth, the proselytes of each generation can warn their generation.' (*Lev.R.*, Wayiḳra, II, 9.)

Balaam, as a prophet, is said to have been superior to Moses (see **Note 7** at the end of this book): he—and six others—were sent to the

Gentiles. Possibly this is why Balaam may have been used as a designation of Jesus. On this see R. Travers Herford, *Christianity in Talmud and Midrash*, London, 1903; pp. 63 ff. deal with these Balaam-Jesus passages. But Bacher, in his review (*J.Q.R.*, O.S., vol. XVII, 1905, pp. 171 ff.), does not always agree with Herford's identification, and I believe that Herford has—at least in some instances—accepted Bacher's view that Balaam does not invariably refer to Jesus.

The odd mixture is observable. The particularist doctrine of the Rabbis was that the heathen nations could not be 'saved'. They were doomed to hell. Yet sometimes the heart of the Rabbis smote them for this cruel doctrine, even as the heart of some Christian theologians smote them for a similar teaching. For if the heathen knew no better, and had never heard of the one true God, how could their doom be justified? (Cp. the Roman Catholic doctrine of Invincible Ignorance.) Hence the theory of the 'seven prophets' who 'warned' them. But these prophets had ceased long ago. What then? Well, then came the Law which arranged for the reception of proselytes. Ever since, the nations could become Jews if they chose. The proselytes of each generation are a warning to all their contemporaries. The warning is unheeded; therefore the doom of hell is justified.

[1604] A woman came to R. Eliezer, and said to him, 'Bring me near' [i.e. accept me as a proselyte]. He said to her, 'Specify your deeds.' She said, 'My youngest son's father was my eldest son.' He rebuked her. She went to R. Joshua, and he received her. His disciples said, 'R Eliezer drove her away, and you draw her near!' He said, 'When she made up her mind to become a proselyte, she was no longer of this world,' as it is said, 'All who come to it [i.e. to the true faith] shall not return [i.e. to sin]' (Prov. II, 19). (*Eccles.R.* I, § 8, 4 on I, 8 (4*a*).)

[1605] 'And many nations shall be joined to the Lord on that day' (Zech. II, 11). R. Ḥanina b. Papa said: This verse refers to the day when God will judge all the nations in the time to come. Then will He bring forward all the proselytes in this age, and judge the nations in their presence, and say to them, 'Why have you left me to serve idols in which there is no reality?' The nations will reply, 'Sovereign of the Universe, had we come to thy door, thou wouldst not have received us.' God will say to them, 'Let the proselytes from you come, and testify against you.' At once will God bring forward all the proselytes, who will judge the nations, and say to them, 'Why did you abandon

God, and serve idols that are unreal? Was not Jethro a priest of idols, and when he came to God's door, did not God receive him? And were *we* not idolaters, and when we came to God's door, did God not receive us?' At once all the wicked will be abashed at the answer of the proselytes. And God will judge them, and they will depart from the world, as it is said, 'They are altogether brutish and foolish; the instruction of idols, it is but a stock' (R.V. Jer. x, 8). (*Pes.R.* 161 *a.*)

[1606] Solomon said, 'I saw the wicked buried, and they came' (Eccles. VIII, 10). How can the wicked who are buried come? The wicked, generally speaking, are buried while they live [by reason of sin], and therefore do not come:...but the wicked who are buried, and who do come, are the proselytes [whose wickedness is buried and] who come, and repent, and 'go to and fro from the holy place' (*ib.*), i.e. from Synagogues and Houses of Study; 'and they are forgotten in the city' (*ib.*), i.e. their evil deeds are forgotten. (*Tanḥ.B.*, Yitro, 35 *a.*)

[1607] They who desire to become proselytes from love of a Jewess or of a Jew are not received. Nor are would-be proselytes from fear, or because of worldly advantage, received. But Rab said: They are to be received; this is the *Halakah* [i.e. the established rule]: they *are* to be considered as proselytes; they are not to be repelled, as would-be proselytes are repelled at the outset [to test their sincerity], and they must have friendly treatment, for, perhaps, after all, they have become proselytes in purity of motive. (*T.J.Ḳid.* IV, § 1, f. 65 *b*, line 55 (cp. *Yeb.* 24 *b* and Moore I, 337, 348).)

[1608] After the return of the spies, there arose contention between Israel and the *gerim*. God said to Moses, 'Wherefore do the Israelites contend with the proselytes?' Moses said to God, 'Lord, thou alone knowest.' God replied, 'Did I not say one statute, one Torah, for Israel and for *gerim* alike?' Hence they say: There are three types of proselytes, some are like Abraham, some like Hamor, son of Shechem, some like a pagan in every respect. How is this? The last named is the man in whose house is flesh of animals found dead, or killed by wild beasts, or creeping things, or other abominations, and he thinks, 'If I become a proselyte, I should eat good food as the Jews do, and the nasty food would cease in my house; and the Jews, moreover, have Sabbaths and festivals. I will prevail upon myself, and become a proselyte.' But then he relapses to his original leaven, yet in the end sufferings come upon him for his good, and to deliver him from the evil he has wrought. And God says, 'Just as he loved you, so do you love him.' Then there is the proselyte like Hamor, who wants to marry a Jewess, and they say to him, 'You cannot marry her unless you become a proselyte.' Then he prevails upon himself, and becomes a proselyte. He too relapses, and he too is delivered by suffering. God says of him, 'My sons, just as he sought for rest among you, so do you grant him rest, for the proselyte shall you not oppress' (Exod. XXII, 20). Finally, there is the proselyte like Abraham, who says, 'When can I become a proselyte, and dwell beneath the wings of the Shechinah,' as it is said, 'Let not the son of the foreigner say, I am separated from God's people' (Isa. LVI, 4). (*Tan.d.b.El.* p. 146.)

[1609] R. Samuel b. Naḥmani said in the name of R. Yudan b. R. Ḥanina: Three times it says, 'Return',[1] according to the three times that one must repel him who seeks to become a proselyte; but if he continues to press to be received, then they receive him. But R. Isaac said, quoting Job XXXI, 32: 'The stranger [=proselyte] did not lodge in the street.' Always repel with the left hand, and draw near with the right (cp. [875]). (*Ruth R.* II, 16, on I, 12, f. 5*a*.)

Even in dark days, men were still found who desired to become Jews. The last passage about proselytes is important and famous:

[1610] The Rabbis say: If anyone comes nowadays, and desires to become a proselyte, they say to him: 'Why do you want to become a proselyte? Do you not know that the Israelites nowadays are harried, driven about, persecuted and harassed, and that sufferings befall them?' If he says, 'I know it, and I am not worthy,' they receive him at once, and they explain to him some of the lighter and some of the heavier commandments, and they tell him the sins connected with the laws of gleaning, the forgotten sheaf, the corner of the field and the tithe for the poor; and they tell him the punishments for the transgressions of the commandments, and they say to him,

[1] The proof text is Ruth I, 12.

'Know that up till now you could eat forbidden fat without being liable to the punishment of "being cut off" (Lev. VII, 23); you could violate the Sabbath without being liable to the punishment of death by stoning; but from now you will be liable.' And even as they tell him of the punishments, they tell him also of the rewards, and they say to him, 'Know that the world to come has been created only for the righteous.' They do not, however, tell him too much, or enter into too many details. If he assents to all, they circumcise him at once, and when he is healed, they baptise him, and two scholars stand by, and tell him of some of the light and of some of the heavy laws. When he has been baptised, he is regarded in all respects as an Israelite. (*Yeb.* 47*a*–47*b*.)

It will be noted that the commands selected as illustrations are mainly agricultural and that these precede even the Sabbath: from this emphasis, one is inclined to assign an early date to the material contained in this passage. (**Note 18.**)

[For the defiant or arrogant proselyte who seeks to impose conditions on which he will accept Judaism, cp. [422] and [1585–6]. For sincere proselytes, admission was facilitated as the famous story of Hillel in [458] shows. (H. L.)]

Chapter XXXI

THE LIFE TO COME: RESURRECTION AND JUDGMENT

I propose now to close this anthology with some quotations concerning the Rabbinic views about the life beyond the grave. These extracts will not be very numerous, because while the Rabbis knew no more about the future than we, they thought about it in terms and conceptions most of which have become obsolete and remote for us to-day, and so their ideas are of small interest or profit.

[1611] When Moses heard his doom, he urged every argument to secure a remission of his sentence. Amongst other things he said, 'Sovereign of the universe, arise from the judgment seat, and sit on the throne of mercy, so that I die not. Let my sins be forgiven by reason of bodily sufferings which may come upon me. But put me not in the power of the angel of death. If thou wilt do this, then will I proclaim thy praise before all the inhabitants of the world, as David said, I shall not die, but live, and declare the works of the Lord' (Ps. CXVIII, 17). Then God said to Moses, 'Hear the rest of the verse, "This is the gate of the Lord, through which the righteous shall enter."' For all creatures death has been prepared from the beginning.

(*Tanḥ.B.*, Wa'etḥanan, 6*a*.)

[1612] The ministering angels said to God, 'Why did Adam die?' God said, 'Because he disobeyed my command.' Then they said, 'But Moses obeyed thy command?' God replied, 'It is a decree of mine, which falls upon all mankind,' for it says, 'This is the law—when a man dies' (Num. XIX, 14).

(*Sifre Deut.*, Ha'azinu, § 339, f. 141 *a fin.*)

[1613] God said to Moses, 'Behold thy days draw near to die' (Deut. XXXI, 14). Samuel bar Naḥmani said: Do days die? But it means that at the death of the righteous, their days cease from the world, yet they themselves abide, as it says, 'In whose hand is the soul of all the living' (Job XII, 10). Can this mean that the living alone are in God's hand, and not the dead? No, it means that the righteous even after their death may be called living, whereas the wicked, both in life and in death, may be called dead. (*Tanḥ.B.*, Berakah, 28*b fin.*)

It may be pointed out that there is a good deal of confusion in the rabbinic literature about 'the world to come'. The phrase may refer to the days of the Messiah and to a purified earth: an earth of prosperity, righteousness and peace, an age when Israel shall live in its own land under the rule of its Messiah-King. But this age is not to last for ever: it is to be succeeded by the *real* End: the resurrection of the dead and the last Judgment. Then begins the *true* world to come. And, again, there is another confusion: for, according to one doctrine, when you die, you sleep till you 'rise' again at the general resurrection and for the last Judgment. According to another doctrine, when you die, you may, if you are righteous or repentant (and more especially if you are an Israelite), straightway enjoy in happy blessedness the life of the blessed world to come, and if you are wicked and an idolater and an enemy of Israel, you may, when you die, go straightway to hell. How long you will remain in hell is another matter; it may be for a shorter or a longer period, or again it may be for ever. Or, again, at the end of a period in hell, you may be annihilated. Or, again, you may be annihilated at your earthly death. Passages which imply or express all these various bizarre conceptions and confusions abound, and there is no one accepted theory or conception. My extracts are purposely given in a haphazard way, partly to illustrate these contradictions and confusions.

The views of the Rabbis, for example, as to the length of time during which Israelite and Gentile sinners will have to endure the pains of hell vary considerably. M. Israel Lévi says not unjustly that 'la théologie rabbinique surtout en matière d'eschatologie n'avait rien d'arrêté: elle se mouvait dans le domaine de la *agada*, où toutes les libertés se donnaient carrière. Seule la croyance en la résurrection est de dogme....En même temps que les écoles de Hillel et de Shammaï promettent aux pécheurs des grâces nouvelles, infinies, elles prodiguent aux déserteurs de toute espèce, hérétiques et délateurs, comme aux ennemis qui ont détruit le Temple, la menace de la rigueur implacable du Juge suprême.' ('Les Morts et l'avènement de l'ère messianique,' *Revue des Études Juives*, 1919, LXIX, 125, 126.)

It will also be seen that if there is narrowness among the old Rabbis, there is also broadness. There are many indications of universalism. The appalling self-delusion which could glibly talk of a God of love and yet believe in an eternal hell was, I think, sooner and more prevailingly lost in Judaism than in Christianity. There is nothing in the rabbinic literature, I think, to equal in horror the words of the Italian poet about the inscription on the gates of hell, 'Abandon hope, all ye who enter here.' And (still worse) just before, 'The divine Power, the supreme wisdom, and the primal love made me' (i.e. hell). Few Israelites were destined for an abiding hell or for annihilation. Only very high-handed criminals, and very outrageous and unrepentant heretics and apostates, would incur such a doom. And the view of R. Joshua that the righteous of all nations (that is, of all non-Jews) would inherit the world to come became the accepted doctrine of the Synagogue. But the modern Synagogue has moved forward, and has realised that if one single soul were ultimately left out of the bliss of the world to come, the purposes of a God of love would be frustrated for ever.

For a more systematic account of rabbinic views about the Messiah and the Messianic age, about the resurrection, the last Judgment, and about heaven and hell, the excellent and carefully worked out chapter on 'the hereafter' in Dr Cohen's book may usefully be consulted (pp. 367–412). I use the words 'more systematic'. But, happily, as I have said, there is little system in the rabbinic sayings and imaginings about the future life. The belief in God's mercy and lovingkindness constantly breaks through. There is no gloating over hell; no elaborate and 'systematic' theories and justifications about endless punishment and material burnings in a physical fire. If anybody reads carefully the twenty-first book of Augustine's *City of God* about hell and eternal punishment, he will be glad that the Rabbis, after all, were no philosophers, and did not attempt to 'systematise' and 'justify' their casual utterances about the retribution of the wicked after death. Certainly, as between them and St Augustine, the advantage is very much on their side, and very much against the Saint. The *City of God* was written between A.D. 413 and 426, and so, as regards time, we may fitly compare Augustine and the Rabbis.

[1614] The raiment with which God will clothe the Messiah will shine from one end of the world to the other. And the Israelites will make use of his radiance, and they will say, 'Happy the hour in which Messiah was created. Happy the womb from which he came. Happy the generation which sees him. Happy the eye that is worthy to behold him. The opening of his lips is for blessing and peace. His talk is appeasement of spirit. Glory and majesty are in his raiment. Confidence and restfulness are in his words. His tongue gives pardon and forgiveness; his prayer is a sweet savour; his supplication is holy and pure. Happy are you, O Israelites, in what is laid up in store for you,' as it is said, 'How great is thy goodness which thou hast stored up for them that fear thee' (Ps. XXXII, 19). (*Pes.K.* 149 *a fin.*–149 *b init.*)

[1615] 'The Lord permits the forbidden' (Ps. CXLVI, 7) (A.V. and R.V. 'looses the prisoner'; the word 'forbidden' is got by a pun). What does this mean? Some say that in the time to come all the animals which are unclean in this world God will declare to be clean, as they were in the days before Noah. And why did God forbid them [i.e. make them unclean]? To see who would accept His bidding and who would not; but in the time to come He will permit all that He has forbidden.

(*Midr.Ps.* on CXLVI, 7 (268*a*, §4).)

[1616] Our teachers have said: His name shall be the Leprous One of the house of Rabbi [perhaps in reference to Rabbi's sufferings for the thirteen years], as it says, 'Surely he bore our sicknesses, and carried our pains: yet we esteemed him as one stricken with leprosy, and smitten of God' (Isa. LIII, 4). (*San.* 98*b*.).

A more familiar passage in the same tractate runs thus:

[1617] R. Joshua b. Levi met Elijah at the mouth of the cave of R. Simeon b. Yoḥai. He said to Elijah, 'Shall I enter the life to come?' Elijah replied, 'If it so please the Master [=God].' Then he asked him, 'When will the Messiah come?' Elijah replied, 'Go, and ask him.' 'But where is he?' 'At the gate of Rome.' 'And what is his mark?' [How shall I recognise him?] 'He sits among the wretched who are laden with sicknesses [sores and wounds are meant, and it is implied that he, too, has sores and wounds]; all the others uncover all their wounds, and then bind them all up again, but he uncovers and binds up each one separately, for he thinks, "Lest I should be summoned and be detained."' Then R. Joshua went and said to him, 'Peace be with thee, Master and Rabbi.' He replied, 'Peace be with thee, son of Levi.' He said, 'When is the Master coming?' He replied, 'To-day.' Then R. Joshua returned to Elijah, who said, 'What did he say to you?' He replied, 'Peace be with thee, son of Levi.' Elijah said, 'Then he assured to you and to your father [a place in] the world to come.' The Rabbi said, 'He spoke falsely to me, for he said he would come to-day, and he has not come.' Then Elijah said, 'He meant to-day, if ye hearken to my voice' (Ps. XCV, 7). (**Note 54.**)

(*San.* 98*a* (cp. [821]).)

Here too Messiah's sufferings may, perhaps, be regarded as undergone for the sake of Israel. The fullest and most interesting passages of those dealing with Messiah's sufferings and collected by Strack-Billerbeck in their *Kommentar zum Neuen Testament* (Vol. II, pp. 284–291) come from the Midrashic compilation known as the Pesikta Rabbathi. Thus:

[1618] Our Rabbis [the phrase is not *Teno Rabbanan*] have said: There is no end to the sufferings with which he [the Messiah] is afflicted in every generation according to the sins of each generation. Therefore God says (Isa. XLIX, 8), 'In that hour I create thee anew, and will not afflict thee any more.'...'All the good which I will do unto you I do through the merit of the Messiah who was kept back all those years. He is righteous and filled with salvation' (Zech. IX, 9). That is the Messiah, who recognises that God's judgment upon Israel is righteous, when they laugh at him when he sits in the prison: therefore is he called 'righteous'. And why is he called 'filled with salvation?' Because he says, 'You are all my children.' Are ye not all saved only by the mercies of God? 'Afflicted and riding on an ass.' That is the Messiah. Why is he called afflicted? Because he was afflicted all those years in the prison, and the transgressors in Israel laughed at him. And why riding upon an ass? Because the transgressors have no merit,...but through his merit God protects them, and leads them on a level way, and redeems them....'In thy light we shall see light.' What is this light which the congregation of Israel looks for? That is the light of the Messiah, as it is said, 'God saw the light and it was good.' God looked at the Messiah and his deeds before the world was created, and He hid the [primal or archetypal] light for His Messiah and for His generation under the throne of His glory. Then Satan said to God, 'Lord of the world, for whom is this light which thou hast hidden under thy throne of glory?' God replied, 'For him who will put thee to shame.' Satan said, 'Show him to me.' God said, 'Come and see him.' When Satan saw him, he was appalled, and he fell on his face, and he said, 'Verily this is the Messiah who will cast me and all the princes [i.e. the angels] of the nations of the world into hell.' In that same hour, all the nations assembled together, and said to God, 'Who is this into whose hands we are to fall, what is his name and his excellence?' God said, 'It is the Messiah, and his name is Ephraim, the Messiah of my righteousness' (Jer. XXXI, 9, 20)....Then God began to make a bargain with the Messiah, and said to him, 'The iniquities of these souls who are stored away beside thine are destined in the future to bring thee under a yoke of iron, and they will make thee as a calf whose eyes have become dim, and they will strangle thy breath under the yoke, and thy tongue will cleave to thy cheek. Dost thou accept this?' [Is this thy will?] The Messiah said, 'Will this anguish last many years?' God said, 'Seven years have I decreed. If thy soul is grieved, I will cast them out forthwith' [i.e. I will annihilate all these pre-existent souls]. The Messiah replied, 'With rejoicing of heart and soul I accept all this, but under the condition that not one [soul] from Israel is lost. And not only the living shall be saved in my day, but those too who are hidden in the dust, and not only they, but also all the dead who have died from the days of Adam till now, and not only these, but even the abortions shall be saved in my day, and not only they, but also all whom thou hadst intended to create, but who were not created. On these conditions I am ready.'...When the Son of David appears, they will bring beams of iron, and put them on his neck, till his frame is bowed down. And he will cry and weep, and his voice will ascend on high. He will say to God, 'How great are my spirit, my strength, my limbs? Am I not flesh and blood?' Then God will reply, 'Ephraim, my righteous Messiah, long ago didst thou accept all this at the time of the creation. Now let thy pain be as my pain, for since the days when Nebuchadnezzar, the wicked [probably, Titus], burnt my Temple, and caused my children to go into exile among the nations, by thy life, and by the life of my head, I have not ascended my throne. If thou believe it not, look upon the dew upon my head' (Cant. v, 2). Then the Messiah will say, 'I am appeased; it is enough for the slave to be as his master.'...In the time to come, in the month of Nissan, the Patriarchs will say, 'Ephraim, our righteous Messiah, though we are thy ancestors, thou art greater than we. For thou hast borne the sins of our children, and thou hast borne heavy punishments, such as neither the former nor the latter generations have endured, and thou becamest the laughter and the mocking of the nations for Israel's sake, and thou didst sit in darkness, and thine eyes saw no light. And thy skin shrank upon thy bones, and thy body withered like a tree, and thine eyes grew dark from fasting, and thy strength dried up like a potsherd, and all this befell thee because of the sins of our children. Is it thy will that thy children should enjoy the felicity, which God has destined to give them in abundance? Perhaps, because of the pains which thou hast endured in overflowing measure for their sakes, and because thou hast lain fettered in prison, thy mind is not at rest because of them?' Messiah will reply, 'Patriarchs, all that I have done, I have done only for your sakes and for your children, and for your honour and theirs, so that they may enjoy the felicity which God has destined to give them in abundance.' Then they reply, 'May thy mind be appeased, for thou hast appeased the mind of thy Creator and our mind.'

(*Pes.R.* 146*b*, 159*b*, 161*a fin.*–161*b*, 162*a*, 162*b*–163*a*.)

In connection with this paragraph, it may be well to quote the following from Moore (I, p. 551). Mr Loewe, however, while agreeing that the passage, as a whole, is exceptional, considers that Moore's judgment is somewhat too dogmatic, since all the material is not necessarily as late as the date of editing the entire work.

'The acceptance of Isaiah of the hardships of his calling which has been quoted above, has in fact a counterpart in a mediaeval Midrash, in a compact between God and the Messiah at the creation, in which the Messiah agrees to endure the sufferings that are set before him on condition that no Israelite of all the generations to come shall perish.

'The work is late, and it is not certain that the messianic homilies were originally a part of it. To take its testimony for authentic Rabbinic Judaism would be like taking that of a Carolingian author for primitive Christianity. Moreover, the passage in question is palpably an appropriation of Christian doctrine for a Jewish Messiah. The same imitation appears also in the following homily, when it is said that in the days of the Messiah, when God pours out floods of blessing on Israel (Ps. XXXI, 20), the patriarchs will stand and say to him' (as just quoted).

[1619] At the creation of the world King Messiah was born, for the spirit of God hovered over the face of the waters, and the spirit of God is King Messiah, as it says, 'And the spirit of God rests upon him' (Isa. XI, 2). (*Pes.R.* 152*b*.)

With regard to the removal of the Spirit of God because of slanderers see [1116].

[1620] It says in Lev. XVIII, 5 about the commandments of the Torah, 'If a man do them, he shall live by them.' That is, he shall live in the world to come. For in *this* world man's end is that he dies; how then can it be said that 'he shall live by them'? The 'living' must refer to the world to come. I am the Lord, faithful to give reward. (*Sifra* 85 *d.*)

[1621] Fear the earthly tribunal, even though witnesses against you can be bribed: fear yet more the heavenly tribunal, for pure witnesses will testify against you there, and, moreover, they proclaim continually, 'If you have fulfilled my words with joy, my servants will come to greet you, and I myself will go forth to meet you, and say to you, May your coming be in peace.' (*Der.Er.Z.* IV, 6.)

The reading in the Wilna ed. is 'Fear *not* the earthly tribunal... *but* fear, etc.'

[1622] R. Johanan said: The Jerusalem of the world to come is unlike the Jerusalem of this world. The Jerusalem of this world all can enter who will; the Jerusalem of the world to come they only can enter who are appointed for it. (*Bab.B.* 75 *b.*)

[1623] It is said that even Doeg and Ahithophel shall have a part in the life to come. The angels of the Service say, 'If David complains of this, what wilt thou do?' God replies, 'It is my business to make them friends with one another.' (*San.* 105 *a.*)

[1624] 'My soul thirsts for the living God' (Ps. XLII, 2). That is, for the time, Israel says, when thou wilt restore that Godhead [fullness of God] which thou didst make for me at Sinai, when I said, 'Gods are ye' (Ps. LXXXII, 6).... Hasten the time, proclaim the Unity of thy Godhead throughout the world, and let the Lord be king over all the earth. (*Pes.R.* 1 *b.*)

[The meaning of the difficult words is: 'My soul thirsts for its early innocence, to be as it was when, at Sinai, it was declared divine by God.' The idea is that at Sinai, Israel, by their obedience, were like gods. God Himself says so, for 'I said' in Ps. LXXXII is referred to God. It is for this lost virtue that Israel sighs. 'My heart thirsts for God,' i.e. to be 'God' once more. This extraordinarily strong pronouncement, 'to be "God" once more' and not 'to be like God', is a bold adaptation of the Psalm just cited. Its extreme boldness is strange and exceptional. It is not even tempered by the usual *kebayakol* (see **Note 69**), 'if one might venture so to say', a common deprecation of a too hardy anthropomorphism. (H. L.)]

[1625] *This* world is an inn, and *that* world is the permanent house. (*M.K.* 9*b*.)

[1626] R. Joshua's son fell sick and swooned. His father asked him what he had seen. He replied, 'I saw a topsy turvy world.' R. Joshua said, 'No, a purified world. How fares it with us Rabbis?' He said, 'As we are honoured here, so we are honoured there. And I heard it said, "Blessed is he who comes hither with his study fresh upon him." Yet none can attain to the division of the martyrs.' (*Bab.B.* 10*b*.)

For the division or class of the martyrs (i.e. the martyrs of the Hadrianic persecution) cp. [746], [1640] and [1644].

['Division of the Martyrs.' The word for 'division' is *meḥiẓah*: in the extract from the *Yalkuṭ* [1644] the ordinary word *battim*, houses, is used. *Meḥiẓah*, from the root *ḥuẓ*, outside, means a *partition*, or *division*, something which puts a person *outside* or, as here, *inside*, i.e. *outside* when regarded from the other side of the partition. Goldschmidt would derive the word from the biblical root *ḥaẓah*, to divide. The term is used not infrequently of divisions in Paradise. It was, no doubt, adapted from the Priestly and Levitical divisions (*meḥiẓot*) in the camp of Israel (*Num.R.* IV, 13). So also is it used in *Deut.R.* I, 12, where the division of the righteous in Paradise is protected by being within the division of the angels. In *Lev.R.* XXVI, 7 Samuel speaks of his division in Paradise. It is sometimes used, as here, of special divisions reserved for martyrs, especially the martyrs of Lyd. This same curious phrase, 'Blessed is he who comes with his study in his hand,' occurs again with reference to the martyrs of Lyd elsewhere, e.g. *Eccles.R.* IX, 10, 'R. Aḥa wished to see R. Alexandri in a dream.[1] He appeared and showed him two things, the (two?) martyrs of Lyd—no one is fit to be within their division—Blessed be He who removed the reproach of Pappus and Lulianus (i.e. who vindicated their good name or who buried their corpses) and happy is he who comes here with his learning in his hand.' The last phrase occurs in *M.K.* 28*a*, also of appearance after death, in this case to R. Ashi, and it means 'happy is he who has studied while alive and who does not need to make up in heaven for opportunities lost on earth.'

The variants and parallels of the stories of the martyrs of Lyd are given in *Mattenot Kehunnah* to *Eccles.R.* IX, 10. See also *J.E.* s.v. Pappus. They were probably two brothers from Alexandria who were executed under Hadrian. According to one account they gave themselves up, though innocent, to save the city from massacre. (H. L.)]

[1] The dream was evidently somewhat confused and the commentators can hardly be said to have interpreted it satisfactorily. Hence it has here been rendered literally.

[1627] As the praise of God rises from Paradise out of the mouths of the righteous, so it rises from Gehinnom out of the mouths of the wicked, as it says, 'Passing through the valley of weeping, they make it a place of wells' (Ps. LXXXIV, 6). For they [the wicked] let their tears flow like wells, till they cool hell by their tears. Thence the praise of God arises. And what do they say? Thou hast spoken rightly; thou hast judged rightly; thou hast declared clean and unclean rightly; thou hast condemned rightly; thou hast taught rightly. (*Exod.R.*, Wa'era, VII, 4.)

[1628] We have learnt that the judgment upon the wicked in hell lasts twelve months. R. Eliezer asked R. Joshua, 'What should a man do to escape the judgment of hell?' He replied, 'Let him occupy himself with good deeds.' R. Eliezer said, 'If that be so, then the nations can do good and pious deeds, and so escape the judgment of hell.' R. Joshua said, 'My son, the Torah speaks to the living and not to the dead.' [The meaning is that the nations *can* 'live', that is, *can* escape 'hell' by doing deeds of goodness and charity.] R. Joshua added, 'Shall I tell you how I deduce my opinion?' R. Eliezer said, 'Say on.' R. Joshua replied, 'Once I heard you teaching in the House of Study and expounding Prov. XIX, 1, "Better is the poor who walks in his integrity", thus: Everyone who walks in blamelessness before his Creator in this world will escape the judgment of hell in the world to come.'

(*Midr.Prov.* XVII, 1, f. 42*b*.)

[1629] On the Day of Judgment after the wicked have been condemned, the righteous will arise and say to God, 'Sovereign of the Universe, when we were in that former world, those men [whom Thou hast condemned] would go early and late to the House of Prayer and Study, they would read the *Shema*, and recite the prayers, and do other commands of thine.' Then will He say unto them, 'If it is thus that they have done, go and heal them.' At once will the righteous go and stand by the dust of the wicked, and entreat mercy for them. And the Holy One will raise them on their feet from their dust, as it is said, 'And ye shall make [by a slight alteration of the Hebrew] the wicked anew' (Mal. IV, 3). [The reference must be to those who pray hypocritically. H. L.] (*Tan.d.b.El.* p. 15.)

[1630] Why has God created paradise and hell? That the one might deliver from the other. (*Pes.K.* XXX, 191*b*.)

[1631] 'There is a righteous man who perishes in his righteousness, and a wicked man who prolongs his life in his wickedness.' They asked Samuel the Little the meaning of this verse. He said, 'God knows that the righteous may totter in his righteousness; therefore God says, "While he is yet righteous, I will take him away." As for the wicked, "So long as a man lives, God awaits his repentance; when he dies, his hope is lost,"' as it is said, 'When the wicked man dies, his hope perishes' (Prov. XI, 7). Like a robber band bound in a prison; one dug a hole, and all escaped but one. When the jailer came, he began to beat him, and he said to him, 'Miserable wretch, hapless fellow; the hole lay before you, and you did not run away.' So God in the time to come will say to the wicked, 'Repentance was before you, and you did not repent.' R. Josiah said: For three reasons God is long-suffering to the wicked; perhaps they will repent; or perhaps they will fulfil some commands, the reward of which He may pay to them in this world, and perhaps some righteous sons may issue from them, as Josiah of Amon, Hezekiah of Ahaz, and Mordecai of Shimei.

(*Eccles.R.* VII, § 15, 1, on VII, 15, f. 20*b*.)

[1632] R. Phinehas, in the name of R. Reuben, told this parable: A king made a banquet, and he invited guests to it, and he decreed that each guest should bring what he was to lie on. Some brought rugs, some brought mattresses, some brought coverlets, others sheets, others chairs, and some brought logs and some stones. The king examined everything, and said, 'Let every man lie on what he has brought.' They that sat on logs and stones were angry with the king, and said, 'Is it fitting for the king's honour that his guests should lie on logs and stones?' When the king heard what they said, he said, 'Not enough that you have polluted my palace, upon which I spent so much, but you are impudent and accuse me. I did not injure your honour; you injured it yourselves.' So in the world to come, when the wicked are condemned to hell, they will murmur against God, and say, 'We hoped for thy salvation, and now this has come upon us.' God will say, 'In the other world were you not quarrelsome, slanderous, evil doers, men of strife and violence, as it says, "All ye that kindle a fire, that compass yourselves about with sparks: walk in the light of your fire, and in the sparks which ye have kindled"? Do ye say that this is from *my* hand? Nay, you did it to yourselves; therefore: "in pain shall ye lie down"' (Isa. L, 11).

(*Eccles.R.* III, § 9, 1, on III, 9, f. 10*a*.)

[1633] There was a man in Sepphoris whose son had died. A heretic sat by his side. R. Jose b. Ḥalafta came to visit him. The heretic saw that he was smiling. He said to him, 'Rabbi, why do you smile?' He replied, 'I trust in the Lord of heaven that the man will see his son again in the world to come.' Then that heretic said, 'Is not his sorrow enough for the man that you should come and sadden him yet more? Can broken sherds be made to cleave again together? Is it not written, "Thou shalt break them in pieces like a potter's vessel"?' (Ps. II, 9). Then R. Jose said, 'Earthen vessels are made by water and perfected by fire; vessels of glass are both made by fire and perfected by fire; the former, if broken, cannot be repaired; the latter, if broken, can be repaired.' The heretic said, 'Why?' He replied, 'Because they are made by blowing. If the glass vessel which is made by the blowing of a mortal man can be repaired, how much more the being who is made by the blowing of God.'

(*Gen.R.*, Bereshit, XIV, 7 (Th. p. 131; Cohen, *E.T.* p. 382).)

[1634] R. Akiba once chanced to be walking through a graveyard, when he met a charcoal-burner who was carrying wood on his shoulders, and running about like a horse. Akiba gave an order, and brought him to a halt. He said to him, 'My son, wherefore such heavy toil? If you are a bondsman, and your master imposes such a yoke upon you, I will redeem you and set you free. If you are poor, I myself will enrich you.' The man replied, 'Sir, let me be, for I cannot stay.' Akiba asked, 'Are you a human being or a demon?' He said, 'I am of the dead: day after day I am fated to gather wood and to be burnt.' Akiba asked, 'What was your trade when you were living on earth?' He replied, 'I was a tax-gatherer, and I used to favour the rich and slay the poor: and I even seduced an affianced virgin on the Day of Atonement.' Akiba said, 'My son, have you heard from those who are set over you that there is any remedy for you?' The man answered, 'Do not hinder me, lest those set in charge of my punishment grow wrathful with me. For me there is no remedy, and of redemption have I heard nothing. Yet I did hear them say that my punishment would be relaxed if I had a son who could stand up in the congregation and proclaim, publicly, "Bless ye the Lord, who is worthy to be blessed." But I had no son. Yet on my death I left my wife with child, but whether she bore a boy or a girl, I do not know. And if indeed she did bear a son, who will teach him Torah?' Akiba said to him, 'What is your name?' He told him. 'And your wife's name?' He said, 'Susmida.' And your city? 'Alduka.' Then was Akiba troubled on account of the charcoal-burner, and he travelled from city to city till he came to the one where the man lived. He asked for the man and for his household. People answered, 'May his bones be ground in hell.' Then he asked for the wife, and they said, 'May her name and remembrance be blotted out of the world.' Then he asked for his son. 'He is not even circumcised!' Not even this command had his father observed. At once Akiba took the boy, and began to teach him Torah, but first he fasted because of him for forty days. A heavenly voice went forth, saying, 'Because of this boy do you fast?' Akiba said, 'Yes.' He taught the boy the alphabet even before he brought him home, then grace after meals, the *Shema* and the *Tefillah*. Then he made the boy stand up [in Synagogue], and pray, 'Bless ye the Lord who is worthy to be blessed! Blessed be the Lord who is worthy to be blessed for ever and ever!' Then was the charcoal-burner's punishment relaxed, and he came to Akiba in a dream and said, 'May you repose in Paradise, even as you have rescued me from hell.' Akiba replied with the verse, 'O Lord, thy Name is for ever; thy memorial is for every generation' (Ps. cxxxv, 13).

(*Sed.El.Z.* (Pirḥe Derek Ereẓ), p. 22.)

[This is from an enlarged parallel given in Friedmann's note, for the story occurs in many varying versions.

The blessing which Akiba taught the boy may be found in *P.B.* p. 68. The implication is that Akiba, in the father's place, taught the boy till his religious majority at the age of thirteen. Till that age a father is responsible for his son; hence the father's blessing in *P.B.* p. 148. (H. L.)]

[1635] R. Naḥman b. Ḥisda quoted Eccles. VIII, 14, 'There are just men, unto whom it happens according to the work of the wicked; and there are wicked men to whom it happens according to the work of the righteous,' and he said: On the contrary; happy are the righteous whose lot in *this* world is as the lot of the wicked in the next world, and woe to the wicked whose lot in this world is like the lot of the righteous in the next world. Raba replied: Are we then to object if the righteous enjoy both worlds? Rather say, Happy are the righteous whose lot in this world is like that of the wicked, and woe to the wicked whose lot in this world is like that of the righteous. (*Hor.* 10*b*.)

[With the following passage students may compare *San.* 90*a* ff. and *Gen.R.* XCV, 1 (Th. p. 1185). In these parallels more stress is laid on the efforts to prove biblical authority for the future life in order to confute opponents of the belief. The interest in the *Tanḥuma* is in the argument that a resurrection of the body illustrates God's justice. (H. L.)]

[1636] Whatever God has smitten in this world is healed in the world to come, e.g. the blind, the lame and the halt, as it says, 'Then [i.e. in the next world] shall the eyes of the blind be opened, and the ears of the deaf be unstopped etc.' (Isa. XXXV, 5). As a man goes, so he returns. If he dies blind or deaf or lame, he lives again blind or deaf or lame. If he dies clothed, he arises clothed (Job XXXVIII, 14), as the case of Samuel proves, for the witch of Endor saw him rising in a 'mantle' (I Sam. XXVIII, 14), and it was a mantle that his mother made for him (*ib.* II, 19). Why [is there no change]? Lest if He healed them *after* they died, the wicked should say: They may not be the same people at all! Therefore, says God, let them arise just as they departed, and then only will I heal them (Isa. XLIII, 10).
(*Tanḥ.B.*, Wayiggash, 104*b* (cp. for a slightly different version, *Eccles.R.* I, § 4, 2, on I, 4; f. 2*b*).)

[1637] When God confused the speech of the builders of the Tower of Babel, He said, 'In this world, by reason of the evil inclination, my creatures are at variance; they are divided into seventy tongues. But in the world to come they will all be equal. All with one accord will call upon my name and serve me, as it says, "For then will I restore to the nations one pure tongue that they may call, all of them, upon the name of the Lord and serve Him unanimously"' (Zeph. III, 9).

(*Tanḥ.*, Noaḥ, § 19, f. 24*a*; cp. *Tanḥ.B.*, 28*b*.)

[1638] It is written, 'The virgins love thee' (Cant. I, 3). [The word 'virgins', in Hebrew '*alamot*, can be punctuated to mean, 'thou hast hidden', or to mean 'worlds', or it can be split up into two words, and mean 'unto' or 'beyond death'.] Thou hast hidden from them the reward of the righteous, for R. Berechiah and R. Ḥelbo said: In the world to come God will lead the dance with the righteous; the righteous on one side and the righteous on the other, and God in their midst, and they will dance before Him with vigour ['*alimut*, another pun], and they will point with the finger and say, *This* God is our God for ever and ever; He will lead us beyond death; in two worlds He will lead us, in this world and in the world to come.

(*Cant.R.* I, § 3, 3, on I, 3; f. 7*a*.)

[1639] 'They had no comforter' (Eccles. IV, 1). Daniel, the tailor, applied this to bastards—to bastards themselves and not to their fathers. A man has been unchaste, and has begotten a bastard. But how has the bastard sinned, and what concern is it of *his*? R. Judah b. Pazzi said: Even the bastard will enter the life to come; for God says, 'In this world they are regarded as unclean, but in the world to come I look at them as all gold,' even as it is said, 'Behold a candlestick all of gold' (Zech. IV, 2).

(*Eccles.R.* IV, § 1, 1, on IV, 1, f. 12*b*.)

In relation to the difficult verse, Zech. XIV, 6:

[1640] R. Joshua b. Levi said: These are the people who in this world are valued, but in the next world are light [unimportant, of no account]. R. Joseph, the son of R. Joshua b. Levi, fell ill, and drew near to death. His father said, 'What did you see?' He said, 'I saw a topsy turvy world; for those who here are above were there below, and those below were above.' His father replied, 'A purified world have you seen.' He asked his son, 'What did you hear them say?' The son replied, 'I heard them say, "Happy is he who arrives with his study in his hand"' (cp. [1626]). (*Pes.* 50*a*.)

[The last words probably mean: 'Happy is he who until death has never given incorrect or heretical teaching.' (H. L.)]

[1641] The Gemara of the Jerusalem Talmud discusses the Mishnah which says that he who *does* one good deed, or fulfils one command, will be rewarded by God. Does this contradict a teaching that he who *abstains* from evil will be rewarded, even as if he had done good and fulfilled commands? One explanation is that the Mishnah really refers to the man whose good and bad deeds are equal. Then, if he does one good or bad deed, he is rewarded or punished. As to the mere abstention from sin being rewarded, R. Ze'era says it refers to a man who has had full opportunity to transgress, and has not done so. R. Jose b. R. Bun says: The Mishnah means a man who has concentrated on one particular commandment, and never transgressed it in his life. What kind of a case can that be? Mar Ukba says: One who has always sought to honour father and mother. Other Rabbis take the view that to abstain from evil is regarded as in itself equivalent to doing good. Thus in Ps. I, 1 that man is regarded as blessed and happy (and therefore rewarded by God) who has *not* walked in the way of the wicked; and in Ps. CXIX, 3 those are said to walk in the ways of God who do no iniquity.

These two biblical quotations are used to prove that one sin—when the number of sins and good deeds is equal—may cause a man to lose all the benefit of his good deeds, and that the lack of one good deed may prevent the balance going in his favour.[1] Then a great transition is made. It is said that this very serious result of one sin over and above an equality of sins and good deeds applies only to a man's retribution in this world, but not to the world to come. At the judgment in the world to come God is much more merciful. For *there*, 999 sins may be brought forward against a man, and only one good deed in his favour, and yet for this one good deed God will make the balance go in his favour. This is proved by Job XXXIII, 23, 24, where the 'angel intercessor' is taken to mean a good deed. This view was held by R. Elazar b. Jose, the Galilean. He went even further, and said [by a strained interpretation of the text] that if but a thousandth part of a good deed could be pleaded for him, God would regard it as his ransom from punishment.

At this point there seems a further transition, and a very

[1] The curiously mechanical view of human character here taken is one of the weaknesses of Rabbinic legalism.

different statement appears to be made. It is said that the assertion of the Mishnah that he who does one good deed will be rewarded, and he who does one transgression will be punished, applies only to this world. At the judgment in the world to come, paradise or hell is given according to the majority of good deeds or evil, but when there is equality, then [and only then] does God's mercy come in. God seizes [as R. Akiba says] one of the sins and removes it from the scales, and so makes the good deeds heavier, or, as R. Elazar says, if a man has none, then God gives him some of His own. Or, He inclines towards mercy.

R. Samuel b. Isaac then raises a difficulty based upon three biblical texts which seem to show that God specially preserves the righteous *from* sin, and specially drives the wicked *to* sin. Shall an enclosure be yet more enclosed? Shall a breach be yet more broken into? How is this consonant with divine justice? The explanation is that if a man keeps aloof from sin two or three times, then God will guard and protect him from sin henceforward. This view is proved by Job XXXIII, 29. But R. Ze'era says: Provided that he does not return to his sin, for the triple cord will not '*never*' be broken, it will not '*easily*' be broken (Eccles. IV, 12). If you strain the cord too much, it breaks. R. Abbahu says: With God there is no forgetfulness; yet, in the case of Israel, God does forget its sins [proved by Mic. VII, 18 and by a pun on the word *nose*' read as *nosheh*].

(*T.J.Ḳid.* I, § 10, 61*d*, line 23.)

[I agree with Mr Montefiore's footnote, with the following modifications. First, I am not certain how far this was meant to be taken seriously: this is just the kind of logical argument, of which we have had examples, that delights in exhausting every possibility, for the sake of dialectics. Secondly, the crudity is more of style than of thought. He who reads the passage for the first time must be shocked at the system of 'book-keeping' that it seems to describe. But in reality, is not the passage, if we sum it up, rather a plea for the value of man's every act? 'Sow an act and reap a habit'; 'For want of a nail, the shoe was lost,' etc.: these adages and fables point the same moral. It is when we look for the clear understanding and fine distinction of a Platonic dialogue, that the crudity strikes home most forcibly. But the Rabbis did their best with the resources available. They were not philosophers, they could not think philosophically, they lacked a philosophical vocabulary and their audience was composed of simple men. To tell such men that a single act may make or mar them may be weak ethics and bad psychology, but it is a good evangelistic argument. If we think of these Rabbis as Salvationists rather than as trained theologians, we can, perhaps, make allowances for their rough-hewn methods. (H. L.)] (**Note 13.**)

The imagination of the Rabbis was allowed to run riot freely as to the divisions of 'heaven' and the 'classes' of the righteous. Thus:

[1642] The first class is alluded to in the text, 'Surely the righteous shall give thanks unto thy name; the upright shall dwell in thy presence' (Ps. CXL, 13). The second is alluded to in, 'Blessed is the man whom thou choosest and causest to approach that he may dwell in thy courts' (Ps. LXV, 4). The third is alluded to in, 'Blessed are they that dwell in thy house' (Ps. LXXXIV, 4). The fourth is alluded to in, 'Lord, who shall sojourn in thy tent?' (Ps. XV, 1). The fifth is alluded to in, 'Who shall dwell in thy holy hill?' (*ib.*). The sixth is alluded to in, 'Who shall ascend the hill of the Lord?' (Ps. XXIV, 3), and the seventh in, 'Who shall stand in His holy place?' (*ib.*).

(*Sifre Deut.*, Debarim, § 10, f. 67*a* (H. p. 18).)

The seven divisions, counting downward, are therefore designated as: Presence, Courts, House, Tent, Holy Hill, Hill of the Lord, and Holy Place.

Another version reads:

[1643] Seven classes will stand before the Holy One, blessed be He, in the Hereafter. Which is the highest of them to receive the presence of the Shechinah? It is the class of the upright; as it is said, 'The upright shall behold their face' (Ps. XI, 7). It is not written 'His face', but 'their face', i.e. the presence of the Shechinah and His retinue.[1] The first class sits in the company of the King and beholds His presence; as it is said, 'The upright shall dwell in thy presence' (Ps. CXL, 13). The second dwells in the house of the King; as it is said, 'Blessed are they that dwell in thy house' (Ps. LXXXIV, 4). The third ascends the hill to meet the King, as it is said, 'Who shall ascend into the hill of the Lord?' (Ps. XXIV, 3). The fourth is in the court of the King; as it is said, 'Happy is the man whom thou choosest, and causest to approach that he may dwell in thy courts' (Ps. LXV, 4). The fifth is in the tent of the King; as it is said, 'Lord, who shall sojourn in thy tent?' (Ps. XV, 1). The sixth is in

[1] For retinue in this connection see [913].

the holy hill of the King; as it is said, 'Who shall dwell in thy holy hill?' (Ps. xv, 1). The seventh is in the place of the King; as it is said, 'Who shall stand in His holy place?' (Ps. xxiv, 3). (*Midr.Ps.* on xi, 7 (51*a*, §6) (cp. *Sifre Deut.*, Debarim, § 10, f. 67*a* (H. p. 18); *Pes.K.* 179*b*; *Lev.R.* xxx, § 2, f. 43*b*).)

[1644] R. Naḥman b. Isaac said: To the scholars who make their foreheads wrinkled because of their study of the Law in this world, God will reveal mysteries in the world to come. (*Ḥag.* 14*a*.)

[The ideas in the foregoing passages are considerably developed in the *Yalkuṭ* and the following extract (from paragr. 20 on Gen. ii, 8, f. 7*a*) is interesting: 'In paradise there are seven classes of the righteous. The first consists of the slain of the government [i.e. the martyrs], such as R. Akiba and his fellows. The second consists of those drowned in the sea [i.e. the youths and maidens who jumped into the sea rather than be dishonoured]. The third consists of R. Johanan b. Zakkai and his disciples. The fourth consists of those upon whom the cloud descended as a covering. The fifth class are the repentant, for where they stand even the completely righteous stand not. The sixth class consists of the bachelors who have remained sinless all their lives. The seventh class consists of the poor who studied the Bible and the Mishnah, and had a worldly occupation. Of them it is written, "Let all who trust in thee rejoice" (Ps. v, 11). God sits in their midst, and explains to them the Law, as it is said, "Mine eyes shall be upon the faithful of the land, that they may dwell with me" (Ps. ci, 6). And God discloses the glory which is appointed for them more and more, even as it is said, "Eye has not seen nor ear heard what God has prepared for them who wait for him"' (Isa. lxiv, 4) (cp. [1626]). (H. L.)]

A clear distinction between the days of the Messiah and the world to come is made in the following brief passage:

[1645] R. Johanan said: Every prophet prophesied only for the days of the Messiah; but as for the world to come, no eye has seen what God has prepared for those who wait for Him. (*Ber.* 34*b*.)

[1646] 'Happy art thou, O Israel' (Deut. xxxiii, 29). All Israel assembled near to Moses and said to him, 'Our master, Moses, tell us what goodness the Holy One, blessed be He, will give us in the world to come.' He replied to them, 'I do not know what I can tell you. Happy are you for what is prepared for you.' (*Sifre Deut.*, Berakah, § 356, f. 148*b*.)

[1647] Even when, for their sins, God slays Israel in this world, there is healing for them in the world to come, as it is said, 'Come, let us return unto the Lord, for it is He who has torn us, and He will bind us up; after two days He will revive us; on the third day He will raise us up' (Hos. VI, 2). The two days are this world and the days of the Messiah; the third day is the world to come. (*Tan.d.b.El.* p. 29.)

[1648] R. Ḥanina taught that all who go down to hell [Gehenna] will come up again except three: the adulterer, he who puts his fellow to shame in public, and he who calls his fellow by an opprobrious nickname. [It is added cleverly:] Surely the third class is merely an example of the second. [The reply is,] Even if the man was accustomed to the nickname (i.e. even then he who uses it will never come up out of hell). (*Bab.M.* 58*b*.)

It is clear that these utterances are not to be taken too dogmatically or literally. They are bits of sermons. At any rate they show a tendency, illustrated by other extracts, to limit eternal punishment to a very great degree. And only *moral* baseness is the test.

Strange—that is, strange to us—attempts were made to prove that the resurrection of the dead was taught in the Pentateuch and in the Bible, e.g. in biblical Hebrew the particle 'then' (*az*) takes the imperfect or future tense when referring to the past. Thus it says: 'Then Moses and the children of Israel sang,' etc. (in the Hebrew 'will sing') (Exod. XV, 1). So we have (Cohen, *E.T.* p. 380 *fin.*):

[1649] R. Me'ir said: Whence is the Resurrection derived from the Torah? As it is said, 'Then will Moses and the children of Israel sing this song unto the Lord' (Exod. XV, 1). It is not said 'sang', but 'will sing'; hence the Resurrection is deducible from the Torah. Again, R. Joshua b. Levi asked: Whence is the Resurrection derived from the Torah? As it is said, 'Blessed are they that dwell in thy house, they will be still praising thee' (Ps. LXXXIV, 4). It is not stated, 'They will have praised thee', but 'will be still praising thee' [in the Hereafter]; hence the Resurrection is deducible from the Torah. [Note, Torah here means the Psalms.] (*San.* 91*b*.)

[The Pharisaic doctrine of the Resurrection rapidly became an unchallenged dogma. It was introduced into the second blessing of the *Amidah*. A favourite proof-text was to divide, in defiance of grammar, Deut. XXXI, 16 and make it read, 'Behold, thou shalt sleep with thy fathers, but shalt arise.' These homiletical methods may seem strained, but they achieved their result. The price was worth paying. Where would Judaism and Christianity have been, had the Sadducees who denied the Resurrection, triumphed?

In the *Mishnah Sanhedrin* (cited below, [1655]) among those who are excluded from the world to come is he who denies that the doctrine of the future life is contained in the Pentateuch. But the famous Cambridge MS. of the *Mishnah*, edited by W. H. Lowe, does not contain the final words *min ha-Torah*: nor did Maimonides know them. The original reading clearly was that he who denied the future life was excluded from it. Only when no one denied the belief were the last two words added, which gave an entirely new meaning to the sentence (cp. [1655]). (H. L.)]

Curiously casual is the way in which the Rabbis speak of those who will, and those who will not, 'live again', i.e. rise at the Resurrection. In the great passage in the *Mishnah Sanhedrin* (X, 1), it is categorically asserted that all Israelites, except certain special sinners and unbelievers, shall have a share in the world to come. Therefore, they will all rise again. But various Rabbis exclude whole classes of Israelites. Thus:

[1650] R. Elazar said: Those who die outside Palestine will not live again. The *Amme ha-Aretz* will not live again. Whoever is slack about Torah will not live again. Whoever makes use of the light of Torah, the light of Torah will revive [after death]; and whoever does not make use of the light of Torah, the light of Torah will not revive. (*Ket.* 111 *a*, *b*.)

How other Rabbis got round this strange idea about the dead buried outside Palestine is given in Cohen, *E.T.* p. 384:

[1651] R. Simai said, The Holy One, blessed be He, will burrow the earth before them, and their bodies will roll through the excavation like bottles, and when they arrive at the land of Israel, their souls will be reunited to them.

(*T.J.Ket.* XII, § 3, f. 35*b*, line 13; *Ket.* 111*a* (by Abbaye).)

We may wonder whether they made these amazing assertions seriously. And yet why should they have made them in jest? One never seems to get to the bottom of the oddity of the Rabbis. See, however, **Note 10**.

Here is one of the two or three more dogmatic passages about the world to come and about those who are to enter heaven or hell (cp. *R.T.* p. 333):

[1652] We have learnt in a *Baraita* (*T.San.* XIII, 3, p. 434): The School of Shammai say, On the day of judgment there will be three classes, one consisting of the perfectly righteous, one of the perfectly wicked, and one of the intermediates. The first are straightway inscribed and sealed for perfect life, and the third are likewise straightway sealed for Gehinnom, as it is said, 'And many of them that sleep in the dust of the earth shall awake, some to everlasting life and some to shame and everlasting contempt' (Dan. XII, 2). The intermediates descend to Gehinnom, and cry out, as it is said, 'And I will bring the third part through the fire, and will refine them as silver is refined, and will try them as gold is tried: they shall call on my name, and I will hear them: I will say, It is my people: and they shall say, The Lord is my God' (Zech. XIII, 9), and of them Hannah said, 'The Lord it is that slays and quickens; though He bring down to Sheol, He raises up' (I Sam. II, 6). Beth Hillel taught: 'Abundant in lovingkindness' (Exod. XXXIV, 6) means that He inclines towards the direction of lovingkindness. About them David said, 'I love the Lord because He has heard the voice of my supplications' (Ps. CXVI, 1): with reference to these intermediates also did David compose the whole section, 'I was brought low and He helped me' (*ib.* 6). Those Jews and those Gentiles who sin with their bodies descend to Gehinnom and are judged there for twelve months. After twelve months their bodies are wasted away, their breath (soul) is burnt; the wind scatters them under the feet of the righteous, as it is said, 'And ye shall tread down the wicked: for they shall be ashes under the soles of your feet in the day that I shall do [this], says the Lord of Hosts' (Mal. III, 21). But the *Minim*, the Informers, the Atheists who repudiate the Law, and deny the Resurrection, and who separate themselves from the ways of the congregation, and who [for their own purposes] cause panic in the land of the living, and who cause the multitude to sin, e.g. Jeroboam, son of Nebat, and his fellows,—these descend to Gehinnom, and are judged there for generation after generation, as it says, 'And they shall go forth, and look upon the carcasses of the men that have transgressed against me: for their worm shall not die, neither shall their flesh be quenched, and they shall be an abhorring unto all flesh' [Isa. LXVI, 24]. Gehinnom shall come to an end, but they shall not come to an end, as it says, 'And their beauty shall consume the grave so that it shall not be their dwelling' (Ps. XLIX, 14). Why all this? Because they put forth their hand against the dwelling [of God], as it says *miz-zebul lo* [*lo* = His, i.e. God's], His dwelling [not their dwelling]. For *zebul* is used of the sanctuary, as Solomon said, 'I have indeed built for thee a dwelling' (*zebul*, I Kings VIII, 13). Of them Hannah says, 'As for the Lord, His adversaries shall be broken into pieces' (I Sam. II, 10). R. Isaac b. Abin said: And their faces shall be likened to the bottom of a pot. Raba said: These are some of the fops of Maḥoza who are termed [nicknamed] hell's sons. Mar[1] said: Beth Hillel says, 'He is abundant in lovingkindness,' i.e. He inclines in the direction of lovingkindness. But [how do they reconcile this with what follows when] it says, 'I will bring the third part into the fire?' Well, that refers to the Israelites who sin with their bodies. Israelites who sin with their bodies! But you just said that there was no 'straightening' at all possible for these (see Eccles. I, 15; VII, 13, 29). [Yes] but that referred to those whose sins were [far and away] more than their virtues; here we are speaking of the intermediates [lit. those who possess half merits and half sins]: even if these are in the category of Israelites who sin with their bodies, they must inevitably be in the category of, 'And the third will I bring into the fire' [i.e. they must ultimately be healed of sin]. But even if they are not, then 'Abundant in lovingkindness' applies to them, and about them David said, 'I loved the Lord' etc. (Ps. CXVI *ad init.*). Raba expounded this verse thus: What does 'I loved', etc., mean? The congregation of Israel say to God: Sovereign of the universe! When am I beloved to thee? When thou hearest my supplications. It continues: 'Though I be made poor [brought low], yet He will save me,' that means, though I be poor in *miẓwot* [commandments], to me is it fitting to be saved. Who are the Israelites who sin with their bodies? Rab says: The head that is not clad with *tefillin* [phylacteries]. Who are the Gentiles who sin with their bodies? Raba says: Those who sin with transgression [i.e. probably those who commit incest]. Who are those who spread panic in the land of the living? Rab Ḥisda says this refers to the Archisynagogos

[1] Mar is not a proper name, but means 'the first-named teacher' (cp. [1554] note).

[head of the synagogue], who puts great fear into his congregation, but not for the name of heaven. R. Judah says: No man who does this will see his son a scholar, as it says, 'Men do therefore fear him, but he shall not see any that are wise of heart' (Job XXXVII, 24). Beth Hillel says: Abundant in lovingkindness, i.e. inclining towards lovingkindness. How does God act? R. Eliezer says: He treads it [i.e. the pan of the virtues in the balance] down, as it says, 'He will once again have mercy on us, and tread down our sins' (Mic. VII, 19). R. Jose b. Ḥanina said: He lifts up [the pan with sins], as it says, 'He lifts up [pardons] sin and transgression.' In the School of Ishmael it was taught: He causes the sins to pass away one by one, from first to last: this is His attribute. Raba says: But the sin itself is not wiped away, for if there are many other sins, He reckons them with it [and then the man comes under class three, i.e. he is perfectly wicked]. Raba said: Whosoever overlooks his attributes [i.e. does not stand upon his rights when others sin against him], all his sins are overlooked, as it says, 'He forgives sin and overlooks transgression' (Exod. XXXIV, 7). For whom does He forgive sin? For him who overlooks transgression [by others].

(*R.H.* 16*b*–17*a* (cp. [104], and [849]).)

Moore says: 'Professor Ginzberg understands the opinion of the School of Shammai to be that these "betwixt and betweens" will go down to hell and *be singed* by its fires, and after this experience arise thence and be healed' (vol. III, p. 198).

[Mahoza, on the Tigris, was largely inhabited by proselytes and their descendants (*Ḳid.* 73*a*). They were noted for their luxury and drunkenness (*R.H.* 17*a* and *Keth.* 65*a*) and were called 'Sons of Hell'. But this condemnation was by no means universal (*Ta'an.* 24*b*; *Ber.* 59*b*). The discussion, at the beginning of this extract, about the 'Three classes', is surely academic: in practice, the third class alone was of importance. I doubt whether the Rabbis really believed that any human being was 'perfectly' righteous or 'perfectly' wicked. Just like other hypothetical cases that we have had before, this was an exercise in logic, all rhetorical arguments and possibilities being taken into account. Could one not find, occasionally, similar extensions, beyond the bounds of ordinary experience, of the discussions of the nature or essence of a given thing, irrespective of its practical use? (H. L.)]

The following passage gives the famous utterance of R. Joshua: 'The righteous of all nations will have a share in the world to come,' which became the official doctrine of the synagogue.

[1653] R. Eliezer said: All the nations will have no share in the world to come [i.e. no heathen or non-Jew will have a share in the world to come], even as it is said, 'The wicked shall go into Sheol, and all the nations that forget God' (Ps. IX, 17). 'The wicked shall go into Sheol' [=hell]: these are the wicked among Israel. R. Joshua said to him: If the verse had said, 'The wicked shall go into Sheol and all the nations,' and had stopped there, I should have agreed with you, but as it goes on to say, 'who forget God', it means that there *are* righteous men among the nations who have a share in the world to come.

(*T.San.* XIII, 2 (Z. p. 434, line 6; Danby's translation, p. 122).)

There is adequate evidence to show that the assertion of R. Joshua was very soon interpreted to mean, not merely that *some* righteous Gentiles would enjoy the felicities of the world to come, but that *all* righteous Gentiles would enjoy them.

[1654] As to those who perished with Korah, the arch-rebel, it is said in one place that they will return from hell. R. Judah b. Bathyra said: They will have a share in the world to come: for what is lost will, at the last, be sought for. [A play upon, and a combination of, the two verses Num. XVI, 33 and Ps. CXIX, 176.] So too did Hannah pray for them, as it is said, 'The Lord casts down to Sheol (=hell) and brings up again' (I Sam. II, 6). (*Num.R.*, Ḳoraḥ, XVIII, 13.)

[1655] All Israel will have a share in the world to come. The biblical proof is Isa. LX, 21, 'They shall all be righteous.' The following have no share in the world to come. He who says the Resurrection of the dead is not indicated in the Law (see p. 600), he who says the Law is not from heaven [i.e. divine], and the Epikouros. R. Akiba said: Also he who reads the alien books, and he who whispers over a wound, and says the words of Exod. XVI, 26. Abba Saul said: He too who pronounces the Divine Name [Yahweh] out loud. Three kings and four private persons have no share in the world to come. The three kings are Jeroboam, Ahab and Manasseh. R. Judah said: Manasseh has a portion in the world to come (II Chron. XXXIII, 13). The four private persons are Balaam, Doeg, Ahithophel and Gehazi. [In the Gemara many rather trivial explanations of 'the Epicurus' are given; thus it is suggested that 'the Epicurus' is the man who despises (or mocks at) the learned. Or it is he who says,

'What use are the Rabbis to us? They learn for themselves, and teach for themselves.' As regards the man who says that the Law is not from heaven, the sentence, 'For he has despised the word of the Lord' (Num. xv, 31) is quoted. Some include under it those who speak insultingly of (or who make false interpretations in) the Torah; others those who (artificially) violate the Abrahamic covenant (cp. I Macc. I, 15).]

Three kings and four private persons have no share in the world to come. The three kings are Jeroboam and Ahab and Manasseh. R. Judah said: Manasseh has a share in the world to come, as it is said, 'And he prayed unto God, and God was intreated of him, and heard his supplication, and brought him again to Jerusalem into his kingdom' (II Chron. XXXIII, 13). They said to R. Judah: God brought him again to his kingdom, but He did not bring him to the life of the world to come. The four private persons are Balaam and Doeg and Ahithophel and Gehazi. [Now it does not escape the notice of the Gemara that Balaam was not an Israelite at all. So it says,] 'Balaam is not to enter the life to come.' Then, are *other* gentiles [=heathen] to enter it. Our Mishnah represents the opinion of R. Joshua. For we are taught in a *Baraita*, R. Eliezer said: The wicked shall go into Sheol and all the nations that forget God: these are the peoples of the world [i.e. the heathen]. R. Joshua said to him: Does it say, '*All* the nations?' Does it not say, 'All the nations that forget God?' Hence: the wicked shall go into Sheol: who are these? They are all the nations who forget God. (*San.* XI, 1, 2 and 99*b* and 105*a* (cp. [818]).)

['Alien books.' These may be non-canonical books, heretical books or foreign books. Various explanations are given and different readings occur. In *T.B.Sab.* 116*b* the books may be Sadducean or Judaeo-Christian. The 'margins', probably containing proof texts, or unorthodox interpretations, are mentioned (*gilyonot* = *Evangelion*). In *T.J.San.* x, § 1, f. 28*a*, lines 17–18, the 'external' or 'alien' books are Ecclesiasticus, Ben Laanah or Homer (**Note 20j**). Elsewhere Tagla is found for Laanah. Laanah, however, may be a deliberate alteration, as the word can mean *curse* or *wormwood*: it may be an allusion to Revelations (*galah*=to reveal) since this apocalypse is said to have been a Jewish book adapted for Christian use. Fürst holds that Laanah stands for Apollonius of Tyana, the pagan philosopher, and Tagla for Empedocles. Perles holds that both are corruptions of *Ta'alah*=*Shu'al*, i.e. 'Fox stories' or the fables of Bidpai. (H. L.)]

With regard to this famous passage from *Sanhedrin*, Moore says: 'A lot in the World to Come is ultimately assured to every Israelite on the ground of the original election of the people by the free grace of God, prompted not by its merits, collective or individual, but solely by God's love, a love that began with the Fathers. For this national election Paul and the church substituted an individual election to eternal life, without regard to race or station. These facts are ignored when Judaism is set in antithesis to Christianity, a "Lohnordnung" over against a "Gnadenordnung". "A lot in the World to Come" is not wages earned by works, but is bestowed by God in pure goodness upon the members of His chosen people, as "eternal life" in Christianity is bestowed on the individuals whom He has chosen, or on the members of the church. If the one is grace, so is the other' (vol. II, p. 95).

Again he says: 'What the Jew craved for himself was to have a part in the future golden age of the nation as the prophets depicted it, the Days of the Messiah, or in the universal Reign of God, or in the Coming Age—always in the realisation of God's purpose of good for His people. It was only so, not in some blissful lot for his individual self apart, that he could conceive of perfect happiness. The idea of salvation for the individual was indissolubly linked with the salvation of the people. This continued to be true in the subsequent development of eschatology, and gives its peculiar character to Jewish ideas of the hereafter' (vol. II, p. 312).

As regards the exceptions to the general rule, he observes: 'These somewhat numerous restrictions of the general proposition at the head of the Mishnah are of the nature of midrash. The significant part of the dogma is in the first sentence, with the exceptions immediately noted, the deniers of the resurrection, of revelation, and of providence or retribution. It is to be noted that they have incurred their fate by denying fundamental articles of orthodoxy—by misbelief, not by misconduct. The amplifications of what is to be regarded as the original anathema are of an essentially different character' (vol. II, p. 388).

[1656] [He judges them] through [the uprightness of] Rahab, Jethro and Ruth.

(*Pes.R.* 167*b*. For the conclusion of this passage see [1568].)

[1657] In the hour when King Messiah is revealed, he will come and stand on the roof of the Temple, and proclaim to Israel, saying, 'Ye meek ones, the time for your redemption has come, and if ye believe not in me, look at my light which shines upon you,' as it says, 'Arise, shine, for thy light has come, and the glory of the Lord is risen upon you' (Isa. LX, 1). And upon you alone has it arisen and not upon the nations, for it says, 'For behold the darkness covers the earth, and gross darkness the peoples, but upon thee does the Lord shine' (*ib.* 2). At that hour will God brighten the light of King Messiah and of Israel, so that all the nations who are in darkness and in gloom, will walk in the light of the Messiah and of Israel, as it says, 'And the nations shall come to thy light.' (*Pes.R.* 162*a fin.*–162*b.*)

[1658] It was a favourite saying of Rab: 'Not like this world is the world to come.' In the world to come there is neither eating nor drinking; no procreation of children or business transactions; no envy or hatred or rivalry; but the righteous sit enthroned, their crowns on their heads, and enjoy the lustre of the Shechinah. (*Ber.* 17*a.*)

Moore says: 'To Rab's (a Babylonian teacher of the third century) description of the World to Come no Tannaite parallel is found, and it does not appear to have been popular. It is echoed in *Ab.R.N.* (vers. I), I, f. 3*a* foot, where the title of Ps. XCI, "A Hymn for the Sabbath Day," is taken, "A day that is all sabbath, in which there is no eating and drinking, and no trading, but the righteous sit with their crowns on their heads, and are nourished by the effulgence of the Shekinah, as it is written, 'and they beheld God, and ate and drank' (Exod. XXIV, 10 f.) like the ministering angels." The blessed hereafter was usually "imagined by the Jews in much more concrete and picturesque fashion"' (vol. II, p. 392).

[1659] R. Simai used to say: There is not a single chapter of the Torah which does not contain the doctrine of the Resurrection, but it is we who have not the power to discern its [true] interpretation. (*Sifre Deut.*, Ha'azinu, § 306, f. 132*a fin.*)

[1660] R. Aḥa b. Ḥanina said: The world to come is not like this world. In this world, on hearing good tidings, a man says, 'Blessed art thou who art good, and dispensest good'; and on hearing sad tidings he says, 'Blessed art thou, the true Judge.' But in the world to come he will only say, 'Blessed art thou, who art good and dispensest good' (cp. *P.B.* p. 292). (*Pes.* 50*a.*)

[1661] R. Jacob said: This world is like a vestibule before the world to come; prepare thyself in the vestibule, that thou mayest enter into the hall. He used to say, 'Better is one hour of repentance and good deeds in this world than the whole life of the world to come; and better is one hour of blissfulness of spirit in the world to come than the whole life of this world.'

(*Aboth* IV, 21, 22; *P.B.* p. 197.)

The final quotation is a great favourite of mine.[1] Yet we must not analyse its exact meaning too closely. The paradox seems to indicate, with a wonderful, yearning graciousness, that there may be a blissful experience in this world which not even the glories of the world to come can rival, but that the fullness of bliss in the world to come is far beyond the best experience which life in this world can offer.

[1] I note with pleasure that E. K. Dietrich (*Die Umkehr*, p. 444) says of this passage: 'Ohne Zweifel gehört dieser Ausspruch über die Umkehr zu den schönsten der rabbinischen Literatur.'

EXCURSUS I

THE USE OF THE ADJECTIVES 'JEWISH' AND 'CHRISTIAN' IN ENGLAND

C. G. Montefiore

In the course of the last thirty years there has been a considerable change in the estimate of the 'Pharisees' and Rabbis by Christian scholars. As I see things, the change has been for the better. The attack upon the Scribes and Pharisees in the Synoptic Gospels is no longer taken 'at the foot of the letter'. It is agreed that in A.D. 28 there were doubtless many black sheep among them, but it is also allowed that there were many white ones, as well as a large number of mixtures —grey sheep, not wholly white, but by no means completely black. Such a view of these old gentlemen is, I am convinced, much nearer to history and truth. It is not unnatural—it is indeed inevitable—that Christian scholars should think that even the good Rabbis were rather dense and foolish to oppose Jesus and his teaching, and should assume that, in their contests with him, they (as the Gospels would lead us to believe) were, historically, always in the wrong, and that Jesus was always in the right. One cannot legitimately object to this. It is sometimes suggested that excess of light can sometimes dazzle. That is an excuse for the wrong-headed Rabbis.

Again, while there used to be a tendency among English scholars, meekly following the lead of German Lutherans, to assume that the Rabbis were ethically a shabby and shoddy lot of creatures, because they were legalists, and a legal religion is a bad religion, and can produce only bad people (formalists, hypocrites, self-righteous men and the like), seeing that the Law, or even law, is the strength of sin—here, too, there has been a vast alteration (see **Note 59 *a***). A beloved and distinguished theologian hazarded the theory that 50 B.C.–A.D. 50 was a specially bad century, so far as Rabbis were concerned—bad ethically and bad religiously—and that the purgations of A.D. 70 and A.D. 135 produced a great change. Thus Jesus (as recorded in the Gospels, and more especially in Mark) was justified, but Paul was thrown over, for the Rabbis after A.D. 135 were certainly not less legalists, but even more confirmed and thorough-going legalists, than their predecessors of 50 B.C.–A.D. 50, and yet *ex hypothesi* they were religiously and ethically far superior.

This advance in impartiality and in historical detachment is the more noteworthy, because Christian scholars are *ab initio* debarred from saying, 'There were faults on both sides', for where Jesus is concerned there can be no faults. He makes the one exception to the otherwise universal rule. Christian scholars can take refuge every now and then, as Dr Martineau did, only in the perilous hypothesis of editorial exaggeration and unauthenticity. All the gentle and beautiful and loving things in the Gospels are authentic; all, or most, or many, of the fierce invectives and of the commitments to hell and to its aeonian flames are either unauthentic, or they do not mean what they seem to mean.

The advance must be gratefully acknowledged by Jews, and especially by those Jews who reverence both Jesus and Hillel, both Paul and R. Johanan b. Zakkai.

Yet, perhaps, in the use of the words Jewish and Christian, there is still room for improvement. Incidentally it may be mentioned that whereas Jewish estimates of Jesus and Paul were often inadequate (the fault has been by no means all on one side), yet, as regards the two adjectives, Jews sin less than Christians. For the Jews do not habitually use the adjective 'Jewish' to mean 'ethically and religiously perfect' (see **Note 59 *b***): Christians are much more inclined to use the adjective Christian in this sort of way. Nor would such a use much matter, if it were not for the human love of foils and contrasts. And what better and more obvious contrast to Christian than Jewish?

The primary meaning of the two adjectives is purely neutral. If I speak of the Jewish religion or of the Christian religion, I pronounce no verdict as to their goodness or badness any more than if I speak of the Buddhist or the Mahommedan religion.

Gradually, however, I suppose, Christians began to use the adjective (as the substantive) Christian in a special sense. Small blame to them if things had stopped there. The great Oxford Dictionary says that 'Christian' is used to mean 'showing character and conduct consistent with discipleship to Christ; marked by genuine piety; following the precepts and example of Christ; Christlike'. Similarly the substantive is used for 'one who exhibits the spirit, and follows the precepts and example, of Christ; a believer in Christ who is characterised by genuine piety'. The first example given of this use of the adjective is from Hooker, 1597; one would have thought that earlier instances could have been discovered (see **Note 59 *c***).

But if, in addition to its obvious neutral sense, 'Christian' means something very excellent and mature, what must 'Jewish' mean? Clearly something poor, immature or even bad, for the two adjectives almost inevitably tended to be used as opposites. A parallel was at hand in the common contrast between the Old Testament and the New. For instead of what I venture to think is the proper and historic way of looking at these two collections—namely that each has its own excellences, and each has its own defects, the usual line taken is to find a series of contrasts (see **Note 59 *d***) to the following effect. The O.T. is preparation; the N.T. is fulfilment. In the first is immaturity, in the second perfection. Or, again, the virtue of the first is justice, of the second, love; in the one is found revenge, in the second, forgiveness; in the one, narrow tribalism, in the other, all-embracing charity. The God of the one is, on the whole, a fierce and cruel God; the God of the other is always a God of mercy, forgiveness and love. The last contrast is, perhaps, the queerest of all when one remembers the many sayings about lovingkindness and forgiveness in the O.T., and the not infrequent denunciations and imprecations in the New. (In some ways it is rather a pleasant thing that in the O.T. Sheol has not yet developed into hell.)

Now far be it from me to deny that there are passages in the O.T.—sayings e.g. about God, or put into the mouth of God—which are cruel, particularistic, revengeful and immature. But it is inaccurate, as well as insulting, to stamp these passages as specifically Jewish. Yet this is what frequently happens. For as Jewish has become the foil and the contrast to Christian, and as Christian can connote only perfection, the more narrow, revengeful and particularistic a given O.T. passage is, the more is it specifically Jewish. Thus Esther becomes the most Jewish book in the O.T., and Jonah the least (see **Note 59 *e***).

But is not the fine ore of a religion its characteristic and essence (if there is an adequate amount of it) rather than its dross? Is not a religion most itself when at its best? Am I to judge the religion of Jesus by 'ye fools and blind', 'ye hypocrites', 'fill up the measure of your fathers, serpents, brood of vipers, who shall not escape the judgment of hell; it shall be more tolerable for Tyre and Sidon at the day of judgment than for you; depart from me, ye cursed, into everlasting fire, prepared for the devil and his angels', or shall I appraise his religion rather by 'love your enemies', 'there is nothing from without, that, entering into a man, can defile him', 'her sins, which are many, are forgiven, for she loved much; ye know not what manner of spirit ye are of, for the son of man is not come to destroy men's lives, but to save them'. In spite of all the specious excuses of the centuries, the one set of sentences are just dross; the others are the essence and the ore.

Again, Christian is an adjective to denominate a living religion, with its millions of adherents. But the adjective is used also to indicate the perfect religion. For hell and eternal punishment, and the virulence of hatred towards heretics and infidels, have all retreated into the background. Christian means sweet reasonableness, toleration, charity, love. But have those Christian writers who still use the word Jewish in a bad sense any vivid recollection of the fact that Judaism, in this feature, at any rate, like Christianity, is also a living religion? Do they suppose that Judaism to-day is 'Jewish' in the 'low' sense of the word, or that it culminated with the writer of Esther? Let us for the moment assume that the O.T. really deserved those strong condemnations which are applied to it. But how far has Judaism to-day freed itself from any O.T. dross? How far does it cherish the ore, and overlook or ignore the dross?

Am I to call the horrors of the Crusades Christian? Or the burnings and tortures of the Inquisition, or for that matter the burnings of Anabaptists and Catholics by Protestants? Are those Christian? Surely not.

A gifted Jewish writer has just called Esther the most *un-Jewish* book in the Hebrew Bible. I think that there is far more justification for this unusual pronouncement than for any stigmatisation of it in the opposite sense. At all events, let the same tests be applied to both religions. If Christian means only what is good, and if all the evil is ignored, forgotten or explained away, let Judaism profit by the same processes. For the second is a living religion no less than the first.

I do not so much mind the contrast between law and grace; law with its servitude over against grace with its freedom. On the whole, the Law is much better understood to-day than forty years ago, though we find no less distinguished a scholar than Dr Oesterley (really Bousset: see **Note 59*f***) writing as follows: 'In the later Greek period Judaism, as is well known, had, in comparison with the religion of the prophets and earlier psalmists, deteriorated through the blighting influence of the Law.'[1] The historic truth is that while there was some deterioration, there was also some advance. Monotheism was becoming more definite, the Law was becoming less priestly, ethics were becoming

[1] *The Age of Transition*, p. 194.

more complete. On the whole, the religion of the Rabbis, inferior to that of the Prophets in some respects, was in others—e.g. in refinement, delicacy, pervasiveness—superior. And as to the Psalter, it is quite on the cards that some of the noblest psalms were by no means the earliest.

It might, indeed, be argued that the O.T. is so much more often particularistic than universalist, so much more often, as regards enemies and God's relations to the enemies of Israel, revengeful and cruel than tender and forgiving, that it is not unfair to use O.T. as an adjective to signify these disagreeable qualities, either absolutely, or in contrast to the predominating N.T. character of sweetness and love. Moreover, as Jews persist in limiting *their* Bible to the O.T., and in regarding that O.T. as religiously and morally perfect and divine, it is not unreasonable to speak of the bad passages and qualities of the O.T. as specifically Jewish. Have they ever been repudiated by Jews till quite modern times (see **Note 59 *g***), and are they not even now repudiated only by a handful of Jews, namely by the Modernists and Liberals? Is not Purim, among all Orthodox Jewish communities, still one of the most popular of Jewish festivals? Is not the scroll on which it is written called *the* scroll, *the* Megillah, as if it were of all the scrolls the dearest and the best?

There are, I think, several lines of reply to these arguments.

(1) I am not clear that, as regards the percentage of good and bad passages, it is numbers which should count, even if it be true, and even if we assume (which I refuse to do off-hand) that the bad passages in the O.T. largely outnumber the good ones. The O.T. religion, in my judgment, is then most distinctive, and is then most true to itself and to its own evolving excellence, if we regard the 'good' passages as more of its essence than the 'bad' ones. The bad ones are the defects and the dross; and do not all religions have their defects and their dross which it may take them long to get rid of and to purge away? It may have taken, or it may take, the Jewish religion a long while fully and openly to divest and cleanse itself of its impurities.

(2) It is true that a most unfortunate 'fundamentalism'—a most unfortunate conception of the Pentateuch and of the whole Hebrew Bible—compelled, and still compels, Orthodox Jews to regard all its teachings as perfect and divine; but, nevertheless, with that delightful inconsistency which is so customary in human nature, the doctrine actually put forward by Jewish theologians and divines became gradually purified. While the 'bad' biblical passages were theoretically

unrepudiated, they were either carefully ignored, or ingeniously, if not very ingenuously, explained away. Today (see **Note 59 *h***) it may safely be asserted that what constitutes Judaism, and what influences the immense majority of Jews, are the 'good' teachings of the O.T. and the good teachings alone. It may even be said with truth that, as regards the very evils for which the O.T. is attacked, and the word Jewish is employed, a great deal is 'read into' the good passages, which tends to make them as universalist and as 'loving' as the most ardent Christian could desire. And Judaism is a living religion, not a museum curiosity. As to Purim, what is really celebrated is the great deliverance. But there is no real hatred of enemies brought in; no virulent cursings and imprecations. At the worst, Haman has become a sort of Jewish Guy Fawkes.

(3) I do not deny that the old Rabbis' religion was prevailingly particularist. The enemies of Israel were the enemies of God. From one point of view to regard the enemies of your nation or of your religious community as being also the enemies of God is a gross offence, but from another point of view it paves the way to the gradual realization of the fact that God, if He be indeed the All-Father, *can* have no enemies. The very idea is ludicrous and absurd. It may, moreover, be noted that, in certain ways and in some passages, there is a fuller and more delicate universalism in the Rabbinic literature than in any portion of the O.T.

Thus to use the word Jewish to mean something religiously and morally imperfect and bad, and to use the word Christian to mean something religiously and morally perfect and good, seems to me to measure two living religions with unequal weights. What would be thought of a Jew who, writing a history of Christianity, spoke of cruelty, persecution and intolerance as specifically Christian? And yet, what endless examples he could find and give of ardent Christians who in deed and writing were cruel, persecuting and intolerant! 'In the tortures and auto-da-fe's of the Inquisition, in the blood bath which accompanied the capture of Jerusalem by the Crusaders, in the fires of Smithfield, in the doctrine of everlasting hell fire, in the deaths of Bruno and Servetus, the true character of Christianity is conspicuously revealed.' What a shocking sentence.

But something of the same sort can be said about Judaism, and it would hardly be noticed. To take a modern instance almost at random. In 1937 there was published an excellent and most useful little Introduction to the O.T. by a Methodist, Dr W. L. Northridge. In the pages about Esther we have the usual business, and the author lets himself go in the easiest and simplest manner. 'The intensity of the hatred which the book reveals is indicated in IX, 13–16, where the demand is made for a second butchery of the non-Jewish population. Here, and in VIII, 7–14, we see Jewish vindictiveness at its worst.' Nevertheless, Esther 'serves a useful purpose at least in setting the contrast between unworthy elements in Judaism and the Christian spirit of love to all, even to one's enemies'. And how often has the Christian spirit of love to all been displayed in fact? Is it displayed in Matthew XXIII or XXV, 41, 46? Is it displayed in John VIII, 44, XVII, 9? Is it displayed in the Christian attitude to heretics and infidels and unbelievers from the days of the Athanasian Creed almost down to eighteen hundred years after the death of the Founder? There is a good deal of glass in both our houses. We had better not throw stones at one another.

If 'Jewish vindictiveness' is intended to mean only that vindictiveness which Jews, like Christians or Mahommedans, or any other body of men, have shown or can show, no exception could be taken to the phrase. But would Dr Northridge write equally facilely about Christian vindictiveness? I doubt it. I think he means by 'Jewish vindictiveness' that vindictiveness is characteristically Jewish, a characteristic mark of Jews and of Judaism. And against such a meaning I must protest. 'Unworthy elements in Judaism': doubtless there have been such; but have there been no unworthy elements in Christianity? It may be the result of powerlessness or of constant oppression, but, as a matter of fact, cruelty to enemies has been far more conspicuously displayed in *deed* during the last 1800 years by Christians than by Jews. As to *words*, I have already called attention in this 'Anthology' to Augustine's appalling chapters about hell, and yet those chapters have found their equals and even their superiors, if one may use the word, in many Christian writings throughout the ages. Whereas, if one wished for 'contrasts', it would be possible to quote remarkable words of forgiveness and gentleness from Jewish sufferers at Christian hands (see **Note 59 *i***).

Nevertheless, the ideal remains. Christians have every right to quote with pride the sayings of Jesus about the love of enemies. And Jews have no less right to quote with pride the Rabbinic sayings that he who is not merciful and kind cannot be of the true seed of Israel, or that he who is reviled and does not revile, returning good for evil, is like the sun when he sets forth in his might. For the adjectives

Jewish and Christian, if used in a non-neutral sense, can and should mean only that which is good and tender and pure. God may be conceived as a hater of sin, but not of the sinner. In that respect Beruria [1290–1] was more 'Jewish', and spoke more according to the true, emerging essence or 'nature' of Judaism (as also of Christianity) than the Psalmist (CXLV, 20).

EXCURSUS II

RABBINICAL AND EARLY CHRISTIAN ETHICS

R. H. Snape

The conspectus of Rabbinical ethics to which I am privileged to add a few pages of historical comparison and contrast is free alike from history and from geography. Changes of time and of place left, it would seem, small trace upon the thought of the Rabbis; it was, with some allowance for personal differences of character and opinion, in the main of one piece. It is unfortunately not possible so to regard the ethical writings of the Fathers of the Church. Second century or third, Greek or Latin, Alexandrian or Syrian or African, are questions that must be answered before we can handle the material which the Fathers provide. Yet some generalisation may prove possible.

One exception, indeed, may perhaps be made immediately; weeds are much the same weeds in any century, in any surroundings, and, it may be added, in most religions. If, under the stress of persecution, some Rabbis saw the nations cast into hell, persecution in Africa of the early third century brought to Tertullian the thought of the joy and exultation to come when the world around him met its rapidly approaching fate. He speaks with grim power and glee of the deified emperors groaning in darkness, of provincial governors in fires more fierce than those of persecution, of philosophers burning together with their deluded victims, and poets under the judgment of Christ. 'I shall have a better opportunity then of hearing the tragedians, louder-voiced in their own calamity; of viewing the play-actors, made more "dissolute" in the dissolving flame; of looking upon the charioteer, all glowing in his chariot of fire; of viewing the wrestlers, not in their gymnasia but tossing in the fiery billows.'[1]

The fruit of patience, which, as Tertullian recognised, he sadly lacked, was vengeance—such vengeance as he depicted above.[2] His gentle and humane pupil, Cyprian, when Africa was again under persecution in the days of Decius, wrote to the proconsul Demetrianus to the same effect. 'Souls with their bodies will be reserved in infinite tortures for suffering. Thus the man will be for ever seen by us who here gazed on us for a season; and the short joy of those cruel eyes in

[1] Tert. *de Spectac.* 30; Gibbon (vol. II, ch. XV) cites the passage with quiet satisfaction.
[2] *Adv. Marc.* IV, 16.

the persecutions that they made for us will be compensated by a perpetual spectacle.'[1]

Lactantius recorded with a fierce joy and, it would seem, no great regard for strict truth, the sufferings and death of the last great persecutors, that all might learn 'how the Almighty manifested His power and sovereign greatness in rooting out and utterly destroying the enemies of His Name'.[2] And Hilary of Poitiers, the great link between East and West in Nicene days, could find no better reason for obeying the difficult commandment to turn the other cheek than that fuller satisfaction would be given if the wrong were stored up against the Day of Judgement.[3] We should do well not to interpret general Christian feeling in the light of these exhibitions of 'the natural man'; there is evidence on the other side.[4] But it is only fair to notice the weeds. We must include among them that very conception of hell which lent its peculiar sting to the melancholy of Samuel Johnson[5] and tormented the gentle spirit of William Cowper.[6] It is well to remember Mill's refusal, even at the risk of damnation, to call evil good.

The whimsies and trivialities of Rabbinical thought may be paralleled to some extent from the writings of the Fathers. There is something very quaint in the moralisation of fourth century natural history by Basil of Caesarea in the true spirit of the medieval bestiaries. The crab, when he catches the oyster sunning himself with shell half-open, throws in a pebble and devours the prey; he is the image of those who

[1] *Ad Demetr.* 24; cf. *Ad Fortunat.* 11: 'how great, how substantial a comfort in his sufferings not to consider his own torments, but to predict the penalties of his tormentor!' Cf. II Clem. XVII ('But the righteous...when they see how those who have done amiss and denied Jesus...are punished with terrible torture in unquenchable fire, shall give glory to their God'). The date is probably about 150: it is uncertain whether the writer belonged to Rome, Corinth or Alexandria. This is the earliest suggestion I have met of the medieval belief that the bliss of the blessed will be increased by their sight of the agonies of the damned, 'as a dark colour', says Gregory the Great (*Mor.* XXXIII, 29), 'is laid on a picture, that the overlying white or red may show more fair'. See G. G. Coulton, *Five Centuries of Religion*, I, 441 ff., III, 6.

[2] *De Mort. Persec.* 1.

[3] *Tractatus super Psalmos*, CXXXII, 16. Lord Herbert of Cherbury (*Autobiography*, ed. W. H. Dicks, p. 40) never took revenge, 'for God, the less I punish mine enemies, will inflict so much the more punishment on them'.

[4] See H. M. Gwatkin, *Early Ch. Hist.* I, 275.

[5] *E.g.* Boswell, *Life of Johnson* (ed. Napier, III, 390), for his view at 75: '"Madam, I do not forget the merits of my Redeemer, but my Redeemer has said that he will set some on his right hand and some on his left"—He was in gloomy agitation and said, 'I'll have no more on't."'

[6] See, *inter alia*, the hideous set of English Sapphics written after his first attempt at suicide.

take advantage of their neighbours' misfortunes. The squid matches the colour of the rock to deceive the fish on which it lives; such are men who court ruling powers. But 'fish do not always deserve our reproaches; often they offer us useful examples'. Each kind of fish remains within its own proper region, unlike men, who move their ancient landmarks and add field to field at the expense of their neighbours.[1] It might come into a Rabbi's mind that but for Israel there would be no sun or rain or that a great Rabbi could bring rain. Just so Tertullian ascribed to Christian prayer a control over the weather. In time of drought the heathen offer sacrifice to Jupiter; 'We, dried up with fastings...rolling in sackcloth and ashes, assail heaven with our importunities—touch God's heart—and, when we have extorted divine compassion, why, Jupiter gets all the honour!'[2]

But most of the whims arise in connection with the ruling system of exegesis. So long as an allegorical interpretation might be found almost at will for any passage of Scripture, strange discoveries were inevitable. Barnabas, late in the first century, found that Abraham foresaw Christ, for he circumcised from his household eighteen men and three hundred. In Greek numerals eighteen is IH or Jesus, and three hundred is T—the cross. 'No one has heard a more excellent lesson from me' says the writer.[3] Yet this preposterous interpretation of a non-existent statement in Genesis[4] was accepted by a formidable array of the Fathers—Clement of Alexandria, Tertullian, Ambrose, Augustine, Paulinus and Gregory the Great, as well as Isidore and Bede.[5]

The home of Christian allegory was Alexandria; there are coincidences of interpretation between Barnabas and Philo which show the immediate connection between Christian and Hellenistic Judaism.[6] The motive for the adoption of this method of interpretation is shown by the parallel use of allegory in Hellenistic philosophy, which it permeated from the early Stoics onward.[7] Failing a modern historical outlook, allegory was the only available method of eliminating the

[1] *Hexaemeron*, Hom. VII, 3.

[2] *Apologeticus*, 40. The Christian soldiers of the Melitene legion obtained rain by prayer for Marcus Aurelius in battle (Euseb. *Ecc. Hist.* V, 5).

[3] Barn. IX, 7, 8.

[4] It is produced by a combination of Gen. XIV, 14 and XVII, 23, 27.

[5] So Farrar, *Hist. Interp.* 168; Clement, *Strom.* VI, 11; I have not troubled to verify the statement further.

[6] Hatch, *Influence of Greek Ideas*, p. 72.

[7] Gilbert Murray, *Five Stages of Greek Religion*, pp. 199 ff. It had already been used by the Cynics.

crudities, anthropomorphisms and immoralities of early religions. What Greek interpretation did for Homer, for religious traditions and ancient rituals, Rabbinical and early Christian thought attempted, and by much the same method, for the Old Testament. The principle once established, allegorical interpretations were sought also in the New Testament. Clement of Alexandria, at the beginning of the third century, implies throughout the existence of a double sense in Scripture, and holds that the primary sense is only for babes in religion.[1] His great successor Origen defended the method against the philosopher Celsus; 'Are the Greeks alone at liberty to convey a philosophic meaning in a secret covering?'[2] Distinguishing three meanings of Scripture, historical, moral, mystic or spiritual,[3] he pointed out that some events in Scripture were physically impossible, as the existence of morning and evening before the sun, or the carrying up of Christ into a mountain by Satan to view the kingdoms of the earth. Some were morally impossible, as the punishment of the child for the sins of the father, the Jewish wars of extermination, the command to pluck out the offending eye, or to turn the left cheek to him who has smitten the right—for are not nearly all men right-handed?[4] But the very impossibility meant that the hidden meaning was all-important. It was not that Origen neglected the primary sense; it was to Origen's homily on 'Abraham commanded to sacrifice his son' that Erasmus was to appeal in favour of the plain words of Scripture as against the medieval development of the text: 'The letter killeth, but the spirit maketh alive.'[5] But he found that the nations whom the Israelites were to overcome in Palestine typified the sins which occupy the soul of man,[6] and discovered in the list of the camps of the Hebrew army through the desert evidence of the pre-existence of the soul;[7] and such interpretation, fascinating if arbitrary, won the day against the cooler historico-grammatical exegesis of the school of Antioch. Protest was of little avail. Methodius (martyred 312) objected to Origen's allegorizing, and yet found an ascetic meaning for Ps. CXXXVII: the harps are the bodies, hung upon the branches of chastity, typified by the willow.[8] Basil of Caesarea in the later fourth

[1] E.g. *Strom.* V, 4.
[2] *Contra Cels.* IV, 38; cf. I, 12.
[3] E.g. *Hom. in Levit.* V.
[4] *De Princ.* IV, i, 18; cf. II, v, 1 ff. and *Contra Cels.* VII, 61; C. Bigg, *Origins of Christianity*, p. 427.
[5] Seebohm, *Oxford Reformers*, XV, 2.
[6] T. B. Strong, *Christian Ethics*, pp. 260, 216.
[7] Bigg, *Origins of Christianity*, p. 438.
Banquet, IV, 3.

century might say that Origen was wrong in seeing in the separation of the waters above and below the firmament the division of good spirits from bad. 'Let us understand that by water water is meant.'[1] But the principle was firmly established, and Basil too used allegory where it suited his purpose.

It was with the New Testament almost as with the Old. Victorinus of Petau (martyred *c.* 303) comments thus on 'and he was girt about the paps with a golden girdle' (Rev. I, 13): 'His paps are the two Testaments and the golden girdle is the choir of saints, as gold tried in the fire.'[2] The West learned the method from the East; the Homilies of Hilary of Poitiers (fourth century) on the Psalms provide perhaps the most influential example.[3] Ambrose borrowed freely from Hilary in his commentary on certain Psalms; and Ambrose leads on to Augustine with a fourfold sense of Scripture, and to Gregory the Great, interpreting the Book of Job with complete disregard of its poetical character and finding in it the whole teaching of the Christian Church, its sacraments and a universal moral philosophy.[4]

So much must be said of the undesirable and the outworn in the writings of the Fathers. A few facts may be given to redress the balance. If the fruit of patience for Tertullian was revenge, it was Tertullian who wrote magnificently 'You have seen a brother, you have seen your Lord.'[5] This was brotherhood between Christian and Christian, the brotherhood marked by the 'kiss of peace' which formed part of every service. The philosopher Celsus, writing in the later second century, was scandalised by the width of this brotherhood. 'Those who invite to other mysteries make proclamation as follows: "Everyone who has clean hands and a prudent tongue"; others again thus: "He who is free from all pollution, and whose soul is conscious of no evil, and who has lived well and justly,"...But let us hear what kind of persons these Christians invite. "Every one", they say, "who is a sinner, who is devoid of understanding, who is a child, and, to speak generally, whoever is unfortunate, him will the Kingdom of God receive."'[6] Origen points out that the invitation is an invitation to be healed, and that God will accept the unrighteous man if, 'after passing condemnation on himself for his past conduct, he walk humbly on account of it, and in a becoming manner for the time to come'.[7] But even this broad brotherhood, which until after

[1] *Hexaemeron*, Hom. III, 9.
[2] Comm. on Apoc. I, 13.
[3] E. W. Watson, *Nicene and Post-Nicene Fathers*, N.S. IX, XI ff.
[4] See F. H. Dudden, *Gregory the Great*, I, 192 ff.
[5] *De Orat.* 26.
[6] Orig. *Contra Cels.* III, 59.
[7] *Ibid.* 62.

the close of the third century gave to Christians their name of 'the brethren',[1] did not stand in the way of the broader conception, shared by Rabbi and Stoic and Christian alike, of the brotherhood of mankind. 'Your brethren, too, we are,' cries Tertullian to the rulers of the Empire, 'by the law of one mother nature, though ye are hardly men, because brothers so unkind.'[2] Origen's view was wider still. He maintained, indeed, that the heretic whose moral life is good is worse, because more dangerous, than one whose moral life is evil.[3] But in him burned the trust 'that somehow good will be the final goal of ill', that 'not one life shall be destroyed, or cast as rubbish to the void'. The object of future punishment is remedial; the fire of hell is the spiritual consequence of sin. 'When the soul shall be found to be beyond the order and connection and harmony in which it was created by God for the purposes of good and useful action and observation, and not to harmonise with itself in the connection of its rational movements, it must be deemed to bear the chastisement and torture of its own dissension, and to feel the punishments of its own disordered condition, and when this dissolution and rending asunder of soul shall have been tested by the application of fire, a solidification undoubtedly into a firmer structure will take place and a restoration be effected.'[4] And the present age is only one of a series of world-orders following one another in an upward direction: 'after this age . . . there will be other ages to follow.' The end will be the restitution of all things, when the whole universe shall come to a perfect termination.[5] Evil spirits have fallen as man has fallen; they too improve.[6] From the logical consequence that the Devil, as Burns wished, would repent and be saved, Origen seems to have drawn back: 'a thing', he wrote, 'which no man can say even if he has taken leave of his senses.'[7] Yet this is the logical consequence of the noblest of theories.

[1] Harnack, *Expans. of Christianity*, II, 10 (1905). The title was then restricted for use between ecclesiastic and ecclesiastic, or was given by ecclesiastics to a layman as a mark of honour.

[2] *Apologeticus*, 39.

[3] *In Ezech.* Hom. VII, 3; Bigg, *Origins of Christianity*, p. 427.

[4] *De Princ.* II, x, 5; so too the Origenist, Gregory of Nyssa, *On the Soul and the Resurrection*. See W. R. Inge, *Philos. of Plotinus*, I, 202, II, 17 ff. for Origen's conflict with traditional eschatology: spirits have no need to masticate, and we need not suppose that God will supply new teeth to gnash with. 'All religious eschatology is a mass of contradictions' (*ib.* II, 7).

[5] *De Princ.* II, iii, 5; cf. III, vi, 3; W. R. Inge, *Philos. of Plotinus*, II, 19.

[6] *De Princ.* I, vi, 3.

[7] See his letter given by Rufinus, *De Adult. Lib. Orig.*; he complains of mutilation and falsification of his writings by heretics in Palestine, Ephesus and Antioch.

Down to the middle of the third century, it may be said, the Christian Church, as in Pauline days, contained not many of the rich, powerful or highly educated classes. It consisted, mainly, of the traders, craftsmen, slaves, of the cities. It was obscure and universalist, intolerant and persecuted. On most of its members little conscious influence was as yet exercised by Greek philosophy. They came from those strata of the population which still clung to the old paganism, or were attracted by the mystery religions or by the barbaric intermixture of Orientalism and Platonism which produced Gnosticism in its many forms. The church from which II Clement emanated half-way through the second century may have been that of Rome, of Corinth or of Alexandria; its antecedents in any case were pagan. 'We were maimed in our understanding, worshipping stone and wood and gold and silver and copper, the works of men.'[1] And again, 'We who are living do not sacrifice to the dead gods and do not worship them.'[2] Paganism had strengthened itself during the first century, which saw new temples, new priesthoods, new rites and new festivals.[3] Reinforced by a syncretic monotheism, and by Roman patriotism, it survived among the aristocracy of the West until the fall of the Western Empire;[4] and in Gaul, St Martin (d. 400) struggled against paganism among the country folk, who could be met carrying about through their fields 'the images of demons vested with a white covering'.[5] It is probably a mark of the severity of the struggle that, while the Rabbinical view of idolatry coincided with that of St Paul[6] in holding that idols are nothing, the Christian apologists—and indeed almost all Christian writers—held that the gods are not empty names, but demons who, dwelling in the idols, filled them with the powers of hell.[7] The belief persisted; in Gaul, when the Western Empire was

[1] II Clement I, 6.

[2] *Ib.* III, I.

[3] Lightfoot, *Apostolic Fathers* (1883), II, 449.

[4] Dill, *Roman Society in the Last Century of the Western Empire*, I, ii, iii. The patrician families of Rome were only beginning to adopt Christianity in the fourth century (W. Bright, *Age of the Fathers*, I, 361).

[5] Sulp. Severus, *Life of St Martin*, p. 12. The African Arnobius (*adversus Gentes*, I, 39) was converted from paganism in the later third century.

[6] I Cor. VIII, 4.

[7] E.g. Justin Martyr, *Apol.* I, 5; Minucius Felix, *Octavius*, 27; Athenagoras, 24–27; Theophilus, *ad Autolycum*, I, 10; Tatian, *ad Graec.* 16–19; Tertullian, *Apologeticus*, 22; *de Spect.* 13; Cyprian, *de Idol.* 7; of the Alexandrians Clement (Exhortation 4) seems to reckon the idols as naught, but Origen (*Contra Cels.* VII, 69) holds that they who worship the gods worship demons. In a commentary on Isaiah (sect. 236) attributed to Basil of Caesarea, it is alleged that the devils, liking rich fare, crowd the temples to enjoy the sacrifices offered to the idols; Gregory of Nazianzus holds the same view (*Carm.* II, *Epig.* 28).

tottering, St Martin was in the habit of rebuking the demons by their names as they came to him. 'He found Mercury a cause of special annoyance, while he said that Jupiter was stupid and doltish.'[1] Centuries afterwards Diana was still summoning the witches to their nightly feasts.[2]

But for those for whom the old pagan beliefs had broken down, there was help in the mystery religions. The Hellenistic world turned from the Olympian Deities to the contemplation of Chance, or Fortune or Fate, whose last stroke was death. The stars, at first inexorably pronouncing man's fate, became evil, malignant and pitiless. On earth we are the sport of Fate, or of Chance which rules beneath the moon. Above the moon reigns Necessity; and further above still lies the realm of true Being, of freedom, and of ultimate union with God.[3] The mystery religion offered, as its salvation, delivery from the tyranny of Fate, an immortality reached by a process of regeneration, a divine life imparted by the transformation of essence described as deification.[4]

Into this world came Christianity, offering, among other things, the Old Testament, the Law and the Prophets together. The Pauline 'gospel *about* Jesus', setting the historic Jesus within the scope of a great cosmic drama, offered, like the mystery religions, immortality and a divine life; and, though these religions had an ethical side, it offered a greater gift, a share in a divine love and holiness which implied an incessant moral demand, and a complete surrender of self to Jesus.[5] The gospel *of* Jesus, therefore, was implied in Paulinism, and this gospel the Church would not and did not separate from the Law and the Prophets. The belief that the Old Testament, through and through, was divine and perfect, was taken over bodily from Judaism.

Before the middle of the third century, it may be said, Christianity was fighting not only its own battle, but that of Judaism also. The very philosophers who accepted Christianity—and most of the Apologists wrote as philosophers—attributed the best that the heathen had

[1] Sulp. Severus, *Dial.* II, 13.

[2] T. Wright, *Proceedings against Dame Alice Kyteler* (Cam. Soc.), IV, and refs.; G. G. Coulton, *A Medieval Garner* (1910), p. 125; Michelet, *La Sorcière*, 55, 141.

[3] Gilbert Murray, *Five Stages of Greek Religion*, pp. 163 ff., 180 ff., 'We are above Fate.' (Tatian, *ad Graec.* 9.)

[4] H. A. A. Kennedy, *St Paul and the Mystery Religions*, p. 198; S. Angus, *The Mystery Religions and Christianity*, pp. 139, 227 ff. Writers of the Alexandrian school did not hesitate to speak of the 'deification' of man by Christianity; the West was more cautious (W. R. Inge, *Christian Mysticism*, pp. 356 ff.).

[5] Kennedy, *op. cit.* pp. 21 ff., cf. Hatch, *Influence of Greek Ideas*, pp. 291 ff.

learned to acquaintance with the Jewish Scriptures. The appeal to antiquity was a strong argument in itself, and Moses was more ancient than any Greek philosopher. Christ, the Divine Word, declared Justin Martyr, was with every race of men; and 'those who lived "with the Word" are Christians, even though they have been thought atheists; as among the Greeks, Socrates and Heraclitus'. But Plato was indebted to Moses for his finest thoughts.[1] Even Clement of Alexandria, who attached the greatest value to Greek philosophy, took exactly the same position. Clement ridicules those who are frightened of classical culture and thought.[2] But he ascribes the wisdom of the Greeks in part to tradition derived from the knowledge which angels betrayed to the women they loved, in part to plagiarism from Moses and the prophets.[3] Origen, arguing against the philosopher Celsus, is more restrained. He admits that Plato, for example, has said things well, 'for it is God who revealed to men these, as well as all other, noble expressions'.[4] He defends the Jewish Scriptures against the attacks of Celsus, and cites from Josephus the report of Hermippus that the Pythagorean philosophy was Jewish in origin.[5] The antiquity of Moses is cited to prove that he cannot have borrowed from Greek philosophy;[6] but the general indebtedness of the Greeks to Judaism is not asserted. Even Origen, who made the widest use of Greek philosophy, was not concerned to exalt it by giving it a close connection with the Old Testament.

By most Christian writers, especially in the West, there was little love wasted on the culture of the pagan world which persecuted the Church. The calm Minucius Felix sees divine inspiration in the view of Thales that God was that mind which from water framed all things.[7] But he can find no better term for Socrates than that attributed to Zeno—'scurra Atticus'—and calls his 'demon' most deceitful. 'We despise the bent brows of the philosophers, whom we know to be corrupters and adulterers and tyrants.'[8] For Tertullian philosophers are merely 'the patriarchs of heresy'. 'What indeed', he cries,

[1] Justin Martyr, *Apol.* I, 44, 46, 59; cf. Theophilus, *ad Autolycum*, III, 9, etc. The theory of borrowing went back to Aristobulus, the Alexandrian Jew of the second century B.C. and to Philo (Lecky, *Hist. Eur. Morals*, I, 344). It was still an open question in Augustine's time.

[2] *Strom.* I, 1; B. H. Streeter, *Prim. Ch.* p. 234.

[3] *Strom.* V, 1. For his theory of plagiarism, cp. *Strom.* V, 14, etc. Miltiades learned from Moses the strategy by which he won the battle of Marathon (*Strom.* I, 24).

[4] *Contra Cels.* VI, 3.

[5] *Ib.* I, 16: *Jos. c. Apionem*, I, 22.

[6] *Contra Cels.* IV, 11, 36.

[7] *Octav.* 19.

[8] *Ib.* 55.

'has Athens to do with Jerusalem? What concord is there between the Academy and the Church?...Away with all attempts to produce a piebald Christianity of Stoic, Platonic and dialectic composition! We want no curious disputation after possessing Christ Jesus, no inquiry after enjoying the Gospel.'[1] 'Abstain from all the heathen books,' say the Apostolic Constitutions[2] in the fourth century. 'For what hast thou to do with such foreign discourses or laws or false prophets?' The Books of Kings provide history, the Prophets, Job and Proverbs provide wisdom and poetry, there are psalms to sing, Genesis gives knowledge of the origin of things, and for laws and statutes there is the Law of God, with due distinction between precepts still binding and those relaxed. The Old Testament was regarded as a repository of all knowledge and culture. The way was open for Jerome to ask how Horace could go with the psalter, Virgil with the Gospels and Cicero's epistles with Paul's.[3] Sulpicius Severus[4] points on to the famous letter in which Gregory the Great expresses his horror at hearing that a bishop teaches 'grammar', or Latin literature in all its branches. All this, however, even in its later stages, implies the repulsion, not of ignorance but of knowledge. Gregory the Great himself received the usual education of a Roman boy of high rank, and, according to Gregory of Tours, was held eminent in grammar, rhetoric and logic. Tertullian's ultimate objection was not so much to philosophy as to the particular doctrines of current philosophy. Willy-nilly, Gentile Christians thought in a method and in terms more or less philosophic.

It was not without difficulty that the Church retained its hold on the Old Testament. Christianity inherited the struggle which the Hellenic world had seen in pre-Christian days between Judaism and Gnosticism. Most of the Gnostic sects were violently anti-Jewish, speaking of 'the accursed God of the Jews' and identifying him with Saturn, most evil of the planets, or with the Devil.[5] Christianised Gnosticism identified its expected Saviour in one way or another with Jesus, but maintained its earlier attitude towards the God of the Old Testament. The main strength of Gnosticism lay in the primitive and obsolete parts of the Jewish Scriptures. The conflict was at its height in the second half of the second century. Marcion, Tertullian's

[1] *De Anima*, 3; *Adv. Hermog.* 8: *De Praes. Haer.* 7.

[2] 1, 6.

[3] *Ad Eustoch.* 29.

[4] *Life of St Martin*, 1. There can be no profit in reading of Hector or Socrates; it is absolute madness not to treat them with the utmost severity.

[5] Gilbert Murray, *Five Stages of Greek Religion*, pp. 196 ff.

'Pontic mouse' who 'gnawed the gospels to pieces'[1] at Rome about 140, may be taken as representative of the Gnostic attitude in general. The God of the Old Testament is the creator and ruler of the world. But nature and the revelation to Israel alike show that this God cannot even be regarded as absolutely just, still less absolutely good and merciful.[2] There is, however, far above creation, a God truly perfect, whose essential attribute is Love; Christ revealed Him and wrested the world from the Creator, or Demiurge.[3] Although his church admitted to baptism only those willing thenceforward to remain celibate,[4] Marcion established a flourishing organisation which still existed at the close of the seventh century.[5] Closely akin were the Manicheans, whose more overt dualism also involved a rejection of the God of the Old Testament. 'Him again who spake with Moses and the Jews and the priests, he [Manes] declares to be the prince of the darkness.' 'It is a thing not without peril, therefore, for any one of you to teach the New Testament along with the Law and the Prophets, as if they were of one and the same origin.'[6] But in East and West, Christian theology, holding fast to the historical connection between Christianity and Judaism, held also that the God of Old Testament and New was one, a perfect God of justice, wisdom, love and mercy, the God, says Origen, of all just men—of Adam, Abel, Seth, Enos, Enoch, Noe, Sem, Abraham, Isaac, Jacob, the twelve Patriarchs, Moses and the Prophets.[7]

The Law, then, and the Prophets were accepted by the Church as divinely and completely inspired. The use of the prophetical books in early Christian literature may be set aside here; they became too often sources for quotations, atomistically detached from their context and supplied, by a forced interpretation, with a literal fulfilment.[8] It is of more moment to see what early Christianity made of the Law. To Paul not merely were the Mosaic ordinances, though divine, temporary; all codes of precepts and systems of restraint involved a bondage which

[1] *Adv. Marc.* I.

[2] *Ib.* I, 2, 13, 14, 'I am He that createth evil' (Isa. XLV, 7); there must be another God.

[3] Hippolytus, X, 17; F. J. Foakes Jackson, *Christian Difficulties in the Second and Twentieth Centuries*, pp. 28 ff.; cf. Hatch, *Influence of Greek Thought*, p. 227; B. H. Streeter, *Primitive Church*, p. 179.

[4] Tert. *adv. Marc.* IV, 11.

[5] Hatch, *op. cit.* p. 227; F. C. Burkitt (*Early Eastern Christianity*, p. 141) suggests that baptism was no doubt delayed till late in life.

[6] Archelaus, *Disputation with Manes*, pp. 10, 13.

[7] *De Princ.* I, i, 4.

[8] Justin Martyr is fairly typical: e.g. Gen. XLIX, 10 is interpreted of Christ.

was dissolved by Christ.[1] Conscience is supreme; the only Law is the voice of the Spirit within, the inner convictions of a man's own heart. It is very like the Quaker's belief in the Inner Light, a prophet's conception, closely paralleled by Jeremiah: 'After those days, saith the Lord, I will put my Law in their inward parts and write it in their hearts; and will be their God and they shall be my people. And they shall teach no more every man his neighbour, and every man his brother, saying Know the Lord: for they shall all know me, from the least of them unto the greatest of them.'[2] But the great mystic had himself to combat antinomianism and sin committed 'that grace may abound'. The sub-apostolic Church, more timid, less conscious of the inspiration of the Spirit, fell back upon the conception of Christ as another Moses, a lawgiver laying down commandments for a new righteousness. The Canon of the New Testament was shaped, first by Marcion's violent determination of its content at Rome, and then by the orthodox rejection of Phrygian prophecy in the hands of Montanus and his successors. By about 180 a New Testament stood definitely over against the Old; and first of all its books was Matthew, written by one who was, 'so to speak, a Christian Rabbi',[3] with the Sermon on the Mount as a parallel to the Law given on Sinai, a persistent emphasis on the necessity of good works, and, for its great aim, insistence that all men should 'observe whatsoever Jesus commanded'.[4]

What, then, was the Law of Christ? The study of a character will yield principles; but principles do not, by themselves, constitute a code, and the gospels gave little more. There was a strong tendency to look in some way or other towards the older Law. Part of it, as Paul had held, was temporary; but the whole Law, as Paul had said, was spiritual[5]—susceptible, that is, of a symbolical or allegorical interpretation on the lines indicated in Hebrews. Barnabas, about the beginning of the second century, was sure that circumcision was never intended to be observed literally: 'They erred because an evil angel was misleading them.'[6] He found a meaning for the red heifer which the Rabbis left unexplained. It was comparatively easy to deal with the Law as to food. 'Moses spoke in the spirit. He mentioned

[1] Lightfoot, *Galatians*, p. 118; C. Bigg, *Origins of Christianity*, p. 81.

[2] Jer. XXXI, 33–4; W. R. Inge, *Truth and Falsehood in Religion*, p. 49.

[3] F. C. Burkitt, *Gospel History*, p. 191.

[4] B. W. Bacon, *The Making of the New Testament*, pp. 150 ff.

[5] Rom. VII, 14; cited, e.g., by Novatian, *de Cib. Jud.* 2; Origen, *de Princ.* (preface).

[6] Barnabas IX, 4, 74*a*; *ib.* VIII.

the swine for this reason; you shall not consort, he means, with men who are like swine, that is to say, when they have plenty they forget the Lord, but when they are in want they recognize the Lord.'[1] But Barnabas draws a further distinction. There were two Laws. The Decalogue, written on tables of stone, was not given to the Jews, for the tables were broken, 'but the Lord Himself gave it to us'.[2] Irenaeus, nearly a century later, worked out the idea differently. The natural precepts are all common to Christians and to Jews, though by the former more fully developed.[3] These precepts are written in the Decalogue. But by reason of the worship of the calf God instituted a second Law, to which Moses added some precepts 'on account of their hardness' of heart;[4] the Jews themselves looked upon the ceremonial Law as of secondary importance.[5] And the ceremonial Law was in part typical,[6] if in part it was penal. Christ Himself (Matt. XXIII, 23) ordered the Law to be observed while Jerusalem was still in safety; His blame of the Scribes and Pharisees arose not from their respect for the words of the Law, but from their lack of love. Christ brought down from heaven no greater commandment than the greatest of the Old Covenant: the precepts of a perfect life are the same in both Testaments—love of God, and love for a neighbour as thyself.[7]

In Africa, at the opening of the third century, Tertullian, lawyer and Puritan, went further. The Law adds to the 'prime counsels of innocence, chastity and justice and piety' recorded in the Decalogue, prescriptions of humanity—the freeing of slaves every seventh year, the unmuzzling of the ox, and so forth. Even the *lex talionis* had its value for a people too impatient to await the vengeance of God; and the minute prescriptions as to the common transactions of life ensured that the people 'might not be at any moment out of the sight of God'. The Law 'simply bound a man to God, so that no one ought to find fault with it except him who does not choose to serve God'.[8] The Law which deals with piety, sanctity, humanity, truth, chastity, justice, mercy, benevolence, modesty, remains in its entirety, and blessed is the man who shall meditate upon it day and night.[9]

[1] *Ib.* x, 2–3. See also Novatian, *de Cib. Jud.* (Rome, middle of third century), where the swine becomes an emblem of a life 'delighting in the garbage of vice' (III); Clem. Alex. *Paed.* III, 11, *Strom.* II, 15, for the East; and Origen, *de Princ.* IV, i, 17—who ever ate a vulture?

[2] Barnabas XIV, 1–5.

[3] Iren. IV, xiii, 4. Irenaeus, born in Asia Minor, was bishop of Lyons and wrote between 182 and 188.

[4] *Ib.* IV, xv, 1, 2.

[5] *Ib.* IV, xvii, 3.

[6] *Ib.* IV, xviii, 16, 5.

[7] *Ib.* IV, xii, 4, 2.

[8] Tert. *adv. Marc.* II, 17–19.

[9] *De Pud.* 6.

Tertullian has no hesitation in tracing a connection between those parts of the Sermon on the Mount given in Luke—he is arguing against Marcion, who recognised no other gospel—and the Old Testament. 'Love your enemies' is a renewal and republication of Isaiah's 'Say, Ye are our brethren, to those who hate you.' Christ added, no doubt, the command to turn the other cheek, but this, and other additions, are quite in keeping with the discipline of the Creator.[1] It is not surprising to find Tertullian's more orthodox disciple, Cyprian, also an African and a lawyer, appealing to the Law on quite everyday matters. Wages should be paid quickly (Lev. XIX, 13); divination must not be used (Deut. XVIII, 10); a tuft of hair is not to be worn on the head and the beard must not be plucked (Lev. XIX, 27); we must rise when a bishop comes (Lev. XIX, 32).[2]

Another example of the same tendency, of historical importance in England, is afforded by the acceptance by the Council of Neocaesarea (*c.* 315) of the Levitical prohibition of marriage with a husband's brother. The general view of Christianity taken in the fourth and later centuries reflects the conclusions of the earlier period. Constantine, attempting to heal the discord between Alexander, bishop of Alexandria, and Arius, argued that they do not differ on 'any important precept contained in the Law'.[3] His son Constantius wrote in 359 of Christianity as 'the divine and adorable Law'.[4] In 386 the Emperor Maximus wrote to his co-ruler Valentinian warning him of the danger of violating Catholic churches and overturning 'the most holy Law'.[5]

Alexandrian theology tended to present Christianity as a philosophy rather than as a Law. Clement of Alexandria was ethically a Greek; but for him the Mosaic Law was the fountain of all ethics; it was humane and the teacher of righteousness. It commanded us to love strangers not only as friends and relatives, but as ourselves, both in body and in soul. It honoured the nations and bore no grudge against those who have done evil, for 'thou shalt not abhor an Egyptian'—that is, any one in the world. The whole system of Moses is suited for the training of such as are capable of becoming good and noble men, and for hunting out men like them.[6] The Jew who be-

[1] *Adv. Marc.* IV, 14, 16.

[2] *Test.* III, 81–5. The common title, 'Testimonies against the Jews' is erroneous: Cyprian, as his preface shows, was merely preparing a summary of 'heavenly precepts' to refresh the memory, and had no controversial purpose.

[3] Socrates, *H.E.* I, 7.

[4] Athanas. *de Syn.* 55.

[5] W. Bright, *Age of the Fathers*, I, 497.

[6] *Strom.* II, 18; I, 26.

comes a Christian, Origen protested, does not abandon the usages of his fathers: the introduction to Christianity is through the Mosaic worship and the prophetic writings—of course, allegorically interpreted.[1]

But Alexandria and the sphere of Alexandrian influence was not the whole of the East. From Antioch, it is probable, there was spread, before the close of the first century,[2] the book known as the Didache —'the Lord's Teaching, by the Twelve Apostles, to the Gentiles.' It is, as we have it, a manual of Church instruction, and its first part, 'the Two Ways', deals with Christian ethics, as taught to those willing to be baptized. Until the fourth century, the doctrine of the 'Two Ways' was of the greatest importance. Barnabas knew and used it about the close of the first century; the writer of II Clement a little later was acquainted with it. In Syria and in Egypt the Didache had a prestige which led, when the church organization which it describes was out-of-date, to revised versions being produced—the Didascalia and the Apostolic Constitutions, Book VII.[3] A Latin version exists, either of parts of the Didache, or of some cognate work; so that the West also must have come under its influence.

The 'Two Ways' is, in the opinion of many scholars, pre-Christian—a Jewish document; and even if this is not the case, there is no doubt that the ethics which, according to the Didache, the Gentiles learned through the Apostles, and which Gentile catechumens received in places where the Didache prevailed, were of a sort with which few Rabbis would not have sympathised.

'The Way of Life is this: "First thou shalt love the God who made thee, secondly, thy neighbour as thyself; and whatsoever thou wouldst not have done to thyself, do not thou to another."'[4] 'There is none other commandment greater than these', Jesus had said of the first clause and the second, and of the third, 'for this is the Law and the Prophets'.

There follows a commentary, based on the Sermon on the Mount

[1] *Contra Cels.* II, 3, 4.

[2] B. H. Streeter, *Primitive Church*, p. 145: the date assigned is A.D. 90.

[3] Streeter, *op. cit.* pp. 285–6.

[4] Didache I, 2; Barnabas XIX, 5. 'Thou shalt love thy neighbour more than thine own life.' He omits the Golden Rule. The Apostolic Constitutions, like the Didache, give the negative form of the Golden Rule as do some MSS. in Acts XV, 29. Theophilus (*ad Autol.* I, 35), Irenaeus (III, xii, 14). Rabbula, bishop of Edessa in the fifth century (Burkitt, *Early Eastern Christianity*, p. 110) gives both forms. The source of the negative form is apparently Tobit IV, 15. Tertullian (*Adv. Marc.* IV, 16) remarks that the positive form no doubt implies the negative.

and the Decalogue. Love those that hate you—the heathen, said the writer of II Clement, when they see that we do not even love those who love us, laugh us to scorn[1]—turn the other cheek; if any man take thy coat, give him thy shirt also. Give to everyone who asks; the penalty falls on the receiver if he receives without need. But—in a different vein—it was also said 'Let thine alms sweat into thy hands until thou knowest to whom thou art giving.'[2] Do not hesitate to give or grumble when giving, 'for thou shalt know who is the good Paymaster of thy reward'. Share everything and claim nothing as your own.[3] Great importance was attached to almsgiving, which was organised by the Church.[4] 'Fasting is better than prayer, but the giving of alms is better than both.'[5] To Cyprian, in Africa of the mid third century, almsgiving had a propitiatory value; it extinguished sin. He rested his proof on the Jewish Apocrypha in the African version: 'As water [baptism] extinguishes fire [hell], so almsgiving quenches sin' (Ecclus. III, 30) and 'By almsgiving and faith sins are purged' (Prov. XVI, 6).[6] He has no hesitation in dwelling on the reward—mainly, of course, in the next world, but in this, too. There is no need to fear poverty; he that giveth to the poor shall never lack (Prov. XXVIII, 27).[7] As Basil of Caesarea put it in the fourth century, when you supply a poor man's need, the transaction is at once a gift and a loan.[8] We are well on the way towards Leo the Great (*c.* 450) and the Middle Ages: 'Let no one...flatter himself in any merits of a good life if works of charity be wanting in him, and let him not trust in the purity of his body if he be not cleansed by the purification of almsgiving.'[9]

The Didache then turns to the Decalogue; do not murder, nor commit adultery, nor steal, nor covet, nor bear false witness, nor speak evil. Do not be double-minded or double-tongued. Hate no

[1] II Clement XIII, 41.

[2] Didache I; Hermas II, *Mandatum* II: 'Give to all the needy in simplicity, not hesitating as to whom you are to give or not to give'; the receiver will have to give an account. Basil the Great, bishop of Caesarea in the later fourth century, thought otherwise: 'For whoever gives to the afflicted gives to the Lord and from the Lord shall have his reward; but he who gives to every vagabond casts to a dog' (*Epist.* 150, 4).

[3] Didache IV, 7, 8. Barnabas repeats the passage about the Paymaster.

[4] Tertullian, *Apol.* 39, describes the administration of the common fund; it is this charity which compels the enemies of the Christians to say 'See how they love one another.'

[5] II Clement XVI, 4.

[6] Cyprian, *On Works and Alms*, 2. He cites also Dan. IV, 27 and Tobit XII, 8, 9.

[7] *Ib.* 8.

[8] *Hom. in Ps.* XIV (XV).

[9] *Serm.* X, 4.

man; some you shall reprove and for some pray, and some love more than life. Pride, jealousy, contention and passion lead to murder; base words and lifting up of the eyes lead to adultery; astrology and magic to idolatry; lying, love of money and vainglory to theft; grumbling, stubbornness and thinking evil to blasphemy. Be long-suffering, merciful, guileless, quiet and good: 'receive the accidents that befall thee as good, knowing that nothing happens without God.'[1] 'The Jews', said Tertullian, 'into whose wild olive-tree we have been grafted':[2] these ethics are not Greek. Nor is the moralism mechanical; the ideal is of a new heart, a changed character.[3]

It may be worth while to turn aside here. The Catechism of the Church of England, drawn up in the later sixteenth century for the instruction of children, confined its ethics even more closely than the Didache to the Decalogue and to the famous summary of the Law and the Prophets—love of God, love of a neighbour as yourself. In modern use these precepts are expanded, supplemented and interpreted by the clergy, as is done, to some extent, in the Catechism itself; but from what is known of the clergy of the later sixteenth century, it seems probable that they were originally taught simply. Despite the emphasis which Luther laid on the Decalogue, and its wide use as a summary of Christian ethics, there seems in some way to be a connection between this English use and the pleasant idea which John Selden expressed in the seventeenth century. The Jews, he said, 'held that themselves should have the chief place of happiness in the other world; but the Gentiles that were good men should likewise have their portion of Bliss there too. Now by Christ the Partition-Wall is broken down, and the Gentiles that believe in him are admitted to the same place of Bliss with the Jews; and why then should not that portion of happiness still remain to them, who do not believe in Christ, so they be morally Good? This is a charitable opinion.'[4] Ideas acquired in childhood cling very closely; the ethics of the Church of England catechism may perhaps help to explain the history of Judaism in England.

We have seen how, as regards almsgiving, a legalist position was established by the time of Cyprian. Other traces of a similar attitude are to be found. 'Fast for those that persecute you' said the Di-

[1] Didache II, III.
[2] *De Test. An.* 5.
[3] Hatch, *Influence of Greek Ideas*, p. 336.
[4] Table-Talk, *s.v.* Salvation.

dache.[1] 'If thou canst bear the whole yoke of the Lord, thou wilt be perfect, but if thou canst not, do what thou canst.' As regards food, 'bear what thou canst, but keep strictly from that which is offered to idols, for it is the worship of dead gods'.[2] The full Christian food law forbade also the eating of things strangled and of blood. The persecution at Lyons and Vienne in 177 shows the law in full force: 'How can these devour children who are not allowed even to eat the blood of animals?'[3] Tertullian bids the heathen blush before the Christians, who do not eat the blood of animals or things strangled, 'that they may not contract pollution'.[4] But not to eat things offered to idols was apparently considered the weightier commandment; it was on this that Novatian laid stress in the West in the mid third century,[5] and Clement of Alexandria in the East.[6] Cyril of Jerusalem, in the middle of the fourth century, recites the full obligation, but emphasizes only the first point: 'Guard thy soul safely lest at any time thou eat of things offered to idols.'[7] The usual accompaniment of such legalist distinction between that which must be observed and that which need not, is the doctrine of supererogation, and of merit acquired by doing more than is necessary. The history of the development of this belief during the period before 250 is obscure, but it was evidently present as early as the middle of the second century. Hermas states it succinctly: 'If you do any good beyond what is commanded by God, you will gain for yourself more abundant glory, and will be more honoured by God than you would otherwise be.'[8]

In close conformity with such beliefs, those Christian theologians who, during the period before 250, considered the problem of evil, pronounced it to be the result of free will, in which they believed as firmly as the Rabbis. 'God,' said Justin Martyr about 150, 'wishing men and angels to follow His will, resolved to create them free to do righteousness....But if the word of God foretells that some angels and men shall be certainly punished, it did so because it foreknew that they would be unchangeably [wicked], but not because God had created them so.'[9] So with Justin's pupil Tatian—'We were not created to die, but we die by our own fault. Our free will has de-

[1] Didache I, 3. [2] Didache VI, 3. [3] Euseb. *H.E.* V, 1.
[4] *Apolog.* 9. [5] *De Cib. Jud.* 7. [6] *Paed.* II, i.
[7] *Catech. Lect.* IV, 27. Things offered to idols revived in importance with the barbarian invasions. See, for example, Leo the Great to Nicætas, bishop of Aquileia (*Ep.* 159, 6), on Christians polluted with things offered to idols during the Vandal invasion under Genseric.
[8] Pastor, *Sim.* V, 3. [9] *Dial. with Trypho*, 141, cf. 102.

stroyed us'[1]—and, at the opening of the third century, with Tertullian, who affirmed not only that man's will is free—'what happens to him should be laid to his own charge and not to God's'—but that, though his liberty might prove injurious, man was rightly so constituted.[2] Origen alone drew a distinction. Man has indeed free will, but not a free will which allows of independent action. He has the power of receiving or of rejecting the help which he needs and which is offered to him.[3]

Down to approximately 250, then, Christian ethics were in the main Judaic. Christian and Jew might share a mutual animosity, but the types of life which each regarded as the highest were closely akin. Without political power, subjected to outrage and persecution, without a firm hold upon the highly educated Gentiles, Christianity and Judaism alike could have little concern in Greek ethics, which, in their classical form, were more concerned at bottom with a satisfactory political life than with the inward fortunes of the soul.[4] But the steady growth of Christianity, even if its converts were in part of unsatisfactory quality, pointed to a different future. The intellectual pressure of Greek thought grew stronger. Christian writers of the latter half of the second century and the first half of the third were already concerned with intellectual problems rather than with moral behaviour.[5] The school of Alexandria was steeped in Greek philosophy. Origen held 'that there could be no genuine piety towards the Lord of all in the man who despised this gift of philosophy'.[6] The 'heavenly virtues' were for him the four cardinal virtues of Plato—prudence, temperance, righteousness or justice, and fortitude, the guardian of the other three.[7] It was on the lines of these virtues that he moulded the lives of his scholars; a new type of Christianity was the result, just as the nature of Stoicism has at one time been reflected in Calvinism,[8] and as, at another time, the code of honour and chivalry has been superadded to the ethics of the New Testament.[9] Nor was the process necessarily a deterioration. A religion must satisfy the whole man, including his mind, and a re-

[1] Tatian, *ad Graec.* XI.

[2] *Adv. Marc.* II, 6.

[3] See Origen's discussion of the question in *De Princ.* III, i, 1 ff.; B. F. Westcott, *Religious Thought in the West*, p. 234.

[4] Cf. T. B. Strong, *Christian Ethics*, p. 136.

[5] Hatch, *Influence of Greek Thought*, pp. 164 ff.

[6] Gregory Thaumat. *Paneg.* 6.

[7] *Ib.* 9.

[8] W. R. Inge, *Christian Ethics and Modern Problems*, p. 60.

[9] *Ib.* p. 344.

ligion without a satisfactory philosophy is at a serious disadvantage. Religion, it has been said, must cover not merely the relationship of God and man, but of God, man and the world, and for an examination of any of the three terms metaphysics seems inevitable. Nor can Greek ethics be set aside as negligible or un-Christian. But the integration of Greek and Jewish ethics was not an easy task; the two tended to exist side by side and disconnected.

The period after 250, then, is marked by the gradual inclusion in the Church of the highly educated classes as well as the rank and file of heathendom. The last great persecution ended with the official toleration of Christianity. It was accompanied by State assistance in the persecution and suppression of heresy, and before the end of the fourth century pagan religion was proscribed. It was a period of philosophic definition of Christian doctrine with the assistance of, and in terms borrowed from, Hellenic philosophy. It was a period, also, in which, while for the educated philosophy and religion were reconciled, the simple and uneducated introduced, with the tacit assent of their educated brethren, a considerable amount of paganism. One element of pagan thought, the asceticism which had been borrowed by both Greek religion and philosophy from Oriental thought, established itself firmly among all sections of the Church, in East and West alike. There is little to be expected in the way of parallels with Rabbinical thought in such a period, and it may be dismissed briefly.

A word must be said as to the assertion by the Council of Nicaea of the Divinity of Christ as against the Arian invitation to worship a creature. From the beginning Christians had worshipped Christ, not in word only but in life. Orthodox thought had recognised in Him the Logos, or Word of God, the Son of God. Heresy had denied His manhood, had set Him in strange gnostic theologies, had identified Him with the Father, and had also worshipped Him. The defence which orthodoxy had set up rested on the record of what was believed to be historical fact in the gospels; but it rested also on the Old Testament revelation to Israel, and the ethical monotheism which distinguished it. Judaism bade men worship one God; Christianity, aware of the worship involved in the love its adherents felt for Jesus, was bound to reply that Jesus was indeed God. To pagan invitations to worship a subordinate deity or a demigod, its reply was as uncompromising as that of Judaism. The attitude of orthodoxy to heresy, intolerant and persecuting, was coloured also by the monotheism of Israel; the God of the Old Testament was a jealous God and the Christian God was, in his worshippers' eyes, as jealous. The Church was the new Israel, the chosen and favourite race. Cyprian's famous phrase, 'Extra Ecclesiam nulla salus' covered heretics and schismatics, pagans and Jews with a condemnation as particularist as anything in Rabbinical thought.[1]

The Church of the East now delivered itself up to a consideration of the minute implications of Nicene Christology. Each new problem involved a new heresy and a new heresy hunt. New definitions might become the watchword of the mob, but popular religion slid steadily towards superstition and magic. Nationalist tendencies allied themselves with heresies and weakened the Empire in the East; Christianity in most of the provinces of the East fell before Islam in its early fervour and purity. The West, where the Empire collapsed entirely, accepted, but was not greatly concerned in, the results of the East's philosophic inquiries. The century before Rome fell to the Vandals saw, indeed, philosophic activity in the West which was of the greatest importance for the future. Western Europe in the Middle Ages owed a knowledge of the main ideas of classical antiquity to the acquisitions made by the Fathers in this period.[2] Under the guidance of Ambrose, a Stoical strain was firmly rooted in the Western Church, which, confirmed by the influence of Roman Law, and, to some extent, of Augustine,[3] became the basis of moral philosophy in the Middle Ages. But, faced with the problem of transmitting Christianity to the barbarians, with popular Christianity more and more paganised, the Western Church found in practice no other way than of presenting it as a Law, enforcing it by penitentials backed by the power of kings and princes. The content of the Christian Law included a good deal that came from the Old Testament. The cardinal virtues might be those which Ambrose, Augustine and Gregory the Great received from Origen and Origen from the Greeks. But when Alfred the Great made laws for his English subjects he said nothing of these civic virtues of the ancient world, but turned instead to the Old Testament. He bade his people observe the additions to their folk law which had been made by Ine of Wessex, Offa of Mercia and Ethelbert of Kent.[4] He ordered

[1] Cyprian, *Epist.* IV, 4: H. M. Gwatkin, *Early Church History*, I, 273.

[2] A. Harnack, *Monasticism* (E. trs. 119).

[3] T. B. Strong, *Christian Ethics*, pp. 136 ff.; Hatch, *Influence of Greek Thought*, p. 169. Ambrose follows closely Cicero's *De Officiis*, which was itself a compilation from Panaetius. Augustine learned from Ambrose, but reached Christianity by way of Neoplatonism.

[4] *Dooms of Alfred*, p. 9 (Introduction).

the enforcement of the penitentials and synodal decrees in which Church law had been embodied.[1] But his own contribution to the law which was to guide his subjects opened with a recital of the Decalogue and proceeded with a recital of much of the Mosaic legislation contained in Exodus. The buyer of a Christian slave must free him without payment. His wife, if he was married while a slave, remains his lord's, together with the children. No man may sell his daughter into slavery with a strange nation. He who slays a man intentionally shall die; but, if the slaying is involuntary, then he may offer the man's price according to folk-right, if he seek a sanctuary. If a man smites out his male or female slave's eye, leaving the slave with only one eye, or if he knocks a tooth out, the slave is to be free.[2] So the Law proceeds: foreigners and strangers must not be oppressed, 'for you were once strangers in the land of Egypt'. This appreciation of the social side of the Mosaic system persisted: Aquinas defended these provisions of the Law on the ground that they are based throughout on the idea of fellowship.[3] As for the ceremonial side of the Christian Law, we may let Erasmus speak. 'Read the New Testament through, you will not find in it any precept which pertains to ceremonies. Where is there a single word of meats or vestments? Where is there any mention of fasts and the like? Love alone He calls His precept. Ceremonies give rise to differences; from love flows peace....And yet we burden those who have been made free by the blood of Christ with all these almost senseless and more than Jewish constitutions!'[4]

'The Great Mystery', said the pagan Symmachus, in defence of his paganism, 'cannot be approached by one avenue alone.'[5] Men satisfy their ethical beliefs by observing a law, by ascetic renunciation, by love; the legalist and the mystic are in no position to judge one another. When Christianity has been made a law, its historical connection with Judaism, and the value which the Church has set upon the Old Testament, have made the written Law of Israel one of the main sources of Christian law. Puritanism in all its forms has looked to the written Law.[6] Of the developments of the oral Law, it may be said, the Church knew nothing. Hostilities between Christian and

[1] *Dooms of Alfred*, 7, 9.
[2] *Ib.* 1 (11, 12, 13, 20).
[3] J. N. Figgis, *City of God*, p. 95.
[4] *Ratio Verae Theologiae*; cited by F. Seebohm, *Oxford Reformers*, xv, 2.
[5] S. Dill, *Roman Society in the Last Century of the Western Empire*, p. 30.
[6] John Wesley (*Journal*, 9 May, 1752) commends the Methodists of Sunderland for their religious liveliness. 'This is the effect of their being so much under the law, as to scruple, one and all, the buying even milk on a Sunday.'

Jew, intolerant alike, prevented any mutual understanding; any parallelism of thought depended, it would seem, on the interpretation of the Old Testament by men under similar circumstances. An early Christian heretic—an Essene Ebionite who regarded the Law as still binding[1]—has given utterance to a thought which even to-day has perhaps its value. 'Neither, therefore, are the Hebrews condemned on account of their ignorance of Jesus, by reason of Him who concealed him, if, doing the things commanded by Moses, they do not hate him whom they do not know. Neither are those from among the Gentiles condemned who know not Moses on account of Him who has concealed him, provided that these also, doing the things spoken by Jesus, do not hate him whom they do not know.'[2] If men on both sides had been able to advance so far, some of the most painful pages of European history need never have been written.

[1] Hort, *Clementine Recognitions*, pp. 83 ff.
[2] *Clementines*, VIII, 7.

R. H. SNAPE

NOTES

by H. Loewe

Note 1 [2]. Considerable difficulty is presented by the questions of the credal use of the *Shema* and its composition. The choice of passages is of no little theological importance. These problems cannot be isolated from similar ones connected with the contents of the *mezuzah* (door-post text) and the *tefillin* (phylacteries). Here it must suffice to refer to *Sifre Deut.*, Wa'ethanan, f. 74*a*, line 20 (on 'And thou shalt teach them diligently to thy children'): *ib.* 74*b*, line 15 (on 'And thou shalt bind them') and to *Men.* III, 7. The *Sifre* argues against the inclusion, in the *Shema*, of the Decalogue and of Exod. XIII, 1–10 and 11–16. These last two passages, together with the first two of the *Shema*, are in the phylacteries. It further rejects the inclusion of the Decalogue in the phylacteries. (See also **Note 77**.)

The evidence in *Menaḥot* makes it clear that the *mezuzah* contained two extracts. All this discussion is not theoretical, but practical. We infer that there must have been great controversy on these points, and the cause of the controversy was no doubt sectarianism. We know that the daily recitation of the Decalogue was abrogated in the Synagogues (but not in the Temple) because of the 'cavilling' of the *Minim*, here probably Judaeo-Christians (*Ber.* 12*a*), who maintained that the Decalogue, alone of the Mosaic Laws, was still valid. No doubt sectarianism lay at the root of the choice of the passages for the *Shema*, *tefillin* and *mezuzah*, all of which would readily become declarations of faith, if only by their prominence in the daily life of the Jew. It is quite possible that the Nash papyrus, in the University Library, Cambridge, is a surviving specimen of a heretical or sectarian *mezuzah*: it contains the Decalogue as well as the *Shema*, with a verse not found in the Hebrew (see *J.Q.R.* XV, April 1903, pp. 392–408 and XVI, April 1904, pp. 559–60). The presence of the Decalogue is interesting in view of the objections in the *Sifre*. Josephus (*Ant.* IV, 8, § 13 (213)) speaks of *tefillin* and *mezuzah* as old institutions, and his vague description of their contents implies that the selection of their passages was both long established and well known. The sectarian motive underlying the choice of extracts accounts for the dropping of the Decalogue in the Synagogue and the emphasising of the *Shema*. But it is difficult to see why the *Shema*, which was used by Jesus (Mark XII, 29, 30), should have been dropped by the Church. Jesus uses the *Shema* as a creed, and there seems no adequate reason for the Church's rejection of it. The wording of the first introductory blessing to the *Shema* (*P.B.* p. 37 and Abrahams' note, p. XLIII) suggests that possibly as far back as the Exile the *Shema* had become a Jewish creed as a monotheistic declaration against dualism; hence the adaptation of Isa. XLV, 7. This is all the more probable since it is recited at dawn, when the light emerges from the darkness, and it proclaims the Divine

Supremacy over both. R. Levy, who discusses this point in his Commentary, *Deutero-Isaiah* (Oxford, 1925, p. 186), dissents, but in spite of his cogent and well-reasoned arguments, I feel that the conclusion is so inevitable and natural that it must stand.

Canon Knox, in *Judaism and Christianity*, pp. 85–6, deals, on the Christian side, with the importance of the choice of the Decalogue as a credal symbol.

Note 2 [2]. The angels are said (*P.B.* p. 38 foot) to 'take upon themselves, one from another, the yoke of the Kingdom of Heaven', and to 'give sanction, one to another' to do so. This means that angels join with Man in rendering the divine service, though elsewhere (*Ḥull.* 91 *b*) we have examples which maintain that human praise is superior to that of the angels. The taking of the yoke 'one from another' and the 'giving sanction' are technical terms of the liturgy. The latter possibly means the invitation to act as precentor: the former points to the antiphonal recitation of the *Shema* which is suggested by Elbogen. (For this interesting but highly controversial subject, see pp. 114 f. of J. Rabbinowitz's *Mishnah Megillah*, Oxford, 1931, where the arguments for and against Elbogen are admirably summarised and where a bibliography will be found.) The introduction of the angels is particularly appropriate. The *Shema* was recited at dawn, for Man's first act of daily life was to take the yoke of the Kingdom on himself, and since artificial illuminants were costly, people retired early and rose early. Only royalty and nobility rose at later hours (*Ber.* I, 2: cp. also Eccles. X, 17; Isa. V, 11). Hence the contrast between light and darkness was both obvious and striking. It has been suggested, in Note 1, that the recital of the *Shema* was a monotheistic declaration against dualism, and that it proclaimed the sun and luminaries to be God's handiwork. Hence the emphasis on the time when the *Shema* might be begun: the light must be adequate and appreciable (*Ber.* I, 2 and *T.Ber.* I, 1 etc.). R. Judah said: He who has never seen rays of light may not act as precentor (in the public recitation) of the *Shema* (*Meg.* IV, 6 and *Meg.* 24*a*). According to *T.J.Meg.* IV, § 7, f. 75*b*, line 72, this refers not to a blind man but to one (immured) in a dark house. For such a man, says R. Judah, would 'appear to be giving false testimony if he proclaims that God has formed the luminaries which he has never seen' (*Tanḥ.*, Toledot, f. 46*a* top: see also comm. '*Etz Yoseph, in loc.*): yet the *Halakah* is against R. Judah, since the blind man can, in fact, appreciate the light vicariously, for he is guided by those who see it (see also *Bab.Ḳ.* 87*a* top, for R. Judah's consideration for the blind).

At the moment when the rays of the sun are warming and illumining the earth, Man is engaged in thanking God for this gift and asserting His supremacy over it. The rays, then, are declared to be God's Angels and they, too, praise Him by performing their allotted functions. Here, no doubt, is the reason for this interpolation of the angels in the first blessing of the *Shema*. Quite a considerable part of this interpolation is of late growth, since age after age would increase the sentences of praise. But the original introduction of the angels may well be old, especially if the reference in *T.Ber.* I, 9 (Z. p. 2), is to the *Ḳedushah* (*trisagion*) of the *Yoẓer* (*P.B.* p. 39) not of the *Amidah* (*P.B.* p. 45). For these questions, see Abrahams' notes on the *Angelology of the Prayer Book* (p. XLIV) and on the *Ḳedushah* (p. XLVII).

Note 3 (p. 15). Mr Montefiore thinks it strange that the Rabbis should have witnessed, without disgust, the blood and killings of goats, sheep and bulls. This does not seem so strange to me, though my reaction to bloodshed should be much stronger than his, since I have—and he has not—seen Kali's temple at Calcutta and I therefore have a much more vivid idea of what sacrifice looks like than he can possibly have. It is a terrible sight, and much time is needed before the mind is freed from this most harrowing reminiscence. Even at this long interval of time, I would not try to recall the scene. Nevertheless, the dilemma put by Mr Montefiore does not trouble me, and I will give my reasons in writing, rather than in private verbal explanation to him, since there must be others to whom the sacrificial system at Jerusalem must have caused much moral perplexity.

My answer is simple: our perplexity arises from the fact that we have, and they, the men of old, had not always, such a commonplace product of civilisation as a butcher's shop, where we can buy a joint or a steak when we so desire. The shop is a clean, white-tiled room, not, perhaps, as attractive as a fruiterer's, still less as enticing as a bookseller's, but in no sense is it revolting to our delicacy. The abattoir—a very different affair—is round the corner, carefully hidden and unsuspected. It may even be a high-class municipal institution, with the latest improvements. But we do not see it. We are pleased to ignore its existence. Some of us may, perhaps, never have entered even the tidy shop—the threshold of the slaughter-house, of course, we have never crossed—and our sole knowledge of meat is derived from the daintily cooked chop that appears on our dining table. Yet between our dinner plate and the abattoir there is an unbroken—if unostentatious—line of connection. And so, to us, the thought of the abattoir is horrible: how much more horrible is the association of the abattoir with public worship!

Now the men of the Temple did not possess this modern convenience to the extent that we do. I am not an economist, and I do not know when the butcher's shop was invented. Trading from shops was an institution that grew up spasmodically. This is not the place for an investigation of the system; I would merely refer, in passing, to the survival, till now, of the fair, of the market and of the pedlar. That shops existed in early times in certain places—e.g. towns—is undoubted. But even in Rome itself, the trade of a baker was unknown until the time of the war against Perseus (172 B.C.), the bread of each family being baked by the female slaves (Rod. Lanciani, *Manual of Roman Antiquities*, 15th ed., London, 1894, p. 491). In Rome, too, animal food was chiefly used on holidays, 'after a sacrifice, when those who had assisted at the rite partook of the flesh of the victim' (*ib.*). This does not mean that there were no butchers in Palestine.

References to them (*ṭabbaḥim*) occur in the *Mishnah* (e.g. *San.* VI, 4; *Ḥul.* V, 4). R. Me'ir held, against the majority, that butchers could not be trusted to remove the prohibited ischiatic nerve (*ib.* VII, 1) and the proverb, not to be taken *au pied de la lettre*, declared that the most decent (*Kasher*) of them was a partner of Amalek (*Ḳid.* IV, 14). They were, in fact, not uncommon, since a comparison between the numbers of Jewish and Gentile butchers, in a city of mixed population, occurs in *Makshirin* II, 9. Nevertheless, the butcher's shop was not universal. Such an inference may be drawn from the huge corpus of slaughtering laws in *Ḥullin*, which would seem to apply as much to private as to commercial cattle-killing, and from such passages as *Beẓah* III, 7, which states that, on a festival, a man should not ask a butcher to sell him a dinar's worth of meat, but that he, i.e. the private individual, might slaughter the animal and divide the flesh with the butcher. Such a passage as this would be meaningless in present-day society.

Nor is this the place to discuss the origin and development of sacrifice. It is, however, generally acknowledged that sacrifice legitimised the eating of meat and marked the passing from a vegetarian to a carnivorous stage. It is further admitted that, subsequently, the Deuteronomic law of the single altar allowed, what had hitherto been forbidden, the killing of animals by laymen. No longer was it possible to eat meat only after a sacrifice, but sacrifice was restricted to a central sanctuary and to the ecclesiastical system, while anyone could kill and eat meat when and where he wished. The magnitude of this far-reaching innovation demands more consideration than it usually receives. It had the effect of associating sacrifice more intimately with religion, since it now became rarer but, correspondingly, more impressive: it also had the effect of making the private killing of animals more common, and it therefore marked the first stage in the evolution of the butcher's shop. These stages are clearly differentiated. (i) No meat at all; (ii) meat only from sacrifices; (iii) sacrifices only at one place, but meat as desired; (iv) meat as desired, but no sacrifices at all.

Shall we ever revert to the first stage? Shall we refrain from taking animal life to give us food? Who can foresee the ethical trend of the future? It seems to me that we cannot have it both ways. Either we must become vegetarians and go back—or forward, perhaps, some may say—or we must refrain from thinking it strange if those to whom the abattoir was a commonplace of daily life did not shrink from the sight of blood. Because we do our slaughtering in private, we can no more evade the responsibility of taking life than we can plead guiltless to acquiescence in capital punishment merely because we no longer witness executions. Privacy is no palliation. The blood of the murderer, however justly he be put to death, is on the hands of every citizen, and it is not cleansed by the circumstance that all that he knows of the tragedy is the small, unostentatious newspaper report telling that the black flag has been hoisted. The system which many of us, as individuals, accept, is our system, and we must answer directly for what is done by us, even though it be done vicariously and out of our sight, while the Law remains unchanged. In our society as at present constituted, both these unhappy necessities, the abattoir and the gallows, seem inevitable, and we should feel justly aggrieved if a new era, which, merely through the effect of ethical progress, found itself able to abolish the death penalty, were to arraign us for something which, most of us feel, it is not in our power to alter.

We can now return to the Temple and the Altar. In the first place, then, the householder was so familiar with the slaughter-house that the sight of blood would not have affected him as it affects us. Would he notice the difference in kind between the meat offerings, the shewbread and the first-fruits? Were not all gifts from God? Do we not put flowers in the Synagogue at Pentecost and fruit in churches for harvest festivals? If a joint of meat is ugly, is an onion or a vegetable-marrow more aesthetic? It is surely a subjective and a relative question. We choose to say that to a shoulder of mutton the adjective 'fine' may be applied if we see it in a shop and 'hideous' if we were to see it in the Synagogue. But we must not apply our criteria to different circumstances. We give a donation to our place of worship in the form of a cheque, but that is merely because this happens to be our form of currency. In olden times, when *pecunia* was connected with *pecus* and *Vieh* with *Fee*, we should have given animals, live or dead. But the possession of a banking system, which we have inherited and not invented, does not entitle us to pat ourselves unduly on the back.

I fully agree with Mr Montefiore's remark that the Law ordained Sacrifices and this sufficed. But that is not the end of the matter. I have tried to show, very briefly and inadequately—and without paying due regard to chronology or discriminating documentary strata—that the law of Sacrifices progressed and, in each stage, satisfied the needs of that stage. The Temple received what the people could give, and what the people could give was conditioned by their method of life and environment. We cannot expect them to show a mentality in advance of their age. What is far more important, to my mind, than the aesthetic ugliness—as we, but not they, would say—of the sacrificial system is the vast mass of legislation insisting on humane slaughter and kindness to animals: of this I shall have occasion to speak elsewhere (see p. xci ff.).

If the association of animal slaughter with public worship tended to diminish pain and suppress brutality, it was a great gain. But this point, though important, is a side-issue. That the Torah ordained sacrifices is often stated by the Rabbis to have been a concession to man [63]. People are not all of the 'perfectly righteous' category, and each was to give 'according to the gift of his hand'. Lucky are we when we can discriminate and reject. Very few preachers to-day can scrutinise their offertory, and it may well be that the most generous response to a temperance sermon comes from the pockets of brewery shareholders. The psalmists and prophets condemn sacrifices, but it would be difficult to maintain that they are thinking entirely of animals. 'The blood of bulls and he-goats I desire not', but the context goes on to reject incense and meal offerings as well. It is the sacrificial system as a whole, or as some hold, sacrificing while sinning, that is reprobated.

I said before that the question of feeling disgust at the sight of blood was relative and subjective. This raises another interesting fact. The association of blood with public worship has had a result just the contrary of what might have been anticipated. For if there is a religious community, to whom blood, in every aspect, is supremely abhorrent, it is the Jews. Pouring out the blood is ordained over and over again: to eat the blood is a heinous sin. I am not now concerned with the anthropological origin of the prohibition in primitive ages, which is not entirely explained by the affixing of a contemptuous label such as 'taboo' (on this easy way of dealing with a problem, see G. F. Moore's *Judaism*, II, 21): I am concerned merely with the development of the prohibition in historical times and with its effect, which is that the Jew has an innate and unconquerable aversion to food in which there is the slightest particle of animal blood, more, I fancy, than the Christian has, and it is a crowning irony that up to the present day the Jew should be the victim of the blood accusation.

But, it will be asked pertinently, if we say that the Rabbis felt no disgust at the blood of sacrifices owing to what can be conveniently called their lack of a butcher's shop, how can we, who have the luxury of such a shop, still retain references to the sacrificial system in our Liturgy? There are, I think, several answers to this question. There are some Jews who believe literally in the restoration of the sacrifices, as mentioned in the Bible—e.g. Mal. III, 4—and in the *P.B.*, e.g. p. 50. The late Mr Morris Joseph was inhibited by the late Chief Rabbi from being a Minister of the United Synagogue on account of an expression of disbelief in the literal restoration of the sacrifices. The Chief Rabbi's action and the belief in the physical restoration were eloquently upheld by Dr M. Hyamson in a cogent article in the *J.Q.R.*, O.S., v, April 1893, pp. 469 f., in reply to one by the late Oswald J. Simon (*ib.* Jan. pp. 231 f.). There are other Jews who deny the restoration and who eliminate all passages referring to sacrifices from the Liturgy. There are still others who retain these passages, but reinterpret them. The sacrificial era is past: prayer takes its place. But the recital of the sacrificial accounts is of immense historical value. It preserves touch with the past: it teaches the lesson of progress. There are, in addition to the accounts of the sacrifices, definite prayers for their restoration. These prayers are so old and so time-honoured that they cannot be touched. But their real object is the Messianic Era, and this was so intimately connected by the authors with the rebuilding of the Temple that the two are intertwined. But we to-day may justifiably concentrate on the larger and permanent element. This is in our minds, the other is a metaphor. To recast the prayer-book would be so gigantic a task that a ruthless cut with tradition would be involved. As ideas change, in course of time, fresh alterations would be necessitated and so there would be no stability: continuity would be lost. The Rabbinic legislation makes a clear-cut division, in many ritual and liturgical matters, between Temple and

Synagogue: it recognised the new era and welded the new to the old by means of recollection, by inculcating history. No age can rest on its laurels. What we need is not a simple prayer-book, perfectly adjusted and requiring no intellectual effort for its comprehension, devoid of any heritage from the past, but the prayer-book of our fathers, studied, understood and loved. Hence those Jews who retain the old bottles do indeed fill them with new wine, but the wine and the bottles alike stand the test.

Finally, there is the Christian answer. Christianity retains and exalts the principle of sacrifice. Enter a Synagogue and a Church, and the contrast is instantaneous and striking. In the latter you are confronted by the Altar, symbol of sacrifice, daily repeated in the Eucharist; in the former, by a lamp burning before a scroll. We can leave out of account certain sacrificial manifestations which very few Christians nowadays retain—such a hymn as 'There is a fountain fill'd with blood, drawn from Emmanuel's veins', was the work of poor, melancholy, pathological Cowper: it is little used to-day. But the sacrifice with all thereby implied is the outstanding difference between Judaism and Christianity: Jews shudder at certain passages in Hebrews and Romans, and the Gospel verses describing the institution of the Eucharist are painfully repugnant to them. This is due to the blood element which is so prominent and, indeed, essential. In modernist Christianity this theme is treated far differently, and, if one may be allowed to say so, as noble and uplifting symbolism. But this is beyond the scope of this note, which was concerned merely with Mr Montefiore's remark that the Rabbis did not find it strange that there was blood on the Altar; I imagine that a Christian writer, seeking to understand the acquiescence of Jesus in the sacrificial system, would follow a line of thought not very dissimilar from mine.

Note 4 (p. 15). With regard to the question of sacrifices, there is little to add to note 3. I agree with Mr Montefiore that the scriptural authority for the sacrificial system was adequate sanction, and ensured its unquestioned acceptance. But, none the less, the prophetical passages against sacrifice also received full consideration, more in the past than, sometimes, in the present, when they are not infrequently taken to be repudiations, not of sacrifice as a whole, but of sacrifice devoid of the accompaniments of prayer and repentance. An examination of *Men.* 110*a* makes this clear: 'He who reads the sacrificial portions is as worthy as though he had offered the sacrifices.' The historical motive was strong: to read the past, and what it stood for, was a salutary study. Unconsciously it induced reflections about progress from past to present, and about future improvement to a still higher stage. This was not the only object of the kindergarten use of the Leviticus chapters. Practically, they possessed educational advantages, for they had a varied vocabulary of useful words not common elsewhere, and they contained frequent repetitions. The normal child in an infant class—to-day, no less than in the time of the Talmud—would prefer to learn the Hebrew word for 'Pancake' (Lev. II, 5) than the kings of Judah and Israel.

Because, in our changed educational circumstances and needs, such chapters are not used in the infant school, it does not follow that they were not once properly in their place as reading lessons. Possibly the use may go back to distant ages when the ritual itself was still in existence, and so there was a practical reason for studying it.

It may be remarked that Buber's note number 90 on *Pes.K.* 60*b* points out that the text is not certain: indeed, he gives this passage as an example of the mistakes made by copyists. The *Lev.R.* parallel makes it possible that the Mishnaic, and not the Pentateuchal, chapters were meant: i.e. 'he who studies the Mishnah [on the sacrifices] etc.' If so, the same may be intended in the case of the children, who would, in that case, be older than the kindergarten age. The Mishnaic chapters still form part of the daily private study—so as to keep the memory of the Temple fresh, and also because, at the time when their study was recommended, the Messianic age was associated with their restoration. (On this see *P.B.* pp. 9–13 and Abrahams' notes, *Companion*, pp. XXIV–XXV.) They are retained as a duty to history, and in order to preserve continuity.)

As a conclusion to this note I would like to add an extract from a very remarkable book that has just appeared, *The Jewish School*, by N. Morris. The author is, presumably, an orthodox Jew, since he is the Education Officer of the Jewish Religious Education Board. He deals, on pp. 89 ff. with Rabbi Assi's remark (see [57]) that school-children began their instruction by learning to read Leviticus. Mr Morris says:

'Now this is on the face of it an after-thought, intended to supply a reason for a custom which had become, or was becoming prevalent. It quite obviously holds no water, and with a little ingenuity, of which the rabbis had no lack, no less cogent reasons could be discovered why children should begin with almost any other part of the Bible. But the explanations of modern writers are scarcely more satisfactory. Bacher, who like other writers considers the custom to have originated before the destruction of the Temple, suggests that it arose in the schools of Jerusalem, where the pupils were priestly children. The teaching of Leviticus was intended as a means of initiating them into priestly life. But even if one could imagine schools of the kind suggested in Jerusalem, for which there is no evidence at all, it would still fail to explain the general acceptance of the custom and its remarkable hold on Jewry throughout the ages. Jewish religious life found its expression mainly in the Synagogue with its various activities. For the communities outside of Jerusalem—and especially for the Diaspora —this must have been so even in Temple times. It is most unlikely that parents and teachers would ignore the demands of their immediate environment and teach the children first of all the least suitable part of the Bible because the priests in Jerusalem might find it useful for their sons.

'Another recent writer expresses the view that the narrative of Genesis might be considered "as unfitting for the natural innocence and piety of children". But this is an ultra-modern thought which would hardly occur to a Jew of the first or second century. Besides, it would be a reason only for not beginning with Genesis. It does not attempt to explain the preference over all other books given to Leviticus.

'Now the difficulty in finding a satisfactory explanation for this custom arises from the assumption that its origin goes back to Temple times. Once this assumption is dropped the custom almost explains itself. The first time we hear of it in connection with a discussion in the second century C.E. about special scrolls for children. At that time, it seems clear, there was no uniform practice: some began with Genesis, others with Leviticus. All other passages where this custom is mentioned are of a later date.

'Its origin must be sought in post-Temple times—probably after the defeat of Bar-Kochba. The efforts for the recovery of political independence ended in disaster. With these also went the hope for the rebuilding of the Temple. There was the danger that the chapters of the Pentateuch which dealt with the sacrificial ceremonial—now fallen into disuse—might be entirely forgotten. And so children were made to begin their studies with "the law of the priests", securing for that part of the Bible an honoured place in the religious life of the community. It was one of the numerous practices of a similar kind affecting the religious, social and domestic life of the Jew, that took their rise in the critical days following the disastrous Roman wars.'

Note 5 (p. 29). In my prefatory note I have made it clear that I am not afraid of admitting that amid the vast mass of Talmudic and Midrashic material which is extant, instances of particularism may sometimes be found. If a thing is true, it must not merely be admitted, but it must be admitted unhesitatingly. Yet it must not be exaggerated. Certain sentences of Mr Montefiore seem to me to imply that particularism is general and habitual. I think this is going too far. To support this charge one would have to show that it was characteristic of the Rabbis to insist on the arbitrary selection of Israel, that this selection was an unmerited privilege, not depending on obligation, and that the Gentiles were categorically and universally condemned. But many of the seemingly particularist passages appear in a different light if viewed in their historical perspective. If an Englishman despises a foreigner as 'an alien', if an Indian subject of His Majesty is treated by his white fellow-subject as a social inferior, this is particularism. If Hitler holds that the 'Aryan' race is magically superior to every other, that is particularism. If a Jew talks contemptuously of a '*Goi*', if the compliment is returned with interest, we have obvious cases of particularism. The essential test is that the two parties must be equal in culture and morality, and that one, without justification, assumes a position of superiority, and decries the other. A man is particularist when he fails to regard his brother-man as an equal. But this does not mean that unequals are equal, or that good and bad are meaningless divisions. If we oppose particularism, we are not particularist. If we maintain that a sin is bad, and a sinner is to be condemned, we are not guilty of self-righteousness. Now the moral condition of the Pagan World was notoriously bad. I shall have to speak of this elsewhere. Here I would merely remark that many passages expressing disapproval or even hatred of Gentiles, opposition to them, God's rejection of them, God's future punishment of them, are in reality protests against idolatry, immorality, persecution, oppression and all forms of wickedness. They are not idle denunciations of respectable fellow-citizens who belong to another faith.

God, as the source of good, must actively be opposed to sin, and must fight the sinner. In so far as naïve and crude parables or phrases describe this vindication as vindictiveness—both come from the same Latin root—or as revenge, it is the form of the thought, rather than the thought itself, which is at fault. There is all the difference in the world between the Hebrew and the Babylonian deluge stories in this respect. But the moral sense of the Hebrew writer always demanded that the victim should be wicked. Agag's fate was stern—cruel if you will—but it was an execution for habitual murder, not a personal vendetta. It is true that there is always a real danger of confusing one's own personal enemies with God's. On the other side, there is the danger of apathy, of condoning sin, and of cowardice in resisting evil-doers. Conscience is the only guide to right action: intelligence is the trustworthy discriminator between passages which are legitimate and necessary, and those which are mischievous and of low ethical character. There are not, I think, very many of these, and it is easy to over-emphasise them. That is my point.

It was, I believe, Dr Johnson, who uttered the warning against allowing the faculty of indignation to atrophy. To-day the danger of this is great. In our desire for peace we sometimes tend to overlook shameful breaches of the moral law. Manchuria, Abyssinia—and now Austria! Complacency, expediency and indifference to conscience are sometimes conveniently concealed under the cloak of forgiveness or pacifism. It is easy to forgive wrongs done to others but without justice there can be no real peace. Justice must be vindicated without vindictiveness.

Now as regards nationalism. The Rabbis put God first, and politics a long way second. They were indifferent to imperialism. But they loved their country. There is no crime in doing so. Mr Baldwin in his address to the Peace Society (October 1935) gave the country a lead on the compatibility of love for Empire and of support of the League of Nations, and the country, a fortnight later, endorsed his speech by returning him to power with a substantial majority. For Britain and Geneva, substitute Palestine and Universalism. As a matter of fact, it was only when religion was jeopardised, that the Pharisees took up arms, and it is noteworthy that when Akiba supported Bar Kokba, he encountered opposition from his colleagues. Now to-day, some clergymen are prepared to pray for the success of their country's forces, and to promote resistance to evil and defend the weak. Others are pacifists, in the extreme sense of the word, and consider that, in no case, is the resort to force justified. Unless we are prepared to limit the term 'patriot' to the second category, we are not entitled to disparage the Rabbis who loved their country, and were ready to fight for Judaism when it was threatened with extinction.

This evening, 13 December 1936, the day after Edward VIII left these shores, the Primate has just broadcast a moving address to the nation, to recall everyone to God who has guided the country during the crisis. The final hymn which he chose on this occasion contained these words:

Lord, while for all mankind we pray,
  Of every clime and coast,
O hear us for our native land—
  The land we love the most.[1]

Is there any particularism in these words?

Note 6 (p. 37). This extract, bizarre as it seems in isolation, becomes less strange if placed within its proper environment.

There were two subjects, cosmogony and revelation, which gave rise to much speculation and debate. The biblical narratives of the Creation and the Theophany in themselves presented many difficulties. But in their exegesis of these themes, the Rabbinic teachers were confronted by many external views, old and contemporary, as to the origin of matter and the contact between the divine and the human. These views were examined, and sometimes approved, but more often rejected, when they proved incompatible with scriptural teaching. Various Greek cosmological theories were more or less known to the Rabbis, just as were the ancient Babylonian and Phoenician cosmogonies to the Israelites of earlier ages. The Stoic theory that the world was due to the transition of a constructive fire or breath (πῦρ τεχνικόν) through air into water and so into solids may be at the bottom of the Midrashic etymology of heaven, i.e. *Shamayim* = *esh*, fire, + *Mayim*, water, which the breath of God vivified and congealed until earth was produced. The Epicurean theory that the world arose from fortuitous combinations of indestructible atoms was doubly repugnant to the Rabbis, because it left no room for a Creator, and because it implied, or seemed to imply, the eternity of matter. When R. Abbahu, in *Gen.R.*, Bereshit, III, 7 (Th. p. 23), maintained that before the Creation there was time, and that this world was the climax of previous ones, he may well have been thinking of Heraclitus, to whom the fundamental uniform fact in nature is constant change (πάντα χωρεῖ καὶ οὐδὲν μένει); hence all phenomena are in a state of continuous transition from non-existence to existence, or, as Abbahu put it, 'God created worlds and destroyed them, until he said, "This one is suitable".' Here it is impossible to discuss this subject; the reader is referred to the various encyclopaedia articles on cosmogony and cosmology. It is sufficient to remark that many apparently strange Rabbinic sayings about God and the world become intelligible if we can trace their background. These subjects were not treated philosophically by the Rabbis, who were not philosophers, and who elaborated no system of their own. We find single utterances and quaint sayings, their reaction to *clichés*, clothed in simple speech for the ready comprehension of a simple

[1] By J. R. Wreford in *Songs of Praise*, no. 320.

audience. But this does not lessen their interest. The same must be said of the relation of God to man, or of revelation. But here an additional factor comes into consideration, the Christian answer of the Incarnation. It was vital for the Rabbis to maintain that God had contact with man: it was equally vital to maintain His Incorporeality. Many solutions were propounded, to meet ever-recurring objections and new presentations of the Incarnation. Among these the present passage may possibly be reckoned. Mr J. Sanders, of Peterhouse, kindly informs me that the idea of 'innumerable worlds' was known to early Greek philosophers. Cicero (*Deor. Nat.* I, 25) says that Anaximander believed 'innumerabiles esse mundos'. On the basis of Pseudo-Plutarch, *Strom.* p. 2 Zeller argued that there was a belief in an endless succession of single worlds, not as in the teaching of the Atomists, an unlimited number of co-existent ones. Cornford (*Class. Quart.* XXVIII, Jan. 1934, 1) supports Zeller against Burnet and Nestle, Zeller's editor. There is nothing in Anaxagoras' system inconsistent with an 'innumerable worlds' theory, but there is no evidence for it.

Aristotle says that those who hold that worlds are limitless, some growing and some perishing, maintain that there is motion perpetually. He is quoting from Democritus (see Ritter and Preller, *Historia Philosophiae Graeciae*, 10th ed. § 21, 198).

There is no reason to doubt that these Greek ideas came to the Rabbis from wandering disciples of the Greek masters or from Jewish travellers. The Rabbis had no hesitation in adopting such ideas as seemed consistent with Judaism.

Note 7 [212]. As regards God's partiality for Israel, it is well to remember that the message of Amos (III, 2), 'You only have I known, therefore will I punish you for your sins', was prominent in Judaism. The chapter forms part of the prophetical lesson for the portion of the Pentateuch contained in Gen. XXXVII–XL and in my opinion is meant to counterbalance Jacob's partiality for Joseph (Gen. XXXVII, 3) with which that portion opens. And the selection from Amos begins at II, 6, with the sins of Israel, omitting the sins of the nations previously recorded. But it is equally necessary to remember that Mal. I, 2 ('I have loved you...I have hated Esau') is read as the prophetical lesson, three Sabbaths earlier, to the story of Jacob and Esau (Gen. XXV, 19–XXVIII, 9). The defence against this charge of divine partiality took several forms. One of these Mr Montefiore has explained. Another was the belief that the Gentiles had not been left without revelation, that they had, in fact, had prophets of their own, and that therefore they were given as good a chance as Israel. Balaam was regarded as a prophet, sent directly to the Gentiles, and his choice is easy to explain. For he bears a double character in the Bible. In E and J, no blame attaches to him. No reason is given for God's anger with him in Num. XXII, 22. In the end, Balaam declared that for no money would he oppose God's will and curse Israel. However in D (Deut. XXIII, 4; Josh. XXIV, 9) the idea first emerges that Balaam wished to curse for hire, but was prevented by God from doing so and this is repeated in Neh. XIII, 2. Only in P is Balaam's terrible sin mentioned, and on the P narrative are based the stories to the discredit of Balaam in the Midrashic and Apocryphal literature. But it is with the earlier documents that we are concerned, for from them proceeded the idea that Balaam was an apostle to the Gentiles. In the *Sifre* (§ 357, f. 150*a*) we read, on the verse at the end of Deuteronomy (XXXIV, 10), 'There arose not in Israel a prophet like Moses', the following comment: 'but among the Gentiles, one did arise. Who was this? Balaam. What was the difference between the prophetical powers of Moses and Balaam? Balaam knew who was speaking with him, Moses did not, for Balaam described himself as "he that heareth the words of God and knoweth the knowledge of the Highest"' (Num. XXIV, 4). Moses did not know when God would speak with him until God actually spoke: but Balaam knew in advance. When God spake to Moses, Moses stood (Deut. V, 31); but Balaam lay down when God spoke to him (Num. XXIV, 4). Here we see that Balaam is regarded as superior to Moses: it is no doubt a later addition to the *Sifre* passage which makes Moses, the prince in the palace, too grand to bother about culinary details, which concern the menial cook, i.e. Balaam. In *Num.R.* XIV, 20, where the account in the *Sifre* is elaborated, it is distinctly stated that Balaam was as (great as) Moses, so that the Gentiles should not have an excuse for saying, 'if only we had had a prophet like Moses, we would have served God' (cp [1603]).

That the morality of the Jews was higher than that of their pagan neighbours would have struck the Rabbis, who differentiated between different classes of idolaters, esteeming those who lived virtuously, e.g. who kept the Noachide laws, far above those whose lives were immoral and vicious. Hence we find such sayings as that 'Gentiles outside Palestine are not idolaters: they follow their ancestral customs' (*Ḥul.* 13*b*: this was repeated by R. Ḥiyya bar Abba, who lived at the end of the third century, in the name of his master Johanan), or that the abandonment of idolatry was tantamount to fulfilling the Torah (*Ḳid.* 40*a*) or even of being reckoned as a Jew, or that there must be no distinction between Jews and Pagans with regard to the treatment of the poor, the sick and the dead (*Giṭ.* 61*a*). The particularist passages, of which there are not a few, refer, one would imagine, to immoral Pagans. The contrast between evil and good living was obvious, and if the Rabbis did not always, like Valeria (Beruriah), Me'ir's wife, distinguish between the sin and the sinner, it may be remarked that many to-day—if not the majority—do likewise. If, then, we get human particularism, due, if you will, to inadequate discrimination, we can see why the Rabbis explained the problem of the divine partiality by asserting that God loved the good and hated the wicked. But as Mr Montefiore says, they more usually took the higher standard as their pattern.

Note 8 [144]. In view of the theory of progressive revelation which I have discussed in my prefatory note, there is not much to add in this place.

I agree with what Mr Montefiore has written, but I would like to add something else. It is obvious that there is inconsistency in a chapter which declares (verse 29) that the Eternal One of Israel does not lie or change—that is, maintain varying standards of ethics—and which also attributes to God an alleged command to slaughter infants in arms. One cannot expect the writer who recorded the Amalekite war to be in advance of his age, still less, of our own. In modern warfare if often happens that women and children suffer. All combatants do not follow the example of our Indian air-force in bombing a village which conducts murder campaigns only after it has been evacuated as a result of aerial warnings. There are still plenty of instances of the callous and deliberate killing of women and children *en masse*, e.g. Abyssinia. When, therefore, we read I Sam. XV, 3 to-day, our first impulse must be to say that it belongs to a primitive age, when the vendetta was not merely normal but obligatory, before the publication of the Deuteronomic code and the teaching of Jeremiah and Ezekiel about personal responsibility. If I were a Fundamentalist, I would say that the vendetta was due to the disappearance of the Mosaic Law during the Monarchy until the time of Josiah. In any case, the Fundamentalist and I would agree that we are here dealing with a lower level of ethics, one incompatible with verse 29, and that the command in verse 3 was what the scribe thought that God had ordered, not what God really did order. We should, therefore, both agree with what Mr Montefiore has written.

But the matter does not end here. Other considerations arise. What are we to make of this command? Is it history or story? History it cannot be, for the facts do not bear it out. According to verses 8 and 9, all that the people spared were the flocks and herds, in other words, Amalek, with the exception of Agag, was exterminated. On the other hand, shortly afterwards, in Chap. XXX, 1, the Amalekites invaded the south and David conducted a campaign against them. Clearly the compiler of the books of Samuel, who, incidentally, includes duplicate and mutually incompatible accounts both of Saul's appointment as King and of David's introduction to Saul, was no modern historian. We have a similar example in the command to root out the seven nations of Canaan, who, as a matter of fact, were not rooted out, since they appear in later times.

It has been argued, not convincingly, that the excavations at Gezer justify the ruthless command, since the evidence of cannibalism and other horrors show that a surgeon's knife was necessary. But this will not do. It does, however, serve to explain the standpoint of the compiler. Amalek, in his eyes, stood for the personification of absolute evil, and the campaign was, by him, regarded as impersonal. He was thinking not of the children as children, but of the extirpation of evil, root and branch. In the days of corporate responsibility—e.g. Korah and Achan—such a view was inevitable. Amalek was the typical sinner, he had met Israel treacherously, fighting from behind (*va-ye-zanneb*, Deut. XXV, 18), homiletically taken as tempting to sin. Though he was the first of nations, Balaam's prophecy marks him for utter destruction (Num. XXIV, 20). The compiler of Samuel had in mind the complete elimination of the power of evil: the fate of the innocent children did not enter his mind.

But the case of Agag is different, and here the compiler must be absolved from unjust blame. Agag was judicially executed for wholesale murder (I Sam. xv, 33) and until we have abolished capital punishment, we have no right to impugn Samuel's action. The Midrash draws a lesson from false mercy. Through Saul's clemency, Agag begat the ancestor of Haman (*P.B.* p. 277; *Meg.* 13*a*; *Targ. Sheni* to Esther, IV, 13, ed. Moritz David, Berlin, 1898, p. 29), and persecution came upon Israel generations afterwards.

Kimḥi, in his commentary on I Sam. xv, 3, endeavours to palliate the command by pointing out that the words 'thou shalt not spare' were inserted to warn Saul against 'sparing' (verse 9). This may well have been done intentionally by the compiler, but it does not solve the difficulty: the command is still attributed to God, and that we cannot accept.

It is interesting to note that Origen skilfully evades the dilemma by making the whole story a metaphor, thus:

'It does not behove us to spare...that invisible Amalek, who withstands those wishing to ascend from Egypt and escape from the darkness of this world into the promised land, and who attacks us' (*Hom. in Num.* XIX, 1; Migne, Col. 722, B). Or again: 'Therefore when you read in Holy Scripture of the battles of the just, of the carnage and heaps of slaughter, and that the saints scarcely ever spare their foes—or rather, if they do spare them, it is reckoned to them as a sin, as it was reckoned to Saul who spared Agag... then, understand all this to refer to the battles of the saints who wage warfare against sin' (*In Lib. Jesu Nave*, VIII, 7; Migne, Col. 870, B *init.*).

The Rev. W. L. Knox, to whom I am indebted for the references from Origen, kindly sends me the following, as well:

'Cornelius a Lapide (a Jesuit of the counter-Reformation) holds that as the infants of Amalek were in any case doomed to perdition, as born in original sin, it was an act of mercy to order that they should be killed, since, had they lived and sinned, they would be doomed to yet hotter torment.' (See **Note 72**.)

Dr Hertz, in his commentary on Samuel (in the Leviticus volume of his edition of the Pentateuch) sees the moral difficulty. He points out the heinous sin of the Amalekites, and suggests that the strictest justice is sometimes the truest mercy. But while this argument might apply to the adults, it is hard to see how it could justify the slaughter of sucklings and infants.

The truth must prevail. Step by step it has led us forward to a greater insight of righteousness. If we do not believe that we are better than our fathers, then, like Elijah, we must proclaim that our death were better than our life. As I have said in my Introduction, the foundation of the doctrine of the Messiah and of progress is this recognition, in no spirit of pride but in thankful humility, that God has helped us and does help us to improve the heritage which our fathers bequeathed to us. We shall be false to that heritage and to our trust, if we conceive of God as ordering the massacre of infants, but we have to show ourselves capable of a very high moral standard, if we condemn, self-righteously, the scribe who once thought otherwise.

Note 9 (p. 507). Mr Montefiore's view is supported by the famous saying, 'Every controversy that is in the Name of Heaven is destined to endure.' There is a profound truth in this adage, for controversies that go deep into the root of religious conceptions do not readily subside: their problems are incidental to human nature, which is constant, generation after generation. Questions like the problem of evil are unanswered, because they are unanswerable. Questions like the equipoise of Immanence and Transcendence, as typified in the doctrine of the Real Presence, recur with regularity. The Pharisees and the Sadducees disputed about it on much the same lines as High and Low Churchmen to-day. For the same frame of mind, on both sides, is to be found in most periods. It is a good thing that interest in fundamentals should be perennial, lest they sink to the level of the commonplace, accepted truth. Truth unchallenged and not revitalised by argument tends to lose its influence. The most fecund controversy is the conflict between Old and New; it will endure till Elijah's coming, to turn the hearts of the children to the fathers; until he come, the struggle must continue, the effort to reconcile progress and tradition. Only so can the equipoise be kept, otherwise 'the earth will be smitten with the curse' of indifference. 'These and those are, each, the words of the Living God' (*'Erub.* 13*b*).

The point raised by Mr Montefiore belongs to this class. Truly, as he says, argument is endless, neither side being convinced by the other's words. The question is twofold, the wording of the benediction and the larger one, of the status of women. I have no new arguments to adduce.

A Jewess is exempt from every religious duty—every positive command, that is to say—which has to be fulfilled at a specific time. She is never free from prohibitions, which are equally incumbent on man and woman. Why is she exempt from certain—only from certain—of the positive commands?[1] Because her first duty is to her children, these have the first call on her time. Not even an angel is given two missions simultaneously. This duty to the children is not merely physical, though the fact that the foster-mother is rare in Judaism is not without significance. But it is from the mother that the infant learns religion. The father, it is true, teaches the child, but the influence of the mother is the ultimate determining factor. The child of a Jewess by a mixed marriage is considered a Jew, but not so the child of a Jew by a non-Jewish mother. It is from the mother that the religious impulse comes: she moulds the sensitive mind of the infant. When public worship is to be held, it often happens that one member of the statutory quorum of ten (*minyan*) is wanting, and service is delayed while people rush round to find a worshipper. In such circumstances it is a high moral duty, incumbent on every Jew, to complete the minimum for congre-

[1] *T.J.Ḳid.* 1, § 8, f. 61*c*, l. 11 (cp. [1468] and **Note 76**).

gational worship, and from this conflict of duties the mother is exempt, because it is a duty to be carried out at a specific moment. Hence, as Dr Abrahams says in his excellent note (p. XVI), man returns thanks for his privilege.

But this is not all. There is, I quite agree, another side. First of all, the blessing, in its present form, readily lends itself to misinterpretation. I should reckon that about once every term I am asked to explain the meaning, and to defend it, by intelligent Christian inquirers. And if this holds good with friends, *a fortiori* with enemies: one can imagine the use made of the wording by Nazis. Certain rites have our blessing in a positive form (see Abrahams' note). On the whole, however, our wording is universal. It is not from 'lack of courage' that orthodox Judaism refuses to remove the blessing. Nor is it altogether obstinacy. There is no general veto on alterations. The Prayer for the King has been altered in the English orthodox Synagogues, which no longer asks that the King's foes should be defeated, but which, instead, substitutes a prayer for universal peace. Again, certain references to angels have been expunged in these same Synagogues. But there are three reasons against altering this blessing. First, its antiquity: to-day such a reason would not be generally accepted. On the contrary, it might well, *eo ipso*, be an argument for change. But Jews are fundamentally conservative. Secondly, and this will, I think, win more general consent, an alteration would imply that the charge was true. Thirdly, it is far better to tell people what their ancient prayers mean, to enlist their sense of history, tradition and continuity, and to induce them to use their intelligence, than to make the Prayer Book something new, simple and not calculated to stimulate thought. No one who says his daily prayers recites this blessing in arrogant superiority. Nothing but the true sense ever occurs to him. From his earliest days the true meaning has been dinned into him. The danger arises from those, alas, so-called orthodox Jews, who do not put on their phylacteries, and who do not begin the day with morning prayer. To them large tracts of the Prayer Book are *terra incognita*. If then, those who recite the benediction invariably use it in its true sense, why alter it for the benefit of those who do not recite it at all and who would not recite an amended one?

Still, you may say that this is special pleading. Our Prayer Book should not need a commentary: it should bear its meaning on its face. This is a strong and sincere argument. I cannot deny its efficacy. My morning prayers would not, by one whit, be disturbed, if some change were made: *per contra*, they would not in the least be benefited by the change, for the idea would remain. I should still thank God for having called me to the highest responsibility and duty, and I should still glory in the recognition of the trust given to my keeping. Nor is this reasoning mere theory, divorced from practice. In the latest Orthodox Prayer Book, that of the American *Sephardim* (New York, 1936, p. 2), the translator, de Sola Pool, renders the words 'Blessed art Thou...who hast set upon me the obligations of a man.' This exactly represents the sense of the words, for they are recited, theoretically, in the process of dressing, before putting on the phylacteries and the fringes, which women do not wear. These blessings (*P.B.* pp. 5 and 6) have now been incorporated in the public liturgy; their primitive use was personal. On rising, one thanked God for the gift of sight, the power of motion, and so on, each bodily function and each act of daily life having its appropriate formula. As Abrahams points out (*P.B.* p. XVI), some rites 'give the formulae *positively*, "Who hast made me an Israelite etc."' Dr Pool's method is not exceptional. It is that followed by the compiler of the *Liberal Jewish Prayer-Book* (see Preface to vol. I), in dealing with old material, the antiquity of which precludes alteration in the Hebrew, 'We have [in the English paraphrase] here and there read a new meaning into an old prayer, one, however, not unrelated to its original meaning' (p. I). The same applies to Dr Pool: his translation is 'not unrelated to the original meaning'. Is it worth while to change the Hebrew? Will it be productive of good to do so?

So we see that on the question of changing the wording, I have an open mind. I can come to meet Mr Montefiore there. But I can definitely not agree that the old formula implied a degradation of women. Again, I join issue on his words 'different from our own'. No one denies that the position of women to-day differs from their position five hundred, a thousand, or even two thousand years ago. In the course of ages, the position of women has obviously changed and, in many respects, improved. But his contrast implies that whereas the outside world has advanced, Judaism has remained stationary. Now here are two distinct issues. We can take women as a whole and compare their position now and in the past, or we can separate Jewesses from Christians at the same periods of history and examine each group. But we must not compare Jewesses of the year 1 C.E. with Christians of the year 1936, nor must we suggest that the position of the Jewess to-day is lower than that of her Christian sister. I would take the home and woman's position in it as a test. Again, it is not fair to ignore environment. No doubt the Rabbi's wife in a Polish village is worse off than the wife of a Rural Dean. But you must compare the Rabbi's wife with her Christian social equal in Poland, and the Dean's wife with her Jewish equal. Again, take the law. In spite of all the difficulties of the Jewess in regard to divorce, the level of the Jewish Law has only just been reached by the Married Woman's Property Act, and the difficulties of the Jewess arise not so much from Jewish Law as from the fact that Jewish Law is not operative. No, given like for like and a fair comparison, I do not agree that 'the Rabbinic attitude of women was very different from our own': I will substitute 'bygone' for 'Rabbinic' with alacrity. But that even the 'bygone attitude' is preserved in Judaism by the continuance of the blessing, I cannot concede, though I can concede a case for altering the formula.

Note 9a (p. xxxviii). To Mr Montefiore's appreciative comment on *Greek Ideals*, I would add the following remarks, not indeed to pay a tribute to that remarkable book, for this would be an impertinence on my part, but to raise an issue arising out of the contrast between the gift of philosophical inquiry which the Greeks possessed to such a supreme degree and the absence of that gift among the Hebrews. For the Hebrew Wisdom literature is but a series of aphorisms; it cannot be said to construct a connected system, save in relation to the problem of evil. On reading pp. 56 and 57, where Sir R. W. Livingstone speaks of the Greeks 'starting from the bottom of the ladder' in science, this contrast forces itself poignantly on the mind. He reminds us of Aristarchus' discovery of the heliocentric theory, of Archimedes' statement of the fundamental principle of hydrostatics, of Eratosthenes' calculation of the earth's circumference at 7850 miles, of anticipations of the modern theory of atoms, of Darwinism, and so on. The first Greek scientist, he reminds us, was born into a world which believed that the sun and moon were gods, and that Zeus released the winds from a leather bag. And then we remember that the Hebrews could scarcely differentiate cause and effect. Their vocabulary included words which possessed both meanings, e.g. 'sin' and the consequence of sin, i.e. a 'sin offering'. 'Blessed is the man who trusts in the Lord, and the Lord shall be his protection': so we read in Jeremiah (XVII, 7), but the Hebrew root for 'trust' and 'protection' is the same. To the ancient Hebrews, *post hoc ergo propter hoc*. It took many centuries before the Jews attained to an adequate understanding of primary and secondary causes. In many respects they remained at the elementary stage of thinking from which the Greeks started. But not in all respects. The Hebrews, it is true, had but one word for 'sin' and 'punishment', but that is true only so far as the words represent philosophical concepts. Where morality was concerned, their vocabulary even in the O.T. was wonderfully subtle and delicate. When Hannah said, 'My heart exults in the Lord,' she used the root '*alaẓ* (I Sam. II, 1). When the fields 'exult' before the Lord, the root becomes '*alaz* (Ps. XCVI, 12). But when 'exult' is used with a sexual connotation, the final sibilant is altered to *s*, '*alas* (cf. Prov. VII, 18). Similarly, the lovers of God are his *Ohabim* (ḳal participle); adulterous lovers are *meahabim* (pi'el participle). The principles underlying inquiry differed profoundly among Hebrews and Greeks. Heraclitus said, 'I searched myself': the Hebrew said, 'The beginning of wisdom is the fear of the Lord.' Between the two seekers, there is a great difference, but the desire for knowledge is equally keen in each. The results in each case are noteworthy. On the philosophical side, the Greeks had all and the Hebrews had nothing. But on the other side! Take the question of human sacrifices. For Hebrew religion, that issue was determined by Gen. XXII. That chapter is generally assigned to the Elohist, about 750 B.C. The Greek tragedians accepted Agamemnon's sacrifice of his daughter. Euripides was the first to rebel, but the *Iphigenia in Tauris* was not produced till after his death in 404 B.C. It is true that even later than 750 B.C. references to human sacrifices occur in the Bible, but they are denounced by the prophets; when performed, they were in opposition to God's will, not in obedience to it. Again, take the doctrine of personal responsibility, as proclaimed by

Ezekiel and Jeremiah. The ghost of inherited sin was laid in Israel: no longer should the children's teeth be blunted by the sour grapes which the fathers had eaten. Against this, consider Orestes. It is true that the Greek and the Hebrew envisaged this problem from different angles. The former was concerned with the undeniable fact that the innocent do, sometimes, suffer in consequence of the parents' misdeeds; the latter were concerned with God's care of the individual. And if the later Rabbis occasionally discuss the case of a sinner who is the son of a sinner, they would never admit that God forces an innocent man to sin, which is, surely, the case with Orestes. Again, note what Plutarch, writing as late as the first century of this era, has to say of the relations between Alcibiades and Socrates. It is no use leaving this—and other things—out of account deliberately, as Sir R. W. Livingstone does (p. 8). We are entitled to ask what compensations, if any, the Hebrew had for his ignorance of science, for his deficiency of the spirit of keen inquiry. This is one compensation, and a valuable one: it is worthy of note. Moreover, when Christianity emerged from Judaism, its contact with Greek philosophy produced a theology which was, for its day, a triumph of intellectual achievement. But, as time progressed, it proved a not altogether welcome legacy. No Jew could have created so wonderful an exposition of the combination of the human and divine as resulted in the Athanasian creed, when Greek dialectics were called to the aid of the Church. But no Jew needed such an exposition, and his simple declaration of the Unity has endured.

Note 10 [1651]. The assertion is indeed so 'amazing' that I may venture to offer an alternative translation, which has long been in my mind, but which I have always hesitated to put forward, just because it is so obvious and so extremely simple. It cannot have escaped the notice of others, and if they have refrained from offering it, who am I to do so? But there are limits to the 'oddity of the Rabbis', and one finds, not infrequently, that at the bottom of the oddness, there is something else, not quite so bizarre.

This passage, [1651], is not isolated: parallels will be considered in a moment. As it stands, it certainly appears to indicate that the dead have a method of transit not very different from our habitual means of crossing London. The connection of the dead with the lower world is obvious, and one might, at first sight, think of Charon or Aeneas's visit to the shades. Something like this was, no doubt, in R. Simai's mind. But where did he get it from? We have had instances (see **Note 6** above) where particles of Greek philosophy were known to the Rabbis and not very critically investigated. Sometimes they were tolerantly accepted, sometimes they were misunderstood. This, I believe, is a case of misunderstanding. The word translated 'roll' *saute aux yeux*, it is *mitgalgelin*, and I venture to suggest that it is here used in the common medieval sense of *gilgul*, or 'transmigration', in other words, what was at the back of Simai's mind was metempsychosis. He may not have understood it, he may well have rejected it, but it was the ultimate source of his remark.

I have said that this use of *gilgul* was medieval, and I shall revert to this obvious objection to my suggestion. First let us consider another word in Simai's statement, 'bottles'. Why 'bottles'? The Hebrew is *nodot*, or so, at least, it is usually read. It is the word which in the Bible (e.g. Ps. LVI, 9 and often) is spelled with *alef*, i.e. *n'od*: in Rabbinic Hebrew, the *alef* is omitted. But the word can be read, both in biblical and in Rabbinic Hebrew, as *nudot*, wanderings. In Ps. LVI, 9 it is used in word-play on *n'od*. The original sense of the passage, as I conceive it to have been, was this. The Holy Land has an atoning influence, based on a Midrashic interpretation of Deut. XXXII, 43, 'And His land shall atone for His people' (A.V. 'And [God] will be merciful unto His land, *and* to His people'). In *Yalkuṭ* on Ps. CXVI, 9 (§ 874) the words 'I will walk before the Lord in the land of life' are applied to the streets of Jerusalem which are considered there to promote the Resurrection. What about the Saints who die outside Palestine? God, by successive transmigrations and wanderings will bring them there, and reunite their original souls to them.

Typical parallels are the following: According to R. Eliezer, the righteous outside Palestine will not live [the future life].

According to R. Ila they will live, by the agency of *gilgul*. Abba Sala objected, saying, '*gilgul* is a pang (*ẓa'ar*) to the righteous.' Abbai said: 'God will make for them holes (*meḥilot*) in the ground etc....' This comes from *Ket.* 111*a* and Rashi here says that the word *meḥilot* means 'underground' tubes. But, here, too, the word might be taken differently: it might be rendered 'pardonings'.

On the other hand, in the Targum to Cant. VIII, 5, it says that the righteous who have died in the *Diaspora* will come by way of graves (*Kukaya*) beneath the earth, and emerge from under the Mount of Olives. *Kokim* are vaulted sepulchres in galleries. The Targum to Canticles is, like that to the other Rolls, very haggadic and paraphrastic: it is presumed to be late in date. Here, the definite term *Kukaya* replaces *Mehiloth*, and the idea of subterranean transit seems clearly intended.

In *Pes.R.* 147*a*, God makes many holes (*mechilim*) for the Ten Tribes and for others who were 'swallowed up' at Riblah, and they undermine (*meḥaledin*) till they reach beneath the Mount of Olives, which is split (Zech. XIV, 4). But *meḥaledin* could also mean 'survive', 'endure' (cp. Ps. LXXXIX, 48 (M.T.)).

In *Gen.R.* XCVI, 5 (Th. p. 1239), the righteous suffer loss, who are buried outside Palestine....God makes for them holes (*meḥilot*), which are like caves (*me'arot*, burial caves, e.g. Macpelah), so that they *mitgalgelin* etc. Theodor's note should be studied.

In these and similar passages we have, it seems to me, the confusion of two ideas. (1) Corpses of the righteous are to be taken to Palestine for re-burial, a practice which survives to-day. Sometimes, *terra santa* is placed in the coffin in England. (2) Metempsychosis. It is the confusion of these two ideas that has given rise, through literal interpretation, to the bizarre conception of tubes below the earth.

Now this belief found no favour in the sight of the Rabbis and it may well have been misunderstood. In each of the examples that have been cited, ambiguous terms occur.

But it is usually said that there is no trace of metempsychosis in Jewish literature till Saadya's time: the word *gilgul* and its root cannot, therefore, have this meaning in the Midrash. Now it is true that we have to wait for Yedaya Bedaresi, Crescas, Shemtob Falakeira, Moses Alsheykh (on Prov. XXXI, 10) and others for a discussion of the *doctrine*, but the use of the term is another matter. The word has many connotations. Some of these are very close to this sense, e.g. in *T.J.Soṭ.* I, § 2, f. 16*c*, l. 56. Akiba speaks of a certain period as 'long enough to incubate (or possibly, to roast) an egg' in *T.J.Pes.* III, § 3, f. 30*a*, l. 33, or *Men.* 67*a*, where it is used of the rolling out of dough. Josephus seems to have known of metempsychosis; even if *War*, II, 8, 14 (162) ff. is ambiguous, his training and environment must have made him acquainted with it. With regard to Philo, Canon Knox kindly tells me, 'Philo (*de Gigantibus*, 4, Cohn-Wendland 13, Mangey I, 264) describes how the souls of true philosophers (τῶν ἀνόθως φιλοσοφησάντων, a phrase copied from Plato, *Phaedo*, 69*c*) escape from the whirl (*Gilgul*?) of things and return to heaven, while those who cling to the material, remain sunk in matter. The whole conception is that of the *Phaedo*. Hence Philo must have known of transmigration, though here, at least, he does not commit himself to it. He does, however, definitely commit himself elsewhere: in *De Cherubim* 32 (114; Mangey, I, 114), he has incorporated a fragment of some book of popular philosophy which clearly demonstrates his belief, with the Stoics, that the soul is reincarnated in each successive world-period.'

In the light of a passage such as *Bab.Ḳ.* 16*a* it seems difficult to assert that metempsychosis is not found in the Talmud. Here the nature of a *pardalis* (panther) is discussed: 'What is a *pardalis*?'...'It is a *nafraza* (? leopard).' 'But what is a *nafraza*?' 'A hyena.' (But this is not certain.) ...A *Baraita* then follows: 'A male hyena changes into a bat in seven years; the bat changes into an *arpad* (? ring-dove) in seven years; the *arpad* changes into a *ḳimos* (? chameleon: others say antelope) in seven years; the *ḳimos* becomes a thorn (?) (probably snake) in seven years; and the snake becomes a ghost in seven years. The human vertebra changes into a snake in seven years—that is to say if the owner of the vertebra has failed to bow at *Modim* ('we give thanks', *P.B.* p. 51; at this blessing, one bows and so should bend the vertebra). Again, in the Jerusalem Talmud (*T.J.Sab.* I, § 3, f. 3*b*, lines 40ff.) R. Jose the son of R. Bun in the name of R. Zabid said that: 'Once in seven years God changes his world; the chameleon becomes a great serpent...the head-louse after seven years becomes a scorpion...the horse worm becomes a human worm...the ox worm is changed into another species of vermin...the male hyena becomes a female...the field-mouse becomes a wild boar...the fish vertebra turns into a centipede...and the human vertebra turns into a serpent, that is, if the owner has failed to bow at *Modim*.'

Joseph Bergel on p. 52 of his *Studien...Naturwiss. Kennt. d. Talm.* (Leipzig, 1880), compares Pliny's remark in *Hist. Nat.* x, 86: 'Unguem [probably *anguem*] ex medulla hominis spinae gigni accipimus a multis.'

The souls of dead sinners are said to become demons (Jos. *War*, Book VII, ch. vi, § 3 (185)): in *Sab.* 152*b* and *Eccles.R.* III, § 21, they are said to be 'slung about' hither and thither, which suggests transmigration. And in *San.* 109*a* it is stated that the men of Babel were transformed into apes, spirits and demons. There was also the belief that the soul could become a bird-demon.

Origen frequently mentions the subject, and it is difficult to believe that it escaped the Rabbis' notice. That Simai and the others were consciously thinking of transmigration, I do not suggest. But the views which they expressed may well have come to them, through various channels, from those who believed in transmigration. This belief became misunderstood and materialised as it was transmitted. In this way, 'wanderings' became 'bottles'; 'pardonings on this earth' became 'holes in the ground'; 'endure' became 'bore through'; and transmigration, as a whole, became converted into subterranean traction.

Note 11. Since this book was in type, Dr L. Finkelstein's *Akiba* has appeared (New York, 1937, Covici Fried). On many of the passages which we have cited, Dr Finkelstein throws very considerable light. For their possible historical setting and occasion of their utterance, the reader is referred to Dr Finkelstein's book, as follows:

(*a*) [4], see p. 252.
(*b*) [89], see p. 204.
(*c*) [137], see p. 207.
(*d*) [139], see pp. 76, 196.
(*e*) [173], see p. 196.
(*f*) [263], see p. 212.
(*g*) [268], see p. 210.
(*h*) [283], see p. 185.
(*i*) [307], see p. 253, note 40 (p. 349).
(*j*) [488], see p. 260, note 52 (p. 349).
(*k*) [659], see p. 261, note 53 (p. 349).
(*l*) [1319], see p. 268, note 67 (p. 350).
(*m*) [1320], see p. 268, note 67 (p. 350).
(*n*) [1401], see p. 261, note 53 (p. 349).

Note 12 [8]. It seems difficult to believe that this Pappos or Pappias was the man of that name who was brought to trial together with Akiba (cp. [368]). For the Pappos of this passage [8] is a Rabbi who discusses theology with Akiba on equal terms. The Pappos b. Judah of [368] attempted to discourage study. In contrast to Akiba, he was arraigned for 'vain things'. This cannot mean that he lost his faith, like Elisha b. Abuyah. For 'vain things', in the Roman sense, would have implied sedition, i.e. Akiba's crime, that of teaching. And this was exactly what Pappos deprecated.

Finkelstein (pp. 195 ff.) points out with great acumen that Akiba's theology developed with his years. 'In his student days he retained the simple anthropomorphic conception of God which as a shepherd he had shared with the other untutored peasants.' Thus, he interpreted the 'thrones' of Dan. VII, 9 as referring to God and David. In later years he abandoned these anthropomorphic ideas. Hence he opposed Dosa b. Horkinas, who took Exod. XXXIII, 20 ('Man cannot see Me and live') to mean that only in the hour of death can man see God. Akiba, however, said that the verse meant that neither man nor angel could see God. 'This new conception of God led Akiba into a series of conflicts with the provincial scholar, Pappias, whose ideas were as naïve and as primitive as Dosa's. For instance, the verse, "I have compared thee, O my love, to a steed in Pharaoh's chariot" (Cant. I, 9), seemed to Pappias a suitable text for the following fancy: "When Pharaoh rode a male horse, God appeared against him on a male horse; when Pharaoh exchanged the horse for a mare, God too appeared on a mare." Again, Pappias explained that the words, "Behold, man is become as one of us" (Gen. III, 22), meant that Adam had become like an angel. Akiba decried both of these interpretations. The first passage has nothing to do, according to Akiba, with any appearance of God as horseman; the second merely implies that man had obtained freewill: "God put before him two ways, the way of death and the way of life, and he chose the way of death." (*Mekilta*, Beshallaḥ, *Vayeḥi*, chap. 6, Horowitz-Rabin, p. 112, Lauterbach, I, p. 247; *Gen.R.* XXI, 5; *Cant.R.* on I, 9; cf. Job IV, 18; V, 1; XV, 15; XXV, 3 and the speeches of Elihu in XXXIII, 23.)'

Note 13 (p. 597). On this passage, Finkelstein (p. 185) observes: 'Taking a position somewhat akin to that developed a millennium later by Maimonides, Akiba seemed to hold that the future life is a privilege to be gained through positive upright living, rather than an inherent right which can only be forfeited as a penalty. Sometimes he asserted God's mercy to be such that a single meritorious act will win a man admission to the future world. He found support for this view in a fanciful interpretation of Isa. V, 14, which he rendered, "Therefore hath the netherworld enlarged her desire and opened her mouth—*for the lack of an observance.*" "It does not say for the lack of observances", he remarked, "but of an *observance*; only those who possess no good deeds at all will descend into the netherworld."'

Note 14 [283]. Finkelstein (p. 185) points out that this was the only occasion when Akiba is known to have inflicted a punishment that seems unduly severe. 400 *zuz* was twice the normal dower of a virgin. For another severe fine (imposed by Resh Lakish) see [1427].

Note 15 [583]. In connection with these utterances of Simeon b. Yoḥai and his son Elazar, the following passage may be compared:

Simeon b. Yoḥai is reported to have said: 'I am able to free the whole world from punishment, from the time that I was born until to-day. If my son Elazar be joined with me, then we can free the world [*sc.* by our merit] from the Creation till now. And if to us twain there be joined Jotham, son of Uzziah, then we can do so till the world comes to an end.... I have considered the sons of the Upper Chamber [i.e. those destined for reward in the future] and they are but few. If they are a thousand, then I and my son are of them. So, too, if they be but one hundred. If there be but two, then, still, they will be I and Elazar.' This statement is discussed in the Gemara, where astonishment is expressed at the small numbers named. These are then referred to the exceptionally pious, who see the Divine Effulgence, i.e. the 'Thirty-six' (*San.* 97 *b*) mentioned in [617]. (See *Suk.* 45 *b*, parallels in *J.Ber.* IX, § 3, f. 13 *d*, lines 65 ff.; *Gen.R.* XXXV, § 2; *Pes.K.*, Beshallaḥ, 88 *a*. The variants in *Pes.K.* are noteworthy.)

Finkelstein (p. 169) speaks of Simeon's 'megalomania' and his relation to Akiba. Marmorstein (*Doctrine of Merits*..., p. 52 (Jews' Coll. Publ. No. 7, London, 1920)) finds Simeon's 'exaggeration' difficult. Now Simeon's saying is reported by R. Hezekiah, in the name of R. Jeremiah. Is it not possible that the statement was not made by Simeon himself but was said of him by his loving disciples? Thus, in *Gen.R.* XXXV, § 2, in discussing the phrase 'Everlasting generations' mentioned in God's promise of a covenant after the Flood (Gen. IX, 12) it states that R. Hezekiah 'removed' the generation of the Men of the Great Synagogue and substituted that of Simeon b. Yoḥai. If his admiration for Simeon was so great, he may well have thought of him as the Saviour of the world—just as Shela's pupils spoke of their master as the Messiah (cf. *Judaism and Christianity*, vol. II, p. 26*; other instances occur there). Marmorstein (p. 155, *ib.*) gives instances of Rabbis who 'were regarded as men whose merits were beneficial to the world'. A pupil may well have thought his master's merits all-powerful. The reason for this suggestion is that such self-aggrandisement seems alien to Simeon's nature. True, he was a mystic, and there may have been in his utterance an esoteric meaning which escapes us. The saying is not unlike that of Hillel [25], where *Ani*, 'I', is a cryptic equivalent of *Adonai*. Taken literally, Simeon's saying is not in keeping with Simeon's character. It does not suit the man who said that the world cannot exist without thirty-six hidden saints or who held that Israel could be redeemed by keeping two Sabbaths properly (*Sab.* 118 *b*). How could Simeon have meant that his merit would save the world indefinitely when he held the view that 'the words of the righteous endure during their lifetime and are null after their death' (*Sifre Deut.*, 'Eḳeb, § 38, f. 77 *b*) and when his son (*ib.*) taught that the world was created by reason of the righteous (i.e. of the righteous generally)? In *San.* 103 *a* he argues from the histories of Jehoiakim and Zedekiah that the righteous men of a generation protect it against the wickedness of one great sinner and conversely, but he does not mean in this way to arrogate to himself the title of saviour.

The saying is difficult and is most probably not to be taken literally.

Note 16 [661]. This refusal to disobey the lightest precept in order to avoid martyrdom is illustrated by the well-known story of Akiba in prison (*'Erubin* 21 *b*) (Finkelstein, pp. 275–6, note 8 (p. 351)):

The Rabbis have taught: When R. Akiba was in prison, R. Joshua

Ha-Garsi [the grits-dealer] used to attend on him. Every day they [*sic*, probably he] would bring in to him a fixed measure of water. Once the gaoler met him and said: 'You have too much water to-day; do you wish to swamp [lit. undermine] the prison?' He spilt half of the water, and gave the rest back to him. When Joshua came to Akiba, he said to him: 'Joshua, do you not know that I am old, and that my life depends on yours; why have you brought me so little water?' Joshua told him what had happened. Then Akiba said to him: 'Give me the water to wash my hands.' Joshua replied: 'Even for drinking there is not enough water, should it then suffice for washing as well?' Akiba rejoined: 'What can I do, seeing that the penalty for intermitting the washing of the hands is death [according to the Rabbis]; it is better that I should die of my own accord than transgress the words of my colleagues.' It is said that he would taste nothing until Joshua brought him water with which to wash his hands. When the sages heard of this they said: 'If he in his old age acted thus, *a fortiori* would he have acted thus in his youth. And if he acted thus in prison, *a fortiori* would he have acted thus when in liberty.'

Note 17 [1534]. See Finkelstein, p. 258, note 48 (p. 349). He gives the parallel in *Semaḥot* VIII (f. 30*a*, foot of inner col. in Vienna Talmud), where the wording is somewhat different.

Note 18 (p. 579). The famous declaration in Deut. X, 18, that God loves the proselyte, was much used by the Rabbis, as has been seen. The universal application of the verse might seem to be modified by XXIII, 7, which states: 'Thou shalt not abhor an Edomite...(or) an Egyptian...the children of the third generation shall enter the congregation.' Finkelstein (p. 210) points out that Akiba 'extended the principle laid down by Joshua b. Hananiah that the various limitations prescribed in Scripture against proselytes from Ammon, Moab (Deut. XXIII, 3), Egypt and Edom no longer applied. "Sennacherib", he said, "came up and confused all the races. None of these peoples are any longer in their own land."'

The relevant passages are: *Sifre*, Ki Teẓe, f. 120*a*, § 253; *Yebamot* 78*a*; *J.Ḳid.* IV, § 3, f. 66*a*, line 13; *T.Ḳid.* V, § 4 (Z. p. 342, line 1). The last passage runs thus:

Nethinim and bastards are pure [with regard to their origin, i.e. can join the congregation] in the future [world], according to R. Jose. R. Me'ir rejected this view. R. Jose, in response, cited Ezek. XXXVI, 25, 'and I will sprinkle on you pure waters and ye shall be pure'. R. Me'ir objected, saying that this applied to sin, as the following words showed, i.e. 'from all your impurities and from all your abominations'. It is remarkable that both Rabbis, without hesitation, extend to the *Nethinim* the force of the promise made to Israel. R. Jose retorted that the words 'I will purify you' covered the impurity of *Nethinuth* and bastardy. Thus, if an Egyptian married an Egyptian wife, or an Edomite an Edomite wife, the first and second generation were excluded from, but the third admissible to the Congregation. R. Judah said: Minyamin, an Egyptian proselyte, was my associate [*Ḥaber*] among Akiba's pupils. Minyamin said: 'I am an Egyptian proselyte and my wife is an Egyptian proselyte, and I am seeking for my son a wife who is an Egyptian proselyte, so that my grandson shall be admissible according to scripture.' Akiba said: 'Minyamin, you are in error. Sennacherib went up and confused all the races. Neither Ammonites nor Moabites are in their old places: nor are Egyptians and Edomites: they have all intermarried: all goes according to the offspring....'

Note 19 [32]. With regard to low conceptions of God and anthropomorphisms, Finkelstein (p. 196) remarks:

'In his later years, Akiba not only abandoned, but opposed, such interpretations. Dosa ben Arkenas, who adhered to the simple provincial belief in an anthropomorphistic God, said that the verse "For a man cannot see Me and live" (Exod. XXXIII, 20), implies that "men do not see God during their life, but they see him at the moment of death".

'To this Akiba responded: "The passage must be explained thus: 'Neither man nor any other living creature can see Me.' This means that even the Holy Beings who bear the Throne of Glory do not see the Glory itself."

'Ben Azzai said: "I am not challenging the words of my master, but rather paraphrasing them. Even the angels, who live for ever, do not see the Glory." (See *Sifre Num.*, Beha'aloteka, § 103, 27*b*–28*a* (H. p. 101); *Sifra* 4*a*.)

'This new conception of God led Akiba into a series of conflicts with the provincial scholar, Pappias, whose ideas were as naïve and primitive as Dosa's.'

For these ideas see [7], [8] and [139]; Finkelstein (p. 196) gives others. Finkelstein renders the Hebrew *mosif* in Ben Azzai's reply by 'paraphrasing'; possibly 'amplifying' may be suggested as an alternative rendering.

Note 20. The following extracts are discussed and illustrated in *Judaism and Christianity*, vol. I, *The Age of Transition*, ed. by Professor Oesterley and Vol. II, *The Contact of Pharisaism...*, ed. by H. Loewe:

(*a*) [612]. On this see vol. II, p. 134.
(*b*) [688]. For the question of 'burdens' on the Congregation, see vol. II, pp. 302 ff.
(*c*) [708]. On this see vol. II, p. 319.
(*d*) [898]. See vol. II, p. 162.
(*e*) [951]. See vol. II, p. 44.
(*f*) [952]. See vol. I, p. 110 and note 5, *ib.*
(*g*) [1270]. On this see vol. II, p. 309.
(*h*) [1558]. For a Messiah from the Gentiles, see vol. II, p. 40.
(*i*) [667]. See vol. I, p. 172.
(*j*) P. 145, line 14 from foot and p. 605: 'Books of Homer' should probably be 'Books of Hermes', see vol. II, pp. 31 and 105.
(*k*) [1234] ff. For Luther's doctrine of the 'Calling' see vol. II, pp. 267 ff.

Note 21 [134]. For the question of *'Ormah* (clever evasion), see *Judaism and Christianity*, vol. II, p. 312.

Resh Laḳish contrasts God's action with the *'Ormah* of an earthly ruler who is פלימיטום, i.e. πολύμητις. The ruler makes the subject work six days for the ruler and one for the subject. But God does the reverse. He asks only for the Sabbath (*Pes.R.* XXIII, f. 116*a*, and note 16 *ib.*).

Note 22 (p. 69). See *Judaism and Christianity*, vol. II, p. 33. There is a touching legend of Metatron teaching Torah to school-children (possibly, to those who die prematurely) (*Ab. Zar.* 3*b*).

Note 23 [357]. This conception of the Torah as an active agent may be compared with *Soṭ.* 47*b*, where the Torah is said to 'beg from house to house' (lit. go round the doors) in order to get students. See *Judaism and Christianity*, vol. II, p. 244.

Note 24 [368]. It was commonly believed that fidelity to the Law was one of the reasons why Jews were persecuted. Such a passage as *Num.R.* XXII, § 2, is typical:

'Sovereign of the world! Were we uncircumcised or idolaters or disobedient to thy Commandments, they would neither hate nor persecute us; it is only for the sake of thy Torah and commandments that we suffer.'

Note 25 [389]. To illustrate the zeal of teachers one may note the famous answer of Akiba, in prison, to Simeon b. Yoḥai: 'My son, more than the calf wishes to suck does the cow yearn to suckle' (*Pes.* 112*a*).

Note 26 [431]. On this passage is based one of the Jewish arguments against the claim of the Christians to be the true Israel, because they, too, possessed the Torah; the Jews maintained that they had the spirit, while the Christians had the letter, or, as they put it, the Christians had only the Torah *Shebbiketab*, the 'Written Law'. The Jews had the Oral Law, which was God's μυστήριον. This differentiated them from the Gentiles—no doubt here the Christians are meant. On this see *Judaism and Christianity*, vol. II, p. 126.

Note 27 (p. 160). In connection with this development or plasticity, one important phenomenon must be borne in mind, i.e. the growth of local custom and its tendency to modify law. But the custom had to be well founded. 'Custom annuls *halakah*' (e.g. *J. Yeb.* XII, § 1, f. 12*c*, line 20, with regard to levirate marriage; *J.Bab. Meṣ.* VII, § 1, f. 11*b*, line 41, with regard to labourers' overtime). But the custom had to be based on valid tradition. In *Soferim* XIV, 18, the adage just cited has the following corollary: 'This applies to a custom which became general at the instance of the *Wethiḳin* (possibly Essenes; certain specially distinguished and conscientious men of old were so called: see A. Cohen, *Berakot*, pp. 55, 166, 172, 202 n.). But a custom which is devoid of proof from the Torah is to be regarded as an erroneous decision.' On the general applicability of the adage, see Joel Müller's note on p. 202 of his edition of *Soferim*. R. Ḥinna said: Custom is everything (*J.Pes.* IV, § 1, f. 30*d*, line 5; also f. 30*c*, line 76). R. Ḥanina said: Do not change ancestral custom (*ib.* f. 30*d*, line 7). For women's customs, regarding working after Sabbath, cf. *ib.* f. 30*d*, line 4. The phrase 'The custom of their fathers is in their hands', i.e. they are but following ancestral custom in a practice which seems contrary to law, illustrates this tendency (*Sab.* 35*b*, on Babylonian variation from the general procedure of blowing the ram's horn; *'Erub.* 104*b*, on drawing water from a well; *Ta'an.* 28*b*, on saying the Hallel Psalms on New Moon; *Bezah* 4*b*, on the two days of festivals). In the *Tosafot* (*additamenta*) to *Menaḥot* 20*b* (comment on *nifsal*) the phrase is 'Ancestral custom is Torah'.

This tendency of custom to modify law was particularly noticeable in the sphere of social relations between Jews and Gentiles. More especially did it help to make life possible under a gentile government. Most important is the saying *Dina de-Malkuta Dina*, i.e. the civil law of the country, takes precedence. For this see *Judaism and Christianity*, vol. II, pp. 175 and 211; also *Giṭ.* 10*b*.

Note 28 [448]. The reference to the Law in the World to Come raises the question of the immutability of the Law, its expansion, or its abrogation. It was held that in Messianic times, mankind would gradually improve and that certain prescriptions would become obsolete. The prohibition against burning witches has no longer any force: that against perjury, alas, is still needed. In a sense this idea is similar to that of Paul's conception of the Torah as a *paidagogos*. But it is not Antinomian. It implies a spontaneous evolution, as a result of the outpouring of the Holy Spirit, which shall regenerate mankind, not a violent or abrupt abolition. Even in the days of the Messiah, certain obligations must remain, ingrained though they be in human nature. This was Jeremiah's teaching, 'After those days I will put my law in their inward parts...and they shall teach no more every man his neighbour...saying, Know the Lord...for they shall all know me...' (XXXI, 33–4). But which commands will survive? The question was often discussed. See *Judaism and Christianity*, vol. I, pp. 176 ff., and the following citations:

'All the Torah learnt in this world will be vanity compared with the Torah in the world to come (*Eccles.R.* II, 1, on "I said in my heart"). Israel will not need the teaching of the Messiah in the world to come but the Gentiles will need him, for "him shall the Gentiles seek" (Isa. XI, 10). But the Messiah will give Israel thirty commandments (Zech. XI, 12; *Gen.R.* XCVIII, § 9). Many ceremonial laws, e.g. sacrifices and prayers, will cease but the song of thanksgiving will endure for ever (*Lev.R.* IX, 7; *Pes.K.* 79*a* and note; *Midr. Ps.* f. 148*a* on Ps. LVI, and Buber's important note No. 16). "Ye shall draw water in gladness from the fountains of salvation" (Isa. XII, 3) is interpreted by the Targum as referring to new

Messianic teaching. But the sentence "the commandments are annulled in the time to come" (*Niddah*, 61*b*) would, from the context, appear to mean that a dead man is exempt from the Commandments, as in *Sabbath*, 30*a*, 151*b*, though, on the face of it, the ordinary meaning of the sentence would appear more normal.'

Note 29 [1137]. The importance of secrecy in almsgiving has been emphasised in all times. For the Middle Ages, the following extract, from the ethical testament of Elazar b. Isaac of Worms, who lived in the middle of the eleventh century, is typical: 'My son! shew honour to the poor and draw out thy soul unto him (Isa. LVIII, 10). Be punctilious to offer thy gift in secret, not in the public gaze. Give him food and drink in thy house but do not watch him while he eats. His soul famishes and perchance he swoops upon the viands (Job IX, 26; cf. Maimonides, *Hilkot Berakot*, VII, 6).' This extract is taken from I. Abrahams, *Hebrew Ethical Wills*, I, 41. See *Judaism and Christianity*, vol. II, pp. 242 ff.

Note 30 [1139]. It is interesting to note that Maimonides divides those who give charity into eight categories (in descending order) (see *Judaism and Christianity*, vol. II, p. 243):

(1) He who helps the poor man to sustain himself by giving him a loan or by taking him into business.
(2) He who gives to the poor without knowing to whom he gives, while the recipient also is ignorant of the giver.
(3) He who gives secretly, knowing the recipient, but the latter remains ignorant of his benefactor.
(4) He who gives, not knowing the recipient, but the recipient knows from whom the gift comes.
(5) He who gives before he is asked (giver and recipient know each other).
(6) He who gives after having been asked.
(7) He who gives inadequately, but with a good grace.
(8) He who gives with a bad grace.

Note 31 [1178]. Similarly, saving of life takes precedence of the Sabbath, in case of Jew and Gentile alike (*Yoma* 85*a*), and where danger to life is concerned one does not inquire whether more Jews or Gentiles are involved (*Ket.* 15*b*). See *Judaism and Christianity*, vol. II, p. 307.

Note 32 [1178]. On the question of the relation between Jews and Gentiles, see *Judaism and Christianity*, vol. I, pp. 112 ff., where instances of friendship and intercourse, commercial and social, are given. 'Thus, R. Judah sent a present to Abidarna, a Gentile, on a heathen festival, saying: "I know well that he does not serve idols"' (*Ab. Zar.* 65*a*, top)....'I testify heaven and earth that if anyone, Gentile or Israelite, man or woman, slave or handmaid, read this verse (Lev. I, 5, referring to the daily sacrifice), God remembers the sacrifice of Isaac and pardons' (*Tanna de Be Eliyahu*, ed.

Friedmann, Vienna 1904, p. 36). Several other passages from the *Tanna* are cited there.

According to some views, the Messiah himself was to be a Gentile: the passage is given in *Judaism and Christianity*, on p. 40 of vol. II. See also vol. II, p. 41.

Note 33 [1564]. The foregoing is cited in a *Baraita* in *Ber.* 57*b*, where question is raised whether the blessing should be recited outside Palestine 'because most of the people there are Gentiles'. R. Simeon b. Elazar held that it should be recited, because 'in the future they will be converted, as it says, "For then will I turn to the Gentiles a pure language"' (Zeph. III, 9). See *Judaism and Christianity*, vol. II, p. 29. 'God does not rejoice at the destruction of the wicked' (*Meḳ.*, Shiratha, I, Lauterbach, II, 6).

Note 34 [1570]. 'The righteous among the Gentiles are priests of God' ...'Whosoever it be that answers "Amen", his decree (for punishment) is sent by God....Even if he is tainted by idolatry, God pardons him' (references in *Judaism and Christianity*, vol. II, p. 41).

Note 35 [320]. R. Simeon b. Ḥalafta said: If a man learns Torah but does not practise it, his punishment is more severe than that of one who has not learnt at all. A king had a garden, into which he brought two labourers. The one planted trees but subsequently cut them down: the other neither planted nor cut down. With whom was the king wrath? Surely with the former! In the same way is it with the words of the Torah, for it says in Isaiah (XXVI, 10) 'Grace will be shown to the wicked man who has not learnt righteousness' [A.V. is different]. But if he has learnt, then grace will not be shown him. (*Deut.R.*, Tabo, VII, § 4.)

With this may be compared Matt. XXI, 31, 'which of them twain did the will of his father?'

Note 36 [1215]. The strangeness of the extract is all the more marked when we bear in mind the stress laid upon the duty of comforting mourners and the touching stories which deal with this theme. One of the most famous of these is that related of Beruriah (or Valeria), the daughter of R. Ḥananya b. Teradyon, the martyr, who married R. Me'ir, and her conduct when her two sons died on the Sabbath. It would appear that the earliest—if not the only source—of the story, is the *Yalḳuṭ* to Proverbs, § 964, on 'A woman of worth' (XXXI, 10). For the form of the story as given in *Midrash Proverbs* see [1547]. Note the paronomasia in 'Rabbis, because they gave light': the Hebrew *me'irin* suggests the name of Me'ir, 'the enlightener'.

The beauty of Beruriah's words are enhanced by their cleverness if we see in her question an allusion to Me'ir's decision on the question of liability for deposits in *Bab. Meṣ.* III, 11. See also **Note 40.**

The metaphor of returning a deposit is somewhat akin to that in the parable of the Taleṇts (Matt. XXV, 14).

Another beautiful story relating to this theme is told in connection with the 'five disciples of R. Johanan b. Zakkai', who are enumerated and 'arranged in order of merit' in *Aboth*, II, §§ 10 ff. (*P.B.*, p. 188). It is related in *Aboth de R. Nathan* (Version I, ch. XIV, f. 29*b*) that when Johanan lost his son, the five disciples came to console him. First came Eliezer b. Hyrcanus, who sat before him and said: 'My master, is it your will that I say a word in your presence?' Johanan said 'Speak'. Thereupon Eliezer said: 'Adam had a son who died, yet he allowed himself to be comforted in his loss, since we read that he "knew" his wife subsequently and begat children' (Gen. IV, 25). Johanan rejoined: 'Is not my own sorrow enough for me, that you have to make mention of Adam's?' Then Joshua b. Hananiah used the same argument as Eliezer had done, referring to Job (IV, 21): he met with the same rejoinder. Then came the third disciple, Jose the Priest, who drew the same parallel from Aaron the Priest (Lev. X, 3), for Aaron's silence, mentioned there, implies acquiescence and comfort. [One must assume that the disciples came in one by one, each ignorant that his line of approach had previously been tried without success: Johanan's irritation must have increased with each successive attempt.] Johanan bade Jose desist, as he had bidden his colleagues. Then came R. Simeon b. Nathaniel, who cited the case of David (II Sam. XII, 24), using the same analogy as before and eliciting a similar rebuff. Finally the fifth disciple, Elazar b. Arak, entered. When Johanan saw him, he called his attendant to take his clothes to the bathroom, for 'Elazar', he said, 'is a great man and I cannot appear before him as I am' (i.e. in mourner's garb, shoeless, etc.). Then Elazar came in and sat before him. 'Let me tell you a parable', he said to Johanan. 'A king gave a man an object in trust. Day by day the man wept and cried out, "Woe is me, when can I be free from the responsibility of this trust?" You, too, my Master, had a son, a scriptural scholar, [learned in] Pentateuch, Prophets and Hagiographa, in Mishna, *Halakot*, *Haggadot*. He has departed sinless from this world. You should receive comfort (reading *yesh 'aleyka le-ḳabbel*, not *yesh le-ḳabbel 'aleyka*) for having restored your trust whole.' Johanan said to him, 'You have comforted me, as men can comfort' (i.e. so far as any man can, or, in a manly way).

Note 37 [312]. Commentators on this somewhat obscure passage (and on its parallel in *Lev.R.* XXIII, § 6) offer the following remarks:

Lev.R., according to *Mattenot Kehunnah*, means: 'Just as the lily does not die until her scent goes, for the scent will not depart so long as the lily lives, so Israel....' Einhorn (*in loc.*) renders: 'If it were not for the scent which the lily gives, men would not handle it, and it would be useless, for men do not trouble to sow it.' He thus takes the word *beṭelah*, which we have rendered 'dies', in its literal sense of 'useless'. Another difficulty lies in the words '*al gav*, literally 'upon' or 'together with'. According to Jacob Moses Hellin (*in loc.*) the sentence means: 'Although the lily is plucked, still its scent remains. So, though Israel is in exile, yet they have Torah and good deeds.'

The wording in the Canticles passage is somewhat different. Here *Matt.K.* says that the meaning is that the scent does not leave the lily until the lily is completely dead. *Yefeh Ḳol* remarks: 'It appears to mean that just as the lily is "taken" only for its smell, so Israel is "taken" only by reason of Torah and good deeds, i.e. that the purpose of the lily is to spread scent and the purpose of Israel is to spread Torah and good deeds.'

Note 38 [842]. The important and valuable book of Erich Kurt Dietrich, *Die Umkehr (Bekehrung und Busse) im Alten Testament und im Judentum* (1936), reached me too late for me to make any use of it in my chapter on Repentance. The Rabbinic section (pp. 314–457) seems, on the whole, to be, usually, objective and fair. But it is amazing that of such a beautiful and pathetic story as that of Elazar b. Durdaya [842] (and the quaint tale of Jakim [681]) the author could say: 'An diesen Beispielen sieht man deutlich, dass es allein um eine äussere selbstquälerische Leistung geht. Von einer wahren inneren Umkehr ist keine Rede' (p. 371). Is this sheer prejudice, or dull lack of insight? To any ordinary reader it is surely obvious that Elazar's repentance (like Jakim's) was not merely outward, but deeply and sincerely inward—as true a repentance as could be conceived or imagined. It is as such that Rabbi Judah appraises it, and it is as such that God accepts and rewards it. [C. G. M.]

Note 39 [1279]. The ordinary observer might naturally imagine that the bath was in consequence of sexual intercourse, to which the other actions of R. Joshua seemed to point, but the disciples took the more charitable, and, as it turned out, the correct view.

Note 40 [1290] and [1291]. In [1290] *yittammu* is taken as 'they shall become perfect', not 'they shall come to an end'. Cp. [989] end. Nehemiah took *resha'im* as the plural of *resha'*, wickedness, not of *rasha'*, wicked. In [1291] the consonants of *ḥaṭṭa'im* (sinners) are read as *ḥaṭa'im* (sins). Beruriah, probably Valeria, was the daughter of the martyr, R. Hananiah b. Teradion, and wife of R. Me'ir. She was noteworthy for her virtues and talents. For an excellent account of her by Henrietta Szold see *J.E.* III, 109. See also **Note 36**.

Note 41 [332]. Comparisons of the Torah with a drug are common. For example: 'R. Hananeel b. Papa, citing Prov. VIII, 6, "Hear, for I will speak of princely (*negidim*: A.V., excellent) things", said, "Why are the words of Torah compared with a prince? [In this chapter, wisdom, i.e. the personified Torah, is speaking.] Because, just as a prince has the power of life and death, so has the Torah." This is as Raba has said, "For those who turn to the right in it, it is a drug (*samma*) of life: for those who turn to the left, it is a drug of death."' (*Sab.* 88*b*.)

But the saying is older than Raba's day, for in *Yoma* 72*b*, where it occurs again, it follows a saying of R. Joshua b. Levi, who derives the same lesson in another way, i.e. from Deut. IV, 44, 'And this is the Torah which Moses set (*sam*) before the children of Israel.' Joshua says, 'If a man be worthy, the Torah becomes for him a life-giving drug: if not, a deadly poison.'

The argument occurs so frequently that it evidently formed a basis for Jewish-Christian controversy.

Note 42 [415]. [The 'mouth' from which Torah issues is not the priests' but the Israelites'. The argument is as follows: (*a*) Israel are likened to priests, as has been mentioned on the basis of Isa. LXI, 6; (*b*) Since now priests = Israel, Israel is likened to the angels, because the priests, i.e. Israel, are compared by Malachi to the angels.

Actually the passage in Malachi refers to the Levites, who according to Malachi (writing from a Deuteronomic standpoint) are all priests. C. G. M.]

Note 43 [898]. 'God said to Israel, "with regard to my πρόσταγμα, I have not burdened by ordaining that you must read the *Shema* when standing...but rather when sitting in your houses or walking by the way"' (Deut. VI, 7) (*Lev.R.* XXVII, 6: see also *Judaism and Christianity*, vol. II, p. 302).

Note 44 [446]. In connection with the question 'Why was the Law given in the wilderness?' Canon Knox kindly points out that it was considered also by Philo (*De Decalogo* I, sqq. (Mangey, II, 180)). Philo's reasons are as follows:

(1) Cities are full of vice, luxury, idolatry, etc.; this point is discussed at some length.
(2) The soul that is to receive the Law must be cleansed from the vices which it acquires in the city.
(3) It was necessary that the Law should be given before the Israelites were occupied with settling into their new land.
(4) It was necessary that the miracles of the manna and the water from the rock should be worked as a preliminary guarantee of the divine origin of the Law.
(5) These are but probable reasons; God alone knows the true (presumably the absolutely true) explanation.

Note 45 [1459]. Abnimos is probably the pagan philosopher Oenomaus who belonged to the school of the Younger Cynics. As he lived in Gadara probably the correct reading should be *ha-Gadri* not *ha-Gardi*, or weaver. See the article in *J.E.*, vol. IX, p. 386 and bibliography there given; also *Encyc. Judaica*, vol. I, col. 340; and S. Krauss, *Griech. u. latein. Lehnwörter...*, Berlin, 1899, vol. II, p. 6.

Note 46 (p. 219 and [1465]). The following passage illustrates the doctrine of *Zekut Banim*, that the merit of the children avails the parents:

At the beginning of the sacrificial regulations in Leviticus it says 'And the sons of Aaron shall put fire upon the altar and lay the wood in order upon the fire' (Lev. I, 7). All kinds of wood were suitable for use on the wood-pile except the wood of the vine and the olive, which produce praiseworthy fruit. Hence we learn that through the merit (*Zekut*) of the children, the parents derive honour. (*Tanḥ.*, va-yiḳra, § 5, f. 181*b*.) The blessing with which [1465] concludes is that recited at the reading of the Torah, see *P.B.* p. 68. See further below, **Note 95**.

Note 47 [586]. To the foregoing, the following may be added, as showing the atoning efficacy of the good works of the patriarchs: 'How many prayers did not Elijah offer on Mount Carmel that fire should descend! For it says "Answer me, O Lord, answer me" (I Kings XVIII, 37). But he was not answered. When, however, he made mention of the dead and said, "Lord God of Abraham, Isaac and Israel" (*ib.* 36) he was immediately answered, for "Then the fire of the Lord fell" (*ib.* 38). So, too, was it with Moses, when Israel committed that [heinous] deed and he interceded for them for forty days and forty nights, without answer. But when he made mention of the dead, "Remember Abraham, Isaac and Israel thy servants" (Exod. XXXII, 13), he was answered immediately, for "The Lord repented of the evil which He had thought to do unto His People" (*ib.* 14). Just as a vine thrives, supported by dead wood, so Israel lives and thrives, supported by the patriarchs, who are dead, for "A vine didst thou bring out of Egypt" (Ps. LXXX, 8).' (*Exod.R.* XLIV, § 1.)

Here, then, we have an instance where the dead may, so to speak, be said to intercede for the living. Conversely, the living may intercede for the dead. This assertion, that the living can redeem the dead, is associated with a parable about the Zodiac, narrated on Deut. XXXI, 28: 'I will call heaven and earth to testify against them.'

'God made heaven and earth witnesses. For it says in the *Pesiḳta* that man is compared with the twelve signs of the Zodiac. When he is born, he is tender as a ram. He grows up like an ox. When he is (fully) grown, he becomes as twins, because of the evil inclination which develops with him; at first, he is puny as a crab, and finally he becomes as strong as a lion. If a man sins, he becomes like a virgin [the proof of this comparison, given in the commentary '*eẓ Yosef*, is not clear]. If he continues in transgression, he is weighed by God in the scales. If he remain obdurate in his obstinacy, God sends him down to Sheol in the depths, to Sheol and Gehinnom, like a scorpion cast to earth and into the ditches. If he repent, he is shot forth as an arrow from a bow. Hence people are accustomed to mention the dead in memorial prayers on Sabbath [*P.B.* Pool, p. 178], so that they should not return to Gehinnom [after Sabbath], as it says in *Torat Kohanim* "Pardon Thy people Israel—these are the living—"whom thou hast redeemed" (Deut. XXI, 8)—these are the dead. Hence we learn that the living can redeem the dead. Hence we have established the rite of holding a memorial service for the dead on the Day of Atonement (Davis and Adler, *Atonement* vol., p. 118) and of vowing charity in their name, as we have learnt in *Torat Kohanim*. One might infer that once a man is dead, charity avails not, but this deduction is wrong, for the verse says "Whom thou hast redeemed". Hence we see that one should vow to give charity. For God brings them out of Sheol and they are shot forth as an arrow from a bow. Straightway a man becomes tender and innocent as a kid. God purifies him as at the hour of his birth, sprinkling pure water on him from a bucket. Then man grows up and increases in happiness like a fish (*Dag*, fish; paronomasia with *Dagah*, he increases) which draws happiness from the water. So is a man baptised every hour in rivers of balsam, milk, oil, honey: he eats of the tree of life continuously, which is planted in the division (*Meḥizah*, see p. 588) of the righteous and his body reclines at the (banquet) table of every single saint and he lives for eternity.' (*Tanḥ.*, Ha'azinu, § 1, f. 339*b*.) The *Meḥizah* of the righteous is said to be above that of the angels (*T.J. Sab.* VI, § 9, f. 8*d*, lines 22 and 27).

This section is marked in the Stettin edition as additional: it contains numerous difficulties. To begin with, it is not impossible that the *Tanḥuma* should cite the *Pesiḳta*, since Buber's contention that the *Tanḥuma* is older than the *Pesiḳta* is not certain (Moore, I, 170): but such a citation is, at all events, curious, if not suspicious. Secondly, the phrase *Torat Kohanim* (lit. Torah of the Priests) occurs twice: this phrase means either Leviticus or the *Sifra*. The citation is from Deuteronomy. Possibly some other book —and some other *Pesiḳta*—is intended. The style of the parable and the reference to prayers and vows for the dead are unusual.

Note 48 [591]. 'So great is the *Zekut* of Abraham that he can atone for all the vanities committed and lies uttered by Israel in this world. This is deduced by R. Naḥman from Josh. XIV, 15, "A great man among the Anakims".' (*Pes.K.* 154*a*.) (But contrast **Note 95**.)

The protective force of the *Zekut* of Moses and others is deduced from Cant. IV, 4, 'Thy neck is like the tower of David, builded for an armoury, whereon there hang a thousand bucklers, all shields of mighty men.' This is interpreted as follows: '"A thousand bucklers": To all those thousands and myriads that stood at the Red Sea did I act as a buckler, and I protected them [against Pharaoh] only for the *Zekut* of that which is to come after a thousand generations [i.e. the Torah; so the commentary *Yefeh Ḳol*: cf. [96]]: "All shields of mighty men", this is to include [i.e. to indicate] him who will arise and subdue his passion and prevail over it, such as Moses in his hour [when he abstained from conjugal intercourse and sent his wife away, Exod. XVIII, 2] or David [who spared Saul] and Ezra [who trained his heart to seek the Law of God]. And the Jordan was crossed through thy two "breasts" (Cant. IV, 5), that is, Joshua and Elazar.' (*Cant.R.* IV, § 4 on IV, 4.)

Note 49 [1524]. The connection of sufferings with atonement may be exemplified by the following: 'Isaac sought for sufferings for himself. He said to God, "Sovereign of the universe, if a man dies without having experienced suffering, the attribute of justice is stretched out towards him [i.e. he incurs suffering in the next world for his sins in this world]. But if Thou bring sufferings on him here, he is free from them hereafter." God said, "As you live, a boon have you sought and you shall be the first to obtain it." For from the beginning of Genesis up till this point, the word suffering has not been mentioned. But when Isaac arose, God gave him suffering, as it says, "When Isaac was old, his eyes grew dim" (Gen. XXVII, 1).' (*Gen.R.* LXV, § 9.)

Note 50 [12]. It says in Lev. V, 1, 'If a soul sin and hear a voice of adjuration...' [*Alah*, A.V. swearing]. On this R. Aḥa observes, that 'after the sin of the golden calf, Israel heard the voice, which was the Holy Spirit, interceding (offering *συνηγορία*) for Israel to God and saying to God, "Say not 'as he did to me, so will I do to him'."' Here the distinction between God and the Holy Spirit is clear: it is unusual. (*Lev.R.* VI, § 1.) (Cp. [913].)

For the Shechinah see [184] and [216].

The scope of the Holy Spirit is ever increasing. It says: 'The Lord God will do nothing but he revealeth his secret unto his servants the prophets' (Amos III, 7). For God's secret counsel was first limited to those who fear Him (Ps. XXV, 14). Then He gave it to the upright (Prov. III, 32). Then He gave it to the Prophets (Amos III, 7). For all that the righteous have accomplished, they have done through the Holy Spirit. (*Tanḥ.*, Vayeḥi, § 14, f. 78*a*.)

The degrees of sanctity are interesting.

Note 51 [312] and [453]. The Torah may be personified and intercede for Israel, thus: 'R. Levi said: Two things did Israel ask from God [at Sinai]. First, that they should see His glory; secondly, that they should hear His words. They saw His glory, as it says, "Behold, the Lord our God has shown us His glory" (Deut. V, 24). And it says also "and His Voice have we heard from the midst of the fire" (*ib.*). Then there was no strength to stand left in them, for when they came to Sinai and God revealed Himself to them, their soul fled, for that He spake with them, as it says, "My soul failed when He spake" (Cant. V, 6). But the Torah interceded for them with God, saying "Does a king, when he gives his daughter in marriage, slay the sons of his house? All the world rejoices and Thy sons are dying!" At once their souls were restored, as it says, "the Torah of the Lord is perfect, it restores the soul" (Ps. XIX, 7). But did not God foresee that the sight of His glory and the sound of His words would overpower Israel? [Yes, but] He also foresaw that they would, in the future, commit idolatry, and He revealed Himself lest they should then say, "Had He shewn us His glory, we would not have made idols", hence it says, "Hear, my people, and I will testify against (A.V. 'unto') thee" (Ps. LXXXI, 8).' (*Exod.R.* XXIX, § 4.)

Note 52 (p. 245, line 2). With regard to intercession the following may be noted:

(*a*) The privilege of intercession is associated also with those who may be termed the minor heroes of scripture. This may be seen in the case of Gideon. In Judges VI, 12, his 'might' is mentioned ('the Lord is with thee, thou mighty man of valour') and in verse 14 the angel says to him, 'Go in this thy might and thou shalt save Israel.' This passage is discussed in the *Tanḥuma*. First it is stated that a judge must have physical power: Law must possess sanction. But this is deduced from Samuel, not from Gideon. In Gideon's case, strength is regarded from the moral rather than from the physical aspect. The passage treats of the appointment of Judges in Deut. XVI, 18, and links this with the story of Gideon. '"They shall judge the people rightly": this means that they should incline the people to a sense of right. But R. Judah b. Shalom said: They must also intercede with them before God. This we deduce from Gideon, son of Joash, in whose days Israel was in stress. God sought for a man who should intercede for them but He found none, for that generation was "poor in commandments and good works". But when merit was found in Gideon, who was able to urge their merit [i.e. to intercede for them] at once the angel revealed himself and said, "Go in this thy strength, for thou hast interceded for my sons": thus we see that the judges, who judge rightly, intercede for their generation.' (*Tanḥ.*, Shofeṭim, § 4, f. 325*a.*)

This is possibly deduced from 'and he sat' in Judges VI, 11, which really refers to the angel, but which is applied to Gideon and interpreted as 'he judged'.

(*b*) For intercession by the Holy Spirit see **Note 50**, and by the Torah **Note 51**.

(*c*) For intercession by the living for the dead and vice versa see **Note 47**.

Note 53 [201]. 'R. Aḥa and R. Tanḥum, in the name of R. Ḥiyya, in the name of R. Johanan, said: In Joel II, 13 it says that God is long-suffering [the Hebrew word is the unusual singular, *af*, not the more usual dual, *appayim*]. This denotes that God is long-suffering with the righteous, punishing them in this world for the few sins which they have committed, so as to reward them in the future. Conversely, the wicked prosper in this world.' (*Pes.K.* f. 161*b.*)

Note 54 [1617]. With reference to Elijah's raising the dead, it is said, 'Three keys have been entrusted to no deputy, the key of birth, the key of rain and the key of the resurrection.' (*Sanh.* 113*a.*)

Note 55 [1457]. This passage is very carefully examined by Dr N. Morris in his book cited in **Note 4**.

Note 56 [404]. On this cp. I Cor. IX, 9, discussed above, in Introduction, p. xcii.

Note 57 [569]. This interpretation of I Sam. XIII, 1 is based on the Targum. For a discussion of the passage see Driver's commentary *in loc.*

Note 58 [665]. In connection with the citation from I Macc. II, 34 ff. (on p. 258, line 2), the following reference may be quoted from Josephus. In *Contra Apionem*, I, §§ 209, 210, he cites Agatharcides, who wrote of events in the year 312 B.C. and whose evidence therefore goes to prove the antiquity of the objection to fighting on the Sabbath: 'There are a people called Jews and they dwell in a city which is the strongest of all cities and which the inhabitants call Jerusalem. And they are accustomed to rest on the seventh day: at these times they do not take up arms, nor do they follow agricultural pursuits, nor do they occupy themselves with the affairs of life; but they lift up their hands in their holy places and pray until the evening. Now it came to pass that when Ptolemy the son of Lagus entered into this city with his army that these people in observing their foolish custom, instead of guarding their city suffered their country to submit to a cruel master and their law was thus clearly proved to command a foolish practice.'

Note 59. On the "Excursus on the use of the adjectives Jewish and Christian in England", pp. 609–16.

(*a*) For example, see Prof. D. C. Simpson's remarks on the alleged ethical antithesis between priest and prophet (pp. x foll., of his *Foreword* to S. H. Hooke's *Myth and Ritual*, Oxford, 1933). He says: 'Our debt to continental—especially German—Protestant Scholarship is very great and manifold. But in one respect some English critics in the past have been, and others still are, in danger of becoming indebted to a certain section of it for a presupposition that is not good. The section in question is obscured by a presupposition partly underlying, and partly resulting from, its use of the terms "priestly" and "prophetical"....Is not the term "priestly"—that is in the disparaging sense in which some critics use it—a very doubtful, and indeed untrue, compliment to pay to the latest of the Pentateuchal Sources?' The whole of the argument, developed by Prof. Simpson in detail, should be carefully studied. The alleged antithesis is really 'Law versus prophets' and the unreality of the contrast is strikingly demonstrated.

(*b*) L. Baeck points out that 'Judaism speaks about the good *man*: the words "a good Jew" are foreign both to the Bible and to the Oral Law. It is *man* who is set before God (*Essence of Judaism*, London, 1936, p. 65).'

(*c*) The dictionary reflects popular usage and is no more to be held responsible for it than is a clinical thermometer for the patient's temperature. Similarly, instructive definitions may be seen *s.v.* Welsh, Jesuit, etc. Compare 'Dutch courage', 'French leave', *filer à l'anglaise*, 'the Bulgarian disease', etc.

(*d*) In this connection see Mr Montefiore's remarks on Matthew XXV, 41, in *Synoptic Gospels*, 2nd ed. II, p. 326.

(*e*) I have already pointed out on p. 100 that what Esther asked from the king was the right of self-defence and not of attack. It seems to me an extraordinary perversion of evidence to take the phrase the right 'to stand up for their lives' (VIII, 11) in any other sense. We are not now concerned with the historicity of the book, but if we take the description of the events narrated at its face value, we have a situation not very different from that which confronts the Jews in Germany to-day. It is now well known that on 1 April 1933, it was only the intervention of the British and French Governments that averted wholesale massacre, an intervention repeated recently when the Goga Government took office in Roumania. Now, the terrible persecutions to which the Jews are subject in Germany and Austria to-day would not cease automatically with the death of Hitler; the poison which he has infused into a large mass of the population would continue effective for some time, and the Jews would have to be prepared to resist attack for a brief period at least. This exactly tallies with the account in the Book of Esther. The Jews had one thing in mind, their safety, they were not out to plunder, for 'on booty they laid not their hand', a phrase repeated and reiterated. Dr Northridge's judgment of the Book of Esther reminds one of the famous condemnation of the wicked lamb which defends itself when attacked by the good wolf.

But what seems so terrible about Dr Northridge's arguments is the fact that they were written in 1937, when current events should have taught him to take a different view. One would like to ask Dr Northridge this question. Let us assume that the Book of Esther 'typifies Jewish vindictiveness at its worst'. That is his thesis. Let us grant it. Shall we go on to say that Hitler's barbarity typifies 'Christian vindictiveness at its worst'? I am proud to think that, in spite of the intense provocation which Jews have had, in spite of their shameful betrayal by their colleagues in business, at the Universities and in the professions, in spite of their repudiation by great ecclesiastics, by Catholics like Archbishop Faulhaber and by Protestants like Gerhard Kittel, in spite of all these strong temptations to dogmatism, no Jew, to my knowledge, has yet said that Hitlerism is typical of Christianity.

(*f*) As one of the editors of these two volumes I think it only right to point out that this citation was marked for correction by Prof. Oesterley but that through an error in proof revision, it was left untouched. The words are not those of Prof. Oesterley himself, they are an adaptation of Bousset's remarks and they should be attributed to him and not to Prof. Oesterley.

(*g*) The 'imprecatory' Psalms are not included in the Liturgy, see p. 53.

(*h*) For 'to-day', it would be fair to say 'generally in the past'.

(*i*) Dr Northridge and those who agree with his contentions, seem not to realise what these logically involve. Assuming that N.T. is superior to O.T., i.e. that O.T.$+x=$N.T. It should follow that Judaism, being deficient of this x, should possess lower ethical conceptions than does Christianity. But surely it is only Nazi exponents who have asserted that Judaism lacks the ordinary virtues of truth, love, etc., or that the Jew has anything to learn from the Christian in this regard. If then, Jews and Christians possess the same heritage of fundamental virtues, whence did the Jews derive them, if they were absent from the Jewish source? To suggest that the Synagogue adopted them from the Church would imply a borrowing for which there is no evidence in history. To argue that Judaism is but an incomplete Christian ethic is as futile as the co-relative, sometimes heard on the Jewish side, i.e. that Christianity is but a corrupted Judaism.

Note 60 (p. 411). Even now the memory of this day survives; in *P.B.* Pool, p. 61, the rubric ordains that on 15th Ab (Reconciliation Day) *Teḥinnot* (supplications) are to be omitted.

Note 61 [14]. These words are the formula of the blessing uttered on hearing thunder (*P.B.* p. 290; Abrahams, p. CCXII). See *Ber.* 59*a* for the formula and for an interesting description of the causes of thunder and lightning. For lightning, a different blessing is now used, see *P.B. ib.*

Note 62 (p. 264). The Krotoschin and Petrikov editions have *Miktobim* or *Maktobim* (with *waw*). This form is not recognised in the biblical Hebrew dictionaries, nor in Levy or Jastrow. Buxtorf, however, accepts it and renders it by *Scalpellum, scalprum librariorum, stylus sculptorius*: he points the word *Miktobim*. Levy and Jastrow have *Mekatteb*, which the former translates by *Schreibgriffel* and the latter by *pencil, stylus*. L. Löw (*Graphische Requisiten*, Leipzig, 1870, I, 174, also adopts the rendering *stylus*. This is based on the commentary *Ḳorban 'Edah* ('wooden or stone stylus, for writing on tablets of stone or wax'). But the commentary in the Krotoschin edition explains the word as pen-knives ('small knives used by scribes'). No doubt stylus is correct.

For the number of schools and colleges in Jerusalem, see *J.Ket.* XIII, § 1, f. 35*c*, line 62. For children learning Greek and Hebrew, see *Soṭ.* 49*b*.

Note 63 (pp. 145 and 444). In *Soṭ.* IX, 14 it is said that a decree was made against teaching Greek to boys. This was an exceptional measure. It was enacted after the *polemos shel Titus*, according to the ordinary reading. But such a date cannot be correct, since the passage deals with three separate disasters, i.e. the war of Vespasian, the war of Titus, and the 'last' war (Bar Kokba). It is obvious that the 'wars of Vespasian and Titus' cannot be separated. Goldschmidt (based on Krauss, *J.E.* vol. X, p. 287) points out that the proper reading should be Quietus (*Ḳiṭus* in Hebrew). This name was not very familiar to the Rabbis and *Ṭiṭus* was an obvious emendation. He remarks that Lowe's Mishna and *Seder 'Olam* have *Ḳiṭum*, but certain MSS. and Neubauer's edition read *Ḳiṭus* correctly. The date of the decree would therefore be 117 C.E.

In *Soṭ.* 49*b*, in the discussion on the Mishnah passage just cited, a distinction is drawn between the Greek language and Greek learning. Simeon b. Gamaliel relates that in his father's house, five hundred children were taught Torah and five hundred Greek learning. This was considered exceptional, because of Gamaliel's relations with the Government.

Note 64 [84]. The parable may possibly refer to the palace built on a ship designed to fall in pieces, in order to drown Nero's mother Agrippina. The only objection to such a suggestion is the date. Poppaea Sabina and Anicetus arranged this plot at Baiae in A.D. 58. Simeon b. Yoḥai flourished about half a century later. But the memory of such an enormity may well have lingered. Moreover, Simeon is referring merely to the ships and not to the crime. Ziegler (*Königsgleichnisse*, p. 271) accepts the interpretation suggested and points out that Suetonius relates that Caligula built palaces on yachts.

Note 65. Pp. 1–16 in Zuckermandel are paginated twice (see his Preface, p. 6); in the following extracts the pagination is that of the first series: [696], [920–1], [926], [994] and [999].

Note 66 [343]. Cf. R. Jeremiah said to R. Ze'era: Whoever makes himself a slave for the Torah in this world, will be free in the world to come. (*Bab.M.* 85*b*.)

Note 67 [345]. Cf. R. Jeremiah said to R. Ze'era: Whoever makes himself small for the Torah in this world, will be made great in the world to come. (*Bab.M.* 85*b*.)

Note 68 (p. 222). Sometimes the doctrine 'tit for tat' was used to exemplify the divine justice. A good example of this use is furnished by the biblical Book of Esther. It is not always realised that this book—as well as others in the canon—exhibits very distinct traces of Greek influence. In my opinion, a historical incident, in which a Jewish community was saved from massacre, is related in the form of a Greek drama, and that, too, in the Persian environment, on purpose to make the venue unrecognisable; in the same way, Daniel has recourse to a Babylonian environment. If the Book of Esther were written in the Seleucid period, such a disguise would be intelligible enough. The form of the drama is that of Euripides, with his vivid action and short speeches, almost *stichomythia*, in contrast to the slower movement of the Aeschylean play. The subject is *Hubris*, and it is noteworthy that Haman is punished precisely in respect of those things of which he boasted. Thus, in Esther v, 11, Haman tells his wife and friends (1) of his riches, (2) of the multitude of his children, and (3) of his rank at court. Now these are precisely the three things in which he is smitten, and his sin is clearly his boastfulness: of this there are many indications. The whole action of the play is directed to this *dénouement*. It is to be noted that the construction of the play, with its introduction, its episodes, its catastrophe, follows the typical plan of the Euripidean drama. It is no accident that Racine and others have utilised this theme for the stage.

Note 69 (p. 587). Levy and Jastrow have the form *kibyakol* but Buber (*Pes.K.* f. 120*a*, note 24) prefers Elijah Levita's form *kebayakol*. The common *kabyakol* would appear to be incorrect. (Cp. [173], [256] and p. 68.)

Note 70 (pp. xxxiii and 159). Mr Montefiore's remarks at the end of [428] and on p. xxxiii should be read in succession. It is, perhaps, desirable to add that, as Travers Herford emphasises, Torah should never be translated 'law', in fact it is best not to translate it at all. For the word has many senses, and misconceptions easily arise if the wrong sense is chosen. Professor Kennett used to point out that the word comes from the root *yarah*, to shoot. The shooting of arrows was sometimes symbolic (e.g. I Sam. xx, 20–2, 35–8; II Kings XIII, 15–19) or, sometimes, a means of obtaining a decision (Ezek. XXI, 21). A 'shooting', or Torah, thus became, successively, first precedent and then law. But in process of time the meaning was extended still more widely. When used in such connections as on p. xxxiii, the word stands for the highest conception of fundamental goodness, for that basic morality which is a prerequisite of civilisation. It certainly does not mean detailed legislation, such as rules of Sabbath or linsey-woolsey. These were not intended for Gentiles, whereas the Torah of p. xxxiii is of universal application. Hence it is inseparable from God [455] and God Himself is bound by it [454].

It may be odd to speak of the world as dependent on a book or as preceded by a book. It is not odd to say that goodness is the foundation of the world and its essential prerequisite.

Note 71 (pp. 163 and xliii). The famous declaration that the words of the Hillelites and Shammaites were equally inspired is not unique. *Aboth* v, 20 declares that every controversy which is 'for the sake of Heaven' is destined to endure. When two aspects of truth are advocated, neither can be suppressed. The same thought is to be found in Acts v, 38–9, where its author is Gamaliel, and Travers Herford suggests that he may likewise have been the author of the saying in *Aboth*. Now the principle laid down in *Aboth* is carefully delimited. An enduring controversy is one like that of the Schools of Hillel and Shammai: a transitory controversy is one of the type of Korah's with Moses.

This exemplification is of some importance. It bears on Mr Montefiore's remark on p. xliii about the 'bourgeois' character of Rabbinic ethics. This remark is true. Because the Rabbis were imbued with the necessity of making their teaching practical, they sometimes seem to be drab and uninspired, though, it must be observed, paradox and height are not wanting, in the proper place. But the common-sense outlook of the Rabbis led them to regard hygiene as a more pressing object of study than astronomy (*Aboth* III, 23; *P.B.* p. 195). This view of life has saved Judaism from the dangers of uncontrolled ecstasy. It is significant that Judaism has had no Montanist movement of magnitude, and where such tendencies have occurred, e.g. among the *Ḥasidim*, they have been allied to antinomianism. It has been the Law that has safeguarded Judaism from wild and uncontrolled enthusiasm.

Hence it is desirable to point out that the correlative to '*Erub*. 13*b* (cited on pp. 163 top and 656) is such a passage as *Soṭ*. 47*b*, which declares that controversies between incompetent scholars of the Schools of Hillel and Shammai produce two Torahs. The principle of *Aboth* v, 20 has its bounds and does not justify every would-be innovator. It is the 'bourgeois' common sense of the Rabbis that has steered between Scylla and Charybdis. Hence local custom (*Minhag*) has grown up. Reality in religion has not given place to a lifeless, conventional uniformity; sanity and not excess has prevailed. But the cord, though free, is not broken. Continuity and cohesion have held the House of Israel together; common sense, combined with a tolerance of the views of others, are responsible for this.

Note 72 (p. 655). The argument of Cornelius a Lapide may be compared with *San.* VIII, 5, where the case of the 'stubborn and rebellious son' (Deut. XXI, 18 ff.) is discussed. But there is a difference. The 'son' is not foredoomed to perdition before birth, through original sin. He has already begun a career of sin. The reasoning is this. It is so heinous to steal from a parent that a son who does this will certainly go from sin to sin and commit the worst sin of all. But the Rabbis were greatly perplexed over the case, and every conceivable means was employed to circumscribe the definition, until finally it would have been impossible to secure a conviction. The whole question was, as a matter of fact, academic and hypothetical. In the Gemara (*San.* 72*a*) it is argued that the execution of the son prevents murder and protects his potential victim: that there would be a victim was taken for granted.

All this goes to support what I have stated previously (p. lxxxii), that moral difficulties caused very great perplexity and every effort was made to prevent a 'lower view' from acquiring influence. Each generation must find better answers than those of its predecessor. And this applies to Jewish and Christian exegesis equally.

Note 73 (p. lxxv). With regard to Congregationalism it may be observed that the obvious disadvantage, i.e. lack of unity and diffusion of energy, has not been striking. Far more important is it to remember the advantages. Persecution has never been universal and so Judaism has been preserved. Had Jews been concentrated in a single locality, one persecution would have been disastrous. In the same way there have not been identical levels of ignorance or of learning everywhere. One part has saved another. International Jewry is a figment of the anti-Semites. In the financial world it is a myth, and where it has been attempted in the political world it has failed. Modern nationalism is but one in a series of such failures. Whenever Jews have suffered persecution, they have had 'recourse to the weapons of their ancestors' [893], that is to say, they have been thrown back on their Judaism and not on artificial centralisation and political assimilation, and thus has Judaism survived.

Note 74 (p. xci). The weekly Pentateuchal portion *Ẓaw* (Lev. VI, 8–VIII, 36) deals exclusively with sacrifices. It is to be noted that the Prophetical lesson is from Jer. VII, beginning at verse 21: 'Put your burnt offerings unto your sacrifices and eat meat.' And *Lev.R.* on *Ẓaw* (VII, § 2) declares that a man who repents is accounted as though he had sacrificed.

Note 75 (p. xciii; cp. pp. xlvii–xlviii, xxviii). Since the foregoing was written, a statement by the Catholic Advisory Council appeared in *The Times* of 2 April 1938. In this statement 'the eternal punishment of the finally impenitent' was reaffirmed. It is by no means clear how far this view is held. The correspondence in the subsequent issues of the *Church Times*, and the leading articles in that paper dealing with the subject, would indicate that the number of people supporting this idea is small and that the article is not representative of Anglo-Catholic opinion or of Church opinion in general.

Attention is drawn to this article, however, because of the sentence with which Mr Montefiore began to discuss this topic on p. xxviii. It would seem safe to say that the belief in eternal damnation has virtually disappeared. In *Judaism and Christianity*, II, 28, a suggestion was put forward that Jesus did not envisage a perpetual hell, and that to him, as to the Rabbis, 'eternity', when applied to punishment, meant 'a long time'; when applied to reward, 'perpetuity'.

It is, however, necessary to say that the extracts cited by Mr Snape indicate the thoroughness and the tenacity with which this belief was held in Patristic circles. On the Rabbinic side it would be difficult to find anything comparable with pp. 617–18.

Note 76 (p. 656 n.). I think it needs emphasising that this argument is in no sense modern, artificial or *ex post facto*, but it is old, spontaneous, and in accordance with the facts. In every case where this blessing is discussed this explanation is put forward. There is no reason to doubt its sincerity. The sources may be seen in S. Baer's Prayer Book *in loc.*

It should be remembered that the common collocation 'women, children and slaves', shows that the basis for the association of these three classes is their restricted freedom of action: they are not independent politically. The exemption of woman never occurs in ethical connections, but only in regard to acts which she may or may not have the power of performing. It is a question therefore of *caput*. When we are considering subjects like penitence or justice, differentiation of the sexes never occurs, except that we sometimes find man subordinated to woman. Thus we have read several times that woman's charity 'is more direct than man's' (cp. pp. 375 and 419). We read, too, that the woman who fears God is as happy as the man who does so [334] and that the faith of the women in Egypt was greater than that of the men [1440]. Is it correct to say that England underestimated women until they were given the vote?

Note 77 (p. 3). There are several indications that the *Shema* at first consisted only of the opening verse. On *P.B.* p. 8, this verse alone occurs; the other passages are absent and may therefore be regarded as additions. They clearly did not belong to the *Shema* when it was inserted at this early part of the Morning Service. This insertion was due to the circumstances that on Sabbath and other occasions Psalms and hymns were included. It might therefore happen that the *Shema* proper (*P.B.* p. 40) would not be reached until after the statutory time for reading it; this should be as early as possible. See Abrahams' note on p. XXII (where the Talmudic sources are given), and *Sifre Num.*, Shelaḥ, § 115, f. 34*b* (H. p. 126).

This circumstance explains why 'intention' (*Kawwanah*) was more necessary for the first verse of the *Shema* than for the other passages (see p. 273).

Note 78 (p. lxxxvi). One of the reasons why Esau came to be regarded as the prototype and representative (*a*) of wickedness in general and (*b*) of Rome, was that Herod was an Idumean (Esau = Edom, Gen. XXXVI, 43) and a great friend of Rome. Nevertheless, the fact that Esau was Isaac's son occasionally breaks through the more general attitude of condemnation; consideration for Esau is sometimes found. For examples of these two views see [906], [631], [569] and [5].

Note 79 [45]. Compare the Logion, 'Cleave the wood...split the rock...there am I.'

Note 80 [575]. The Hebrew word rendered 'reward' is *Paras*, the etymology and signification of which are doubtful. It is not clear whether the word means (1) 'wages', i.e. a sum of money to which the recipient is legitimately entitled or (2) a 'reward', i.e. an *ex gratia* payment given purely as an act of charity. See the views of Charles Taylor and Travers Herford in their editions of *Aboth*, and Krauss, *Griech. u. Latein. Lehnwörter...*, s.v.

Generally the word *Sakar* (hire) is used in this connection (cp. [579] and **Note 88**).

Compare the Logion of Jesus 'see that you do not lose the wage (τὸν μισθόν)', cited from E. Klostermann's *Apocrypha* III (*Agrapha*), Bonn, 1904, p. 19.

Note 81 ([62] and p. 230). In this passage the idea of a new birth or regeneration is to be noted. Similar examples will be found in the index under *Ḥaddeshu* ('renew'), *Ḥadash* ('New'), *Shofar* (*Shafar*, make fair, pp. 237–8). All these passages occur in connection with the New Year and acquittal from sin. The anti-Pauline character of the end of this extract should be noted. See also **Note 99.**

Note 82 [276]. Sometimes the value of an individual Israelite is stressed, sometimes that of an individual human being (cp. [269], [486], and [617–18]).

Note 83 [297]. For condemnation of astrology, etc., see *Sifra*, Ḳedoshim, f. 91*c*, foot, cited in [633].

Note 84 ([341], pp. xlv, 138, 252). It is in the highest degree unlikely that Eliezer b. Zadok meant his words to be taken literally; he was at the moment emphasising the sanctity of holy things. Had his topic been God's overpowering mercy, his conclusion would have been very different. We have had other examples of this failure of a Rabbi to note the logical implications of his words, e.g. [655] and [374]. In fact Mr Montefiore has drawn attention to this phenomenon in his witty, and essentially true, remarks on p. xlv–xlvi.

Note 85 [374]. The use of the metaphor 'leaven' in a good sense is indeed remarkable, but the reading is doubtful.

Note 86 [481] and [1104]. The term ass-driver is sometimes tantamount to costermonger. Thus in [1104] the ass-driver is looking for wares to purchase for re-sale.

Note 87 (p. 204). I venture to think that it is not quite exact to describe Rabbinic remarks about the well-being of the Gentiles and the sufferings of the Israelites as doctrines. They were hardly items of belief. They were rather attempts to explain very patent but very difficult facts. Such explanations come naturally to the under-dog: in the over-dog such attitudes seem strange. Hence it is surprising to find them in Patristic sources at the time when the Church was triumphant. The worse the disaster and the less in apparent keeping with the Divine justice, the more desperate were the attempts to find a solution of the problem. One could parallel this dilemma in other connections, e.g. in [1215], where the death of an innocent child seemed to baffle explanation and defy consolation.

Note 88 [579]. Instead of 'The day is short (*Kaẓer*)', it is conjectured that the correct reading should be 'To-day is harvest (*Kaẓir*)'.

For 'reward' cf. **Note 80**.

Note 89 (p. 412). With regard to giving alms to deceivers, that is to say to fraudulent or unworthy recipients, cp. [1157–8] and [1160]. On the other hand, in some versions of the Prayer for sustenance (*P.B.* 87), the petition to God 'that I may have the means of giving alms' contains the addition 'but may I not be deceived by unworthy men'. This clause will be found in S. Baer's Prayer Book.

In this connection see also **Note 91**.

Note 90 [1168], [986]. It seems extraordinary that the Gemara should raise the question whether Nicodemus practised charity. The incident related of him in [986] must have been forgotten very soon.

This Nicodemus may have been the Nicodemus of John III, 1–21; VII, 50; XIX, 39. He was a wealthy man and a prominent member of the Sanhedrin. During the war against Titus, he, together with two others, Kalba Sabua' and Ben Ẓiẓit ha-Keset, accumulated a large store of provisions, which would have enabled Jerusalem to hold out. Because he was suspected of siding with Rome, the Zealots burnt the food, thus hastening the fall of the city (*Giṭ.* 56*a*).

Note 91 [490], [1159], [1182], [1218], [1244] and [1519]. In connection with the mutual relation and obligations of rich and poor, Mr I. Foster, of Trinity College, to whom I am already indebted for other references and help, kindly draws my attention to parallels in *The Shepherd of Hermas*. The passage to which he refers is Parable 2 (p. 440 in Lightfoot, *Apostolic Fathers*, ed. J. R. Harmer, 1891). Here the rich and the poor are compared respectively to an elm and a vine, the unfruitful elm supporting the fruit-bearing vine. The relevant passage is this:

'The vine beareth fruit, but the elm is an unfruitful stock. Yet this vine, except it climb up the elm, cannot bear much fruit when it is spread on the ground: and such fruit as it beareth is rotten, because it is not suspended upon the elm. When then the vine is attached to the elm, it beareth fruit both from itself and from the elm. Thou seest then that the elm also beareth fruit, not less than the vine, but rather more....

'The vine, when hanging upon the elm, bears its fruit in abundance, and in good condition: but, when spread on the ground, it beareth little fruit, and that rotten....This parable therefore is applicable to the servants of God, to poor and to rich alike....

'The rich man hath much wealth, but in the things of the Lord he is poor, being distracted about his riches, and his confession and intercession with the Lord is very scanty: and even that which he giveth is small and weak and hath not power above. When then the rich man goeth up to the poor, and assisteth him in his needs, believing that for what he doeth to the poor man he shall be able to obtain a reward with God—because the poor man is rich in intercession and his intercession hath great power with God—the rich man then supplieth all things to the poor man without wavering. But the poor man, being supplied by the rich, maketh intercession for him, thanking God for him that gave to him. And the other is still more zealous to assist the poor man, that he may be continuous in his life: for he knoweth that the intercession of the poor man is acceptable and rich before God. They both then accomplish their work: the poor man maketh intercession, wherein he is rich: this he rendereth again to the Lord Who supplieth him with it. The rich man too in like manner furnisheth to the poor man, nothing doubting, the riches which he received from the Lord. And this work is great and acceptable with God, because the rich man hath understanding concerning his riches, and worketh for the poor man from the bounties of the Lord, and accomplisheth the ministration of the Lord rightly. In the sight of men, then, the elm seemeth not to bear fruit, and they know not, neither perceive, that if there cometh a drought, the elm having water nurtureth the vine, and the vine, having a constant supply of water, beareth fruit twofold, both for itself and for the elm. So likewise the poor, by interceding with the Lord for the rich, establish their riches, and again the rich, supplying their needs to the poor, establish their souls. So then both are made partners in the righteous work.'

For the metaphor of the *Amme ha-Aretz* giving shade to scholars as the vine's leaves shade the clusters, cp. *Lev.R.*, Beḥuḳḳotai, XXXVI, § 2.

Note 92 (p. 445). With regard to '*grinding* poverty (*diḳduḳe 'aniyut*)' it is said ('*Erub.* 41 *b*): 'Three things drive a man out of his mind and mindfulness of his Creator, Gentiles, evil spirits, and grinding poverty.... Three things keep a man from the sight of hell, grinding poverty, stomach ache and [annoyances from] the Government: some say, a termagant wife.'

Note 93 [1399]. The following rendering of this extract appeared in *the Transactions of the Jewish Historical Society*, Vol. XI, 1928, p. 230:

Sons of the Wise, they know not rest
  Throughout this life,
And when they rise, amid the blest
  Renew the strife.

The path they trod before them lies,
  They view their goal:
By grace of God with eager eyes
  They see life whole.

Earth's dreams proved true, earth's phantoms laid,
  Earth's labours done,
To visions new, to words unsaid
  Now call them on.

The books of old, the empty lines
  They might not write,
Rewrit in gold from heaven's own mines
  Now send us light.

Door after door they open wide,
  But not alone:
They go before, but side by side
  We face the throne.

Note 94 [196]. For the collocation 'Scripture, Mishnah, Talmud, Halakot and Haggadot', cp. *Exod.R.*, Beshallaḥ, XXIII, 10; Mishpaṭim, XXX, 14; also [356], [431], [468] and [1265–6].

Note 95 (p. 219). With regard to the attitude of Paul to the doctrine of the merits of the Patriarchs (Rom. XI, 16–24), see the excursus on the subject on p. 330 of W. Sanday and A. C. Headlam's *Commentary on Romans* in the I.C.I. series.

The idea of the merits of the children [*Zekut banim*] is discussed at some length in *Lev.R.*, Beḥuḳḳotai, XXXVI, §§ 4, 5: here, for example, Abraham is delivered from Nimrod's furnace through the merits of Jacob, his descendant.

Note 96 ([643]; cp. pp. 219 and 306). To some extent the Golden Calf, as the worst of all sins, fills the place of Adam's sin in Christian theology, in that its taint endures for subsequent generations. This might be inferred from passages like [643], p. 306, p. 219 note. But such evidence must not be pressed. Far more characteristic is [805], with the declaration, ascribed to God, 'I am pure and the soul which I have given you is pure'. The belief in the inherent purity of the soul predominated. It is re-echoed on *P.B.* p. 5 (as cited on p. 312), and the passage in question was intended to be recited on awakening from sleep (Abrahams, p. xv). The concluding benediction (see above, p. 312, line 7) asserts a belief in the Resurrection, originally, no doubt, understood as bodily Resurrection and, subsequently, as spiritual immortality. But the last two words of the Hebrew (*pegarim metim*) are curious and redundant. The English version, 'dead bodies' (so Singer and Gaster), conceals the redundancy, for the literal meaning is 'dead corpses'. It may be suggested that the word *peger*, in this instance, originally meant the body when unconscious in sleep, and that the blessing was, first of all, a thanksgiving for the awakening of the senses and the restoration of the dormant faculties without which man's frame may well be compared with a lifeless corpse. The subsequent blessings of the series are of this type, thus one formula gives thanks for the power of standing erect; another, for freedom of movement, etc. When the blessing was extended so as to include the Resurrection, the word *metim* may have been added. Pool (*P.B.* p. 1) renders 'who dost restore the soul to the dead'.

Note 97 [558, 560]. In connection with [558] and [560], Mr Montefiore suggests that a short excursus on miracles and miraculous legends in the Rabbinic literature 'would be of much interest and value. Take two stories like those in [558] and [560]; how did they originate? Did somebody sit down and deliberately invent these two stories about the two Rabbi Simeons? What is the nucleus of fact on which they may be based? How did they grow up? Are such stories told only of certain Rabbis and not of others?'

The answer to Mr Montefiore's queries would require not a brief excursus, but a lengthy treatise. Here, only a short note can be offered. Of the three main divisions of the subject, namely, Biblical, Rabbinic and Medieval, only the second can be considered. Nor can even this be treated fully. This present note deals almost exclusively with extracts contained in the Anthology.

There is plenty of material. It needs classification according to certain characteristics, and evaluation according to its significance for life and thought in the Midrashic period.

First of all we note miraculous stories of what may be called the 'fanciful' type. Examples of these are [558], the story of Simeon b. Yoḥai's pupil and the valley of gold coins, and [560], the story of Simeon b. Ḥalafta and the precious stone, with its ending reminiscent of the story of Excalibur. Both these Rabbis were heroes of stories of this type. Thus Simeon b. Ḥalafta was miraculously saved from lions (*San.* 59*b*), while about Simeon b. Yoḥai and his son a story is told in *J. Shebi'it* IX, § 1, f. 38*d*, lines 25 ff., similar to the legend of the Sleepers of Ephesus (*Ḳur'an*, XVIII, 8 ff.;

Gregory of Tours, *De glor. mort.* c. 95). Here, no doubt, the element of the miraculous is to be explained by the saintly character of the persons for whom the miracles were said to have been performed. Legends gather round saints in all parts and at all times. In [364], where Moses contends with the Seraphim, we have an example of legend attaching itself to a biblical hero, and it is easy to see how a process beginning with heroes of the Bible could and would continue to contemporary saints. Among these 'fanciful' stories are those concerning the future life, described with fabulous details in *Ket.* 111*b*–112*a* and elsewhere. Here, too, we may include a large series of the Sindbad the Sailor, Barlaam or Bidpai type, associated with Rabbah bar bar Ḥana. Of these our Anthology gives no examples, but they can be read in *Bab.B.* 73*b*–74*a*. Some may not be Jewish in origin; thus the Aḥiḳar story, which has been found in Aramaic in Elephantine, is said to be a Buddhist Jataka which travelled across Asia and reached the Jews in Egypt by the fourth century B.C. Again, many of Aesop's fables occur in the Talmud, some in their original Eastern form, and some from the collections of Jatakas edited by Kybises, Nicostratus or Babrius. R. Me'ir knew three (or three hundred) fables of foxes (*San.* 38*b* foot). Sometimes such stories told about Rabbis are purely fanciful exaggerations, as, for example, that narrated of R. Ḥaninah and Osha'ya, who, it is said, used to sit and study every Friday and create a three-year-old calf which they ate for their Sabbath meal (*San.* 65*b*). Sometimes, again, these stories may have had a substratum of fact. As examples we may cite the story of the well-digger's daughter in [889], or the cycle of stories about animals connected with Phinehas b. Jair mentioned below. Again, Simeon b. Ḥalafta may have thrown a piece of meat at the pursuing lions and thus escaped (*San.* 59*b*). Simeon b. Yoḥai's sojourn in a cave saved him from Rome and is simple to understand.

These last examples suggest a process of rationalisation. Thus in the numerous stories of successful prayers for rain, e.g. [984] or [986], it is clear that, on the one hand, unsuccessful petitions have been forgotten, and, on the other, generalised rules have been deduced from instances where prayers were answered. So the miraculous enters. The same can probably be said in other cases, e.g. Simeon b. Yoḥai's protracted sojourn in a cave, mentioned above, and the stories about Phinehas b. Jair, told to drive home a moral [120–1], [889], [1066]. We may include in this category certain developments of biblical stories into the miraculous, e.g. the legend of the well which followed Israel in the Wilderness (*Num.R.*, Ḥuḳḳat, XIX, 26 end: but see also *Ta'an.* 9*a*), to which legend there are Christian parallels (e.g. I Cor. X, 4). Perhaps the best example in the Anthology of rationalisation is [889], where two explanations are offered for the escape of the well-digger's daughter who fell into the well; either that her clothes caught on a peg and held her up, or that her father extricated her from the bottom after her fall. In the parallel [1548] the miraculous element is lacking altogether.

Now Paul (I Cor. I, 22) declared that 'Jews seek signs, Greeks seek wisdom' and Jesus is reported (Matt. xii, 39) to have upbraided the Scribes and Pharisees as 'An evil and adulterous generation that seeks after a sign'. With regard to the latter quotation, see Mr Montefiore's remarks in his *Synoptic Gospels, in loc.* (vol. ii, p. 201). Similarly, with regard to the former, it may be said that the charge is not established. Popular superstition, folk-lore and fairy stories there were in plenty, but their effect was not great. Simeon b. Sheṭaḥ was so furious with Onias' rain-miracle [984] that he wished to excommunicate him: for the sin of witchcraft he (Simeon) is said to have had eighty women executed at Ascalon (*San.* vi, 4). We may say that the Rabbis made determined attempts to stamp out sorcery, witchcraft, superstition and credulity in the miraculous: the practice of ocular illusions (*'aḥizat 'eynayim*) and other modes of sorcery were condemned vigorously (*San.* 65*b* foot) and the man who used Exod. xv, 26 as a charm was excluded from the future life, because of his lack of faith (*San.* x, 1). Judges were to be experienced, *inter alia*, in dealing with such things (*San.* 17*a* foot). Appeals to miracles were no argument in law [890], they were the signs of a weak case, for 'moving walls' prove nothing (p. lxxii). One must not rely on a miracle ([580] and [891]). Hillel declared that the process by which man gets his daily bread is a greater miracle than the cleaving of the Red Sea [115].

Biblical miracles stood, naturally, in a different category. But faith without miracles is superior to faith based on them ([881], [731]). Since Israel accepted the Torah at Sinai because of the miracles, it follows that the proselyte, who comes under the wings of the Shechinah without the inducement of miracles, is greater than Israel [1577] (cp. 'Blessed are they that have not seen, and yet have believed', John xx, 29). The miracles at the Theophany were intended to impress the Gentiles (see **Note 51** *ad fin.*): for Israel, faith sufficed, 'We will do, we will hear.' Philo said that the miracles of the manna and the rock had to be performed as a preliminary guarantee of the Divine origin of the Torah (p. 674): such exegesis would seem to be Alexandrian rather than Palestinian. The sayings of Paul and Jesus just cited are all the harder to understand when it is recalled how conspicuous a place miracles hold in the New Testament and in the history of Christianity, whereas in Rabbinical literature they were subsidiary. Efforts were made to harmonise miracles with the scheme of creation. Thus God foreordained the cleaving of the Red Sea (see p. 171, also *Exod.R.* xxi, 6). The order of creation was held thereby not to have been interrupted. God is bound by His own laws (p. 171). Similar attempts at harmonisation can be seen in *Aboth* v, 9 (*P.B.* p. 200: see Singer's note *ib.*), where a list of things created on Friday is given. These are all objects which cannot be fitted into the natural order. They are therefore described as having been planned and executed after the actual work of the Creation was finished, and before Sabbath began. Nevertheless, the miracles of the Bible were not underestimated, but stress was laid on those which could be explained naturally; thus the term 'publishing the miracle' (p. 442) was applied, for example, to the Maccabaean victories; the Jews were bidden to celebrate their deliverance in the eyes of all and thereby express their gratitude to God: 'Tell forth among the Gentiles that the Lord reigneth.'

It was a common tendency to relegate miracles to the distant past. In the 'good old days' no doubt miracles were common. *Aboth* v, 8 (*P.B.* p. 200) speaks of those which happened regularly in the Temple and in *Ta'an.* 21 *a* ff. we have a whole series of stories of people to whom miracles happened. But the men of old were holy and deserved miracles. Thus, an old tradition ('Hence they said') records, in *Ber.* 4 *a*, that the Israelites, 'in the days of Ezra, would have been as worthy of miracles as they were in the days of Joshua, son of Nun, had not sin intervened'. Again, R. Papa remarks (*Ber.* 20 *a*), 'Why were the men of old (*Ri'shonim*) different from us in that miracles were done for them?' Among the answers offered is that the men of old were martyrs. Similarly, in *San.* 94 *b*: 'These were as worthy that a miracle be wrought for them, as those who crossed the Red Sea and trod the Jordan dry-shod.'

The following tentative conclusions may be suggested:

(1) Of the fanciful, harmless 'fairy story' type of miracles there was a fair amount. Certain Rabbis were noted *raconteurs*: the use of the parable was one contributory cause: the desire to amuse and attract, another: around Saints, legends tend to cluster.

(2) There is evidence of the existence of superstition and credulity, both popular and also among certain Rabbis. Dr Büchler has shown that Galilee was more prone to such beliefs and practices than was the South. So also, in the N.T. we find the miracle of the swine located in Gadara which, though actually in Decapolis, may be said to be in Galilee rather than in Judaea: it is in Galilee that Jesus walks on the lake.

(3) But from the earliest times, the opposite tendency can be observed, as in the examples cited of Simeon b. Sheṭaḥ and Hillel. Faith without miracles was exalted: the use of Exod. xv, 26 as a charm was condemned. Attempts at rationalisation may be noted. Biblical miracles, when possible, were given a natural explanation. The use of miracles or *Bat Ḳol* to establish precedents was deprecated, and the place of miracles in Jewish theology became secondary.

Note 98 [563]. For nature's praise of God, cp. p. lxix. An interesting parallel may be seen in *Lev.R.*, Beḥuḳḳotai, xxxv, which deals generally with God's statutes. In § 4 God's statutes are said to be both for man and for nature. This is, in fact, one argument deduced from the text 'If ye walk in my statutes', and would indicate that Torah and the regularity of nature can equally be termed God's statutes.

Note 99 [871], [872]. For the idea of rebirth see also *Lev.R.*, Beḥuḳḳotai, xxxv, § 7, which deals with the keeping of God's statutes and the reward for doing so. The idea of a new birth is derived by a pun: 'If ye keep my commands and do them [*otam*], I count it to you as though ye had made yourselves [*attem*] anew.' (See also **Note 81**.)

EXCURSUS III

THE RABBIS, THEIR 'GENERATIONS' AND THEIR COUNTRIES

H. Loewe

The general reader, being unfamiliar with Rabbis and Rabbinic terminology, may desire to have some explanation of such words as *Tanna*, *Amora*, etc., since an understanding of their meaning, and of the chronological significance of the 'generations' and 'countries' under which the Rabbis are grouped, may be helpful to him in fixing in his mind where and when some of the men lived whose sayings are recorded in the Anthology. The following note serves as an introduction to the tables and lists which follow.

The date of Ezra is usually given as 444 B.C. The chronology of the period is as obscure as its history. But it can with safety be said that its task was to codify the Scriptures, to interpret them and to make them the norm of daily life. Although the first translation (the Septuagint) was made in Egypt during this period, the amount of Palestinian influence thereon is a matter of dispute: the Aramaic versions (*Targumim*) were the work of later generations. During this early age we hear of a mysterious body called the 'Men of the Great Synagogue' who had a good deal to do with the formulation of the liturgy (see *Judaism and Christianity*, vol. I, p. 109; vol. II, pp. 7ff.). The medium of study was oral and constant repetition was necessary. Hence 'to repeat' meant 'to study'. 'Say not, "When I have leisure I will *repeat*", peradventure thou wilt never have leisure': this saying of Hillel in *Aboth* II, 5 is rendered by Singer (*P.B.* p. 187), 'When I have leisure I will *study*'. *Repetitio est mater studiorum*. The Hebrew verb 'to repeat' is *Shanah* and the noun is *Mishnah*. This word was applied to the Corpus of traditions accompanying the Scriptures and termed the 'Oral Law': it was preserved orally. The Aramaic equivalent of the verb *Shanah* is *Tena* and the noun-agent, meaning *teacher*, is *Tanna* (plural, *Tanna'im*) from which the Anglicised adjectives 'Tannaite', 'Tannaitic' are permissible derivatives. The *Tanna'im* are usually divided into six 'generations', from A.D. 10 to 220. The pre-Tannaitic period is usually reckoned from 200 B.C. to A.D. 10, but the starting point is a subject of controversy, since it depends on the identification of Simeon the Just (*Aboth* I, 2; *P.B.* p. 184). He may be one of two men; either the High Priest from 310 to 291 B.C. (or 300 to 270) or his grandson, who was High Priest from 219 to 199 B.C. Both are mentioned by Josephus (*Ant.* Book XII, Chap. II, § 5 (43) and *ib.* Chap. IV, § 10 (224)), who, however, applies the epithet 'Just' only to the older man. The Tannaitic period ends with the final reduction of the Mishnah to writing by Judah the Prince.

The academies in which these studies were carried on were numerous. The seat of the Sanhedrin was in the 'Chamber of Hewn Stone' in Jerusalem. When the fall of the city was imminent, Johanan b. Zakkai obtained leave from Vespasian to found an academy at Jamnia (Jabneh, near Jaffa). After the defeat of Bar Kokba in 135, the scholars moved to Sikhnin (north of Jotapata). Among other schools, mention may be made of Usha (east of Haifa), Peḳi'in (near Lyd), Bene Beraḳ (near Jaffa), Shefar'am (near Usha), Sepphoris (north-west of Nazareth), Tiberias and Beth Shearim (east of Sepphoris), where Judah the Prince taught. The removal of the Judaean schools to Galilee (Jamnia to Usha) was due to the persecution under Hadrian.

The pre-Tannaitic period ends with five 'pairs' (*zugot*, ζεῦγος) of scholars, whose sayings are recorded in *Aboth* I, 4 ff. (*P.B.* p. 184). These included Antigonus of Soko, whose motto (*Aboth* I, 3; *P.B.* p. 184) was 'Be not as servants who serve the Master for the sake of reward', Simeon b. Shetaḥ [1065] and others. The last 'pair' was that of Hillel, whose 'Golden Rule' is cited in [539], and Shammai. After Hillel, the Tannaitic period begins: the sixth descendant of Hillel was Judah the Prince, thus:

(1) Hillel,
(2) Simeon,
(3) Rabban Gamaliel I (Acts V, 34),
(4) Rabban Simeon I b. Gamaliel I,
(5) Rabban Gamaliel II,
(6) Rabban Simeon II b. Gamaliel II,
(7) 'Rabbi' = Rabbi Judah the Prince.

In consequence of persecution, the danger of studies being forgotten was great. Therefore, various attempts at codification were made: these attempts are associated with the names of certain Rabbis, such as Akiba and Me'ir. The following tables give the conventional dates of the Tannaitic generations:

PRE-TANNAITIC	*Temple period*	*circa* 200 ? B.C.–A.D. 10
Typical Scholars:	Simeon b. Sheṭaḥ Hillel Shammai	
TANNAITIC I	*Destruction of Jerusalem*	A.D. 10–80
Typical Scholars:	Johanan b. Zakkai (founded Jamnia Academy, Gamaliel I (Acts v, 34)	
TANNAITIC II	*Trajan's offer to rebuild the Temple*	A.D. 80–120
Typical Scholars:	Pappos [7–8] Gamaliel II	
TANNAITIC III	*Bar Kokba War*	A.D. 120–140
Typical Scholars:	Akiba Ṭarfon Elazar of Modi'im	
TANNAITIC IV	*Me'ir's Mishnah*	A.D. 140–165
Typical Scholars:	Judah b. Ilai Me'ir Simeon b. Yoḥai	
TANNAITIC V	*Codification of Mishnah*	A.D. 165–200
Typical Scholars:	Judah the Prince Phinehas b. Jair	
TANNAITIC VI		A.D. 200–220
POST-TANNAITIC		*circa* A.D. 240

The centre of gravity soon shifted from Palestine to Babylon. In 219, Rab (Abba Areka, 160–247), a fellow-student and subsequent disciple of Judah the Prince, returned from Sepphoris to Babylonia. He settled at Sura, on the Euphrates, and founded an academy there: at Naharde'a, also on the Euphrates, north of Sura, an academy, founded by Samuel, was already in existence. Some decades later, yet a third was founded at Pumbeditha (north of Naharde'a). These were followed by others at Maḥoza (p. 180 n.) (on the Tigris, south of Ctesiphon) and elsewhere. Here the codified Mishnah was studied. The teachers were therefore not known as *Tanna'im*, since that term was associated with the growth of the Mishnah. They were called *'Amora'im* (sing. *'Amora*). This Aramaic word originally meant a speaker and was used of one who repeated the teacher's words to the people: it then became used of the teacher himself and not merely of his mouthpiece. Those who were ordained in Palestine were called 'Rabbi': those ordained in Babylon, 'Rab' or 'Mar'. The work of the *'Amora'im* was to 'complete' the Mishnah and this 'completion' is called *Gemara*, therefore Gemara + Mishnah = Talmud (lit. 'study'). The Gemara exists in two recensions. That of the Tiberias Schools is called the 'Jerusalem' or Palestinian Talmud: neither the date of completion nor the name of its redactor is certain. It was first codified by Johanan b. Nappaḥa (*d.* 279), but it was finished probably by 425, when the Schools of Palestine fell into decay. The other recension is the Babylonian Talmud. R. Ashi, head of the Sura Academy (*circa* 367), began the codification: the final version was complete probably by 500.

The *'Amora'im* are divided into countries (Palestine and Babylonia) and generations: the dates are not always certain and different systems of classification exist. The one followed here is based, with modifications, on Aaron Hyman, *Encyclopedia Judaica*, and the *Jewish Encyclopedia*. For the sake of completeness the arrangement in the *Jewish Encyclopedia* (s.v. *'Amora*) is also given with that of the Anthology.

CLASSIFICATION FOLLOWED IN THE ANTHOLOGY

Palestinian

Generation I. Ḥiyya (mid. 2nd cent.)
" II. Johanan (*d.* 279)
" III. Ammi (3rd cent.)
" IV. Mana (Mani) (4th cent.)
" V. Tanḥuma b. Abba (4th cent.)

Babylonian

Generation I. Huna I (*c.* 260)
" II. Ḥisda (*d.* 309)
" III. Rabbah b. Naḥmani (*d.* 339)
" IV. Raba (*d.* 352)
" V. Papa (*d.* 375)
" VI. Mar Zuṭra (*d.* 417)
" VII. Rabina b. Huna (*d.* 499; the last Amora in Sura)

CLASSIFICATION OF *JEWISH ENCYCLOPEDIA*

Palestinian		*Babylonian*			
Gen. I.	A.D. 219–279	Gen. I.	A.D. 219–257	Gen. IV.	A.D. 375–427
" II.	" 279–320	" II.	" 257–320	" V.	" 427–468
" III.	" 320–359	" III.	" 320–375	" VI.	" 468–500

The foregoing may therefore be summarised thus:

The quotations in this Anthology come from Rabbis who lived between the years 200 B.C. and A.D. 500 and mainly between the years

A.D. 100–350. Of the Rabbis mentioned by name, some lived in Palestine, some in Babylonia. We can gain a fair idea of their geographical distribution by consulting two maps. For Palestine, let us turn to that given on p. 496 of the *Jewish Encyclopedia*, vol. IX, depicting Palestine according to Talmudic sources. It will be observed that the places therein indicated fall into two groups, sundered by a well-defined interval. First, in Judaea, there is a band of towns on the map running south-east, from Joppa to Engedi on the Dead Sea. Many of the names marked here, such as Bene Beraḳ, Lyd, Antipatris, Modi'im, Bethar, Ascalon, Emmaus, etc., will have been noticed by readers of the Anthology as being connected with Rabbis whose names are mentioned. In the centre of the map is a gap, in which the name of Caesarea stands prominent. The northern group, in Galilee, extending down to the banks of the Kishon, is similarly familiar to the reader. Here he will find Sepphoris, Beth Shean, Tiberias, Gush Ḥalab, etc. This map will give the reader ample guidance for Palestine. For Babylonia, let him turn to the frontispiece of Rabbi J. Newman's *Agricultural Life of the Jews in Babylonia* (London, 1932) or to J. Obermeyer's *Die Landschaft Babyloniens*. Here the courses of the Euphrates and the Tigris, the names Bagdad, Ctesiphon, Kut-al-Amara, Wasit, etc., will be fixed lines and points to help localise names like Sura, Maḥoza, etc., which occur in the Anthology.

The Rabbis were not salaried officials: they had their own occupations or possessed private means. Hillel was a wood-cutter; Shammai, a mason; Abba Hosha'ya, a laundryman; Huna, a water-carrier; Abba b. Zemina, a tailor; R. Joshua and R. Isaac Nappaḥa, blacksmiths; R. Ḥisda and R. Pappa were brewers. Some were farmers, some were traders, some were artisans. They were to be found in all social classes.

Palestine, from 301 to 198 B.C. remained, with short intervals, under the rule of the Ptolemies. It then passed to the Seleucids. The Maccabaean struggle for freedom (165 B.C.) was successful, and independence, more or less complete, was established. Pompey captured Jerusalem in 63 B.C. Gradually the grasp of Rome grew tighter until, at the death of Herod, the kingdom was dismembered and came under direct Roman control. In A.D. 70 the state fell and in A.D. 132–5 Bar Kokba's fight for freedom was abortive. The conversion of Constantine to Christianity gave rise to persecution of the Jews. On the partition of the Roman Empire in A.D. 395, Palestine fell to the Emperor of the East. For the next two hundred years, there was comparative tranquillity in the country, but there were periods of severe persecution.

The people among whom the Jews lived were heterogeneous. It is unnecessary to enumerate their neighbours. Palestine must, at different times, have seen Greek traders and philosophers, Roman officials, and soldiers, Egyptian priests and 'soothsayers from the East', worshippers of idols, drawn from every cult and from syncretistic sects. There were Gentiles, Gentile Christians and Jewish Christians. Some of the non-Jews led decent lives, others were noted for unmentionable vices. The intercourse between the Jews and their fellow-citizens of other faiths was conditioned by this and by other circumstances, such as peace or war, persecution or friendship, economic plenty or famine, etc.; uniformity must not be looked for.

Similar variety prevailed in Babylonia. One of the main reasons for the shifting of the religious and academic centre to that country was the fact that, for the most part, the lot of the Jews there was far better than in the West. Under the Arsacide Parthian kings, the Jews enjoyed freedom, and that, too, at a time when there was cruel oppression in Palestine. In 226 the Sassanians rose to power, and this change caused severe suffering to the Jews. The Magi were often their enemies and interfered with Jewish religious practices. After the death of Ardashir I conditions improved. His son, Shapur I, was a just and tolerant monarch. But the Jews suffered during some—but not during all—of the wars with the Romans. The tolerance of Yezdegird I (399–420) and of Bahram Gur (420–38) was followed by the era of persecution initiated by Yezdegird II (438–57) and continued by his son Firuz (457–84): at the death of Firuz the sufferings of the Jews abated.

The main difference between the social conditions of Jews in Palestine and Babylonia was that in Babylon Jews lived in large homogeneous groups and enjoyed autonomy. The rule of the Rabbis consequently possessed greater authority than in Palestine and their decisions were more easily enforced. These circumstances should be borne in mind in comparing Palestinian and Babylonian extracts cited in the Anthology.

LIST OF RABBIS

The references in this index are to extracts

(*a*) Pre-Tannaitic

(*b*) Tannaitic

The generation to which each Rabbi belonged is indicated by the number following his name

The references in this index are to extracts

The references in this index are to extracts

The references in this index are to extracts

(*c*) Amoraic

B = Babylonian; P = Palestinian.

The references in this index are to extracts

Abba b. Zemina (P. IV), 661.
Abbahu (P. III), 1, 21, 87, 129, 212, 274, 299, 350, 389, 482, 491, 578, 722, 727, 775, 867, 979, 1105, 1157, 1232, 1292, 1396, 1422, 1424, 1546, 1573–4, 1582, 1641.
Abbaye (or Abbai) (B. IV, *d.* A.D. 339), 483, 501, 580, 615, 617, 636, 782, 1210, 1315, 1396, 1466, 1503, 1516.
Abdimi of Ḥaifa (P. II), 805.
Abimi b. Abbahu (P. III), 1422.
Abin or Abun (B.-P. IV), 312, 555, 727, 773, 849, 888, 1179, 1423, 1641.
Abin ha-Levi (P. III), 94.
Abun, *see* Abin.
Adda b. Ahabah (Aḥwai) (B. II), 1365.
Aḥa I (P. II), 147, 157, 617, 718, 726, 849, 1573.
Aḥa II (P. IV), 38, 136, 163, 227, 253, 299, 328, 471, 491, 555–6, 624, 913, 927, 1001, 1423, 1442, 1626, 1630 (?), Note 50.
Aḥa b. Abdan (B. II or B.-P. III, probably latter), 711.
Aḥa b. Ḥanina (P. III), 796, 1539, 1660.
Aibu (P. IV), 36, 225, 550, 778, 1329, 1563.
Alexander or Alexandri (P. I–II), 327, 707, 825, 1286, 1295, 1305, 1360, 1443, 1535, 1568, 1626, 1656.
Ammi (P. III), 40, 59, 288, 603, 662, 746, 773, 915, 1181, 1460, 1553.
Amram (B. II), 334, 770, 1123.
Anan (B. II), 814, 1390.
Annaniel (P. III), 29.
Annaniel b. Papa (B. IV), Note 41.
Aristo (P. IV–V), 671.
Ashi (B. VI), 1478, 1626.
Assi I (B. I), 941 [see *J.E.* vol. II, p. 231 inner col., top].
Assi II (P. III), 4, 598, 741, 1138, 1181, 1460, 1556.
Awira (B. and P. III–IV), 1181.
Azariah (P. IV–V), 79, 134, 725, 1449, 1527.
Baruka of Ḥuza (B. IV–V), 484.
Bebai (P. III), 829(?), 1209.
Bebai b. Zabdai (P. II), 831.
Benjamin b. Levi (P. III), 559, 1110.
Berechiah (P. IV–V), 22, 66, 157, 209, 232, 242, 274, 436, 632, 646, 671, 784, 861, 885, 1145, 1335, 1588, 1638.
Bisna (P. III–IV), 1538.
Daniel the Tailor (Ḥayyaṭa) (period uncertain, probably P. III), 1639.
Dimi, brother of Safra (B. III–IV), 1125, 1457.
Dimi of Nehardea (B. IV), 1256.
Elazar b. Menahem (P. III–IV), 394.
Elazar b. Pedat (B.-P. III), 55, 72, 126, 140, 142, 192, 243, 266, 301, 389, 479–80, 492, 516, 531, 553, 564, 575, 580, 588, 618, 631, 650, 704, 756, 801, 836, 868, 910, 919, 938, 961–2, 990, 1003, 1008, 1022, 1048, 1069, 1104–5, 1108, 1137, 1160, 1197, 1242 n., 1312, 1332, 1390, 1397, 1432, 1436, 1445, 1485, 1493, 1505, 1510, 1542–3, 1554(?), 1556, 1575, 1589, 1641, 1650.

The references in this index are to extracts

Gamaliel b. Inninia (Ḥanina?) (P. III), 739.
Gorion (P. III), 610.
Haggai (P. IV), 61, 88, 237, 531, 568, 781, 889, 1069, 1094–5.
Ḥama b. Ḥanina (P. II), 91, 107, 129, 203, 274, 295, 299, 500, 715, 722, 756 1180, 1304, 1332, 1535.
Ḥama b. Osha'ya (Hoshaiah) (P. I), 1025.
Hamnuna (B. III), 496, 516, 972, 1396, 1458, 1478.
Ḥana (B.-P. III), 1002, 1510.
Ḥana b. Aḥa (B. I–II), 776.
Ḥanan (B. III or V), 891, 1482.
Ḥanan b. Pazzi (P.), 1455.
Ḥanan b. Raba (P. II), 1393.
Hananiel, *see* Annaniel
Ḥanilai (P. III), 1432.
Ḥanin b. Adda (P., period uncertain), 397.
Ḥanin of Sepphoris (P. IV), 1535.
Ḥanina b. Abba (P., period uncertain), 249, 786(?).
Ḥanina b. Ḥama (P. I–II), 783, 786, 1065, 1556.
Ḥanina b. Idi (B. III), 1348.
Ḥanina b. Isaac (P. IV), 810, 816.
Ḥanina b. Papa (P. III), 10, 594, 677, 773, 1524, 1605.
Ḥelbo (B.-P. III–IV), 22, 296, 814, 1433, 1588 n., 1638.
Hezekiah (P. I), 277, 1095.
Hezekiah b. Ḥiyya (period uncertain, probably P.), 849.
Hilkiah (P. III–IV), 805, 1519.
Ḥinena b. Papa, *see* Ḥanina b. Papa.
Ḥisda (B. III), 516, 592, 748, 960, 1105, 1272, 1332, 1393, 1652.
Ḥiyya b. Abba (P. III), 14, 63, 350, 361, 520, 522, 567, 617, 654, 676, 749, 798, 867, 925, 968, 982, 1215, 1471.
Ḥiyya b. Ashi (B. II), 517, 769, 1399.
Ḥiyya b. Gamda (P. I), 1430.
Ḥiyya b. Rab of Difte (B. III), 1021.
Huna I (B. II), 57, 460(?), 461, 485, 613, 742, 887, 929, 1065, 1188, 1272, 1315, 1385, 1464, 1471, 1510, 1529, 1584.
Huna II (P. IV), 40, 147, 157, 374, 644, 726, 816, 1087.
Huna b. Aḥa (P. III), 1463.
Ḥunya (Ḥuna b. Abbin ha-Kohen), *see* Neḥunya.
Idi (B.-P. III), 62, 737, 1444.
Isaac (P. II–III), 18, 39, 51, 61, 88, 188, 237, 303, 329, 427, 502, 643, 686, 773, 881, 892, 895, 982, 1347, 1396–7, 1415, 1474, 1479, 1609.
Isaac b. Abin (B. III–IV), 1652.
Isaac b. Elazar (P. III), 1015.
Isaac the Smith, or Isaac Nappaḥa (B.-P. III), 260, 365.
Isa'i (B. II–III), 58.
Ishmael b. Naḥman (P. III), 805, 1589.
Issachar (P. II), 1470.
Issi (period uncertain), 821.
Jacob (B.-P. III), 530, 727, 1220, 1430, 1445, 1573, 1661.

The references in this index are to extracts

The references in this index are to extracts

The references in this index are to extracts

EXCURSUS IV

THE DATING OF RABBINIC MATERIAL

H. Loewe

The following table attempts to supply approximate dates to some of the passages cited in the Anthology. The task is one of extreme difficulty, because the method of editing Rabbinical books differed in many ways from modern methods and because, as has been stated before, Rabbinical traditions were intended to be preserved orally. For a long period it was considered impious to write down formulas for prayer, legal decisions and arguments, parables and translations of scriptures. With regard to each of these subjects we are told that to write them down was tantamount to burning the Torah. 'From the mouth of Scribes (*Soferim*) and not from (the mouth of) books (*Sefarim*).' For so alone could spontaneity in prayer be maintained and rote avoided; so alone could law develop according to growing needs; so alone would parables remain ever fresh and inspiring; so alone would Bible translations neither oust the original nor become stereotyped. Hence 'the letter killeth, the spirit giveth life'; this phrase was probably not Paul's invention. He seems to have adapted a well-known thought and given to it a new significance. Yet he recognised exceptions. Paul, who disparaged the 'letter', was one of the greatest writers of 'letters' that the world has known. For he used this means of reaching those to whom his voice could not carry. Similarly, when the Rabbis felt that their voices were failing, when study was proscribed and ordination punishable by death, when the danger of the wholesale massacre of scholars and the consequent decay of tradition became imminent, they had recourse to the pen; the process of codification began.

Like the Gospels, Rabbinic traditions underwent an era of oral transmission, so that arrangement for mnemonical purposes proved inevitable, and so it happened that parallel accounts of a saying or parable were handed down. We may talk even of a Rabbinic *Formgeschichte*: readers will often come upon examples illustrating and justifying this assertion. Thus, in [642] the remarks of Elazar and of Issi may have been contemporary, but it is just as likely that they are separate, parallel sayings, possibly earlier in date than either of the Rabbis who record them here. Considerable caution, therefore, must be exercised in dating passages by authors or by persons or events with which they deal. And considerable skill is necessary. Anonymous passages present still greater problems. Parallel accounts have to be examined: phrases scrutinised; legal development and historical events must all be taken into account. Small wonder, then, that some people, especially certain non-Hebraists, take the line of least resistance. All Hebrew evidence, these people declare, is late and, in addition, unreliable. For, as illustrating Christianity, it is biased; whereas Christian evidence about Jews and Judaism, being written in Greek, in intelligible sentences, in attractive style, in properly edited documents and by authors of undisputed impartiality, may be admitted without question.

Similarly, on the Jewish side one can sometimes find reasoning about the date and value of Christian material that is just as reprehensible. On both sides the same causes may be traced: these causes are two. First, there is idleness: it needs a great deal of patience to familiarise oneself with knotty problems in someone else's sphere; short cuts are tempting, generalisations convenient. I know no more glaring example of this than Aḥad Ha'am's facile pronouncements about the Christian theory of divorce on pp. 244 ff. of Leon Simon's *Ten Essays by Achad Ha-am* (London, 1922). It takes a Hillel to summarise the whole Law while standing on one foot, and Hillel knew the Law from *alef* to *tau* whereas Aḥad Ha'am clearly had but a superficial knowledge of the Christian conception of marriage, an enormous and complicated subject about which he wrote so dogmatically. The fact that his essay is a polemic makes the parallel with similar errors on the Christian side the more striking. It corresponds to the statement, made not infrequently in Christian polemics, that Jewish husbands divorce their wives for spoiling their soup. It is so easy to write this if you have never heard of *Giṭṭin* and cannot read a line of it. The second cause of which mention has been made, is the desire to score points, and it can be seen how easily the first cause glides into the second. When scoring points, subjective intuition is as good as argument: the ever ready 'of course it is well known that' serves as proof. Thus, as Mr Montefiore shows on p. 612, Bousset can with consummate ease talk of 'the blighting influence of the Law', without attempting to show how the influence was blighting. What would be said of a Jewish writer who assumed 'the blighting influence of the Gospels'? Dates are similarly abused. Chronological investigation in the cause of truth is valuable and important, but when the quest for priority is undertaken with the sole object of equipping an armoury with weapons of offence, then such a quest is barren and harmful: the table hereafter presented will serve no useful purpose.

With proper precautions the attempt to date documents is of extreme value: it is essential. One must bear in mind that the date of a saying is that of the man who first uttered it, not of the transmitter who reported it, still less of the later editor who recorded it. Gospels may be used to illustrate Rabbinic sources and vice versa. Let us take a case in point. 'The Sabbath is made for man, not man for the Sabbath.' We find this in Mark II, 27 and in the Mekilta *Ki Tissa*', Shab. § 1 (*Mek.*[1] 109*b*; *Mek.*[3] vol. III, p. 198; *Mek.*[4] 104*a*), where the speaker is Simeon b. Menasya. Now Mark is generally dated just before the war with Titus (J. Weiss favours A.D. 64–66), while Simeon b. Menasya lived about A.D. 180. Small wonder, then, that people say that Simeon cites Mark. One might as well expect the Pope to cite Luther! A moment's reflection shows that such a suggestion is impossible, for at once the incident of R. Eliezer b. Hyrcanus, recorded in *T.Ḥull.* II, 24 (Z. p. 503, lines 18 ff.) comes to mind. He had been arrested, as being a Christian, during the persecution of the Christians under Trajan. He was, however, released. Puzzled as to the cause of his arrest, he consulted Akiba, who remarked: 'Perhaps a Christian once told you some Christian saying of which you approved?' Eliezer replied: 'By Heaven, you remind me that once in Sepphoris Jacob of Kefar Sikhnin told me a saying of Jesus....'[1] The horror of Eliezer at such an occurrence is adequate proof that Rabbis did not cite Christian sayings.

What, then, is the answer? Surely that both Mark and Simeon are repeating ancient Pharisaic exegesis of Exod. XXXI, 14 which was directed against the strict Sadducean observance of the Sabbath.[2] The material is far older than Simeon and older than Mark; each authority preserves an independent line of transmission. So, New Testament and Talmud can be compared to their mutual advantage.

It does not follow that, as is sometimes asserted on the Jewish side, all Rabbinic material is old. Two examples may be cited to illustrate the need of care in dating and the dangers of generalisation. The first concerns a relatively unimportant matter and the second something much more serious.

There is a well-known passage in *Genesis Rabbah* (Bereshit, I. § 4,

[1] The passage is discussed by Travers Herford on pp. 137 ff. of his *Christianity in Midrash and Talmud*, London, 1903.

[2] See *Judaism and Christianity*, vol. I, p. 167.

Th. p. 10, where the parallels are cited) which relates that on a rainy day, the teachers were unable to come to their classes and so the children played at school. The place in question must have been a kindergarten, since the children are called *Tinoḳot* and since their game was about the alphabet, in fact, about the origin of the final letters. Two explanations are offered. According to one reading, the Prophets were said to be the inventors; according to the better reading (see Theodor's note), the final letters were *Halakah le-Mosheh mis-Sinai*. The literal translation of these words is 'A law [given] to Moses from Sinai'. But this phrase has a special signification, which has been discussed by Bacher in *Studies in Jewish Literature issued in honor of Kaufmann Kohler*, Berlin, 1913, pp. 56–70. He proves that the object of this formula was to invest Halakah, for which no scriptural support was evident, with the stamp of revelation (*Ueberlieferungs-charakter*). In other words the phrase covered customs and institutions of unknown antiquity.

Now in the case which is under consideration, the authority for the tradition in one of the sources (*J.Meg.* I, § 11, f. 71 d, line 34) is Mattitya b. Ḥeresh, a Tanna who lived before the time of Hadrian: the other authorities need not here be taken into account. The point is that at the beginning of the second century, the date when the final letters were introduced was unknown.

But this happens to be a question on which epigraphy has something to say. In the well-known Benê Ḥezîr inscription, which is written over the so-called tomb of James at the foot of the Mount of Olives, the script, as G. A. Cooke (*Text-Book of North Semitic Inscriptions*, Oxford, 1903, p. 341) remarks, 'is advancing towards the square character'. Here, probably for the first time, *nun* has a final form. The inscription is said to belong to the first pre-Christian century.

Here, then, we have a striking illustration of the weakness of popular memory. About two hundred years suffice for the origin of a custom to be lost in dim antiquity.

It may be said that the question of the final letters is relatively unimportant. But this verdict cannot be applied to the problem of divergences in the text of the Bible. To this question attention has already been drawn (see p. lxiii, footnote). On almost any page of the Hebrew Bible there will be found a footnote that a certain word has a 'pause form' but is 'out of pause'. This means that, according to another tradition, the sentence once ended at a different place: the present ending represents another school of Massorah: the divisions between the verses were unknown. And if we turn to *Ḳid.* 30*a* we find the lament that 'in our day we have no definite knowledge of *plene* and defective spellings and of the beginnings and ends of verses'. Here the contrast is between the *Soferim* (Scribes or 'Counters', who counted the verses of the scriptures), who are described as 'Men of Old' (*Ri'shonim*), and the speakers, who are Rabbah b. bar Ḥana and R. Aḥa b. Ada. The latter was an Amora of the fourth century, born in Palestine but an emigrant to Babylonia: the former was a Babylonian Amora of the Second Generation.

Here, again, generalisations must be avoided. The reliability of Rabbinic tradition is attested in many ways. It is the essentials, the subject-matter, that are transmitted with care. Chronology was not always regarded as an essential. But when we take Halakah and history into account, we have sure criteria as to antiquity. With such safeguards, the following tables will be found of use.

TABLE OF DATES OF EXTRACTS

The extracts are given in numerical order as indicated by the numbers in square brackets. The names and dates of Rabbis associated with each extract are here given in the order in which they occur therein.

The generation to which each Rabbi belonged is indicated by the number following his name.

The following abbreviations are used:

T. = Tanna A. = Amora
P. = Palestinian B. = Babylonian

[1] Abbahu (A.P. III); Johanan (A.P. II)
[2] Joshua b. Ḳarḥa (T. IV)
[3] Judah (A.B. II); Rab (T. VI or A.B. I)
[4] Assi II (A.P. III)
[5] Simeon b. Laḳish (A.P. II)
[6] Levi (A.P. III)
[7] Pappias (T. II); Akiba (T. III)
[8] Akiba (T. III)
[9] Abba b. Memel (A.P. III)
[10] Ḥanina b. Papa (A.P. III); Levi (A.P. III); Jose b. Ḥanina (A.P. II)
[11] Anon.
[12] Anon.
[13] Anon.
[14] Ḥiyya b. Abba (A.P. III); Levi (A.P. III)
[15] Anon.
[16] Simlai (A.B. or P. II)
[17] Simlai (A.B. or P. II)
[18] Isaac (A.P. II–III)
[19] Anon.
[20] Anon.
[21] Abbahu (A.P. III)
[22] Elazar b. Aḥwai (T. III); Samuel b. Naḥmani (A.P. III); Berechiah (A.P. IV–V); Ḥelbo (A.B.-P. III–IV)

[23] Jose b. Halafta (T. IV)
[24] Joshua b. Ḳarḥa (T. IV)
[25] Hillel (*d. c.* 10 B.C.)
[26] Rabbah b. Bar Ḥanah (A.B. III); Johanan (A.P. II); Ṭarfon (T. III); Judah b. Ilai (T. IV); Rab (T. VI or A.B. I)
[27] Joshua of Sikhnin (A.P. IV); Levi (A.P. III)
[28] Phinehas b. Ḥama (A.P. III–IV)
[29] Annaniel (A.P. III)
[30] Anon.
[31] Anon.
[32] Azzai, Ben (T. III)
[33] Me'ir (T. IV)
[34] Me'ir (T. IV)
[35] Anon.
[36] Aibu (A.P. IV)
[37] Anon.
[38] Aḥa II (A.P. IV)
[39] Isaac (A.P. II–III); Jose b. Ḥalafta (T. IV); Resh Laḳish (A.P. II)
[40] Ammi (A.P. III); Huna II (A.P. IV); Abba b. Yudan (A.P. IV)
[41] Anon.
[42] Anon.
[43] Anon.
[44] Joshua b. Levi (A.P. I)
[45] Anon.
[46] Judah b. Simon (A.P. IV)
[47] Ze'era (A.B.-P. III)
[48] Yudan (A.P. III–IV)
[49] Judah b. Simon (A.P. IV)
[50] Ḥanina b. Teradion (T. III)
[51] Isaac (A.P. II–III)
[52] Anon.
[53] Joshua b. Levi (A.P. I)
[54] Anon.
[55] Samuel b. Naḥman (A.P. III); Zerika (A.P. III); Elazar b. Pedat (A.B.-P. III)
[56] Jose b. Ḥalafta (T. IV)
[57] Huna I (A.B. II)
[58] Isa'i (A.B. II–III)
[59] Ammi (A.P. III)
[60] Anon.
[61] Haggai (A.P. IV); Isaac (A.P. II–III)
[62] Elazar b. Jose (T. VI); Jose b. Ḳaẓrata (T. VI); Mesharshiya (A.P. V); Idi (A.B.-P. III)
[63] Simeon b. Pazzi (A.P. III); Ḥiyya b. Abba (A.P. III)
[64] Anon.
[65] Anon.
[66] Berechiah (A.P. IV–V); Johanan (A.P. II)
[67] Anon.
[68] Anon.
[69] Anon.
[70] Levi (A.P. III)
[71] Johanan (A.P. II)
[72] Elazar b. Pedat (A.B.-P. III)
[73] Anon.
[74] Anon.
[75] Anon.
[76] Johanan (A.P. II); Levi (A.P. III); Jose b. Abin (A.P. IV); Joshua b. Levi (A.P. I)
[77] Anon.
[78] Anon.
[79] Azariah (A.P. IV–V); Judah b. Simon (A.P. IV)
[80] Anon.
[81] Anon.
[82] Anon.
[83] Anon.
[84] Simeon b. Yoḥai (T. IV)
[85] Simeon b. Elazar (T. V)
[86] Anon.
[87] Abbahu (A.P. III)
[88] Haggai (A.P. IV); Isaac (A.P. II–III)
[89] Akiba (*d.* A.D. 132)
[90] Anon
[91] Ḥama b. Ḥanina (A.P. II)
[92] Anon.
[93] Anon.
[94] Abin ha-Levi (A.P. III)
[95] Anon.
[96] Yudan (A.P. III–IV); Joshua b. Nehemiah (A.P. IV)
[97] Joshua b. Ḳarḥa (T. IV); Azariah (T. IV)
[98] Nehemiah (T. IV)
[99] Anon.

[100] Joshua b. Ḳarḥa (T. IV)
[101] Anon.
[102] Josiah (T. IV)
[103] Anon.
[104] Anon.
[105] Anon.
[106] Judah (A.B. II); Rab (T. VI or A.B. I)
[107] Ḥama b. Ḥanina (A.P. II)
[108] Joshua b. Levi (A.P. I); Men of Great Synagogue (200 B.C.)
[109] Anon.
[110] Anon.
[111] Abba b. Kahana (A.P. III)
[112] Ḥiyya (T. VI)
[113] Joshua b. Nehemiah (A.P. IV)
[114] Johanan (A.P. II)
[115] Hillel (*d. c.* 10 B.C.); Joshua b. Levi (A.P. I)
[116] Anon. (reported by Joshua b. Levi)
[117] Anon.
[118] Judah the Prince (T. V)
[119] Anon.
[120] Phinehas b. Jair (T. V)
[121] Phinehas b. Jair (T. V)
[122] Joshua b. Torta (T. III)
[123] Judah (A.B. II); Rab (T. VI or A.B. I)
[124] Tanḥuma b. Abba (A.P. III)
[125] Zadok (T. II)
[126] Elazar b. Pedat (A.B.-P. III); Samuel b. Naḥmani (A.P. III)
[127] Anon.
[128] Phinehas b. Ḥama (A.P. III–IV)
[129] Ḥama b. Ḥanina (A.P. II); Abbahu (A.P. III)
[130] Anon.
[131] Me'ir (T. IV)
[132] Levi (A.P. III)
[133] Judah b. Simon (A.P. IV)
[134] Yudan (A.P. III–IV); Azariah (A.P. IV–V)
[135] Ḥanina (T. VI)
[136] Ḥanina (T. VI); Aḥa II (A.P. IV); Jose (A.P. IV)
[137] Akiba (*d.* A.D. 132)
[138] Elazar ha-Ḳappar (T. V)
[139] Akiba (*d.* A.D. 132); Pappias (T. II)
[140] Elazar b. Pedat (A.B.-P. III)
[141] Jose b. Dosetai (T. IV–V)
[142] Johanan (A.P. II); Elazar b. Pedat (A.B.-P. III)
[143] Anon.
[144] Anon.
[145] Judah the Prince (T. V); Gamaliel II (T. II)
[146] Judah the Prince (T. V); Nathan (T. IV)
[147] Huna II (A.P. IV); Aḥa I (A.P. II); Judah (A.B. II)
[148] Anon.
[149] Anon.
[150] Anon.
[151] Anon.
[152] Samuel b. Naḥmani (A.P. III)
[153] Anon.
[154] Anon.
[155] Anon.
[156] Anon.
[157] Berechiah (A.P. IV–V); Levi (A.P. III); Huna II (A.P. IV); Aḥa I (A.P. II); Judah b. Ilai (T. IV)
[158] Joshua b. Nehemiah (A.P. IV)
[159] Anon.
[160] Simeon b. Yoḥai (T. IV); Elazar or Eliezer b. Jose the Galilean (T. IV)
[161] Judah b. Ilai (T. IV)
[162] Anon.
[163] Aḥa II (A.P. IV); Johanan (A.P. II)
[164] Yudan (A.P. III–IV); Simeon b. Yoḥai (T. IV)
[165] Anon.
[166] Anon.
[167] Yannai (T. VI); Joshua of Sikhnin (A.P. IV); Levi (A.P. III)
[168] Anon.
[169] Anon.
[170] Anon.
[171] Anon.
[172] Joshua b. Hananiah (T. II)

[173] Akiba (*d.* A.D. 132); Judah b. Ilai (T. IV)
[174] Anon.
[175] Anon.
[176] Ḥanina [T. VI]
[177] Anon.
[178] Anon.
[179] Anon.
[180] Anon.
[181] Anon.
[182] Judah b. Ilai (T. IV)
[183] Anon.
[184] Anon.
[185] Reuben (A.P. III–IV)
[186] Anon.
[187] Anon.
[188] Levi (A.P. III); Isaac (A.P. II–III)
[189] Joshua b. Levi (A.P. I)
[190] Anon.
[191] Levi (A.P. III)
[192] Johanan (A.P. II); Elazar b. Pedat (A.B.-P. III)
[193] Nehorai (T. IV)
[194] Resh Laḳish (A.P. II)
[195] Anon.
[196] Simeon b. Yoḥai (T. IV)
[197] Hananiah b. Gamla (T.)
[198] Anon.
[199] Anon.
[200] Anon.
[201] Jonathan (A.P. I); Jonathan (A.P. II)
[202] Samuel b. Naḥmani (A.P. III)
[203] Ḥama b. Ḥanina (A.P. II); Osha'ya (A.P. I)
[204] Anon.
[205] Anon.
[206] Anon.
[207] Anon.
[208] Samuel b. Naḥmani (A.P. III)
[209] Berechiah (A.P. IV–V)
[210] Simeon b. Elazar (T. V)
[211] Anon.
[212] Anon.; Abbahu (A.P. III)
[213] Anon.
[214] Joshua b. Levi (A.P. I)
[215] Joshua b. Levi (A.P. I)
[216] Anon.
[217] Zabda b. Levi (A.P. I)
[218] Jose b. Simon (A.P. III)
[219] Nathan (T. IV)
[220] Samuel b. Abba (A.P. II–III)
[221] Anon.
[222] Anon.
[223] Samuel b. Naḥmani (A.P. III)
[224] Anon.
[225] Aibu (A.P. IV)
[226] Simeon b. Yoḥai (T. IV)
[227] Tafdai (A.P. ?); Aḥa II (A.P. IV)
[228] Joshua b. Levi (A.P. I)
[229] Resh Laḳish (A.P. II)
[230] Elazar b. Simeon (T. V)
[231] Judah the Prince (T. V); Simeon b. Menasya (T. V)
[232] Berechiah (A.P. IV–V); Ḥanina (T. VI); Simeon b. Pazzi (A.P. III)
[233] Anon.
[234] Anon.
[235] Anon.
[236] Anon.
[237] Haggai (A.P. IV); Isaac (A.P. II–III)
[238] Judah b. Shalom (A.P. IV–V)
[239] Elazar b. Azariah (T. III)
[240] Anon.
[241] Anon.
[242] Berechiah (A.P. IV–V)
[243] Elazar b. Pedat (A.B.-P. III)
[244] Johanan (A.P. II); Levi (A.P. III)
[245] Anon.
[246] Joshua b. Levi (A.P. I)
[247] Anon.
[248] Ḥanina (T. VI)
[249] Ḥanina b. Abba (A.P.)
[250] Anon.
[251] Tanḥuma b. Abba (A.P. V)
[252] Joshua b. Levi (A.P. I); Johanan (A.P. II)
[253] Aḥa II (A.P. IV)
[254] Judah b. Ilai (T. IV); Me'ir (T. IV)
[255] Anon.
[256] Anon.
[257] Simeon b. Ḥalafta (T. VI)
[258] Ḥalafta b. Dosa (T. II)
[259] Jose (A.P. IV)

[260] Isaac Nappaḥa (A.B.-P. III); Ishmael (T. III)
[261] Anon.
[262] Anon.
[263] Akiba (*d.* A.D. 132)
[264] Anon.
[265] Anon.
[266] Johanan (A.P. II); Elazar b. Pedat (A.B.-P. III)
[267] Anon.
[268] Akiba (*d.* A.D. 132)
[269] Anon.
[270] Me'ir (T. IV)
[271] Nathan (T. IV)
[272] Zadok (T. II)
[273] Eliezer b. Hyrcanus (T. II)
[274] Yudan (A.P. III–IV); Ḥama b. Ḥanina (A.P. II); Berechiah (A.P. IV–V); Abbahu (A.P. III)
[275] Simeon b. Yoḥai (T. IV)
[276] Anon.
[277] Hezekiah (A.P. I); Simeon b. Yoḥai (T. IV)
[278] Anon.
[279] Rabbah b. Bar Ḥana (A.B. III); Jose b. Ḥanina (A.P. II)
[280] Anon.
[281] Anon.
[282] Anon.
[283] Akiba (*d.* A.D. 132)
[284] Anon.
[285] Elazar b. Jose the Galilean (T. IV)
[286] Anon.
[287] Abba b. Kahana (A.P. III)
[288] Johanan (A.P. II); Ammi (A.P. III)
[289] Phinehas b. Ḥama (A.P. III–IV)
[290] Anon.
[291] Anon.
[292] Levi (A.P. III)
[293] Judah b. Shalom (A.P. IV–V)
[294] Samuel b. Naḥmani (A.P. III)
[295] Ḥama b. Ḥanina (A.P. II); Simeon b. Pazzi (A.P. III); Ishmael (T. III)
[296] Ḥelbo (A.B.-P. III–IV)
[297] Ḥanina (T. VI); Johanan (A.P. II); Rab (T. VI or A.B. I); Judah (A.B. II)
[298] Me'ir (T. IV)
[299] Ḥama b. Ḥanina (A.P. II); Abbahu (A.P. III); Aḥa II (A.P. IV)
[300] Anon.
[301] Elazar b. Pedat (A.B.-P. III); Osha'ya (A.P. I)
[302] Phinehas b. Ḥama (A.P. III–IV)
[303] Isaac (A.P. II–III)
[304] Joshua b. Levi (A.P. I)
[305] Judah b. Simon (A.P. IV)
[306] Anon.
[307] Ishmael (T. III)
[308] Anon.
[309] Anon.
[310] Anon.
[311] Anon.
[312] Abin (A.B.-P. IV)
[313] Anon.
[314] Anon.
[315] Abba b. Kahana (A.P. III); Johanan (A.P. II)
[316] Johanan (A.P. II)
[317] Anon.
[318] Anon.
[319] Anon.
[320] Anon.
[321] Anon.
[322] Hananiah b. Ḥakinai (T. III); Reuben (A.P. III–IV)
[323] Anon.
[324] Anon.
[325] Anon.
[326] Johanan (A.P. II)
[327] Alexander (A.P. I–II)
[328] Aḥa II (A.P. IV); Tanḥum b. Abba (A.P. V); Jeremiah (A.B.-P. IV)
[329] Isaac (A.P. II–III)
[330] Anon.
[331] Levi b. Ḥama (A.P. III); Resh Laḳish (A.P. II)
[332] Anon.
[333] Abba b. Kahana (A.P. III)
[334] Amran (A.B. II); Rab (T. VI or A.B. I)

[335] Antigonus of Soko (3rd cent. B.C.); Simeon the Just (? *c.* 200 B.C.)
[336] Johanan b. Zakkai (T. I); Jose the Priest (T. II); Judah (A.B. II); Rab (T. VI or A.B. I)
[337] Hillel (*d. c.* 10 B.C.); Zadok (T. II)
[338] Anon.
[339] Raba (A.B. IV, *d.* A.D. 352)
[340] Anon.
[341] Eliezer b. Zadok (T. II, ? IV)
[342] Anon.
[343] Joshua b. Levi (A.P. I)
[344] Jeremiah (A.B.-P. IV); Ze'era (A.B.-P. III)
[345] Jose b. Ḥalafta (T. IV)
[346] Simeon b. Elazar (T. V)
[347] Anon.
[348] Anon.
[349] Resh Laḳish (A.P. II)
[350] Johanan (A.P. II); Resh Laḳish (A.P. II); Abbahu (A.P. III); Ḥiyya b. Abba (A.P. III)
[351] Samuel b. Naḥmani (A.P. III); Judah b. Ilai (T. IV); Nehemiah (T. IV)
[352] Resh Laḳish (A.P. II)
[353] Anon.
[354] Anon.
[355] Phinehas b. Ḥama (A.P. III–IV)
[356] Anon.
[357] Judah (A.B. II)
[358] Judah b. Ilai (T. IV); Elazar b. Shammua (?) (T. IV) or b. Azariah (?) (T. III)
[359] Anon.
[360] Josiah (T. IV)
[361] Johanan (A.P. II); Ḥiyya b. Abba (A.P. III)
[362] Me'ir (T. IV); Simeon b. Elazar (T. V); Nehorai (T. IV)
[363] Azzai, b. (T. III)
[364] Anon.
[365] Isaac Nappaḥa (A.B.-P. III)
[366] Resh Laḳish (A.P. II)
[367] Anon.
[368] Pappos b. Judah (T. III); Akiba (*d.* A.D. 132)
[369] Anon.
[370] Jonathan (A.P. I); Ishmael, school of (T. IV)
[371] Ḥanina (T. VI)
[372] Anon.
[373] Elisha b. Abuyah (T. III)
[374] Dosa (T. V); Sumah b. Katbah (A.); Huna II (A.P. IV)
[375] Anon.
[376] Ḥanina b. Dosa (T. I)
[377] Ḥanina b. Dosa (T. I)
[378] Me'ir (T. IV); Joshua b. Levi (A.P. I)
[379] Anon.
[380] Anon.
[381] Anon.
[382] Jose b. Ḳisma (T. III)
[383] Anon.
[384] Anon.
[385] Anon.
[386] Bag Bag, b. (T. I); He He, b. (T. I)
[387] Anon.
[388] Me'ir (T. IV); Nathan (T. IV)
[389] Resh Laḳish (A.P. II); Elazar b. Pedat (A.B.-P. III); Abbahu (A.P. III); Tanḥum b. Ḥanilai (A.P. II)
[390] Johanan (A.P. II)
[391] Anon.
[392] Anon.
[393] Rab (T. VI or A.B. I)
[394] Phinehas b. Ḥama (A.P. III–IV); Elazar b. Menahem (A.P. III–IV); Levi (A.P. III)
[395] Anon.
[396] Jonathan (A.P. I); Resh Laḳish (A.P. II)
[397] Ḥanin b. Adda (A.P.); Hillel (*d. c.* 10 B.C.); Abtalion (1st cent. B.C.); Shemaiah (1st cent. B.C.); Elazar b. Ḥarsom (T.)
[398] Judah b. Ilai (T. IV)
[399] Raba (A.B. IV, *d.* A.D. 352)

[400] Raba (A.B. IV, *d.* A.D. 352); Samuel b. Naḥmani (A.P. III); Jonathan (A.P. I); Yannai (T. VI); Joshua b. Levi (A.P. I); Resh Laḳish (A.P. II)
[401] Anon.
[402] Yudan (A.P. III–IV); Simeon b. Pazzi (A.P. III)
[403] Anon.
[404] Rab (T. VI or A.B. I)
[405] Anon.
[406] Anon.
[407] Johanan b. Zakkai (T. I)
[408] Anon.
[409] Anon.
[410] Azzai, b. (T. III)
[411] Akiba (*d.* A.D. 132)
[412] Anon.
[413] Anon.
[414] Anon.
[415] Anon.
[416] Anon.
[417] Anon.
[418] Anon.
[419] Judah b. Ilai (T. IV); Jacob b. Ḥanina (A.P. I); Judah the Prince (T. V)
[420] Johanan (A.P. II)
[421] Anon.
[422] Elazar of Modi'im (T. II)
[423] Elazar of Modi'im (T. II)
[424] Anon.
[425] Anon.
[426] Ḥanina (T. VI)
[427] Isaac (A.P. II–III)
[428] Anon.
[429] Anon.
[430] Anon.
[431] Anon.
[432] Anon.
[433] Joshua b. Ziruz (T. IV); Me'ir (T. IV); Judah the Prince (T. V)
[434] Judah b. Pazzi (A.P. III–IV); Judah b. Shalom (A.P. III–IV)
[435] *Doreshe Reshumot*
[436] Berechiah (A.P. IV–V)
[437] Anon.
[438] Akiba (*d.* A.D. 132)
[439] Anon.
[440] Anon.
[441] Anon.
[442] Anon.
[443] Anon.
[444] Anon.
[445] Anon.
[446] Matnah (A.B. II)
[447] Anon.
[448] Anon.
[449] Anon.
[450] Anon.
[451] Elazar b. Modi'im (T. II)
[452] Joshua b. Levi (A.P. I)
[453] Anon.
[454] Anon.
[455] Anon.
[456] Azzai, b. (T. III); Akiba (*d.* A.D. 132); Tanḥuma b. Abba (A.P. V)
[457] Akiba (*d.* A.D. 132); Azzai, b. (T. III)
[458] Akiba (*d.* A.D. 132)
[459] Anon.
[460] Elazar b. Peraṭa (T. III); Ḥanina b. Teradion (T. III)
[461] Huna I (B. II); Judah, brother of Sala Ḥasida (B. III)
[462] Gamaliel III, son of Judah the Prince (T. VI)
[463] Anon.
[464] Anon.
[465] Johanan b. Zakkai (T. I)
[466] Ḥanina b. Dosa (T. I); Elazar b. Azariah (T. III)
[467] Rabbah b. Bar Huna (A.B. III, *d.* A.D. 322)
[468] Anon.
[469] Elisha b. Abuyah (T. III)
[470] Anon.
[471] Ḥiyya (T. VI); Johanan (A.P. II); Aḥa II (A.P. IV)
[472] Elisha b. Abuyah (T. III)
[473] Osha'ya (A.P. I)
[474] Anon.
[475] Anon.
[476] Jabneh, Rabbis of (till A.D. 132)
[477] Anon.
[478] Joshua b. Hananiah (T. II)

[479] Elazar b. Pedat (A.B.-P. III)
[480] Simeon b. Pazzi (A.P. III); Elazar b. Pedat (A.B.-P. III); Jacob b. Aḥa (A.P. III–IV)
[481] Anon.
[482] Abbahu (A.P. III)
[483] Abbaye (A.B. IV, *d.* A.D. 339); Raba (A.B. IV, *d.* A.D. 352)
[484] Baruka of Ḥuza (A.B. IV–V)
[485] Rab (T. VI or A.B. I); Huna I (A.B. II)
[486] Anon.
[487] Anon.
[488] Ṭarfon (T. III); Akiba (*d.* A.D. 132)
[489] Zuṭra b. Tobia (A.B. II–III); Rab (T. VI or A.B. I)
[490] Resh Laḳish (A.P. II)
[491] Aḥa II (A.P. IV)
[492] Elazar b. Pedat (A.B.-P. III)
[493] Akiba (*d.* A.D. 132)
[494] Naḥman b. Isaac (A.B. IV); Ḥanina (T. VI) or Judah the Prince (T. V)
[495] Jose the Galilean (T. III)
[496] Raba (A.B. IV, *d.* A.D. 352); Hamnuna (A.B. III); Jeremiah (A.B.-P. IV); Ze'era (A.B.-P. III)
[497] Anon.
[498] Anon.
[499] Anon.
[500] Ḥama b. Ḥanina (A.P. II)
[501] Abbaye (A.B. IV, *d.* A.D. 339)
[502] Judah the Prince (T. V); Isaac (A.P. II–III)
[503] Levi (A.P. III)
[504] Anon.
[505] Joshua b. Hananiah (T. II); Elazar of Modi'im (T. II)
[506] Jose b. Ḥanina (A.P. II); Johanan (A.P. II); Resh Laḳish (A.P. II)
[507] Anon.
[508] Phinehas b. Ḥama (A.P. III–IV); Hananiah b. 'Akashyah (T. IV)
[509] Banna'ah (T. VI)
[510] Naḥman (A.B. III)
[511] Anon.
[512] Joshua b. Hananiah (T. II)
[513] Anon.
[514] Jose b. Judah (T. V)
[515] Ḥanina (T. VI); Simlai (A.B.-P. II)
[516] Ḥisda (A.B. III); Hamnuna (A.B. III); Elazar b. Pedat (A.B.-P. III); Johanan (A.P. II); Jonathan (A.P. I); Manasseh, school of (A.B.-P. III)
[517] Rab (T. VI or A.B. I); Judah b. Samuel (A.B. II–III); Ḥiyya b. Ashi (A.B. II)
[518] Joshua b. Levi (A.P. I)
[519] Ḥanina (T. VI); Yannai (T. VI); Rabbah b. Bar Huna (A.B. III, *d.* A.D. 322); Rabba b. R. Naḥman (A.B. III)
[520] Simeon b. Yoḥai (T. IV)
[521] Ḥanina (T. VI)
[522] Ḥiyya b. Abba (A.P. III); Samuel b. Naḥmani (A.P. III)
[523] Anon.
[524] Phinehas b. Ḥama (A.P. III–IV)
[525] Judah the Prince (T. V); Simeon b. Gamaliel (T. I and IV)
[526] Anon.
[527] Judah b. Shalom (A.P. IV–V); Judah b. Simon (A.P. IV); Eliezer b. Hyrcanus (T. II)
[528] Anon.
[529] Anon.
[530] Jacob (A.B.-P. III)
[531] Elazar b. Pedat (A.B.-P. III); Haggai (A.P. IV)
[532] Azzai, b. (T. III)
[533] Me'ir (T. IV)
[534] Anon.
[535] Anon.
[536] Judah the Prince (T. V)
[537] Anon.
[538] Simlai (A.B.-P. II)
[539] Shammai (T. I); Hillel (*d. c.* 10 B.C.)
[540] Anon.
[541] Anon.

[542] Anon.
[543] Bar Ḳappara (T. VI)
[544] Judah b. Ilai (T. IV)
[545] Anon.
[546] Anon.
[547] Anon.
[548] Anon.
[549] Anon.
[550] Aibu (A.P. IV)
[551] Jonah (A.P. V)
[552] Eliezer b. Hyrcanus (T. II); Joshua b. Hananiah (T. II); Johanan (A.P. II)
[553] Rab (T. VI or A.B. I); Elazar b. Pedat (A.B.-P. III)
[554] Judah the Prince (T. V)
[555] Aḥa II (A.P. IV); Abba b. Kahana (A.P. III); Abun (A.B.-P. IV)
[556] Elazar b. Azariah (T. III)
[557] Jose b. Ḥalafta (T. IV)
[558] Simeon b. Yoḥai (T. IV)
[559] Benjamin b. Levi (A.P. III); Samuel b. Naḥmani (A.P. III)
[560] Simeon b. Ḥalafta (T. VI); Judah the Prince (T. V)
[561] Levi (A.P. III)
[562] Phinehas b. Ḥama (A.P. III–IV); Simeon b. Pazzi (A.P. III)
[563] Anon.
[564] Elazar b. Pedat (A.B.-P. III)
[565] Anon.
[566] Aḥa II (A.P. IV)
[567] Ḥiyya b. Abba (A.P. III); Ulla (A.B.-P. II)
[568] Haggai (A.P. IV); Eliezer b. Hyrcanus (T. II); Akiba (*d.* A.D. 132)
[569] Ze'era (A.B.-P. III)
[570] Menaḥema (A.P. III); Tanḥum b. Ḥiyya (A.P. III); Mana (Mani) (A.P. IV); Jose b. Zebida (A.P. IV–V)
[571] Gamaliel II (T. II)
[572] Nathan (T. IV); Ḥiyya (T. VI)
[573] Anon.
[574] Gamaliel II (T. II); Elazar b. Azariah (T. III); Joshua b. Hananiah (T. II); Akiba (*d.* A.D. 132)
[575] Elazar b. Pedat (A.B.-P. III)
[576] Antigonus of Soko (3rd cent. B.C.)
[577] Anon.
[578] Abbahu (A.P. III)
[579] Ṭarfon (T. III)
[580] Judah (A.B. II); Shemaiah (A.B. III); Abbaye (A.B. IV); Jacob (T. IV); Elazar b. Pedat (A.B.-P. III)
[581] Anon.
[582] Judah (A.B. II); Rab (T. VI or A.B. I); Akiba (*d.* A.D. 132)
[583] Elazar b. Simeon (T. V); Simeon b. Yoḥai (T. IV)
[584] Ḥanina b. Gamaliel (T. III); Simeon b. Yoḥai (T. IV); Simeon b. Rabbi (T. VI)
[585] Hananiah b. 'Aḳashyah (T. IV)
[586] Phinehas b. Ḥama (A.P. III–IV)
[587] Anon.
[588] Elazar b. Pedat (A.B.-P. III); Ḥiyya (T. VI)
[589] Anon.
[590] Anon.
[591] Gamaliel III, son of Judah the Prince (T. VI)
[592] Raba (A.B. IV, *d.* A.D. 352); Rabbah b. Naḥmani (A.B. III); Ḥisda (A.B. III)
[593] Anon.
[594] Ḥanina b. Papa (A.P. III) or Ze'era (A.B.-P. III)
[595] Johanan (A.P. II)
[596] Jose b. Ḥalafta (T. IV)
[597] Anon.
[598] Assi II (A.P. III)
[599] Yudan (A.P. III–IV)
[600] Judah b. Ilai (T. IV)
[601] Jose b. Ḥalafta (T. IV)
[602] Abba b. Ḥanina (A.P. II)
[603] Ammi (A.P. III)
[604] Simai (T. VI)
[605] Jonathan (A.P. I); Osha'ya (A.P. I)

[606] Osha'ya (A.P. I)
[607] Anon.
[608] Anon.
[609] Anon.
[610] Gorion (A.P. III); Joseph (A.B. III)
[611] Judah b. Ilai (T. IV)
[612] Johanan (A.P. II)
[613] Huna I (A.B. II); Jose b. Zimra (A.P. I)
[614] Anon.
[615] Simeon the Pious (T.); Abbaye (A.B. IV, *d.* A.D. 339)
[616] Akiba (*d.* A.D. 132)
[617] Ḥiyya b. Abba (A.P. III); Johanan (A.P. II)
[618] Elazar b. Pedat (A.B.-P. III); Abba b. Kahana (A.P. III); Azzai, b. (T. III) or Zoma, b. (T. III)
[619] Simeon b. Gamaliel (T. I and IV)
[620] Anon.
[621] Judah b. Naḥmani (A.P. III)
[622] Ishmael (T. III)
[623] Abba Ḥanin (T. III); Eliezer b. Hyrcanus (T. II)
[624] Simeon b. Yoḥai (T. IV); Yudan (A.P. III–IV); Aḥa II (A.P. IV); Ḥanina (T. VI); Onias (A.P. IV)
[625] Johanan (A.P. II); Elazar b. Jose the Galilean (T. IV)
[626] Anon.
[627] Abba b. Kahana (A.P. III); Resh Laḳish (A.P. II)
[628] Johanan (A.P. II)
[629] Anon.
[630] Anon.
[631] Elazar b. Pedat (A.B.-P. III)
[632] Berechiah (A.P. IV–V)
[633] Anon.
[634] Anon.
[635] Anon.
[636] Abbaye (A.B. IV, *d.* A.D. 339); Raba (A.B. IV, *d.* A.D. 352)
[637] Johanan (A.P. II)
[638] Anon.
[639] Anon.
[640] Anon.
[641] Anon.
[642] Elazar b. Azariah (T. III); Issi b. 'Akabyah (T. IV)
[643] Isaac (A.P. II–III)
[644] Huna II (A.P. IV)
[645] Nehemiah (T. IV)
[646] Berechiah (A.P. IV–V); Levi (A.P. III)
[647] Johanan (A.P. II)
[648] Anon.
[649] Samuel b. Naḥmani (A.P. III)
[650] Elazar b. Pedat (A.B.-P. III)
[651] Samuel b. Naḥmani (A.P. III); Gamaliel II (T. II)
[652] Gamaliel II (T. II)
[653] Anon.
[654] Naḥman (A.B. III); Rabbah b. Abuha (A.B. II); Ḥiyya b. Abba (A.P. III); Johanan (A.P. II)
[655] Anon.
[656] Johanan (A.P. II)
[657] Anon.
[658] Phinehas b. Ḥama (A.P. III–IV)
[659] Ishmael (T. III); Akiba (*d.* A.D. 132)
[660] Anon.
[661] Abba b. Zemina (A.P. IV)
[662] Ammi (A.P. III)
[663] Anon.
[664] Johanan (A.P. II); Joshua b. Levi (A.P. I)
[665] Raba (A.B. IV, *d.* A.D. 352)
[666] Joshua b. Hananiah (T. II)
[667] Elazar b. Peraṭa (T. III)
[668] Anon.
[669] Anon.
[670] Judah (A.B. II)
[671] Aristo (A.P. IV–V); Berechiah (A.P. IV–V)
[672] Anon.
[673] Anon.
[674] Nathan (T. IV)
[675] Judah the Prince (T. V); Johanan (A.P. II); Judah b. Ilai (T. IV); Simeon b. Yoḥai (T. IV); Bar Kokba (soldier, *d.* A.D. 135); Akiba (*d.* A.D. 132); Johanan b.

Torta (T. III); Elazar of Modi'im (T. II); Simeon b. Gamaliel (T. I and IV)
[676] Ḥiyya b. Abba (A.P. III)
[677] Ḥanina b. Papa (A.P. III)
[678] Anon.
[679] Anon.
[680] Johanan b. Zakkai (T. I); Eliezer b. Hyrcanus (T. II); Joshua b. Hananiah (T. II)
[681] Phinehas b. Ḥama (A.P. III–IV); Jose b. Joezer (B.C.)
[682] Simeon b. Gamaliel (T. I and IV); Ishmael (T. III)
[683] Ḥanina b. Teradion (T. III)
[684] Akiba (*d.* A.D. 132)
[685] Anon.
[686] Isaac (A.P. II–III)
[687] Gamaliel II (T. II); Akiba (*d.* A.D. 132)
[688] Joshua b. Hananiah (T. II)
[689] Tanḥuma b. Abba (A.P. V); Jose b. Ḥanina (A.P. II)
[690] Anon.
[691] Anon.
[692] Me'ir (T. IV); Raba (A.B. IV, *d.* A.D. 352)
[693] Judah b. Ilai (T. IV) (?) or Rab (T. VI or A.B. I) (?); Samuel (?) (A.B. I)
[694] Anon.
[695] Anon.
[696] Anon.
[697] Raba (A.B. IV, *d.* A.D. 352)
[698] Johanan (A.P. II)
[699] Anon.
[700] Eliezer b. Jacob (T. II, ? IV)
[701] Nehemiah (T. IV)
[702] Simeon b. Menasya (T. V); Azzai, b. (T. III); Eliezer b. Jacob (T. II, ? IV); Jacob (T. IV); Me'ir (T. IV)
[703] Joshua b. Levi (A.P. I)
[704] Elazar b. Pedat (A.B.-P. III)
[705] Banna'ah (T. VI)
[706] Banna'ah (T. VI)
[707] Alexander (A.P. I–II); Rab (T. VI or A.B. I); Johanan (A.P. II); Levi b. Sisi (A.P. III)
[708] Dosetai b. Yannai (T. V)
[709] Ṭarfon (T. III)
[710] Rabbah b. Bar Ḥana (A.B. III); Johanan (A.P. II)
[711] Aḥa b. Abdan (? A.B. II)
[712] Anon.
[713] Naḥman b. Isaac (A.B. IV)
[714] Ishmael (T. III)
[715] Ḥama b. Ḥanina (A.P. II)
[716] Abba Saul (T. IV)
[717] Simeon b. Yoḥai (T. IV)
[718] Levi (A.P. III); Samuel b. Naḥmani (A.P. III); Joshua of Sikhnin (A.P. IV); Abba b. Abin (A.P. III–IV); Aḥa I (A.P. II); Tanḥuma b. Abba (A.P. V)
[719] Levi (A.P. III)
[720] Me'ir (T. IV)
[721] Simlai (A.B.-P. II)
[722] Abbahu (A.P. III); Ḥama b. Ḥanina (A.P. II)
[723] Anon.
[724] Resh Laḳish (A.P. II)
[725] Azariah (A.P. IV–V)
[726] Huna II (A.P. IV); Aḥa I (A.P. II); Judah b. Palia (A.P. ?)
[727] Abbahu (A.P. III); Johanan (A.P. II); Ḥanina (T. VI); Jonathan (A.P. I); Abin or Abun (A.B.-P. IV); Jacob of Neboria (A.P. II); Men of Great Synagogue (200 B.C.); Jacob (A.B.-P. III)
[728] Johanan (A.P. II)
[729] Ḥanina (T. VI)
[730] Simeon b. Judah the Prince (Transition T.-A.)
[731] Anon.
[732] Anon.
[733] Anon.
[734] Samuel b. Sustra (A.P. III–IV)
[735] Anon.
[736] Ḥanina (T. VI)
[737] Idi (A.B.-P. III)
[738] Akiba (*d.* A.D. 132); Joshua ha-Garsi (T. IV)

[739] Resh Laḳish (A.P. II); Judah b. Ḥanina (A.P. I); Gamaliel b. Inninia (A.P. III); Mana (Mani) (A.P. IV); Jeshebab (T. IV); Gamaliel II (T. II)
[740] Anon.
[741] Assi II (A.P. III)
[742] Huna I (A.B. II)
[743] Simeon b. Yoḥai (T. IV)
[744] Anon.
[745] Nahman (A.B. III)
[746] Ammi (A.P. III)
[747] Anon.
[748] Anon.
[749] Ḥiyya b. Abba (A.P. III); Johanan (A.P. II)
[750] Ḥanina (T. VI)
[751] Levi (A.P. III)
[752] Azzai, b. (T. III)
[753] Azzai, b. (T. III)
[754] Resh Laḳish (A.P. II)
[755] Resh Laḳish (A.P. II); Ishmael, school of (T. IV)
[756] Elazar b. Pedat (A.B.-P. III); Ḥama b. Ḥanina (A.P. II)
[757] Johanan b. Nuri (T. III)
[758] Simeon b. Levi (A.P. II)
[759] Anon.
[760] Raba (A.B. IV, *d.* A.D. 352)
[761] Yannai (T. VI)
[762] Anon.
[763] Judah b. Naḥmani (A.P. III)
[764] Anon.
[765] Samuel b. Naḥmani (A.P. III)
[766] Simai (T. VI)
[767] Ishmael, school of (T. IV)
[768] Simeon the Just (? *c.* 200 B.C.); Mana (Mani) (A.P. IV)
[769] Ḥiyya b. Ashi (A.B. II)
[770] Amram (A.B. II)
[771] Me'ir (T. IV)
[772] Akiba (*d.* A.D. 132); Mattithiah b. Ḥeresh (T. III); Me'ir (T. IV)
[773] Akiba (*d.* A.D. 132); Isaac (A.P. II–III); Ammi (A.P. III); Abin or Abun (A.B.-P. IV); Ḥanina b. Papa (A.P. III)
[774] Anon.
[775] Abbahu (A.P. III)
[776] Ḥana b. Aḥa (A.B. I–II); Rab (T. VI or A.B. I)
[777] Ḥiyya (T. VI); Abba Jose the Potter (T. VI)
[778] Aibu (A.P. IV)
[779] Anon.
[780] Anon.
[781] Haggai (A.P. IV); Mana (Mani) (A.P. IV)
[782] Abbaye (A.B. IV, *d.* A.D. 339)
[783] Ḥanina b. Ḥama (A.P. I–II); Jonathan (A.P. I)
[784] Simeon b. Yoḥai (T. IV); Berechiah (A.P. IV–V)
[785] Zadok (T. II); Kahana (A.P. II)
[786] Johanan (A.P. II); Safra (A.B.-P. III–IV); Raba (A.B. IV, *d.* A.D. 352); Ḥanina b. Ḥama (A.P. I–II); Osha'ya (A.P. I)
[787] Joshua b. Levi (A.P. I)
[788] Naḥman b. Samuel (A.P. III)
[789] Ilai (T. III); Joseph (A.B. III)
[790] Ḥanina (T. VI)
[791] Zuṭra, Mar (A.B. IV or VI); Mar b. Rabina (A.B. III–IV)
[792] Anon.
[793] Johanan b. Baroḳa (T. III)
[794] Rab (T. VI or A.B. I)
[795] Anon.
[796] Aḥa b. Ḥanina (A.P. III); Joseph (A.B. III)
[797] Anon.
[798] Ḥiyya b. Abba (A.P. III); Akiba (*d.* A.D. 132); Joshua b. Hananiah (T. II); Samuel b. Naḥmani (A.P. III)
[799] Anon.
[800] Johanan (A.P. II)
[801] Jonathan (A.P. I); Jose b. Ḥanina (A.P. II); Elazar b. Pedat (A.B.-P. III)
[802] Eliezer b. Zadok (T. II, ? IV)
[803] Anon.
[804] Johanan (A.P. II)

[805] Phinehas b. Ḥama (A.P. III–IV); Hilkiah (A.P. III–IV); Simeon b. Pazzi (A.P. III); Ishmael b. Naḥman (A.P. III); Abdimi of Ḥaifa (A.P. II)
[806] Anon.
[807] Ishmael (T. III); Ḥiyya (T. VI)
[808] Anon.
[809] Simai (T. VI)
[810] Ḥanina b. Isaac (A.P. IV)
[811] Hillel (*d. c.* 10 B.C.)
[812] Raba (A.B. IV, *d.* A.D. 352)
[813] Anon.
[814] Ḥelbo (A.B.-P. III–IV); Samuel b. Naḥmani (A.P. III); Anan (A.B. II)
[815] Anon.
[816] Huna II (A.P. IV); Ḥanina b. Isaac (A.P. IV)
[817] Anon.
[818] Sumah b. Katbah (A.); Resh Laḳish (A.P. II)
[819] Jose b. Tartas (A.P. ?)
[820] Judah (A.B. II)
[821] Issi (A.); Levi (A.P. III)
[822] Anon.
[823] Anon.
[824] Samuel b. Naḥmani (A.P. III)
[825] Alexander (A.P. I–II)
[826] Anon.
[827] Me'ir (T. IV)
[828] Anon.
[829] Bebai (A.P. III ?); Rab (T. VI or A.B. I); Johanan (A.P. II)
[830] Anon.
[831] Bebai b. Zabdai (A.P. II); Ṭanḥum b. Ḥanilai (A.P. II); Josiah (A.P. III)
[832] Judah Nesia (T. VI); Judah b. Simeon (T. V ?)
[833] Judah the Prince (T. V)
[834] Anon.
[835] Anon.
[836] Elazar b. Pedat (A.B.-P. III)
[837] Phinehas b. Ḥama (A.P. III–IV)
[838] Anon.
[839] Joshua b. Hananiah (T. II); Eliezer b. Hyrcanus (T. II)
[840] Anon.
[841] Simeon b. Pazzi (A.P. III)
[842] Elazar b. Durdaya (T. V); Judah (ha-Nasi) the Prince (T. V)
[843] Anon.
[844] Anon.
[845] Anon.
[846] Me'ir (T. IV)
[847] Anon.
[848] Anon.
[849] Hezekiah b. Ḥiyya (A.P. ?); Phinehas b. Ḥama (A.P. III–IV); Abin (A.B.-P. IV); Aḥa I (A.P. II); Simeon b. Pazzi (A.P. III)
[850] Anon.
[851] Anon.
[852] Anon.
[853] Akiba (*d.* A.D. 132)
[854] Eliezer b. Hyrcanus (T. II)
[855] Anon.
[856] Anon.
[857] Anon.
[858] Anon.
[859] Joshua b. Levi (A.P. I); Simeon b. Yoḥai (T. IV)
[860] Rab (T. VI or A.B. I)
[861] Berechiah (A.P. IV–V)
[862] Johanan (A.P. II); Resh Laḳish (A.P. II)
[863] Phinehas b. Ḥama (A.P. III–IV)
[864] Anon.
[865] Anon.
[866] Anon.
[867] Ḥiyya b. Abba (A.P. III); Johanan (A.P. II); Abbahu (A.P. III); Rab (T. VI or A.B. I)
[868] Yudan (A.P. III–IV); Elazar b. Pedat (A.B.-P. III)
[869] Judah b. Ḥiyya (A.P. II); Joshua b. Levi (A.P. I)
[870] Johanan (A.P. II)
[871] Anon.
[872] Anon.
[873] Anon.

[874] Ze'era (A.B.-P. III)
[875] Anon.
[876] Anon.
[877] Anon.
[878] Anon.
[879] Nehemiah (T. IV)
[880] Judah the Prince (T. V)
[881] Nehemiah (T. IV); Isaac (A.P. II–III); Simeon b. Abba (A.P. III)
[882] Anon.
[883] Anon.
[884] Anon.
[885] Samuel b. Naḥmani (A.P. III); Berechiah (A.P. IV–V)
[886] Elazar of Modi'im (T. II); Eliezer b. Hyrcanus (T. II)
[887] Huna I (A.B. II); Levi b. Sisi (A.P. III)
[888] Abin or Abun (A.B.-P. IV)
[889] Phinehas b. Jair (T. V); Haggai (A.P. IV); Naḥman (A.B. III)
[890] Eliezer b. Hyrcanus (T. II); Joshua b. Hananiah (T. II); Jeremiah (A.B.-P. IV); Nathan (T. IV)
[891] Yannai (T. VI); Ḥanan (A.B. III or V)
[892] Isaac (A.P. II–III)
[893] Anon.
[894] Anon.
[895] Isaac (A.P. II–III)
[896] Anon.
[897] Anon.
[898] Eliezer b. Hyrcanus (T. II)
[899] Judah (A.B. II)
[900] Johanan (A.P. II)
[901] Anon.
[902] Phinehas b. Ḥama (A.P. III–IV)
[903] Johanan (A.P. II)
[904] Anon.
[905] Ḥiyya (T. VI); Kahana (A.P. II)
[906] Anon.
[907] Simeon the Pious (T.)
[908] Anon.
[909] Anon.
[910] Judah b. Shalom (A.P. IV–V); Elazar b. Pedat (A.B.-P. III)
[911] Rab (T. VI or A.B. I); Ḥanina (T. VI)
[912] Samuel b. Naḥmani (A.P. III)
[913] Aḥa II (A.P. IV)
[914] Anon.
[915] Ammi (A.P. III)
[916] Anon.
[917] Anon.
[918] Ishmael b. Jose (T. V)
[919] Elazar b. Pedat (A.B.-P. III)
[920] Judah the Prince (T. V)
[921] Anon.
[922] Me'ir (T. IV)
[923] Eliezer b. Hyrcanus (T. II)
[924] Eliezer b. Hyrcanus (T. II)
[925] Ḥiyya b. Abba (A.P. III); Johanan (A.P. II)
[926] Akiba (*d.* A.D. 132)
[927] Aḥa II (A.P. IV)
[928] Elazar b. Shammua (T. IV); Jacob b. Idi (A.P. III); Osha'ya (A.P. I); Rabbah b. Naḥman (A.B. III); Joseph (A.B. III)
[929] Huna I (A.B. II)
[930] Phinehas b. Ḥama (A.P. III–IV); Levi (A.P. III); Johanan (A.P. II); Menahem of Galilee (T. V)
[931] Rab (T. VI or A.B. I)
[932] Nathan (T. IV)
[933] Judah b. Ilai (T. IV); Akiba (*d.* A.D. 132); Elazar b. Azariah (T. III)
[934] Anon.
[935] Anon.
[936] Nathan (T. IV)
[937] Simeon b. Yoḥai (T. IV)
[938] Elazar b. Pedat (A.B.-P. III)
[939] Hillel (*d. c.* 10 B.C.)
[940] Anon.
[941] Assi I (A.B. I)
[942] Anon.
[943] Anon.
[944] Jeremiah (A.B.-P. IV)
[945] Nehemiah (T. IV)
[946] Lulianus (A.P. III)
[947] Anon.
[948] Johanan (A.P. II); Judah the Prince (T. V)

[949] Jose b. Ḥalafta (T. IV)
[950] Anon.
[951] Anon.
[952] Anon.
[953] Anon.
[954] Anon.
[955] Anon.
[956] Yannai (T. VI)
[957] Anon.
[958] Anon.
[959] Anon.
[960] Ḥisda (A.B. III)
[961] Elazar b. Pedat (A.B.-P. III)
[962] Elazar b. Pedat (A.B.-P. III)
[963] Eliezer b. Zadok (T. II, ? IV)
[964] Johanan (A.P. II)
[965] Safra (A.B.-P. III–IV)
[966] Rab (T. VI or A.B. I)
[967] Tanḥum b. Eskolastika (A.P. II–III)
[968] Ḥiyya b. Abba (A.P. III)
[969] Pedat (A.P. III)
[970] Mar b. Rabina (A.B. III–IV)
[971] Zuṭra, Mar (A.B. IV or VI)
[972] Hamnuna (A.B. III)
[973] Anon.
[974] Anon.
[975] Anon.
[976] Anon.
[977] Anon.
[978] Rab (T. VI or A.B. I)
[979] Abbahu (A.P. III)
[980] Anon.
[981] Joshua b. Hananiah (T. II); Tanḥum b. Ḥiyya (A.P. III)
[982] Osha'ya (A.P. I); Isaac (A.P. II–III); Tanḥum b. Ḥanilai (A.P. II); Ḥiyya b. Abba (A.P. III); Joshua b. Ḳarḥa (T. IV)
[983] Anon.
[984] Ḥoni the Circle-drawer (1st cent. B.C.); Simeon b. Sheṭaḥ (B.C.)
[985] Eliezer b. Hyrcanus (T. II); Akiba (*d.* A.D. 132)
[986] Naḳdimon b. Gorion (time of Temple)
[987] Ḥanin ha-Neḥba (before A.D.); Ḥoni the Circle-drawer (1st cent. B.C.)
[988] Rab (T. VI or A.B. I)
[989] Abba Ḥilkiah (a few years B.C.); Ḥoni the Circle-drawer (1st cent. B.C.)
[990] Elazar b. Pedat (A.B.-P. III); Levi b. Sisi (A.P. I)
[991] Anon.
[992] Anon.
[993] Judah (A.B. II)
[994] Anon.
[995] Anon.
[996] Anon.
[997] Anon.
[998] Anon.
[999] Me'ir (T. IV)
[1000] Anon.
[1001] Aḥa II (A.P. IV)
[1002] Johanan (A.P. II); Ḥana (A.B.-P. III)
[1003] Elazar b. Pedat (A.B.-P. III)
[1004] Anon.
[1005] Eliezer b. Hyrcanus (T. II); Akiba (*d.* A.D. 132)
[1006] Judah b. Tema (T. V)
[1007] Raba (A.B. IV, *d.* A.D. 352)
[1008] Elazar b. Pedat (A.B.-P. III)
[1009] Judah b. Tema (T. V)
[1010] Anon.
[1011] Anon.
[1012] Anon.
[1013] Anon.
[1014] Gamaliel III, son of Judah the Prince (T. VI)
[1015] Isaac b. Elazar (A.P. III)
[1016] Anon.
[1017] Men of Great Synagogue (200 B.C.)
[1018] Simeon b. Gamaliel (T. I and IV)
[1019] Simeon b. Gamaliel (T. I and IV)
[1020] Judah (ha-Nasi) the Prince (T. V)
[1021] Ḥiyya b. Rab of Difte (A.B. III)
[1022] Elazar b. Pedat (A.B.-P. III)
[1023] Anon.

[1024] Anon.
[1025] Ḥama b. Osha'ya (A.P. I)
[1026] Anon.
[1027] Judah b. Ilai (T. IV)
[1028] Anon.
[1029] Anon.
[1030] Anon.
[1031] Anon.
[1032] Akiba (*d.* A.D. 132)
[1033] Anon.
[1034] Levi (A.P. III)
[1035] Anon.
[1036] Anon.
[1037] Simeon b. Sheṭaḥ (B.C.)
[1038] Anon.
[1039] Anon.
[1040] Akiba (*d.* A.D. 132)
[1041] Anon.
[1042] Samuel b. Naḥmani (A.P. III); Jonathan (A.P. I)
[1043] Anon.
[1044] Anon.
[1045] Anon.
[1046] Samuel b. Naḥmani (A.P. III)
[1047] Anon.
[1048] Judah b. Ilai (T. IV); Elazar b. Pedat (A.B.-P. III); Samuel b. Naḥmani (A.P. III)
[1049] Jose b. Elisha (T.)
[1050] Anon.
[1051] Anon.
[1052] Samuel (A.B. I)
[1053] Papa (A.B. V, *d.* A.D. 375)
[1054] Ishmael (T. III)
[1055] Jonathan (A.P. I)
[1056] Yannai (T. VI)
[1057] Nehemiah (T. IV); Jose b. Ḥanina (A.P. II)
[1058] Anon.
[1059] Gamaliel II (T. II); Johanan b. Nuri (T. III); Elazar or Eliezer Ḥisma (T. III)
[1060] Rabbah b. Bar Ḥana (A.B. III); Rab (T. VI or A.B. I)
[1061] Joshua b. Ḳarḥa (T. IV)
[1062] Anon.
[1063] Johanan (A.P. II)
[1064] Anon.
[1065] Simeon b. Sheṭaḥ (B.C.); Huna I (A.B. II); Ḥanina b. Ḥama (A.P. I–II)
[1066] Phinehas b. Jair (T. V)
[1067] Anon.
[1068] Anon.
[1069] Elazar b. Pedat (A.B.-P. III); Simeon b. Kahana (A.P. II); Haggai (A.P. IV); Ze'era (A.B.-P. III)
[1070] Joshua b. Hananiah (T. II)
[1071] Anon.
[1072] Johanan (A.P. II)
[1073] Elazar or Eliezer Ḥisma (T. III)
[1074] Hananiah (or Ḥanina) b. Gamla (T.)
[1075] Anon.
[1076] Eliezer b. Hyrcanus (T. II); Johanan (A.P. II)
[1077] Anon.; Bag Bag, b. (T. I)
[1078] Anon.
[1079] Eliezer b. Jacob (T. II, ? IV)
[1080] Ze'era (A.B.-P. III)
[1081] Rab (T. VI or A.B. I)
[1082] Simeon b. Gamaliel (T. I and IV)
[1083] Simeon b. Yoḥai (T. IV)
[1084] Anon.
[1085] Anon.
[1086] Gamaliel II (T. II)
[1087] Huna II (A.P. IV); Samuel b. Isaac (A.B.-P. III)
[1088] Anon.
[1089] Simeon b. Yoḥai (T. IV)
[1090] Raba (A.B. IV, *d.* A.D. 352); Tabyomi (A.B. VI)
[1091] Levi (A.P. III)
[1092] Anon.
[1093] Anon.
[1094] Jonah (A.P. V); Jose (A.P. IV); Haggai (A.P. IV)
[1095] Simeon b. Pazzi (A.P. III); Samuel b. Naḥmani (A.P. III) or Menaḥema (A.P. III); Hezekiah (A.P. I); Haggai (A.P. IV)
[1096] Anon.
[1097] Anon.
[1098] Anon.

[1099] Anon.
[1100] Me'ir (T. IV)
[1101] Samuel (A.B. I)
[1102] Me'ir (T. IV)
[1103] Anon.
[1104] Judah b. Ilai (T. IV); Johanan (A.P. II); Elazar b. Pedat (A.B.-P. III); Samuel b. Naḥmani (A.P. III)
[1105] Elazar b. Pedat (A.B.-P. III); Ḥisda (A.B. III); Abbahu (A.P. III)
[1106] Anon.
[1107] Anon.
[1108] Elazar b. Pedat (A.B.-P. III)
[1109] Ḥiyya (T. VI)
[1110] Benjamin b. Levi (A.P. III)
[1111] Gamaliel II (T. II)
[1112] Shammai (T. I)
[1113] Anon.
[1114] Anon.
[1115] Joshua b. Hananiah (T. II ?)
[1116] Anon.
[1117] Samuel b. Naḥmani (A.P. III)
[1118] Joshua b. Levi (A.P. I)
[1119] Jose (A.P. IV); Johanan (A.P. II)
[1120] Mana (Mani) (A.P. IV)
[1121] Joshua b. Levi (A.P. I)
[1122] Anon.
[1123] Amram (A.B. II); Rab (T. VI or A.B. I)
[1124] Anon.
[1125] Dimi, brother of Safra (A.B. III–IV)
[1126] Resh Laḳish (A.P. II)
[1127] Samuel b. Isaac (A.B.-P. III)
[1128] Anon.
[1129] Johanan (A.P. II); Simeon b. Yoḥai (T. IV)
[1130] Simeon b. Yoḥai (T. IV)
[1131] Naḥman b. Isaac (A.B. IV)
[1132] Simeon b. Gamaliel (T. I and IV)
[1133] Levi (A.P. III); Resh Laḳish (A.P. II)
[1134] Eliezer b. Jacob (T. II, ? IV)
[1135] Osha'ya (A.P. I)
[1136] Anon.
[1137] Elazar b. Pedat (A.B.-P. III)
[1138] Assi II (A.P. III)
[1139] Levi (A.P. III)
[1140] Ḥiyya (T. VI)
[1141] Yannai (T. VI)
[1142] Elazar b. Jose (T. VI)
[1143] Anon.
[1144] Anon.
[1145] Anon.
[1146] Jose b. Johanan (B.C.)
[1147] Anon.
[1148] Anon.
[1149] Anon.
[1150] Anon.
[1151] Anon.
[1152] Ishmael (T. III)
[1153] Joshua of Sikhnin (A.P. IV); Levi (A.P. III)
[1154] Abba b. Abba (A.B. I)
[1155] Anon.
[1156] Anon.
[1157] Johanan (A.P. II); Resh Laḳish (A.P. II); Abbahu (A.P. III)
[1158] Samuel (A.B. I)
[1159] Tanḥum (A.P. III)
[1160] Ḥanina (T. VI); Elazar b. Pedat (A.B.-P. III)
[1161] 'Ukba (Mar) (A.B. II)
[1162] 'Ukba (Mar) (A.B. II); Ilai (T. III)
[1163] Anon.
[1164] Anon.
[1165] Raba (A.B. IV, *d.* A.D. 354)
[1166] Anon.
[1167] Anon.
[1168] Johanan b. Zakkai (T. I)
[1169] Nehemiah of Siḥin (A.P. V)
[1170] Nathan b. Abba (A.B.-P. II–III); Rab (T. VI or A.B. I)
[1171] Nahum of Gimzo (T. II); Akiba (*d.* A.D. 132)
[1172] Anon.
[1173] Ṭarfon (T. III); Akiba (*d.* A.D. 132)
[1174] Judah b. Ilai (T. IV)
[1175] Anon.
[1176] Eliezer b. Hyrcanus (T. II); Joshua b. Hananiah (T. II); Akiba (*d.* A.D. 132)

[1177] Anon.
[1178] Anon.
[1179] Abin or Abun (A.B.-P. IV); Mana (Mani) (A.P. IV)
[1180] Ḥama b. Ḥanina (A.P. II); Osha'ya (A.P. I)
[1181] Awira (A.B.-P. III–IV); Ammi (A.P. III); Assi II (A.P. III); Ishmael, school of (T. IV)
[1182] Joshua b. Hananiah (T. II)
[1183] Anon.
[1184] Resh Laḳish (A.P. II); Ishmael (T. III)
[1185] Anon.
[1186] Judah b. Ilai (T. IV); Simeon b. Yoḥai (T. IV)
[1187] Jonah (A.P. V)
[1188] Huna I (A.B. II)
[1189] Anon.
[1190] Mana (Mani) (A.P. IV)
[1191] Simeon b. Yoḥai (T. IV)
[1192] Anon.
[1193] Anon.
[1194] Me'ir (T. IV); Simeon b. Yoḥai (T. IV)
[1195] Anon.
[1196] Akiba (*d.* A.D. 132)
[1197] Elazar b. Pedat (A.B.-P. III)
[1198] Johanan (A.P. II)
[1199] Anon.
[1200] Simeon the Just (? *c.* 200 B.C.); Johanan b. Zakkai (T. I); Joshua b. Hananiah (T. II)
[1201] Judah (A.B. II)
[1202] Johanan (A.P. II)
[1203] Abba Taḥna (? T.)
[1204] Elazar b. Shammua (T. IV)
[1205] Joshua of Sikhnin (A.P. IV); Levi (A.P. III)
[1206] Anon.
[1207] Judah (A.B. II)
[1208] Bar Ḳappara (T. VI)
[1209] Bebai (A.P. III); Akiba (*d.* A.D. 132)
[1210] Joseph (A.B. III); Abbaye (A.B. IV, *d.* A.D. 339); Raba (A.B. IV, *d.* A.D. 352); Akiba (*d.* A.D. 132); Rab (T. VI or A.B. I)
[1211] Ṭarfon (T. III)
[1212] Hillel, school of (T. I–II); Shammai, school of (T. I)
[1213] Samuel b. Isaac (A.B.-P. III); Ze'era (A.B.-P. III)
[1214] Judah b. Ilai (T. IV)
[1215] Ḥiyya b. Abba (A.P. III); Resh Laḳish (A.P. II)
[1216] Jose b. Ḥalafta (T. IV)
[1217] Anon.
[1218] Tanḥum b. Ḥiyya (A.P. III)
[1219] Anon.
[1220] Jacob (A.B.-P. III)
[1221] Judah b. Ilai (T. IV); Simeon b. Yoḥai (T. IV)
[1222] Anon.
[1223] Nehorai (T. IV)
[1224] Bar Ḳappara (T. VI); Judah (A.B. II); Judah (ha-Nasi) the Prince (T. V); Me'ir (T. IV)
[1225] Rab (T. VI or A.B. I); Kahana (A.P. II)
[1226] Akiba (*d.* A.D. 132)
[1227] Ulla (A.B.-P. II)
[1228] Anon.
[1229] Dosetai b. Yannai (T. V); Me'ir (T. IV)
[1230] Me'ir (T. IV); Johanan b. Zakkai (T. I)
[1231] Judah (ha-Nasi) the Prince (T. V); Jose b. Ḥalafta (T. IV); Simeon b. Yoḥai (T. IV)
[1232] Joshua b. Hananiah (T. II); Ishmael (T. III); Abbahu (A.P. III); Johanan (A.P. II)
[1233] Simeon b. Elazar (T. V); Ṭarfon (T. III)
[1234] Judah b. Ilai (T. IV); Gamaliel II (T. II)
[1235] Elazar b. Azariah (T. III)
[1236] Shemaiah (1st cent. B.C.); Eliezer b. Hyrcanus (T. II); Judah b. Ilai (T. IV); Me'ir (T. IV)
[1237] Jose b. Ḥalafta (T. IV)
[1238] Anon.
[1239] Anon.

[1240] Samuel (A.B. I); Joseph (A.B. III)
[1241] Anon.
[1242] Anon.
[1243] Anon.
[1244] Anon.
[1245] Anon.
[1246] Anon.
[1247] Anon.
[1248] Anon.
[1249] Anon.
[1250] Anon.
[1251] Anon.
[1252] Jose b. Ḥalafta (T. IV); Simeon b. Elazar (T. V); Akiba (*d.* A.D. 132)
[1253] Jose b. Ḥalafta (T. IV); Simeon b. Elazar (T. V); Akiba (*d.* A.D. 132)
[1254] Anon.
[1255] Anon.
[1256] Dimi of Nehardea (A.B. IV); Judah (A.B. II); Rab (T. VI or A.B. I)
[1257] Anon.
[1258] Anon.
[1259] Anon.
[1260] Zoma b. (T. III)
[1261] Eliezer b. Jacob (T. II, ? IV)
[1262] Simeon b. Gamaliel (T. I and IV)
[1263] Anon.
[1264] Anon.
[1265] Yannai (T. VI)
[1266] Anon.
[1267] Judah b. Ezekiel (A.B. II); Rab (T. VI or A.B. I)
[1268] Judah (ha-Nasi) the Prince (T. V); Ḥiyya (T. VI)
[1269] Shammai (T. I)
[1270] Anon.
[1271] Hillel (*d. c.* 10 B.C.)
[1272] Huna I (A.B. II); Rabbah b. Bar Huna (A.B. III, *d.* A.D. 322)
[1273] Eliezer b. Hyrcanus (T. II)
[1274] Eliezer b. Hyrcanus (T. II)
[1275] Anon.
[1276] Azzai, b. (T. III)
[1277] Anon.
[1278] Joshua b. Peraḥyah (B.C.)
[1279] Joshua b. Hananiah (T. II)
[1280] Anon.
[1281] Nittai of Arbela (B.C.)
[1282] Gamaliel II (T. II)
[1283] Anon.
[1284] Anon.
[1285] Anon.
[1286] Abba (A.P. III); Alexander (A.P. I–II)
[1287] Nehemiah (T. IV)
[1288] Gamaliel II (T. II)
[1289] Jose b. Durmaskis (T. III); Samuel b. Naḥmani (A.P. III)
[1290] Judah b. Ilai (T. IV); Nehemiah (T. IV)
[1291] Me'ir (T. IV)
[1292] Abbahu (A.P. III)
[1293] Anon.
[1294] Judah b. Tema (T. V)
[1295] Alexander (A.P. I–II)
[1296] Anon.
[1297] Anon.
[1298] Anon.
[1299] Anon.
[1300] Johanan b. Torta (T. III)
[1301] Anon.
[1302] Anon.
[1303] Anon.
[1304] Ḥama b. Ḥanina (A.P. II)
[1305] Johanan (A.P. II); Simeon b. Abba (A.P. III); Alexander (A.P. I–II)
[1306] Akiba (*d.* A.D. 132)
[1307] Samuel b. Naḥmani (A.P. III); Jonathan (A.P. I)
[1308] Rabbah b. Bar Huna (A.B. III, *d.* A.D. 322)
[1309] Jeremiah of Difte (A.B. V)
[1310] Naḥman b. Isaac (A.B. IV)
[1311] Hillel (*d. c.* 10 B.C.)
[1312] Elazar b. Pedat (A.B.-P. III)
[1313] Samuel the Little (T. II)
[1314] Joshua b. Levi (A.P. I)
[1315] Huna I (A.B. II); Abbaye (A.B. IV, *d.* A.D. 339)
[1316] Anon.
[1317] Judah (ha-Nasi) the Prince (T. V); Jonathan (A.P. I)

[1318] Jose b. Ḥanina (A.P. II); Resh Laḳish (A.P. II)
[1319] Ḥanina (T. VI); Ṭarfon (T. III)
[1320] Ṭarfon (T. III); Elazar b. Azariah (T. III); Akiba (*d.* A.D. 132); Johanan b. Nuri (T. III); Gamaliel II (T. II)
[1321] Anon.
[1322] Anon.
[1323] Anon.
[1324] Ḥanina b. Dosa (T. I)
[1325] Hillel (*d. c.* 10 B.C.)
[1326] Anon.
[1327] Anon.
[1328] Simeon b. Elazar (T. V)
[1329] Tanḥum b. Abba (A.P. V); Aibu (A.P. IV)
[1330] Me'ir (T. IV)
[1331] Judah (A.B. II); Rab (T. VI or A.B. I); Hillel (*d. c.* 10 B.C.); Resh Laḳish (P. II)
[1332] Simeon b. Yoḥai (T. IV); Johanan (A.P. II); Ḥama b. Ḥanina (A.P. II); Ulla (A.B.-P. II); Elazar b. Pedat (A.B.-P. III); Ḥisda (A.B. III)
[1333] Anon.
[1334] Anon.
[1335] Berechiah (A.P. IV–V)
1336] Anon.
[1337] Yudan (A.P. III–IV)
[1338] Hillel (*d. c.* 10 B.C.)
[1339] Resh Laḳish (A.P. II) or Joshua b. Levi (A.P. I); Ḥiyya (T. VI)
[1340] Johanan (A.P. II)
[1341] Joseph (A.B. III); Raba (A.B. IV, *d.* A.D. 352)
[1342] Joshua b. Levi (A.P. I)
[1343] Anon.
[1344] Anon.
[1345] Anon.
[1346] Anon.
[1347] Isaac (A.P. II–III); Gamaliel II (T. II); Joshua b. Hananiah (T. II)
[1348] Ḥanina b. Idi (A.B. III)
[1349] Osha'ya (A.P. I)
[1350] Abba b. Aḥa (A.P. I); Simeon b. Ze'era (A.P. III)
[1351] Anon.
[1352] Levitas of Jabneh (T. II)
[1353] Anon.
[1354] Anon.
[1355] Anon.
[1356] Anon.
[1357] Samuel b. Naḥmani (A.P. III); Simeon b. Yoḥai (T. IV)
[1358] Anon.
[1359] Phinehas b. Jair (T. V)
[1360] Abba b. Yudan (A.P. IV–V); Alexander (A.P. I–II)
[1361] Nittai of Arbela (B.C.); Simeon b. Yoḥai (T. IV)
[1362] Johanan b. Zakkai (T. I)
[1363] Johanan (A.P. II); Josiah (A.P. III)
[1364] Johanan (A.P. II); Josiah (A.P. III); Jeremiah (A.B.-P. IV)
[1365] Adda b. Ahabah (A.B. II)
[1366] Anon.
[1367] Jose b. Joezer (B.C.)
[1368] Anon.
[1369] Anon.
[1370] Anon.
[1371] Gamaliel II (T. II); Joshua b. Hananiah (T. II); Akiba (*d.* A.D. 132); Dosa b. Harkinas (T. II)
[1372] Dosa b. Harkinas (T. II)
[1373] Joshua b. Hananiah (T. II)
[1374] Anon.
[1375] Ilai (T. III)
[1376] Anon.
[1377] Anon.
[1378] Anon.
[1379] Anon.
[1380] Anon.
[1381] Anon.
[1382] Joshua b. Hananiah (T. II)
[1383] Anon.
[1384] Johanan (A.P. II)
[1385] Huna I (A.B. II)
[1386] Elazar b. Shammua (T. IV); Simeon b. Yoḥai (T. IV)

[1387] Anon.
[1388] Zoma, b. (T. III)
[1389] Levi (A.P. III)
[1390] Anan (A.B. II); Elazar b. Pedat (A.B.-P. III)
[1391] Anon.
[1392] Joshua b. Levi (A.P. I)
[1393] Ḥanan b. Raba (P. II); Rabba b. Shela (A.B. IV); Ḥisda (A.B. III); Naḥman b. Isaac (A.B. IV)
[1394] Anon.
[1395] Anon.
[1396] Abbaye (A.B. IV, *d.* A.D. 339); Abbahu (A.P. III); Hamnuna (A.B. III); Ulla (A.B.-P. II); Isaac (A.P. II–III); Simeon b. Abba (A.P. III); Ḥanina (T. VI); Judah b. Ilai (T. IV); Raba (A.B. IV, *d.* A.D. 352)
[1397] Raba (A.B. IV, *d.* A.D. 352); Judah (A.B. II)
[1398] Anon.
[1399] Ḥiyya b. Ashi (A.B. II); Rab (T. VI or A.B. I)
[1400] Jonathan (A.P. I); Ḥiyya (T. VI)
[1401] Judah (ha-Nasi) the Prince (T. V)
[1402] Anon.
[1403] Anon.
[1404] Simeon b. Yoḥai (T. IV)
[1405] Anon.
[1406] Anon.
[1407] Azzai, b. (T. III)
[1408] Anon.
[1409] Anon.
[1410] Anon.
[1411] Anon.
[1412] Elazar b. Azariah (T. III); Elazar or Eliezer b. Jose the Galilean (T. IV)
[1413] Johanan b. Zakkai (T. I)
[1414] Anon.
[1415] Isaac (A.P. II–III)
[1416] Anon.
[1417] Anon.
[1418] Judah (ha-Nasi) the Prince (T. V)
[1419] Ṭarfon (T. III); Joseph (A.B. III)
[1420] Eliezer b. Hyrcanus (T. II)
[1421] Elazar b. Mattai (T. III–IV); Issi b. Judah (T. IV); Samuel (A.B. I); Judah (A.B. II)
[1422] Abbahu (A.P. III); Abimi b. Abbahu (A.P. III)
[1423] Ṭarfon (T. III); Ishmael (T. III); Mana (Mani) (A.P. IV); Ze'era (A.B.-P. III); Abin or Abun (A.B.-P. IV); Simeon b. Yoḥai (T. IV); Aḥa II (A.P. IV); Abba b. Kahana (A.P. III)
[1424] Abbahu (A.P. III); Eliezer b. Hyrcanus (T. II)
[1425] Anon.
[1426] Judah b. Ilai (T. IV)
[1427] Resh Laḳish (A.P. II); Judah b. Ḥanina (A.P. I)
[1428] Me'ir (T. IV)
[1429] Jose the Galilean (T. III); Simeon b. Elazar (T. V); Issi b. Judah (T. IV)
[1430] Jacob (A.B.-P. III); Joshua of Sikhnin (A.P. IV); Levi (A.P. III); Ḥiyya b. Gamda (A.P. I)
[1431] Judah b. Bathyra (T. III)
[1432] Ḥanilai (A.P. III); Raba b. 'Ulla (A.B. III–IV); Elazar b. Pedat (A.B.-P. III)
[1433] Rab (T. VI or A.B. I); Ḥelbo (A.B.-P. III–IV)
[1434] Phinehas b. Ḥama (A.P. III–IV); Jose (A.P. IV)
[1435] Anon.
[1436] Elazar b. Pedat (A.B.-P. III)
[1437] Anon.
[1438] Neḥunya (Ḥunya) (A.B.-P. IV)
[1439] Anon.
[1440] Nathan (T. IV)
[1441] Rab (T. VI or A.B. I); Ḥiyya (T. VI ?)
[1442] Aḥa II (A.P. IV)
[1443] Johanan (A.P. II); Alexander (A.P. I–II); Samuel b. Naḥmani (A.P. III)

[1444] Idi (A.B.-P. III); Simeon b. Yoḥai (T. IV)
[1445] Jacob (A.B.-P. III) or Jacob b. Aḥa (A.P. III–IV); Elazar b. Pedat (A.B.-P. III); Jose the Galilean (T. III); Elazar b. Azariah (T. III)
[1446] Tanḥuma b. Abba (A.P. V)
[1447] Resh Laḳish (A.P. II)
[1448] Yaḳum (A.)
[1449] Resh Laḳish (A.P. II); Bar Ḳappara (T. VI); Azariah (A.P. IV–V); Judah b. Simon (A.P. IV)
[1450] Me'asha, son of Joshua (A.P. II)
[1451] Anon.
[1452] Anon.
[1453] Anon.
[1454] Anon.
[1455] Ḥanan b. Pazzi (A.P.)
[1456] Anon.
[1457] Judah (A.B. II); Rab (T. VI or A.B. I); Joshua b. Gamla (time of Temple); Dimi Nehardea (A.B. IV)
[1458] Hamnuna (A.B. III)
[1459] Abba b. Kahana (A.P. III)
[1460] Yuda Nesia (T. VI); Ḥiyya (T. VI); Assi II (A.B. I); Ammi (A.P. III)
[1461] Jonathan (A.P. I)
[1462] Judah b. Ilai (T. IV)
[1463] Huna b. Aḥa (A.P. III)
[1464] Huna I (A.B. II)
[1465] Anon.
[1466] Resh Laḳish (A.P. II); Judah Nesia (T. VI); Papa (A.B. V, *d.* A.D. 375); Abbaye (A.B. IV, *d.* A.D. 339)
[1467] Anon.
[1468] Anon.
[1469] Anon.
[1470] Issachar (A.P. II); Neḥunya (Ḥanya) (A.B.-P. IV)
[1471] Ḥiyya b. Abba (A.P. III); Joshua b. Levi (A.P. I); Huna I (A.B. II)
[1472] Jose b. Judah (T. V); Judah (ha-Nasi) the Prince (T. V); Joshua b. Ḳarḥa (T. IV)
[1473] Anon.
[1474] Isaac (A.P. II–III)
[1475] Anon.
[1476] Elazar ha-Ḳappar (T. V)
[1477] Joshua b. Hananiah (T. II); Ishmael (T. III)
[1478] Mar b. Rabina (A.B. III–IV); Ashi (A.B. VI); Hamnuna (A.B. III); Simeon b. Yoḥai (T. IV); Johanan (A.P. II); Resh Laḳish (A.P. II)
[1479] Isaac (A.P. II–III); Me'ir (T. IV)
[1480] Anon.
[1481] Anon.
[1482] Ḥanan (A.B. III or V)
[1483] Anon.
[1484] Elazar ha-Ḳappar (T. V)
[1485] Samuel (A.B. I); Elazar ha-Ḳappar (T. V); Elazar b. Pedat (A.B.-P. III)
[1486] Judah (A.B. II); Rab (T. VI or A.B. I); Jose b. Halafta (T. IV)
[1487] Jeremiah b. Abba (A.P. III); Resh Laḳish (A.P. II)
[1488] Zoma, b. (T. III)
[1489] Tanḥuma b. Abba (A.P. V)
[1490] Simeon b. Gamaliel (T. I and IV)
[1491] Anon.
[1492] Simeon b. Elazar (T. V)
[1493] Elazar b. Pedat (A.B.-P. III)
[1494] Anon.
[1495] Ishmael (T. III); Me'ir (T. IV)
[1496] Anon.
[1497] Resh Laḳish (A.P. II); Simeon b. Ḥalafta (T. VI)
[1498] Simeon b. Yoḥai (T. IV); Bar Ḳappara (T. VI); Yudan b. Jose (T. ? V)
[1499] Bar Ḳappara (T. VI); Me'ir (T. IV)
[1500] Simeon b. Ḥalafta (T. VI)

[1501] Judah (ha-Nasi) the Prince (T. V)
[1502] Hillel (*d. c.* 10 B.C.)
[1503] Abbaye (A.B. IV, *d.* A.D. 339)
[1504] Me'ir (T. IV)
[1505] Elazar b. Pedat (A.B.-P. III); Ḥanina (T. VI)
[1506] Anon.
[1507] Anon.
[1508] Johanan b. Zakkai (T. I)
[1509] Anon.
[1510] Neḥunya b. ha-Ḳanah (T. I); Ḥana (A.B.-P. III); Huna I (A.B. II); Zuṭra, Mar (A.B. IV or VI); Elazar b. Pedat (A.B.-P. III); Raba (A.B. IV, *d.* A.D. 352)
[1511] Simeon b. Rabbi (T. VI); Simeon b. Yoḥai (T. IV)
[1512] Hillel, school of (T. I–II); Shammai, school of (T. I)
[1513] Levi (A.P. III)
[1514] Judah (ha-Nasi) the Prince (T. V)
[1515] Levi (A.P. III)
[1516] Samuel b. Naḥmani (A.P. III); Jonathan (A.P. I); Joseph (A.B. III); Abbaye (A.B. IV, *d.* A.D. 339)
[1517] Judah (A.B. II); Rab (T. VI or A.B. I)
[1518] Jonathan (A.P. I); Johanan (A.P. II)
[1519] Phinehas b. Ḥama (A.P. III–IV); Simeon b. Pazzi (A.P. III); Hilkiah (A.P. III–IV)
[1520] Simeon b. Yoḥai (T. IV)
[1521] Joshua b. Levi (A.P. I)
[1522] Anon.
[1523] Anon.
[1524] Ḥanina b. Papa (A.P. III)
[1525] Anon.
[1526] Anon.
[1527] Yudan (A.P. III–IV); Azariah (A.P. IV–V)
[1528] Anon.
[1529] Huna I (A.B. II)
[1530] Eliezer b. Jacob (T. II, ? IV); Me'ir (T. IV); Jose b. Judah (T. V)
[1531] Nehemiah (T. IV); Eliezer b. Hyrcanus (T. II); Ṭarfon (T. III); Joshua b. Hananiah (T. II); Elazar b. Azariah (T. III); Akiba (*d.* A.D. 132)
[1532] Anon.
[1533] Elazar b. Peraṭa (T. III)
[1534] Anon.
[1535] Phinehas b. Ḥama (A.P. III–IV); Ḥanin of Sepphoris (A.P. IV); Alexander (A.P. I–II); Joshua b. Levi (A.P. I); Ḥama b. Ḥanina (A.P. II); Yudan (A.P. III–IV)
[1536] Anon.
[1537] Me'ir (T. IV); Judah b. Ilai (T. IV)
[1538] Joshua b. Hananiah (T. II); Bisna (A.P. III–IV)
[1539] Jacob b. Idi (A.P. III); Aḥa b. Ḥanina (A.P. III)
[1540] Raba (A.B. IV, *d.* A.D. 352)
[1541] Anon.
[1542] Johanan (A.P. II); Ḥanina (T. VI); Jose b. Ḥanina (A.P. II)
[1543] Elazar b. Pedat (A.B.-P. III); Johanan (A.P. II)
[1544] Simeon b. Gamaliel II (T. IV)
[1545] Anon.
[1546] Abbahu (A.P. III); Jonah (A.P. V); Jose (A.P. IV)
[1547] Me'ir (T. IV)
[1548] Ḥanina b. Dosa (T. I); Abba (A.P. III); Ḥanina (T. VI)
[1549] Anon.
[1550] Anon.
[1551] Jose b. Ḥanina (A.P. II)
[1552] Nathan (T. IV)
[1553] Ammi (A.P. III)
[1554] Anon.
[1555] Anon.
[1556] Elazar b. Pedat (A.B.-P. III); Simeon b. Yoḥai (T. IV); Jeshebab (T. IV); Assi II (A.P. III); Ḥanina b. Ḥama (A.P. I–II)

[1557] Anon.
[1558] Phinehas b. Ḥama (A.P. III–IV)
[1559] Johanan (A.P. II)
[1560] Judah (ha-Nasi) the Prince (T. V)
[1561] Anon.
[1562] Jonathan (A.P. I)
[1563] Aibu (A.P. IV)
[1564] Johanan (A.P. II)
[1565] Ḥanina, *Segan ha-Kohanim* (T. I)
[1566] Anon.
[1567] Johanan (A.P. II)
[1568] Alexander (A.P. I–II); Levi (A.P. III)
[1569] Reuben (A.P. III–IV)
[1570] Jeremiah (A.B.-P. IV)
[1571] Johanan (A.P. II)
[1572] Anon.
[1573] Jacob (A.B.-P. III); Abbahu (A.P. III); Aḥa I (A.P. II)
[1574] Abbahu (A.P. III)
[1575] Elazar b. Pedat (A.B.-P. III)
[1576] Anon.
[1577] Anon.
[1578] Eliezer b. Hyrcanus (T. II)
[1579] Elazar of Modi'im (T. II)
[1580] Resh Laḳish (A.P. II)
[1581] Anon.
[1582] Judah b. Ilai (T. IV); Joshua b. Levi (A.P. I); Abbahu (A.P. III)
[1583] Rab (T. VI or A.B. I)
[1584] Elazar b. Simeon (T. V); Huna I (A.B. II)
[1585] Jose (A.P. IV); Judah b. Shalom (A.P. IV–V)
[1586] Jose b. Judah (T. V)
[1587] Anon.
[1588] Berechiah (A.P. IV–V)
[1589] Ishmael b. Naḥman (A.P. III); Elazar b. Pedat (A.B.-P. III)
[1590] Jose b. Ḥalafta (T. IV)
[1591] Anon.
[1592] Anon.
[1593] Anon.
[1594] Anon.
[1595] Simeon b. Yoḥai (T. IV)
[1596] Aquila the Proselyte (*c.* 100–130, T. III); Eliezer b. Hyrcanus (T. II); Joshua b. Hananiah (T. II)
[1597] Anon.
[1598] Levi (A.P. III)
[1599] Anon.
[1600] Anon.
[1601] Jose b. Ḥalafta (T. IV)
[1602] Anon.
[1603] Simeon b. Gamaliel (T. I and IV)
[1604] Eliezer b. Hyrcanus (T. II); Joshua b. Hananiah (T. II)
[1605] Ḥanina b. Papa (A.P. III)
[1606] Simeon b. Pazzi (A.P. III)
[1607] Rab (T. VI or A.B. I)
[1608] Anon.
[1609] Samuel b. Naḥmani (A.P. III); Judan b. Ḥanina (A.P. IV–V); Isaac (A.P. II–III)
[1610] Anon.
[1611] Anon.
[1612] Anon.
[1613] Samuel b. Naḥmani (A.P. III)
[1614] Anon.
[1615] Anon.
[1616] Anon.
[1617] Joshua b. Levi (A.P. I); Simeon b. Yoḥai (T. IV)
[1618] Anon.
[1619] Anon.
[1620] Anon.
[1621] Anon.
[1622] Johanan (A.P. II)
[1623] Anon.
[1624] Anon.
[1625] Simeon b. Yoḥai (T. IV)
[1626] Joshua b. Levi (A.P. I). In note: Samuel (A.B. I); Aḥa II (A.P. IV); Alexander (A.P. I–II); Ashi (A.B. VI)
[1627] Levi (A.P. III)
[1628] Eliezer b. Hyrcanus (T. II); Joshua b. Hananiah (T. II)
[1629] Anon.
[1630] Aḥa II (A.P. IV)
[1631] Samuel the Little (T. II); Josiah (A.P. III)

[1632] Phinehas b. Ḥama (A.P. III–IV); Reuben (A.P. III–IV)
[1633] Jose b. Ḥalafta (T. IV)
[1634] Akiba (*d.* A.D. 132)
[1635] Naḥman b. Ḥisda (A.B. IV); Raba (A.B. IV, *d.* A.D. 352)
[1636] Anon.
[1637] Anon.
[1638] Berechiah (A.P. IV–V); Ḥelbo (A.B.-P. III–IV)
[1639] Daniel the Tailor (A.P. III); Judah b. Pazzi (A.P. III–IV)
[1640] Joshua b. Levi (A.P. I); Joseph, son of Joshua (A.P. III)
[1641] Ze'era (A.B.-P. III); Jose b. Abin (Bun) (A.P. IV); 'Ukba (Mar) (A.B. II); Mana (Mani) (A.P. IV); Abin or Abun (A.B.-P. IV); Jose b. Abin (Bun) (A.P. IV); Elazar or Eliezer b. Jose the Galilean (T. IV); Akiba (*d.* A.D. 132); Elazar b. Pedat (A.B.-P. III); Samuel b. Isaac (A.B.-P. III); Ze'era (A.B.-P. III); Abbahu (A.P. III)
[1642] Anon.
[1643] Anon.
[1644] Naḥman b. Isaac (A.B. IV); Akiba (*d.* A.D. 132); Johanan b. Zakkai (T. I)
[1645] Johanan (A.P. II)
[1646] Anon.
[1647] Anon.
[1648] Ḥanina (T. VI)
[1649] Me'ir (T. IV); Joshua b. Levi (A.P. I)
[1650] Elazar b. Pedat (A.B.-P. III)
[1651] Simai (T. VI)
[1652] Shammai, school of (T. I); Hillel, school of (T. I–II); Isaac b. Abin (A.B. III–IV); Raba (A.B. IV, *d.* A.D. 352); Ḥisda (A.B. III); Judah (A.B. II); Eliezer b. Hyrcanus (T. II); Jose b. Ḥanina (A.P. II); Ishmael, school of (T. IV)
[1653] Eliezer b. Hyrcanus (T. II); Joshua b. Hananiah (T. II)
[1654] Samuel b. Naḥmani (A.P. III); Judah b. Bathyra (T. III)
[1655] Akiba (*d.* A.D. 132); Abba Saul (T. IV); Judah b. Ilai (T. IV); Joshua b. Hananiah (T. II); Eliezer b. Hyrcanus (T. II)
[1656] Alexander (A.P. I–II)
[1657] Anon.
[1658] Rab (T. VI or A.B. I)
[1659] Simai (T. VI)
[1660] Aḥa b. Ḥanina (A.P. III)
[1661] Jacob (A.B.-P. III)

GLOSSARY

Ab, Babylonian name for the fifth month. *Ninth of*, Fast to commemorate the Destruction of Jerusalem and the Temple by the Babylonians (586 B.C.) and the Romans (A.D. 70). It is possible that Zech. VII, 5 and VIII, 19 refer to this day. *Fifteenth of*, popular holiday (see pp. 409–10).

Abaḳ, 'dust', used of a tinge or taint of something, e.g. 'dust of slander' or gossip (see p. 407).

Abinu malkenu, 'Our Father', 'Our King' (*P.B.* pp. 55 ff.; Abrahams, p. LXXIII), a Litany used on Penitential Days, attributed to Akiba.

Aboth, 'Patriarchs', first blessing of *Amidah* (*P.B.* p. 44; Abrahams, p. LIX); *see also Pereḳ*.

Abudarham, David, son of Joseph, of Seville; wrote a commentary on the Jewish Prayer-Book in 1340.

'Af: (1) Particle = 'also'; (2) Noun = 'anger'. These words are often used in paronomasia.

Agudah, 'band', see *Aboth* III, 7 (*P.B.* p. 193) (see p. 97).

Aḥenu bet Yisrael, 'Our brethren', the house of Israel, a phrase equivalent to 'Catholic Judaism' (*P.B.* p. 70).

'Al 'aḥat kammah we-kammah, '[If] with one, how much more [sc. with two]?' A form of argument similar to 'If they do these things in the green tree what shall be done in the dry?'

'Al ha-rishonim we-'al ha-'aḥaronim, 'For the first and for the last' (*P.B.* p. 42).

'Alenu, 'It is our duty to praise...': now used as concluding prayer at all services (*P.B.* p. 76; Abrahams, p. LXXXVI), but taken from New Year *Musaf* (Additional Service, *P.B.* p. 247). Date: either adapted by Rab (A.D. 365) from a pre-Christian prayer or composed by him.

Am ha-Aretz, 'people of the land'. In the Bible represents agricultural population; in Rabbinic times, probably class of people ethically debased, not, as is sometimes thought, simple pious folk, suffering from the contempt of the learned (see p. 107).

Amidah, 'standing', also called *Shemoneh 'Esreh* or 'Eighteen (Benedictions)' or *Tefillah*, prayer. Probably earliest statutory prayer (*P.B.* pp. 44 ff.; Abrahams, p. LV). The prayer is said three times daily. Parts of it are pre-Christian.

Aramaic, see Abrahams, p. LXXXIV. *See also Chaldee*.

Ashkenaz-(i)-(ic)-(im), proper name occurring in Gen. X, 3, applied to Germany in Middle Ages, now used of the rite of N. Europe (mainly).

Azazel, 'scape-goat' (Lev. XVI); the spelling '*Aza'-zel*, which has no particular meaning, would seem to be a deliberate alteration for '*Azaz-'el*, evidently a primitive demon of the wilderness.

Baraita, Aramaic word meaning 'external', used generally of a tradition of the *Tanna'im* (*q.v.*) which was not incorporated in the *Mishnah* (*q.v.*) (Abrahams, p. XXV).

Bat Ḳol, 'daughter of a voice', i.e. a supernatural voice [890] sometimes compared with that of a dove as in John I, 32.

Bekol peraṭeyha we-diḳduḳeyha, 'In all its details and particulars' (*P.B.* p. 218).

Bi'ah, 'coming', i.e. cohabitation, legal marriage without a religious ceremony.

Biryah, or *beriyyah*, 'creature'. Prayers or passages containing this word are always universalist in character, e.g. *P.B.* p. 17.

Chaldee, old term for Aramaic.

Denarius (*dinar*), *see* List of coins.

Derek ereẓ, 'way of earth'. Used in several senses, such as decency [1149], or secular occupation (*Aboth* II, 2; *P.B.* p. 187), or even anxiety (cp. *Aboth* III, 6; *P.B.* p. 191 foot) (see p. 176).

Din, 'judgment, justice' (*P.B.* p. 320), hence law: *Bet Din* is a Jewish Tribunal: *see also Ẓidduḳ ha-din*.

Dinar, *see* List of coins.

'Edah, 'congregation', cp. *Aboth* III, 7; *P.B.* p. 192 (see p. 97).

Eleh Ezkerah, 'These I remember'. First words of a dirge relating to the death of 'the Ten Martyrs', recited on Ninth Ab or Day of Atonement according to rite.

Ephah, *see* List of measures.

Gedilim, 'fringes' (not the usual term, *Ziẓit*), used in Deut. XXII, 12.

Gemara, Aramaic, 'completion'; term applied to the discussions on the *Mishnah* (*q.v.*) in the Rabbinical schools.

Ger, 'sojourner', 'resident alien', in Biblical usage, but 'proselyte' in Rabbinic usage.

Goi, 'nation'; plural (*goyim*) used for Gentiles.

Habdalah (*Havdalah*), 'distinction', prayer (*P.B.* p. 94*d* top, old ed. p. 46) and ceremony (*P.B.* p. 216) at the conclusion of Sabbaths and Festivals. See Abrahams, pp. LXII and CLXXXII (see p. lix and [502] and [1547]).

Ḥaber (*Ḥaver*), 'fellow', member of Rabbinic brotherhood (see *Ḥaberim*, p. 107).

Ḥaberim kol Yisrael, 'All Israel are brothers' (*P.B.* p. 154).

Hafṭarah, the second or Prophetical lesson (*P.B.* p. 148 foot; Abrahams, p. CLVI).

Haggadah, *see Halakah*.

Halakah, 'going', 'conduct', hence 'canon law'. Sometimes opposed to *Haggadah*, 'narrative' or homiletical exegesis (see p. xvi).

Ḥaliẓah, 'drawing off' (of the shoe): ceremony performed when levirate marriage is not carried out (see Deut. xxv, 5–10).

Ḥallah, 'dough'. The separation of the priest's portion of dough is commanded in Num. xv, 20, and a commemorative ceremony is still performed by the housewife (see *P.B.* Gaster, p. 79, where rubric and formula of benediction are given).

Hallel, series of Psalms sung on festivals (*P.B.* pp. 219 ff.; Abrahams, p. CLXXXIV).

Ḥillul ha-Shem, 'profanation of the Name' (of God), i.e. public scandal: opposed to *Ḳiddush ha-Shem*, *q.v.*

Hin, *see* List of measures.

Ḥuppah we-Ḳiddushin, 'canopy and separation (or sanctification)': term signifying religious as opposed to civil marriage (*Bi'ah*, *q.v.*) (*P.B.* p. 298; Abrahams, p. CCXV).

Ibn Ezra, Abraham. Famous commentator and grammarian: born at Toledo before 1100, visited London (? in 1158).

'*Iḳḳar*, 'root' or 'essential': to 'deny the root' means to repudiate God or to commit a cardinal heresy.

'*Iḳḳar shel parnasah* 'root of sustenance'. Fundamental declaration of God's providence, applied to Ps. CXLV, 15, 16 (see p. lxxxvii).

Issar, *see* List of coins.

Ḳabbalah, 'tradition', originally applied to Hagiographa or Prophets. In later times used generally of tradition and finally applied to the well-known mystic philosophy of that name.

Ḳaddish, Aramaic, 'holy'; term applied to an ancient Aramaic prayer extant in several versions (*P.B.* pp. 37, 75, 77, 86; Abrahams, p. XXXIX; see p. 112).

Ḳal wa-ḥomer, 'light and heavy'; term of logic applied to the inference from minor to major (*P.B.* p. 13).

Kasher, 'fit': the adjective occurs in the Bible only once (Esther VIII, 5); now generally used in the sense of 'pure' as applied to food (*kosher*) which is ritually permissible.

Kawwanah, 'attention' or 'attuning of the mind', see Chapter X: the term is also applied to meditations before performing certain ceremonies (*P.B.* p. 218; Abrahams, p. CLXXXIV).

Ḳeba', 'fixed' measure or place, used in a good sense (regularity) and in a bad sense (rote) (see p. 349).

Kebayakol, 'If it were possible (so to say)'; term used to deprecate an anthropomorphism (see pp. xcvi and 587).

Ḳedushah, 'sanctification'; portion of the *Amidah* (*q.v.*) containing the threefold 'holy' (*P.B.* p. 45; Abrahams, p. LX).

Kelal Yisrael, 'United Israel'.

Ḳere', *see Ketib*.

Ketib, Aramaic, 'written': used of the *written* or *received* text of the Bible; sometimes, in cases of difficulty, another form is substituted in public reading (*Ḳere'*) (*P.B.* p. 20; Abrahams, pp. XXXIII, LXXXI and CCXXVII).

Ketubbah, 'written', marriage covenant or contract (*P.B.* p. 299 top; Abrahams, p. CCXVI) (see p. c).

Ḳiddush, 'sanctification' (of Sabbath or Festival); pronounced over bread and wine (*P.B.* p. 124; Abrahams, p. CXXXIX).

Ḳiddush ha-Shem, 'sanctification of the Name', usually applied to martyrdom (*P.B.* p. 155, line 3 of Hebrew). *See Ḥillul ha-Shem*.

Kohanim (plural of *Kohen*), descendants of Aaron who pronounce the Priestly Benediction on Festivals (*P.B.* pp. 238*a*, 308; Abrahams, p. CCXXII).

Letek, *see* List of measures.

Lishmah, 'for its name', to do a thing for proper and not for ulterior motives (see Chapter x).

Lulab, 'palm-branch', used on Tabernacles (*P.B.* p. 218; Abrahams, p. CLXXXIV).

Ma'amadot, division of lay representatives of villages, sent to Jerusalem to accompany the daily sacrifices with prayers, corresponding to the divisions of Priests and Levites (*Mishmarot*). The term now signifies a series of extra-liturgical prayers and extracts.

Mafteaḥ shel parnasah, 'key of sustenance' (*see* '*Iḳḳar shel parnasah*).

Maḥshabah ke-ma'aseh, 'thought is like act', i.e. God takes the will for the deed (see p. ci).

Maḳom, 'place', used of God, in sense of 'the Omnipresent' (*P.B.* p. 70; Abrahams, p. LXXX).

Megillah, 'scroll', applied to the Five Rolls (Canticles, Ruth, Lamentations, Ecclesiastes and Esther), particularly to the last-named (*P.B.* p. 276; Abrahams, p. CCVI).

Meḥiẓah, 'division', so screen or compartment. Sometimes used of special place in heaven reserved for martyrs, etc. (see p. 588).

Menaḥot, plural of *Minḥah* (*q.v.*) 'sacrifices': name of tractate in the Talmud.

Metatron, name of Angel (see p. 68).

Meturgeman, translator (see *Targum* and p. 437).

Mezuzah, 'door-post', 'side-post' (Exod. XII, 22); text written on door-post in accordance with Deut. VI, 9 (*P.B.* p. 291, also p. 40 foot; Abrahams p. CCXII).

Middah, 'measure'; sometimes used in sense of 'measure for measure' (pp. 222–5); or, nature, quality (pp. 21, 27); or attribute, especially the 'Thirteen Attributes of God' (pp. 43–4) and the 'Thirteen measures of scriptural exegesis' (*P.B.* p. 13; Abrahams, p. xxv).

Midrash, 'exposition', from *darash*, 'to expound'. A term applied to scriptural expositions. It occurs in II Chron. XIII, 22 and XXIV, 27.

Mina, *see* List of coins, *also* List of weights.

Minhag, 'leading' or 'driving'; used of Jehu in II Kings IX, 20; hence ceremonial custom, or liturgical rite.

Minḥah, in Bible 'present' or 'sacrifice', or 'afternoon', especially the 'Afternoon Sacrifice'; in later times 'Afternoon Service' (*P.B.* p. 94; Abrahams, p. CV).

Minim, plural of *Min*, in Bible 'kind' or 'sort' (Gen. I, 11); in post-biblical Hebrew 'sectarian'; sometimes, Jewish-Christian (*P.B.* p. 48; Abrahams, p. LXIV).

Mishnah, 'repetition', from *Shanah*, to repeat. A code compiled by Judah the Prince about A.D. 200.

Miẓwah, plural *Miẓwot*, 'commandment', often used in sense of 'good deed' or 'privilege'.

Musaf, in Bible 'additional offering' (Num. XXVIII–XXIX), brought on Sabbaths, etc. Hence in post-biblical Hebrew used of additional services in Synagogue on those days (*P.B.* p. 159; Abrahams, p. CLXIV).

Neẓaḥ, 'eternity', or 'victory' (see [103] and [78]).

'Ona'ah, 'unfriendly behaviour' or 'oppression' (see pp. xciv and 403 ff.).

Onḳelos, author of a *Targum*, *q.v.*

Parnas, from Greek πρόνοος, one having *forethought* for: hence *Parnasah*, 'sustenance'; *Parnas* comes to mean Head of a Synagogue.

Parush (plural *Perushim*) 'separated', 'abstemious', 'pious'; sometimes Pharisee: the quality is *Perishut*.

Pereḳ, 'division' or 'chapter', hence *Pirḳe Aboth* or 'Chapters of the Fathers' (*P.B.* pp. 184–209; Abrahams, p. CLXXVI).

Perishut, *Perushim*, *see Parush*.

Pondion, *see* List of coins.

Prosbul, Greek term, etymology uncertain. Name of system introduced by Hillel under which debts made over to the Court were not cancelled by the year of release (see pp. lxxvi and c).

Pseudo-Jonathan: name of a *Targum* on the Pentateuch, popularly but incorrectly ascribed to Jonathan b. Uzziel, pupil of Hillel.

Purim, 'Lots', name of the feast of Esther (*P.B.* p. 276; Abrahams, p. CCVI).

Rashi, initials of Rabbi Solomon, son of Isaac, of Troyes (1040–1105), commentator on Bible and Talmud.

Se'ah, *see* List of measures (see p. 275).

Seder, 'order'; used also of the 'orders' or divisions of the Mishnah or of the domestic ritual of the Passover, etc. The word will be found in *P.B.* pp. 243 top and 238*a* top.

Sela', *see* List of coins.

Sephardi (*Sefardi*, Spaniard). Sepharad in Obadiah 20 was later identified with Spain, hence *Sephardim*, Spaniards. The Sephardic liturgy is mainly that of southern Europe.

Sepphoris, capital of Galilee, so called because it was perched like a 'bird (*Ẓippor*) on a mountain'; seat of Talmudic Academy, probably modern Saffuriyyah, north-west of Nazareth (Neubauer, *Géogr.*, pp. 191–5).

Sforno, Obadiah b. Jacob, Italian exegete, philosopher and physician; born at Cesena about 1475, died at Bologna in 1550.

Shema, 'Hear O Israel' (*P.B.* p. 40; Abrahams, p. L) (see [2]).

Shemoneh 'Esreh, see Amidah.

Shofar, 'ram's horn', used on New Year (Abrahams, p. CXCVII).

Shulḥan 'Aruk, 'Prepared Table', name of code, compiled by Joseph Karo, 1488–1575.

Shurat ha-Din, the 'line of the Law', i.e. the strict letter of the Law.

Sukkah, 'tabernacle' (*P.B.* p. 232; Abrahams, p. CXCV).

Ṭallit, mantle with fringes (Abrahams, p. XXVI)

Talmud, 'teaching', consists of *Mishnah* (*q.v.*) and *Gemara* (*q.v.*). The Palestinian (so-called Jerusalem) rescension was compiled about the end of the fourth century, the Babylonian rescension about a century later.

Tanna'im, Rabbis who lived before the completion of the *Mishnah* (*q.v.*); singular *Tanna*, adjective Tannaitic.

Targum, Aramaic translation of the Hebrew Bible (*P.B.* p. 73; Abrahams, p. LXXXIV).

Tefillah, see Amidah.

Tefillin, phylacteries (Abrahams, p. XXVII; see also *Judaism and Christianity*, I, 152–3).

Ṭerephah, 'torn', of a beast (Gen. XXXI, 39); now used of food which is not *kasher* (*q.v.*).

Tishri, first month of the year, beginning in autumn. The first two days are celebrated as New Year, the tenth as Day of Atonement, the fifteenth to twenty-third as Tabernacles, and Eighth Day of Assembly.

Torah min ha-Shamayim, 'law from Heaven', i.e. Divine Revelation.

Wa'ad 'Arba' 'Araẓot, 'Council of the Four Lands'. Jewish autonomous Council in Poland from the middle of the sixteenth to the middle of the eighteenth centuries.

Yetzer, 'formation', 'inclination', or 'imagination', for good (*yetzer ha-ṭob*) or evil (*yetzer ha-ra'*), see Chapter XI.

Yigdal, opening hymn in the Daily Service (*P.B.* p. 2; Abrahams, p. vii).

Ẓa'ar ba'al ḥayyim, 'cruelty to animals' (see p. 47).

Ẓaw, name of a weekly portion of the Pentateuch (Lev. vi–viii).

Ẓedaḳah, 'righteousness', often used in sense of almsgiving.

Zekut, 'merit' (see Chapter viii).

Zekut Aboth, 'Merits of the Fathers' (see p. 219).

Ẓidduḳ ha-din, 'justification of the judgment'. Name of a prayer in the Burial Service (*P.B.* p. 318; Abrahams, p. ccxxvi) in which the mourner expresses his acquiescence in God's decree.

Zuz, *see* List of coins, *also* List of weights.

List of coins

1 perutah (widow's mite)			
8 perutahs	= 1 issar	roughly	½*d*.
2 issars	= 1 pondion	"	1*d*.
12 pondions	= 1 dinar or zuz	"	1*s*.
2 dinars	= 1 shekel	"	2*s*.
2 shekels	= 1 sela	"	4*s*.
25 selas		"	£5

List of liquid and dry measures

1 log	= contents of 6 eggs		
1 log	=		1 pint (roughly)
12 logs	= 1 hin	=	1½ gallons (roughly)
2 hins	= 1 seah	=	3 gallons (roughly)
3 seahs	= 1 ephah	=	approx. 1 bushel
5 ephahs	= 1 letek	=	approx. 6 bushels

---

1 zuz = approx. 54 grains troy

LIST OF EDITIONS USED

As has been explained on p. vii the sources consulted have been subject to limitations. Thus, certain texts, such as *Midrash Tannaim*, have been cited very sparingly; others, such as the *Yalkuṭ*, occur only in H. L.'s notes. The following editions have been used:

Aboth de Rabbi Nathan, ed. S. Schechter, London, etc., 1887.

Mekilta: in most cases references to all four editions of the *Mekilta* have been given in the Rabbinic index, if not in the text of the book. These editions are: (1) *Mek.*[1] = ed. I. H. Weiss, Vienna, 1865; (2) *Mek.*[2] = ed. H. S. Horovitz, Berlin, 1931; (3) *Mek.*[3] = ed. J. Z. Lauterbach, Philadelphia, 1933–5; (4) *Mek.*[4] = ed. M. Friedmann, Vienna, 1870.

Midrash Proverbs (*Mishle*), ed. S. Buber, 1893. Also D. Z. Ashkenazi, Stettin, 1861 (shorter text).

Midrash Psalms (*Shoḥer Ṭob*), ed. S. Buber, Wilna, 1891.

Midrash Rabba, ed. Romm, Wilna, 1878.

Midrash Tannaim, ed. D. Hoffmann, Berlin, 1908–9.

Pesikta Kahana, ed. S. Buber, Lyck, 1868.

Pesikta Rabbati, ed. M. Friedmann, Vienna, 1880.

Sifra, ed. I. H. Weiss and J. Schlossberg, Vienna, 1862; also ed. M. L. Malbim, Bucharest, 1860.

Sifre, ed. M. Friedmann, Vienna, 1864; also ed. H. S. Horovitz (on Numbers), Leipzig, 1917; (on Deuteronomy), ed. H. S. Horovitz and L. Finkelstein, Breslau, 1935– .

Talmud Jerusalem, ed. Krotoschin, 1866.

Tanḥuma, ed. Stettin, 1865; and ed. S. Buber, Wilna, 1885.

Tanna de Be Eliyyahu, ed. M. Friedmann, Vienna, 1902.

Tosefta, ed. M. S. Zuckermandel, Pasewalk, 1880. The attention of readers is directed to **Note 68**.

LIST OF BIBLICAL PASSAGES

Note. References as a rule are according to chapter and verse of A.V.

Figures in black type in this index refer to extracts

Genesis I, 2, **449**; 4, lix; 7, lix; 11, p. 742; 31, **91**, **788**, **1518**, **1566**; II, 2, **1235**, **1236**; 7, **1486**; 15, **1233**, **1236**; 16, **1233**; 18, **1454**; 22, **721**, **722**, **1214**; III, 3, **421**; 14, **1121**; 22, **780**, p. 664; IV, 7, **773**; 10, **486**; 16, **816**; 25, p. 672; 26, **649**; V, 1, xl, **456**, **457**; 24, **184**; VI, 5, **757**; 6, **156**, **775** (twice), **778**; 7, **110**; 9, **1412**, **1483**; 12, **1076**; 13, **1076**; VII, 1, **1412**; 8, **1392**; VIII, 1, **110**; 21, **648**, **757**, **774**, **777**; IX, 6, **268**, **1271**; 12, p. 665; X, 3, p. 738; 6, lxiv; 25, **345**; XI, 1–9, **1325**; 5, **1050**; XII, 3, **893**, **1267**; 5, **1584**; XIII, 4, **893**; XIV, 1, **1496**; 14, p. 619 n.; 19, cii, **97** n.; 22, **727**; XV, 1, **1600**; 5, **297**; 6, **804**, **879**, **880**, **882**; 8, **1465**, **1524**; 9, **59**; 12, **395**; 13, **1524**; 15, **1499**; 16, **861**; XVI, 12, **210**; XVII, 5, **1582**; 17, **1534**; 23, p. 619; 27, p. 619; XVIII, 1, 2, **70**; 1, **52**, **721**; 16, **1172**; 19, **257**, **725**, **804**; 23, **616**; 24, **147**; 25, **132**, **133**; 27, **285**, **883**; XIX, 1, **616**; 27, **948**; 36, **210**; XX, 17, **1282**; XXI, 1, **1444**; 7, **1598**; XXII, ci, p. 659; 3, **359**; 12, **1097**; 17, **259**; 18, **101**; XXIV, 2, 3, **637** n.; 50, **1437**; 63, **893**, **948**; XXV, 19–XXVIII, 9, p. 652; XXVI, 4, **215**; 12, **1229**; 24, **1229**; XXVII, 1, **784**, **1524**, p. 677; 22, **675**, **1459**; 28, **906**; 39, **906**; 40, **210**; XXVIII, 9, **569**; 11, **893**, **948**; 12, **885**; 13, **784**; 14, **231**; 20, **1596**; XXXI, 24, **1228**; 30, **675**; 39, p. 743; 42, **1228**; XXXII, 11, **891**; XXXIII, 4, lxiii; XXXV, 22, lxiii; XXXVI, 3, **569**; 10, **1581**; 12, **1581**; 29, **1581**; 43, p. 686; XXXVII-XL, p. 652; XXXVII, 3, p. 652; 4, **1264**; XXXIX, 10, **397**; XLII, 3, **280**; 18, **1097**; XLIII, 27, **1264**; XLIV, 13, **593**; XLV, 3, **347**; XLVII, 29, **491** n.; XLVIII, 14, **345**; 14, **416**; 16, **126**; XLIX, 1, 2, **6**, **22**; 10, p. 627; L, 16, 17, **1497**

Exodus I, 6, **1267**; II, 15, **667**; III, 6, **454**, **979**, **1357**; 7, **151**; 13, **409**; 15, **26**; IV, 3, **23**; 18, **1257**; 22, **651**; 31, **879**, **881**; V, 23, **408**; VI, 13, **947**; VIII, 5, **1489**; XII, 13, **876**; 22, p. 741; 29, **119**; 38, **1170**; XIII, 1–10, p. 641; 11–16, p. 641; 17, 18, **218**; 21, **1602**; XIV, 1–3, **880**; 10, **893**; 15, **924**; 19, **161**; 31, **879**, **880**; XV, **879**; 1, **94**, **1649**; 2, **82**, **84**, **262**, **311** n., **714**; 3, **68**, **77**; 9, **1404**; 11, **262**; 13, **235**; 23, **408**; 25, **923**; 26, **329**, **477**, **534**, **752**, p. 693; XVI, 8, **285**; 16, **509**; 26, **1655**; XVII, 2, **720**; 5, **720**; 6, **45**; 7, **158**; 11, **695**; 15, cii, **158**; 16, **637** n.; XVIII, 2, **647**, p. 676; 20, **505**; 21, **1058**; 27, **1579**; XIX, 1, **213**, **369**; 2, **1506**; 4, **162**; 18, **442**; 19, **689**; 20, **447**; 21, **276**; XX, 1, **73**, **431**; 2, **320**; 3, **658**, **670**; 5, **1550**, **1551**, **1552**; 6, **674**; 7, **1095**, **1096**; 9, **1236**; 12, **333**, **1417**, **1418**, **1423**; 20, **284**; 21, **205**; 24, **25**, **258**, **670**; 25, **222**, **1508**; XXI, 1, **1022**; 6, **202**; 17, **1423**; 26, **153**; 26–7, **1535**; XXII, 1, **1230**; 20, **670**, **1608**; 25, **1151**, **1152**, **1184**; 27, **19**; 20, **670**; XXIII, 2, **890**; 4, **1298**; 5, **1295**, **1305**; 7, **1212**; XXIV, 1, **205**; 7, **209**, **210**, **320**, **651**; 10, **69**, **1658**; 17, **287**; XXV, 2, **455**; 8, **33**, **223**, **1233**; 13, **34**; 34, **1456**; XXVI, 1, **223–4**; 7, **223–4**; 15, **606**; 18, **31**; 20, **31**; 25, **31**; 35, **55**; XXVII, 20, **402**; XXX, 34, **171**; XXXI, 14, p. 711; 18, **1397**; XXXII, 4, **643**; 7, **938**; 9, **288**; 11, **206**, **644**; 13, 14, **586**, p. 675; 16, **343**; 28,

Figures in black type in this index refer to extracts

Figures in black type in this index refer to extracts

Figures in black type in this index refer to extracts

Figures in black type in this index refer to extracts

Figures in black type in this index refer to extracts

LIST OF GREEK AND LATIN PASSAGES

Cited from: (*a*) New Testament
(*b*) Apocrypha
(*c*) Hellenistic writers
(*d*) Patristic writers

Figures in black type in this index refer to pages

(*a*) New Testament

(*b*) Apocrypha

(*c*) Hellenistic Writers

Figures in black type in this index refer to pages

(*d*) Patristic Writers

Figures in black type in this index refer to pages

LIST OF RABBINIC PASSAGES

These passages have been classified alphabetically as follows:

Mekilta
Midrash: 'Aseret ha-Dibrot
Proverbs
Psalms
Tanna'im
Mishnah (treatises in alphabetical order)
Pesiḳta: Kahana
Rabbati
Pirḳe de R. Eliezer
Prayer Books (various)
Rabbot: Gen., Exod., Lev., Num., Deut. Cant., Ruth, Lam., Eccles., Esther
R. T. (Rabbinic Literature and Gospel Teaching)
Ruth Zuṭa
Seder Eliyyahu Zuṭa
Sekel Ṭob
Sifra
Sifre Num., Sifre Deut.
Talmud: Babylonian (treatises in alphabetical order)
Jerusalem (treatises in alphabetical order)
Tanna de be Eliyyahu
Tanḥuma
Tanḥuma (Buber's edition)
Targum
Tosefta (treatises in alphabetical order)
Yalḳut

Figures in black type in this index refer to pages

Figures in black type in this index refer to pages

	ed. Weiss	ed. Horovitz	ed. Lauterbach	ed. Friedmann	Page of Anthology
Beshallaḥ, Amalek, § 1	f. 61*b*	p. 178	II, 140	f. 53*b*	**482**
	62*a*	180	II, 144	54*a*	**334**
Yitro, Amalek, § 1	66*a*	193	II, 172	58*a*	**569**
	67*a*	195	II, 177 (§ 3)	59*a*	**474**
	67*a*	195	II, 178 (§ 3)	59*a*	**48**
§ 2	67*a*	196	II, 179 (§ 4)	59*a*	**383**
	67*b*	198	II, 182 (§ 4)	59*b*	**189**
	68*a*	199	II, 185 (§ 4)	60*a*	**569**
Yitro, Baḥodesh, § 1	69*b*	204	II, 196	61*b*	**333**
	70*a*	205	II, 198	62*a*	**166**
	70*a*	206	II, 199	62*a*	**224**
§ 2	70*b*	207	II, 202	62*b*	**60**
	71*b*	210	II, 209	63*b*	**546**
§ 4	72*b*	215	II, 221	65*a*	**24**
	73*a*	216	II, 224	65*b*	**25**
	73*a*	217	II, 225	65*b*	**106**
§ 5	74*a*	221–2	II, 234	67*a*	**78**
	74*a*	222	II, 236	67*a*	**166**
	74*a*	222	II, 237	67*a*	**166**
§ 6	74*b*	222	II, 238	67*a*	**121**
	75*b*	226	II, 244	68*a*	**54**
	75*b*	226	II, 245	68*a*	**250**
	75*b*	226	II, 246	68*b*	**554**
	75*b*	227	II, 247	68*b*	**261**
§ 10	79*b*	240–1	II, 280	72*b*	**546**
§ 11	80*b*	243	II, 287	73*b*	**417**, **426**
Mishpaṭim, Neziḳin, § 18	101*a*	311	III, 138	95*a*	**573**
Ki Tissa', Shab. § 1	109*b*	—	III, 198	104*a*	**711**

Midrash, '*Aseret ha-Dibrot*, pp. 10–19, **519**

Midr.Prov. (ed. Buber): VI, 12, f. 28*a*, **405**; 30, f. 29*a*, **332**; IX, 2, f. 31*a fin.* **287**; XI, 21, f. 34*b fin.*–35*a*, **240**; XIV, 28, f. 38*a*, **112**; 34, f. 38*b*, **311**, **563**; XVII, 1, f. 42*b*, **589**; XXIV, 31, f. 48*b*, **124**; XXV, 21, f. 49*b*, **464**; XXXI, 10, f. 54*b*, **552**

Ed. Stettin: XXV, 21, f. 25*b*, **53**

Midr.Ps. (references to A.V. (chapter and verse) and to Buber's ed. (folio and section)): On V, 1 (26*a*, § 3), **146**; 4 (27*a*, § 7), **342**; IX, 9 (44*a*, § 11), **563**; XI, 7 (51*a*, § 6), **598**; XIX, 1 (82*b*, § 3), **283**; XXII, 8 (96*b*, § 22), **319**; XXIII, 1 (99*b*, § 3), **440**; XXIV, 1 (103*a*, § 5), **16**; 3 (102*b*, § 3), **202**; XXV, 2 *fin.* (106*a*, § 5 *fin.*) **321**; 4 (106*a*, § 6), **28**; XXVI, 1 (108*a*, § 2), **547**; XXIX, 2 (116*b*, § 2), **388**; XXX, heading, (117*a*, § 2), **48**, (118*a*, § 4), **275**; XXXI, 23 (120*b*, § 8), **335**, (120*b*, § 9), **278**; XXXVI, 6 (125*b*, § 5), **40**; XXXVII, 1 (126*b*, § 1), **422**; 3 (127*a*, § 3), **208**; XXXIX, 1 (128*b*, § 4), **407**; XL, 1 (129*a*, § 1), **334**; 4 (129*a fin.* § 3), **321**; XLI, 1 (130*b*, § 3), **427**; XLIV, 1 (134*b*, § 1), **92**; XLV, 1 (135*b init.* § 3), **330**, (135*b*, § 4), **322**; L, 1 (139*b*, § 1), **10**; 8 (140*a fin.* § 2), **414**; LI, 1 (140*b fin.* § 2), **89**; 4 (141*a*, § 3), **324**; LII, heading, (142*b*, § 3), **404**; LV, 22 (147*a*,

Figures in black type in this index refer to pages

Figures in black type in this index refer to pages

Figures in black type in this index refer to pages

Figures in black type in this index refer to pages

Figures in black type in this index refer to pages

Figures in black type in this index refer to pages

Figures in black type in this index refer to pages

Figures in black type in this index refer to pages

Figures in black type in this index refer to pages

Figures in black type in this index refer to pages

Figures in black type in this index refer to pages

Figures in black type in this index refer to pages

Figures in black type in this index refer to pages

Figures in black type in this index refer to pages

* Numbers to which an asterisk is affixed indicate pages in the duplicated first sheet printed by Zuckermandel at the beginning of the book (see his Preface, p. 6); these are numbered in the same type as the rest of the book.

GENERAL INDEX

The references in this index are to pages

* Words to which * is prefixed are explained in the glossary.

The references in this index are to pages

The references in this index are to pages

Age no obstacle to proselytisation, 572
Age limit for deputy, 437
Age of the Fathers, 623
Aged, honouring the, 506
Aggereia, 93
Agnus Dei, ci
Agrippina, 682
**Agudah*
Aḥa, R., and God's patience, 678; and the Holy Spirit, 677; and the thirty righteous, 232; dream of, 588
Aḥa b. Ada, 713
Ahab, 256; excluded from Resurrection, 604–5
Ahabah, confused with *Aybah*, 183
'Ahabah rabbah and *'Ahabat 'Olam*, 63
Aḥad Ha-'am, 710
'Aḥare-Mot-Ḳedoshim-'Emor, 471; *see also* 303
Ahasuerus, 98
Ahaz, father of the righteous Hezekiah, 590; the sinner, 76
**Aḥenu bet Yisrael*, lxxx
Aḥiḳar, 401, 691
Ahitophel, 492; and future life, 587, 604–5
'Ahizat 'eynayim, 692
Ahran (for Aaron), 521
Akabya b. Mahalalel differed from his colleagues, 353
Aḳedah and *zekut*, ci
Akiba, 695–6; abandons anthropomorphisms, 667; and alien books, 604; and cushions, 181; and Ecclesiastes, 495; and Eliezer b. Hyrcanus, 711; and future life, 664; and hand washing, 666; and his disciples, 217; and 'love thy neighbour', xl; and man who unloosed woman's hair, 108; and proselytes, 666; and roasting an egg, 662; and Simeon b. Yoḥai in prison, 668; and the charcoal burner, 591; and the restoration of sacrifices, lxxxix, xc; and the shipwrecked sage, 434; and zeal of teachers, 668; appointed Parnas, 209; arguments with Pappos, 4–5, 51, 663–4, 667; best pupil of, and the harlot, 325; burial of, 286; closed schools early on Eve of Atonement, 522; consulted by R. Joshua, 483; controversy with Johanan b. Torta, 262; dies saying the *Shema*, 269; 'estates' of, 422; fasting of, 592; gave nuts to children, 522; imposes severe fine, 664; in heaven, 598; in prison, 665–6; interpretation of Num. (xxiv, 7), 282; martyrdom of, xc, 155, 217; parable of fox and fishes, 136; romantic wooing of, 185; shortened congregational prayer, 348; tempted and the palm tree, 298; theology of, 663; torture of, 269; use of *Miḳweh Yisra'el*, 152; whipped by order of Gamaliel, 467
Akiba, by L. Finkelstein, xcix
'Akum, 366; *see also* Gentiles *and* Nations
**'Al 'aḥat kammah we-kammah*
'Al Gav, 672
**'Al ha-Ri'shonim...*
'Alah, 677
'Alamot (*'alimut*), 594
'Alas, *'Alaz*, *'Alaẓ*, 659
Alcibiades and Socrates, 660
Alcimus, 268
Alduka, 592
Alef, omission of, 661; stands for *'Anoki*, 246
Alef Bet, 307, 592
Alef to *Tau*, 307, 511
**'Alenu* prayer, 365
Alexander, Bp. of Alexandria, 630
Alexander Jannaeus, 4, 488
Alexander of Macedon and questions to Elders of South, 494
Alexandri (R.), seen in dream, 588
Alexandria and Greek thought, 635
Alexandrian, allegory, 619; theology, 630
Alexandrine Logos, 68
Alfred the Great and the Old Testament, 637
Al-Hidr, 257
Alien books, 604–5
'All depends on the woman', 509
'All flesh', includes some of the heathen, 557
'All flesh, not all men', 343
'All is in hand of heaven...', 291
'All Israel will have a share in the world to come', 604
'All' Israel mourned for Aaron, 537
'All that scholars are destined to ask...', 159
'All the days' = world to come, 548
'All the divisions of hell...', 464
'All things' includes 'evil', 125
All-present, *see Maḳom*
Allegorical interpretation, 619, 628

The references in this index are to pages

The references in this index are to pages

The references in this index are to pages

The references in this index are to pages

The references in this index are to pages

The references in this index are to pages

The references in this index are to pages

The references in this index are to pages

The references in this index are to pages

The references in this index are to pages

The references in this index are to pages

The references in this index are to pages

The references in this index are to pages

The references in this index are to pages

The references in this index are to pages

The references in this index are to pages

The references in this index are to pages

The references in this index are to pages

The references in this index are to pages

The references in this index are to pages

The references in this index are to pages

The references in this index are to pages

The references in this index are to pages

The references in this index are to pages

The references in this index are to pages

The references in this index are to pages

God (*cont.*)
of house, metaphor of, 214; material representations of, lii; merits of, 61; mercy of, 41; mercy of, overpowering, 664; more lenient to idolatry than to contempt of Torah, 138; mourns because of Flood, 57; mourns over man's heart, 300; myrrh, bundle of, as metaphor, 277; mystery of, 191; mystery of (Oral Law), 161; name of, always in our mouths, 543; Nature and Character of, chap. 1; nature of, and sin, xxxiv; nearness of, xxv, liii, 11, 81, 230, 325, 568; needs comfort, 69; needs no lamp, 25, 148; new conception about character of, xxviii; not absolutely good, 627; not priests, blesses Israel, 153–4; nourishes the whole world, 22; oath of, 585; offers Torah to 70 nations, 79; omnipotence of, 334; omnipresence of, lii ff., 12, 16; pain of, 585; partiality of, for Israel, 77, 652; partner of, 383; partnership with, 115; permits a man to sin, 291; pleads with Moses at burning bush, 474; power of, 30, 34, 270, 535 (*see also* Capacity of God); praise of Noah, 498; praise of, to be limited, 283, 498; prayer of, 368; presence of, in Synagogue, 18; preserves proselytes, 335; priests of, 671; proclaims the virtue of three types, 304; promises to receive the Gentiles, 565; promise of, to women, 510; provides, 28; purity of, 280; puts the leaven in the dough, 300; reconciles David and Doeg, 587; regarded as Demiurge, 627; rejects no penitent, 323; relation of, to Torah, xxxiii; Relations of, to Man, chap. 1; repents, 301; reproaches Moses for length in prayer, 348; retinue of (*familia*), 346; reverence of, and parents, 503; right hand of, 34; rod of, 550; sanctified through Israel, xxxiii; says Israel shall be partner of Sabbath, 195; seal of (*emet*), 307; separates the Sabbath, 195; shows Moses treasuries of reward, 223; slays Israel in this world, 599; son of, Israel, 103–4, 341, 348, 351; spatial conceptions of, xxviii, xcviii; stands before school-children, 24; studies and teaches Torah, 167; studies Torah, 41; supports the sick, 435; takes Israel back, 318; taught by Moses, 76; teaches the Torah, 598; tells Moses Israelites are troublesome, 354; tests all, 448; thinks thought, 167; three gifts of, 447, 542; three possessions of, 244; throne of, 37, 90, 482; to the world, relation of, 21; 'trade' of, 57; transcendence of, liii, 19, 72; tries the righteous, xlii; uniqueness of, 5, 497; unites His name to marriage, 509–10; unites His name to righteous men when they die, 303; unity of, 587 (*see also* Unity of God); unlikeness to man, 28, 30; visits Abraham after circumcision, 23, 281; visits the barren, 512; voice of, 677; wants the heart, 492–4; warnings by, 325, 329; ways of, 468; ways of, are not man's, 33; wears *ṭallit*, 324; weaves crowns for letters of Torah, 24; weeps, 67; weeps daily because of three classes, 470; weeps for Israel, 96; weighs merits against sins, 72; will make Jerusalem a mother city, 464; will of, 34–5, 58, 69–71, 103, 193, 234, 358–64, 367–8, 380, 495, 561; witnesses of, 34; work of, all through the day, 41; wrath of, xxxi, 93; *see also* Father, Immanence, Longsuffering *and* Shechinah
'God changes his world', 662
'God did not descend', lxi
'God inclined the heavens like a vault', lxi
'God needs us all', xxxiv
'God of Abraham, Isaac and Israel', 675
'God of Abraham, Isaac and Jacob', 369
'God of our Fathers', lxxxv
'God of the living, not of the dead', 369
Godfather (*Sandeḳ*), 257
God-fearers alone may take oaths, 401, 492
'God-fearing Pharisee', 488
'God-loving Pharisee', 488
Godhead at Sinai, 587
Godlo, 521
**Goi*, *see* Gentile
Gol (*galah*, *galal*), 319
Gold (fine), 505
Gold takes a man out of this world, 445
'Golden age', xliii

The references in this index are to pages

The references in this index are to pages

The references in this index are to pages

The references in this index are to pages

The references in this index are to pages

The references in this index are to pages

Hosea, children of, 244; controversy of, with God, 243
Hoshaiah (R.), blind teacher for his son, 411; *see also* Osha'ya
Hospitality, chap. XVIII, 214, 451 ff.; must be sincere, 452; to strangers, 380
Host, blessed by guest, 454; children of, behaviour towards, 522; who had only three eggs for three guests, 452
Hot-tempered, 451
Hour (good fortune), 475; of God's wrath, 465
Hours of rising, 642
'House' (third division of heaven), 597
House = wife, 511
House, collapses, 481; of Israel, 337; with four doors, 415; with four stories catches fire, 553
House(s) of Study, 112, 119, 121, 146, 163, 187, 189, 292, 296, 326, 340, 398, 420, 424, 440, 451, 501–2, 518, 552, 577; early attendance at, 482; walls of, 340
'Household above' (*famalya*), 362
Householders (*Ba'ale Battim*), 108, 183; delivered over to Rome, 498; duties of, 397
'How can a man escape hell?' 497
'How hard is the evil inclination?' 296
'How heavy is my head?' 49
Hubris in Esther, 682
Hügel, Baron von, 137
Human, character, mechanical view of, 595; life, 182 (*see also* Life)
Human being, *see* Man
Human race, and hell, xlviii; ultimate improvement of, lxx; unity of, xl
Human sacrifices, *see* Sacrifices, human
Humanism, Jewish and Greek, xxxvii ff.
Humiliation, *see* Asceticism
Humility, 109, 210, 379, 497; imprint of Torah's heel, 170, 380; making oneself small, 129; of God, 30; of Moses, 170–1, 462; of Samuel, 462; of students of Torah, 165
Humility and Bride, chap. XX
Ḥummashim, 82
Ḥummesh, 82
Huna (water-carrier), 698
Huna I, 697
Huna, and hypocrisy, lxxix; and his tenants, 175; and Judah b. Ilai, 274; wine of, goes sour, 175
Hunger, death by, in old age, 440
**Ḥuppah we-Ḳiddushin*, lxxvi
Husband and wife, 515; reconciled, 537 (*see also* Aaron)
Husband's brother, marriage with, 630
Ḥuẓ, 588
Ḥuzpit, Amora of Rabban Gamaliel II, 438
Hyamson, M., cited, 106, 646
Hydrostatics, 659
Hyenas, 488, 662
Hygiene more important than astronomy, 353, 683
'Hymn for the Sabbath Day', 607
Hyperbole, ci, 138
Hypocrisy, 404; and R. Elazar, 489
Hypocrites, as oppressors, 404; cannot see God, 405; fall into Gehinnom, 404; may be exposed, 404; who pretend to be saints and scholars, 404
Hypocritical, prayers, 589; woman, 487
Hyrcanus, John, 108; became Sadducee, 304
Hyrcanus II and Aristobulus, 372
Hyssop cleanses leper, 473

'I am your Father', 62
'I call heaven and earth to witness...', 486
'I created myself', 9
'I have seen two things', 56
'I need no offerings', 27
'I rise before the Shechinah', 501
'I searched myself', 659
'I was victorious but I suffered loss', 34
Iakeimos, 268
*Ibn Ezra, Abraham, cited, 44, 493–4; and criticism, lxiv
Ibn Gabirol, xxi, xxii
Ideal scholar, 484
Ideals of Judaism and Hellenism, xxxvii
Idiom ('tongue of men'), 253
'Idle rich', 388
Idleness, 440 ff.
Idolaters, conversion of, 561; sustained by God, 48, 474
Idolatrous intentions, 215
Idolatry, chap. IX, 122, 253–5, 260, 464; abandonment of, 653; abetting of, 463; and almsgiving, 413; and contempt of Torah, 138; and environment, 250; and evil inclination, 296; and groundless hatred, 463; and martyrdom, 253; and Noachides, 556; and peace, 530, 533, 535; and pride, 470; and

The references in this index are to pages

The references in this index are to pages

The references in this index are to pages

The references in this index are to pages

The references in this index are to pages

The references in this index are to pages

The references in this index are to pages

The references in this index are to pages

The references in this index are to pages

The references in this index are to pages

The references in this index are to pages

The references in this index are to pages

The references in this index are to pages

The references in this index are to pages

The references in this index are to pages

The references in this index are to pages

The references in this index are to pages

The references in this index are to pages

The references in this index are to pages

The references in this index are to pages

The references in this index are to pages

The references in this index are to pages

The references in this index are to pages

The references in this index are to pages

The references in this index are to pages

The references in this index are to pages

The references in this index are to pages

The references in this index are to pages

The references in this index are to pages

The references in this index are to pages

The references in this index are to pages

The references in this index are to pages

The references in this index are to pages

The references in this index are to pages

The references in this index are to pages

The references in this index are to pages

The references in this index are to pages

The references in this index are to pages

The references in this index are to pages

The references in this index are to pages

The references in this index are to pages

The references in this index are to pages

The references in this index are to pages

The references in this index are to pages

The references in this index are to pages

The references in this index are to pages

C. G. MONTEFIORE

C(laude) Joseph G(oldsmid) Montefiore (1858-1938) was educated at Balliol College, Oxford, under Benjamin Jowett and T. H. Green. In the characteristic spirit of Liberal Judaism, the English equivalent of Reform, he sought to establish the interconnection of Judaism and Christianity by exposing the Jewish sources of the Gospels. Among his major works are: *The Origin and Development of the Religion of the Ancient Hebrews* (1892), *The Synoptic Gospels* (1909; revised edition, 1927), and *Rabbinic Literature and Gospel Teaching* (1930).

H. LOEWE

H(erbert) Martin James Loewe (1882-1940) was Reader in Rabbinics at Cambridge University from 1931 until his death. He was, as he described himself, "an Orthodox Jew . . . but not a fundamentalist." As a student Loewe had been deeply influenced by Israel Abrahams, his predecessor at Cambridge, and later also by Abrahams's friend and collaborator, Claude Montefiore. Loewe worked closely with Montefiore on the latter's *Rabbinic Literature and Gospel Teaching*. Among Loewe's many works of scholarship are: *Render unto Caesar* (1940) and an unpublished catalogue of Hebrew manuscripts in the Cambridge University Library.